Date Due

HANDBOOK OF SEMIOTICS

Advances in Semiotics
THOMAS A. SEBEOK, GENERAL EDITOR

HANDBOOK

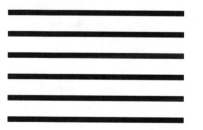

Winfried Nöth

OF SEMIOTICS

Indiana University Press

Bloomington and Indianapolis

This English-language edition is the enlarged and completely revised version of a work by Winfried Nöth originally published as *Handbuch der Semiotik* in 1985 by J. B. Metzlersche Verlagsbuchhandlung, Stuttgart.

Manufactured in the United States of America

Library of Congress Cataloging-in-Publication Data

Nöth, Winfried.
  [Handbuch der Semiotik. English]
  Handbook of semiotics / Winfried Nöth.
  p. cm. — (Advances in semiotics)
  Enlarged translation of: Handbuch der Semiotik.
  Bibliography: p.
  Includes indexes.
  ISBN 0-253-34120-5
  1. Semiotics—handbooks, manuals, etc. 2. Communication —Handbooks, manuals, etc. I. Title. II. Series.
P99.N6513 1990
302.2—dc20   89-45199
                                    CIP

1 2 3 4 5 94 93 92 91 90

C O N T E N T S

III. Semiosis, Code, and the Semiotic Field

IV. Language and Language-Based Codes

V. From Structuralism to Text Semiotics: Schools and Major Figures

VI. Text Semiotics: The Field

VII. Nonverbal Communication

VIII. Aesthetics and Visual Communication

PREFACE

A handbook with the ambitious objective of dealing with a vast field of research ranging from *A*(esthetics) to *Z*(ooethology) may be excused for beginning with a few apologetic remarks on the design of such a daring undertaking.

1. A Topography of Semiotics

Imagine you should have to describe [. . .] the topography of a country about which there is hardly any certain knowledge. Neither the frontiers of this country are known, nor do we know whether it is a country in the traditional sense at all. Many claim that it is indeed a genuine country, even one that surpasses all known countries in beauty and riches, a country whose possession, once gained, would end all need. Others not only call this hope into question, but also consider the very existence of the country a mere utopia. But let us see further. Sources available for a topographic description are on the one hand certain reports by different authors. Every one of the authors lays claim to having discovered a new country, but it is uncertain whether they have the same country in mind. Indeed, they not only use different names for the newly discovered country, but also describe it in diverging ways. Moreover, several historians are of the opinion that the country

in question has been discovered not only by these modern pioneers but much earlier, even in antiquity. There are still further sources in an immense number of writings giving a detailed description of some regions supposedly belonging to this country. But since these descriptions are mostly quite diverse—some, for example, presenting the landscape of a moorland or a rugged highland, others an urban landscape, and still others describing its flora and fauna—therefore one does not really know whether these are different regions and ecological areas of one and the same country or whether these are, instead, different countries.

With this poetic image, Peter Schmitter (*Kratylos* 32 [1987]: 1) described the situation in which the author of this handbook found himself, embarking on the adventure of writing a *Handbuch der Semiotik* in the early 1980s (Nöth 1985). This handbook once more aims at the adventurous goal of a topographical survey of the main areas of theoretical and applied semiotics. The survey of the history and the present state of the art in this domain of research intends to be systematic, comprehensive, and up to date. Wherever limitations of space prevent a more extensive discussion, bibliographical references indicate further sources of orientation. Readers with particular terminological questions may find answers with the aid of the index of terms. With its comprehensive bibliography and detailed indexes of subjects and names, this handbook is intended to be useful as an encyclopedic reference book in semiotics.

2. A Pluralistic Approach

A project of such ambitious scope is likely to attract criticism from two opposing directions. Some will find that this handbook covers too little, neglecting areas of the semiotic field which they might find more important. These critics may occasionally be satisfied with the explicit acknowledgment of lacunae and appropriate further references (see, for example, Introduction 2.). Others will object that the handbook covers too much, including many topics or approaches that are not "semiotic enough" or perhaps are no longer sufficiently relevant to current developments in semiotics. Such criticism is expected from the disciples of particular schools of semiotics. Against these critics, it must be emphasized that the approach to semiotics adopted in this handbook is basically descriptive and pluralistic. Current trends in semiotics are quite heterogeneous, and it is not the intention of this handbook to conceal the great variety in approaches to the study of signs. Wherever necessary, differences will be emphasized. But wherever possible, the common foundations of these approaches and the interconnections among them will be pointed out.

This handbook is not a collection of critical review articles. A critical evaluation of the semiotic research under discussion is not one of its primary objectives. The critical reader should have ample opportunity to draw his or her own critical conclusions. On the other hand, the author is well aware of the impossibility of a totally value-neutral account of the state of the art. According to a principle of structuralist semiotics, any selection is an implicit evaluation, since it implies the rejection of all nonselected items. In this sense, this volume cannot escape being evaluative. However, the author hopes that the choice of the chapters and their comparative length is motivated less by his own personal preferences than by the degree of attention which the topics under discussion have attracted during the last few decades of semiotic research. Necessarily remaining lacunae are not always intended. Apart from the fact that a still more comprehensive account of the state of the art in semiotics exceeds the capabilities of an individual scholar, the author admits frankly that a report on some of the more specialized areas of semiotics, such as the semiotics of mathematics, is beyond his own qualification. For the same reason he has been unable to consult in the original the rich semiotic literature published in East European languages.

3. Handbook and *Handbuch*

This handbook has a precursor in my German *Handbuch der Semiotik* (Stuttgart: Metzler 1985). The very positive and sometimes enthusiastic (Sebeok 1986a, Bär 1987) assessment of this publication in no fewer than twenty-five reviews has resulted in a Serbo-Croation translation (Belgrad: Globus) and the invitation for an English translation. In 1986, Thomas A. Sebeok and John Gallman of Indiana University Press persuaded me to take care of the English translation myself. However, beginning to work as my own translator, I soon discovered the truth of the Italian proverb "Translator, traitor!" (*traduttore tradittore*). It obliged me to completely rewrite the *Handbuch* of 1985. The result is this totally reworked, updated, and largely expanded *Handbook*.

4. The Encyclopedic Landscape of Semiotics

My German handbook was the second publication of this title in the history of semiotics.

However, the earlier *Handbuch der Semiotik,* which Konrad Sprengel published in 1801, has little in common with this project: it was a treatise in medical symptomatology (cf. History 1.2.2).

There have been two different approaches to the project of an encyclopedic guide to semiotics, which may be characterized as monistic and pluralistic. Monistic approaches are guides to the foundations and basic concepts of a particular school of semiotic research. The advantage of such approaches is that they can aspire to terminological and systematic coherence. Their disadvantage is that they usually neglect most of the results of other approaches to semiotics. A few early dictionaries and glossaries of semiotics have pursued this monistic goal, providing guides to a sometimes hermetic terminology of a particular system of semiotics. Thus, Morris wrote a glossary to his own writings in semiotics (1946: 359–68). Bense & Walther (1973) published a small dictionary as a guide to the Peircean foundations and Bense's own school of semiotics. Greimas & Courtés (1979) published an analytical dictionary as a guide to their own Paris School of Semiotics (with the sequel in Greimas & Courtés 1986).

A first comprehensive pluralistic attempt at an encyclopedic guide to semiotics was my *Handbuch* of 1985. Precursors in this direction were a number of smaller glossaries (Rey-Debove 1979, Krampen et al., eds. 1981: 211–58) and various encyclopedic dictionaries of linguistics. Most of the latter deal only marginally with topics of theoretical and applied semiotics. An exception is Ducrot & Todorov's *Encyclopedic Dictionary of the Sciences of Language* (1972), which covers many topics of linguistic semiotics and text semiotics. In 1986, a new pluralistic guide to semiotics appeared with Sebeok's monumental *Encyclopedic Dictionary of Semiotics* (ed. 1986), which brings together 380 articles written by no fewer than 132 authors. (For the project of a new systematic international encyclopedia of semiotics, announced by Posner & Sebeok to appear toward the end of this millennium, see Wulff 1988.)

5. Bibliographical References

References to the bibliography are of the type AUTHOR (YEAR [of first publication]: PAGE), for example "Morris (1946: 87)." The only exception is the references to the *Collected Papers* by Peirce, which indicate volumes and paragraphs; for example, "(Peirce § 4.521)" refers to vol. 4, § 521. Several publications by one author in one year are differentiated by a, b, c, etc., for example "(Saussure 1916b)."

The bibliography contains only titles explicitly referred to in the text. To save publication costs, references are abbreviated. In the case of reeditions, reprints, or translations, only two publication dates are given, for example "Saussure (1916b) 1972." The first year, in parentheses, indicates the year of the first publication of this title. The second year indicates the edition used in the text. Only when later editions of a title are considerably different from first editions does the first year indicate the publication date of the revised edition. Further information on the number of the edition or a possible translator or translation is usually omitted. Wherever available, English translations are quoted. When an English quote refers to a title in a foreign language, the translation is the author's own. When a translation was known to exist but was not available, it is listed in brackets after the original title.

6. Personal Acknowledgments

I would like to begin with a word of thanks to Walter A. Koch. He introduced me to semiotics in the late 1960s and eary 1970s. Without his always inspiring teaching and the extraordinary breadth of his semiotic horizon, this handbook would not have been written.

For the initiatives taken to make this publication possible, I thank Jean Umiker-Sebeok, who invited me to Bloomington, Thomas A. Sebeok, who proposed to include the handbook in his series Advances in Semiotics, John Gallman for his very reliable care of the project on the behalf of Indiana University Press, Inter Nationes, Bonn, who promised a partial translation grant, and Bernd Lutz of Metzler, Stuttgart, who ceded the copyright of the German *Handbuch*.

For helpful suggestions and corrections in the articles on theology and information, I am indebted to Erhardt Güttgemanns, Bonn, and Friedrich Wille, Kassel. Thanks are due to Jerrold Rodesch, Green Bay, and Michael Morrissey, Kassel, who read the manuscript, discovered mistakes, and suggested stylistic improvements. Nobody is responsible for possibly remaining deficiencies except for the author alone.

The University of Kassel provided me with resources to prepare this book. For much bibliographical and technical assistance I thank Volker Zähme. He also prepared the drawings of most of the diagrams. Four figures (SL 1, SL 3, SL 4, and SL 5) are hand drawings by Ortraud Nöth, Berlin. For further major assistance in editing the manuscript and preparing the indexes, I thank Christine Brinkmann. Special thanks is due to Renate Förster-Fernández. With indefatigable readiness and always without mistakes, she did a magnificent typing job.

---

7. Copyright Acknowledgments

Permission to reproduce photographs, diagrams, and a quotation was kindly given by the following authors and publishers (in the order of appearance in text): For the quote in Preface (1.): Peter Schmitter (Münster). Fig. P 1: The Peirce Edition Project (Indiana University, Indianapolis). Fig. Mo 1: Indiana University Press (Bloomington). Fig. Mo 2: Mouton de Gruyter (Berlin). Fig. S 1: Bibliothèque publique et universitaire de Genève. Fig. S 2: Editions Payot (Paris). Fig. H 1: Det Kgl. Bibliotek (København). Fig. J 1: Walter A. Koch (Source: Koch 1986a: 131). Fig. Z 3: Springer-Verlag (Heidelberg). Fig. Z 4: Plenum Press (New York). Fig. C 1: University of Illinois Press (Champaign). Fig. C 2: Springer-Verlag (Heidelberg). Fig. C 3: Editions Payot (Paris). Fig. C 4: Springer-Verlag (Heidelberg). Fig. F 1: Gustav Fischer Verlag (Stuttgart). Fig. W 1: Scientific American, Inc. (New York). Fig. W 2: Mouton de Gruyter (Berlin). Fig. W 3: VEB Deutscher Verlag der Wissenschaften (Berlin, GDR). Fig. W 4: Mouton de Gruyter (Berlin). Fig. W 5: Brockhaus (Mannheim). Fig. W 6: Scolar Press (Oxford). Fig. U 2: Scolar Press (Oxford). Fig. SL 2: Scolar Press (Oxford). Fig. SL 4: Southern Illinois University Press (Carbondale). Fig. SL 5: Harvard University Press (Cambridge, Mass.). Fig. B 1: Editions du Seuil (Paris). Fig. G 1: Algirdas J. Greimas. Fig. G 2: Indiana University Press (Bloomington). Fig. G 3: Larousse (Paris) and University of Nebraska Press (Lincoln). Fig. K 1: Editions du Seuil (Paris). Fig. E 1: Gruppo Editoriale Fabbri Bompiani (Milano). Fig. N 2: Mouton de Gruyter (Berlin) and Claude Bremond (Paris).

HANDBOOK OF SEMIOTICS

Introduction

In Walter Abish's piece of experimental prose entitled *Ardor/Awe/Atrocity,* in a passage under the heading "Zoo[76]/Zodiac[77]/Zero[78]," one character, upon announcing his marriage, tells his friend: "She's very bright and attractive. She's got a Ph.D. in semiotics. Her father is in oil" (1977: 57). Is this heroine an expert in an unusually difficult, perhaps even esoteric discipline (for which one has to be "very bright"), is her field of specialty perhaps as "attractive" as the heroine herself, or does she follow her father's trail by working in a discipline that promises to be particularly successful? Whatever the answer may be, it is evident that semiotics is no longer the *terra incognita* which Saussure characterized it as toward the beginning of this century, when he postulated it as a "science that studies the life of signs within society" (1916b: 16).

1. Semiotics

At a time when semiotics has entered the realm of fiction and when countless publications and journals from *A(merican Journal of Semiotics)* to *Z(eitschrift für Semiotik)* are deciphering the secret messages of semiosis, the question "What is semiotics?", still asked by authors *In Search of Semiotics* (Toussaint 1978, Sless 1986: 1–9), need no longer be the first one to be answered in a handbook of semiotics. On the other hand,

there are now so many definitions of the "science of signs," some even refusing to define semiotics as a science of signs (cf. Greimas 1.2), that a preliminary word on the view of semiotics adopted in this handbook is inevitable.

1.1 Pluralism in Semiotics

Semiotics has become neither that unified science nor that "unifying point of view" which Morris had in mind when he delineated "the contours of the science of signs" for Otto Neurath's *International Encyclopedia of Unified Science* (Morris 1938: 1). Today, there are many schools and branches of both theoretical and applied semiotics. Pelc enumerates no fewer than sixteen different definitions given to semiotics by the diverse schools of this discipline (1984a) and distinguishes five major current meanings of the notion of semiotics (1981b). Most of these will be discussed later in this handbook. Their scope ranges from narrow to broad. In the present topography of semiotics (cf. Preface), the broadest possible view of semiotics will be adopted. The following survey of the semiotic field investigates both explicitly and implicitly semiotic research.

Explicitly semiotic research covers not only semiotics but also semiology (whenever a difference between the two domains is still assumed, cf. History 1.2 or Hjelmslev 2.). It covers theoretical and applied semiotics and extends from zoosemiotics to anthroposemiotics, including the various branches of cultural and text semiotics. It explores the threshold between the semiotic and the nonsemiotic in biosemiotics, photosemiotics, endosemiotics, and the semiotics of objects (see also Sign), studying processes of both signification and communication.

Implicitly semiotic research covers the many semioticians *avant la lettre* who have contributed to the theory of signs since Plato and Aristotle but also includes semiotically relevant current studies in the many neighboring fields of semiotics. However, since, in Peirce's words, "the entire universe is perfused with signs," it is impossible to give a comprehensive survey of all implicitly semiotic research. For this reason (further discussed in Language 1. and Semantics 1.), not even the basic outlines of central domains of the semiotic field, such as linguistics and logic, could be included in this handbook. Fortunately, there are already excellent manuals and surveys of research in those domains.

1.2 Science or Movement?

"It is doubtful if signs have ever before been so vigorously studied by so many persons and from so many points of view. The army of investigators includes linguists, logicians, philosophers, psychologists, biologists, anthropologists, psychopathologists, aestheticians, and sociologists" (Morris 1938: 1). This characterization of interdisciplinary research activities in the field of semiotics is today even more valid than it was in the days of Morris. However, toward the end of this millennium, the scientific status of semiotics is still a topic of debate.

1.2.1 FASHION OR REVOLUTION?
Assessments of the state of the art in research within the *Semiotic Sphere* (Sebeok & Umiker-Sebeok, eds. 1986) range from "activity," "movement," and "project" to "field," "approach," "method," "discipline," "doctrine," "metadiscipline," "theory," and "science" (cf.

Withalm 1988: 159–61). Whereas some are confident that semiotics today "attempts to become a discipline rather than simply an area of interest" (Culler 1981b: 78), others already believe themselves to be witnesses of a "crisis" and even the "agony" of semiotics (Blonsky, ed. 1985: xiii). In the assessment of Deely et al., eds. (1986: viii), the extreme positions of this variegated spectrum are characterized by "*fad* vs. *revolution*." Deely et al. believe that the "fad" view is associated with the history of structuralist semiology (as revived by Blonsky, ed. 1985), whereas the revolutionary aspect is achieved in a much broader field of research in semiosis in culture and nature. Whichever place semiotics may occupy in this spectrum, the poetic images chosen by both its apocalyptists and its apologetics are quite dramatic, be it "semiotics at the crossroads," "semiotics out of the ivy tower" (Blonsky, ed. 1985: xviii, xxvvii), *Frontiers in Semiotics* (Deely et al., eds. 1986), *Semiotics Unfolding* (Borbé, ed. 1984), or simply *Silence, on parle* (Pesot 1979).

1.2.2 A PROJECT, A DOCTRINE?
The Saussurean dictum of the "science that does not yet exist" (1916b: 16) has remained a *topos* in the historiography of semiotics until very recently (cf. Withalm 1988: 163–68). According to Todorov, semiotics is still "more a project than an established science," and "this is due not only to the necessarily slow rhythm of a science at its inception, but also to a certain uncertainty as to its basic principles and concepts" (Ducrot & Todorov 1972: 90).

Among those who hesitate to call semiotics a science or at least a theory are also Greimas and Sebeok. Greimas & Courtés, while seeing "signs of health and vitality" in current semiotic research, conclude that "semiotics proposes itself both as a project for research and as already on-going research" (1979: 291). Sebeok characterizes general semiotics as a "scientific discipline [. . .] still in its infancy," which "even today [. . .] lacks a comprehensive theoretical foundation but is sustained largely as a consistently shared point of view [. . .], having as its subject matter all systems of signs irrespective of their substance and without regard to the species of the emitter or receiver involved" (1976: 64). Sebeok's own proposal for characterizing the scientific status of semiotics is to adopt Locke's definition of semiotics as a "doctrine of signs" (ibid.:ix; cf. History 3.2.3). However, for Locke, a doctrine was not a system of established principles but hardly more than a body of "tenets loosely constituting a department of knowledge" (ibid.).

1.2.3 THEORETICAL AND APPLIED SEMIOTICS

There have been many proposals for a systematic subdivision of semiotics. Morris proposed the subdivision into *pure, descriptive,* and *applied* semiotics (1938: 9; 1946: 366), Carnap added the branches of *general* and *special* semiotics (cf. Lieb 1971), and Hjelmslev distinguished between *semiology* as the metalanguage of semiotic systems and *metasemiology* as the metadiscipline of the various scientific semiologies. Whether a *pure* semiotic is ever possible or whether the science of signs is necessarily an "impure" study, affected in its impurity by the very content of signs, as Moles (1976) maintains, the distinction between the two levels of *theory* and *application* (or *analysis*) in semiotic research is generally acknowledged.

However, these are not two separate branches of semiotics. Since the theory of signs is a language of its own and thus a system of signs itself, this theory should ideally be applicable to itself, being able to analyze the very system of signs used for the investigation of signs. In the discovery of this self-reflexivity of semiotics, there has been surprising alliance between the otherwise antipodean semioticians Morris and Kristeva. Morris describes semiotics as being both a science and an instrument of the sciences, a metascience and a "science coordinate with the other sciences" (1938: 2; Morris 2.1.3). Kristeva discovers this self-reflexivity when she describes semiotics as being both a metalanguage (being a "science of the text") and an object language (being a "signifying practice" like other languages). More recently, in the context of mathematics and logic, Hofstadter has characterized this type of

antinomy as "bootstrapping," the necessity of having to lift oneself by one's own bootstraps (1980: 24). Kristeva's proposal for an escape from this antinomy was to turn semiotics into "an open path of research, a constant critique referring to itself in *autocriticism.*"

---

2. The Semiotic Field

The field of research in theoretical and applied semiotics which is outlined in the sixty-five chapters in the eight parts of this handbook need not be outlined here once more. However, possible alternative subdivisions and regrettable lacunae may be of interest. Several main areas of the semiotic field not dealt with in chapters of their own are nevertheless discussed extensively under various other headings. Such topics from alternative subdivisions of the semiotic field include

— semiotics of culture (cf. Umiker-Sebeok 1977, Winner & Umiker-Sebeok 1979, Serrano 1980, Berger 1984, Fawcett et al., eds. 1984, Koch 1986a, Eschbach & Koch, eds. 1987, Bystrina 1989),

— semiotics of multimedia communication (cf. Hess-Lüttich, ed. 1982), popular culture (Berger 1984; 1987, Blonsky, ed. 1985), and the mass media (see Text Semiotics 1.2, Film, Advertising, Comics, etc., but not included in this handbook: the semiotics of television (cf. Cerbrián-Herreros 1978, Fiske & Hartley 1978, Eco 1980b, Berger 1982: 40–42),

— semiotics and anthropology (cf. Singer 1984, Mertz & Parmentier, eds. 1985, and Zoosemiotics, Magic, Structuralism, Narrative, Myth) and ethnosemiotics (cf. MacCannell & MacCannell 1982: 68–84 and *Semiotica* 46.2–4 [1983], Sebeok, ed. 1986: 235–37).

Topics only partially covered in the chapters of this handbook are:

— philosophy and logic in relation to semiotics (cf. Klaus 1963, Pelc, ed. 1971, Deely 1982, Descombes 1983, Parret 1983, Eco

1984b, Pelc et al., eds. 1984, Kalinowski 1985, Martin, ed. 1988; see History, Meaning, Structuralism 4., Ideology),

— psychosemiotics (Ullmann 1975, *Zeitschrift für Semiotik* 3.4 [1981], Mininni 1982, Watt 1984, and Darrault 1985,

— medical semiotics (see History 1.2.2; Typology 4.2.4),

— sociosemiotics and semiotic sociology (Koch 1971b, Delahaye 1977, Halliday 1978, Greimas & Courtés 1979: 302–304, Zito 1984, Jules-Rosette 1986, MacCannell 1986, Ventola 1987) including feminism (de Lauretis 1984),

— semiotics and economics (see Objects 4., Advertising),

— semiotics of folklore (Bogatyrev 1937, Mesnil 1974, Ben-Amos & Goldstein, eds. 1975, Marcus, ed. 1978, Sebeok, ed. 1986: 255–67; see Myth),

— the semiotics of opera and ballet (see Music 1.4).

Remaining lacunae are:

— semiotics of mathematics (Hermes 1938, Klaus 1963: 133–51, Zellmer 1979, Bense 1981, Sebeok, ed. 1986: 487–97; but see Information and Code 5.2),

— semiotics of law (but see Text Semiotics 1.2),

— semiotics of history (but see Text Semiotics 1.2, Structuralism 4.2.2),

— semiotics of psychoanalysis, psychiatry, and psychotherapy (cf. Sebeok et al., eds. 1964, Shands 1970; 1977, Ruesch 1972, Bär 1975, Gear & Liendo 1975, Verdiglione, ed. 1975, Coward & Ellis 1977, Rancour-Laferrière 1980, Silverman 1983; but see Structuralism 3. on Lacan).

For further topics see also Index of Subjects.

---

3. Resources in Semiotics

The following brief survey of introductory and bibliographical material in semiotics is necessarily incomplete.

3.1 Introductions

There are several introductions to semiotics in the English language. Hervey (1982) introduces the broadest scope of topics from the semiotic field. Deely (1982) and Clarke (1987) focus on historical and philosophical foundations. Guiraud (1971) and Hawkes (1977) introduce structuralist semiology and aspects of text semiotics. Berger (1984) and Sless (1986) discuss a variety of topics in applied cultural semiotics. Eco (1976), often quoted as an introduction, is more a pluralistic *Theory of Semiotics*. An introductory anthology is Innis, ed. (1985). Krampen et al., eds. (1981) introduce the *Classics of Semiotics*. Other anthologies available as paperbacks are Blonsky, ed. (1985) and Deely et al., eds. (1986).

French introductions to semiotics are Mounin (1970a), J. Martinet (1973), Carontini & Péraya (1975), Toussaint (1978), Hénault (1979), Pesot (1979), Carontini (1983), and Helbo (1983b). German introductions are Walther (1974), Nöth (1975b), Trabant (1976a), and Bentele & Bystrina (1978). Italian introductions are Calabrese & Mucci (1975) and Casetti (1977). Spanish and Dutch introductions are Serrano (1981) and Zoest (1978). For earlier introductions in various languages (until 1975) see Sebeok (1976: 164–67).

3.2 Bibliographies, Journals, and Yearbooks

Bibliographies of semiotics are Eschbach, comp. (1974), Eschbach & Rader, comps. (1976), Eschbach & Eschbach-Szabó, comps. (1986), and *Bulletin du groupe de recherches sémio-linguistiques* 22 (1982) and 29 (1984). The journal *Semiotica* (1 [1969]ff.) has meanwhile appeared in more than seventy volumes. Other semiotic or semiotically oriented journals are *Versus (VS)* 1 (1979)ff., *Canadian Journal of Research in Semiotics* 1 (1973)ff., *Degrés* 1 (1973)ff., *Semiosis* 1 (1976)ff., *Bulletin* (1 [1977]ff.), and *Documents* (1 [1979]ff.) *de recherche du groupe de recherches sémio-linguistiques* (Paris), *Kodikas/Code* 1 (1979)ff., *Zeitschrift für Semiotik* 1 (1979)ff., *American*

Journal of Semiotics 1 (1981)ff., and *Recherches Sémiotiques/Semiotic Inquiry* 1 (1981)ff.

A series of state-of-the-art yearbooks in semiotics is Helbo, ed. (1979), Sebeok & Umiker-Sebeok, eds. (1986; 1987). Interdisciplinary relationships of semiotics to no fewer than forty other areas of research are surveyed in an edition by Koch, ed. (1989c). The state of the art in semiotics is further documented by the proceedings of congresses or conventions such as Chatman et al., eds. (1979), Lange-Seidl, ed. (1981), Borbé, ed. (1984), Oehler, ed. (1984), and Deely, ed. (1986), and in numerous book series, such as Aachener Studien zur Semiotik (Aachen: Rader), Bochum Publications in Evolutionary Cultural Semiotics (Bochum: Brockmeyer), Actes Sémiotiques (Paris: Hadès), Advances in Semiotics (Bloomington: Indiana University Press), Approaches to Semiotics (Berlin: Mouton de Gruyter), Applications/Theory of Semiotics (Amsterdam: Benjamins), Kodikas/Code Supplement (Tübingen: Narr), Probleme der Semiotik (Tübingen: Stauffenburg), Studia Semiotica (Hildesheim: Olms), and Topics in Contemporary Semiotics (New York: Plenum). See also Sebeok (1976: 171–76), the *Bulletin* of the *International Association for Semiotic Studies,* and History (4.3) on surveys of international semiotic activities.

PART I

History and Classics of Modern Semiotics

History of Semiotics
Peirce
Morris
Saussure
Hjelmslev
Jakobson

History of Semiotics

In spite of the increasing number of contributions to many of its branches, it is still true that "the history of semiotics as a whole yet remains to be written," as Morris observed (1946: 335; cf. Deely 1982: 7, Schmitter 1983: 3). One of the problems of semiotic historiography is the uncertainty of its field. While semiotic ideas on the nature of signs and meaning were developed in antiquity and the Middle Ages, a general theory of signs under the name of semiotics did not arise before the period of modern semiotics. The classics and the major schools of semiotics since Peirce will be introduced in chapters of their own. A historical survey is also part of the chapters on signs and meaning.

1. Historiography of Semiotics

The delimitation of the field of semiotics in relation to other sciences is one of the central concerns in the current efforts at constituting a history of semiotics. The terminological history shows that the history of the theory of signs does not coincide with research that has traditionally been associated with the label "semiotics."

1.1 Scope and State of the Art of Semiotic Historiography

What belongs to the history of semiotics? Progress in the historiography of the theory of signs presupposes answers to the delimitation of its field.

1.1.1 ROOTS OR GOLDEN LEGEND?

According to Todorov (1977: 15–31; cf. also Morris 1946: 335), four traditions have contributed to the "birth of Western semiotics," semantics (including the philosophy of language), logic, rhetoric, and hermeneutics. But what about the histories of other subjects of the semiotic field such as linguistics, aesthetics, poetics, nonverbal communication, epistemology, or even biology? Trying to incorporate the histories of all disciplines related or belonging to the semiotic field would have the undesirable effect of making the history of semiotics coextensive with the history of philosophy or even of science in general.

On the other hand, the history of semiotics cannot be reduced to research which has explicitly been placed under the heading of semiotics (cf. Schmitter 1983). There is a much older tradition of implicitly semiotic studies concerned with the nature of signs and communication. It is therefore not a "fictitious genealogy" or "golden legend," as Bouissac claims (1976b: 371–72), to begin the history of semiotics with the ancient theories on the nature of the sign.

1.1.2 DELIMITATION OF THE FIELD

The delimitation of the scope of semiotic historiography has been discussed in papers by Bouissac (1976b), Romeo (1979b), Trabant (1981b), Schmitter (1983), Rey (1984), and

Dutz (1986), and in the contributions by Eco, Dascal, Malmberg, and Sebeok to Borbé, ed. (1984). Different interpretations of the scope of semiotic historiography are often a mirror of different views of the scope of semiotics. Trabant therefore argues that "an 'objective' history of semiotics is not possible, but that there will be different histories of semiotics" (1981b: 41).

Eco (1984a) discusses the outline of three possible directions for the future of semiotic historiography, one following a restricted, the second a moderate, and the third an encyclopedic approach to the history of semiotics. While the first approach restricts its attention to authors who have explicitly dealt with the theory of signs or even with "semiotics," the second also takes into account implicit or even "repressed" theories of semiotics. In this tradition, semioticians have endeavored to broaden the historical background of semiotics by focusing on "neglected figures of semiotics" (cf. Deely 1986b: 267 and Deely, ed. 1986: 219ff.). Eco points out that this approach "involves an impressive re-reading of the whole history of philosophy and maybe of many other disciplines" from a semiotic point of view (1984a; 80). The third, the encyclopedic, approach, according to Eco, "should consider not only theories but also practices" (ibid.). Aspects of this third historiographic dimension of semiotics are discussed in various chapters of this handbook, such as Theology, Theater, Gesture, Sign Language, and Universal Langauge.

The pluralistic position adopted in this handbook presupposes a broad scope, but excludes the more specific histories of its branches, such as logic or the history of linguistics. Other restrictions, besides those imposed by space, are due to the presently still underdeveloped state of the historiography of semiotics. In particular, the semiotic traditions of India (but see Rey 1973: 45–62), China, and Islam are excluded for these reasons.

1.1.3 STATE OF THE ART IN THE HISTORIOGRAPHY OF SEMIOTICS

Outlines of the history of semiotics since its origins are so far available only in the form of articles or as chapters in introductions to our surveys of semiotics. For many topics, chapters from the history of linguistics (cf. Robins 1951; 1967, Verburg 1952, Arens 1969, Sebeok, ed. 1975, Padley 1976, Parret, ed. 1976) and of logic (Bocheński 1956; 1968, Kneale & Kneale 1962) may be consulted. A very informative survey is Kretzmann's encyclopedic article entitled "History of Semantics" (1967). Although restricted to language, it deals with many theories concerning the nature of the sign. A brief but influential panorama of the history of semiotics was outlined by Jakobson (1975). Monographs with chapters on the history of semiotics are Walther (1974: 9–43), Sebeok (1976: 3–26), and Clarke (1987: 12–42). Deely (1982), Eco (1984b), and Kalinowski (1985) deal with various topics of ancient, medieval, and modern semiotics. A reader with annotated texts from the history of semiotics since Plato is Rey (1973 & 1976). A shorter anthology of excerpts from the history of semiotics is included in Calabrese & Mucci (1975: 207–285). The volume on *Classics of Semiotics* (1981) by Krampen et al., eds. deals only with semioticians since Peirce.

Collected papers on the history of semiotics were published by Eschbach & Trabant, eds. (1983), by Dutz & Schmitter, eds. (1985; 1986), in the book series by Sulowski, ed. (1971; 1973; 1976; only this latter volume is in English), and in congress proceedings such as Lange-Seidl, ed. (1981: 62–145), Borbé, ed. (1984), and Deely, ed. (1986). Several issues of *Zeitschrift für Semiotik* deal with topics of semiotic historiography. A book series with reprints and other volumes focusing on the origins of semiotics (and other topics) is Foundations of Semiotics (ed. A. Eschbach, Amsterdam).

1.2 The Terminological History of Semiotics

The history of the term *semiotics* and of its congeners has been investigated by Sebeok (1976: 47–58), Romeo (1977), and Deely (1985; see also Deely et al., eds. 1986: 236–71). In its oldest usage, *semiotics* referred to a branch of medicine. Only later did philosophers and linguists adopt the term to designate a general theory of signs.

1.2.1 SEMIOTICS AND ITS TERMINOLOGICAL RIVALS

The etymology of *semiotics* is related to the Greek words σημεῖον 'sign' and σῆμα 'signal, sign.' The related roots *semio-* (the Latinized transliteration of the Greek form *semeio-*), *sema(t)-* and *seman-* have been the basis for the derivation of various terms in the field of semiotics and semantics. Among the precursors and terminological rivals of *semiotics* are *semasiology* (since 1825; cf. Kronasser 1952: 9, and resumed by Gomperz 1908), *sematology* (Smart 1831; 1837), *semantics* (since Bréal 1897; cf. Read 1948), *sensifics* and *significs* (Welby 1903; 1911), *semology* (ca. 1903 by Noreen; cf. Lotz 1966; later resumed by Joos 1958), *semiology* (since Saussure; cf. Arrivé 1974), *semeiotic* or *semiotic* (Peirce, Morris), and *sematology* (Bühler's [1934] version of semiotics; cf. Camhy 1984). Some of these terms are now restricted to the field of language studies (*linguistic semantics* and *semasiology*). Others are restricted to the theories of meaning proposed by their authors (*sematology*, *significs*, and *semology*), and still others have been forgotten or are out of use (*sensifics* and *semeiotic*). The plural form *semiotics* (instead of *semiotic*) seems to have been adopted in analogy to forms such as *semantics* and *physics*. One of the earliest occurrences of this form is in the volume by Sebeok et al., eds. *Approaches to Semiotics* (1964).

The major rival to the term *semiotics* has been *semiology*. For some time, these two terms used to be identified with the "two traditions" of semiotics (Sebeok 1979: 63). The linguistic tradition from Saussure to Hjelmslev and Barthes was usually defined as *semiology*. The general theory of signs in the tradition of Peirce and Morris was called *semiotics*. Today, *semiotics* is generally accepted as a synonym of *semiology* or as a more general term, which includes semiology as one of its branches (see also 1.2.4).

1.2.2 THE MEDICAL TRADITION

Semiotics is an ancient branch of medical science, even though the term itself may be of a more recent date (cf. Barthes 1972, Romeo 1977, Bär 1988). The physician Galen of Pergamum (139–199), for example, referred to diagnosis as a process of *semeiosis* (σημείω-σις). By the eighteenth century *semiotica*, *semiotique*, or *Semiotik* had been officially adopted as a medical term for the doctrine of symptoms in various European languages (Metzger 1785: 3; Barthes 1972). In Italian, the term *semeiotica* is still used in medical science (cf. Romeo 1977: 48). Broadly, its scope corresponds to *symptomatology* (cf. Bär 1983; 1988), although Michaelis draws certain distinctions between medical semiotics and symptomatology (1940: 3). According to Sprengel, the author of a medical *Handbook of Semiotics*, medical semiotics "can also be called *semiology* ['Semiologie'], but in this case the term refers rather to the theories of signs than to the whole doctrine of it" (1801: 3).

The traditional manuals of medical semiotics (Metzger 1785, Sprengel 1801, Michaelis 1940: 9) subdivide the field of semiotics into three branches, *anamnestics*, the study of the patient's medical history, *diagnostics*, the study of the present symptoms of disease, and *prognostics*, concerning the predictions about future developments of a disease. For points of contact between modern semiotics and medical science, see Typology (4.2.4).

1.2.3 THE PHILOSOPHICAL TRADITION

The first explicit mention of semiotics as a branch of philosophy is in Locke's *Essay concerning Human Understanding* (IV. 21.4), where the "doctrine of signs" is defined as Σημειωτική (1690: 443; see 3.2.3). While Locke only proposed this term without himself using it systematically, the word reappears more frequently in the writings of Johann Heinrich Lambert (1764). The second volume of his *Neues Organon* is entitled *Semiotik* [*Semiotics, or the Doctrine of the Designation of Ideas and Things*] The tradition of explicit semiotic philosophy was continued by Bolzano (1837a–c), who deals with semiotics in his *Theory of Science* (see 4.1.4). From Locke's σημειωτική, Peirce adopted the term *semeiotic*. Sometimes he uses the form *semiotic* or *semeiotics*, rarely *semeotic*, but never *semiotics* (cf. Sebeok 1976: 48). *Semiotic* is the form adopted by Morris.

1.2.4 THE LINGUISTIC TRADITION:
FROM SEMIOLOGY TO SEMIOTICS

In the branch of semiotics which developed from the Saussurean heritage of semiology, the term *semiotics* has now been widely adopted instead of, or as a synonym of, *semiology* (for example, Ducrot & Todorov 1972: 84). However, earlier distinctions between the two concepts have still been retained by some scholars. These distinctions and the history of the gradual replacement of *semiology* by *semiotics* have been outlined by Rey (1976: 285–303), Sebeok (1976: 53–57), and Arrivé (1982a: 127–31).

I. *Semiotics vs. Semiology.* Those who have continued to distinguish between semiotics and semiology have done so either to distinguish different traditions of research or to specify different fields of study.

(1a) Often, *semiotics* is used to refer to the philosophical tradition of the theory of signs since Peirce, while *semiology* refers to the linguistic tradition since Saussure (see 1.2.1 and Sebeok 1976: 55).

(1b) Mounin, however, rejects adopting the term *semiotique* with reference to the general theory of signs even in the American tradition because he believes that *sémiologie* is "a better translation" of *semiotics* (1970a: 57). Others who have retained *semiology* include Toussaint (1978).

(2a) Rossi-Landi, among others, defines semiotics as the "general science of signs," linguistics as "the science of all verbal sign systems," while semiology "deals with post-linguistic (post-verbal) sign systems," such as ritual and ceremonial "languages" or literature (1975a: 103). In a similar tradition (cf. Rey 1976: 295), semiotics is conceived of as the theory of nonlinguistic signs in contrast to semiology, the study of textual structures (see Text Semiotics). Wunderli gives a somewhat different delimitation of the two fields

(1981a: 18). In his view, semiology studies only human sign systems, while semiotics is only concerned with the study of nonhuman and natural signs.

(2b) For Hjelmslev's definition of semiology as a metasemiotic, see Hjelmslev (2.2). His terminology has also been adopted by Greimas (cf. Greimas & Courtés 1979).

II. *Semiology as Semiotics.* In 1969, the initiators of what was to become the International Association of Semiotic Studies, among them Barthes, Benveniste, Greimas, Jakobson, Lévi-Strauss, and Sebeok (cf. Eco 1976: 30, Rey 1976: 301, Arrivé 1982a: 128), decided to adopt *semiotics* as the general term that should henceforth comprise the whole field of research in the traditions of both semiology and general semiotics. This terminological decision has been followed widely in international semiotic research.

2. Ancient, Medieval, and Renaissance Semiotics

Romeo proposes a subdivision of the early history of Western semiotics into three periods, the Graeco-Roman period until Augustine, the Middle Ages until Dante, and the Renaissance, ending with Campanella (1979a: 98). This was the period of the origins and the heyday of logic, rhetoric, poetics, and hermeneutics (cf. Todorov 1977), but the following survey will have to be restricted to the development of semantics and the early theories on the nature of the sign and meaning. The authority of the ancients, especially Aristotle's philosophy, remained a common foundation until the period of humanism and the Renaissance.

2.1 The Ancient Graeco-Roman Period

From the Graeco-Roman period, five theories on the nature of the sign will be discussed in the following sections. Other authors from the period who have been considered to belong to the history of semiotics (Romeo 1979b, Oehler 1982, Deely 1982, Eco 1984a) include Heraclitus (544–483) (pace Schmitter 1983: 8; 1984; 1987: 1–18), Parmenides (540–after 480) (cf. Detel 1982), Gorgias of Leantinos (ca. 480–ca.380) (cf. Rodríguez Andrados 1981), Porphyry (232–ca. 305) (cf. Sebeok, ed. 1986), and Boethius (ca. 480–524) (cf. ibid.), and in medical semiotics, the physicians Hippocrates (460–377) (cf. ibid.) and Galen (ca. 139–199) (cf. ibid.). From the Roman period, Oehler (1982) includes Varro, Cicero, Quintilian, Gellius, and Lucretius.

2.1.1 PLATO (427–347)

Semiotic topics from Plato's writings are discussed in various other chapters of this handbook. For details, see his definition of the sign (q.v. 3.1.3) and of meaning (q.v. 3.1), his phonocentric view of writing (q.v. 5.2.1), his dialogue "On the Correctness of Names" (see Arbitrariness 1.1), and his theory of iconicity in mental images (see Image 2.) and of mimesis in literature (q.v. 2.1.1). The central theses of Plato's semiotics may be summarized as follows (cf. Coseriu 1970: 58–59, De Lacy 1986): (1) Verbal signs, whether natural or conventional, are only incomplete representations of the true nature of things. (2) The study of words reveals nothing about the true nature of things since the realm of ideas is independent of its representation in the form of words. (3) Knowledge mediated by signs is indirect and inferior to immediate knowledge, and truth about things through words, even if words are excellent likenesses, is inferior to knowing the truth itself (cf. Cratylus 439 A, B).

2.1.2 ARISTOTLE (384–322)

Aristotle's ideas on the nature of the sign have been studied in detail by Bocheński, Coseriu (1970: 68–122), Kretzmann (1974), Lieb (1981a), Weidemann (1982), and Kalinowski (1985: 22–31). For other semiotic topics in his writings, see also Rhetoric (2.1.1) and Metaphor (2.2).

In Peri hermeneias (De interpretatione), Aris-

totle gives his definition of the sign (quoted in Sign 3.2 [2]), which may be summarized as follows (cf. Kretzmann 1974: 4): (1) Written marks are symbols of spoken sounds. (2) Spoken sounds are (in the first place) signs and symbols of mental impressions. (3) Mental impressions are likenesses of actual things. (4) While mental events and things are the same for all mankind, speech is not. This definition of the sign contains the roots of a theory both of meaning (in [2]) and of reference (in [3]), but unlike modern semioticians (cf. Hjelmslev), Aristotle believes that the difference in the structures of sign systems is only a matter of the expression-plane, not of the content-plane (since the mental events are the same; see [4]). Aristotle also takes sides in the debate on the arbitrariness and conventionality of the sign. In Peri hermeneias (chap. 2 [16a 19; 26–29]), he argues: "A name is a spoken sound significant by convention. [. . .] I say 'by convention' because no name is a name naturally but only when it has become a symbol."

2.1.3 THE STOICS (CA. 300 B.C.–A.D. 200)

Stoicism began with Zeno of Citium (ca. 336–264) and Chrysippus (ca. 280–206) and lasted until the reign of the Roman emperor Marcus Aurelius (121–180) (cf. Polenz 1948). Much has been written about the Stoic theory of the sign and of meaning (cf. Barwick 1957, Mates 1953, Melazzo 1975, Graeser 1978, Eco 1984b: 29–33). Following Bocheński (1968: 83–84), the main theses of the Stoic theory of signs are: (1) The sign "links together" three components: the material signifier (σημαῖνον), the signified or meaning (σημαινόμενον), and the external object (τυγχάνον), (the definition is quoted in Sign 3.2 [3]). (2) While the signifier and the object were defined as material entities, meaning (also called λεκτόν, 'that which is meant' or 'said') was considered incorporeal. (3) Signs (σημεῖα) were divided into commemorative and indicative (ἐνδεικτικά) signs. The former reveal something else which has previously been observed in conjunction with the sign; the latter indicate something nonevident.

The Stoic theory of the sign was the foundation of Stoic logic. According to Sextus Empiricus (*Adv. math.* II, 245), the sign in Stoic philosophy "is an antecedent proposition in a valid hypothetical major premise, which serves to reveal the consequent." Semiosis, in this view, is a process of syllogistic induction. From the observable signifier, we infer by mediation of the signified in a process of drawing a logical conclusion about what the sign stands for. As to language signs, the Stoics distinguished two aspects of their phonetic representation which anticipate the modern semiotic distinction between unstructured expression-matter and structured expression-form (see Hjelmslev) (Kretzmann 1967: 364):

> The Stoics distinguished vocal sound generally, "which may include mere noise," from the sort that is articulate (ἔναρθρος), that is, capable of being embodied in written symbols (ἐγγράμματος). Articulate sound, in turn, may be nonsignificant—for instance, "blityri"—or significant (σημαντική); but for any articulate sound to be considered a sentence (λόγος) it must be significant *and* a product of someone's reason (Diogenes Laërtius 7.55–57).

2.1.4 THE EPICUREANS (CA.300–0)

Under the influence of Democritus (ca. 460–ca. 370), the school of Epicurus (341–270) defended a materialist epistemology according to which sensations are impressions made on the soul by images of atoms from the surface of physical objects (*eidola*). The Roman poets Horace and Lucretius (99–55) belonged to the Epicurean School, which was influential through the first three centuries B.C. The Epicurean logic and theory of semiosis was also described in a treatise by Philodemus of Gadara (cf. De Lacy & De Lacy, eds. 1941 and Sebeok, ed. 1986: 701–702) of the first century B.C., to which Peirce made several references. See also De Lacy (1938).

The Epicureans defended a dyadic model of the sign, rejecting the Stoic *lekton,* the domain of intensional meaning. The referent of a sign was identified with a sense impression or feeling (cf. Kretzmann 1967: 365). Plutarch (*Adversus Coloten* 1119F) describes the Epicureans as "completely doing away with the category of lekta, leaving only words and objects and claiming that the intermediate things conveyed by the signs simply do not exist."

The Epicureans also rejected the inferential account of semiosis of the Stoics. They objected that the capacity for semiosis is not reserved to those who have studied "logical technicalities" (Sextus Empiricus, *Adv. math.* VII, 269–71), "but often illiterate pilots, and farmers unskilled in logical theorems interpet by signs excellently. [. . . Even] the dog, when he tracks a beast by footprints, is interpreting by signs; but he does not therefore derive an impression of the judgement 'if this is a footprint, a beast is here.' [. . .]Therefore the sign is not a judgement, which is the antecedent in a valid major premiss." Such reflections on zoosemiotics and related speculations on gestural origins of language belong to the most interesting contributions of the Epicureans to the history of semiotics. In *De rerum natura,* Lucretius gives one of the earliest phylogenetic accounts of anthroposemiotics (cf. Mauro 1975: 39). After an outline of the various human and nonhuman, verbal and nonverbal systems of communication, Lucretius concludes that man's verbal language, like animal behavior and the infant's gestures, has its origins not in an intellectual convention but in *natura* and *utilitas.*

2.1.5 AURELIUS AUGUSTINE (354–430)

To some historiographers, St. Augustine still belongs to the period of late antiquity (Coseriu 1970, Simone 1972, Oehler 1982); others see in his work the beginning of the Middle Ages (Chydenius 1960, Kretzmann 1967, Clarke 1987). Many agree with Coseriu, who evaluates Augustine as "the greatest semiotician of antiquity and the real founder of semiotics" (1970: 123). Studies of Augustine's semiotics are Kuypers (1934), Markus (1957), Chydenius (1960), Jackson (1969), Mayer (1969), Simone (1972), Todorov (1977: 13–

33), Ruef (1981), Güttgemanns (1983: 101–170), Eco (1984b), and Clarke (1987: 19–25). See also Sign (1.3.2, 2.1.1) and Typology (1.1.1). The writings in which Augustine develops his theory of signs are *De magistro* (389), *De doctrina christiana* (397), and *Principia dialecticae* (ca. 384).

Augustine accepts the Epicurean view of the sign as a sense datum representing something that is not presently perceivable. However, following the Stoics, Augustine's definition of the sign also makes reference to the interpreter's mind as a third correlate of semiosis (see Sign 2.1.1). In contrast to the theories of his Roman predecessors, Augustine's has a further Christian dimension in his interpretation of the sign: the objects of semiosis are interpreted as indexical signs revealing God's will in earthly creation (cf. Simone 1972: 9 and Theology).

Augustine's definition of the sign also anticipates the medieval *aliquid pro aliquo* formula: "Signum est enim res, praeter speciam quam ingerit sensibus, aluid aliquid ex se faciens in cogitationem venire" (*De doctr. Christ.* 2.1.1; see Sign 2.1.1 for the translation). He distinguishes between *natural* and *conventional* signs (cf. Typology 1.1.1) and specifies that signs and things are not different classes of objects since every material entity can possibly function as a sign for another object (see Sign 1.3.2).

A particularly modern dimension in Augustine's semiotics is his extension of the scope of studies in signs from language to other modes of semiosis. As summarized by Eco et al., "With Augustine, there begins to take shape this '*doctrina*' or 'science' of *signum,* wherein both symptoms and the words of language, mimetic gestures of actors along with the sounds of military trumpets and the chirrups of cicadas, all become species. In essaying such a doctrine, Augustine foresees lines of development of enormous theoretical interest" (1986: 65).

2.2 Medieval Semiotics

Medieval semiotics developed within theology and the trivium of the three liberal arts of grammar, dialectic (logic), and rhetoric. The theology and philosophy of this period is also called *scholasticism* (after the schools [Lat. *schola*] of medieval universities in which they were taught). Major studies of scholastic semiotics have appeared in the context of the history of philosophy (Maritain 1938, Kretzmann et al., eds. 1982, Eco, ed. 1984, Eco and Marmo, eds. 1989), logic (Bocheński 1956, Rijk 1967, Pinborg 1972), and linguistics (Verburg 1952, Saarnio 1959, Pinborg 1967, Bursill-Hall 1971, Parret, ed. 1976, Jakobson 1980: 39–60).

2.2.1 TOPICS OF SCHOLASTIC SEMIOTICS

Major topics of medieval semiotics are the Christian pansemiotic views of the universe (see Theology 1.3) and of textual exegesis (see Hermeneutics 1.2), the *realism-nominalism* dispute, and the doctrines of *suppositions* and of the *modes of signifying*. Further topics in scholastic semiotics are the typology of signs (cf. Eco et al. 1986 or, concerning Bacon's treatise *De Signis,* Howell 1987) and the theory of *representation* (cf. Zimmermann, ed. 1971, Kaczmarek 1986). Apart from these topics of the mainstream schools of medieval philosophy, the Spanish philosopher Raymond Lully (Ramón Lull, 1232–ca. 1316) developed a somewhat esoteric theological semiotics in his *Ars Magna* and *Ars Generalis Ultima* (Lull 1308). Based on an "alphabet" of predicates reflecting God's nature, he proposed a logical calculus and *ars inventiva* which he considered to be a key to the intepretation of the universe (cf. Universal Language 2.1.1). In the more rational seventeenth century, Leibniz was influenced by Lully's ideas in his universal language project (cf. Yates 1954, Bocheński 1956: 318ff.).

2.2.2 REALISM VS. NOMINALISM:
THE PROBLEM OF UNIVERSALS

The Scholastic dispute about the nature of the universals concerns the question of the ontological status and the relationship between the signs for general concepts and their objects of reference. *Universal* was the term used to designate concepts (ideas) of a general nature. While the empirical objects of the world, for example flowers or trees, are always experienced as individual entities, the predicates ascribed to them in the form of words, such as *flower* or *red,* are universals. Thus, whereas the object is particular, the general term designating it is universal. What is, then, the nature of these universals? Do they have any reality outside the system of signs?

Plato maintained that universals were ideas existing independently of particular objects. *Universalia sunt ante res* ('u. exist before the things') was the medieval characterization of this Platonian position. The early Scholastics maintained that universals are in fact real things whose substantial existence could be observed in the plurality of objects (such as flowers or trees). *Universalia sunt in rebus* ('u. are in the things') was the characterization of this position, as a consequence of which it was assumed that every individual thing participates in the universals of its class. William of Champeaux (1070–1120) and Anselm of Canterbury (1033–1109) were among the proponents of this so-called extreme realism.

The nominalists, by contrast, argued that only individuals exist in nature. In their view, the universals do not refer to anything and are only names (*nomina*) or vocal emissions (*flatus vocis*). The motto of this school was *universalia sunt post res* ('u. come after the things'). Roscelin (1050–1125) and later William of Ockham (1285–1349) were proponents of a nominalist theory of universals. Ockham considered universals to be signs without an existence of their own, but standing for individual objects. In his view, real existence had to be individual and could not be universal. On Ockham's nominalist semiotics, see also Panaccio (1985).

A moderate realism, also called *conceptualism,* was accepted as a synthesis between nominalism and realism by Peter Abelard (1079–1142), Albert the Great (1200–1280), and Thomas Aquinas (1225–1274). In the conceptualist view, the universals are also mind-dependent, but it was maintained that the concepts of the mind were formed by real similarities between things of a common form. For the origins of nominalism and realism in scholastic philosophy, see Geyer, ed. (1951), Edwards, ed. (1967). For nominalist and realist models of the sign in other periods of the history of semiotics, see Sign (1.4.2–4).

2.2.3 SUPPOSITION THEORY

The Scholastic theory of supposition was developed in treatises by William of Sherwood (ca. 1200–ca. 1272), Peter of Spain (ca. 1210–1277), Ockham, and Vincent Ferrer (1400) (cf. Arnold 1952, Rijk 1967, Pinborg 1972, Leff 1975, Ducrot 1976, Ebbesen 1983; for a modern interpretation of the theory of supposition, see Geach 1962). The theory of supposition is a contextual theory of meaning and reference. From about 1200, the relation of *supponere pro aliquo* had become a synonym of *stare pro aliquo* (cf. Geyer, ed. 1951: 578 and Sign 2.1), but more specifically, supposition characterizes the mode of meaning of the subject term in a sentence within the context of its predicate. Supposition was thus meaning in context. It was opposed to *signification* (*significatio*), which was the context-independent general meaning of a word (cf. Pinborg 1972: 59, Kaczmarek 1983, and Sign 2.1.1). In the terminology of modern linguistics, *significatio* is the lexical meaning of a word.

Up to ten modes of supposition were distinguished (cf. Arnold 1952: 110ff., Rijk 1967: 589ff.). The most important type of supposition is reference to an empirically existing entity. For example, in "FIDO is an animal," "Fido" suppones for an existing entity. This mode of reference is called *suppositio personalis.* Subtypes include *s. confusa* ("Every DOG is an animal"), *s. determinativa* ("Some DOG is running") and *s. discreta* ("FIDO is running" or "F. is an animal"). Two other main modes of supposition are *suppositio simplex,* where the term stands for a concept or "suppones for" a universal, as in "DOG is a species," and *suppositio materialis,* where reference is made to the word as a sign, such as in "DIO is disyllabic" or "MAN is a noun."

Material supposition corresponds to what is today known as metalanguage. The distinction between object- and metalanguage had earlier been discussed by the Scholastics under the designation of *first* and *second imposition.* Words of the object language, such as *dog, animal,* or *man,* were defined as conventional signs by first imposition ("name giving"). Metalinguistic words, such as *noun, syllable* or *species,* were defined as being the result of a second imposition.

2.2.4 MODIST SEMIOTICS

The theory of the modes of signifying (*modi significandi*) was developed within the *ars grammatica* of the late thirteenth and early fourteenth centuries. Among the Modistae, the grammarians who wrote treatises on the subject, were Martin of Dacia (ca. 1270), Boethius of Dacia (ca. 1270), John of Dacia (ca. 1280), Radulphus Brito (ca. 1300), Siger of Courtrai (ca. 1300), and Thomas of Erfurt (ca. 1310). The tractatus by Thomas of Erfurt was for a long time ascribed to John Duns Scotus. Studies of the Modistae are O'Mahony (1964), Pinborg (1967; 1982; 1984), Bursill-Hall (1971; 1976), and Gabler (1987).

The Modist grammarians were convinced of an essential iconicity between things of the world and the structure of language. Because of this iconic dependence on the nature of things, all languages, according to the Modists, have an underlying universal structure. In Aristotelian terms, Roger Bacon (ca. 1214–1292) declared that "with respect to its *substance,* grammar is one and the same in all languages, although it does vary *accidentally*" (cf. Gabler 1987: 23). The universal grammar developed by the Modists was also called *speculative* (*grammatica speculativa et universalis*). This term, derived from Lat. *speculum* 'mirror,' expresses the assumption of language being an icon of reality.

The Modists distinguish three dimensions of linguistic semiosis, *res* (thing), *intellectus* (understanding), and *vox* (vocal noise) (see also Sign 2.1.1). Three types of modes are associated with these dimensions, *modus essendi, mo-* *dus intelligendi,* and *modus significandi.* The mode of being (*m. essendi*) provides the ontological foundation of semiosis. It characterizes the categorial nature of things (their substance, quality, etc.). These "essential" structures are perceived by the human mind by means of the mode of understanding (*m. intelligendi*). Since, in the Aristotelian tradition, concepts were the same for all men, being the result of external sense impressions, the modes of being were declared to precede the modes of understanding as a cause precedes its effect (cf. Kretzmann 1967: 375). The act of perception and conceptualization is performed by the *active* mode of understanding (*modus intelligendi activus*). The resulting mental entities belong to the *passive* mode of understanding (*m. int. passivus*).

In the third dimension of linguistic semiosis, the thing and the concept are designated by means of words as a result of acts of imposition. The word is composed of a vocal signifier (*vox*) which is associated with a referent (called *significatum*). Only by the association of the phonetic sound with a specific referent does the *vox* become a verbal sign (*dictio*). The semantic functions of this verbal sign are the modes of signifying. By a first imposition, the vocal signifier is connected with a specific referent. This process constitutes a relation called *signification* (*ratio significandi*). Today, *designation* would be the appropriate semiotic term. The resulting word (*dictio*) is arbitrary and language-specific.

By a secondary act of imposition, the word is associated with various modes of signifying which derive from its grammatical form. All grammatical categories or parts of speech are interpreted as having general semantic features which combine with the basic lexical meaning of the word. The semantic relation of these modes is therefore called *consignification* (*ratio consignificandi*). These "consignified" meanings are not arbitrary. They correspond to modes of understanding of the concept and are therefore universal. The modes of signifying are thus a form created by the intellect, which relates the word to the mode of being of the things (cf. Pinborg 1984). The study of these universal categorical dimensions of language forms the core of modist semiotics. Examples of modist views of language as an icon of reality are their interpretations of word classes such as nouns, verbs, or pronouns: "The noun is defined by reference to its 'essential' mode of signifying substances, permanent states or entities. The verb is the part of speech that signifies by the modes of change, becoming, movement of existence. The pronoun signifies substance without reference to any qualities" (Robins 1951: 83).

2.3 Renaissance Semiotics

The period of the Renaissance and humanism is a rather unexplored chapter of the history of semiotics. Many historiographers have claimed that it was not a period of important innovations in the theory of signs (for example, Kretzmann 1967: 375). Most research in the semiotics of this time is part of the historiography of linguistics (cf. Verburg 1952, Percival 1975, Padley 1976). Some studies have appeared in the context of the history of logic and philosophy (Apel 1963, Ashworth 1974; 1985, Kretzmann et al., eds. 1982: 785ff.). On the one hand, it was a period of break with medieval scholasticism, in particular because of the discovery of the historicity and arbitrariness of language and the rejection of universal grammar, for example in the works of Juan Luis Vives (1492–1540) (cf. Coseriu 1970: 161, Brekle 1985: 88–115 with special reference to semiotics, pp. 101ff.), Julius Cesar Scaliger (1484–1588) (cf. Stéfanini 1976), Petrus Ramus (1515–1572), and Franciscus Sanctius Brocensis (ca. 1552–1632) (cf. Percival 1975, Padley 1976). On the other hand, there was a return to Aristotelian semiotics and, particularly in Spain and Portugal, a revival of scholasticism (cf. Kretzmann et al., 1982: 808ff.).

The central figure of semiotic historiography of this period is the Portuguese John Poinsot (1589–1644), who called himself João de São Tomás or Johannes a Sancto Thoma. After earlier studies by Maritain (1938) and Herculano

de Carvalho (1961), Poinsot's *Treatise on Signs* (1632) has appeared in a critical edition (1985) with several supplementary studies by Deely (1974; 1982; 1988). However, there is disagreement about the degree of originality of Poinsot's semiotics. While Deely (1988) evaluates Poinsot as a central or even revolutionary figure in the history of semiotics, other historiographers have interpreted Poinsot's work as standing in the tradition of the Scholastics (Coseriu 1970: 160, Kretzmann et al., eds. 1982: 818ff., Kaczmarek 1986, Ashworth 1988).

Further authors of the Renaissance period whose contributions to semiotics have been studied are Domingo de Soto (1494–1560) (cf. Ashworth 1988), Pedro de Fonseca (1528–1599) (cf. Romeo 1979b, Deely 1982: 52ff.), and Thomas Campanella (1568–1639) (Padley 1976, Romeo 1979a). New discoveries in the semiotic historiography of this period are the works of Clemens Timpler (1563–1624), who was the author of an elaborate typology of signs (cf. Freedman 1986), and of Emanuele Tesauro (1592–1675), whose contributions to semiotics are in the field of the theory of signs and in rhetoric (cf. Speciale 1986).

3. Rationalism and Enlightenment

A new era of interest and research in the nature of signs began in the ages of rationalism and British empiricism. During the seventeenth century, the ancient and medieval traditions of semiotics, including the work of Poinsot, had fallen into oblivion, so that Locke's (1690) postulate of semiotics as a branch of science appeared as an innovation (Coseriu 1970: 160). Only during the period of Enlightenment in France and Germany was this postulate taken up, and an explicit theory of signs began to develop. General outlines of this development are given by Haller (1959), Kretzmann (1967), Rey (1973), Walther (1974: 17–39), and Malmberg (1977: 31–77). Schmidt (1968), Mauro (1969: 29–82), Holenstein

(1978b), and Aarsleff (1982) deal with selected topics. Foucault's (1966a) panorama of the history of the idea of representation since the seventeenth century is in many respects an implicit history of semiotics. Many aspects of the theory of signs have been studied within the framework of the history of linguistics and the philosophy of language (Cassirer 1923:I 1, Coseriu 1972, Parret, ed. 1976). For the seventeenth century in particular, see Formigari (1970), Brekle (1975), and Salmon (1979); for the eighteenth and nineteenth centuries, see Land (1974), Aarsleff (1975), and Gipper & Schmitter (1975).

3.1 The Age of Rationalism

The age of rationalism, with its emphasis on the powers of the human intellect, developed two topics of specifically semiotic relevance, the mentalist account of the sign and the search for a rational universal grammar common to all languages, whose practical alternative was the universal language project.

3.1.1 FROM DESCARTES TO THE UNIVERSAL LANGUAGE PROJECT

René Descartes (1596–1650) was not a semiotic philosopher, but his work contains a number of topics of semiotic relevance (cf. Coseriu 1972: 43–56, Niebel 1984, Joly 1986). Cartesian rationalism is strictly anthropocentric. Descartes maintained that animals are characterized not only by their lack of language, but also by a lack of reason (*raison*). These principles are characteristic of an antievolutionary semiotics which, in consequence, denies the theoretical relevance of zoosemiotics.

Descartes's axiom of *innate ideas,* which presupposes the priority of intellectual knowledge over perceptual experience, and his mind-body dualism are the basis of a theory of meaning which emphasizes *sense* (the concepts) over *reference* (the things). Since thought, in his view, is prior to language, the diversity of languages is only a surface-structural phenomenon. Whereas sounds are variable, ideas are not. The structure of thought and reason is

common to all men (cf. Joly 1986: 184). This philosophy is the foundation of research in semiotic universals and the beginning of the project of a universal language. For this chapter of the history of semiotics, whose central figures are Comenius (1592–1670), Dalgarno (1626–87), Wilkins (1614–72), and Leibniz, see Universal Language (2.).

3.1.2 PORT-ROYAL

Antoine Arnauld (1612–1694), Claude Lancelot (1616–1695), and Pierre Nicole (1625–1695), of the school of Port-Royal, developed an influential rationalist semiotics in the context of their *Grammaire générale et raisonnée* (1660, by Arnauld & Lancelot) and *Logique ou l'art de penser* (1662, by Arnauld & Nicole). For studies of the semiotic aspects of these works, see Brekle (1964), Kretzmann (1967: 378–79), Padley 1976: 210–59), and Swiggers (1981; 1986). The basis of Port-Royal semiotics is a mentalist and dyadic model of the sign. In the definition of Arnauld & Nicole's *Logic* (I, chap. 4 of the editions since 1683), "the sign comprises two ideas—one of the thing that represents, the other of the thing represented—and its nature consists in exciting the second by the first." This semiotic dyad does not consist of a material signifier related to a conceptual meaning, but of two conceptual entities, of which the signifier is an "idea" or "image of the sound" (*Logic* I.1, cf. Swiggers 1986: 125). This characterization clearly anticipates Saussure's definition of the signifier as an "acoustic image."

Port-Royal semiotics distinguishes four main types of sign (*Logic* I.4; cf. Brekle 1964: 110–13 and Swiggers 1981: 276). In modern terminology, these are (1) *indexical natural signs,* which can be either "certain," such as "breathing" as a sign of 'life,' or only probable, such as certain medical symptoms; (2) (indexically or iconically) *motivated symbols,* such as the iconographic symbols of Christianity; (3) *natural icons,* such as mirror images; and (4) arbitrary or motivated *conventional signs* ("signs by institution"), such as the words of a language. Only the latter are the subject of the

Port-Royal grammar. In addition to such typological distinctions, Port-Royal semiotics introduces a number of basic concepts of semantics (cf. Kretzmann 1967: 378–79), including a distinction between *proper* and *accessory signification,* which corresponds to the *denotation-connotation* dichotomy of modern semiotics, and the distinction between *comprehension* and *extension,* which corresponds to the *intension-extension* dichotomy of modern theories of meaning.

The relation of *arbitrariness,* which Port-Royal semiotics considers a characteristic of verbal signs, is specified as a relation between the signifier and the signified and not the referent (cf. Kretzmann 1967: 378, Swiggers 1981: 275). However, arbitrariness is wholly on the side of the signifier. While "it is purely arbitrary to join one idea to one sound rather than to another, the ideas, at least those that are clear and distinct, are not arbitrary" (*Logic* I.1). Thus, arbitrariness is a mere surface structural phenomenon. The sphere of meaning or of rational ideas, by contrast, is subject to universally valid laws of the human mind. It is not affected by what later generations of semioticians were to call *semantic relativity.*

3.1.3 LEIBNIZ

Gottfried Wilhelm Leibniz (1646–1716) is one of the classics in the history of semiotics. His ideas on the theory of signs have been the topic of intensive research (Couturat 1901, Schnelle 1962, Aarsleff 1975, Heinekamp 1976, Dascal 1978, Poser 1979, Burkhardt 1980, Dutz 1985, Widmaier 1986, Dascal 1987). Leibniz extended his interest in signs to a broad scope of semiotic phenomena: "In the number of signs I include words; letters; chemical, astronomical, Chinese and hieroglyphical figures; musical, stenographic, arithmetic and algebraic marks; and all the others we use for things when thinking" (Dascal 1987: 181).

His definition of the sign (of 1672) is in the tradition of the Scholastics: "A *sign* is that which we now perceive and, besides, consider to be connected with something else, by virtue of our or someone else's experience" (ibid.:

31). Semiosis is thus based on the association of perceptions, and the sign is an instrument of human cognition. This broad definition includes natural and conventional signs, but Leibniz's special attention was devoted to the latter. He studied written and other visual signs as *characters* and defined these as visible marks representing concepts: "Characterem voco notam visibilem cogitationes representantem" (Burkhardt 1980: 175). Characters are arbitrary by themselves, but the principles of their connection to rational discourse are not. There is a relation (*proportio sive relatio*) between the structures of rational discourse and the things of the world which is the foundation of truth (*fundamentum veritatis;* see Haller 1959: 124). In Peircean terms, the syntactic structure of signs according to Leibniz is related to reality by a relation of diagrammatic iconicity. The foundation of this semiotic theory is Leibniz's metaphysical principle of *prestabilized harmony* (cf. Poser 1979: 312): the whole world is virtually represented in every individual mind as a *facultas cogitandi.* This implies an indirectly triadic model of the sign. In the first place, the sign represents an idea, but secondly it also stands for things, since ideas (*regio idearum*) "correspond by themselves with their objects" (ibid.: 312).

In the process of reasoning, signs fulfill the function of useful and necessary tools since they serve as an "abbreviation" of the more complex semantic concepts which they represent: "All human reasoning is performed by means of certain signs or characters. Indeed, it is neither possible nor desirable that the things themselves or even the ideas of them be always distinctly observed by the mind. So, for reasons of economy, signs are used for them" (Dascal 1987: 181). For these reasons of rational economy, the sign is a tool "for the attainment of new discoveries." Leibniz developed these general ideas on the nature of the sign more specifically in the three branches of his project of a universal language, which comprises a theory of signs (*ars characteristica*), a *rational calculus,* and an *ars inveniendi* (see Universal Language 2.4).

3.2 British Empiricism and Precursors

Locke, Berkeley, and Hume are the main representatives of British empiricism, but the discovery of natural science as a foundation of an empirically based philosophy begins with Bacon and Hobbes. In contrast to the rationalists' confidence in reason and the method of deduction as the foundation of human knowledge, the empiricists turned to the experimental sciences and with them to the method of induction as their model of philosophical inquiry. Besides Bacon, Hobbes, Locke, and Berkeley, there are two further philosophers of semiotic interest during this period, David Hume (1711–1776) (cf. the article in Sebeok, ed. 1986) and Thomas Reid (1710–1796) (cf. Clarke 1987).

3.2.1 BACON

There are three topics of special semiotic interest in the writings of Francis Bacon (1561–1626) (cf. Funke 1926, Odgen 1934: 9–34, Eberlein 1961, Kretzmann 1967: 375–76, and Brekle 1975: 281–87): (1) skepticism against and criticism of language, (2) the variety of signs besides words, and (3) the discovery of the binary code. According to Bacon, "words are but the current tokens or marks of popular notions of things" (1605: 126). They may lead to correct or to distorted models of understanding. The latter are caused by words that "impose upon us false appearances" (ibid.: 134), and these are the *Idols of the Marketplace*. There are two kinds of such idols, words of nonexistent things ("resulting from a fantastic supposition") and confused or ill-defined words hastily abstracted from the things (*Novum organum* I, 43ff.; cf. Ogden 1934: 22).

Bacon's skepticism against language and his observation that "it is not of necessity that cogitations be expressed by the medium of words" led to an investigation of signs other than spoken or written words (1605: 136–37). He discussed gestural sign language and the real characters of Chinese writing and Egyptian hieroglyphics (cf. Universal Language 2.2.1) and claimed that these latter types of writing

signify "things and notions" by direct semiosis, i.e., without the intervention of words (cf. Kretzmann 1967: 376).

Bacon distinguished between iconic signs ("when the note hath some similitude or congruity with the notion") and arbitrary signs ("ad placitum, having force only by contract or acceptation") (1605: 139). In a comment on the variety of signs and the criteria of semiosis, Bacon seemed to anticipate the Saussurean principle of semiotic value as structural difference: "For whatsoever is capable of sufficient differences, and those perceptible by the sense, is in nature competent to express cogitations" (ibid.: 137). Bacon's interest in the cryptography of his time (see Universal Language 2.1.2) led to his discovery of a binary cipher alphabet (cf. Code 1.2.2, 5.3) very similar to the modern teletype alphabet (cf. Information 2.2). Using the two elements a and b combined into signs of five sign elements, his alphabet begins as follows: A $= a\,a\,a\,a\,a$, B $= a\,a\,a\,a\,b$, C $= a\,a\,a\,b\,a$, D $= a\,a\,a\,b\,b$ (*De augmentis scientiarum* VI. 1).

3.2.2 HOBBES

With Thomas Hobbes (1588–1679), the theory of signs takes an explicitly mentalistic and associationistic direction. (For studies of his semiotics, see Ogden 1934: 35–45, Verburg 1952: 234–53, Formigari 1970: 141–55, and Sebeok, ed. 1986: 315–17). "Names [. . .] are signs of our conceptions, [. . .] they are not signs of the things themselves," is one of Hobbes's dyadic and mentalist definitions of the sign (1655: 2.5). Elsewhere, Hobbes described signs as the relata in the association of an antecedent with a consequent (1640: 17; 1655: 2.2; see Sign 2.2.2). If this relationship is independent of the human will, the sign is *natural*. Otherwise, the sign is "arbitrary," that is, based "upon *agreement*" (1655: 2.2; and *Philos. Rudiments* 15.16). Among the natural signs, Hobbes considered signs of nonverbal communication, which he called signs of *action*. These "do not signify by men's appointment but naturally; even as the effects are signs of their causes" (ibid.).

In Hobbes's account of semiosis, memory and mental association play a central role: "The *succession* of conceptions in the *mind* are caused [. . .] by the succession they *had* one to another when they were produced by the senses" (1640: 5.1). The use of memory requires semiotic tools, which Hobbes called *marks,* that is, "*sensible objects* which a man erecteth voluntarily to himself, to the end to *remember* thereby somewhat past, when the same is objected to his sense again" (ibid.). Hobbes distinguished between marks and signs. Whereas marks are sign vehicles "for our own use" only, signs serve for the purpose of communicating with others. By means of signs, "what one man finds out may be made known to others" (1655: 2.2). Marks of "conceptions," according to Hobbes, are names. "A *name* [. . .] is the *voice* of a man *arbitrary,* imposed for a mark to bring into his mind some conception concerning the thing on which it is imposed" (1640: 5.2). Names given to many things are universal, and Hobbes emphasized that "universals are not in *rerum naturae*" and that *"There is nothing universal* but *names"* (ibid.: 5–6).

3.2.3 LOCKE
The historiography of semiotics has given much attention to the semiotic ideas developed by John Locke (1632–1704) (cf. Zobel 1928, Schmidt 1968, Coseriu 1970: 164–75, Formigari 1970: 173–95, Land 1974, Kelemen 1976, Kretzmann 1976, Aarsleff 1982, Deely 1982, Ashworth 1985, Paetzold 1985). For Locke's early postulate of a doctrine of signs called Σημειωτικὴ, see 1.2.3. For his definitions of ideas as signs of things and words as signs of ideas, see Sign (2.3 [4]) and Meaning (3.2).

In the evaluation of Kretzmann, "no work had a greater influence over the development of semantics during the Enlightenment than did Book III" of Locke's *Essay concerning Human Understanding,* "yet its semantic theories were neither novel in principle nor clearly and thoroughly developed" (1967: 379; cf. 1976). Among Locke's views

adopted from the tradition of semiotics (cf. 2.2.2 and 3.3.2) is his nominalism, which he expressed as follows: "Universality belongs not to things themselves, which are all of them particular in their existence, even those words and ideas which in their signification are general" (1690: 3.3, 11).

Signs, according to Locke, are "great instruments of knowledge," and there are two kinds of them: ideas and words ("articulate sounds") (ibid.: 4.21.4; see Sign 2.3). Locke rejected Descartes's axiom of innate ideas, maintaining that "all ideas come [either] from *sensation,"* which is "about external sensible objects," or from *reflection,* which is "about the internal operations of our minds perceived and reflected on by ourselves" (ibid.: 2.1.2). That class of sign, which Locke called idea, is "whatsoever the mind perceives in itself, or is the immediate object of perception, thought, or understanding" (ibid.: 2.8.8). Words, according to Locke, "stand for nothing but the ideas of him that uses them" (ibid.: 3.2.2; cf. Sign 2.3 [4]). However, Locke admitted a pragmatic exception to this semantic principle, namely, that words are "marks of the ideas in the minds also of other men, with whom they communicate; for else they should talk in vain, and could not be understood" (ibid.: 3.2.4).

Since ideas are signs and words are signs of ideas, Locke thus interpreted words as signs of signs, i.e., *metasigns.* However, Locke's artificial separation of words and the ideas they stand for into two classes of signs led to a semiotic aporia which Kretzmann has called "one of the classic blunders in semantic theory." It was his failure to recognize "that words are themselves ideas and the signification of words is a special case of the connection of ideas" (1976: 332, 347). It was Saussure who expressed the antithesis to Locke's view of the sign in his simile of the word and idea (signifier and signified) being inseparably connected like the front and the back of a sheet of paper.

3.2.4 BERKELEY
The semiotics of George Berkeley (1685–1753) is characterized by an extreme nominal-

ism and an ontological idealism, whose ultimate foundation lies in theology. For studies of semiotic aspects of his philosophy, see Ogden (1934: 50–87), Coseriu (1972: 58–66), Land (1974: 139–48), Pfeifer (1981), and Paetzold (1985). The point of departure of Berkeley's semiotics is his thesis that *matter* is an ontologically meaningless term, whereas sensations or ideas are the only proper subject of philosophical investigation: "The various sensations, or *ideas imprinted on the sense* [. . .] cannot exist otherwise than in a mind perceiving them. [. . .] Their *esse* is *percipi,* nor is it possible they should have any existence out of the minds or thinking things which perceive them" (1710: § 3). The consequence of this principle is a radically dyadic model of the sign. The assumption of a referential object is rejected as being semiotically meaningless. Locke had already admitted that the essence of material substances is for the most part unknowable. Nevertheless, he duplicated the sphere of semiotics by assuming one world of ideas that we perceive and, behind it, another inaccessible world of "external bodies" (cf. Warnock, in Berkeley 1710: 21 [= introduction]). Berkeley went a step further by abandoning altogether the distinction between the objects of cognition and the objects of the external world, or as he called it, the "difference between *things* and *ideas*" (1710: § 87).

Berkeley developed his nominalism in an attack against the doctrine of abstract general ideas which he attributed to Locke (ibid.: §§ 5–10). In Berkeley's view, all ideas are particulars, and universals are only derived from particulars: "A word becomes general by being made the sign, not of an abstract general idea, but of several particular ideas, any one of which it indifferently suggests to the mind" (ibid.: § 11). Against Locke, Berkeley maintained that words do not always stand for ideas. There are other functions of words, such as "the raising of some passion, the exciting to or deterring from an action, [and] the putting the mind in some particular disposition" (ibid.: § 20).

Berkeley's principle of *esse est percipi* ("to be is to be perceived") leads to a reinterpretation of nature in terms of semiosis:

> The connexion of ideas does not imply the relation of *cause* and *effect,* but only a *mark* or *sign* with the *thing signified.* The fire which I see is not the cause of the pain I suffer upon my approaching it, but the mark that forewarns me of it. In like manner the noise that I hear is not the effect of this or that motion [. . .], but the sign thereof. (1710: § 65)

But this pansemiotic view of the world has its ultimate foundation in God, from whom all signs emanate, for "we do at all times in all places perceive manifest tokens of the Divinity—everything we see, hear, feel or anywise perceive by Sense, being a *sign* or *effect* of the power of God" (ibid.: § 148).

3.3 French Enlightenment

Port-Royal semiotics (of 1660; cf. 3.1.2) remained influential in France throughout the Age of Reason. Only after the middle of the eighteenth century did new developments take place in the history of French semiotics. A new interest in the nature of signs was professed by three philosophical movements, the *sensualists,* the *encyclopedians,* and the *idéologues.* Apart from these mainstream developments in the history of semiotics, Alphonse Costadeau (1667–1725) published a *Treatise on Signs* in 1717. This encyclopedic inquiry into the nature of various sign systems from language to music and from gestures to zoosemiotics remained unknown to most historiographers of semiotics until its new edition in 1983.

3.3.1 CONDILLAC

The French version of empiricism became known as sensualism. Its most influential representative was Etienne Bonnot de Condillac (1715–1780). For his contributions to semiotics, see Verburg (1952: 357–67), Kretzmann (1967: 385–86), Coseriu (1972: 223–38), Rey (1973: 154–57), Land (1974), Parret (1975), Tort (1976), Auroux (1979), Aarsleff (1982: 146–224), and Sebeok, ed. (1986: 145–46).

In his *Essai sur l'origine des connaissances humaines,* Condillac expressed his conviction "that the use of signs is the principle that discloses the source of all our ideas" (1746: Intro., last par.). He developed his account of semiosis in a genetic and psychosemiotic framework. Condillac set up a semiogenetic hierarchy of semiotic operations, beginning with lower and extending to higher levels of semiosis in the order of *sensation* (immediate sensual experience), *perception, conscience, attention, reminiscence, imagination, contemplation, memory,* and *reflection* (ibid.: pt. 1, sec. 1–2; cf. Coseriu 1972: 229, Tort 1976: 492). In correlation with these levels of semiosis, Condillac distinguished three categories of signs: *accidental signs* (where "objects are connected to some of our ideas by particular circumstances"), *natural signs* ("or the cries which nature has established for the feelings of joy, fear, pain, etc."), and *signs by institution* ("which we ourselves have chosen and which have only an arbitrary connection with our ideas") (ibid.: pt. 1, sec. 2, chap. 4, § 35). The lowest levels, from sensation to conscience, are only passive modes of semiosis and are not yet associated with any of the three categories of signs. Only the level of reminiscence is the origin of accidental and natural signs. Natural signs are also the signs from which language has originated, but a fully developed language is always founded on arbitrary signs, which presuppose the level of memory. Between natural and arbitrary signs there is also the dividing line between animal and human communication.

Condillac distinguished language proper from a prelinguistic developmental stage of human semiosis which he called the *language of action* (ibid.: pt. 2, sec. 1, chap. 1). "This language of action is the germ of [spoken] language and of all arts that are appropriate to express our ideas" (ibid.: chap. 15, § 163): the art of gestures, dance, speech, declamation, the art of notation, pantomime, music, poetry, eloquence, and writing. Man is born with the semiotic faculties of this language of action. Although Condillac rejected the assumption of innate ideas, he postulated the innateness of the language of action as a necessary prerequisite for the development of language proper, and this development is a gradual transformation of natural and accidental into arbitrary signs.

3.3.2 MAUPERTUIS

The evolution of signs is also the subject of semiotic inquiry in the writings of Pierre Louis Moreau de Maupertuis (1698–1759) (cf. Kretzmann 1967: 384–85, Rey 1973: 146–53, Formigari 1976). His *Essai sur l'origine des connaissances humaines* (1746) contains two arguments of particular relevance to the history of semiotics. The first is a prestructuralist account of the evolution of signs as a development of progressive differentiation of perceptions (anticipating Saussure's account of the sign as a structural difference; cf. Structure 2.1). The second is a holistic account of the genesis of language, according to which language originates in global messages corresponding to whole phrases (such as "I see a tree" and not simply "tree!") and not to elementary, simple words, as Locke and Condillac had maintained.

3.3.3 DIDEROT AND THE ENCYCLOPEDIANS

Denis Diderot (1713–1784) developed his ideas on the nature of the sign in several of his articles for the *Encyclopédie* (of 1751–80), in his *Lettre sur les aveugles* (1749), in his *Lettre sur les sourds et muets* (1751), and in his writings on subjects of poetry, painting, and other topics of aesthetics. For semiotic aspects of Diderot's and other contributions to the *Encyclopédie,* see Auroux (1979); for semiotic aspects of Diderot's aesthetics, see Walther (1974: 25–26), Todorov (1977), Droixhe (1983), and Fischer-Lichte (1983b: 117–30).

One of Diderot's topics was the specific difference between linguistic and nonlinguistic signs. Among other things, Diderot claimed that the language of gestures is not only more expressive but also more logical than verbal language, because in his view the linearity of spoken language leads to a distortion of reality.

The background of this claim for the superiority of nonverbal communication was the eighteenth-century theory of mimesis, whose basis is a general belief in the aesthetic superiority of iconic and natural signs in comparison to arbitrary signs.

3.3.4 THE IDEOLOGUES

Toward the end of the eighteenth century, the philosophical interest in the nature of signs reached a climax in the writings of the so-called idéologues. The major semioticians in this group of scholars, whose program was the "study of the origins of ideas" (cf. Ideology 1.), were Pierre Cabanis (1759–1808), Antoine Louis Claude Destutt de Tracy (1754–1836), and Marie-Joseph Degérando (1772–1842). For studies of the semiotic theories of this group, see Kretzmann (1967: 387–89), Rastier (1972a), Knowlson (1975), Dascal (1983), and Sebeok, ed. (1986: 332–34).

In 1795, the *Institut National* set up a prize for the best essay on the topic of "the influence of signs on the faculty of thought." Among the questions to be answered in this contest were: (1) Do our first ideas depend essentially on signs? and (2) Would the art of thinking be perfect if the art of signs were perfected? The prize-winning essay was Degérando's *Des signes et de l'art de penser*. In his reply, Degérando maintained that signs are not yet needed at the lowest level of semiosis, where attention is sufficient for the act of transforming a sensation into a perception. According to Degérando (1800: vol. 1, 62ff.), sensations as such are not yet signs, but signs are sensations connected with certain functions. A sign is "every sensation that excites in us an idea, by virtue of the association that obtains between them" (cf. Dascal 1983: 178). Examples of sensations fulfilling the function of signs are "the smell of the rose [which] is the sign of the idea of color and of form that the smell excites" or the sight of a mansion that indicates those who inhabit it. Whereas such *prelinguistic signs,* according to Degérando, "excite" ideas in us but attract attention to themselves, *language signs* direct our attention away from themselves to the ideas which they signify (1800: vol. 1, 62ff.). Degérando pointed out that the natural, prelinguistic signs may be non-communicative, so to speak "mute," being based on associations caused by external factors. On such considerations, Degérando developed a typology of signs distinguishing between primitive prelinguistic "first signs," *indicative* signs, *natural* signs, *arbitrary* signs, *analogue* (iconic) signs, and *figurative* signs (ibid.: 64–67).

3.4 German Enlightenment

The philosophy of German enlightenment after Leibniz has its most important representatives in Wolff and Lambert. Herder, concerned mostly with language, literature, and the arts, had a poetic vision of the future of semiotics. In the philosophy of Kant, the theory of signs plays only a marginal role. Other eighteenth-century topics in semiotics were developed in the context of hermeneutics and aesthetics. An early survey of the semiotics of this period is Roeder (1927). For further literature on the semiotics of German enlightenment, see Haller (1959), Coseriu (1972), Walther (1974), and *Zeitschrift für Semiotik* 1.4 (1979).

3.4.1 WOLFF

Christian Wolff (1679–1754) is still a representative of rationalism. In his theoretical interest in the project of an ideal language or *ars characteristica* (cf. Universal Language), Wolff was a direct follower of Leibniz. For his contributions to the theory of signs, see Roeder (1927), Coseriu (1972: 129–39), Arndt (1979), and Ungeheuer (1981).

Wolff developed his theory of signs in his treatise *Vernünfftige Gedancken* (1720: §§ 291–324) and in chapter 3, "De signo," of his *Philosphia prima sive ontologica* (1730: §§ 952–67). According to Wolff (§§ 292 and 952), "a sign is that entity from which the present, the future, or the past existence of another entity can be recognized." On the basis of these three temporal dimensions of semiosis, Wolff (§§ 953–54) distinguished three classes of *natural signs* (§§ 294–95). A *signum demonstrativum* refs to a present *signatum* (smoke to fire, e.g.), a *signum rememorativum* refers to a past *signatum* (wet ground to rain, e.g.), and a *signum prognosticum* refers to a future *signatum* (clouds to rain, e.g.). All these signs are natural (§§ 956–57) and necessary because the reason (*ratio*) of the *significatus* is contained in the very notions of the things (*in ipsius rerum notionibus continetur*).

Natural signs are opposed to *artificial signs* (§§ 958–59), whose "signifying force" depends on arbitrariness. Words, for example, are arbitrary, since "the author of the universe" is called "Gott" in German, "Deus" in Latin, and "Bog" in Polish. Other arbitrary signs are sign boards or folkloristic costumes (§§ 294–96). The relation of these signs to their object is "not necessary because it could be different." Arbitrary signs are either primitive or they are derived from primitive signs (§ 964).

3.4.2 LAMBERT

Johann Heinrich Lambert (1728–1777) was the first philosopher to adopt the title *Semiotik* for an extensive treatise on the theory of signs. For studies of his theory of signs, see Coseriu (1972: 140–49), Brinkmann (1975), Jakobson (1975), Nef (1976), Holenstein (1978b), and Hubig (1979). Lambert developed his *Semiotik* as one of four branches of a general theory of knowledge whose other branches are *dianoiology* (doctrine of the laws of thought), *alethiology* (doctrine of truth), and *phenomenology* (doctrine of appearance). Within this framework, "semiotics, or the doctrine of the designation of thoughts and things, is to investigate how language and other signs influence the cognition of truth and how these signs can be made to serve for this purpose" (Lambert 1764: Preface).

Symbolic cognition, according to Lambert, is an "indispensable tool of thought" (ibid.: § 12). Its advantage is that it permits the renewal of sensations, whereas immediate, and hence nonsemiotic, sensations cannot be repeated at will. The renewal of sensations by means of signs is necessary for clarity in cognition.

Without such renewal, those notions remain necessarily obscure (§§ 6–11). The signs available in such processes of cognition are of four kinds (§§ 47–51): *natural* signs, *arbitrary* signs, "mere *imitations*," or (iconic) *representations,* which are characterized by various "degrees of similarity" (cf. Iconicity). "In our languages, the arbitrary, the natural, and the necessary are blended" (§ 71).

Lambert investigated no fewer than nineteen sign systems, from musical notes, gestures, and hieroglyphics to chemical, astrological, heraldic, social, and natural signs, with respect to their arbitrariness, motivation, semiotic "necessity," systematicity, and reliability (§§ 25–48; cf. Nef 1976: 173). These various sign systems evince different degrees of approximation to the reality of things. The highest degree of approximation can be attained by means of *scientific* signs. Such signs not only represent concepts, but indicate relations in a way that "the theory of things and the theory of signs become interchangeable" (§§ 23–24). The background of this view of iconicity in scientific sign systems is Leibniz's ideal of a universal alphabet isomorphic with the facts of nature (see Universal Language 2.4.1). In his pursuit of this ideal, Lambert postulated that scientific signs should be based on a semiotic theory which replaces arbitrariness in signs, and that those signs are more perfect which embody a mark of their own meaning within themselves (§ 58). Lambert postulated similar principles for the project of a universal grammar (§ 71). The task of this project should be the investigation of "the natural and necessary in language," whereas "the arbitrary should be partly abolished, partly placed in closer connection with the natural and necessary."

3.4.3 HERDER

Johann Gottfried Herder (1744–1803) was primarily a philosopher of language (cf. Schmidt 1968: 36–65), poetics, and aesthetics. According to Herder, the cognitive capacity of man has access only "to the *exterior* marks of things" and can designate only these by means of words. There is "no organ for the sensation and expression of the *interior* existence of individual things." Language therefore "does not express things, but only names," and "our poor reason is but a signifying reckoner" [*bezeichnende Rechnerin*], calculating with "sounds and ciphers" (1784: 358–59). Herder briefly discussed Lambert's philosophical project of a *"semiotics a priori"* and defended it against critics who deplored the necessary lack of poeticalness in an ideal philosophical language (1768: 91). Herder's own view on the future of semiotics is that

> there is a symbolism common to all men—a great treasury in which the knowledge is stored that belongs to all mankind. The true way of speaking, which, however, I do not know yet, has the key to this dark chamber. When this key is available, it will open the chamber, bring light into it, and show us its treasures. This would be the semiotics that we can now find only in the registers of our philosophical encyclopedias: a decipherment of the human soul from its language. (ibid.: 13)

3.4.4 KANT

The place of Immanuel Kant (1724–1804) in the history of semiotics remains to be determined. In the context of semantics and the semiotics of language, Mauro talks about Kant's "great silence" (1969: 62–69). In his *Critique of Pure Reason* (1781), Kant postulated twelve basic conceptual categories of human thought as being our *a priori* tools for making sense of the world. Whereas these categories—among them are quantity, quality, and relation—have no significance apart from their application in perception, they nevertheless exist independently of our experience. Ricœur interprets this theory of *a priori* judgments, which do not derive from acts of semiosis, as a "powerful model where meaning is not derived from the sign" (1975b: 882). Other historiographers of semiotics believe that Kant's writings contain many topics of semiotic relevance (Rey 1973: 175, Walther 1974: 30–31, Oehler, ed. 1984: 335–59, Sebeok, ed. 1986: 415–17). Haller discusses Kant's remarks on the human *facultas signatrix* (in a passage of Kant's *Anthropology* of 1789), where the sign is defined as a

"custodian" (*custos*) that merely accompanies the concept, only in order "to reproduce it occasionally" (1959: 133).

It was Kant who established the basic semiotic distinction between *analytic* and *synthetic judgments*. In analytic judgments, the predicate is already semantically included in the meaning of the subject. (Example: "All triangles have three angles.") Thus, analytic judgments cannot provide new information about the subject. In synthetic judgments, by contrast, the predicate adds new information to the subject. (Example: "All bodies are heavy.")

Another topic of semiotic interest is Kant's theory of "symbolic cognition," which he develops in § 59 of his *Critique of Judgement* (1790). Kant explains that "the reality of our concepts" can be demonstrated only by *Anschauungen* (perceptions). In the case of "empirical concepts," these *Anschauungen* are *examples*. The a priori concepts of pure reason, on the other hand, are represented either directly by means of *schemata* or indirectly by means of *symbols*. The former represent by immediate demonstration, the latter by means of an analogy. Elsewhere (in his *Critique of Pure Reason* I, sec. 1, bk. 2, pt. 1), Kant draws a further distinction between the *schema,* which is a category of pure reason, and the *image* (*Bild*), which is a category of perception, a kind of perceptual icon (cf. Walther 1974: 30–31).

3.4.5 MINOR FIGURES OF EIGHTEENTH-CENTURY GERMAN SEMIOTICS

Several minor figures in eighteenth-century German philosophy have become known for their contributions to the theory of signs. Roeder (1927), Verburg (1952), Haller (1959), Walther (1974), and Eschbach (1986) have studied contributions by authors such as Hermann Samuel Reimarus (1694–1768), Johann Andreas Segner (1704–1777), the Wolffian Georg Bernhard Bilfinger (1693–1750), Hegel's teacher Gottfried Ploucquet (1716–1790), the mathematician and logician Leonard Euler (1707–1783), the theological pansemiotician Johann Georg Hamann (1730–1788), Georg Jonathan Holland (1742–1784), and Salomon

Maimon (1753–1800). On the whole, however, there was a shift of interest after Lambert from the general theory of signs to other topics of philosophy or to the more specific fields of semiotic inquiry, in particular to the field of aesthetics and hermeneutics. Another special topic of semiotic investigation was the origin of language. Participants in a debate on this topic were Johann Peter Süßmilch (1707–1767), Dietrich Tiedemann (1748–1803), and Herder.

3.4.6 SEMIOTIC HERMENEUTICS

The theory of signs played an important role during the rise of hermeneutics and aesthetics in this century. In hermeneutics, Georg Friedrich Meier (1718–1777) wrote an *Essay on the General Art of Interpretation* (Meier 1756) (cf. Szondi 1975: 98–134). It begins with an investigation of the nature of signs in general (§§ 7–34). A sign, according to Meier, is "a means by which the reality of another thing may be recognized" (§ 7). It is "the ground of cognition [*Erkenntnisgrund*] of the thing designated." Meier then continues with the investigation of *natural* signs (§§ 35–83) and *arbitrary* signs (§§ 84–102), before turning to the principles of the interpretation of discourse (§§ 103–248). Before Meier, Johann Martin Chladenius (1710–1759) had already written a major work in hermeneutics in 1742 (cf. Szondi 1975: 27–97, Fischer-Lichte 1980), but in contradistinction to his precursor, Meier placed special emphasis on the role of natural signs in interpretation. His pansemiotic view of the world may be considered a link between medieval and Romantic hermeneutics. Meier accounts for it as follows: "In this world, because it is the best, there is the greatest general signifying coherence that is possible in the world. Consequently, any real part in this world can be immediate or mediate, a distant or proximate natural sign of any other real part of the world" (§ 35). Ultimately, Meier's theory of natural signs is based on the conviction that "any natural sign is an effect of God, and with respect to God an arbitrary sign, and thus a consequence of the wisest choice of the best will" (§ 38).

3.4.7 SEMIOTIC AESTHETICS

The rise of aesthetics in German enlightenment is closely associated with the works of Alexander Baumgarten (1714–1762), Gotthold Ephraim Lessing (1729–1781), and Moses Mendelssohn (1729–1786). For the semiotic foundations of the theories of these authors, see Aesthetics (1.1) and Literature (2.1.1) (see also Todorov 1977). On Lessing's semiotics, see further Bayer (1975) and Hardenberg (1979); on Mendelssohn, see Franke (1979). A lesser-known *Ästhetik* on semiotic foundations was published in 1785 by Philip Gäng (cf. Eschbach 1980: 45). A further important contribution to the semiotic aesthetics of the time is the work of Johann Jakob Engel (1741–1802). For his *Ideen zu einer Mimik* (1785) in the context of the semiotics of theater, see Fischer-Lichte (1983b: 156–76). This work is also a milestone in the history of the semiotics of nonverbal communication.

The predominant topic of the aestheticians of this period was the iconicity of the arts. The principle of imitation in painting was considered to be the paradigm of this aesthetic iconicity. As to poetry, the aestheticians sought explanations to reconcile the aesthetic ideal of iconicity with the noniconic arbitrariness and linearity of the language sign. (For Lessing's solution, see Literature 2.1.1) A precursor to this idea of iconicity in the arts is Vico. Besides the theory of aesthetic iconicity, the eighteenth century saw the rise of a quite different account of aestheticity, namely, the theory of the autotelic nature of the aesthetic sign. It was expressed in Kant's formula of "disinterested pleasure" (see Aesthetics 3.1.) and led to the aesthetics of "art for art's sake," of which Jakobson's poetic function (see Function 3.2) is a variant.

With respect to poetry, a third account of the semiotic nature of the aesthetic sign was proposed in this epoch by Herder (cf. 3.4.3). Herder rejects the assumption of the autotelic nature of the poetic sign when he claims that in poetry "the natural in signs, such as letters, sound, or melody, contributes little or nothing to the effect of poetry" (1769: 136). Herder, by contrast, locates the essence of poetry in its semantic dimensions (Jakobson's referential function). In poetry, "no sign has to be perceived in itself. Only its signification [Sinn] is important. The soul does not have to perceive the *vehicle* of force, [namely] the words, but force itself, [which is in its] signification" (ibid.: 137).

3.4.8 EXCURSUS ON VICO

In the context of eighteenth-century hermeneutics and aesthetics, an excursus on the Neapolitan Giambattista Vico (1668–1744) may be permitted. He certainly does not belong to the history of German thought, but in his own country as well as in all of Europe, Vico remained a rather isolated thinker until his rediscovery by Croce (cf. Mauro 1969: 54) and Cassirer. On Vico's place in the history of linguistics and semiotics, see Apel (1963), Mauro (1969), Aarsleff (1975: 427–30), Hawkes (1977), Burke (1985), and Sebeok, ed. (1986). According to Hawkes (1977: 11–15, 160), Vico's *New Science* (1725) is a direct precursor of Piaget's and Lévi-Strauss's structuralism and of semiotics in general. Whether these and similar evaluations of Vico's originality are justified or not (cf. Aarsleff 1975: 427–30, Burke 1985), there are certainly elements in his evolutionary and non-Cartesian approach to the science of man that point to later developments in semiotics.

Poetry, myth, metaphor, language, and the evolution of signs and humanity are the topics of semiotic relevance in Vico's work. Vico believed in an "ideal eternal history" during which mankind has gone through three phases of development called the divine age, the heroic age, and the human age. These phases constitute cycles which may result in phases of return (*recorso*) to earlier stages of development. During the divine age, men "thought everything was a god or was made or done by a god" (Vico 1725 § 922). It was an age of ritual semiosis with "mute religious acts or divine ceremonies" (§ 929). Before developing articulate speech, men communicated by means of divine hieroglyphics (§ 933) or "expressed themselves by means of gestures or physical objects which had natural relations with the ideas" (§ 431). Spoken language was developed from onomatopoeia and interjections (§§ 447–48). It was "a language with natural significations" (§ 431).

The dominant mode of communication during the heroic age was by means of visual emblems, coats of arms, ensigns, and other symbols of ownership (§§ 484–87). Abstract ideas were expressed in the anthropomorphic form of mythical heroes. The meaning of 'valor,' for example, was expressed in the form of the mythical hero Achilles (§ 934). Both ages were a period of poetic wisdom. The peoples of these ages were genuine poets. Poetry, metaphor, and myth are thus archaic modes of thought.

The third age, the age of men, is the age of reason and of civilization. Signs are now arbitrary, literal, and abstract at the price of the decline of poetry and imagination. It would be wrong, however, to assume that only this rational age has access to truth. On the contrary, Vico postulated that the ancient mythologies are not mere fictions or even distortions of reality but early poetic expressions of human wisdom (§ 352). Therefore, "it follows that the first science to be learned should be mythology or the interpretation of fables; for [. . .] all the histories of the gentiles have their beginnings in fables" (§ 51).

4. From the Nineteenth Century to Modern Semiotics

This period in the history of semiotics can be dealt with more briefly because the major figures and developments in modern semiotics since Peirce and Saussure are discussed in chapters of their own.

4.1 Nineteenth-Century Semiotics

The nineteenth century saw the rise of modern theories of meaning, sense, and reference of linguistic semantics and the beginning of the scientific inquiry into language. However, the major developments in linguistics in the narrower sense have to be excluded from this survey focusing on general semiotics (cf. 1.). For the dominant figure of the later part of this century, see Peirce.

4.1.1 THE ROMANTICS

The period of romanticism (between 1790 and 1830), in particular the writings of Friedrich Wilhelm Schelling (1775–1854), Novalis (=Friedrich von Hardenberg, 1772–1801), and Friedrich Daniel Ernst Schleiermacher (1768–1834; cf. Hermeneutics 2.2.1), is a neglected chapter of the history of semiotics. A survey from the point of view of linguistics is Gipper & Schmitter (1975). From the point of view of the general theory of signs, the interpretation of the concepts of symbol, image, and sign in this period is of special interest (see also Fiesel 1927). Oehler (1981b) studies Fichte's idealist definition of the image (*Bild*), which is a key concept in the romantic interpretation of the relation between the individual and reality. According to Fichte, human cognition has an iconic nature, since "all knowledge is only representation (*Abbildung*) and requires something corresponding to the image. [. . .] A system of knowledge is necessarily a system of mere images, without any reality, meaning, and purpose" (quoted in Oehler 1981b: 78).

A climax of romantic semiotics is Novalis's pansemiotic view of nature (quotes from Haller 1959: 136). The "theory of signs," according to Novalis, is the "main subject of a true philosophy." Adopting the medieval doctrine of signatures, Novalis maintains that "the universe speaks" and that "all things are mutually symptoms of each other." However, between the symbol and the symbolized there is a dialectics of contrast since "the sign and the signified belong to different spheres in mutual determination."

4.1.2 HEGEL

The work of Georg Wilhelm Friedrich Hegel (1770–1831), although not a primarily semi-otic one, contains a number of topics of semiotic interest (cf. Haller 1959, Coseriu 1970: 188–89, Cook 1973, Walther 1974: 32–33, Malmberg 1977: 66–68, Gutterer 1983, Steinfeld 1984) and of influence to later developments in semiotics (cf. Sebeok, ed. 1986: 300–301). Hegel defined the sign (*Zeichen*) as "any immediate perception (*Anschauung*) representing a content quite different from the one it has by itself" (1830: § 458). In contrast to a perception whose "matter is immediately given (such as the color of a cockade)," the perception in the case of a sign "is not valued positively and by itself, but as representing *something else.*" By this difference between the signifier and the signified, the sign is distinguished from the symbol. The symbol is "a perception which, by its own nature, is more or less the content that it expresses as a symbol. In the sign, by contrast, the perceptual content proper and the content of which it is a sign are unrelated. With *signs,* the intelligence exhibits a freer arbitrariness and control in the use of perception than with symbols."

In his reflections on the semiotic foundations of aesthetics (1817: I, 25, 51–52 = *Lect. on Aesth.* I, introd. 2.1 and 3.2.d), Hegel defined art as a phenomenon whose essence is neither in the perception of an immediately given signifier, nor in the awareness of the signifier-signified difference which characterizes signs: "In our consideration of a work of art we begin with that which is directly presented to us, and after seeing it we proceed to inquire what its significance or content is [. . .] We assume that there is a [. . .] significance behind it, in virtue of which the external appearance is made alive with mind or spirit." Art, according to Hegel, is thus not an autonomous sign, nor does the essence of art lie in its semantic dimension alone. Its semiotic status is situated between these two semiotic dimensions: "The sensuous presence in the work of art is transmuted to mere semblance or *show,* and the work of art occupies a midway ground, with the directly perceived objective world on one side and the ideality of pure thought on the other."

4.1.3 HUMBOLDT

Wilhelm von Humboldt (1767–1835) was a pioneer in the science of language (cf. Arens 1969, Coseriu 1970: 184–88, Gipper & Schmitter 1975: 532–68, Conte 1976). Among his seminal contributions to the history of linguistics, there are five of special relevance to the semiotics of language: (1) his definition of language as a dynamic process and activity (*energeia*), not as a static, a "dead" product (*ergon*), (2–3) his doctrines of the differences between the *inner forms* of individual languages and of language as the "formative organ of thought" (cf. Schmidt 1968: 66–79), which are precursors of the principle of *linguistic relativity* (cf. Brown 1967), (4) his distinction between *form* and *stuff* in language, which is the origin of Hjelmslev's *form-substance* dichotomy (Coseriu 1975: 157ff.), and (5) his doctrine of the genetic primacy of the text in relation to its elements, according to which "the words issued from the totality of discourse" (cf. Kretzmann 1967: 392).

Whereas Humboldt's place in the history of linguistics is well established, his contributions to the general theory of signs have only more recently been investigated by historiographers of semiotics. In this context, Trabant (1983; 1986) developed the thesis of Humboldt's *antisemiotic* approach to language, because Humboldt, in his latter writings, defined words as *not* belonging to the class of signs. The basis of this definition was Humboldt's thesis of the inseparability of language and thought, of the signifier (word) and the signified (concept). In this respect, words are different from signs, since signs, according to Humboldt, are tools for referring to entities existing independently of the signifier (cf. Trabant 1986: 72–74). But Humboldt also developed ideas on language which are semiotic in a broader sense, particularly when he defined language as being both iconic and arbitrary. In view of this twofold characterization of language as being sign and transcending the nature of signs, Schmitter (1985; 1986; 1987) concludes that Humboldt's approach to language and the arts is based on a *transsemiotic* model.

4.1.4 BOLZANO

Bernard Bolzano (1781–1848) was the first philosopher after Lambert to resume the tradition of explicitly semiotic research. Bolzano (1837a; b) developed a general "doctrine of signs" (*Zeichenlehre*), which includes a branch of applied studies in *Semiotik,* mainly in the third and fourth volumes of his *Theory of Science (Wissenschaftstheorie* §§ 637–98, but also §§ 285ff. and §§ 334–45, the latter included in Bolzano 1837a; Bolzano 1837c is only a partial English translation of the original German text). For short assessments of Bolzano's place in the history of semiotics, see Haller (1959: 139–40), Walther (1974: 37–39 and her introduction to Bolzano 1937a), Jakobson (1975: 5–6), and Sebeok, ed. (1986: 86–88).

Bolzano emphasized the syntactic dimension of semiosis when he considered it "a characteristic of our minds [. . .] that ideas once associated will mutually revive each other" (1837c: § 285, p. 308). On this basis, Bolzano defined the sign according to an additional pragmatic criterion as "an object we use [. . .] with the intention of reviving an idea associated with it in a thinking being" (ibid.). Bolzano further distinguished between the *meaning* (*Bedeutung*), which the sign has in general, and its *sense* or *significance* (*Sinn*), which it has in the partiular circumstances of its use.

The pragmatic dimension of semiosis is not a prerequisite in Bolzano's ontology of signs (1837b: 77), since he believed in signs as an objective category (*Zeichen an sich*) so that misinterpreted or even unnoticed signs remain still signs. Nevertheless, the pragmatic topics of the "perfection or utility of signs" were central to his investigation, and Bolzano enumerated nine advantages of using signs for the discovery of truth and thirteen rules for the use and the invention of signs (§§ 334 & 344).

Bolzano defined "the set of all signs conventional to a man" as "that man's *language*" (1837c: 309). As such he discussed *visual* and *auditory* signs, gestural and verbal signs. *Universally applicable* signs are "used by all men," in contrast to *particular* signs, which are used by only few. Signs used for reasons "that lie in human nature" are *natural* signs, in contrast to *accidental* signs, which do not apply universally. An accidental sign is *arbitrary* when object and idea are associated by intentionality (*Willensentschluß*). Signs are *expressions* when they are exterior objects where "the thing signifies something internal to us." In addition to these semantic and pragmatic distinctions, Bolzano (§ 285) furthermore classified signs according to syntactic (single vs. composite signs) and semantic (unisemic vs. polysemic, proper vs. figurative, metonymical vs. metaphorical signs) criteria.

4.1.5 ADDENDA TO NINETEENTH-CENTURY SEMIOTICS

Further nineteenth-century authors of relevance to the historiography of semiotics can be mentioned only briefly. Eschbach (1978) has done much for the rediscovery of Benjamin Humphrey Smart (1786–1872), the author of a theory of signs and a semiotic logic, rhetoric, and grammar, which he called *sematology* (Smart 1831; 1837). Walther (1974) includes Karl Christian Friedrich Krause (1781–1832), author of a metaphysical theory of signs and language, and J. L. Boeckmann, an early writer on the theory of telegraphic codes, in her history of semiotics.

In his history of semantics, Kretzmann (1967) discusses further semiotically relevant philosophers and logicians of the nineteenth century, such as Jeremy Bentham (1748–1832), a follower of the idéologues in the theory of language, Alexander Bryan Johnson (1786–1867), the earliest American philosopher of language, the logicians John Stuart Mill (1806–1873) and Gottlob Frege (cf. Meaning 1.1.2), the language critic Fritz Mauthner (1849–1923), and Husserl's teacher Franz Brentano (1838–1917) and his other students of meaning, Anton Marty (1847–1914) and Alexius Meinong (1853–1920) (for Brentano and Meinong see also Sebeok, ed. 1986). An addition to this field of semioticians of language is the Polish philosopher Joseph Maria Hoëne-Wronski (1778–

1853), whom Jakobson (1975) includes in his brief history of semiotics. Other philosophers of this century who have been studied for their contributions to the theory of signs are the positivist and evolutionary sociologist Auguste Comte (1789–1857) (cf. Rey 1971), the semiotic epistemologist Oswald Külpe (1862–1915) (cf. Henckmann 1985), and Ernst Schröder (1841–1902), author of a treatise on *The Sign* (1890).

Among the linguists of the century, William Dwight Whitney (1827–1894) and Michel Bréal, the founder of semantics, have been studied as figures in the history of semiotics (cf. Bailey 1978, Aarsleff 1982: 382–98, Sebeok, ed. 1986). From the point of view of applied semiotics, the work of Rud. Kleinpaul (1845–1918) on visual and nonverbal signs in various fields of culture and society deserves special mention (Kleinpaul 1888, cf. Sebeok 1976). Andrea de Iorio (1769–1851), Charles R. Darwin (1809–1882), Garrick Mallery (1831–1894), and Wilhelm Wundt (1832–1920) laid empirical and theoretical foundations for the study of gestures, sign languages, and ethnosemiotics (cf. Darwin 1872, Mallery 1881; 1893, Wundt 1900, Sebeok, ed. 1986).

A nineteenth-century student of meaning whose writings and influence in semiotics began in the early twentieth century is Victoria Lady Welby (1837–1912). Today, Lady Welby's major works, *What Is Meaning?* (1903), and *Significs and Language* (1911), are less well known than her correspondence with Peirce. In her writings, she postulates a new science of meaning and communication under the name of *significs,* "the study of the nature of significance in all its forms and relations" (1911: vii). Her influence extended from Ogden & Richards (1923) to the philosopher and sociologist Ferdinand Tönnies (1855–1936) and culminated and survived in the so-called signific movement in the Netherlands until the mid-twentieth century. For the rediscovery of Lady Welby's significs, see Eschbach's introduction to the reprint of Welby (1903), and Schmitz (1985).

4.2 Twentieth-Century Semiotics

Since the major authors and developments in modern semiotics are discussed in chapters of their own, the purpose of this section is only to provide additions and to give further bibliographical references which might be of interest to the future elaboration of a more complete history of modern semiotics.

4.2.1 HUSSERL AND PHENOMENOLOGICAL SEMIOTICS

Edmund Husserl (1859–1938) inaugurates twentieth-century semiotics with his phenomenological theory of signs and meaning developed in the second volume of his *Philosophical Investigations* (Husserl 1900–1901). His earlier paper, "On the Logic of Signs (Semiotics)," was not published until 1970 (Husserl 1890). For aspects of Husserl's semiotics, see Meaning (3.1.3), Typology (1.2.1), Gillan (1982), Klein (1983), and Descombes (1983: 49ff.). Holenstein (1978b: 53ff.), Kalinowski (1985), and Sebeok, ed. (1986: 324–27) give surveys of Husserl's contributions to semiotics. Holenstein (1974: 82; 1975) shows that Jakobson, in his search for linguistic universals and distinctive features of phonology, was influenced by Husserl's theory of eidetic abstraction, which aims at uncovering the invariant traits of an object or a meaning. For Husserl's influence on Prague School structuralism and Mukařovský's theory of aesthetic autonomy, see Chvatík (1984).

Phenomenological semiotics rejects the empiricist and pansemiotic assumption that sensory data are the foundation of cognition and semiosis. Husserl, instead, postulated a semiotic threshold that begins above a level of presemiotic intuition of the phenomena (1913: 99). This threshold lies between the spheres of immediate perception and symbolic conception (*Vorstellung*). At the level of perception, an object is given in its immediate appearance. Although perceptual cognition is based on sense impressions, it occurs without the mediation of signs. At this level, the essence of things (*eidos*) can be grasped only by phenomenological intuition (*Wesensschau*). Above the semiotic threshold, by contrast, a phenomenon is no longer perceived "in itself," but "with the awareness (*Bewuβtsein*) that it represents something else or indicates it signitively" (ibid.). The distinction between the semiotic and the nonsemiotic world (cf. Sign 1.3) is thus a distinction between the immediate awareness of the phenomena and the awareness of the "otherness" of the perceived object, which implies the cognition of a difference between the signifier and the signified.

Later approaches to phenomenological semiotics have been developed and studied in the works of Martin Heidegger (1889–1976) (cf. Apel 1976, Rey 1976: 271–83, Emanuele 1982, Lanigan 1972, Sebeok, ed. 1986: 301–303, and the poststructuralism of Derrida), Alfred Schütz (1899–1959) (cf. Bentele & Bystrina 1978: 64–74), and Maurice Merleau-Ponty (1908–1961) (cf. Lanigan 1972; 1977 and Malmberg 1977: 218–24). See also the special issues of *Semiotica* (41 [1981]) on semiotics and phenomenology.

4.2.2 CASSIRER'S PHILOSOPHY OF SYMBOLIC FORMS

The *Philosophy of Symbolic Forms* by Ernst Cassirer (1874–1945), in spite of its early propagation by Susanne Langer (1942), has only recently been rediscovered by historiographers of semiotics (cf. Malmberg 1977: 146–48, George 1978, Steiner 1978, Krois 1984a; b, Göller 1986, Ranea 1986, Sebeok, ed. 1986, Roggenhofer 1987, Sign 2.3 [10], Typology 1.2.2, and Cassirer 1922–38; 1923–29; 1935–45; 1944). Whereas Morris found Cassirer's work "more suggestive than scientific" (1946; 229) and Steiner criticizes his "imprecision of discourse and toleration of quasi-mystical notions" (1978: 103), Ducrot & Todorov evaluate Cassirer's work as one of the four "major sources of modern semiotics" (1972: 87).

Cassirer advocated a pansemiotic epistemology. Man is essentially an *animal symbolicum* No cognition of a reality beyond the one of symbols is possible. According to Cassirer, the "metaphysical dualism" between the worlds of the senses and of the spirit is bridged by means of symbols, since "the pure *function* of the spirit itself must seek its concrete fulfilment in the sensory world" (1923: 87). Like Saussure, Cassirer considered the sign to be an indivisible unity of the sensory signifier and the intellectual signified: "The sign is no mere accidental cloak of the idea, but its necessary and essential organ. [. . .] The conceptual definition of a content goes hand in hand with its stabilization in some characteristic sign. Consequently all truly strict and exact thought is sustained by the *symbolics* and *semiotics* on which it is based" (ibid.: 86).

The world of symbolic forms, which comprises everything that has meaning (cf. Sign 2.3 [10]), is reflected in language, myth, art, religion, science, and history. Each of these domains is based on symbolic laws of its own, which are essentially independent of nature. Symbolic forms therefore do not imitate, but *create* the reality of man: "Myth and art, language and society are in this sense configurations *towards* being: they are not simple copies of an existing reality" (Cassirer 1923: 107). The "thing in itself" (*Ding an sich*) is inaccessible, according to Cassirer's dyadic view of the sign (q.v. 2.3 [10]).

Cassirer (1929) distinguished three modes or functions of perception which correspond to three stages of the evolution of human semiosis. The first is the function of *expression* (*Ausdruck*). It is a semiotic sphere of "immediacy and mere presence," where the symbolic signifier and signified are not yet sufficiently differentiated. The world of myth is dominated by this function (cf. Magic and 3.4.8). The second is the function of *representation* (*Darstellung*). Here, a distinction between signifier and signified begins to emerge. This function is characteristic of ordinary language. The third is the function of *signification* (*Bedeutung*). This mode of perception, which is typical of scientific symbolism, allows a complete abstraction of the perceptual signifier and the conceptual signified. In language itself, Cassirer distinguished three similar phases in the evolution from predominantly sensual to more abstract modes of representation. He defined them as *mimetic,* *analogical,* and *symbolic expression* (1923: 186ff.).

4.2.3 OTHER CLASSICS OF TWENTIETH-CENTURY SEMIOTICS

Krampen et al., eds. (1981) have ventured to determine the *Classics of Modern Semiotics*. In addition to articles on Peirce, Morris, Saussure, Hjelmslev, and Jakobson, their volume introduces three further semioticians as classics of twentieth-century semiotics: Bühler, Uexküll, and Sebeok.

Karl Bühler (1879–1963), pioneer in the psychology of language, has been influential in semiotics with his work on the expressive functions of nonverbal communication (Bühler 1933a), his contributions to the theory of metaphors and to the semiotic foundations of language (Bühler 1933b; 1934), and his proposals for a general theory of signs, which he called *sematology* (see 1.2.1). On Bühler's definition of the sign and his structuralist "principle of abstractive relevance," see Sign (3.1). On his organon model and its influence on Jakobson, see Function (3.1). Bühler's (1934) "two field theory of language" is a further significant contribution to the semiotics of language. It emphasizes the difference between two elementary functions of language called *index field* (*Zeigefeld*) and *symbol field*. The index field refers to the speech situation by means of pointing or presenting (deixis, anaphora, etc.). The symbol field refers to the contextual or syntactic dimension of linguistic semiosis. For studies in Bühler's semiotics, see Innis (1982), Sebeok (1981: 91–108), Eschbach, ed. (1984), and Graumann & Herrmann, eds. (1984).

The theoretical biologist Jakob von Uexküll (1864–1944) was discovered as a pioneer in biosemiotics and phytosemiotics by Sebeok (1979: 187–207 and earlier), Krampen (1981c), and T. von Uexküll (1981a; see also the special issue of *Semiotica* 42.1 [1982] on Uexküll's *Theory of Meaning*). A central topic of his research was the role of environmental (*Umwelt*) factors in human and animal semiosis (see also Zoosemiotics 3.2.1 for Uexküll's functional cycle). Cassirer, who referred to Uexküll as a source of support of his own view of the specificity of human semiosis, summarized Uexküll's theory of environmental semiotics as follows:

> Every organism has its special *Umwelt* and its special *Innenwelt*—a specific mode of its outward life and its inward life. [. . .] The anatomical structure of an animal gives us the clue to the reconstruction of its inner and outward experience. Animals that widely diverge in this respect do not live in the same reality. [. . .] There exists, therefore, no common world of objects that is one and the same for men and for all animal species. "In the world of a fly," he says "we find only fly-things; in the world of a sea-urchin we have only sea-urchin things." (1935–45: 168)

Uexküll thus shows that organisms in general do not perceive an object in itself (*Ding an sich*), but signs, "and from these signs, each according to its pre-existing *Bauplan,* or blue print, build up mental models of the world" (Sebeok 1979: 195).

Thomas Albert Sebeok (b. 1920), one of the most frequently quoted authors in this handbook, is a major figure in twentieth-century semiotics not only because of his own semiotic tetralogy (Sebeok 1976; 1979; 1981; 1986b), but also because of his seminal activities as editor-in-chief of the more than seventy volumes of *Semiotica* (1969ff.), the book series Approaches to Semiotics (1968ff.), Studies in Semiotics (1975–78), Advances in Semiotics (1974ff.), and Topics in Contemporary Semiotics (1984ff.), and numerous editorships of other publications in the field of semiotics (see Bär 1981 and Bouissac et al., eds. 1986). Sebeok's special merit in the history of semiotics is his contribution to the extension of the field of semiotics from its mainly philosophical and linguistic tradition to a larger biosemiotic field covering not only anthroposemiotics, "the totality of man's species-specific signalling systems," but also zoosemiotics and, as its third domain, endosemiotics, "which studies cybernetic systems within the body" (Sebeok 1976: 3), including semiotic interpretations of immunological reactions and of the metabolic and genetic codes (see Code 5.1).

4.2.4 ADDENDA TO TWENTIETH-CENTURY SEMIOTICS

Two psychologists and philosophers of the sign from the first decades of the twentieth century whose contributions to semiotics have not yet been forgotten are Gätschenberger and Gomperz. Richard Gätschenberger (1865–1936) wrote a *Psychology of the Sign* in 1901 and later several other treatises on sematology (cf. Eschbach's introduction to the 1987 reprint of Gätschenberger 1901). Heinrich Gomperz (1873–1942) wrote a treatise on semasiology (Gomperz 1908, cf. Kiesow 1986) which contains a semiotic triangle similar to the more famous one from the influential classic of semantics by Charles Kay Ogden (1889–1957) and Ivor Armstrong Richards (1893–1979) (see Sign 3.1.2).

From the fields of logical semantics and linguistic philosophy, authors who have been included in the history of semiotics (cf. Sebeok, ed. 1986) are Alfred North Whitehead (1861–1947), Bertrand Russell (1872–1970), Ludwig Wittgenstein (1889–1951) (for Wittgenstein and semiotics, see Rossi-Landi 1984 and Sebeok, ed. 1986), and the logical positivists Moritz Schlick (1882–1936), Otto Neurath (1882–1942), and Rudolf Carnap (1891–1970). Some aspects of the works of these authors are discussed in the chapters on sign, symbol, meaning, and image.

In the field of cultural semiotics, it is less well known that Paul Valéry (1871–1945) wrote on topics of "sémeiologie" and "sémiotique" from 1901. In his theory of signs, Valéry dealt among other things with language, writing, gestures, the poetic sign, myth, signs, and systems. For details see Malmberg (1977: 218–40) and Schmidt-Radefeldt (1984; 1987). Among those who followed Saussure in the project of developing a general theory of signs on a linguistic basis, Eric Buyssens (b. 1900) has been accorded a special chapter by historiographers of semiotics (cf. Sebeok 1976, Caprettini 1980: 180–93, Swiggers 1907). Buyssens's (1943; 1967) studies in structures and functions of nonlinguistic codes and systems, sign languages, and language substitutes have been influential in a direction of modern semiotics which is known as *functional semiotics* (cf. Hervey 1982: 154–83), and whose main other representatives are G. Mounin, L. Prieto, and A. and J. Martinet (see especially Code 4.1). A descendant of this school of semiotics is Hervey's own *axiomatic semiotics* (ibid.: 184–218).

A further addition to the other main representatives of current schools of semiotics, dealt with in other chapters, is Walter A. Koch (b. 1934) and his Bochum school of semiotics. Koch's influential semiotic research began as early as the late 1960s as a sociosemiotic structuralism (Koch 1971b) with investigations in the field of art, literature, and the mass media and has since then developed into a theory of *evolutionary cultural semiotics* (Koch 1986a) studying *semiogenesis* (Koch, ed. 1982) with special attention to analogies in the evolution of culture and nature (Koch 1983; 1986b; c).

Another school of modern semiotics not dealt with in a separate chapter is Marxist semiotics (cf. Coward & Ellis 1977, Bentele & Bystrina 1978: 50–63, Heim 1983, the special issues of *Versus* 23 [1979] and *Zeitschrift für Semiotik* 10.1–2 [1988]). Besides Lasar O. Resnikow (cf. 1964; 1977) and Adam Schaff (b. 1913) (cf. 1960 and Fischer-Lichte 1979: 81–98), the major representatives of Marxist semiotics are Georg Klaus (1912–1974) (cf. Kalkofen 1979) and Ferruccio Rossi-Landi (1921–1985) (cf. Bernard & Withalm 1986, Sebeok, ed. 1986: 482–83). See also Ideology and Morris (2.3.5).

4.3 Appendix: *Geography of Modern Semiotics*

Today, at the end of the history of modern semiotics, the historiographer of the theory of signs is faced with worldwide semiotic research activities. Even a merely bibliographical survey of these expanding international activities would go beyond the scope of this handbook. Helbo, ed. (1979) has reports on semiotic activities in fifteen countries. Nöth gives bibliographical information on semiotics in twenty-two countries (1985: 9–10). Sebeok & Umiker-Sebeok, eds. (1986; 1987) have reports on the state of the art in current semiotic research in thirty-one countries, bibliographically supplemented (and expanded to thirty-seven countries) by Withalm (1988). The latter three publications also give a comprehensive survey of the activities of the International Association for Semiotic Studies and of other semiotic associations around the world. Current activities in the field of semiotics are most comprehensively documented in the international "calendar" of projects, meetings, and conferences regularly published by *Zeitschrift für Semiotik*.

Peirce

Charles Sanders Peirce (1839–1914; pronounced "purse") was early recognized as "one of the great figures in the history of semiotics" and as "the founder of the modern theory of signs" (Weiss & Burks 1945: 383). A universal genius in many sciences, Peirce, who was largely ignored by his contemporaries, is now unanimously acclaimed as America's greatest philosopher. His writings, consisting of thousands of papers, can be discussed here only with respect to three topics of central semiotic concern: Peirce's pansemiotic view of the universe, and his definition and classification of signs. An appendix to this chapter investigates the relevance of Peircean semiotics to text semiotics.

Fig. P 1. Portrait of Charles Sanders Peirce (1839–1914). Courtesy of the Peirce Edition Project (Indiana University, Indianapolis).

1. Foundations and Survey of Peircean Semiotics

In the history of modern semiotics, Peirce is the major figure of its philosophical branch, which first developed rather independently of the linguistic branch represented by the Saussurean and Hjelmslevian tradition. In contrast to this linguistic branch, Peirce's semiotics aims at epistemological and even metaphysical universality.

1.1 Peirce and the History of Modern Semiotics

The importance of Peirce's work was first recognized in the philosophical branch of semiotics, and only much later in linguistic semiotics.

1.1.1 PEIRCE AND GENERAL SEMIOTICS

In the field of general semiotics, Morris was among the first to pursue the Peircean heritage. But Morris left his debt to Peirce largely unacknowledged, and his behaviorist approach is based on positions which are often irreconcilable with Peirce's philosophy (cf. Rochberg-Halton & McMurtrey 1983: 141; see also Fisch 1978: 58–60). An influential school of general semiotics, whose goal has been a systematic "reconstruction" of the Peircean theory of signs and its "further development" to a "Basistheorie" of semiotics, is Bense's Stuttgart School of Semiotics (cf. Bense 1967; 1975; 1981; 1983; 1986, Walther 1974, and Bense & Walther, eds. 1973, critically reviewed by Ketner & Kloesel 1975). The forum of the Stuttgart School of Semiotics is the journal *Semiosis* (1 [1976]ff.). For their contributions to the field of applied semiotics, see 4. and Aesthetics (2.1.1).

Other centers of studies in Peirce's general semiotics are the Peirce Edition Project (Indiana–Purdue University at Indianapolis), the Institute for Studies in Pragmatism at Texas Tech University (editor of the book series Peirce Studies 1 [1979], 2 [1984]), and the *Seminaire de Sémiotique* at Perpignan (cf. Deledalle 1979; 1987). A forum of American research in Peircean semiotics is *Transactions of the Charles S. Peirce Society* 1 (1965)ff. For further references see 1.2.

1.1.2 PEIRCE AND LINGUISTIC SEMIOTICS

In linguistic semiotics of the Saussurean tradition, Peirce's theory of signs remained undiscovered for many years. Although Ogden & Richards's classic of semantics, *The Meaning of Meaning*, contained a brief outline of Peircean semiotics (1923: 279–90; see also Fisch 1978: 57), the linguistic discovery of Peirce's theory of signs is generally attributed to Jakobson (1965; cf. Malmberg 1977: 93, Bruss 1978, and Language 2.3.1). Since Eco (1968: 198), the basic concepts of Peirce's typology of signs have had a firm place in structuralist accounts of semiotics. A number of authors have focused on the differences between and the few common elements of the semiotic theories of

Peirce and Saussure (cf. Köller 1977, Deledalle 1979, Stetter 1979, Vigener 1979, and Hervey 1982). For a comparison of Hjelmslev's and Peirce's semiotics, see Parret (1983).

1.2 Survey of Peirce's Writings and Peircean Studies

The project of a complete edition of Peirce's works is still far from its completion. The survey of Peircean scholarship must be restricted to his semiotic writings.

1.2.1 EDITIONS OF PEIRCE'S WRITINGS

The standard edition of Peirce's works, from which his writings are usually quoted in this handbook (by volume and paragraph), is his *Collected Papers* (Peirce 1931–58). However, this edition, in spite of its eight volumes (in four), is still incomplete and is not a chronological edition. Peirce's *Complete Published Works* (1977a) are so far available only in a microfiche edition, together with the bibliography of his writings and of secondary studies (Ketner et al., comps. 1977). His unpublished manuscripts are also available on microfilm (Peirce 1963–66). A new and more complete chronological edition of Peirce's writings has so far appeared in four volumes (Peirce 1982–89). Some writings on semiotic topics are also included in the four-volume edition of Peirce's mathematical writings (Peirce 1976). Two other important editions are his *Contributions to "The Nation"* (Peirce 1975–79) and his letters to Victoria Lady Welby (Peirce 1977b). Selections from his writings are Peirce (1940; 1958; 1972).

1.2.2 SURVEY OF PEIRCEAN SEMIOTIC STUDIES

Access to Peirce's semiotics is difficult because the founder of modern semiotics never wrote a coherent outline of his complete theory of signs. Furthermore, there have been many terminological changes in the numerous papers on semiotic topics which Peirce produced during the half century of his semiotic research, and these changes have often raised the question whether they also involve a change of theory (cf. Weiss & Burks 1945: 383). These difficulties make good guides to Peirce's semiotic writings indispensable. Introductory articles are Zeman (1977), Fisch (1978; also in 1986), Savan (1980), Oehler (1981a), Skidmore (1981), Rochberg-Halton & McMurtrey (1983), and Parmentier (1985). Introductory monographs and general studies of Peirce's theory of signs are Fitzgerald (1966), Greenlee (1973), Walther (1974), Deledalle (1979), Calvet de Magalhaes (1981), Scherer (1984), Pharies (1985), and Callaghan (1986). See also the series Peirce Studies 1 (1979)ff., Ketner et al., eds. (1981), and the special Peirce issues of *Languages* 58 (1980) and *American Journal of Semiotics* 2.1–2 (1983). Most monographs in Peirce's philosophy in general and his philosophical pragmatism are also concerned with Peirce's theory of signs (cf. Goudge 1950, Kempski 1952, Murphey 1961, Gallie 1966, Apel 1967, Ayer 1968, Feibleman 1970, Almeder 1980, Esposito 1980, Freeman, ed. 1983, Hookway 1985, Fisch 1986, Deledalle 1987, and Kevelson 1987).

1.3 Peirce's Pansemiotic View of the Universe

The point of departure of Peirce's theory of signs is the axiom that cognition, thought, and even man are semiotic in their essence. Like a sign, a thought refers to other thoughts and to objects of the world so that "all which is reflected upon has [a] past" (§ 5.253). Peirce even went so far as to conclude that "the fact that every thought is a sign, taken in conjunction with the fact that life is a train of thought, proves that man is a sign" (§ 5.314; on this thesis, see also Burks 1981 and Singer 1984: 53–73). This semiotic interpretation of man and cognition has a present, a past, and a future dimension:

A man denotes whatever is the object of his attention at the moment; he connotes whatever he knows or feels of this object, and is the incarnation of this form or intelligible species; his interpretant is the future memory of this cognition, his

future self, or another person he addresses, or a sentence he writes, or a child he gets." (§ 7.591)

Peirce defended a pansemiotic view of the universe. In his view, signs are not a class of phenomena besides other nonsemiotic objects: "The entire universe is perfused with signs, if it is not composed exclusively of signs" (§ 5.448, fn.). Semiotics in this interpretation turns out to be a universal science about which Peirce wrote to Lady Welby on December 23, 1908: "It has never been in my power to study anything,—mathematics, ethics, metaphysics, gravitation, thermodynamics, optics, chemistry, comparative anatomy, astronomy, psychology, phonetics, economics, the history of science, whist, men and women, wine, metrology, except as a study of semeiotic" (1977b: 85).

1.4 Universal Categories

An essential philosophical foundation of Peirce's semiotics is his system of categories (§§ 1.300ff. and 8.328ff.). While Aristotle had postulated ten, and Kant twelve, ontological categories, Peirce developed a phenomenology based on only three universal categories called *firstness*, *secondness*, and *thirdness* (cf. Zeman 1977: 23–24, Esposito 1980: 163). "*Firstness* is the mode of being of that which is such as it is, positively and without reference to anything else" (§ 8.328). It is the category of the unreflected feeling, mere potentiality, freedom, immediacy, of undifferentiated quality and independence (§§ 1.302–303, 1.328, 1.531). Secondness involves the relation of a first to a second (§§ 1.356–59). It is the category of comparison, facticity, action, reality, and experience in time and space: "It meets us in such facts as another, relation, compulsion, effect, dependence, independence, negation, occurrence, reality, result." Thirdness brings a second in relation to a third (§§ 1.337ff.). It is the category of mediation (cf. Parmentier 1985), habit, memory, continuity, synthesis, communication (semiosis), representation, and signs.

2. The Sign as a Triadic Relation

As a phenomenon of thirdness, the sign participates in the three categories as follows (Peirce § 2.274): there is a first, called *representamen*, which stands in a triadic relation to a second, called its *object*, "as to be capable of determining a third, called its *interpretant*." For partial terminological equivalents to this triad in other triadic models of the sign, see Sign (3.).

2.1 The Sign and the Process of Semiosis

Peirce defined the sign in terms of a triadic process, called semiosis.

2.1.1 PEIRCE'S DEFINITION OF THE SIGN

In his definitions of the sign, Peirce introduced an idiosyncratic and often changing terminology which has been adopted by few of his followers. In neutral terms, Peirce once referred to his sign model as consisting of a "triple connection of *sign, thing signified, cognition produced in the mind*" (§ 1.372). One of his more elaborate definitions is:

> A sign, or *representamen*, is something which stands to somebody for something in some respect or capacity. It addresses somebody, that is, creates in the mind of that person an equivalent sign, or perhaps a more developed sign. That sign which it creates I call the *interpretant* of the first sign. The sign stands for something, its *object*. It stands for that object, not in all respects, but in reference to a sort of idea. (§ 2.228)

One of the central tenets of Peirce's semiotics is its relational or *functional* character of the sign (see also Greenlee 1973: 23–33). Signs are not a class of objects. They exist only in the mind of the interpreter: "Nothing is a sign unless it is interpreted as a sign" (§ 2.308).

2.1.2 SEMIOSIS

Peirce (§ 5.472) defined this triadic "action of the sign," this process in which the sign has a cognitive effect on its interpreter (§ 5.484), as *semiosis* (or *semeiosis*). Strictly speaking, semio-sis, and not the sign, is thus the proper object of semiotic study (cf. Fisch 1978: 42). In one of his definitions, "*semiotic* is the doctrine of the essential nature and fundamental varieties of possible semiosis" (Peirce § 5.488). The term *semiosis* is derived from a treatise of the Epicurean philosopher Philodemus (cf. Fisch 1978: 41). Peirce explained that "Σημείωσις [. . .] meant the action of almost any kind of sign; and my definition confers on anything that so acts the title of a 'sign' " (§ 5.484).

2.2 The Representamen

Representamen is Peirce's term for the "perceptible object" (§ 2.230) functioning as a sign. Other semioticians have designated this correlate of the sign as the *symbol* (Ogden & Richards), the *sign vehicle* (Morris), the *signifier* (Saussure), or *expression* (Hjelmslev). Peirce also described it as "a vehicle conveying into the mind something from without," as the sign in its "own material nature" or "as in itself" (§§ 1.339, 8.333–34). Theoretically, Peirce distinguished clearly between the sign, which is the complete triad, and the representamen, which is its first correlate. Terminologically, however, there is an occasional ambiguity because Peirce sometimes also used the less technical term *sign* instead of *representamen* (for example, §§ 2.230, 8.332). Once, Peirce even speaks of the "sign or representamen" (§§ 2.228–29), but in this context his term for the sign vehicle is *ground*.

2.3 Object

Peirce's second correlate of the sign, the object, corresponds to the *referent* of other models of the sign (see Sign 3.2; cf. also Meaning).

2.3.1 DEFINITION OF THE OBJECT

The object is that which the sign "represents," usually "something else," but in the borderline case of *self-reference*, representamen and object can also be the same entity (Peirce §§ 2.230). This correlate can be a material "object of the world" with which we have a "perceptual acquaintance" (§ 2.330) or a merely mental or imaginary entity "of the nature of a sign or thought" (§ 1.538). It can be a "single known existing thing" (§ 2.232) or a class of things. "The Sign can only represent the Object and tell about it. It cannot furnish acquaintance with or recognition of that Object. [. . .] It presupposes an acquaintance in order to convey some further information concerning it" (§ 2.231).

2.3.2 IMMEDIATE AND DYNAMICAL OBJECT

Peirce distinguished between two kinds of objects (cf. Eco 1976a and Deledalle 1981), the *immediate* and the *mediate* or *dynamical* object. The immediate object is the "Object within the Sign" (1977b: 83), the object "as the Sign itself represents it, and whose Being is thus dependent upon the Representation of it in the Sign" (§ 4.536). It is thus a mental representation of an object, whether this object actually "exists" or not. The mediate, real, or dynamical object is the "Object outside of the Sign" (1977b: 83). It is "the Reality which by some means contrives to determine the Sign to its Representation" (§ 4.536) or that "which, from the nature of things, the Sign *cannot* express, which it can only *indicate* and leave the interpreter to find out by *collateral experience*" (§ 8.314). Peirce's definitions of the dynamical object seem to have committed him to an ontological realism, but in fact, his semiotic philosophy has overcome the realism-idealism dichotomy (cf. Oehler 1981a). Hesitating to use the term *real object*, Peirce added "perhaps the Object is altogether fictive" (§ 8.314).

2.4 The Interpretant

Interpretant is Peirce's term for the meaning of a sign. Occasionally, Peirce defined it as "significance" (§ 8.179), "signification," or "interpretation" (§ 8.184).

2.4.1 PRAGMATIC AND SIGN NATURE OF THE INTERPRETANT

Peirce gave a pragmatic account of the nature of meaning (cf. Gentry 1952, Alston 1956: 82–

85) when he defined the interpretant as "the proper significate outcome" or "effect of the sign" (§§ 5.474–75), or as "something created in the Mind of the Interpreter" (§ 8.179). In accordance with his theory of thought being a sign and his view of interpretation as a process of semiosis, Peirce also defined the interpretant as a sign: "A sign addresses somebody, that is, creates in the mind of that person an equivalent sign, or perhaps a more developed sign. That sign which it creates I call the *interpretant* of the first sign" (§ 2.228).

2.4.2 UNLIMITED SEMIOSIS

Since every sign creates an interpretant which in turn is the representamen of a second sign, semiosis results in a "series of successive interpretants" *ad infinitum* (Peirce §§ 2.303, 2.92). There is no "first" nor "last" sign in this process of unlimited semiosis. Nor does the idea of infinite semiosis imply a vicious circle. It refers instead to the very modern idea that "thinking always proceeds in the form of a dialogue—a dialogue between different phases of the *ego*—so that, being dialogical, it is essentially composed of signs" (§ 4.6). Since "every thought must address itself to some other" (§ 5.253), the continuous process of semiosis (or thinking) can only be "interrupted," but never really be "ended" (§ 5.284). As Gallie points out, "this endless series is essentially a *potential* one. Peirce's point is that any actual interpretant of a given sign *can* theoretically be interpreted in some further sign, and that in another without any necessary end being reached. [. . .] The exigencies of practical life inevitably cut short such potentially endless development" (1966: 126).

2.4.3 THE THREE INTERPRETANTS

Differentiating between the effects of the sign on the interpreter's mind, and in application of his triadic categorial principles, Peirce distinguished three main types of interpretant (§§ 4.536, 5.475–76, 8.314–15, 8.343; cf. Gentry 1952, Greenlee 1973: 117ff., Eco 1976a, Almeder 1980: 28). The first category is the *immediate* interpretant. It is "the *Quality* of the

Impression that a sign is fit to produce, not any actual reaction" (§ 8.315). In accordance with his definition of firstness, Peirce defined the immediate interpretant as a semantic *potentiality*: "I understand it to be the total unanalyzed effect that the Sign is calculated to produce, or naturally might be expected to produce [. . .], the effect the sign first produces or may produce upon a mind, without any reflection upon it." It refers to the "peculiar Interpretability" of the sign "before it gets any Interpreter" (1977b: 110–11). The second category is the *dynamical* interpretant. It is the "direct effect actually produced by a Sign upon an Interpreter of it, [. . .] that which is experienced in each act of Interpretation and is different in each from that of any other" (ibid.).

The third category, the *final* interpretant, is associated with the third category of habit and law. "It is that which *would finally* be decided to be the true interpretation if consideration of the matter were carried so far that an ultimate opinion were reached" (§ 8.184) or "the one Interpretative result to which every Interpreter is destined to come if the Sign is sufficiently considered" (1977b: 111). Meaning as studied in lexicology would be a study of final interpretants. Peirce furthermore distinguished between the *emotional*, the *energetic*, and the *logical* interpretant. This typology has been interpreted by some as synonymous with the above trichotomy (cf. Greenlee 1973: 117), while others (cf. Fitzgerald 1966: 80, Almeder 1980: 28) have interpreted it as a subdivision of the dynamical interpretant.

---

3. Peirce's Classification of Signs

Peirce developed an elaborate typology of signs (§§ 2.233–71), beginning with a triadic classification of the sign correlates representamen, object, and interpretant into three trichotomies. Considering the possibilities of combining firstness, secondness, and thirdness, he arrived at ten major classes of signs. Later, Peirce postulated ten trichotomies and sixty-six and even 3^{10}

= 59,049 classes of signs (§§ 1.291, 4.530, 8.343; cf. Sanders 1970).

3.1 First Trichotomy

From the point of view of the representamen, Peirce subdivided signs into *qualisigns* (belonging to the category of firstness; cf. 1.4), *sinsigns* or *tokens* (secondness), and *legisigns* or *types* (thirdness) "according as the sign in itself is a mere quality, is an actual existent, or is a general law" (§ 2.243). "A *Qualisign* is a quality which is a Sign. It cannot actually act as a sign until it is embodied" (§ 2.244), but in this case it is already a sinsign. The representamen of a sinsign or token is "an actual existent thing or event" (a "*singular*" sign) (§ 2.245).

"A *Legisign* is a law that is a Sign. [. . .] Every conventional sign is a legisign. It is not a single object, but a general type which, it has been agreed, shall be significant." Thus, every word of a language is a legisign. But in an individual utterance, the word is also a sinsign. Peirce defined such sinsigns which are occurrences of legisigns as *replicas*: "Every legisign signifies through an instance of its application, which may be termed a *Replica* of it. Thus, the word 'the' will usually occur from fifteen to twenty-five times on a page. It is in all these occurrences one and the same word, the same legisign. Each single instance of it is a Replica. The Replica is a Sinsign" (§ 2.246). In linguistics, Peirce's distinction between legisigns and replicas has been widely adopted, but the terms generally used are *type* (for *legisign*) and *token* (for *replica*).

3.2 Second Trichotomy: Icon, Index, Symbol

This trichotomy classifies signs with respect to the relation between the representamen and object (cf. Burks 1949). Peirce referred to this trichotomy as "the most fundamental division of signs" (§ 2.275). The three members of this trichotomy are *icon* (firstness), *index* (secondness), and *symbol* (thirdness). Peirce's definition of the first class is discussed in detail in Icon (1.). For his criteria of indexicality, see Typology (4.2.2). The symbol, according to Peirce, is the category of arbitrary and conventional signs: "A *Symbol* is a sign which refers to the Object that it denotes by virtue of a law, usually an association of general ideas" (§ 2.449). "Any ordinary word as 'give,' 'bird,' 'marriage,' is an example of a symbol" (§ 2.298). "Every symbol is necessarily a legisign" (§ 8.335).

3.3 The Third Trichotomy

According to the nature of the interpretant, a sign is either a *rheme*, a *dicent*, or an *argument*. This trichotomy "corresponds to the old division [of logic], Term, Proposition, and Argument, modified so as to be applicable to signs generally" (§ 8.337). A term is "simply a class-name or proper-name," while a rheme is "any sign that is not true nor false, like almost any single word except 'yes' and 'no' " (§ 8.337). A rheme (Gr. 'ῥῆμα—'word') is a "simple or substitutive sign" (§ 2.309). It is a "Sign of qualitative Possibility [. . .] representing such and such a kind of possible Object" (§ 2.250).

A dicent (or *dicisign*) "is a Sign of actual existence" (§ 2.251). Like a proposition, it is an "informational sign" (§ 2.309), but it "does not assert" (§ 8.337). "The readiest characteristic test showing whether a sign is a Dicisign or not is that a Dicisign is either true or false, but does not directly furnish reasons for being so" (§ 2.310). An argument is "a Sign of law" (§ 2.252), "namely, the law that the passage from all such premises to such conclusions tends to the truth" (§ 2.263). While a dicent only affirms the existence of an object, the argument proves its truth.

3.4 Ten Principal Classes of Signs

Since every sign is determined by its three correlates, and there are three ways in which every correlate may be characterized, as summarized in Figure P 2, there are theoretically $3^3 = 27$ possible classes of signs. However, some of the possible combinations are semiotically impossible. For example, a qualisign can be only iconic and rhematic, a sinsign cannot be a symbol, and an index cannot be an argument. Such restrictions reduce the number

of valid combinations to the following ten principal classes of signs (§§ 2.254–63, 8.341). The semiotically superfluous (presupposed) characterizations are placed in parentheses:

Trichotomy / Category	I. of the representamen	II. of relation to *object*	III. of relation to *interpretant*
Firstness	qualisign	icon	rheme
Secondness	sinsign	index	dicent
Thirdness	legisign	symbol	argument

Fig. P 2. Peirce's three trichotomies of signs.

I: 1. (Rhematic Iconic) *Qualisign*, for example: "a feeling of 'red.' "
II: 2. (Rhematic) *Iconic Sinsign*: "an individual diagram."
   3. *Rhematic Indexical Sinsign*: "a spontaneous cry."
   4. *Dicent* (Indexical) *Sinsign*: "a weathercock."
III: 5. (Rhematic) *Iconic Legisign*: "a diagram, apart from its factual individuality."
   6. *Rhematic Indexical Legisign*: "a demonstrative pronoun."
   7. *Dicent Indexical Legisign*: "a street cry," traffic signs, commands.
   8. *Rhematic Symbol*(ic Legisign): "a common noun."
   9. *Dicent Symbol*(ic Legisign): "an ordinary proposition."
   10. *Argument* (Symbolic Legisign): "a syllogism."

4. Text Semiotic Studies on Peircean Foundations

Parallel to Peircean approaches to language and linguistics, there have been text semiotic studies on Peircean principles since the 1960s. These studies have shown that semiotic features of texts can be revealed with respect to all three correlates of the Peircean sign, its representamen, its object relation, and its interpretant.

4.1 Survey of Research

The earliest Peircean approaches to the study of texts were proposed in the framework of Bense's (1962) Stuttgart School of Semiotics. A paper by Walther (1962), entitled *Textsemiotik*, was the first in a series of studies concerned with the application of Peirce's typology of signs to mostly literary texts (Walther 1965a; 1965b; 1971, Gerhardt 1969). The foundations of this approach are outlined in Bense (1967: 73–79; 1969: 91–96). Other analytic studies of literary texts on Peircean principles are Browne (1971), Pignatari (1974), Zoest (1974), Nöth (1980: 66–100), and Eco & Sebeok, eds. (1983). The theory of literature and literary semiotics is examined from the point of view of Peircean semiotics by Köller (1977; 1980), Sheriff (1981), and Johansen (1986a). Other areas in the field of text semiotics which have become topics of research from a Peircean point of view are rhetoric, stylistics (Kirstein 1982, Podlewski 1982), and the theory of metaphor (Gumpel 1984).

The main concern of Bense's text semiotic research was the classification of texts in aesthetic and semantic respects (cf. 1967: 73). However, the essence of textual, and particularly literary, signs cannot be exhausted by a merely taxonomic approach. Within the Peircean framework, a given sign cannot be assigned unambiguously to one class only. Its classification can change with its function, history, the perspective and process of its interpretation. An essential insight into the nature of texts gained from Peirce's semiotics is that "language signs do not have a static structure but form a dynamic event, and that language cannot be adequately studied from the perspective of *system*, but only from the perspective of *process*" (Köller 1977: 73). The following quote can therefore be taken as a motto of text semiotic research in the spirit of Peirce: "Symbols grow. They come into being by development out of other signs, particularly from icons, or from mixed signs partaking of the nature of icons and symbols. [. . .] A symbol, once in being, spreads among the peoples. In use and in experience, its meaning grows" (§ 2.302).

4.2 Textual Representamen

As Bense points out (1967: 73–74), the textual representamen can be qualisign, sinsign, or legisign. Only the study of the particular case can reveal the dominant sign character of a given text. Texts, like all language signs, consist in the first place of legisigns, since they are signs that belong to the repertoire of a general code. This is the most general characterization of textuality. However, in every specific act of text production and text reception, the representamen is a sinsign, being unique in time, space, and communicative situation. More specific features which make a text a sinsign are its characteristics of style, textual originality, and creativity (cf. ibid.).

The focus is on the text as a qualisign, whenever its phonetic-graphemic quality, its visual or sound effects, are considered. In a Peircean interpretation, the Jakobsonian poetic function ("focus on the message for its own sake"; cf. Poetry 1.2) is one of a qualisign. Poeticalness of deviation (see Poetry 2.2), by contrast, is based on sinsigns. The legisign character of poetry and literary texts lies in their historical codification through the codes of rhetoric and poetic theory. In Peirce's own aesthetics, art and literature are essentially associated with the category of firstness. The essence of aesthetic creation has to do with "qualities of feelings" (Peirce § 1.43, cf. Sheriff 1981: 66), thus with qualisigns.

4.3 Icon, Index, Symbol

Also from the point of view of its object relation, the textual sign is polyfunctional (see also Johansen 1986a: 115). The text is a symbol insofar as it consists of arbitrary signs. It is predominantly indexical when its primary function is conative (appellative), as in commands, instructions, questions (cf. Bense 1967: 74). Dramatic texts are predominantly indexical (cf. Theater 3.3.3). Indexicality is furthermore characteristic of realism in literature (cf. Bettetini 1971) because of the textual reference to persons, objects, and events in a (more or less) precise temporal, spatial, and social setting.

Textual iconicity can have the form of an *image*, a *diagram*, or a *metaphor* (cf. Icon 1.3). Visual poetry, depicting its objects in the form of its typography (cf. Whiteside 1988), and onomatopoeic poems are examples of texts functioning as images. A case of diagrammatic iconicity is the *ordo naturalis*, the natural order in a narrative (cf. Browne 1971: 337): the sequence of the textual signs is a linear icon of the sequence of events depicted in the text. Jakobson (1965: 27) quoted Caesar's "veni, vidi, vici" ('I came, I saw, I conquered') as an example. For further aspects of textual iconicity, see Literature (2.1) and Metaphor (4).

4.4 Interpretant and Interpretation

From the point of view of its interpretant, the text is a rheme when it is incomplete, when it has a predominantly expressive function, or when its structure is open to many interpretations (cf. Bense 1967: 75). The rheme, as the sign of possibility, and not of factuality, is characteristic of literary and poetic textuality. The essence of fiction and imagination is of a rhematic nature (cf. Johansen 1986a).

Descriptive texts, whether fictional or nonfictional, have the character of a dicent, since they are informational, but nonassertive (cf. 3.3). Scientific and legal texts are predominantly arguments as to their interpretant. From a pragmatic point of view, texts can further be characterized as having different interpretants according to their effects on their interpreters (cf. Kirstein 1982). In this respect, the categories of the dynamical and final interpretant are particularly relevant. Texts that arouse emotions or provoke immediate action, such as larmoyant novels, literature of agitation, and partly advertising, have a dynamical interpretant. The final interpretant is predominant in legal texts and in texts that tend to result in new habits, such as ideologies or fashions.

Morris

Charles William Morris (1901–1979) is a "classic of semiotics" (Posner 1981), whose influence on the development of the history of semiotics was decisive in the 1930s and 1940s. With roots in the semiotics of Peirce, George H. Mead's (1934) social behaviorism and symbolic interaction theory (cf. Posner 1981), American pragmatism (cf. Morris 1970 and Eschbach 1977), empiricism, and logical positivism, Morris developed a general theory of signs by which

Fig. Mo 1. Portrait of Charles W. Morris (1901–1979).

he intended to contribute to the project of a "Unified Science" (cf. Morris 1938). While the behaviorist foundation of his theory of signs became a focus of criticism in the postbehaviorist era of semiotics (cf. Mounin 1970a: 57–76, Kutschera 1971: 80–88), Morris's broad definition of the scope of semiotics and his threefold subdivision of approaches to semiotics have remained a cornerstone of the foundations of semiotics. In applied semiotics, Morris's theory of signs has been influential in semiotic aesthetics and in the theory of iconicity. His pragmatic typology of discourse is of special interest to text semiotics.

1. Survey of Morris's Semiotic Writings

Morris showed a continued interest in the theory of signs after his dissertation on *Symbolism and Reality* (1925). His most important contributions to semiotics have been reissued under the title *Writings on the General Theory of Signs* (1971). The core of these writings are *Foundations of the Theory of Signs* (1938) and *Signs, Language, and Behavior* (1946). Morris discussed the reaction to the latter work in the article "Signs about signs about signs" (1948) and published a new *summa* of his semiotics under the title *Signification and Significance* (1964; only chap. 1 is included in Morris 1971). His semiotic aesthetics is formulated in Morris (1939) and Morris & Hamilton (1965). For bibliographies of Morris's writings and the critique of his work, see Eschbach (1975b) and Fiordo (1977: 191–95).

Surveys of and introductions to Morris's semiotics include the papers by Spang-Hanssen (1954), Mounin (1970a: 57–76), Apel (1973), Eschbach (1975a), Rossi-Landi (1975b), Bentele & Bystrina (1978), Posner (1981), Hervey (1982), and Dutz (1983). Monographs on Morris's semiotic work include Rossi-Landi (1953), Fiordo (1977), the collection of studies by Eschbach, ed. (1981), and the dissertations by Müller (1970) and Eakins (1972). Dutz (1979) is a glossary of Morris's terminology. Bentley (1947), Dutz (1983), and Rochberg-Halton & McMurtrey (1983) are mostly critical accounts of Morris's work.

2. Semiotics and Its Three Dimensions

The "science of signs," as Morris (1938: 1–2) defined semiotics, has a broad scope, ranging from language to animal communication. The factors participating in *sign processes* determine the three-dimensional framework of semiotic studies.

2.1 The Scope of Semiotics

The scope of semiotics, according to Morris, is both broader and narrower than the science of signs outlined by Peirce.

2.1.1 PEIRCE AND MORRIS
Both founders of semiotics defined the theory of signs as the study of signs of any kind, including language and any other signs (cf. Morris 1946: 79), but while Peirce conceived of semiotics basically as a science of man, Morris (1946: 83, 366) extended the scope of the gen-

eral theory of signs to include sign processing by animals (see Zoosemiotics) or, more generally, by organisms. However, while similar in the broad scope of subjects of research, the science of signs conceived by Morris is characterized by a "fundamental departure from the Peircean tradition" (cf. Hervey 1982: 38). While Peirce envisioned a semiotic philosophy based on universal categories of perception and the assumption that "every thought is a sign" (Peirce § 2.253), Morris wanted to develop a science of signs "on a biological basis and specifically within the framework of the science of behavior" (1946: 80). For further differences between Peirce and Morris, see Dewey (1946) and Rochberg-Halton & McMurtrey (1983).

In spite of their difference in approach, Morris agreed with Peirce in the assumption that "something is a sign only because it is interpreted as a sign of something by some interpreter [. . .]. Semiotic, then, is not concerned with the study of a particular kind of object, but with ordinary objects in so far (and only in so far) as they participate in semiosis" (1938: 4; cf. 2.2.1).

2.1.2 THE INTERDISCIPLINARY SCOPE OF SEMIOTICS
The science of signs, according to Morris, has the following scope: "Semiotic has for its goal a general theory of signs in all their forms and manifestations, whether in animals or men, whether normal or pathological, whether linguistic or nonlinguistic, whether personal or social. Semiotic is thus an interdisciplinary enterprise" (1964: 1). As investigators interested in this enterprise, Morris enumerated "linguists, logicians, philosophers, psychologists, biologists, anthropologists, psychopathologists, aestheticians, and sociologists" (1938: 1).

2.1.3 SCIENCE AND INSTRUMENT OF SCIENCE
As the theory of signs, semiotics, according to Morris, has a twofold relation to all other sciences (1938: 2): "It is both a science among the sciences and an instrument of the sciences." As individual science, semiotics stud-

ies "things or the properties of things in their function of serving as signs." But "since every science makes use of and expresses its results in terms of signs, metascience (the science of science) must use semiotic as an organon" (cf. Language 2.2.1). Morris was convinced that "since it supplies the foundations for any special science of signs," semiotics is "a step in the unification of science" (ibid.).

2.2 Semiosis and the Dimensions of Semiotics

Morris derived his theory of the three dimensions of semiotics from his model of semiosis.

2.2.1 THE THREE COMPONENTS OF SEMIOSIS

Semiosis, a term coined by Peirce, was defined by Morris as "a sign process, that is, a process in which something is a sign to some organism" (1946: 366). Semiosis, according to Morris, involves three main factors: "that which acts as a sign, that which the sign refers to, and that effect on some interpreter in virtue of which the thing in question is a sign to that interpreter. These three components in semiosis may be called, respectively, the *sign vehicle*, the *designatum*, and the *interpretant*" (1938: 3). For the further definition of semiosis, see 3.1.

2.2.2 THE THREE DIMENSIONS OF SEMIOSIS

From the three correlates of the triadic relation of semiosis, Morris derived three dyadic relations, which he considered to be the basis of three dimensions of semiosis and semiotics. Accordingly, *syntactics* studies the relation between a given sign vehicle and other sign vehicles, *semantics* studies the relations between sign vehicles and their designata, and *pragmatics* studies the relation between sign vehicles and their interpreters (1938: 6–7). In addition, Morris distinguished two further subdivisions of semiotic studies: *pure semiotic*, which elaborates "the metalanguage in terms of which all sign situations would be discussed," and *descriptive semiotic*, which applies this language to the study of instances of semiosis (ibid.: 9). For the interrelation of these five branches of

semiotics, see Lieb (1971). The model of the three basic dimensions of semiosis according to Morris is shown in Figure Mo 2.

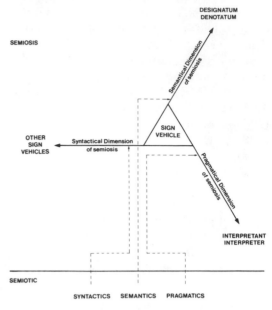

Fig. Mo 2. Three correlates of semiosis and three dimensions of semiotics according to Morris (1939: 417, redrawn).

2.2.3 HISTORY OF THE THREE DIMENSIONS

Posner discusses two historical precursors of Morris's triadic subdivision of semiotics (1985b: 75). One is the medieval trivium of the three language arts (see Rhetoric 1.2); the other is Peirce's triadic reinterpretation of this trivium. Peirce distinguished "three branches" of the science of semiotics "in consequence of every representamen being connected with three things, the ground, the object, and the interpretant" (§ 2.229). The first branch is called *pure grammar*. "It has for its task to ascertain what must be true of the representamen used by every scientific intelligence that they may embody any *meaning*." The second branch is called *logic proper*. "It is the science of what is quasi-necessarily true of the representamina of any scientific intelligence in order that they may hold good of any *object*, that is, may be true." The third branch is *pure rhetoric.* "Its task is to ascertain the laws by which in every scientific intelligence one sign gives birth to another, and especially one thought brings forth another" (ibid.). The parallel to Morris's three dimensions is apparent. "Pure grammar" is the precursor of syntax, "logic proper" of semantics, and "pure rhetoric" of pragmatics. For further aspects of Peirce's subdivision of semiotics in the light of Morris's three dimensions, see Deledalle (1979: 71–79) and Rochberg-Halton & McMurtrey (1983: 147–52).

2.3 Syntactics, Semantics, Pragmatics

Do Morris's three dimensions of semiotics give an analytically exhaustive subdivision of semiotics? This is so only if the concepts of syntax, semantics, and pragmatics are defined more broadly than they often are in semiotics.

2.3.1 SYNTAX AND POSSIBLE GAPS IN THE TRICHOTOMY

In the history of semiotics after Morris, the three dimensions were soon renamed *syntax* (instead of syntactics), semantics, and pragmatics (thus, for example, Reichenbach 1947: 15, Carnap 1954: 79). This terminology, however, gave rise to the impression that the three dimensions are insufficient to subdivide the whole field of semiotic research.

Particularly in linguistics, there are branches of study which seem to be excluded from Morris's three dimensions. Thus, linguists have criticized Morris's trichotomy for not providing a framework for the disciplines of phonology and graphemics (see Writing) and for other reasons (cf. Althaus & Henne 1971: 3–4, Trabant 1976a: 42, Lyons 1977: 114–19). A further question is whether Morris's scheme provides a framework for describing the two basic types of relations in language (cf. System 2.1): while the syntagmatic relations can clearly be subsumed under Morris's dimension of syntactics, the place of the paradigmatic dimension is questionable in Morris's scheme. However that may be, the claim for analytic exhaustiveness of Morris's trichotomy can be

maintained only if syntactics is defined more broadly than syntax in linguistics, where it is only the study of the rules for combining words into sentences. It is a mere matter of terminology whether this redefined branch of semiotics should be called syntactics, as proposed by Morris, or syntax, as named by his followers.

2.3.2 SYNTACTICS

In contrast to linguistic and logical syntax, Morris generalized his syntactics to cover more than only language signs: "There are, then, syntactical problems in the fields of perceptual signs, aesthetic signs, the practical use of signs, and general linguistics" (1938: 16). Posner (1985b) gives an interpretation of Morris's dimension of syntactics which closes the gaps that have been criticized by the linguists. He points out that Morris actually used three different definitions of syntactics: (1) syntactics as "the consideration of signs and sign combinations in so far as they are subject to syntactical rules" (Morris 1938: 14), (2) syntactics as the study of "the way in which signs of various classes are combined to form compound signs" (Morris 1946: 367), and (3) syntactics as the study of "the formal relations of signs to one another" (Morris 1938: 6).

Posner interprets the scope of syntactics according to definition (3) as including both syntagmatic and paradigmatic relations in language (1985b: 1982). He furthermore claims that syntactics studies the "formal aspects of language" in the sense of Hjelmslevian relations of form, that is, semiotic structure in general (ibid.: 79). In this sense, syntactics comprises most branches of structural linguistics, including syntax, morphology, and even phonology. Whether this expanded scope of syntactics is compatible with Morris's definitions or not, it is important to recognize that paradigmatic relations in text and system are relations of possible substitution in opposition to syntagmatic relations, which are relations of possible combinations of signs. If syntactics is extended to comprise the study of paradigmatic relations, syntactics is defined in a much broader sense than as the study of sign combinations only.

2.3.3 SEMANTICS

In Morris's early definition, "semantics deals with the relation of signs to their designata," that is, "that which the sign refers to" (1938: 21,3). In this definition, semantics covers only the aspect of reference, not that of sense (cf. Meaning). Later, however, Morris gave a broader definition of semantics. It is "that branch of semiotic which studies the signification of signs" (1946: 366). See further 3.3 and the chapters on semantics and meaning.

2.3.4 PRAGMATICS

Morris defined "the science of the relation of signs to their interpreters" as "that branch of semiotic which studies the origin, the uses and the effects of signs" (1938: 30; 1946: 365). Morris proposed a scope of pragmatic studies which is much broader than that of pragmatics in current language studies (1938: 30). While the linguist Leech, for example, defines it as "the study of how utterances have meanings in situations" (1983: x), Morris envisioned a study which "deals with the biotic aspects of semiosis, that is, with all the psychological, biological, and sociological phenomena which occur in the functioning of signs" (1938: 30). In this handbook, the chapters on communication, function, hermeneutics, rhetoric, and partly those on zoosemiotics and meaning focus on pragmatic aspects of semiosis. Pragmatics has only recently become a major branch of linguistics (cf. Leech 1983) and of the philosophy of language. For pragmatics in the framework of semiotics, see especially Parret (1983).

2.3.5 EXCURSUS ON SIGMATICS

In the framework of Marxist semiotics, Klaus (1963; 1964) proposed to extend Morris's three-dimensional framework of semiotics by a fourth dimension called *sigmatics*. Klaus describes sigmatics as a dimension parallel to semantics (1963: 60). In this definition, semantics is the study of the sign and its conceptual dimension (that is, sense; cf. Meaning),

while sigmatics is the study of the referential dimension of signs. Based on his Marxist copy theory of cognition (see Image 2.1.2), Klaus defines this sigmatic dimension as the study of dyadic relations R (S, O) between signs (S) and their "objects of reality" (O) (1964: 14). For the foundations of this semiotic theory in Marxist philosophy, see Bentele & Bystrina (1978: 70–79).

While many semioticians have acknowledged the theory of reference as a constitutive branch of semantics (cf. Meaning 2.), most have rejected the possibility of isolating the study of dyads of the type R (S, O) from the semiotic triad which includes the dimension of sense as the third correlate of semiosis (cf. Meaning). Thus, even the Marxist semiotician Resnikow (1964: 98) refuses to accept sigmatics as a semiotic dimension apart from semantics.

3. Sign and Typology of Signs

In the course of his writings from 1938 to 1964, Morris revised or differentiated several of his basic concepts (cf. Dutz 1979 and Hervey 1982), but his behavioristic approach remained a common denominator of his varying definitions of basic concepts of semiotics.

3.1 The Sign

Signs, in Morris's definition, are constituted in situations of sign use involving the three components of semiosis. Morris interpreted such processes in terms of *semiotic mediation* and in terms of *behaviorism*.

3.1.1 SEMIOTIC MEDIATION

In a preliminary definition, Morris described semiosis as a process of semiotic mediation (cf. Sign 1.3.3): "A sign is used with respect to some goal if it is produced by an interpreter as a means of attaining that goal; a sign that is used is thus a means-object" (1946: 368). The three terms of semiosis, the *sign vehicle* (S), the *designatum* (*D*), and the *interpretant* (*I*), constitute the following mediational relation: "*S* is a sign of *D* for *I* to the degree that *I* takes account of *D* in virtue of the presence of *S*" (Morris 1938: 4). Sign vehicles are thus *mediators*, and "semiosis is accordingly a mediated-taking-account-of" (ibid.).

3.1.2 THE BEHAVIORIST DEFINITION OF THE SIGN

Morris wanted to overcome the shortcomings of the mentalist tradition of semiotics and pursued the goal of developing an "empirical science of signs" which abandons "terms whose reliability cannot be checked by observation" (1946: 105–106). His scientific ideal was behaviorism and a science on a biological basis. Within this framework, the sign is "roughly: something that directs behavior with respect to something that is not at the moment a stimulus" (ibid.: 366). A prototype of semiosis is observable in the conditioned response of a dog trained to seek food at a certain place on hearing a buzzer (ibid.: 83–84). Early behaviorists such as Pavlov had described the buzzer as a substitute stimulus evoking the same response (namely, salivation) as the original stimulus (food). Morris refused to equate the sign generally with a substitute stimulus (ibid.). He knew that signs do not necessarily evoke a direct response in the sense of "an action of a muscle or gland" (ibid.: 365) and that signs are not mere substitutes of their designata. The stimulus in semiosis is rather a *preparatory-stimulus*, one that influences reactions to other stimuli in other situations, and the response is not a singular event, but an empirically observable class of similar events called a *behavior-family*. The sign is then defined as follows: "If A is a preparatory-stimulus that, in the absence of stimulus-objects initiating response-sequences of a certain behavior-family, causes in some organism a disposition to respond by response-sequences of this behavior-family, then A is a sign" (ibid.: 366).

3.2 Signification and Denotation

The semantic dimension of the sign is also defined in behavioristic terms (cf. Meaning 4.1

for other behaviorist approaches to semantics). Morris reinterpreted the Peircean interpretant as "the disposition in an interpreter to respond, because of the sign" (1946: 93). As semantic correlates of the sign vehicle, Morris distinguished between *significatum* and *denotatum* (ibid.). These terms correspond closely to the *sense-reference* dichotomy (see Meaning 1.1.2) in the version adopted in logical semantics, namely, the distinction between *intension* ("the property designated by a predicate") and *extension* ("the class of individuals having this property"; cf. Carnap 1954: 40). Morris, however, reinterpreted both categories in behavioristic terms:

> Anything which would permit the completion of the response-sequences to which the interpreter is disposed because of a sign will be called a *denotatum* of the sign. A sign will be said to *denote* a denotatum. Those conditions which are such that whatever fulfills them is a denotatum will be called a *significatum* of the sign. A sign will be said to *signify* a significatum (1946: 93–94).

Returning to the example of Pavlov's dog, Morris interpreted the buzzer as the sign, the dog as the interpreter, the disposition to seek food at a certain place as the interpretant, "food in the place sought which permits the completion of the response-sequence" as the denotatum, and "the condition of being an edible object in a given place" as the significatum (ibid.: 94). In his earlier writings, Morris wanted to give a purely referential account of meaning at the neglect of the aspect of sense. At that time, he distinguished between the *denotatum* (an actually existing member of a class of objects of reference) and the *designatum* (the class of referential objects—where a class may have many, one, or no members) (1938: 5).

3.3 Typology of Signs

Morris developed an elaborate typology of signs, some based on pragmatic, others on semantic criteria (1946: 20ff.). Only a few characteristic examples of his typology can be given below.

3.3.1 SOME PRAGMATICALLY DETERMINED TYPES OF SIGN

Since signs, according to Morris (1946: 96–97), are formed by assigning similar sign vehicles to sign-families (see 3.1.2), signs usually belong to the class of *plurisituational* signs. These signs signify in many situations, while *unisituational* signs have signification in only one situation. In another pragmatic category, the criterion is the sign user: "To the degree that a sign has the same signification to a number of interpreters it is an *interpersonal sign*; to the degree that this is not so the sign is a *personal sign*" (ibid.). According to the degree to which the user can rely on finding a denotation in connection with a sign vehicle, Morris distinguished between *reliable* and *unreliable* signs (ibid.: 98).

A subclass of interpersonal signs is called *comsigns* (ibid.: 111). A comsign "has the same signification to the organism which produces it that it has to other organisms stimulated by it." These pragmatic criteria are the basis for Morris's definition of language or, as he calls it, *lansign-systems*: "A language is a set of plurisituational comsigns restricted in the ways in which they may be combined" (ibid.: 113).

3.3.2 SOME SEMANTICALLY DETERMINED TYPES OF SIGN

Several of Morris's typological categories are based on semantic criteria, for example:
Vague sign: "its significatum does not permit the determination of whether something is or is not a denotatum; otherwise it is *precise*."
Unambiguous sign: "it has only one significatum"; otherwise it is *ambiguous*.
Singular sign: "a sign whose signification permits only one denotatum; otherwise it is *general*."
Synonymous signs "belong to different sign-families and yet have the same signification" (1946: 359–68).

3.3.3 ICON, INDEX, AND SYMBOL

Morris gave the following reinterpretation of the famous Peircean trichotomy (1938: 24): "An indexical sign designates what it directs attention to." The index is opposed to a sign which "characterizes that which it can denote. Such a sign may do this by exhibiting in itself the properties an object must have to be denoted by it, and in this case the *characterizing sign* is an *icon*; if this is not so, the characterizing sign may be called a *symbol*" (ibid.). Instead of the category of index, Morris later introduced the sign type of *identifior* (see Typology 4.2.3). For Morris's theory of iconicity, see Icon (2.1).

3.3.4 SIGNALS VS. SYMBOLS

Morris also discussed the distinction between signals and symbols, which—sometimes under the designation of sign vs. symbol—many semioticians have considered the most basic one in the theory of signs (cf. Typology 1.2.2, 3.1). In his definition, "a *symbol* is a sign produced by its interpreter which acts as a substitute for some other sign with which it is synonymous; all signs not symbols are *signals*. [. . .] A person may interpret his pulse as a sign of his heart condition [. . .] such signs are simply signals; his resulting words—when substitutes for such signals—would however be symbols" (1946: 100–101).

4. Morris's Semiotic Typology of Discourse

On the basis of a theory of modes of signifying and a theory of sign use, Morris developed a typology of discourse which has had some influence within applied text semiotics (1946: 140ff., 203ff.; cf. Klaus 1964, Fiordo 1977).

4.1 Modes of Signifying

According to the nature of the environment in which an organism operates, Morris distinguished three major pragmasemantic modes of signifying (1946: 142). The buzzer, for example, "designates food in a certain place, appraises this positively in relation to hunger, and prescribes the response of acting in a certain way." This case of semiosis illustrates the *designative*, *appraisive*, and *prescriptive* modes of signifying. All three modes may be involved to varying degrees in any act of semiosis, but statements are predominantly designative, valuations predominantly appraisive, and imperatives predominantly prescriptive.

Two further less important modes of signifying distinguished by Morris are the *identificative* mode—it designates locations in space and time—and the *formative* mode designating formators. Formators are language signs having only contextual functions, such as conjunctions, quantifiers, other function words, and punctuation marks. All of these modes are defined in behavioristic categories. Formators, for example, are "signs that dispose their interpreters to modify in determinate ways the dispositions to response occasioned by other signs in the sign combinations in which the formator appears" (ibid.: 362).

4.2 Dimensions of Sign Use

While the modes of signifying characterize the sign predominantly in its semantic dimension, the dimensions of sign use focus on the pragmatic aspects of semiosis, the "question of the purpose for which an organism produces the signs which it or other organisms interpret" (Morris 1946: 172). Four primary sign usages are distinguished which evince a certain parallelism to the main modes of signifying. Depending on the or-

ganism's behavioral goals, there is (1) *informative* usage when the sign is used to inform about something, (2) *valuative* usage when it is intended to aid in the preferential selection of objects, (3) *incitive* usage when it incites response-sequences, and (4) *systemic* usage when it organizes sign-produced behavior into a determinate whole (cf. ibid.: 174–75). When the goal of these modes of usage is attained, the informative usage was *convincing*, the valuative usage was *effective*, the incitive usage was *persuasive*, and the systemic usage was *correct* (cf. ibid.: 176).

4.3 Discourse Typology

Morris was convinced that the major types of discourse in everyday life can be distinguished by two dimensions of criteria, the characteristic mode of signifying and the primary mode of sign use (1946: 203–205). In every discourse type there is one dominant mode of signifying and a primary usage. Fictive discourse, for example, is predominantly designative in the way it signifies the events of a story. It minimizes appraisals and prescriptions. The communicative purpose of fiction, according to Morris, is valuative since it aims to induce the reader to evaluate the events represented in the story. It does not inform or tell us how to act. Altogether, Morris gave sixteen examples of discourse types distinguished by the criteria of use and signification (Fig. Mo 3).

Mode \ Use	Informative	Valuative	Incitive	Systemic
Designative	Scientific	Fictive	Legal	Cosmological
Appraisive	Mythical	Poetic	Moral	Critical
Prescriptive	Technological	Political	Religious	Propagandistic
Formative	Logico-mathematical	Rhetorical	Grammatical	Metaphysical

Fig. Mo 3. Morris's examples of the major types of discourse (1946: 205).

Saussure

Ferdinand de Saussure (1857–1913) is the undisputed founder of modern linguistics (cf., e.g., Lyons 1968: 38). Moreover, the basic principles of his theory of language have profoundly influenced the development of structuralism. The importance of Saussure's work in the history of semiotics, however, has received a mixed evaluation. The core of Saussure's contribution to semiotics is his project for a general theory of sign systems which he called *semiology*. A basic element of this theory is Saussure's *sign model*. Other important principles of the Saussurean semiotic tradition are discussed in the chapters on arbitrariness, structure, and system. It should be emphasized that the whole range of Saussure's contributions to linguistics cannot be outlined in a handbook dealing with the broader scope of semiotics.

1. Saussure's Work and Saussurean Studies

With his semiotic antipode and contemporary Charles Sanders Peirce, whose work remained unknown to him (cf. Sebeok 1979: 183–86), Saussure shared the fate of having become world famous only posthumously. Unlike Peirce, however, Saussure was successful in an academic career. After study in Leipzig (1876–80) and a teaching position at the Sorbonne (1881–91), he taught Indo-European and general linguistics at the University of Geneva (1891–1912). For Saussure's biography see Sebeok, ed. (1966: 87–110), Mounin (1968b), Godel (1957), de Mauro (1972, in Saussure 1916c: 319–89), Koerner (1973: 20–37), and Culler (1976).

Saussure developed his ideas for a general theory of language and sign systems in three courses given between 1907 and 1911. Since

Fig. S 1. Ferdinand de Saussure (1857–1913).

many of the manuscripts for these courses were destroyed by the author himself, Saussure's *Cours de linguistique générale* was published in 1916 from notes taken by his students Bally and Sechehaye. This edition (1916a) was supplemented with critical notes to a new standard edition (1916c) by de Mauro in 1972. The first English translation by W. Baskin (Saussure 1916b) appeared in 1959. The new translation of 1986 by Roy Harris presents Saussure's (1916e) *Course* in a revolutionized terminology (for example: the *signifiant-signifié* dichotomy is translated as *signification-signal*). This new terminology has not been adopted in this handbook. It differs too much from the tradition of Saussurean exegesis which has become the current semiotic terminology. Text critical research by Godel (1957), and the monumental critical edition by Engler (Saussure 1916d), which gives a synopsis of all available notes by Saussure and his students, have contributed to the reconstruction of Saussure's original system of thought.

Most European introductions to linguistics give a good account of Saussure's contributions to the theory of language (e.g., Lyons 1968). A bibliography on Saussure's work and its study is Koerner (1972a; b). Monographic studies are Derossi (1965), Mounin (1968b), Koerner (1973), Calvet (1975), Culler (1976), Scheerer (1980), and Wunderli (1981a). Studies with particular interest in Saussure's contribution to the development of semiotics are Godel (1975), Engler (1975b; 1980), Culler (1976: 90–117), Vigener (1979), Krampen (1981b), Percival (1981), and Wunderli (1981a: 11–49). For the reception of Saussure's work in England and the United States see, e.g., Wells (1947), de Mauro (in Saussure 1916c: 371–73), and the special issue of the journal *Semiotext[e]* (vol. 1, no. 2, 1974) entitled "The Two Saussures."

2. Saussure's Semiological Project

Semiology was at first only the project of a future science of sign systems, but Saussure indicated its place within a general system of the sciences. For the terminological equivalence between *semiology* and *semiotics* since the 1970s, see History (1.2.4).

2.1 Definition and Concept of Semiology

The term *sémiologie* was apparently coined by Saussure himself to designate the "not yet existing" general science of signs (cf. Engler 1980). An alternative term suggested in a different context was *signologie* (1916d: § 3342: 6). Semiology is not to be confounded with semantics, the study of meaning in language (see History 1.1.3). Saussure gave the following outline of his project of a future semiology:

> A science that studies the life of signs within society is conceivable; [. . .] I shall call it *semiology* (from Greek *sēmeîon* 'sign'). Semiology would show what constitutes signs, what laws govern them. Since the science does not yet exist, no one can say what it would be; but it has a right to existence, a place staked out in advance. (1916b: 16)

2.2 Saussure's Program for Semiological Research

Saussure commented frequently on the "mass of semiological data" (1916b: 19) to be studied within the framework of semiotics without giving a detailed analysis of most of those sign systems.

2.2.1 EXAMPLES OF SEMIOLOGICAL SYSTEMS

Saussure gave the following examples for sign systems besides language: "Language is a system of signs that express ideas, and is therefore comparable to the system of writing, the alphabet, the alphabet of deaf-mutes, symbolic rites, polite formulas, military signals, etc. But it is the most important of all these systems" (1916b: 16). Other sign systems mentioned elsewhere by Saussure as further topics of semiological research are Braille, the maritime flag code, military trumpet signals, cipher codes, and the Germanic myths (cf. Wunderli 1981a: 20–21).

2.2.2 SAUSSURE'S CONTRIBUTION TO LITERARY SEMIOTICS

Only in the field of literature did Saussure undertake more extensive studies of sign systems other than language. In his mythological studies (cf. Avalle 1973a; b) the Germanic *Nibelungen* legend is described as a "system of symbols" and "part of semiology," where "these symbols are unconsciously subject to the same variations and laws as any other series of symbols, for example, the symbols which are the words of language" (Starobinski 1971: 5). Besides this mythological study, Saussure has become noted for a second study in the semiotics of literature, dealing with anagrams in Latin poetry (cf. Starobinski 1971, Culler 1976: 106–114). Both studies were discovered only in the 1970s. For Saussure's influence on structuralist and poststructuralist theories of literature, see especially Tallis (1988).

2.2.3 SEMIOLOGY AS ANTHROPOSEMIOTICS

Although Saussure's outline of semiological research is only sketchy, his examples show that his concept refers to a semiotics of culture, or perhaps to the field of anthroposemiotics (see Semiotics 1.1). Zoosemiotic phenomena or even natural signs as discussed within Peirce's universal semiotics have no place in Saussure's program of semiology, for one of the fundamental tenets of Saussurean semiology is the principle of *arbitrariness* and *conventionality* of signs. The importance of this principle for semiological research is emphasized in the following passage:

> When semiology becomes organized as a science, the question will arise whether or not it properly includes modes of expression based on completely natural signs, such as pantomime. Supposing that the new science welcomes them, its main concern will still be the whole group of systems grounded on the arbitrariness of the sign. In fact, every means of expression used in society is based, in principle, on collective behavior or—what amounts to the same thing—on convention. [. . .] Signs that are wholly arbitrary realize better than the others the ideal of the semiological process. (1916b: 68)

2.3 *Semiology and Linguistics within the System of Sciences*

At various points in his lectures, Saussure showed a great interest in the classification of the sciences. Within semiology, a dominant role is assigned to linguistics.

2.3.1 SEMIOLOGY AS A BRANCH OF SOCIOLOGY AND PSYCHOLOGY

Saussure's semiology was already mentioned in 1901 in the classification of the sciences by the Genevan contemporary Adrien Naville (cf. Saussure 1916c: 352; Engler 1980: 4–5). Naville classified semiology as an essential part of sociology and defined the latter, and thus also semiology and linguistics, as sciences of laws. Saussure later assigned semiology to social psychology, suggesting that it is the task of the psychologist to determine the exact place of semiology within the sciences (1916b: 16). At various other points, however, Saussure referred to semiology as a science of social institutions, a discipline related to the study of judiciary institutions (1916d: 45, 49, 51).

2.3.2 LINGUISTICS AS THE *PATRON GÉNÉRAL* OF SEMIOTICS

Within semiology, Saussure attributed a special role to linguistics. Since

> signs that are wholly arbitrary realize better than the others the ideal of the semiological process, that is why language, the most complex and universal of all systems of expression, is also the most characteristic; in this sense linguistics can become the master-pattern [*patron général*] for all branches of semiology although language is only one particular semiological system. (1916b: 68)

This famous thesis of linguistics as the *patron général* of semiotics has often been misinterpreted. Influential schools of semiotics held that language is a sign system that is dominant in relation to other semiotic systems. From this (and for other reasons), Barthes even drew the conclusion that semiology should be considered a branch of linguistics (see Language 2.2). However, this was not Saussure's own argument. Elsewhere (1916d: 48), Saussure even argued that the special place of linguistics within semiology is only a matter of chance, since theoretically language is only one among many semiological systems.

The special role of linguistics within semiology is, however, not purely due to chance. Following the *Course* and Naville's account of Saussure's semiology (Engler 1980: 4), there are three arguments which characterize language in relation to other sign systems: (1) The first argument is practical or empirical: Language is the most important of all sign systems. (2) The second argument is from the history of science (and semiotics): Linguistics is the most advanced of all semiological sciences. (3) The third argument is heuristic: "Language, better than anything else, offers a basis for understanding the semiological problem" (1916b: 16).

2.4 "Design Features" of Language

One of Saussure's main interests was the attempt to define the distinctive features of language in relation to other sign systems. Thus, long before the semiotic discussion about the design features of language (see Language 3.1), Saussure arrived at a list of semiotic characteristics of language, which Wunderli summarizes as follows (1981a: 33): (1) highest degree of *arbitrariness*; (2) *social institution*: dependence on the whole of the social community that uses the language; (3) *immutability*: independence from individual acts of volition or social legislation; (4) *no predetermined units*: lack of any *a priori* delimitation in the linguistic form of expression; (5) *productivity*: unlimited semantic possibilities with a limited inventory of signs; (6) *acoustic* manifestation.

3. Saussure's Theory of the Sign

Saussure (1916b: 65–70; 102–103; 114) elaborated his sign model only in order to analyze the "nature of the *linguistic* sign." In the semiological tradition following Saussure, this lin-

guistic sign model was also transferred to nonlinguistic signs. This transfer seems to be compatible with the semiological program. Fundamental aspects of Saussure's theory of the sign are its bilateral structure, its mentalistic conception, the exclusion of reference, and the structural conception of meaning. Another basic aspect is the arbitrariness of the linguistic sign. With these features, Saussure's sign theory is opposed both to unilateral and to triadic models of the sign. For research in Saussure's theory of the sign, see Derossi (1965), Koerner (1972b; 1973), Avalle (1973b), Vigener (1979), Jäger & Stetter, eds. (1986).

3.1 The Bilateral Model

Saussure's two-sided or bilateral sign model comprises three terms, the *sign* and its constituents *signifier* and *signified*. The distinctive feature of its bilaterality is the exclusion of the referential object.

3.1.1 THE TWO-SIDED SIGN

According to a simile given by Saussure, the linguistic sign can be compared with the two sides of a sheet of paper: "Thought is the front and the sound the back; one cannot cut the front without cutting the back at the same time" (1916b: 113). This simile of the two-sided sign has led to the designation of the Saussurean sign as bilateral or dyadic. In this sense, Saussure defined the linguistic sign as a "two-sided psychological entity" consisting of a *concept* and a *sound-image* (ibid.: 66; for these terms see 3.2). Figure S 2 represents these two sides within an ellipse which stands for the sign as a whole. An exemplification of the model shows the Latin word *arbor* as a sequence of sounds referring to the concept 'tree.' The arrows indicate the "psychological association" between sound-image and concept. Their directions refer to the processes of speech production and reception within Saussure's speech circuit (see Communication 3.2.1).

Fig. S 2. Saussure's model of the linguistic sign (*left*) with Saussure's exemplification (*right*). The *concept* is illustrated by the image of a 'tree,' the *sound-image* ("image acoustique") by the Latin word *arbor* (1916a: 99).

3.1.2 SIGN, SIGNIFIER, AND SIGNIFIED

For the two sides which constitute a sign, Saussure later introduced the new terms *signifié* (for *concept*) and *signifiant* (for *sound-image*) (1916b: 67; the English translation is *signified* and *signifier*). The reason for this terminological innovation was that these two terms "have the advantage of indicating the opposition that separates them from each other and from the whole of which they are parts" (ibid.). Thus, three notions are involved in Saussure's dyadic sign model. The sign [*signe*] designates the whole which has the signified and the signifier as its two parts (see Fig. S 3). For Saussure's use of signification as a fourth term in his semiological theory, see Wunderli (1981b). (The termi-

sign	signified (concept)
	signifier (sound-image)

Fig. S 3. The three terms in Saussure's dyadic sign model.

nological triad of sign, signifier, and signified led Stetter [1979: 126] to the assumption that Saussure actually proposed a triadic sign model. This argument is hardly convincing. If the characterization of the sign models were always to include the superordinate term, Peirce's model [sign = representamen + object + interpretant] would have to be called a tetradic model.)

Incidentally, in spite of his objection to the colloquial identification of the term *sign* with the signifier, Saussure himself occasionally used the term *sign* when referring to the signi-

fier (cf. Wells 1947: 5–6). The same inconsistency occurs in the writings of Peirce, where *representamen* and *sign* are not always distinguished.

3.2 *The Mentalistic Conception*

Both the signified and the signifier are mental entities and independent of any external object in Saussure's theory of the sign. The mentalistic conception of the signifier is already apparent in Saussure's term and definition of *sound-image*: "The latter is not the material sound, a purely physical thing, but the psychological imprint of the sound, the impression that it makes in our senses" (1916b: 66). However, this psychological view of the two sides of the sign is not conceived of as a matter of individual psychology, for the study of "the sign-mechanisms in the individual [. . .] does not reach the sign, which is social" (ibid.: 17). Since semiology, according to Saussure (ibid.), studies signs as social institutions, the signified and the signifier are not individual but collective concepts and sound images.

The mentalistic sign model is opposed to empiricist and materialist theories of the sign (for the latter see Morris 2.3.5). A typical antipode to Saussure in this respect is Morris. In his theory, the sign-vehicle is a physical event and the denotatum is (at least potentially) a physically existing stimulus object. Saussure's mentalist and system-based semiology is also incompatible with semiotic theories which describe semiosis as a cognitive process of interaction between individual and world, a process in which signs play the role of a mediator between thought and reality (cf. Mertz & Parmentier, eds. 1985).

3.3 *The Exclusion of the Referential Object*

The dyadic character of the sign was emphasized by Saussure in his explicit rejection of the referential object as an element in his semiology, for "the linguistic sign unites, not a thing [chose] and a name, but a concept and a sound-image" (1916b: 66). For Saussure, nothing existed (structurally) beyond the signifier and the signified. His semiology operated totally within the sign system. Since only a semiological system gives structure to the otherwise amorphous world, the referential object is excluded from semiotic consideration.

One of the objections which have been raised against the exclusion of the referential object is that Saussure's argument of the arbitrary nature of signs (see Arbitrariness 2.1) necessarily requires reference to characteristics of objects in the world. Helbig even argues that in this respect Saussure's argumentation changes to a triadic sign model (1974: 40). It is true that Saussure claimed that arbitrariness is a relation between signifier and signified, and not the object (1916b: 69). But when he argues that "the signified 'ox' has as its signifier *b-ö-f* on one side of the border and *o-k-s* (*Ochs*) on the other" (ibid.: 68), the *tertium comparationis* of these French and German signifiers cannot be one and the same signified. It must be the extrasemiotic object after all, for there are two signifieds involved, since these are determined by their value in two sign systems (cf. Arbitrariness 2.3.2).

3.4 Meaning as Semantic Structure

Concept and *signified* are terms which lead into the semiotic dimension of semantics. Apparently, these concepts closely correspond to the more general semiotic terms *meaning* and *content*. What is the "meaning of meaning" in Saussure's semiology? Besides his mentalistic interpretation of meaning and his exclusion of the referential object from the sphere of semantics, Saussure's main contribution to this question lies in his view of meaning as form or as a differential value.

3.4.1 MEANING: NOT SUBSTANCE BUT FORM

Parallel to his rejection of an "objective world," Saussure also objected to the notion that "ready-made ideas exist before words" (1916b: 65). For Saussure, nothing existed outside of the semiological system of signifiers and signifieds. Thought, considered before language, "is only a shapeless and indistinct mass.

[. . .] Without language, thought is a vague, uncharted nebula. There are no pre-existing ideas, and nothing is distinct before the appearance of language" (ibid.: 111–12).

These arguments are part of Saussure's (cf. 1916b: 113) thesis that semiology is a science of forms, not of substances, a theory which was further elaborated by Hjelmslev. Form, in this context, means structure. It does not refer to the signifier, as the popular form-content dichotomy might suggest. Form can exist only as structure within a system. Outside of the semiological system, ideas belong to an amorphous presemiotic substance. Within the sign system, both signifiers and signifieds are therefore form, not substance.

3.4.2 MEANINGS AS DIFFERENTIAL VALUES

According to Saussure's structuralist view of semantics, meaning is the *value* of a concept within the whole semiological system (see System 2.2.1). These semantic values form a network of structural relations, in which not the semantic concepts as such, but only the differences or oppositions between them are semiotically relevant (see Structure 2.1). Although it was Hjelmslev who systematically elaborated this idea of structural semantics, Saussure set the guidelines of this structuralist view of language with arguments such as:

> Language is a system of interdependent terms in which the value of each term results solely from the simultaneous presence of the others. [. . .] Content is really fixed only by the concurrence of everything that exists outside it. Being part of a system, it is endowed not only with a signification but also and especially with a value." (1916b: 114–15)

An exemplification of the semantic theory of value given by Saussure (ibid.) is the meaning of French *mouton* compared to English *sheep*. The value of the English term is different from the French one because English opposes *sheep* to *mutton*, while French does not have this difference of semantic value. Thus, the different place of *sheep* within the English language system also accounts for the difference in meaning.

4. The Dyadic Tradition: Between Semiotic Monads and Triads

In contradistinction to Peirce, whose philosophy is imbued with triadic ideas, most of Saussure's basic concepts are based on dyads. He rejected monadic sign models and established a dyadic tradition (with Hjelmslev as his most important follower). There are few precedents to this strictly dyadic semiology in the history of semiotics.

4.1 Rejection of Monadic Sign Models

Bilateral sign models are opposed both to monadic (or monolateral) and to triadic models of signs. Monolateral concepts of the sign are without much theoretical importance in semiotics. They occur in colloquial language when the sign is identified with its sign vehicle or signifier (cf. Helbig 1974: 38). Saussure criticized this colloquial use of the term *sign*: "In current usage the term [*sign*] generally designates only a sound-image, a word, for example (*arbor*, etc.). One tends to forget that *arbor* is called a sign only because it carries the concept 'tree' " (1916b: 67). (For his own inconsistencies in this point, see 3.1.2). But monadic sign models also occur in certain theories of semantics which consider meaning *and* the referential object as extralinguistic facts to which the sign vehicle is correlated (cf. Wiegand 1970). It was one of these approaches to meaning which Saussure criticized as naive when he argued that the elements of language should not be regarded as a nomenclature, a list of terms, each corresponding to objects (1916a: 97; 1916b: 65).

4.2 The Dyadic and the Triadic Traditions

Many semioticians consider Saussure's dyadic sign model, with its exclusion of the referential object, one of the most distinctive features of Saussurean semiology. While many have followed this dyadic tradition, some have argued that the triadic model proposed by Peirce is superior for the solution of semiotic problems (cf. Köller 1977: 25–33).

The dyadic model has certain precursors in the history of semiotics (cf. Koerner 1973: 312–24). In the dialectics of the Stoics, it appears as the dichotomy of *sēmáinon* (σημαῖνον) and *sēmainómenon* (σημαινόμενον) (cf. Brekle 1985: 51). With reference to this tradition, Jakobson (cf. 1965: 345) introduced the Latin translation of these terms, *signans* and *signatum*, as the equivalent of Saussure's *signifier* and *signified* (with *signum* as the superordinate term for the whole sign). But it is in fact controversial whether this tradition is a genuinely dyadic one, or whether it is only part of an essentially triadic model which includes the referential object as a third category. While Jakobson considered the dyadic sign concept "more than a bimillenary model" (ibid.), Coseriu (1970) and Lieb (1981a) emphasize the triadic character of this tradition. Foucault discusses the sign model of Port-Royal as a precursor of the dyadic tradition, quoting Arnauld's definition (see History 3.1.2): "The sign encloses two ideas, one of the thing representing, the other of the thing represented" (1966a: 63–64). But Rey argues that with the referential object, which is mentioned elsewhere in the *Port-Royal Logic*, a third dimension is also implied in this sign theory (1973: 119). However, the question whether a sign model has a dyadic or a triadic character cannot be resolved on the basis of terminological comparison, as some studies suggest. (For such a comparison, see Sign, Fig. Si 1.) It is irrelevant whether Saussure or other sign theoreticians use a term such as *object* or *chose* somewhere in their discussion. The question is whether this term has a systematic place within the semiotic theory. For Saussure's system of semiology this is certainly not the case.

5. System, *Langue-Parole*, Synchrony-Diachrony

Another major contribution of Saussure to the history of semiotics is his analysis of sign phenomena *qua* system. These aspects of Saussurean semiology are discussed in detail in the chapters on system and structure, but two related Saussurean dichotomies have to be mentioned here as an addendum, *langue* vs. *parole* and *synchrony* vs. *diachrony*. Saussure's primary interest was in language as a system or a code, and a social phenomenon. He called this linguistic system language (*la langue*) and opposed it to speech (*la parole*). Speech is the individual's use of the social sign system in speech acts and texts.

Saussure's concept of language is a rather static one. In order to isolate linguistic structures from their historical evolution, Saussure introduced the dichotomy of *synchrony* and *diachrony*. Synchronic analysis studies a sign system at a given point of time, irrespective of its history. Diachronic analysis studies the evolution of a sign system in its historical development. Since linguists before Saussure were concerned primarily with the history of language, Saussure's suggestions for the study of language in a synchronic perspective meant a new paradigm in the history of linguistics.

---

6. Saussure and the Development of Semiotics

Saussure's contribution to the development of semiotics has received a mixed evaluation.

6.1 Saussure as a Founder of Semiotics

In the Romance countries, Saussure was for a long time considered the real founder of semiotics (e.g., Prieto 1968: 93). Hardly any semiotic study in these countries fails to pay tribute to Saussure's project of semiology (e.g., Buyssens 1943: 5–6; and see Barthes).

6.2 Saussure as a Precursor of Semiotics

Yet, Mounin gives a restrictive evaluation of Saussure's place in the history of semiotics (1968b: 33). He argues that Saussure's concern for semiology was motivated primarily by his

interest in the classification of the sciences (pace Godel 1975: 3). In his opinion, Saussure's *Cours* is important for linguistics, but the semiological project is only a rough outline from which neither theoretical nor methodological consequences are drawn. Thus, Mounin evaluates Saussure not as the founder but only as an initiator or a precursor of semiotics. Saussure's contribution to progress in semiotics is also estimated as modest by Jakobson (1975: 12), and Sebeok (1976: 153) likewise considers the high evaluation of Saussure's achievement for the history of semiotics "a downright distortion of true historical equilibrium."

6.3 Heuristic Importance of Saussure

In fact, Saussure's contribution to a general theory of signs has been only minor. He had little to say about nonlinguistic signs and was not concerned with questions such as the general typology of signs. Nevertheless, his historical influence in semiotics has been considerable in two respects, heuristics and systematics of semiotics.

As to heuristics, Saussure's idea of linguistics as a *patron général* of semiology has been most influential in the structuralist-semiological tradition. With this guideline, nonlinguistic sign systems have been analyzed according to principles derived from linguistics. The model of language served as a heuristic instrument in the analysis of other sign systems. As to semiotic systematics, Saussure has drawn the researchers' attention to the necessity of studying signs within systems. His ideas in this respect have had a decisive influence on the development of the semiotic theory of codes. Ideas of semiotic structure and systematicity have little precedent in the more philosophical tradition of semiotics represented by Peirce. Thus, it is probably justified to agree with Hervey, who designates both Peirce and Saussure as pioneers of modern semiotics (1982: 9).

Hjelmslev

Louis Hjelmslev (['jɛlmsleu], 1899–1965) was the founder of a school of radically structuralist linguistics, known as *glossematics* or the Copenhagen School of Linguistics. Language, in the theory of glossematics (from γλῶσσα 'language'), comprises both "linguistic" and "nonlinguistic languages," and this extended scope of research made glossematics an important school of semiotics. Hjelmslev's model of

the sign and of language and his concepts of structure, text, and system have had considerable influence on later developments in general semiotics. His theory of connotation is the foundation of a glossematic theory of literature and aesthetics. For Hjelmslev's academic biography, see Fischer-Jørgensen (1965).

1. Hjelmslev's Contribution to Semiotics

In spite of objections that have been raised against Hjelmslev's structuralist formalism in linguistics, the founder of the Copenhagen School has meanwhile been acknowledged to be a classic of semiotics (cf. Krampen et al., eds. 1981).

1.1 Survey of Hjelmslev's Work

The foundations of Hjelmslev's semiotics lie in Saussure's structural linguistics and semiology. In the context of linguistic structuralism, glossematics is distinguished by its formalism from the functionalism which characterizes the Prague School structuralism. Another distinctive feature of glossematics is its theory of structural homology between the expression and the content planes of language, which A.

Fig. H 1. Portrait of Louis Hjelmslev (1899–1965).

Martinet found to be incompatible with his theory of *double articulation* (cf. Language 4.1.1). See also Christensen (1967), Helbig (1974: 60–72), Lepschy (1975), and Metz (1977a: 11–30) for further differences between glossematics and other schools of linguistics.

Hjelmslev's most influential semiotic study is his *Omkring sprogteoriens grundlæggelse*, translated by F. J. Whitfield as *Prolegomena to a Theory of Language* (1943). For further developments in his semiotic structuralism, in particular his ideas on structural semantics, see Hjelmslev (1959; 1973; 1975). Uldall, who collaborated closely with Hjelmslev in the development of the Copenhagen School, wrote an *Outline of Glossematics* (1967). Critical studies and surveys of Hjelmslev's linguistic and semiotic research are Siertsema (1954), Haas (1956), Coseriu (1962: 156–88), Fischer-Jørgensen (1966), Spang-Hanssen (1966), Mounin (1970c), Barth & Harras (1974), Helbig (1974: 60–72), Gutiérrez López (1975: 95–122), Malmberg (1977: 344–60), Trabant (1981a), and Johansen (1986 a and b). Hjelmslev's work in contrast to Peircean semiotics is the topic of a study by Parret (1983: 23–87).

1.2 Hjelmslev's Influence in Semiotic Studies

Hjelmslev's place in the history of semiotics has been disputed. On the one hand, there has been criticism of his abstract formalism and "terminological extravagance" (Haas 1956: 110). Among others, Mounin misses the empirical relevance of Hjelmslev's theory and criticizes his "rather naive axiomatic, based on a no less naive logic" (1970c: 99). On the other hand, Coseriu likens Hjelmslev's place in the history of linguistics to that of W. von Humboldt (1962: 156), while according to Trabant, "the truly original aspect of his work is the development of a semiotic rather than a linguistic theory. For he is nothing less than the originator of that Saussurean desideratum, namely a *general* science of signs (*sémiologie*) based on immanent and structural linguistics" (1981a: 90).

Hjelmslev has had the greatest influence on Greimas and his School of Paris, but Eco's theory of semiotics is also based on central Hjelmslevian principles. To a lesser degree, Barthes's *Elements of Semiotics* and Metz's (1971; 1977a) semiotics of film are founded in Hjelmslev's semiotics. The element of Hjelmslev's theory which has been most popularized in applied semiotics is his theory of connotation. A Hjelmslevian theory of theater is Jansen (1968). For the semiotics of literature, see 4.2. An evaluation of Hjelmslev's work which does justice to the influence of the Danish linguist in modern semiotics, without concealing its limits, is given by Eco:

> The only author who could have succeeded in proposing a general theoretical framework for a semiotic theory was Hjelmslev, but his theory was too abstract, his examples concerning other semiotic systems very limited and rather parenthetical, and his glossematic jargon impenetrable. Hjelmslev as a semiotician has been highly influential in the last two decades. (1977a: 41)

2. Language, Semiotic(s), and Semiology

Glossematics is a formal and abstract theory, studying the immanent factors of semiotic systems without considering a pragmatic dimension of semiosis. By abstracting from structures of the material substance of language, glossematics aims at a level of descriptive generality which makes this theory of language applicable to the study of sign systems in general.

2.1 Language and Semiotic

The heuristic point of departure for Hjelmslev's semiotics is language, which in his definition is not only "natural" language but "language in a far broader sense," including "any structure that is analogous to a language and satisfies the given definition" (1943: 102, 107). Hjelmslev introduced the term *semiotic* for language in this broad sense. The "given definition" to which Hjelmslev referred is, "a *semiotic* is a *hierarchy, any of whose components admits of a further analysis into classes defined by mutual relation*" (ibid. 106). Thus, a natural language, in this terminology, is a semiotic, but since "structures analogous to language" belong to the class of language in the broad sense, the distinction between language and semiotic, and with it the distinction between linguistics and semiotics, tends to dissolve itself in Hjelmslev's glossematics (cf. Mounin 1970c: 96). The German translators of Hjelmslev's *Prolegomena* (1943a) even translate *semiotic* generally as *language* (*Sprache*), justifying this terminology with reference to the text of the Danish original (1943a: 105).

Nevertheless, Hjelmslev attributed a special place to language in relation to other semiotic systems: "In practice, a language is a semiotic into which all other semiotics may be translated—both all other languages, and all other conceivable semiotic structures" (1943: 109). Quoting S. Kierkegaard, Hjelmslev added: "In a language, and only in a language, we can 'work over the inexpressible until it is expressed.'"

2.2 Semiology and Metasemiotic

Hjelmslev placed his semiotic project of establishing a "linguistics in the broader sense" on an "*immanent* basis" in the tradition of the Saussurean project of a general semiology (1943: 108). The goal of his new project was "to establish a common point of view for a large number of disciplines, from the study of literature, art, and music, and general history, all the way to logistics and mathematics, so that from this common point of view these sciences are concentrated around a linguistically defined setting of problems" (ibid.).

Hjelmslev defined semiology as a *metalanguage* (cf. Function 3.2) of semiotic systems, "as a metasemiotic with a nonscientific semiotic as an object semiotic" (ibid.: 120). In this sense, linguistics is a semiology whose object (semiotic) is natural language. Besides linguis-

tics, there are other semiologies whose object of study is other sign phenomena. The common principles of these semiologies, according to Hjelmslev, form the field of *metasemiology*, "a meta-(scientific) semiotic whose object semiotics are semiologies" (ibid.).

3. Hjelmslev's Sign Model

Hjelmslev's theory of the sign is a further development of Saussure's bilateral sign model and of the Saussurean distinction between *substance* and *form*. The outline of Hjelmslev's model is in chapter 13 of his *Prolegomena*. A more elaborated account is Hjelmslev (1954).

3.1 Outline of the Stratified Dyadic Model

Signifier ("sound-image") and signified ("concept") are the two sides of Saussure's sign model. Hjelmslev renamed them *expression* and *content* and called these two sides *planes* of the sign. Both the *expression plane* and the *content plane* are further stratified into semiotic form and substance. This makes four strata: *content-form*, *expression-form*, *content-substance*, and *expression-substance*.

In accordance with Saussure's thesis that semiotics is a science of forms (or structures) and not of substances, Hjelmslev restricted the use of the term *sign* to the two strata of expression-form and content-form (1943: 58; cf. Fig. H 2). However, unlike Saussure, Hjelmslev considered the two strata of substance not as being amorphous, but as being semiotically formed, i.e., structured by the system of sign forms. For the presemiotic sphere of the semiotically unstructured world, Hjelmslev introduced the concept of *purport*. This term causes some terminological difficulties (cf. Metz 1971: 2), and the distinction between substance and purport is not always consistent (cf. Fischer-Jørgensen 1966: 7). It translates the Danish word *mening*, which has been rendered as *sense* in French translations. A terminological equivalent is *matter* (cf. Eco 1984b: 44–45). Hjelmslev himself specified "matière ou sens" as equivalent to *purport* (1954: 50).

Only the sphere of purport corresponds to Saussure's "amorphous substance." But while Saussure discussed this presemiotic sphere only in relation to the content plane of language, Hjelmslev also postulated an unstructured sphere of *expression-purport* (see 3.2.2). With this parallelism in the stratification of expression and content and in other respects, the two planes are formally homologous, but for the differences in the structures of expression and content, which derive from the principle of arbitrariness; see 3.3.3. Figure H 2 shows a model representing Hjelmslev's stratification of the bilateral sign.

3.2 *Form, Substance, and Purport*

The ancient dichotomy of substance and form appears in quite a number of variants in semiotics and linguistics, but Hjelmslev's definition, which distinguishes matter (purport) as a third term, has been the most influential one.

3.2.1 PRELIMINARIES ON SUBSTANCE, FORM, AND MATTER

The terms *substance*, *form*, and *matter* are central concepts in the history of philosophy. They were used to translate Plato's and Aristotle's concepts of οὐσία ('substance'), εἶδος ('form,' Plato's *idea*), and ὕλη ('matter'). Traditionally, substance was defined as the essence of a

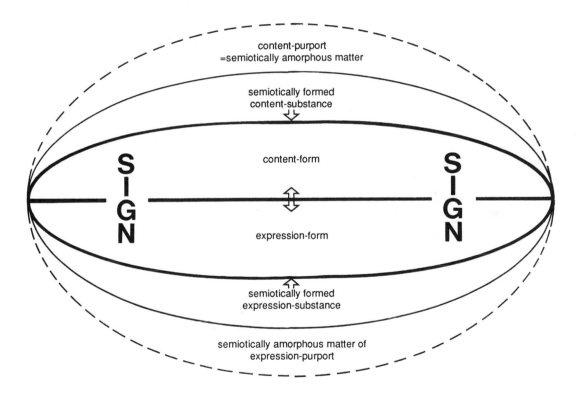

Fig. H 2. Hjelmslev's stratified dyadic sign model. ⟷ symbolizes a relation of *interdependence*: content-form and expression form are two constants which depend mutually on one another. ⟶ symbolizes the relation *determination* between a necessary functive (the constant), which is the form of content or expression, and a nonnecessary functive (the variable), which is the substance of content or expression.

thing, that which remains the same, whereas its appearance, the form, changes. According to Aristotle, substance consists of both matter and form, but has an existence independent from the thing and its matter. In this sense, substance is essentially unknowable. Matter is the basic stuff, the raw material of which the objects of the world are composed. It has traditionally been contrasted with either form or mind. According to Aristotle, matter, in contrast to substance, is that which has form. Every concrete object is composed of form and matter. Without form, matter would be "amorphous." Form is the shaping of matter to a perceptible object.

In the history of language studies, the dichotomy of form and matter has become mixed up in various ways with the dichotomy of expression and content (cf. Fischer-Jørgensen 1966: 1–2), and moreover, substance was often used in the sense of matter. In one tradition, the sounds of language were considered to be matter which received its form in linguistic articulation. In another tradition, syntactic structure was considered linguistic form and opposed to its content as its matter. Later, the phonetic manifestation of a language was called its form in opposition to its meaning (or content).

In modern linguistics, form is used in opposition to a variety of other concepts: (1) In opposition to meaning, form is still being used in the sense of phonetic or grammatical structure. (2) In morphology, form is the inflectional variant of a word. (3) In systemic linguistics, form is the organization of the phonetic or written "substance" of language into lexical or grammatical patterns (cf. Joia & Stenton 1980). (4) In a more general sense, *formal* is opposed to *informal*, in the sense of 'intuitive' or 'prescientific.' (5) A further dichotomy is the one between form and function (q.v.).

The main difference between these definitions and glossematic semiotics is that Hjelmslev ascribed substance and form to both meaning (content) and phonetic or graphemic expression, and that substance is distinguished from both matter (purport) and form. As Fi-

scher-Jørgensen points out (1966: 2), the two-fold distinction between form and matter in both sound and meaning was observed by Wilhelm von Humboldt. In his view, "the matter of language consisted partly in sounds, partly in unformed thoughts, the sounds being formed by the 'Lautform,' the thoughts by the 'Ideenform' or 'innere Form' of language."

3.2.2 PURPORT OF CONTENT AND EXPRESSION

At the content plane of language, *content-purport* is that "amorphous thought-mass" (Hjelmslev 1943: 52) which is formed differently by different languages. One of the examples is the "amorphous continuum" of the color spectrum and the color terms in different languages. Into this semiotically amorphous purport, "every language lays down its boundaries" (ibid.: 52). However, when Hjelmslev characterized the sphere of purport as being "unformed" or "inaccessible to knowledge" (ibid.: 76), he refers only to a semiotically amorphous sphere, which cannot be taken as the basis for linguistic description. But this lack of semiotic structure does not preclude the existence of nonsemiotic structures. Therefore, "the description of purport [. . .] may in all essentials be thought of as belonging partly to the sphere of *physics* and partly to that of (social) *anthropology*" (ibid.: 77–78). Later, Hjelmslev even postulated that "purport must be scientifically formed, at least to a degree that permits to distinguish it from other purports (matters)" (1954: 50).

At the expression plane, expression-purport is the phonetic potential of human vocal articulation, which is used differently to form the phonological systems of the natural languages of the world. Expression-purport can also be the potential of graphic communication which is used to form systems of writing, or the potential of gestural communication of which sign languages make use.

3.2.3 FORMED SUBSTANCE

Semiotic substance is the result of a specific structuring of purport by form. "Just as the same sand can be put into different molds," purport is shaped into formed substance (Hjelmslev 1943: 52–53). More specifically, Hjelmslev described the forming of substance out of purport as follows: "By virtue of the content-form and the expression-form, and only by virtue of them, exists respectively the content-substance and the expression-substance, which appear by the form's being projected on to the purport, just as an open net casts its shadows down on an undivided surface" (ibid.: 57). In this metaphor, the "undivided surface" is the purport, the "open net" is the form, and the "shadow" is the substance (cf. Metz 1971: 226).

But if substance always depends on form (ibid.: 50), why is the distinction between the two strata necessary at all? Hjelmslev answered that "substance is not a necessary presupposition for linguistic form, but linguistic form is a necessary presupposition for substance" (1943: 106). Pure form is thus an abstract structure, while formed substance is but "a reflex of pure form, projected onto substance" (Hjelmslev 1957: 108). Thus, substance (and with it matter) turns out to be the variable and nonnecessary functive of semiosis, while form is the constant and necessary functive (cf. Fig. H 2). This view of the primacy of form over substance reverses the traditional Aristotelian view of the primacy of matter (and substance) over form, but this reversal is due to two different perspectives. The traditional view of form being secondary to matter or substance is based on a semiogenetic perspective: substance and matter (Hjelmslev's purport) are prior to semiotic structures. Hjelmslev's view of the primacy of form over substance is true from a synchronically cognitive point of view. According to this view, semiotic or cultural structure determines the perception of the substances.

3.2.4 PURE FORM
Hjelmslev defined the two strata of form as systems of pure relations: "The entities of linguistic form are of 'algebraic' nature and have no natural designation; they can therefore be designated arbitrarily in many ways" (1943:

105). It is this abstract formal system of relations which, according to Hjelmslev, should be the subject of semiotic research: "The real units of language are not sounds, or written characters, or meanings [i.e., substances]; the real units of language are the relata which these sounds, characters, and meanings represent" (1948: 27).

However, the dependence of formed substance on pure form does not always imply a strict 1:1 homology between the two strata. Differences may arise because within the axiomatic system of pure form, "all possibilities must be foreseen, including those that are virtual in the world of experience, or remain without a 'natural' or 'actual' manifestation" (Hjelmslev 1943: 106). This difference between pure form and actual substance corresponds to Hjelmslev's (1937: 158) and Coseriu's (1962) distinction between *system* (q.v. 2.2.3) (~ form) on the one hand and *norm* and usage (~ substance) on the other. A lexical gap, for example the lack of an English lexeme to designate a female cat (in contrast to 'female dog'—*bitch*), is an example of a category of form without one of substance. Other possible differences between substance and form derive from Hjelmslev's postulate that "one and the same form can be manifested in different substances" (1957: 107). However, Hjelmslev's evidence for this postulate is restricted to the level of expression.

3.2.5 CONTENT-FORM AND -SUBSTANCE
Content-form "is independent of, and stands in arbitrary relation to, the *purport*, and forms it into a *content-substance*" (1943: 52). The comparison of lexical fields in different languages gives evidence of the arbitrariness of content-form. Many languages, including English, divide the progression from 'light' to 'dark' into three areas (*white, gray, black*). Some languages have only a twofold distinction (no *gray*); others have more lexical items, distinguishing various values of gray (cf. ibid.: 53). In morphology (ibid.), most languages have only the twofold number distinction between singular and plural, but some languages

impose a different content-form on the content-purport of "plurality," producing further categories of content-substance, such as an additional *dual*, *trial*, or even *quadral* (morphological forms designating groups of two, three, or four entities). From these and other examples of *linguistic relativity*, Hjelmslev concluded that it is impossible to describe language on the basis of substance: "The description of substance depends on the description of the linguistic form. The old dream of a universal phonetic system and a universal content system (system of concepts) cannot therefore be realized" (1943: 76–77).

3.2.6 EXPRESSION-FORM AND -SUBSTANCE

At the expression plane of a spoken language, the phonological system is its expression-substance. The underlying system of abstract relations is its expression-form. In languages with a relatively autonomous orthography, such as English and French, the written language differs from the spoken one both in expression-substance and in expression-form. In other cases, one and the same expression-form can be manifested by various content-forms (Hjelmslev 1954: 49–50), for example, spoken language and its 1:1 phonetic transcription are two substances manifesting one form. Further examples of various substances manifesting one form are "transliterations" of an alphabetically written language into the Morse alphabet, a hand alphabet (see Sign language 2.1.1), or a semaphore (flag) alphabet (cf. Code 5.3).

3.3 Sign Function, Sign, and Symbol

Hjelmslev's definition of the sign as pure form and his concept of sign function are based on a revolution of the traditional semiotic dogma of the sign being something which stands for something else, *aliquid pro aliquo*.

3.3.1 THE SIGN FUNCTION AND REFERRAL

Hjelmslev rejected the common definition of the sign as an expression that points to a content outside the sign itself (1943: 47–48). Following Saussure, he defined the sign as an entity generated by the indissoluble connection between an expression and a content: "An expression is expression only by virtue of being an expression of a content, and a content is content only by virtue of being a content of an expression" (ibid.: 48–49). Hjelmslev called this interdependence between expression-form and content-form a relation of *solidarity*. Expression-form and content-form are also defined as the functives of a *sign function* (ibid.: 47–48, 57).

The traditional semiotic function of reference (cf. Meaning 2.) was reinterpreted by Hjelmslev as a relation between content-form and content-substance: "That a sign is a sign for something means that the content-form of a sign can subsume that something as content-substance" (1943: 57). Thus, extralinguistic reference is projected into the sphere of meaning. This principle has become a dogma of the neo-Hjelmslevians, such as Greimas and Eco. But Hjelmslev went still further in revolutionizing the concept of sign. Based on his assumption of a strict parallelism between the expression and content planes (cf. 3.3.3), he arrived at the conclusion that there is also a referral from expression-form to expression-substance:

> The sign is then—paradoxical as it may seem—a sign for a content-substance and a sign for an expression-substance. It is in this sense that the sign can be said to be a sign for something. [. . .] The sign is a two-sided entity, with a Janus-like perspective in two directions, and with effect in two respects: "outwards" toward the expression-substance and "inwards" toward the content-substance. (ibid.: 58)

3.3.2 SIGN AND FIGURAE

Signs are not the ultimate constituents of sign systems. There are smaller, minimal constituents on both planes of the sign. Hjelmslev defined these semiotic elements, which are not yet signs themselves but only parts of signs, as *figurae* (1943: 46). Elsewhere (1973: 144, 175, 234), Hjelmslev called these elements *sign components*. The sign components of the expression-plane (the *expression-figurae*) of language are its phonemes, but Hjelmslev preferred the term *ceneme* (from Gr. κενός 'empty,' i.e., containing no meaning) (1937: 157). By this terminological innovation, Hjelmslev wanted to express the idea of an entity of pure form, whereas the term *phoneme* is associated with an entity of phonetic substance. Furthermore, cenemes can also be manifested in written or gestural substances. The study of cenemes is called *cenematics*.

At the content plane, the semantic components of signs or *content-figurae* are called *pleremes* (from Gr. πλήρης 'full,' i.e., containing meaning). Structural semantics later adopted the term *seme* (see Greimas 3.2) or *semantic component*. An example of Hjelmslev's decomposition of a sign at two planes is his analysis of the English form *am* (1957: 111; 1973: 145). It consists of two expression-figurae, *a* and *m*, and five content-figurae, namely 'be,' 'indicative,' 'present tense,' 'first person,' and 'singular.'

3.3.3 HOMOLOGY VS. DIFFERENCE OF THE PLANES

Hjelmslev emphasized both homologies and differences between the two planes of language. The homologies consist in the formal parallelisms between the entities which constitute the planes. Both planes have the strata of form, substance, and purport, both have figurae, and there are further formal parallelisms. Hjelmslev concluded: "The two planes of a language have completely analogous categorial structure" (1943: 101). On the other hand, the structures of the two planes of a language sign are necessarily different. The two expression-figurae of the sign *am*, for example, are in no way homologous to the five content-figurae of this sign. Thus, the two planes of the language sign "cannot be shown to have the same structure throughout, with a one-to-one relation between the functives of the one plane and the functives of the other" (ibid.: 112).

3.3.4 SIGN VS. SYMBOL

Not all entities which have been called signs in the history of semiotics have two structurally independent planes. Many nonlinguistic signs cannot be decomposed into minimal elements of content or expression. Examples are chess pieces, traffic lights, telephone numbers, tower-clocks striking quarter-hours and hours, or the prisoner's rapping code (Hjelmslev 1948: 34). In these cases, there is a 1:1 relationship between the forms of content and of expression (Hjelmslev 1943: 113). The "red" of the traffic light corresponds to 'stop,' "green" to 'proceed,' and "amber" to 'attention.' There is no further articulation. Such phenomena are therefore not biplanar, but monoplanar, although these signs have, of course, both content and expression. Hjelmslev defined them as "interpretable *nonsemiotic* entities" (ibid.: 114). In his terminology, these monoplanar entities with an expression-content isomorphy are defined as *symbols*, while the term *sign* is restricted to biplanar, twice-decomposable semiotic entities.

4. Connotative Semiotics and Glossematic Aesthetics

Various semiotic definitions of the connotation-denotation dichotomy are discussed in the chapters on meaning, Barthes, and literature. Many of these definitions are founded on Hjelmslev, whose theory of connotation has become the basis of a semiotic school of aesthetics and literary theory.

4.1 Denotation, Connotation, and Metasigns

Hjelmslev's sign model (Fig. H 2) is the model of a denotative sign (1943: 114). He derived two more complex types of sign from this basic model, the connotative and the metasign, more generally: the models of a connotative semiotic and of a metasemiotic.

4.1.1 STRUCTURE OF CONNOTATIVE AND METASEMIOTICS

Essentially, *connotators*, according to Hjelmslev (1943: 115–16), are semiotic units of style. They belong to semiotic systems called *connotative semiotics*. Examples are the various subcategories of style, including "medium, tone, vernacular, national language, regional language and physiognomy." The common characteristic of these phenomena is that the stylistic value is a semantic addition to a primary semiotic form. Thus, style (and connotation) is interpreted as a semiotic whose expression plane consists of denotative elements of the language and whose content plane consists of the stylistic values: "Thus it seems appropriate to view the connotators as content for which the denotative semiotics are expression, and to designate this content and this expression as a *semiotic*, namely a *connotative semiotic*" (ibid.: 119).

Hjelmslev's concept of metalanguage or metasemiotic corresponds to the logical definition of the term as a language *about* a (primary) language (ibid.: 119–20). The logician calls this primary language an object language. In Hjelmslev's semiotics, it is a denotative language. Every grammar is a metalanguage, because it describes a natural (object) language (see also Language 2.2.1 and Function 3.2). Since a metalanguage forms new terms and terminologies *about* an object language, its specific addition to that first object language consists in a new expression plane. The content-plane associated with this new (terminological) expression plane is precisely the vocabulary of the object language. Metalinguistic terms are "expressions" to designate the signs of a (denotative) object language.

In the difference between connotative and metasemiotics, Hjelmslev discovered the following structural parallelism: a *connotative semiotic* is one "whose expression plane is a semiotic," and a *denotative semiotic* is one "whose content plane is a semiotic" (1943: 114). In other words, connotative and denotative signs are signs which contain a semantically more primitive sign at either the expression or the content plane. Accordingly, a denotative semiotic is "a semiotic none of whose planes is a semiotic (ibid.)." Barthes represented these three semiotic structures in

the form of the box diagrams shown in figures B 2 and B 3 (see Barthes 1.).

4.1.2 HJELMSLEV'S THEORY OF CONNOTATION

Barthes's popular diagram (B 2) is entirely restricted to Hjelmslev's basic scheme of the connotative sign as one "whose expression plane is a semiotic." Hjelmslev, however, gave the outline of a much more elaborated theory of connotation, deriving from the glossematic principle of differentiating between four strata both of the denotative and of the connotative sign (1943: 116ff.).

Accordingly, the connotative extension of the denotative sign may be (1) one of the denotative form, (2) substance, or (3) form and substance (ibid.: 116; see also 4.2.1). The Danish language, for example, is a denotative *form and substance*, and these constitute a connotative expression whose content is the connotator 'Danish' (ibid.: 118). The discovery procedure for connotators is translation. The translation of a Danish text into English changes its connotators, but not its denotational content. The connotator 'Danish' is thus a *connotative content-form* insofar as it is structurally opposed to and forms a semiotic paradigm with other connotators such as 'French,' 'German,' or 'English.' As a science of pure form, glossematic semiotics is restricted to an analysis at this level of content-form. The study of *connotative content-substances* or even *content-purport* is not its task. Hjelmslev mentioned that such connotative content-purport could consist of "the actual notions of social or sacral character that common usage attaches to concepts like national language [. . .] etc." (ibid.: 119).

Connotative contents can furthermore be restricted to one of the two planes of the denotative sign. In this case, Hjelmslev speaks of signals: "A *signal* may always be referred unambiguously to one definite plane of the semiotic," while a *connotator* "is found in both planes of the semiotic" (ibid.: 118). A connotative content associated ("solidary") with the expression plane only, thus forming a signal, may be exemplified by the paralinguistic characteristics of voice set or voice quality; for example, those by which a 'female voice' is distinguished from a 'male voice' or a 'child's voice.' The connotative content of this signal is based on a denotative expression-substance. Only this substance changes with the voice quality, not the expression-form.

4.2 Connotation as an Aesthetic Principle

Johansen (1949), Stender-Petersen (1949; 1958), Sørensen (1958), Jansen (1968), and Trabant (1970) (see also Busse 1971 and Ihwe 1972a) have developed Hjelmslev's theory of connotation further into a glossematic aesthetics of literature. The common denominator of these approaches is the assumption that a text, when considered as a work of art, is an aesthetic expression plane connoting an aesthetic content. There have been several interpretations as to the nature of the elements of the aesthetic expression and content planes.

4.2.1 SIMPLE AESTHETIC CONNOTATORS

Johansen distinguishes between *simple* and *complex aesthetic connotators* in literature (1949: 292–93, 301). Simple aesthetic connotators are signs whose expression consists of only one of the four strata of the denotative sign. (In Hjelmslev's terminology these would be signals; cf. 4.1.2.) The four possible types of simple connotators in Johansen's interpretation are as follows: (1) Simple connotators based on the denotative expression-substance are rhyme and expressive sound values. (2) Simple connotators derived from the denotative expression-form are the effects of rhythm, because these "are expressed by relations between the elements of denotative expression." This interpretation reminds of Peirce's distinction between *images* (icons [see Icon 1.3] based on substance) and *diagrams* (icons based on structural relations, thus on form). (3) Simple connotators based on denotative content form are semantic and syntactic licenses (poetic figures, etc.) insofar as they are independent of the metric structure of the verse. (4) Simple connotators based on denotative con-

tent-substance are obtained from the study of the "material and intellectual idiosyncrasies of the author, his (or her) preferences for certain subjects," and their special effect on the reader.

4.2.2 COMPLEX AESTHETIC CONNOTATIONS

In contrast to simple aesthetic connotators, complex aesthetic connotators, according to Johansen (1949: 292, 298, 302), have the denotative sign with all of its strata as their basis of expression. In addition, the connotative sign is itself structured into four strata: (1) The connotative expression-substance is formed by the denotative sign. (2) The connotative expression-form is its specifically aesthetic verbal structure. (3) The connotative content-form consists of the relations between the elements of connotative content. (4) The connotative content-substance is the "autonomous psychic structure" of "aesthetic experience" (ibid.: 298–99). It is manifested in spontaneous, emotional reactions or in reflected reactions, in the form of interpretations. With this new semiotic perspective, Johansen opens the door from immanent text structuralism to a theory of literary reception. Like Hjelmslev's glossematic sign, Johansen's aesthetic sign is one in which "the form is the constant element and the substance is the variable element" (ibid.: 302). This is so because aesthetic experience varies individually, while "the invariable network is the complex of signs as formal structure." This theory of interpretation as literary content-substance is taken up in Trabant's (1970) semiotics of literature, but Trabant interprets the nature of the literary content-form in a new way. In his view, the aesthetic content-form is an *empty* form "because the [literary] text does not disclose its meaning. Literary meaning exists only in every actual creation of this meaning by individual interpreters. The units, however, which are filled with meaning by the interpretations exist as empty units, independent of the interpretation" (ibid.: 274).

Jakobson

Roman Jakobson (1896–1982) was one of the most influential linguists of this century. Although few of his writings deal with explicitly semiotic topics, Jakobson today counts as one of the "classics of semiotics" (Krampen et al., eds. 1981). Jakobson's contributions to semiotics and the theoretical principles of his re-search are discussed in many sections of this handbook and can be summarized only briefly in this chapter.

1. Universality of Jakobson's Scholarship

Although Jakobson modestly preferred to characterize his work as that of a "Russian linguist" (*Russkij filolog*; cf. Jakobson et al. 1984: 21), the scope of his scholarship is truly universal.

1.1 Survey of Jakobson's Work

A personal bibliography of some one thousand titles (cf. Jakobson 1971, Koch 1981: 232) testifies to the extreme productivity of Jakobson's genius. The eight-volume edition of his main works (Jakobson 1966–88) is so far only a collection of *Selected Writings*. Major writings of semiotic interest published elsewhere include Jakobson (1973a; b; 1975; 1976; 1985). Studies on Jakobson and echoes of his scholarship are Holenstein (1975), Waugh (1976), Armstrong & Schooneveld, eds. (1977), Eco (1977a), Krampen (1981), Schnelle, ed. (1981), Sangster (1982), Halle et al. (1983), Koch (1986a), and Pomorska et al., eds. (1987).

Fig. J 1. Portrait of Roman Jakobson (1896–1982) (Source: Koch 1986a: 131).

1.2 Epochs of Jakobson's Research

Jakobson's teaching has deeply influenced several trends in the evolution of twentieth-century structuralism and linguistics. Koch distinguishes four epochs in the development of his research (1981: 225–26):

1. In his *formalist* period, from 1914 to 1920, Jakobson was both the founder of the Moscow Linguistic Circle and a member of the influential *Opoyaz* poetics group (see Russian Formalism 1.).

2. In his *structuralist* period, from 1920 to 1939, Jakobson was a dominating figure of the Prague School of Linguistics and Aesthetics.

3. In his *semiotic* period, from 1939 to 1949, Jakobson was associated with the Copenhagen Linguistic Circle (Brøndal, Hjelmslev) and was active in the founding of the Linguistic Circle of New York.

4. Jakobson's *interdisciplinary* period began in 1949 with his teaching at Harvard (later also at MIT). Information and communication theory, mathematics (cf. Holenstein 1975), neurolinguistics, biology (cf. Code 5.1), and even physics (Jakobson 1982) were among the fields to which Jakobson extended his interests.

2. Jakobson as a Semiotician

According to Eco, the linguist Jakobson "was semiotically biased from his early years: he could not focus on the laws of language without considering the whole of their behavioral background" (1977a: 43). The semiotic substratum of Jakobson's work appears in his topics of research, in his view of linguistics as part of semiotics, and in the basic tenets of his dynamic structuralism.

2.1 Jakobson's Semiotic Field

The central fields of Jakobson's research were poetics (see also Literature 1.3) and linguistics,

especially phonology, morphology, dialectology, and aphasiology. But from his early years, Jakobson's interest went beyond language and the verbal arts to cover the larger semiotic fields of culture and aesthetics. Jakobson contributed to applied semiotics with papers on music (q.v. 3.1–2), painting, film, theater, and folklore, and to fundamental issues of semiotics such as the concepts of sign (cf. Waugh 1976: 38–53), system (q.v. 2.4), code (q.v. 5.1), structure, function (q.v. 3.2), communication, and the history of semiotics. Moreover, he was one of the first scholars to discover the relevance of Peirce's semiotics to linguistics (cf. Jakobson 1965; 1980: 31–38). In particular through his influence on Lévi-Strauss, Jakobson's semiotic principles became highly influential to the development of structuralism. For Jakobson's influence in text semiotics, see also Culler (1975: 55–74) and Hawkes (1977: 76–87).

2.2 Semiotic Systems and Language

Jakobson determined the scope of semiotics in relation to linguistics as follows:

> The subject matter of semiotic is the communication of any messages whatever, whereas the field of linguistics is confined to the communication of verbal messages. Hence, of these two sciences of man, the latter has a narrower scope, yet, on the other hand, any human communication of nonverbal messages presupposes a circuit of verbal messages, without a reverse implication. (1973a: 32)

Based on the relationship to spoken language, Jakobson distinguished three types of sign systems (1973a: 28–31):

(1) *language substitutes*, including writing, drum and whistled languages, and the Morse code (which is a case of second-order substitution, secondary to writing); (2) *language transforms*, which are formalized scientific languages; and (3) *idiomorphic systems*, such as gestures or music, which are only indirectly related to language.

2.3 The Interdisciplinary Framework

In spite of the universality of his research, Jakobson did not propose a pansemiotic view of the sciences. The place of linguistics and semiotics, according to Jakobson, is within a larger framework of communication studies: "Three integrated sciences encompass each other and present three gradually increasing degrees of generality:

1. Study in communication of verbal messages = linguistics;
2. Study in communication of any messages = semiotic (communication of verbal messages implied);
3. Study in communication = social anthropology jointly with economics (communication of messages implied)" (1973a: 36).

Following Lévi-Strauss (cf. Objects 4.1), Jakobson distinguished three levels of social communication: exchange of messages, of commodities, and of women (more generally, of mates): "Therefore, linguistics (jointly with the other semiotic disciplines), economics, and finally kinship and marriage studies, approach the same kinds of problems on different strategic levels and really pertain to the same field (ibid.: 33)."

3. Some Jakobsonian Principles of Semiotic Research

In his own words, Jakobson's research was a lifelong attempt "to overcome mere short-sighted empiricism on the one hand and ab-stract speculative dogmatism on the other" (Jakobson et al. 1984: 8). In this and in many other respects, Jakobson was a spirit of synthesis (cf. Koch 1986a: 130–39). He objected to the antinomic nature of structuralist dichotomies such as *langue* vs. *parole*, variants vs. invariants, code vs. message, and competence vs. performance, which he strove to overcome by principles of a dynamic structuralism (cf. Jakobson et al. 1984: 10). Many of the methodological principles developed by Jakobson in the field of language studies proved to be fruitful guidelines for research in other semiotic systems (cf. Eco 1977a, Krampen 1981). Some of the most influential ones are:

1. *pertinence* (see Structuralism 1.1.3, Function 2.1.1)

2. *binarism* and *distinctive feature* analysis (see Structuralism 1.1.4)

3. The axes of *selection* and *combination* in semiotic systems (see Structure 2.1)

4. The *metaphor-metonymy* dichotomy and their foundation in the opposition between *similarity* and *contiguity* (see Rhetoric 2.3.1)

5. The *code-message* dichotomy (see Code 3.2.1)

6. The theory of semiotic *functions*

7. The theory of *markedness*: according to this principle, the two poles of a semiotic opposition consist of an unmarked and a marked form. The unmarked form is the genetically earlier, the more natural and often more frequent one. The marked term has an additional and more specific morphological feature, as, e.g., the plural vs. singular, the female vs. male, the passive vs. active form, or the past vs. present form.

PART II

Sign and Meaning

Sign

In this handbook, the concept of sign is generally used in its broadest sense of a natural or conventional semiotic entity consisting of a *sign vehicle* connected with *meaning*. Many narrower definitions of the term *sign* have been given during the history of semiotics (cf. Typology 1.) The most important models of the sign are discussed in the chapters on the classics of semiotics (Peirce, Saussure, Morris, and Hjelmslev). In this chapter, a synopsis of these and other sign models will be given based on the standard distinction between dyadic and triadic sign models. A few theoretical and terminological preliminaries deal with various distinctions between signs in the context of related semiotic and nonsemiotic phenomena. Two dimensions of the sign, namely, *sense* and *reference*, are discussed in the chapter on meaning. For further aspects, see Typology and Arbitrariness.

1. Preliminary Distinctions and Theoretical Foundations

The definition of the sign begins with problems of terminology and the ontological question of the nature of the sign and its signifier as opposed to the nonsemiotic world. These are terminological and theoretical preliminaries to a typology of sign models.

1.1 *Terminological Preliminaries*

There is a considerable terminological vagueness in the distinction between the sign, its signifier, and its minimal elements.

1.1.1 THE SIGN IS NOT THE SIGN VEHICLE

The sign is more than its constituent sign vehicle (cf. Peirce's *representamen*, Saussure's *signifier*), but this distinction is often neglected. In everyday language, there are no words to distinguish between sign vehicle and the sign. The word *sign* is ambiguous. It has either the broader sense of a semiotic entity which unites a sign vehicle with a meaning, or it has the narrower sense of a sign vehicle only. Both senses are probably implied when we talk about "traffic signs." (The German language has two words to distinguish between the sign vehicle [*Verkehrsschild*] and the sign [*Verkehrszeichen*].) The narrower definition referring only to the sign vehicle is given in *Webster's Third International Dictionary*: "Sign is a very general term for any indication to be perceived by the senses or reason."

In semiotics, the distinction between sign vehicle and sign was introduced in various terminological versions (see the synopses in figs. Si 1 and 3). But because of the ordinary language usage, this distinction has never been strictly observed. Even Saussure and Peirce did not consistently distinguish between signifier and sign or representamen and sign.

1.1.2 THE SIGN IS NOT A PHYSICAL SIGNAL

In information theory, the term *signal* corresponds to the *sign vehicle* of semiotics (cf. Communication 3.1.2). This signal or information vehicle (cf. Nauta 1972: 282, 294) is opposed to the sign since it is only its physical embodiment. According to Klaus's *Dictionary of Cybernetics*, "signals are only *potential* sign vehicles. Insofar as they fulfil the function of signs, this transcends their physical properties. Only those signals are signs which transmit a message" (1969: 569, 721). In linguistics, Hockett adopted the term *speech signal* to characterize the linguistic signifier in its physical form (1958: 115). Roy Harris, in his translation of Saussure (1916e), translates *signifiant* as *signal*. For other definitions of the signal, see Typology of Signs (4.).

1.1.3 THE SIGN IS NOT A SIGN ELEMENT

In sign systems with a second level of articulation (see Language 4.1), the elements of (the minimal) signs are not signs themselves. Phonemes, for example, are not signs since they mean nothing. Terminologically, this difference is neglected in definitions which extend the term *sign* to include nonsignifying sign elements. Resnikow, for example, states: "A material object which has no sign function of its own, being only one of the elements in the process of designation, is usually also called sign. In this sense, the term 'sign' is also used with respect to phonemes or letters" (1964: 14).

This use of *sign* as a term for *sign element* has even been adopted in the German industrial norm DIN 44 300, which gives terminological recommendations in the field of information technology. It defines *sign* only as the minimal element of a sign repertoire, such as letters, ciphers, etc., and introduces the term *symbol* for the meaningful units of the message (which are signs in the terminology adopted here). For other terminological distinctions between sign and symbol, see also Typology of Signs (3.1).

1.2 Ontology of the Sign

What is the mode of existence of the sign and its signifier? Do they have a real existence in the form of a physical object or event, or do they exist only as the perceptum in an act of semiosis? While this paragraph focuses on the ontology of the signifier, the question of the ontology of sense and reference will be resumed in the excursus on realism, conceptualism, and nominalism in semiotics.

1.2.1 THE NATURE OF THE SIGN VEHICLE

The signifier of the sign has been characterized as a concrete object, an abstract entity, or both (cf. Pelc 1981a: 2–3). Morris defined the sign vehicle as "a particular physical event or object" (1946: 96, 367). Saussure had the mentalist concept of the signifier as a "psychological imprint." Hjelmslev differentiated with respect to the sign vehicle further between a physical and physiological *expression-substance*, whose study should be the subject of physics and psychology, and an *expression-form*, which is the conceptional structure of the signifier.

In Peirce's semiotics, the sign vehicle or representamen is either a concrete object, a perceptum, or an idea or "thought." In one of his definitions, where he neglected the terminological distinction between sign and representamen, Peirce defined the sign vehicle as "an Object perceptible, or only imaginable, or even unimaginable in one sense—for the word '*fast*,' which is a Sign, is not imaginable, since it is not *this word itself* that can be set down on paper or pronounced, but only *an instance* of it" (§ 2.230; cf. 1.2.3).

1.2.2 THE SIGN IS NOT A CLASS OF SEMIOTIC OBJECTS

In everyday language, there is a tendency to identify signs (as opposed to nonsigns) with a class of prototypical signs. These are never employed except as signs and belong to the sign repertoire of a code (cf. the technological definition discussed in 1.1.3). Words, characters, or conventional gestures are such prototypical signs which can be listed as the sign repertoire or lexicon of a code. Against this view, Morris objected that "semiotic is not concerned with the study of a particular kind of object, but with ordinary objects in so far (and only in so far) as they participate in semiosis'' (1938: 4). Every object, event, or behavior is thus a potential sign. Even silence can have the semiotic function of a *zero sign* (cf. Sebeok 1976: 118, Chronemics 4.2.1). Everything can thus be perceived as a natural sign of something else, and by prior agreement between a sender and a receiver, every object can also serve as a conventional sign. This does not mean that every phenomenon of the world is semiotic. It only means that under conditions of semiosis every object can become a sign to a given interpreter.

1.2.3 ACTUAL AND POTENTIAL SIGNS, TOKEN, AND TYPE

If, as Morris argued, ''something is a sign only because it is interpreted as a sign of something by some interpreter'' (1938: 4), it must be concluded that signs cease to exist as signs when no interpreter perceives them. Does this mean that words in a lexicon or the characters of an extinct language are usually nonsigns? Two semiotic concepts have been developed to avoid a simple negative answer to this question, *type* and *potential sign*.

Kamlah & Lorenzen distinguish between *actual* and *potential* signs (1967: 58). Words in a lexicon which are actually not read can thus be described as potential signs. In the world of natural semiosis, the number of potential signs is unlimited (cf. 1.2.1). When signs belong to a code, there are as many potential signs as there are elements in the sign repertoire of the code. Peirce introduced the distinction between *token* and *type*. A sign in its singular occurrence is a token, whereas the sign as a general law or rule underlying its use is a type. An example is the word *fast* in the passage from Peirce quoted above (1.2.1). As a word of the English language it is a type. Every written or spoken instance of it is a token. The linguistic dimensions corresponding to the token-type dichotomy are text and system. In terms of these semiotic categories, signs do not exist only as tokens in actual processes of semiosis. They also exist as types, as the user's semiotic potential of lawful sign use.

1.3 The Sign and the Nonsemiotic World

The nonsemiotic world is related to the sphere of semiotics in two ways. One has to do with the process of reference. The other has to do with the delimitation of signs from nonsigns. Before the definitions of the sign are discussed, an outline of the main views of semioticians on the nature of the nonsemiotic world will be given. There seem to be six main approaches to this problem, *transsemiotic agnosticism, pansemiotism, naive realism, pragmatic mediationalism, functionalism,* and *integrative holism*. Some of these approaches have parallels in the semiotic approaches to the problem of reference (see Meaning 2.).

1.3.1 TRANSSEMIOTIC AGNOSTICISM AND PANSEMIOTISM

Orthodox structuralism defends a transsemiotic agnosticism. According to Saussure, the nonsemiotic world is ''a vague, uncharted nebula.'' Since ''nothing is distinct before the appearance of language'' (Saussure 1916b: 111–12), nothing can be said about the nonsemiotic world. Pansemiotism seems to maintain the opposite view: the whole world is a semiotic sphere. Peirce is the crown witness of this approach: ''The entire universe [. . .] is perfused with signs, if it is not composed exclusively of signs'' (§ 5.448, fn.). Under quite different premises, pansemiotism was also defended in medieval theology (q.v. 1.3; see also Eco 1973b: 111 for pansemiotic metaphysics). Variants of pansemiotism occur also in information theory (see Information 4.1.1: perception as information), communication theory (see Communication 2.6.2: the metacommunicative axiom), semiotic epistemology (cognition as semiosis; cf. Gutiérrez López 1975), endosemiotics (see Communication 2.2.2), and semiotic views of molecular biology (cf. Prodi 1988 and the discussion of the genetic code in Code 5.1).

The difference between pansemiotism and transsemiotic agnosticism is not as fundamental as it seems. Both refuse to assume a nonsemiotic sphere. An attempt to bridge the gap between the two approaches is Greimas's theory of a natural semiotics (cf. Meaning 1.3, 2.3.2). In this theory, the nonsemiotic world becomes semiotized in a natural semiotics, and the relation between the semiotic and the nonsemiotic is reinterpreted in terms of intersemioticity.

1.3.2 NONSIGNS IN NAIVE REALISM

St. Augustine represents a naive realism (see below, 1.4) in his division of the world into things and signs (*res* and *signum*) (397: 624–25). In *De doctrina christiana* I. 2, he gave the following account of "What a Thing Is, and What a Sign: [. . .] I use the word 'thing' in a strict sense to signify that which is never employed as a sign of anything else: for example wood, stone, cattle or other things of that kind." But Augustine also knew that signs are not a class of objects which is ontologically distinct from things (cf. 1.2.2): "Every sign is also a thing; for what is not a thing is nothing at all. Every thing, however, is not also a sign." Although logically separate, the spheres of things and signs are not epistemologically unrelated, for according to Augustine, "things are learnt by means of signs."

1.3.3 NONSIGNS IN MEDIATIONAL AND FUNCTIONAL THEORIES OF ACTION

Implicitly or explicitly, the theories of semiotic *mediation* (cf. Mertz & Parmentier, eds. 1985) characterize human interaction with the nonsemiotic world from the point of view of a general theory of perception or behavior. The key to the difference between signs and nonsigns is the dichotomy of mediated vs. nonmediated perception. Whitehead characterizes the world below the "semiotic threshold" as a sphere of perceptive immediacy: "The immediate world around us [is] a world decorated by sense-data dependent on the immediate states of relevant parts of our bodies. [. . .] 'Sense-datum' is a modern term: Hume uses the word 'impression.' " In contrast to such "presentational immediacy," "the human mind is functioning symbolically when some components of its experience elicit consciousness, beliefs,

emotions, and usages, respecting other components of its experience" (1928: 16, 9). When Morris defined semiosis as "a mediated-taking-account-of" (1938: 4), he also characterized nonsemiotic behavior as an unmediated interaction with objects of the world.

One of the most explicit theories of semiotic mediation has been proposed by Vygotsky (1930: 137–38; cf. Rissom 1979: 11). Vygotsky distinguishes two elementary forms of human behavior: *natural* and *artificial* or *instrumental* acts. In natural acts, there is a direct associative (conditioned reflex) connection between a stimulus A and a response B. In instrumental acts, "two new connections, A-X and B-X, are established with the help of the psychological tool X." According to Vygotsky, such a tool X is a stimulus which functions "as a means of influencing the mind and behavior" (ibid.: 141). In other words, the mediating stimulus X is a sign, while direct acts are forms of nonsemiotic behavior.

In the framework of his functional structuralism, Mukařovský also draws a dividing line between signs and nonsigns by means of the criterion of immediacy of action (1942: 41–42; cf. Function 3.3). Nonsemiotic behavior, in his theory, is the immediate (practical or theoretical) interaction with reality, while a sign presupposes a mediated interaction, where the sign is the mediator between two realities.

1.3.4 THE PRESEMIOTIC SPHERES IN INTEGRATIVE HOLISM

Some philosophers and semioticians have proposed holistic world models in which the sphere of signs is assigned a place beside a nonsemiotic (or several such) world(s). Popper & Eccles's three worlds are a prominent example of such an approach (1977: 16ff.). World 1, the world of physical objects, is clearly the nonsemiotic sphere. Worlds 2 and 3 are spheres of increasing semioticity. World 2 is the world of subjective experience, and World 3 comprises the products of the human mind. In the framework of his *Evolutionary Cultural Semiotics*, Koch (1986a; b; c) develops a holistic world model in which the dividing line between the semiotic and the nonsemiotic worlds is drawn according to evolutionary principles. Within the presemiotic sphere, the following five "worlds" are distinguished as evolutionary stages: (1) the cosmic, (2) the galactic, (3) the geological, (4) the biological, and (5) the sociological world (1986b: 12).

1.4 The Typology of Sign Models

Sign models can be classified according to several semiotic dimensions. Most of the criteria discussed in the context of the typology of theories of meaning are also valid with respect to the typology of sign models. This chapter will survey the major models of the sign on the basis of the distinction between dyadic and triadic models. Criteria of an alternative classification are discussed in the following paragraphs on realism, conceptualism, and nominalism in semiotics. These aspects of the typology of sign models are especially relevant to the history of semiotics. The framework provided by the philosophical distinction between realism and nominalism is coextensive neither with the dyadic-triadic dichotomy nor with the typology of theories of sense and reference outlined in the chapter on meaning (but see Meaning 3.1). For interpretations of sign models in terms of the nominalism-conceptualism-realism tradition, see Woozley (1967), Kutschera (1971: 31–78, only on realism), Trabant (1976a: 23–27, only on nominalism and realism), Lyons (1977: 109–114), and Jadacki (1986).

1.4.1 DYADIC, TRIADIC, AND OTHER MODELS OF THE RELATA

A standard typology of sign models distinguishes dyadic and triadic models on the basis of the number of relata characterizing the sign in its semantic dimension (cf. Meaning). Triadic models distinguish between sign vehicle, sense, and reference as three relata of the sign. Dyadic models ignore either the dimension of reference or that of sense. Dyadic models are sometimes developed into tetradic models by a further dyadic subdivision of the two into four

components (or planes) of the sign. Hjelmslev's sign model is an example of such an extension of a dyad to a tetrad. Auroux's suggestion that most other semiotic dyads are essentially based on a tetrad (1979: 24) is not very convincing.

The distinction between dyadic and triadic sign models has been interpreted as being both fundamental and unbridgeable, although there has not always been a clear-cut distinction between these two types of models in the history of semiotics (cf. 2.1.1). Followers of the dyadic tradition have elaborated on the aporias of a triadic theory of the sign (cf. Fischer-Lichte 1979: 38–51), while followers of the triadic tradition have criticized the inadequacy of the dyadic model (cf. Köller 1977: 25–33). It must be emphasized that the option for either one of the two models does not imply the neglect of the pragmatic dimension of semiosis (pace Schaff 1960: 205; cf. Meaning 4.). In any case the interpreter is an additional relatum of the sign (see also Lieb 1981a: 144).

Are there sign models proposing less or more than two or three relata of the sign? A monadic view of the sign which neglects to differentiate between sign vehicle and meaning occurs only outside of the theory of signs. It is characteristic of magic and unreflected modes of sign manipulation. General Semantics warns against this view of the sign with the slogan "The symbol is not the thing symbolized" (Hayakawa 1941: 27; cf. Semantics 1.5). A tetradic model of the linguistic sign has been proposed by Hockett (1977: 82), who argues that the triad of word-idea-thing should be extended by an additional conceptual unit of the "image of the word." (Notice that Saussure's signifier is also a mentalist "acoustic image.")

In linguistic lexicology, K. Heger's semiotic trapezium is a sign model with more than three relata. It extends the classical triad to a trapezium which specifies the following six relata of the linguistic sign (Baldinger 1970: 135–36). (1) *phonic substance*, (2) *moneme* (sum of sememes and phonemes), (3) *sense* or *signified* (sum of all meanings associated with one signifier), (4) *sememe* (one particular meaning), (5)

concept or *seme* (a language-independent, elementary meaning), and (6) *reality* (thing). Syn-
optic surveys of dyadic and triadic sign models
from the history of semiotics are given by Eco
(1973b: 30), Nattiez (1979: 391), and Faltin
(1985: 30).

1.4.2 REALIST MODELS OF THE SIGN
Semiotic realism in its most genuine form
originates from the philosophy of Plato (cf. History 2.2.2). The correlates of the sign are assumed to be nonmental entities. The extreme
realist believes that both sense and reference
(cf. Meaning 2.–3.) exist in themselves and
would exist even if there were no minds to be
aware of them. In a mindless world, they
would be available for discovery, even if there
were nobody to discover them (cf. Woozley
1967: 194–95). Plato, Aristotle, Augustine,
Bolzano, and Frege are counted among the
realists in the history of semiotics. For Husserl's semantic realism, see Meaning (3.1).

1.4.3 CONCEPTUALIST MODELS OF THE SIGN
In semiotic conceptualism, the semantic dimension of the sign is assumed to be mind-dependent. For the conceptualist, meanings exist
in the mind in a subjective sense, such that if
there were no minds, there could be no meanings (cf. Woozley 1967: 195). Conceptualism
raises the question of the referential correlate
of the sign and its reality only insofar as this
"reality" provides the sense data to the mind.
The main representatives of conceptualism are
the British empiricists Locke, Berkeley, and
Hume. John Stuart Mill and Franz Brentano are
modern (nineteenth-century) conceptualists in
logical semantics. See also Meaning (3.2) for
mentalism in modern semantics.

1.4.4 NOMINALIST MODELS OF THE SIGN
Semiotic nominalism rejects the idea of a reality of general concepts or referents (cf. History
2.2.2). Nominalists acknowledge only the existence of singular objects and deny the reality of
universals, i.e., the property predicated of all

the individuals of a certain class, such as "red-
ness." In its extreme form, nominalism argues
that objects having the same quality have nothing in common but their name (Lat. *nomen*,
therefore: nominalism). William of Ockham,
for example, taught that universals are only
signs without an existence of their own, standing for individual objects or sets of objects (cf.
Geyer, ed. 1951: 576 and Woozley 1967:
203). These signs are thus only names without
any correlate in reality.

According to Jadacki, "recent tendencies to
'semiotize' all areas [. . .] concerned with the
formal or empirical aspects of meaning and
reference, can be interpreted as expressing the
fact that nominalism today is, more or less, the
dominant school of thinking: everything conceptual only exists in the use of its sign" (1986:
1136). Modern semiotic nominalists, according to this interpretation, are thus the structuralists, and semioticians in the line from
Saussure to Hjelmslev, Greimas, and Eco.
However, this modern semiotic nominalism
tends to be still more nominalist than the traditional one which acknowledged at least the referential reality of individuals.

2. Dyadic Models of the Sign

The most general dyadic characterization of
the sign is given in the medieval formula *aliquid stat pro aliquo*, "something stands for
something else." According to Eschbach
(1980: 44), one of the first explicit quotations
of this formula is in the writings of Albert the
Great (thirteenth century), but the Scholastics
usually used a different formulation, *supponit
aliquid pro aliquo*, "something serves in place
of something else" (cf. Kneale & Kneale 1962:
250). Definitions of the sign using the *aliquid
pro aliquo* formula may be dyadic or triadic. If
the *aliquo* is subdivided into sense and reference (see Meaning), the definition is extended
from a dyadic to a triadic one.

2.1 Aliquid pro Aliquo

The representative function (*stare pro*) of the sign has been a criterion of the definition of the sign from Augustine to Jakobson. What is the nature of the relata and of the relation?

2.1.1 DYAD OR TRIAD IN THE HISTORY OF SEMIOTICS

One of the earliest explicitly dyadic models of the sign was proposed by the Epicureans (see History 2.1.4), who rejected the Stoic *lekton* as the third correlate of semiosis. The *aliquid pro aliquo* formula of medieval semiotics suggests a dyadic model with the two correlates of the sign vehicle (*aliquid*) and its referent (*aliquo*). However, a closer look at the definitions often reveals reference to a third correlate. In Augustine's definition (*De doctrina christiana* 2.1.1; cf. History 2.1.5), "a sign is a thing which, over and above the impression it makes on the senses, causes something else to come into the mind as a consequence of itself" (397: 636). Markus (1957: 71–72) and Simone (1972: 16) have interpreted this definition of the sign as a triadic one, consisting of (1) the sign vehicle, (2) its referent, and (3) the mind to whom the sign stands for the object. However, the model is not triadic in the tradition of a systematic distinction between sense and reference (cf. Meaning), as it was postulated by the Stoics (see 3.2). The focus is on the sign vehicle and the referent. The interpreter is a necessary prerequisite of any sign model even though it may not always be mentioned explicitly. The decisive difference between triadic and dyadic models remains the distinction between sense and reference, which seems to be of no concern to Augustine.

The Scholastics developed the theory of *stare pro* further in their theories of representation (cf. Kaczmarek 1986) and supposition (see History 2.2.3). Ockham's definition of the sign is still very similar to Augustine's: "A sign is that which makes something else come to one's mind" ("ille, quod aliquid facit in cognitionem venire," quoted in Geyer, ed. 1951: 578). Almost the same definition is used by Poinsot: "A sign is something that makes

something other than itself present to knowledge" (1632: 25).

The question whether this *aliquid-aliquo* dyad involves a semiotic dyad or a triad has been interpreted differently in the course of the history of medieval semiotics. Coseriu gives evidence for a triadic conception in early medieval semiotics consisting of the three terms *vox-conceptiones-res*. He quotes Boethius (480–524) as follows: "The voice (*vox*) signifies the concepts (*conceptiones*) of soul and intellect, but the same intellect conceives of the things (*res*) and is signified by the voices" (1970: 153). (See also History 2.2.4.) In early Scholastic semiotics, this Stoic triad was broken up into two dyads. Thus, Anselm of Canterbury (1033–1109) distinguished two semantic relations, *significatio* and *appellatio* (Pinborg 1972: 43): *appellatio* is the relation between word and thing, while *significatio* is the relation between word and its conceptual content. In the later development of the semiotics of the Modistae, there was a shift from the triad to a word-thing dyad, although the mediating role of the intellect was still acknowledged (cf. Bursill-Hall 1971: 97, Ebbesen 1983: 73, Gabler 1987: 48).

2.1.2 *ALIQUID PRO ALIQUO* IN MODERN SEMIOTICS

With reference to H. Gomperz, Bühler resumes the *aliquid pro aliquo* formula as an element in his theory of representation (1933b: 93–96). He describes the *aliquid* (the sign vehicle) as a *concretum* which can stand for (function as a representative of) the *aliquo* only by a process of abstraction. Bühler calls this the principle of *abstractive relevance*. Jakobson follows this tradition when he states, "Each and every sign is a *referral* (*renvoi*)" (1975: 22). Even Peirce accepts the *aliquid pro aliquo* formula, although his general semiotic framework is triadic: "A sign, or *representamen*, is something which stands to somebody for something in some respect or capacity" (§ 2.228).

2.1.3 THE RELATA

The *aliquid pro aliquo* formula is open to both dyadic and triadic interpretations. The following relata of the "*stat pro*"-relation are characteristic of different types of sign models (cf. Meaning 2.–3. and Wiegand 1970: 249–51): (1) signifier-referent (the "nomen significat rem-" theory of Roman grammarians; cf. Padley 1976: 164), (2) (Saussure's) signifier-signified (sense), (3) the unity of signifier plus signified-referent, (4) a triad as a coupling of two dyads (cf. 2.1.1 and Locke in 2.3), and (5) the (triadic; see 3.) signifier-signified-referent model.

2.2 *The Relation of "Standing for"*

Peirce's specification that the "standing for" must be "for something in some respect" has the advantage of precluding a common misinterpretation. It says clearly that the relation of "standing for" is not one of substitution (cf. Wells 1977: 6, pace Morris 1946: 84). The more precise nature of the "standing for" relation depends, of course, on the nature of the relata. The class of natural signs, where the interpreter relates the sign vehicle (the symptom or index) to its referent by means of an inference, raises the question whether it is still appropriate to call this relation one of "standing for."

2.2.1 SIGNIFICATION AND DESIGNATION
If the *aliquo* is the referent, the relation is one of *designation* or *reference*; if it is sense, the relation is one of *signification* (see Meaning 1.2). The medieval distinction was between *appellatio* and *significatio*. If the signifier refers to the referent via the relatum of sense, this triadic relation is one of *mediation* (see 1.3.3). For representation as a semiotic relation, see Meaning (1.2.3). The nature of the *aliquid-aliquo* relation can furthermore be specified as being *arbitrary* (symbolic) or *motivated* (iconic or indexical; cf. Peirce 3.2).

In the framework of their triadic sign model, Ogden & Richards specify the relation of the sign vehicle ("symbol") and the referent as being without any "relevant relation other than an indirect one," while they see relations of psychological or social "causality" between the relata sign vehicle-sense ("thought or reference") and sense-referent (1923: 10–11). Today, the concept of causality is certainly

inappropriate in this context. A modern successor is the concept of inference.

2.2.2 THE DYAD IN NATURAL SIGNS
According to Augustine's definition of the natural sign, natural signs are the object of unilateral observation, in contradistinction to signs in bilateral communication. The sign vehicle (A) and the referent (B) in this type of natural semiosis are related in two ways. At an extrasemiotic level, the level of natural events, A is the effect of the cause B. At the semiotic level, the effect A becomes an index or symptom which an interpreter connects by inference to B. Hobbes explains the genesis of natural signs (and moreover of signs in general) as a process of interpreting the consequent as an effect of its antecedent or vice versa:

> When a man hath *so often* observed like antecedents to be followed by like consequents, that *whensoever* he seeth the antecedent, he looketh again for the consequent; or when he seeth the consequent, maketh account there hath been the like antecedent; then he calleth both the antecedent and the consequent *signs* of one another, as clouds are signs of rain to come, and rain of clouds past. (1640: 4.9)

Later, Wolff was to divide this field of natural signs into demonstrative, prognostic, and rememorative signs depending whether the referent is a present, future, or past event (1720: §§ 953–54; cf. History 3.4.1). For a more recent theory of natural signs, see Clarke (1987).

2.2.3 INFERENCE AND SEMIOSIS
Is the inference by which an interpreter connects the antecedent with its consequent a sign relation (cf. Pelc 1984b)? Critics of a broad concept of the sign have argued that clouds do not *mean* rain and that therefore the distinction between indication and signification, indices and symbols is a fundamental threshold from nonsigns to signs (cf. Savigny 1974: 1788, Clarke 1987). From a pragmatic point of view, Alston argues that "there is a sharp distinction between the two groups of facts. One is a matter of certain *de facto* correlations holding and not a matter of

the x's being used in a certain way. The other is a matter of the way the x in question is used and not a matter of correlations in which it stands with the y" (1967: 440). Clarke proposes to exclude inferences from natural evidence from the definition of signs (1987: 49–50): "Clouds may signify rain [. . .], but they clearly do not refer to anything at all. To assign them a reference to the rain is to collapse the crucial distinction between the significance and reference of a sign." According to his own proposal, a natural sign should "be defined as an event having significance for an interpreter which is not produced for the purpose of communication and whose interpretation does not require an inference from a linguistic generalization." This proposal is an attempt to mediate between two ancient rival theories of the sign, those of Stoic and Epicurean semiotics.

The Epicureans defended a realist view of the natural sign. According to Sextus Empiricus (*Against the Logicians* II: 269–71), natural signs can be apprehended by direct observation and do not require the mediation of language. Even animals can thus interpret natural signs. This view of natural semiosis has been accepted in the pansemiotic tradition from Augustine to Peirce and Morris.

An early nominalist view of natural semiosis was the Stoic theory of signs. The nominalist Eco (1976: 17; 1984b: 31) sympathizes with this view because it makes natural semiosis depend on a criterion of "cultural recognition." According to the Stoics, the natural sign is not the association between a natural event A ("smoke") and a physically related event B ("fire"), but the result of a process of hypothetical reasoning. Instead of being events, A and B become propositions. The sign A is the antecedent of a hypothetical reasoning ("If there is smoke . . . ") and B is its inferred consequent (" . . . then there must be fire"). This rationalist view of natural semiosis is untenable within the larger framework of general semiotics. Its consequence would be the exclusion of zoosemiotics and large sectors of anthroposemiotics (for example, the semiotics of music) from the semiotic field.

2.3 The Dyadic Sign: A Synopsis

A clear-cut distinction between dyadic and triadic sign models is not always possible (see also 2.1.1). There is a zone of vagueness whenever a third correlate is mentioned but not systematically incorporated into the semiotic theory. Saussure's model is the prototype of a dyadic model. Although he mentions the "chose" in addition to the signifier and the signified, he rejects it as a third correlate of the sign. Hjelmslev, while discussing reference in the domain of content-substance, also remains essentially dyadic in his concept of the sign. Furthermore, there are semioticians who postulate two aspects of the sign but consider the relation between sign vehicle and meaning to be the third component.

Major dyadic definitions of the sign from the history of semiotics are summarized in the synopsis of Figure Si 1. The definitions on which this survey is based are as follows:

1. Augustine, see 1.3.2, 2.1.1, and History (2.1.5).

2. Albertus Magnus and the Scholastics, see 2.1.1.

3. Hobbes, see 2.2.2 and History (3.2.2).

4. Locke (1690) distinguishes two types of signs, (I) ideas as signs of things and (II) words as signs of ideas (see also Meaning 3.2): (I) "For, since the things the mind contemplates are none of them, besides itself, present to the understanding, it is necessary that something else, as a sign or representation of the thing it considers, should be present to it: and these are *ideas*" (Locke 1690: IV.21.4). (II) "Words [. . .] stand for nothing but the *ideas in the mind of him that uses them*. [. . .] That then which words are the marks of are the ideas of the speaker" (Locke 1690: III.2.2). See also History (3.3.3).

5. Port-Royal (= Arnauld & Nicole 1685), see Rey (1973: 112), Auroux (1979: 22), Swiggers (1981), and History (3.1.2).

6. Wolff (1720: § 293; cf. Coseriu 1967: 98 and Trabant 1976a: 17): "Thus, if two things occur always simultaneously or one always after the other, then one is always a sign of the

other. Such are called *natural* signs." See also History (3.4.1).

7. Degérando (1800: I, 63), cf. History (3.3.4).

8.–9. See Saussure and Hjelmslev.

10. Cassirer (1922–38: 175; cf. Krois 1984b: 440): "Under the term symbolic form should be understood each energy of human spirit through which an intelligible content and meaning is joined with and internally adapted to a concrete sensible sign." On Cassirer's theory of the sign and symbol, see History (3.6.2) and Typology (1.2.2).

11. Bühler (1933b; 1934), cf. 2.1.2.

12. Bloomfield (1933), cf. Meaning (4.1) on behaviorism in semiotics.

13. Buyssens (1943: 12, 34–41), cf. System (4.2).

14. Jakobson (1959a: 260; 1961: 575; 1975: 10ff.; cf. Waugh 1976: 38–53).

15. Goodman (1968: xi, 5) does not differentiate between sign and sign vehicle. His term *symbol* "covers letters, words, texts, pictures, diagrams, maps, models, and more." His referential view of the "symbol" is apparent in this quote: "The plain fact is that a picture, to represent an object [footnote: I use 'object' indifferently for anything a picture represents, whether an apple or a battle], must be a symbol for it, stand for it, refer to it." See also Image (3.4).

Goodman's *representation, description, exemplification,* and *expression* (1968: 256) are not

	Sign	Correlates of the Dyad	
		① sign vehicle	② meaning
(1) Augustine (397)	sign	sign (as thing)	(other) thing(s), something else
(2) Albertus Magnus and Scholastics (13th cent.)	signum	aliquid (vox)	aliquo (res)
(3) Hobbes (1640)	sign	antecedent experience	consequent experience
(4) Locke (1690)	sign (1) sign (2)	idea word	thing idea
(5) Port-Royal (Arnauld & Nicole 1685)	sign	idea of the representing thing	idea of the thing represented
(6) Wolff (1720)	sign	one thing	another thing
(7) Degérando (1800)	sign	sensation	idea
(8) Saussure	sign (signe)	signifier (signifiant)	signified (signifié)
(9) Hjelmslev	sign	expression	content
(10) Cassirer (1923ff.)	symbol(ic) form	concrete sensible sign	content, meaning
(11) Bühler (1933b)	sign	representative (concrete thing)	meaning
(12) Bloomfield (1933)	linguistic form	speech sound, signal	response in hearer
(13) Buyssens (1943)	seme	semic act	meaning, signification
(14) Jakobson (1959ff.)	sign(um)	signans	signatum
(15) Goodman (1968)	symbol	[words, pictures, models, etc.]	denotatum, object

Fig. Si 1. Synopsis of dyadic models of the sign. (See also the synopsis M 3 on meaning, and History of Semiotics.)

variants of *sense* (see Meaning 3.), as Faltin claims (1985: 30), but four types of referential function.

---

3. Triadic Models of the Sign

Triadic sign models comprise a nonhomogeneous group of semiotic theories distinguishing three correlates of the sign, sign vehicle, sense, and referent (cf. Meaning). In some cases, there is no clear-cut distinction between dyadic and triadic models (cf. 2.1.1). For surveys of triadic sign models see Gomperz (1908: 76–91) and Lieb (1981a).

3.1 *Some Types of Triadic Sign Models*

The nonhomogeneous character of these sign models can be illustrated in a tentative typology of triadic models. The basic distinction will be between triads that are reducible to dyads and genuine triads.

3.1.1 TRIADS REDUCIBLE TO DYADS

Some triadic sign models are actually reducible to two dyads. These may be either subsequent or alternative dyads. Locke's definition implies two subsequent but still potentially independent dyads: words are signs of ideas and ideas are signs of things. Anselm's distinction between *significatio*, the relation between word and concept, and *appellatio*, the relation between word and thing, implies two alternative dyads. In modern semantics, too, the distinction between sense and reference is sometimes taken to be a matter of alternative dyads. This is the theory that words have *either* sense *or* reference (cf. Meaning 1.). Others have postulated a genuine triad claiming that there is always some sense *and* reference in signs.

3.1.2 GENUINE TRIADS AND THE SEMIOTIC TRIANGLE

Genuine triads are based on the concept of mediation (cf. 1.3.3): a third correlate is related to a first via a second. After Gomperz (1908: 77), Ogden & Richards (1923: 11) have repre-

sented the triadic structure of the sign by means of a triangle. This diagram (cf. Fig. Si 2) has become known as the *semiotic triangle* (cf. Lyons 1977: 96, Lieb 1981a). It shows the three correlates of the sign in the order (1) sign vehicle, (2) sense, and (3) referent (Ogden & Richards use different terms; cf. synopsis in Fig. S 3). The dotted base line indicates the indirect nature of the relationship between the sign vehicle and the referent and thus the path of mediation from (1) to (3). However, the order of the relata in the process of triadic mediation has been interpreted in different ways.

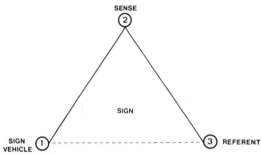

Fig. Si 2. The semiotic triangle (cf. text).

Aristotle's definition of words as signs of the soul, and the latter as likenesses of actual things, gives the outline of the standard order of the triad: (1) sign vehicle-(2) sense-(3) referent (Fig. Si 2). Sense is the mediator of the referent. In medieval semiotics: "Vox significat rem mediantibus conceptibus" (cf. Lyons 1977: 96). This is also the order of Ogden & Richards's triad and of Vygotsky's mediational view of the sign. Peirce's definition of the sign (§ 2.228) enumerates the three relata representamen-interpretant-object in the same order, but within his categorial system, the object is a phenomenon of secondness, and the interpretant is one of thirdness.

In contradistinction to this standard order of the triad, Plato's and Aristotle's sign models also suggest a different interpretation of the sequence of the relata (cf. Schmidt 1969: 13). Since in the Platonic tradition, ideas are "likenesses" of actual things, this early picture theory of meaning (cf. Image 2.2) assigns the object in a way the first place within the triad:

the thing (1) evokes the idea (2) which names the word (3). A still different order is suggested by Husserl's phenomenology of meaning (q.v. 3.1.3). Husserl's theory of the "meaning endowing act," in connection with his Platonic view of sense, assigns the first place within the semiotic triad to sense: sense (1) "gives life" to a "name-Thing" (2) which refers to the object (3). More generally, the order (1) sense-(2) sign vehicle-(3) object is the order of semiosis from the point of view of sign production, while the order (1) sign vehicle-(2) sense-(3) referent is the order of semiosis from the point of view of the interpreter.

3.2 The Triadic Sign: A Synopsis

The semiotic triangle (Fig. Si 2) is the framework of the following synopsis of major triadic definitions of the sign (Fig. Si 3). The synopsis is based on the following definitions:

1. Plato: *Cratylus* (cf. Arbitrariness 1.1.1, Meaning 3.1.1, Gomperz 1908: 79, Schmidt 1969: 19, Coseriu 1970: 46, Schmitter 1987: 28, 32). The Greek terms are name—ὄνομα,

νόμος, idea, notion—εἶδος, λόγος, διανόημα, sound, voice—φθόγγος, φθέγμα, and thing—πρᾶγμα, οὐσία.

2. Aristotle: *De interpretatione* (16a trans. J. L. Ackrile; cf. Lieb 1981a): "Now spoken sounds (φωνῇ) are symbols (σύμβολα) of affections (παθήματα) in the soul (ψυχῇ), and written marks symbols of spoken sounds. And just as written marks are not the same for all men, neither are spoken sounds. But what these are in the first place signs of (σημεῖα)—affections of the soul—are the same for all; and what these affections are likenesses of—actual things (πράγματα)—are also the same."

3. The Stoic sign model is described by Sextus Empiricus (*Adversus mathematicos* 8.11–2; cf. Kretzmann 1967: 364): "The Stoics [. . .] said that three things are linked together: (1) what is conveyed by the linguistic sign (τὸ σημαινόμενον) (2) the linguistic sign itself (τὸ σημαῖνον) and (3) the object or event (τὸ τνγχάνον) [. . .] Two of these are corporeal—viz. the sound and the object or event—and one is incorporeal—viz. the matter of discourse conveyed by the linguistic sign, the

	Sign	Correlates of the Triad		
		① sign vehicle	② sense	③ referent
(1) Plato (ca. 400 B.C.)	name	sound	idea, content	thing
(2) Aristotle (ca. 350 B.C.)	[sign]	sound	affections	thing (pragma)
(3) Stoics (ca. 250 B.C.)	[sign]	sēmaínon	sémainómenon, lektón	object or event
(4) Boethius (ca. 500)	[word]	voice	concept	thing
(5) Bacon (1605)	[word]	word	notion	thing
(6) Leibniz (ca. 1700)	[sign]	sign character	concept	thing
(7) Peirce	sign	representamen	interpretant	object
(8) Husserl (1900)	sign	expression	meaning	thing
(9) Ogden & Richards (1923)	—	symbol	thought or reference	referent
(10) Morris	sign	sign vehicle	significatum	denotatum

Fig. Si 3. Synopsis of triadic models of the sign. (See also the synopsis of Meaning (Fig. M 3) and History of Semiotics.)

lekton." Cf. Robins (1967: 16): "The Stoics formalized the dichotomy between form and meaning, distinguishing in language 'the signifier' and 'the signified,' in terms strikingly reminiscent of de Saussure's *signifiant* and *signifié*." See also Robins (1951: 26ff.) and Eco (1984b: 29–33) and History (2.1.3).

4. Boethius: see 2.1.1: voice-*vox*, concept-*conceptio*, thing-*res*.

5. Bacon: see Universal Language (2.2.1).

6. Leibniz; see Poser (1979): sign-*signum* or *character*, concept-*conceptio* (also *notio*, *cogitatio*, *idea*), thing-*res*.

7. See Peirce.

8. Husserl; see Meaning (3.1.3).

9. Ogden & Richards (1923: 11; cf. Lieb 1981a).

10. See Morris.

Meaning, Sense, and Reference

The meaning of *meaning* is a semiotic labyrinth both on theoretical and on terminological grounds. In this chapter, the term *meaning* will be used in a very broad sense, covering both of the two more specific dimensions of *sense* (or content) and *reference* (object or denotatum). Many semanticians, however, define the term *meaning* in a narrower sense which excludes the aspect of reference. The major accounts of meaning will be classified into theories of reference, theories of sense, and pragmatic theories. Some theories are reductionist, defining meaning in only one of these semiotic dimensions. Other theories are pluralist, taking both sense, reference, and possibly also other semiotic dimensions into account. In addition to these definitions of meaning, two types of meaning, nonsemiotic and connotative meaning, are complementary and not rival accounts of the nature of meaning.

This chapter on meaning, sense, and reference is a continuation of the one on the sign. Semiotic models of meaning are further discussed in the chapters on Peirce, Saussure, Hjelmslev, and Morris. Textual meaning is the topic of Greimas's structural semantics and other chapters in the section on text semiotics. Major schools of research in linguistic and nonlinguistic meaning are the topic of the chapter on semantics and semiotics.

1. Terminological and Theoretical Preliminaries

According to Morris (1938: 43–44), the term *meaning* "has had such a notorious history" that "it is well to avoid this term in discussions of signs." In Morris's opinion, "semiotic does not rest upon a theory of 'meaning'; the term 'meaning' is rather to be clarified in terms of semiotic." Such a clarification presupposes both terminological and theoretical considerations.

1.1 *The Meanings of* Meaning, Sense, *and* Reference

No fewer than twenty-three meanings of *meaning* were distinguished by Ogden & Richards (1923: 186). The understanding of these and other meanings of *meaning* requires a terminological clarification. The guide through the jungle of terms takes the three key terms, *meaning*, *sense*, and *reference*, as marks of orientation.

1.1.1 MEANING
Meaning has become adopted as the general term covering both sense and reference in linguistics (Lyons 1977, Allan 1986) and in the philosophy of language (Dummett 1976: 74). Figure M1 illustrates this meaning of *meaning*.

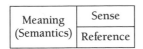

Fig. M 1. *Meaning* in the broader sense.

The major terminological rival to this broad definition is a narrower definition according to which *meaning* is a synonym of *sense* or *content* (cf. Schmitter 1987: 205–212). The basic dichotomy of semantics is then not sense vs. reference but meaning vs. reference (cf. Kempson 1977: 12). Sometimes this narrower definition can be found with the same authors who later adopted the broader definition (thus Lyons 1963: 50ff. vs. Lyons 1977, and Dummett 1973: 84 vs. 1976: 74). This meaning of *meaning* is represented in Figure M2.

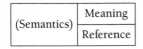

Fig. M 2. *Meaning* in the narrower sense.

1.1.2 SENSE VS. REFERENCE

Terminologically, the sense-reference dichotomy is derived from M. Black's standard translation of Frege (1892). Frege pointed out that the two expressions *morning star* and *evening star* have the same reference (Ger. *Bedeutung*) since both refer to the same planet (namely, Venus). But *morning star* is not a synonym of *evening star* since one is the name of the planet Venus "when seen in the morning before sunrise" and the other "when it appears in the heavens after sunset" (ibid.: 119; cf. Linsky 1967: 129–30).

The history of the sense-reference dichotomy before and after Frege is a Babylonian confusion (cf. Frisch 1969, who examined the terms used by no fewer than 200 authors). In the history of logic before Frege, the dominant terminological distinction was between *comprehension* and *extension* (cf. ibid.). Besides the standard translation of Frege's terms, there is Russell's (1905) discussion of Frege in which the terms *meaning* and *denotation* are used. Furthermore, in German, Frege's original ter-

minology, *Sinn* vs. *Bedeutung*, has by now been replaced in part by its terminological opposite, *Bedeutung* vs. *Bezeichnung* (cf. Brekle 1972: 63). Notice that similar terminological reversals have occurred with the terms originally proposed by Mill (1843) and Ogden & Richards (1923).

The major terminological conventions which have been adopted for the distinction between the dimensions of sense and reference are surveyed in the synopsis of Figure M 3. This survey has to neglect many theoretical differences, in particular the relational aspect of meaning, which is usually defined in the additional categories of signification and designation. See also the synopsis of the components of the sign.

1.2 Signification vs. Designation

In the dimensions both of sense and of reference, meaning has been defined either as a conceptual or even real entity, or as a relation between semiotic entities (cf. Schaff 1960: 210–75). In the former perspective, meaning is an idea, a concept, an object, or a thing. In the latter perspective, meaning is a function, a relation between the signifier and its signified, the signifier and its user, or the signifier and other signs. A variety of terms have been introduced to describe the relational aspects of meaning. The most common distinction is between *signification* for the intrasemiotic relation and *designation* for the extrasemiotic relation (thus, Coseriu & Geckeler 1974: 147). Frege used the dichotomy *expression* and *designation*: "By means of a sign we express its sense and designate its reference" (1892: 123).

1.2.1 SIGNIFICATION

Ullmann defends a relational theory of meaning, which he defines as "a reciprocal and reversible relationship between name and sense" (1962: 57). More commonly, this relation is not identified with meaning but is defined as only one aspect of the semantic dimension, namely, signification. Thus, Ducrot & Todorov define the relationship between the

	Dimension of Sense	Dimension of Reference
Mill (1843; cf. 5.2.1)	connotation	denotation
Frege (1892)	Sinn	Bedeutung
Frege (Black's trans.)	sense	reference
Russell (1905, quoting Frege)	meaning	denotation
Peirce	interpretant	object
Husserl (1900)	Bedeutung (meaning)	Gegenstand (thing)
Saussure	signifed or concept	[thing]
Ogden & Richards (1923)	thought or reference	referent
Hjelmslev (1943: 57)	content	[content-substance]
Carnap (1942; 1947)	intension	extension
Ullmann (1962: 67)	sense or meaning	[thing]
Brekle (1972)	Bedeutung	Bezeichnung
Eco (1976)	meaning or content	[referent]
Greimas (see 1.3)	signification	[meaning, referent]
Lyons (see 1.2.2)	sense	referent, denotation
Malmberg (1977)	content	referent
Quine (1981: 43ff.)	meaning	designation

Fig. M 3. Sense and reference: a terminological synopsis. Aspects whose study is explicitly characterized as being extrasemiotic are indicated in brackets. For the further differentiation of the relational aspect, see 1.2. See also the synopses of the models of signs (Sign 2.3, 3.).

signifier and the signified as signification (1972: 100). Barthes emphasizes the dynamic aspect of this correlation. To him, "*signification* can be conceived as a process; it is the act which binds the signifier and the signified, an act whose product is the sign" (1964a: 48).

Within the domain of sense, Baldinger (1970: 111) draws a further distinction corresponding to the semasiology-onomasiology subdivision of semantics. In this terminology,

sense (the signified) studied from the perspective of the signifier (the relationship "signifier→ signified") is called signification, while the study of the signifiers associated with one signified (the relationship "signified→ signifier") is called designation. More commonly, however, the latter term is used for the relationship of reference.

1.2.2 DESIGNATION OR REFERENCE

Designation is only one of the terms used to describe the semiotic relationship between sign and object. More precisely, it is not a dyadic relationship but a triadic one, involving the interpreter as the third term in the act of referring (Linsky 1967) to the referential object. Other terms are *denotation* and *reference* as opposed to the *denotatum* and the *referent*, which characterize the entity referred to. Lyons adopts the term *reference* for the relation and *referent* for the entity referred to (1977: 177). But he restricts these terms to the utterance-bound occurrence of signs, the usages of an expression "on particular occasions of its utterance" (ibid.: 174). For the usage- or utterance-independent aspect of meaning he introduces a new dichotomy (ibid.: 207–208): *denotation* for the context-independent relation and *denotatum* for the relatum of meaning.

1.2.3 REFERENCE VS. REPRESENTATION

The function of *reference* is related to, but sometimes also distinguished from, *representation*. This latter term is far from being clearly defined in semiotic terminology (cf. Foucault 1966a: 46–77, Parret 1969, Kaczmarek 1986). Sometimes, *representation* (Ger. *Darstellung*) is a synonym of the referential function of semiosis in general. Cassirer uses the term in this way (cf. Ranea 1986: 306). Hockett opposes representation and signification (1977: 82). In his definition, representation is the relation between the mental signifier and the referential object (the idea represents the thing) and also between the mental signifier and the actual utterance (the image of the word represents the utterance of the word). Signification, according to Hockett (ibid.), is then the relation between the word (mental and acoustic) and its sense and reference (idea and thing). Often, representation means simply "reference" in the domain of pictorial semiotics (see Image 3.4). Goodman defines representation (besides description, exemplification, and expression) as a type of referential function (1968: 256).

Bunge discusses similarities and differences between *pictorial* representation as in art and *conceptual* representation as in scientific theories (1974: 84–85). In a way, both aim at depicting referents, but while pictures are concrete sensual images of reality, theoretical representations are conceptual reconstructions of reality. Bunge draws the following distinction between representation and reference: while reference relates a construct to a thing as a whole, representation matches a construct with some aspect or property of the thing (ibid.: 87). Reference is possible without representation and vice versa. The statement "There are no green people" refers to people but represents nothing. From theoretical physics, he gives examples of representing but nonreferential concepts.

1.3 Meaning and Signification According to Greimas

Greimas draws a nonstandard distinction between meaning and signification.

1.3.1 MEANING
According to Greimas & Courtés, meaning "is undefinable" and "anterior to semiotic production": "Nothing can be said about meaning, unless metaphorical presuppositions full of implications are introduced" (1979: 187, 298). There are only *meaning effects* "produced by our senses in contact with meaning," and this effect is "the sole graspable reality, but one which cannot be apprehended directly." These arguments for the inscrutability of meaning stand clearly in the tradition of the philosophical debate on the inscrutability of reference (Quine 1968). The dimension of semantics which Greimas defines as meaning is evidently the referent (cf. Fig. M 3).

1.3.2 SIGNIFICATION
Whereas meaning remains inscrutable, signification "is the key concept around which all semiotic theory is organized" (Greimas & Courtés 1979: 298). In this definition, signification is *articulated meaning*. It comprises both a dynamic and a static aspect. The former is the "process of producing meaning," the latter is "meaning already produced" (ibid.). According to the neo-Hjelmslevian semiotics of Greimas, signification (Fr. *signification*) is a transformation of a meaning (Fr. *sens*) which is given prior to signification:

> Man lives in a signifying world. To him, meaning is not a problem, meaning is given [. . .] . In a "white universe" where language were the pure denotation of objects and gestures, it would be impossible to inquire about meaning. [. . .] The production of meaning is meaningless unless it is the transformation of the given meaning. Consequently, the production of meaning is in itself the putting into a significant form, a process which is indifferent to the contents to be transformed. (1970: 12–15)

1.4 Typologies of Theories of Meaning

The major theories of meaning have been developed in the context of linguistics and the philosophy of language (cf. Schaff 1960: 196–284, Kretzmann 1967, Black 1968: 150–67, Schmidt 1969, Katz 1971: 84–122, Kutschera 1971, Pelc 1971, Fischer-Lichte 1979, Kalinowski 1985, Runggaldier 1985, Allan 1986: 75–135). The typology of meaning has its more general background in the typology of sign models (see Sign 1.4).

1.4.1 CRITERIA OF CLASSIFICATION
The typological characteristics of theories of meaning can be classified according to several criteria. Schaff draws a basic distinction between theories that conceive of meaning as an entity and those that define it as a relation between entities of semiosis (1960: 210–75). Fischer-Lichte (1979) sets up a typology of meaning distinguishing between syntactic, semantic, and pragmatic theories. However,

purely syntactic theories of meaning are rare and have actually developed only in early distributional linguistics. The following discussion distinguishes pragmatic theories and the theories of reference and of sense as two types of semantic theories. For a different typology of approaches to meaning, based on the various disciplines concerned with the study of meaning, see Semantics (1.1).

1.4.2 MONIST AND DUALIST THEORIES OF MEANING

Among the various semantic theories, some explain the nature of meaning in terms of only one semiotic dimension, reference, sense, or use. Others take two or even more dimensions into consideration. The former will be called monist, the latter are dualist (or pluralist) theories of meaning. In semiotics, monist theories of meaning are defended in the tradition of the dyadic sign models of Saussure and Hjelmslev (see Sign 2.). In this tradition, Eco attacks vigorously the pitfalls of the "referential fallacy" (1976: 58). The triadic sign model of Peircean semiotics (see Sign 3.) provides a framework for a dualist account of meaning taking both sense (Peirce's interpretant) and reference (Peirce's object) into consideration (cf. Deledalle 1979: 147–57).

In linguistics, *structural semantics* followed the monist path of locating meaning in the sphere of sense only. Since no structure was admitted beyond the semiotic system of language, the dimension of reference was excluded from semantic investigation. Against this immanent view of meaning, there has been a new development of semantics which emphasizes the impossibility of studying phenomena of temporal, local, or personal deixis without having recourse to the dimension of reference. For this pragmatically oriented *referential semantics*, see Wimmer (1979).

2. Meaning as Reference

The problem of reference and of the referent is closely connected with the ontological problem of the existence of the entities referred to. Referential theories of meaning usually do not question the existence of the referent as an external entity. Their philosophical foundation is an ontological realism (cf. Runggaldier 1985).

2.1 Meaning as the Referent

The identification of meaning with the thing (or class of things) referred to is one of the oldest theories of meaning (cf. Black 1968: 151–52). In this view, the meaning of "moon," for example, is the actual object which moves around the world as its satellite. This approach to meaning is also called *extensionalism* (Kempson 1977: 13, derived from Carnap's terminology). Russell's theory of denotation is representative of a theory which derives meaning from reference (or denotation). In his view, "meaning cannot be got at except by means of denoting phrases" (1905: 151). Wittgenstein in his early writings advocates a referential theory of meaning when he argues, "The name means the object. The object is its meaning" (1922, § 3.203), but in the same *Tractatus*, he also develops an idea which leads to his later pragmatic theory of meaning (cf. 4.2): "In order to recognize the symbol in the sign we must consider the significant use" (§ 3.326). With logical positivism, the search for meaning in the dimension of reference reached a climax (cf. 2.2.1, 2.3.1).

A more recent author who develops a monist referential theory of meaning which excludes the dimension of sense is Quine (1960, cf. chap. VI: "Flight from Intensions"). In Marxist semiotics (cf. Morris 2.3.5), a dualist theory of reference is proposed which distinguishes between the *sigmatic* dimension of an "objective reality" and the *semantic* dimension of a materialist copy of this reality in human consciousness (cf. Lorenz & Wotjak 1977).

2.2 Meaning as Empirical Truth

To some philosophers of language, meaning is the determination of the referent and implies the search for empirical truth (cf. Evans &

McDowell, eds. 1976). Allan distinguishes two variants of this view of meaning, *verificationism* and *truth-conditional semantics* (1986: 79–82; cf. also Evans & McDowell, eds. 1976: 42ff.).

2.2.1 VERIFICATIONISM

Ayer defines meaning according to the positivist "principle of verification," postulating that "a statement is held to be literally meaningful if and only if it is either analytic or empirically verifiable" (1936: 12).

2.2.2 TRUTH-CONDITIONAL SEMANTICS

Davidson explains meaning in terms of truth, since "to give truth conditions is a way of giving the meaning of a sentence" (1967: 456). The background to this view is the "correspondence theory of truth" (cf. Tarski 1944), according to which a sentence is true if it designates an existing state of affairs.

2.3 Expansion and Deconstruction of the Referent

As a monist account of meaning, referential theories fail to give a comprehensive account of meaning (cf. Black 1968: 152, Fischer-Lichte 1979: 39, Runggaldier 1985). While the referent of *Paris* or *dog* may still be easy to determine, the referents of *Pegasus*, *morning star*, or the article *the* cause difficulties. Two kinds of proposals have been made to solve these problems of referential semantics, extending the scope of reference and eliminating the referent.

2.3.1 EXTENDING THE SCOPE OF REFERENCE

The prototype of a referential determination of meaning is a (proper) name designating an object or class of objects. From this prototype and from the so-called singular descriptions, logical semantics proceeded to extend the scope of reference to include also *predicates* and *functors* (of negation, conjunction, etc.) (Carnap 1947). Strawson (1950) shifts the scope to the pragmatic dimension by investigating the act of referring and by defining the referential object as a function of the use of an expression. Linsky investigates the referents of and reference to fictional and imaginary objects (1967: 125–26). He extends the study of reference by including the dimension of *modality*. In his description, words in the context of legends, dreams, or movies occur within the scope of special operators. An "in-the-movie" operator, for example, characterizes the mode of reference in a movie.

Jakobson's theory of the referential function of language reflects the pragmatic extension of the scope of reference (1960: 353). In his definition, the referent is the context. He rejects the idea that *morning star* and *evening star* have the same referent since reference is the contextualization of a sign (cf. Holenstein 1975: 88). This view, however, comes close to an elimination of the referent (as Waugh [1983: 189–91] sees it).

2.3.2 ELIMINATING THE REFERENT

The exclusion of the referent from the investigation of meaning is characteristic of the monist theories of meaning as sense. The semiotic foundations of this approach were laid by Saussure and Hjelmslev. In linguistics, Ullmann (1962: 57–58) and the tradition of structural semantics defended a theory of meaning without recourse to reference.

Eco (1968; 1976) rejects any semiotic relevance to the referent by defining meaning as a purely cultural unit, a structure generated by a cultural code. Since in his view, every sign function implies the possibility of lying, the investigation of referential truth conditions cannot be a matter of semiotics (1976: 58). Eco does not refute the idea of the existence of an extrasemiotic reality of objects, but avoids any ontological commitment in this respect: "Within the framework of a theory of codes it is unnecessary to resort to the notion of extension, nor to that of possible worlds; the codes [. . .] set up a 'cultural' world which is neither actual nor possible in the ontological sense; its existence is linked to a cultural order, which is the way in which a society thinks and speaks" (ibid.: 61).

A different proposal for the semiotic elimination of the referent is made by Greimas & Courtés (1979: 260; cf. above, 1.3). Following Hjelmslev, Greimas first defines the sphere of "common sense" reality as being semioticized. Within this framework, reference from language to the semioticized world turns out to be a matter of *intersemiotic translation*:

> The extralinguistic world [. . .] is given form by human beings and constituted by them as signification. Such a world, far from being the referent [. . .] is itself, on the contrary, a bi-planar language, a natural semiotics (or a semiotics of the physical world). The problem of the referent is then reduced to the question of the correlation between two semiotic systems (for example, natural languages and natural semiotics; pictorial semiotics and natural semiotics). This is a problem of inter-semioticity. [. . .] The referent loses its need to exist as a linguistic concept.

3. Meaning as Sense

Four theories of meaning as sense will be distinguished, *semantic realism, mentalism, contextualism,* and *substitutional equivalence theories.* A further mentalist approach to meaning is implied in the psychosemantic theory of meaning (see Semantics 1.1). For further major theories of meaning as sense, see Saussure, Hjelmslev, and Greimas. While the discussion focuses on monist theories which neglect the dimension of reference, some theories of meaning are also included in which reference is an additional dimension besides sense.

3.1 Semantic Realism of Sense

The prototype of semantic realism in the dimension of sense is platonism. Plato's theory of ideas is as realist as the referential theories of meaning, since both conceive of meaning in terms of entities believed to exist independently of the sign and its user (cf. Kutschera 1971: 32; see also Sign 1.4.2–4 and History 2.2.2 on the distinction between realism and nominalism). Semantic theories based on se-

mantic realism are not necessarily committed to a monist approach to meaning. Both Plato and Husserl clearly distinguish between the idea (sense) and the referential object (or thing) as a second correlate of meaning.

3.1.1 THE PLATONIC HERITAGE
In the Platonic tradition, ideas are something objective, independent of our minds, existing in a spiritual world beyond ours. Meaning in this framework is the approximative and never perfect access we have to the truths of these immortal ideas (cf. Nehring 1945: 29–30, Arbitrariness 1.1).

3.1.2 NEO-PLATONISM IN LINGUISTIC PHILOSOPHY
Allan interprets the philosophical semantics which Katz developed in the context of generative grammar as a neo-Platonic approach to meaning (1986: 89). Katz, too, considers meaning to be an abstract object existing separately from the speaker or hearer. The neo-Platonic views are apparent when Katz concludes: "The actual speaker's knowledge of the meaning of words and sentences is, then, an imperfect facsimile of their meaning in the language, which is given by an idealized grammar" (1971: 122).

3.1.3 HUSSERL'S PHENOMENOLOGICAL THEORY OF MEANING
In spite of Husserl's explicit assertions to the contrary, his phenomenological concept of meaning has a Platonic foundation, since meanings are also conceived of as ideal entities (1900: 322) apart from the human mind (cf. Schaff 1960: 213–26, Schmidt 1969: 13–17). Husserl distinguished three ingredients of meaningfulness (cf. Kretzmann 1967: 399): (1) a "meaning-endowing act" or *"meaning intention"* on the part of the producer of the expression corresponding to a "meaning-fulfilling act" on the part of the interpreter, (2) the *content* or *meaning* of these acts, and (3) the *object* meant by the expression.

To Husserl, meanings were subject to *a priori* laws. They did not have to be expressed in the form of signs. He even envisioned meanings beyond the limits of human cognition:

> As numbers—in the ideal sense that arithmetic presupposes—neither spring forth nor vanish with the act of enumeration, and as the endless number-series thus represents an objectively fixed set of general objects, sharply delimited by an ideal law, which no one can either add to or take away from, so it is with the ideal unities of pure logic, with its concepts, propositions, truths, or in other words, with its meanings. They are an ideally closed set of general objects, to which being thought or being expressed are alike contingent. There are therefore countless meanings which, in the common, relational sense, are merely possible ones, since they are never expressed, and since they can, owing to the limits of man's cognitive powers, never be expressed. (1900: 333)

But this ideal entity of meaning is associated with human consciousness through the intentional *act* of meaning (ibid.: 289). Only by this act is meaning bestowed upon the object. This aspect gives Husserl's semantics a pragmatic dimension (cf. 4.). In this perspective, meaning appears as a "lived experience," a movement of metamorphosis and interpretation: "It is only in those movements that the sign signifies. Isolated and by itself in a solitary relationship to things, as the name of the Thing, and hence a name-Thing, the sign is mute, without life, requiring an animation from without" (Gillan 1982: 9). Only the intentional act of consciousness confers meaning on the sign, although the sense of the sign lies in the sign itself. For further aspects of Husserl's theory of meaning, see Kalinowski (1985: 47–81).

3.2 Mentalist Theories of Meaning

Mentalist theories of meaning continue the historical tradition of semiotic conceptualism (see Sign 1.4.3). They are sometimes also called ideational theories of meaning (Pelc 1971: 61–63), but the term *idea* is not the Platonic one in this context. Meaning, according to these theories, is a concept in the sense of a mental event. Locke gave the following conceptualist or mentalist definition of meaning: "The use, then, of words, is to be sensible marks of ideas; and the ideas they stand for are their proper and immediate signification" (1690: III.2.1). Since meaning is defined as the thought associated with signs, such mentalist approaches to semantics are called associationist theories of meaning.

A mentalist account of meaning is also apparent in Saussure's definition of the signified as a concept. But this is, of course, only one aspect of Saussure's theory of meaning, the other being the aspect of value and structure. Another variant of mentalist semantics is the image theory of meaning, which identifies meaning with an image arising in the speaker's or hearer's mind. For details see Image (2.2). Behaviorism condemned the mentalist accounts of meaning as unscientific because concepts are unobservable entities, but modern linguistics with developments such as cognitive semantics has resumed the study of meaning in a mentalistic fashion.

3.3 Substitutional Equivalence Theories of Meaning

These theories account for the meaning of a word in terms of its substitutional equivalent. In contradistinction to the syntagmatic approach of the contextual theory, this approach has its discovery procedure in the paradigmatic dimension of language. The view that the meaning of a word can be equated with its intralingual or interlingual translation, i.e., a synonym, a paraphrase, or a foreign-language equivalent, has been the foundation of practical lexicography for centuries. The semiotic foundation of this principle was made explicit by Peirce, who defines meaning as "the translation of a sign into another system of signs" (§ 4.127). Jakobson called this "one of the most felicitous, brilliant ideas which general linguistics and semiotics gained from the American thinker" and points out that "many fruitless discussions about mentalism and anti-mentalism would be avoided if one approached the notion of meaning in terms of translation" (1980: 35–36).

A more recent variant of the theory of meaning is proposed by Quine. In his definition, meaning is accounted for in terms of substitutional and cognitive equivalence: "The meaning of an expression is the set of all expressions that mean like it," and the criterion of likeness is cognitive equivalence, "that is, the sameness of truth conditions" (1981: 46, 48).

3.4 Contextual Theories of Meaning

According to the contextual theory of meaning, meaning is ultimately derivable from its observable context (cf. Leech 1974: 74). The theory was first proposed in the framework of the British school of contextualism by J. R. Firth (1937; 1957). Other variants of this theory were developed in the framework of distributional linguistics. In this tradition, Nida sets up the "semantic principle" that "meaning is definable by environment" (1952: 126). The contextual theory of meaning follows a syntactic (or syntagmatic) approach when it considers the meaning of a sign a function of its relation to other signs in its context. It belongs to the pragmatic theories of meaning when it defines meaning as a function of its situational context.

Firth emphasizes both modes of context. His syntactic concept of meaning actually transcends semantics proper, covering all other branches of linguistic description (cf. Palmer 1981: 54–55). In this definition, meaning is "the whole complex of functions which a linguistic form may have" and contextual relations at all levels, phonology, grammar, or lexicography, are manifestations of meaning (Firth 1957: 33, 19). Firth's key concept, the *context of situation*, refers to the pragmatic aspects of meaning. This context comprises the following factors of meaning (ibid.: 182):
A. The relevant features of participants: persons, personalities.
  (i) The verbal action of the participants.
  (ii) The nonverbal action of the participants.
B. The relevant objects.
C. The effect of the verbal action.

4. Pragmatic Theories of Meaning

In most typologies of semantics, pragmatic theories of meaning are only those based on the tradition of ordinary-language philosophy (Wittgenstein, Austin, Strawson, Searle) and the further developments in linguistic pragmatics. But the now historical behaviorist account of meaning is also pragmatic because it studies meaning in relation to the sign user. In a further subdivision of pragmatic theories of signs and meaning, a distinction between sender- and receiver- (speaker-/hearer-) related theories can be made (Savigny 1974). From this perspective, the theory of meaning as effect or use is receiver-related. A sender-related theory is Husserl's theory of intentionality in meaning (cf. 3.1.3).

4.1 Behaviorist Theories of Meaning

The behaviorist approach to semantics has its classical representative in Bloomfield, who defines "the *meaning* of a linguistic form as the situation in which the speaker utters it and the response which it calls forth in the hearer" (1933: 139). Meaning is thus identified with the speaker's and the hearer's response. Such semantic theories have also been defined as causal theories of meaning (Black 1968: 156), since meaning is seen as the cause of stimuli or responses.

The difference between behaviorist and mentalist semantics is not as radical as has been claimed. Ogden & Richards, for example, gave an earlier behaviorist account of meaning which was clearly mentalist as well. In their definition, meaning is the engram of a stimulus: "A sign is always a stimulus similar to some part of an original stimulus and sufficient to call up the engram formed by that stimulus. An engram is the residual trace of an adaptation made by the organism to a stimulus" (1923: 53). While both mentalism and behaviorism identify meaning as an event within an interpreting organism, behaviorism has emphasized the necessity of external empirical evidence for the discovery of these events. The impasse of behavioristic semantics is reached where meanings are understood but no reaction of the interpreter can be observed.

4.2 Meaning as Use

The pragmatic theories study meanings of signs in relation to the sign users. Peirce proposes such a theory when he defines meaning as the "proper significate effect of a sign" (§ 5.475). Morris is another semiotician who gives a pragmatic account of meaning.

Wittgenstein is the crown witness of a different pragmatic theory of meaning. In his *Philosophical Investigations*, Wittgenstein explains meaning in terms of *use*: "For a *large* class of cases—though not for all—in which we employ the word 'meaning' it can be defined thus: the meaning of a word is its use in the language. And the *meaning* of a name is sometimes explained by pointing to its *bearer*" (1953: § 43). This Wittgensteinian approach to semantics is also called the operational theory of meaning (cf. Hallett 1967, Mauro 1967, Schmidt 1969: 19–32). A further variant of pragmatic semantics wants to account for meaning in terms of *ostension* (pointing to the object, as mentioned by Wittgenstein). Although ostension plays a role in the acquisition of meaning, Allan rightly concludes that ostension explains nothing about the nature of meaning (1986: 77).

5. Further Types of Meaning

The typology of theories discussed so far has been concerned with mostly mutually exclusive accounts of the nature of meaning. To these accounts of meaning, a discussion of two further meanings of meaning, namely, non semiotic and connotative meaning, will be added. These are not rival accounts but rather complementary dimensions of the theory of meaning.

5.1 Nonsemiotic Meaning

According to Pelc, the term *meaning* is used semiotically when it is attached to any type of sign, not only words, sentences, texts, but also symptoms, signals, symbols, representative pictures, or sculptures (1982: 1–2). But metaphorically, meaning is also attached to nonsigns, such as existence, activity, sacrifice, suffering, life, or history (ibid.: 18). In these cases, Pelc distinguishes three major types of nonsemiotic meaning: (1) *finitistic* concepts, comprising intentional, teleological (m. = aim, purpose), functional, and result-concepts (m. = result) of meaning, (2) *explicatory* concepts, including motivational (m. = motive), causal, and genetic (m. = origin) concepts, and (3) *axiological* concepts, which are evaluative (m. as value), importance concepts, or essence concepts (m. as "something crucial") (ibid.).

5.2 Connotative Meanings

Connotation has become a key concept in semiotics, stylistics, and the theory of literature. The origins of this concept and of its dichotomic counterpart, *denotation*, date back to medieval semantics. Its development in modern semiotics has been outlined by Molino (1971), Kerbrat-Orecchioni (1977), and Rössler (1979). Hjelmslev's and Barthes's theories of connotation have been particularly influential. For connotation as a principle of literariness, see Literature (3.2).

5.2.1 CONNOTATION AND DENOTATION

In Scholastic semantics, the concepts of connotation (from Latin *con-* 'together' and *notare* 'to designate') and denotation were first used in the analysis of the distinction between *abstract* and *concrete terms* (cf. Molino 1971: 5–6, Pinborg et al. 1974). Only abstract terms were interpreted as having an absolute meaning ("per modum per se stantis"), signifying directly a substance or quality (for example, "whiteness," "humanity," or "blindness"). Concrete terms ("white," "human," or "blind"), on the other hand, were said to be connotative, signifying (denoting) not only a substance or quality, but in addition, connoting the carrier of this substance (the white *house*, the blind *man*). Later, Ockham defined *connotatio* as a term whose primary signification is the object for which it stands, while the quality to which the concept refers is its connotation, and thus a secondary meaning. Mill follows this tradition. In his definition, "a non-connotative term is one which signifies a subject only, or an attribute only. A connotative term is one which denotes a subject, and implies an attribute" (1843: 25). The modern successors to denotation and connotation in this sense are the terms *extension* and *intension* of logical semantics (see 1.1.2 and Fig. M 3).

5.2.2 CONNOTATIONS AS SECONDARY MEANINGS

In traditional semantics, connotative meaning is a secondary meaning which a sign may have in addition to a primary, standard, or core meaning, called denotative meaning. Bloomfield defines connotations as "supplementary values." He gives examples of personal, social, local, archaic, technical, learned, foreign, and slangy connotations, concluding that "connotations are countless and indefinable" (1933: 151–55). This field of connotations has meanwhile become the subject of more systematic research in the linguistics of language varieties, registers, and styles (cf. Gregory & Carroll 1978).

Leech defines denotative meaning as *conceptual* meaning and distinguishes six additional varieties of meaning (1974: 10–27): (1) *connotative* (in a narrower sense of "additional, non-criterial or even putative" aspects of meaning), (2) *stylistic*, (3) *affective*, (4) *reflected* ("what is communicated through association with another sense of the same expression),", (5) *collocative* (contextual m.), and (6) *thematic* (a kind of rhetorical) meaning. For further aspects of the typology of connotations, see Rössler (1979: 59–103).

5.2.3 THE DECONSTRUCTION OF DENOTATION AND CONNOTATION

The difficulty with a clear distinction between primary and secondary aspects of meaning has led many semioticians to reject the denotation-connotation dichotomy altogether. Geach proposes to "withdraw" these terms "from philosophical currency" (1962: 56). Barthes, in his later writings, saw in the denotation of a sign nothing but one of its many connotations. Eco (1968: 101–116; 1976: 54–57, 84–90) retains the basic dichotomy, but since his theory of meaning rejects the dimension of reference, his concepts of denotation and connotation cover much of the traditional sphere of connotation. Denotation, according to Eco, is a "cultural unit, [. . .] the culturally recognized property of a possible referent." A connotation is also "a cultural unit," but it is "conveyed by its denotation and not necessarily corresponding to a culturally recognized property of the possible referent" (1976: 85–86). Elsewhere, Eco defines a connotation as the "set of all cultural units which are institutionally associated in the receiver's mind with the signifier" (1968: 108). On this basis, Eco sets up the following typology of connotations which essentially comprises both primary (1, 5) and secondary (2–4, 6–9) meanings (ibid.: 108–116):

1. connotation as definitional meaning (e.g., *Venus* = *Morning Star*)
2. connotations of the constituent elements (e.g., Lat. *luna* connotes 'feminine')
3. ideological connotation
4. emotional connotation
5. connotations derived from hyponymy (*tulip* connotes 'flower'), hyperonymy (*flower* may connote 'tulip') or antonymy (*husband* connotes 'wife')
6. connotations by intersemiotic translation (a word sign connoting a picture sign, e.g.)
7. connotations of rhetorical figures (metaphors, e.g.)
8. rhetorical-stylistic connotations
9. global axiological connotations (referring to values).

Semantics and Semiotics

Semantics is the study of meaning. Historically, it was one of the precursors of modern semiotics. Today it is a branch of both semiotics and linguistics. This chapter deals with trends in and directions of semantics, in particular their relationship to general semiotics. The foundations of semantics are the topic of the chapter on meaning. The section on linguistic semantics is an addendum to the chapter on language in a semiotic frame. Discourse semantics is the subject of Greimas's structural semantics and of other chapters of the section on text semiotics.

1. Semiotics and Semantics

Different approaches to questions of meaning are characteristic of a number of different types of semantics within or perhaps also beyond the scope of semiotics.

1.1 Some Types of Semantics

Coseriu & Geckeler distinguish three major types of semantics, linguistic semantics, logical semantics, and General Semantics (1974: 103). Other traditions of semantics which have acquired some degree of (inter)disciplinary autonomy are philosophical, anthropological, and psychological semantics (cf. Palmer 1981:

12–16). For the typology of the theories of meaning according to semiotic criteria of meaning, sense, and reference, see Meaning (1.4).

Philosophical semantics is an extension of logical semantics, merging partly with semiotics (cf. Schaff 1960) and partly with language philosophy. Anthropological semantics has a tradition founded by Malinowski (1925; cf. Ogden & Richards 1923 and Schmidt 1984) and later resumed in linguistics by J. R. Firth's British school of contextualism. More recently, anthropological semantics has merged with a semiotic anthropology (Ardener, ed. 1971 and Singer 1984).

In psychology, Osgood et al. (1957; Osgood 1976) have developed a further approach to the *Exploration of Semantic Space*, the *Measurement of Meaning* by means of the *semantic differential* technique. In this type of *psychosemantics*, people's subjective connotations of words are investigated. The test person's evaluation of a given concept (such as 'father' or 'freedom') is rated according to the dimensions of a semantic space. Its coordinates are semantic axes whose end points are semantic opposites, such as 'good' vs. 'bad,' 'hard' vs. 'soft,' etc. The method of measuring these semantic differentials is related to the techniques of word association tests. In semiotics, this technique has been applied in studies which Krampen (1979b) defines as *psychosemiology*. For semantics within the theory of information, see MacKay (1969) and Information (3.2).

1.2 Semantics as Semiotics

In the history of semiotics, the term *semantics* can be found as a synonymous precursor of the term *semiotics*. Kretzmann's *History of Semantics* (1967) reflects this tradition. It is essentially a history of the theories of meaning since the Stoics. This broad scope of the term *semantics* has a long tradition. Read (1948) showed that *semantics* in seventeenth-century England was a term referring to the study of divination. In his account, *semasiology*, *sematology*, *significs*, *semiotics*, and *semiology* are "rival terms of *semantics*." As late as 1946, Morris introduced the term *semiotics* as a terminological successor to *semantics*. With reference to the traditional doctrine of signs, Morris remarks: "Today this discipline is frequently known as semantics; we shall call it *semiotic*" (1946: 80).

1.3 Semantics as Linguistic Semantics

Today, the term *semantics* is often used in the abbreviated sense of linguistic semantics, mostly, though, without opposing it to semantics in the broader semiotic sense. Some linguists, however, prefer to define semantics as the science of meaning in language, as opposed to semiotics as the study of semiotic systems in general (Mounin 1968a: 148, Toussaint 1978: 30). Both terminological conventions are motivated by the history of linguistics, where semantics is an autonomous discipline with a tradition older than any influence from general semiotics.

1.4 Semantics in Semiotics

Most semioticians accept Morris's definition of semantics as a branch of general semiotics, which was also adopted within logic. A minor trend in semiotics defines both fields as mutually exclusive.

1.4.1 SEMANTICS AS A BRANCH OF SEMIOTICS

In Morris's classical definition, syntax, semantics, and pragmatics are the three dimensions of semiotic study. Semantics, in Morris's first definition, studies "the relations of signs to the objects to which the signs are applicable" (1938: 6). In Morris's later definition, "semantics deals with the signification of signs in all modes of signifying" (1946: 302).

1.4.2 LOGICAL SEMANTICS

Morris's semiotic definition of semantics was also adopted in logic, where the scope of semantics is restricted to language. According to Carnap, "if we abstract from the user of the language and analyze only the expressions and their designata, we are in the field of *semantics*" (1942: 9). He furthermore distinguishes between *descriptive* semantics, "the empirical investigation of the semantic features of historically given languages," and *pure* semantics, the abstract "construction and analysis of semantical systems" (ibid.: 11–12).

1.4.3 BENVENISTE: SEMANTICS VS. SEMIOTICS

Benveniste (1969: 241–43; 1974: 224–25) opposes the semantic and the semiotic within general semiology (see also Malmberg 1977: 194–98 and Descombes 1983: 148–56). One is the domain of the system, the other is the domain of the text. Semiotics studies the sign as an element of the signifying system, "in the midst of a constellation or among an ensemble of signs." Here, "the sign is pure identity itself, totally foreign to all other signs, the signifying foundation of language. [. . .] It exists when it is recognized as signifier by all members of a linguistic community, and when it calls forth for each individual roughly the same associations and oppositions" (Benveniste 1969: 242). Semantics, on the other hand, is the specific domain of "meaning which is generated by *discourse*" (ibid.). At this level, the signs are transformed into elements of a new, more global contextual meaning. Reference begins only at this level of semantics, "while semiotics is in principle cut off and independent of all reference" (ibid.).

Benveniste claims that a hiatus separates the

semantic from the semiotic: "In reality the world of the sign is closed. From the sign to the sentence there is no transition." Semantics and semiotics are "two separate domains, each of which requires its own conceptual apparatus" (ibid.: 243). While the dimensions of text and system remain fundamental to semiotic research, Benveniste's terminological distinction has not been generally adopted.

1.4.4 GREIMAS: SEMANTIC VS. SEMIOLOGICAL LEVEL

Greimas draws a similar basic distinction between the *semiological* level pertaining to the system and the *semantic* level to the discourse. However, his conclusion as to the place of reference within these domains is quite the opposite. In his view, the semiological, not the semantic, level is the one of reference. The semiological level is directed outward toward the world, while the semantic level is directed inward toward language itself (see also Schleifer 1987: 75).

1.5 Excursus on General Semantics

General Semantics is the name of a popular movement of ideological language criticism and practical rhetorical therapy which began in 1933 with the publication of *Science and Sanity* by Alfred Korzybski (1879–1950). It is not connected with linguistic or logical semantics and is usually not considered a trend in semiotics, although there are some points of contact (cf. Morris 1946: 322, 333; 1957: 456). One of the most influential works in General Semantics is Hayakawa (1941). An introductory survey is Rapoport (1952). General Semantics is based on the assumption that historical languages are only inadequate tools for the cognition of reality, are misleading in verbal communication, and may have negative effects on our nervous system. From these premises, General Semantics develops a practical philosophy and didactic program (cf. Bühring 1973) of rhetoric with the goal of protecting the individual against the *Tyranny of Words* (Chase 1938), which is believed to be a result of the pitfalls inherent in language.

In Hayakawa's interpretation (1941: 27),

Korzybski's General Semantics is based on three "non-Aristotelian" principles: (1) the principle of *nonidentity* ("The map is not the territory," the signifier not the signified; cf. Magic 3.2), (2) the principle of *non-allness* ("The map is not all of the territory," there is a semantic loss in every general or abstract expression), and (3) the principle of *self-reflexivity* and *multiordinality* ("An ideal map contains the map of the map, etc.," therefore orders of abstraction must be distinguished and the difference between language and metalanguage must not be confused).

The remedy recommended by Korzybski against traditional Aristotelian language is a language reform. For example, he recommends the use of indices to specify uniqueness in time and space, of quotes to specify inadequate terms, or of "*etc.*" to indicate the incompleteness of sentence meanings. As critically summarized by Morris, "the follower of Korzybski sees the task of language to be an ever more adequate mapping of the world, and looks to science to supply this language. The general semanticist talks, or wishes to talk, as a scientist. And he gives the impression at times of believing that all men at all times should talk the same way" (1957: 456). Tarski also satirizes General Semantics (without mentioning it explicitly) when he characterizes philosophical semantics as follows: "You will not find in semantics any remedy for decayed teeth or illusions of grandeur or class conflicts. Nor is semantics a device for establishing that everyone except the speaker and his friends is speaking nonsense" (1944: 681). For a critique of General Semantics from a Marxist point of view, see also Neubert (1962).

2. Linguistic Semantics

A comprehensive account of linguistic semantics is beyond the scope of this handbook (cf. Verbal Communication 1.). For the foundations and methods of this branch of linguistics, see Ullmann (1962), Lyons (1977), and Allan

(1986). Only a rough outline and some semiotic aspects of linguistic semantics can be given here.

2.1 Semantics of Language

Linguistic semantics in the modern sense began in the nineteenth century under the designation of *semasiology*, introduced by C. K. Reisig in the 1820s (cf. Gordon 1982; some linguists have retained this term, instead of *semantics*, until recently [cf. Schippan 1972]). Only with Bréal (1897) did semantics become an integral part of the sciences of language. To Bréal, semantics was still a diachronic discipline dealing with change of meaning. Modern semantics is primarily synchronic in its orientation. Its core field is word semantics or lexicology (Schwarze & Wunderlich, eds. 1985). Extensions of this traditional core are sentence semantics (or syntagmatic semantics) and text semantics.

Structural semantics, the main approach to modern linguistic semantics, began with the decomposition of word meanings into elementary semantic components (*componential analysis*), analogous to the decomposition of the phoneme into its distinctive features (see Structuralism 1.1). While this structural semantics in the narrower sense is basically a semantics of words studied within the system of language, Greimas's structural semantics is actually a semantics of the text.

2.2 Semasiology and Onomasiology

Within traditional lexical semantics, two subfields, *semasiology* and *onomasiology*, are sometimes distinguished (cf. Baldinger 1970, Wiegand 1970), reflecting two different approaches to word meaning. Although many linguists have not adopted this distinction, it seems to be useful in historical and dialectal studies of words. According to this distinction, semasiology is that branch of semantics which begins with the word form (the linguistic signifier) and studies the meanings which were associated with it in the course of its history or which are associated with it in various dialects and related languages. An example of a semasiological study would be a study of the meanings of *democracy* in communist and in capitalist countries (same word form, different meanings). In onomasiology, the point of departure is the level of content. Beginning with a particular signified or object, the study proceeds to investigate the various signifiers (lexemes) designating this meaning. An example of the onomasiological approach would be a study of the various names (in different dialects) used to designate a particular plant or animal species.

2.3 Semiotic Approaches to Linguistic Semantics

Answers to the question of the specific nature of a semiotic approach to linguistic semantics are given implicitly in the chapter on language, insofar as semiotic semantics is a branch of semiotic linguistics. Only a few explicitly semiotic approaches to meaning in language can be reviewed here. Brekle (1972) and Lyons (cf. 1977: xi) extend the scope of linguistic semantics to its more general semiotic framework by giving an outline of the sign theoretical and pragmatic dimensions of meaning in human and nonhuman communication. Guiraud's *Semiologie de la sexualité* (1978: 7) is a lexicological study, which the author himself describes as semasiological in its orientation. In this and in other semiotic contributions to lexicology (cf. Oehler, ed. 1984: 527–638), there is little difference between semiotic and other linguistic approaches to word meaning. Norrick (1981, reviewed by Droste 1985) develops *Semiotic Principles* in linguistic semantics in a study of iconic, indexical, metaphoric, metonymic relationships in language. For these topics, see Arbitrariness and Motivation, Icon and Iconicity, and Metaphor.

Typology of Signs: Sign, Signal, Index

Semioticians have not yet agreed on a general typology of signs. The problem is only partly one of finding a common terminology. Partly it is also due to the multidimensionality of the criteria on which typologies of signs can be based. Some proposals for a typology of signs are an integral part of the semiotic theory of their authors. Such proposals are discussed in the chapters on Peirce and Morris (partly see also History of Semiotics). This chapter discusses some common typological distinctions and major dimensions of typologies of signs. It gives a survey of common restrictive definitions of the term *sign* and discusses definitions of the signal and of the index. For further major types of sign, see Symbol and Icon.

1. Some Proposals for a Typology of Signs

Medieval semioticians had a great interest in the typology of signs. Modern semioticians concerned with this topic are Peirce, Morris, Husserl, Cassirer, Eco, and Sebeok. For further discussions of the typology of signs, see Schaff (1960: 145–80), Resnikow (1964: on indices, signals, and symbols), Lyons (1977: on indices, icons, symbols, and symptoms), Nattiez (1979), and Clarke (1987: on signals and

natural and conventional signs). For Bühler's distinction between symbols, symptoms, and signals, see also Function (3.1).

1.1 Natural and Nonnatural Signs

Medieval semiotics began by distinguishing *natural (signum naturale)* from *conventional (signum ad placidum)* or *intentional* signs. Modern semiotics has raised several objections against this dichotomy.

1.1.1 NATURE VS. CONVENTION AND INTENTION
Augustine opposed natural and conventional signs (cf. Sign 2.2.2; for further aspects of Augustine's typological system, see Todorov 1977: 45–54):

> *Natural* signs are those which, apart from any intention or desire of using them as signs, do yet lead to the knowledge of something else, as, for example, smoke when it indicates fire. For it is not from any intention of making it a sign that it is so, but through attention to experience we come to know that fire is beneath, even when nothing but smoke can be seen. [. . .] *Conventional* signs, on the other hand, are those which living beings mutually exchange for the purpose of showing [. . .] the feelings of their minds, or their perceptions, or their thoughts. (397: 637 = II. 1–2)

Augustine's definition already mentions the criterion of intentionality. Roger Bacon later considered this criterion to be the most fundamental one. His basic distinction was between natural and intentional signs (for his complete typological system, see Howell 1987).

1.1.2 OBJECTIONS AGAINST NATURE

In modern semiotics, two kinds of objections have been raised against accepting the nature vs. convention dichotomy as fundamental in the typology of signs: (1) objections claiming that any kind of semiosis must be based on some degree of conventionality (Eco's position, for example), and (2) objections pointing out that the basic dichotomy is insufficient because icons and pictures, for example, are neither simply natural nor conventional. A solution to the latter objection is Peirce's index-icon-symbol trichotomy. For a modern theory of natural signs, see Clarke (1987).

1.2 Symbol vs. Signal or Index

The fundamental dichotomy established by medieval semiotics reappears in new theoretical contexts in some modern theories of semiotics.

1.2.1 HUSSERL

Husserl (1890; 1900–1901: 269) drew a basic distinction between *expressions* (*Ausdruck*), which presuppose an intentional meaning-endowing act (cf. Meaning 3.1.3), and *indices* (*Anzeichen*, translated as *indication*), where "we usually feel the connection" of the sign vehicle with the simultaneously or successively present object (Husserl 1900: 274).

1.2.2 CASSIRER AND LANGER

In Cassirer's *Philosophy of Symbolic Forms*, the primary distinction is between *signals* (or signs; cf. 3.1) and *symbols*: "a signal is a part of the physical world of being; a symbol is a part of the human world of meaning. Signals are 'operators'; symbols are 'designators.' Signals [. . .] have a sort of physical or substantial be-

ing; symbols have only a functional value" (1944: 32). In Cassirer's tradition, Langer divides the realm of signs into those which *indicate* (signals, symptoms, natural signs) and those which *represent* (symbols, names, pictures, etc.) (1942: 35–39, 54–67).

1.3 Sebeok's Six Signs

Sebeok establishes a typology comprising six species of signs (1976: 117–47). His definitions are:

1.3.1 SIGNAL

When a sign token mechanically or conventionally triggers some reaction on the part of a receiver, it is said to function as a *signal*.

1.3.2 SYMPTOM

A *symptom* is a compulsive, automatic, nonarbitrary sign, such that the signifier is coupled with the signified in the manner of a natural link.

1.3.3 ICON

A sign is said to be *iconic* when there is a topological similarity between a signifier and its denotata.

1.3.4 INDEX

A sign is said to be *indexic* insofar as its signifier is contiguous with its signified, or is a sample of it.

1.3.5 SYMBOL

A sign without either similarity or contiguity, but only with a conventional link between its signifier and its denotata, and with an intensional class for its designatum, is called a *symbol*.

1.3.6 NAME

A sign which has an extensional class for its designatum is called a *name*.

2. Criteria and Typological Dimensions

The typology of signs is multidimensional. Since the sign is not a class of objects, and one and the same signifier may have many semiotic functions, a single sign vehicle may be perceived from several perspectives as belonging to several classes of sign. As Peirce observed, "It is a nice problem to say to what class a given sign belongs; since all the circumstances of the case have to be considered" (§ 2.265).

Various dimensions of the typology of signs have been discussed by Eco. A possible general framework for distinguishing typologies of signs is Morris's syntax-semantics-pragmatics trichotomy. However, the syntactic dimension will be extended to sign- and code-related criteria, thus comprising not only the aspect of sign combination, but also the dimensions of structure and system.

2.1 Eco's Typological Dimensions

Eco discusses ten semiotic criteria which underlie ten different typologies of signs (1973b: 37–77). Among his typological dimensions are the following ones: (1) *source* and *channel* (cf. Communication 3.1.3), (2) *semiotic specificity* (signs with exclusively semiotic functions against those which also fulfil other functions), (3) *replicability* of the signifier (unique vs. repeatable, etc.), (4) degree of the sender's and receiver's *intentionality*, (5) receiver's behavior, (6) relation between signifier and signified, and (7) the "alleged" relation between signifier and referent. Below, dimensions (1) to (3) are discussed as sign- and code-related, (4)–(5) as semantic, and (6)–(7) as pragmatic criteria. Having come to the conclusion that "there is a radical fallacy in the project of drawing up a typology of signs," Eco himself develops an elaborate multidimensional typology of sign production instead (1976: 217ff.). It distinguishes four modes of sign production: *recognition* (as with symptoms), *ostension* (sam-

ples, etc.), *replica* (signs taken from the repertoire of a code), and *invention* (of uncoded expressions).

2.2 Pragmatic Criteria

Pragmatic criteria are related to the sender or to the receiver of a message. A first example of such a classification is Bühler's distinction between *symptoms*, which he defines as sender-related, and *signals*, which are receiver-related signs in his definition (cf. Function 3.1). In Morris's semiotic typology, several classes of signs are based on pragmatic criteria. For example, his *prescriptor* signifies an obligation, his *valuator* causes a "preferential behavior," and his *pathic sign* "gives satisfaction" to the interpreter (Morris 1946: 359–68). Some of his criteria refer to both sender and receiver and to the whole situation of semiosis, for example, his distinction between *uni-* vs. *plurisituational* and *personal* vs. *interpersonal* signs. Most traditional criteria of sign classification are sender-related, in particular the divisions into natural vs. conventional or intentional signs and most definitions of the index and signal. For semiosis without a sender, see also Communication (2.1).

2.3 Semantic Criteria

The most widely used typology based on the semantic criterion of the sign-object relationship is Peirce's division of signs into *icons*, *indices*, and *symbols*. Morris classified several types of signs according to semantic criteria (1946: 359–68). With respect to criteria of *sense* (cf. Meaning), he distinguished between *vague* and *precise*, *ambiguous* and *unambiguous*, or *reliable* and *unreliable* signs. With respect to criteria of *reference*, Morris distinguished between *singular* and *general* signs (one vs. many denotata), *indicators*, *descriptors*, *namors* (referring to locations in space or time), *designators* (referring to "characteristics" of objects), and further types of signs. A semantic typology from the history of semiotics is Wolff's distinction between *signum demonstrativum*, *prognosticum*, and *rememorativum* (referring to present, future, or past objects).

2.4 Sign and Code-Related Criteria

Among the criteria related to the sign vehicle are those which classify signs according to the nature of their source (for example: organic or inorganic) or their channel (visual, acoustic, etc.). On the basis of other characteristics of the sign vehicle, Peirce distinguished between *qualisigns*, *sinsigns* (or *tokens*), and *legisigns* (or *types*). Eco adopts similar criteria in his dimension of replicability (cf. 2.1).

According to their syntactic structure, signs have traditionally been classified into *simple* and *compound* or *primitive* and *derivative* signs (cf. History 3.4.1). The theory of codes provides a framework for a typology of signs from a systematic point of view. On this basis, Mulder & Hervey develop a typology distinguishing between *simple signs*, *complex unarticulated signs*, *signs with two articulations*, and *signs with one articulation* (with further subtypes) (1980: 176; cf. Hervey 1982: 199).

3. "Sign" as a Class of Sign

In the Peircean and Morrissean tradition adopted in this handbook, the sign is the most general semiotic category, whose subtypes are symbols, indices, and others. However, this terminological convention has not always been accepted during the history of semiotics. There are many more restricted definitions of the term *sign*. Often the sign is opposed to the symbol, occasionally also to the index. When such restricted definitions are given, a general term for the category comprising all significant entities is usually missing.

3.1 Sign and Symbol

Various traditions define signs as a class *besides symbols* or even as a class *of symbols*. Occasionally, the sign is also opposed to the index.

3.1.1 SIGN AS AN INDEX OR SIGNAL

In the tradition of Cassirer's *Philosophy of Symbolic Forms*, *sign*, sometimes used synonymously with *signal*, comprises natural and animal signs or similar types of indices as opposed to human symbols (cf. Sign 2.3 [10]). An author who also developed a theory of signs and symbols based on this terminological convention is Price (1953: 144: 97).

3.1.2 ARBITRARY SIGNS VS. MOTIVATED SYMBOLS

In the tradition of Saussurean terminology, Durand (1964: 15) and Todorov (1972: 275–76) define signs as *arbitrary* in opposition to symbols, which are *motivated*. Wallis draws a distinction between signs and symbols which is partly similar to this tradition, partly also different from it. In his definition, signs represent either by convention or by resemblance, but in opposition to such conventional or iconic signs, symbols signify "on the basis of an analogy, often vague and difficult to grasp" (1975: 88). While both definitions oppose signs to the iconic concept of symbol, only Saussure and Todorov insist on arbitrariness as a characteristic of the sign in the narrower sense.

3.1.3 HJELMSLEV'S DEFINITION OF THE SIGN

Hjelmslev (1943: 113–14) opposed signs and symbols according to the criterion of *double articulation* (see Language 4.1): only signs have biplanar semiotic structure and are thus further structured into smaller figures of expression and of content. Symbols are elementary meaningful entities without this biplanar structure (see Symbol 2.3).

3.1.4 SIGNS AS A CLASS OF SYMBOLS

Similar to Hjelmslev, Malmberg defines signs as those semiotic entities which are produced intentionally and are based on a system of double articulation (1977: 21). But in contradistinction to Hjelmslev, Malmberg opposes the sign to a different concept of symbol. To him, *symbol* is the general term for any semiotic entity representing something else (see also Eco 1984b: 18). Signs are thus a class of symbols.

Other authors who have adopted this terminology are discussed by Price (1953: 161ff.).

3.1.5 CONTEXT-FREE VS. CONTEXT-BOUND SIGNS

In neurosemiotics, Pribram distinguishes between signs and symbols by defining signs as context-free and symbols as context-bound "signs" (1971: 305; see also Pesaresi 1981). Pribram's distinction has the following neurosemiotic relevance:

> To some considerable extent the parts of the brain involved in constructing "signs" are different from those involved in constructing "symbols." In man, however, a higher order relationship develops. Linguistic signs are used symbolically in propositional language and linguistic symbols are used significantly in thinking. (1971: 305–308)

Pribram's terminology is unusual. In the tradition of behaviorist semiotics, one finds an almost opposite definition (by R. M. Yerkes, quoted in Morris 1946: 99): "The sign sooner or later loses its meaning apart from its context; the symbol does not" (see also 3.2.1).

3.2 Sign and Index

The term *sign* is occasionally opposed to *index*, but the index has also been defined as the general class which includes the sign.

3.2.1 SIGN VS. INDEX

Occasionally, signs are opposed to indices by authors who want to emphasize the fundamental difference between *indication* and *signification* or *representation* (for example, Savigny 1974: 1788). In these cases, there is no general term covering both types of semiotic phenomena. Indices and natural signs are simply excluded from semiotic consideration.

3.2.2 SIGN AS A CLASS OF INDEX

In the history of semiotics, there have been attempts to reduce symbols to indices. Alston interprets Locke's view of words as signs of ideas (cf. Sign 2.3 [4]) as an example of this tradition (1967: 441). More recently, a definition of the sign as a class of index has been proposed by

Prieto (1966; 1975b: 15–16) and in the framework of the semiotics of Mulder & Hervey (1980: 177; earlier also in *Semiotica* 4 [1971]; see also Hervey 1982: 178–79). These authors define *index* as the generic term for any entity which "conveys some information outside itself." Prieto defines the index or indicator in terms of the *aliquid pro aliquo* relationship of the sign as follows: "A fact provides an indication and consequently constitutes an index when, from the observation of its belonging to a certain class, one can deduce the belonging of another fact to another given class" (1975b: 15). From these premises, Prieto distinguishes between intentional and nonintentional indices, such as natural signs based on cause-effect relations between sign vehicle and meaning.

Indices, according to Mulder & Hervey, are subdivided into natural indices (symptoms or signaling devices) and arbitrary *signa* (1980: 177). The sign is then only one of two subclasses of *signum* (besides the symbol). Signs are "signa whose information value depends wholly on fixed conventions" (ibid.: 183). Examples of signs in this sense are written or spoken words and the elements of the Morse code. Symbols are "signa whose information value is not wholly determined by fixed conventions, but at least partly by separate definitions." Examples of symbols in this definition are variables in algebraic notations or the units of a secret code. This terminological proposal has also been adopted in anthropology by Leach (1976).

4. Signal, Index, and Symptom

Signal, *index*, and *symptom* are three terms which are often taken as representing one category of sign, especially when opposed to *symbol* or to *sign* in one of its narrower definitions. Klaus enumerates *signal*, *index*, and *symptom* as synonyms (1963: 88). When these terms are differentiated as three classes of sign, the symptom is usually subsumed under the general class which Peirce defined as index. The signal, however, is sometimes not a class of sign at all, but only a term designating the sign vehicle.

4.1 Signal

General criteria for the definition of the signal have been discussed by Schaff (1960: 168–71), Resnikow (1964: 143–77), Pazukhin (1972), and Sebeok (see 1.3). There are four main groups of criteria, which define the signal as a signifier, as a semiotic stimulus, as a type of index, or as a certain type of elementary sign. In a pluralistic definition, several of these criteria are combined.

4.1.1 A PLURALISTIC DEFINITION
Resnikow proposes a pluralistic definition of signal which combines several criteria which other authors take as single defining criteria of this species of sign. According to Resnikow, the signal is (1) an artificially created sign with a conventional meaning (2) which is intended to induce a certain behavior or modification of behavior; (3) they are created for future events and are precise in their assignments; (4) they are usually rather simple in their structure, but striking and easily remembered (1964: 177).

4.1.2 SIGNAL AS THE SIGN VEHICLE
To define *signal* as a technical term for the sign vehicle or signifier is common in information theory (see also Sign 1.1.2). In Cherry's definition, the signal is "the physical embodiment of a message (an utterance, a transmission, an exhibition of sign events)" (1957: 308). In this definition, the signal is not a type of sign but only the token of a sign type (cf. Sign 1.2.3).

4.1.3 SIGNALS AS A PRIMITIVE SEMIOTIC STIMULUS
Morris defined the signal as being semiotically more primitive than the symbol. A signal is "a sign that is not [. . .] produced by its interpreter and not a substitute for some other sign with which it is synonymous" (1946: 366). (See Symbol 2.2 for further discussion.) In Sebeok's definition, the signal "mechanically or conventionally triggers some reaction on the part of the receiver" (1976: 121). This crite-

rion of "mechanical triggering" permits inclusion of machines as senders and receivers of signals. Behaviorists have tended to take this view of the signal as a general principle of semiosis. Thus, Bloomfield defines language as a system of signals (1933: 162).

From the point of view of genetic epistemology, Piaget defines signals (and indices) as semiogenetic precursors of arbitrary signs and symbols (1946: 68, 278). Signals and indices have the nature of a more primitive semiotic stimulus. They are signs whose signifiers are still undifferentiated from their signifieds. They are still "linked with the immediate action" (ibid.: 19) and are "merely certain aspects of the object or of the schema of action" (ibid.: 278).

In linguistics, Benveniste is among those who adopt a definition of the signal as a primitive semiotic stimulus. In his view, there is an opposition between signals and symbols which allows one to explain the distinction between animal and human communication. In contradistinction to the anthroposemiotic symbol, Benveniste defines the signal as "a physical fact *bound to another physical fact* by a natural or conventional relationship" (1966: 24). While signals have only a sensory-motor function, symbols have a representative function. Between the two "there is a threshold which only human beings have been able to cross" (ibid.). This very threshold is also central to Cassirer's distinction between signal and symbol.

However, not every stimulus in a stimulus-response sequence has been defined as a signal. Most semioticians postulate that only those stimuli to which the *aliquid pro aliquo* criterion of the sign applies should be called signals. Natural or causal stimuli which give rise to immediate responses should be excluded from the class of signals. Pazukhin therefore specifies that the signal is "a physical phenomenon which provokes reactions in mechanisms and organisms, *without being the cause* of these reactions" (1972: 41).

4.1.4 SIGNAL AS INTENTIONAL INDEX
All of the definitions discussed in the preceding paragraph belong to the class of index in the

sense of Peirce, but in Peircean semiotics, the category of index also comprises intentional indices in human communication. Two authors who define indices in such terms are Bühler (1933b) and Prieto (1966; 1975b). Bühler defines the signal as a receiver-related sign, one in which the function of appeal dominates. A verbal sign is a signal "by reason of its appeal to the hearer, whose outer or inner behavior it directs just as other traffic signs do" (1933b: 164). This definition comes close to the ordinary language usage of the term according to which a signal is "a sign with the communicative goal of pressing the hearer to perform, change or refrain from an action" (Schaff 1960: 169). According to Prieto, a signal is an instrument for the transmission of messages (1966: 13). Prieto defines the signal as an intentional index (in the general sense of sign; cf. 4.2) which is autonomous in being neither a mere fragment of a sign nor a whole group of signs (1975b: 17). Most traffic signs are signals in this sense. Signals are the foundation of Prieto's semiotics of communication.

4.1.5 SIGNAL AS AN ELEMENTARY UNIT OF COMMUNICATION

Prieto's definition postulates that a signal is an elementary semiotic unit (neither compound nor part of a sign). This criterion of being an elementary unit of communication is also postulated in other definitions. Hjelmslev (1943: 137; 1975: 79) defined the signal as an indicator which admits no further analysis and belongs only to one plane of the semiotic (in contrast to a connotator, which belongs to two planes). Clarke defines signals as those signs of communicative intent which, unlike complete sentences, lack a subject-predicate structure. Simple gestures, warning cries, a drawing, and single word utterances are his examples of signals (1987: 90).

4.2 Index and Symptom

Index and symptom are modern successors to the ancient class of natural signs. The general class of indices comprises those signs which

many semioticians have described as being fundamentally opposed to the symbol, but Peirce and Morris have given a still more extended definition of this species of sign. For discussions of the index and the symptom as species of sign, see Resnikow (1964), Goudge (1965), Gale (1967), Sebeok (1976: 124–34; 1984), and Lyons (1977: 105–109). For the terminological aspects of differentiating between *index*, *sign*, and *symbol*, see 1.2. For *index* as a general synonym of *sign*, see 3.2.

4.2.1 NATURAL AND NONINTENTIONAL INDICES

Resnikow defines the index as a natural sign based on a "natural link" between sign vehicle and referent (1964: 138–39). As such, the index can be only observed, not reproduced. Eco divides the class of natural signs into symptoms and indices, distinguishing two kinds of the latter: *traces* and *indices* (1973b: 67). Both are based on a relation of contiguity, but traces are inferences from an assumed relation of causality to a nonactual contiguity with the referent, while indices are inferences from a relation of contiguity to causal dependence. In contrast to this tradition, Husserl defines indices (*Anzeichen*) as natural *or* artificial signs which are produced without intentionality (1900: 31).

4.2.2 PEIRCE'S INDEX

Peirce defined the index in opposition to symbols and icons as a category comprising not only natural, but also many conventional signs. A sign vehicle is an index if it is "really affected" (Peirce § 2.248) by its referential object. "The index is physically connected with its object; they make an organic pair, but the interpreting mind has nothing to do with this connection, except remarking it, after it is established" (§ 2.299). Other features of Peirce's index are (cf. Goudge 1965: 53–54): it focuses the interpreter's attention on the object; it involves the existence of the object as an individual entity; it asserts nothing, but shows the object. From these premises, Peirce included the following diverse phenomena in the class of indices (cf. ibid.): a weathercock, a yardstick, a photograph, a rap on the door, a pointing finger, an appellative cry, and the field of linguistic deixis, including proper names and possessive, relative, personal, and selective pronouns. For indexical expressions in language, see also Bar-Hillel (1954) and later studies in the field of linguistic pragmatics. Lyons (1977: 106–108), following Abercrombie (1967: 5–9), adopts the term *index* to designate stylistic features of language use "which characterize the source of the signal as a particular individual" or member of a sociolinguistic group.

4.2.3 MORRIS'S IDENTIFIOR

Morris did not adopt the term *index*, but his category of *identifiors* corresponds to Peirce's index (1946: 154, 362). But in contrast to Peirce, Morris restricted the class of identifiors to spatio-temporal deixis. Identifiors signify "locations in space and time (locata) and direct behavior toward a certain region of the environment." The identifior "has a genuine, though minimal, sign status; it is a preparatory-stimulus influencing the orientation of behavior with respect to the location of something other than itself." Morris distinguished three kinds of identifiors: *indicators*, "which are non-language signals," *descriptors*, which "describe a spatial or temporal location," and *namors*, which are "language symbols, and hence, substitute signs synonymous with other identifiors."

4.2.4 SYMPTOMS

The term *symptom* has its origins in the history of medical semiotics (cf. History 1.2.2, Bär 1982; 1988, Sebeok 1984, Schonauer 1986, Staiano 1986). In ordinary English, the term designates an outwardly observable sign of disease. In metaphorical usage, the word means 'a sign of a usually bad condition or event.' Bühler extended the sense of the term still further by defining all signs having an expressive function as symptoms (1934: 28). Elsewhere, Bühler defines this same species of sign "by reason of its dependence on the sender, whose interiority it expresses," as index (*indicium*) (1933b: 164).

Peirce described symptoms as a type of index, distinguishing between the symptom as part of the general medical knowledge (and thus code) and the symptom of an individual patient: "The symptom itself is a legisign, a general type of a definite character. The occurrence in a particular case is a sinsign" (§ 8.335). Langer observes a "fine distinction between sign and symptom, in that the object signified by a symptom is the entire condition of which the symptom is a proper part; e.g., red spots are a symptom of measles, and 'measles' is the entire condition begetting and including the red spots" (1942: 58). An index, on the other hand, may refer only to a part of a total condition.

Among those phenomena which are called symptoms in ordinary English, medical diagnostics differentiates between signs and symptoms proper (cf. Barthes 1972: 38–39, Sebeok 1984: 213–15, Staiano 1986: 2–5). In this special sense, the symptom is only the mark of illness as observed by the patient ("subjectively"), while the mark of illness as observed in the physician's examination ("objectively") is called a sign.

Symbol

Symbol is one of the most overburdened terms in the field of the humanities. In its broadest sense, symbol is a synonym of sign. In spite of the vagueness of terminology, the narrower definitions, which specify symbols as a class of signs, can be grouped into three categories: symbol as a conventional sign, symbol as a kind of iconic sign, and symbol as a connotational sign. In the latter two definitions, the symbol is a key concept of aesthetics and cultural studies. (Sub)types of symbols in this field (cf. Sebeok 1976: 135) are verbal symbols, graphic and other pictorial symbols (such as signets, logos, marks, or brands; cf. Code 5.4), flags, coats of arms (see Code 5.6), emblems (symbolic pictures or figures with an explanatory motto; cf. Hill 1970), attributes (of the emblematic figures, such as Justitia's scales or Death's scythe), and allegories (also opposed to the symbol; cf. Gombrich 1972: 183ff.).

1. Symbols as Signs

The term symbol is used in many fields of research. Its ubiquity suggests that symbol and symbolic are often synonyms of sign and semiotic.

1.1 The Ubiquity of Symbols

Symbol has been a key concept in anthropology (Douglas 1970, Firth 1973, Sperber 1974, Turner 1975, Lewis, ed. 1977, Foster & Brandes, eds. 1980, Wagner 1986), sociology (Mead 1934, Bourdieu 1970), theology (Eliade 1952), philosophy and hermeneutics (Cassirer 1922–38; 1923–29, Whitehead 1928, Durand 1964), poetics (Pohl 1968, Todorov 1972; 1974; 1977, Wellek 1973), aesthetics (Ferguson 1954, Gombrich 1972, Wallis 1975, Pochat 1982), and psychoanalysis (Arrivé 1982b and Gillan 1982). Societies of symbolism (cf. Paulus 1969: 8) and of symbol research (Gesellschaft für Symbolforschung, ed. 1984) and bibliographies and dictionaries of symbols and symbolism (Ferguson 1954, Lurker 1968; 1979, Chetwynd 1982, Moser 1986) testify to the ubiquity of symbols in everyday life and scholarly research. If semiotics seems to have paid less attention to the study of symbols (except for Resnikow 1964, Malmberg 1977, Arrivé 1981–82b, and Eco 1984b: 130–63), this is in part a terminological phenomenon, since the concept of symbol in its broadest definition tends to be synonymous with that of sign.

1.2 Symbol as a Synonym of Sign

According to Whitehead (1928), every act of nonimmediate perception is a symbol (cf. Sign

1.3.3). Still more generally, neurosemioticians have described the symbol as the instrument of cognition (cf. Laughlin & Stephens 1980: 327). In such definitions, *symbol* is a synonym of *sign*.

1.2.1 VERBAL AND VISUAL SYMBOLS

Other examples of the broad definition of symbol are the following: Ogden & Richards define symbols as signs used in human communication and give "words, images, gestures, drawings or mimetic sounds" as examples (1923: 23). In other contexts, the authors use *symbol* as a synonym of the signifier of a sign (Fig. Si 3). In the field of literary criticism, N. Frye uses symbol as a passe-partout concept for "any unit of any work of literature which can be isolated for critical attention." A sign is then "a symbol in its aspect as a verbal representative of a natural object or concept" (1957: 36). In aesthetics, Goodman uses *symbol* "as a very general and colorless term. It covers letters, words, texts, pictures, diagrams, maps, models, and more, but carries no implication of the oblique or the occult" (1968: xi). Pohl, who studies the symbol as a "key to the human," plainly reduces the essence of the symbol to the ancient *aliquid pro aliquo* formula discussed in the chapter on the sign (1968: 30–31). The German industrial norm DIN 44 300 defines symbol as "a sign or word which has meaning" (cf. Sign 1.1.3).

1.2.2 LACAN'S AND KRISTEVA'S DEFINITIONS

Lacan and Kristeva use a broad concept of symbol which is practically synonymous with sign. In the writings of Lacan (1956: 29–52; 1966), the symbolic is part of a triad comprising the *real*, the *imaginary*, and the *symbolic*. The real is a sphere of primitive, inexpressible experience. The imaginary is the realm of images, mirrors, and specular identification (see Structuralism 3.2). The order of the symbolic is the order of language and visual signs. It constitutes the semiotic essence of man: "Man speaks therefore, but it is because the symbol has made him man" (Lacan 1956: 39). Kristeva also adopts this broad definition of the

symbolic and opposes it to a prelinguistic domain which she calls the *semiotic*.

1.2.3 THE WORLD AS A SYMBOL

Medieval hermeneutics and theology considered not only the scriptures but also the phenomena of the world to be symbols of divine meanings. In our century, Jaspers interprets the totality of the natural world as an encoded system of symbols to be deciphered by man (1947: 1032).

---

2. Symbol as a Conventional Sign

Peirce's definition of the symbol as an arbitrary and conventional sign has been widely adopted in semiotics (see also Sebeok's definition, Typology 1.3.5). In this sense, symbol is opposed to various nonconventional types of sign (see also Typology 1.1–2, 3.1.2). A variant of this class of definitions is the one that characterizes the symbol as being a substitutive sign. According to a rarer terminological usage, symbols are a type of elementary arbitrary sign.

2.1 Symbols vs. Nonconventional Signs

Peirce opposed the symbol to the *index* and the *icon*. Bühler contrasts it with the *index* and the *signal* (1933b: 164): the symbol is the sign with a referential function, while index and signal have expressive and appellative functions (see Function 3.1). The Philosophy of Symbolic Forms opposes the symbol to *signals*, *symptoms*, and *indexical natural signs*. For Cassirer's definition of the symbol(ic form), see Sign (2.3) [10] and Typology (1.2.2). Langer specifies that "symbols are not proxy for their objects, but are *vehicles for the conception of object*" (1942: 61).

Although Piaget defines the symbol as an iconically motivated (cf. 3.) and thus not a conventional sign (1946: 68), he interprets this type of symbol as being more arbitrary than the index or signal, which in his definition are signs where the signifier is still undifferentiated from the signified (see Typology 4.1.3). In contrast to these signs, symbols, according to Piaget, are genetically more developed (1946: 163). They have a genuine signifier-signified differentiation, which is only more fully developed in noniconic conventional signs. In this interpretation, arbitrariness and conventionality of signs increase in the order signal, index, (iconic) symbol, arbitrary sign. For definitions of symbols based on the criterion of context dependence and other definitions of the signal-symbol dichotomy, see also Typology (3.1.5) and (4.1.3).

2.2 Symbol as a Substitutive Sign

From definitions which emphasize the sign-object differentiation in the symbol in contradistinction to the more natural types of connection in other types of sign, it is but a small step to substitutional theories of the symbol: the general idea is that the symbol, in a way, replaces the absent object. If the mode of "replacement" is not sufficiently differentiated from the general *aliquid pro aliquo* relation, the substitutional theory makes the symbol a synonym of sign. Morris gives a substitutional definition of the symbol:

> Where an organism provides itself with a sign which is a substitute in the control of its behavior for another sign, signifying what the sign for which it is a substitute signifies, then this sign is a *symbol*; [. . .] when this is not the case the sign is a *signal*. [. . .] A symbol is a sign produced by its interpreter which acts as a substitute for some other sign with which it is synonymous; all signs not symbols are signals. (1946: 100)

Thus, symbols are substitutes for signals. Symbols can occur in the absence of the signals which they denote, while signals require the presence of their denotatum: "A person may interpret his pulse as a sign of his heart condition [. . .]; such signs are simply signals; his resulting words—when substitutes for such signals—would however be symbols" (ibid.: 101). An author who follows Morris in this substitutional view of the symbol is Schaff (1960:

168–80), but he postulates, in addition, that symbols are conventional signs representing abstract concepts in a sensuous form.

2.3 Symbols as Elementary Signs

Hjelmslev (1943: 113–14; cf. Hjelmslev 3.3.4) defined symbols as signs whose expression- and content-structures cannot be further analyzed into smaller components. In the interpretation of such symbols "there is an entity of content corresponding to each entity of expression." Symbols in this sense can be arbitrary (for example, traffic signs), iconic, or indexical. According to this unusually restricted definition, words of a language are not symbols because they have the feature of double articulation (see Language 4.1).

3. Symbol as an Iconic Sign

The iconic definition of the symbol has its roots in the history of aesthetics and has had influence in semiotics through Saussure's terminology.

3.1 The Symbol in Aesthetics

In the history of semiotics, Kant and Hegel defended an iconic theory of the symbol (cf. Resnikow 1964: 178, Wellek 1973, Todorov 1977, Eco 1984b).

3.1.1 KANT AND HEGEL

In his *Critique of Judgement* (1790), Kant defines symbols as "indirect representations of the concept through the medium of analogy" (cf. History 3.4.4). In his *Philosophy of Fine Art* (1817: II, 8–9), Hegel opposes the symbol to arbitrary signs, in which "the bond between the signification and the sign is one of *indifference*" or in which there is no "necessary connection between the thing signified and its modus of expression." In Hegel's definition, the symbol is "a significant fact which in its own external form already presents the content of the idea which it symbolizes" (ibid.: 10). But iconicity, according to Hegel, does not exhaust the essence of the symbol: "Though the content which is significant, and the form which is used to typify it in respect to a *single* quality, unite in agreement, none the less the symbolical form must possess at the same time still *other* qualities entirely independent of that *one* which is shared by it, and is once for all marked as significant" (ibid.).

3.1.2 THE CRITERION OF ANALOGY
The criterion of analogy, and thus iconicity, has been widely adopted in the field of aesthetics and cultural studies (cf. Turner 1975: 151). The definition of the *Concise Oxford Dictionary* quoted by Turner (ibid.) expresses it as follows: [a symbol is] "a thing regarded by general consent as naturally typifying or representing or recalling something by possession of analogous qualities or by association in fact or thought." Maritain adopts this criterion when he defines "a symbol as a *sign-image* (both *Bild* and *Bedeutung*), a sensible thing *signifying* an object by reason of a presupposed relation of *analogy*" (1957: 87).

3.2 *The Saussurean Tradition*

Quite in accordance with Hegel's aesthetics, Saussure defined the symbol as a *motivated* sign, contrasting it with *arbitrary* signs: "One characteristic of the symbol is that it is never wholly arbitrary; it is not empty, for there is the rudiment of a natural bond between the signifier and the signified. The symbol of justice, a pair of scales, could not be replaced by just any other symbol, such as the chariot" (1916b: 68). These examples show that the type of motivation Saussure had in mind is motivation by iconicity (for a more comprehensive account of Saussure's concept of symbol, see Todorov 1977: 255–70). The Saussurean definition of the symbol has been widely adopted in linguistics and the theory of literature. Thus, Todorov defines the symbol as a motivated sign (1972: 275–76; cf. Typology 3.1.2). At the same time,

he points out that the Saussurean symbol is an icon in the terminology of Peirce.

---

4. Symbol as a Connotative Sign

The connotational theory of the symbolic is the one which defines the symbol as a sign to whose primary signifier a secondary meaning is added. There have been countless interpretations of the nature of this secondary meaning.

4.1 *The Symbolic as the Connotative*

The connotational view of symbolism characterizes symbols in contradistinction to other signs as having a "surplus of meaning." This theory is not incompatible with the iconic theory of the symbol, but the criterion of similarity is not essential to the nature of the connotation in this definition. The connotational interpretation also explains the difference between symbols and metaphors.

4.1.1 SURPLUS OF MEANING
According to Todorov, "linguistic symbolism is defined by that excess of meaning with which the signified overflows the signifier" (1974: 111). This formula epitomizes the connotational view of the symbol. Creuzer, in his *Symbolik* of 1810, expressed this interpretation of the symbol as connotation as follows: "It is precisely through its lack of harmony between form and meaning and through its superabundance of content as compared to its expression that the symbol becomes significant" (Gombrich 1972: 187).

In contradistinction to normal connotations (cf. Meaning 5.2), where the connotative sense is only an addition to the primary denotative sense, the connotation of the symbol is essential in contrast to its denotational meaning. This aspect of the symbolic is also expressed by the criterion of indirect representation (cf. Kant's definition, 3.1.1). The symbolic meaning is indirect because it signifies primarily a connotative and only in the second place a denotative meaning.

4.1.2 SYMBOL VS. METAPHOR

According to Ricoeur, "there is a symbol where language produces compound signs whose meaning, not contented with designating one thing, designates another meaning which can only be realized by and from its own internal organization" (1965: 25). This definition as well as Kant's criteria of "indirect meaning" and "analogy" brings the symbol in close proximity to the metaphor. Although it is true that symbols are often not differentiated from the metaphor and other tropes, the following distinction is in accordance with the tradition of poetics (cf. Eco 1984b: 141). While in the interpretation of a metaphor, the literal sense has to be abandoned and to be replaced by the figurative sense, the symbol retains its primary sense and acquires its connotation in addition. "We read what is said as if that were what is meant, but are made to infer [. . .] something more or something else as the additional or true meaning" (Friedman 1965: 833).

4.2 The Nature of Symbolic Meanings

What is the semantic nature of the connotative "surplus" by which the symbol is characterized? At the risk of oversimplification, four major interpretations will be distinguished which seem to have dominated in the history of symbol studies: the essential, the cryptic, the irrational, and the unconscious meaning.

4.2.1 SYMBOL AS AN ESSENTIAL MEANING

This view of the symbol postulates that the symbolic connotation evinces some deeper layer of meaning as opposed to its more trivial surface content. "Hammer and sickle" representing communism is an example of such a symbol. Thus, in symbolic signs, a concrete, sometimes ordinary signifier symbolizes an immaterial content of importance to human life (cf. Resnikow 1964: 183). Goethe gave this essentialist interpretation of the symbol in his *Maximen und Reflexionen* (§ 314): "True sym-

bolism is where the particular represents the more general, not as a dream or shadow, but as a living momentary revelation of the Inscrutable."

In a much-quoted definition, Firth specifies the range of essential contents occurring in symbols as follows: "*Symbol*—where a sign has a complex series of associations, often of emotional kind, and difficult (some would say, impossible) to describe in terms other than partial representation. [. . .] No sensory likeness of symbol to object may be apparent to an observer, and imputation of relationship may seem arbitrary" (1973: 75). Goethe and Firth also refer to the cryptic aspect of the symbol.

4.2.2 SYMBOL AS A CRYPTIC MEANING

This interpretation assumes that the symbol has some hidden, cryptic, and inscrutable content. Whether this meaning may be discovered or not, the symbologists agree in that it calls for interpretation. (Ricoeur [1965: 30] raises this point to a defining criterion of the symbol; see also Frye's definition, 1.2.1.) Following a long symbologic tradition, Durand gives special emphasis to the cryptological criterion in his definition of the symbol. To him, it is "a sign referring to an inexpressible and invisible content which is hence obliged to incarnate concretely that missing adequacy, and that by means of the mythical, ritual and iconographic redundancies which inexhaustibly correct and complete that inadequacy" (1964: 14). In psychoanalysis, C. G. Jung emphasizes the cryptic view of the symbol as follows: "A symbol does not define or explain; it points beyond itself to a meaning that is darkly divined yet still beyond our grasp, and cannot be adequately expressed in the familiar words of our language" (1956: vii, 336).

4.2.3 SYMBOL AS AN IRRATIONAL MEANING

The irrational interpretation of the symbolic has played a role in cultural anthropology. In his critique of the theory of symbolism in ethnography, Sperber discusses two criteria which have dominated the traditional interpretations: "According to the first criterion, the symbolic is the mental minus the rational; according to the second, it is the semiotic minus language" (1974: 1–4). The first is the criterion of irrationality. It was emphasized in nineteenth-century anthropology (Frazer, Tylor). As a reaction, those who adopted the second criterion (Lévy-Bruhl and others) claimed that "there is no irrational symbolism, there is only poorly-interpreted symbolism." The irrational was simply a hidden meaning which could be revealed by interpretation. In this controversy, Sperber rejects both views, to adopt an entirely different view of the symbolic. Accordingly, "symbols are not signs. [. . .] Their interpretations are not meanings [. . .] Symbolism is a non-semiological cognitive system," a system of "conceptual representations" (1974: 85–87, 109).

4.2.4 THE SYMBOL AND THE UNCONSCIOUS

According to Freud, dream symbols are only a small part of the "immensely wide field of symbolism" (1916: 351; see also Arrivé 1982b). This wider field of symbolism "is not peculiar to dreams, but is characteristic of unconscious ideation, in particular among the people, and it is to be found in folklore, and in popular myths, legends, linguistic idioms, proverbial wisdom and current jokes" (Freud 1900: 351).

Freud defined the symbol as an "indirect method of representation" based on a comparison (1916: 331). However, "the common element between a symbol and what it represents [. . .] is often concealed" (1900: 352; 1916: 332). The interpretation of dream symbols, according to Freud (1916: 330), is therefore a process of translation: there are nonsymbolic dream elements, for which "we never obtain constant translations," and symbols of the unconscious dream thought, for which there are such constant translations "just as popular 'dream-books' provide them for everything that appears in dreams." Although Freud (1900: 353) rejected the ancient method of decoding dreams by means of dream-books and "arbitrary judgement," since dreams can be interpreted adequately only with reference to the personal history of the individual, he nevertheless tried to find a symbolic code (cf. Eco 1984b: 140) to interpret the meanings of (mostly sexual) dream symbols, such as sticks, staircases, umbrellas, and so on. Within this code, there are many symbolic signifiers which designate relatively few meanings so that one meaning can be expressed by many symbols (Freud 1916: 333). The rules for the decoding of dream symbols can be derived from a knowledge of symbolism in ordinary language and culture, in myths, fairy tales, jokes, folklore, customs, or poetry (ibid.: 338).

Freud envisioned a unity of the symbolic signifiers and signifieds in archaic times: "Things that are symbolically connected to-day were probably united in prehistoric times by conceptual and linguistic identity. The symbolic relation seems to be a relic and a mark of former identity" (1900: 352). Later, C. G. Jung was to develop a theory of the symbol specifying its relation to the archaic and unconscious thought in the framework of a theory of archetypes and of the collective unconscious. In Jung's definition, the symbols created by the collective unconscious are

> always grounded in the unconscious archetype, but their manifest forms are moulded by the ideas acquired by the conscious mind. The archetypes are the numinous, structural elements of the psyche and possess a certain autonomy and specific energy which enables them to attract, out of the conscious mind, those contents which are best suited to themselves. The symbols act as *transformers*, their function being to convert libido from a "lower" to a "higher" form. (1956: 232)

Thus, Jung's symbols are the conscious forms given to the unconscious archetypes to which we have no direct access. As Chouinard puts it, "A symbol would then be an allomorph of an archetype" (1970: 159).

Icon and Iconicity

Iconic signs, according to the classical definitions of Peirce and Morris, have a sign vehicle which is similar to their denotatum, but the validity of this criterion of similarity has frequently been questioned. Icons not only are signs of visual communication, but exist in almost any area of the semiotic field, including language (see also Metaphor, and Arbitrariness and Motivation). Literature on iconicity can be found in the bibliography by Huggins & Entwistle (1974), articles by Eco (1972b; 1976: 191–217), Volli (1972b), Krampen (1973), and Sebeok (1979: 107–127), and especially the collected papers in Bouissac et al., eds. (1986). For iconicity in language, literature (see the special issue of *Word & Image* 2.3 [1986]), and the arts, see the special issues of *Communications* 29 (1978), *Degrés* 15 (1978), and Hasenmueller (1981), Steiner, ed. (1981a), and Baron (1984).

1. Peirce's Definition of the Icon

Peirce gave various definitions of the icon which focus on different criteria valid for a large class of semiotic phenomena (cf. Greenlee 1973: 70–84, Elling 1978, Scherer 1984: 67–74, Pharies 1985: 34–39, Ransdell 1986). One of his main criteria is based on his semiotic category of *firstness*. Another is the crite-

rion of similarity between the sign vehicle and its object. From his triadic system of semiotics, Peirce derived a triple subclassification of the icon.

1.1 Immediacy of the Icon

Peirce's icon is a sign which signifies by its own quality, in contrast to the index, which depends on its object, and the symbol, which depends on conventions between interpreters.

1.1.1 FIRSTNESS OF THE ICON

In Peirce's universal categorial system, the icon belongs to the category of firstness, in contrast to the index and symbol, which belong to secondness and thirdness. Firstness is the mode of being which represents "the absolute present [. . .], something which is what it is without reference to anything else" (§ 2.85). The icon participates in firstness because it is "a Sign whose significant virtue is due simply to its Quality" (§ 2.92), or: "An *Icon* is a Representamen whose Representative Quality is a Firstness of it as a First. That is, a quality that it has *qua* thing renders it fit to be a representamen" (§ 2.276).

1.1.2 THE PURE ICON

However, since every *genuine sign* always participates in secondness (*qua* object) and thirdness (*qua* interpretant), a *pure icon* (cf. § 2.92) or *iconic qualisign* (see Peirce 3.1) is only a hypothetical possibility. It cannot really exist, for: "A sign by Firstness is an image of its object and [. . .] can only be an *idea*. For it must produce an Interpretant idea [. . .]. But most strictly speaking, even an idea, except in the case of a possibility, or Firstness, cannot be an Icon. A possibility alone is an Icon purely by virtue of its quality; and its object can only be a Firstness" (§ 2.276).

A pure icon would be a noncommunicative sign, since "a pure icon is independent of any purpose. It serves as a sign solely and simply by exhibiting the quality it serves to signify" (Peirce 1976: vol. 4, p. 242). Pure icons therefore represent only a hypothetical borderline case of semiosis. Peirce envisioned such a case under the following circumstances: "In contemplating a painting, there is a moment when we lose the consciousness that it is not the thing, the distinction of the real and the copy disappears, and it is for the moment a pure dream—not any particular existence, and yet not general. At that moment we are contemplating an *icon*" (§ 3.362). Since pure icons are signs by themselves and do not depend on an object, "a pure icon can convey no positive or factual information; for it affords no assurance that there is any such thing in nature" (§ 4.447).

Thus, no actual sign is a pure icon (cf. Ayer 1968: 150). A pure icon "can only be a fragment of a completer sign" (Peirce 1973: § 4.422). To characterize real and material iconic representations in contrast to pure icons (iconic qualisigns), Peirce introduced the term *hypoicon* (§ 2.276). A hypoicon is either an *iconic sinsign* or an *iconic legisign* (see Peirce 3.4).

1.1.3 SEMIOTIC DEGENERACY OF THE PURE ICON

The pure icon is a semiotic paradox. As a sign it should participate in a semiotic triad; as a pure icon it participates only in firstness. Peirce (§§ 2.91–92, 3.360–62, Peirce 1976: vol. 4, pp. 241–42) described this as a case of *semiotic degeneracy*. Unlike genuine signs, which presuppose a complete triad of sign (representamen), object, and interpretant, degenerate signs are reduced to a semiotic dyad or even monad (cf. Buczyńska-Garewicz 1984). Since the icon consists of a sign vehicle which has a relation to its object not depending on an interpreter's mind and thus on an interpretant, the semiotic triad of the icon is reduced to a dyad. If, as in the pure icon, the relation to the object is absent, the dyad is even reduced to a monad. Peirce considered such cases of degeneracy to be less perfect modes of semioticity. However, since most "real" icons have some degree of conventionality, these icons do participate in a semiotic triad. The field of iconicity is thus not completely dominated by semiotic degeneracy.

1.2 The Icon in Relation to Its Object

Actual icons (hypoicons or iconic sinsigns and iconic legisigns; cf. 1.1.2 and Peirce 3.4) are defined by the criterion of similarity between sign (representamen) and object.

1.2.1 THE CRITERION OF SIMILARITY

Peirce characterized the icon as "a sign which stands for something merely because it resembles it" (§ 3.362), as "partaking in the characters of the object" (§ 4.531), or as a sign whose "qualities resemble those of that object, and excite analogous sensations in the mind for which it is a likeness" (§ 2.299). His examples of icons are portraits, paintings (§ 2.92), photographs (§ 2.281), ideographs (§ 2.280), metaphors, diagrams, logical graphs (§§ 4.418–20), and even algebraic formulas (§ 2.279). Many of these icons are not based on similarity in the ordinary sense of the word. Algebraic formulas, for example, only "*exhibit*, by means of the algebraic signs (which are not themselves icons), the relations of the quantities concerned" (§ 2.282), and "many diagrams resemble their objects not at all in looks; it is only in respect to the relations of their parts that their likeness consists" (§ 2.282).

Thus, iconicity includes similarity of abstract relations or structural homologies, and many icons also participate in other modes of semiosis. An ideograph, for example, is also symbolic, because it is a conventional sign of writing; and photographs, according to Peirce, are also indexical, "having been produced under such circumstances that they were physically forced to correspond point by point to nature" (§ 2.281).

1.2.2 ICONIC OPENNESS

Similarity, according to Peirce, implies referential openness to a degree that the referential object does not even have to exist:

> Each Icon partakes of some more or less overt character of its Object. They, one and all, partake of the most overt character of all lies and deceptions—their Overtness. Yet they have more to do with the living character of truth than have either Symbols and Indices. The Icon does not stand unequivocally for this or that existing thing, as the Index does. Its Object may be a pure fiction, as to its existence. (§ 4.531)

1.2.3 THE PRAGMATIC DIMENSION OF SIMILARITY

In a way, Peirce anticipated the later critique of the validity of the criterion of similarity. He admitted that there are no logical limits to the discovery of similarity and thus iconicity: "Anything whatever, be it quality, existent individual, or law, is an Icon of anything, in so far as it is like that thing and used as a sign of it" (§ 2.247). But instead of a logical delimitation of iconicity, which seems impossible, Peirce gave a pragmatic interpretation of the relevance of similarity in semiosis:

> Any two objects in nature resemble each other, and indeed in themselves just as much as any other two; it is only with reference to our senses and needs that one resemblance counts for more than another. [. . .] Resemblance is an identity of characters; and this is the same as to say that the mind gathers the resembling ideas together into one conception. (§ 1.365)

1.3 Images, Diagrams, and Metaphors

Within his triadic categorial system, Peirce further distinguished three modes of firstness and accordingly subdivided icons (or hypoicons; cf. 1.1.2) into three types:

Hypoicons may be roughly divided according to the mode of Firstness of which they partake. Those which partake in simple qualities, or First Firstnesses, are *images*; those which represent the relations, mainly dyadic, or so regarded, of the parts of one thing by analogous relations in their own parts, are *diagrams*; those which represent the representative character of a representamen by representing a parallelism in something else, are *metaphors*. (§ 2.277)

Thus, the three types of icon represent three degrees of decreasing iconicity and also semiotic degeneracy. Images are immediately iconic, representing simple qualities, as in a color picture. Diagrams are icons of relations and thus depend on indices and conventions (§ 4.418). Metaphors are metasigns whose iconicity is based on the similarity between the objects of two symbolic signs, the *tenor* and the *vehicle* of the metaphor (see Metaphor 1.2).

---

2. The Scope of Iconicity

The concept of iconicity was first proposed by Morris. The scope of iconicity extends over all areas of the semiotic field including language.

2.1 Iconicity

Morris reduced Peirce's criteria of the icon to the single criterion of "shared properties" and believed on this basis in a quantifiability of iconicity.

2.1.1 MORRIS'S DEFINITION OF THE ICON

According to Morris, "a sign is *iconic* to the extent to which it itself has the properties of its denotata," and "iconicity is thus a matter of degree" (1946: 98, 273). Morris illustrated his quantitative view of iconicity as follows:

> A portrait of a person is to a considerable extent iconic, but it is not completely so since the painted canvas does not have the texture of the skin, or the capacities for speech and motion, which the person portrayed has. The motion picture is more iconic, but again not completely so. A

completely iconic sign would always denote, since it would itself be a denotatum. (ibid.: 98–99)

Thus, a complete icon is a borderline case of semiosis, since the sign is identical with its denotatum. Iconicity, in this view, is the degree of material difference between sign vehicle and denotatum.

2.1.2 DEGREES OF ICONICITY

Several authors have followed Morris in the attempt at establishing scales of iconicity (cf. also Morris & Hamilton 1965: 361). Wallis argues that iconicity is a matter of "many intermediate stages" between two extremes, which he calls *schemata* and *pleromata* (1975: 7). *Pleromata* are icons representing their objects in great detail, as in naturalistic painting or photography. Schemata are more abstract representations, such as diagrams or pictograms. Moles develops a most elaborate scale of visual iconicity (1972b: 52). He distinguishes thirteen degrees of iconicity, beginning with maximum iconicity (the object itself), followed by three-dimensional models of original scale and several types of progressively more simplified schemata, and ending with verbal descriptions as examples of a zero iconicity. Attempts at a quantification of iconicity remain problematic. Similarity is multidimensional, depending on many independent factors, such as form, color, size, material and situational variables, and these cannot be projected onto a two-dimensional scale. Nevertheless, the idea of iconicity being a matter of degree remains a useful tool of semiotic description.

2.2 Ubiquity of Iconic Signs

In the context of visual communication, the topic of iconicity has been discussed in the chapters on images, paintings, and photography. However, iconicity is not restricted to visual communication (pace Huggins & Entwistle 1974). There is auditive iconicity in music (q.v. 2.2.5) or in radio plays (cf. Knilli 1970: 46ff.) and multimedial iconicity in film and theater.

In aesthetics, poetics, and the theory of literature (see Literature 2.1), iconicity has been discussed since Aristotle first postulated the principle of mimesis.

Iconicity is not necessarily restricted to similarities within the same channel of perception. Morris included intersensory phenomena, such as *synaesthesia* between sounds and visual impressions, among the modes of iconicity (1946: 273). Iconicity exists in verbal and nonverbal communication (see Bouissac, ed. 1986: 437–525), dancing (cf. Wallis 1975: 4), gestures (cf. Ekman & Friesen 1969: 60), and sign languages (cf. Klima & Bellugi et al. 1979: 9–34). In zoosemiotics and phytosemiotics (Krampen 1981c), visual and olfactive icons occur in the form of mimicry (cf. Sebeok 1979: 116), evolutionary adaptations to the environment, and there is acoustic iconicity in bird calls (cf. Wescott 1971: 417).

3. Iconicity in Language

Structural linguistics has for a long time adhered to the Saussurean dogma of *arbitrariness*. Only recently has the importance of the opposed principle of iconicity become a topic of more intensive research.

3.1 Research Fields

The history of the idea of iconicity in language studies has been outlined by Genette (1976). Iconicity is relevant to both synchronic and diachronic research in language.

3.1.1 TOPICS IN SYNCHRONIC LINGUISTICS

General aspects of the topic have been discussed by Jakobson (1965), Wescott (1971), Woolley (1977), Toussaint (1983), Baron (1984), and Pharies (1985). The special branches of linguistics in which iconicity has been studied are phonology (Jakobson & Waugh 1979, Pesot 1980), morphology (Mayerthaler 1981, Plank 1981, Toussaint 1983, Dressler et al. 1987), lexicology (Ross

1983), syntax (Haiman 1980, Haiman, ed. 1985, Posner 1986), and text linguistics (Enkvist 1981). For metaphorical icons and noniconicity in language, see Metaphor and Arbitrariness. For iconicity in the relationship between verbal and nonverbal communication, see McNeill (1980).

3.1.2 ICONICITY AND THE ORIGINS OF LANGUAGE
The hypothesis of an iconic origin of language inspired the theoreticians of language evolution until the nineteenth century (cf. Jespersen 1894: 328ff.). According to the ancient bow-wow theory, primitive words were believed to be imitations of sounds. Another variant of original iconicity in language, the ding-dong theory, was based on the assumption of a somewhat mystic correspondence between sound and sense, the belief that every substance "has its particular ring" (ibid.: 330). Opponents of these theories set up the antitheses of the pooh-pooh and the yo-he-ho theories, which assume an indexical origin of language based on various kinds of exclamations associated with elementary human activities. All of these theories of iconicity or indexicality in the origins of language have remained purely speculative. For current research on the theories of language origin, see Wescott (1984) and Gessinger & Rahden, eds. (1988). For less speculative inquiries into the iconic origins of nonvocal languages, see Writing (1.) and Sign Language (2.2).

3.1.3 ICONICITY IN LANGUAGE CHANGE
In the evolution of historical languages, there has been both an increase and a decrease of iconicity (cf. Anttila 1972 and Plank 1979). The laws of regular sound and grammatical change often have an effect of *deiconization*. The phonetic iconicity of a word becomes lost with the change of its pronunciation. Against this evolution toward arbitrariness, there is an opposed trend toward *iconization*, by which language gains new forms of expressivity. Bolinger argues that "most change in language that is not due to accident arises from the underlying iconic drive to make sound conform to sense" (1975: 218). In the sound structure of language, such iconizations result in new imaginal icons. In morphology and syntax, the result is more typically diagrammatic iconicity. Lexical or semantic change (cf. Anttila 1972) results not only in new iconicities (including metaphors), but also in metonymies (thus: indexicality) and other forms of motivation (see Arbitrariness 3.2).

3.2 Imaginal and Diagrammatic Iconicity

A semiotic basis for research in linguistic iconicity is the Peircean distinction between linguistic icons which are images and those which are diagrams and metaphors. Linguists who have adopted and applied this distinction in the study of language are Jakobson (1965), Anttila (1972), Todorov (1972: 286–92), Bolinger (1975), Plank (1979; 1981), Haiman (1980), Shapiro (1983), Pharies (1985), and Dressler et al. (1987). The distinction between imaginal and diagrammatic iconicity is related to the two types of language motivation distinguished by Gamkrelidze (1974). His "vertical" motivation, the motivation of a signifier by a signified, is primarily a form of imaginal iconicity. "Horizontal" motivation, the influence of one signifier of the language system on another, is largely based on diagrammatic iconicity.

3.2.1 IMAGINAL ICONICITY
Images "partake in simple qualities" of their referent (see 1.3). As an acoustic medium, language exhibits such forms in the most direct form in onomatopoeia, i.e., words representing similar sound events. Examples are the words designating the cry of the rooster in many languages (cf. Pharies 1985: 72); *kukuruku* in Basque, *kukeleku* in Dutch, or *kokoriko* in Turkish. Such forms of onomatopoeic iconicity in language have also been defined as *primary iconicity* in contrast to various other modes of *secondary iconicity* (Lyons 1977: 102–105). For further research in onomatopoeic iconicity, see Pesot (1980), Pharies (1985), and Sornig (1986: 66–84).

A much larger field of imaginal iconicity is based on isomorphisms between the phonetic mode of articulation and expression on the one hand and various nonacoustic designata. These occur in *sound symbolisms* (cf. Marchand 1960: 397–428, Jakobson & Waugh 1979: 181ff.) and *phonaesthemes* (nonmorphemic groups of phonemes having some common semantic characteristic, such as initial *gl-* in *glitter, gleam, glisten, glimpse,* etc.; cf. Firth 1930: 184, Marchand 1960: 397ff., Bolinger 1975: 218–20, Pharies 1985). The effect is one of synaesthesia (cf. Jakobson & Waugh 1979: 191–98). The impressionistic distinction between ''light'' and ''dark'' vowels, which suggests some correspondence between auditory and visual or weight perceptions, exemplifies this case of secondary iconicity. Other examples of such imaginal iconicity are synaesthetic correspondences between articulatory movements or duration and kinetic or temporal properties of referents, e.g., long vowels denoting length vs. short vowels denoting shortness.

3.2.2 DIAGRAMMATIC ICONICITY

Isomorphisms between structural relations in language and relational patterns of its referents constitute diagrammatic linguistic iconicity. Such correspondences exist in texts and within the language system. In texts, the correspondence between the order of words and the sequence of the events described is a case of diagrammatic iconicity (cf. Caesar's *veni, vidi, vici*). Ancient rhetoric defined this form of textual iconicity as *ordo naturalis* in contrast to the noniconic *ordo artificialis* (cf. Enkvist 1981). A rich source of textual (or syntagmatic) iconicity is the field of binomials and idiomatic phrases. As Cooper & Ross (1975) have shown, the *ordo naturalis* in the sequence of idiomatic phrases corresponds to various forms of referential order: the perceptually, biologically, or culturally more salient or important referent is linguistically expressed before the less important element.

Examples of diagrammatic iconicity in the language system are isomorphisms between grammatical paradigms and their referents.

Thus, the gradual increase of the number of phonemes in comparative (*high-higher-highest*) and plural forms (*girl-girls, child-children*) depicts a corresponding gradation in the referential domain (cf. Jakobson 1965: 352). Besides such quantitative iconicities, there are also diagrammatic iconicities related to qualitative aspects of sound patterns. Thus, Tanz (1971) has described statistically significant correlations between sound and meaning of word pairs denoting physical, temporal, or personal proximity vs. distance. The phonetic parallels are high - front vs. low - back vowel contrasts (cf. English *here* vs. *there, this* vs. *that, freeze* vs. *froze, see* vs. *saw,* etc.). For further studies in such patterns of diagrammatic iconicity, see Todorov (1972: 286–92), Haiman (1980), Mayerthaler (1981, who calls it constructional iconicity), Plank (1981), Haiman, ed. (1985), Pharies (1985), and Dressler et al. (1987).

4. The Semiotic Critique of the Iconic Sign

The concept of iconicity has been the subject of much semiotic criticism. The main objection is directed against the validity of the criterion of similarity.

4.1 Relativism and Conventionalism

Since everything has in principle some feature in common with something else, it has been argued that ''there are no iconic signs'' (Bierman 1962). Goodman rejects the concept of similarity entirely after an examination of ''Seven Strictures of Similarity'' (1972: 437–47). His position is one of complete relativism: almost any picture may represent almost anything (cf. Gombrich 1981: 12). Gombrich (1960; 1981) is less radical in his criticism of the notion of likeness. He emphasizes the relative conventionality of pictures and rejects the idea of a natural likeness.

4.2 Eco's Critique of Iconism

One of the most influential semiotic critiques of iconism is Eco's (1972b; 1976: 191–217). Eco rejects not only all variants of the "naive" criterion of similarity (such as analogy, motivation, and common properties), but also the opposite thesis of arbitrariness of icons (1976: 191). In his own interpretation, iconism is based on *cultural convention*, and "similarity does not concern the relationship between the image and its object, but that between the image and a previously culturalized content" (ibid.: 204). This reinterpretation of iconicity in terms of a sign vehicle-content (and not referent) relation is one of the logical consequences of Eco's semiotic elimination of the referent (cf. Meaning 2.3.2). But Eco also wants to eliminate the iconic sign itself (ibid.: 216–17). While objecting to the idea of signs as units of fixed correlations, he wants to replace the typology of signs by a theory of the modes of *sign production*. Within such a framework, Eco reinterprets the semiotic opposition of arbitrariness vs. iconicity by this dichotomy of *ratio facilis* vs. *ratio difficilis*. A sign production by *ratio facilis* takes place according to a preexisting code. The sign production in this case is *facilis* because it can be predicted according to the rules of the code (cf. ibid.: 183). The individual sign token has a conventional and arbitrary correlation to the sign type within the code. In a sign production by *ratio difficilis*, both expression and content are not yet coded; they must be invented (therefore: *difficilis*; cf. ibid.: 188). *Ratio difficilis* is Eco's reinterpretation of semiotic motivation and iconicity. A sign production ruled by *ratio difficilis* is one in which "the form of the expression maps (or is determined by) the spatial organization of the content" (Eco 1984b: 176).

4.3 In Defense of Iconism

Sebeok (1979: 115) and others have defended the pragmatic validity of the concept of iconicity (see also 1.2.3). While the naive notion of a quantifiability of iconicity according to the number of common features has generally been abandoned in favor of a more differentiated approach (among others by Knowlton 1966: 165ff.), there has also been evidence for a cognitive relevance of the perception of similarities (cf. Tversky 1977). It is true that iconicity, unlike logical truths, depends on judgments of similarity, and these are codified according to persons, places, and time of judgment (cf. Metz 1970a: 3). But this does not mean that there is no relevance to similarity judgments. Perceptions of similarities are a common cognitive process, and its effect is heuristically relevant (cf. Greenlee 1968: 762) insofar as "it is likely to guide further inquiry constructively" (ibid.).

Metaphor

The topic of metaphor lies at the root of semiotics, both historically and analytically. Historically, there is the long tradition of theories of metaphor, which dates back to Aristotle (384–321 B.C.). Analytically, metaphors concern the study of figurative signs and also raise the more fundamental question of whether "literal" meaning is possible at all. Topics such as arbitrariness, conventionality, motivation, and iconicity have dominated the semiotic discussion of metaphors. Some controversies about the subject seem to be due to the terminological ambiguity of the concept of metaphor. Most research in metaphors has so far been concerned with verbal tropes (see Rhetoric 2.3.1). For visual metaphors as deviations from standard modes of depiction, see Kennedy (1982) and Advertising (2.2).

1. The Concept of Metaphor

Traditionally, *metaphor* has been used as a term for two clearly different concepts, but only the criteria for metaphors in the narrower of the two senses will be discussed in this chapter.

1.1 The Traditional Concept of Metaphor

The term *metaphor* has been used in both a narrow and a broad sense since ancient times (cf. Lieb 1964). While *metaphor* in the narrow sense represents a particular trope among others, e.g., metonymy, synecdoche, hyperbole, etc., *metaphor* in the broad sense amounts to a cover term for all figures of speech. In contemporary theories of language and literature, the narrow term is more customary, although its separation from the broader one is often ignored. In the following, therefore, the term *metaphor* is used only in the narrow sense.

1.2 Definitional Criteria for Metaphor

Despite many differences in detail, two central concepts reappear as criteria of most traditional definitions of metaphor, *transfer* and *similarity*. Major variants of the former concept are replacement, substitution, and translation. Variants of the latter are likeness, comparison, and analogy. A typical definition (from *Webster's Third New International Dictionary*) combines these criteria as follows: "a figure of speech in which a word or a phrase denoting one kind of object or action is used in place of another to suggest a likeness or analogy between them."

While the criterion of transfer holds for all tropes (metaphors in a broad sense), similarity is the distinguishing criterion of metaphors in the narrow sense. The idea of transfer is already expressed in the etymology of the term. Μεταφορά (*metaphorá*) means precisely 'transfer,' 'a carrying from one place to another.' The two "places" implied in this definition refer to the spheres of literal and of figurative meaning. Both are said to be related by similarity or implicit comparison. Richards (1936) introduced the terms *tenor* and *vehicle* for the two domains of meaning interacting in the metaphorical process. When Shakespeare refers to the 'sun' as "the eye of heaven," the 'sun' (which is in certain respects like an eye) is the tenor, the underlying idea of this metaphor, and "the eye" is the vehicle, that is, the image which is used to represent or "carry" the tenor. Pelc (1971: 148) argues that the metaphor is a semantic constellation which actually involves three and not only two terms: the metaphorical expression E ("eye of heaven") and two literal expressions E_1, the proper sense (of "the eye"), and E_2, the tenor ('the sun'). Pelc defines this triadic constellation E E_1 E_2 as the *metaphoric triangle*.

2. Theories of Metaphor

Since Aristotle, the subject of metaphor has been dealt with in thousands of treatises (cf. Shibles 1971, Noppen 1985). And yet, in the mid–1980s, with a new journal (*Metaphor* 1ff. [1986ff.]), collected papers (Papprotté & Dirven, eds. 1985), and new "reexaminations" of the topic (Gumpel 1984), no end of this scholarly tradition is in sight (cf. Cooper 1986, Köller 1986). The long history of metaphorology, for which the establishment of a Museum of Metaphors has been proposed (Gumpel 1984: 231–38), has created a *Myth of Metaphor* (Turbayne 1962, Scheffler 1986). Some claim that only a few have added anything of substance to Aristotle's first analysis of the topic (Eco 1984b: 88). A more recent study proposes a new theory which divides the world of metaphorology into two realms, the one with an Aristotelian, the other with a non-Aristotelian approach. More traditional typologies of metaphor theories have proposed other divisions.

2.1 Substitution, Comparison, and Interaction Theories

Black (1962) reduces the multiplicity of metaphor theories to three types: the *substitution theory*, the *comparison theory*, and the *interaction theory*. Each of these theories alone can probably illuminate only one side of metaphor. Thus, with respect to the definitional criteria for metaphor in the narrow sense, the substitution and comparison theories must be seen as complementary. Both theories describe metaphor primarily from a paradigmatic point of view. The interaction theory proposed by Black (1962) and earlier by Richards (1936), on the other hand, explains metaphor primarily from a syntagmatic point of view as the resolution of a semantic tension between the metaphoric expression and its context. But even the syntagmatic structure of metaphor necessarily presupposes a paradigmatic dimension, so that the two aspects are again complementary.

Criticism of the substitution theory of metaphor stems from different views of the substitution process. Todorov critically notes among other things that metaphor theory has often failed to recognize that only signifieds are replaced in the metaphoric process, while the signifiers of the linguistic sign remain constant (1970c: 28). Only in the metalinguistic analysis is this process indirectly illuminated by the exchange of two signifiers, e.g., "*Bean* can metaphorically stand for *head*."

2.2 Monistic and Dualistic Theories of Metaphor

A typology of metaphor which skews Black's (1962) classification is proposed by Mooij (1975: 259). According to whether a simple or a double reference is attributed to metaphors, Mooij differentiates between monistic and dualistic theories of metaphor. Monistic descriptions see substitution as a process of complete deletion of the literal sense in favor of the figurative one (cf. 'feature deletion' in semantic componential analysis). Dualistic theories attribute a double reference to metaphor: the literal sense of the metaphorical expression is not completely deleted but instead remains as a semantic background for the figurative meaning and creates a semantic conflict with it.

The comparison theory of metaphor is one such dualistic theory. Aristotle argues in the sense of a dualistic metaphor theory when he stresses in the *Poetics* (xxii): "For the right use of metaphor means an eye for resemblances." A typical dualistic view also appears in Samuel Johnson's thesis (as quoted by Richards 1936: 93), according to which a metaphorical expression "gives you two ideas for one." In other variants of dualistic theories of metaphor, the metaphoric process is described as the result of a "mixture of semantic spheres" (Bühler 1934) in combination with a "filter function" (ibid. and Black 1962: 39) or as the result of a "cognitive synergy" (Apter 1982).

2.3 From Semantics to Syntax and Pragmatics

The similarity and substitution criteria for metaphor concern primarily its semantic dimension. Two general semiotic problems are bound up with these definitional criteria, and only they are directly at issue in the following, viz., the conventionality and the iconicity of metaphor. Beyond the semantic definitional criteria for metaphor, recent discussion stresses the necessity of describing metaphors contextually (Ricoeur 1975a; see also 3.3) and in their communicative function (Köller 1975, Mack 1975). This enlarges the analysis of metaphor through addition of the syntactic (for which see Brooke-Rose 1958) and the pragmatic dimensions.

3. On the Conventionality of the Metaphoric Sign

If metaphor can be defined as an uncharacteristic or uncustomary use of a word in a particular context, then this means that the metaphoric sign departs from the semiotic structure of the language system in its conventionality. This departure involves two aspects of linguistic conventionality in the broad sense: arbitrariness and conformity with the linguistic norm, which can be called conventionality in the narrow sense. The view of metaphor from the point of view of the language system has to be complemented by a (con)textual view.

3.1 Arbitrariness and Motivation

Saussure's thesis of the arbitrariness of the linguistic sign claims that a linguistic expression is not motivated by its content. This arbitrariness in principle is restricted by a number of motivations which have been discussed as "relative arbitrariness" (see Arbitrariness 3.1). One of these is semantic motivation (cf. Ullmann 1962: 91, Todorov 1970c: 33), a principle which explains the origin of metaphors and tropes in general. When an expression has a literal and a metaphorical meaning, it is only the metaphor which is said to be motivated, while the literal expression remains arbitrary. The cause of motivation is the similarity between the two contents.

The explanation of metaphors by semantic similarity relations presupposes a broad theory of semantics, which must comprise not only lexical but also encyclopedic knowledge. For theories with an approach restricted to lexical semantics, not all similarity relations in metaphors are explicable. Thus, Levin excludes referentially motivated metaphors from his semantics of metaphor (1977: 94ff.). Other authors have developed a theory of metaphor which includes encyclopedic knowledge (cf. Eco 1984b: 87–129). Frame semantics and the general theory of cognition have further contributed to this broader approach to metaphor. The most convincing step in this direction has been taken by Lakoff & Johnson (1980).

3.2 Conventionality

Metaphoric departure from the codified linguistic norm can be unique, but it may also recur. So-called poetic or more generally creative metaphors are unique. They are semantically innovative in appearing for the first time as a departure from the historically determined convention of the language norm. Through multiple recurrence metaphors can themselves finally become conventionalized and therewith a part of the language norm. This process takes place diachronically in several stages of conventionalization: At first there is the original, *creative* metaphor. When it becomes part of everyday language, it is a lexicalized metaphor (e.g., *bottleneck*). With the vanishing of the original literal meaning, an *opaque* metaphor appears (e.g., *radical*: literally 'from the root'). Finally, with *dead* metaphors (e.g., *news magazine*: originally *magazine* meant 'storehouse') the literal meaning is known only to the etymologist. These four stages of demetaphorization differ in their degree of innovativeness and in the decreasing *semantic transparency* of their figurative vis-à-vis their literal meanings.

The process of conventionalization can also be reversed in the poetic device of *remetaphorization* or *resurrection* of a dead metaphor (cf. Shapiro 1983: 204–206, Nieraad 1977: 47ff.). This shows that the dead metaphor retains a potential, revivable image which goes unnoticed in our everyday use of language. Imagery is in general a matter of linguistic awareness: only then is a linguistic sign produced and understood as a metaphor when the speaker/hearer is aware of the tension between the literal and figurative meanings of the sign. By contrast with simple polysemy, metaphor presupposes semantic transparency (Pelc 1961: 334).

It can be determined empirically that language users recognize different language norms and hence view metaphors differently. But the difficulty in determining the language norm in the face of metaphoric usage does not necessarily entail reference to the empirical study of *parole* for its solution. It also presents a problem for lexicography, a branch of linguistics necessarily oriented toward the *langue*. The lexicographer's difficulties with the distinction between literal and metaphorical meanings are illustrated by Leisi (1973: 174–75), who shows that the expression "foot of the mountain" is not metaphor if the word *foot* is defined as 'the lowest portion on which someone or something stands.' Thus, the determination of the literal meaning of a lexeme sets a precedent for the decision about the metaphorical status of its other meanings.

3.3 *Metaphors in Texts and in the Language System*

Some philosophers of language tend to define metaphors as speech acts occurring only in *parole*, and hence as being irrelevant for the semantics of the *langue*. In doing so, they assume a static word or sentence semantics according to which metaphors can never occur in the language system (e.g., Searle 1979: 100) and in which word and sentence meaning exist independently of particular contexts of occurrence (Davidson 1978: 33). Davidson even takes the extreme monist position that a metaphor contains nothing besides its literal meaning (ibid.: 32).

Such a strict division of text and language system turns out to be especially unfruitful for the analysis of metaphor. A static semantics would allow neither language change nor lexicalized metaphors. The analysis of metaphor requires instead a dynamic text semantics which includes the text and the situation of metaphoric communication over and above the level of the word. But even within the norm of the language system, metaphors are contained in the lexicon. Like all structures of the system, metaphors are potential structures, which may or may not be realized in texts.

4. On the Iconicity of Metaphor

Although the similarity criterion is the only one which distinguishes metaphor in the narrow sense from other figures of speech, precisely this criterion is especially disputed within metaphor theory.

4.1 Classical Similarity Theses

Quintilian's thesis of metaphor as an abbreviated comparison (cf. Lausberg 1960: §§ 558ff.) is among the best-known versions of the comparison theory of metaphor. The concept of comparison, however, exhibits, as Le Guern notes (1973: 52), a certain ambiguity, inasmuch as it functions as a collective term for two clearly distinct concepts in classical grammatical theory, viz., *comparatio* and *similitudo*. While *comparatio* concerns the quantitative relations of "larger/smaller than" or "just as large as," *similitudo* involves a qualitative judgment about two similar properties. Only the latter type of comparison is relevant for metaphor.

Crucial aspects of a similarity theory of metaphor appear especially in Aristotle's work. In his *Poetics* (xxi), metaphors are defined as "transferences by analogy." For Aristotle (*Rhetoric* III, 4), the difference between metaphor (μεταφορά) and simile (ἐικών [eikōn]) was slight. While Quintilian viewed the comparison as fundamental and the metaphor as derived from it, Aristotle considered the metaphor fundamental and the comparison simply an elaborated metaphor (cf. Ricœur 1975a: 25).

For Aristotle, the recognition of similarity in metaphor did not presuppose an especially high degree of iconicity at all. Instead, metaphor appears as a creative process of establishing similarities: "Metaphors must be drawn [. . .] from things that are related to the original thing, and yet not obviously so related—just as in philosophy also an acute mind will perceive resemblances even in things far apart" (*Rhetoric* III, 11). So similarity is seen before a background of dissimilarities from which it need not *a priori* clearly distinguish itself in all cases. Where Aristotle postulated a relationship between the metaphor and the riddle, it becomes obvious that the dissimilarity in a metaphor can be quite severe and the iconicity consequently rather slight (e.g., *Rhetoric* III, 2): "For metaphors imply riddles, and therefore a good riddle can furnish a good metaphor."

4.2 Criticism of Similarity Theory

As to its semiotic foundation, criticism of the similarity theory of metaphor is identical with the more general discussion of iconicity in signs as a whole. The criticism is justified to the degree that it is directed toward several "naive ideas about iconicity" (cf. Eco 1976: 191ff.). It is unjustified where it takes account of neither the more sophisticated versions of semiotic iconicity theory nor the subtle distinctions of the comparison theory of metaphor.

Two arguments make up the central portion of the criticism of the comparison theory of metaphor: the first is of a logical and the second of an ontological nature. The logical argument has been put forth by philosophers of language, such as Davidson (1978: 39) and Searle (1979: 106); it maintains that similarity amounts to a "vacuous predicate" because "any two things are similar in some respect or other." The ontological argument attacks the naive view of comparison theory according to which metaphoric similarity must be based on objectively given similarities or on common properties of the literal and metaphorical reference objects. The most extensive criticism of the objectivist myth of the similarity inherent in referential objects is to be found in Eco's theory of the iconic sign (see Icon 4.2). Within recent metaphor theory, Lakoff & Johnson especially have criticized the objectivist similarity theory (1980: 153–54). But before touching on the modifications of comparison theory which these authors suggest, a few semiotic fundamentals of iconicity relevant to metaphor should be discussed.

4.3 Peirce on Metaphors

One of the first theories of metaphor to stress the iconic character of the metaphoric sign on the basis of Peirce's semiotics is Henle's (1958: 177–81). For a more recent comprehensive theory of metaphor on the basis of Peirce's semiotics, see Gumpel (1984). Among other things, Henle notes that linguistic metaphors are not directly metaphoric because they initially signify their literal meaning symbolically, i.e., as arbitrary signs. Then, in a second semantic relation, the metaphor functions iconically in representing the similarity of two objects or situations. So the metaphor contains only an indirect icon which is not shown but only described.

The indirectness of metaphorical iconicity noted by Henle was already differentiated by Peirce himself in his theory of the iconic sign; for Peirce (§§ 2.276–77), metaphors exhibited a sort of third level of iconicity. The first level of signs which represent their objects by means of similarity is occupied by pictures (*images*). They signify their objects by means of simple, qualitative similarity. The second level contains diagrams, which manifest a structural similarity between the relations of their elements and those of their objects. Finally, at the third level of iconicity, metaphors are defined as "signs which represent the representative character of a representamen by representing a parallelism in something else" (§ 2.277). Apparently this formulation is intended to characterize the metaphor as an *iconic metasign*, whereby its iconicity is described as a "parallelism" and the indirectness of the metasign as the representing of the representative character.

In no way did Peirce interpret the similarity of the iconic sign in the way that the objectivist theory does. He defined likeness as "a mental fact, and the sensation of it is of no consequence except as an advertisement of that fact" (§ 7.467). "Anything whatever [. . .] is an Icon of anything, in so far as it is like that thing and used as a sign of it" (§ 2.247). The object of an icon may even be a "pure fiction" (§ 4.531). These theses contain a clear rebuttal of the "myth of objectivism"; they define the perception of similarity as a process dependent not on logic but rather on cognitive psychology.

4.4 Summarizing Theses on Metaphorical Iconicity

The five following theses are intended to summarize and in some cases to elaborate and refine the arguments presented for a differentiated theory of the iconicity of the metaphoric sign.

1. The iconicity of metaphor is based on the facts of experience (cf. Lakoff & Johnson 1980: 154). It is neither a logical truth (cf. Pulman 1982: 85) nor an ontological reality (cf. Weinrich 1963: 337).

2. The iconicity of metaphors implies similarities whose perception depends to various degrees on cultural codes (Eco 1976: 191ff., Lakoff & Johnson 1980): metaphors are not natural and universal, but rather culturally determined.

3. The iconicity of metaphor arises in a creative process (cf. Lakoff & Johnson 1980: 15, Pulman 1982). Metaphors can point out previously unrecognized similarities and thereby create new congruencies. They can thus become "cognitive instruments" (Black 1979: 39).

4. Any linguistic sign at all can become a metaphor for another linguistic sign. This thesis follows from the ontological theses and the thesis of creativity 1 and 3: the metaphoric relation presupposes no particular level of objectively given similarity or of shared features (pace Leisi 1973: 172). Creative metaphors can arise even from apparently completely dissimilar objects.

5. Metaphorical iconicity can be based on qualitative or on structural similarities. Qualitative similarities are not only visual; they can also be perceived by means of other sensory channels. Similarity can even be perceived between distinct perceptual fields (cf. synaesthetic metaphor).

Information

Information in its everyday sense is a qualitative concept associated with meaning and news. However, in the theory of information, it is a technical term which describes only quantifiable aspects of messages. Information theory and semiotics have goals of similar analytic universality. Both study messages of any kind, but because of its strictly quantitative approach, information theory is much more restricted in its scope.

1. The Meaning of Information

The meaning of information in everyday language is different from the technical sense which the term has in the mathematical theory of information. However, both concepts have a common basis in the notion of novelty.

1.1 The Ordinary Meaning of Information

In everyday language, information is "communication of the knowledge or 'news' of some fact or occurrence" (*Oxford English Dictionary*). The history and development of the term has been explored by Seiffert (1968: 23ff.) and Capurro (1978). The concept of "news" is central to its meaning: what is known already is not information. Only a message of a certain news value is informative to its receiver. In this

sense, the term has a semantic and a pragmatic dimension (cf. Cherry 1957: 228). Information is a semantic property of a message because only meaningful messages can be informative. Informativity depends on pragmatic factors of communication, namely, a sender, who informs, and a receiver, who notices a certain degree of novelty in the message.

1.2 The Probabilistic Definition of Information

Essentially, the mathematical theory of information defines information merely as a statistical property of a message, irrespective of its meaning. There have been proposals for an extension of the investigation to semantic and pragmatic characteristics of messages, but these have not advanced beyond the first outlines.

1.2.1 INFORMATION AS STATISTICAL RARITY

In terms of information theory, a signal has information insofar as it excludes the occurrence of alternative signals which could occur in its stead (cf. Martinet 1960: 173). In the fragmentary message "Give me the a- . . . ," the word fragment *a-* has no meaning, but it has information because it excludes words such as *banana* or *orange*. In this definition, information is not a semantic concept since every single letter has information although it is itself without meaning. If the letters -pr- are added in continuation of our message ending in a-, we have again information without meaning, but now more words are excluded as a possible continuation. Only two lexical items, *apricot* or *apron*, can be expected in English when the word begins with the letters *apr-*.

The quantification of information from this perspective depends on the number of excluded alternatives and the probability with which a signal can be expected to occur. Rare signals and signals to which there are only few alternatives have more information than frequent signals and signals to which there are many alternatives. Thus, the letters -icot after *apr-* are low in information since there is only one possible alternative in this context, namely, the -on of *apron*. The amount of information of the word fragment *a-* after the message "Give me the . . ." was much higher since it excluded all English nouns not beginning with the first letter of the alphabet. Information is thus a measure of the improbability of a message. The unexpected and rare signal is the one that carries most information.

In this definition of information, novelty is as criterial as in the everyday usage of the word, but in a different sense. In the everyday sense, the information value of a message depends on the pragmatic conditions of the receiver's interest and prior knowledge. Mathematical information theory, on the other hand, calculates the information value of a signal only according to the probability of its occurrence at a given point in the message chain: a frequent signal has little information, but a rare signal is considered to be very informative. In the mathematical sense, information is thus measured in terms of the statistical rarity of signs (Cherry 1957: 14). The statistical property of frequency or rarity is a signal characteristic of the sign repertoire or code. Information is thus measured as a relation between the textual occurrence and the code value of a signal.

1.2.2 SYNTACTIC OR SIGNAL INFORMATION

The mathematical concept of information, which describes information as the probability of a selection from a code, is *asemantic*. It studies only the relation between signs in messages and codes. This type of information is therefore usually defined as *syntactic information* (Cherry 1957: 228, Nauta 1972: 39). However, information in this sense is not derived from the syntagmatic structure of a message, i.e., the probabilities of sign combination. Every single occurrence of a sign has already an information value of its own, which is derived only from the values indicated by the code. Code values, however, are in the first place paradigmatic structures and indicate in the second place only a syntagmatic characteristic. As an alternative to *syntactic information*, Lyons proposes the term *signal information* (1977: 41). Both terms are opposed to a semantic view of information, which is also possible within a probabilistic framework.

2. The Quantification of Information

The quantification of information is based on probability calculus. The measure adopted within information theory requires the transformation of codes into systems of binary structures.

2.1 Information, Frequency, and Probability

The mathematical measurement of information depends on the complexity of the code. The number of signals, their probability, and combinatorial restrictions have to be considered.

2.1.1 INFORMATION AS THE RECIPROCAL OF PROBABILITY

The amount of information conveyed by a signal increases with its rarity, and the more frequent a signal is, the less informative it is (cf. 1.2.1). These basic ideas lead to a first approximation to the quantification of information: the amount of information (I) transmitted by a signal is the reciprocal value of its probability (p). In a very first approach, we could therefore write: $I = \frac{1}{p}$ to express that information increases with a decrease of probability. However, in a more precise method of calculation (cf. 2.1.2), information theory has adopted the logarithmic formula

$$I = \log_2 \frac{1}{p}$$

which also indicates that the value of I is higher when p is smaller.

The probability of a signal depends essentially on two factors: the number of other signals that belong to the same code and the relative frequency at which the signal usually occurs in a message. The method of calculation is relatively simple when the codes consist of equally frequent and thus equally probable signals. The mathematical laws by which this type of information may be calculated were formulated by Hartley (1928).

2.1.2 CODES WITH EQUIPROBABLE SIGNALS

An example of a code with N signals occurring with equal probability in a message of the length m is a Dutch lottery. The equiprobable signals are the 10 decimals between 0 and 9 ($N = 10$). The message is the lottery number consisting of $m = 7$ signals. This can be any number from 1 to 9,999,999. For such a code, the probability p_i ($i = 1, \ldots, N$) of occurrence of any particular signal i at any position of the 7–place lottery message is always

$$p_i = \left(\frac{1}{N}\right).$$

Every single lottery number will thus have a probability of $\frac{1}{10}$. In the sequence of such signals, the numbers are independent and remain equally likely. The probability of getting a particular sequence of two signals is not the sum but the product of the individual probabilities, i.e., $\frac{1}{10} \times \frac{1}{10}$ or $\left(\frac{1}{10}\right)^2$. More generally, the chance (q) of a particular sequence of m signals in a row is

$$q_m = \left(\frac{1}{N}\right)^m.$$

Instead of multiplying the quotients $\left(\frac{1}{N} \times \frac{1}{N} \ldots\right)$, it is mathematically simpler to add their

logarithms to the base of two ($\log_2$) m times (see also 2.2). The above probability of q_m can therefore be translated into a logarithmic form as $m \log_2 N$.

As discussed above, the information (I) of a message is measured by the logarithm of its reciprocal probability ($\log_2 \frac{1}{p}$). In the case of a message of m signals, we thus obtain these formulations of its information value:

$$I_m = \log_2 \frac{1}{q_m} = \log N^m = m \log_2 N,$$

thus:

$$I_m = m \log_2 N.$$

2.1.3 CODES WITH UNEQUAL PROBABILITIES

Every language is a code whose signals occur with unequal probabilities. The information of the signals in such a code is the statistical average value of their probabilities, which is derived from the relative frequency of the signals. Consider the following text

$$T = a\,a\,a\,a\,b\,b\,c\,d$$

as an example of a message generated by a code according to which a is four times as frequent as c or d and twice as frequent as b. The text consists of eight signal tokens (individually occurring signals), but there are only four signal types (a, b, c, d) (see Peirce 3.1 for the type-token distinction). The relative frequency h_x of any token x is the absolute frequency H_x of this token divided by the quantity M, the sum total of all tokens of this text:

$$h_x = \frac{H_x}{M}$$

In our example, where $M = 8$, $H_a = 4$, $H_b = 2$, $H_c = 1$, and $H_d = 1$, the value of h_x is identical with the probability (p_x) of x in the text T, so that $h_x = p_x$. The individual values for the signal types to occur in T are $h_a = \frac{4}{8} = 0.5$, $h_b = \frac{2}{8} = 0.25$, and $h_c = h_d = \frac{1}{8} = 0.125$. The probability of every signal type is thus a value from 0 up to 1, where 0 corresponds to 0% and 1 to 100%. The sum total of all token probabilities of the text will always be 1 (= 100%). According to the logarithmic formula of calculating the information value discussed above, the information value (I_x) of every token x is thus:

$$I_x = \log_2 \frac{1}{h_x}$$

It happens that the value obtained by this calculus, measured in terms of logarithms to the base of two, is identical with the value obtained by information measurement in elementary binary units called *bits* (see below, 2.2). In our example, the values are: $I_a = 1$ bit, $I_b = 2$ bits, $I_c = I_d = 3$ bits. Thus, the token d has three times as much information as the token a.

For the theory of information transmission, it is important to know the average information associated with every individual signal occurrence. This value is obtained by weighting the *I*-values of each type with its probability. Thus in our message T, the average information associated with every signal occurrence is: $I = 1 \times 0.5 + 2 \times 0.25 + 3 \times 0.125 + 3 \times 0.125 = 1.75$ bits. More generally, for a message with m signal types, where $p_i = h_i$ (as in the message T discussed above), the formula is (cf. Attneave 1959: 7):

$$I = p_1 I_1 + p_2 I_2 \ldots + p_i I_i \ldots + p_m I_m$$

or

$$I = \sum_{i=1}^{m} p_i h_i$$

Replacing I_i by its equivalent value $\log_2 \frac{1}{p_i}$ or $-\log p_i$ (the negative sign appears because the logarithm of a fraction is a negative value), one obtains a formula of the average information value entirely in terms of p:

$$I = -\sum_{i=1}^{m} p_i \log_2 p_i$$

This is the so-called Shannon-Weaver measure of information. It can be applied to calculate the economy or cost of a code, i.e., the amount of information a transmitter can send per second by using this code.

2.1.4 CONDITIONAL PROBABILITIES

Conditional probabilities are contextual restrictions on the probability and information value of a signal. In the code of traffic lights, the signal "yellow" has a 100% probability after the signal "green," and after the sequence *apric-*, the letters *-ot* have a 100% probability according to the vocabulary of English. A code which produces a sequence of signals according to certain probabilities is called a *stochastic process*. The special case of a stochastic process in which the probabilities depend on the previous events is called a *Markoff process* or *Markoff chain* (cf. Shannon & Weaver 1949: 11).

2.1.5 REDUNDANCY

Unequal and conditional probabilities of signals are sources of *redundancy*, i.e., an information surplus whose value can be predicted (or guessed) from the context. Only codes with equally probable signals generate messages without redundancy. Redundancy can then be measured as a difference between the maximum information rate which a message could possess (I_{max}) and the average of the actually transmitted information (I_x). The precise formula is (Cherry 1957: 185):

$$\text{Redundancy} = \frac{I_{max} - I_x}{I_{max}} \times 100\%$$

Redundantia was a technical term in ancient rhetoric, designating the stylistic defect of prolixity (cf. Dubois et al. 1970), a violation of the virtue of *brevitas*. The term connotes superfluity. However, redundancy is a desirable and technically necessary feature of signal transmission since it protects the message against distortion by mistakes. Messages generated by the code of natural numbers (cf. the lottery example in 2.1.2) are nonredundant. It is impossible to correct a single cipher from its context. Natural languages have a redundancy of about 50% (cf. Moles 1958: 54), which allows the correction of a high number of transmission mistakes or errors (see also 3.1.3).

2.1.6 COST AND ECONOMY

Redundancy is a factor of cost in signal transmission because the channel, for example a telex cable, is occupied for a longer time. But in addition to the factor of material length, there is a second factor which has to be taken into consideration by the technician interested in economy of signal transmission, namely, the effort necessary to produce the individual signals. This effort increases with the number of elementary signals to be transmitted. A transmitter who has to distinguish one hundred different signals is more expensive and requires a higher skill of operation compared to a transmitter of only two signals.

The economy of length (or redundancy) has to do with the syntagmatic dimension of the messages. The economy of effort is concerned with the paradigmatic dimension of messages. Prieto (1966) distinguishes these two dimensions as *economy of quantity* and *economy of cost* and studies their relevance to a semiotic theory of codes. For further applications of these principles in functional semiotics, see J. Martinet (1973) and Hervey (1982). For language, see 3.1.3.

2.2 Binary Codes and Binarization of Messages

For reasons of technological economy, information theory has adopted a code with only two elementary signals, for example a positive and a negative electrical impulse. In writing, these will be represented by 0 and 1. Codes such as alphabets or the system of decimal ciphers have to be translated into such binary codes. This binarization is effected by successively subdividing the sign repertoire into halves and numbering these halves by 0 or 1. An alphabet of thirty-two letters could be subdivided and the letters translated into a binary form as shown in Figure I 1.

In successive binarization, the number of choices (*C*) correponds to the number of signals (*N*) as follows:

number of choices $C =$ 1 2 3 4 5 . . .
number of signals $N =$ 2 4 8 16 32 . . .

Mathematically, this relation is expressed by the formula

$$C = \log_2 N$$

The resulting value expresses the number of binary selections which are necessary to choose

a signal from a sign repertoire. This value has been adopted in information theory as the elementary unit of information measurement. It is called a bit (binary digit). As shown in Figure I 1, the information value of a letter from our alphabet is 5 bits. The information value of the code of the 10 decimal ciphers is 3.32 bits (= $\log_2 10$), since we need more than three but fewer than four dual choices to select one number out of ten.

2.3 Information, Entropy, and Order

Information is closely related to *entropy*, a concept of physics which has to do with the notions of order and disorder.

2.3.1 ENTROPY AS DISORDER
In physics, entropy describes the order of particles in a closed thermodynamic system. According to the second law of thermodynamics, gas particles in a closed system move irreversibly toward a state of completely random distribution, which means complete disorder in space. This state of disorder is defined as *maximum entropy*. A minimum of entropy would mean a state of maximum order, for example, a state where all gas molecules are in the left-half side of the container. But gas cannot remain in such a state. Entropy always increases according to a statistical law which is similar to the Shannon-Weaver measure of information.

2.3.2 INFORMATION AS NEGATIVE ENTROPY
Following these premises, the process of increasing entropy in physics is the reverse of the process of information increase in communication. Information has therefore also been defined as *negative entropy*. In the thermodynamic process, there is a steady increase of disorder, while communication is a process of bringing increasing order out of chaos. At the beginning of signal transmission, the receiver is in a high state of uncertainty about the message to be received. This state of uncertainty corresponds to disorder or maximum entropy. Since every signal is still equally probable, the receiver's "mes-

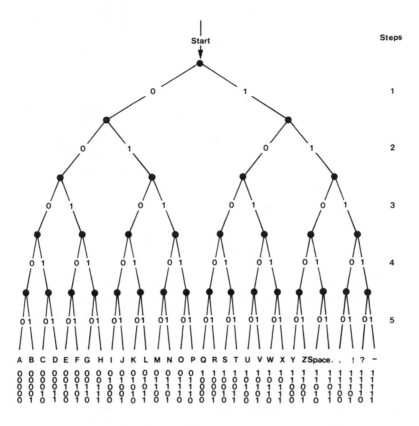

Fig. I 1: The translation of the alphabet into a binary code.

sage space" is still unstructured and thus unordered. The process of communication begins with a high amount of information transfer since every signal initially excludes a huge number of alternative messages. As the message develops, information decreases because the signals become more and more predictable from previous signals. At the end of the message, uncertainty is completely removed. Ideally, the receiver has a completely structured message space. The received signals have been integrated into a state of semiotic order. In this view, information theory presents communication as a process of decrease of information paralleled by an increase of order. A critique of this idealized and mechanistic view of text processing need not be given here, but for alternative models see Text Semiotics.

3. Information and Language

A number of information theoretical aspects of language have already been discussed above, in particular the asemantic nature of the probabilistic approach, the conditional probabilities of linguistic signals, and the redundancy of language. The following section will give a more detailed account of syntactic and semantic aspects of information in language.

3.1 Syntactic or Signal Information

The quantity of linguistic information can be calculated either at the level of first articulation, mostly in terms of words, or at the level of second articulation, in terms of phonemes or letters. The results are quite different. The information quantity calculated on the basis of word probability is much lower than the sum of the information values calculated on the basis of letters or phonemes.

3.1.1 INFORMATION VALUE OF PHONEMES OR LETTERS

At the level of second articulation of the English language, information and redundancy values are determined by the frequency of the individual phonemes or letters, restrictions on their combination, and their position within the word. According to a frequency count of English phonemes (cf. Miller 1951: 86), the most frequent English phoneme is /ɪ/ (8.53%) and the least frequent one is /ʒ/ (0.05%). Counted individually, the information value of these speech sounds is 3.42 bits for /ɪ/ and 10.97 bits for /ʒ/. Taking contextual restrictions into account, the values change considerably. Since /ʒ/ occurs almost exclusively after /d-/, its information value is much lower in this context, but higher in other positions. The probabilities are also different for initial and final phonemes in words: /ŋ/, /z/, and /v/ are more frequent and thus less informative in word-final positions, while /w/, /j/, /h/, and /ð/ are more frequent in initial positions.

In written English, the letter u is completely predictable after q-. In this context, u has an information value of zero. After th-, e has a frequency of about 83%, i about 8%, and a about 3% (Gleason 1955: 381). Taking these and other conditional probabilities into consideration, the average information rate of letters in English tends toward a limit of only 1.5 bits per letter, while the noncontextual average value is 4.14 bits (cf. Cherry 1957: 186). The difference between the two values indicates a relatively high degree of redundancy per letter in context.

3.1.2 INFORMATION VALUES OF WORDS

Information calculus on the basis of the code of words is extremely difficult because of the great amount of variation in the vocabulary of speakers and language varieties. The *Oxford English Dictionary* (OED) has about half a million ($\sim 2^{19}$) entries. At equal frequency, every word would thus have an information value of nineteen bits, which is less than the average information quantity of five letters (5×4.14; see 3.1.1), although most of the OED entries are much longer words. However, the number of words which form the active or passive vocabulary of an average speaker of English is much smaller than the number of the OED entries, and also the frequencies of words vary greatly. For example, the fifty most commonly used word types make up about 60% of the word tokens of spoken and 45% of written English (Miller 1951: 89).

According to a law discovered by J. B. Estoup and G. K. Zipf (1935), the frequency distribution in any large corpus of words is (approximately) such that the frequency (f) of every individual word multiplied by its rank, i.e., its order in the frequency list (r), forms a constant (C):

$$f \times r = C$$

If, for example, the most frequent word (= rank 1) occurs 10,000 times ($10,000 \times 1 = 10,000$), the second most frequent will occur about 5,000 times ($5,000 \times 2 = 10,000$) and the tenth word about 1,000 times ($1,000 \times 10 = 10,000$). In addition to vocabulary size and individual frequencies, the contextual probabilities are a third factor which reduces the average amount of information associated with individual words.

3.1.3 ECONOMY AND COST

Economy of language (cf. 2.1.6) is one of the central topics of study in functional linguistics. Martinet (1955; 1960) describes it as the effect of an equilibrium between two types of pressure on the act of communication. On the one hand, there is the speaker's tendency toward minimizing his or her syntagmatic and paradigmatic effort (or cost). This pressure goes in the direction of reducing redundancy. But an excessive reduction of redundancy is a threat to effective communication because the information of any nonredundant message will be changed and thus endangered by the slightest disturbance (noise or misprint). Since a certain amount of redundancy is thus necessary, this necessity to secure the intelligibility of the message is the second pressure at work in every act of communication, a pressure whose direction is opposed to the force of redundancy reduction. Based on the assumption that the speaker aims at producing a maximum amount of information at a minimum effort (and redundancy), linguistic economy is thus the equilibrium between the two pressures of production and reduction of effort and redundancy.

Linguistic redundancy is a major force of language change. Codes without redundancy, such as the mathematical code of numbers, cannot change in structure. In language, the sphere of redundancy is the space within which speakers can introduce linguistic changes and innovations (cf. Guiraud 1968: 165).

3.2 Semantic Information

Bar-Hillel & Carnap (1953), MacKay (1969), and Bar-Hillel (1964: 221–310) have given a first outline of an extension of the theory of information to the investigation of meaning. Instead of letters and words, the units of analysis in Bar-Hillel & Carnap's study are basic statements describing events. The probabilities under investigation are logical probabilities, calculating the uncertainty of events on the basis of given evidence. The semantic information of a statement is the class of all propositions which are logically implied by this statement. The frame of reference for the measurement of informativity, according to Bar-Hillel (1964: 224), is the universal knowledge of an ideal receiver, and this knowledge is represented by the propositions of a logical language. Carnap's calculus of logical probabilities is the instrument for the measurement of semantic information. Accordingly, logically true, and thus tautologous, propositions have a minimum amount of information, while logically false sentences convey theoretically an unlimited amount of informativity. The information quantity of synthetic sentences lies between these two extremes. This measure of semantic information reflects the idea that the knowledge obtained from a statement increases with the number of alternative state-descriptions excluded by the statement. There are no logical alternatives to a tautologous statement. For further aspects of the logical theory of information, see Hintikka (1968).

3.3 Pragmatic Information

It is doubtful whether a mathematical theory of pragmatic information may ever become possible. It would have to quantify economic, social, emotional, or ethical value expectations. Possible studies of pragmatic information would have to investigate degrees of interest and belief in messages (cf. Cherry 1957: 244), their utility and reliability (cf. Nauta 1972: 220–25, 267–71), and their innovative or confirmative impact (cf. Weizsäcker 1984).

4. Information, Communication, and Semiosis

Information theory is a neighboring discipline of semiotics insofar as it is also concerned with studying signs (as signals), codes, and communication.

4.1 Information in Semiosis and Communication

The processing of information in a probabilistic sense has been studied both in unilateral semiosis and in bilateral communication. In communication from a sender to a receiver, the measurement of information can be based on a general code or on the individual codes of sender and receiver.

4.1.1 INFORMATION IN UNILATERAL SEMIOSIS
Unilateral semiosis has been interpreted in probabilistic terms in the framework of information psychology (Frank 1964) and information theoretical psychology (Attneave 1959,

Klix 1971, Berlyne 1974). In this framework, every act of perception is an act of information processing. The stimuli of the exterior world are the information source. Information processing proceeds in a process of reducing the theoretically unlimited number of sensorial stimuli to the limited number of perceived sense data. The actual quantity of input and storage of sensorial information is the difference between the units (bits) of information stored by the perceiver before and after sensorial stimulation.

4.1.2 INFORMATION AND GENERAL CODE

Shannon & Weaver's (1949) study of information relates signals to a general code of statistical averages. In studies of language, the code values are derived from frequency dictionaries which represent a kind of statistical *langue*.

4.1.3 INFORMATION AND RECEIVER'S EXPECTATIONS

From the receiver's point of view, information is "that which removes or reduces *uncertainty*" (Attneave 1959: 1). The code of an individual receiver is conceived as a store of information which generates structures of expectation. One who is very ignorant about a certain topic and thus has a low quantity of stored information in this field will be very uncertain about the possible content of a message. His or her expectation and uncertainty correspond to the number of possible alternatives which might occur as a message. Once the message has been received, the uncertainty is removed. Information is then the difference between the informational content of the message and the amount of knowledge stored in the receiver's code before the act of communication. The individual code itself expands with every informational input. This view of information processing is able to give a general account of the receiver's expectation, curiosity, boredom (cf. Berlyne 1974), surprise, tension, and suspense (for the latter see Koch 1985), but a reliable quantification of these semantic and pragmatic aspects of information is hardly possible.

4.1.4 INFORMATION AND THE SENDER SELECTION

From the perspective of text production, "information is a measure of one's freedom of choice when one selects a message" (Shannon & Weaver 1949: 9). Information is thus measured as the difference between the sender's code and the produced message. Highly unpredictable choices in this process of selection characterize creativity and innovation in text production, but these modes of text production also reflect unpredictability from the receiver's point of view. Information as the probability of selection from a code is also defined as *selective information* (Schnelle 1976, Krippendorff 1986: 13–15).

4.2 *Information Theory, Communication Theory, and Semiotics*

Besides mathematics, the theory of communication is a main source of information theory. In its broad scope of possible applications, information theory is concerned with many areas of research which also belong to the semiotic field.

4.2.1 INFORMATION AND COMMUNICATION THEORY

The original concept of information theory as outlined in Shannon & Weaver's *Mathematical Theory of Communication* (1949) was a research program concerned with the possibilities of maximizing the efficiency of signal transmission in terms of cost and reliability. The distinction between the theories of information and communication has never been clear-cut. Pierce (1962) considers both terms essentially synonymous. Cherry wants to "reserve the title 'theory of information' for a broader field of scientific method, including communication" (1957: 249). The extensions beyond the field of communication (including language and aesthetics; see 3., 4.2.2) lie in various applications of information theory in fields such as psychology (Frank 1964, Klix 1971, Berlyne 1974), neurophysiology (Pinsker & Willis 1980), physics (cf. Pierce 1962), and biology. A field closely associated with information theory is cybernetics. Wiener (1948) defined it as the science of *Control and Communication in the Animal and the Machine.*

Classics of information theory are Shannon & Weaver (1949), Cherry (1957), Meyer-Eppler (1959), and MacKay (1969). Surveys and introductions are Pierce (1962), Flechtner (1966), Jaglom & Jaglom (1967), Peters (1967), Seiffert (1968), Maser (1971), Krippendorff (1986), and Escarpit (1976).

4.2.2 INFORMATION THEORY AND SEMIOTICS

The semiotic framework of information theoretical research has been outlined by Cherry (1957), Bense (1965a; 1969; cf. Bense & Walther, eds. 1973), Maser (1971), and Nauta (1972). Major points of contact between semiotics and information theory are in their common fields of study: language, texts, style, poetics, and aesthetics. For the fields of the fine arts, see especially Moles (1958), Frank (1959), Gunzenhäuser (1962), Pierce (1962), Bense (1965a; 1969), Marcus (1970), Maser (1970; 1971), and Aesthetics (1.2.4). It was the idea of a possible quantification of style, originality, and creativity which made information theory attractive to many scholars in this field. In language studies, the information theoretical paradigm was adopted by Miller (1951), Gleason (1955: 373–90), Apostel et al. (1957), Martinet (1960: 172–87), Jakobson (1961), Osgood & Sebeok eds. (1965), Hörmann (1967), Guiraud (1968), and Hockett (1974) (see also Mounin 1964). For points

of contact between information theory and rhetoric, see Frank-Böhringer (1963) and Rosenfeld (1971).

4.2.3 AN OBSOLETE PARADIGM?

The brief chronology of information theoretical research in the fields of interest to semiotics shows that interest and progress in information theory seem to have declined since the 1960s. Partly this decline is due to the fact that the quantitative approach to the study of communication "has not so far justified all the claims that were made for it by some of its early enthusiastic proponents" (Lyons 1977: 42). Partly, it is also because scholars in the field of information research have abandoned the scientific paradigm of information theory in favor of other more powerful technological paradigms such as systems theory and artificial intelligence. For the latter field and its relationship to semiotics, see the special issue of *Bulletin du groupe de recherches sémio-linguistiques* 36 (1985) and Beaugrande (1986). In spite of justified critique of exaggerated hopes concerning the quantifiability of communicative processes, the basic insights which information theory has provided into the nature of meaning remain valid in semiotics. In the field of text semiotics, Beaugrande (1980) has more recently adopted a nonquantitative principle of *informativity* as one of the essential features of textuality.

Zoosemiotics, Ethology, and Semiogenesis

Zoosemiotics, the study of the semiotic behavior of animals, is a transdisciplinary field of research. Situated between biology and anthropology, it investigates a domain located between nature and culture. Zoosemiotics reinterprets the age-old question of the language of animals in the light of modern linguistics and animal communication studies. It has a synchronic branch studying pragmatic, syntactic, and semantic aspects of animal communication and a diachronic branch investigating the evolution of animal semiosis. The latter branch falls into the domain of ethology. Whereas there has hardly ever been any doubt about the existence of signs in the animal kingdom, the assumption of semiosis in the sphere of plants, defended by the proponents of a new branch of semiotics called *phytosemiotics*, is still controversial.

1. Survey of Zoosemiotics

Although zoosemiotics was not conceived of as a branch of semiotics until 1963, studies in animal communication systems have, of course, a much older tradition and are certainly not restricted to research carried out from an explicitly semiotic perspective.

1.1 The Zoosemiotic Branch of Semiotics

Zoosemiotics is distinguished from other approaches to animal communication by its specific perspective, which has its foundation in the general theory of signs. There is some degree of vagueness in the delimitation of this branch of research from other branches of semiotics.

1.1.1 DEFINITION OF ZOOSEMIOTICS
The term *zoosemiotics*, with the pronunciation [zo:ə] as in *zoological*, was coined in 1963 by Sebeok (cf. 1972: 178–81). According to its first definition, zoosemiotics is "the discipline, within which the science of signs intersects with ethology, devoted to the scientific study of signalling behavior in and across animal species" (ibid.: 178). Later, Sebeok gave this somewhat extended definition: "Zoosemiotics [. . .] is that segment of the field which focuses on messages given off and received by animals, including important components of human nonverbal communication, but excluding man's language, and his secondary, language-derived semiotic systems, such as sign language or Morse code" (1981: 109).

1.1.2 ZOOSEMIOTICS AND ANTHROPOSEMIOTICS
According to Sebeok's own subdivision of semiotics, zoosemiotics is one of the three major branches of semiotics, along with anthro-

posemiotics and endosemiotics (1972: 163; 1976: 2–3; 1979: 38; cf. History 4.2.3). Sebeok adopts a very broad definition of zoosemiotics and includes paralinguistic, proxemic, and other nonverbal modes of human semiosis among the "zoosemiotic components of human communication" (1972: 133; 1979: 35). In contrast to this outline of the field, this handbook draws a different dividing line between anthroposemiotics and zoosemiotics by excluding human nonverbal communication from the scope of zoosemiotics. However, there is certainly an overlap between these two domains, especially in the field of human ethology.

1.1.3 ZOOSEMIOTICS AND BIOSEMIOTICS

Biosemiotics is sometimes used as a synonym, and sometimes defined as a neighboring field, of *zoosemiotics*. Tembrock (1971; 1973) investigates the field of "animal information transfer" under the designation of *biocommunication* and considers zoosemiotics a subfield of this study. Rothschild defines *biosemiotic* as the study of "the psychophysical nexus within the central nervous system and in other structures possessed of psychophysical functions within organisms" (1968: 163). In the field of molecular biology, Florkin (1974) studies among other things the biosemiotics of the flux of information from DNA and the biosemiotic characters of amino acids. These biosemiotic investigations cover essentially the field which Sebeok has defined as endosemiotics (cf. Code 5.1) and which also includes the field of neurosemiotics (cf. Ivanov 1978a; 1979).

Koch describes biosemiotics as a field covering both endosemiotics and zoosemiotics, distinguishing between *semiobiology* (research with emphasis on the biological perspective) and biosemiotics proper (research from the semiotic perspective) (1974a: 318; 1986a). Krampen defines biosemiotics as the discipline studying the three areas of zoosemiotics, anthroposemiotics, and phytosemiotics (1981c: 187; cf. 6.). Similarly, Jander defines biosemiotics as the study "concerned with living semiotic systems" (1981: 226–27), but Jander

excludes cultural semiotics from biosemiotics as a semiotic domain of its own.

1.1.4 ZOOSEMIOTICS AND ETHOLOGY

Zoosemiotics is closely related to ethology, but there are different interpretations of the relationship between these two fields. Whereas ethology focuses on evolutionary aspects of animal semiosis only, zoosemiotics also studies the synchronic systems and processes of animal communication. Sebeok characterizes ethology as "diachronic semiotics on a phylogenetic scale" (1979: 260). Whereas Tembrock restricts his survey of zoosemiotics only to synchronic aspects of animal communication (1971: 39–58), Sebeok (1972; 1976) and Smith (1974) also include ethological topics in their survey of zoosemiotics. Sebeok, ed. (1986), by contrast, has two separate articles, one on ethology and one on zoosemiotics.

Sebeok explains that his coinage of *zoosemiotics* was "intended as a mediating concept for reconciling these two seemingly antithetical spheres of discourse, ethology and semiotics" (1976: 86). Although ethology has not simply become a branch of modern semiotics, it is true that zoosemiotics has emerged as a dominant theme in ethology and has contributed to a synthesis in the field of animal behavior (cf. Sebeok 1972: 134–35).

1.2 Systematics of Zoosemiotics

Following Morris, Sebeok (& Ramsay, eds. 1969: 202; Sebeok 1972: 124), Tembrock (1971: 39–58), and Smith (1974: 568–614; 1977) subdivide zoosemiotic research into syntactics, semantics, and pragmatics. *Zoosyntactics* determines the sign repertoires of animals, investigates their temporal and spatial elements, and studies the rules of their combination into messages. An example of zoosyntactic research is the segmentation and classification of bird songs into their minimal elements and their combination into strophes (cf. Tembrock 1971: 42–45). Zoosemantics deals with the meaning and modes of reference of animal signs, whereas *zoopragmatics* studies the processes of propagation, the determinants of communication, and the function of animal signs. From a different point of view, the field of research can be subdivided into *pure* zoosemiotics, the study of theoretical models of animal signaling, *descriptive* zoosemiotics, the study of individual animal communication systems, and *applied* zoosemiotics, dealing with "the exploitation of animal communication systems for the benefit of man" (Sebeok 1972: 132).

1.3 Survey of Zoosemiotic Research

In addition to explicitly semiotic research, literature of relevance to zoosemiotics can be consulted in various domains of animal behavior studies as well as in the often speculative traditional writings on the "language of animals."

1.3.1 HISTORY OF ZOOSEMIOTIC INVESTIGATIONS
The history of zoosemiotics has not yet been written. Elements of this history are introduced by Tembrock (1971: 6–12) and Sebeok (1979: 75ff.). Prescientific observations on the nature of animal semiosis have been known since Aristotle. They culminated in Descartes's rationalist and unsemiotic equation of animals with machines (cf. History 3.1.1). As a reaction against this mechanist view, several eighteenth-century scholars, among them figures from the history of semiotics such as G. F. Meier, began to speculate on the topic of the language of animals. A milestone of zoosemiotics is Darwin's *The Expression of the Emotions in Man and Animals* (1872), which was the birth of ethology proper.

1.3.2 STUDIES IN ZOOSEMIOTICS
An early annotated guide to the literature of zoosemiotics and its background is Sebeok (1972: 134–61). Sebeok (1976; 1979; 1981; 1986b) has further contributions to various topics in the field. Other monographs with an explicitly zoosemiotic approach are Tembrock (1971) and Smith (1977a). Readers adopting an explicitly zoosemiotic approach are Sebeok,

ed. (1968; 1977), Sebeok & Ramsay, eds. (1969), Sebeok & Umiker-Sebeok, eds. (1980), and Sebeok & Rosenthal, eds. (1981). Survey articles on zoosemiotics and other papers with an explicitly zoosemiotic approach are Marler (1961), Tembrock (1973), Smith (1974), Sebeok (1981: 109–116), Hervey (1982: 244–65), Kalkofen (1985, with information on relevant film material), and Sebeok, ed. (1986: 1178–79). Related surveys are those included in introductions to or readers in linguistics, such as Marshall (1970), Russell & Russell (1971), Aitchinson (1976: 33–50), Fromkin & Rodman (1983: 346–61), and Akmajian et al. (1979: 52–66). For further linguistic approaches, see 2.

From the perspective of nonverbal communication studies, approaches to zoosemiotics are included in Hinde, ed. (1972), Cranach & Vine, eds. (1973), Krames et al., eds. (1974), Argyle (1975), and Petrovich & Hess (1978). General animal behavior studies of relevance to zoosemiotics are Frings & Frings (1964), McGill, ed. (1965), Evans (1968), Thorpe (1974), and the studies concerning individual species discussed below (see 2.2). For approaches from the point of view of ethology, see 5. Other related fields of study are behavioral ecology (cf. Krebs & Davies, eds. 1978), the branch of ethology concerned with the study of the animal-environment relationship, hence a kind of animal proxemics, and sociobiology, the study of the biological basis of social behavior in animal societies (Wilson 1975, Barash 1981).

2. The "Language of Animals" and "Animal Languages"

The "language of animals" is a metaphor referring to a variety of animal communication systems. To what degree do these systems have features in common with human languages? Is the comparative anatomy of human and animal "languages" relevant to the question of the origins of human language?

2.1 Language, Animals, and Man

The "language of animals" is an archaic topic in myths and narratives (cf. Thompson 1966: 396–401). As a transdisciplinary subject of investigation and sometimes of popular speculation, the topic has been approached in the frameworks of philosophy (cf. Kainz 1961: 1–2, Schaff 1964: 205–219), psychology (Kainz 1961), anthropology (Bronowski 1967, Count 1973), biology and ethology (Hediger 1970, Russell & Russell 1971, Schauenberg 1972, Bright 1984, Premack 1986), psycholinguistics (Morton, ed. 1971, Aitchinson 1976: 33–50), and general linguistics (Hockett; cf. 2.4, Mounin 1970a: 41–56, Benveniste 1966: 49–54, Chomsky 1979, Sommerfeld 1980, Marquardt 1984, and the survey in Fromkin & Rodman 1983: 346–61).

In the history of anthropology, the essence of man has been associated with various modes of human semiosis (cf. Romeo 1979d): the use of "wisdom" (homo [sapiens] sapiens), the use and the making of tools (homo faber or homo habilis), the use of fire (homo prometheus), the ability to laugh and play (homo ridens, homo ludens), or activity in politics (homo politicus), but the use of language (homo loquens) has always been the first candidate in the search for a feature characterizing the distinguishing feature of man. However, whether language is the exclusive property of the human species depends on the definition of language. Some philosophers and linguists have drawn the dividing line between human and animal semiosis by a petitio principii. Thus, Sapir defines language as "a purely human and noninstinctive method of communicating ideas, emotions, and desires by means of a system of voluntarily produced symbols" (1921: 8). Nonhuman semiosis is thus by definition excluded from being considered as a language.

If, by contrast, language is defined very generally as a system of communication, then obviously many species have languages. If, on the other hand, language is defined as "a system of arbitrary vocal symbols" (Trager 1950: 4), then not only very highly developed animal codes,

but also human sign languages must fail to qualify as language. The standard method of determining the nature of human language in comparison to animal languages has so far been strictly anthropocentric (cf. Marler 1961: 296). The design features of language are taken as a measure for determining features missing in animal codes. Only few have so far adopted a more general semiotic perspective showing that there are features of animal communication missing in language and by which some animal codes are partially superior to human language.

2.2 Selected Animal "Languages"

Bees, birds, and apes are among the species whose systems of semiosis have been investigated most closely in comparison to human language. Other species which have been discussed as candidates for having a "language" are dolphins, horses, and dogs. For the controversial results of Lilly's (1967; 1978) claims concerning the "language" of dolphins, see Russell & Russell (1971: 173–80), Sebeok (1972: 53–61; 1981: 169–70), Sebeok & Rosenthal, eds. (1981), Herman et al. (1984), and Premack (1986). For the "language" of horses and other hooved mammals, see Schäfer (1974) and Walther (1984). A semiotic investigation of the communicative behavior of dogs is Fleischer (1987). For semiosis in other selected species, see McGill, ed. (1965), Burkhardt et al., eds. (1966), Evans (1968), Sebeok, ed. (1968; 1977), Bright (1984), and Schult (1986: on spiders).

2.2.1 THE "LANGUAGE" OF THE HONEY BEE
The sensational discovery of The Dance Language and Orientation of Bees (Frisch 1965; see also Lindauer 1961) in the 1920s, for which Karl von Frisch was awarded the Nobel Prize in 1973, has attracted much attention from linguists and semioticians (cf. Benveniste 1966: 49–54, Hervey 1982: 252–59, Figge 1986). The dance of the honey bee is a semiotic means of informing the hive about places to find food (nectar or pollen), water, resin, or a nesting

site. The message is transmitted by the olfactive and tactile channels. Smell indicates the quality of the object to search. By repeatedly touching the dancing messenger ("scout") bee in the dark of the hive and by sensing the vibrations caused by this dance, the other bees perceive the form and content of this message. Two types of dance are performed for different purposes. The *round dance* indicates a location up to 50–100 m in the vicinity of the hive. The fellow bees find this source by simply following the scout bee. The figure eight–shaped *waggle dance* indicates sources between 0.1 and 13 km. This message, performed vertically along the honeycomb of the hive, informs about the direction and the distance of the source. The distance is indicated by the speed of the dance: the greater the distance, the slower is the dance. The direction is indicated by the angle formed between the middle axis or straight part of the figure eight (or double zero) and a vertical line crossing the center of this dance figure (cf. Fig. Z 1). This angle corresponds to the angle formed between the two lines connecting the hive with the feeding place and the sun.

From a semiotic point of view, the "language" of the bee is a code by which indefinitely many messages can be transmitted. The creativity of this code is restricted to the ecological needs of this species. There is, for example, no sign to indicate a location above or below the hive. The type of sign performed in a waggle dance is primarily indexical, since it indicates a location and a distance. However, there is also some diagrammatic iconicity due to the relation of correspondence between the distance of the source and the speed of the dance. Finally, the signs are also arbitrary and thus symbolic, since Frisch (1965) was able to discover various "dialects" in the different subspecies of *apis mellifica*. Thus, certain species indicate intermediate distances by performing a *sickle dance*, which has the form of a semicircle. Further "dialectal" differences relate to the exact distance indicated by a given speed of dance.

2.2.2 BIRDS

Sources for the study of vocal communication in birds are Thorpe (1961; 1972b), Armstrong (1963), Bremond (1963), Smith (1977b), Kroodsma & Miller, eds. (1982), and Wiener (1986). Bird vocalizations are divided into calls and songs. Bird calls consist of short notes which serve to convey messages about referential objects in the animal's environment (Thorpe 1961: 17): food, nesting places, or sources of danger. Many species, for example, have different calls for aerial and ground predators (cf. Wiener 1986: 161). Besides such referential functions, bird calls also have expressive functions (pleasure calls, distress calls, general alarm calls) and the phatic function of maintaining contact with the flock. Russell & Russell point out that the numbers of basic call units in bird calls "fall roughly into the same range as do the numbers of phonemes of human languages" (1971: 162). For example, the European finch has twenty and the white-throated warbler has twenty-five basic vocal signals. However, it is important to notice that these call units, unlike phonemes, are complete messages, and thus equivalent to elements of first articulation (words or sentences), without having a second articulation of merely distinctive elements (see Language 4.1).

Bird songs are more complex in structure and can be segmented into units such as strophes, verses, syllables or phrases, and impulses (Tembrock 1971: 160), but there is no semantic structure corresponding to these segments (cf. Smith 1977b: 563–65). Only the song as a whole is a message. Its meaning is territorial defense or mate attraction. Whereas bird calls are largely innate, bird songs have been discovered to depend on learning. Like human language, the acquisition of bird songs occurs during a certain early sensitive period. Another striking parallel between human and bird "languages" is the phenomenon of geographical dialects in bird songs. In some species, its function seems to be assortive mating. For details see Wiener (1986).

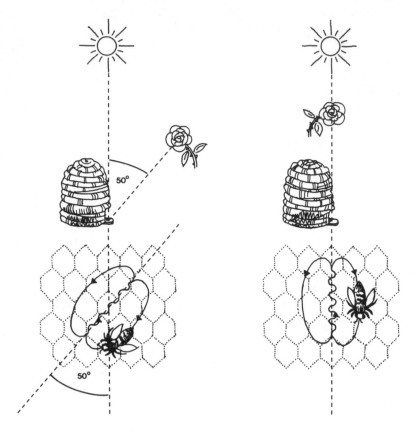

Fig. Z 1. Indication of the direction of a food source by the wagging dance of the honey bee (adapted from Frisch 1965). *Right:* when the source is exactly in the direction of the sun, the axis of the figure eight is vertical. *Left:* when the triangle source, hive, sun forms an angle of 50, the angle between the vertical and the bee's wagging direction is also 50.

2.3 The "Languages" of Apes

Chimpanzees, gorillas, and other nonhuman primates, being the closest phylogenetic relatives of man, have early been investigated as the most hopeful candidates for true animal language. Ape communication research was greatly intensified in a number of projects beginning in the 1960s. For the state of the art of these studies, see Linden (1976), Sebeok & Umiker-Sebeok, eds. (1980), Sebeok & Rosenthal, eds. (1981), Premack & Premack (1983), Premack (1986), and Savage-Rumbaugh (1986).

In most of these recent projects, the semiotic behavior of apes has been investigated under the artificial conditions of training by interspecific (man-animal) teaching. For the "language" of apes in their natural ecology, see DeVore, ed. (1965), Altmann, ed. (1967), Ploog (1974), and Goodall (1986). In contrast to studies with artificial sign systems, the study of natural ape semiosis has given special attention to the various "nonverbal" channels (visual, tactile, auditory, and olfactory) which are often used simultaneously in ape communication (cf. Marler 1965, Goodall 1986). For facial messages and other modes of nonverbal communication in apes and their relation to human communication, see in particular Chevalier-

Skolnikoff (1973), Cranach & Vine, eds. (1973), Hinde (1974), and Argyle (1975).

2.3.1 THE "SPEECH" OF APES

Apes in captivity may be taught to respond to as many as sixty different words (cf. Russell & Russell 1971: 182). This passive language competence stimulated two early projects of teaching spoken English to two infant chimpanzees called Gua (Kellogg & Kellogg 1933) and Viki (Hayes 1951). Linguistically, both projects resulted in failure. As a result of several years' teaching, these apes were unable to articulate with difficulty more than four English words, although they attained a passive vocabulary of some one hundred words. It is now clear that the anatomy of the vocal tract of nonhuman primates is unsuited for the distinct articulation of sounds such as human phonemes (cf. Lenneberg 1967, Lieberman 1972; 1984).

2.3.2 SIGN LANGUAGE LEARNING

A breakthrough in primate language teaching was Gardner & Gardner's (1969) project with the chimpanzee Washoe. In view of the great manual dexterity of apes as contrasted with their inability to produce articulated sounds, the Gardners decided to use the English sign language ASL as a medium of language teaching. As result of three and a half years' teaching, Washoe in fact acquired an active ASL vocabulary of 132 words (cf. Terrace 1979: 11). A later project showed that a gorilla was able to learn as many as 224 ASL words in four years (Patterson 1978). For other results in the history of teaching ASL to apes, see Peng, ed. (1978), Fouts et al. (1978), Terrace (1979), Sebeok & Umiker-Sebeok, eds. (1980), and Savage-Rumbaugh (1986).

The most significant results of these projects are the discoveries concerning the degree to which apes are able to generalize and abstract in the use of signs. The ASL gestures used by Washoe were not only context-dependent indices or imitative icons (for which apes are proverbially famous), but true symbols, arbitrary signs used in the absence of the refer-ential object, occasionally even in creative generalizations and sometimes for no other purpose than naming the object.

Although Washoe and her successors were able to combine ASL signs into utterances, the investigation of thousands of such two- and three-word utterances has made it seem questionable whether these utterances are based on a syntax in the sense of a system of word-order rules, by which grammatical sentences can be distinguished from ungrammatical sentences (cf. Terrace 1979). Another drawback in the history of ape language research was the discovery that many of the linguistic utterances of signing apes seemed to be generated in response to the teacher's signing. This raised the suspicion that much of what had been thought to be proof of ape intelligence might really be due to the so-called Clever Hans phenomenon: the solving of a difficult semiotic problem by merely responding to some undetected nonverbal cue of the trainer (cf. Sebeok & Rosenthal, eds. 1981). New generations of projects tried to avoid this source of error by investigating apes relatively isolated from human trainers.

2.3.3 THE LEARNING OF ARTIFICIAL VISUAL SYMBOLS

In his study of the intelligence of the chimpanzee Sarah, Premack (1976; 1986; Premack & Premack 1983) developed a special artificial language consisting of plastic tokens used on a magnetic board. These tokens are arbitrary symbols, which are distinguished by shape and color. For example, a blue triangle means 'apple' and a pink square means 'banana.' The system is thus a language without second articulation. Sarah acquired a vocabulary of about 130 such symbols. The focus of this investigation was on syntax and logic. Premack demonstrated that Sarah was able to perform rudimentary semiotic operations, such as using and understanding quantifiers, designating colors and shapes by arbitrary symbols, drawing if-then conclusions, performing meta-linguistic operations, and constructing sentences and questions in correct word order.

A different artificial language, called "Yerkish," was developed for language learning with the chimpanzee Lana (Rumbaugh, ed. 1977, Savage-Rumbaugh 1986). The symbols of this language consist of geometric configurations embossed on the keys of a computer keyboard of 124 keys (cf. Savage-Rumbaugh 1986: 48). Each symbol (called a *lexigram*) corresponds to a word of human language. It represents an object, action, color, or location. To produce a message, Lana had to push the word keys in a correct syntactic order. The receiver was an experimenter outside the room who provided appropriate rewards for correct requests. The use of this type of animal-machine dialogue instead of animal-man communication was motivated by the attempt to eliminate undesired influences such as the Clever Hans phenomenon.

Technically, Yerkish is a language with two levels of articulation (cf. Hervey 1982: 263). Each lexigram consists of one, or a combination of two or three, minimal meaningless elements such as a triangle, a circle, or a vertical line. These elements are figurae and correspond to the phonemes of a language (see Code 4.2.1). However, since each lexigram has a fixed place on the keyboard, it is doubtful whether the lexigrams are decoded as a combination of elements of second articulation. They could also be decoded from their position on the keyboard, which would make the identification by figurae redundant. The semiotic capabilities of apes discovered in these projects are summarized as follows by Savage-Rumbaugh:

> Apes can learn words spontaneously and efficiently, and they can use them referentially for things not present; they can learn words from one another; they can learn to use words to coordinate their joint activities and to tell one another things otherwise not known; they can learn rules for ordering their words; they do make comments; they can come to announce their intended actions; and they are spontaneous and not necessarily subject to imitation in their signs. (1986: 379)

2.4 Design Features of Animal "Languages"

The theory of the design features of language was originally developed from the comparison of human and vocal languages with various animal communication systems. Whereas the definition of these design features is introduced and discussed in the chapter on language (q.v. 3.1), the following paragraphs focus on the possible presence of these features in various animal "languages." Hockett's sixteen design features were an attempt to determine the specificity of human communication. However, many of these design features are in fact present in animal communication, and only some of them are candidates for the specificity of human language. For a survey see 2.4.3.

2.4.1 DESIGN FEATURES OF HUMAN AND NONHUMAN "LANGUAGES"

Hockett's view of language is a phonocentric one. His first three design features therefore relate to the *vocal-auditory channel* (DF 1). These design features not only are common to all acoustic modes of communication in animals (see 3.4.3), but also are nondefining for such human modes of language as writing and sign language. Whereas the feature of *broadcast transmission and directional reception* (DF 2) is not applicable to visual "languages" (since these cannot be used in the dark), *rapid fading* (DF 3) is characteristic of gestural, but not of written languages. Other features depending on the phonocentric definition of language are *discreteness* (DF 9), *interchangeability* (DF 4), and *complete feedback* (DF 5). Bird calls, for example, are also characterized by all of these features. For visual modes of communication, several modifications have to be considered. The messages of bees are interchangeable, but not immediately. While every forager bee is a potential sender *and* receiver, the sending and receiving activities are two different phases of their work, separated by time.

The features which have traditionally been considered to be characteristic of culture (and thus of man), in contrast to nature (and animals), are especially those of the semantic and semiogenetic dimensions of language (see Language 3.1.3–4). Only recent zoosemiotic research has shown that many of these features are also present in animal "languages." The fact that birds and bees develop regional dialects testifies to the presence of *tradition* (DF 13) and *learnability* (DF 16) in these "languages." The projects in ape language research have shown that apes can even learn a "foreign language." For the design features of the semantic dimension (DF 7–8, 10, 14), see 4. The presence of these DFs in animal "languages" is a matter of degree.

2.4.2 CENTRAL DESIGN FEATURES OF HUMAN LANGUAGE

The design features which have been isolated as central properties of human language are discussed in detail in the chapter on language (q.v. 3.2). The presence of these features in animal communication is a matter of degree and depends on whether artificial "ape languages" are included. Among these features, *double articulation* (DF 12) most certainly does not occur in natural animal communication systems. Most probably, not even the "ape language" Yerkish is decoded as a system with double articulation. Some authors who ascribe the feature of double articulation to bird calls and other animal "languages" (Thorpe 1972a) seem to take the mere segmentability of acoustic signals for a level of second articulation (see Language 4.1). However, a prerequisite of a truly phonemic patterning is that the same minimal but meaningless elements are combined to form new messages. When they are substituted for each other, the substitution results in a semantic difference. This type of patterning seems to be absent from animal communication systems.

Reflexiveness (DF 15) or the metasemiotic use of signs occurs as a feature in trained ape "languages," but it is doubtful whether this feature occurs in natural environments. *Productivity* and *displacement* (DF 10–11) are two design features whose presence in animal communication is a matter of degree. To some degree, both occur in the language of bees. Bees can indicate an indefinite number of directions and distances, but the productivity of this "language" is restricted to this one dimension. This "language" is certainly capable of referring to remote objects, but this type of displacement is restricted to objects at a local distance. It is questionable whether reference to objects remote in time is possible in animal communication. True reference to past events seems highly improbable.

2.4.3 SYNOPSIS OF DESIGN FEATURES IN ANIMAL "LANGUAGES"

Following Hockett (1960: 160), several other authors have given surveys of the design features of communication systems of various animal species (Altmann 1967, Marler 1969, Tembrock 1971: 35, Thorpe 1972a, Hinde 1975, Kalkofen 1983). As a summary, Figure Z 2 shows the design features of the "languages" of six selected species.

2.5 Zoosemiotics and Human Semiogenesis

The biological history of language is a topic whose discussion is currently being intensified after more than fifty years of dogmatic silence (cf. Révész 1946, Rosenkranz 1961, Lenneberg 1967, Wescott 1967, Schwidetzky, ed. 1973, Fouts 1974, Zisterer 1975, Harnad et al., eds. 1976, Sommerfeld 1980, Grolier, ed. 1983, Lieberman 1984, Marquardt 1984, Müller 1987, Gessinger & Rahden, eds. 1988, Landsberg, ed. 1988, Koch, ed. 1989b). Can the comparative study of animal communication give answers to the questions of the phylogeny of language? Whereas it is controversial whether zoosemiotics is relevant to the problem of the phylogeny of spoken language, zoosemiotic research is indispensable in the study of human semiogenesis in general.

2.5.1 PHYLOGENY OF SPEECH

Since Darwin, it is apparent that not only the anatomy of man but also human behavior and communication must have antecedents in earlier animal species. However, it is a matter of dispute whether these antecedents can be observed in animal species still living today. With respect to spoken language, Lenneberg distinguishes two approaches to this problem, one postulating continuity, the other discontinuity in the evolution of speech (1967: 227 ff.).

Design Features \ Species	Man: spoken language	Trained chimpanzees	Gibbon calls	Dogs: vocal & nonvocal	Finches & crows	Honey bee
1 Vocal-auditory ch.	+	−	+	+	+	−
2 Broadcast transm.	+	p	+	+	+	p
3 Rapid fading	+	+	+	+	+	p
4 Interchangeability	+	+	+	+	p	p
5 Total feedback	+	+	+	+	+	−?
6 Specialization	+	+	+	+	+	−?
7 Semanticity	+	+	+	+	+	+
8 Arbitrariness	+	+	+	−	+	p
9 Discreteness	+	+	+	−	+	−
10 Displacement	+	+	−	−	p	+
11 Productivity	+	+	−	−	p	p
12 Duality	+	−?	−	−	−	−
13 Tradition	+	+	?	?	+	p
14 Prevarication	+	+	−	+	−	−
15 Reflexiveness	+	p	−	−	−	−
16 Learnability	+	+	−	+	+	p

Fig. Z 2. The design features of the communication systems of selected animal species, compared to the design features of the vocal language of man (adapted from Hockett 1960 and Thorpe 1972a; see text). + and − indicate relevant and absent features, p and ? indicate partly relevant and questionable features.

The continuity theory of language evolution rests on the belief that there is no essential difference between human and animal communication: human language is merely quantitatively different from animal "language," and many design features of language can also be observed in still living animal species. The discontinuity theory, defended by Lenneberg himself, argues that "no living animal represents a direct primitive ancestor of our own kind and, therefore, there is no reason to believe that any one of *their* traits is a primitive form of any one of *our* traits" (1967: 234–35).

The fact that animals share certain traits with man does not prove continuity. A variant of this discontinuity thesis is the analogy theory proposed by Kainz (1961: 271). It admits "systematic analogies" between human and animal communication but rejects a genetic interpretation of these relationships.

A third approach to the problem of the evolution of speech steers a middle course between the continuity and discontinuity theories. It is the theory of *parallel evolution* (Wiener 1986: 170). According to this theory, similarities between features of human and animal "languages" are the result of parallel developments under similar ecological and biosocial conditions of evolution.

2.5.2 HUMAN AND ANIMAL SEMIOGENESIS

Glottogenesis, the evolution of a fully developed phonemic language, is now generally assumed to have begun only about fifty thousand years ago (cf. Harnad et al., eds. 1976). By contrast, semiogenesis in general, the evolution of nonlinguistic semiotic behavior, and with it, the evolution of culture, has a much older history (cf. Koch 1986a). The nonlinguistic modes of human semiosis have also much clearer parallels in animal behavior than language. Therefore, the study of semiogenesis depends much more closely on zoosemiotics than the study of glottogenesis. Bonner even argues that not only can the evolution of culture be explained with reference to animal behavior, but culture in fact begins in animals. In his definition, culture is already "passing information by behavioral rather than genetic means" (1980: 4).

Semiotic investigations of "sub-human culture beginnings" (see Kroeber 1928) have so far focused on various modes of nonverbal communication such as laughter, smiling (Hooff 1972), other facial expressions (Vine 1970, Chevalier-Skolnikoff 1973), gestures, body posture, and so on (cf. Eibl-Eibesfeldt 1967, Hinde 1974, Argyle 1975). In this context, the theory of the gestural origin of human language deserves special mention (see also Gesture 2.5.2). Hewes (1973), one of the main proponents of this theory, believes that prelinguistic human semiosis must have been a highly developed gestural sign language because human cognition is based to a higher degree on vision than on audition. Whether this assumption is right or not, it is certainly true that nonverbal communication in nonhuman primates is much more developed than vocal communication. It also appears that the shift to the vocal channel brought advantages to man which visually communicating animals do not have, namely, to communicate more quickly and across visual barriers, including darkness (cf. Valsiner & Allik 1982). In addition to nonverbal communication, the evolution of aesthetic semiosis is another topic of prehuman semiogenesis. On antecedents to art in animal behavior, see Sebeok (1981) and Koch (1984).

3. Zoopragmatics: Elements of Communication

According to Sebeok, "zoopragmatics is concerned with the manner in which an animal encodes a message, how this is transmitted in a channel, and the manner in which the user decodes it" (1972: 124). Zoopragmatics thus investigates various semiotic aspects of the relationship between the animal and its environment. Where is the beginning of semiosis in the animal-environment interaction, what are the criteria and modes of communication between animals, and what is the nature and function of the channel in animal communication?

3.1 Definition and Criteria of Animal Communication

What is communication in animals? Is it any interaction between an animal and its environment or only the intentional exchange of messages between animals of the same species? How can we verify the occurrence of an act of communication between animals? Most biologists have tried to solve the problem of defining animal communication by adopting a behav-

ioristic position. According to Frings & Frings, "communication between animals involves the giving off by one individual of some chemical or physical signal, that, on being received by another, influences its behavior" (1964: 3). Cullen postulates that animal communication should "evoke a change of behavior in another individual" (1972: 103). Wilson defines biological communication as "the action on the part of one organism (or cell) that alters the probability pattern of behavior in another organism (or cell) in a fashion adaptive to either one or both of the participants" (1975: 176). Finally, Dawkins & Krebs argue that "communication is said to occur when an animal, the actor, does something which appears to be the result of selection to influence the sense organs of another animal, the reactor, so that the reactor's behavior changes to the advantage of the actor" (1978: 283).

Problems discussed in these and other definitions of animal communication (cf. Halliday & Slater, eds. 1983a) include the question whether *mutualism* (Marler 1974: 28–30), *intraspecificity* or sameness of sender-receiver species (Frings & Frings 1964: 4), *goal-directedness* (MacKay 1972), *purposiveness* (criticized by Marler 1961: 296–97), or even *intent* (Burghardt 1970: 17) should be adopted as a criterion. In contrast to many of these definitions, which postulate a clear-cut distinction between communication and noncommunicative behavior, the pluralistic approach to semiosis and communication adopted in this handbook is based on the assumption that communication and semiosis exist in various modes and at various levels of interaction between the animal and its environment. Whether all these levels of interaction should be defined as communication is a mere question of terminology.

3.2 Roots and Levels of Animal Semiosis

Models for the description of the roots of semiosis and levels of animal-environment interaction have been proposed by Uexküll and Tavolga.

3.2.1 UEXKÜLL'S FUNCTIONAL CIRCLE

In his biological theory of meaning, Jakob von Uexküll (1928: 158, 1940: 32; see also History 4.2.3 and Sebeok 1979) proposes a model which focuses on the lowest possible level of semiosis, the mere interaction of an organism with its *Umwelt* (environment). *Umwelt*, according to Uexküll, is not any objective physical or biological environment of an organism, but a subjective world consisting of the organism's specific perceptual field or world (*Merkwelt*) and the sphere of its practical interaction, the operational field (*Wirkwelt*). Only those perceptual and operational factors of the environment form an *Umwelt* which are of significance to the survival of an organism.

Uexküll's functional circle (Fig. Z 3) represents an animal or biological organism involved in semiosis as a *subject* or "receiver of meaning." This animal is confronted in its environment with an *object* which functions as the subject's "counter-structure." The animal is connected with this object perceptually and operationally. The subject perceives the object with *receptors* such as eye or ear and processes the sense data (*Wirkzeichen*) neurologically by its inner *perceptual organ*. This organ is neurologically connected with the animal's inner *effector organ*, a neurological network which steers the muscles of the subject's *effectors* such as hands, paws, or the masticatory organs. By means of these effectors, the animal interacts practically with its "operational field." The object functions as a "carrier of meaning," insofar as it sends both perceptual and operational messages to the receiver (subject). As a "carrier of a perceptual signal" or "perceptual cue," such as color, light, sound, or odor, it is a potential message to be perceived by the subject's receptor. As a "carrier of an effect signal" or "operational cue," the object influences the subject

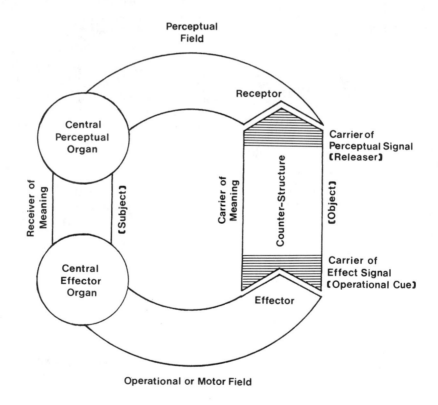

Fig. Z 3. Uexküll's model of the functional circle of semiosis in organism-environment interaction (see text).

by controlling its operational or motor behavior. As soon as the object is acted upon by the animal in some manner, the perceptual cue is thereby eliminated. More generally, the perceptual signal is terminated by the animal's operation, for example, in the act of feeding.

3.2.2 TAVOLGA'S LEVELS OF INTERACTION

Tavolga (1974: 57) proposes a hierarchical model of zoosemiosis distinguishing six phylogenetic levels of interaction between organisms (Fig. Z 4). At the lowest level of interaction, the *vegetative* or *trophic* level, organisms such as multicellular plants interact by mere physical contiguity, by growth and tropism. The *tonic* or *organismic* level of interaction involves metabolism, homeostatic regulations, and other continuous physiological processes of energy exchange of a more complex organism. At this level, relations of symbiosis become possible. At the next level, that of *phasic* interaction, the exchange of information between organisms is no longer permanent, but occurs at more or less regular intervals (phases) or in response to particular events. The interactions are primarily taxic.

Higher forms of semiosis, and communication in the narrower sense, begin at the *signal* or *message* level. At this level, signals are primarily intraspecific and based on a code shared by receiver and emitter. Higher forms of communication at this level occur in *biosocial* or even *psychosocial* modes of interaction. According to Tavolga, only vocal and nonverbal communication of primates has attained the next higher level of semiosis, the *symbolic* or *goal-directed* level. This level comprises further design features of communication, such as interchangeability and intentionality. The complete set of design features, however, appears only at the *linguistic* level. Only *homo sapiens* attains this level of interaction.

3.3 Levels and Typology of Animal Communication

Focusing on the higher modes of zoosemiosis, the various zoosemiotic forms of communica-

tion may be subdivided into *proprioceptive*, *intraspecific*, and *interspecific* communication. A special subtype of the latter, which lies at the lower threshold of communication, is semiotic interaction between plants and animals (see 6.).

3.3.1 PROPRIOCEPTIVE COMMUNICATION

The processing of signals whose sender is at the same time the receiver forms the lowest level of communication, between endosemiotics (see Code 5.1) and zoosemiotics. In contrast to unilateral communication, such as observation or diagnosis, where the sender remains passive, proprioceptive or *auto-communication* requires the active participation of the sender-receiver in the act of semiosis. Bats and porpoises use proprioceptive communication in the form of echolocation. They emit ultrasonic sounds which are reflected by their prey, and in receiving the retransmitted sound they locate the prey. For details see Sebeok, ed. (1977: 252–62).

3.3.2 INTRASPECIFIC COMMUNICATION AND MUTUALISM

The mutual exchange of messages between members of the same species, based on a common code, characterizes a fully developed system of communication. Complete *mutualism* (Marler 1974: 28–30), *reciprocity* (Burghardt 1970: 9), or *symmetry* (Kalmus 1962: 15) is not attained by all animal species. The highest degree of mutualism permits true dialogic interaction. The receiver of a message must be able to give immediately a new message in reply to the former one. The "language of bees" does not attain this degree of mutualness. As Benveniste points out, "the bee's message does not call for any reply from those to whom it is addressed, except that it evokes a particular behavior which is not strictly an answer" (1966: 52).

3.3.3 INTERSPECIFIC COMMUNICATION

Communication is not only restricted to intraspecific exchange of signals. There are many varieties of interspecific communication (cf.

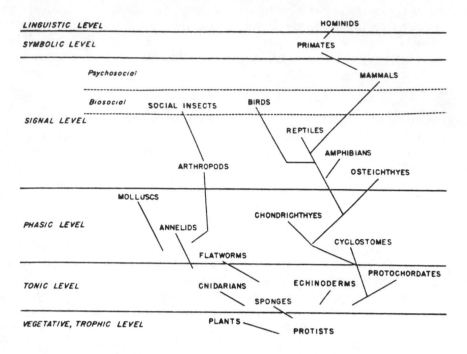

LINGUISTIC LEVEL   HOMINIDS

SYMBOLIC LEVEL   PRIMATES

Psychosocial   MAMMALS

Biosocial   SOCIAL INSECTS   BIRDS

SIGNAL LEVEL

REPTILES

AMPHIBIANS

ARTHROPODS   OSTEICHTHYES

MOLLUSCS

CHONDRICHTHYES

PHASIC LEVEL   ANNELIDS

CYCLOSTOMES

FLATWORMS

PROTOCHORDATES

TONIC LEVEL   CNIDARIANS   ECHINODERMS

SPONGES

VEGETATIVE, TROPHIC LEVEL   PLANTS

PROTISTS

Fig. Z 4. Tavolga's phylogenetic levels of interaction between organisms. Allocation of a species to a particular level is based on the highest level achieved in the course of its evolution.

Sebeok 1981: 136–43). In natural ecology, such communication between different species occurs in various forms of predation symbiosis, territorial defense, and self-defense. Threats, protective deception (mimicry; cf. 4.2.1), and requests to perform certain desired actions are typical messages in interspecific semiosis. Interspecific communication between man and animal has developed under various conditions of domestication, taming, and training.

Some biologists prefer to exclude interspecific interaction from communication, arguing that the messages often have different meanings for the members of the two species involved (cf. Burghardt 1970: 8). Thus, the wax-eating African bird *indicator indicator* (honey guide) attracts the attention of the honey-eating badger by calling certain notes and flying toward the bee's nest (cf. Sebeok 1986b: 136–39). To the badger, this message means 'honey,' whereas to the honey guide,

the same message is a request to the badger to follow the bird, destroy the bee's nest, and leave the wax for the bird. A still greater difference between the sender's intended and the receiver's decoded meaning exists in mimicry (see 4.2.1). However, there is also interspecific communication in which the message means the same to the sender and to the receiver, for example threat behavior directed at predators.

3.4 Channel and Medium

Compared to human semiosis, animals exploit a greater variety of channels in communication. What advantages and disadvantages do these diverse channels have (cf. Frings & Frings 1964: 11–21, Marler 1965, Sebeok, ed. 1968: 73–164; 1977: 137–292, Sebeok & Ramsay, eds. 1969, Tembrock 1971, Sebeok 1972: 124–28, Argyle 1975: 27–38)?

3.4.1 CHEMICAL COMMUNICATION

The most elementary and at the same time most common zoosemiotic signals are those transmitted via chemical channels (cf. Sebeok, ed. 1968: 103–126, Johnston et al., eds. 1970, Sebeok 1972: 93–105, Tembrock 1971: 96–123, Shorey 1976). The branch of biochemistry which studies substances by means of which organisms interact chemically is called *semiochemistry* (Albone 1984, Acree & Soderlund, eds. 1985). Chemical substances which serve as sign vehicles of communication between organisms in the shared natural environment are called *semiochemicals*. Semiochemicals used in intraspecific communication are defined as *pheromones* (cf. Shorey 1976: 3). Some species have two chemoreceptors for taste and smell; others do not distinguish clearly between the gustatory and olfactive channels (cf. Frings & Frings 1964: 12).

In contrast to acoustic signals, chemical messages have the advantage of being relatively permanent. They can act at great distances and are decodable in the future, but there is a slow variability and a high susceptibility to inferences (cf. ibid.). Chemical signals are indexical signs (see Typology 4.2). They serve to indicate territories or to identify the individuals of a group. Basically, they are nondirectional, but with a moving source they can be decoded directionally (as trails). For gustatory and olfactory signals in human communication, see Nonverbal Communication (1.2).

3.4.2 TACTILE, THERMIC, AND ELECTRICAL SIGNALS

Tactile signals are transmitted by direct body contact or by vibrations produced in the close vicinity of the receiver. The signals are variable in time and intensity, but cannot be transmitted at distance. Messages transmitted via the tactile channel are related to sexual contact, the raising of young, social position, group affiliation, or danger. The honey bee's use of the tactile channel for messages referring to distant places is a rarer example of the potential of tactile communication. Many tactile forms of information processing are nonmediated, and in this sense nonsemiotic, modes of behavior (see Sign 1.3.3). They are either proprioceptive, as

in tactile orientation in the environment, or they represent immediate modes of social interaction, such as aggression, protection, nutrition, or sexual affiliation.

Whereas little is known concerning the potential of thermic information transfer (cf. Tembrock 1971: 123–24), the use of the electrical channel, particularly in various fish species, but also in some insects using electromagnetic fields for purposes of orientation, is well explored (Hopkins 1977). Electric fish produce signals for a variety of purposes, such as the detection of objects, indication of social status, threat, submission, or courtship.

3.4.3 THE ACOUSTIC CHANNEL

The branch of zoosemiotics studying acoustic systems of communication is also known as *bioacoustics* or *biophonetics* (Lanyon & Tavolga, eds. 1960, Busnel, ed. 1963, Sebeok, ed. 1968: 127–53, Trojan 1975, Tembrock 1971: 147–203; 1973, Busnel 1977, and see 2.2.2). Acoustic signals are produced vocally or nonvocally. They can be transmitted and received through the media of air and water. The vocal signals of mammals are produced by vocal cords in the larynx. Birds also produce sounds in an air chamber called the syrinx, which is located at the lower end of the trachea (cf. Thorpe 1961: 106–128). Nonvocal signals are produced as percussion sounds by tapping against something, by scraping comblike organs together, or by the vibration of membranes.

Some of the advantages of the acoustic channel are listed in Hockett's system of design features of language (see Language 3.1; cf. 2.4): *broadcast transmission* (signals can travel in the dark and around corners) *and directional reception* (DF 2), *rapid fading* (DF 3), which makes a fast continuation and response possible, potential *discreteness* (DF 9) due to the linear character of sounds, immediate *feedback* (DF 5), and *specialization* (DF 6), the advantage of needing little effort in signal production. Rapid fading is at the same time the main disadvantage of the acoustic channel. Man has overcome it by the invention of writing. Many animal species explore the chemical channel for more permanent messages.

3.4.4 THE VISUAL CHANNEL

Surveys and studies of visual or optical systems in animal semiosis are given by Marler (1968) and Hailman (1977a; b). Most animals have to rely on reflected light for visual communication. Some species have a capacity for vision which surpasses that of man. Eagles can see small objects at several miles' distance. Bees can see ultraviolet light which remains invisible to man. Only a few species, such as lightning bugs and some fish species, have photophoric organs with which they can produce signals on their own, even in the dark. For details on communication by bioluminescence, see Lloyd (1977).

Hailman (1977a; b) distinguishes between *extrinsic* and *intrinsic* visual signals. Extrinsic signals are produced in the animal's environment. Tracks, nests, traces of feeding, or the colored objects with which bowerbirds decorate their bowers are examples. Intrinsic signals are part of the animal's body or behavior. Three main modes of intrinsic visual signaling according to Hailman are orientation toward the intended receiver, body shape and color, and movement patterns (1977a: 186). The various forms of nonverbal communication in animals (see 2.5.2) belong to the latter category of intrinsic visual signals.

Optical signals are superior to acoustic ones for the purpose of orientation in space. Visual messages can transmit a greater quantity of information than messages of other channels. The main disadvantage of the visual channel is that it requires light (except for bioluminescent signaling). Static extrinsic and intrinsic visual signals have the advantage of permanence, but only dynamic visual signals such as gestures allow flexibility and transience in time.

4. Zoosemantics

From the point of view of zoosemantics, the varieties of meanings in animal communication, the functions of animal signs, and the relationship of their meanings to the sign vehicles of animal semiosis have to be investigated. Although the difference between human and "animal" languages is also apparent in the semantic dimension of semiosis, there are few types of signs and few functions of semiosis that are completely absent in nonhuman semiosis.

4.1 Meanings and Functions of Animal Semiosis

With respect to acoustic and visual modes of animal semiosis, Tembrock (1971) and Argyle (1975: 20–27) distinguish a variety of zoosemantic functions. These belong to three major zoosemantic fields: identity, and the social and ecological environment. Signals of identity show the individual as belonging to a certain species, group, sex, or age group in contrast to rival groups or predators. These are a special class of the signals of social relationship, which include signals of courtship and mating, signals of parental care, affiliative signals between siblings and friends, play signals, threat, attack, flight, submission, and appeasement signals. The function of these signals is expressive when the focus is on identity and conative when the focus is on social interaction. In addition, there are many forms of phatic signalization which indicate the establishment and maintenance of contact between animals.

The third major semantic field represents the referential function in animal semiosis. It comprises reference to sources of food or danger, reference to territory, weather, orientation, and other environmental conditions. In addition to these main functions, bird songs and the artful constructions of the bowerbirds even testify to the presence of rudiments of the poetic function in animal semiosis (cf. Sebeok 1981). For a semantico-pragmatic classification of signs in zoosemiosis in terms of Morris's typology of signs, which distinguishes between *designators*, *appraisors*, *prescriptors*, and *identifiors* in animal semiosis, see Marler (1961: 300–302; 1965: 566–67).

4.2 *Object Relation*

Peirce distinguished between icons, indices, and symbols according to the semantic criterion of the signifier-referent relationship. The symbolic or arbitrary sign has often been considered a distinguishing feature of human in contrast to animal communication. However, arbitrariness is not restricted to human semiosis. There are iconic, indexical, and symbolic aspects of signs in animal semiosis (cf. Bronowski 1967: 377, Hailman 1977b: 250–61, Nöth 1977a: 20–22, Sebeok 1979: 13–19).

4.2.1 ICONIC ASPECTS OF ZOOSEMIOSIS

The most impressive examples of iconicity in zoosemiosis are found in interspecific communication. In the various modes of *anti-predator adaptation*, iconic imitation has developed for purposes of predator deception and self-protection (cf. Heymer 1977). In *protective adaptation* we find camouflage coloring and morphological resemblances to animals or objects naturally avoided by the animal's predator, thus resulting in an advantage for the potential prey species. In *mimicry* (cf. Wickler 1971), such imitations also develop with the result of mutual benefit between the interacting species, as with the orchid *ophrys* that resembles, and thus attracts, the bumblebee. Whereas most forms of mimicry are visual, there is also vocal mimicry in many bird species (cf. Armstrong 1963: 70–87). A further example of iconicity in animal semiosis is *sham behavior*, by which animals imitate attacks, infirmity, or even death for the purpose of detracting rival or predator species (cf. Hailman 1977b: 179ff.).

For nondeceptive purposes, iconicity is relatively rare in animal semiosis. Nondeceptive vocal imitation, as with mockingbirds, although hardly communicative (cf. Wescott 1971), is one of the rarer examples. However, animal signals often evince diagrammatic (or relational) iconicity (see Icon 1.3). In this respect, the bee's dance is iconic (cf. Hockett 1960: 144) since the speed of the dance is inversely proportional to the distance to the target location, and the angle of the dance corresponds to the angle between the line of sight to the sun and the direction toward the source of nectar. Another example of diagrammatic iconicity is alarm calls, whose loudness is proportional to the degree of threat felt by the animal (cf. Altmann 1967: 340).

4.2.2 INDEXICAL ASPECTS OF ZOOSEMIOSIS

The design feature of *displacement* is only weakly developed in animal semiosis. Animal messages are essentially dependent on the temporal presence or spatial proximity of or some material influence from their referential object. By these features, animal signals are characterized as indices. Examples of indexical animal signs are the identifiors and other group signals discussed above, territorial markers, the various behavioral indicators of direction, signal colors (cf. Hailman 1977b: 250–55), and all acoustic signals insofar as they indicate the sender's location. The bees' dance is indexical insofar as it is an indicator of direction. Except for some iconic ethological modes of semiosis, it is hard to find signs in animal communication devoid of indexicality. The degree of indexicality in animal semiosis is definitely higher than in human semiosis.

4.2.3 SYMBOLIC ASPECTS OF ZOOSEMIOTICS

Animal alarm calls are as unrelated to the source of danger as are human cries of alarm. The same lack of signal-object dependency occurs in most visual signals of animal semiosis. Thus, a fearful rhesus monkey carries its tail stiffly out behind, whereas in baboons, fear is expressed by a vertical tail; tail movements in a dog mean friendship, in a cat hostility (cf. Sebeok 1976: 137, 44). Based on these and other observations, zoosemioticians have concluded that there is arbitrariness and that there are thus symbols in animal semiosis (cf. Hockett 1960: 144, Bronowski 1967: 376, Marler 1974: 34–37; 1977: 51). Arbitrariness of animal signs is indeed convincing wherever there are geographical dialects in the animal signals of one species (cf. 2.2.1–2 and Sebeok 1979: 216–20).

However, the discussion of the symbolic element in animal communication is often based on the mere ascertainment of their noniconicity. If it is taken into consideration that signs are motivated not only by similarity (see Iconicity), but also by factors of spatio-temporal contiguity (indexicality), the symbolic element in animal semiosis turns out to be much lower than maintained by those who restrict their observations to a dichotomy of arbitrariness and iconicity. By Peircean triadic criteria, there are certainly no genuine symbols in zoosemiosis, since indexicality is always involved in arbitrary animal signs (cf. Nöth 1977a: 22).

5. Ethology and Semiogenesis

Ethology, the study of the biological and phylogenetic roots of human and animal behavior, extends the predominantly synchronic horizon of zoosemiotics to a diachronic dimension (cf. 1.1.4). Only a few basic concepts of ethology which are of particular relevance to research in semiosis, semiogenesis (cf. 2.5.2), and especially the evolution of culture can be discussed in the following.

5.1 Survey of Ethological and Semiogenetic Research

With its two branches of animal and human ethology, the evolutionary study of behavior is relevant to both zoosemiotics and anthroposemiotics. The founders of modern ethology are Julian Huxley (1887–1975), Oscar Heinroth (1871–1945), Erich W. von Holst (1908–1962), Konrad Lorenz (1903-1989), Karl von Frisch (see 2.2.1), and Niko L. Tinbergen (1907–1988). For the state of the art in ethology, see Eibl-Eibesfeldt (1967), Klopfer & Hailman, eds. (1972), Wickler (1972), Bateson & Klopfer, eds. (1973–81), Hinde (1974), Thorpe (1974), Immelmann (1976), Heymer (1977), Smith (1977a; and Smith's article in Sebeok, ed. 1986: 237–45), Bonner (1980), and Halliday & Slater, eds. (1983b). Closely related fields of study are be-

havioral ecology, sociobiology, neuroethology (Ewert 1976), and psychobiology (Davidson & Davidson, eds. 1980). For human ethology and its branch of (human) cultural ethology, see in particular Eibl-Eibesfeldt (1967), Ardrey (1967), Koenig (1970), Desmond Morris (1978; 1985), and Cranach et al., eds. (1979). Within semiotics, Koch (1986a; b, Koch, ed. 1989a) has developed an integrated theory of cultural evolution in which the study of semiogenesis and glottogenesis (cf. 2.5) is placed in a larger framework of *sociogenesis, psychogenesis, biogenesis* (cf. 1.1.3), and *cosmogenesis*.

5.2 Basic Concepts of Ethology

The basis of ethological research in animal behavior is the *ethogram*, a comprehensive catalog of all behavior patterns occurring in an animal species. For the study of such behavioral patterns, the distinction between innate and learned behavior is particularly relevant. Only some of the most central concepts in the ethological study of innate behavior and of innate bodily signals of animals can be discussed below. For mimicry, which is one class of such signals, see 4.2.1.

5.2.1 THE SEMANTICS OF INNATE BEHAVIOR
In contrast to schools of anthroposemiotics which consider arbitrariness (q.v. 4.1) and intentionality as distinguishing features of semiosis in general (cf. Communication 2.4.2, Code 3.2–3), ethologists have a wider concept of semiosis, assuming that even innate behavior has various semantic implications. However, ethological interpretations of behavior, at least in the field of anthroposemiotics, are often concerned only with evolutionary semantic motivations, describing archaic meanings which may no longer correspond to actual meanings conveyed today. In the course of their evolution, the original meanings of behavior have been subject to many semantic changes. For example, when Eibl-Eibesfeldt (1967) interprets laughing as ritualized aggression, it is clear that the archaic meaning of 'aggression' is lost in modern human com-

munication. In a way, such ethological interpretations of behavior are similar to etymological interpretations of language. These are relevant to the origins of modern words, but often do not explain their present meaning.

5.2.2 FROM STIMULUS TO INNATE SIGNALS

In the ethological interpretation of Lorenz and his school, semiosis has an innate foundation in a process in which certain exterior stimuli cause a specific instinctive response. These occur in a *fixed action pattern* which the animal performs without learning. No organism responds to all stimuli in its environment. There is a central filter, called a *releasing mechanism*, which processes only species-specific *key stimuli*. In unilateral semiosis, when the stimulus is evoked by environmental objects, and in interspecific communication, these *perceptual stimuli* are called *signal stimuli* or key stimuli proper. An example of such a key stimulus is the odor of butric acid to which the tick responds by dropping from the twig onto a mammal. In intraspecific communication, when the stimulus is a morphological structure or innate behavior of a member of the same species, this stimulus is defined as a *releaser*. Releasers may be colors, shapes, vocalizations, or movement patterns, for example in courtship or fighting behavior. When this intraspecific stimulus is a behavior pattern and not only a morphological body feature, the releaser is defined as a *signal*.

5.2.3 DISPLACEMENT ACTIVITY

Displacement activities are instinctive actions released in situations of excitement or indecision, particularly in conflicts between opposing drives, such as flight and attack. Displacement activities are apparently irrelevant as far as their biological survival value in the actual situation is concerned. They are, so to speak, performed by mistake. Examples are the grass-pulling of herring gulls in situations of fight or the human scratching of the head in embarrassment. The biological function of displacement behavior is uncertain.

5.2.4 DISPLAY BEHAVIOR

The term *display* is a central ethological concept describing certain stereotyped patterns of behavior. There are a narrower and a broader definition of this term. In the narrower sense, display behavior is "behavior which may impress or intimidate the partner or rival and which is frequently directed at a rival or rivals in the presence of the mate" (Ger. *Imponierverhalten*) (Heymer 1977: 91). Striking examples are parades and display running and/or swimming, which occur in birds and mammals. Human forms of display are parade uniforms or military parades. For an example of human nonverbal display behavior, see Gesture (2.5.1).

Broader definitions of display begin when the criterion of "impressiveness" of the action in question is modified or dropped altogether. Simpson replaces it with a criterion of "conspicuousness" when he defines display "as a conspicuous (to the observer) action made by an animal, whose conspicuousness led me to believe that he could, through the display, be having some effect on his companions" (1973: 230). Smith defines display behavior still more generally as behavior that deviates from immediate practical or biological needs. In his view, displays are stereotyped behavioral patterns which "often produce no obvious results, at least by acting directly on things in the environments of the individuals who perform them" (1977a: 7). In this sense, displacement activities are a subclass of display behavior. From this definition, it is only a small step to the still broader definition given by Wilson, who focuses on the evolutionary history of these signals: "Display [is a] behavior pattern that has been modified in the course of evolution to convey information. A display is a special kind of signal, which in turn is broadly defined as *any* behavior that conveys information regardless of whether it serves other functions" (1975: 582).

5.2.5 RITUALIZATION

Ritualization is a key concept of ethology introduced by J. Huxley (1914; see further Blest

1961, Wickler 1975, and D'Aquili et al., eds. 1979). Its ethological definition is only loosely related to the meaning of ritual in the social and cultural sciences (for these, see Gesture 2.4.2). Ritualization is an evolutionary modification of a behavior pattern to serve a communicative function (cf. Wilson 1975: 594, Heymer 1977: 148). According to Wickler (1970: 233), this process results, through natural selection, in improved conditions of communication, since the behavioral change increases the clarity and distinctiveness of the signal for the receiver. Huxley defined ritualization as

> the adaptive formalization or canalization of emotionally motivated behavior, under the teleonomic pressure of natural selection so as: (a) to promote better and more unambiguous signal function, both intra- and interspecifically; (b) to serve as more efficient stimulators or releasers of more efficient patterns of action in other individuals; (c) to reduce intraspecific damage; and (d) to serve as sexual or social bonding mechanisms. (1966: 250)

Examples of ritualizations from the phylogeny of human gestures (see Gesture 2.5.1) are the greeting etiquette of bowing as a ritualized form of submission, the man's taking off his hat in greeting as the ritualization of his taking off his helmet, military greeting as the ritualization of the lifting of the knight's visor, etc. (cf. Koenig 1970). Sebeok gives a semiotic interpretation of ritualization, redefining it as

> the semiosis of *gene-dependency*, in order to emphasize the fact that here we are dealing with the progressive elaboration, in the course of evolution, of instructions stored not in the memory but in the genetic make-up of animals and man, in brief, the shaping of signs according to the requirements of natural selection. (1979: 29)

5.3 The Meme and the Evolution of Culture

If culture is semiotic "behavior transmitted from one individual to another by teaching and learning" (Bonner 1980: 18; cf. 2.5.2), it is defined in opposition to the innate forms of semiosis described in ethology and to all other biological structures of an organism. From this point of view, the propagation of information by teaching and learning (culture) seems to be radically opposed to the transmission of information by genetic inheritance (nature). Nevertheless, Dawkins (1976) has postulated far-reaching analogies between the evolution of culture and nature. In analogy to the gene, the carrier of genetic messages in biological evolution (cf. Code 5.1), Dawkins postulates an equivalent for the evolution of culture, which he defines as the *meme*. A meme, according to Dawkins, is

> a unit of cultural transmission, or a unit of *imitation*. [. . .] Examples of memes are tunes, ideas, catch-phrases, clothes fashions, ways of making pots or of building arches. Just as genes propagate themselves in the gene pool by leaping from body to body via sperms or eggs, so memes propagate themselves in the meme pool by leaping from brain to brain via a process which, in the broad sense, can be called imitation. (1976: 206)

Koch lists the following analogies between the gene and the meme (1986b: 11): (1) *storage of information* (gene: through aperiodic sequences of nucleotides; meme: through protein synthesis in the brain), (2) *Self-replication* (gene: within and between individuals by growth and sexual recombination; meme: within and between brains by thinking and communication), (3) capacity for *mutation* (gene: through alteration of nucleotides; meme: through error or misinterpretation), and (4) *transfer of information*. Bonner enumerates these differences between genetic and cultural evolution (1980: 19): (1) Genes can be passed only once from one individual (the parent) to another (the offspring), whereas memes can be taught by one individual to many individuals. (2) Genetic evolution is very slow, whereas cultural evolution may be very rapid. (3) Memes are utterly dependent upon genes, but genes can exist and change quite independently of memes.

The idea of an analogy between the evolution of life and culture has also been elaborated by Lumsden & Wilson (1981: 368, 372). Their parallel to the biological gene is the *culturgen* [ˈkʌltʃərdʒen]. These "basic units of culture" are defined as being the result of a process of "gene-culture coevolution" (cf. 6.2) in which "culturgen changes alter the gene frequencies as well."

6. Excursus on Phytosemiotics

Krampen (1981c; 1986) has proposed to extend the semiotic field to include the new domain of phytosemiotics, the semiotics of plants.

6.1 Do Plants Communicate?

Krampen argues that there is semiosis and even communication in the vegetable kingdom. The basis of this assumption is Uexküll's biological theory of meaning and the definition of biocommunication as the "seeking of confirmation of environmental information via other individuals" (Krampen 1986: 728). Krampen distinguishes three main cases of phytosemiosis, plant-plant interaction, plant-animal interaction, and plant-human interaction, such as the "green thumb" phenomenon, caring for and learning from plants. Deely (1986a) argues that these cases of interaction are only presemiotic, involving no (triadic) signification but only (dyadic) communication (see Communication 2.4.3; in Eco's terminology). An example of plant-plant semiosis is the symbiotic interaction between the rose and the lavender, which "may form an alliance for mutual benefit against mildew" (Krampen 1986: 729).

The occurrence of semiosis in plant-animal and plant-man interaction is perhaps more convincing at first sight. Examples are the coloration of many fruits which has evolved as a signal perceptible at a distance to animals which disperse them (Marler 1974: 29), the orchid which imitates and thus attracts the bumblebee, or the yucca plant which opens its flower only at nighttime when the yucca moths are active (Frings & Frings 1964: 3–4). For plant-man interaction, there is Wickler's example of mimetic weeds which are not as easily pulled by the gardener because they resemble useful plants (1971: 34–39).

6.2 Is Coevolution Semiosis?

These and other examples of plant-animal/man interaction are all cases of *coevolution*, that is, evolutionary selective changes "in a trait of the individuals in one population in response to a trait of the individuals of a second population, followed by an evolutionary response by the second population to the change in the first" (Janzen 1980). Count characterizes such processes of mutual adaptation as "phylogenetic learning," (1973: 157), an interpretation which also suggests a process of semiosis.

The parallels between communication and the above examples of coevolution are: a "sender" (the plant) emits a visual "message" (in the plant's own morphology) toward a receiver (animal or man) that reacts in a way which is to the sender's benefit (or disadvantage). The "message" is moreover taken from a large repertoire of morphological structures (colors, forms, etc.). However, there are two main differences between these forms of phytosemiosis and genuine bilateral communication (see Communication 2.3): (1) The morphological repertoire from which the "message" is selected is not a synchronic code, available at the moment of semiosis. The "message" is selected from a diachronic sign repertoire consisting of the morphological forms from which the present "message," the plant's present morphology, has evolved phylogenetically by natural selection. (2) The "message" does not have the same "meaning" to the "sender" and the "receiver." Whereas the plant's evolutionary "message" to the bird is to carry the berry far away, the bird will interpret it as 'food.' In mimicry, the message is not only different but even deceptive.

Communication and Semiosis

Communication is a key concept in semiotics and many of its neighboring disciplines. Yet, the meaning of this term is extremely diffuse. The concept is used to designate human and animal (see Zoosemiotics), direct (face-to-face) and indirect, intentional and unintentional, verbal and nonverbal, auditory, visual, and otherwise coded flows of information and thus exchange of signs. But while some semioticians define communication as any kind of information processing, others restrict this term to particular forms of semiosis. One of these restrictions has led to the distinction between communication and signification as two classes of semiosis.

Communicative processes are represented in models of communication. These give an outline of the semiotic dimension of pragmatics (see Morris 2.3.4). The founders of modern semiotics, however, rarely used the term *communication*. In the terminology of Peirce and Morris, communicative processes are generally discussed under the term *semiosis*.

1. Communication in Neighboring Disciplines

The following outline of neighboring disciplines in which the concept of communication is a key term does not intend to suggest a clearcut division between semiotics and nonsemiotic disciplines. While all of the following fields of communication research have at some point been subsumed under the more general framework of semiotics (cf. Thayer 1982), some have remained relatively independent of semiotics.

1.1 Various Interdisciplinary Connections

In a number of sciences, the concept of communication is basic to subfields which appear as independent areas of semiotic research in this handbook. Thus, the field of nonverbal communication is an academic branch of social psychology. The delimitation of communicative and noncommunicative forms of behavior is one of its most fundamental problems. Zoosemiotics, institutionally a branch of biology, and more particularly ethology (cf. Smith 1977a) raise the problem of the phylogenetic origin and the "design features" of communication (see Language 3.). Tembrock (1971) defines this field under the term *biocommunication*.

Basic research in the field is pursued by the disciplines of information and communication theory (cf. Bormann 1980). The models of communication discussed below have their origin in these theories. The discipline which imprinted its character on the earlier of these models is communications engineering. Its further development takes place within cybernetics, cognitive science, and systems theory (cf. Nöth 1989).

1.2 Cultural Anthropology and Social Science

In a tradition initiated by anthropologists and anthropological linguists, such as Sapir, Whorf, Malinowski, Firth, Leach (1976), and Lévi-Strauss (cf. Schmitz 1975), *communication* has become a key term for the analysis of societies and cultures. The thesis proposed by G. Bateson (cf. La Barre 1964: 191) that "all culture is communication" epitomizes the broad scope of the concept in cultural anthropology. This tradition was particularly influential for the development of modern semiotics. Significantly, it was the anthropologist Margaret Mead who at the 1962 Indiana University Conference on Paralinguistics and Kinesics introduced *semiotics* as a new term for the study of "patterned communications in all modalities" (cf. Sebeok et al., eds. 1964: 5).

A branch of anthropological linguistics which has been influential for sociolinguistics is Hymes's *ethnography of communication* (cf. Schmitz 1975). Its objects of study are communication situations and the functions of speech. In a critical extension of Chomsky's concept of competence, Hymes (1972) develops a theory of *communicative competence* to study the varieties of language codes in sociological groups and the command of these codes by individual speakers.

In sociology, Habermas further extends the theory of communicative competence to cover all "general structures of possible speech situations" (1971: 102). This research is dedicated to the rule system "according to which we generate situations of possible discourse in general" (ibid.). For Habermas, communication is not restricted to verbal and nonverbal "discourse" but also includes *communicative acts* without actual exchange of information (ibid.: 114–15).

1.3 Journalism and Mass Media Research

In mass media research, interdisciplinary studies in propaganda analysis, content analysis, and public opinion research have formed the field of communication research. Techniques of persuasion, information transfer, and opinion leading are among the topics of this field of research (cf. Schramm, ed. 1963, Corner & Hawthorn, eds. 1980). More recently, a discipline called communication science has emerged from this field of study which "seeks to understand the production, processing, and effects of symbol and signal systems by developing testable theories, containing lawful generalizations" (Berger & Chaffee, eds. 1987: 17). For semiotic aspects of this field of research, see ibid.: 130–32, Kroepsch (1976), and Bentele, ed. (1981).

1.4 Communication Theory in Psychology

In the areas of psychotherapy, psychiatry, and psychoanalysis, Bateson et al. (1956), Ruesch (cf. 1972), Watzlawick et al. (1967), and others have developed a general theory of human behavior based on a theory of communication. Within this approach, psychopathologies, especially schizophrenia, are defined as a disturbance of communication, and their analysis and therapy are seen as a particular communication situation. As the title of Ruesch's collection of earlier papers, *Semiotic Approaches to Human Relations* (1972), indicates, research in this area, which was first developed within communication theory, was later placed within the framework of a semiotic theory of behavior. A key concept of this direction of research, *metacommunication*, is discussed below.

2. Communication and Semiosis

Before an analysis of the process of communication, the field of communicative phenomena has to be separated from the sphere of noncommunicative events. The diversity of approaches to this fundamental problem is similar to that encountered in the discussion of the delimitation of signs from nonsemiotic phenomena (see Sign 1.3). In a pansemiotic perspective, communication is any form of semiosis. In contrast to this view, there are many narrower definitions of communication which introduce additional criteria and define communication as a particular mode of semiosis. Also, the concept of the communicative function of language is used in a narrow and a broad sense.

Instead of postulating a clear-cut boundary between communicative and noncommunicative phenomena, a gradual transition may be conceived going from the more rudimentary to the more complex modes of interaction. The order of the following sections suggests such a field beginning with unilateral semiosis and continuing with simple endosemiotic interactions, bilateral, intentional, linguistic, and finally metacommunication. However, a unified integration of the diverse concepts discussed here is not intended. The discussion is resumed in the chapter on nonverbal communication. Elsewhere, within the framework of zoosemiotics, the theories of the biological levels of interaction and of the design features of communication also suggest a gradual transition from noncommunicative to communicative modes of interaction. From a different perspective, Kelkar gives an outline of the field of semiosis which distinguishes various degrees of "primitivity" of communicative events (1984: 112–14).

2.1 *"Unilateral" Semiosis*

A representative of a pansemiotic idea of communication, according to which the most elementary forms of semiosis are already "communicative," is Meyer-Eppler. In his definition, communication is the "reception and processing of physically, chemically or biologically detectable *signals* by a living being" (1959: 1). According to this theory, any information processing by individual organisms (but not by machines) constitutes an instance of communication. Active cooperation of the signal source is not required. The source can even be an inanimate object. Most semioticians would reject applying the term *communication* to this type of *unilateral semiosis*. Semiosis without any activity on the side of the signal source certainly constitutes the lowest threshold of the semiotic field. The role of the participant in this one-sided communication situation is that of an observer. Meyer-Eppler (ibid.) defines it as unilateral communication and distinguishes between *observation* and *diagnosis* as its two subtypes (for bilateral communication see 2.3). In observational communication, an observer perceives and processes signals from an inanimate source. This communicative situation is typical of semiosis in physics and chemistry. In diagnostic communication, the signals originate with an animate emitter of signals. This form of unidirectional semiosis from one organism to another is typical of observations in biology, medicine, and psychology.

The nonstandard expansion of the concept of communication to include unilateral semiosis makes communication largely synonymous with semiosis in general as defined by Peirce and Morris. When Morris defines semiosis as a "process in which something is a sign to some organism" (1946: 366), no second participant is implied in this situation either.

2.2 *Bilateral Interaction between Machines or Cells*

Among those who define communication as mutual interaction between two entities, some researchers propose a still very broad concept which includes entities such as machines or biological cells.

2.2.1 SYSTEMIC INTERACTION

In cybernetics and systems theory, communication is often the interaction between any two systems. Thus, Klaus (1969) in his dictionary of cybernetics defines communication as "the exchange of information between dynamic systems capable of receiving, storing, or transforming information." This definition of communication also includes processes of interaction between machines.

2.2.2 ENDOSEMIOTIC INTERACTION

For other systems theorists, the origins of communication are located within the biological sphere of life. Thus, Rosnay describes the molecules of life as "informational individuals" with memory and the capability of recognition (1975: 135). The exchange of information in this chemical process of communication takes place on the basis of the genetic code (see Code 5.1). According to Rosnay (ibid.), the "history of communication" reaches from communication between molecules and biological cells to interactions between organisms and finally between human beings. This concept of communication in the biological sphere refers to the concept of semiosis which Sebeok describes as the field of endosemiotics (1976: 17), while the following concepts of communication, which define the term as interaction between two organisms, fall into the domains of zoosemiotics or anthroposemiotics. For an endosemiotic interpretation of molecular biology, see also Prodi (1988).

2.3 Bilateral Communication

The inclusion of unilateral interaction in the definition of communication is not very typical of communication theory on the whole. For the most part, communication is defined as a bilateral interaction between at least two organisms.

2.3.1 FROM UNILATERAL SEMIOSIS TO COMMUNICATION

A communication theorist who objects to a pansemiotic concept of communication which includes endosemiotic or unilateral events is Cherry (1957: 63). For him, observation and diagnosis are not yet communication because "Nature as a source of information is uncooperative" and incapable of any response to semiotic stimuli. An observed signal in unilateral semiosis, according to Cherry, is only a *causal sign*, since "not all signs are communicative signs. For example, black clouds are a sign of rain, but we do not communicate with Mother Nature [. . .]. The clouds do not in turn respond to us; we share nothing with them" (1980: 252).

Thus, communication is only a part of the larger field of semiosis, and causal semiosis is its other major area. However, the distinction between these two forms of semiosis is not clearcut. Cherry himself suggests a gradual transition from semiosis by direct causation with inevitable and automatic responses (causal semiosis), to semiosis with semi-automatic responses (animal semiosis), to still more flexible and finally to free manners of response (human semiosis) (1957: 221). For a more recent proposal to distinguish between (unilateral) semiotic events and (bilateral) communicative events, see Kelkar (1984).

2.3.2 BILATERAL INTERACTION BETWEEN ORGANISMS

A very broad concept of communication based on the criterion of mutual interaction between organisms is represented by Shannon & Weaver. They define communication as "all the procedures by which one mind may affect another. This, of course, involves not only written and oral speech, but also music, the pictorial arts, the theatre, the ballet, and in fact all human behavior" (1949: 3). Any form of nonverbal behavior can thus become communicative. Ruesch describes this process of transformation from behavior to communication as follows:

An action becomes a message when it is perceived, either by the self or by other people. In other words, signals in transit become messages when there is a receiver which, at the destination, can evaluate the meaning of these signals. Such a definition includes communication between human beings and animals, as well as between animals. As a matter of fact, all biological organisms, including plants, receive, evaluate and send messages. In brief, *communication is an organizing principle of nature.* (1972: 82–83)

2.3.3 CONGRUENCE IN BILATERAL INTERACTION

Bilateral semiotic interaction as defined by Shannon & Weaver or Cherry does not yet imply any *congruence* between the sender's message and the receiver's interpretation. But this feature of congruence is an additional distinctive criterion set up in some definitions of communication. It is a feature which is already suggested by the etymology of the word, which implies "a common sharing of information." A clear formulation of the criterion of congruence is given by Richards, who writes: "Communication [. . .] takes place when one mind so acts upon its environment that another mind is influenced, and in that other mind an experience occurs which is like the experience in the first mind, and is caused in part by that experience" (1928: 177). However, Richards has to admit that congruence in communication is a matter of degree: "The two experiences may be more or less similar, and the second may be more or less dependent upon the first" (ibid.).

2.4 Intention, Communication, and Signification

A still stronger criterion for the definition of communication is *intentionality*. This criterion has been used to divide the semiotic field into two large areas, semiotics of communication and semiotics of signification. But it has to be pointed out that other differentiations between communication and signification have been made in semiotics.

2.4.1 INTENTIONALITY

Intention involves volition and goal-directed activity. In communication, intention is the addresser's conscious attempt to influence the addressee by means of a message, and the addressee's response is a reaction based on the assumption of intentions on the part of the addresser. Most visible bodily expressions of emotion are unintentional. For a more detailed discussion of intentionality and awareness, see also Nonverbal Communication (3.2).

In a semiotic tradition reaching from Buyssens (1943) to Prieto (1966; 1975a) and Mounin (1970e; 1981), intentionality has been discussed as a distinctive feature of communication. For Prieto (1966: 20; cf. Hervey 1982), every communicative act presupposes an intention on the part of the sender, which has to be identifiable on the part of the receiver. Only under these conditions are signs—in Prieto's terminology *signals*—transmitted. Without a sender's intention, information observed by the receiver is not a signal but only an index. While the transmission of signals is defined as communication, the transmission of indices is called signification (Prieto 1975c).

2.4.2 SEMIOTICS OF COMMUNICATION AND OF SIGNIFICATION

Both communication and signification are described as parts of the semiotic field in this tradition. The two areas of research are discussed as semiotics of communication and of signification. While semiotics of communication studies only intentional semiosis, semiotics of signification includes processes of observation and diagnosis (see 2.1). However, there are many difficulties with the criterion of intentionality in semiotic research. For the psychological and philosophical problems with the determination of intentionality, see Kalkofen (1983: 149–54).

2.4.3 OTHER CONCEPTS OF COMMUNICATION AND SIGNIFICATION

The terminological differentiation between *communication* and *signification* in the sense of Prieto has not become generally accepted in semiotics (cf. also Rey 1978a, Culler 1981b). Remarkably, Eco gives an almost opposite definition of the two terms. For Eco, any flow of information from a source to a destination is a process of communication, even the passage of a signal from machine to machine (1976: 8–9). But signification is the higher form of semiotic interaction, where the destination must be a human being and "the signal is not a mere stimulus but arouses an interpretive response in the addressee" (ibid.: 8). This process also presupposes a code.

Thus, for Eco the semiotics of communication is the more comprehensive field which includes the semiotics of signification. Communication is possible without signification, but signification presupposes communication. The relationship between communication and signification for Prieto is thus quite the reverse of that for Eco. But for the latter, the criterion of intentionality is irrelevant.

2.5 Communication and Language

Language use is evidently always a process of communication according to all definitions discussed above. Yet, when linguists discuss the communicative function of language, they often imply that language may also be used with noncommunicative functions. For some linguists, verbal interaction *is* communication, and *communication* is the general cover term for all functions of language. In this sense, Jakobson speaks of the six functions of verbal communication (see Function 3.2).

Other linguists restrict the term *communication* to only one of several functions of language, generally the most important one. In this sense, Martinet defines communication as the central function of language, which refers to "the necessity of making oneself understood" (1960: 18). Other functions include the expressive and the appellative function, and these are explicitly defined as being noncommunicative (François 1969: 75). For another important distinction between the communicative and other functions of language which has been proposed by Leont'ev, see Gröschel (1983: 25). See also Function (3).

2.6 Appendix on Metacommunication

The concept of metacommunication was first developed in the context of psychopathology. In the form of the *metacommunicative axiom* it was expanded to be an inevitable factor in any act of human semiosis. Yet, for the semiotic relevance of this principle, the difference between actual and only potential semiosis should be taken into consideration.

2.6.1 METACOMMUNICATION
In their theory of schizophrenia, Bateson et al. first introduced the term *metacommunication* to refer to "the ability to communicate about communication, to comment upon the meaningful actions of oneself and others" (1956: 208). Thus, metacommunication is not scientific metalanguage (cf. Schlieben-Lange 1975) but a principle of everyday social interaction. Metacommunication is often not a verbal message (for the latter see Jakobson's metalinguistic function in Function 3.2) but a form of nonverbal communication. For example, by winking at the hearer, a speaker may turn the meaning of his or her verbal message into its ironic opposite.

2.6.2 METACOMMUNICATIVE AXIOM
Bateson et al. (1956) argue that the ability for metacommunication is an essential factor of social interaction and that its loss may be the cause of schizophrenia. Watzlawick et al. go further and claim that metacommunication is omnipresent in any instance of social interaction. With their metacommunicative axiom, Watzlawick et al. postulate the thesis of the impossibility of not communicating (1967: 48–51). After emphasizing the fact that communication occurs verbally and in many nonverbal modalities, the inventors of this axiom argue: "Behavior has no opposite. There is no such thing as nonbehavior. . . . One cannot *not* behave" (ibid.: 48). Thus, any form of behavior in social interaction is of semiotic relevance. "One cannot *not* communicate" (ibid.: 49). Even silence and "nonbehavior" have the character of a message.

2.6.3 ACTUAL AND POTENTIAL METACOMMUNICATION
The metacommunicative axiom of the impossibility in any situation not to communicate gives an incomplete account of communicative processes. It describes the act of communication primarily from the perspective of the emitter of signals and does not reflect adequately the receiver's activity. A permanent process of message transmission, as suggested by Watzlawick et al., presupposes a receiver with a permanent

attention to those messages. Such a receiver is evidently an idealistic abstraction. At most, it may describe the attention of an ideal psychotherapist. In everyday situations, however, no receiver is capable or willing to register all messages which an analyst might be able to discover. Since it is doubtful whether unintentional signals which are not perceived by anybody should be described as communicative processes at all, the metacommunicative axiom should be reduced to a potential factor in communication according to which all behavior may have a communicative function.

3. Models of Communication

Communication models are graphic representations of the elements of communication and the process of their interaction. The totality of these elements and their interrelation constitutes a communication system. Most traditional models represent communication as a sequence of semiotic events. Functional models of communication, as discussed by Bühler and Jakobson (see Function 3.), are alternatives to sequential representations. The following survey of communication models begins with the traditional linear model, continues with circular models, and finally discusses models that reject the concept of information flow and emphasize the autonomy of the interacting organisms. Only the most basic elements of communication will be discussed. For an attempt to incorporate neurological, psychological, sociological, referential, and many other factors into a comprehensive model of communication, see, for example, Meier (1969) and Dingwall (1980). For further determinants of communication, see also Firth's "context of situation" (Meaning 3.4).

3.1 Basic Elements: the Communication Chain

The basic elements of a communicative process can be illustrated from Shannon &

Weaver's (1949) model. This communication model is deficient because of its linear character (cf. Thayer 1972, Köck 1980). But in the history of communication theory, Shannon & Weaver's model has been so influential that it cannot be ignored in a handbook of semiotics.

3.1.1 SHANNON & WEAVER'S COMMUNICATION CHAIN

Shannon & Weaver (1949: 7) represent a communication system in the linear form of a *communication chain* (Fig. C 1). They emphasize that this model is restricted to the technical process and excludes semantic aspects and the pragmatic aspect of effectiveness (ibid.: 4). Taking the example of vocal communication, the stations of the information flow in this chain are as follows: The *information source* is the speaker's brain. His or her vocal organs are the *transmitter*. The *signals* are the sound waves of the voice. Their *channel* is the air. On the way to their *destination*, the hearer's brain, the signal is received by the hearer's organs of hearing. They are defined as the *receiver*. Undesired distortions of sound may come from a *noise source*.

3.1.2 SIGNAL, MESSAGE, AND SIGN

From a semiotic point of view, Shannon & Weaver's model and most other communication models do not represent signs as one of their elements. Not signs but signals are transmitted in the process of communication. Signals are only the energetic or material vehicles of signs, their physical form. In this sense, a signal is a physical event, while a sign is a mental process (see Sign 1.1.2).

Implicitly, however, signs do appear in Shannon & Weaver's model, namely, as an element of the *message*. The message (ibid.: 10) is defined as a sequence of elementary symbols (where symbols in this terminology refer to signs; see Sign 1.1.3). Thus, the message is equivalent to a text (see Text Semiotics 3.1). Messages are associated with meanings and require the mental process of encoding and decoding (see Code 2.1.2), and this is why the message in Shannon & Weaver's model appears between source and transmitter and be-

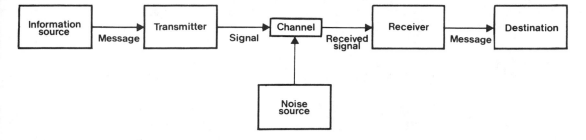

Fig. C 1. The communication chain according to Shannon and Weaver (1949: 7; modified drawing).

tween receiver and destination. This location indicates the cognitive process of the communicator's transformation of physical signals into en- or decoded signs. For a broader concept of communication, beyond the exchange of messages, see Objects (4.1).

3.1.3 CHANNEL AND MEDIUM

According to Shannon & Weaver (1949: 7), the *communication channel* is defined as the physical or technical medium of transmission, in which the signal moves from the transmitter to the receiver. Examples of such channels are the air in speech or the wire in telephony. Later models of communication define the channel in terms of the physical characteristics of the signal instead of its medium. Thus, for example, the channel in telephony would be defined more generally as "electrical," not as "the wire." In this sense, Sebeok (1976: 30) gives the outline of a typology of communication channels distinguishing between *material* (gases, liquids, or solids) and *energetic* (chemical or physical) channels with *optical*, *tactile*, *acoustic*, *electric*, *thermal*, and other channels as the major subtypes of the physical channel (see Zoosemiotics 3.4). For further discussion of this typology of channels, see Wulff (1979). Other typologies of channel are based on the organs of perception with which the destination receives the signals. This leads to a classification into *visual*, *auditory*, *tactile*, *olfactory*, *thermal*, and *gustatory* channels (e.g., Scherer 1970: 3–4).

Closely related to the concept of channel is the term *medium*. (For a discussion of this concept see Posner 1985a.) With many authors the two concepts are interchangeable in meaning. Thus, Tembrock uses the term *medium* in the sense of *channel* as discussed above (1971: 135). In terms of the general theory of signs, the medium has been equated with the *expression-form* (see Hjelmslev 3.) of a sign system (cf. Wulff 1979). Less appropriate is the use of *medium* as a term to designate a code. This sense is implied when some authors refer to the written or spoken language as a medium (e.g., Maser 1971: 9).

A much extended definition of medium is common in media research, where the concept refers to the distinctive features of radio, film, television, photography, the comics, the book, news magazines, or other mass media (cf. Knilli 1979). A medium is here broadly defined as the technical and socioeconomic apparatus of the propagation of messages (which comprises Shannon & Weaver's transmitter, channel, and receiver). For the semiotics of the mass media, cf. also Bentele, ed. (1981).

3.1.4 SENDER-RECEIVER, ADDRESSER-ADDRESSEE

Many communication models do not represent the distinction between the mental and the physiological (or technical) processes in communication which Shannon & Weaver (Fig. C 1) make in their dichotomies of source/transmitter and receiver/destination. When within each communicating organism no such distinctions are made, a different terminology is used. The most neutral concepts for the two communicating organisms were suggested by Morris (1946: 360), namely, *communicator-communicatee*. These terms, however, are rarely used. The terms introduced by Jakobson in his model of communicative functions (see Function 3. 2), *addresser-addressee*, have been very successful.

The word formations chosen by Morris and Jakobson for the designation of the receiver/destination side, *communicatee* and *addressee*, suggest, with their suffixes *-ee*, a somewhat passive participant in the communication process. This connotation is avoided by the next most frequent terminological alternative, which is the dichotomy *sender-receiver*. These terms for the two participants in the communication process should not be confused with Shannon & Weaver's terminology, where the "receiver" refers only to half of the second participant's activities. A survey of other terms used to designate the two organisms in communicative interaction (cf. Stappers 1966) gives the following dichotomies which will be listed without further comment:

communicant A-communicant B
(Cherry 1957)
communicator-recipient
emitter-receiver
source-receiver
source-destination
encoder-decoder
speaker-listener/hearer
writer/author-reader

3.1.5 SIGN REPERTOIRE

An important expansion of the linear communication chain is the sign repertoire, often also identified with the code (q.v. 2.2). The first models with this element were introduced by Moles (1958: 163) and Meyer-Eppler (1959: 2). Figure C 2 is a modification of the version given by Meyer-Eppler, whose terms are adapted here in accordance with the above terminological discussion (but Shannon & Weaver's *receiver* has been replaced by the term *receptor* to avoid confusion with the term chosen for the addressee).

According to this model, both sender and receiver have their own individual sign repertoires SR_1 and SR_2. The sender performs a selection of signs from his repertoire SR_1 in order to form a message. The receiver performs a correlation of the received signals with elements of his sign repertoire. Both the sender's selection and the receiver's correlation are processes of understanding. Thus, the semantic dimension appears in the communication model. Communication as a process of mutual understanding is possible only where the sender selects signs from his repertoire (SR_1) which are also elements of the receiver's repertoire (SR_2). This common repertoire SR_3 is represented as the intersection of the sets SR_1 and SR_2 in Figure C 2.

3.2 Circular Processes in Communication

In communication theory, the linearity of the technological model was soon criticized as being an inadequate representation of the process of communication. Linearity suggests simple causality. The sender's activity appears as a cause which has a calculated effect on the receiver's mind. This suggests the interaction of an active with a passive participant. From an ideological perspective this is a model which suggests an almost total potential for the manipulation of the receiver. The only factor that seems to endanger this process is the element of noise. Evidently, communication is a more complex process than one of linear causality. The sender is not unaffected by the receiver's information processing. Thus, linearity becomes circularity.

3.2.1 SAUSSURE'S MODEL OF THE SPEECH CIRCUIT

A first circular communication model was outlined by Saussure (1916a: 28). His model of the speech circuit is represented in Figure C 3. Saussure described the path of acoustic signals (sound waves) as an information flow in two directions from a speaker to a hearer and back to the speaker. This is the model of a dialogue.

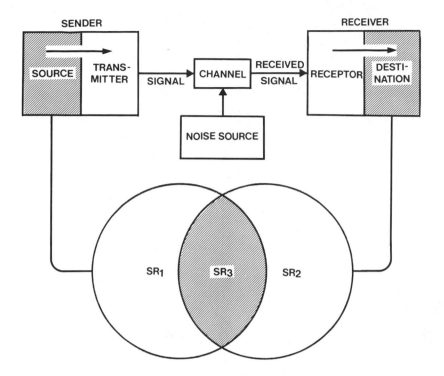

Fig. C 2. The sign repertoire (SR) in the communication process: SR_1: the sender's (active) sign repertoire, SR_2: the receiver's (passive) sign repertoire, SR_3: the common sign repertoire of both.

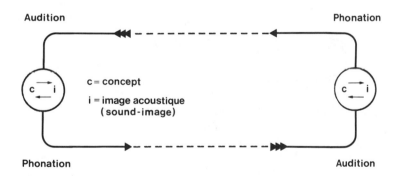

Fig. C 3. Saussure's model of the "speech circuit" (1916a: 28; redrawn) (cf. Saussure 3.1.1 and Fig. S 2).

As Figure C 3 shows, this circularity is still only the connection of two simple linear communication chains. However, Saussure also suggested a second circularity occurring in the mental process. It is indicated by the two arrows within the circles standing for the speaker and the hearer. These go both from c (the concept) to i (the sound-image) and from i back to c. It remains unclear, however, whether this circularity represents only a consecutive linearity occurring with the change of roles (speaker/hearer) in dialogue or whether it represents the simultaneous process of feedback, where the outgoing signal is checked by its sender for accuracy and efficiency.

3.2.2 FEEDBACK LOOPS

With cybernetics and systems theory, new concepts of circularity were introduced into the model of communication. *Feedback*, the sender's monitoring and adaptation of his or her own message by observation of its effects on the recipients, became a key term of systems theoretic communication theory (cf. Watzlawick et al. 1967, Nöth 1975a; 1977a: 83ff.; 1989). Feedback loops in communication models show that the information flow not only leads away from the sender but also is "fed back" into his or her own information-processing system. Several major types of feedback loops can be distinguished in communication. One classification concerns the path, the other the quality and effect of information.

With respect to the path of the information flow, three feedback loops are distinguished in the expanded communication model in Figure C 4. The first path is located in the participant's neurological system: The effects of the transmitter's activity (the muscular movements in writing or speaking, e.g.) are reported back to its source, the central nervous system. This process is called *proprioceptive feedback*. *Exteroceptive feedback* reports the signal output back to the sender's receptors and from there back to the source. It describes, for example, the sender's acoustic or visual self-control of his or her own speech or writing in a constant process of self-adaptation and self-correction. *Communicative feedback* occurs when the sender observes a reaction of the receiver and adjusts his or her message accordingly. The receiver's reaction is then a message, which is "fed back" as a signal to the original sender. This message can be verbal but is often also

nonverbal. The receiver's reaction can actually be observed (and thus cause corrections with the sender) or it can be anticipated. For the latter case of influence on the signal production by the sender's assumptions about potential effects, the term *feedforward* has also been suggested (cf. Mysak 1970).

With respect to the quality and effect of the message, the distinction between positive and negative feedback is relevant. *Negative feedback* influences the sender to correct or change the message because of observed undesired effects. It thus contributes to communicative homeostasis, the maintenance of a steady state. *Positive feedback* reinforces existing structures of the message and can thus, by uncontrolled repetition, lead to disturbances of communication or, if successful, to a change of the sign repertoire or code.

3.3 *Aspects of the Receiver's Autonomy*

In the course of the development from linear to circular models, communication theory has overcome the misleading idea of communication as an almost undisturbed flow of signals from a source to a destination. Yet, the improvements introduced by cybernetics and systems theory have attracted new criticism. Two objections are most notable in the field of semiotics. The first has to do with the concept of *control*, which is implied in the systems theoretical model, and which suggests a process of optimization, efficiency, and the goal of congruence between sender and receiver (cf. also Laszlo 1972: 251). Closely related is the second objection, which criticizes the still inadequate representation of the role of the receiver. To overcome these objections, models have been developed which emphasize the receiver's autonomy in communication processes first in text semiotics, and more recently also in communication theory.

3.3.1 AUTOPOIESIS IN COMMUNICATION
The theory of autopoietic systems (see System 1.2.4) was originally developed within the framework of a biological theory of cognition

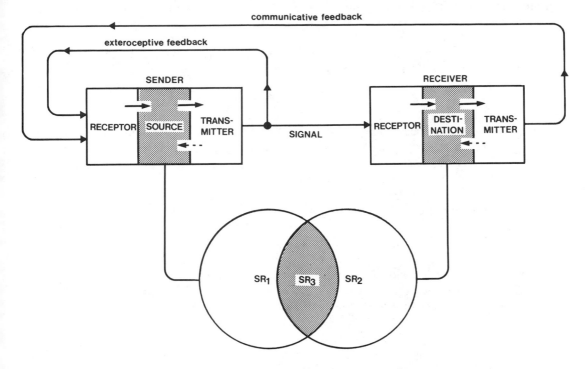

Fig. C 4. Feedback in communication (adapted from Meyer-Eppler 1959: 4; the broken arrow represents proprioceptive feedback).

(Maturana & Varela 1972). Its model of communication is radically opposed to both the linear and the circular paradigms (cf. Jantsch 1980, Köck 1980). Communication, according to this theory, is not a transfer of "in-formation" and implies neither instruction nor representation as a mapping of the environment (Varela 1981: 21). Communication is rather seen as a process of interaction between structurally coupled autonomous organisms in which "the domain of possible states of the emitter and the domain of possible states of the receiver must be homomorphic, so that each state of the emitter triggers a unique state in the receiver" (Maturana 1978: 54). Congruence of the cognitive domains of sender and receiver is thus not the goal, but so-called consensual domains are a prerequisite of the process of communication. Cognition here coincides with re-cognition, presentation becomes representation: "The verbal description of a colorful

sunset transmits nothing of the real experience, if not by way of remembering a comparable experience of one's own" (Jantsch 1980: 203). Thus, autopoietic systems behave self-referentially. They form *semiotically closed systems* (Uexküll 1978; 1981b, Köck 1980: 100), since their cognition takes place only as the triggering of neural processes that are specified by the system's own structure.

This solipsistic account of communication as interaction between two closed systems appears to be revolutionary. It seems to conflict radically with the traditional circular paradigm according to which dialogic exchange, conversation in the etymological sense of a "turning around together," appears as the prototype of communication. Yet, on closer examination this apparently revolutionary account turns out to incorporate elements of the traditional theories of communication. Evidently Maturana's and Varela's concept of closure refers, in the last analysis, to the dependence of communication on a common code, which is the semiotic equivalent of the "consensual domain." Semiotics, too, claims that only those signals can be emitted by the sender and understood by the receiver which were previously internalized in the communicators' codes. Thure von Uexküll (1981b: 14) demonstrates that both Jacob von Uexküll's biosemiotic functional circle (1940: 8; see Zoosemiotics 3.2.1) and Wiener's cybernetic control system already have this feature of autonomous closure: both the biological and the cybernetic systems react to their environment only according to their inner needs, that is, their desired state.

But how are processes such as creativity and learning compatible with the principle of autonomous closure? The difficulty of this aspect of the theory of autopoiesis is partially of a terminological nature. These processes are eminently communicative phenomena in terms of information theory. However, Maturana defines creativity and dialogical exchange (expansions of consensual domains) as "pre- or anticommunicative interactions" (1978: 54–55). Nevertheless, these phenomena are dealt with in the theory of autopoiesis. Maturana and Varela describe them as strictly state-determined processes of self-generation and -transformation of the autonomous system: The autonomous organism develops in "an endless sequence of interactions with independent entities that select its changes of state but do not specify them" (1972: 35, 51).

3.3.2 THE TEXT SEMIOTIC ROLE OF THE RECEIVER

Aesthetics, semiotics of literature, and text semiotics have a longer tradition of theories which emphasize the autonomous role of the recipient (or more traditionally the interpreter) in textual and aesthetic processes of communication. With growing skepticism about the "intentional fallacy" of focusing on the author as the hermeneutic key to the work of art, text semiotics and the *theory of reception* have turned to the reader (or viewer) in the process of interpretation (cf. Eco 1979; for a survey of reception theory see Warning, ed. 1975, Fokkema & Kunne-Ibsch 1977). Textual *openness* has become a key term which presupposes the potential autonomy of the recipient in this process (see Aesthetics 4.1.2, Literature 4.2).

A text semiotic communication model which is based on this assumption of an autonomous receiver is the one developed by Koch (1971b: 112). In its core it shows a reversal in the direction of the arrows which traditionally indicate the flow of information which leads to the constellation *sender* → *text* ← *receiver*. Instead of information flow, the arrows here represent the participants' focus, their attention and selective behavior in view of the *a priori* undetermined potential of semiotic structures in the text. For a theory of literature which analyzes literary texts as a social system with autonomous agents in communicative interaction, see Schmidt (1980) and System (3.1.4).

Function

Function is a key term in the study of texts, communication, and semiotic structures and systems. However, definitions of the term are often vague or quite divergent, ranging from a strictly formal concept to a quasi-synonym of *meaning*. This broad semantic spectrum is paralleled by definitions given to the term in mathematics, linguistics, and the social sciences. In this chapter, two main concepts of semiotic function will be distinguished: *structural functions* and *functions of use* or *pragmatic functions*. The former are functions *in* language, the latter are functions *of* language and communication. Both concepts are central to a direction or even school of semiotics which has been designated as *functional semiotics* (Hervey 1982). Main proponents of functional semiotics are the Prague School semioticians, Jakobson, Buyssens, Martinet, Prieto, and Mounin.

1. The Concept of Function

Definitions of function, as established in various sciences, are based on criteria such as relation, purpose, and instrumentality. They range from a purely formal or structural notion to a pragmatic, use-oriented concept.

1.1 Function as Instrumentality and Finality

Function in a general sense is the specific contribution of a part to a whole. The term connotes instrumentality, utility, or even finality and presupposes the holistic framework of a system. The particular contribution of a function to the system is often defined as a purpose, but the latter concept is occasionally criticized for its teleological and vitalistic connotations (cf. Stegmüller 1969b). An example of this general notion of function is its definition in physiology, where the function of an organ is defined as the normal and specific performance which the organ fulfils within and for the body as a whole.

1.2 Function in the Social Sciences

Functionalism was a trend in sociology (R. K. Merton), anthropology (A. Radcliffe-Brown, B. Malinowski), and psychology (W. James, J. Dewey) in the first half of this century. By functions, these approaches to the social sciences understand structures which fulfil a task for the maintenance of the social system. According to Stegmüller, a functional analysis wants to explain the existence of structures, processes, or features of the system by specifying their tasks or functions for the adequate functioning of the system (1969b: 558). The effect of a function on a social or psychological system can be intended by or unconscious to the individual or group. The former are called *manifest functions*, the latter are called *latent functions*. For a semiotic functionalism in ethnography, see Bogatyrev (1937).

1.3 Mathematical and Logical Functions

In mathematics, a function is a relation between two variable quantities, a set of arguments (*A*) and a set of values (*B*) for every argument (cf. Klaus & Buhr, eds. 1964: 437). If *x* is an element of *A*, and *y* an element of *B*, the function $y = f(x)$ indicates that to every *x* there is a relation of correspondence that associates a value *y* to *x*. Set theoretically, functions are also defined as operations of *mapping* by which the elements of *A* are mapped into the class of *B*.

In symbolic logic, expressions such as "the capital of" can be defined as standing for a function which, for a country as argument, gives a city as its value. Thus, Reichenbach (1947: 81–82) interprets the function $f(x)$ as a proposition consisting of function-name (or propositional function, *f*) with a certain syntactic relation to an argument-name (*x*).

1.4 Linguistic Functions

The concept of function in linguistics has been investigated by Gardiner (1932: 141), Verburg (1952), Mounin (1967), François (1969), Helbig (1969), Pelc (1971), Busse (1975), Holenstein (1978a), Martinet (1978), Jachnow (1981), and Gröschel (1983). For *function* as a key term in systemic linguistics, see Joia & Stenton (1980: 27–55) and Ellis (1987). Although by no means a homogeneous school of research, functionalism in linguistics generally defines itself in opposition to formalism. However, linguists have not only adopted "functionalist" definitions of function, as in the social sciences, but there is also a "formalist" definition, as in mathematics and logic.

1.4.1 HJELMSLEV'S FORMALIST CONCEPT OF FUNCTION
Hjelmslev defined function in a logico-mathematical sense as a relation of dependence be-

tween language entities called *functives* (1943: 33–41). Such functions exist within the text and within the system. An entity has a function insofar as it "has dependences with other entities." An entity functions in a certain way, insofar as it fulfils a certain role or assumes a certain position in the text (cf. ibid.: 34). A *sign function* (ibid.: 47–48) is a relation between two functives called *expression* and *content* (cf. Hjelmslev 3.1).

1.4.2 FUNCTIONAL APPROACHES TO LANGUAGE
According to Martinet, "a linguistic functionalist is one who tries to determine how speakers manage to reach their communicative ends by means of a language and who is ready to classify and hierarchize facts accordingly, even at the expense of formal identities" (1979: 142). Functional as opposed to formalist or autonomous theories of language explain linguistic form or structure in relation to meaning, situational use, text, or context and its role within the system. There are functional approaches to phonology and morphology (cf. Martinet 1962), syntax (Kuno 1987), grammar in general (Dik 1978, Halliday 1985), semantics (cf. Coppieters & Goyvaerts, eds. 1978), text or discourse analysis (cf. ibid. and Halliday 1973; 1978; 1985), and linguistic change (Martinet 1955). The study of language function as language use merges in many respects with linguistic pragmatics (cf. Beck 1980). For the functionalism of Prague School linguistics, see also Structuralism (1.1).

1.5 Structure and Function

Form (or structure) and function as well as structuralism and functionalism are occasionally opposed in a false dichotomy: structures are seen as merely static, while functions are seen as dynamic entities (but see Structure 1.1.2). However, as Koch points out (1983: 40), there are no forms or structures without function and there is no function without structure. All semiotic structures are defined by their functions in text, system, and communication, and functions can only be described as relations between structures. Benveniste even defines structure in terms of functions: "That which gives the character of a structure to the form is that the constituent parts serve a function" (1966: 20–21). Thus, both in synchrony and in diachrony, structures and functions are interdependent.

2. Structural Functions

The role which a semiotic element or relation has for the constitution, maintenance, and adequate functioning of the sentence, text, or semiotic system is its structural function. Ultimately, every structural function also depends on communicative functions, i.e., the use of signs and texts in communicative situations.

2.1 Functions within the System

A semiotic system functions adequately as long as its elements and structures remain sufficiently distinct or differentiated. The semiotic principle which guarantees this functional differentiation is called the *principle of pertinence* (or *relevance*). It was first established in linguistics and later also applied to the study of nonlinguistic systems.

2.1.1 PERTINENCE IN LINGUISTICS

The principle of pertinence was first formulated in the framework of functionalist phonology (see Structuralism 1.1.3). It was later extended to other levels of linguistic analysis from the *morpheme* to the *texteme* (cf. Koch 1971a). In phonology, pertinence is the property by which a speech sound (a *phone*) is structurally opposed and thus distinct from another speech sound of the same system. This property is called the *distinctive feature* of the phoneme. Phonological distinctiveness has a phonetic basis (the difference must be audible), but the decisive test of distinctiveness in *phonemes*, the commutation test (see Structuralism 1.1.2), has to relate the difference in sound to a difference in meaning, which is a feature of a higher level of linguistic analysis, the morpheme. Structural function is

thus "the link between a unit of a lower level and a unit of a higher level of analysis" (Buyssens 1967: 8).

In the opposition between /b/ and /p/, the feature 'voiced' is the distinctive feature which constitutes the pertinence of the English phoneme /b/ in opposition to /p/ because it has the function to distinguish between words such as *pin* and *bin*. From this primary phonological function, which is related to the paradigmatic axis of language, Martinet distinguishes a further function, related to the syntagmatic axis of language (1960: 53). Its purpose is to differentiate sounds as successive elements of the phonetic chain of sounds. This function of phonetic demarcation is called the *function of contrast*.

The principle of pertinence is related to Pike's (1967) *emic-etic* dichotomy (for which see Structuralism 1.1.3), but *emic* is not a synonym of *pertinent*. An emic unit, such as a phoneme or morpheme, is an invariant form obtained from the reduction of a class of variant forms to a limited number of abstract units. The etic unit, the phone or *morph*, consists of individual and contextual variants of this abstract unit. Thus, the emic unit comprises a whole class of pertinent features.

2.1.2 STRUCTURAL FUNCTIONS IN OTHER SEMIOTIC SYSTEMS

Prieto extends the principle of pertinence to the study of nonlinguistic codes (1966: 63–71; 1975b). In his analysis, there are distinctive features differentiating structures of the level both of expression (signifier) and of content (signified). Taking the example of the traffic sign "No Cycling," he shows that the features 'white disk' and 'red circle' are distinctive at the expression-plane. Their function is opposed to the 'blue disk' of the traffic sign indicating "Route for Cyclists." Nondistinctive features of the expression-plane are features such as '172 cm high' vs. '180 cm high.' At the content-plane, the instruction 'for cyclists' is distinctive as opposed to the instruction 'for motor vehicles,' while the contextual information 'for this road going south' would be a nondistinctive content element of this traffic sign.

The principle of pertinence has been applied in the search for emic structures in a variety of semiotic codes. Among the functional units which have been postulated in various fields of semiotics are the *choreme* in architecture (q.v., 3.2.2), the *chereme* in sign languages (q.v., 2.3.2), the *kineme* in kinesics, the *proxeme* in proxemics, more generally the *figura* as the distinctive feature of second articulation in nonverbal codes (q.v., 4.2.1), and the *narreme*, *motifeme*, or *mytheme* in narrativity (q.v., 2).

2.2 Functions in Syntagmatic Structure

In the syntagmatic structure of language, structural functions have been described at the level of syntax and text.

2.2.1 SYNTACTIC FUNCTION
In traditional grammar, the function of a word was opposed to its nature (cf. Martinet 1979: 143). While *nature* refers to the value of a word by itself (for example, verb or noun), irrespective of its context, *function* describes the role and the additional values of this element within the sentence, for example, its being predicate or subject. *Function* is thus a purely relational term. Syntactic function is the relation between two or more elements of a sentence. Syntactic functions in this sense have also been studied under other designations. Fillmore (1968) speaks of cases (Agent, Object, etc.) as playing "roles" in sentences. For further approaches to functional syntax, see 1.4.2.

2.2.2 STRUCTURAL FUNCTIONS IN TEXTS
The term *textual function* (cf. Lotman & Pjatigorskij 1977), similar to *stylistic function*, is often used in the pragmatic sense of function as use. In a syntagmatic sense, function is a key concept in the text linguistic theory of *Functional Sentence Perspective*, in Halliday's functional text linguistics, and in a different sense in the theory of narrativity. The theory of Functional Sentence Perspective studies the function of textual elements by setting the knowledge they activate into a 'perspective' of textual importance or *informativity* (cf.

Beaugrande & Dressler 1981 for a survey). Halliday (1970: 143; 1973; cf. Ellis 1987) uses the term *textual function* in a partially syntagmatic-relational sense, defining it as follows:

> Language has to provide for making links with itself and with features of the situation in which it is used. We may call this the *textual* function, since this is what enables the speaker or writer to construct "texts," or connected passages of discourse that is situationally relevant [. . .]. One aspect of the textual function is the establishment of cohesive relations from one sentence to another in a discourse.

In Propp's theory of *narrativity* (1928: 21–23), a function is understood as "an act of a dramatis personae defined from the point of view of its significance for the course of the action of a tale as a whole." Function is thus an element of meaning defined in its narrative context. For details see Narrative (2.2).

3. Pragmatic Functions

While structural functions refer to the functions of elements within the code or message, pragmatic functions refer to the use of messages in communicative situations. Such functions are occasionally called *communicative functions* (cf. Uhlenbeck 1978, Kolschanski 1984), but this term is also used in a narrower sense (Mounin 1967), in which it is a primary function of semiotic interaction opposed to other secondary or even noncommunicative functions (see Communication 2.5).

Three theories of pragmatic functions have been especially influential in semiotics, Bühler's *organon model*, Jakobson's *functions of verbal communication*, and Mukařovský's *system of semiotic functions*. The theory of language functions developed partly on the basis of Jakobson (Hymes 1962, Leech 1974: 47–68), partly on the basis of a critique of Jakobson (Leont'ev 1969, Beck 1980, Gröschel 1983), and in part on the basis of additional independent proposals for taxonomies of speech functions (Halliday 1970; 1973; 1978,

Robinson 1972, Condon 1977). In contrast to Bühler and Jakobson, the taxonomic approaches to speech functions seem to be less fundamental. Thus, Robinson (1972: 50) distinguishes fourteen and Halliday, in various phases of his work, distinguishes no fewer than twenty-five language functions (cf. Joia & Stenton 1980: 27–55).

3.1 Bühler's Organon Model

Plato was the first to discuss an instrumentalist definition of language. In his quotation of Socrates' words, "a name is an instrument (ὄργανον) of teaching and of separating reality" (Cratylus 388b). From this theory of language as an instrument, "an *organum* for one person's communicating with another about things," Bühler derives the name of his schema of language functions (1933b: 147, 164): the organon model of language (Fig. F 1; Bühler 1934: 28, and for further discussions see Hörmann 1967: 18–23, Wunderlich 1969a, Busse 1975: 213–16, Beck 1980: 164–76, Veltruský 1984, and various other papers in Eschbach, ed. 1984).

Bühler's organon model distinguishes three characteristic functions of language, which are also functions of signs in general: *representation*, *expression*, and *appeal*. These functions are determined according to the dominance of one of the three relata of the sign in a given situation of communication. The function of representation dominates whenever the focus of the message is on the referential object. When the focus is on the sender and the sign expresses his or her "interiority," the function is expression. The function of appeal dominates when the message focuses on the hearer "whose outer or inner behavior it directs just as other traffic signs do" (Bühler 1934: 28). The dominance of the function is also the criterion of a typology of signs. The sign is *symbol* when there is a predominantly representative function, it is *symptom* (or *index*) when the dominant function is expression, and it is *signal* when the dominant function is appeal.

Bühler's *principle of dominance* precludes a monadic view of sign and communication (1934: 30–33). Every factor of the organon is to some degree present in any act of communication. Although he does not dispute the general dominance of the representational function of language, Bühler restricts its functional relevance, emphasizing that the sign does not always refer to objects or states of affairs:

> Rather, the opposite is true, namely, that in the structure of the speech situation a special position is occupied just as much by the sender [. . .] as by the receiver [. . .]. They are not simply a part of what the communication is *about*, but they are the partners in the exchange, and therefore, in the last analysis, it is possible that the medial sound product indeed exhibits its own specific sign relation to the one and to the other. (1933b: 153)

3.2 Jakobson's Functions of Verbal Communication

Jakobson extended Bühler's organon model to a model of six "constitutive factors of verbal communication" (1960: 355), to which he correlated six corresponding functions of language (Fig. F 2). For further discussions of this model see Hymes (1962), Busse (1975), Holenstein (1975: 153–63), Beck (1980: 197–208), Coseriu (1981: 56–65), and Veltruský (1984). For applications of the model in other areas of the semiotic field, see Architecture (2.1), Advertising (4.), Zoosemiotics (4.1), and Poetry (1.2). Jakobson's six factors of speech events constitute a model of verbal communication, of which he gave the following outline:

> The ADDRESSER sends a MESSAGE to the ADDRESSEE. To be operative the message requires a CONTEXT referred to ("referent" in another, somewhat ambiguous, nomenclature), seizable by the addressee, and either verbal or capable of being verbalized; a CODE fully, or at least partially, common to the addresser and addressee (or in other words, to the encoder and decoder of the message); and, finally, a CONTACT, a physical channel and psychological connection between the addresser and the addressee, enabling both of them to enter and stay in communication. (1960: 353)

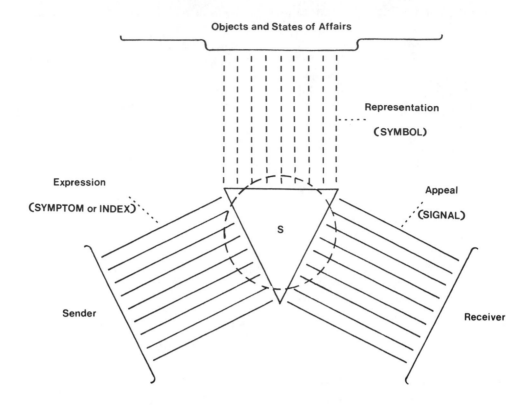

Fig. F 1. Bühler's organon model of language: "The circle in the middle symbolizes the concrete sound phenomenon. Three variable moments on it are capable of raising it in three different ways to the rank of a sign. The sides of the drawn-in triangle symbolize these three moments. The triangle encompasses, in one respect, less than the circle (principle of abstractive relevance). In another direction, however, it surpasses the circle, in order to indicate that the sensibly given constantly experiences an apperceptive enlargement. The bundles of lines symbolize the semantic functions of the (complex) language sign" (1934: 28; cf. 1933b: 164).

CONTEXT
(referential function)

ADDRESSER _ _ _ _ MESSAGE _ _ _ _ ADDRESSEE
(emotive function) (poetic function) (conative function)

CONTACT
(phatic function)

CODE
(metalingual function)

Fig. F 2. Jakobson's model of the constitutive factors and the corresponding functions of verbal communication (1960: 353, 357).

The functions of messages corresponding to each of these basic elements of communication are determined according to the communicative "orientation," the predominant focus on the respective factor of the communicative situation. In this respect, Jakobson followed Bühler's principle of dominance: every message may have several functions, but one function is often predominant or primary, while other functions play only a secondary role. A message with "a set (*Einstellung*) toward the referent, an orientation toward the context," has a predominantly *referential* function. Its information focuses on the cognitive aspect of language. This is Bühler's function of representation, but Jakobson's situational correlate is not an "object" but the context (see Meaning 2.3.1).

The *emotive* or *expressive* function focuses on the speaker's own attitude toward the content of the message. Interjections and emphatic speech are examples of language use with a predominantly emotive function. The *conative* function, Bühler's function of appeal, is oriented toward the addressee. Its purest grammatical expression is in the vocative and imperative (see also Isačenko 1964). The *phatic* function was discovered by Malinowski (1923: 315), who defined *phatic communion* as "a type of speech in which ties of union are created by a mere exchange of words" without conveying meaning (see also Laver 1975, B. Schmidt 1984). Jakobson adopted the term to describe "messages primarily serving to establish, to prolong, or to discontinue communication, to check whether the channel works ('Hello, do you hear me?'), to attract the attention of the interlocutor or to confirm his continued attention ('Are you listening?')" (1960: 355).

The *metalinguistic* function is exemplified by language referring to language and communication. Here, Jakobson resumed the distinction drawn by logicians between two levels of language use: object language is discourse about the nonlinguistic world, and metalanguage is discourse about language, grammar, or questions of terminology. Every definition fixing the usage of a term and every spelling rule is metalinguistic. Questions such as "What do you mean?" or "I don't follow you" exemplify the metalinguistic function in everyday communication. For Jakobson's *poetic* function, see Poetry (1.2).

3.3 Mukařovský's Semiotic Functions

Mukařovský develops his structuralist aesthetics within the framework of his functional theory of action (see Prague School Semiotics and Aesthetics 3.2). According to Mukařovský, "a function is the mode of a subject's self-realization vis-à-vis the external world" (1942: 40). Such behavior toward reality can be either direct or indirect, i.e., "by means of another reality" (ibid.). Mukařovský defines the direct modes of interaction with reality as *immediate* functions and distinguishes among these the *practical* and the *theoretical* functions:

> In *practical functions* the object is in the foreground, because the subject's self-realization is directed at a reorganization of the object, that is, reality. In the *theoretical function*, on the other hand, the subject is in the foreground, because its general and ultimate goal is the projection of a reality into the subject's consciousness.

In opposition to these immmediate functions, the mediated modes of "self-realization" are defined as *semiotic* functions (ibid.: 41):

> These also divide spontaneously for us if we apply to them the duality of orientation according to subject and object. A function in which the *object* is in the foreground is a *symbolic function*. In this case attention is focused on the effectiveness of the relation between the symbolized thing and the symbolic sign. [. . .] The semiotic function foregrounding the *subject* is the *aesthetic function*.

Elsewhere, Mukařovský had characterized the aesthetic sign as being represented by an autonomous and noncommunicative message (see Aesthetics 3.2). How is this aspect of autonomy compatible with the aspect of subjectivity (cf. Fietz 1982: 61–69)? By "focus on the subject" (1942: 42), Mukařovský does not refer to an emotional or expressive sign in the sense of Bühler and Jakobson. In his definition, the subject "is not an individual, but man in general." Therefore he can substantiate his view of aesthetic subjectivity as follows: "An aesthetic sign [. . .] is not an instrument [. . .]. It does not affect any particular reality as does a symbolic sign, but instead it reflects in itself reality as a whole [. . .]. Reality reflected as a whole is also organized in an aesthetic sign according to the image of the subject's organization" (ibid.). Reflection of reality is thus a reflection of collective consciousness, and from this point of view, the aesthetic function focuses on the subject in the sense of man in general.

Magic

Magic is a form of semiosis. Its origins are closely connected with the early history of semiotics. Its semiotic structure is determined by general semiotic principles. But according to the criteria valid for normal communicative acts, magic is based on a semiotic fallacy, a misjudgment of the pragmatic effect of signs and their semantic object relation. Viewing magic as a semiotic fallacy, however, is inadequate without taking the complementary perspective of magic as a potentially effective form of communication, according to which it may be seen as a semiotic therapy.

1. Origins of Semiotics in Magic

In the earliest beginnings of culture, magic was closely associated not only with science in general (Thorndike 1923, Hansen 1986) but also with semiotics in particular. The etymology of several basic semiotic concepts indicates that the origin of the science of signs may be found in the context of magic rituals. The English word *spell* still means both 'to name or print in order the letters of (a word)' and 'a spoken word believed to have magic power.' The old Germanic *rune* is not only a sign from the code of the runic alphabet, but the word also means 'charm,' 'magic incantation.' Another interesting case is the etymology of *glamor*, in the origi-nal sense of 'a magic spell,' 'bewitchment.' This word is a derivation from the word *grammar*, from the popular association of semiotic erudition with occult practices. The etymology of the German word *Bild* ('image') also contains a magic element, namely, the Germanic etymon *bil-, 'miraculous sign.'

This etymological evidence indicates that in the origins of our cultural history, the knowledge and use of letters, writing, and later also grammar was closely related to acquaintance with magical practices. Evidently such a connection continued to be assumed for many centuries. The cultural origins of pictures and art in general (cf. Kris 1952: 47–56, Koch, ed. 1982) are also to be found in the sphere of magic.

2. Magic as a Form of Semiosis

Magic practices operate by means of signs, and these signs are motivated by the same general principles valid for other forms of semiosis. For further aspects of magical semiosis see Lange-Seidl, ed. (1988).

2.1 Examples of Magical Semiosis

An Old English charm prescribes the burning of a dog's head as a remedy for a headache (cf.

Nöth 1977b). A more recent folkloristic formula (cf. Nöth 1986) recommends the utterance of the following conjuration as a therapy against fever: "Fever, fever, stay away. / Don't come in my bed today." These examples show that magic is a form of semiosis. In the first case there is a nonverbal icon representing the destruction of the disease. In the second case there is the speech act of a request, addressed to the disease. In both cases there is an addresser communicating a message to an unusual addressee.

2.2 Semantic Motivation of the Magical Sign

Magical signs are often semantically motivated by the kind of effect they are assumed to have. Frazer distinguished between magic according to the "law of similarity" (homeopathic magic) and magic based on the "law of contact" (contagious magic) (1922: 16). Jakobson reinterpreted these "laws" in terms of the metaphoric and metonymic poles of semiosis (1956: 258; cf. Rhetoric 2.3.1; see also Leach 1976: 29). In the semiotic categories of Peirce these types refer to iconic and indexical signs. Besides these two types of magic semiosis, there are also arbitrary, i.e., symbolic, magic signs (cf. Nöth; 1977b; 1986).

The forms of motivation of the magical sign have often been interpreted as the result of semantic fallacies. The magical icon has been interpreted as a case of the sophism *similia similibus evocantur* (like produces like). The magical index has been associated with the fallacies *post hoc, ergo propter hoc* (after it, therefore because of it) and *pars pro toto* (part for whole). This iconic or indexical motivation of signs, however, is so universal that it cannot be regarded as a specific feature of magic.

2.3 Forms and Typology of Magic

The following typology of magic from semiotic points of view gives only a general survey of the field.

2.3.1 BLACK AND WHITE MAGIC

According to the criterion of the assumed magic effect, folklorists distinguish between black and white magic. With white magic the agent calls for a positive event or wants to prevent a negative one. Black magic aims at negative effects or wants to avoid positive ones.

2.3.2 NONLINGUISTIC MAGICAL SIGNS

There are linguistic and nonlinguistic magical signs. Nonlinguistic magical signs have the form of nonverbal acts, visual images (magic icons), semiotic artifacts such as iconic amulets and talismans, and natural signs (indices), especially indexical (*pars pro toto*) amulets.

2.3.3 VERBAL MAGIC

Verbal magic can be explicit or implicit. The former is the overt use of language for magical purposes. The latter appears as the avoidance of language because of magical beliefs. Charms are examples of explicit magic. They either contain a speech act of conjuration or they are mere descriptions of nonverbal magical practices like instructions for magico-medical therapies. Another form of explicit verbal magic is the "magic of names." It is based on the assumption that the adoption, the knowledge, and the use of a name have an influence on the person bearing it. The major forms of implicit verbal magic are linguistic taboo and euphemism (cf. Bruneau 1952, Todorov 1973). Taboo is the avoidance of words because of the fear of their effect in use. Euphemism is the corresponding substitution for a tabooed word.

2.3.4 MANTIC CODES

Related to natural magical semiosis are the signs of *mantic codes* (cf. Guiraud 1971: 59–65), divination by the constellation of stars (*astrology*) or of earth (*geomancy*; cf. Jaulin 1970), by playing cards (*cartomancy*; cf. Lekomceva & Uspenskij 1977, Aphek & Tobin 1986), by the migration of birds (*auspices*), by water (*hydromancy*) and coffee reading, by the examination of the hand (*chiromancy*), or by other natural phenomena and artifacts. While magic semiosis aims at an active, although supernatural, influence on the world, mantic semiosis operates in the reverse direction. Mantic signs are interpreted as an index of supernatural forces determining the world. Unlike magic, the semiotic anomaly of mantic is not so much in the pragmatic dimension of the effect of signs but in the anomaly of a mantic addresser (the star, the hand, etc.) and the correspondence between the message and events in the world.

3. Magic as a Semiotic Fallacy

Since the end of the nineteenth century, several schools of anthropology have attempted to give an explanation of the phenomenon of magic (cf. Petzoldt, ed. 1978). With some simplification, two major approaches may be distinguished. The first approach, taking the "exterior" perspective of a scientific observer, wants to explain magic as a semiotic fallacy. The second approach, taking the "interior" perspective of the magic agents, describes magic as a potentially successful act of communication. Beginning with the first perspective, magic acts appear as forms of semiosis which in comparison to normal communicative acts show anomalies in their pragmatic and their semantic dimension.

3.1 Pragmatic Anomaly in the Magical Act

The specific pragmatic feature of magic is the magician's attempt to use signs with the goal of obtaining an immediate effect on the nonsemiotic world. An additional anomaly concerning the addressee is observed in magic conjurations, where the signs are addressed to entities which are normally not potential partners in communication at all, e.g., a material object, a disease, or an absent person (cf. Todorov 1973: 41, Nöth 1986).

3.1.1 ANOMALY OF THE IMMEDIATE EFFECT
The anomaly in the magician's attempt to attain an immediate effect on the world by means of signs can be elucidated with refer-

ence to the normal conditions under which a speaker may influence the nonsemiotic world of objects or organisms. The normal effect of signs is always a *mediate* one. Signs are a means or a tool (see Function 3.1) for influencing the world. Semiosis, according to Morris's early definition, is a "mediated-taking-account-of" (1938: 4). Thus, the communicator must first direct a message to a receiver before a successful act of semiosis can result in an act with any influence on the world. While in normal semiosis only a mediate practical effect on the world is possible, magic semiosis is expected to have an immediate practical effect. The magic sign, says Maritain, "not only makes men know, it makes things be; it is an efficient cause in itself" (1957: 96). (On the similarities and differences between magic and everyday practical acts, see also Leach's discussion of "techno-magic in the home" [1976: 32]).

3.1.2 SCIENTIFIC IMPOSSIBILITY
According to Tylor, the magician "attempts to discover, to foretell, and to cause events" (1871, vol. 1: 104). In genuine magic these effects must neither be the result of a practical act nor be caused by a natural event, which would seem to occur independently of the magician's action. This prerequisite has led many anthropologists to postulate an opposition between science and magic. Magic depends on the belief that its assumed effect cannot possibly be obtained by nature and science. Thus, magic depends on the limits of the scientifically possible, as Todorov (1973: 41) pointed out. Morris even considered factual inefficiency the specific feature of magic in general: "What is often called 'magic,'" he writes, "is the persistence of techniques when there is evidence that the practices do not in fact influence the attainment of the goal, especially when these practices are symbolic in nature" (1946: 221).

3.2 Semantic Anomaly and the Theory of Word Magic

Considered from the semantic point of view, the anomaly in magic consists in a fallacious assumption about the relation between sign and object (cf. Nöth 1977a: 65). Frazer, for example, evaluated this semantic anomaly as follows (quoted by Freud 1913: 83): "Men mistook the order of their ideas for the order of nature, and hence imagined that the control which they have, or seem to have, over their thoughts, permitted them to exercise a corresponding control over things." In contradistinction to normal communication, where signs can at most be motivated by their object, the magician assumes that the manipulation of a magic signifier can influence the object to which the sign refers.

The semantic anomaly of the assumed direct or even causal relation between sign and object is a central topic of the theory of "word magic" developed by Ogden & Richards (1923) in collaboration with Malinowski (see also Ogden 1934). The further elaboration of this principle with extension to everyday language and to the mass media is of central concern to Korzybski's General Semantics (1933; cf. Semantics 1.5). The assumption of an immediate connection between sign and object in magic has also been defined as a denotative fallacy (Tambiah 1968: 187). A much expanded generalization of the principle of magic thinking was proposed by Izutsu (1956). This author's connotative theory of word magic argues for the omnipresence of magical thought in all spheres of discourse.

4. Magic as a Semiotic Therapy

After Tylor (1871), the "exterior" view of magic from the scientific point of view reached its climax with Frazer's work. In his judgment, magic was an "erroneous system" or even "one great disastrous fallacy" (1922: 26). From the "interior" point of view, however, magic is a communicative act which is potentially successful for the magic agents. This perspective was opened up by authors such as Mauss (1902), Malinowski (1925), Evans-Pritchard (1937), Lévi-Strauss (1958), and Boesch (1983). Malinowski, for example, interprets magic action as a semiotic activity with the function of bridging gaps in the pursuit of practical activities in life (1925: 79, 90). This view of magic as an escape from and alternative to practical deadlocks leads to more recent psychotherapeutic interpretations of the phenomenon (cf. Schmidtbauer 1971, Hsu 1983). Also in this perspective, magic has no immediate effect, but there is an indirect influence of the sign on the unconscious of the magic agents. Thus, the effect of magic is a semiotic therapy for the body or for practical actions of the participants.

Structure

The concept of structure has a static and a dynamic dimension. In semiotics, there are a "minimalist" and a holistic definition of the term. In the static sense, structure is often opposed to function. In the holistic sense, structure is closely related to the concept of system. Structure has become a basic concept in mathematics, biology, sociology, psychology, linguistics, and philosophy (cf. Bastide, ed. 1962, Piaget 1968, Naumann, ed. 1973, Robey, ed. 1973). The relevance of the concept to the theory of sign systems becomes apparent with regard to the roots of semiotics in structural linguistics (see 2., Saussure, Hjelmslev) and more generally in structuralism (q.v.). The analysis of structures in sign systems raises the question of the ontological status of these structures.

1. General Definitions of Structure

Since its origins, the concept of structure has experienced a semantic expansion which, besides various precise scientific definitions, has also resulted in a conceptual degeneration to a vogue word (cf. Lévi-Strauss 1958: 278). In its current use in semiotics, two versions of the term can be distinguished, a minimalist and a holistic one. While the minimalist definition reduces structure to a relation between two en-

tities, the holistic definition describes structure as an organic whole, which brings this concept very close to that of system.

1.1 Origins and Dimensions of the Concept

Structuralism has often been criticized for its allegedly static way of thinking. But, although it is true that the term *structure* is often used in a static sense, a dynamic interpretation of the concept has a considerable tradition. Structure is opposed to chaos. It refers to the order of entities (in the static sense), or to the regularities in their development (in the dynamic sense). The minimalist and the holistic views of structure have both received static and dynamic interpretations.

1.1.1 THE STATIC PARADIGM

The static paradigm derives from the etymology of the concept: Latin *structura* first refers to the 'construction of a building,' the ordered arrangement of materials to build up an architectonic whole. Structure in this sense implies statics and synchrony. Today, this connotation is particularly evident when architectonic frameworks or crystalline and geological formations are referred to as structures. Besides this material sense, there is also an early conceptual sense of the term *structure*. Thus, in ancient grammar and rhetoric and in medieval hermeneutics (cf. Scholz 1969), structure is the organization of sentences or the composition of speeches and texts. An example of a modern version of a static and synchronic conception of structure is the definition given by Kröber:

> When we analyze the structure of a system we generally not only disregard the concrete material of its elements but also the movement, change, and development of the system. Structure in this respect is the relatively invariable side of the system; it is curdled dynamics, a cross section through the development of the system at a given point of time $= t_x$. (1968: 1314)

1.1.2 THE DYNAMIC PARADIGM

The dynamic paradigm has its origins in biology and physiology, where the term *structure* has been used in an organic-functional sense since the eighteenth century (Nykrog 1968). Dynamic structures refer to regularities of processes and evolutions. Cybernetics and systems theory have developed structural matrices and other models for the formalization of dynamic structures (cf. Klaus 1969: 625–28). With his criteria of *transformation* and *self-regulation*, Piaget (1968) raises dynamics to a constitutive factor of structures in general. Thus even history has been studied as a science of dynamic structures (cf. Born 1973). In text semiotics, this dynamic dimension of structural analysis was particularly propagated by the Czech School of Semiotics (cf. Günther 1972). For the genetic and evolutionary aspects of structure in other disciplines, see especially Gandillac et al., eds. (1965).

1.2 The Minimalist Definition

The minimalist definition of structure has its roots in mathematics. There, a structure is essentially a net of relations.

1.2.1 STRUCTURE AS SYSTEMIC RELATIONS

The mathematical definition of structure has been developed within the theory of sets (cf. Wunderlich 1971, Figge 1973). In set theoretical terms, a structure is "the set of relations connecting the elements of a system" (Klaus 1969: 625). A system in this context is both a set of objects or elements and the set of relations between these elements. Thus, system is clearly differentiated from structure. The system has objects as its constitutive elements, while these objects are disregarded in the analysis of structure. Nevertheless, a structure presupposes a system. Structure is always the structure of a system. In the critical assessment of Wald, structuralism "idolizes the structure at the cost of its components" and considers the elements, which support the structure, to be simple illusions (1969: 20). What is the analytic status of those elements which are neglected by the structuralist? Elements are entities which are irreducible, not further analyzable by criteria of the system (cf. Klaus 1969: 173). Since objects can be analyzed within the framework of several systems and subsystems, the analytic status of an element depends on the systemic perspective. Thus, for example, a morpheme is a linguistic element which is irreducible within the linguistic subsystem of morphology. No segments of the English morpheme *soon* have any morphemic relevance. (*Soon*, e.g., is not the combination of *so + on*.) Thus, the whole morpheme is an irreducible element of the morphological system. But, of course, within a different system, that of phonology, further analysis is possible and new (phonemic) elements and structures become apparent. Thus, both the irreducibility of elements and the structural relations depend on the system within which they are analyzed.

1.2.2 OPPOSITION, DIFFERENCE, AND STRUCTURE

The most fundamental structural relation within a semiotic system is that of *opposition*. Following Saussure's theory of value, elements of a semiotic system are constituted only by the "differences that make it possible to distinguish [them] from all others, for [only] differences carry signification" (Saussure 1916b: 118). Oppositions thus have a negative characterization. They refer to what an element is not. More precisely, they refer to the feature(s) of other elements from which they are distinguished within the system: "In language there are only differences *without positive terms*" (ibid.: 120).

In structuralism, opposition and difference have become the fundamental principles for the explanation of cognitive processes. "When we perceive differences," writes Greimas, "the world 'takes form' in front of us and for us" (1966: 19). Thus, to structure is to perceive differences and oppositions. The perception of differences is possible only according to cognitive schemata in the percipient's mind. To structure is therefore to correlate elements and relations with perceptual schemata. This means that structuring is a process of creating order (cf. Koch 1971b: 7). With this idea of structure as order (vs. chaos), the concept of structure approaches that of information, being a measure of order (vs. entropy as disorder).

1.2.3 ELEMENTARY STRUCTURES
Elementary structures are the basic components of Greimas's structural semantics (1966: 20). Within this theory, the concept of structure is reduced to its absolute essentials, the "presence of two terms and the relation between them." In a typically structuralist way, Greimas further argues for the priority of the relations before the elements within a structure (Greimas & Courtés 1979: 314): Elements "are not knowable in themselves." The property of an element or the meaning of a term becomes apparent only by its opposition to the other element with which it forms an elementary structure (cf. Greimas 1.1).

1.3 The Holistic Definition

The holistic and the minimalist definitions of structure are not necessarily mutually exclusive. The difference is often only one of emphasis. Holistic definitions generally accept the minimalist criteria, but in addition they postulate criteria such as wholenesss or totality. With these criteria, the definition of structure comes very close to that of system. Often no difference between the holistic definitions of structure and system is made (but see 1.2.1).

Three typically holistic definitions of structure, from Dilthey to Piaget, will be discussed.

1.3.1 DILTHEY'S CONCEPT OF STRUCTURE
In the context of *Geisteswissenschaften*, the introduction of the concept of structure is generally attributed to Dilthey. Within his *Strukturlehre*, Dilthey developed a holistic concept of structure in opposition to earlier atomistic schools of psychology. His idea of structure is based on the dialectics of the part-and-whole relation: "Structure [. . .] is an order in which psychic facts are connected by inner relations. Any of those correlated facts is part of the structural connection. Thus, the regularity exists here in the relation of the parts within a whole" (1905: 15). Thus, structure is the holistic organizing principle which determines the interpretation of its constitutive elements. But at the same time, both element and structural wholeness are in dialectic interaction within a *hermeneutic circle*: in structure, the part becomes meaningful only within the whole, but the whole can derive its significance only from its parts.

1.3.2 LÉVI-STRAUSS'S DEFINITION
In a definition adopted and discussed by many structuralists (cf. Sperber 1968: 237–49), Lévi-Strauss defines structure as a model and postulates the following holistic criteria which leave little difference between structure and system:

First, the structure exhibits the characteristics of a system. It is made up of several elements, none of which can undergo a change without effecting changes in all the other elements.

Second, for any given model there should be a possibility of ordering a series of transformations resulting in a group of models of the same type.

Third, the above properties make it possible to predict how the model will react if one or more of its elements are submitted to certain modifications.

Finally, the model should be constituted so as to make immediately intelligible all the observed facts. (1958: 279–80)

1.3.3 PIAGET'S CRITERIA

Piaget's *genetic structuralism* develops the concept of structure further in a systems theoretic direction (1968: 8). In his definition, structure has the three characteristics of *totality, transformation*, and *self-regulation*. Totality is the holistic factor by which structure is differentiated from an unordered agglomeration of elements. Second, structure is defined by the set of transformations which determine its invariance. This invariance of a structure consists of the features which remain constant in a range of permissible transformations (cf. Laszlo 1983: 102). Third, self-regulation is the process of the maintenance of a structure against disturbances from outside. The means of self-regulation is usually that of feedback (see System 1.2.3). With these systems theoretical criteria, Piaget departs considerably from the minimalist concept of structure. In his definition, a structure is identical not only with a system, but also with a particular type of system, namely, the dynamic system.

2. Structure in Linguistics

In linguistics, the concept of structure is also used in a minimalist and in a holistic way (cf. Hudson 1968). The holistic concept of structure dominates where *gestalt, form, design, organization*, or *pattern* is used as a synonym of *structure* and even more so when Piaget's criteria are postulated as constitutive of structure in language (as with Dubois et al. 1973). Since *structure* in these definitions is a synonym of *system*, these structural aspects of language are discussed elsewhere (see System 2.). The following discussion focuses only on minimalist definitions of structure in language.

2.1 Saussure's Concept of Structure

The fact that Saussure hardly ever used the concept of structure (cf. Benveniste 1966: 79) is merely a matter of terminology. The idea of structure was in fact fundamental to his concept of language as a system of values (see System 2.2.1). He expressed this idea in his metaphor of chess. Saussure pointed out that only two things matter in chess: the values of the pieces according to the rules of the game, and their positions on the chessboard. Likewise "each linguistic term derives its value from its opposition to all the other terms" (1916b: 88). With this metaphor, Saussure argued for the priority of the relations before the elements of a structure. Elsewhere (1911, in Engler 1968: 20), Saussure concluded: *There are no signs, there are only differences between signs.*

Besides difference and opposition, Saussure distinguished two more special types of structural relations in language, namely, syntagmatic and paradigmatic relations (which he called "associative relations"). Paradigmatic relations exist between linguistic elements which may structurally occupy the same position within the same context. Substitution is the test for this potentiality of occurrence. For example, the phoneme /g/ may be substituted for /s/ in *go* so that in the context of *-o*, /s/ and /g/ are in a paradigmatic relation in English. Whole classes of words can be related paradigmatically, e.g., the adjectives *horrible* and *dreadful*, which may be mutually substituted in *Horrible Harry!* Thus, paradigmatic relations are relations of *equivalence*. They form the *vertical* axis of sign system.

Syntagmatic relations are the relations between elements in the sequence or combination, e.g., the relation that holds between *Horrible* and *Harry* or between /g/ and /o/ in *go*. Owing to the linear character of language, syntagmatic relations form the second major dimension of linguistics, so to speak, the *horizontal* dimension. Jakobson (1960) later called the paradigmatic dimension the *axis of selection* and the syntagmatic dimension the *axis of combination*.

2.2 Hjelmslev's Concept of Structure

Linguistic structuralism reached a climax in the work of Hjelmslev (q.v.). According to

Hjelmslev, language is not only an object of structural investigation, but language is "a mere structure" itself (1948: 33; 1957: 100). With reference to Carnap (1928: 15), Hjelmslev defined structure as "a purely formal and purely relational fact" and claimed that "a scientific statement must always be a statement about relations without involving a knowledge or a description of the relata themselves" (1948: 32). In language, these relata are the sounds, letters, or words, and it is not the substance of these elements, but only their relationships which are studied in structural linguistics. Hjelmslev emphasized the minimalist concept of structure, but had a holistic component in his definition:

> Structure is an autonomous entity of internal dependencies. [Following A. Lalande], structure is used "to designate, in opposition to a simple combination of elements, a wholeness formed by interdependent [solidary] phenomena, so that every element depends on the other ones and can only be what it is in and by its relation to them." (1957: 100)

3. Ontology of Structures

Structuralists have questioned not only the "objective reality" of the elements within a structure, but also the reality of the structure itself. Do structures exist in reality or only within a scientific model? This question about the ontological status of structures divided the philosophers of the Middle Ages into two camps, the realists and the nominalists. While the realists believed in an objective reality and thus in structures beyond the investigator's mind, the nominalists refused to accept this idea of an objective reality. (For a more complete survey of structuralist views about the ontology of structure, see Petitot-Cocorda 1985: 23–26).

3.1 "Realist" Concepts of Structure

A typically "realist" answer to the question about the existence of structures is given by the

American linguist Hockett: "For a scientist, then, 'linguistic structure' refers to something existing quite independently of the activities of the analyst: a language is what it is, it has the structure it has, whether studied and analyzed by a linguist or not" (1948: 280).

3.2 Reality vs. Structural Model

European structuralists have shown more reluctance concerning the ontology of structures. An influential position with respect to this problem is that of Lévi-Strauss. His answers to the question of the objective reality of structures are based on the distinction between *reality* and *model*. Structures in his view are not part of reality, but they constitute models of reality. In his discussion of social structures, Lévi-Strauss argues that " 'structure' has nothing to do with empirical reality but with models which are built after it" (1958: 279). Thus, social relations are also only "the raw materials out of which the models making up the social structure are built" (ibid.).

3.3 Methodological Concept of Structure

A modified thesis of the reality of structures is defended by semioticians who, according to Eco, represent a *methodological structuralism* (1968: 361). This structuralist position dispenses with any claim concerning the ontological status of structure but considers structures a useful and necessary instrument of thought. Eco himself favors this position in his book on the "absent structure" (see Eco 2.). One of its central theses is:

> A structure is a model constructed according to operations of simplification which allow the unification of different phenomena from a single point of view. [. . .] From this perspective it is useless to ask whether the thus identified structure exists *as such*. Structure is a technical means to designate different objects in a homogeneous way. (1968: 63)

A quite similar position is proposed within Greimas's structural semantics (q.v.). For

Greimas & Courtés, "structure is an entity [. . .] whose ontological status does not need to be questioned. On the contrary, it must be put between brackets, so as to render the concept operational" (1979: 313). With this argument, structural semantics rejects the question "whether structures are immanent to the object examined or whether they are constructions resulting from the congnitive activity of the knowing subject" (ibid.).

3.4 Potential Reality of Semiotic Structures

Within text semiotics, Koch poses the question of the reality of structure with respect to the participants in the communicative process (1976: 26). According to Koch, a text has no semiotic structure without a receiver who structures its message. Irrespective of the interpreting receiver, the text may at most have structures which are universally perceptible (such as phonic or graphic signals) or structures which only indicate the probability and the potentiality of a semiotic structure. Hence, the analyst in semiotic research can discover only *potential* semiotic structures. These are based on assumptions about possible interpretations of potential recipients. While the activity of the analyst is concerned with potential structures only, *actual* structures occur in the (primary) processes of text production and reception. Thus, the ontology of actual structures depends on parameters of the communicative situation. The reality of structures is the reality of semiotic activities in processes of semiosis.

System

The concept of system most generally implies the idea of elements forming an ordered whole. The relations among these elements form the structure of the system. The elements may have common features, but their systemic character appears only in their function within the system. Etymologically, the word *system* refers to somewhat less coherent entities. Gr. *sýstēma* (σύστημα) means 'that which is put together,' 'a composite whole,' 'an assembly.' Most scholars agree that sign systems are the major object of semiotic research. While the systemic character of language is generally acknowledged, there is less agreement about texts and nonlinguistic phenomena being systems. Terminologically, the concept of (sign) system is often not clearly differentiated from the concepts of structure and code.

1. General Characteristics of Systems

General characteristics of systems have been studied in the theory of science and especially in the interdisciplinary research of systems theory (cf. Bertalanffy 1968, Laszlo 1972, Nöth 1989). The definition of system has to be specified particularly in relation to the concept of structure. The complexity of systems increases as systems theoretical research is extended from physical to biological, sociological, and even metaphysical systems.

1.1 Definition of System

An attempt to reduce the characteristics of a system to a minimum of features has been made in the mathematical theory of sets. But this definition neglects the important feature of wholeness which has been elaborated within the framework of gestalt psychology.

1.1.1 ELEMENTS, RELATIONS, AND STRUCTURES

One of the most frequently quoted definitions of systems was proposed by Hall & Fagen: "A system is a set of objects together with relationships between the objects and between their attributes" (1956: 18). In pure terms of the theory of sets, Klaus gives an even more reduced characterization of the minimal features of a system. In his definition, a system is a "set of elements and [the] set of relations existing between these elements" (1969: 634). If structure is defined as "the set of relations connecting the elements of a system," the only distinguishing criterion between system and structure is "the set of elements," which is part of a system but not of a structure.

1.1.2 WHOLENESS AND ORDER

Both system and structure are characterized by the feature of *unity* or *wholeness* (cf. Strombach 1983). This characteristic evidently escapes the possibilities of a set theoretic formalization. At most, it is referred to as one of the "relations existing between the elements" in the set theoretic definition. The concept of wholeness was elaborated within the framework of gestalt psychology in opposition to atomistic and mechanistic views of the sciences. Wholeness is that relation which makes a system "more than the sum of its elements." But this structural "more" cannot be derived from the elements. The holistic approach postulates an analysis which has to consider the level of wholeness in order to determine the elements and their function within the structure. This principle can be illustrated with a simple example from linguistics, where it has always been acknowledged in practice: A sentence ('the whole') is more than the sum of its lexemes ('the elements'). Its structure (such as subject + predicate) cannot be determined from the lexical information alone.

The negative characterization of systems by 'the impossibility of reducing its wholeness to the sum of its elements' is avoided when the unity of a system is described as its permanence in dynamic change. This criterion appears in Laszlo's definition of order, a concept closely related to that of wholeness: "*Order* in a system refers to the invariance that underlies transformations of state, and by means of which the system's structure can be identified" (1983: 28).

1.2 Complex Systems and Their Typology

With the increasing complexity of systems, further features appear, from which a typology of systems (cf. Boulding 1968, Laszlo 1972: 36ff.) can be derived.

1.2.1 STATIC AND DYNAMIC SYSTEMS

Static systems occur in the world of objects in material structures that are relatively resistant to change, e.g., in crystals or in technical constructions. An example of a conceptual static system is Linnaeus's taxonomy of plants. Static systems are stable and in equilibrium. The stability of a system is its capacity to keep its variables unchanged within defined limits. The state of a system in which its variables remain unchanged by any perturbation is called equilibrium. A good steel construction has a stable equilibrium. Children's building-block constructions usually have an unstable equilibrium. In *dynamic* systems, the structure changes with time. There are various degrees of complexity of dynamic systems. The simplest dynamic systems are predetermined in their mechanical motions, as is the case with clockworks. The dynamic complexity increases from closed to open systems.

1.2.2 CLOSED AND OPEN SYSTEMS

Closed systems are physically isolated from their environment. All static systems are closed systems, but there may also be dynamical processes within closed systems. According to the second law of thermodynamics, isolated physical systems having no exchange of matter and energy with their environment tend to a state of thermodynamical equilibrium, in which eventually all mechanical processes come to a stop. This state of the closed system is determined by *maximum entropy*, i.e., the most probable distribution and thus maximum disorder of its molecules. In opposition to this concept, information is defined as *negative entropy*, a measure of improbability and thus unpredictability of signals.

Open systems exchange energy and matter with their environment. There are many degrees of complexity in open systems. Flames and rivers are very simple physico-chemical systems, which maintain themselves in a constant throughput of atoms (cf. Boulding 1968: 7). In biological organisms, the property of self-maintenance in constant exchange with the environment becomes dominant. Such open systems evade decay to the state of entropy by "feeding on negative entropy" through metabolism and by drawing information from their environment (Schrödinger

1947: 70–72). Open systems are capable not only of *self-stabilization* but also of *self-organization*.

1.2.3 SELF-STABILIZING AND SELF-ORGANIZING SYSTEMS

Self-stabilization is the distinctive property of all cybernetic systems. These systems are capable of counteracting perturbations of the system by means of control processes. These processes require the transmission and evaluation of information within the system. Negative feedback signals (see Communication 3.2.2) give information to counteract and eliminate a perturbation and restore the desired state of a system. Maintaining a constant desired state is thus the goal of such a system.

In open organic systems, the capability for dynamic self-stabilization of given desired states is called *homeostasis* (Cannon 1932). These systems are in a *flow equilibrium* or *steady state* (Bertalanffy 1975: 127) since after absorbing environmental influences (e.g., in metabolism), they do not return to their former state but attain a new state of equilibrium. When the self-stabilization is directed at variable desired states prescribed by a genetically determined developmental path, such as in biological growth, this process is called *homeorhesis* (Waddington 1957: 43).

Self-organization and *morphogenesis* are the more general processes of system change in the evolution of open systems (cf. Maruyama 1963, Laszlo 1972, Jantsch 1980). While self-stabilization maintains the system in a desired state by means of negative feedback (*morphostasis*), self-organization proceeds basically by means of positive feedback: The system develops (*morphogenesis*) by amplifying inner changes or adapting to outer perturbations of its former equilibrium, thus attaining new stages of development. In each phase of this process, there are nonequilibrium states requiring an enforcement of the mechanisms of self-stabilization (cf. Laszlo 1972: 42–45). Self-organization necessarily involves an open system that has multiple equilibria and thus several strata of potential stability (Laszlo 1983: 32).

1.2.4 AUTOPOIESIS AND DISSIPATIVE SELF-ORGANIZATION

Autopoiesis emphasizes the autonomy of living systems in their interaction with the environment (Varela 1981). In the process of their self-maintenance, autopoietic systems (e.g., biological cells) are capable of continuous self-renewal. Since such a system fulfils only functions given by its own structure, it is also called *self-referential* (Maturana & Varela 1972). Autopoietic systems are the opposite of *allopoietic* systems (example: machines), the functions of which are determined externally.

Classical systems theory focuses on processes of equilibration in the context of perturbations and increasing entropy. A new systems paradigm is Prigogine's theory of *nonequilibrium dynamics* and *dissipative self-organization* in open systems (Prigogine & Stengers 1979) and Haken's (1981) theory of *synergetics*. Their work led to the discovery of spontaneous processes, which originate in higher states of order and stability out of fluctuations and *disorder far from equilibrium*. Prigogine, whose research was first concerned with chemical processes, calls the resulting processes *dissipative structures*, since their stability depends on the use (dissipation) of energy and matter.

With this discovery of the emergence of order out of nonlinearity, instability, and fluctuation, the emergence of order out of chaos (Prigogine & Stengers 1979), the theories of nonequilibrium dynamics and synergetics set up a new paradigm of systems evolution overcoming the thermodynamical principle of progressive deterioration to the entropic state of disorder. Both the loss and the gain of structures of order consequently occur in the processes of systemic evolution (cf. also Makridakis 1977). From the point of view of this new systems theoretical paradigm, the goal of stability and equilibrium maintenance is supplanted by the goal of permanence of dynamic nonequilibrium states giving rise to self-organizing evolution.

2. Language as a System

The history of modern linguistics has long been dominated by structuralist paradigms which developed some rather static concepts of system. Some linguists restrict the concept of system to the very elementary idea of a paradigm, although a more holistic view of the language system has already been developed by Saussure. Only in diachronic linguistics was language early referred to as a dynamic system. But characteristics of a dynamic system can also be observed in language from a synchronic perspective.

2.1 System as a Paradigmatic Structure

Two very different schools of structuralist linguistics, Hjelmslev's *glossematics* and Halliday's *systemic linguistics*, have developed a rather minimalist and static concept of system. Hjelmslev defined a system as a hierarchy of either-or functions between language elements (1943: 38–39, 132). In language use such either-or relations exist whenever a choice between different elements is possible in one and the same context. Phonologically, for example, after an initial s-, the speaker of English has the choice between vowels (as in *so*) and some consonants (as in *slot* or *spot*, but *g, r,* and other consonants are not possible choices (no English word can begin with *sr-* or *sg-*). Hjelmslev defined these relations of choice as the paradigmatic relations within a language and opposed them to the syntagmatic relations which exist in the combination of linguistic elements in a given (con)text. Thus, system and text are two fundamental and complementary categories of language in glossematic linguistics. The system exists in the paradigmatic and the text exists in the syntagmatic dimension of language. The text is the semiotic process which

becomes possible because of the possible choices inherent in the system of language.

Also in Halliday's systemic linguistics (cf. Berry 1975: 142), systems refer to the paradigmatic axis of a language. They are defined as "lists of choices which are available in the grammar of a language" (ibid.). Thus, the categories of number, person, and tense are examples of systems in English. System in this sense refers to the potentiality of structures but does not yet imply any holistic ideas such as totality or gestalt.

2.2 Holistic Views of the Language System

While a language has innumerable systems in the minimalist definition of the term, holistic conceptions refer to the totality of language as *a* system. Following the set theoretic model, the language system is described holistically as the class of elements and structures of a language, and the class of rules which generate these structures is called the *rule system.*

2.2.1 SAUSSURE'S HOLISTIC CONCEPT OF SYSTEM

The adoption of the concept of system in structural linguistics is largely due to Saussure. While in the nineteenth century Wilhelm von Humboldt preferred the biological term *organism* to refer to language (cf. Gipper 1978: 62), Saussure's view of language as a system was a new paradigm which was more closely related to logic than to biology.

Although it was the term *structure* which became the key concept of the new paradigm of linguistic structuralism, Saussure almost always used the term *system* to describe the "mechanism" of language. In his theory, language is a sign system. Its elements are signs, and its structure is a network of oppositions, differences, and values. Saussure speaks of a *tight system* (*système serré*), "characterized by the precision of the values, the multiplicity of the kind of values, the immense multiplicity of terms or units of the system, and their strict reciprocal dependence" (Godel 1957: 71). The holistic view in Saussure's idea of a semiological system becomes apparent in this characterization of the place of the linguistic sign within the language system:

> To consider a term as simply the union of a certain sound with a certain concept is grossly misleading. To define it in this way would isolate the term from its system; it would mean assuming that one can start from the terms and construct the system by adding them together when, on the contrary, it is from the interdependent whole that one must start and through analysis obtain its elements. (1916b: 113)

2.2.2 SYSTEMIC AUTONOMY IN SUBSYSTEMS

The holistic conception of the language system also acknowledges that a language is a complex system with various subsystems. Standard versions of linguistics distinguish subsystems such as the phonological, the graphemic (see 2.2.4; Writing 4.), the morphological, the lexical, the syntactic, and the semantic subsystems of language. In extension of this standard division, text linguistics and text semiotics have explored the text as an autonomous level of analysis. The idea of wholeness in the definition of these subsystems of language is represented by the criterion of their *relative autonomy*. For example, the structures of the phonological system are relatively independent of the syntactic subsystem of a language because the phonemes are practically unaffected by the structures of syntax. But there is no total autonomy of the subsystems. The language system as a whole integrates its subsystems in two characteristic ways, *hierarchy* and *simultaneity*. Hierarchical integration exists between subsystems which are included in other subsystems; for example, the lexical subsystem includes the morphological one. Simultaneous or parallel integration exists between the semantic and the other subsystems except for phonology.

2.2.3 SYSTEM AND NORM

Coseriu (e.g., 1973: 44) extends the concept of language system and introduces a new distinction between *system* and *norm*. Accordingly, the system is not only the sum of all actually occurring structures of a language, but also the class of all potential structures which could oc-

cur according to its general rules. In actual language use, however, not all those potential structures occur. The class of those structures of the language system which are actually used by its speakers constitutes the language norm. For example, the phonological (sub)system of English allows a word such as [su:m] (possible spelling: "soom"), but no such word occurs in the norm of the English language.

2.2.4 HOMOGENEITY AND HETEROGENEITY

In his analysis of alphabetic writing systems, Watt (1983) discusses the more general question of the distinctive characteristics of a semiotic system. He argues that such a system is constituted by the homogeneity of its elements. In this view, the homogeneity of a sign repertoire and, with it, its "systemhood" increase in proportion to the increase of the number of elements in agreement over those in discord between the sign elements. In this interpretation, the basically synchronic fact of homogeneity is only diachronically affected by the opposing forces of inertia, facilitation, and heterogenization.

Although homogeneity may be a significant factor in the structure of relatively closed semiotic systems with a limited sign repertoire, it cannot be accepted as a distinctive criterion of systems analysis in semiotics (cf. Posner et al. 1983). Systemhood cannot be determined from the (visual) features of semiotic elements alone. Also in a phonemic system, the phonemes cannot be determined merely on the basis of their acoustic properties. Their function within the higher context of meaning must be taken into consideration. Thus, what constitutes a systemic whole is necessarily more than the sum of the distinctive features of its elements. Posner thus argues that semiotic functions, and not the structures of the elements, constitute the unifying factor of a semiotic system, which may consist of quite heterogeneous elements (ibid.: 402).

2.3 Dynamics of the Diachronic System

Language change was the first field of linguistics to be described in dynamic categories of systems theory. Central to the first interpretations is the cybernetic model of self-stabilization (see 1.2.3; for a critical survey see Schweizer 1979). From a synchronic perspective, every language change is a systemic perturbation. The acceptance of a diachronic innovation as a new language norm occurs through a process of positive feedback (cf. Nöth 1975a; 1983b). This process, however, must not lead to a loss in the functional requirements of the language system. Otherwise, perturbation compensating mechanisms of negative feedback in the form of new linguistic changes will be the homeostatic reaction of the system. Since this process results from the system's own needs, it may also be termed self-organization and autopoiesis. When new systemic stability arises irreversibly from linguistic nonequilibrium states, an interpretation in categories of *nonequilibrium dynamics* is also suggested (cf. Mottron & Wildgen 1987: 86-215). In contradistinction to the general application of this model in the general theory of evolution, the development of historically documented languages does not show examples where language change can be said to have resulted in systems of a higher stage of evolution. Even if the prehistoric phylogenesis of language makes the assumption of a development from the simple to the complex imperative, such processes cannot be documented from known histories of languages.

2.4 *Dynamics of the Synchronic System*

Language shows the features of a dynamic system not only from the point of view of language change (diachrony) but also in ahistorical processes of language use (synchrony). The synchronic dynamics of language, however, requires the perspective not of a static but of a *dynamic synchrony*. Although already postulated by Jakobson (1959b: 275), this perspective has not yet become a dominant paradigm of current linguistics. First approaches to this perspective were determined by the systems theoretical paradigms of information theory and statistics, mathematical catastrophe theory, and the model

of dissipative self-organization. For a more detailed discussion see Nöth (1989).

3. Texts as Semiotic Systems

The histories of literature and the arts have already been interpreted from structuralist points of view in terms of the dynamic evolution of systems (cf. Günther 1972 on the Prague structuralists, and Guillén 1971). The new paradigms of systems theory have mostly been applied to the analysis of aesthetic texts and their evolution.

3.1 *Textual Synchrony*

The study of texts as synchronic systems is still in its beginnings. Systems theoretical paradigms which have been applied in this field are information theory, general systems theory, mathematical catastrophe theory, and the theory of autopoietic systems.

3.1.1 ORDER AND CHAOS
Information theory provides a new framework for the question, already much discussed in traditional aesthetics (cf. Peckham 1965), whether order or chaos is the essence of art. Some theoreticians of information believe in the statistical calculability of aesthetic states of order (see *Aesthetics* 1.2.4). Arnheim (1971), however, shows that aesthetic perception cannot be described in categories such as information, entropy, equilibrium, or homeostasis alone. A more differentiated semiotics of texts based on information theory is developed by Lotman (1970) (cf. *Soviet Semiotics*). Art is here described as being "capable of transforming noise into information" (ibid.: 75).

3.1.2 EQUILIBRIUM, HOMEOSTASIS, AND STABILITY
According to the paradigm of general systems theory, Oomen (1972) outlines a systems theory of texts. The author defines texts as complex systems of subsystems controlled by communicative functions and in which the system tends to a holistic equilibrium integrating

the various equilibrium states of the subsystems. Also for the text linguist Beaugrande (1980: 17; 111), the cybernetic paradigm of the self-stabilizing system is the model of textuality. Nöth (1977a; 1978b) interprets narrative texts as homeostatic processes but also shows from the examples of a literary epoch the possibility of the dominance of phases of *instability* in texts.

3.1.3 TEXTUAL CATASTROPHES
On the basis of René Thom's mathematical catastrophe theory, Wildgen (1983) studies the dynamics in textual systems. His applications of this systems theoretical model are concerned with narrative and dialogical texts.

3.1.4 TEXTS AS AUTOPOIETIC SYSTEMS
A systems theoretical theory of literature based on the theory of autopoietic systems is being developed by S. J. Schmidt (1984; cf. Hauptmeier & Schmidt 1985). Within this new paradigm, literary communication is no longer considered a unilinear process but a process of social interaction in which the autonomy of the interacting subjects plays a decisive role (see Communication 3.3).

3.2 Textual Diachrony

The evolution of literature and the arts occurs in dynamic processes which can be interpreted in systems theoretical categories of self-organization and nonequilibrium dynamics. In the cyclical process of literary and artistic evolution (cf. Nöth 1977a: 145; 1983b), any aesthetic innovation represents a perturbation with respect to established styles and "ways of seeing." The propagation of the innovation means positive feedback and self-organization when it leads to a new style. The establishment of the new style then leads to the self-stabilization of a new system by means of negative feedback (cf. also Laszlo 1972: 225). In every new phase of innovation, order arises out of fluctuation. As in language evolution, however, in spite of cyclical oscillations, no evolution to higher stages of

development can be discerned. (Joyce's *Ulysses* is not more highly developed, not a more "valuable" work of art, than the Old English *Beowulf* epic.) And yet, there is a basic difference between language change and literary evolution (cf. Nöth 1977a: 146; 1983b): While the degree of innovation and hence self-organization is limited in the process of language change because of the speakers' communicative needs, innovation and hence systemic perturbances can be much more important for literary and aesthetic evolution. Disequilibrium can become the systemic goal of the arts.

4. Nonlinguistic Semiotic Systems

In the field of nonverbal and visual communication, systems have also been defined according to the criterion of paradigmatic relations between semiotic elements (cf. 2.1). But some semioticians deny the idea that all visual and nonverbal signs are elements of semiotic systems. Since semiotic systems are often referred to as codes, their systematicity is discussed in the section on code structures.

4.1 Cultural Systems as Paradigms

Barthes (1964a) discussed various cultural phenomena as systems: the garment system, the food system, the car system, the furniture system, and the architecture system. The concept of system in this discussion is a minimalist one. System here refers to a paradigm, and the paradigmatic axis of analysis is, in Barthes's terminology, the *systematic plane*, which he opposed to syntagmatic relationships. For example, in the garment system, the system is "the set of pieces, parts or details which cannot be worn at the same time on the same part of the body and whose variation corresponds to a change in the meaning of the clothing: toque—bonnet—hood, etc." (ibid.: 63). Here, the rules for the combination of these elements (in *syntagms*) are not included in the garment system.

4.2 Systematic and Asystematic Sign Repertoires

Saussure was the first to refer to phenomena such as military signals, symbolic rites, or the sign language of the deaf as semiotic systems. Although he did not elaborate on the structure of these systems, his concept of language system suggests a holistic view of such nonlinguistic semiotic systems. But can *any* nonverbal act of communication be traced back to signs which constitute a semiotic system?

Buyssens denies this and argues that sign repertoires (*sémies*, in his terminology) can be *systematic* or *asystematic* (1943: 34–36). For Buyssens, a sign repertoire is a system only when it is constructed out of complex semantic units (*sèmes*) which can be further decomposed into a constant and stable set of smaller meaningful components (which he calls *signes*; cf. Code 4.1.2). A nonlinguistic systematic sign repertoire in this sense is the code of traffic signs, where the recurrent forms, colors, and pictures are meaningful components which combine into the individual road signs.

Asystematic sign repertoires in this conception are made up of uncombinable and unanalyzable units (*sèmes* without *signes*). The system of the traffic lights is asystematic in this sense because its elements (e.g., "red light" = 'stop') are not further decomposable (cf. Hervey 1982: 160). More complex examples for asystematic sign repertoires given by Buyssens are art, advertising, and codes of politeness (1943: 37). For further research in the systematicity of nonlinguistic sign systems, see also Mounin (1970a: 17–39).

4.3 Sign System or Code?

The concepts of semiotic system and code are often used interchangeably. Buyssens calls a systematic sign repertoire a system *or* a code (1967: 52). Prieto (1966) discusses nonlinguistic sign systems *as* codes. Eco, however, differentiates between systems and codes. (For a more detailed discussion, see Language 4.2.) Whenever sign systems are differentiated from codes, the concept of system emphasizes the ideas of order, wholeness, and structural potentiality, while a code has the additional characteristic of the correlation or correspondence between sign repertoires or signs and their meanings.

Code

The term *code* was adopted as a key concept of semiotics under the influence of information theory. A large field of diverse phenomena, from phoneme systems (cf. Language 4.2) to aesthetic conventions, was soon studied under the designation of code, but this terminological expansion did not remain without criticism. The semiotic concept of code has inherited a fundamental ambiguity from its presemiotic usage. Accordingly, a code is defined either as an autonomous system of signs or as a mere instruction for the translation of signs from one to another system of signs. The search for code structures in the nonlinguistic field of sign phenomena was an important step in the development from Saussurean linguistics to a general theory of signs.

1. Two Meanings of *Code*

The polysemy of the semiotic term *code* has its roots in the general history of the word, which has its origins in two quite opposed domains: the public sphere of laws and the secret sphere of cryptography. The two meanings have different semiotic implications.

1.1 Institutional Codes

From the language of law, codes are known as sets of rules prescribing forms of social behav-

ior. Originally, such codes had the form of a book (a *codex*). Examples are the Napoleonic Code or the Code of the Laws of the United States. Later, unwritten traditional rules of social conduct were also called codes, for example the code of decorum or the fashion code. From a semantic point of view, codes of social institution are autonomous semiotic systems. In contrast to cryptographic codes, they generate a system of social signs and meanings which do not exist except by this very social convention. From a pragmatic point of view, institutional codes belong to *deontic semiotics* (cf. Greimas & Courtés 1979: 73) since they influence behavior by prescription, prohibition, permission, and optionality.

1.2 Cryptographic Codes

Cryptographic codes, by contrast, are only secondary sign systems. They are instructions for translating a message of a given, primary code into a secret message. The secret code is then a correlational device for substituting the signs or sign elements of the primary code, usually a natural language, into a secret code.

1.2.1 CRYPTOLOGY AND CRYPTOGRAPHY
Cryptology has two branches (cf. Kahn 1966, Friedman 1974). The first branch, *cryptography*, is concerned with the task of developing secret codes and of encoding or enciphering

messages in a way that guarantees signal security against interception. The second branch, cryptanalysis, develops methods of "code breaking," that is, discovering keys to secret codes. A person who is in legitimate possession of this secret key is said to decipher or decode the secret message. The message to be encoded is called the *plaintext*. It may be transformed by *steganography*, that is, methods of concealing the plaintext—for example, by using secret inks—or by cryptography proper, either by *transposition*, the disarrangement of plaintext signals in their serial order, or by *substitution*.

1.2.2 CIPHERS AND CLOAKS
There are two basic substitutional systems for cryptographic encoding, called *ciphers* and *cloaks*. A cipher is a system which replaces plaintext letters with equivalent secret letters or numbers. The key or code book which gives the equivalences between plaintext letters and cipher letters is called the *cipher alphabet*. Several language substitutes, such as the Morse and the Braille code, have the structure of a cipher alphabet. A cloak is a code that replaces plaintext elements of the extension of words, phrases, or sentences. The code book consists of a plaintext lexicon correlated with secret code words or code numbers (see also Language Substitutes 2.2). The early universal languages were devised on the principle of word substitution. In the terminology of cryptology, cloaks are usually defined as codes proper and distinguished from ciphers, which are not termed codes. In nontechnical usage, however, cloaks and ciphers are both called codes. Notice that the Morse alphabet is usually called Morse code, not Morse cipher.

2. Code, Information, and Communication

The two historical meanings of the term *code* have also influenced the terminology of information theory, where the concept is defined ei-

ther as a correlational device or as a sign repertoire.

2.1 Correlational Device

Defined as a correlational device in the process of encoding and decoding, the code is a secondary sign system, developed for reasons of economy in signal transmission.

2.1.1 SIGNAL TRANSFORMATION AND CORRELATION
In the definition of the German Industrial Norm DIN 44 300 (Berlin, 1972), a code is "a rule for the unambiguous correlation ('coding') of the signs of one sign repertoire to those of another sign repertoire." This correlational definition of code presupposes a primary sign repertoire, such as numeral ciphers or the letters of the alphabet, and a secondary sign repertoire into which the primary signals are translated. Coding is thus a process which occurs after messages are already expressed by means of signs. In the definition of Cherry, a code is then "an agreed transformation, usually one to one and reversible, by which messages may be converted from one set of signs into another. Morse code, semaphore, and the deaf-dumb code represent typical examples" (1957: 8).

2.1.2 ENCODING AND DECODING
Shannon & Weaver's communication chain (Fig. C 1) does not yet represent codes and coding as elements and processes in communicative events. For example, Shannon & Weaver describe a telephone conversation as communication without coding, since the telephone merely transforms the audible voice signal into equivalent electrical impulses (1949: 17). Only when the message is enciphered into a different form, such as Morse code, does communication occur via a process of encoding and decoding.

Later, however, communication theory considered a code to be a constitutive element of any process of communication, not only in the sense of a sign repertoire, as shown in Figure C 2 (see Communication), but also in the sense of signal transformation. Neurolinguists, for example, describe language production and reception as involving various phases of coding (cf. Crystal 1980: 56). At first, there is *neurological coding*. The message is encoded in signals capable of being sent through our nervous system. Then there is *physiological coding*. The neurological signals are transformed into physiological signals which control the movements of the speech organs. Finally, *anatomical coding* is the phase of actual speech production or reception, which involves the performance of articulatory movements and the receptive transformation of acoustic or visual signals in the human ear or eye. The programs which control these processes are the neurological, physiological, and anatomical codes.

2.1.3 THE SIGN IN INDIRECT AND DIRECT SEMIOSIS
According to Shannon & Weaver's account of coding, there are uncoded and coded messages. From a semiotic point of view, the uncoded message is a mode of direct semiosis, while the coded message is a mode of indirect or substitutive semiosis. In the evolution of codes, however, a shift from indirect to direct semiosis can develop. Writing, for example, was substitutive of speech in the age of oral communication. With the advent of the Gutenberg galaxy, it has become a mode of direct semiosis.

In indirect semiosis, every element of the sign repertoire of the code is a sign, even if it represents only letters or phonemes of the direct code. For example, the Morse signal • ━ is a sign of the letter *A*, the signal ━ • • • is a sign representing the letter *B*. More precisely: there is a signifier "• ━" whose signified is '*A*.' This mode of substitutive semiosis is *metasemiotic*: every indirect signal is a secondary sign of a direct or primary one.

From the point of view of the Morse *message*, however, the Morse letters are not signs, but only sign elements. The Morse letter • • •, for example, is just as incapable of expressing a meaningful message as is its alphabetical counterpart, *S*. Only when combined into a message, such as • • • ━ ━ ━ • • • (S O S), do the Morse

signals acquire direct meaning ('Help!'). From this perspective of direct semiosis, the Morse alphabet consists only of sign elements. (For more details see 5.3.3–4.) To the degree that a substitutive code becomes independent from being transformed into spoken or written language, the code acquires semiotic autonomy (cf. Writing 3.2, Language Substitutes 3.).

2.1.4 ECONOMY IN CODING AND BINARY CODES
The technical advantage of transforming linguistic messages into a different code consists in the economy of transmission (see Information 2.1.6). Technically, the most economic code is a binary code. It employs only two distinguishable sign elements. All computer signals, for example, are coded binarily. They consist of innumerable combinations of the two elements "electrical impulse" and "no impulse" (cf. Information 2.2). Neurological coding is also based on binary coding (cf. Cherry 1957: 35): "The electrical signals which pass along the nervous systems of animals and men, both from the sense organs (receptors) and to the controlled organs and muscles (effectors), take the form of triggered pulses which are either *on* or *off*; there is no half measure."

2.1.5 ANALOGIC AND DIGITAL CODING
Pictures and alphabetically written messages illustrate two different principles of coding, analogic and digital coding. Analogic coding generates messages in a continuous space, such as images, models, or nonverbal signs. Digital coding generates messages with discrete signals in a linear but segmented form, as in the form of letters, numbers, or binary signals.

Many scholars have described the distinction between analogic and digital coding as fundamental in semiotics (cf. Ruesch 1972, Verón 1970; 1973a). However, the difference may be less crucial than has been maintained. It may be argued that ultimately every act of semiosis involves a digital transformation of messages, namely, at the neurologic level. Technological evidence of the decreasing importance of the difference between analogic and digital coding has been the invention of digital recording of music. While sound was formerly believed to be codable in the analogic form only, it can now be recorded digitally. Even at higher levels of semiosis, the distinction cannot be maintained as fundamental. Written language, for example, is often quoted as the prototype of digital coding, but handwriting shows many points of convergence between digital and analogic coding. While spoken language has, at its lowest level, the digitally analyzable system of phonemes and distinctive features, the perception and transmission of speech is, at the perceptive level, largely analogic. The transmission of sound waves by telephone, for example (cf. Flechtner 1966: 146), is based on a process of the analogic transformation of continuous sound waves into continuously modulated electric current.

2.2 Sign Repertoire and Semiotic System

Whenever the code is defined as a sign repertoire, there is a shift of analytic focus from the secondary nature of the coded signals to their own systemic properties.

2.2.1 THE CODE AS A SEMIOTIC SYSTEM
Greimas & Courtés quote Wiener with the naive (perhaps only ironic?) statement that Chinese is only American coded into Chinese (1979: 32). Jakobson, by contrast, proposed to study language *as* a code (cf. Language 4.). These two positions characterize the terminological shift from the code as a correlational device to the code as a sign system.

In the expanded version of Shannon & Weaver's model of communication (see Communication 3.1.5, Fig. C 2), communication is represented as a process in which the sender encodes and the receiver decodes signals on the basis of a common sign repertoire or code. In this sense, the code is no longer a rule for the transformation of signs, but a sign system in its own right. In this sense, not only the Morse alphabet, but also language, is a code. To study Morse code as a sign system is to investigate the structure of its minimal units and the rules for their combination. In spite of the essential difference between the correlational and the systemic definitions of the concept of code, there is a common denominator in the fact that sign systems may also be said to correlate two semiotic structures, namely, those of expression and those of form (in the sense of Hjelmslev).

2.2.2 SIGNIFICANT AND NONSIGNIFICANT CODES
The information theoretical study of codes distinguishes between *significant* (or *representative*) and *nonsignificant* (or *selective*) codes (cf. Elias 1958: 16–05, Nauta 1972: 134). This distinction corresponds to the semiotic distinction between codes with or without the level of first articulation. The principles according to which a garment may be registered in a warehouse catalog can serve as an example: if the code number consists of groups of decimal digits, the first group denoting the type of garment, the second the size, and the third the color, there is significant coding. A code that assigns only simple serial numbers to the items of the catalog is called nonsignificant. Such a number does not give any information about the listed item. It only selects it from the catalog (therefore: selective code).

3. Semiotic Definitions

The introduction of the term *code* in semiotics had a terminological "landslide effect" (cf. Eco 1984b: 166). Only few scholars adhered to the narrower definition of code as a correlational device. Mostly, the term became a synonym of *sign system*. The original concept from the field of information technology became widely adopted in the field of text semiotics and aesthetics and even with respect to the sphere of natural semiosis. This expansion of the term did not remain without criticism, at least in the field of language studies (cf. Kurz 1976, Gipper 1978: 173–77).

3.1 Correlational and Narrower Definitions

Among those who adhere to a correlational definition of the term *code* are Mounin and Prieto.

3.1.1 CODE AS A SUBSTITUTIVE SYSTEM

Buyssens (1967: 46–47) and Mounin (1970a: 83) define codes as secondary or indirect semiotic systems (with the function of substituting for a primary semiotic system; cf. Language Substitutes 3.). Codes are thus opposed to languages, which are direct semiotic systems. While spoken language is not a code in this sense, writing is a coding of spoken language, and the Morse alphabet is a substitutive code of the Latin alphabet.

3.1.2 PRIETO'S CORRELATIONAL DEFINITION OF SEMIOTIC SYSTEMS

Prieto (1966) also adopts a correlational concept of code but extends his definition to include not only secondary but also primary semiotic systems. According to Prieto, "the code which is used in a semiotic act is that semiotic structure on which the sender's and receiver's knowledge of the signals is based" (1975b: 129). In Prieto's definition, codes consist of correlations between two "universes of discourse," called the *semantic field* (the field of signifiers) and the *noetic field* (that of signifieds) (1966: 43–45). In the code of traffic signals, for example, the red, green, and amber lights form the "semantic field," and the corresponding stop-go commands belong to the "noetic field" (cf. Hervey 1982: 72). Only intentional signals can form codes, according to Prieto (1966: 44–45; cf. Communication 2.4). Indices of natural semiosis are not elements of codes.

3.1.3 PRIETO'S CRITERIA OF NONLINGUISTIC CODES

Although Prieto extends the concept of code to include language, his definition of nonlinguistic codes is a narrow one, which comes close to the technological definitions of information theorists. Nonlinguistic codes, in Prieto's definition (1975b: 130–31), are codes with signs (in his terminology: *sèmes*) whose meanings (*signifiés*) are always in a relation of logical exclusion. Language, by contrast, is a code with signs whose meanings are in a relation of either logical exclusion, inclusion, or intersection. In other words, Prieto studies only simple, highly conventional systems with strictly unambiguous signs as nonlinguistic codes. His examples include such codes as traffic signs and numerical codes, but most of the field of nonverbal communication does not belong to his field of semiotic codes.

3.2 Codes and Semiotic Systems

In the sense of a semiotic system, the term *code* has its origins in the development of semiotics from the Saussurean theory of language to a general theory of signifying systems.

3.2.1 FROM *LANGUE* AND *PAROLE* TO CODE AND MESSAGE

Saussure only briefly used the term *social code* with reference to the language system (*langue*) (1916d: 41). It was Jakobson who, under the influence of information theory, adopted the dichotomy of *code* and *message* to replace the Saussurean *langue* and *parole* (for details see Language 4.2). As summarized by Martinet, the code is "the organization which permits the composition of the message. It is to this code that each element of a message is referred in order to elicit sense" (1960: 34). After Jakobson, Lévi-Strauss (1962) adopted the concept of code as a key term in his semiotic anthropology (cf. Structuralism 2.) to describe the underlying rules of culture and social behavior (see also Eco 1984b: 167–68).

3.2.2 CODE AS SYSTEM OF CONSTRAINTS

Ducrot & Todorov use a very narrow concept of code, defining it as a mere "system of constraints," whose elements do not have to be meaningful (1972: 104). "Thus, music is a code: all the elements of a composition are interrelated, but they do not signify." In contrast to such elementary codes, sign systems fulfil the additional criterion of having signs associated with meanings. Finally, language is a sign system with additional properties of "secondness," by which the authors understand various modes of metalinguistic functions. Most signifying systems are described as being of a mixed type. Literature, for example, "illustrates the imposition of a second code on a language (for example, the formal constraints of poetry or the narrative)." Most other semiotic definitions of code include the feature "system of constraints" as a minimum criterion, but usually additional criteria are postulated by which languages are included in the category of code.

3.2.3 CONVENTIONALITY

One of the most common criteria in semiotic definitions of code is that of conventionality. Focusing on this criterion, Guiraud defines a code as a system of explicit social conventions (1971: 41). Guiraud opposes codes in this sense to "systems of implicit, latent and purely contingent signs," which he calls *hermeneutics*. Guiraud's field of semiotic codes covers a broad spectrum including aesthetic and poetic codes. Therefore, his distinction between the criteria *explicit-implicit* seems somewhat questionable. The evolution of the arts, for example, is certainly not made by explicit conventions. There are conventions in the arts, but these are rather implicit than explicit. Guiraud therefore admits that codification is ultimately a matter of degree:

> Signification is more or less codified, and ultimately we are left with open systems which scarcely merit the designation "code" but are merely systems of hermeneutic interpretation. Here, too, we have the frontier between *logic* and *poetics*; though it is true that certain poetic systems are, as we shall see, highly codified. What is fundamental is the notion of a *more* or *less* codified sign or system of signs. (1971: 24)

3.3 Eco's Definition of Codes

Eco developed his influential semiotic theory of codes in several phases (Eco 1968; 1973b; 1976; 1984b). Cultural convention is the basic

criterion of his definitions. Although this theory is characterized by an extraordinary expansion of the field of phenomena studied as codes, Eco excludes systems from his definition of codes. For Eco's delimitation of the semiotic field, see 3.4.2.

3.3.1 CULTURE AND CONVENTION

Conventionality is Eco's basic criterion of codes. As a first approach, Eco (1968: 19) accepts Miller's (1951: 7) definition of codes as "any system of symbols that, by prior agreement between the source and destination, is used to represent and convey information." More specifically, Eco defines the code as a system of significant units with rules of combination and transformation. In sum, a code is "a system of rules given by a culture" (1968: 130, 134).

3.3.2 ECO'S EXPANSION OF THE SEMIOTIC FIELD OF CODES

Eco gives an outline of the semiotic field which comprises codes of various degrees of conventionality and complexity (1968: 20–27; 1976: 9–14). This semiotic field is symptomatic of an extremely broad concept of code. It comprises "codes" from zoosemiotics, tactile communication, paralinguistics, medical semiotics, kinesics, music, languages, visual communication, including architecture and paintings, systems of objects, narrativity and other branches of text semiotics, cultural codes such as systems of etiquette and primitive religions, aesthetics, mass communication, and rhetoric. In contrast to the narrower definitions of codes, Eco (1973: 171) includes in his definition *vague* codes, *weak* codes (changing rapidly), *incomplete* codes (with few signifiers associated with large complexes of content), *preliminary* codes ("soon to be replaced") and even *contradictory* codes. He mentions the *fashion* code as one that is imprecise, weak, incomplete, and preliminary.

3.3.3 CODES VS. SYSTEMS

Eco distinguishes between codes and systems by pointing out that every code comprises two correlated systems of paradigmatic structures, one of content structures and one of expression structures (1973: 85–86). The code of traffic lights, for example, consists of a system of visual expression elements in which "red" is opposed to "green," "amber," and "red plus amber." It is arbitrarily correlated to the system of content elements 'stop,' 'go,' 'prepare to stop,' and 'prepare to go.' A code is thus a rule coupling elements from an expression system with elements from a content system. Since this distinction between codes and systems is not generally accepted in semiotic terminology, Eco later proposes the equivalent terms *code* (proper) and *s-code* ("or code as system") (1976: 37–38; 1984b: 169). In linguistics, the so-called phonological code is an example of an s-code since it is merely a system of expression elements (distinctive features with rules of combination) without a correlated system of content elements (phonemes have no meaning).

3.3.4 OVERCODING AND UNDERCODING

According to Eco, "the mobility of semantic space makes codes change transiently and processually" (1976: 129). The interpretation of messages therefore requires continuous *extra-coding*, the challenging and hypothetical modification of existing codes. Eco distinguishes two modes of extra-coding in text interpretation, *overcoding* and *undercoding* (ibid.: 133–36, 155). Overcoding is the interpretative process of modifying a preestablished code by proposing a new rule which governs a rarer application of the previous rule. Stylistic and ideological conventions are examples of such rules used in overcoding. According to Eco, overcoding proceeds in a twofold direction:

> It may be that, given a code assigning meaning to certain minimal expressions, overcoding will assign additional meanings to more macroscopic strings of these expressions. Rhetorical or iconological rules are of this sort. But it may also be that, given certain coded units, overcoding will analyze these units into more analytical entities, as when, given a word, paralinguistics establishes that different ways of pronouncing it [. . .] correspond to different shades of meaning. (1976: 134)

Undercoding, according to Eco (1976: 135–36), is a kind of rough, imprecise, and hypothetical coding, a "movement from unknown texts to codes." The discovery of meanings in the acquisition of a foreign language or culture is an example:

> So undercoding may be defined as the operation by means of which in the absence of reliable pre-established rules, certain macroscopic portions of certain texts are provisionally assumed to be pertinent units of a code in formation, even though the combinatorial rules governing the more basic compositional items of the expression, along with the corresponding content-units, remain unknown. [. . .]
>
> Thus, overcoding proceeds *from existing codes to more analytic subcodes* while undercoding proceeds *from non-existent codes to potential codes*.

3.4 Codes and the Semiotic Field

The field of phenomena which have been studied as codes has an enormous breadth extending from the genetic code to codes of painting and music. While this field can be only summarily surveyed in this section, special attention will be given to codes that demarcate its "lower threshold."

3.4.1 CODES IN THE SEMIOTIC FIELD

Eco introduces the term *semiotic field* as a metaphor for the plurality of codes which are possible subjects of semiotic research (1968: 20–27; 1976: 9–14). For his own, rather unsystematic, list of codes in the semiotic field, see 3.3.2. One of the most ambitious attempts at a taxonomy of semiotic codes is Fabbri et al. (1976: 167, 203. 222). Based on the writings of Barthes, Jakobson, Lévi-Strauss, Lotman, and Bernstein, it distinguishes up to one hundred types of codes. A less ambitious subdivision of the semiotic field is the following one proposed by Guiraud (1971 and modified 1973: 478–83):

I. LOGICAL CODES
   —*language-based* (substitutive) *codes* including language substitutes and

speech-related nonverbal communication.

— *practical codes*: signals and programs to coordinate action by means of injunctions, instructions, notices, or warnings.

— *epistemological codes* including *scientific codes* (taxonomies, algorithms, symbols of chemistry, etc.) and *mantic codes* (astrology, etc.).

II. SOCIAL CODES

These codes use signs to establish social status or relations, such as

— *insignia*: signs of social identity, such as flags, totems, uniforms, decorations, tattoos, names, shop signs, trademarks.

— *protocols* and *etiquettes* including various codes of politeness.

— *rituals, fashions, games*—and one should add to Guiraud's list *legal codes*; cf. Seibert, ed. (1980) and Text Semiotics (1.2).

III. LANGUAGE AND AESTHETIC CODES

For the study of these phenomena as codes, see Language (4.), Language Substitutes (2.–3.), Aesthetics (4.), and Literature (3.1).

3.4.2 ECO'S SEMIOTIC THRESHOLDS

Eco delimits the semiotic field by setting up a lower and an upper threshold beyond which the topics of research fall into the domain of sciences other than semiotics (1972: 31–39; 1976: 16–28). From his standpoint of cultural semiotics, only communication based on codes and conventions is studied within the semiotic field. Roughly, the lower threshold of semiotics is "that which separates signs from things and artificial signs from natural ones" (Eco 1972: 19). Physiological stimuli, most natural indices, physical information, neurophysiological and genetic "codes" are below his semiotic threshold, since they are not based on social conventions. But this threshold is not a sharp boundary. Zoosemiotics, for example, is included in the semiotic field insofar as it provides evidence "that even on the animal level there exist patterns of signification which

can, to a certain degree, be defined as cultural and social" (ibid.: 9).

Eco's upper threshold of semiotics is that between the semiotic and various nonsemiotic points of view. Women (in anthropological studies of marriage rules), tools, and commodities (cf. Objects) do not function primarily as signs although they may be studied *sub specie semioticae* (cf. Eco 1976: 27). When studied as signs, these phenomena belong to the semiotic field. When studied from other (biological, mechanical, or economic) points of view, they are beyond the upper threshold of semiotics.

3.4.3 THE DECODING OF NATURAL SEMIOSIS

Although phenomena of natural semiosis are below Eco's lower threshold of semiotics, Eco nevertheless considers the interpretation of medical symptoms to be based on a code and thus to belong to the semiotic field (1976: 10, 17). In Eco's view, this semiotic transformation of nonsemiotic phenomena occurs as follows:

> The first doctor who discovered a sort of constant relationship between an array of red spots on the patient's face and a given disease (measles) made a [nonsemiotic] inference: but insofar as this relationship has been made conventional and has been registered as such in medical treatises, a *semiotic convention* has been established. There is a sign every time a human group decides to use and to recognize something as the vehicle of something else. (ibid.: 17)

What Eco describes is not really culture *in* nature, but the shift from natural semiosis to its cultural interpretation, which is a shift between two levels of semiosis. While events of natural semiosis remain unaffected by cultural conventions, their interpretation changes with time and culture. Even that mode of interpretation which comes closest to the reality of the facts of natural semiosis, namely, scientific explanation, is still affected by culture, as the changes in the world models of physics show. In archaic times, for example, lightning was once understood as the gesture of a supernatural being. Modern meteorology explains it as an electrical phenomenon. These two modes of explanation exemplify the shift from a mythic code to a scientific code as the basis of the interpretation of natural semiosis (cf. Scholes 1982: 143). For other approaches to determine the threshold from the nonsemiotic to the semiotic, see Sign (1.3).

4. Code Structure and Typology

There are several criteria according to which codes can be classified. One possible criterion is the channel of communication (see Communication 3.1.3). Accordingly, Guiraud distinguishes between visual, auditory, tactile, olfactive, and gustatory (or culinary) codes (1973; 460–64). Other typologies focus on the semantic dimensions of the signs of a code and distinguish between arbitrary, iconic, indexical, and other types of coding (cf. Verón 1970; 1973a). Two of the most influential typologies of codes, those by Buyssens and Prieto, are based on structural principles. Both authors are concerned only with highly conventional codes, based on intentional communication. These types of code allow an analysis in close analogy to the structure of language.

4.1 Buyssens's Typology of Codes

Buyssens's (1943; 1967) contribution to the history of semiotics has been outlined by Mounin (1970a: 18–20, 235–41), Caprettini (1980: 180–93), Hervey (1982: 155ff.), and Martin (1986). His studies in functional semiotics were an important step in the realization of the Saussurean program of extending structural linguistics to a general theory of sign systems. His direct successor in this project was Prieto.

4.1.1 SEME AND SÉMIE

Buyssens studies codes under the designation of *sémies*; later he also uses the terms "*system* or *code*" (1967: 52). A *sémie* is a system of *sèmes* (semes). A seme, according to Buyssens, is a semiotic unit which can function as a message in a "semic act" of communication. Basically it corresponds to a message at the level of a proposition, a combination of a subject plus a predicate. Semes must be conventional and intentional, and they are members of a set of equivalent semes, the *sémie*. Buyssens distinguishes three dimensions in the classification of *sémies* or codes.

4.1.2 SYSTEMATIC VS. ASYSTEMATIC CODES

The first class of codes is divided into *systematic* and *asystematic* or *articulated* and *unarticulated* codes (cf. Buyssens 1943: 34–37; 1967: 50). In systematic codes, the semes can be segmented into elementary semiotic units, called signs. Buyssens defines a sign as the "indivisible element common to several semes with respect to both form and signification" (1943: 37). A *sémie* is not a system of such signs, but a system of semes. Words and morphemes in language, being only elements of messages, correspond to the level of signs. Asystematic codes produce messages which cannot be segmented in this way.

4.1.3 INTRINSIC AND EXTRINSIC CODES

Intrinsic and *extrinsic* codes are distinguished by the criterion of the conventionality of their elements (Buyssens 1943: 44–46; 1967: 63–65). Codes whose semes are iconic or indexical are called intrinsic (because "the link between signifier and signified is inherent to the nature of the signifier"). Codes with arbitrary semes are called extrinsic.

4.1.4 DIRECT AND SUBSTITUTIVE CODES

Buyssens's distinction between direct and indirect codes (1943: 49–52; 1967: 45–48) is relevant to the theory of language and language-related codes (see Language Substitutes 3.1.1, Writing 3.). In Buyssens's view, only the spoken mode of language is a direct code. Writing, being derived from speech, is thus a substitutive code. Morse code, being derived from writing, is classified as substitutive to the second degree. Direct coding also occurs in the field of nonlinguistic communication. More generally defined, direct codes "directly link perceptible facts to facts of consciousness," while indirect codes "regularly substitute certain perceptible facts for other perceptible facts which are used as a form for another *sémie*" (Buyssens 1943: 49). For a different perspective of substitution in coding, see 2.1.3 and 5.3.1.

4.2 Prieto's Theory of Code Articulation

Prieto (1966; 1968; 1975a; b), followed by Eco (1968: 236ff; 1976: 231ff.), Mounin (1970a; 1985), J. Martinet (1973; 1982), and Hervey (1982), develops a theory of codes whose basic concepts are derived from the model of language.

4.2.1 CODE WITH DOUBLE ARTICULATION

The basic principle of Prieto's theory of codes is derived from the model of *double articulation* in language (see Language 4.1). The structure of the nonlinguistic codes is compared to this model and, accordingly, various types of code are distinguished: some have no articulation; some have only the first, others only the second articulation. Since Prieto deals with nonlinguistic signs, he uses general semiotic terms for the description of the levels and elements of codes. His terminology is derived partly from Hjelmslev and partly from Buyssens. Accordingly, messages of codes with two levels of articulation are structured into *figurae*, *signs*, and *semes*. Figurae are the distinctive, but not yet meaningful, units, corresponding to phonemes or graphemes in language (cf. Hjelmslev 3.3.2). Signs and semes are meaningful elements corresponding to words and complete sentences (cf. 4.1.1). A *message* consists of one or several semes.

Codes with two levels of articulation other than language can be found in the domain of cataloging and registration. In section 2.2.2, an example of a warehouse catalog was given in which garments were indicated by three groups of code numbers. To specify this example, let us assume the number is "28/40/07" and means 'shirt,' 'size 40,' color 'yellow.' This total information is the seme. The three se-

mantic elements are its signs, which proves that there is first articulation. If "28" is one of 65 possible garments, "40" one of 12 possible sizes, and "07" one of 18 possible colors, these three code groups prove that there is second articulation. Each of the three two-digit numbers is composed of figurae, the single numerals which in themselves are unrelated to the meaning of the sign. The figura "8" in the group "28" is as unrelated to the meaning of 'shirt' as is the letter s to the word *shirt* of which it is a grapheme. Structurally, the message "28/40/07" is similar with its two levels of articulation to the verbal message "yellow shirt of size 40," which can be segmented into 4 words (first articulation) and 23 graphemes (including spaces) (second articulation).

The principle of single or double articulation represents a principle of coding, which Prieto describes as *economy* (cf. 2.1.4). The coding is economic because it reduces the number of minimal elements necessary to generate a message (cf. Information 2.1.6). Instead of sixty-five different symbols to designate sixty-five garments, we only need the ten numerals from zero to nine, combined in groups of two.

4.2.2 CODES WITHOUT ARTICULATION

Codes without articulation exemplify a code structure which is uneconomical: there are as many signs as there are semes. No seme is further decomposable into elements which occur elsewhere. In praxis, such codes are used only in very restricted domains or situations of communication. The "language of flowers," as described by Billig & List, eds. (1974), is a code without articulation. Its signifiers are about five hundred flowers, each of which is ascribed a different meaning (such as "red rose"—'victory is yours' or "salad"—'give me advice').

Eco (1973: 10) and Martinet (1982: 170) refer to traffic lights as a code without articulation. The messages "red-green-amber" cannot be segmented into smaller components, neither signs, which compose a seme, nor figures. However, if the "yellow + red" combination is taken into consideration, which in some countries signalizes 'prepare to go,' there is at least one seme composed of two signs. Prieto discusses codes with only one seme as a special case of an unarticulated code (1966: 49, 158). Examples are the white walking cane of the blind or the emblem of the Olympic rings.

4.2.3 CODES WITH SECOND ARTICULATION ONLY

Any cataloging system registering items consecutively with arbitrary numbers, for example a code which identifies 843 books with numbers from 1 to 843, is a code without first, but with second articulation. A nonnumerical example of a code with second articulation only is an international maritime flag code quoted by Bühler (1933b: 138). It combines three elementary but meaningless figurae, a round ball, a triangular pennant, and a square flag, into messages such as:

    ○ △ You are in danger.
    △ ○ Shortage of food. Suffering hunger.
    ○ □ Fire or leak. In need of immediate help.
    □ ○ Aground. In immediate need of help.
  △ ○ □ Stop or heave to. Important messages.
  □ ○ △ Do you have telegrams or news for me?
  ○ □ △ Yes.
  ○ △ △ No.

Each of these eight messages represents one or two semes, but there are no signs, only the three figurae: triangle, circle, and square.

4.2.4 CODES WITH FIRST ARTICULATION ONLY

In this type of code, the messages (or semes) can be segmented into smaller meaningful signs, but there are no figurae. Prieto's example is the code of traffic signs. For example, the circular traffic sign with the profile of a cyclist against a white background with a red edging is a seme which has two signs, "white circle with red edging" (meaning 'interdiction') and "profile of a cyclist" (meaning 'for cyclist'). The code does not combine smaller and nonsignifying elements into signs.

4.2.5 CODES WITH MOBILE ARTICULATION

Eco extends Prieto's typology of codes by postulating codes with *mobile articulation* (1976: 233). In these codes, there are both signs and figurae, but with flexible functions. The signs can become figurae and vice versa. The figurae can even assume the value of a seme. His examples are tonal music, where the timbre of a melody can be either figura (in distinction from other variants of the same melody) or sign, bearing cultural connotations ("such as rustic bagpipe-pastoral"). Another example is the code of playing cards. The units of the suits such as "hearts" or "clubs" are figurae. They are combined into signs, such as "the seven of hearts," and these in turn are combined into semes, such as "full" or "royal flush." But there are also signs without figurae, such as "king" or "queen," and moreover, there is a general fexibility of the figurae, whose value can change from game to game: "Thus, in a game in which hearts are of greater value than spades, the figurae are no longer without meaning, but can be understood as signs" (ibid.). For other aspects of the semiotics of playing cards, see Magic (2.3.4). It should be added, however, that a certain degree of mobility of articulation is also characteristic of language, since there are phonemes which can become semes, as in the exclamations "ah!" or "eh!"

4.2.6 THIRD ARTICULATION

Prieto doubts the possibility of a code with three articulations, in which the third level consists of structural units without correspondence to the first and second levels (1966: 99–100). Eco considers the film to be such a code with a third level of "hyper-units" (1968: 257ff.; 1976: 233–34). This third articulation of cinematographic language lies in the dynamic (or kinetic) dimension of film. Double articulation, according to Eco (1976: 234), is already characteristic of the structure of the static image (see Image 3.3.2–3). When the pictures begin to move, there is a third articulation:

In passing from the frame to the shot, characters perform gestures and images give rise, through a temporal movement, to kinesic signs that can be broken into discrete kinesic *figurae*, which are not portions of their content (in the sense that small units of movement, deprived of any meaning, can make up diverse meaningful gestures). (ibid.)

4.2.7 THE TEXT AS A LEVEL OF ARTICULATION

Martinet's model of language considered only two levels of articulation to be basic, the level of distinctive and the level of meaningful units. With the levels of figura, sign, and seme, Prieto and Eco distinguish three levels of message analysis. Koch (1971a; b) postulates further levels of articulation and analogies between language and nonlinguistic codes. In his theory, five autonomous levels of language articulation have to be distinguished, (1) the phoneme, (2) the morpheme, (3) the word, (4) the sentence, and (5) the text. He distinguishes analogous levels in the study of messages of visual and nonverbal communication.

5. Survey of Code Structures and Sample Analyses

The following discussion is restricted to the semiotic field which Guiraud classifies as logical and social codes (see 3.4.1; see ibid. for references to codes from other areas of the semiotic field). It is intended as a survey of semiotic studies in this area and in part as an illustration of the semiotic principles of code analysis discussed above. For specialized semiotic research in this field, in addition to the studies quoted earlier and below, see Lucas (1974, on practical codes in work and industry), Mestrallet (1980, on chemical symbolism; cf. Mounin 1985: 177–88), and Toumajian (1986, on numerical codes and computer languages).

5.1 *The Genetic Code*

While Eco excludes it from the semiotic field, Sebeok includes the study of the genetic and the metabolic codes as belonging to endosemiotics (1976: 3), and Jakobson variously discussed the analogies between the structures of language and the genetic code (1973a: 49–51; Jakobson & Waugh 1979: 67–73). For further discussions of these analogies see Masters (1970), Jakob (1974), Tomkins (1975), Lees (1980), Lumsden & Wilson (1981), Eco (1984b: 182–84), Bastide (1985), Koch (1986b), and Lumsden (1986).

The most striking parallelism between language and the genetic code is *duality of patterning* (see Language 4.1–2). As Jakobson has shown (1973: 49–51; and Jakobson & Waugh 1979: 69–71), both codes have discrete minimal components, devoid of meaning. In language, these elements of second articulation are the phonemes or graphemes. In the genetic code, the corresponding units are the nucleotides or nucleic letters. There is an ''alphabet'' of four different nucleic letters, by which meaningful genetic ''words'' are formed. Each genetic code word (or ''triplet'') consists of three letters. All possible combinations of these letters generate a lexicon of sixty-four genetic words. Sixty-one of them have individual meanings. The three remaining triplets fulfil the ''syntactic function'' to demarcate the beginning or ending of a message. Genetic messages are transmitted in sequences of words (the chromosomes). Further homologies exist at a level below that of the phonemes or nucleic letters; both are composed of distinctive features forming pairs of binary oppositions.

5.2 *Numerical Codes*

The semiotic study of numbers is a part of the larger field of *semiotic mathematics* (cf. Hermes 1938, Zellmer 1979, Bense 1981, Pogorzelski & Ryan 1982, Ard 1983, and Thom & Marcus 1986). In addition to its relevance to the foundations of mathematics, the topic has semantic, linguistic, and cultural dimensions. For the study of number words and other numerical symbols, see Menninger (1958), Lamizet (1984), and Posner (1984). In this section, only the code structure of numerical systems can be discussed (see also Prieto 1966, Metz 1967, Martinet 1974, and Toumajian 1986). The semiotics of numerical codes has two branches, the study of the system of natural numbers as a primary code and the study of derived or secondary numerical codes, which have a semantics of their own.

5.2.1 NUMERALS AS A PRIMARY CODE

As a primary code, the system of decimal numbers, written in Arabic or Roman *number signs* (numerals), is a code with first articulation only (cf. Prieto 1966: 105–108). From 0 to 9, the system of numerals is still unarticulated, unless one accepts proposals which have been made for a segmentation of numerals into distinctive features (Holenstein 1980). The level of first articulation begins with the two-digit numerals. Every element of multidigit numerals is twice signifying, first by its numerical, second by its positional value. The seme that is composed by multidigit cardinal numbers is a set; in the case of ordinal numbers, it is a position in a sequence. In spite of its relatively limited number of elements, the code of natural numerals is a code which can generate an unlimited number of semes (cf. Prieto 1975b: 137–38). Thus, the code of numerals is characterized by the design feature of creativity or *productivity*, which is often ascribed to language (q.v. 3.1.5) only.

5.2.2 SECONDARY NUMERICAL CODES

Secondary numerical codes are used for the purpose of registering and cataloging. There are significant and nonsignificant numerical codes. An example of a nonsignificant code is the code of book acquisition numbers which are assigned daily and consecutively to the newly acquired titles of a library. Since every acquisition number signifies a different book, the user interprets this code as one without first articulation. At the level of content, it is unstructured, since there is only one seme for every message, without smaller signs. At the expression level, however, the numbers are structured. They have as many figurae as there are digits in the number. Thus, there is second articulation. Notice the difference between the semiotic value of numbers in nonsignificant codes and the numerals in the primary code, which is a code with first articulation.

The acquisition numbers discussed above are nonsignificant only from the ordinary perspective of the library user. From the librarian's perspective, there may be some degree of first articulation if he or she interprets it as indicating the place in which the book is registered in the acquisition book (for example, numbers beginning with a 4 are registered in vol. 4 of the acquisition book). Similarly, the number may also be indicative of the date of the acquisition of the book (high numbers indicating recently acquired books). A special case of a nonsignificant code is one that consists of fewer than ten numbers, for example the code of bus line numbers in a smaller town. Such a code is one without articulation (cf. Eco 1976: 232).

Significant codes have either double articulation or only first articulation. Hotel room numbers are often of the latter type (cf. Prieto 1966: 98–108), if their first digit indicates the floor and the second digit the serial number of the room on that floor, for example: 53 = third room, fifth floor.

5.3 Substitutive Codes of the Alphabet

Figure Cd 1 shows three alphabetical codes which are usually interpreted as substitutive codes of the alphabet. However, it is possible that some of these alphabets may also serve in situations of direct semiosis.

5.3.1 SUBSTITUTIVE CODING

Considered substitutes of letters (cf. 2.1.3), the elements of the three substitutive codes are signs, consisting of signifiers whose signifieds are Roman letters. As substitutive codes, all three alphabets have no first articulation since no further semantically relevant segmentation of the substitutive letters is possible. However, there is a difference as to the second level of articulation. The naval flag code has no second articulation. There are no recurrent minimal

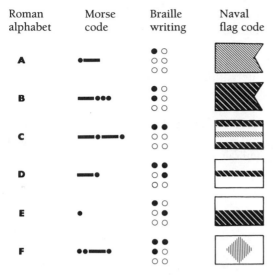

Roman alphabet	Morse code	Braille writing	Naval flag code
A	•—	● ○ / ○ ○ / ○ ○	
B	—•••	● ○ / ● ○ / ○ ○	
C	—•—•	● ● / ○ ○ / ○ ○	
D	—••	● ● / ○ ● / ○ ○	
E	•	● ○ / ○ ● / ○ ○	
F	••—•	● ● / ● ○ / ○ ○	

Fig. Cd 1. Three alphabetical codes (see text).

units by which the signal flags are distinguished from each other. The Braille and Morse alphabets, by contrast, have a level of second articulation, consisting of distinctive features: dots and dashes (Morse), or dot size and position within a pattern of six dots (Braille).

5.3.2 DIRECT CODING

An experienced blind reader of Braille does not transliterate the Braille letters into Roman letters while interpreting a Braille message. To him or her, the Braille letter has the same function as the grapheme in writing for seeing language users. To the reader of Braille, the single Braille letter is a figure, an element of second articulation. It is a nonsignifying element of Braille words, and these words are the signs which form messages at the level of first articulation of the Braille language code. Only in its origin is this code a substitutive one. (For the substitutive interpretation of this code, see 2.1.3).

5.3.3 MORSE CODE

Morse code was developed by Samuel F. B. Morse in 1832. With its dots and dashes, which are the figurae of this code, it seems to be a binary code. However, Morse code is not a truly binary code because there are two additional distinctive elements (figurae): a pause of two-dot length, to mark the limits between letters, and a five-dot pause, to mark word boundaries. Without these pauses, it is impossible to decide whether the message •• — •• means FE, EAEE, or EED (cf. Fig. Cd 1). Thus, Morse code is a digital code with four figurae. The signs are made up of combinations of one to four, the numbers of five, and punctuation marks of six figurae. While this code is essentially without first articulation, there are a few code-specific semes which testify to a partial first articulation. Among these are:

•— ••• Wait
•••••••• Error
••• — • Understood

5.3.4 CODE ECONOMY

Morse code was devised according to principles of code economy. The length of the Morse signs was determined in consideration of the frequency of the letters in English texts. The most frequent letters in English, *E* and *T*, are transliterated by only one figura: • and —. Rarer letters have up to four figurae (cf. Cherry 1957: 367). Thus, the economy of Morse code is a syntagmatic one (cf. Information 2.1.6), since with the shortness of frequent letters the total length, and with it the costs, are reduced.

The disadvantage of Morse code consists in its lack of paradigmatic economy, since it requires four figurae instead of two. A binary coding is much more economical (cf. 2.1.4). As Figure I 1 (see Information 2.2) shows, a genuinely binary coding of the alphabet (including space and punctuation marks) requires signs of five digits. The loss in syntagmatic economy (5 instead of 1–4 figurae) is compensated by a gain in paradigmatic economy (2 instead of 4 figurae).

5.4 Systems of Graphic Symbols

The so-called graphic symbols (which include iconic and indexical signs) are a semiotically still largely unexplored field of research. Sources for the study of religious, botanical, astrological, or folkloristic symbols, marks, brands, signets, and logos are Koch (1930),

Lehner (1950), Bühler-Oppenheim (1971), Croy (1972), Dreyfuss (1972), Schwarz-Winkelhofer & Biedermann (1972), Kuwayama (1973), and Frutiger (1981). See also the bibliographical references in Symbols (1.1). For the development of graphic symbols for universal communication or at least international public orientation, see Krampen (1965), Modley (1966), Aichler & Krampen (1977), and Krampen (1983: 162–94). See also the pictographic languages discussed in Universal Languages (3.2). A study in the semiotics of diagrams, networks, and maps, especially in the field of cartography, is Bertin (1967).

Many of the signs in question, in particular trademarks and signets, do not form a system of recurrent units. They can be interpreted either as codes with one seme (every symbol is a new code; cf. 4.2.2) or as a global but unarticulated code (comprising the class of all signets, for example). However, there are some special areas of graphical symbolism, such as the Olympic sports pictograms, which have partially recurrent meaningful elements and thus elements of a first articulation. Another example of a graphic code with first articulation is the symbols for textile care (cf. Martinet 1973: 215–17).

5.5 Traffic Signs

The study of traffic signs has been approached from various semiotic perspectives. From semantic and syntactic points of view, Studnicki (1970) and Droste (1972) have studied the grammar and the normative function of traffic regulations. The basis of these studies is verbal paraphrases of the meaning of traffic signs. A comprehensive pragmatic analysis of the code of nonverbal (gestural) and visual signs (such as light signals) used by drivers on public roads is Savigny (1980).

On the basis of Peircean semiotics, Kiefer studies theoretical and typological aspects of traffic signs (1970: 64ff.). Mounin investigates traffic signs from the perspective of French semiology (1970: 155–68). A comprehensive historical and comparative semiotic study of international road signs is Krampen (1983). Prieto (1966) describes traffic signs as a code of a mixed type: there are some groups with first articulation, some (using words) with second articulation, and some (pictorial ones) without articulation.

5.6 Coats of Arms and Flags

Semiotic aspects of coats of arms have been studied by Mounin (1970a: 103–115; 1986) and, under the guidance of Karl Bühler, by Klanfer (1934; 1935). Semiotic studies of national flags are Firth (1973: 328–67), Weitman (1973), and Pasch (1975). Both coats of arms and national flags are clearly codes since they form classes of substitutable signs. In their code structure, both codes have a mobile articulation (cf. 4.2.5).

The code of coats of arms has been subject to historical changes. It is more strongly conventionalized in its syntax, the rules for the combination of its elements, than in its semantics. In the course of the history of heraldry, the symbolic value of the elements of coats of arms was interpreted in many different and sometimes quite arbitrary ways (cf. Klanfer 1934: 122ff.). Some epochs of heraldry developed certain dominant paradigms of interpretation (for example Christian genealogic, political, or even "realistic" ones). National flags constitute a system of recurrent units (colors, forms, and emblems) of an extremely variable semantics (mobile articulation). Thus, the single color "red" in fifty-one national flags of the UN is ascribed no fewer than thirty different meanings, according to official sources (cf. Weitman 1973: 349).

Teaching

The semiotics of teaching and the teaching of semiotics are the two areas of research which intersect in the broader field of semiotics and education. Only a brief survey of research activities in this field can be given in this chapter.

1. Semiotics and Education

The state of the art in semiotic research in education shows a growing interest in a broad spectrum of topics, ranging from the theoretical foundations of education to methodological and practical aspects of teaching in the classroom.

1.1 State of the Art

The general relationships between semiotics and education have been investigated in a number of programmatic articles and state-of-the-art reports (Bense 1977b, Imbert 1980, Bettetini 1986, Cunningham 1987a; b, Sebeok et al. 1988), in anthologies (Brög, ed. 1977, Bernard, ed. 1983), and in the special issues of the journals *Bulletin du groupe de recherches sémio-linguistiques* 7 (1979), *Degrés* 38 (1984), *Langue Française* 61 (1984), *Zeitschrift für Semiotik* 7.4 (1985), and *American Journal of Semiotics* 5.2 (1987). For contributions of

semiotics to individual subjects of the curriculum, see 2.

1.2 Semiotics of Teaching

The semiotics of teaching studies educational interactions as processes of semiosis. Investigations into these communicative processes belong to the foundations of pedagogy. The results of these investigations are relevant to the choice of methods and media in teaching.

1.2.1 TEACHING AS SEMIOSIS

Bense argues that semiotics is fundamental to pedagogy because it develops cognitive faculties at all levels of perception and provides the general theory of communication and of the media necessary to the methodology of teaching (1977b: 23). For the contributions of semiotics to the study of media in the methodology of teaching, see also Schanze (1974) and Suhor (1984). Similarly, Regan (in Sebeok et al. 1988: 1–2) considers semiotics to be fundamentally relevant to education insofar as semiotics is a theory of "mind, meaning, learning, and information" and provides a broader perspective by extending interest "beyond the verbal into the nonverbal." Semiotic foundations of the theory of learning are further investigated by Rossi (1987) and by Cunningham (1985; 1987b: 214), who argues that "education based upon semiotic insights" influences our conceptions of curriculum by regarding knowledge "as a process, not a static structure to be learned and remembered."

Bense (1977b), Zellmer (1979), and Houser (1987) investigate teaching as a process of semiosis in terms of Peircean semiotics. Zellmer describes education as a "guidance to semioses" in a process involving communication, cognition, and behavior. He further considers the Peircean triad of firstness (cognition of *elements*), secondness (cognition of *structures*), and thirdness (*influence* of elements on structures) to be constitutive of three successive phases of learning (1979: 43, 18).

1.2.2 TEACHING AS COMMUNICATION

Teaching is a highly asymmetric mode of communication (cf. Dobnig-Jülch et al. 1981). The ideological force of the subject, particularly in the natural sciences (cf. Lemke 1987: 221), and the teacher's own authority characterize the situation in the classroom as an interaction between unequal partners. From the point of view of linguistic pragmatics, these and other aspects of verbal classroom interaction have been outlined by Wunderlich (1969b) and Zarcadoolas (1984). The role of nonverbal behavior in classroom interaction is described by Ward & Raffler-Engel (1980) and Smith (1984). For the semiotics of the visual media in teaching, see Metz (1970b) and Jacquinot (1977). Focusing on text semiotic features of educational interaction, Greimas (1979) and other members of the Paris School of Semiotics investigate the persuasive strategies in teaching and describe semiotic didactics as a "normative meta-discourse." Greimas envisions the semiotics of teaching as a future branch of semiotics which, "once constituted, will essentially be a *maieutic*" (that is, a Socratic method of eliciting and clarifying the ideas of others) (ibid.: 8).

2. Semiotics in the Teaching of School Subjects

The role of semiotics in the curriculum of secondary schools has been investigated by Imbert (1980), Suhor (1984), and Cunningham

(1987b). Topics and results of applied semiotics have been introduced in the teaching of primary language, secondary language, and a number of other subjects.

2.1 Language Teaching

Apart from the proposal for teaching elements of applied semiotics in the framework of language courses and with the exception of a few semiotic approaches to topics such as vocabulary development (cf. Brög, ed. 1977: 79–104, Zarcadoolas 1984), the main proposals for introducing elements of semiotics in language teaching have been in the field of text semiotics, particularly in literary semiotics (cf. Schuh 1977, Spinner 1977, Mariani 1980: 14–16, Landowski 1980, Kiefer 1982, Fontanille, ed. 1984, and Zarcadoolas 1984). The semiotic theories of literature adopted in these approaches range from Greimas's structural semantics (Landowski 1980) to structuralist theories of aesthetic openness (Spinner 1977) and Derrida's theory of deconstruction (cf. Structuralism 4.3) (Kiefer 1982). In addition to providing models for the teaching of literary text analysis, semiotics contributes to the broadening of the scope of language teaching by offering analytic tools for the study of language in the context of visual communication (cf. Image 3.–4.) and for the study of texts from the mass media, such as advertising, the comics, or film and television (see also Brög, ed. 1977, Bernard, ed. 1983, Bettetini 1986).

2.2 Foreign Language Teaching

There are three main areas of contact between semiotics and the theory of foreign language teaching: nonverbal and visual communication, cultural semiotics, and the methodology of vocabulary teaching. A general review of these and other aspects of foreign language teaching is Baur & Grzybek (1989).

2.2.1 NONVERBAL AND VISUAL COMMUNICATION IN THE FOREIGN CULTURE

Communicative competence in a foreign culture requires more than the correct use of the foreign language grammar. To explore the relevance of nonverbal communication to the understanding of communication in the culture of the target language, research in kinesics (cf. Hayes 1964) and in the semiotics of gestures has begun to lay the foundations of a contrastive theory of nonverbal behavior (see especially Gesture 2.2.2). For the role of visual communication in foreign language learning, see also Corder (1966), Réthoré (1978), Faber (1981), Brown (1984), and Bettetini (1986).

2.2.2 THE SEMIOTICS OF CULTURE IN FOREIGN LANGUAGE TEACHING

Foreign language teaching should pursue the goal of providing the learner not only with a linguistic, but moreover with an intercultural competence (cf. Baur & Grzybek 1989). To attain this goal, the teaching of a foreign language must also be the teaching of a foreign culture. Proposals for adopting cultural semiotics as a foundation in the domain of cultural and area studies in foreign language learning have been made by Köhring & Schwerdtfeger (1976), Melenk (1980), and Baur & Grzybek (1989).

2.2.3 SEMIOTIC FOUNDATIONS OF TEACHING METHODOLOGY

The two major methods of foreign language teaching, the indirect (or translation) method and the direct method, with its variants, the audiolingual and the audiovisual methods, make use of a variety of semiotic strategies in teaching verbal signs (cf. Nöth 1985: 314–17). Whereas the traditional indirect method taught words of the foreign vocabulary primarily as arbitrary symbols, the strategies of the direct method avail themselves predominantly of indexical and iconic signs. Indexicality occurs both in ostension and in contextualization in foreign language teaching. The element of iconicity in the learning of a foreign vocabulary is discussed by Peirce (§ 8.183). He argues that the teacher who introduces a new word in foreign language teaching uses a pure icon of it: "He virtually says 'our word is like this:' and makes the sound. He informs the pupil that the word [. . .] has an effect which he pictures acoustically." Besides these and other seman-

tic topics in the methodology of foreign language teaching, current trends in the didactics of secondary languages focus in particular on the pragmatic dimension of teaching (cf. Neuner, ed. 1979, Zarcadoolas 1984, Baur & Grzybek 1989). The problems of teaching syntax have so far only rarely been approached from a semiotic perspective (but see Engels 1978).

2.3 Art and Other School Subjects

Besides language teaching, the visual arts and media studies are subjects whose teaching has been approached from semiotic points of view (cf. Ehmer, ed. 1971; 1973, Brög, ed. 1977, Busse & Riemenschneider 1979, and see also Comics 1.). On the integration of semiotic elements into secondary school programs in visual communication and the arts, see Wichelhaus (1979). A high-school textbook in visual communication based on semiotic principles is Kerner & Duroy (1977). Other subjects whose methodology has been investigated from semiotic points of view are mathematics (Zellmer 1979), science (Lemke 1987), economics (Komar 1985, with special emphasis on trademarks, trade names, samples, and other signs in marketing semiosis), and religious instruction (Stock 1978). For semiotic aspects of the teaching of the deaf, see Sign Language.

3. Teaching Semiotics

Semiotics as an explicit subject of teaching is primarily a matter of courses or programs at the university level, but elements of semiotics are also being introduced in teaching programs of secondary schools.

3.1 University Programs

Centers of semiotic research and university chairs explicitly dedicated to semiotic studies have already been established all over the world (for example: Bloomington, Bochum,

Bologna, Buenos Aires, Montevideo, Montreal, Toronto, Urbino, and Paris—for details and further institutions see Sebeok & Umiker-Sebeok, eds. 1986; 1987). Nevertheless, semiotics remains a mostly transdisciplinary enterprise, whose teaching is institutionally associated with many other university programs, such as philosophy, linguistics, language, literary or media studies, aesthetics, communication research, anthropology, or cultural sciences. Courses in semiotics taught in the framework of these various disciplines in German-speaking countries have regularly been surveyed in a series of articles by Lange-Seidl (1985 and 1988). Summer courses—among them the traditional Urbino Summer Institute in Semiotics and the Summer Institute for Semiotic and Structural Studies (now Toronto)—and related international teaching activities in semiotics are regularly announced in the section "Institutions" of *Zeitschrift für Semiotik*, in the semiannual *Bulletin* of the *International Association for Semiotic Studies* (Vienna), and in the *International Semiotic Spectrum* (Toronto). Teaching programs and syllabi for semiotics as a major or minor in university studies are described by Sebeok (1976: 176–80; 1979: 272–79) and Koch (1971b: 571–600: 1987). For textbooks developed for introductory courses to semiotics at university level, see Introduction (3.1).

3.2 Teaching Semiotics in the Schools

In his programmatic theses on "Semiotic and the School," Morris observed that "semiotic as a separate discipline need not be introduced into the early levels of the school system [. . .]. Skill in the use of signs would not be best served in the early years of education by the too early introduction of a technical semiotical vocabulary (1946: 325)." However, at every stage of the educational process teachers, particularly of the native language, should

> show what signs appear in an utterance, how they serve various ends, how they are inadequate or adequate in actual communication. [. . .] At the level of higher education, a specific and detailed study of semiotic can serve to raise to fuller awareness the training in the adequate use of signs which should have occurred throughout the earlier levels. (1946: 326)

Today, elements of semiotics are being taught in various high-school programs. After first proposals for introducing basic concepts of semiotics in language courses of secondary schools (Kleinschmidt 1973, Pütz 1973) and a secondary-school textbook in visual communication beginning with an introduction to semiotics (Kerner & Duroy 1977), there is now an Italian *Guide to a Semiotics for School* (Mariani 1985) and an American five-volume series of anthologies for the use as textbooks in the teaching of semiotics courses in high schools (Thomas, ed. 1980–83). The high-school teaching project in which these materials were developed is described in more detail by Thomas (1984; 1987). Concerning the place of semiotics within the teaching curriculum of schools, Imbert (1980) argues that

> from an ideal semiotic point of view, a true and complete methodology of pedagogy should lead to a program that would allow, at the same time, both the freedom of a being mastering (consciously or unconsciously) the rules of the manifold systems giving him the possibility to communicate, and also the freedom of the being who would be able to break the rules and to "see" beyond the systems.

Language and Language-Based Codes

Verbal Communication: Introduction

The chapters on language and language-based codes form both the most central and the most incomplete section of this handbook.

1. Language and the Center of Semiotics

The articles on verbal communication are central to the field of semiotics because language is the most highly developed and culturally most important of all semiotic systems. They are necessarily incomplete because an adequate treatment of language would require a more comprehensive survey of linguistics, the science of language. There are two reasons why this more complete survey of language studies cannot and need not be given here: economy of research and the actual research situation.

For reasons of research economy and the history of linguistics, semiotics does not simply include linguistics. A handbook of semiotics therefore need not contain another handbook of linguistics. Although semiotics does include the field of language, linguistics with all its subdisciplines from phonetics to text linguistics has its own autonomous research tradition. Central topics of language study, such as morphology or syntax, therefore cannot be introduced in this handbook. The focus will be only

on *semiotic linguistics*, approaches to language with a specific semiotic background. For reasons of the actual research situation, a handbook of semiotics can afford to omit central topics of linguistics since the reader can be referred to a number of excellent introductions (Bolinger 1975, Lyons 1981, Fromkin & Rodman 1983) or encyclopedic handbooks of language and linguistics (Ducrot & Todorov 1972, Althaus et al., eds. 1980, Crystal 1987).

2. Translinguistic Topics of the Semiotics of Language

The semiotic interest in language is directed both at the foundations of language and at translinguistic extensions of verbal communication. The choice of the topics in this section results from these two directions of research. Topics concerning the semiotic foundations of language are discussed in the chapters on language and on arbitrariness and motivation of language signs, but the structures and functions of the semiotic system of language are also discussed in many other chapters of this handbook.

As a translinguistic field of research, semiotics extends the scope of study from vocal verbal communication (language in the narrower sense) to nonvocal modes of language and to language phenomena traditionally neglected or even ignored by linguists. This translinguistic scope is the reason for including the chapters on paralanguage, writing, universal language, sign language, and language substitutes in this section. There are other chapters in this handbook whose topic is the scope of "translinguistics." Verbal communication beyond language as a system is the topic of the sections on text semiotics, while nonverbal and visual communication are two further sections in which the relationship between language and nonlinguistic phenomena is discussed.

Language in a Semiotic Frame

To study language in a semiotic frame is to investigate language in relation to semiotic systems in general. This investigation raises the question of the scope of linguistics in relation to semiotics. Explicitly semiotic approaches to language generally aim at some extension of the scope of linguistics. In particular, semiotics is interested in determining the features of language in comparison to other sign systems or codes. Addenda to this chapter are the chapters on linguistic semantics, discussed in the broader context of semantics and meaning. The chapters on linguistic structure, system, iconicity, and linguistic structuralism discuss further aspects of linguistics which have become paradigmatic for the study of other semiotic systems.

1. Linguistics and Semiotics

The relationship between linguistics and semiotics can be interpreted as one of mutual exclusion, one of a part-whole relationship, one of interpenetration, and one of heuristic relevance.

1.1 Semiotics Excluding Linguistics

The least fruitful view is the one that considers linguistics and semiotics to be two mutually exclusive disciplines. Explicitly, Guiraud expresses this view as follows:

> Semiology is the science which studies sign systems: language, codes, sets of signals, etc. According to this definition, language is part of semiology. However, it is generally accepted that language has a privileged and autonomous status, and this allows semiology to be defined as the study of non-linguistic sign systems, which is the definition we shall adopt here. (1971: 1)

Similarly, Mounin claims that semiotics "constitutes itself by differentiation from linguistics" and warns against the confusion of semiotics with linguistics (1970a: 18; 1970d: 67). One of the reasons why linguistics is thus considered a discipline apart from semiotics is the historical autonomy of linguistics in relation to the more recent discipline of semiotics (cf. Mauro 1975). For different reasons, the view of semiotics and linguistics as two separate domains is also shared implicitly by Chomsky (1979) when he claims that the study of nonlinguistic sign systems contributes little or nothing to the study of language.

1.2 Linguistics as a Part of Semiotics

According to Cassirer, "linguistics is a part of semiotics" (1945: 115). This view is accepted by those who refuse to restrict semiotics in its scope and exclude certain sign systems from it (cf. Jakobson 1980: 19). To study linguistics as part of semiotics is to consider semiotics as the general theory of signs and linguistics as one of its special subfields. Sebeok supports this view: "If the subject matter of semiotics encompasses any messages whatsoever, the subject matter of linguistics is confined to verbal messages only" (1979: 37; see also 1988). This view is in accordance with the semiotic theories proposed by Peirce, Saussure, and Morris. In this view, a semiotic approach to language is an extension of linguistics, provides a particular general perspective in the study of language, or contributes to the discovery of the specific characteristics of language.

1.3 Semiotics as Part of Linguistics?

Barthes proposed the provocative theory of semiotics as being a branch of linguistics. In this view, linguistics is extended to include the level of the text (cf. 2.2.4), but at the same time, semiotics is reduced to the study of textual structures only (cf. Engler 1970: 64–65). From the point of view of general semiotics, this theory is generally rejected as being logocentric. The view of semiotics as a part of linguistics has also been attributed to Hjelmslev, who argued that "a language is a semiotic into which all other semiotics may be translated" (1943: 109), but Hjelmslev, in this context, did not refer to natural language but rather to semiotic systems in general (cf. 2.1).

A linguist who also argues that semiotics is in a way derived from linguistics is Benveniste (1969: 239, 241). Discussing the relationships between language and nonlinguistic sign systems, he argues that

> no semiology of sound, color, or image can be formulated or expressed in sounds, colors, or images. Every semiology of a nonlinguistic system must use language as an intermediary, and thus can only exist in and through the semiology of language. Whether language serves here as an instrument rather than as an object of analysis does not alter this situation which governs all semiotic relationships; language is the interpreting system of all other systems, linguistic and nonlinguistic.

> [. . .] Language alone can — and, in fact, does — confer on other groups the rank of signifying system by acquainting them with the relationship of the sign.

While it is true that language is the only possible instrument of semiotic analysis, this does not prove the semiotic dependence of nonlinguistic signs on language. It is a logical mistake to neglect the distinction between object- and metalevels of analysis, as Benveniste does expressly. Concerning the aspect of translatability of nonlinguistic signs into language, Sebeok correctly observes that such *intersemiotic transmutation* "is, at best, likely to introduce gross falsification, or, like most music, altogether defy comprehensible verbal definition" (1979: 38). For further arguments against this axiom of translatability, see also Prieto (1975a: 134).

1.4 Perspective Interpenetration

If semiotics is accepted as the general theory of signs, a general sign theoretical perspective can in principle be applied to every field of language. Almost every branch of linguistics can therefore be studied from a general semiotic perspective. The broad scope of linguistic topics which have thus come under consideration in a semiotic context is evident in the sections on "language and semiotics" of congress proceedings such as Chatman et al., eds. (1979: 377–416), Borbé, ed. (1984: 1059–1269), Oehler, ed. (1984: 527–638), and Deely, ed. (1986: 597–648). Even topics which traditionally belong to the core of linguistics have been interpreted from a semiotic perspective. Thus, Andersen (1979) studies "phonology as semiotic," Shapiro (1983) interprets topics of phonology, morphophonemics, and morphology from a Peircean semiotic perspective, and Shaumyan (1987) extends his semiotics of language from phonology and morphology to syntax. In addition to linguistic semantics, another field of linguistics which has increasingly attracted a semiotic attention is the study of translation (cf. Lawendowski 1978, Wilss, ed. 1980).

However, core fields of linguistics, such as phonology, morphology, lexicology, and syntax, have a tradition which is largely independent of general semiotics. Semiotics only adds a specific perspective to these fields of research or contributes to the theoretical foundations of these branches of linguistics. But there are fields of linguistics which are more naturally dependent on semiotics. Among these fields which essentially require a semiotic extension are linguistic semantics and pragmatics.

1.5 Linguistics as the Pilot Science of Semiotics

Saussure proposed to take linguistics as the *patron général* for the study of other sign systems, and Lévi-Strauss considered phonology a paradigm of the sciences of man (see Structuralism 2.1). The tradition of functional semiotics (Buyssens 1943, Prieto 1966; cf. Hervey 1982) has followed most closely such guidelines for the discovery of *isomorphisms* (cf. Marcus 1974: 2871) between language and the structure of nonlinguistic sign systems (see also Code, Music 3.1, Architecture 3.2.1, Objects 2.1, and Film 1.2.2). For warnings against the dangers of transferring the model of language to the study of nonlinguistic systems see Mounin (1970d: 69), Garvin (1977: 103), and Sebeok (1979: 38).

The views of the heuristic relevance of linguistics to semiotics have been supported by historical, genetic, and structural arguments. From the perspective of the history of semiotics, it has been argued that linguistics as a discipline has a higher degree of development than semiotics and therefore merits being taken as a guideline in the more recent field of semiotics. Both genetically and structurally, others have argued that language is the most highly developed sign system and that language can therefore best explain the principles of semiosis in general. Bloomfield represents this view when he argues that "linguistics is the chief contributor to semiotic" (1939: 55). Similarly, Weinreich refers to natural language as "the semiotic phenomenon par excellence" (1968: 164).

Structurally, Benveniste distinguishes three types of relationship between semiotic systems, each of which implies a type of heuristic relevance of language in relation to other semiotic systems (1969: 239–41). (1) There is a *generative* relationship: language can generate other semiotic systems, such as scientific and artificial languages or religious and legal systems (see also Greimas 1974b). (2) There is a relationship of *homology* (or isomorphism; cf. above). (3) There is a relationship of *interpretance*: language is the interpreting system of all other semiotic systems (see 1.3).

2. Semiotic Linguistics

What is a semiotic approach to language? The answer to this question requires a preliminary definition of language and depends very much on the basic positions adopted by the various schools of semiotics. There are usually two reasons why approaches to language are characterized as being semiotic: either the study is concerned with a particular field of language study which is being considered as an extension of traditional linguistics, or the study is based on the theories of a scholar whose work is considered to belong to semiotics.

The following discussion of semiotic approaches to language and linguistics is mainly restricted to explicitly semiotic approaches, i.e., language studies by authors who characterize their particular approach as semiotic. The field of implicitly semiotic approaches to language is much larger. It certainly includes most of linguistic semantics (and pragmatics; cf. 2.2.3), and, since language is a semiotic system, all of linguistics could be considered as being implicitly semiotic (but see Verbal Communication).

2.1 Linguistic and Nonlinguistic "Languages"

The term *language* is commonly used both for linguistic and for nonlinguistic sign systems. In the latter, metaphorical sense, there is a language of music (q.v. 3.1), architecture (q.v. 3.2.1), objects (q.v. 2.1), and film (q.v. 1.2.2), a language of space (see Proxemics 3.1), and animal languages (see Zoosemiotics 2.). Hjelmslev defined language in this "far broader sense" of a semiotic system generally (1943: 102). This metaphorical extension of the concept of language has given rise to some confusion concerning the scopes of semiotics and linguistics (cf. Mounin 1970a: 18, Chomsky 1979: 32). Therefore, it must be clarified that the following discussion deals only with human vocal language in a nonmetaphorical sense (cf. Verbal Communication).

2.2 Semiotic Extensions of Linguistics

The extensions of traditional linguistics which are usually characterized as representing a semiotic approach to language may be grouped in seven categories.

2.2.1 SEMIOTICS AS THE THEORY OF LANGUAGE

In the tradition of logical empiricism, semiotic (mostly not semiotics) is a philosophical theory of language. This view is best expressed by Carnap as follows:

> In the investigation of languages, either historical natural ones or artificial ones, the language which is the object of study is called the *object language*. [...] The language we use in speaking *about* the object language is called the *metalanguage*. [...] The entire theory of an object language is called the *semiotic* of that language; this semiotic is formulated in the metalanguage. (1954: 78–79)

In this tradition of logical semiotics, Pelc (1971) investigates the semantic foundations of language, Bobes Naves (1973) discusses semiotics as a theory of language, Martin (1978) entitles his primer of formal logic and metalogic *Semiotics and Linguistic Structure*, and

others (cf. 2.3) study language from the perspective of Peirce's philosophy.

2.2.2 SIGN THEORETICAL FOUNDATIONS OF LANGUAGE

One of the characteristics of semiotic linguistics is its special interest in the structure of the language sign. Sign theoretical aspects of language are discussed in several chapters of this handbook (Saussure, Hjelmslev, Arbitrariness, Icon 3.). Classics in the semiotics of the linguistic sign are Spang-Hanssen (1954) and Rey (1973 & 1976). On the history of this topic see also Schmitter (1987). More recent contributions are Mulder & Hervey (1972), Lange-Seidl, ed. (1981: 147–201), and Waugh (1984). The language sign and its role in the cognition of reality is the topic of a study by Gutiérrez López (1975). Pharies (1985) studies Peirce's semiotic views of the linguistic sign. Clarke (1987) focuses on the specific differences between natural and language signs.

2.2.3 THE PRAGMATIC FRAMEWORK OF LINGUISTICS

Pragmatics, according to Morris, studies "the relation of signs to their interpreters" (1938: 30). While syntax and semantics belong to the traditional core fields of linguistics, the extension of language studies in the direction of pragmatics is a more recent development which presupposes a semiotic foundation (cf. Frier 1977, Lieb 1981b, Hervey 1982: 93–125, Hüllen 1989). The development of linguistic pragmatics was strongly influenced by Austin's and Searle's "theory of speech acts." Although, as Hervey points out, there is a conspicuous lack of semiotic terms in this tradition of linguistic pragmatics, "the correct framework of the theory of speech acts is that of communication in general and semiotics in particular" (1982: 93). Aspects of this framework are discussed in the chapters on communication, function, and magic and in the section on nonverbal communication. On the differences between and the common bases of linguistic pragmatics and semiotics, see also Parret (1983).

2.2.4 THE TEXT SEMIOTIC EXTENSION OF LINGUISTICS

To some semioticians, the specifically semiotic approach to language begins with text semiotics (cf. 1.3). *Semiolinguistics* is a term which is sometimes applied to this semiotic direction of linguistic research (Hendricks 1973, Charaudeau 1983). For details see Text Semiotics (2.2.1) and Greimas (1.1–2).

2.2.5 THE CULTURAL FRAMEWORK OF LANGUAGE

According to Bateson, "to deal with linguistics in a semiotic frame, we must assume that coded linguistic communication is concurrent with little known types of communication in other modalities" (1968: 10–11). In this view (see also Ramat 1975), semiotic linguistics extends the study of language to its cultural framework. This framework is the one of the codes of visual and nonverbal communication (see especially Film, Comics, Advertising). The relationship between language and those nonlinguistic cultural codes is either one of *contiguity* (as in theater or film: language in the context of nonlinguistic modes of communication) or one of *representation* (as in literature: language depicts other modalities of culture). See also Nöth (1978a).

If the extension of language studies to the cultural and behavioral framework of language is characteristic of a semiotic approach to language, Pike's *tagmemics*, the theory of *Language in Relation to a Unified Theory of the Structure of Human Behavior* (1967), must be considered a classic of semiotics although Pike himself does not use an explicitly semiotic terminology in his studies. For further aspects of the cultural framework of a semiotic linguistics, see also Fawcett et al., eds. (1984).

2.2.6 THE STUDY OF NONVOCAL LANGUAGES

The view of semiotic linguistics as an extension from the traditional concern of linguistics for the study of vocal language to nonvocal language systems is discussed in the other chapters of this section (see also Verbal Communication 2.).

2.2.7 SEMIOGENESIS AND LANGUAGE

A specific semiotic extension of linguistics is the study of the evolutionary roots of language (cf. Koch 1974a, McNeill 1979, Sommerfeld 1980, and Koch, ed. 1982). The study of the biological foundations of language (Lenneberg 1967, Lieberman 1984, and Marquardt 1984) and the phylogenetic principles of *glossogenetics* (Grolier, ed. 1983) presupposes research in nonlinguistic sign systems. For some of these aspects see Nonverbal Communication, especially Gesture (2.5.2) and Zoosemiotics.

2.3 Semioticians as Linguists and Linguists as Semioticians

Some language theories are usually considered and sometimes declared to be semiotic because either their authors are major figures in semiotics or they are linguists whose work is associated with semiotics (cf. Hüllen 1989). For "semiolinguists" such as Greimas, who could also be mentioned in this paragraph, see 2.2.4 and Text Semiotics.

2.3.1 SEMIOTICIANS IN LINGUISTICS

The major figure in general semiotics whose work has been of influence to linguistics is Peirce (cf. Romeo 1979a). Jakobson called him a "pathfinder in the science of language" (1980: 31). Bense made an early attempt at determining the structure of sentences, linguistic categories, and text types on the basis of Peirce's typology of signs (1967: 58–72; see Peirce 3.4). Shapiro (1983) elaborated the foundations of a Peircean linguistics. From an orthodox semiotic point of view, Walther (1984) criticizes this approach as not being Peircean enough, but unfortunately, Walther's (1985) own contributions to the field are devoid of a linguistic foundation. Deledalle (1979) proposes a reinterpretation of standard theories of modern linguistics and deals extensively with the differences between the Peircean and the Saussurean approach to language (see also Peirce 1.1.2). Further aspects of a Peircean theory of language are discussed by

Ransdell (1980) and Pharies (1985). For a Peircean text semiotics, see Peirce (4).

Another semiotician of relevance to linguistics is Morris. As the founder of the famous tripartition of semiotics into syntax, semantics, and pragmatics, Morris might have been expected to be particularly influential in linguistic pragmatics, but this branch of linguistics developed largely independently of his semiotics. For Morris's contribution to text semiotics see Morris (4).

2.3.2 CLASSICS OF SEMIOTIC LINGUISTICS

Classics in linguistics whose work is generally considered to be semiotic are Saussure, Hjelmslev, Jakobson, and the psycholinguist Karl Bühler (1879–1963). In part, this is an evaluation *post festum*: Saussure, for example, considered semiotics (semiology) an extension of linguistics. Nevertheless, because of his concern for the semiotic foundations of language, it is certainly justified to interpret Saussure's work as one of semiotic linguistics (cf. Fawcett 1982). Hjelmslev's semiotic linguistics ("glossematics") became particularly influential in the field of structural semantics (cf. Greimas, whose work is sometimes characterized as "neo-Hjelmslevian"). More recently, a synthesis of Hjelmslev's semiotics with the stratificational approach to linguistics has been proposed by Lamb (1984). For Bühler's contributions to semiotic linguistics see especially Innis (1982), Sebeok (1981: 91–108), Eschbach, ed. (1984), and Function (3.1).

2.3.3 HALLIDAY AND SHAUMYAN

Two more recent authors who have proposed a semiotic theory of language are Halliday and Shaumyan. Halliday characterizes his studies in first language acquisition as *sociosemiotic* (1978: 1; see also Fawcett et al., eds. 1984). He wants to study language as a product of a social process in which "the construal of reality is inseparable from the construal of the semantic system in which the reality is encoded." In Halliday's interpretation, "a social reality (or a 'culture') is itself an edifice of meanings — a semiotic construct," and "language is one of the semiotic systems that constitute a culture; one that is distinctive in that it also serves as an encoding system for many (though not all) of the others" (1978: 2). The dimensions of Halliday's sociosemiotic theory of language are the text, the situation, the text variety, the code, the linguistic system, and the social structure (ibid.: 108).

Shaumyan proposes *A Semiotic Theory of Language* (1987) whose core is his theory of applicative universal grammar. He defines language as a sign system with six properties (ibid.: 2): (1) two semiotic strata, called *sign stratum* and *diacritic stratum* (basically double articulation; cf. 4.1), (2) sequencing, (3) use of rules, (4) structure, (5) hierarchical stratification, and (6) semiotic relevance. His *principle of semiotic relevance* is inspired by the Humboldt-Whorf principle of linguistic relativity: "The only distinctions between meanings that are semiotically relevant are those that correlate with the distinctions between their signs" (ibid.: 11–12). But neither are signs determined by their meanings nor are meanings determined by their signs. Only the sign-meaning correlation is semiotically primitive. However, Shaumyan also admits the relevance of what he calls *extrasemiotic* aspects of meaning, meanings rooted in culture (ibid.). Thus, what is relevant from a semiotic point of view may be irrelevant from an "extrasemiotic" point of view and vice versa (ibid.). In this terminology, *semiotic* is apparently synonymous with *linguistic*, while *extrasemiotic* refers to *semiotic* in the broader sense, as used throughout this handbook.

A basic principle of Shaumyan's semiotic linguistics is his distinction between *genotype* and *phenotype grammar* (1987: 19, 284). The linguistic genotype is the common semiotic basis of all natural languages. It is a simple sign system which controls the functioning of language and explains the unconscious process of language acquisition. The linguistic phenotype varies with different languages. The same basic genotype structure can be represented by a variety of grammatical phenotype structures. Language universals are part of the genotype. Genotype grammar comprises formal units (predicates, terms, modifiers) and abstract operator-operand relations between these units. Phenotype grammar comprises morphemes, words, and their syntactic structure (ibid.: 97).

---

3. Design Features of Language

According to Mauro, semiotics draws the attention of linguistics to the new frontier of a theory "capable of explaining the specific characteristics of human language" (1975: 46). Several attempts have been made to attain this goal by contrasting human language with nonlinguistic semiotic systems. The most influential proposal in this context is Hockett's list of design features. Other definitions of language in a semiotic frame can only be discussed more briefly (see 3.2–4.).

3.1 Hockett's Design Features (DF) of Language

Hockett (1960; 1963; Hockett & Altmann 1968) developed a list of sixteen *design features* of human language (DF) by comparing language with communicative systems of various animal species (see Zoosemiotics 2.4). This method of characterizing language within a zoosemiotic framework has become highly influential in interdisciplinary semiotic studies by anthropologists, linguists, and biologists (cf. Altmann 1967, Bronowski 1967, Marler 1969, Householder 1971: 24–42, Tembrock 1971: 35, Thorpe 1972a, Hinde 1975, Lyons 1977: 70–85, Hervey 1982: 247–52, Kalkofen 1983, and Clarke 1987: 96–103). Hockett first introduced his DFs as an unordered list. Only later, Hockett & Altmann (1968) proposed a subclassification within five "frameworks." The following survey retains Hockett's original list numbers (DF 1–16) but classifies the features further according to their common semiotic characteristics.

3.1.1 DFS RELATING TO THE CHANNEL
Language in Hockett's characterization is only vocal verbal communication and does not include written or sign language (cf. the DFs of writing in Writing 2.2). Three of his DFs relate to the vocal channel:

DF 1: *Vocal-Auditory Channel.* Language is produced by means of the vocal tract. The signals are received through the ears.

DF 2: *Broadcast Transmission and Directional Reception.* Sound moves in all directions from its source and can pass around obstacles. The receiver is able to locate the direction of the source of speech.

DF 3: *Rapid Fading.* Spoken signals vanish quickly, leaving the channel free for further messages.

3.1.2 DFS OF THE PRAGMATIC DIMENSION
Three features characterize the social setting of linguistic communication and its behavioral implications:

DF 4: *Interchangeability.* Adult members of a speech community can be both senders and receivers of messages.

DF 5: *Complete Feedback.* The speaker can hear immediately, and thus monitor by feedback, his or her own message. Together with DF 4, total feedback has also a social dimension (cf. Communication 3.2.2 on proprio-exteroceptive and communicative feedback).

DF 6: *Specialization.* The act of speaking is specialized to the communicative functions of language. Speaking does not serve any additional physiological functions. It requires little physical effort, and its energetic consequences are biologically irrelevant. The speaker is free to perform other activities while speaking.

3.1.3 DFS OF THE SEMANTIC DIMENSION
Five DFs characterize language in its semantic dimension:

DF 7: *Semanticity.* Hockett (1960: 141) considers only the referential function of language. In his view, human language is a semantic system of communication because its elements have "associative ties with things and situations, or types of things and situations, in the environment of its users." This is an insufficient characterization of the semantic dimension of language (cf. Lyons 1977: 79–80), which comprises both sense and reference (cf. Meaning).

DF 8: *Arbitrariness*. The signal-object relationship is arbitrary and not iconic.

DF 10: *Displacement*. The language sign can refer to objects remote in time and space.

DF 14: *Prevarication*. We can say things that are false or meaningless. Eco considers this feature to be characteristic of semiosis in general.

DF 15: *Reflexiveness*. Language can be used to communicate about language. This is Jakobson's metalinguistic function.

3.1.4 SEMIOGENETIC FEATURES

Two features relate to the conditions of language acquisition:

DF 13: *Tradition*. The conventions of language are passed down by teaching and learning, not through the germ plasm. Language is thus acquired by culture, not by nature.

DF 16: *Learnability*. The speaker of one language can learn another language.

3.1.5 CHARACTERISTICS OF THE CODE

Three features relate to language as a code (for further aspects see 4.):

DF 9: *Discreteness*. The sign repertoire consists of discrete and recurrent units. There is no gradation of linguistic elements in terms of more or less. The units of language are not continuous.

DF 11: *Productivity* or *Openness*: "New linguistic messages are coined freely and easily, and, in context, are usually understood." Productivity is primarily due to the syntax of language. New messages are generated by the creative combination of linguistic signs.

DF 12: *Duality of Patterning*. This is the feature which semioticians, following Martinet (1949), also refer to by the term *double articulation*. The discussion of this key concept of linguistics and the semiotic theory of codes requires a separate paragraph (see 4.1).

3.2 Central Properties of Language

Zoosemiotics is only one framework within which the specific features of language may be determined. Other features can be obtained by comparing language to human nonverbal communication, to the "languages" of music, the visual arts, or other nonlinguistic codes. Of the many approaches to this topic, only three additional proposals can be discussed in this chapter.

3.2.1 THE ZOOSEMIOTIC FRAMEWORK

Within his zoosemiotic framework, Hockett showed that many of his sixteen design features of language also occur in systems of animal communication. Nevertheless, he regards four features to be central properties of language: openness, displacement, duality, and traditional transmission (Hockett 1963: 177).

3.2.2 THE SEMIOGENETIC FRAMEWORK

From a semiogenetic perspective, Bronowski isolates the characteristic of *delay* between the incoming auditory message and the outgoing response as a "central and formative feature in the evolution of human language" (1967: 381). He furthermore distinguishes four consequences of this delay of human linguistic response: (1) *separation of affect*, (2) *prolongation* ("the ability to refer backward and forward in time"), (3) *internalization* ("the effect of producing an inner discussion of alternatives before the outgoing message is formed"), and (4) *reconstitution* (analysis and synthesis of messages).

3.2.3 THE ANTHROPOSEMIOTIC FRAMEWORK

In an attempt at determining the essence of language against the background of other modes of human communication, Mounin (1970d), based on Buyssens (1943) and Benveniste (1969), singles out the following six features of language: (1) the function of *communication* (not present in symptoms or indices), (2) *arbitrariness*, (3) being a *system* (unlike the visual arts or spontaneous gestures), (4) *linearity* (unlike visual communication), (5) *discreteness*, and (6) *double articulation*.

3.2.4 A UNIVERSAL SEMIOTIC FRAMEWORK

In extension of Hockett's list of design features, Osgood (1980) proposes a system of defining characteristics of language based on additional code theoretical, behavioristic, and comparative linguistic considerations. Osgood distinguishes (I) defining features of language generally (considering the possibility of semiotic systems of creatures from outer space) from those of human language. He further classifies some of the latter as (II) defining and others as (III) nondefining features of human language.

I. Language in general has six defining characteristics: *nonrandomly recurrent signals*, a syntactic, a semantic, and a pragmatic criterion ("dependencies between signals and their users"), and the DFs of interchangeability and productivity.

II. The defining criteria of human language, according to Osgood, are either *structural* or *functional*. The structural criteria include the DFs of the channel, feedback, plus a new criterion called *integration-over-time* (similar to Bronowski's feature of delay; see 3.2.2). His functional criteria include arbitrariness, discreteness, and the features of *hierarchical* and *componential organization* (similar to the DF of duality of patterning).

III. While all defining characteristics of human language are, *ipso facto*, language universals, Osgood specifies that most of the nondefining characteristics are only statistical universals (1980: 26). In addition to Hockett's DFs 14–16, these include such criteria as *translatability*, *propositionalization* (language creates propositions testable as to their truth or falsity), *progressive differentiation*, *a least effort* principle (G. K. Zipf's law), and two principles related to Jakobson's theory of *markedness* (see Jakobson 3.).

4. Language as a Code

There are two directions of heuristic influence between the semiotics of language and the theory of codes. One is that the linguistic model of the double articulation of language has become paradigmatic for the study of other semiotic systems (see Code 4.2.1); the other is that the metaphor of language as a code has led to specific views of language derived from the more general theories of codes and information. Since *code* is largely synonymous with semiotic *system*, the topic of this chapter overlaps with those on linguistic system and structure. Those chapters, however, focus on specifically linguistic models and their relevance to semiotics in general.

4.1 Double Articulation

The principle of double articulation or duality of patterning has often been considered to be the principal or even the single distinguishing feature of human language (thus Martinet 1949: 8). Its formulation is generally attributed to Martinet's functional linguistics. Jakobson claims that the principle has a tradition dating back to medieval speculative grammar, where the Modistae distinguished between *articulatio prima et secunda* (1980: 40), but according to Pinborg (1967: 43–44), this medieval distinction refers to the difference between the lexical and grammatical levels of language.

4.1.1 MARTINET'S DOUBLE ARTICULATION
In Martinet's (1949; 1960) theory, articulation means structuring. In language, there is a twofold structuring (double articulation) by two types of units. At the level of first articulation, a message is structured into meaningful units. These units are linguistic signs consisting of a signifier and a signified. The minimal units at this level are defined as *monemes* (corresponding to *morphemes* in American linguistic terminology). The English word *in-act-ive* is composed of three distinguishable units of meaning and has thus three monemes. The level of second articulation structures the phonetic signifiers of the monemes into nonsignifying but distinctive units, the *phonemes*. The corresponding units of written language are the *graphemes* (see Writing 4.1). Their only function is to distinguish monemes. The structure (articulation) is determined by the laws of the phonological system.

4.1.2 HOCKETT'S DUALITY OF PATTERNING

In Hockett's version of the same principle (1960: 151–52), duality of patterning means that the semiotic system of language consists of two types of elements: (1) smallest meaningful elements and (2) minimum meaningless but differentiating elements. In language, these units are (1) the morphemes (Martinet's monemes) and (2) the phonemes. For the study of other semiotic systems, Hockett adopts Hjelmslev's glossematic terminology and calls the differentiating elements *cenemes* and the meaningful elements *pleremes* (1963: 172) (see Fig. L 1). However, in Hjelmslev's glossematics, the fundamental dualism of language is *not* the double articulation into phonemes and morphemes but between the two planes of *expression* and *content* (cf. Martinet 1957: 106). Hjelmslev's expression plane comprises both phonemes and morphemes, while the content plane comprises only conceptual units of sense (see Meaning).

Units Levels	in language (Martinet)	in semiotic systems (Hockett)
1st articulation	monemes (or morphemes)	plereme
2nd articulation	phonemes (and graphemes)	ceneme

Fig. L 1. Double articulation according to Martinet and Hockett.

4.1.3 EXTENSIONS OF THE PRINCIPLE

Some linguists have criticized the principle of double articulation for providing only an insufficient characterization of the basic structural levels of language. The proposals for extending this principle have essentially taken two directions: either lower or higher structural levels are proposed (see also Code). Hjelmslev's semiotic linguistics introduces lower levels of linguistic structure, namely, the levels of figurae, which he postulates both for the content and

for the expression plane of language. His model of language can therefore be interpreted to consist of four articulations. Other linguists want to extend the principle of double articulation by introducing higher levels of linguistic patterning. Thus, Henne & Wiegand propose a level of third articulation to describe the rules of combining morphemes into higher syntagmatic units (1973: 133–34). Koch (1971a) even postulates further levels of articulation by ascribing structural autonomy to the levels of the word, the sentence, and the text.

4.2 The Language Code

The term *code* has been adopted in linguistics as a synonym of *system*. There are homologies and differences between language and artificial codes which are both sign repertoires and systems of semiotic transformation.

4.2.1 TERMINOLOGICAL PRELIMINARIES

The designation of language as a code is of a relatively recent date (cf. Mounin 1970a: 77–86). Although Saussure talked about the *language code* once (1916b: 14), a wider dissemination of the term in linguistics began only in the 1950s. In the context of developments in the theories of information and communication, Martinet (1960: 34) and Jakobson (1961: 573) proposed to restate the Saussurean *langue/parole* dichotomy by the terms *code* and *message*, "the code being the organization which permits the composition of the message." Under the influence of Jakobson, the new concept was adopted by Hymes and Bernstein in sociolinguistics, where it became a key term in the sociology of language.

Several scholars have criticized (Mounin 1970a, Kurz 1976) or even rejected (Cherry 1957: 8, Gipper 1978: 173–77) the term *language code*, emphasizing the differences between natural languages and artificial codes. Although *code* is also used as a synonym of *system* (cf. Buyssens 1967: 52), the two terms have different terminological connotations. *Code* implies reference to the psycholinguistic processes of encoding, storage, and decoding of language, but has the inadequate connotations of artificial closure. The term *system* places more emphasis on aspects of structure, relations, and rules in language (see further System 4.3).

4.2.2 THE LANGUAGE CODE AS SIGN REPERTOIRE

As sign repertoires, codes consist of a homogeneous and closed set of unambiguous symbols. Language, however, is an open system of semantically flexible signs. To overcome these implications of statics and closure, Jakobson and the sociolinguists have introduced two modifications of the concept of code in linguistics. Jakobson proposed "the dynamic view of [language as] a diversified, *convertible code*" (1973a: 37–38), emphasizing that "language is never monolithic," that "its overall code includes a set of subcodes [. . .] with fluctuations from subcode to subcode" resulting in dynamic changes in language (1961: 574). The subcodes of language according to Jakobson are its *functional varieties* (dialects, ideolects, styles, etc.) (1973a: 37).

Bernstein's sociolinguistic "code theory" of the 1960s (cf. Hager et al. 1973) distinguishes between the *general code* of a national language and the *speech codes* of individuals or social groups. In this theory, the latter is defined as a selection from the sign repertoire of the former. Since individuals or groups select differently from the repertoire of the general code, this results in code differences between different speakers in a language community. (The communication model in Fig. C 2 represents these differences as SR_1 and SR_2, the partial sign repertoires not shared by speaker and hearer.) Bernstein considered the differences between the *elaborated* code of middle-class speakers and the *restricted* code of lower-class speakers to be one of the most important facts in the sociology of language. The assumption that the difference between these sociolinguistic codes is only a matter of the degree of "elaboration," however, has been rejected by the generation of sociol inguists following Bernstein. The mere differential view of the subcodes of a language is static and neglects the dynamic principle of convertibility postulated by Jakobson.

4.2.3 CODES AS RULES OF SEMIOTIC TRANSFORMATION

The second main aspect of the definition of artificial codes is that they are "systems of transformation," whereby the signs of one sign repertoire, for example the letters or words of a language, are substituted for those of a second sign repertoire. Does language have characteristics of this kind? Language is not a substitutive system in the way Morse code is. Messages of vocal language are not the transformation of messages of some other code. Not even writing, sign languages, or language substitutes are mere 1:1 transformations of vocal language since they have various degrees of semiotic autonomy.

From a psycho- and neurosemiotic perspective, however, language processing has often been described as involving transformations between different modes of coding. Thus, early psycholinguistic models of communication (cf. Hörmann 1967: 7) describe linguistic encoding and decoding as processes of translation: the speaker transforms intentional behavior into acoustic signals, the hearer transforms the signals into interpretative behavior. Jakobson described encoding as a transformation of meanings (*signata*) into sounds (*signantia*) (1961: 575). These models characterize semiosis at the levels of content and expression as two successive stages of the communicative process. It is true that a dogma of the semiotics of language claims that the expression and content planes of the linguistic sign cannot be separated. According to Saussure, the signifier and the signified are inseparable like the front and the back of a sheet of paper: "One can neither divide sound from thought nor thought from sound" (1916b: 113). But the perspective from the logic of signs is not the same as that from psychology or neurology. Research in neurosemiotics (cf. Ivanov 1978) has meanwhile given evidence that a disconnection of signifier and signified can occur in aphasia (Linke 1981). These data suggest that the en- and decoding of linguistic sound and meaning are probably different cerebral processes.

Arbitrariness and Motivation: The Language Sign

"The linguistic sign is arbitrary." This thesis is Saussure's "first principle of the nature of the linguistic sign" (1916b: 67). Hockett considers arbitrariness to be a defining property of language, but traces of this feature also appear in nonlinguistic sign systems. A precursor to the Saussurean dogma of arbitrariness is the thesis of the conventionality of words. Both theories have their antitheses in views emphasizing the natural and motivated character of language. But the two dichotomies are not altogether equivalent. While arbitrariness and motivation primarily relate to the semantic dimension of the sign (its relation to the object), the convention-nature dualism focuses on its pragmatic dimension. For further aspects of motivation in language see also Icon (1.2), Metaphor and Universal Language.

1. Nature and Convention

The dualism of nature and convention is only a segment of a larger semantic network including semantic oppositions such as conventional vs. motivated, conventional vs. universal, and also natural vs. artificial (cf. Hołówka 1981). From Plato to modern philosophy, the dualism of nature and convention has been a fundamental issue of the philosophy of language. Aristotle, Augustine, William of Ockham, Port-Royal, Malebranche, Locke, Leibniz, Berkeley, Hume, de Brosses, Wilhelm von Humboldt (cf. Trabant 1986), Heidegger, Dewey, Wittgenstein, Austin, Grice, and Lewis (1969) are some of the landmarks in the history of this semiotic principle (cf. Coseriu 1967, Formigari 1970, Genette 1976, Rollin 1976, Schrader 1976). Saussure's dogma of arbitrariness is part of this history but has developed its own tradition within linguistics and semiotics.

1.1 Cratylus vs. Hermogenes

The dualism of nature (φύσις) and convention (νόμος and θέσις) in language was discussed by the pre-Socratic philosophers Heraclitus (cf. Coseriu 1970, Schmitter 1987) and Democritus (Rollin 1976: 15–16). It became the central topic of Plato's *Cratylus or on the Correctness of Names*. In this dialogue, the topic of linguistic conventionality is discussed dialectically from the perspectives of two philosophical schools (cf. Goldschmidt 1940 and Coseriu 1970).

1.1.1 NATURE

Cratylus, follower of Heraclitus, maintained that "everything has a right name of its own, which comes by nature" [φύσει], not "by agreement" [ξυνθέμενοι] and that "there is a kind of inherent correctness in names" (383A). In this view, the "true" [ἔτυμοσ] meaning of words could be revealed by the study of their etymology. The *primitive names* resulting from etymological analysis of words are signs which correctly describe the "reality of the things named and *imitate* their essential nature" (424A). "Correctness of a name is the quality of showing the nature of the thing named" (428 E), and "he who knows the names knows also the things named" (435D).

1.1.2 CONVENTION

Hermogenes, follower of Parmenides, expressed the antithesis (384D): "I cannot come to the conclusion that there is any correctness of names other than convention and agreement" [ξυνθήκη καὶ ὁμολογία] and "no name belongs to any particular thing by nature, but only by the habit and custom [νόμῳ καὶ ἔθει] of those who employ it and who established the usage."

1.1.3 PLATO'S SYNTHESIS

Socrates mediated between thesis and antithesis by admitting that "both like and unlike letters, by the influence of custom and convention, produce indication," i.e., meaning (435A). Words cannot be totally arbitrary since "in naming we cannot follow our own will" (387D). The giving of names is "the work of a lawgiver" (390D). While he thus admitted that there is conventionality in language, Socrates nevertheless argued for the superiority of the names "representing by likeness" over "representations by chance signs" (434A). But ultimately, "no man of sense can put himself and his soul under the control of names, and trust in names and their makers to the point of affirming that he knows anything" (440C).

1.2 Pragmatics of Conventions and Rules

While Plato discussed the nature-convention dualism primarily from the semantic perspective of the correctness of words in relation to their referential objects, the pragmatic dimension of linguistic conventionality, its role in social semiotic behavior, is a main topic of modern language philosophy (cf. Wunderlich 1972, Rollin 1976, Schrader 1976).

1.2.1 WITTGENSTEIN

According to Wittgenstein, "if language is to be a means of communication there must be agreement" (1953: § 242). Language "is founded on convention" (ibid.: § 355), and grammatical rules are based on grammatical conventions (Wittgenstein 1964: 55). But the social agreement on which linguistic correctness is founded "is not agreement in opinions but in form of life" (Wittgenstein 1953: § 241).

1.2.2 AUSTIN AND SEARLE

Austin defines only the class of illocutionary acts as "done conforming to a convention" (1962: 105). These are speech acts such as promising, commanding, baptizing, or arresting, which produce social effects and establish social consequences at the very moment of being uttered. The conventionality of illocutionary acts lies in the social conditions to which the speaker has to conform before the speech act can be successful.

Searle distinguishes between conventions and rules, defining the difference as a matter of surface vs. deep structure (1970: 39–40): English and French are "different conventional realizations of the same underlying rules." The difference between "je promets" and "I promise" is a matter of convention, but the promising device common to both utterances is a matter of rules. Searle furthermore distinguishes two types of rules relevant not only to language, but also to semiotic behavior in general (ibid.: 33–34). *Regulative* rules regulate an activity whose existence is independent of the rule, for example, most rules of etiquette or clothing regulations. *Constitutive* rules create and regulate new forms of behavior whose existence depends on these rules, such as the rules of chess or football. (For further aspects of language rules see Heringer, ed. 1974.)

1.2.3 LEWIS

A most general definition of convention is proposed by Lewis (1969: 58). To him, conventions are any regularities of behavior in recurrent situations, when this behavioral pattern conforms to general expectation. In this definition, conventions are essential pragmatic determinants of semiotic behavior in general insofar as signs presuppose a code, which is a system of semiotic expectations.

2. Saussure's Theory of Arbitrariness

Saussure's dogma of arbitrariness has led to a flood of semiotic exegesis (Benveniste 1939, Ege 1949, Engler 1962, Coseriu 1967, Fónagy 1971, Koerner 1972b, Lindemann 1972, Gamkrelidze 1974, Hiersche 1974, Normand 1974, Genette 1976, Wright 1976, Toussaint 1983). Two questions have come to the fore of the discussion: what is the nature of arbitrariness, and is arbitrariness a matter of sense or of reference?

2.1 Saussure's First Principle

Saussure did not claim originality for his "first principle," since "no one disputes the principle of the arbitrary nature of the sign" (1916b: 68).

2.1.1 PRECURSORS
In fact, the term had already been used by Locke, who wrote that words "signify by a perfect arbitrary imposition" (1690: III, 2.8). The direct source of Saussure's thesis was Whitney, who discussed the concept in the context of language learning and evolution, stating that "an internal and necessary tie between word and idea is absolutely non-existent for the learner" (1875: 18). Whitney also distinguishes between arbitrariness and convention:

> Every word handed down in every human language is an arbitrary and conventional sign: arbitrary, because any one of the thousand other words current among men, or of the tens of thousands which might be fabricated, could have been equally well learned and applied to this particular purpose; conventional, because the reason for the use of this rather than another lies solely in the

fact that it is already used in the community to which the speaker belongs. (ibid.: 19)

2.1.2 THE SAUSSUREAN THESES
Saussure formulated his "first principle of the nature of the sign" as follows (1916b: 67–68; see also Saussure 3.1):

> The bond between the signifier and the signified is arbitrary. Since I mean by sign the whole that results from the associating of the signifier with the signified, I can simply say: *the linguistic sign is arbitrary*.
>
> The idea of "sister" is not linked by any inner relationship to the succession of sounds s-ö-r which serves as its signifier in French; that it could be represented equally by just any other sequence is proved by differences among languages and by the very existence of different languages: the signified "ox" has as its signifier *b-ö-f* on one side of the border and *o-k-s* (*Ochs*) on the other.

2.2 Nature of Arbitrariness

The exegetic dispute about Saussure's first principle has in part its roots in the term *arbitrary*, which is associated with the idea of free choice, but Saussure warned that "the term should not imply that the choice of the signifier is left entirely to the speaker" (1916b: 68–69). His own explanation of arbitrariness focuses on the unmotivated nature of the sign. Against the false association of arbitrariness with semiotic freedom of choice, Saussure postulated the complementary principle of the *immutability* of the sign.

2.2.1 THE UNMOTIVATED AND OPAQUE SIGN
Saussure specified that the term *arbitrary* means *unmotivated* (1916b: 69). In an arbitrary sign, the signifier "actually has no necessary connection with the signified." Unlike (iconic) signs which have a "rational relationship with the thing signified," language lacks this necessary basis: "There is no reason for preferring *soeur* to *sister*" (ibid.: 73). This lack of motivation thus describes the semantic dimension of the linguistic sign, i.e., the relation of sense or reference. To characterize the sign as arbitrary

or unmotivated is to describe the phenomenon from the perspective of encoding. From the perspective of decoding, arbitrary words are also defined as being *opaque*.

2.2.2 CONVENTIONALITY AND IMMUTABILITY

Arbitrariness, according to Saussure, also accounts for the conventionality of the language system: "The arbitrary nature of the sign explains in turn why the social fact alone can create a linguistic system. The community is necessary if values that owe their existence solely to usage and general acceptance are to be set up; by himself the individual is incapable of fixing a single value" (1916b: 113). This idea of the binding force of conventionality is expressed in Saussure's principle of the immutability of the (linguistic) sign: "The signifier, though to all appearances freely chosen with respect to the idea that it represents, is fixed, not free, with respect to the linguistic community that uses it. [. . .] The signifier chosen by language could be replaced by no other. [. . .] No individual could modify in any way at all the choice that has been made" (ibid.: 71).

The principle of immutability is thus the pragmatic counterpart to the semantic principle of arbitrariness. However, it is a strictly synchronic principle. Saussure did not ignore the fact that the linguistic sign does change in its historical evolution (ibid.: 74). He called this diachronic universal of language the principle of linguistic *mutability*.

2.2.3 NECESSITY OF THE SIGN

Against the Saussurean principle of arbitrariness, Benveniste postulates the principle of the necessity of the linguistic sign: "Between the signifier and the signified, the connection is not arbitrary; on the contrary, it is *necessary*. The concept (the "signified") *boeuf* is perforce identical in my consciousness with the sound sequence (the "signifier") *böf* [. . .] Together the two are imprinted on my mind, together they evoke each other under any circumstance" (1939: 45). This principle of semiotic necessity is not as anti-Saussurean as Benveniste pretends (cf. 2.3.1). Saussure's the-

ory of immutability acknowledges at least the social aspect of this close association between signifier and signified. The remaining difference between Benveniste and Saussure is one of perspective: Saussure's arbitrariness focuses on the *logical* (lack of a) relation between the linguistic signifier and signified, while Benveniste's principle of necessity describes the *psychological* association between the two sides of the linguistic sign.

2.3 Arbitrariness: Relation of Sense or Reference?

A major exegetical dispute concerning the nature of arbitrariness arose from the question whether arbitrariness is a relation between the linguistic signifier and extralinguistic reality (reference) or between the signifier and its conceptual signified (sense). The Saussurean dyadic sign model seems to permit only the interpretation of arbitrariness as a relation of sense, but some of Saussure's own examples as well as the history of the principle of arbitrariness suggest that arbitrariness is a matter of reference.

2.3.1 ARBITRARINESS AND SENSE

Since Saussure's theory of the sign strictly excludes any semiotic consideration of extralinguistic reference (see Saussure 3.3), the orthodox interpretation of his principle (Godel 1957: 254–55, Engler 1962: 49–61) states that arbitrariness is a matter of sense only, i.e., a relationship between the signifier and the signified. In which respect can this necessary relationship between the two sides of a "psychological entity," the sign (see Saussure 3.1.1), be unmotivated? Meaning, according to Saussure, is a differential value, determined only by the structures of the language system and not by any extralinguistic reality. Since languages differ both in phonetic (*soeur* vs. *sister*; cf. 2.2.1) and in semantic (*mouton* vs. *sheep*; cf. Saussure 3.4.2) structure, the language sign is an arbitrary combination of arbitrary segments of semantic (conceptual) and phonetic substances (cf. Engler 1962: 58). This conclusion does not contradict

Benveniste's principle of the necessity of the signifier-signified relationship. Since the sign, according to Saussure, is only form, not substance, neither the signifier nor the signified can be said to exist before the creation of the sign (cf. Malmberg 1977: 140). Arbitrariness, in Saussure's semiology, is thus closely related to his theories of system and structure: "The choice of a given slice of sound to name a given idea is completely arbitrary. If this were not true, the notion of value would be compromised, for it would include an externally imposed element. But actually values remain entirely relative, and that is why the bond between the sound and the idea is radically arbitrary" (1916b: 113).

2.3.2 ARBITRARINESS AND REFERENCE

According to Benveniste, Saussure's examples of linguistic arbitrariness betray

> an unconscious and surreptitious recourse to a third term which was not included in the initial definition. This third term is the thing itself, the reality. [. . .] It is only if one thinks of the animal *ox* in its concrete and "substantial" particularity, that one is justified in considering "arbitrary" the relationship between *böf* on the one hand and *oks* on the other to the same reality. (1939: 44)

Since Benveniste himself follows Saussure insofar as he, too, considers linguistics a science of forms and not of substances, his own conclusion is that the principle of arbitrariness should be abandoned altogether. Against this conclusion, Gardiner expresses the traditional view of those who consider arbitrariness a relation of reference: "Does Benveniste deny that reality is at the base of every concept? Would he dispute the old scholastic doctrine *Nihil est in intellectu quod non prius fuerit in sensu*? What else is a concept than the mental precipitate left over from countless experiences of similar realities?" (1944: 109)

2.3.3 ARBITRARINESS IN A TRIADIC MODEL OF THE SIGN

To consider arbitrariness (also) a relation of reference is conclusive within a triadic theory of signs (cf. Peirce 2.). It must be specified,

though, that the referential object in relation to which the signifier is unmotivated is not the physical object as such. It is superfluous to refute an impossible influence of the physical object "ox" on the linguistic signifier. The correlates of arbitrariness can only be those between which motivation is imaginable (see 3.). Within a triadic framework of semiotics, referential arbitrariness must therefore be considered a relationship between two emic percepta, the emic perceptum of the referential object (cf. Lindemann 1972: 179–83), whose perceptual structure may already be culture-specific to a certain degree (cf. Eco 1976: 193–95), and the acoustic perceptum of the phonetic signifier.

Within a triadic framework of the sign, arbitrariness (and motivation) exists as a relation both of sense and of reference. Arbitrariness of reference is mostly demonstrated with examples of words standing for physical objects. Arbitrariness of sense is preferably demonstrated with abstract nouns. But both aspects are inseparable in semiosis, as Descombes observes: "If the signifier is arbitrary with respect to the referent and if the signified is necessarily linked to the signifier, the signified must also be considered arbitrary. [. . .] Signifying differences elicit conceptual differences. [. . .] Yet the semiological demonstration does unintentionally bear upon the referent. It engenders the referent" (1983: 171).

3. Motivation

The principle of arbitrariness cannot be taken as an absolute law of language. Besides the unmotivated and opaque sign, there is also the motivated or, from the perspective of decoding, the *transparent* sign (cf. Ullmann 1962). Since Cratylus, linguists have defended this aspect of language motivation against the principle of arbitrariness (Genette 1976). Some have even gone so far as to raise motivation to a constitutive principle of language and reject the principle of arbitrariness altogether (Toussaint 1983).

3.1 Absolute vs. Relative Arbitrariness

Saussure admitted that onomatopoeia and interjections are phonetically motivated signs but considered such *phonetic motivation* to be marginal in language (1916b: 67). He attributed more importance to motivation in morphology. Examples of word formation, according to Saussure, testify to a *relative motivation* in language (ibid.: 131): while simple forms, such as *ten*, *sheep*, or *apple*, exhibit *absolute arbitrariness*, compound forms, such as *fifteen*, *shepherd*, or *apple tree*, are examples of *relative arbitrariness* since their structure is derived from the simple forms. In addition to such motivation in morphology, it can be argued that all rules of grammar restrict arbitrariness and introduce motivation into the system of language.

3.2 Types of Motivation in Language

Ullmann (1962; 1975) distinguishes three types of motivation: *phonetic*, *morphological*, and *semantic*. From a more general semiotic point of view, some of these forms of motivation are discussed in the context of linguistic iconicity (see Icon 3.). Phonetic motivation or onomatopoeia is *primary* when the word imitates an acoustic phenomenon (as in *crack*, *plop*, or *whizz*). It is *secondary* when the referent is nonacoustic and the vowels or consonants imitate such dimensions as size (small vs. big), weight (light vs. heavy), color (light vs. dark), or speed (quick vs. slow). For these modes of motivation in language, see especially Jakobson & Waugh (1979). Even nonsense words can have secondary onomatopoetic effects, as studies in psychophonetics have shown (Ertel 1969). Morphological motivation accounts for the transparency of derivatives, compounds (cf. 3.1), and other morphological patterns (Mayerthaler 1981). Semantic motivation occurs in figurative language, especially in metaphors and metonymies whose motivational bases are similarity and contiguity (see Rhetoric 2.3.1).

Some linguists consider etymology to be a type of linguistic motivation (cf. Pohl 1968:

127). But since every word has its own history, one would have to say that all linguistic signs are etymologically motivated. On the other hand, there are certainly various degrees of *etymological transparency* depending on our knowledge of the history of a word. In the evolution of language, the transparency of words can decrease (as after sound changes) or increase. Arbitrary words can be transformed into a more motivated form. *Folk etymology* (also *popular etymology*) is the most striking case of such acquisitions of motivation (Ullmann 1962: 101–105). The history of the English word *sovereign* is an example: its French etymon *souverain* was transformed by the popular assumption of a semantic connection with English *reign*. The unetymological *-g-* in *sovereign* results in a new form which is partially motivated.

4. Arbitrariness in the General Theory of Signs

Arbitrariness is not only a feature of the linguistic sign. Saussure acknowledged it as a general semiological principle, and the classification of signs according to Peirce is also essentially connected with this criterion. For arbitrariness in animal communication, see Zoosemiotics (4.2.3).

4.1 Arbitrariness as a Semiotic Principle

According to Saussure, the linguistic signifier "is not phonic but incorporeal—constituted not by its material substance but by the differences that separate its sound image from all others" (1916b: 118–19; cf. Saussure 3.4.2, Structure 2.1). Since arbitrariness is thus not a matter of sound structure, it is also not restricted to language alone. It is a general principle of sign systems. Even if the future science of semiology should include the study of "completely natural signs," Saussure predicted that "its main concern will still be the whole group of systems grounded on the arbitrariness of the sign. In fact, every means of expression used in society is based, in principle, on collective behavior or—what amounts to the same thing—on convention." Therefore, "signs that are wholly arbitrary realize better than the others the ideal of the semiological process" (ibid.: 68; cf. Saussure 2.2.3).

4.2 Degrees of Arbitrariness

Peirce classified signs with respect to their referential dimension in the categorial order of I. icon, II. index, and III. symbol, but his categorial principles are not based on the criterion of arbitrariness (cf. Peirce 1.4). In fact, the degree of arbitrariness and conventionality in these three classes of signs may be said to decrease in the order of symbol, icon, and index (Nöth 1977a: 14–16).

Peirce defined symbol explicitly as "a conventional sign, or one depending upon habit" (§ 2.297). This necessity of social convention characterizes symbols as signs of the highest degree of arbitrariness. The class of indices includes most of the so-called natural signs ("smoke" as an index of "fire," for example). It is based on relations of causality or contiguity between the sign and its object. Since the object has a direct, often physical effect on the sign, the index proves to be the sign of minimal arbitrariness. The arbitrariness of an icon is higher than that of an index. Decoding the similarity of an icon or image with its object presupposes a higher degree of cultural conventionality than decoding signs which "direct the attention to their objects by blind compulsion," as Peirce (§ 2.306) defines the index.

These degrees of arbitrariness may be corroborated by considering the number of semiotic alternatives available with the three types of signs. The alternatives available for arbitrary conventions permit an almost infinite number of symbolic signs to be agreed upon for a given referent. The number of alternatives for the production and recognition of icons is restricted by the criterion of similarity, but all icons have elements of conventionality. The semiotic alternatives in the case of an indexical sign are strictly reduced by the singularity of the individual object to which it refers. While icons may even refer to fictional objects, no index can exist without the presence of its object. It must be added, though, that there are also degrees of arbitrariness within the three classes of signs. Symbols vary in arbitrariness as well as icons (see Icon 3.2) or indices.

Paralanguage

Paralinguistics is the study of vocal signals beyond (Gr. παρά 'beside') the verbal message in the narrower sense. This is why some scholars classify paralinguistics as a branch of nonverbal communication. But *paralanguage* raises the problem of the extension of the field of linguistics. From a holistic and semiotic point of view, it seems rather arbitrary to separate the study of linguistic messages from the accompanying paralinguistic signals. Paralanguage is therefore introduced as a branch of language studies in this handbook. A precursor of paralinguistics is Sievers's *Schallanalyse* (1924). One of the first explicit discussions of paralinguistics was in the context of stylistics (Hill 1958: 408). According to Weitz, ed., "paralinguistics sets great store on *how* something is said, not on *what* is said" (1974: 94). This definition shows clearly that paralanguage has a stylistic function. Paralinguistics may thus also be defined as a kind of *phonostylistics*.

1. Language and Paralanguage

Paralinguistics has been conceived in a narrower and in a broader sense. The distinction between language and paralanguage raises the question of the scope of linguistics and phonetics in the study of verbal and vocal messages.

1.1 The Scope of Paralanguage

The term *paralanguage* suggests a vast field of communicative phenomena beyond language, but this chapter adopts a narrower view of this field.

1.1.1 PARALINGUISTICS IN THE BROADEST SENSE

In his survey of current trends in paralinguistics, Crystal shows that the scope of paralanguage has been defined in seven different ways, as including
1. nonhuman as well as human vocalizations,
2. nonvocal as well as vocal features of human communication,
3. all nonsegmental ('suprasegmental') features and some segmental ones,
4. voice quality as well as (all or most) nonsegmental features,
5. only nonsegmental features, but excluding prosodic phonemes and voice quality,
6. only a subset of nonsegmental features other than prosodic phonemes and voice quality, and
7. certain communicative functions, such as the expression of emotions or personality (1975: 47–64).
1 and 2 are very broad definitions of paralanguage. While the first includes acoustic modes of zoosemiotic communication, the second covers the whole field of nonverbal communication. This broad view of paralinguistics is

shared by linguists such as Abercrombie (1968), Laver (1976), and Lyons (1977: 57–67) but is not adopted in this handbook.

1.1.2 PARALANGUAGE IN THE NARROWER SENSE

In this handbook, the term paralanguage will be restricted to human vocalizations only, whereas zoosemiotic and nonverbal communication are ascribed a more independent status within the semiotic field. Paralanguage in this narrower sense is outlined in Crystal's definitions 3–7. These characterize paralanguage as being "vocal," "human," and "nonphonological" communication. The differences between these definitions indicate different views of the scope of linguistics.

1.1.3 PARALANGUAGE AND NONVERBAL COMMUNICATION

Some scholars have proposed another narrower view of the place of paralinguistics within the field of communication studies (cf. Harrison 1974, Weitz, ed. 1974, Key 1975, Poyatos 1976, Harper et al. 1978). These authors describe paralanguage as a mode of nonverbal communication. This view is terminologically plausible since paralinguistic messages are mostly suprasegmental (see 1.2.1) and thus not inherent in the words, i.e., the verbal message in the narrower sense. Nevertheless, paralanguage is more closely connected with verbal communication than, for example, nonverbal gestures. While gestural, proxemic, and other modes of nonverbal communication can be used to transmit messages independently of language, paralanguage is communication which always occurs simultaneously with verbal messages.

1.2 Linguistics and Paralinguistics

The field of paralinguistics remains to be delimitated against the still linguistic field of phonology, on the one hand, and against possibly no longer paralinguistic modes of human acoustic communication, on the other.

1.2.1 SEGMENTAL AND SUPRASEGMENTAL PHONEMES

The segmental and suprasegmental phonemes of language belong to the "still linguistic" elements of language. They constitute the phonological system of language, which is the domain of phonology (or phonemics). Segmental phonemes are vowels and consonants, sounds which can be studied isolated from their context. Suprasegmental elements are modifications of these speech sounds in extended discourse. Among such suprasegmentals of language are stress (word accent or sentence stress), juncture (markers of word boundaries), pitch (tone), intonation patterns, and partly also length (quantity). These suprasegmentals are phonemic whenever they have the function to differentiate meanings (cf. Structuralism 1.1.2–3). For example, juncture and intonation differentiate between "I don't know" and "I don't, no," and accentual patterns differentiate between the compound "blackbird" (with the primary stress on the first syllable) and the noun phrase "black bird" (with level stress or a primary stress on the second syllable). Special subfields of phonology concerned with suprasegmentals are called *intonation* and *prosody*. For details see Crystal & Quirk (1964), Crystal (1969; 1975), and Bolinger, ed. (1972).

1.2.2 PARALINGUISTIC PHONATIONS

The boundary between language and paralanguage lies in the field of prosody. Suprasegmentals, such as stress, pitch, or length, can be both linguistic (phonemic; cf. 1.2.1) and paralinguistic. Nonphonemic stylistic exaggerations or other variations of pitch, length, or stress, e.g., extra-low pitch in bored speech and extra-high pitch in excited speech, are usually described as paralinguistic phenomena. Paralinguistic suprasegmentals with other stylistic functions are tempo and rhythm. Crystal, however, describes all of these prosodic features as "not yet" paralinguistic because they may enter into functional (stylistic) contrasts. Based on this criterion of functionality, Crystal distinguishes between *prosodic* and *paralinguistic* features of language (1969: 128–31; 1975: 94–95).

Definitely paralinguistic modes of phonation include less systematic variations of speech, such as slurred vs. precise articulation, whispering, nasalization, and husky vocalization (see 2.2.3). Less clear cut is the classification of voice quality (see 2.2.2). Since these features of phonation are beyond the speaker's control, Crystal classifies them as being beyond both linguistics and paralinguistics (1969: 131). On the other hand, voice quality can be interpreted functionally as an indicator of personality (cf. Harper et al., 1978: 26–31, Scherer & Giles, eds. 1979, Scherer, ed. 1982), a fact which has to be observed in the choice of speakers in radio plays or in theater. This is why most other scholars consider voice quality a paralinguistic feature of phonation. Pike even discovers subsegmental phonemes in voice quality (1967: 525–27).

1.2.3 BEYOND PARALANGUAGE

Not all vocal signals beyond language belong to paralanguage. For example, sneezing, yawning, coughing, and snoring are vocal signals that are usually excluded from paralinguistics. These vocal signals are defined as "vocal reflexes" (Crystal 1969: 131) because they are usually uncontrolled and physiologically determined. Lyons characterizes the semiotic status of such vocal reflexes as follows:

> Although they are signals, in the sense that they are transmitted (for the most part involuntarily) and can be interpreted by the receiver, no one would wish to regard them as being other than external to language. When they occur as physiological reflexes during speech, they merely introduce noise into the channel; and when, by prior individual or cultural convention, they are deliberately produced for the purpose of communication (when, for example, we cough to warn a speaker that he might be overheard by someone approaching), they operate outside and independently of language. (1977: 58)

Human acoustic communication beyond paralanguage (and, of course, music) includes some further phenomena which have not yet been (and perhaps will never be) recognized as an area of semiotic study. Only Wescott has so far

proposed to study this area of "communicative body noise" under the designation of *strepistics*. Among his examples of "strepitative behavior" are hand-clapping, foot-stamping, face-slapping, tooth-gnashing, whistling, and spitting (1966: 350–51).

2. Survey of Paralanguage

The scope of paralinguistic phonation can be illustrated from Trager's "classical" typology of paralanguage, one of the first systematic studies in the field.

2.1 State of the Art in Paralinguistics

A notable precursor of modern paralinguistics is Sievers (e.g., 1924), who developed a phonetic theory ("Schallanalyse") of individual physiognomic sound curves. Paralinguistics in its current research tradition has its origins in the late 1950s. The term *paralanguage* was first introduced by Hill (1958: 408; cf. Trager 1958: 4). On the early history of paralinguistic research, see Birdwhistell (1961).

Surveys of paralinguistics are given by Pittenger & Smith (1957), Trager (1958; 1961), Fährmann (1960), Birdwhistell (1961), Mahl & Schulze (1964), Renský (1966), Abercrombie (1968), Kendon et al., eds. (1975: 251–314), Key (1975; 1977), Poyatos (1976: 89–115), Harper et al. (1978: 20–76), Knapp (1978: 322–75), and Siegman & Feldstein, eds. (1978: 183–244). Important monographs and collections of papers are Crystal & Quirk (1964), Crystal (1969; 1975), Bolinger, ed. (1972), Laver & Hutcheson, eds. (1972), Ostwald (1973), Scherer & Giles, eds. (1979), Laver (1980), and Scherer, ed. (1982).

2.2 Typology of Paralanguage

An early influential classification of paralanguage was proposed by Trager (1958; 1961). Trager also developed a system of notation of paralinguistic behavior which has been applied in the transcription of psychiatric interviews (cf. Pittenger et al. 1960, McQuown, ed. 1971; cf. Poyatos 1976 for a more recent proposal for paralinguistic transcription). Trager's system distinguishes three domains of vocal behavior: *voice set*, which he considers prelinguistic, *voice quality*, and *vocalizations*, all of which he describes as paralinguistic (1958: 3–4; cf. Pittenger & Smith 1957).

2.2.1 VOICE SET

Voice set, according to Trager (1958), is the idiosyncratic background of speech. It comprises the permanent or quasi-permanent voice characteristics which are due to the speaker's physiology (age, sex, health, etc.), e.g., timbre, natural pitch height, or volume of the voice. Laver & Trudgill (1979) characterize these voice features as "informative" but not "communicative." The domain of voice set is not always distinguished from that of voice quality (cf. Fährmann 1960, Crystal 1975: 53).

2.2.2 VOICE QUALITY

Voice qualities are speech variables which characterize a speaker's "tone of voice" in adjustment to situational factors. Trager classifies them as follows (1958: 5):
— pitch range and control (spread or narrowed [as in monotone speech])
— vocal lip control (from hoarseness to openness)
— glottis control (sharp or smooth transitions)
— articulatory control (forceful vs. relaxed speech)
— rhythm control (smooth or jerky)
— resonance (from resonant to thin)
— tempo (increased or decreased)

For further paralinguistic studies in voice quality, see Crystal (1969; 1975), Ostwald (1973), Laver (1980), Scherer & Giles, eds. (1979), and Scherer, ed. (1982).

2.2.3 VOCALIZATIONS

Vocalizations, according to Trager, are "actual specifically identifiable noises (sounds) or aspects of noises" which do not belong to the general background characteristics of speech (1958: 5–6). Trager distinguishes three kinds of vocalizations: (1) *vocal characterizers*, such as laughing, crying, yelling, whispering, moaning, etc., (2) *vocal qualifiers*, i.e., variations of intensity (overloud, oversoft), pitch height (overhigh, overlow), and extent (drawl, clipping), and (3) *vocal segregates*, segmental sounds, such as English "uh-uh" for negation, "uh-huh" for affirmation, or the "uh" of hesitation (ibid.). Vocal segregates are considered paralinguistic since they do not fit into the ordinary phonological frame of a language (ibid.: 6), but there is a fuzzy border between these segmental sounds and lexicalized interjections. For details see also Key (1975: 42–45) and Scherer, ed. (1982: 281ff.).

3. Paralinguistics and Semiotics

In the history of language studies, paralinguistics was one of the first steps in the extension of structural linguistics toward a semiotic theory of human communication. Sebeok et al., eds. (1964) consequently introduced paralinguistics (beside kinesics) as one of the *Approaches to Semiotics*. Rauch (1980) locates paralinguistics "between linguistics and semiotics." From the point of view of a general theory of signs, paralanguage consists mostly of *indexical signs* (cf. Abercrombie 1967: 7–9, Laver 1968, Laver & Trudgill 1979: 1–4). In addition to the verbal content, paralanguage is an index of personality traits, affective states, or even regional or social group membership (cf. Scherer & Giles, eds. 1979, Scherer, ed. 1982). These dimensions of paralinguistics have led to an interdisciplinary interest in paralanguage which extends from social psychology (Laver & Hutcheson, eds. 1972, Scherer & Giles, eds. 1979), psychiatry (Pittenger & Smith 1957, Crystal 1969: 80–90, Ostwald 1973, Harper et al. 1978: 26–46), and pedagogy (Hayes 1964 and see Teaching) to musicology (Crystal 1969: 94–95, Bolinger, ed. 1972: 269–312, Ostwald 1973: 176–214).

Writing

Except for its historical dimension, the study of writing has been a neglected field of language studies. Etymologically, the terms *language* and *linguistics* are related only to spoken language (Lat. *lingua* 'tongue'). Although languages have traditionally been studied mainly on the basis of written records, many linguists have shared Bloomfield's view that "writing is not language, but merely a way of recording language by means of visible marks" (1933: 21). Against this phonocentric view of language, Derrida has recently argued that a new semiotics should henceforth be based on the study of writing and no longer on speech.

Within a semiotic framework, the specific features of writing in relation to other signs and the semiotic structures of writing systems have to be determined. The semiotics of writing has further dimensions of interest to philosophy, cultural anthropology, and (mass) media studies. For related topics in the psychology and pedagogy of writing, see Kolers et al., eds. (1979–80) and Assmann et al., eds. (1983). For some explicitly semiotic approaches to the study of writing, see also Watt (1975; 1980; 1981, 1988), Baron (1981), *Zeitschrift für Semiotik* 2.4 (1980), and *Kodikas/Code* 9.3–4 (1986).

1. The Evolution of Writing and the Basic Options

Studies in the history of writing have a long scholarly tradition (Jensen 1935, Février 1948, Gelb 1952, Cohen 1958, Diringer 1962, Földes-Papp 1966, Friedrich 1966, Trager 1974, Schmitt 1980, and Harris 1986). According to the standard interpretation, writing systems have evolved in progressive stages from primitive pictography to alphabetic writing. The general validity of this account and the related claim for the general semiotic superiority of alphabetic writing has more recently been contested.

1.1 Precursors of Writing

The earliest precursors of writing are iconic or symbolic signs designating individual concepts of a specialized vocabulary or giving a holistic pictorial representation of a scene of social life. In both cases, the messages do not yet correspond systematically to spoken language, being either too specialized or too global in their correspondence to speech. These precursors of language are either three-dimensional artifacts or graphic representations.

1.1.1 OBJECT SIGNS AND EARLIEST PRECURSORS OF WRITING

Examples of message-carrying artifacts which belong to the precursors of writing are counting stones, notched tally sticks (cf. Menninger 1958: 223–56), quipus (knotted strings of the Incas), and wampum belts (of the Iroquois). Among these object signs are the earliest known precursors of writing: Mesopotamian clay tokens dating back to the ninth millennium B.C. According to Schmandt-Besserat (1978), these object signs were used as a system of accounting. These early counting stones represent numerals or objects, such as cow, wool, granary, or oil. Their shape is very similar to the characters of Sumerian writing which were developed later, toward the end of the fourth millennium B.C. (cf. Fig. W 1). Schmandt-Besserat points out that a large proportion of these early counting stones are not iconic. From this observation, she derives the theory that writing had symbolic elements from its very beginnings.

1.1.2 PICTOGRAMS

Examples of two-dimensional precursors of writing are paleolithic petrograms (rock paintings), petroglyphs (rock engravings), pictographs, and pictograms, i.e., pictorial messages corresponding to whole propositions or texts (cf. Gelb 1952: 250). The prelinguistic character of pictograms, for example, is illustrated in Figure W 2, which is included in Mallery's (1893) documentation of pictograms of the North American Indians.

1.2 The Basic Options and Evolutionary Stages

The writing systems of the world have evolved from several independent sources. This evolution has not always led to the development of an alphabetic script. There are other types of writing in the world, and some of them have proved to be equally valid options for the visual representation of languages.

1.2.1 PLEREMIC AND CENEMIC WRITING

There are two basic options for the development of a writing system: the signs of writing, the graphemes, may refer either to semantic or to phonetic units of the language. In the first case, the graphemes are pictographs, ideographs, or logographs; in the second case, the graphemes represent phonemes or syllables. Based on this distinction, Trager distinguishes between *sememographic* and *phonemographic* writing (1974: 382–83). Sampson, following

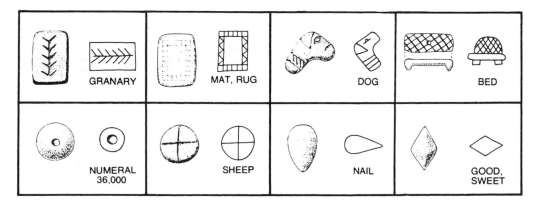

Fig. W 1. Symbolic (*1st row*) and iconic (*2nd row*) Mesopotamian counting stones. Clay tokens of this kind date back to the ninth millennium B.C. The counting stones (*left*) correspond to characters of Sumerian writing of the fourth millennium B.C. (*right*). (From Schmandt-Besserat 1978: 44–45, drawings by Alan D. Iselin, copyright © 1978 by Scientific American, Inc. All rights reserved.)

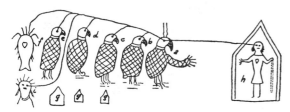

Fig. W 2. A colored pictogram sent as a letter from the chief of the Eagle Totem [*a*] to the President of the United States [*h*, a white man in a white house]: "I [*a*] and a few of my warriors [*b-e*], together with some other mighty chiefs of other totems [*f*, *i*], are gathered together and offer you friendship through me. We are all of one mind with you. Three sections of my tribe [*c*, *d*, *e*] want to live from now on in houses" (from Wundt 1900: 141).

Haas, ed. (1976), introduces the terms *semasiographic* writing ("for systems which indicate ideas directly") and *glottographic* writing (for "systems which provide visible representations of spoken-language utterances") (1985: 29–32). But according to this definition, only pictographs and ideographs are semasiographic, while logographs are defined as glottographic. This classification is motivated by the origins of logographs, which are more directly derived from words than from concepts.

From a structural semiotic point of view, a terminological alternative based on Hjelmslev (cf. Language 4.1.2) has been proposed (cf. French 1976: 118). In this terminology, graphemes representing meaningful segments of language belong to *pleremic* writing systems, and graphemes representing phonetic (meaningless) elements belong to *cenemic* writing.

1.2.2 THE THEORY OF EVOLUTIONARY STAGES

The evolution of writing is often described as a history of progressive stages beginning with the iconic signs of pictography and culminating in the symbols of the alphabet (cf. Jensen 1935, Gelb 1952, Diringer 1962). While this interpretation is valid for many elements of writing systems, the general evolutionary validity of this assumption may be contested. Neither are

the origins of writing always pictographic (cf. Fig. W 1), nor is the alphabet in principle superior to pleremic modes of writing. Thus, the standard theory of the general superiority of alphabetic writing systems has been rejected by authors such as Schmitt (1980) and Coulmas (1981). They have shown that the semiotic adequacy of a writing system depends on the structure of the language to be written. Some languages, among them the Chinese, have structures whose alphabetic transcription would cause serious difficulties, so that pleremic writing is more appropriate to the language. One of the advantages of pleremic writing is its potentially greater universality: a pleremic writing system is structurally independent of historical sound changes and dialectal variations of the language.

1.3 Pleremic Writing

Three major types of pleremic writing are usually distinguished in the historiography of writing, but no common terminology has been adopted.

1.3.1 PICTOGRAPHY

Pictographs are iconic characters. They represent pictures of visible objects or actions. For example, in Egyptian hieroglyphs, two "legs" are a pictograph of 'walking,' an "eye with tears" represents 'to weep,' and a "bird with extended wings" means 'to fly' (cf. Jensen 1935: 51; see also 1.3.5). No language can be written with pictographs only since many concepts cannot be represented iconically (see also Universal Language 3.2 for modern pictographic languages). Therefore, ideographs, symbolic characters representing abstract concepts, are necessary in any genuine writing system.

1.3.2 IDEOGRAPHY

The ideal of a truly ideographic writing has been pursued in universal language projects from Descartes to Leibniz. In the history of writing, ideographs are those graphemes which symbolize elements of content. In principle, elements of ideography do not have to correspond to the units of phonetic expression of the same linguistic sign (cf. Alarcos Llorach 1968: 552–54). In its ideographic representation, the spoken word may become semantically decomposed. For example, the word *mother* may be expressed by two ideographs, one for 'parent' plus one for 'female.' Ideographic writing has often been interpreted as the second stage (after pictography) in the evolution of writing (cf. Diringer 1962: 22), but the earliest writing systems already had both types of characters. The Sumerian characters shown in Figure W 1 are partly ideographs (1st line) and partly pictographs (2nd line).

The term *pictograph* is sometimes used as a synonym of *pictogram*, and *ideographs* are also called *ideograms*. Some authors even reject the terminological distinction between *picto-* and *ideography* (Gelb 1952: 35) because of the low degree of iconicity in true writing systems. For this reason, Jensen prefers the term *ideography* for both modes of writing (1935: 34). Today's traffic signs are often referred to as modern pictographs and ideographs, but these signs are not elements of writing systems.

1.3.3 THE REBUS PRINCIPLE

An important technique of reducing the number of the characters in a writing system is the *rebus principle* (cf. Jensen 1935: 151–57, Ehlich 1980: 113, Baron 1981: 165). A rebus character is a pictograph or ideograph whose original usage is extended to another homophonous word. An example adapted to the English language: the pictograph of an eye might also be used to represent the pronoun *I*. The pictograph of a sun might also serve to represent the concept 'son.' The rebus principle appears both in the Egyptian hieroglyphic and in the Chinese writing systems.

1.3.4 LOGOGRAPHS

Logographs (or logograms) are characters representing words. The distinction between logographs and ideographs is partly a matter of linguistic convention (cf. 1.2.1). Some linguists even use the terms *ideography* and *logography*

interchangeably (e.g., Alarcos Llorach 1968: 523). Chinese characters are usually described as being logographic. Like logographs, ideographs often also represent units corresponding to spoken words (though not necessarily; cf. 1.3.2). But characters formed by the rebus principle and the so-called phonetic compounds are more closely related to the phonetic than to the semantic structure of the word. At least in their origin, these characters are not directly ideographic. This is one of the reasons for the adoption of the term *logograph* (cf. Trager 1974: 383). Logographs are also used in modern alphabetic typography: $, £, §, &, %, +, and – are logographs which are available on most alphabetic typewriters. All single-digit Arabic number symbols (from 0 to 9) are logographic symbols.

1.3.5 THE CHINESE WRITING SYSTEM

An illustration of pleremic writing is the Chinese writing system (cf. Jensen 1935: 153–59, Chao 1968: 103–104). The number of Chinese graphemes varies between two thousand (sufficient for basic literacy) and fifty thousand (for very elaborate writing, including archaic and specialized characters). Traditionally, the following six types of characters are distinguished (Fig. W 3 illustrates four of them):

1. *Pictographs* (*hsiang hsing*). Only a relatively small number of characters are pictographic. The iconicity of these graphemes is mostly apparent only in their oldest form. The ancient Chinese writing system is said to have had about six hundred such characters.

2. *Ideographs* (*chih shih*). Chao defines these characters as "diagrammatic indications of ideas." In Peircean categories, the examples shown in Figure W 3 are diagrammatic icons, i.e., icons of relations.

3. *Compound ideographs* (*hui i*). These consist of a combination of two or more characters motivating the meaning of a new concept.

4. *Phonetic compounds* (*hsing sheng*). This is the largest class of Chinese characters. The characters consist of a semantic element, called *signific* (or *radical*), plus a phonetic element to indicate its pronunciation, sometimes

TYPE	Character: ancient modern	Pronun-ciation	Meaning	Motivation/Components
Pictograph (hsiang hsing)	子	tsi	child	head, arms
	雨	yü	rain	rain drops from sky
	木	mù	tree	branches (above), roots (below)
Ideograph (chih shih)	方	fang	region	the four cardinal points
	中	chung	middle	disc with arrows
	畺	chiang	boundary	line between two fields
Compound ideograph (hui i)	孖	tsi	twins	2 x child
	炎	yen	very hot	2 x fire
	囚	chin	prison(er)	man in enclosure
Phonetic compound (hsiang hsing)	A + B = C			A (phonetic indicator) + B (signific) = C (phon. compound)
	皇 + 火 = 煌			huang³ ('majestic') + huo ('fire') = huang² ('bright')
	分 + 言 = 訜			fen ('divide') + yen ('speak') = fen ('gossip')
	巫 + 言 = 誣			wu ('wizard') + yen ('speak') = wu ('to lie')

Fig. W 3. Four types of Chinese characters (examples from Jensen 1935: 154–58).

1. THE EVOLUTION OF WRITING AND THE BASIC OPTIONS ▌ 255

only by approximation. Because of this large class of characters, Chinese writing is no longer a genuinely ideographic writing system.

5. *Loan characters* (*chia chieh*) are graphemes generated by the rebus principle, for example: the character for 'dustpan' came to be used for the formerly homophonous pronoun *his*.

6. *Chuăn chù* characters are a small group of graphemes formed by modifying another character (e. g., deleting one of its elements) to represent a related meaning.

1.4 Cenemic Writing

The basic options of cenemic writing are syllabic and alphabetic writing.

1.4.1 SYLLABIC WRITING

Writing systems whose graphemes represent syllables are called *syllabaries*. Partially syllabic systems have been traced back to the cuneiform writing of the third millennium B.C. (cf. Gelb 1952: 120). Phoenician writing (2nd millenium B.C.), the precursor of the Greek alphabet, was a syllabic system. But, like other Semitic writing systems, the Phoenician syllabary symbolizes only the consonants and not the vowels of a syllable. (Some linguists therefore prefer to describe this writing system as alphabetic-consonantic.) Only one syllabic grapheme, for example, was used to write the five syllables *ra, re, ri, ro*, and *ru* (cf. Schmitt 1980: 310).

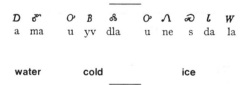

water   cold   ice

Fig. W 4. A sample line in Cherokee syllabic writing with Latin transcription and English translation (from Trager 1974: 472).

An early genuine syllabic script with characters indicating both consonants and vowels is the Cypriote syllabary (sixth to third century B.C.). A modern syllabary of eighty-five graphemes was invented in 1821 by the Cherokee Indian Sequoya. It became widely used in the

nineteenth century. A sample line of Cherokee writing is quoted in Figure W 4. The only major modern language that employs a syllabic script (*kana*) is Japanese, but Japanese writing also consists of ideographic characters of Chinese origin (*kanji*). There are two types of Japanese syllabaries: *hiranaga* characters are used for grammatical morphemes, while *katakana* characters are used to write foreign words.

The utility of a syllabary as a writing system depends on the phonetic structure of the language to be written. The Semitic languages which employ a syllabary have a relatively simple syllable structure, and in Japanese, for example, the number of possible syllables is limited to 102 (cf. Paradis et al. 1985: 1). The Greek and other Indo-European languages have a much more complicated syllable structure. This is one of the reasons why the Greeks, after 1,000 B.C., transformed Phoenician writing into the first genuine alphabet of the world.

1.4.2 ALPHABETIC WRITING

The ideal of an alphabetic writing system is to represent each phoneme by one grapheme. But every language has its own phonemic system. A truly international alphabet therefore cannot exist. For this and other reasons, the alphabets of the world vary in size between eleven (the Rotoka alphabets of the Solomon Islands) and seventy-four letters (the Khmer alphabet).

The Roman letters (since about 600 B.C.) descended from the Greek by way of the Etruscan alphabet (ca. 800 B.C.). Another direct derivative from Greek is the Cyrillic alphabet (ninth century A.D.). The major derivatives of the Roman alphabet are its many variants of handwriting, calligraphy, and typography. In the British Isles, two non-Roman alphabets had been used before the adoption of the Roman alphabet, the Germanic runes and the Celtic Ogham script (Fig. W 5). Both alphabets differ in their form and order from the Roman alphabet. *Futhork* (or *futhark*), the name of the runic alphabet, is derived from the order of its letters. Earliest runic inscriptions date from the third century A.D. Ogham script was used in Irish and Pictish inscriptions of the fourth century A.D. The letters are usually cut into the edge (middle line, Fig. W 5) of a stone.

1.4.3 TRANSLATION OF ALPHABETS

There are two main cases of the translation of alphabets, transliteration and intersemiotic translation. Transliteration is the translation from one alphabet to another (as in Fig. W 5). The transliterated grapheme is a secondary sign which represents the same phonetic value as the primary grapheme. Intersemiotic translation replaces a primary grapheme with other visual (flag or hand), acoustic (Morse alphabet), or tactile (Braille) media. For details see Code (1.2.2), Sign Language (2.1), Language Substitutes (2.1, 3.2).

1.4.4 ORTHOGRAPHIES

The adoption of foreign alphabets and later sound changes are two causes of discrepancies between the alphabetic and phonemic structures of languages. The Roman alphabet adopted by the English had no letter to represent the phonemes /θ/ and /ð/. Therefore, the medieval scribes borrowed the Germanic letters thorn and eth to write these phonemes in Roman script. But these nonclassical letters were later abandoned in favor of the Latin letters *th*, which individually serve to represent other phonemes.

Once a writing tradition has been established, the orthography of a language begins to develop a structure which evolves independently of the spoken language. This is particularly evident in the conservative orthography of modern English, which basically represents the language as it was pronounced about five hundred years ago. For this reason, Cohen has even maintained that the orthography of English has now developed from a phonographic to an ideographic system of writing (1954: 51).

1.4.5 EXCURSUS ON PHONETIC WRITING

Phonetic alphabets or scripts are systems of writing which have been developed by linguists for the purpose of transcribing phonemes or by language reformers for the purpose of a spelling reform. In England, early proposals for systems of phonetic transcription were made in the sixteenth century in the context of language teaching, spelling reform (cf. Scragg 1974: 88–117), and universal language projects. In America, the Mormons developed a new phonetic script in the 1850s for the purpose of spelling reform (cf. Thompson 1982). The history of phonetics distinguishes three main types of phonetic notation (Abercrombie 1967: 111–32; 1981): *analphabetic, iconic alphabetic,* and *Roman-based alphabetic* notations.

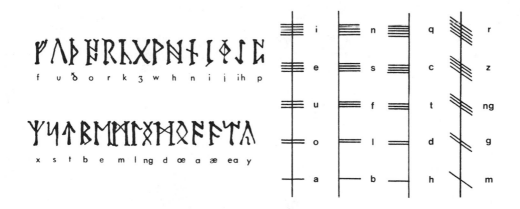

Fig. W 5. The Germanic futhork (Vienna codex) and the Celtic Ogham script and their Latin transliteration. (Source of the futhork: *Brockhaus Enzyklopädie,* vol. 16 [1973: 249].)

Fig. W 6. Wilkins's phonetic characters (*upper right*) are simplified icons of the corresponding position of the speech organs (lips, air stream, tongue, etc.; the representation of N and G is mirror-inverted) (1668: 378).

1. Analphabetic notations represent the articulatory features of speech sounds by a composite formula of symbols indicating the active speech organs. One of the phoneticians who have developed such a system is Pike (1943: 155). His formula for the phoneme /t/, for example, is:

[t]: Ma*I*lDe*C*Vve*I*c*AP*paat*d*t*l*tn*r*ansfs*Si*FSs

The key to the first of these features is: *M* mechanism, *a* air stream, *I* initiator, *l* lung air, *D* direction, *e* egressive.

2. Iconic phonetic alphabets have newly designed phonetic characters whose graphic features correspond systematically to the phonetic features of articulation. The Ogham alphabet (Fig. W 5) is a partially iconic alphabet since all vowels are distinguished from the consonants by a common graphemic feature. An early proposal for an iconic notation of phonemes was made by Wilkins (1668: 378–80; cf. Universal Language 2.3.2). His "natural pictures of letters" (Fig. W 6) are an attempt at representing the speaker's vocal organ in profile.

A different principle of iconicity has been the basis for the design of *organic alphabets*, which have been proposed in a tradition from Lodwick (1686, *Essay towards an Universal Alphabet*; cf. Abercrombie 1948), de Brosses (1765, *Traité de la formation mécanique des langues*; cf. Genette 1976: 108–118), Alexander M. Bell (1864, *Visible Speech*), and Henry Sweet (1890) until the Shaw alphabet (Shaw

1962). In organic alphabets, the letters are composed of graphic elements which are an arbitrary representation of the articulatory features of the sound which they represent. But there is a diagrammatic iconicity in the systematic combination of these elements into letters: related articulatory features are represented by graphic elements of similar shapes (cf. Fig. W 7). The alphabet is thus a code with first and second articulation.

3. Roman-based alphabetic notations make use of Roman letters, sometimes with diacritical marks, graphic transformations, and other letters added. The alphabet adopted by the International Phonetic Association (IPA) in 1888 is Roman-based. This system has become widely recognized as the international phonetic alphabet. Following Daniel Jones (1914), phoneticians have distinguished between the more detailed narrow and the less specific broad transcription. Among the latter systems are phonemic notations, which transcribe only phonemes and no phonetic variants.

ᑌ ᑍ   ᗡ ᗴ   ᑐ ᗰ   ᑕ ᑐ
[k] [g] [p] [b] [t] [d] [f] [v]

Fig. W 7. Characters from the Jones-Passy (1907) organic alphabet based on the principle of diagrammatic iconicity: articulatory features, such as velar (k/g), labio-dental (f/v), or voiced (g, b, d, v), are represented by the same graphic elements.

2. Semiotic Features of Writing

Within a semiotic framework, the specific features and functions of writing have to be determined in comparison to spoken language and to nonlinguistic visual messages.

2.1 Definitions of Writing

Standard definitions of writing have focused on the symbolic, graphic, and linguistic characteristics of writing.

2.1.1 VISUAL SYMBOLS

In the definition of Gelb, writing is "a system of human intercommunication by means of visible marks" (1952: 12). Later, Gelb defines writing in its broadest sense as "a recording system or device by means of conventional markings or shapes or color of objects, achieved by the motor action of the hand of an individual and received visually by another" (1980: 22). While these definitions exclude acoustic signs as well as nonsystematic images, they do not distinguish between writing and other graphic symbol codes, such as traffic signs and other pictorial symbols.

2.1.2 EXPRESSION-SUBSTANCE AND COMMUNICATIVE FUNCTION

A definition of writing given by Jensen (1935: 18) emphasizes two different aspects: (1) writing is fixed on a "solid writing ground by means of a graphic (drawing, scratching) activity," and (2) writing has a communicative function and is addressed to another person or, as a memory aid, to the writer himself. The first of these criteria refers to the expression-substance of writing, distinguishing it from messages in the form of objects which have been among the precursors of writing. Jensen's second criterion, the communicative and mnemonic purpose of writing, is a functional criterion. It characterizes first of all the difference between writing and spoken language and secondly, to a certain degree, also the difference between writing and archaic images or magico-religious symbols. But this definition does not yet exclude the graphic precursors of writing, such as archaic pictograms, which may be deciphered without any knowledge of the encoder's spoken language.

2.1.3 WRITING AS LANGUAGE

According to Chao, "visual symbols do not begin to be writing until they have a close correspondence to language" (1968: 101). This standard definition identifies language with spoken language and characterizes writing as a secondary semiotic system derived from speech. A similar definition of writing is the one by Trager: "A writing system is any conventional system of marks or drawings or analogous artifacts which represents the utterances of a language as such" (1974: 377). Whether it is necessary to characterize writing as semiotically secondary to spoken language will be discussed below, but the systematic correspondence between the written and spoken modes of language is certainly a central criterion for the definition of writing. This correspondence need not be a 1:1 relationship (cf. 3.). But systems of graphic symbols can be writing systems only if they have the same communicative potential as spoken language. A writing system "must be so constructed as to make possible the writing of any utterance of the language" (Trager 1974: 377). This is the criterion which excludes both specialized visual codes, such as traffic signs, and general modes of graphic representation, such as archaic pictograms.

2.2 Design Features of Writing

If writing is a medium or channel of linguistic communication, the design features of language cannot be set up on the basis of speech only. One of the specific features of writing is its multilinearity or even multidimensionality.

2.2.1 SPECIFIC DIFFERENCES OF CHANNEL

The design features (DF) of language set up by Hockett (1960) characterize language as a spoken medium only.

DF 1: In the medium of writing, the *vocal-auditory channel* of speech is replaced by the *visual channel*. Compared to acoustic communication, the visual channel has the disadvantage that reading and writing are not possible in the dark. This may have been important in the evolutionary preference of the acoustic over the visual channel in human communication (cf. Gesture 2.5.2). But writing cannot make use of the whole potential of the visual channel. Because of the time lag between the acts of reading and writing, the encoder's nonverbal visual messages are lost in the act of transmission.

DF 2: While speech is characterized by *broadcast transmission*, writing allows *directional reception* only. One of the consequences of this restriction in the spatial range of writing is that reading, in comparison to hearing, requires a higher degree of attention to the source of information. This is closely connected with

DF 6, *specialization*: writing is more specialized than speech since writing and reading require a higher energetic effort and technical skill in comparison to speaking and hearing (cf. the problem of analphabetism in literate cultures). One aspect of this specialization is the higher degree of revising and editing connected with writing.

DF 3, *rapid fading*, refers to the most important difference between writing and speech. In contradistinction to this feature of speech, writing may be characterized by its capacity of *permanent recording* and *information storage* (cf. Hockett 1960: 133). These features characterize the most important advantages of the written over the spoken mode of language.

2.2.2 THE MULTIDIMENSIONALITY OF WRITING

In its acoustic surface structure, speech has a strictly unilinear character. While writing is also basically linear in its nature, it is more flexible in its dimensionality. Its linearity may take several directions and may even be overcome by two-dimensional patterns. The direction of writing is one of the characteristics of the individual writing system. Besides the left-to-right direction of writing in the tradition of the Roman alphabet, there is the right-to-left writing of Arabic. Top-to-bottom writing from right to left is used in ancient Chinese, and an example of the rarer bottom-to-top mode of writing can be found in Ogham inscriptions (cf. Fig. W 5). While in these types of writing the direction of writing remains the same from line to line, the ancient Greeks and other early cultures also used a method of writing, called *boustrophedon*, where the lines were written in alternate directions, for example: first line left to right, second line right to left, etc.

Besides these conventional patterns of linearity, writing and reading can also make use of the two-dimensionality of the writing surface. Writing in tables, columns, matrices, block patterns (paragraphs), tree diagrams, or circular and other patterns (as in visual poetry or advertising) is a mode of linguistic expression which cannot be translated into speaking. Nonlinear (rapid) reading, which is typical of newspaper reading, is a process which has no analogy in the hearing of language. These examples illustrate that writers and readers have a higher degree of choice in the processing of language than the speakers and listeners.

2.3 Semiotic Functions of Writing

The primary function of both spoken and written language is the communicative function. In addition to this primary function of communicating verbal messages, there are two major secondary functions of writing, a magic and a poetic function (cf. Glück 1987: 203–250). A magic function of letters is apparent in the use of writing by the ancient Egyptians and Germanic peoples. The Egyptian hieroglyphics are etymologically "sacred carvings," and the runes, the letters of the Germanic alphabet, were also more than mere signs of phonemes. They were secret and magic signs (see Magic 1). The magic incantations called spells equally refer in their etymology to the art of writing ("spelling"). In ancient Tibet, the religious practice of *grapholatry*, the adoration of written texts, illustrates another magic dimension of writing (cf. Glück 1987: 206). Very elaborate magical codes for deciphering written texts were developed within the medieval *Kabbala*: exegetic codes ascribed esoteric meanings, sometimes to be deciphered by the assignment of numerical values, to the letters and even punctuation marks of biblical and Thora texts (cf. Crystal 1987: 59).

Parallel to the acoustic poetic dimension of spoken language, there is a visual poetic dimension in the calligraphy of handwriting and the graphic design of printed letters. For details see Vachek (1948, from the point of view of functional linguistics), Berger (1979, on graphic design), and Oechslin (1982, on letter forms in architecture and aesthetics).

3. Writing and Speech: Autonomy vs. Heteronomy

The structural study of alphabetic writing is of a much more recent date than the study of speech. Many linguists have thought that writing is structurally secondary to speech, but there are other types of interrelationship between the two modes of linguistic expression.

3.1 Graphemics: A New Field of Study

After decades of neglecting the written mode of language, linguists have begun to approach writing in close analogy to phonetics and phonemics (cf. Venezky 1970, Augst, ed. 1985; 1986, Sampson 1985). In analogy to phonemics (or phonology, cf. Structuralism 1.1.2), the new discipline began to be established under the designation of *graphemics* (Althaus 1973, Harweg 1973, Augst, ed. 1985; 1986). Most British linguists (cf. Gimson 1962: 5, Crystal 1987: 185) prefer the term *graphology*, which has the unfor-

tunate traditional association with "the study of handwriting, esp. for the purpose of character analysis" (*Webster's Third New Int. Dict.*). In analogy to the established distinction between phonemics and phonetics (see Structuralism 1.1.2), some linguists have proposed to study writing from the two complementary perspectives of graphemics and *graphetics* (Veith 1973). While graphemics "is the study of the linguistic contrasts that writing systems convey," graphetics "is the study of the physical properties of the symbols that constitute writing systems" (Crystal 1987: 185).

3.2 Autonomy vs. Heteronomy of Writing

Semioticians of writing are divided into two camps. Some consider writing as a secondary, substitutive, or heteronomous (Harweg 1973) semiotic system, derived from the primary system of spoken language. Others propose to study writing as an autonomous semiotic system, a system *sui generis*, which may be studied without reference to speech (cf. Language Substitutes 3.1). The two views are based on different concepts of the semiotic function of signs in written language.

3.2.1 HETERONOMOUS GRAPHEMICS
The view of the substitutive character of writing is associated with the classics of linguistics, such as Saussure, Sapir (1921: 20), and Bloomfield (cf. 2.1.3). While Saussure describes writing as being secondary to spoken language (1916b: 23), Bloomfield warns against confusing writing with "language itself" and characterizes writing as "an external device which happens to preserve for our observation some features of the speech of past times" (1933: 282). Under the influence of Saussure, linguistics and semiotics (cf. Buyssens 1943: 49, Jakobson 1973a: 29) have for a long time upheld the dogma of the substitutive character of writing (cf. Code 2.1.3, 3.1.1, Language Substitutes 3.1.2). It is this dogma which came under heavy attack in Derrida's grammatology.

An early outline of an autonomous science of writing was given by Uldall (1944), based on Hjelmslev's glossematics. Uldall argues that the substitution of a written expression for a spoken one does not change the content of the message. Therefore, he considers speech and writing equivalent manifestations of language. The difference is only one of the expression-substance. Since, in the view of glossematics, language is a semiotic system whose structure consists only of form, and not of substance, writing and speech must be alternative representations of one and the same language system. A variant of the autonomy theory of writing is the theory of writing as a parallel code of speech (Prieto 1975a: 85–93).

3.3 Interdependence and Complementarity

While the autonomous perspective of writing is a strictly synchronic and structural view, the heteronomous view is motivated by evolutionary considerations. In addition to these two views of dependence or independence between speech and writing, there are further relations between the two modes of language which are of concern to the semiotics of writing.

Figure W 8 gives the outline of five possible relations between linguistic meanings, writing, and speech. The arrows represent structural or genetic dependence. Relation I characterizes the heteronomous view of writing, while III represents the view of writing as an autonomous mode of language. A genuine dependence (type I) of writing on speech exists only for phonetic alphabets (see 1.4.5). All orthographies of cenemic writing systems (see 1.4) have developed some degree of independence between Ph and Gr. A genuine independence (type III) between speech and writing is true for pleremic writing systems and for written universal languages (*pasigraphies*). A priority of written over spoken language (type II) exists in the reconstruction of dead languages on the basis of written documents, in reading, spelling pronunciations, and the primitive belief in the authority or even magic power of the written word (cf. Coulmas 1981: 13).

Relation IV represents a view of writing which acknowledges both an autonomy of writing (as in III) and some dependence of writing on speech (as in I). Those who insist on the structural autonomy of writing (III) cannot deny some genetic influences of Ph on Gr (I). Examples are historical changes or even reforms of orthography following sound changes

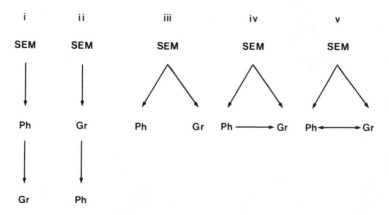

Fig. W 8. Five types of relation between the phonetic (Ph) and graphemic (Gr) representation, and the semantic level of language (SEM): I heteronomy, III autonomy, II spelling pronunciations, IV writing as a semi-autonomous system, V interdependence.

or the interferences of speech in orthography in learning to write a first language. Relation V is the comprehensive model of an interdependence between writing and speech in linguistic communication (cf. Günther 1983: 25). In contradistinction to IV, it shows that speech can also be influenced by writing and not only writing by speech. Such interdependences can be discovered in evolutionary, psycholinguistic, and cultural respects.

3.3.2 EVOLUTIONARY INTERRELATIONS

The temporal priority of spoken over written language is a fact in the history and ontogenesis of languages. Nevertheless, the evolution of pleremic writing systems, such as the Chinese script, was basically independent from the spoken language. While alphabetic writing systems are genetically derived from speech, there is a considerable historical influence of writing on speech in languages with conservative orthographies (such as English and French).

3.3.3 PSYCHOLINGUISTIC INTERRELATIONS

Experimental research in the psychology of reading (cf. Scheerer 1983) has shown that the process of reading is neither one of genuine visual perception (Gr → SEM), nor altogether dependent on phonetic mediation (Gr → Ph → SEM). Psycholinguistic studies of reading have discovered that a reader has both direct (Gr → SEM) and indirect access to meaning (SEM). The latter is psychologically explained (cf. ibid.) as a process which is mediated by "inner speaking or hearing" (thus: Gr → inner-Ph → SEM). In the reading of texts, both processes play a complementary role.

3.3.4 CULTURAL COMPLEMENTARITY

Writing and speech have different but complementary sociocultural functions. As Vachek points out, a spoken utterance permits an immediate response to an event, while a written message preserves a possibly permanent record of a statement about an event (1939: 115). Ehlich, too, interprets writing systems as "the result of social efforts to overcome the transient character of speech acts" (1980: 99)

and studies the evolution of writing systems from this premise. For further sociocultural functions of writing see Coulmas (1981: 26ff.), Assman et al., eds. (1983), Günther (1983: 36–39), and 5.1.

---

4. Alphabetic Writing as a Semiotic System

To study writing as a semiotic system is to discover the elements and the structure of written language. Only alphabetic writing systems can be discussed in this context.

4.1 The Grapheme

In analogy to the phoneme, the "smallest contrastive linguistic unit which may bring about a change of meaning" (Gimson 1962: 44; cf. Structuralism 1.1.2), the grapheme has been defined as "the smallest distinctive visual unit of the alphabet" (cf. Pulgram 1951). Every grapheme consists of a class of typographic or chirographic (hand-written) variants called *allographs*.

4.1.1 IS THE GRAPHEME A SIGN?

Depending on the view concerning the autonomy or heteronomy of writing, the grapheme is defined either as a sign or only as a constituent element of a sign. To those who study writing as an autonomous semiotic system, only written segments of the size of a word (or morpheme) are signs of writing. Only units of this size are signifiers related to a signified of language. In this view, the grapheme (letter), like the phoneme in spoken language, is not yet a sign but only an element of a sign in writing. In the heteronomous view of writing, however, the single letter already has the status of a sign: the grapheme (letter) is a sign which refers to a phoneme. By thus referring to another element of language, the heteronomous grapheme has the function of a secondary sign or *metasign* (cf. Code 2.1.3).

4.1.2 THE HETERONOMOUS DEFINITION OF THE GRAPHEME

The differences between the autonomous and heteronomous approaches to graphemics result in different discovery procedures and definitions of the grapheme. In heteronomous graphemics, letters and combinations of letters which correspond to the spelling of a phoneme are defined as one grapheme. Thus, combinations of letters, such as *ng*, *ph*, *mm*, *tt*, *th*, *ea*, *ie*, *oa*, have been defined as compound graphemes of English since they spell single English phonemes (cf. Venezky 1970: 48).

4.1.3 THE AUTONOMOUS DEFINITION

In autonomous graphemics, the discovery procedure of graphemes is a commutation test (see Structuralism 1.1.2), performed on the basis of written texts. The commutation (i.e., exchange) of *h* for *r* in the written word *thick*, for example, results in a new graphemic word with a different meaning. Therefore *h* and *r* are two (autonomous) graphemes of English, and *h* is not a segment of *th*. Graphemes in this definition are not necessarily coextensive with letters. For example, the two Old English letters thorn (Þ) and eth (ð) were allographs which could be employed interchangeably in the same words. Notice that the upper case vs. lower case distinction may have a graphemic relevance which is not reflected in spoken language (e.g., *God* vs. (a) *god*, *mother* vs. *Mother*).

4.2 Segmentation and Articulation of the Grapheme

Is a further segmentation of graphemes into smaller units possible? What are the implications of such a segmentation for the graphemic system?

4.2.1 DISTINCTIVE FEATURE ANALYSIS

Authors who have made proposals for the segmentation of graphemes in analogy to the "atomization" of phonemes into their distinctive articulatory features are Catford (1965: 62–

65), Mounin (1970a: 135–54), Koch (1971a: 74–75), Althaus (1973: 108), Watt (1975; 1980; 1981; 1988), Holenstein (1980), and Boudon (1981: 35–66). Catford, for example, proposes *minimal features* of graphemes, such as vertical $|$, horizontal —, right and left oblique $(/,\backslash)$, right and left semicircle $((,))$, categories of modification (full, low, high, mid), and categories of combination (attached, crossing, connecting) (1965: 62). Examples of graphemic distinctive feature analyses on this basis are:

A = / \ — mid connecting
H = | | — mid connecting
X = / \   crossing
T = | —   high crossing

The methods and results of graphemic feature analysis differ considerably. While Koch (1971a), for example, proposes eleven distinctive features of the Roman alphabet, Althaus (1973) distinguishes nineteen features. One of the problems is that different typographies have different systems of distinctive features. This is the major difference between phonemic and graphemic distinctive feature analysis.

4.2.2 DOUBLE ARTICULATION IN WRITING?

Mounin (1970a: 135–54) and Holenstein (1980) discuss the question whether graphemic distinctive feature analysis can lead to the discovery of a double articulation (see Language 4.1) of alphabetic writing systems. From this point of view, the graphemes would be assigned to the first level and their distinctive features would belong to a second level of articulation. This interpretation is not correct in autonomous graphemics: being an element which serves to differentiate meanings, the grapheme, like the phoneme in spoken language, belongs only to the second level of articulation and not to the first level of meaningful elements. In the heteronomous view, however, the grapheme is a sign (cf. 4.1.2) and can therefore be interpreted as constituting a first level of articulation whose distinctive features belong to a second level of articulation.

4.3 Graphemes of Sentence and Text Structure

At the levels of sentence and text structure, there are specific graphemes to indicate the structure of written messages: space indicates word boundaries, punctuation marks indicate sentence structures, and paragraphs are markers of text structures. The level of the morpheme is usually graphemically unmarked, except for the apostrophe as the marker of the possessive case. In the case of logographs (see 1.3.4) and in one-letter words, the grapheme is coextensive with the levels of the morpheme or word.

5. Semiotic Philosophy and Cultural Criticism of Writing

Philosophy and theories of culture have discussed writing with special attention to the differences between the oral and visual modes of communication.

5.1 Cultural Criticism of Writing

There have been three critical stages in the cultural history of writing (cf. Havelock 1976, Olson 1977, Baron 1981: 178–88): the "invention" of writing by illiterate societies, the invention of the printing press and the development of writing to a mass medium, and the partial replacement of writing by the new audiovisual media.

5.1.1 THE INVENTION OF WRITING
The development from oral to written culture in ancient Greece is discussed by Havelock (1963; 1976), Olson (1977), Rösler (1983), and Glück (1987). The invention of writing resulted in a gain of semantic transparency, made the critical scrutiny of texts possible, and allowed the writer to overcome the limitations of memory. But at the same time, writing brought a loss in textual explicitness, since a writer or scribe was needed to serve as a medi-ator and interpreter of the text (Olson 1977: 265–67).

5.1.2 FROM PRINTING TO THE AUDIOVISUAL MEDIA
Marshall McLuhan (1962; 1964) has discussed the cultural significance of the inventions of book printing and of the audiovisual media in both stimulating and speculative writings. His cultural criticism of the print medium culminates in the claim that "print created national uniformity and government centralism, but also individualism and opposition" (1962: 282). The new phase of cultural revolution by means of the electronic media, according to McLuhan, results in a reversal of the former situation: "The mass media of today are decentralizing modern living, turning the globe into a village, and catapulting twentieth century man back to the life of the tribe" (1964: back cover). From a semiotic point of view, such views seem to imply an overestimation of the expression plane of the media to the neglect of their content plane. Nevertheless, McLuhan conveys numerous insights about how the expression-substance of media may transmit a content of its own. For the future of culture "after the book," see also Steiner (1972).

5.2 Philosophy from Phonocentrism to Graphocentrism

The history of philosophy from Plato to Derrida shows a remarkable shift in the evaluation of writing as compared to speech.

5.2.1 PLATO'S PHONOCENTRISM
In Plato's Phaedrus (§ 274E, trans. H. N. Fowler), Socrates quotes the ancient Egyptian god and king Thamus for having criticized the invention of letters as follows: "This invention will produce forgetfulness in the minds of those who learn to use it, because they will not practise their memory. Their trust in writing, produced by external characters which are not part of themselves, will discourage the use of their own memory within them." This disdain of writing in comparison to spoken language is the origin of a philosophical tradition which

Derrida (1967a; c) has criticized as *phonocentrism*. The modern version of this phonocentrism, according to Derrida, is the Saussurean tradition of emphasizing the linguistic study of the spoken to the neglect of the written language (cf. 3.). However, Derrida's critique neglects a complementary *graphocentristic* tradition in the form of a dogmatic reliance on the written sources, which has been a tradition since the scholastics. As Malmberg points out, Saussure's linguistic phonocentrism was also a reaction to a previous philology which was primarily interested in the study of written language (1974: 197).

5.2.2 DERRIDA'S GRAMMATOLOGY

Derrida (1967a: 51; 1967c; 1968; cf. Structuralism 4.3) introduces his *grammatology* as a poststructuralist "science of writing before speech and in speech." The point of departure of this semiotic philosophy is Saussure's principle of the differential nature of the linguistic sign (cf. Structure 2.1) and his view of the derivative and secondary character of writing (see 3.2.1). Grammatology aims at replacing this phonocentric view of language by its antithesis, a theory of the primacy of writing before speech. Derrida even wants to subsume oral language under writing (1967a: 55), which, of course, presupposes a modification of the concept of writing. In his view, writing is more than the graphemic variant of phonetic language. Writing "signifies inscription and especially the durable institution of a sign." This implies "the very idea of institution—hence of the arbitrariness of the sign" (ibid.: 44). In this definition, writing turns out to be a metaphor of the general concept of sign (cf. Hempfer 1976: 16). In this way, Derrida can argue that "language had itself always been a writing," namely, an *archewriting*. But "this arche-writing, although its concept is *invoked* by the themes of 'the arbitrariness of the sign' and of difference, cannot and can never be recognized as the *object of a science*. It is that very thing which cannot let itself be reduced to the form of *presence*" (1967a: 56–57).

For this writing implies a framework which Derrida calls the *instituted trace* (1967a: 46). It is the result of the *play of differences* within the semiotic system (cf. Structuralism 4.3). Due to its differential character, every semiotic element incorporates in itself the trace of all other elements (and structures) in the form of an "inscription." Since every trace exists only by another trace, there can be no absolute origin of the trace. To Derrida, the metaphysical problem of signification is thus opened to deciphering: "*The trace is in fact the absolute origin of sense in general.* [. . .] *The trace is the differance* [cf. Structuralism 4.3] which opens appearance and signification. [. . .] No concept of metaphysics can describe it" (1967a: 65).

Universal Language

The range and utility of language as a tool of human communication are limited by the geographical and historical diversity of natural languages. The semiotic roots of these shortcomings lie in the linguistic design features of *arbitrariness* and *tradition* (see Language 3.1.3–4). With the aim of overcoming the Babylonian confusion of tongues, about nine hundred universal languages have been proposed or even developed in detail during the history of semiotics. Most of them are practical proposals for an *international auxiliary language*. A more philosophical goal has been pursued in projects aiming at the invention of an ideal language both economic in its structure and isomorphic with the system of nature which it should represent.

For many semiotic, cultural, pedagogical, and political reasons, the future of both projects is questionable, but this perspective does not diminish the interest of theoretical semiotics in the universal language idea, which lies in the search for (optimal) structures of semiotic systems. Among the most notable results of the history of universal language (UL) projects are the procedures of the atomization of meaning, which are an invention not of twentieth-century structural semantics but of eighteenth-century UL philosophers.

1. Semiotic Foundations of Universal Languages

The study of universal languages belongs both to applied and to theoretical semiotics. The languages which have been proposed up to now may be classified with respect to their structure and their relation to natural language.

1.1 Semiotic Dimensions of the UL Idea

In addition to the theoretical question of the structure of an ideal language, the universal language project has three other semiotic dimensions which can only briefly be discussed in this article: mythology, language evolution, and pragmatics.

1.1.1 THE UL MYTH

Mythological, literary, ideological, and religious dimensions of the UL idea have been explored by Cornelius (1965) and Bausani (1970). According to the tradition of Biblical exegesis, *lingua humana*, the first language of mankind, was a natural and universal language. The loss of this language after the confusion of tongues at Babel was a divine punishment for mankind. But there is also a different mythological vision in which a UL lies not in the past but in the future of mankind: the

Persian Manichaeans have the myth of a future kingdom under Ahuramazda in which there will be only one law and one language. Under secular premises, this vision later also appears in the communist ideology of Stalin (cf. Blanke 1985: 56). In literature, the discovery of Chinese and hieroglyphic writing, and proposals for a real character and for secret writing systems, motivated a number of seventeenth- and eighteenth-century authors to invent fictional ULs spoken in imaginary countries (cf. Cornelius 1965; see also Objects 2.1).

1.1.2 LANGUAGE ORIGINS AND LANGUAGE UNIVERSALS

An evolutionary semiotic dimension of the study of ULs lies in the related research fields of onto- and phylogenetic language origins and linguistic universals. From research in language acquisition and pidginizations of natural languages (cf. Valdman, ed. 1977), UL projects can derive insights into the processes of language simplification and regularization. Research in the structures of human protolanguages (cf. Wescott, ed. 1974) could lead to the discovery of elements to be adopted in a universal language. Finally, no universal language project can afford to ignore the results of research in language universals, i.e., those features common to or at least statistically dominant in all languages (see Greenberg 1966, Comrie 1981, Holenstein 1985, Petitot 1987, and the special issue of *Bulletin du groupe de recherches sémio-linguistiques* 14 [1980]. On the other hand, the universality of linguistic evolution itself has provided one of the major objections against the adoption of ULs. Since the history of natural languages shows that every language changes with time, it must be assumed that an international auxiliary language, after being adopted, would lose its universality by its own evolution.

1.1.3 PRAGMATICS OF THE UL PROJECT

From a pragmatic point of view, the UL project raises the question of the ideal conditions of language learnability and communicative effi-

ciency. Articulatory ease, structural transparency, systemic regularity, and economy are among the features which a UL should have for these reasons. There are two major obstacles to the realization of these conditions. One is the relativity of learnability: to adult learners, the grammatical and articulatory simplicity of a second language depends largely on its structural distance from the learner's first language. Thus, Esperanto is relatively simple for native speakers of Romance and Germanic languages. However, it has inflectional characteristics, such as cases and adjective-noun agreement, which are difficult for native speakers of Chinese, although they are relatively easy to learn for speakers of Indo-European languages. The other major obstacle to UL projects is the pragmatic necessity of redundancy (see Information 2.1.5). This feature of practically spoken languages is opposed to the ideal of systemic simplicity. Several early philosophical projects of a universal character were conceived as ideal systems without any redundancy. For this reason, they could never have been adopted in practical use.

1.2 Universal and Natural Languages

A basic decision of any UL project is whether the proposed language should take existing natural languages as its model or whether it should be designed as a completely new semiotic system.

1.2.1 A PRIORI AND A POSTERIORI ULS

The relationship between a UL and existing natural languages is the criterion for the classification of ULs into *a priori* and *a posteriori* languages (Couturat & Leau 1903, Large 1985). *A priori* languages are systems with artificial elements and structures invented independently of the grammar and lexicon of any existing natural language. *A posteriori* languages are composed of elements taken from one or several historical languages with the goal of creating a simpler, more regular, and easier to learn language. For further aspects of the typology of ULs, see Sakaguchi (1983) and Blanke (1985: 99–110).

1.2.2 PRACTICAL AND PHILOSOPHICAL SYSTEMS

Practical ULs are designed for the practical purpose of international communication. They are planned to be learned easily. All *a posteriori* ULs were designed as practical ULs, but there are also practical ULs which were planned as *a priori* systems (cf. Blanke 1985), among them the pictographic *pasigraphies*, which are not derived from spoken languages (cf. 3.2).

Philosophical ULs are generally *a priori* languages. They aim at the discovery of an ideal semiotic system irrespective of any pragmatic concern for pronounceability or learnability. The core of these projects was generally a system for the classification and the logical decomposition of concepts. A theoretical descendant of these projects is the search for the components of meaning in structural semantics. A practical offspring is the development of a thesaurus in lexicography (cf. P. M. Roget's *Thesaurus*).

1.3 The Medium of ULs

Speech, alphabetic writing, and numbers are the major, but not the only, media which have been proposed for ULs.

1.3.1 SPOKEN AND WRITTEN ULS

The spoken and written modes of ULs are either parallel (I) or mutually independent (II) codes. Some ULs were developed for writing only (III).

I. *Speech and Writing as Parallel Codes*: Most alphabetically written ULs are conceived for being spoken. In these languages, speech and writing are parallel codes. Esperanto and other international auxiliary languages are devised in this way. In contrast to historical languages, these artificial languages do not raise the question of the primacy of speech or the derivative nature of writing since both codes were developed at the same time.

II. *Spoken ULs with Autonomous Writing Systems*: Wilkins and some other early UL inventors proposed languages both for speaking and for writing in which the writing system was a completely new invention and not a transliteration of speech (although the spoken version of ULs was, of course, transcribed alphabetically, too). In such ULs, speech and writing are two autonomous codes.

III. *Pasigraphies*: Some ULs were developed for writing only and have no spoken counterpart (cf. 3.2). These languages are called pasigraphies (Gr. 'a writing for all'). The first pure pasigraphy was proposed by Joseph de Maimieux in 1797. Some inventors of pasigraphies were convinced of the superiority and greater universality of the written medium over speech.

1.3.2 NUMERICAL CODES

Numbers were often proposed as the medium of ULs in the early UL schemes (cf. Knowlson 1975: 61–64, Beck 1657; cf. Salmon 1979, Becher 1661, Kircher 1663; cf. McCracken 1948, and Wolke 1797). Essentially, these projects consist of code books, in which the words of the base language(s), mostly Latin, are listed in alphabetical order, sometimes expanded to a multilingual dictionary (as in Becher and Kircher). In a parallel column, the words of the base language are assigned a number which is the symbol to be used in the UL. In addition, there is a grammatical component for the encoding of case, number, tense, or other syntactic characteristics. In Beck's numerical UL project, there is even a proposal for a simplified pronunciation of the code numbers (1 = on, 2 = to, 3 = tre etc.). An example is given in Figure U 1.

English:		Honor	thy	Father	and	thy	Mother
Written UL:	leb	2314		p 2477	&	pf	2477
Spoken UL:	leb	totreónfo	pee	tofosénsen	and	pif	tofosénsen

Fig. U 1. The fifth commandment in Beck's (1657) UL (cf. Salmon 1979: 189): *leb* = imperative plural, *p* = agent noun [male], *pf* = agent noun female, *2314* = honor, *2477* = parent.

The major deficiency of these proposals is that they presuppose a 1:1 correspondence between the vocabularies and grammars of existing languages. For modern numerical ULs see Blanke (1985: 116).

1.3.3 MUSIC

The idea of a UL using musical sounds as elements of expression was discussed by Wilkins (1641: 75–77). In 1638, Bishop F. Goodwin described a language "of tunes and mouth sounds" in his science fiction romance *The Man in the Moon* (cf. Davies 1967). In 1817, Jean-François Sudré proposed the UL *Sorésol*, whose elements were the seven tones do, re, mi, fa, sol, la, si, plus accent (cf. Couturat & Leau 1903: 33–39, Large 1985: 60–63). The author suggested that these elements could be expressed as sounds, as colors, by means of gestures, or by speech (by their names). In Sorésol, function words are expressed by one to two notes, e.g., *re* 'and,' *mi* 'or,' *si* 'if,' *dore* 'I,' *domi* 'you,' *dofa* 'he.' The most common lexical words are formed by three notes (*doresol* 'mouth,' *dorefa* 'week'). Opposites are often expressed by reversing the order of the notes (e.g., *domisol* 'God,' *solmido* 'Satan'). In four-note words, the first note (the "key") indicates the semantic category of the concept. By extending the vocabulary to five-note words, Sudré could have expressed a vocabulary of 11,732 words.

1.3.4 OTHER MEDIA

After speech and writing, pictographs have been proposed most frequently as the medium of ULs. Rambosson (1853), Paget (1943), Magarotto, and others (cf. Damm 1876: iv, Knowlson 1975) have proposed to develop a gestural medium of universal communication (cf. Sign Language 2.1.3). Swift made the satirical proposal to use objects as the medium of a UL (cf. Objects 2.1).

2. The Philosophical Project of a UL

The idea of a UL was one of the central topics in the philosophy of the eighteenth century. Studies of these early projects are Funke (1929), Cohen (1954), Rossi (1960), Formigari (1970), Brekle (1975), Knowlson (1975), Padley (1976), Salmon (1972; 1979), Slaugh-

ter (1982), Asbach-Schnitker (1984), and Large (1985). After precursors which date back to the Middle Ages, the rise of the vernacular languages and the decline of Latin as an international language in the seventeenth century led to a growing interest in the idea of an artificial language for universal communication. *Characteristica universalis* or *characteristica generalis* (χαρακτήρ = 'mark,' 'exact representation') were the terms by which these languages were designated in the seventeenth century. Bacon and Descartes contributed to the philosophical foundations of the UL idea. The first detailed UL schemes fulfilled the philosophical standards set up by Bacon and Descartes only partly. The more ambitious project by Leibniz was never completed.

2.1 Precursors

There are two precursors to the philosophical idea of a UL, medieval *mysticism* and sixteenth-century *cryptography*.

2.1.1 EARLIEST PRECURSORS

Earliest precursors of a UL idea appear in medieval mysticism: St. Hildegard of Bingen (1098–1179) invented an artificial language with a taxonomic vocabulary of nine hundred words representing the assumed order of the world (reprinted in Steinmeyer & Sievers, eds. 1895: 390–420; cf. Asbach-Schnitker 1984: xii–iii). More influential for future UL projects was the *Ars Magna* of Raymond Lully (Ramón Lull, ca. 1232–1316). Lully developed a logical system with sets of elementary notions in alphabetical notation whose combination was to provide new insights into truth (cf. Salmon 1972 and the reprint: R. Lullus, [1645] 1970, *Ars Generalis Ultima*, Frankfurt: Minerva).

2.1.2 CRYPTOGRAPHY, STENOGRAPHY, AND TELEGRAPHY

The development of a *universal character* in the seventeenth century is closely connected with contemporary interests in communication in secret (cryptography), at speed (stenography), and even at distance (telegraphy) (cf. Salmon 1972: 60–68, Knowlson 1975). In 1641, the UL inventor Wilkins investigated all of these topics in a book entitled *Mercury: Or the Secret and Swift Messenger, Shewing How a Man May with Privacy and Speed Communicate His Thoughts to a Friend at Distance* (reprint 1984).

The close relationship between secret and universal encoding of ideas is explicitly discussed in Becher's numerical UL project (cf. 1.3.2). Becher suggested that the numerical messages of his universal code might be turned into cryptographic messages if the sender added and the receiver subtracted a secret number to (or from) every character (1661: 33–34). Another project in which the relationship between universal and secret writing is particularly evident is Kircher's *Polygraphia* (1663) (see 1.3.2). This work was influenced by the cryptographic treatise *Polygraphia* of J. Trithemius (1518).

Between 1588 and 1633 there was a growing interest in stenographic writing in England. A shorthand system, the *Tironian notes*, was already known and used in ancient and medieval times (cf. Boge 1974), but in 1588 Timothy Bright invented a new *Characterie*, followed by other authors who called their systems *stenography*, *brachigraphy*, or *tachygraphy* (cf. Salmon 1979: 157–61). These shorthand writing systems inspired a number of philosophers in their attempts at developing a universal system of writing (cf. 1.3.1).

2.1.3 A BRIEF CHRONOLOGY OF THE EARLIEST PROJECTS

Since the following paragraphs have to remain restricted to only some of the most famous philosophical UL projects, a brief chronology of other UL schemes is added here. For further reference, see especially Formigari (1970) and Knowlson (1975: 224–32).

1548: Theodore Bibliander, *De ratione communi omnium linguarum*, Zurich. This is one of the earliest books dealing with the project of restoring a unified protolanguage (cf. Salmon 1979, Asbach-Schnitker 1984: xi).

1605: Bacon; see 2.2.1.

1617: Hermann Hugo, *De prima scribendi origine et universa rei literariae antiquitate*, Antwerp. Hugo proposes the project of a universal character and refers to Chinese characters and other graphic symbols as examples of signs which denote things directly (cf. Knowlson 1975).

1627: Jean Douet, *Proposition présentée au roy, d'une escriture universelle*, Paris. This was the earliest project of a universal character in France (cf. Knowlson 1975).

1629: Marin Mersenne, *Harmonie universelle*, Paris. Mersenne develops the idea of a natural primitive language whose words should signify directly without convention (cf. Knowlson 1975, Slaughter 1982). In particular, Mersenne emphasizes the role of onomatopoeic sounds in this language.

1647: Francis Lodwick, *A Common Writing: Whereby Two Although Not Understanding One the Others Language, Yet by the Helpe thereof, May Communicate Their Minds One to Another*, London. This is one of the first elaborations of an actual scheme of real characters. It is based on a primarily morphological segmentation of English words into stem and derivational morphemes (cf. Salmon 1972, Knowlson 1975). The scheme is similar to Beck's numerical project (cf. 1.3.2) but instead of numbers, Lodwick uses artificial graphic symbols. The language is an *a posteriori* project. Owing to its morphological approach, it does not yet belong to the philosophical languages, which operate by semantic decomposition (cf. 2.3–4).

1652: Sir Thomas Urquhart, Εκσκυβαλαυρον, London, and

1653: id., *Logopandecteision, or An Introduction to the Universal Language*, London. Urquhart discusses philosophical principles on which a UL should be based and enumerates sixty-six advantages of such a language (cf. Cohen 1954: 55, Asbach-Schnitker 1984: xxii–iii, Large 1985: 19–20).

1654: Seth Ward, *Vindiciae Academiarum*, Oxford. Ward proposes a spoken and written philosophical language with complex notions consisting of simple notions whose elements should be still more elementary concepts (cf.

Slaughter 1982: 139, Asbach-Schnitker 1984: xxiv–v).

1657: Cave Beck, *The Universal Character, by Which All the Nations in the World May Understand One Another's Conceptions: Reading out of One Common Writing Their Own Mother Tongues.* This is an early numerical UL project (cf. 1.3.2).

1661: Johann Joachim Becher, *Character pro notitia*; see 1.3.2, 2.1.2.

1661: George Dalgarno, *Ars Signorum*; see 2.3.1.

1663: Athanasius Kircher, *Polygraphia nova*; see 2.1.2 and McCracken (1948).

1665–66: Johann Amos Comenius, *Panglottia.* Amsterdam. In this book and in his *Via lucis* (written in 1641), Comenius pursues the idea of an ideal language "adapted to the exact and perfect representation of things." This language should be "(1) rational [. . .], (2) analogical, containing no anomaly in any matter, and (3) harmonious, bringing no discrepancies between things and the concepts of things" (Comenius 1668: 168, 191; cf. DeMott 1955, Miškovská 1959, Brekle 1975: 304–305, 323, Padley 1976, Slaughter 1982). One of his topics is the role of sound symbolism in a UL scheme (cf. Miškovská 1962).

1666: Gottfried Leibniz, *Dissertatio de arte combinatoria*; see 2.4.

1668: John Wilkins, *An Essay towards a Real Character*; see 2.3.2.

2.2 Philosophical Foundations

Francis Bacon (1561–1626) and René Descartes (1596–1650) were among the earliest philosophers to discuss the idea of a philosophical language.

2.2.1 BACON'S IDEA OF A REAL CHARACTER

In *The Advancement of Learning* (1605) and *De dignitate et augmentis scientiarum* (1623), Bacon criticized language for being an unreliable tool of human understanding, since "false appearances are imposed upon us by words, which are framed and applied according to the vulgar" (1605: 134 [= § XIV, 11]). In his search for a better tool of human communication, Bacon discussed the idea of a *real character* (cf. Salmon 1972: 78), a system of written symbols "which express neither letters nor words in gross, but things or notions; insomuch as countries and provinces, which understand not one another's language, can nevertheless read one another's writing" (ibid.: 137 [= § XVI, 1.2]). Like many of his contemporaries, Bacon believed that Chinese writing and Egyptian hieroglyphics were such systems of real characters. For the history of the discovery of Chinese and hieroglyphic writing in this time and its influence on contemporary UL projects, see David (1965).

2.2.2 DESCARTES

In his letter of November 20, 1629, to Mersenne, Descartes criticized the UL project of an anonymous contemporary who claimed to have rediscovered the protolanguage of mankind (cf. Knowlson 1975: 48–51). This UL was described as having a completely regular grammar. Its words were to be decoded by means of a multilingual dictionary. Descartes criticized this language for two reasons: its sounds would be "disagreeable" to speakers used to different first languages, and its words would be hard to learn because of the novelty of its dictionary (1629: 913).

As an improvement of the UL project, Descartes recommended the invention of a UL according to philosophical principles (ibid.: 914). Its lexicon should be composed of primitive elements. By systematically combining these elements, one could generate "an infinity of different words" just as numbers can be combined infinitely. Once the primitives have been discovered, the UL would be not only easy to learn but also an instrument for the discovery of truth. In spite of these theoretical proposals, however, Descartes remains skeptical about the practical realization of this project, for "cela présuppose de grands changements en l'ordre des choses, et il faudrait que tout le monde ne fût qu'un paradis terrestre, ce qui n'est bon à proposer que dans les pays des romans" (ibid.: 915).

2.3 The First Philosophical Languages

George Dalgarno (ca. 1626–1687) and John Wilkins (1614–1672) published the first elaborated projects of a philosophical *a priori* language. Based on a scientific taxonomy of concepts and things, the authors gave an encyclopedic outline of the contemporary knowledge of the universe (cf. Slaughter 1982). As Knowlson points out (1975: 91, 95) this encyclopedic approach distinguishes Dalgarno's and Wilkins's UL schemes from the more ambitious philosophical UL projects of Descartes and Leibniz:

> The emphasis in Dalgarno's and Wilkins's philosophical languages is placed upon a description of the order of reality. [. . .] There is no effort to reduce complex ideas to a few philosophical simples. [. . .]. It was essentially because of this difference in conception that Leibniz was later to assert that the schemes formulated by Dalgarno and Wilkins were not philosophical enough.

2.3.1 DALGARNO

Dalgarno's (1661) UL project (cf. Funke 1929: 10–14, Salmon 1979: 157–75, Slaughter 1982: 141–53, Cram 1985) is entitled *Ars signorum, vulgo character universalis et lingua philosophica*. The author characterized this project as a treatise of sematology and defined its goals as follows: "cutting off all Redundancy, rectifying all Anomaly, taking away all Ambiguity and Æquivocation, contracting the Primitives to a few number, and even those not to be of a meer arbitrary, but a rational Institution, enlarging the bounds of derivation and Composition" (1680: Introduction). *Ars signorum* is a written and potentially speakable language. Its words consist of letters of the Latin alphabet (plus Gr. eta [η, H] and y) combined into elementary sequences with the structure of syllables. Since every letter is meaningful, the language has only a first and no second articulation (see Language 4.1). The initial letter indicates the general category (*genus*) to which the concept belongs.

Dalgarno distinguished up to twenty-three genera, such as substance (H), spirit (Y), physi-cal (N) or artifactual entity (F). Each of these categories is divided into *species*, and these in turn are subdivided into *subspecies*. These categories are indicated by the second and third letters. For example, in *fan* ('house'), *f-* stands for the genus 'concrete artifact,' and *-n* for the species 'construction.' There are two other subspecies of this class, *fηn* ('ship') and *fen* ('bridge'). Thus, the second and third letters only indicate the place of the (sub)species within the categorical system. Their value changes within each category. For example, within the category *n-* ('physical entities'), the final letter *-n* indicates 'birds,' while the middle letters *-a-* and *-η-* specify 'carnivore' and 'nocturnal' (birds). This principle shows that Dalgarno's philosophical language is basically a semantic taxonomy and does not yet achieve the systematic atomization of meaning which was later envisioned by Leibniz (cf. 2.4).

2.3.2 WILKINS

In Wilkins's monumental *Essay towards a Real Character, and a Philosophical Language* (1668), the project of a UL based on taxonomic principles reaches its climax (cf. Funke 1929, Knowlson 1975: 98–107, Salmon 1979: 97–126, Slaughter 1982: 157–74). The language is much more elaborate than Dalgarno's, comprising a hierarchy of forty genera. For each genus, a number of taxonomic features can be derived from this hierarchy, for example, that the genus "STONE" is a 'substance' of 'imperfect' and 'vegetative' species being of an 'animate' [sic!] substance (ibid.: 23). The further subclassification into *differences* and *species* and the formation of the written and spoken words are similar to Dalgarno's system except for elaborate definitions which Wilkins adds. In the word *Dibe* = 'flint,' for example, *Di-* indicates the genus STONE, *-b-* the difference 'vulgar . . . or of little or no price,' and *-e* the third species of this class, which is 'unequal, used for the striking of fire' (ibid.: 61, 442). An additional grammatical component specifies the derivational and inflectional morphemes which have to be affixed to these lexemes (ibid.: 443).

In addition to this spoken and alphabetically written version, Wilkins devised a completely new pasigraphic notation of his real character (1668: 387). It consists of an inventory of elementary graphemes to represent the forty genera such as:

God ———

World ╪

Element ╧

Stone ╤

Marks at the left of these categorical symbols indicate the differences, marks at the right indicate the species. Thus, the pasigraphic symbols

↙ (= 'flint') and

↙┤ (= 'sand')

indicate two objects of the genus STONE (╤), both 'vulgar' (↙), but one belonging to the third (↙) species (see above) and the other to the eighth (┤) species, which comprises STONES 'of minute magnitude' (ibid.: 61, 387). An illustration of Wilkins's UL is given in Figure U 2.

2.4 *Leibniz's* lingua rationalis

Gottfried Wilhelm von Leibniz (1646–1716) (see also History 3.1.3) developed the idea of an *ars characteristica*, the UL project of *characteristica universalis* or *generalis* in many of his fragments after 1666 (cf. Trendelenburg 1856, Couturat 1901: 51–118, Lewis 1918: 5–18, Heinekamp 1975, Burkhardt 1980: 175–90). The goal of his project surpassed those of his predecessors in three respects: (1) Leibniz's *ars characteristica* aimed at a more exhaustive semantic decomposition of concepts, (2) the project included a *rational calculus* for the combination of ideas, and (3) Leibniz even envisioned a universal *ars inveniendi* (cf. Rhetoric 2.1.2) for the invention of new truths. With these goals, Leibniz's fragmentary project had to remain utopian. Nevertheless, his work is an important step in the history of semiotics and

contains the foundations of symbolic logic (cf. Lewis 1918).

2.4.1 THE ALPHABET OF HUMAN THOUGHT

As the medium (cf. 1.3) of his universal character, Leibniz considered speech, writing, numbers, pictures (cf. Couturat 1901: 106–114), various graphic-geometrical figures (cf. Schnelle 1962: 15), and even musical tones (cf. Trendelenburg 1856: 53). The basic elements of his ideal language are characters representing unambiguously a limited number of elementary concepts. Leibniz called the inventory of these concepts "the alphabet of human thought." All complex concepts would have to be formed by a combination of these primitive elements and not only, as in Dalgarno's and Wilkins's languages, by assigning them a place in a taxonomic system. On the one hand, the characters were to be isomorphic with the concepts designated by them; on the other hand, the universal signs were to be isomorphic with the facts of nature (cf. Heinekamp 1975: 266).

2.4.2 THE *ARS COMBINATORIA*

Leibniz believed in the possibility of an algebra of thought. At one time, he proposed that by representing primitive concepts as prime numbers, complex concepts might be represented as their product. Thus, if 3 represents 'rational' and 2 'animal,' 6 would be the character for 'man' (Couturat 1901: 62). Leibniz worked on the development of a *calculus rationator*, a system of rules for the combination of the semantic primitives. He was convinced that the application of this calculus would allow the demonstration of the truth of any argument. This rational operation could then terminate any future disputes since errors or truths of reasoning would be demonstrated simply by applying the rules of this calculus. Thus, disagreements would be settled by mathematical operations. Mistakes of reasoning would be revealed by a close scrutiny of the language. Moreover, this UL should even serve as an *ars inveniendi* for the discovery of truths and sciences (cf. Burkhardt 1980). Leibniz was aware of the difficulties of his project and proposed to

The Lords Prayer.

1	2	3	4	5	6	7	8	9	10

Haı́ coba 𝕩𝕩 ıa ril dad, ha babı ıo ſ𝕩ymta

Our Father who art in Heaven, Thy Name be Hallowed,

Our   1. (Haı) This Dipthong (aı) is affigned to fignifie the firſt Perſon plural amongſt the Pronouns, *viz. We.* The Letter *h* prefixed to it, doth denote that Pronoun to be uſed poffeffively, *viz. Our.*

Parent   2. (Coba) Co doth denote the Genus of *Oeconomical Relation* ; the Letter (b) fignifying the firſt difference under that Genus, which is Relation of Confanguinity ; the Vowel (a) the fecond Species, which is *Direct afcending* ; namely, *Parent.*

Who   3. (𝕩𝕩) This Dipthong is appointed to fignifie the fecond of the compound Pronouns, *Who,* perfonal ; or *Which,* Real.

Art   4. (ia) This dipthong is appointed to fignifie the prefent tenfe of the Copula (*eſt*) and being fpoken of the fecond perfon, is to be rendered *Art.*

In   (ril) is a *Prepofition,* the firſt Oppofite of the fourth combination ; and therefore muſt fignifie (*in.*)

Heaven   6. (dad) The Syllable (da) is appointed to fignifie the Genus of *World* ; the addition of the Letter (d) doth denote the fecond difference under that Genus, which is *Heaven.*

Fig. U 2. The beginning of the Lord's Prayer in phonetic and pasigraphic transcription (with annotations) according to Wilkins (1668: 421–22). The diphthong quoted under (3.) is the bilabial semivowel /w-/, as in the beginning of *woo.*

develop a regularized and simplified Latin which should serve as a provisional international auxiliary language until the ideal language was fully elaborated (cf. Couturat 1901: 65–79).

2.5 Later Projects

The history of philosophical UL projects after Leibniz has partially (especially the 18th century) been outlined by Knowlson (1975) and Asbach-Schnitker (1984). After a decline of interest in ULs, Wolff (cf. Arndt 1979) and Lambert (see History 3.4.2) were among the first to resume Leibniz's project of an *ars characteristica.* Most philosophical UL projects since the eighteenth century have been concerned with the development of pasigraphies. A revival of interest in the development of a rational language was characteristic of the semiotic philosophy of the French idèologues (see also History 3.3.4). Although there have been few projects since the nineteenth century, philosophical pasigraphies have still been proposed until this century (Haag 1930). Some notable projects are:

1726: D. Solbrig, *Allgemeine Schrift.*

1772: G. Kalmár, *Praecepta grammatica* (1773 in Italian, 1774 in German).

1779: C. G. Berger, *Plan zu einer allgemeinen Sprache.*

1795: J. Delormel, *Projet d'une langue universelle.*

1797: J. de Maimieux, *Pasigraphie.*

1797: C. H. Wolke, . . . *Pasiphrasie.*

The developments of formal languages in symbolic logic (DeMorgan, Boole, Peirce, Russell, Frege) and in analytical philosophy are only partially successors to the philosophical project of a UL. Although they also aim at the discovery of a universal instrument of pure reasoning, these languages are restricted in their scope to formal operation in fields such as logic, mathematics, or physics and do not pursue the aim of becoming an instrument of universal communication. A notable exception is Freudenthal's *Lincos* (1960), a project of a language for cosmic intercourse.

3. International Auxiliary Languages

The history of international auxiliary languages and the state of the art in *interlinguistics*, the linguistic study of these languages, is well documented by Couturat & Leau (1903), Pei (1958), Rónai (1967), Haupenthal, ed. (1976), Sakaguchi (1983), Blanke (1985), and Large (1985). The most famous projects are spoken languages, but there are also a number of pasigraphic or pictographic UL projects.

3.1 Spoken International Auxiliary Languages

Ironically, the history of interlinguistics is no less reminiscent of the scattering at Babel than the history of natural languages: about nine hundred international artificial languages have

been invented (or at least proposed; cf. Blanke 1985: 66). The most famous of them are *a posteriori* languages derived from Western European languages. Among the best-known are:

Date	International Auxiliary Language	Inventor
1880	Volapück	Johann M. Schleier
1887	Esperanto	Ludwig L. Zamenhof
1903	Latino Sine Flexione	Giuseppe Peano
1907	Ido	Louis de Beaufront, Louis Couturat, and others
1922	Occidental-Interlingue	Edgar de Wahl
1928	Novial	Otto Jespersen
1930	Basic English	Charles K. Ogden
1951	Interlingua	Alexander Gode

There are two major types of planned languages, those of a *polylinguistic* and those of a *monolinguistic* origin. The former type are constructed from elements of various existing languages. Esperanto and Ido, for example, have their sources in Romance languages, English, German, and some Greek and Russian, not only lexically (cf. Esperanto *domo* 'house,' *birdo* 'bird,' *hundo* 'dog') but also grammatically (cf. *lingva* = nom., lingvon = acc. in the sample below).

ULs of a monolinguistic origin are either simplifying transformations of existing languages (such as Latino Sine Flexione) or elementary versions of natural languages preserving the basic structures of their model. Basic (*British American International Commercial*) English is such a language. It is an English reduced to an elementary grammar and a vocabulary of 850 words (plus a number of "international words" and compounds). Words from the vocabulary of natural English which do not belong to the 850 words of Basic English have to be translated by means of paraphrases. The following samples illustrate these structures of Esperanto (source: Blanke 1985:

221) and Basic English (source: Ogden 1930: 378):

Esperanto:
Esperantisto estas nomata ĉiu persono, kin scias kaj uzas la lingvon Esperanto, tute egale por kiaj celoj li ĝin uzas.

English translation:
Esperantist is the name for any person who knows and uses the Esperanto language, no matter for which goal he uses it.

Basic English
Foreign Office and trade representatives in other countries will be requested to do everything possible to get Basic English more widely used as a second language.

(Original) English
Diplomatic and commercial representatives in foreign countries will be asked to do all they can to encourage the spread of Basic English as an auxiliary language.

3.2 Modern Pasigraphies and Picture Languages

More than 120 practical pasigraphies have been invented or proposed so far (cf. the surveys by Monnerot-Dumaine 1960: 11–16 and Blanke 1985: 110–22; see also 2.5 for the earliest philosophical pasigraphies). The characters of pasigraphies are iconic pictograms, symbolic ideograms, letters, numbers, and other graphic symbols, and various types of indices (arrows, etc.). The pasigraphic characters used in most earlier pasigraphies (from Maimieux 1797 until Damm 1876) were mostly arbitrary symbols. The characters proposed in the more recent practical pasigraphies have mostly a certain degree of iconic and indexical motivation. The inventors of these languages often claim that their pasigraphies are particularly universal because of this feature. Some examples are:

Date	Pasigraphy	Inventor
1949	Semantography	C. K. Bliss (1949)
1951	Safo	A. Eckardt
1957	Picto	K. J. A. Janson
1973	LoCoS	Y. Ota

Safo, for example, is a system of about 180 elementary (lexical) characters. By combining these elements, more complex signs can be formed. Further characters represent grammatical and derivational morphemes. The grammar is an *a posteriori* design derived from European languages (cf. Fig. U 3). In most pasigraphies, the principle of combining the elementary characters is linear order. Ota (1973), however, proposed a pasigraphy which makes additional use of the visual potential of the second dimension by combining the elements of complex concepts in a vertical row (cf. Muckenhaupt 1986: 80–85).

The hopes of the inventors of pasigraphies for the discovery of a universal medium of communication have been disappointed, even more so than the hopes of the inventors of spoken ULs. Some of the semiotic reasons for this failure are discussed by Eschbach (1987). A number of picture languages seem to have a certain success as languages for special purposes. Thus, Bliss's *Semantography* (or *Blissymbolics*) (1949) has been used successfully in the teaching of severely handicapped deaf children (cf. Helfman 1981).

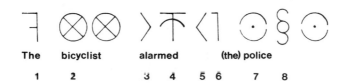

The   bicyclist   alarmed   (the) police

  1   2   3   4   5 6   7   8

Fig. U 3. A sample of Safo pictography (cf. Blanke 1985: 119). The elementary characters are: 1 = man, 2 = wheel, 3 = back, 4 = bell, 5 = breast, 6 = past, 7 = eye, 8 = law.

Some so-called picture languages have been designed for restricted purposes such as cartography, traffic regulation, public orientation, and the visualization of statistical charts (cf. Code 5.4). One of the most successful systems of this type is ISOTYPE, invented by O. Neurath in the context of the positivist unified science project of the 1930s (cf. Eschbach 1987). These (picto)graphic systems, however, cannot be considered ULs. Basically, they are only lexical codes and have no grammatical component to express derivational, logical, or other syntactic relationships between the pictograms.

Sign Language

Sign Languages (SLs) in the narrower sense are semiotic systems of gestural communication with the communicative potential of a spoken language. Such gestural languages have been developed in contexts where speech is not available (as in the SLs of the deaf), in situations where speech is forbidden (as in monastic SLs), or as a universal language for people of different native languages (as in aboriginal SLs). Like writing, SLs communicate via the visual channel. But while writing is basically two-dimensional, thus depicting the linearity of spoken language, SLs are the only full-fledged languages in the three-dimensional medium of nonverbal communication. One of the specific semiotic features of SLs is therefore the higher degree of simultaneity of informational units compared with the more sequential nature of speech.

1. Gestural Communication as Language

In comparison with other modes of nonverbal communication, SLs in the narrower sense are characterized by their communicative equivalence to but relative structural independence from spoken language.

1.1 SL in the Broader and in the Narrower Sense

The designation *sign language* is generally restricted to the narrower usage of the term by most scholars of the field (cf. Stokoe 1980: 365, Kendon 1986b: 8). It must be distinguished from the usage in the broader sense.

1.1.1 SL IN THE BROADER SENSE

In a very broad sense, the term *sign language* is sometimes used as a synonym of semiotic systems in general. *Language* in this usage is only a figurative designation of all kinds of nonlinguistic codes. The metaphorical nature of this term is apparent in studies such as *The Language of Signs* (Voigt et al. 1973), *The Language of Gestures* (Wundt 1900), and *Language without Words* (Kleinpaul 1888). In the field of nonverbal communication, the special gestural codes used by certain groups of people in particular professional or leisure activities are sometimes also designated as sign languages. In this broadest sense, Meissner & Philpott (1975), for example, study the "sign language of the sawmill workers" in British Columbia, and Savigny (1980) the "signal language of the automobilist" (for further gestural systems of this kind, see Gesture 2.2.3).

1.1.2 SLS IN THE NARROWER SENSE

SLs in the narrower sense are not restricted in the domain of their communicative functions.

They must be able to serve as a functional equivalent to spoken language in any situation of life. This communicative potential of SLs is apparent from the size of their sign repertoires. According to Stokoe, the number of signs in the lexicon of American Sign Language is about four thousand (1972: 63). Mallery's (1881) dictionary of the SL of the Plains Indians contains about three thousand entries. Barakat's study of the Cistercian SL (which is not used in all situations of life) lists a lexicon of about five hundred signs (1975: 26).

Being gestural languages, SLs in the narrower sense use the same medium of expression as the codes of nonverbal communication, but there are a number of features which are characteristic of SLs only: (a) SLs show a higher degree of conventionality (cf. 2.2, 3.2.1), (b) gesturing in SLs is restricted to a particular space for signing, normally not extending below waist level or above the head (cf. ibid.: 71–77 and Voegelin 1958: 71), (c) there is a tendency toward symmetry in the use of two-handed signs (cf. ibid.), and (d) SLs are semiotic systems with a grammar of their own (cf. 2.3, 3.2.2).

1.2 SLs and Spoken Language

Can gestural systems of communication be classified as genuine languages, and if so, to what degree are they different from spoken languages?

1.2.1 ARE SLS LANGUAGES?
There has been some debate about whether SLs have the nature of a language at all (cf. Schlesinger & Namir 1978: 4–6, Deuchar 1984: 18–25). While Stokoe (1972; 1974; 1976; 1980), Baron (1981: 207–214), and others have defended the language status of the SL of the deaf, Crystal & Craig (1978) and Schlesinger (1978) have emphasized a number of differences from spoken languages. Their criteria of analysis are derived from Hockett's design features of language (q.v., 3.1), which

are based on an essentially phonocentric view of language. A more affirmative answer to the question of the language status of signing systems can be given if language is understood in a more abstract sense in which writing may be considered a mode of language, too (cf. Deuchar 1984: 24–25). From these premises, Voegelin & Harris compare the structural autonomy of aboriginal SLs to the autonomy of Chinese writing in relation to spoken Chinese, and to the autonomy of Arabic numerals in comparison to their corresponding number words (1945: 459).

1.2.2 SEMIOTIC AUTONOMY OF SLS
The autonomy of SLs in relation to spoken languages is structural, geographical, and functional. SLs are structurally autonomous to the degree to which they have a morphology, lexicon, and grammar of their own. This is one of the major distinctions between SLs and *language substitutes*, which correspond more closely to the sound structure and grammar of their base language. SLs are geographically autonomous since their distribution does not coincide with the language boundaries of spoken languages and since different SLs are to a large degree mutually unintelligible. SLs are functionally autonomous since they differ from spoken language with respect to the circumstances of their use and availability. They substitute the visual for the auditory channel of communication because speech is unavailable or unintelligible, or speaking is prohibited. But this substitution of the auditory channel is not necessarily disadvantageous under all circumstances since visual signs can be transmitted under noisy conditions and over longer distances than vocal signs.

The SL of the deaf is usually acquired as a first language by its users. Aboriginal and monastic SLs are second languages to their users. They are restricted to certain situations of communication and are therefore less universal in their communicative functions than the SL of the deaf.

2. The Sign Languages of the Deaf

The SLs of the deaf are the most highly developed systems of gestural communication. Among them, American Sign Language (ASL) has so far received the most scholarly attention (cf. Stokoe 1972; 1980, Friedman, ed. 1977, Siple, ed. 1978, Klima & Bellugi et al. 1979, Wilbur 1979, Lane & Grosjean, eds. 1980, Liddell 1980, and the dictionaries by Stokoe et al. 1965 and Sternberg 1981). For studies of SLs from other countries see Kröhnert (1966), Cohen et al. (1977), Schlesinger & Namir, eds. (1978), Oléron (1978), Kendon (1980a), Kyle & Woll, eds. (1983), and Deuchar (1984).

2.1 History

The history of the SLs of the deaf has been outlined by Mendelson et al. (1964), Kröhnert (1966), Siger (1968), and Lane (1980). Lane characterizes it as a "chronology of the oppression" of a naturally developed native (sign) language by the users of the dominant (spoken) language. This oppression resulted in attempts to transform or even replace the autonomously developed gestural SLs of the deaf by SLs whose structure corresponds more closely to the spoken national language.

2.1.1 EARLY HAND ALPHABETS
The earliest descriptions of SLs of the deaf were published in Spain (cf. Kröhnert 1966, Alston 1971). The main concern of the early methods was with the teaching of writing and speaking (oral method) the national language.

During this time, manual alphabets were invented as gestural language substitutes for writing. After Lasso (1550), the work of Bonet (1620) became highly influential. His hand alphabet was adopted in Spain and France and is basically still used today by the American deaf population (cf. Mendelson et al. 1964: 183). Figure SL 1 shows the first letters of this hand alphabet. For the complete alphabet see Wilbur (1979: 18).

A quite different hand alphabet, no longer in use today, was proposed by Dalgarno (1680: 75). It was formed by pointing with the right index finger or thumb to certain parts of the left hand, as shown in Figure SL 2. The modern British hand alphabet is a two-handed system. Its first letters are shown in Figure SL 3 (for the full system see Deuchar 1984: 9). The differences between the British and the American alphabets (Fig. SL 1) illustrate the semiotic autonomy of both systems. For a gestural system representing phonemes instead of letters, see Language Substitutes (1.3.2).

2.1.2 DEVELOPMENT OF AUTONOMOUS CODES
Manual alphabets are only a subcode of modern SLs. Most gestural messages of the deaf today are coded without speech-related finger spelling. However, the degree of structural autonomy from spoken language varies considerably with the type of SL. Elements of autonomous SLs of the deaf were first discovered and described in 1774 by Abbé Charles Michel de l'Epée (1712–1789). In his own teachings, however (cf. Stokoe 1974: 356–58, Lane 1980), Epée still impeded the development of an autonomous gestural language by introducing unnecessary signs to represent

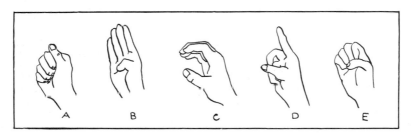

Fig. SL 1. The American manual alphabet from A to E.

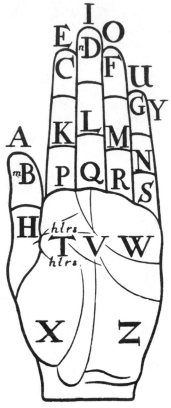

Fig. SL 2. Dalgarno's hand alphabet (1680: 75). Vowels are pointed at by the index, consonants by the thumb of the right hand.

French grammatical morphemes, such as prepositions and articles. In the nineteenth century, teaching of gestural systems was largely abandoned in favor of attempts to teach deaf individuals to speak (oral method) and to read lips.

The various types of modern SLs of the deaf still vary as to their autonomy from spoken lan-

guage. In their typology of current sign systems of the deaf, Crystal & Craig distinguish between "contrived signing systems," which are in close correspondence to a vocal base language, and the more autonomous "natural systems," including ASL (1978: 161–66). An example of an SL with a very close correspondence to the morphology and syntax of spoken English is S.E.E. (Signing Exact English). It was invented to help the deaf student learn English and has signs for articles and suffixes, which are not used in ASL (cf. Liddell 1980: v). The development of ASL was historically influenced by the teachings brought from France by Thomas H. Gallaudet (1787–1851) and Laurent Clerk (1785–1869) (cf. Woodward 1978). For this reason, ASL is more closely related to French SL than to British SL.

2.1.3 THE MYTH OF UNIVERSALITY

An early topic of SL studies was the assumption of the universality of gestures. Sign languages were often considered to be an ideal medium of international communication. Bulwer (1644), who was convinced of the superiority of gestures over spoken language, even believed that gestural communication should be adopted by mankind as a universal language (cf. Knowlson 1975: 212). His illustrations of "natural gestures" expressing human emotions (cf. Fig. SL 4) had their origins in a tradition reaching back to Quintilian's rhetoric. With respect to the structure and development of modern SLs of the deaf, the assumption of a basic universality of gestural communication is no longer justified (cf. Markowicz 1977, Frishberg 1978, Baron 1981: 202–206, Deuchar 1984: 2–7). Their structural and geographic autonomy and

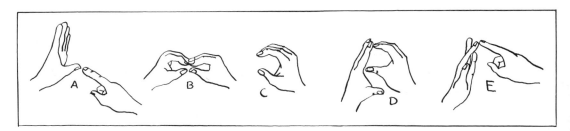

Fig. SL 3. The British manual alphabet from A to E.

Fig. SL 4. Four "chirograms" by Bulwer (1644: 117) illustrating the "natural language" of the human hand (N: shame, O: adoration, P: affirmation, Q: repentance).

their conventionality disprove the persistent myth of SL universality (but see 2.2).

2.2 Arbitrariness, Motivation, and Universality

The assumption of an essential iconicity in SLs is another myth of SL studies (Markowicz 1980: 4; cf. Mandel 1977, Frishberg 1978; 1979, Klima & Bellugi et al. 1979: 10–34, Deuchar 1984: 11–18). Even Bulwer's "natural gestures" (Fig. SL 4) were hardly iconic. The gestures are in no way similar to the meanings they express. The signs of modern SLs are to a large degree arbitrary and conventional and thus symbols in the sense of Peirce. Figure SL 5 illustrates this characteristic in ASL signs.

Nevertheless, there is a considerable degree of motivation and universality in SLs. As ethologists have shown, gestural communication in general has already a certain genetically determined universality (which is not neces-

sarily iconicity; cf. Gesture 2.5). An example is Bulwer's gesture of "shame" (Fig. SL 4), which can be observed with children throughout the world (cf. Eibl-Eibesfeldt 1972). Moreover, as Markowicz points out, "deaf persons from different cultures are usually able to communicate their basic needs to each other better than hearing people because they lack a certain inhibition about using gestures and because they are masters at pantomime" (1980: 2).

In comparison to spoken languages, SLs have a higher degree of iconicity in word fields representing visual phenomena, such as objects, spaces, or movements (cf. Mandel 1977). On the other hand, SLs are also less iconic than spoken languages since they are necessarily uniconic with respect to acoustic phenomena. A certain degree of iconicity is, so to speak, an etymological heritage of SLs, which has become obscured in the course of its history (cf. Frishberg 1979). As Klima & Bellugi et al. have shown, there are productive processes in the

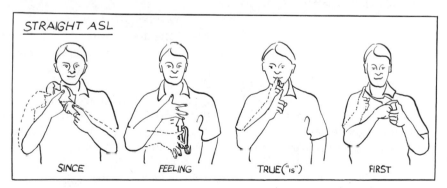

Fig. SL 5. E. E. Cummings's line "since feeling is first" in ASL (adapted from Klima & Bellugi et al. 1979: 345).

expressive use of ASL by which the original transparency of gestures can be reexploited (1979: 34). The motivation of SLs is not only iconic and universal but also indexical to a high degree (cf. Klima & Bellugi et al. 1979, Deuchar 1984). In particular, personal and spatial deixis and other modes of ostension are expressed by indexical gestures which are more universally intelligible than the corresponding morphemes of spoken languages.

2.3 System and Structure of ASL

In the analysis of Stokoe (1960; 1972), ASL is a semiotic system with three major characteristics of a language (q.v., 4.1): first articulation, second articulation, and a syntax of its own.

2.3.1 FIRST ARTICULATION
The level of first articulation in ASL consists of signs corresponding to the morpheme- and word level of spoken language. The repertoire of these signs forms the ASL lexicon (see Stokoe et al. 1965 and Sternberg 1981). Stokoe (1972; 1976; 1980) defines these units of ASL as *signs* or *gSigns* (gestural signs) and characterizes them as the *emic* units of the ASL system in contradistinction to the *etic* units of SL communication, which he defines as *gestures*. There are signs corresponding to verbs, adverbs, adjectives, nouns, pronouns, and prepositions. Among the English words without a correlate in ASL are the articles *the* and *a(n)*, the preposition *of*, and the auxiliary forms of *to be* (*is, was, are*, etc.; cf. Stokoe 1972: 69).

2.3.2 SECOND ARTICULATION
In analogy to the linguistic phoneme (see Structuralism 1.1.2), Stokoe defines the non-signifying differential units of gestural signs as *cheremes* (from Gr. χειρ 'hand') (1972: 69). In analogy to phonology, Stokoe postulates a branch of sign language studies to be called *cherology* (1960: 33–50). Others have continued research in this field under the designation of SL phonology (cf. Friedman 1977, Wilbur 1979, Stokoe 1980, Deuchar 1984).

In contradistinction to phonemes, cheremes

are not elements in a sequence, but basically simultaneous components of a gestural sign. Stokoe distinguishes three types of such elementary components whose combination constitutes a sign: *dez* (designator), the acting (handshape) configuration, *sig* (signation), the performed movement, and *tab* (tabula), the location of action (1980: 369). As an example, the cheremes of the ASL sign for girl (Fig. SL 6) are drawing down (sig) the ball of the thumb (dez) along the cheek (tab) (1972: 27). On the basis of fifty-five cheremes (12 tab, 19 dez, and 24 sig), Stokoe et al. (1965) describe the ASL lexicon of about twenty-five hundred signs.

Fig. SL 6. The ASL sign for 'girl' is composed of the cheremes "drawing down" (sig), "the ball of the thumb" (dez), and "along the cheek" (tab).

Klima & Bellugi et al. have pursued the phonological principles of cheremic analysis one step further (1979: 164–80). At a structural level below the chereme, they distinguish distinctive features of (handshape) cheremes, such as "dual," "radical," "touch," "cross," and others.

2.3.3 SYNTAX OF ASL
For a long time, the autonomous syntax of SLs remained undiscovered. The myth of "ungrammaticality" of SLs (Markowicz 1980) was the assumption of a nonexistent or a base-language-derived and reduced syntax. Meanwhile, the complexity of SL morphology and syntax has been ascertained in studies of ASL (Stokoe 1976, Wilbur 1979, Liddell 1980) and of other SLs (Oléron 1978, Namir & Schlesinger 1978, Kyle & Woll, eds. 1983, Deuchar 1984).

Compared with spoken languages, in which most syntactic information is coded sequentially by means of prepositions, articles, or inflectional morphemes, one of the specific features of SLs is the simultaneous coding of these structural indices together with the lexical signs. While ASL has no "segmental" signs corresponding to articles, plural and past-tense morphemes, these and other grammatical markers are signed "suprasegmentally" in the form of nonmanual signs, such as facial signals or body movements (cf. Liddell 1980). Syntactic information is also expressed by means of a flexible word order in ASL.

3. Aboriginal Sign Language

Semiotic and presemiotic research on aboriginal SLs has been collected in a two-volume edition by Umiker-Sebeok & Sebeok, eds. (1978). There are two areas in the world from which aboriginal SLs have been reported in detail, Australia and the North American Plains. Both differ in their communicative functions. Only the SL of the Indians of the North American Plains and of the Australian Aborigines (Kendon 1989) have so far been studied in detail.

3.1 Communicative Functions

Aboriginal SLs in Australia and North America were developed for essentially different communicative purposes.

3.1.1 PLAINS SL
The Plains SL (PSL) is a universal language whose major function was intertribal communication between speakers of different native languages. It has been used at least since the sixteenth century (cf. Taylor 1975: 330). Other uses of these languages were in public entertainment and oratory. Conversational use has also been reported (ibid.: 335–36). Research in PSL dates back to Mallery (1881; further studies by Mallery are reprinted in Umiker-Sebeok & Sebeok, eds. 1978). There has been a continuous popular interest in the PSL, which has resulted in numerous publications (for example, Fronval & Dubois 1985, with hundreds of color photographs).

Although English became the *lingua franca* of the Plains Indians in the nineteenth century, the PSL is not yet extinct today. Its most general use in this century is for oratorical purposes at the occasion of formal councils, but PSL is also used for storytelling (cf. Taylor 1975: 336–37). The most comprehensive study of PSL of this century is the unpublished work by West (1960, available on microfilm). For a clinical project of using an adapted version of PSL in therapeutical communication with speech-impaired persons, see Skelly (1979).

3.1.2 SL OF THE AUSTRALIAN ABORIGINES
In contradistinction to PSL, the Australian SL is primarily for intratribal communication, although there are also reports of intertribal use (Umiker-Sebeok & Sebeok, eds. 1978: xiv). Among the situations in which SL is used instead of speech by the Australian aborigines are communication at distance, in hunting, and in ceremonies. A major function of SL use with the Australian aborigines is communication during times in which language taboo has to be observed. Thus, Walpiri women use an SL for long periods after they have been bereaved because their culture prohibits speaking during this time (cf. Kendon 1980d; 1989).

3.2 The Semiotics of the Plains SL

Semiotic research on PSL has focused on two major topics, its semiotic features as a language and its grammar.

3.2.1 PSL, SL OF THE DEAF, AND SPOKEN LANGUAGE
In comparison to the SLs of the deaf, PSL signs have a higher degree of iconic and indexical motivation (cf. Umiker-Sebeok & Sebeok, eds. 1978: xvii–xx). But PSL nevertheless has a large percentage of arbitrary signs and is by no means universally understandable (cf. Kroeber 1958: 15). PSL is thus a language, which must be learned. There are even dialectal variations of PSL.

Although PSL is only a second language to its

users, the structure of this SL shows little grammatical influence of the spoken first languages of the Plains Indians (cf. Taylor 1975: 348). Because PSL is a *lingua franca* for speakers of different tongues, its structure is by necessity relatively autonomous in relation to specific spoken languages. In addition to its arbitrariness and double articulation, another design feature of the PSL languages is semantic openness. As Umiker-Sebeok & Sebeok observe, "they may be used to formulate a potentially indefinite number of messages and their lexicon may be enlarged to suit changing demands on the system" (1978: xv).

3.2.2 SYSTEM AND STRUCTURE

While Kroeber was still unable to discover a level of the structure of PSL corresponding to the phoneme (1958: 14), Voegelin (1958) was already defending the hypothesis of a double articulation of PSL. In the analysis of West (1960; cf. Taylor 1975: 340–44, Umiker-Sebeok & Sebeok, eds. 1978: xxvii), PSL has a level of second articulation at which eighty *kinemes* can be distinguished. These structural equivalents of Stokoe's cheremes (cf. 2.3.2) are minimal visual elements characterizing the hand shapes, directions, dynamics, motion patterns, and relational positions. In West's description, the first articulation of the PSL system consists of morphemes, composed of three or four kinemes, and of gestural words, having one or several morphemes. While West's grammar of PSL follows the language model of taxonomic structuralism, Ljung (1965) gives an outline of the PSL grammar based on principles of S. Lamb's stratificational linguistics. His three strata of PSL analysis are *gestemics* (second articulation), *morphemics*, and *lexemics* (first articulation).

4. Monastic Sign Languages

Most research on monastic sign languages, including all publications quoted in the following, has been collected and published by Umiker-Sebeok & Sebeok, eds. (1987). The origin of monastic sign languages is the medieval silence rule of the Benedictine monasteries. Today, this rule is still observed by the Cluniac, the Trappist (cf. Hutt 1968), and the Cistercian (cf. Barakat 1975) orders. Descriptions of the SL developed by the Benedictines were published in medieval manuscripts, mostly in the form of illustrated nomenclatures (cf. Kluge 1885, Rijnberk 1953, and Barley 1974). Semiotic aspects of the systems of monastic SLs have been studied by Buyssens (1956), Hutt (1968), Barley (1974), Barakat (1975), and Baron (1981).

Monastic SLs have many semiotic features in common with SLs such as ASL and PSL (cf. Barakat 1975 and Baron 1981). Their design features include arbitrariness, double articulation, and semantic openness or productivity (cf. 3.2.1). The main difference between ASL, PSL, and monastic SLs is of a pragmatic nature: the communicative function of monastic SLs is restricted to certain topics and situations of life. The Benedictines, for example, are allowed to use spoken language in conversations with laymen and on religious topics. This restriction on SL use explains certain gaps in the vocabulary of monastic SLs. Monastic SLs are thus structurally autonomous, but pragmatically they are semiotic systems whose function is complementary to that of spoken language.

Language Substitutes

Language substitutes are secondary codes whose signs are molded on the model of a primary linguistic code. Since there are several degrees of dependence between verbal languages and other language-based codes, the semiotic field under consideration has been defined in broader and in narrower ways. This handbook adopts the narrower definition: language substitutes include speech surrogates, such as drum and whistle languages, as derivatives of speech, and various alphabetic codes as derivatives of writing. In contradistinction to such heteronomous codes, sign languages, writing systems, and universal languages have a higher degree of semiotic autonomy in relation to the primary code of natural, spoken language and are therefore not included as language substitutes (in contradistinction to definitions proposed by several other authors; cf. 3.).

1. Speech Surrogates

Drum and whistle languages are the speech surrogates which have so far received most scholarly attention, but there are other substitutes of spoken individual languages which may also be classified as speech surrogates.

1.1 Survey of Drum and Whistle Languages

Drum and whistle languages are archaic speech substitutes used mostly for telecommunication. Discovered and studied since the nineteenth century by anthropologists and linguists, these codes seem to be dying out in this century (cf. Busnel & Classe 1976: 108; but see Sebeok & Umiker-Sebeok, eds. 1976: xxiii on new discoveries). A monument of research in this field is the collection of studies by Sebeok & Umiker-Sebeok, eds. (1976). Busnel & Classe (1976) have done a thorough phonetic study of whistle languages.

1.1.1 GEOGRAPHICAL DISTRIBUTION

Drum languages have been reported primarily from Africa, Southeast Asia, and Oceania. Whistle languages were discovered in Africa, Asia, South and Central America, and Europe. Busnel & Classe's (1976) studies deal with systems used in mountainous regions of the Canaries (La Gomera), Turkey (Kusköy), Mexico (Oaxaca), and the Pyrenees (Aas), where the "speakers" are usually in sight of each other but separated by a valley.

1.1.2 COMMUNICATIVE FUNCTIONS

The primary function of these codes is telecommunication. According to Busnel & Classe, whistled signals can be exchanged in valleys over distances from two hundred meters up to two thousand meters (1976: 28). The range can be extended up to ten kilometers by the use of a shell for signal production. Valen reports a range of ten kilometers and more for drum signals (1955: 747). The range of these signals can be extended by continued transmissions of the message via "relay stations." The modern technologies of communication have largely, but not yet completely, replaced signal drums as a means of telecommunication. A few other functions of drum and whistle languages are known. For example, Mexican Kickapoo whistle speech is restricted to courtship (Taylor 1975: 358), and the Cuban ñañigos are said to have used whistled speech as a secret language (Busnel & Classe 1976: 22). Drum languages have a variety of other functions, especially ritual and entertainment (musical or poetic).

1.1.3 TYPOLOGY OF SYSTEMS
Following Stern (1957: 130) and Umiker (1974: 497–98), the major systems of drum and whistle languages can be summarized as follows:

1. *instrumental systems*
   (a) wind instruments (esp. whistles, horns, flutes)
   (b) percussive instruments (membrane drums, slit gongs, xylophones, etc.)
   (c) string instruments
2. *somatic systems*
   (1) without voice (whistling)
   (2) with voice (humming, syllabic calling, falsetto)

1.2 Semiotic Structures of Drum and Whistle Languages

Stern (1957: 125) and Umiker (1974: 499) distinguish two basic principles of speech substitution in drum and whistle systems, which they call *encoding* and *abridgement*.

1.2.1 SYMBOLIC ENCODING
Encoding uses arbitrary acoustic symbols, which have no similarity to the sound structure of the base language (as in Morse; cf. 2.1.1).

Drum languages are only partly based on encoding and are otherwise iconic. Whistle languages are in principle iconic. When a drum language uses signals which represent words ("lexical logograms," as discussed by Umiker [1974: 499–502]) and not only phonemes (or letters, as in Morse), the code might be considered a direct and not a substitutive signaling system (cf. Taylor 1975; see also 3.1.1 on direct and indirect semiosis).

1.2.2 ICONIC ABRIDGEMENT
Speech surrogates based on the principle of abridgement use acoustic signs which resemble the sounds of their base language. This iconic mode of representation always implies a simplification of the phonetics of the base message (not necessarily a shortening, as the term *abridgement* suggests). A high degree of acoustic iconicity is attained in whistle languages. According to Busnel & Classe (1976: 2–3), these speech surrogates are produced by replacing the cord-tone of everyday phonation by a whistle, the factor of articulation remaining basically as it is in ordinary speech. By this technique, even consonants can be substituted. Drum languages attain only a lower degree of phonetic similarity in relation to their base language. Consonants cannot be represented by drumming. The sound imitation is restricted to phonetic features, such as vowel quantity, syllable length, sentence rhythm, intonation curves, and stress (cf. Nketia 1971: 843). Tone languages, where the tone of the message has a phonemic function, are particularly suited for substitution by drums.

1.2.3 SEMANTIC POTENTIAL
The principle of phonetic simplification in speech substitutes implies a loss of semiotic structure, which can result in difficulties of decoding the substitutive message. Many phonetically distinct words of the base language, for example, become homonyms when translated into a drum language. As a semiotic remedy for this problem, the users of drum languages employ a technique of *enphrasing*, where paraphrases and stereotypes are used instead of

words otherwise difficult to identify (cf. Valen 1955: 748, Umiker 1974: 504). Owing to characteristics such as phonetic loss and enphrasing, speech surrogates are not completely iconic and cannot be deciphered by the members of the base language community without some degree of learning. This difference between base language and speech surrogate characterizes the margin of autonomy of the substitutive code. In spite of their reduced semiotic potential, drum languages still have a considerable scope of communicative functions. According to Valen, they serve to transmit messages about commercial transactions, festivities, conflicts, or deaths (1955: 749). Even narratives, poems, proverbs, and riddles are transmitted by drums (cf. Umiker 1974: 509–513).

1.3 Other Speech Surrogates

There are few other language substitutes derived from speech, while there are many more language substitutes derived from writing.

1.3.1 SECRET SPEECH

Spoken secret languages derived from a natural base language have the character of a speech surrogate. Some of them are devised on a principle of distorting the phonology of the base language; others distort the meaning by employing a substitute vocabulary. Examples of phonetic secret languages used by children are described by Opie & Opie (1959: 344–45) and Kirshenblatt-Gimblett, ed. (1976). In *Pig Latin*, for example, the initial consonant (cluster) is transferred to the second position, and "ay" is added as a word ending, thus: "Unejay ithsmay isay igpay" → 'June Smith is a pig.' In *backslang*, the words are simply pronounced backwards, e.g., "Enuj thims" → 'June Smith.' A secret speech substitute based on a semantic principle, antonym substitution, has been discovered by Hale (1971) in Central Australia, where the Walpiri use it in ritual contexts. (Example: "Another is standing in the sky" → 'I am sitting on the ground.') Other examples of

culturally motivated forms of speech disguise are reported by Conklin (1959) and Crystal (1987: 179).

1.3.2 AUXILIARY SPEECH

Most visual derivatives of language, such as writing and sign languages, have developed a relative autonomy in relation to speech and are therefore not classified as speech surrogates in this handbook. But there are systems of auxiliary speech for the deaf which consist of a translation of phonemes (not letters) by means of hand gestures (cf. Wilbur 1979: 225). Cornett (1967), who developed such an auxiliary speech called *Cued Speech*, describes it as a system designed "to enable the deaf children to learn language through exposure to a visible phonetic analog of speech supplied by the lip movements and supplementing hand cues." The system uses thirty-six cues for the phonemes of English. Every cue consists of a hand sign plus a lip shape. There are only twelve hand signs (eight hand shapes for consonants, four hand positions in relation to the face for vowels). Each hand sign is associated with two to four phonemes which are further differentiated by the lip shape which is characteristic of their articulation. For example, the bilabial /m/, the labio-dental /f/, and the alveolar /t/ are associated with one hand shape only.

2. Substitutes of Written Language

There are two semiotic strategies of substituting written language. One is to substitute elements of first articulation (i.e., words; cf. Language 4.1); the other is to substitute elements of second articulation, i.e., letters. Typical examples of these two strategies can be found in the history of cryptography (cf. Kahn 1966: xiii–xiv), where systems of word substitution are called *cloaks* or *codes* (cf. 2.2), and systems of letter substitution are defined as *ciphers* (cf. Code 1.2). (Ciphers are also codes in the more general semiotic terminology.)

2.1 Alphabetic Codes

The substitution of writing on the level of second articulation requires no knowledge of the base language except for its alphabet. A *ciphertext*, for example, can therefore be decoded when the cipher alphabet is known, but the content of the message may still remain unintelligible if the base language is unknown. On these grounds, one might ask whether an alphabetic code should be called a substitute *language*, but this is only a question of terminology (cf. 3.3.1).

2.1.1 EXAMPLES OF ALPHABETIC CODES

While ciphers intend to conceal a message, all other alphabetic codes have the function of extending the range of the medium of writing, either to the benefit of the disabled (b, g) or for the purpose of telecommunication (a, c–f). Examples are:

a. Morse code (see Code 5.3.1, 5.3.3)

b. Braille code (see Code 5.3.1–2)

c. the binary code of the alphabet (see Information 2.2)

d. naval semaphore (cf. Prieto 1966: 113–21)

e. Aleut Wig-wag (arm and body semaphore of Alaskan Aleuts; cf. Taylor 1975: 361)

f. manual alphabets (supplementary codes to the sign languages of the deaf, which are themselves not based on alphabetic substitution; cf. Stokoe 1974: 346–51 and Sign Language 2.1.2)

g. tactile alphabets (see Tactile Communication 3.)

h. cryptographic ciphers

2.1.2 PRINCIPLES OF ALPHABETIC SUBSTITUTIONS

The signals of alphabets (a) to (g) are 1:1 substitutions for the letters of the base alphabet. All of these codes are examples of *intersemiotic translations* (cf. Jakobson 1959a: 261): letters of the Latin (or Cyrillic, as in [e]) alphabet are transposed to a visual or acoustic nonwriting code. Only ciphers are usually *intraalphabetic translation* systems, where letters are substituted for letters of the same alphabet. But for the sake of transmission se-

curity, ciphers cannot rely on simple 1:1 substitutions. They employ, instead, variable principles of substitution, such as *polyalphabetic substitution* (cf. Kahn 1966: xiv), where various ciphers are used in rotation, or substitution by means of a code book, where the order of the letters in a secret book provides the key to the ciphertext.

2.2 Word Codes

There are only few genuine substitutes for written language whose units of translation are words. In cryptography, secret codes give instructions for the replacement of plaintext words by code words. Ideally, such a code must have as many code words as there are words in the lexicon of the base language. This is a technical disadvantage which reduces the practical usefulness of such codes. Apart from cryptography, word substitutive systems were developed for the purpose of message abridgement. Thus, commercial codes were formerly used in business to save on cable tolls (see Meyer-Eppler 1959: 199 for such codes). There are other codes whose signs correspond to words of a base language (cf. Code 5.4–6), but most of these are restricted to the encoding of special types of message, such as traffic regulation. Codes with such a restricted productivity (cf. Language 3.1.5) cannot be classified as language substitutes.

3. Substitution and Semiotic Autonomy

Language substitution implies a process of intersemiotic translation. Divergent opinions about the autonomy of language-related codes have resulted in different definitions of the term *language substitute*.

3.1 Principles of Code Substitution

Substitutive codes are secondary in relation to a primary code. The principles of code substitution and the various degrees of dependence of substitutive languages on spoken natural languages are discussed by Sapir (1921: 19–21), Jakobson (1959a), and Buyssens (1967).

3.1.1 DIRECT AND INDIRECT SEMIOSIS

Substitutive signs are heteronomous, referring to the signs of the primary code. Only the primary code is autonomous, having a direct referential function. Buyssens describes this difference in his distinction between *substitutive* and *direct* semiotic systems (*sémies*): the signified of a substitutive sign is the signifier of another sign, while only the signified of a direct sign has a content of its own (1967: 45). Buyssens also points out that language substitutes are not the only substitutive codes (ibid.: 48). His other examples of codes with signs derived from a primary code are musical notes (referring to the primary code of musical sounds) and spoken mathematical formulas (referring to the primary code of the mathematical writing system).

3.1.2 FIRST-ORDER AND SECOND-ORDER
SUBSTITUTIONS

Buyssens (1967: 45–48) and Jakobson (1973a: 28–32) develop a theory of semiotic substitution which is based on the assumption of the autonomy of speech and the heteronomy of writing (see Writing 3.). In their view, writing and other speech-related substitutive codes, such as stenography or drum and whistle languages, are *first-order* substitutive systems, while codes related to writing (cf. 2.1.1) are *second-order* substitutions. This view is not acceptable to the proponents of an autonomous view of writing. If writing is a primary code, the derivatives of writing are first-order substitutes.

3.2 Intersemiotic Translation and Substitution

Although code substitution is a process of intersemiotic translation (in the sense of Jakobson 1959a: 261), not every translation is a transfer into a substitutive code (cf. Buyssens 1967: 48). In interlingual translation (from German to English, e.g.) or in transliteration

(from Latin to Cyrillic writing, e.g.), the goal language (or alphabet) is not a substitutive code of the source language. Most messages of other sign systems may be expressed by means of verbal signs. Sign languages, for example, may be translated into speech. But this instance of intersemiotic translation does not make speech a substitute of sign language. The distinguishing feature between code substitution and the more general case of intersemiotic translation is the semiotic autonomy of the message in question (cf. 3.1.1). Messages that can be understood without being translated into (another) spoken language are not substitutive messages. Thus, the semiotic systems of mathematical or chemical formulas (cf. Buyssens 1967: 48) and universal or sign languages are autonomous and not substitutive codes (see also 3.3.1).

3.3 Substitution and Complementarity

Since language substitutes cannot replace the code of spoken language in all its semiotic functions, there have been different opinions about the adequacy of the term *language* with respect to these codes.

3.3.1 TERMINOLOGICAL CONSIDERATIONS

Stern (1957), Umiker (1974), and Sebeok & Umiker-Sebeok, eds. (1976) introduced the terms *speech surrogate* and *substitutive system* in their studies of drum and whistle languages. Busnel & Classe, however, object to defining whistle languages as speech surrogates since these codes cannot replace normal speech in all circumstances (1976: 107). These authors propose, instead, to define the sign languages of the deaf as speech surrogates, which they consider to be "true substitutes for normal speech" (ibid.). Adler follows this proposal in his study of "the speech surrogates of the handicapped" (1979: 71ff.).

Most scholars, however, reject the classification of sign languages as substitutive codes. Thus, Buyssens (1967: 46) and Stokoe (1972: 15–18) define the sign language of the deaf as a primary code with a direct semiotic function. Stokoe even postulates the additional criterion of genetic priority as a characteristic of primary codes (1972: 17). This underlines the nonsubstitutive character of sign languages, which are acquired as a first language by those born deaf. For further aspects of the autonomy of semiotic systems, see also Sign Language (1.2).

3.3.2 SUBSTITUTION AND COMPLEMENTARITY

Even though the signs of a substitutive system may be in a 1:1 relationship to those of the base language, as in alphabetic substitutes, this structural homology does not imply a functional equivalence. Every language substitute remains distinguished from its base language by a specific communicative difference. Language substitution results in a communicative loss (cf. 1.2), but it has at the same time some communicative advantage to its users, such as secrecy, the extension of the medium, or the replacement of a defective channel (cf. 1.1.2, 1.3.2, 2.1.1). From this point of view, substitutive languages are not mere replacements of their base languages. They are *complementary codes* to their base language.

From Structuralism to Text Semiotics: Schools and Major Figures

From Structuralism to Text Semiotics: Introduction

This section introduces major schools and figures of text semiotics and argues that structuralism in its various variants is an important source of inspiration for most of these schools. The scope of this section is restricted in two ways: (1) The field of text semiotics is reduced to verbal texts. (For this restriction see also Text Semiotics.) (2) The schools and "major figures" are introduced here only with respect to their contributions to *text* semiotics. Their contributions to other fields of semiotics are discussed in many other chapters. (3) Some important figures in, or precursors of, text semiotics are discussed elsewhere. For related trends in the study of texts, see also Text Semiotics.

1. Text Structuralism

The chapter on structuralism is restricted to the fields of linguistics, anthropology, psychoanalysis, and philosophy. Structuralist approaches to textual and in particular literary studies, sometimes also designated as *text structuralism*, are excluded there since these approaches gradually merge with text semiotics, the field to which two sections of this handbook are dedicated.

1.1 Rules of Structuralist Analysis

In spite of the continuity in the development from structuralism to text semiotics, a number of characteristics may be isolated which have come to be considered typical for the early structuralist approaches to texts. (In the field of literary criticism, this structuralist approach has been discussed extensively by Barthes, Donato 1967, Lane, ed. 1970, Blumensath, ed. 1972, Koch, ed. 1972, Scholes 1974, and Fietz 1976.) In early text structuralism, these characteristics were sometimes formulated as principles of research. Fages programmatically summarized these principles in the form of the following seven rules (1968: 45ff.): (1) *Rule of immanence*: The structuralist analyzes structures within a system, primarily in a synchronic perspective. (2) *Rule of pertinence*: The structuralist analyzes the pertinent (or distinctive) features of the system, those features which have a differential value (cf. Structuralism 1.1.3). (3) *Rule of commutation*: The structuralist applies the commutation test (cf. Structuralism 1.1.2) in order to determine systemic oppositions in minimal pairs. (4) *Rule of compatibility*: The structuralist studies the rules which govern the combination (and thus compatibility) of elements in texts. (5) *Rule of integration*: The elementary structures have to be integrated within the totality of the system. (6) *Rule of diachronic change*: Historical change is studied on the basis of a synchronic analysis of the system. (7) *Rule of function*: The structuralist studies the communicative and other functions of the system (cf. Structuralism 1.1.1).

This "manifesto" of structuralism shows the paradigmatic nature of linguistic methodology for the field of textual analysis. It also makes explicit some of those principles which later critics of text structuralism sought to overcome in new developments of text semiotics, in particular the emphasis on "immanence" and the underlying concept of the text as a closed system.

1.2 The Structuralist Activity

In the heyday of structuralism, Barthes gave the following guideline for those who wanted to know who was a structuralist: "Watch who uses *signifier* and *signified*, *synchrony* and *diachrony*, and you will know whether the structuralist vision is present" (1964b: 214). The Saussurean origin of this terminological characterization was equally evident when Barthes characterized structuralist activity by the operations of *segmentation* and *articulation*, the discovery of the elements and of "the syntax of the arts and of discourse" (ibid.: 216–17). The implicit scientific claim of such procedures has gained text structuralism the reputation of a positivist methodology. Against such criticism, Barthes himself claimed that there are elements of creativity and subjectivity in these procedures:

> The goal of all structuralist activity [. . .] is to reconstruct an "object" in such a way as to manifest thereby the rules of functioning of this object. Structure is therefore a *simulacrum* of the object, but a directed, *interested* simulacrum, since the imitated object makes something appear which remained invisible [. . .] in the natural object. [. . .] There occurs something new, and what is new is nothing less than the generally intelligible. [. . .] Hence one might say that structuralism is essentially *an activity of imitation*, which is also why there is, strictly speaking, no *technical* difference between structuralism as an intellectual activity, on the one hand, and literature in particular, art

in general, on the other: both derive from a *mimesis*, based not on the analogy of substances (as in so-called realist art), but on the analogy of functions (what Lévi-Strauss calls *homology*). (1964b: 214–15)

Such restrictions to the objectivist myth of structuralism soon led to what some have claimed to be the "death of structuralism" (see Structuralism 1.3, 4.3).

---

2. Death of Structuralism and Rise of Text Semiotics

The development from text structuralism to text semiotics and its poststructuralist sequel in the theory of *deconstruction* (see Structuralism 4.3) is documented by Heath et al., eds. (1971), Schiwy (1973), Segre (1973: 26–77; 1979a), Baran, ed. (1974), Culler (1975; 1981a; 1982), Hawkes (1977), and Lindner & Pfister (1984). For those who had diagnosed the "death of structuralism," semiotics became a new paradigm in the field of textual studies. Others, however, emphasized the continuity in this development.

2.1 Continuity

In the field of textual studies, scholars such as Barthes, Riffaterre, Segre, and Todorov have seen no rupture in the development from structuralism to text semiotics. An indicator of the continuity in this transition is the gradual replacement of the term *structural* by *semiotic* in this field, which appears in designations such as "semiotico-structuralist criticism" (Cerisola 1980) or "structuralist-semiotic criticism" (Marchese 1981: 149–76). Proof of this continuity is above all the work of scholars such as Jakobson, Barthes, Greimas, and Eco. Without any methodological rupture, these and other former structuralists in East and West began to be referred to as semioticians in the 1970s. Thus, in the field of textual criticism, text semiotics became the successor to the structuralist heritage.

Even the earlier (text) structuralism was for some critics no longer distinguished from semiotics (e.g., Fages 1968, Baran, ed. 1974, mostly also Hawkes 1977). A typical characterization of structuralism which is no longer distinguishable from semiotics is given by Wahl. In his preface to an introduction to structuralism, Wahl declares: "Structuralism is the name under which the sciences of the sign and of sign systems are classified" (1968a: 10).

2.2 Evolution

In spite of continuity, there were certainly also evolutionary changes in the development from structuralism to text semiotics. The degree of these changes varies with the authors. The chronologists of poststructuralism in the field of literary criticism (e.g., Brütting 1976, Hempfer 1976, and see Structuralism 4.3) have seen revolutionary changes in these developments. Representative of such radical innovations are the studies of the later Barthes (q.v. 6.) and of Kristeva. But these two authors show also that poststructuralism does not mean postsemiotic.

Culler discusses the possibility of differentiating between structuralism and (text) semiotics on the basis of different research interests: One might try to characterize semiotics as being more interested in meaning and signs, and structuralism as being more interested in the networks of relations. Yet, Culler concludes:

"In fact the two are inseparable, for in studying signs one must investigate the system of relations that enables meaning to be produced and, reciprocally, one can only determine what are the pertinent relations among items by considering them as signs" (1975: 4).

3. Schools and Major Figures of Text Semiotics

Only the future will reveal the major schools and figures of text semiotics, but even now necessary additions to the figures and trends discussed in this section have to be pointed out. A number of important contributors to text semiotics are discussed extensively in part I on the major schools of semiotics. That is why a major figure of text semiotics such as Jakobson is discussed outside of the present section. Schools of text semiotics can also be found among the disciples and followers of the founding fathers of modern semiotics. While Saussure (q.v. 2.2.2), in this respect, is perhaps only a precursor of text semiotics, there is certainly a glossematic school of text semiotics following ideas developed by Hjelmslev (q.v. 4.). Peirce has had a considerable influence on various text semiotic studies, which seems to be still increasing (see Peirce 4.). Morris's influence on text semiotics is rather restricted to text pragmatics and typology (see Morris 4.).

Structuralism, Poststructuralism, and Neostructuralism

Structuralism extends over linguistics, anthropology, mathematics, biology, psychology (cf. Piaget 1968), the social sciences, psychoanalysis, history, philosophy, and literary criticism (see Text Semiotics). For general surveys see Ehrmann, ed. (1966), Auzias (1967), Fages (1968), Ducrot et al. (1968), Corvez (1969), Schiwy (1969a; 1971; 1973), Lane, ed. (1970), Millet & Varin d'Ainvelle (1970), De George & De George, eds. (1972), Jameson (1972), Robey, ed. (1973), Pettit (1975), Hawkes (1977), Sturrock, ed. (1979), Kurzweil (1980), Fietz (1982), Füssel (1983), and Mounin (1985). Structuralism has its roots in Saussure's semiology, the Prague Linguistic School, and Russian Formalism. With their interest in structure as a relation among the phenomena rather than in the nature of the phenomena themselves, structuralists have characterized themselves as non-empiricists, non-atomists, and non-positivists (Wilden 1972: 7).

Structuralism became a dominant intellectual paradigm in the 1960s and even a fashion or ideology (cf. Jaeggi 1968, Schiwy 1969a). Not long after having replaced existentialism as the dominant intellectual fashion in France, structuralism was already declared to be dead (Posner 1969: 130, Benoist 1970: 50, pace Koch 1971b: 1; 1986b: 49). Soon after, new paradigms were introduced under the designation of *poststructuralism* (cf. Harari, ed. 1979,

Schiwy 1985). But some of the most prominent poststructuralists (and among them Derrida) are already being discussed as *neostructuralists* (Frank 1984) or even *superstructuralists* (Harland 1987). The gradual development from structuralism to semiotics is particularly evident in the field of literary criticism and mass media analysis. This development is discussed in detail in the chapters on text semiotics.

1. Structuralism in Linguistics

Structuralist linguistics has played the role of the *patron général* of structuralism, a role which Saussure (q.v. 2.3.2) predicted for linguistics with respect to semiology. Within linguistics, two groups of structuralist schools have been distinguished, European structuralism (cf. Engler 1975a, Koerner 1975, Lepschy 1975) and American structuralism. Foundations of European linguistic structuralism were laid by Saussure and Hjelmslev. Since these scholars are discussed in separate chapters, the survey of European structuralism will be restricted to its third major structuralist school, that of the Prague linguists. As a continuation of this genealogy, the French structuralist A. Martinet (b. 1908) must be mentioned at this point. His thesis of the double articulation of language played a decisive role in the development which led from structuralism to semiotics (see Code 4.).

1.1 Prague School Structuralism

The *Cercle Linguistique de Prague* was founded in 1926. Among its major contributors were the Czechs V. Mathesius (1882–1946), B. Havránek (1893–1978), and J. Mukařovský (1891–1975), and the Russians N. Trubetzkoy (1890–1938) and R. Jakobson (1896–1982). It was Jakobson whose structuralist theory of language had the most direct influence on the development of French structuralism. For surveys of the Prague School, see Garvin, ed. (1964), Vachek (1960; 1966), Vachek, ed. (1964), Szemerényi (1971), Helbig (1974), Lepschy (1975), and Bellert & Ohlin, eds. (1978).

In opposition to the "pure" structuralists Saussure and Hjelmslev, the Prague School refused to consider language as an isolated synchronic system of pure form. Their approach to structure in language was based on key terms such as *function* and *communication*. In contradistinction to other structuralisms, Prague School linguists have therefore specified their own approach as *functionalist structuralism* (cf. Vachek, ed. 1964: 469, Ducrot & Todorov 1972: 24). The core of the Prague School contribution to linguistics lies in the field of phonology. The discovery of the *distinctive features* as the "atoms of language" and the functional principles of phonological analysis contributed significantly to structural research in sign systems. But the contribution of the Prague School to semiotics was not restricted to linguistics alone. Jakobson, Mukařovský, and others were influential contributors to aesthetics, poetics, stylistics, and the theory of literature.

1.1.1 FUNCTION, COMMUNICATION, AND SYSTEM

Among the programmatic innovations of the Prague School linguists was their attempt to overcome the antinomy between *statics* and *dynamics* in synchronic and diachronic linguistics. Language is described as a functional system serving the purpose of communication.

Because of this, the language system cannot remain static but has to maintain a dynamic equilibrium. The dynamic approach to language was also extended to the study of syntax and texts. In the theory of *functional sentence perspective*, the distribution of given and new elements of information in sentences and texts is analyzed. The dynamic distribution and progression of these elements within texts is described as a *communicative dynamism*.

1.1.2 THE DISCOVERY OF THE PHONEME

With his research in the field of phonology, Trubetzkoy became, so to speak, the discoverer of the atomic structure of language. Following Saussure's differentiation between *langue* and *parole*, Trubetzkoy introduced the distinction between *phonology* and *phonetics* (1939: 7). Phonetics is the study of the material sounds and their articulation in speech (*parole*), irrespective of their systemic properties. Phonology (American linguists prefer the term *phonemics*) studies the sounds of a language as functional elements in a system of form and content (*langue*).

From a phonetic point of view, an almost unlimited number of phonetic differences can be discovered in the analysis of actually spoken sounds (later also called *phones*). Phonology reduces these differences to those which play a functional role in the system, the so-called phonological oppositions. The criterion of functionality is the effect of phonic differences on meaning. This effect is tested by means of the substitution of sounds in their context (commutation test). Classes of sounds whose commutation (mutual substitution) in words causes differences of meaning are called phonemes. In English, the sounds /s/ and /θ/ are two phonemes because their commutation in the minimal pair *sin* and *thin* causes a difference of meaning. The phonetic difference between the voiceless fricatives /s/ and /θ/ is their place of articulation, which is dental in /θ/ and alveolar in /s/. But it is not the phonic difference as such which differentiates these two sounds as phonemes. The same phonetic difference can never cause a difference of meaning in German. There is no single pair of words in which the substitution of /θ/ for /s/ (which occurs with lisping speakers) changes the meaning of a word. Thus, in German these two phones are not distinguished as phonemes. In spite of their phonetic difference, they are not in phonological opposition.

1.1.3 THE PRINCIPLE OF PERTINENCE: FROM ETIC TO EMIC ANALYSIS

Trubetzkoy's functionalist discovery procedure of the phoneme illustrates the principle of *pertinence* (also *relevance*). Pertinence refers to the feature of distinctiveness of structures within a system. This principle requires the distinction of different levels of analysis. The systemic pertinence on the level of the phonemes can be decided only with reference to a higher level of linguistic structure, namely, the level of the morpheme (and semantics), because only the semantic difference in commutation proves the systemic relevance (pertinence) of the phonetic difference (on the lower level).

To characterize the change of perspective from phonetic to phonological (or in American terminology phonemic) analysis, Pike (1967) later introduced the terms *etic* and *emic*. An etic (from "phon*etic*") approach is nonstructural and studies phenomena in their surface structure. *Emic* is derived from "phon*emic*" and ultimately from "syst*emic*." An emic approach to semiotic phenomena considers elements of sign systems with respect to their function within the code. For the principle of pertinence in the study of semiotic systems and for pertinent and emic structures, see Function (2.1.1–2).

1.1.4 DISTINCTIVE FEATURES AND BINARY OPPOSITIONS

A further step in the atomization of language was Jakobson's reduction of phonemes to a system of distinctive features in binary (i.e., +/−) oppositions. Although phonemes are minimal elements in the sequence of speech sounds, they may be further broken down into their distinctive features of articulation. The number of these features is less than the number of phonemes. Jakobson claimed that a limited list of distinctive features is valid for all languages. These universally valid features are the so-called phonological universals.

Within the binary system of distinctive features, every phoneme is structurally characterized by those features which it has and by those which it does not have. Thus, the phoneme /s/ is characterized not only positively by the presence (+) of features, such as +alveolar, +continuant, and +fricative, but also negatively by the absence (−) of features, such as −vocalic, −voiced, and −nasal. Phonemes are distinguished by at least one distinctive feature. /θ/ and /ð/ are distinguished by the single feature (±) voiced; /θ/ and /s/ by the features (±) dental and (±) alveolar. Thus, it is no longer the phonemes which appear as the irreducible atoms of language but the distinctive features, whose combination makes up the phonemes.

Jakobson himself extended the principles of distinctive feature analysis to morphology. His analytic binarism was most influential on structuralists such as Lévi-Strauss and Lacan. The universality of these principles, however, has been questioned both in phonology and in semiotics. Eco suggests that Jakobson's binarism may have been too influential "because semioticians have frequently superimposed binary networks upon phenomena strenuously resistant to them" (1977: 46).

1.2 American Structuralism

The development of American structuralism in linguistics was relatively independent of the European schools. (For surveys see Bense et al., eds. 1976, Ducrot & Todorov 1972: 31–37, Hymes & Fought 1975). The foundations of American structuralism were laid by Bloomfield (1933), and with Harris (1951) the structuralist methodology in American linguistics reached a climax. Two major characteristics of these approaches to language are their *antimentalistic descriptivism* and their *distributionalism*.

1.2.1 ANTIMENTALISTIC DESCRIPTIVISM

In opposition to nineteenth-century historicism in linguistics, Bloomfield postulated a descriptive approach to language. With this postulate, Bloomfield's approach agrees with the Saussurean shift from diachronic to synchronic analysis. Unlike the European schools, however, Bloomfieldian linguistics is antimentalistic and prefers a behavioristic approach to language. No internal mental facts, such as "ideas," concepts, or intentions, should be taken into consideration in scientific analysis. Instead, linguistics should restrict itself to the analysis of observable behavior, of speech acts in the context of human behavior. The consequence of this antimentalistic point of view was that questions of semantics were long neglected by American structuralists.

1.2.2 DISTRIBUTIONALISM

Distributional analysis is the approach of American structuralists to the systemic aspects of language. The first step of this analytic procedure is to determine a corpus of linguistic data. It should be representative and closed, and its analysis should be complete and exhaustive. In a second step, the relevant elements of analysis are determined by means of segmentation of the corpus (into phonemes, morphemes, etc.). In a third step, the relations among these elements, and thus the structure of the language, are studied. This is the step of distributional analysis: Distribution is the occurrence of language elements in their typical linguistic environment. In a procedure of classification, these elements are determined according to the types of context in which they occur in the corpus. Because of its emphasis on segmentation and classification, this approach to linguistics was later also called *taxonomic structuralism*.

1.3 *Poststructuralism in Linguistics?*

Opinions about the continuity of structuralism in modern linguistics are divided. (Cf. 4.3 for poststructuralist text theories.) Those who diagnosed the "death of structuralism" in the late 1960s considered Chomsky's Generative Grammar to be the new poststructuralist paradigm of linguistic research. With Chomsky, linguistics turned mentalistic again. The closed corpus was rejected as the basis of analysis. Linguists turned toward the deep structures of language, while accusing the distributionalists of having been concerned with the surface structures of language only. After new schools of linguistics entered into the heritage of the generativists, linguists then emphasized again the common structuralist foundations in all trends of modern linguistics (cf. Anttila 1976). If structuralism is recognized as the broad trend which includes such diverse positions as Hjelmslev's glossematics, Prague functionalism, and American distributionalism, there is certainly a continuity of structuralist methods in modern linguistics.

2. Lévi-Strauss's Structural Anthropology

The French anthropologist Lévi-Strauss (b. 1908 in Belgium) has been acclaimed as the "Father of Structuralism" (e.g., Kurzweil 1980). This evaluation may be correct with respect to the so-called structuralist movement in France and Europe of the 1960s (cf. ibid., Auzias 1967, Corvez 1969, Schiwy 1969a, Leach 1970, Macksey & Donato, eds. 1970, Gardner 1973, Clarke 1981). But it must be remembered that Lévi-Strauss himself derived the principles of his structuralism from structural linguistics, particularly from the teachings of Jakobson. From this perspective, Lévi-Strauss is not only a "father" but also a "son" of structuralism. In this section, Lévi-Strauss's methods of analysis are exemplified only by his approach to kinship analysis. His structural approach to the study of myth, which has become a significant contribution to text semiotics, is discussed elsewhere (see Myth 2.). For a comprehensive survey of Lévi-Strauss's structuralism, see Rossi, ed. (1974).

2.1 Phonology as a Paradigm of the Sciences of Man

Through Jakobson, Lévi-Strauss discovered structural phonology and became convinced that structural linguistics should become the *patron général* of the sciences of man. He argues: "Structural linguistics will certainly play the same renovating role with respect to the social sciences that nuclear physics, for example, has played for the physical sciences" (1958: 33). From Trubetzkoy, Lévi-Strauss derives the following four principles of analysis (ibid.): (1) the shift from the study of conscious phenomena to the study of their unconscious infrastructure, (2) the shift from the terms to the relations between them, (3) the study of the whole system, and (4) the discovery of general laws within the system. Lévi-Strauss emphasizes the innovative character of the structural approach within the sciences of man: "The error of traditional anthropology, like that of traditional linguistics, was to consider the terms, and not the relations between the terms" (ibid.: 46). Lévi-Strauss applies the analytic principles of linguistic structuralism to numerous anthropological phenomena: totemism, rites, customs, marriage rules, and kinship patterns. A pervading theme of his studies is the structural analogy between language and culture. Such analogies are discovered by Lévi-Strauss in music, art, myth, ritual, religion, and even the cuisine of different societies (ibid.: 83–87). Within the latter, for example, he discovers systems of semantic oppositions (e.g., raw/cooked, sweet/sour, etc.) and derives from these differential structures minimal culinary elements for which he proposes the term *gusteme*.

2.2 Kinship Structures

Lévi-Strauss's analysis of kinship structure is an example of the analogies which he discovers between language and culture: "Like phonemes, kinship terms are elements of meaning; like phonemes, they acquire meaning only if they are integrated into systems. 'Kinship systems,' like 'phonemic systems,' are built by the mind on the level of unconscious thought" (1958: 34). Kinship systems express rules of prohibited marriages (e.g., incest taboo) and in some cultures prescribe certain categories of relatives who should be married. In primitive societies, these rules form a system of exchange, where women are exchanged by men. Thus, Lévi-Strauss interprets kinship as a system of communication, a language, in which the women are the messages exchanged between clans, lineages, or families (ibid.: 61).

Within these systems, Lévi-Strauss isolates minimal units of kinship as the *elementary structures* of a society (ibid.: 46). These structures, however, are not biologically given, but they represent a cultural symbolism. "What confers upon kinship its socio-cultural character is not what it retains from nature, but, rather, the essential way in which it diverges from nature. A kinship system [. . .] exists only in human consciousness; it is an arbitrary system of representations" (ibid.: 50). Thus, a kinship pattern is not only a system of communication with binary structures (such as father/son, brother/sister, etc.), but it is also, like language, characterized by the feature of arbitrariness.

3. Lacan's Structuralist Psychoanalysis

In psychoanalysis, the structuralist movement is represented by the writings of Jacques Lacan (1901–1981; cf. Lacan 1949; 1956; 1966; 1973; for general surveys cf. Ehrmann, ed. 1966: 94–137, Corvez 1969: 113–48, Bär 1974; 1975, Coward & Ellis 1977: 93–121, Bowie 1979, Kurzweil 1980: 135–64, Silverman 1983: 149–93, Thom 1981, Mac-Cannell 1986a). In this field, too, structuralism manifests itself in the application of concepts and models drawn from linguistics. Like Saussure's, Lacan's thought was dominated by binary oppositions. From Saussure and Jakobson he derived dichotomies, such as *signifier-signified*, *langue-parole*, and *metaphor-metonymy*, as structural tools for his rereading of Freud. Furthermore, Lacan's structuralism is apparent in his adherence to the Saussurean theory of the differential quality of the sign and the semiotic determination of the sign by the structures of the system.

3.1 The Unconscious as a Language

According to Freud's psychoanalytic theory, man uses language on two levels: simultaneously with the message of his conscious I, the subject transmits the conflicting message of his unconscious. For Lacan, this message of the Freudian unconscious is "the discourse of the other" (1956: 27). Not only the messages of the conscious but also those of the unconscious have a linguistic structure: "What the psychoanalytic experience discovers in the unconscious is the whole structure of language" (Lacan 1966: 147; cf. 234). For Lacan, the language of the unconscious is a system of dyadic signs in which the psychoanalytic symptom functions as a signifier that points to the unconscious thought process (cf. Bär 1975: 38). Reinterpreting Saussure's sign model (see Saussure 3.1), Lacan argued that the formula

$$\frac{S(ignifier)}{s(ignified)}$$

indicates two things: (1) a dominance of the signifier over the signified and (2) a primordial barrier between the two sides of the sign (indicated by the line separating the two levels) (1966: 149). For Lacan, this barrier indicates a gulf between the two sides of the sign which prohibits any "access from one to the other" (ibid.: 152). It is an illusion to believe in the signifier as a representation of the signified, since "no signification can be sustained other than by reference to another signification" (ibid.: 150). Since these intrasystemic references develop in speech, Lacan concluded that "it is in the chain of the signifier that the meaning 'insists' but that none of its elements 'consists' in the signification of which it is at the moment capable" (ibid.: 153). According to

Lacan, the dominance of the signifier over the signified also interprets Freud's theories about the function of signs in dreams: "Freud shows us in every possible way that the value of the image as signifier has nothing whatever to do with its signification." The "unnatural images" of dreams "are to be taken only for their value as signifiers, that is to say, in so far as they allow us to spell out the 'proverb' presented by the rebus of the dream" (ibid.: 159). Thus, the meaning of dreams is in the signifying chain itself, and not beyond these signifiers.

3.2 Communication

Besides its duality between the conscious I and the unconscious Other, the subject, according to Lacan, is further divided in another dimension: in this dimension, the I is opposed to its own alter ego, which is the subject's image of the I. This image is ultimately derived from the so-called mirror stage, in which the child first discovers its own external image and learns to differentiate between the person as a subject and an object. The thus twofold-split subject experiences language and communication in a quite subjective way. Lacan described communication as a process "where the sender receives his own message from the receiver in an inverse form. [. . .] For the function of Language is not to inform but to evoke. What I seek in the Word is the response of the other. What constitutes me as subject is my question" (1956: 62–63). With this interpretation of the subject's autonomous role in communication, Lacan proposed a psychoanalytic theory of communication (see Communication 3.3.1) which anticipated the later models developed within the theory of autopoietic systems.

3.3 The Prison House of Language

The idea of the subject's being determined by the structure of language leads to an image of language as a prison house from which there is no escape (cf. Jameson 1972). Since "language and its structure exist prior to the moment at which each subject at a certain point in his

mental development makes his entry to it,"
Lacan concluded that

> the speaking subject, too, if he can appear to be
> the slave of language is all the more so of a dis-
> course in the universal moment in which his place
> is already inscribed at birth, if only by virtue of his
> proper name. Reference to the experience of the
> community, or to the substance of this discourse
> settles nothing. For this experience assumes its
> essential dimension in the tradition that this dis-
> course itself establishes. This tradition [. . .] lays
> down the elementary structures of culture.
> (1966: 248)

Man being thus a slave of language is not the
master of his own thought. Instead of
Descartes's "I think, therefore I am," Lacan's
motto is *ça pense*. It, i.e., the Other, thinks, and
since this Other has the structure of the prison
house of language, Lacan replaced Descartes's
cogito with a "two-sided mystery": "what one
ought to say is: I am not wherever I am the
plaything of my thought; I think of what I am
where I do not think to think" (1966: 166).

4. Philosophical Structuralisms

Among the most prominent philosophers who
have been discussed in the context of structuralism (cf. Wahl 1968b, Corvez 1969, Schiwy
1969a, Sturrock, ed. 1979, Kurzweil 1980) are
the Marxist Althusser, the poststructuralist,
neostructuralist (Frank 1984), or superstructuralist (Harland 1987) Derrida, the historian
Michel Foucault, and in the field of hermeneutics Paul Ricoeur (b. 1913; cf. Esbroeck 1968,
Kurzweil 1980: 87–112). These philosophers
have at times objected to being called structuralists, but their theories nevertheless have
an unmistakable common structuralist
foundation.

4.1 Structuralism and Marxism (Althusser)

Louis Althusser (b. 1918) gives a structuralist
interpretation of the work of Karl Marx (cf.

Corvez 1969: 151–77, Coward & Ellis 1977:
61ff., Kurzweil 1980: 35–56). Lévi-Strauss,
Foucault, Lacan, and the structural linguists
have provided the major influences in Althusser's Marxist research (cf. Althusser 1965,
Althusser & Balibar 1968). Like Lacan, Althusser & Balibar discover "beneath the inno-
cence of speech and hearing the culpable
depth of a second *quite different* discourse, the
discourse of the unconscious" (1968: 16). The
unconscious, structured system of a society
manifests itself in its ideology, and ideologies
are like a *langue* which remains unconscious in
parole (cf. ibid.: 59). A typically structuralist
position is derived from these premises: Man
disappears from the center of world history. In
fact, there is no such center. It is the totality of
the social system which determines the subject
(cf. Althusser & Balibar 1968: II, 8). History is
determined not by a linear but by a *structural
causality* (ibid.: 164). For a more detailed discussion of the relation between structuralism
and Marxism, see Füssel (1983) and Heim
(1983).

4.2 Foucault's Structural History
of Knowledge

In his book *The Order of Things* (1966a), Michel
Foucault (1926–1984) presents a structuralist
history of ideas, an *Archeology of Knowledge*
(1969) in Europe from the Renaissance to
modern structuralism. (For general surveys see
Piaget 1968: 128–35, Corvez 1969: 35–78,
Kurzweil 1980: 193–226, Hoy, ed. 1986.)

4.2.1 FOUCAULT'S STRUCTURALISM
Foucault's structuralism does not manifest itself in the direct application of linguistic for-
malisms which aim at a search for differential
structures, oppositions, emic units, or other
structures in historical systems of ideas. But
like other structuralists, Foucault placed the
sign in the center of his research and emphasized the disappearance of the subject in an
anonymous system. With this latter idea, Foucault retained what Piaget calls "all the negative aspects of static structuralism—the

devaluation of history and genesis, the contempt for functional considerations; and, since man is about to disappear, Foucault's ouster of the subject is more radical than any hitherto" (1968: 134–35).

According to Foucault, "we think within an anonymous and constraining system of thought which is that of an epoch and of a language" (1966b: 15). These constraints on our language and thought make humanism impossible. For humanism, with its concepts of morality and value, wants to introduce meanings into a system of thought from the outside, while according to the structuralists, meaning is always generated within the system itself. As summarized by Silverman,

> Foucault insists that man as we know him is the product of certain historically determined discourses, and that by challenging those discourses we can "dissolve" him. Foucault does not suggest that we will thereby eliminate the category of the human, but that we will deconstruct the conceptions by means of which we have so far understood that category. (1983: 129)

4.2.2 FOUCAULT'S HISTORY OF CULTURAL SEMIOTICS
Foucault's *Order of Things* is also a history of the cultural-philosophical semantics of three periods, the Renaissance, the Enlightenment, and the period from the nineteenth century to modern structuralism. As the French title, *Les mots et les choses*, indicates, the topic is the relation between signs and their objects. The signs are the systems of representation in three areas: in language, the words representing reality; in economics, money representing values; and in natural history, the systems of classification of fauna and flora. Foucault's aim was to determine "on what basis knowledge and theory became possible; [. . .] on the basis of what historical *a priori* [. . .] ideas could appear" (1966a: xxi–ii). He called these conditions which determine the possibility of knowledge epistemological fields or *epistemes* (ibid.) and claimed, "In any given culture and at any given moment, there is always only one *episteme* that defines the conditions of possibility of all knowledge" (ibid.: 168).

In the three periods studied in *The Order of Things*, Foucault discovered such epistemes in semiotic homologies that appear in the fields of language, nature, and economics. In the Renaissance, the relationship between the three semiotic systems and the word designated by them is one of similarity:

> To search for a meaning is to bring to light a resemblance. [. . .] There is no difference between the visible marks that God has stamped upon the surface of earth, so that we may know its inner secrets. [. . .] Knowledge therefore consisted in relating one form of language to another [. . .]; in making everything speak. [. . .] The function proper to knowledge is not seeing or demonstrating; it is interpreting. (Foucault 1966a: 29, 33, 40)

In the classical period, a new epistemic paradigm appears (cf. ibid.: 53–56): Resemblances now have to be subjected to proof by comparison. Order is established without reference to an exterior entity. The word is no longer a sign of truth. It is the task of words to translate that truth if they can. From the Stoics to the Renaissance, signs, according to Foucault, had been triadic (including reference to the exterior world as their third correlate) (ibid.: 42; cf. Sign, Fig. Si 3). But in the age of Port–Royal, signs became dyadic. Being without connection to the external "reality," the sign becomes a connection "between the *idea of one thing* and the *idea of another*" (ibid.: 63). The consequence of this development is a growing importance of signs in classical thought: "Before, they were means of knowing and the keys to knowledge; now, they are co-extensive with representation, that is with thought as a whole" (ibid.: 65). Thus, a cleavage appears between the sign and its object. Since words no longer allow direct access to the things, all that remains is representation, discourse, and criticism (cf. ibid.: 79–80). "Language was a form of knowing and knowing was automatically discourse. Thus, language occupied a fundamental situation in relation to all knowledge: it was only by the medium of language that the things of the world could be known" (ibid.: 295–96). Henceforth, *general grammar* acquires prime importance for philosophy (ibid.: 83). It provides the universal model of all scientific reflection.

In the nineteenth century, historicism and empiricism discover that language has a history and laws of its own. Language is demoted to the status of an object: "To know language is no longer to come as close as possible to knowledge itself; it is merely to apply the methods of understanding in general to a particular domain of objectivity" (ibid.: 296). With the emergence of philology, biology, and political economy, things no longer obey the laws of discourse and general grammar but those of their own historical evolution. This is the end of the epistemic predominance of discourse, and man begins to emancipate himself in a new relation between words and things. Foucault quotes Humboldt: "Language is human: it owes its origin and progress to our full freedom," and concludes: "Language is no longer linked to the knowing of things, but to men's freedom" (ibid.: 291). This origin of freedom is for Foucault the origin of the sciences of man. But "since man was constituted at a time when language was doomed to dispersion," Foucault asks, "will he not be dispersed when language regains its unity? [. . .] As the archeology of our thought easily shows, man is an invention of recent date. And one perhaps nearing its end" (ibid.: 386–87).

4.3 Derrida: From Structure to Deconstruction

Jacques Derrida (b. 1930) examines structuralism on the basis of a philosophy influenced by Nietzsche and Husserl (Derrida 1967a; b; c, Wahl 1968b; cf. Jameson 1972, Norris 1982, Englert 1987). His position is programmatically poststructuralist (cf. Harari, ed. 1979). Not structural analysis, but *deconstruction* is his method and goal of research, a method which has meanwhile been adopted by a highly influential critical theory of literature (cf. Culler 1982, Norris 1982, Ulmer 1985, Tallis 1988).

Nevertheless, the discussion of Derrida's philosophy in the context of structuralism is not inappropriate. The root or at least the point of departure of his text philosophy is structuralism and Saussure's theory of the sign. It is this structuralist foundation which induces some philosophers to discuss Derrida as a neostructuralist (Frank 1984) or even superstructuralist (Harland 1987). For Derrida's grammatology and his deconstruction of the Saussurean sign, see Writing (5.2.2).

Deconstructionist theory rejects the objectivist idea of a structure inherent in the text and also the assumption of textual universals or codes of interpretation. For Derrida, this "absence of the transcendental signified extends the domain and the play of signification infinitely" (1967c: 280). Meanings are generated in a dynamic process which involves both *différence* and what Derrida calls *différance*. *Différence* is the Saussurean principle of structure, according to which a sign acquires meaning only by its difference from other signs of the system (see Saussure 3.4.2, Structure 2.1). For Derrida, this structural principle presupposes that every sign contains a trace of all those other elements in itself with which it stands in a syntagmatic contrast or paradigmatic opposition (1968: 142). This trace implies a temporal dimension. Signs are not only marked by a static presence or absence. The absences marked by the trace, the reference to the other, imply a dynamic process: The effect of differences is one of delay, postponement, or deferring an idea, for which Derrida coins the term *différance* (with the suffix *-ance* referring to the act of 'deferment'). The passive effect of *différence* and the active process of *différance* caused by the traces inscribed in the signs result in a generative movement which makes interpretation a semantic process of infinite regression (cf. Peirce's theory of infinite regress in semiosis). This is why the text, the network of these traces, can have no ultimate meaning. Its interpretation becomes an uncontrollable process.

Russian Formalism, Prague School, Soviet Semiotics

Russian Formalism was at the root of the development from text structuralism to semiotics in Eastern Europe. The schools of Prague and Moscow-Tartu became most influential propagators of text semiotics. For other developments in East European text semiotics, see, e.g., Odmark, ed. (1979–80), and Voigt (1979). An integrating figure in this development was the linguist Roman Jakobson (q.v.).

1. Russian Formalism

Russian Formalism had two centers, the Petrograd Society for the Study of Poetic Language (*Opoyaz*) from 1916 to 1930, and the Moscow Linguistic Circle from 1915 to 1921. Among the most influential Formalists were the literary historians Boris Èjxenbaum, Viktor Šklovskij, Jurij Tynjanov, the linguist Roman Jakobson, and the folklorist Petr Bogatyrev. For surveys see Erlich (1955), Jameson (1972), Eimermacher (1975), Fokkema & Kunne-Ibsch (1977). Anthologies are Todorov, ed. (1965), Striedter, ed. (1969), Matejka & Pomorska, eds. (1971), Stempel, ed. (1972), Bann & Bowlt, eds. (1973), and Matejka (1978).

The Formalists' goal was to develop a scientific approach to literature and art. Opponents of the Formalists accused the school of being interested only in form (in Hjelmslev's sense of expression-form) and neglecting the dimension of content. A major concern was to determine the differential qualities of poetry and art in comparison with "practical" language and artifacts. In this context, Jakobson developed his theory of literariness (*literaturnost'*) (cf. Literature 1.3).

Art and poetry were studied as autonomous systems which attract attention to themselves and cannot be reduced to their content. A specific technique designed to make a text a work of art was called a *device* (*priem*). According to Šklovskij (1916), the devices of art have the central function of "making strange" (*ostranenie*), causing a renewal of perception against the background of the process of *automatization* in which we become used to everyday actions and perceptions. The concept of automatization was later used by Tynjanov (1927) in his theory of literary evolution. He described literature as a system whose devices tend to become automatized, i.e., lose their artistic effect with time. As a consequence, new innovative devices are introduced within the system to guarantee its literariness. Such devices are opposed to the former ones which they replace. Thus, literature develops as a dynamic system by integrating innovations and abandoning its automatized structures.

These pragmatic and functional considerations of art show that the Formalists extended their analysis beyond the level of expression-form (see Hjelmslev 3.). In their contributions to the study of narrativity, the Formalists were even concerned with structures of content. One of the most influential concepts in this field is Šklovskij's distinction between story (*fabula*) and plot (*syuzhet*). Story is the preliterary succession of events and thus the artist's raw material. Plot is the literary transformation of the story in the narrative sequence. Thus, the plot is the way in which the story is "made strange." It is the transformation of actions and events into literature. The most elaborate approach to the study of plot structure at the time of the Russian Formalists is certainly Propp's *Morphology of the Folktale* (see Narrative 2.2, 3.1). But Propp is generally not considered one of the Formalists (cf. Meletinsky & Segal 1971: 89), although he was certainly a pioneer of text structuralism.

2. Prague School Text Semiotics

Within the Prague School of Linguistics (see Structuralism 1.1), scholars such as B. Havránek, R. Jakobson, J. Veltruský, F. Vodička, and, as a central figure, Jan Mukařovský (cf. Winner 1979, Chvatík 1984) developed a structuralist theory of aesthetics and literature with specifically semiotic elements. (For editions, readers, and surveys see Garvin, ed. 1964, Wellek 1969, Osolsobě 1973, Matejka & Titunik, eds. 1976, Fokkema & Kunne-Ibsch 1977, Mukařovský 1977; 1978, Matejka, ed. 1978, Steiner & Volek 1978, Winner 1978, Tobin, ed. 1988.) Important contributions of the Czech structuralists to text semiotics are discussed in detail in the chapters on aesthetics, theater, poetry, and function. Therefore, a summary of their key concepts must suffice here:

1. The Prague structuralists develop a dynamic concept of structure. Cf. Mukařovský (1977: 79): "The basic notion of structuralist thought is that of the interplay of forces, agreeing with and opposing one another, and restoring a disturbed equilibrium by a constantly repeated synthesis."

2. The Prague structuralists emphasize a functional approach to culture (cf. Bogatyrev 1937) and to aesthetics. The aesthetic function originates in a dialectical process of *foregrounding* (*aktualizace*) or *deautomatization* against a background of norms and *automatization*. The importance of the social context in the perception of art is emphasized.

3. The Prague structuralists extend their scope of analysis from linguistic expression to content structures, and from the analysis of verbal to nonverbal and visual media of expression.

4. With Mukařovský's paper of 1934 on "Art as a Semiotic Fact" (in 1977: 82–89), Prague structuralism acquires an explicitly semiotic dimension. The work of art is defined as a sign with both a communicative and an autonomous function.

3. Soviet Semiotics

After the end of the Stalinist era, scholars in the Soviet Union were able to revive their own formalist heritage and to join and pursue structuralist research which meanwhile had taken place in Prague, Copenhagen (see Hjelmslev), Paris, and America (see Structuralism 1.2). In the 1960s, research done under these premises became known as "Soviet structuralism" (e.g., Eimermacher, ed. 1971), but since its beginnings, this structuralism was also designated as "semiotic" (e.g., Meletinsky & Segal 1971, Baran, ed. 1974, Eimermacher 1975). After the mid–1970s, "Soviet semiotics" became the general designation of this new direction of research. For further surveys, see Rewar (1976), Winner & Winner (1976), Fokkema & Kunne-Ibsch (1977), Shukman (1977), Lhoest (1979). Translated anthologies are Lotman & Uspenskij, eds. (1973), Baran, ed. (1974), Lucid, ed. (1977), Prevignano, ed. (1979), Eimermacher & Eimermacher, eds. (1982), Eimermacher, ed. (1986), Grzybek (1988), Fleischer (1989).

For anthologies in Russian see Eimermacher, ed. (1971), Eng & Grygar, eds. (1973), Matejka et al., eds. (1977). Special bibliographies were published by Eimermacher, comp. (1974), Eimermacher & Shishkoff, comps. (1977), and in Eimermacher, ed. (1986). A new journal is *Znakolog—International Yearbook of Slavic Semiotics* (Bochum 1989ff.).

The two dominant research centers of Soviet semiotics are Moscow and Tartu, Estonia. These centers are also known as the Moscow-Tartu Semiotics School. The founder of the Tartu branch of this school is Jurij Lotman (cf. 1970; 1972, Halle & Matejka, eds. 1984, Shukman 1977). Among the members of the Moscow branch are A. M. Piatigorsky, I. I. Revzin, D. M. Segal, the generative linguist S. K. Shaumyan, V. N. Toporov, B. A. Uspensky, A. K. Zholkovsky, and, as a dominating figure, V. V. Ivanov (cf. 1976). Contributions by the Moscow-Tartu semioticians (in particular by Lotman) are discussed in various chapters of this handbook (e.g., Aesthetics 1.2.4, 4.2; Literature 2.1.2; Poetry 2.3.1). The following points summarize some of their major characteristics:

1. Soviet semiotics developed out of earlier projects in machine translation, mathematical linguistics, and cybernetics. It continued to develop semiotics with a strong foundation in information, communication, and systems theory. Among the semioticians who have had a strong influence on the Soviet school are Saussure, Hjelmslev, and Jakobson.

2. Their scope of analysis extended from language and literature to other phenomena of culture, such as nonverbal and visual communication (see Painting, Music, Film), myth, folklore, and religion. With the extension of the field of analysis, the concept of text is largely expanded. Thus, Lotman describes not only linguistic and literary utterances but also films, paintings, and even symphonies as texts.

3. In poetics and aesthetics, a characteristic of Soviet semiotic research is the semantization of the form of expression: Features of style and metric form are frequently given a semantic interpretation.

4. Art and culture in general are considered *secondary modeling systems*. These systems are secondary in relation to the primary system of language because, according to Lotman, "like all semiotic systems, [they] are constructed *on the model of language*" (1970: 9).

Barthes's Text Semiotics

The continuity in the development from structuralism to text semiotics is particularly evident in the works of Roland Barthes (1915–1980). In the 1960s, Barthes was both a leading structuralist and one of the earliest propagators of Saussure's semiological program. In this tradition, he contributed to text semiotics (see Myth, Literature, Narrative, Theology), to the semiotics of

Fig. B 1. Portrait of Roland Barthes (1915–1980) (Photo by S. Bassouls, copyright Seuil).

visual communication (see Architecture, Image, Painting, Film, Advertising), and even to the semiotics of medicine (see History 1.2.2). But structuralism and semiotics, to which this survey is restricted, were only two among several phases in Barthes's studies (cf. Barthes 1975a; 1984; 1985a; b; Culler 1983). After his phase of more systematic research in semiotics, which reached a climax with his *Fashion System*, Barthes returned to more essayistic, sometimes even poetic writings on literature and culture. For recent studies of Barthes's work in semiotics see Culler (1975; 1983), Coward & Ellis (1977), Sturrock, ed. (1979), Kurzweil (1980), Strickland (1981), Hervey (1982), Lavers (1982), Füssel (1983), and Silverman (1983).

1. Connotation and Metalanguage

The concept of *connotation* (cf. Meaning 5.2), in particular Hjelmslev's theory of connotation (see Hjelmslev 4.), is a key to Barthes's semiotic analyses of culture (cf. Baker 1985) and literature (q.v. 3.2.1). Barthes used a greatly simplified version of the glossematic sign model. Neglecting the dimensions of form and substance (see Hjelmslev 3.), Barthes (1957; 1964a; 1967b) defined a sign as a system consisting of E, an expression (or signifier), in relation (R) to C, a content (or signified): E R C. Such a primary

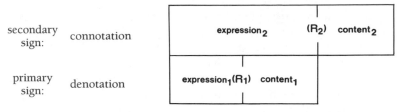

Fig. B 2. Barthes's model of *connotation* as the semantic extension of a denotative sign (cf. Barthes 1957: 115; 1964a: 90; 1967b: 28).

sign system can become an element of a more comprehensive sign system. If the extension is one of content, the primary sign (E_1 R_1 C_1) becomes the expression of a secondary sign system: E_2 (= E_1 R_1 C_1) R_2 C_2 (Barthes 1964a: 89). In this case, the primary sign is one of *denotative* while the secondary sign is one of *connotative* semiotics. Barthes represented these relations in his model of a staggered system (Fig. B 2).

An example of such a semiotic system is a cover photo of the French magazine *Paris-Match* published in the mid–1950s (Barthes 1957: 116). The photo (= expression$_1$) shows ("denotates") 'a black African in a French uniform saluting a French flag' (= content$_1$). But beyond this denotative sign (E_1, R_1, C_1), there is the implicit content (C_2) that "France is a great colonial Empire with loyal black citizens in its army, etc." This content (C_2) is the content of a new (connotative) sign. Its expression (E_2) is the whole of the denotative sign E_1 R_1 C_1.

The extension of a first-level sign system can also occur with the addition of a new expression. This is the case in metalinguistic signs (cf. Fig. B 3), where the primary system is that of an object language, and the secondary system consists of the metalanguage. Scientific terminologies are examples of such metalanguages. For example, the statement " 'house' is a noun" contains the metalinguistic sign (E_2)

"noun." Its content (C_2) is another complete sign on the level of the object language (E_1 = the letters h-o-u-s-e, C_1 the content 'house'). Figures B 2 and B 3 show the structural similarities between connotation and metalanguage. Both are secondary sign systems, but while connotation takes the primary sign as its expression, metalanguage takes it as its content. (In fact, Barthes in his *Mythologies* [1957] still failed to recognize this Hjelmslevian distinction and identifies connotation with metalanguage; cf. Mounin 1970a: 193.)

2. Mythology and Ideology

In his cultural and literary criticism, Barthes used the concept of connotative semiotics to uncover the hidden meanings in texts. In his *Mythologies* (1957: 131), he defined such systems of secondary meanings as myths (q.v. 3.). Later, Barthes described this sphere of connotations as an ideology (q.v. 2.1.1). The mass media create mythologies or ideologies as secondary connotative systems by attempting to give their messages a foundation in nature, considered as a primary denotative system (cf. ibid.). At the denotative level, they express primary, "natural" meanings. At the connotative

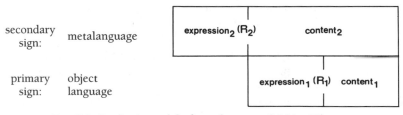

Fig. B 3. Barthes's model of metalanguage (1964a: 90).

level, they conceal secondary, ideological meanings. By referring to a denotative level of content which cannot be questioned (as in his example of the black French soldier), "myth does not deny things; [. . .] it purifies them, it makes them innocent, it gives them a natural and eternal justification" (ibid.: 143).

The idea of an ideologically innocent primary layer of denotation was later abandoned. In *S/Z*, Barthes redefined denotation as the final result of a connotative process, the effect of a semiotic closure: "Denotation is not the first meaning, but pretends to be so; under this illusion, it is ultimately no more than the *last* of the connotations (that one which seems both to establish and to close the reading), the superior myth by which the text pretends to return to the nature of language" (1970b: 9).

3. Research in Semiotic Systems

After his more essayistic semiotic analyses in *Mythologies* (1957), Barthes proposed a program for systematic research in nonlinguistic semiotic systems in *Elements of Semiology* (1964a). Cars, architecture, furniture, food, and garments were among the objects for which he suggested methods of semiotic analysis. In *The Fashion System* (1967b), Barthes made the most detailed and at the same time exemplary attempt at a study of sign systems beyond language and literature. The object of this study is fashion in France according to two magazines of 1958–59. The main features of his structuralist-semiotic approach may be summarized as follows:

1. In accordance with principles of linguistic structuralism, Barthes chose a closed corpus of analysis (namely, the fashion magazines of one season) in order to subject it to a synchronic analysis.

2. Methods of structural linguistics, such as distributional analysis and commutation tests (see Structuralism 1.1.2, 1.2.2), were applied to the data of the corpus in order to determine the pertinent or distinctive features of the fashion system. By these procedures, Barthes set up

classes of paradigmatic elements (see System 4.1), found rules of syntagmatic compatibilities and incompatibilities of these elements, and determined the minimal units of the fashion system, which he called *vestemes* or variants (ibid.: 76). After an inventory of possible categories of clothing, called *genres*, and a typology of possible oppositions in the system of vestemes, Barthes arrived at a comprehensive taxonomy of possible elements of clothing. The limitation of this analysis to a closed corpus of data turns out to be both an analytical virtue (because of the verifiability of the results) and an empirical disadvantage (because data which are not in the corpus may nevertheless be pertinent; cf. Culler 1975: 32–40).

3. In analogy to Saussure's dichotomy of *langue* and *parole*, Barthes distinguished between the *vestimentary code*, the system of fashion elements and rules, and its individual actualization in *garments*. The vestimentary code determines what is fashionable in a given season. This is the level of denotation in the fashion system. In addition to saying what is fashionable, fashion magazines give a whole "mythology" of comments on the social effects, possible occasions of usage, or personal styles connected with the elements of fashion. These are systems of connotation in fashion, which Barthes defined as a *rhetorical* system (see Rhetoric 2.3.2).

Since the only denotative message of fashion is whether a garment is fashionable or out of fashion, the fashion system creates a basic paradox between the simple message of the vestimentary and that of the elaborate rhetorical code: Fashion is "a semantic system whose only goal is to undermine the meaning which it so luxuriantly elaborates. [. . .] Without content, it [. . .] makes the insignificant signify" (Barthes 1967b: 269, 288).

4. Systems of Objects as Secondary Systems

Although fashion is a system of visual objects, Barthes's study was only indirectly concerned with such objects or their photographic representations. Instead of a system of objects, Barthes's corpus of analysis consisted only of "written fashion," i.e., the commentaries beneath the fashion photographs. Barthes argued that clothes in fashion magazines can signify beyond a certain rudimentary level only because their descriptions direct the readers' attention to certain features of the garment, and only the commentary generates meanings by "extracting signifiers" from the objects and by "naming their signifieds" (Barthes 1967b: xi; 1964a: 10). This consideration induced Barthes to deny the semiotic autonomy of nonlinguistic systems:

> It is true that objects, images and patterns of behavior can signify, and do so on a large scale, but never autonomously; every semiological system has its linguistic admixture. Where there is a visual substance, for example, the meaning is confirmed by being duplicated in a linguistic message [. . .], so that at least a part of the iconic message is, in terms of structural relationship, either redundant or taken up by the linguistic system. (1964a: 10)

Those who favor the possibility of an autonomous semiotics of nonlinguistic objects have accused Barthes of logocentrism, the fallacy that messages have semiotic structure only through the mediation of language (cf. Hervey 1982: 132). But for the phenomena studied by Barthes, the question is certainly (a) how "rudimentary" (see above) the immediate meaning of objects can be, and (b) whether the system of those immediate meanings is in accordance with those meanings provided by the ("rhetorical") system of the commentaries.

5. The Relationship between Linguistics and Semiotics

As a consequence of his thesis of the dependence of nonlinguistic semiotic phenomena on language, Barthes concluded that "linguistics is not a part of the general science of signs, even a

privileged part, it is semiology which is a part of linguistics" (1964a: 11). This thesis is the most radical antithesis to Saussure's theory of linguistics as a branch of semiotics (cf. Language 1.3). If this logocentristic position still seems understandable on the basis of iconic texts accompanied by language, it leads to a paradox when Barthes's thesis of semiotics as the study of *translinguistic* (i.e., textual) systems is taken into consideration (see Text semiotics 2.2.1). If translinguistics is a necessary extension of linguistics, how can it be a branch of linguistics, to which it is supposed to provide an extension? For further arguments against this Barthesian doctrine, see also Prieto (1975a: 133–35).

6. Barthes on the Limitations of Structuralist Semiotics

After his work on *The Fashion System*, Barthes abandoned the structuralist project of research in semiotic systems. In 1971, he concluded with reference to his earlier research: "I passed through a (euphoric) dream of scientificity" (1971a: 97). Yet, Barthes's semiotic studies not only continued to have a great influence in later text semiotic studies, he also obtained a professorship in "Literary Semiology" at the Collège de France in 1976. In his inaugural lecture, Barthes gave an outline of his new concept of semiotics (in Sontag, ed. 1982: 467–78). Distinguishing between "semiology [. . .] as the positive science of signs" and "my semiology" (ibid.: 471), he described language as an oppressive system, literature as a revolt against language, and semiotics as a creative activity:

> Semiology [. . .] does not rest on a "semiophysis," an inert naturalness of the sign, and it is also not a "semioclastry," a destruction of the sign. Rather, [. . .] it is a *semiotropy*: turned toward the sign, this semiology is captivated by and receives the sign, treats and if need be, imitates it as an imaginary spectacle. The semiologist is, in short, an artist . . . . (ibid.: 474–75)

Greimas's Structural Semantics and Text Semiotic Project

With his *Structural Semantics* (1966), Algirdas Julien Greimas (b. 1917) introduced a highly influential and productive text semiotics, which has become the core of a semiotic school, the School of Paris (Coquet et al. 1982, Parret & Ruprecht, eds. 1985, Arrivé & Coquet, eds. 1987, Perron & Collins, eds. 1988). In spite of several phases of continuous development, Greimas (1970; 1976a; b; 1983; cf.

Fig. G 1. Portrait of Algirdas J. Greimas (b. 1917).

Coquet 1985) still calls his theory a "semiotic project" (Greimas & Courtés 1979: 291). The influence of Greimas's ideas is noticeable in many areas of the semiotic field (cf. Parret & Ruprecht, eds. 1985), from the semiotics of space and architecture to painting, theology, law, and social sciences (Greimas 1976b), and even to the sciences of documentation (Lagrange 1973) and a semiotics of Eskimo (Collis 1971). The central object of research of this semiotic program, however, is the study of texts, in particular of narrative texts.

1. Greimas's Semiotic Project

Only a rough outline of Greimas's semiotic project can be given here. Access to its basic ideas requires the study of a sometimes idiosyncratic terminology, elaborated in a dictionary of its own (Greimas & Courtés 1979; 1986). A good survey of the development of this project is given by Coquet et al. (1982) and Schleifer (1987). For introductions to and studies and applications of Greimas's text semiotics, see Culler (1975: 75–95), Gumbrecht (1975), Stierle (1975: 186–219), Courtés (1976), Nef (1977), Kritzman (1978), Groupe d'Entrevernes (1979), Hénault (1979; 1983), Hafner (1982), Stockinger (1983), and Parret & Ruprecht, eds. (1985).

1.1 From Structuralism to Structural Semantics

Structuralism in linguistics and in Lévi-Strauss's anthropology, and Propp's and Souriau's early formalist theories of action in the narrative and in drama have influenced Greimas's semiotics. His point of departure is the attempt to apply methods of research from structural linguistics (phonology, semantics, and syntax) to the analysis of texts, which Greimas defines as *discourse*. His linguistic framework is determined by Saussure's concept of structure as difference, the principle of binary oppositions and distinctiveness of functional phonology, and Hjelmslev's glossematic sign model (cf. Greimas 1974a: 58). For the School of Paris, Greimas's *Sémantique structurale* (1966) is the first elaboration of a linguistic semiotics (Coquet et al. 1982: 15). Based on structural lexicology (cf. Coseriu & Geckeler 1974: 136), the goal of this study is the semantic analysis of text structures. *Sémantique structurale* is thus more than structural semantics as represented in the lexical approaches of linguists such as Pottier, Coseriu, Katz & Fodor, and Lyons. Aiming beyond the scope of word semantics, it is a text (or discourse) semantics.

1.2 Greimas's Concept of Semiotics

Against Peirce, Greimas & Courtés object to the concept of semiotics as a theory of signs. In their definition, semiotics should be a "theory of signification" which "becomes operational only when it situates its analyses on levels both higher and lower than the sign" (1979: 287, 147). Two directions of research are indicated in this definition. On the "lower level," analogous to the decomposition of the phoneme into its distinctive features, the structural "atomization" of signs (more precisely: "significations") into their semantic components, called *semes*, yields analytic elements which are not yet signs. On the "higher level," the discovery of textual units yields semantic entities which are more than signs.

2. The Model of Generative Discourse Analysis

The further development of his structural semantics led Greimas to a new semiotic model of text constitution which he defines as the generative trajectory (Greimas & Courtés 1979: 132–34. For discussions and applications see also Courtés 1976, Greimas & Nef 1977, Stockinger 1983, Patte 1984, Schleifer 1987).

2.1 The Generative Trajectory

This generative text semiotic model aims at accounting for the generation of discourses of any semiotic system. While emphasizing the semantic nature of all text semiotic categories (even the so-called syntactic ones), Greimas distinguishes three "autonomous general areas" of interpretation: *semio-narrative structures*, *discursive structures*, and *textual structures* (Greimas & Courtés 1979: 133). Since textual structures in the definition of Greimas are primarily structures of (linear or spatial, phonetic, written or visual) expression and not of content (cf. Courtés 1976: 39–43), they are situated outside of the generative trajectory.

The generative trajectory (Fig. G 2) describes discourse production as a process developing in various stages, each with a syntactic and a semantic subcomponent. The generative process begins at the deep level with elementary structures and extends over more complex structures at the higher levels. The whole trajectory describes structures "which govern the organization of the discourse prior to its manifestation in a given natural language (or in a non-linguistic semiotic system)" (Greimas & Courtés 1979: 85).

2.2 The Semio-Narrative Structures

The semio-narrative structures are postulated as being universal and independent of a spe-

		syntactic component	semantic component
Semiotic and narrative structures	deep level	FUNDAMENTAL SYNTAX	FUNDAMENTAL SEMANTICS
	surface levels	SURFACE NARRATIVE SYNTAX	NARRATIVE SEMANTICS
Discoursive structures		DISCOURSIVE SYNTAX Discoursivization actorialization temporalization spatialization	DISCOURSIVE SEMANTICS Thematization Figurativization

Fig. G 2. Greimas's generative trajectory (according to Greimas & Courtés 1979: 134).

cific code. They describe a semiotic competence of taxonomic and syntagmatic structures which form a *fundamental grammar*, comparable to Saussure's *langue* or Chomsky's *competence*, but both broadened by the dimensions of semantics and discourse (cf. Greimas & Courtés 1979: 83). At the deep level (cf. ibid.: 275, 331), the *fundamental semantics* contains the semantic categories which form the elementary structures of signification, and the *fundamental syntax* contains the relations and transformations which constitute those structures. At the surface level (ibid.: 5, 207, 277, 332), *narrative syntax* analyzes the structure of elementary narrative syntagms (called narrative programs) which are conceived in anthropomorphic categories as relations between *actants*. (For Greimas's *actantial grammar*, see Narrative 3.1.3.) The chainlike organization of narrative programs into narrative trajectories reflects the narrative progress of the discourse.

Narrative semantics is the domain of the actualization of semantic values, selected from the deep structure and attributed to the actants of the surface narrative syntax. Greimas & Courtés distinguish between *descriptive* and *modal* values (1979: 365). The former are either essential or accidental values. The latter refer to categories such as "desire," "obligation," or "knowledge."

2.3 Discoursive Structures

The discoursive structures "are charged with 'putting the surface structures into discourse' " (ibid.: 134). *Discoursive syntax* has the effect of producing an organized group of actors and a temporal and spatial framework (ibid.: 86, 330). It is thus the process of localizing narrative actors in time and space. *Discoursive semantics* (ibid.: 275, 344) is a relatively unexamined field. Its components of *thematization* and *figurativization* describe the isotopic concatenations of abstract themes which may be connected with concrete figures (see 4.).

---

3. Signification and the Semantic Universe

For Greimas, signification is the key concept of semiotics. The totality of significations forms the *semantic universe*. Terminologically, Greimas opposes *signification* to *meaning* by defining the latter term as "that which is anterior to semiotic production," whereas signification is "articulated meaning" (Greimas & Courtés 1979: 298). Greimas elaborated his model of the elementary structure of signification and of semic analysis in his *Structural Semantics* (1966). (For introductions and discussions see Grosse 1971, Dierkes & Kiesel 1973, Culler 1975: 75–95, Courtés 1976, Nef, ed. 1976, Schleifer 1983; 1987). In his later text semiotic program (cf. Fig. G 2), the elementary structures of signification are located at the level of deep and abstract structures, where they form an elementary morphological component (cf. Courtés 1976) besides the fundamental syntax to which the semiotic square is assigned (see 3.4).

3.1 The Elementary Structure of Signification

The starting point of Greimas's semantic theory is his minimalist definition of structure, in which priority is given to relations at the expense of elements, since only the differences (which are relations) between elements constitute a structure (1966: 19). Also in language and other semiotic systems, significations do not exist as autonomous elements. They are constituted only by relations. Hence, the origin of signification is defined as an elementary relation constituted by the difference between two semantic terms. For example, the difference between the lexical items "son" and

"daughter" is due to a semantic opposition which may be described metalinguistically by the features 'male' and 'female.' But for Greimas, this binary semantic structure has already a double aspect (cf. Greimas & Courtés 1979: 314): The difference between 'male' and 'female,' which is a relation of *disjunction*, presupposes the recognition of some semantic "resemblance," such as the so-called semic category of 'sex,' which is common to both 'male' and 'female.' This common category constitutes a relation of *conjunction*. Such a twofold semantic constellation is defined as an *elementary structure of signification*. Its model is a linear *semantic axis* with two elements at its ends. The axis represents the common semantic feature (the semic category). At the end points are the differential terms ('male,' 'female'). These are defined as *semes*.

3.2 Semic Analysis

Semes and semantic axes are abstract entities of the content-substance in the sense of Hjelmslev (Greimas 1966: 27). As Hjelmslev has shown, a semantic axis, like the one designating the color spectrum, may have different "articulations," i.e., form different lexical fields, in different languages. The specific semic articulation in a specific language becomes its content-form.

3.2.1 SEME, SEMEME, AND LEXEME

In lexical semantics, Greimas's semes have a status and function similar to those of the semantic components in other models of structural semantics. The seme is the minimal unit of semantics, whose function is to differentiate significations. Within the semantic universe, semes form hierarchies of *semic systems* (Greimas 1966: 33). Any two semes subsumed under a common semic category form an element of a semic hierarchy.

Semes are conceived as abstract, deep structural entities of metalinguistic description. The universe of semes represents the totality of conceptual categories of the human mind. At this level, which Greimas calls the level of *im-*

manence, the units of signification are still independent of the form they take in any particular language. The actual combination of semes into significations as they appear in lexemes takes place at the level of *manifestation*. Yet *lexemes*, the surface structural units of the lexicon, are not units of semantics in themselves. Only their significations belong to the semantic level of manifestation. These significations, combinations of semes, are defined as *sememes*. Since lexemes can be polysemous, one lexeme may have several sememes. For example, different sememes of the lexeme "table" are 'a piece of furniture,' 'a list of facts,' 'a tablet,' etc.

3.2.2 THE COMBINATION OF SEMES

Within a sememe, Greimas distinguishes two types of semes, *nuclear semes*, which characterize a sememe in its specificity and constitute a permanent, context-independent semic minimum, and *contextual semes*, also called *classemes*, which the sememe possesses in common with other elements of the utterance (1966: 46–60). The delimitation of nuclear semes from classemes, however, is connected with considerable methodological problems. The problems with the attempt at establishing two basic types of minimal semantic elements are similar to the difficulties which Katz & Fodor encountered with their proposal to distinguish between semantic *markers* and *distinguishers* (cf. Bolinger 1965). While sememes are always composed of nuclear and of contextual semes, there are also lexemes whose significations have only contextual semes and no nuclear semes, e.g., conjunctions and relational adverbs. Such combinations of semes are defined as *metasememes* (Greimas 1966: 122).

3.3 *The Semantic and the Semiological Level*

The differentiation between nuclear semes and contextual semes is connected with two further levels of analysis within the signifying universe (Greimas 1966: 53–68, Greimas & Courtés 1979: 282). Semes which form the nucleus of sememes are located at the so-called semiological (or figurative) level. They refer to a univer-

sal, extralinguistic sphere of perception ("sensible world") and form the deepest level of analysis. The systems of contextual semes form the semantic (or nonfigurative, also abstract) level of the signifying universe. In contradistinction to nuclear semes, contextual semes refer to categories of the human mind. Greimas also refers to the dichotomy of semiological vs. semantic in terms of the categories *exteroceptivity* (referring to properties of the exterior world) and *interoceptivity* (referring to data which have no perceptual correspondence) (1966: 120). For the two levels, see also *Semantics* (1.4.4).

3.4 *The Semiotic Square*

The oppositions constituting semantic axes may represent two different types of logical relation. The first type, *contradiction*, is the relation which exists between two terms of the binary category *assertion/negation* (cf. Greimas & Courtés 1979: 60). This relation is described as the opposition between the presence and absence of a seme. In this way, a seme s_1, "life," is opposed to its contradictory non-s_1 ($\bar{s}_1$), "non-life" (in which the seme "life" is absent). The second type is *contrariety* (cf. ibid.). Two semes of a semantic axis are contrary if each of them implies the contrary of the other. The contrary of s_1, "life," is s_2, "death." The two semes presuppose each other. The semantic constellation of three terms at two axes, s_1-$\bar{s}_1$ and s_1-s_2, may now be expanded by the contrary of s_2 which is $\bar{s}_2$ ("non-death"). The result is now a four-term constellation in which a new type of relation, *implication* or *complementarity*, appears between the terms s_1 and $\bar{s}_2$ or s_2 and $\bar{s}_1$. ("Life" implies "non-death." "Death" implies "non-life.") This constellation is visualized as a *semiotic square* (Fig. G 3; cf. Greimas 1970: 160, Greimas & Courtés 1979: 309, and the special issue entitled *Le carré semiotique* of *Bulletin du groupe de recherches sémio-linguistiques* 17 [1981]). This diagrammatic way of representing the four relations is a modern version of a formalization known from Aristotelian and medieval logic, where it was called the *square of oppositions* (cf. Reichenbach 1947: 95, Libéria

1976). The deep-structural character of this se-miotic square is evident from the fact that its four semantic values do not always have a corresponding lexical equivalent in the surface structure. There are, for example, no lexical items expressing the ideas of "non-death" or "non-life."

4. Isotopy

Greimas (1966) borrowed the term *isotopy* (Gr. ἴσος 'the same,' τόπος 'place') from nuclear physics. In structural semantics, isotopy describes the *coherence* and *homogeneity* of texts (cf. Rastier 1972b; 1981, Arrivé 1973, Klinkenberg 1973, Kerbrat-Orecchioni 1976, Greimas & Courtés 1979: 163–65). The concept has been widely accepted as a principle of text constitution within text semiotics (cf. Eco 1984b: 189–201).

4.1 Isotopy in Structural Semantics

Greimas defines isotopy as "the principle that allows the semantic concatenation of utterances" (1974a: 60; cf. 1970: 188). In his first approach, Greimas develops the theory of textual coherence on the basis of his concept of *contextual semes*: The "iterativity" (recurrence) of contextual semes, which connect the semantic elements of discourse (sememes), assures its textual homogeneity and coherence (1966: 69–101). Greimas (cf. 1974a: 60) links this principle to Katz & Fodor's theory of semantic *disambiguation*. Within a text, a polysemous noun such as *bark* ('outer covering on the trunk of a tree,' and 'sailing ship') is disambiguated by a contextual seme such as 'ocean.' The minimal condition of discoursive isotopy is thus a syntagm of two contextual semes. Later, Greimas & Courtés also interpret the semiotic square in terms of discoursive isotopy (1979: 163).

In its syntagmatic extension, an isotopy is constituted by all those textual segments which are connected by one contextual seme. Since texts are usually neither unilinear nor univocal, Greimas describes the overlapping of isotopies at various isotopic strata (1966: 109–115). When a discourse has only one interpretation, its semantic structure is a *simple isotopy*. The simultaneity of two readings, such as in ambiguities or metaphors, is called *bi-isotopy*. The superimposition of several semantic levels in a

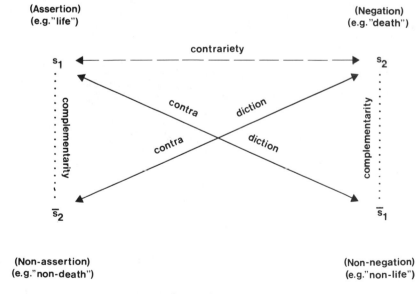

Fig. G 3. Greimas's semiotic square.

text is called *pluri-* or *poly-isotopy* (cf. Arrivé 1973).

4.2 *Toward an Extended Typology of Isotopies*

From the early model of contextual semic concatenation, the theory of isotopy was progressively expanded to cover recurrences at other textual levels. In addition to semantic isotopies, Greimas & Courtés distinguish *grammatical*, *actorial*, *partial*, and *global* isotopies (1979: 164). (The latter two play a role in discoursive *condensations* or *expansions*, such as in summa-rizing.) In a further expansion (cf. ibid. and Rastier 1972b: 84), the typology of isotopies is extended by *semiological* isotopies (cf. 3.3) to cover iterativities in terms of "exteroceptive" world knowledge. These are further subdivided into *thematic* and *figurative* isotopies (cf. Fig. G 2, 2.3). A still further expansion of the concept of isotopy was proposed by Rastier (1972b), who extends his typology of isotopies from the level of content to that of expression and thus describes morphological and phonetic recurrences (e.g., rhyme and assonance) as cases of isotopy. A different typology of isotopies is proposed by Eco (1984b).

Kristeva's Semanalysis

Julia Kristeva (b. 1941) is the author of an influential poststructuralist semiotic text theory which she first introduced under the designation of *semanalysis* (Kristeva 1969c). Although this term is rarely used in her later works, Kristeva's (1969c) project of "Research for a

Fig. K 1. Portrait of Julia Kristeva (b. 1941) (Photo by A. de Brunhoff, copyright Seuil).

Semanalysis" developed into a semiotic theory of remarkable coherence (Kristeva 1969c; 1970; 1974; 1977; 1980; 1982; 1986). Its frame of reference is a critical synthesis of a broad spectrum of scientific disciplines, such as psychoanalysis (Freud, Lacan; cf. Structuralism 3.), philosophy (Hegel, Marx's dialectical materialism, Husserl's phenomenology), logic, mathematics, linguistics (Jakobson, Benveniste, Chomsky's and Shaumyan's generative grammars), the theory of literature of the Russian postformalist Mikhail Bakhtin (1895–1975; cf. Todorov 1981), and semiotics (from the Stoics to Saussure, Peirce, Hjelmslev, and in particular the Moscow-Tartu School [see Soviet Semiotics 3.]; cf. also the survey of semiotics given by Kristeva 1969a: 291–320). For surveys of semanalysis and criticism, see Ducrot & Todorov (1972), Lewis (1974), Barthes (1975b), Carontini & Péraya (1975), Hardt (1975), Brütting (1976), Hempfer (1976), Coward & Ellis (1977), Féral (1978), Adriaens (1981), and MacCannell (1986b).

1. Semiotics as Autocritical Metatheory

Semiotics, according to Kristeva, is concerned with the making of *models*, i.e., "formal systems whose structure is isomorphic or analogous to the structure of another system (the one under study)" (1969c: 29 = 1986: 76). She gives the following outline of the field of semiotic study: "At present, semiotics is not restricted to *discourse*. It takes as its object *several signifying practices* which it considers as translinguistic, i.e., produced by language, but irreducible to linguistic categories" (1969c: 113). In its research, "semiotics uses linguistic, mathematical and logical models" but at the same time "demystifies" the assumed objectivity of scientific discourse (1969c: 32 = 1986: 79). For semiotics not only produces models, it also considers these models as its own object of study.

In Kristeva's view, semiotics should be more than "an empirical science aspiring to the modeling of signifying practices by means of logical [. . .] formulas" (1969b: 196–97). More than a "technical discourse," semiotics should become a science "critical and autocritical" of its own foundations. Being a "science of the text" (Kristeva 1969c: 18), semiotics turns out to be a signifying practice in itself. "At every instant of its production, semiotics thinks (of) its object, its instrument and the relation between them" (Kristeva 1969c: 30 = 1986: 77). Thus, "thinking (of) itself," semiotics is "an open form of research, a constant critique that turns back on itself and offers its own autocritique" (ibid.). In this way, semiotics realizes itself only as a critique of semiotics and of the sciences with which semiotics has interdisciplinary connections. Thus contributing to the "disillusionment that takes place within scientific discourse itself," semiotics could be called both a "science of ideologies" and an "ideology of sciences" (1969c: 31–32 = 1986: 78; cf. Ideology 2.2.3).

2. Semanalysis as a Science of the Text

The text, an object of semiotic research, is a central concept in semanalysis.

2.1 Text and System

Kristeva defines the text

> as a translinguistic apparatus that redistributes the order of language, relating a communicative "parole" aiming at direct information to different types of previous or synchronic utterances. The text is thus a *productivity*, which means: 1. Its relation to the language in which it is situated is redistributive (destructivo-constructive). [. . .] 2. It is a permutation of texts, an intertextuality: In the space of one text several utterances, taken from other texts, cross and neutralize themselves. (1969c: 113)

Thus, text and language (system) are opposed in a dialectical relationship, in which the text appears as the revolutionary transformation of the system:

> Submerged in language, the "text" is consequently [. . .] that which changes it, which dissolves it from the automatism of its habitual development. . . . The (poetic, literary or other) "text" digs into the surface of speech a vertical shaft where the models of that *significance* are sought which the representative and communicative language *does not recite* even if it indicates them. [. . .] The text is not the communicative language codified by grammar. It is not satisfied with representing or meaning the real. Wherever it signifies [. . .] it participates in the transformation of reality, capturing it at the moment of its non-closure. (ibid.: 8–9)

2.2 The Text as Signifying Practice and Productivity

Kristeva refuses to accept the naive notion of a textual understanding between a sender and a receiver suggested by the simplified model of communication. Instead of analyzing the text as a communicative process of social exchange, Kristeva is interested in the analysis of the text as a generative activity, which she calls a *signifying practice* and *productivity*.

Signifying practices are described as the activity of a "plural subject," based on a dialectics of contradiction (cf. Barthes 1975b: 998). The indeterminacy of this activity is particu-

larly evident in view of an object such as literature, which Kristeva characterizes as "plural,
sometimes plurilinguistic, often polyphonic"
and as "presenting a potential infinity"
(1969c: 16, 180). With the concept of textual
productivity, Kristeva wants to focus on "the
dynamics of production over the actual product" (1969c: 39 = 1986: 85). This production
is seen as a process of work, less in the sense of
Marx, who was too much concerned with the
product in social exchange, than in the sense of
Freud's dream work: "Freud revealed production itself to be a *process* not of exchange (or
use) or meaning (value) but of playful permutation, which provides the very model for production. Freud therefore opens up the
problematics of *work as a particular semiotic
system*, as distinct from that of exchange"
(ibid.: 38 = 83).

2.3 Intertextuality

One of the factors determining the textual "polyphony" is its *intertextuality*. Kristeva elaborates this concept under the influence of Bakhtin
(1929), who described the literary text as a mul-
tilayered mosaic of quotations, forming a dialogical and polyphonous structure. For Kristeva, the
text is an intersection of texts and codes, "the
absorption and transformation of another text"
(1969c: 146 = 1980: 37). Intertextuality cannot
be reduced to the question of literary influences.
It comprises the whole field of contemporary
and historical language as reflected within the
text (cf. Barthes 1975b: 998). For the concept of
intertextuality in current literary criticism, see
Broich & Pfister, eds. (1985).

3. Semanalysis and Psychoanalysis

The importance of psychoanalysis for Kristeva's semiotic research is programmatically
expressed in her term *semanalysis*, a portman-
teau word referring to both semiotics and
psychoanalysis.

3.1 Textual Analysis, Genotext, and Phenotext

Kristeva understands the concept of analysis in
the etymological sense as a 'dissolution' (Gr.
ἀνάλῦσις), a decomposition of the sign and
text, a process leading to the discovery of hidden dimensions of meaning (1969c: 278–79).
This analysis takes place in a process of two
stages called *phenotext* and *genotext* (cf. ibid.:
284, Kristeva & Coquet 1972: 335). The distinction is inspired by Shaumyan's genotype
and phenotype grammar (see Language 2.3.3).
The phenotext is the textual surface structure.
It can be described empirically by the methods
of structural linguistics (phonology, syntax,
and semantics). The genotext is the level of
textual deep structure, where the "production
of signification" takes place. It is "unstructured
and non-structuring," "exterior to the subject," "timeless," and contains the possibilities of all languages and signifying practices as
its predisposition "before falling on the phenotext as a mask or censure."

3.2 The Semiotic and the Symbolic

In a later study, Kristeva (1974) elucidates the
psychoanalytic position of semanalysis by introducing a distinction between the *semiotic*
and the *symbolic*, in which the former is related
to Freud's primary and the latter to his secondary processes. The semiotic is the prelinguistic
disposition of instinctual drives. It precedes
the symbolic, with which it is related in a dialectical contradiction. The symbolic is "language as nomination, sign, and syntax." "It
involves the thetic phase, the identification of
the subject and its distinction from objects,
and the establishment of a sign system" (Kristeva 1980: 136, 19).

3.3 Logic of Negativity

Following Freudian psychoanalysis with its
theory of a "psycho"-logic determined by
processes of displacement and condensation,
Kristeva postulates a new "dialectical logic of

contradiction" at work in the signifying practice between geno- and phenotext (1969c: 246–77). She describes the logical operation of *negation*, which Hegel took for the basis of *difference* and *differentiation*, as being at the foundation of any symbolic activity (ibid.: 248). In poetic language, this negation becomes a law, but poetic negativity negates both the *parole* and that which results from this negation (ibid.: 276).

Eco

Umberto Eco (b. 1932) has made significant contributions to many areas of theoretical and applied semiotics, many of which are discussed in detail in several chapters of this handbook. This chapter gives a survey of the main topics of this research and focuses on Eco's development from structuralism to text semiotics and on his definition of semiotics as a theory of culture.

Fig. E 1. Portrait of Umberto Eco (b. 1932) (Photo, Bompiani).

1. Semiotic Theory and Praxis

Eco's writings extend from philosophy (1984b) to popular culture (1964; 1973a), and semiotics is the center of these manifold studies. His major works in theoretical semiotics are Eco (1968; 1973b; 1976; 1984b; 1985b). Many of Eco's topics in theoretical semiotics are discussed in the chapters on meaning, iconicity, typology of signs, codes, structure, and communication. One of Eco's central fields of research is aesthetics (see especially Eco 1954; 1962 [partially in Eco 1979]; 1978; 1984b). In the field of applied semiotics, Eco has studied topics from medieval culture to avant-garde music, from art to kitsch, and from myth to ideology in the mass media (see also Architecture, Image, Comics, and Film). Of special interest to text semiotics is Eco's semiotics of metaphor, iconicity, ideology, and his theory of open form (in Literature 4. and Aesthetics 4.1.2).

Eco has become the world's most famous semiotician because of his best-selling novel *The Name of the Rose* (1980a). In a way, this novel is a creative work of applied semiotics (cf. Hüllen 1987, Kroeber, ed. 1987). Eco himself set store by this assessment when he gave the following comment on his own writings: "Every single thing I've done comes down to the same thing: a stubborn effort to understand the mechanisms by which we give meaning to the world around us" (in Sullivan 1986: 46).

2. Eco's Critique of Structuralism

The development from structuralism to semiotics in Italy (cf. Segre 1979a) was significantly influenced by Eco's work. In 1968, Eco published a work whose title, *The Absent Structure* (*La struttura assente*, Milano: Bompiani), announces an attack on the foundations of structuralism. The French translation of this study, *La structure absente* (Paris: Mecure de France 1972), had a subtitle which places the study within the framework of semiotics: *Introduction à la recherche sémiotique*. The title of the revised German translation of 1972 was only *Einführung in die Semiotik*. This change of titles is indicative of a research program which developed a *Theory of Semiotics* (Eco's 1976 revised version of the former titles) from a critique of structuralism.

The study is a synthesis of various approaches to the analysis of texts, visual communication, and meaning in general. Besides such tools of structuralism as the methods of structural semantics and syntax and Hjelmslev's theory of signs, Eco incorporates methods of communication and information theory, cultural anthropology, and Peirce's theory of signs into his theory of semiotics. The climax of this study (cf. Segre 1973: 37–41) is a philosophical critique of structuralism. Eco attacks structuralists such as Lévi-Strauss for their attempt to discover structures, and for ascribing to them the status of an objective reality. Such an "ontological structuralism," according to Eco, "can only result in an ontological self-destruction of structure" (1968: 395). For, if

there were an ultimate structure, it could not be defined. There would be no metalanguage to achieve such a definition (cf. ibid.: 411), no opposition to constitute the structure itself. For these reasons, Eco advocates a methodological structuralism (see Structure 3.3). It accepts structural models only as operational procedures and is willing to give these up in favor of new models when new evidence calls for new explanations.

3. Eco's Definition of Semiotics

Eco defines semiotics as a research program which "studies all cultural processes as *processes of communication*" (1976: 8). Culture, according to Eco, "can be studied completely under a semiotic profile" (ibid.: 26–27), but cultural entities can also be considered from nonsemiotic points of view. For example, a car can be a sign indicating social status, but at a physical or a mechanical level it has no communicative function, and semiotics is not concerned with these levels. Eco's rejection of ontological realism reappears in his theory of the sign and its referent, on the basis of which he gives the following definition of semiotics:

> Semiotics is concerned with everything that can be *taken* as a sign. A sign is everything which can be taken as significantly substituting for something else. This something else does not necessarily have to exist or actually be somewhere at the moment in which a sign stands for it. Thus, *semiotics is in principle the discipline studying everything which can be used in order to lie*. (ibid.: 7)

This conclusion ultimately derives from a structuralist argument: If something cannot be used to tell a lie, it has no semantic opposition, consequently no structure, and hence no meaning. Without a possible lie there is no possible truth.

Text Semiotics: The Field

Text Semiotics: Introduction

The introduction to this section gives a brief survey of the field of text semiotics, discusses related approaches to the study of texts, and introduces some major definitions of text and criteria of textuality. Although this handbook discusses many other semiotic phenomena as texts, text semiotics in this section is primarily restricted to the study of *verbal* texts. The section is further restricted to approaches and topics which are characterized as explicitly semiotic but includes the major precursors of text semiotics.

1. Survey of the Field

After the discussion of current theories of text semiotic research in the previous section, this section deals with the major topics of text semiotics and its precursors.

1.1 Major Topics of Research

The first chapters deal with the ancient precursors (cf. Todorov 1977) of text semiotics, hermeneutics, rhetoric (with stylistics as its younger descendant), and poetics. A related topic is the semiotics of metaphor. Today, these fields are both branches of text semiotics and also its neighboring disciplines within philosophy and aesthetics. The core of current

text semiotic research is the field of literature. However, instead of the classical subfields of literature, epic, lyric, and drama, text semiotics comprises the much broader areas of narratives, poeticalness, and theater. In relation to traditional literary criticism, the analytic field is expanded in the direction of a multiplicity of nonlinguistic codes and nonliterary texts.

With its interest in myths, ideology, and theology, text semiotics turns to nonaesthetic phenomena. In this field, semiotic research strives to uncover structures common to texts from archaic times to the modern mass media. Such textual phenomena are also studied in fields which are discussed outside of this section, e.g., advertising, film, and comics. These examples show a certain overlap between the field of text semiotics and areas of research discussed in other sections of this handbook. Within this section this overlap is particularly evident in the chapters on theater and theology.

1.2 Lacunae: Law, History, Mass Media

Two major lacunae in this section, the semiotics of law and of history, and a partial lacuna, the semiotics of mass media, can be filled here only by bibliographical references. The semiotics of law is an expanding area of research (cf. Carzo & Jackson, eds. 1985, Jackson 1985, Mertz & Weissbourd 1985, Kevelson 1986; 1987, and the special issues of the journals *Zeitschrift für*

Semiotik 2.3 [1980] and *Text* 4.1/3 [1984]). With roots in ancient hermeneutics and rhetoric (Goodrich 1986; 1987, Schreckenberger 1978), current approaches to legal semiotics are influenced by Greimasian text semiotics (Greimas & Landowski 1976, Jackson 1985) and by Peircean semiotics (Klein 1984, Kevelson, ed. 1987; Kevelson 1988).

The semiotics of history has been debated in several issues of *Semiotica* (1982; 1985, and the special issue *Semiotica* 59.3/4 [1986]) and in the volume by Schmid, ed. (1986). While Uspenskij (1977a) analyzes history as a communication process in which meaning is attributed to events, Haidu (1982, pace Finlay-Pelinski 1982) discusses the transformations of historical codes and the narrative and structural semantic (see Greimas) structures in historical texts. With the semiotic interpretation of historicity and historical truth, Williams (1985) turns to one of the central topics in the current philosophy of history.

The semiotics of the mass media is only a partial lacuna in this handbook because it is the topic of several individual chapters (e.g., Advertising, Comics, etc.). For explicitly semiotic approaches to this vast field of text semiotics, see Eco (1964), Moragas Spa (1976), Peña-Marín and Lozano y Gonzalo Abril (1978), Bentele, ed. (1981), Berger (1982: 14–43; 1984), Bentele (1985), and Bentele & Hess-Lüttich, eds. (1985).

2. Text Semiotic and Related Approaches to Texts

A necessary complement to the previous section on the schools of semiotics and to this section is a brief discussion of related sciences of the text, particularly of the relation between text semiotics and linguistics.

2.1 Sciences of the Text

After rhetoric, hermeneutics, and literary criticism, a number of more recent disciplines besides text semiotics have developed approaches to the study of texts in general. An impressive number of such disciplines, mostly derived from linguistics and artificial intelligence, are enumerated by Petöfi (1986: 1080–81) under designations such as *text* (or *discourse*) *processing*, *text* (or *discourse*) *analysis*, *text linguistics*, *text* (or *discourse*) *grammar*, *text theory*, *theory of discourse*, and *science of texts* (*Textwissenschaft*). Although these approaches may be subsumed under the general heading of text semiotics in its broadest sense (as Petöfi does by including them in an encyclopedic survey of semiotics), most of them are not discussed in this handbook, which focuses on explicitly semiotic fields of study. The research program which is perhaps most closely related to text semiotics because of its interdisciplinary approach and broad scope of topics is discourse analysis (Dijk, ed. 1985).

2.2 Text Semiotics between Linguistics and Literary Criticism

Text semiotics has often been defined as an extension of linguistics into the field of textual analysis or literary criticism. Such delimitations of the text semiotic field depend on the scope of the underlying linguistic model, which is sometimes narrower, excluding the level of the text, and sometimes more extended, including a *text linguistics* (for a survey of the latter see Beaugrande 1985). Depending on the views about the scope of linguistics, three major types of delimitation of the text semiotic field may be distinguished.

2.2.1 TEXT SEMIOTICS AS TRANSLINGUISTICS

The first delimitation, adopted mainly by French semioticians, is based on a narrower model of linguistics extending from phonology to syntax only. (Cf. Martinet's levels of linguistics: phoneme, moneme, and phrase.) From this point of view, structures beyond the sentence are no longer subject to linguistic research. Research at the textual level is then considered semiotic (cf. Heath 1971: 22). Such a delimitation is the basis of Barthes's definition of text semiotics as a study whose units of analysis are

> no longer monemes or phonemes, but larger fragments of discourse. [. . .] Semiology is therefore perhaps destined to be absorbed into a *translinguistics*, the materials of which may be myth, narrative, journalism, or on the other hand objects of our civilization, in so far as they are *spoken* (through press, prospectus, interview, conversation . . .). (1964a: 11)

On this type of delimitation between linguistics and text semiotics, see also Greimas (1.1–2).

2.2.2 TEXT SEMIOTICS AS TEXT PRAGMATICS
The second delimitation departs from a linguistic model which includes the level of the text but considers text linguistics as a discipline concerned mainly with text syntax and text semantics. Text semiotics in this perspective is the extension of analysis into the pragmatic dimension of texts. The focus is on the communicative processes and functions of texts, and special attention is given to the processes of text reception, the role of the reader (e.g., Wienold 1972, Köller 1975, Koch, ed. 1976, Eco 1979, Merrell 1982; 1985; see also Language 2.2.3).

2.2.3 THEORY OF SIGNS AND CODES IN TEXTS
The third delimitation represents perhaps not a major trend in text semiotics but is nevertheless a tendency characterizing many assumptions about the specifically semiotic extension of textual research. According to this view, the semiotic extension of text linguistics in text semiotics begins only with the analysis of nonlinguistic signs and codes in texts. This view of text semiotics is particularly evident in the semiotics of theater, but it can also be maintained in the study of genuinely verbal texts (cf. Nöth 1978a; 1980): The relationship between text linguistic structures and nonlinguistic signs or codes in texts can be one of *iconic mapping* or one of *indexical contiguity*. In the former case, the verbal text describes or tells about nonverbal or visual signs (e.g., in a poem or a narrative). In the latter case, the verbal text is placed in the context of

nonlinguistic signs or codes (e.g., in theater, film, comics, etc.).

---

3. Text and Textuality

Since textuality "is not an inherent property of certain objects, but is rather a property assigned to objects by those producing or analyzing them" (Petöfi 1986: 1080), it is not surprising that semioticians of the text have been unable to agree on a definition and on criteria of their object of research.

3.1 Definitions of Text

Although this section deals only with texts in the narrower sense, a brief reference to the concept of text in the broader sense is appropriate here.

3.1.1 TEXTS AS CULTURAL MESSAGES
The concept of text in its broadest sense refers to messages of any code. In this sense, authors such as Koch (1971b), Nöth (1972), Uspenskij et al. (1973: 6), and Bouissac (1976a: 90) study the most diverse cultural phenomena as texts: films, ballet performances, happenings, pieces of music, ceremonies, or circus acts. In a most programmatic way, the Soviet semioticians define texts in this broadest sense as their field of research. Bakhtin, as quoted by Todorov, calls the text the "primary datum" of the human sciences: "The text is the *immediate reality* (reality of thought and of experience) within which this thought and these disciplines can exclusively constitute themselves. Where there is no text, there is neither object of inquiry nor thought" (1981: 17). More specifically, Uspenskij et al. regard texts as "the primary element (basic unit) of culture" (1973: 6), as a message generated by the systems of cultural codes. (For additional criteria of this definition see 3.2.1.)

3.1.2 TEXTS AS VERBAL MESSAGES
In a narrower sense, the text is a verbal message only. Several variants of this definition relate the text to different semiotic concepts.

1. *Text or discourse*: If *text* is used as a synonym of *discourse*, the verbal messages under consideration are either oral or written. In linguistics, Benveniste preferred the term *discourse* with reference to written *and* spoken messages (1966: 209), while German scholars have preferred the concept of text, and the early American tradition (since Z. Harris) used the concept of discourse for this field of study.

2. *Text vs. (oral) discourse*: Barthes (1975b: 997) and others restrict the concept of text to written messages only. For those who apply this restriction, spoken messages are the domain of discourse (cf. Greimas & Courtés 1979: 340).

3. *Text vs. (empirical) discourse*: In analogy to the distinction between *sentence* and *utterance* in linguistics, Dijk defines text as the abstract structure underlying discourse, defined as the empirical verbal utterance (1972: 3).

4. *Text vs. system*: In the tradition of Hjelmslev, text is the semiotic dimension of process and syntagmatic relations, while system is the paradigmatic dimension of choice (cf. System 2.1, 4.).

5. *Text, utterance, enunciation*: These concepts refer to the pragmatic dimension of the text. Enunciation is the individual act of speech production. The result of this act is an utterance (cf. Dubois et al. 1973). Utterance (*énoncé*) is a prestructural semiotic entity designating the product of a speech act which may be a text or merely a fragment of text. The text as a result of enunciation contains traces of the speech act in the form of indexical words pointing to the participants, time, and space of the enunciation.

6. *Text as corpus*: Some linguists use the concept of text in the sense of a corpus, "the set of linguistic utterances subjected to analysis" (Dubois et al. 1973: 128).

7. *Text as productivity*: see Kristeva (2.1).

3.2 Criteria of Textuality

The etymology of *text*, 'something woven,' refers to a characteristic of textuality that might be circumscribed as a 'coherent whole.' This charac-

teristic of textuality has been studied from text semantic and text syntactic points of view. For many scholars, textual coherence presupposes longer segments of language, which is also implied in the characterization of the text as a *transphrastic* structure. Yet, a text cannot be defined by the extension of an utterance alone. Many text semioticians are willing to accept units of one word or one sentence as texts (e.g., road signs, orders, or proverbs). The criterion of textuality in these cases is a text pragmatic one. Both types of criteria are complementary. There is no single minimal criterion valid for all of these forms of textuality. For the systemic properties of text, see System (3.).

3.2.1 TEXT AS MESSAGE WITHIN A CONTEXT

In the pragmatic view, the text is defined by criteria of communication: it is the (verbal) message of an addresser to an addressee. Hartmann, proposing the thesis of the text as the *original linguistic sign*, argues that language in communication is always primarily text (and only secondarily sentence, word, etc.) (1971: 10–11). Several criteria have been proposed in addition to this basic pragmatic postulate of textuality. A frequent criterion is the *intentionality* of the message (cf. Communication 2.4). Uspenskij et al. restrict textuality to those messages "which possess a certain integral meaning and fulfill a common function" (1973: 6).

The pragmatic criteria determine the text within its situational context. This context comprises textual and extratextual phenomena, which Lotman has tried to differentiate by the two criteria of *expression* and *demarcation* (1970: 51–52). By its being expression, the text is materially fixed in the form of the signs (*parole*) of a system (*langue*). In this sense, the text is opposed to extratextual structures of *langue* which are not expressed within the text. By its demarcation, the text is opposed to all material signs of the context not contained within the text.

3.2.2 TEXT AS A COHERENT STRUCTURE

In its internal text syntactic and text semantic structure, the text is characterized as an autonomous and in certain respects closed system (cf. Ducrot & Todorov 1972: 294). The systemic wholeness of the text is created by a process of the integration of individual signs into an *integral sign* (Uspenskij et al. 1973: 6) or, in the terminology of information theoretical semiotics, into a *supersign* (cf. Posner & Reinecke, eds. 1977: 47–106). Lotman characterizes this process as follows: "A text is an integral sign and all the separate signs of the general linguistic text [i.e., of natural language] are reduced in the text to the level of elements of this sign" (1970: 22).

Various text syntactic and text semantic criteria have been proposed to describe the integration of linguistic elements into the textual whole. Some of them are pronominalization (or other pro-forms), syntagmatic substitution, semantic recurrence, and textual deep structure. Within Greimas's text semiotic model, textual coherence is described by the principle of *isotopy*. A list of no fewer than seven standards of textuality is set up by Beaugrande (1980: 19–20). His criteria are (surface structural) *cohesion*, (conceptual) *coherence*, *intentionality*, *acceptability*, *situationality*, *intertextuality*, and *informativity*.

Hermeneutics and Exegesis

Hermeneutics is both a predecessor and a neighboring discipline of text semiotics. Originally the "art of interpretation," hermeneutics was one of the earliest sciences of the text and thus a precursor of text semiotics. Like rhetoric, hermeneutics has its most important roots in ancient Greece. (But see Rey 1973: 45–62 and Todorov 1978: 47–49 on Sanskrit, Faur 1986 and Güttgemanns 1989 on Jewish hermeneutics.) It reached a first climax with the doctrines of scriptural exegesis developed by Augustine (354–430) and medieval theology. Modern hermeneutics is a neighboring discipline of semiotics (cf. Daube-Schackat 1988). It has become a philosophy of understanding, not only of texts, to which this chapter will be restricted, but moreover of the essence of human existence.

1. Origins of Hermeneutics

The art of interpretation has its traditions in philology (textual commentary on the classics), theology (exegesis), and jurisprudence (cf. Gadamer 1974).

1.1 Ancient Hermeneutics

The principles of ἑρμηνεύειν, of explaining, interpreting, and translating, were a topic of Greek philosophy (cf. Pépin 1975) and mythology. The mythological patron of hermeneutics is Hermes, the messenger of the gods as well as the inventor of speech and writing (cf. Ebeling 1959). Plato (Epinomis 975c) discussed the art of interpretation in connection with that of divination (*mantics*). Both interpretation and divination are hermeneutic arts (cf. Todorov 1977: 31). Both are concerned with the discovery of meaning. Whereas divination reveals meanings in objects that do not seem to have any, interpretation reveals secondary meanings beyond the primary meanings of texts.

A central topic of ancient textual criticism was the allegorical interpretation of Homer's works. Classic criticism was concerned with two levels of textual analysis. At a "surface level," textual commentary had to explain word and sentence meanings. At a "deep level" of analysis, a second, 'hidden sense' (ὑπόνοια) had to be uncovered which became later known as the allegorical sense.

1.2 Scriptural Exegesis

The ancient notion of two levels of textual meaning was developed into a complex system of interpretation by Christian theologians after Origines (185–254). Caught in a permanent conflict between dogmatic interpretation and the revelation of new meanings in the Scriptures, the Church Fathers developed a doctrine of scriptural meanings which has the character of a theory of textual codes (cf. Eco 1984b: 147–53).

Medieval exegesis considered the Bible to have "a *cortex*, or level of surface meaning, covering a *nucleus* of truth" which was to be revealed by the exegete (Robertson 1951: 11). The hermeneutic tradition distinguishes three stages of scriptural analysis (cf. Robertson & Huppé 1951: 1–3): The first stage, called *littera*, was concerned with grammatical structure. At the second stage, called *sensus*, the obvious, literal, or narrative meanings had to be understood. *Littera* and *sensus* form the outer cortex of the text. At the same time, *sensus* comprises the first of four levels of scriptural meanings. As such it is called literal or historical meaning (*sensus litteralis, s. historicus*). The more profound meaning concerning the scriptural nucleus is revealed only at a third stage of exegesis, called *sententia* (see Fig. H 1).

The exegetic stage of *sententia* is that of the spiritual senses of the Holy Scriptures. These were studied according to the elaborate doctrine of the multiple scriptural meanings (see Lubac 1959–64, Esbroeck 1968). Beyond the first (literal or historical) sense, three modes of spiritual meaning were distinguished (with varying designations): *tropology*, *allegory*, and *anagogy*. The tropological (also *moral*) sense is the significance which the Scriptures have for the individual life of man on earth. The allegor-

ical sense reveals the layer of meaning referring to Christ and the Church. Finally, the anagogical sense refers to the heavenly mysteries which will be revealed in the future. In scriptural exegesis, every biblical message was interpreted according to one, two, or all three of these spiritual senses. An example of a fourfold scriptural interpretation is the meaning of Jerusalem according to Dante (Il Convivio II, 1, 2–15): Historically or literally, Jerusalem refers to 'the city of the Jews.' Its tropological sense is 'the soul of man.' The allegorical sense is 'the Church of Christ,' and the anagogical sense is 'the city of God in heaven.'

2. The Problem of Understanding in Modern Hermeneutics

Modern hermeneutics developed from Friedrich Schleiermacher (1768–1834) and Wilhelm Dilthey (1833–1911) to Martin Heidegger (1889–1976), Rudolf Bultmann (1884–1976), Gadamer (1960), Betti (1962), Habermas (1968), Ricoeur (1969), Szondi (1975), and Apel (1976). The history of this (only implicitly semiotic) development and its relevance to text semiotics (with special reference to exegesis) are discussed by McKnight (1978). Seung (1982) and Güttgemanns (1983) give the outlines of an explicitly semiotic hermeneutics. For surveys see Palmer

	Stages of Exegesis	Scriptural Meanings
Cortex (surface structure)	1. *littera* (grammar)	———
	2. *sensus* (semantics)	(1) *sensus litteralis* (*s. historicus*)
Nucleus (deep structure)	3. *sententia* (textual interpretation)	Three spiritual senses (2) *sensus tropologicus* (3) *sensus allegoricus* (4) *sensus anagogicus*

Fig. H 1. Medieval exegetic codes.

(1969), Hauff (1971), Gadamer (1974), Gadamer & Boehm, eds. (1976), Hufnagel (1976), Todorov (1978), Holub (1984: 36–45; only on Gadamer), and Mueller-Vollmer, ed. (1986). For its eighteenth-century precursors see History (3.4.6). From this philosophical tradition, only two central problems of understanding and interpretation can briefly be dealt with here, the *hermeneutic circle* and the ideal of correct understanding.

2.1 The Hermeneutic Circle

For the hermeneutics, textual understanding (and human knowledge in general) is possible neither by *induction*, i.e., by beginning with the textual (or experiential) data and arriving at a general explanation of the text (or law, concerning other phenomena) as a whole, nor by *deduction*, i.e., by beginning with a general law or knowledge of the whole and explaining the data through it. Against these unidirectional models of scientific discovery, the hermeneutics propose an alternative model of understanding, not unrelated to the alternative which Peirce introduced under the designation of *abduction*, the method of explaining data on the basis of assumptions and hypotheses about probable, not yet certain laws (see also Daube-Schackat 1988). The hermeneutic model of understanding is the so-called hermeneutic circle. Dilthey describes it as a central theorem of interpretation:

> From the individual words and their combinations, the whole of a work is to be understood, and yet, the complete understanding of the individual part already presupposes the whole. This circle occurs again in the relation of the individual work to the mentality and development of its author. It reoccurs in the relation of this individual work to its literary genre. (1900: 330)

The determination of understanding by the individual preconceptions and historical predispositions of the interpreter is one of the central topics of hermeneutics. (See also the related problem of ideology in Ideology 2.2.)

According to Hauff's discussion of Gadamer's work,

> this preconception generates a context of meaning into which the text is integrated and from which the text appears as understandable. When the text conforms with the given interpretative frame, this preconception [. . .] is confirmed. When the text conflicts with the preconceived frame, contradicting certain semantic expectations, the reader takes offense: Only this moment creates the situation which requires explicit interpretation. Textual understanding [is] seen as an integration of the strange into the familiar, the as-yet-unknown into the already-known [. . .]. (1971: 24)

Following Heidegger, Gadamer emphasizes that the hermeneutic circle is not a *vicious* circle:

> Being neither subjective nor objective, it describes understanding as the interplay of the movement of tradition and of the movement of the interpreter. The anticipation of signification which determines the understanding of a text is not an act of subjectivity, but is determined by the community which connects us with tradition. (1960: 251, 277)

2.2 Is a Correct Interpretation Possible?

The ideal of interpretative correctness is based on the assumption of textual *monosemy* and emphasizes the importance of the author's intentions. Those who reject this ideal accept the principle of textual *polysemy* and focus mostly on the reader's perspective.

2.2.1 INTERPRETATION AS RECONSTRUCTION
The objectivist goal of a correct and objective interpretation was aimed at in a tradition from Schleiermacher (1838) (cf. Volp 1982), Dilthey (1900), and Betti (1962) to E. D. Hirsch (1967). The ideal of a true understanding, which implies the rejection of alternative interpretations, is pursued in the search for an original sense, corresponding to the author's intention. This goal seemed to be inherent in the theological and legal traditions of hermeneutics. (But the interpretation of laws already

has a traditional dimension of creativity, as Gadamer [1974: 1067] points out.)

For Schleiermacher, interpretation is a reconstruction of the author's thought. It is based on "the linguistic domain common to the author and his original public" and aims at the discovery of "the unity of the work, considered as the principle moving the author, and [at] the outlines of composition, considered as his characteristic nature apparent in that movement" (1838: 101, 167). Dilthey (1892) pursues the ideal of "objective interpretation" (cf. 1900: 320) in a poetics aiming at an explanation of the work on the basis of the psychology and biography of its author. The interpreter's hermeneutic activity is described as a reliving of the author's psychic condition. For Dilthey (cf. 1958: 315), the interpreter can achieve this reliving of the Other only by a referral to the experiences of his or her own Self. Dilthey's critic, Habermas, interprets this hermeneutic ideal of "reliving" as an equivalent of the objectivist ideal of scientific observation, a kind of a picture theory of truth (1968: 226).

The ideal of interpretative objectivity and the rejection of textual polysemy become a programmatic point of discussion in the hermeneutics of Betti (1962) and Hirsch (1967). Betti describes interpretation as the adequate reconstruction of an intended sense. While he acknowledges the role of the interpreter's subjectivity in this process, Betti wants to reduce this factor to a minimum and warns against "subjective arbitrariness," which might falsify the historically correct interpretation (1962: 49).

Hirsch tries to defend a theory of textual monosemy by introducing a distinction between meaning and significance: "*Meaning* is that which is represented by a text; it is what the author meant by his use of a particular sign

sequence; it is what the sign represents. *Significance*, on the other hand, names a relationship between that meaning and a person, or a conception, or a situation, or indeed anything imaginable" (1967: 8). From these premises, he concludes that a text has only one unchangeable meaning, while its significance may vary with time and situation.

2.2.2 PRODUCTIVE INTERPRETATION

Schleiermacher's and Dilthey's hermeneutics contained the germ of a view of interpretation transcending mere reproduction. This germ is the postulate that the goal of interpretation should be to understand better than the author himself (cf. Gadamer 1960: 180–85). However, this early topos of hermeneutics basically referred only to the interpreter's activities in raising unconscious processes to consciousness or to clarify the obscure in the text (cf. Bollnow 1949). It was not yet the acknowledgment of the principle of textual polysemy which has now become a topos of current text semiotic and other trends of research (cf. Kristeva's textual "polyphony," Eco's "open text," Barthes's "semiotropy," and Literature 3.3).

Within hermeneutics, the philosopher who comes closest to the acknowledgment of textual polysemy is Gadamer. While emphasizing the dependency of understanding on the horizons of the interpreter and his or her own historicity, Gadamer pleads for the recognition of the productivity of the hermeneutic situation: "Not only occasionally, but always does the sense of a text surpass its own author. Therefore understanding is not mere reproduction but always a productive behavior. [. . .] Understanding is in reality no better understanding [. . .]. It suffices to say that one understands *differently, if one understands at all*." (1960: 289, 280)

Rhetoric and Stylistics

Rhetoric, the ancient art of persuasion, and stylistics, its younger descendant, are programmatically included in the semiotic field by those who consider semiotics to be the discipline which studies the "life of signs within society" (cf. Saussure 2.1), those who define it as a "translinguistic" science of the text (cf. Barthes 5.), and those who follow Morris's project of a semiotics that transcends syntactics and semantics with pragmatics. Yet, although many have argued that text semiotics has become a modern successor of rhetoric and stylistics, few attempts at a semiotic foundation of those disciplines have been made so far. Also, their place within the sciences of discourse, particularly their relationship to poetics, often remains uncertain.

1. Grammar, Rhetoric, Poetics, and Stylistics

From its birth in Sicily in the fifth century B.C. until its alleged end in the the nineteenth century, rhetoric, in its relation to other sciences of discourse, passed through several phases of "splendor and misery" (see Kennedy 1963; 1972; 1980; 1983, Todorov 1977, Ueding & Steinbrink 1986, and the journal *Rhetorica* lff. [1983ff.] for the history of rhetoric).

1.1 Rhetoric and Poetics

Originally, rhetoric was the art and theory of public speech. Aristotle (ca. 335–34 B.C.) clearly distinguished this discipline from poetics and discussed both in separate treatises (cf., e.g., Herrick 1965). His poetics is a theory of literature, dealing with the epic, drama, and (only indirectly) lyric. The essence of poetry is characterized as *imitation* (cf. Literature 2.1), while *persuasion* is defined as the essence of rhetoric. In terms of semiotics, poetry is thus defined in its semantic and rhetoric in its pragmatic dimension.

The "degeneration" of rhetoric came with a shift of emphasis from a practical art of persuasion in social contexts to an art of mere eloquence or even of deceit. Within a narrower scope, rhetoric developed an elaborate system of ornaments of speech, the so-called rhetorical figures. As such, it took a new direction but also reached a new zenith as *literary rhetoric* (cf. Lausberg 1960). In this form, rhetoric from the thirteenth century until the Renaissance merged with poetics. In this tradition, some modern scholars still define poetics as a branch of rhetoric (cf. Arrivé 1979: J3).

1.2 Rhetoric, Grammar, and Logic

The medieval canon of the seven liberal arts comprised a trivium of three language arts:

grammar, dialectic (= the medieval logic), and rhetoric. While grammar was defined as the art of *correct* speech (*ars recte loquendi*), rhetoric was the theory and praxis of technically and morally *good* speech (*ars bene dicendi*) (cf. Lausberg 1960: 35–40).

In his *Rhetoric* (I, 1–2; II, 20, 22), Aristotle discusses both parallels and differences between the art of persuasion and logic, or dialectic: Both are concerned with methods of reasoning and argumentation. But the methods of giving evidence by means of induction or deduction (syllogism) are different. Logic obtains proofs by means of syllogisms based on premises from which conclusions follow by necessity. But in rhetoric, persuasion is often achieved by apparent proof only. Here, induction proceeds by giving factual or fictive examples, and deduction by incomplete syllogisms (cf. Lausberg 1960: 199–200), based on commonplaces or contingencies. Such rhetorical syllogisms are called *enthymemes*. (For a discussion of their basic forms see Barthes 1970a: 201–206.) Aristotle saw in the enthymeme "the most effective of the modes of persuasion" (I, 1).

1.3 Rhetoric and Stylistics

Ancient rhetoric included stylistics in the branch of *elocutio*. Traditionally, three styles (genera) were distinguished (in various versions; cf. Wimsatt & Brooks 1957: 102–103): the lofty or "sublime," the middle or common, and the plain style. But in a broader sense, ancient stylistics comprises the whole sphere of *elocutio*, in particular the rhetorical ornaments (*ornatus*) of tropes and figures. Significantly, these are now often referred to as stylistic figures.

Today, stylistics has been called "rhetoric's most direct heir" (Ducrot & Todorov 1972: 75) or a "modern rhetoric" (Guiraud 1954: 5; cf. Colin 1973). This judgment places stylistics in the tradition of a rhetoric restricted to the study of *ornatus*. Yet, rhetoric in its original, broader sense differs from stylistics in three typical respects: (1) While stylistics is basically concerned with textual surface structures, mostly variants of lexical and syntactic expression, rhetoric provides rules for the organization of a whole discourse. In this respect, rhetoric is more comprehensive than stylistics. (2) While stylistics is mostly interested in the language characterizing an individual author (or epoch), rhetoric is interested in rediscovering or even recommending structural patterns predetermined by a tradition of ancient norms. (This is why the Romantics opposed stylistic liberty to rhetorical constraints). In this respect, stylistics is more comprehensive than rhetoric because it deals with *any*, and not only traditional, textual features. (3) Rhetoric, with its interest in the effect of discourse on the audience, and stylistics, with its focus on textual uniqueness, focus on different phases of text pragmatics, namely, text reception and text production.

2. Rhetoric

The elaborate system of ancient rhetoric emphasized the pragmatic dimension of persuasive speech (for surveys of traditional rhetorics see Lausberg 1960, Kennedy 1963; 1972; 1980; 1983, Corbett 1965, McCroskey 1968, Barthes 1970a, Jens 1971, Ueding & Steinbrink 1986). Semiotic and other recent approaches to rhetoric either have shown a renewed interest in rhetorical pragmatics or have restricted themselves to the system of rhetorical figures.

2.1 The Pragmatic Dimension of Classical Rhetoric

Morris mentions rhetoric as "an early and restricted form of pragmatics" (1938: 30). To persuade and to convince the public were the pragmatic goals which orators wanted to achieve by means of rhetorical techniques. The functions of discourse and the phases of its production are pragmatic dimensions studied since classical rhetoric.

2.1.1 FUNCTIONS AND TYPOLOGY OF DISCOURSE

Pragmatic dimensions of persuasion were outlined in Aristotle's *Rhetoric* (I, 2). His distinction of three factors of effective persuasion, (a) "the personal character of the speaker," (b) "putting the audience into a certain frame of mind," and (c) "proof" or "subject," circumscribe the expressive, appellative, and referential functions of discourse (see Function 3.2). The appellative function is the dominant one. Aristotle distinguished three modes of appeal related to his three factors of persuasion as follows: (a) ethical appeal (ἦθος), (b) emotional appeal (πάθος), and (c) rational appeal (λόγος) (ibid.). Cicero reduced these to two: the emotional and the didactic function (*movere* and *docere*). Horace added the function of pleasure (*delectare*).

Pragmatic criteria are also the basis of Aristotle's typology of discourse (ibid.: I, 3): *Forensic* or *judiciary* discourse is directed to a judge. Its subject is accusation or defense. *Deliberative* discourse is directed to public assemblies, who are urged "either to do or not to do something." Advice or dissuasion is its appellative function. A discourse with the referential function of praise or censure is called *epideictic* speech.

2.1.2 PHASES OF DISCOURSE PRODUCTION

The system of ancient rhetoric consists of five parts, which correspond to five phases of discourse production:

(1) *Inventio* is the discovery of ideas and arguments. A system of topics (Gr. *topoi*, Lat. *loci*) provided aids for finding arguments and facts (cf. Curtius 1948, Barthes 1970a: 206–213). (2) *Dispositio* is the effective organization of a discourse. Roman rhetoricians recommended six parts: introduction (*exordium*), statement of case and facts (*narratio*), outline (*divisio*), arguments for (*confirmatio*) and against (*refutatio*) the case, and the conclusion (*peroratio*). (3) *Elocutio* is the choice of words and their syntactic arrangement. It is the field of style, tropes, and figures. (4) *Memoria* is the art and technique of memorizing a speech. The

two principal mnemotechnical devices were the association of ideas with places (*loci*) and with images (cf. Rossi 1960, Yates 1966, Blum 1969, Eco 1989). (5) *Pronuntiato* teaches the effective vocal and gestural delivery of discourse (see Gesture 2.3.3).

2.2 *The New Rhetoric: Current Trends*

The revival of rhetoric has led to various schools and trends in current research. For surveys and critical discussions see Steinmann, ed. (1967), McCroskey (1968: 289–302), Jens (1971), Johannesen, ed. (1971), Kopperschmidt (1973), Plett, ed. (1977), Rehbock (1980), Podlewski (1982), Ueding & Steinbrink (1986), and the yearbook *Rhetorik* 1ff. (1982ff.). Besides the literary and the explicitly semiotic approaches, the major trends of new rhetoric are:

1. The new rhetoric of I. A. Richards and K. Burke. In the context of literary theory, semantics, and social psychology, and in opposition to the rhetorical theories of persuasion, Richards redefines rhetoric as "a study of misunderstanding and its remedies" (1936: 3), while Burke (1950) defines it as "the conscious or unconscious use of verbal or nonverbal symbolic strategies to achieve identification between men" (in Johannesen, ed. 1971: 75).

2. The psychology of persuasive communication and communicational effectiveness (Hovland et al. 1953, Schramm, ed. 1963) and the new rhetoric based on communication theory (cf. Frank-Böhringer 1963, McCroskey 1968, Geißner 1969, Johannesen, ed. 1971: 50–62, Bormann 1980: 130–43).

3. The new rhetoric based on the audience-oriented theory of argumentation by Perelman & Olbrechts-Tyteca (1958).

4. The hermeneutic-critical rhetoric (Jens 1971, Kopperschmidt 1973, and in a philosophical tradition H. G. Gadamer, K.-O. Apel, and J. Habermas) focused on the conditions of rational argumentation in social-political interaction emphasizing the aim of rhetorical convincing instead of persuasion.

2.3 Semiotic Approaches to Rhetoric

Existing surveys (cf. Kaemmerling 1973, Chatman 1974, Dupriez 1986, Ueding & Steinbrink 1986: 168–70), readers (such as *Rhétoriques*, *Sémiotiques* [= *Revue d'Esthétique* 1979, no. 1/2]), special issues of journals (such as *Bulletin du groupe de recherches sémio-linguistiques* 20 [1981] and 26 [1983]), and critical discussions (Man 1979, Valesio 1980) of semiotic approaches to rhetoric have generally included approaches based on (text) linguistics (cf. Kalverkämper 1983) and particularly on structural semantics. The latter have dominated the discussion of the semiotics of rhetorical figures. A more recent theoretical topic of the semiotics of rhetoric is the discovery of the rhetoric of Peirce. Besides these theoretical studies there is a growing interest in applied analyses, particularly in the fields of the mass media.

2.3.1 SEMIOTICS OF RHETORICAL FIGURES

Since antiquity, attempts have been made to discover a semiotic system in the field of rhetorical figures. Quintilian first introduced the definition of the figure (and trope) as "a departure from the simple and straightforward method of expression" (*Inst. Orat.*, IX, 1, 3). This concept reappears in modern linguistic rhetoric (and stylistics; see 3.2) in definitions of figures as linguistic anomalies (cf. Todorov 1967: 108) or as a deviation from an ordinary *zero degree* of language (Dubois et al. 1970). In a more global perspective, semiotic theories have described this aspect of rhetorical deviation as the effect of a secondary code (cf. Barthes; 3.1) or as an instance of overcoding (see Eco 1976: 133, 155, 279), i.e., the establishment and generative application of rules which articulate more macroscopic portions of the text, on the basis of a first level of preestablished rules (see Code 3.3.4).

Quintilian also set up four general categories of deviation (*mutatio*) (ibid.: I, 5, 38–41), which reappear with modification in modern semiotic systems of rhetorical figures (Dubois et al. 1970, Plett 1975, Plett, ed. 1977): (1) addition of elements (*adjectio*; e.g., anaphora [= repetition at the beginning of phrases]), (2) omission (*detractio*; e.g., asyndeton [= omission of conjunctions]), (3) *rearrangement* (or permutation) (*transmutatio*; e.g., inversion or metathesis), and (4) *substitution* of elements (*immutatio*; e.g., metaphor, metonymy).

Another elementary ancient classification divided rhetorical figures into *schemes* and *tropes* (cf. Corbett 1965: 426): A scheme is a deviation from the ordinary patterns of words in sentences (as in Quintilian's categories [1] to [3]). A trope involves a semantic deviation (as in Quintilian's category [4]). The distinction underlying this classification can be correlated with the two dimensions of syntagmatic and paradigmatic relations (see Structure 2.1) and Morris's semiotic dimensions of syntactics and semantics. The latter categories are the basis of the typology of figures developed by Todorov (1967) and Bonsiepe (1966; cf. Plett 1975: 141). In addition, Kopperschmidt discusses pragmatic figures as the third semiotic typology (1973: 170).

Within the system of tropes, Jakobson (1956) considered metaphor and metonymy to be two prototypical figures. Dubois et al. (1970), Le Guern (1973), Eco (1976: 280), Shapiro & Shapiro (1976), Metz (1977: 149–297), and others followed Jakobson with this argument. Traditionally, metonymies ("name-changes") are explained as the substitution of a word x for another, y, where the referential objects of x and y are existentially or habitually connected, such as *crown* for 'king,' *White House* for 'U.S. President and his staff,' or *gold* for 'money.' Jakobson explains metaphors as substitutions by *similarity* and metonymies as substitutions by *contiguity* and relates these tropes to the paradigmatic and the syntagmatic axes of language (see Structure 2.1). (For a more comprehensive discussion of these interrelations, see Metz 1977: 187.)

One of the most elaborate semiotic systems of rhetorical figures was developed by the Liège Group μ (Dubois et al. 1970; cf. Merrell 1983). Its point of departure is an ideal *zero degree language*, a language determined by conventional expectations. Compared with this zero degree, rhetorical figures appear as deviations. The basic unit of deviation is defined as *metaboly*. The field of metabolies is further classified according to two categories of criteria, the linguistic level of deviation (basically: word or sentence) and the aspect of the sign (signifier or signified). The resulting categories of figures are *metaplasms* (phonetic or graphemic deviations on the word level, e.g., alliteration), *metataxes* (phonetic or graphemic deviations on the sentence level, e.g., ellipsis or inversion), *metasemes* (semantic deviations on the word level, e.g., metaphor or metonymy), and *metalogisms* (semantic deviations on the sentence level, e.g., irony).

Structural semantics is the method of Group μ rhetoric, but besides the traditional method of semantic feature analysis, which decomposes meanings into components basically derived from predications or definitions (e.g., *oak* = + plant, + tree, + fagaceae . . .), Group μ introduces two new principles of analysis: *conjunctive* feature analysis (e.g., *tree* = trunk + branches + leaves + roots . . .) and *disjunctive* feature analysis (e.g., *tree x* = oak *or* birch *or* willow . . .). On the basis of this system, Group μ defines the semantic (and other) deviations of figures with Quintilian's categories of (feature) adjunction, suppression, substitution, and permutation.

2.3.2 APPLIED STUDIES IN SEMIOTIC RHETORIC

The extension of semiotic analysis from the restricted field of *ornatus* to a broader scope of literary, textual, visual, and other phenomena has resulted in various applied studies. Within text semiotics, Valesio proposes a radical, threefold redefinition of rhetoric as (1) "the whole functional dimension of human discourse" (including any form of communication, even the unconscious one), (2) "an integrated structure" (including topoi, arguments, and figures), and (3) "not merely a technical linguistic description, but a philosophic alternative" (1980: 39).

In the semiotics of law, Schreckenberger (1978) developed a comprehensive semiotic

rhetoric of legal discourse. For a discussion of a legal rhetorics on the basis of the semiotics of Peirce, see also Podlewski (1982: 83–95). In the semiotics of film, Metz discusses the specific rhetorical *dispositio* of the film (1968: 117–19), and the visual rhetorical figures of film are studied by Kaemmerling (1971) and Metz (1977: 149ff.). In the semiotics of painting, Group μ has developed structuralist categories of a rhetoric of the image (Klinkenberg et al. 1980). For the rhetoric of visual tropes, see Metaphor (∅.) and Advertising (2.2).

In his critical studies of the mass media, Barthes discusses rhetoric as the semiotic counterpart of myth and ideology. Barthes defines rhetoric in a nonclassical way as "a set of fixed, regulated, insistent figures, according to which the varied forms of the mythical signifier arrange themselves" (1957: 150). One of seven figures by which he characterizes "the myth of the right" is tautology. ("It is that way because it is that way.") In his *Fashion System* (1967b: 225–75), Barthes studies the rhetorical system as a level of analysis which he characterizes as a semiotic in the sense of Hjelmslev: The rhetorical signifier is the phraseology through which the magazines strive to persuade; the rhetorical signified is the "ideology of fashion." More precisely, Barthes calls these signifiers of ideology "*connotators*" and the set of connotators a *rhetoric*, rhetoric thus appearing as the signifying aspect of ideology" (1964a: 92; 1964c: 49).

2.3.3 PEIRCEAN RHETORIC

A rhetoric on the basis of Peirce's semiotic is being rediscovered and developed further by Deledalle (1979: 157–67), Podlewski (1982), and Fry (1986). Peirce's triadic theory and typology of signs has been used as a model of interpretation for the system of rhetorical figures (cf. ibid., and Metaphor 4.3), but in partially as yet unpublished papers, Peirce also developed a pragmatic theory of rhetoric.

Peirce (§ 2.93) defined *speculative rhetoric* or *methodeutic* ("a method of discovering methods," § 2.108) as a theoretical science which constitutes one of the three branches of semiotics, besides speculative grammar and critical logic. While grammar studies signs (as "grounds" or "representamens") in their semiotic dimension of firstness, and logic studies their correlation with the object, and thus the dimension of secondness, rhetoric is concerned with the dimension of thirdness (see Peirce 1.4; 3.1) since it analyzes how signs are "rendered effective" as interpretants, i.e., in the minds of the interpreters.

Peirce described rhetoric as "the study of the necessary conditions of the transmission of meaning by signs from mind to mind, and from one state of mind to another" (§ 1.444), and as the study of "the formal conditions of the force of symbols, or their power of appealing to a mind" (§ 1.559). Since this outline describes a field which comprises the whole of Aristotelian rhetoric, pragmatics in the sense of Morris, and even psycho- and neurosemiotics, it is not surprising that for Peirce rhetoric "is destined to grow into a colossal doctrine which may be expected to lead to most important philosophical conclusions" (§ 3.454).

3. Stylistics

It has been argued that "it is difficult, if not impossible, to give a semiotic definition of style" (Greimas & Courtés 1979: 318), that style "has never been given a semiotic definition" (Klinkenberg 1986: 1023), and even that the analysis of the existing definitions of style leads to unsolvable aporias, which should result in the abandonment of the very concept (Gray 1969). Yet, if the scope of style and stylistics is restricted to its narrower sense, the notions of semiotic system or code, with their implications of choice, rule, and deviation, presuppose a stylistic dimension of semiosis. For general discussions and surveys of stylistics see Guiraud (1954; 1969; 1974), Enkvist et al. (1964), Ullmann (1966), Crystal & Davy (1969), Guiraud & Kuentz (1970), Todorov (1970a), Enkvist (1973), Sanders (1973), Spillner (1974), Hendricks (1976), Püschel

(1980), Müller (1981), Hervey (1982: 219–33), Schuh (1982), and Klinkenberg (1986). Relevant anthologies are Sebeok, ed. (1960), Freeman, ed. (1970), Chatman, ed. (1971), and Kachru & Stahlke, eds. (1972). A bibliography of stylistics is Bennett (1985). Its index contains references to 117 titles in the field of semiotic stylistics.

3.1 The Scope of Stylistics

A characterization of style, which would include such concepts as *deviation*, *addition*, and *choice*, defines it as the difference between alternative messages. Yet, besides this concept of stylistics and its many variants, style is often defined in a much broader sense (not used in this article). Hill, for example, defines stylistics as the study of language beyond the limits of the sentence (1958: 406). Stylistics thus covers the whole field of text linguistics. Others, in particular literary critics, have adopted definitions of style according to which the scope of stylistics is essentially coextensive with the field of poetics or the interpretation of literature (cf. Spillner 1974: 25–26). Such a broad concept of style is sometimes also the basis of semiotic approaches which discuss the whole field of text semiotics under the heading of stylistics (cf. Blanchard's [1975] "semiostyles," Kirstein 1982, and Schuh 1982).

On the other hand, style and stylistics are not restricted to language or literature. Defined as the difference between alternative messages, style depends on the code. Hence, codes, such as painting, architecture, or fashion, presuppose their own styles (cf. Uspenskij 1971a: 445). This makes style a pansemiotic phenomenon, even if the identification of stylistics and (text) semiotics is rejected.

In an even more pansemiotic view (also adopted by Bureau 1976: 12), Granger, in his "philosophy of style," locates style at the very roots of semiosis and even of human praxis in general. Defining semiosis as a process of work, in which obstacles have to be overcome during the transformation of the amorphous into the structured and of content into form,

Granger describes style as the "individual's mode of integration" into this very process of structuring (1968: 8). Yet, this assumption of an omnipresence of style in every act of semiosis presupposes the communicators' permanent consciousness of the semiotic alternatives to their choices which constitute this style. This unlikely view of semiosis and style can be modified by the ontological assumption of style as a potential structure (q.v. 3.4) in the act of semiosis.

3.2 Semiotic Criteria of Style

According to Barthes (1971b), two semiotic dichotomies have traditionally determined the concept of style, content vs. form (style as *elocutio*, ornament, or "dress," thus: form) and code vs. message (style as a deviation of the message from the coded norm). In both cases, style is connected with some semiotic difference, be it an addition or a deviation.

But what is the semiotic basis on which stylistic features can be determined as a difference? Some have assumed a norm (cf. Fricke 1981) against which the stylistic feature is a deviation, be it everyday language, one of its subcodes, or an abstract code (for a typology see Spillner 1974: 31–40). Some have postulated a neutral or stylistically unmarked (cf. Enkvist 1973: 15) zero degree level of language (cf. 2.3.1). Others have argued that only the (con)text (Riffaterre 1959; 1971) or the semiotic function establishes such a norm. (For the latter theory see Doležel & Kraus 1972 on the Prague School theory of functional styles.) Still others have rejected the norm-deviation dichotomy altogether in order to describe style autonomously as "the internal characteristic of a type of discourse" (Todorov 1970a: 226) or as a language use with a (transformational) grammar of its own (cf. Spillner 1974: 40–45). Those who are willing to abandon the possibility of finding a zero degree language have to accept a variable basis for a differential determination of style(s). A general definition under these premises could describe style as the difference between alternative messages.

3.3 The Semiotic Dimensions of Stylistics

Style has been approached in terms of different elements in the process of semiosis and on different levels of the code. There is a partial overlap of criteria in a taxonomy of concepts of style according to the dimensions of semiosis.

3.3.1 PRAGMATIC APPROACHES

From the pragmatic perspective, style is studied in terms of the participants of semiosis. With respect to the process of encoding, style has been described in the categories of selection or choice (e.g., Prieto 1975a: 99–100; cf. Spillner 1974: 45–49 for a survey). In the tradition of so-called genetic stylistics (cf. Guiraud 1967), these stylistic choices were interpreted as being determined by the author's psychological, sociological, or cultural constitution. Under the motto "Style is man," stylistic features were taken as indexical signs of the author and his time (cf. Thoma 1976: 130–37).

Several authors have analyzed style with respect to the process of decoding, either as their dominant perspective or as one complementary (cf. Spillner 1974: 64) to stylistic encoding. A most consistent stylistics of encoding was developed by Riffaterre (1959; 1971), based on elements of information theory and behavioristic ideas of structural linguistics. Riffaterre proposes to study stylistic effects from the reactions of an average reader, whose activity of decoding is determined by expectations and thus predictabilities of new message elements. Such patterns of expectation exist due to language and genre norms as codes *a priori*, but they are also built up within an individual text, where they form a code *a posteriori* (cf. Riffaterre 1971: 78). Based on these assumptions, Riffaterre defines a *stylistic stimulus* as an element of surprise being the effect of a (con)textually unpredictable, pattern-disrupting element (1959: 171). The basic assumptions of this theory are related to the principles of automatization and deautomatization (or foregrounding) which the Russian Formalists postulated as general determinants of poetry and aesthetics (see Poetry 1.3).

3.3.2 SEMANTIC AND SYNTACTIC APPROACHES

In the semantic perspective, Doležel & Kraus define style as "the study of alternative modes of expressing the same (or approximately the same) content" (1972: 37). The controversial point in this and similar definitions is, of course, the problem of semantic sameness. Linguists are confronted with the same problem when discussing the semantics of synonyms and paraphrases (cf. Spillner 1974: 23). As a solution to this semantic problem of style, Koch (1963) has proposed to acknowledge both sameness and difference in meaning. Accordingly, alternative semiotic items have a common semantic core but also a difference in meaning, which Koch calls the *semantic differential*. It is this differential which constitutes the semantic essence of style.

Several proposals have been made to give semantic interpretations of the stylistic differential in general. Bally defined style as the study of the expressive ("affective") value of language, in contradistinction to its nonstylistic referential ("intellectual") function (1909: 1). Riffaterre continues this tradition when he defines style as "an emphasis (expressive, affective or aesthetic) added to the information conveyed by the linguistic structure" (1959: 155). Hjelmslev founded a semiotic tradition according to which the stylistic differential is a connotative semiotics (1943: 114; cf. Kerbrat-Orecchioni 1977: 94–103).

Syntactic approaches to stylistics were for some time inspired by the model of generative grammar (for a survey see Spillner 1974: 40–45), where stylistic features of sentences were defined on the basis of transformational rules operating on a stylistically neutral deep structure. A syntagmatic approach is also implicit in Riffaterre's contextual view of style. But ultimately, a syntagmatic approach to style is not possible without the paradigmatic dimension of semiosis (see Structure 2.1). Style is a matter both of selection and of combination.

Literature

The semiotics of literature studies the specifics of literary signs and systems. A survey of the state of the art in literary semiotics shows that research in this field overlaps especially with poetic and aesthetic semiotics. Also, literary semiotics is not always clearly distinguished from text semiotics as a whole. This chapter will focus on semiotic theories of *literariness*, the specific features of literature. Other topics concerning particular literary genres (see Poetry, Narrative, Theater) and individual semiotic approaches to literature (e.g., see Hjelmslev 4., Greimas, Kristeva) are therefore excluded from the following discussion.

1. Literature and Semiotics: State of the Art

Semiotics of literature has its roots in linguistics and structuralism since Russian Formalism. In spite of a great variety of semiotic approaches to literature, literary semiotics is only one among several other modern theories of literature. The divergence of semiotic schools and traditions has prevented a general consensus about the essence of literature.

1.1 Semiotics, Poetics, and Theories of Literature

The field of literary research is particularly open both as a discipline and with respect to theories and methods.

1.1.1 POETICS AND THEORY OF LITERATURE

Literary scholarship is an activity whose "scientific" character and designation as a discipline have been a topic of permanent debate (cf. Culler 1982: 21–28). While the discipline is officially called literary science (*Literaturwissenschaft*) in Germany, the Anglo-American tradition usually prefers the more modest designation of literary criticism. Todorov (1968: 69), in continuation of the Aristotelian tradition, proposes a science of literature under the designation of *poetics* (a term which others, e.g., Preminger, ed. 1965: 639, Kloepfer 1975: 24, prefer to restrict to the field of poetry). Scholarly discourse about literature, as Todorov points out (1968: xxi–ii), has traditionally taken two directions, exegesis (or interpretation; cf. Hermeneutics) and theory. The semiotics of literature is a theory of literature (or a group of theories), but in its application it becomes a method of exegesis.

1.1.2 SEMIOTIC APPROACHES TO LITERATURE

The boundaries between semiotic and non-semiotic approaches to literature are particularly fluid. Several reviews of the state of the art in literary semiotics include theories of literature which are not usually characterized as "semiotic" by their authors. Examples are van Dijk's (e.g., 1972) generative poetics and S. J. Schmidt's (e.g., 1973; 1974; 1980) philosophy of literary communication, both presented as prominent semiotic theories of literature in reviews by Kloepfer (1977a) and in Helbo, ed. (1979). Such reviews tend to convey the impression that the theory and semiotics of literature are coextensive fields. Yet, there are major theoretical trends in literary scholarship which prefer to describe their own approaches as being separate from semiotics, e.g., *reception theory* (cf. Holub 1984), or even opposed to semiotics, e.g., poststructuralism (cf. Young, ed. 1981) and deconstruction (cf. Culler 1982, Norris 1982; cf. Structuralism 4.3), even though others have discovered affinities between these theories and the foundations of semiotics (e.g., Culler 1981a; 1982). Faced with this vagueness of the field of literary semiotics, this chapter will primarily discuss studies which have explicitly placed their approach in the framework of semiotics.

1.1.3 BETWEEN LINGUISTICS AND LITERARY CRITICISM

Since its origins, literary semiotics has been situated between linguistics and literary criticism. Some early semioticians of literature have opposed their approaches to those of literary critics. Barthes (1963: chap. III; 1964b: 249–54; 1966b), for example, attacks "academic" historical criticism, while Koch (1971a; b) and Wienold (1972: 27) define literary semiotics as a *meta*theory of literature and literary criticism, not opposed to but essentially different from the latter. But literary criticism and theory soon accepted and adopted semiotics as a method of literary research (e.g., Plett 1975, Fokkema & Kunne-Ibsch 1977, Bohn, ed. 1980). Within literary scholarship, the "semiotic trend" has already resulted in a number of "semiotic" studies whose semiotic substratum is hardly perceivable (e.g., Hantsch 1975). Within linguistics,

the closest neighbor of literary semiotics, and also concerned with the analysis of literary texts, is text linguistics. For text linguistic approaches to literature see Ihwe, ed. (1971), Dijk (1972), Ihwe (1972a), Hendricks (1973), Dijk & Petöfi, eds. (1977).

1.2 The State of the Art

The state of the art in literary semiotics has been reviewed in the following general surveys covering the various schools and mostly including semiotic theories of narrative and poetry since structuralism and Russian Formalism: Scholes (1974), Blanchard (1975), Brütting (1975), Culler (1975; 1981a), Todorov (1975), Wittig (1976), Hawkes (1977), Mignolo (1978), Cerisola (1980), Fellinger (1980), Oldani (1981), Garrido Gallardo (1982), and Tiefenbrun (1984). Several surveys review the state of the art in various countries (Fokkema & Kunne-Ibsch 1977, Helbo, ed. 1979), in Italy (Kapp, ed. 1973, Segre 1979a), in Germany (Kloepfer 1977a, Schmitter 1980), in France (Arrivé 1979; 1982a), or in Spain (Garrido Gallardo 1982).

Besides the various schools of semiotics which have developed their own approach to literature (discussed elsewhere, esp. Hjelmslev 4., Soviet Semiotics, Barthes, Greimas, Kristeva, Eco), several other authors have made general contributions to the semiotics of literature, either in the form of original models of literary semiotics or in pluralistic attempts at a synthesis: Wienold (1972) develops a pragmatic theory of literary text processing. Pignatari (1974), Köller (1980), Eco & Sebeok, eds. (1983), and Johansen (1986a) develop Peircean categories within literary semiotics. Nöth (1980) and Koch (1986c) propose the study of literature on the basis of a transdisciplinary world-text model. MacCannell & MacCannell (1982) discuss the literary sign from the Saussurean perspective. Antezana (1977), Corti (1978), and Marchese (1981) have published introductions to literary semiotics. Segre (1973; 1979a) and Talens et al. (1978) give a pluralistic perspective of the field.

Applied literary semiotic research is documented in several collective volumes and individual monographs. Among the former are Koch, ed. (1976; 1979), Chatman et al., eds. (1979: 583–730), Eschbach & Rader, eds. (1980), Steiner, ed. (1981b), Borbé, ed. (1984: 681–1058), and Oehler, ed. (1984: 453–526). Monographs with literary semiotic analyses are Arrivé (1972), Coquet (1973), Rastier (1973), Segre (1973; 1979b; c; 1980), Avalle (1975), Hardt (1976), Finter (1980), Norrman & Haarberg (1980), Nöth (1980), Tiefenbrun (1980), Carillo (1982), Scholes (1982), Hess-Lüttich (1984), Maddox (1984), and Janik (1985).

1.3 Literature and Literariness

In 1921, Jakobson postulated the following Formalist objective of literary research (quoted in Ejxenbaum 1927: 8): "The object of study in literary science is not literature but 'literariness,' that is, what makes a given work a *literary* work." With this programmatic postulate, Jakobson, as Scholes puts it, "delivered us from 'literature' as an absolute category. 'Literariness,' he has taught us, is found in all sorts of utterances, some of which are not especially literary. And a 'literary work' is simply one in which literariness is dominant" (1982: 19).

The search for literariness has developed in two directions. The first direction assumes a "qualitative difference" (Corti 1978: 50) between literature and nonliterary language which, for some, is even describable by an autonomous grammar (Dijk 1972: 200). Some of the features which have been considered to be specific to literature will be discussed in the following sections. The second direction in the search for literariness has rejected the assumption of a literary grammar as a fallacy (Pratt 1977) because all features which have been described as specifically literary are to be found in other types of discourse as well. Greimas & Courtés, for example, therefore "consider the concept of literariness [. . .] as void of meaning," but nevertheless "grant it, on the other hand, the status of a social connotation" (1979: 178). This solution moves literariness from the dimension of syntax and semantics to that of pragmatics. Such theories are discussed in the context of poeticalness (see Poetry 3.) and aesthetics (q.v. 3.).

---

2. Literariness as a Special Mode of Reference

Implicitly semiotic interpretations of literariness can be traced back to early theories of aesthetics defining the distinctive feature of literature as a particular relation between the literary sign and its referential object. There are three major theories of a specific referential function of literature, the thesis of literary *iconicity* and its antitheses, literary *autonomy* and literary *fictionality*.

2.1 Literary Iconicity

The thesis of iconicity in literature has both traditional and modern variants (see also Morris's theory of the aesthetic sign in Aesthetics 2.2).

2.1.1 LITERATURE AS MIMESIS

Ancient theories of mimesis (Auerbach 1946, Abrams 1953, Lyons & Nichols, eds. 1982) represent the earliest theories of literary iconicity. Socrates illustrated the mimetic, i.e., imitative, function of literature by means of a mirror (Plato, *Republic* X, 596). By this demonstration of mimesis, literature is characterized as an icon of the depicted world.

Ut pictura poesis, "Poetry is like painting." By this thesis, Horace (*Ars poetica*, 361) founded another tradition of literary mimesis. The discussion of the classical thesis of affinity between painting and literature reaches a climax with Lessing's *Laokoon* (1766). Lessing developed an implicitly semiotic theory of literary iconicity (cf. Bayer 1975, Todorov 1977: 129–48, Gebauer, ed. 1984, Wellbery 1984). In his letter to F. Nicolai of 5–26–1769, Lessing wrote:

> Poetry must necessarily seek to raise its signs from arbitrary to natural ones [. . .]. The means by

which it achieves this are: the sound of words, the order of words, length of syllables, figures and tropes, comparisons, etc. All these things bring the arbitrary signs closer to the natural ones [. . .]. The highest genre of poetry is the one which transforms arbitrary signs wholly into natural signs. This is the drama, for in drama words cease to be arbitrary signs and become *natural* signs of arbitrary things.

In this manifesto, Lessing interprets literariness on the basis of a semiotic theory of arbitrariness and relates ideas about degrees of iconicity to corresponding degrees of literariness. The highest iconicity, and with it literariness, is represented by drama, since acting and speaking on the stage appear as the best possible icon of human actions (cf. Theater 3.3.2). Because of the arbitrariness of language, the other literary genres, according to Lessing, have a lower degree of literariness.

2.1.2 LOTMAN'S THEORY OF LITERARY ICONICITY

A modern semiotic variant of literary iconicity is proposed by Lotman (1970; cf. Soviet Semiotics 3.). Based on the premise "that signs in art are iconic and representational rather than conventional," Lotman concludes that in verbal art a sign (as expression) is the model of its content and that in literature a "semantization of the extra-semantic (syntactic) elements of natural language occurs under these conditions" (1970: 21). By this process of semantization of elements on the expression plane, the literary text, according to Lotman, is characterized as a secondary modeling system. On the basis of language, the primary system, literature acquires a supplementary secondary structure in iconic relation to its primary structure. The thesis of literature as a secondary semiotic system is also maintained in French literary semiotics. For further aspects of Lotman's literary semiotics, see Aesthetics (4.2).

2.1.3 APORIAS OF LITERARY ICONICITY

In their discussion of literary iconicity, theorists have often been vague about the component of the literary sign which they claim to be an icon. Is the expression or the content of the literary sign an icon of the depicted world? In either case the thesis would be strictly untenable. On the expression plane, icons actually occur only in onomatopoeic language use. On the content plane, optimum iconicity is also typical of descriptive or scientific language. In any case, there is a rather loose concept of the terms which are said to be related iconically in literature.

2.2 Literary Self-Referentiality

The literary work refers to itself. This thesis has been discussed under such labels as *autonomy* (Mukařovský, Jakobson), *autonymy* (Rey-Debove 1971; 1974), and *auto-reflexivity* (Eco 1968: 145). Literary self-referentiality is related to the more general aesthetic and the more particular poetic autonomy. Its theoretical origin is the classical *l'art-pour-l'art* aesthetics. In the history of English literature, the thesis was defended from A. Pope ("poem *per se* . . . written solely for the poem's sake") to T. S. Eliot ("considering poetry . . . primarily as poetry and not another thing") (cf. Abrams 1953: 27).

In the tradition of literary semiotics, the thesis of literary self-referentiality was discussed in Russian Formalism, Prague Structuralism, and French text semiotics. Barthes, for example, defends this thesis when he argues that the literary author's "raw material becomes in a sense its own end" and that "literature is at bottom a tautological activity, like that of those cybernetic machines constructed for themselves" (1964b: 144). Criticism of the theory of literary self-referentiality has come from various directions. Besides those who reject self-referentiality as a semiotic contradiction in terms (e.g., Laferrière 1979: 309), many refuse to accept the argument that literariness should not also consist in reference to extraliterary reality.

2.3 Fictional Reference

The literary text has no reference because the agents and objects depicted in it have no real-world existence. This thesis (critically discussed by Arrivé 1972: 16 and Lavis 1971) is the point of departure of theories which take the criterion of fictionality as the distinguishing feature of literature. (For a comprehensive discussion of the semantics of fictionality, see Gabriel 1975, Cebik 1984).

2.3.1 LITERATURE AND TRUTH

From the point of view of logical semantics, the referential relation of literary statements has been characterized as lacking truth value and the possibility of empirical verification (cf. Dijk 1972: 336). (For a comprehensive discussion of the semantics of fictionality, see Gabriel 1975.) This negative characterization of literariness, however, requires modifications. Reichenbach restricts the lack of truth value in literature to its factual statements, arguing that "the *laws* assumed for the behavior of the fictitious persons should be *objectively true*" (1947: 282). For Mukařovský, reference is only a secondary function of a literary text, subordinate to its primary aesthetic function (1936: 70–77). However, in literature, reference occurs to "systems of values." Stankiewicz, too, describes "the requirement to relate subject matter to external referents" as "a side line of literary interpretation" (1960: 72).

2.3.2 THE IMAGINARY, "AS IF,"
AND POSSIBLE WORLDS

Todorov ascribes to literature an *imaginary reference* (1967: 117), and Arrivé characterizes the referent of the literary text as a *simulacrum* (1972: 17–18). In a related tradition, Hamburger calls the referential world of literature an "appearance of reality," or an "as-structure" (1957: 55; cf. also Lüthe 1974). Merrell relates the "as-if" view of the literary text to Coleridge's "willing suspension of disbelief" (1982: 88). Finally, Pavel (1976) has resumed the discussion of the semantic autonomy of literary worlds from the point of view of *possible-world semantics*.

2.3.3 PRAGMATIC VIEWS OF FICTIONALITY

From a pragmatic perspective, literariness is analyzed with reference to the author's inten-

tion and the reader's way of interpreting the text. Schmidt ascribes to the literary text a merely potential reference which lacks unequivocal instructions for exhaustive referential mappings onto particular communicative situations (1974: 81). Accordingly, the literary text is polyfunctional and permits reference to several extratextual contexts. Similarly, Gabriel defines fiction as a "non-assertive discourse which does not claim to be capable of making any reference or of being fulfilled" (1975: 27–28). A positive characterization of the pragmatics of literature is given by Segre: Literature "maintains its communicative potential also outside of its pragmatic context: in the literary text an *introjection* of contextual referents occurs, so that the reader can derive these from the text itself" (1979b: 35). (On this thesis see also Marchese 1981: 41.)

3. Literariness as a Structure of Meaning

Semantic definitions of literariness ascribe to literature levels of meaning beyond its primary, textual meaning. Such semantic structures exemplify a phenomenon which Lotman has discussed as *secondary coding*. In generalization of the more particular phenomena of figurative discourse (see Rhetoric 2.3.1) and metaphor, literary semiotics has discussed this semantic feature of literature under the heading of *connotation*. An extension of the theory of literary connotation is that of literary *polysemy*.

3.1 Secondary Meaning as Secondary Coding

Literary connotation and polysemy are a particular case of what Lotman describes more generally as secondary coding (cf. Soviet Semiotics 3.): "Literature speaks in a special language which is superimposed as a secondary system on natural language. Literature is accordingly defined as a secondary modeling system. [. . .] Literature possesses an exclusive, inherent system of signs [. . .] which serve to transmit special messages, nontransmittable by other means" (1970: 21).

3.2 *Connotation as Semantic Feature of Literariness*

Attempts to characterize literature as a language of connotation have led to contentious debates in literary semiotics. For the concept of connotation, see also Meaning (5.2).

3.2.1 FOR CONNOTATION

Connotation (cf. Prieto 1975b: 61–75, Kerbrat-Orecchioni 1977, Rössler 1979) was first discussed as a feature of literariness within the literary theory of glossematics (discussed in Hjelmslev 4.). In the simplified model proposed by Barthes, the principle of connotation became widely adopted in literary semiotic studies (e.g., Todorov 1967: 29–37, Arrivé 1972: 19, 99, Lipski 1976, Segre 1979b: 40). As Barthes pointed out, the secondary content of a connotative sign is added to its primary, denotative content (unlike in metaphor, where primary and secondary contents are usually incompatible in spite of being similar in origin). When, for example, the "cat" in Baudelaire's poem connotes 'voluptuousness,' this content element is part of a secondary connotative system. The connotation extends beyond the primary denotative level of meaning (at which "the cat" denotes 'the feline pet') but still includes the latter.

The sphere of connotations turns out to be unlimited if it is extended from lexicalized and culturally codified secondary meanings to individual associations of ideas (cf. Kerbrat-Orecchioni 1977). Most semioticians have therefore excluded individual, noncodified associations from the class of connotative signs (e.g., Todorov 1967: 30, Barthes 1970b: 14–15). Typologies of connotative signs (cf. Greimas 1970: 93–102, Kerbrat-Orecchioni 1977, Rössler 1979) include dialects, sociolects, idiolects (characterizing individual authors), styles, and cultural symbols (see also Meaning 5.2).

The signifier of a connotative sign can be an element of language or a nonlinguistic object, which, in literature, would be represented linguistically.

3.2.2 AGAINST CONNOTATION

The vagueness of the concept of connotation and the ubiquity of connotations even outside of literature (see, e.g., Myth, Ideology, and Advertising) have resulted in criticism or even in the rejection of connotations as a factor of literariness (cf. Barthes 1970b: 13 and Barthes 1.–2., Gary-Prieur 1971, Spinner 1980, Arrivé 1982a: 137–38). The problem of conceptual *vagueness* is apparent when connotations are characterized in definitions such as "everything which a term can distinctly or vaguely evoke, suggest, excite or imply in every language user individually" (Martinet 1967: 1290). At any rate, since connotations, according to Barthes, are "meanings which are neither in the dictionary nor in the grammar of the language" (1970b: 15), it is evident that connotative analysis cannot hope to reach the scientific standards of precision of lexicology or linguistic syntax.

Another problem with the semiotics of connotation is the impossibility of a clear-cut dividing line between primary denotations and secondary connotations. This problem led some semioticians of literature to abandon the distinction altogether or even to declare that "everything in the text is connotation, including the denotation" (Gary-Prieur 1971: 103; cf. also the revision of the concept by Barthes in Barthes 2.). This criticism of the denotation-connotation dichotomy does not imply the desire to return to the myth of the "definitive text." It is rather an affirmation of the principle of literary polysemy.

3.3 *Literary Polysemy*

The characterization of literature as a polysemic message can be interpreted as an extension of the principle of literary connotation. Corti summarizes this theory as follows:

Every text can support an incalculable number of decodifications or destructuralizations; in effect, every text is many texts in that the very nature of its polysemic complexity prevents identically repetitive readings even in the same cultural context. This explains [. . .] why in our era there has arisen the conception of readings as *variations of a basic invariant*, that is, the text. (1978: 42)

A variant of the theory of literary polysemy is Kristeva's and Bakhtin's theory of the literary text as a *polyphonous* structure. These theories are only one step away from the literary theory of deconstruction (see Structuralism 4.3).

4. Systemic Characteristics of the Literary Text

Closure and openness are two apparently incompatible features which have both been discussed as characteristic of the literary text (cf. Arrivé 1982a: 134–36).

4.1 Closure

Kristeva develops the thesis of the closure of the literary text (1969c: 113–42; cf. Arrivé 1972: 13–16). She sees closure on two levels, those of *story* and of *discourse* (cf. Narrative 1.3). At the level of story, Kristeva discovers closure because by its narrative logic the literary text implies its own end from its very beginning (1969c: 117). The end is present in embryo from the beginning of the literary text. The "oppositional dyads" of action (cf. Narrative 3.1.2) strive toward their logical solution at the end of a narrative (ibid.: 119).

At the level of discourse, Kristeva discovers a *compositional closure* (1969c: 138–39). This type of closure is most evident where the text has explicit boundary signals, e.g., by the words *beginning* and *end*. However, "the explicit termination of a fictional text can often be missing or ambiguous or implicit. But this incompleteness nevertheless underlines the structural closure of the text" (ibid.). Although Kristeva mostly refers to literature in general,

her analyses are concerned only with narrative texts. For the structural closure of poetry see, in addition, B. H. Smith (1968).

4.2 Openness

If one accepts Bremond's principle of alternative functions in narratives (see Narrative 3.1.2), the very logic of action does not mean closure, as Kristeva argues, but implies openness to those countless possibilities of action which guarantee the reader's suspense (cf. Koch 1985). Against the argument of logical closure, Eco (1962; 1979) thus develops the thesis of an "open logic of signifiers [. . .] by which the work fulfills its double function of stimulating interpretations and of controlling the free space of interpretations" (Eco 1968: 162; cf. Aesthetics 4.1.2).

Greimas has indicated two sources of the literary text, the *intertextual* (cf. Kristeva 2.3) and the *semantic universe*: "Every poetic object is thus open toward the universe of poetic forms and has existence only within this universe. The poetic object is, on the other hand, open toward its context, toward the semantic universe" (1972: 22). The thesis of literary openness is closely connected with the analytic shift of perspective from the author's to the reader's perception of the text. Openness characterizes the reader's processes of interpretation. Owing to "a fundamental ambiguity of the aesthetic message it is a constant factor of every work from every time" (Eco 1962: 11; cf. Poetry 2.2.3).

4.3 Dialectics of Openness and Closure

Yet, openness and closure, according to Eco (1979), are not contradictory but rather complementary characterizations of the artistic text referring to different aspects of literary semiosis. While openness characterizes the reader's interpretative potential and activity, closure describes the author's communicative effort, because the author

presents a finished product with the intention that this particular composition should be appreciated and received in the same form as he devised it. [. . .] A work of art, therefore, is a complete and *closed* form in its uniqueness as a balanced organic whole, while at the same time constituting an *open* product on account of its susceptibility to countless different interpretations. (1979: 49)

5. Dynamics of Evolution and Evaluation

Literature is not a static category. The predicate of literariness characterizes aesthetic evaluation, and such evaluations may change with cultures and times. Originally nonliterary (e.g., religious) texts have after centuries been evaluated as literary, and originally literary texts may lose their literariness with time (Lotman 1970: 287–88). Especially radical changes of literary evaluation have been demonstrated by the modern literary avant-garde, where among other texts, cooking recipes have been raised to the status of literariness (cf. Nöth 1977a; 1978a). For these and other evolutionary aspects of literariness, see System (3.2).

Poetry and Poeticalness

The semiotics of poetry and of the more general phenomenon of *poeticalness* is an interdisciplinary project of linguistics (cf. Levin 1962, Cohen 1966, Koch 1966, Baumgärtner 1969, Greimas, ed. 1972, Delas & Filliolet 1973, Kloepfer 1975, Shapiro 1976, Pelletier 1977, Oomen 1979, Posner 1982, Hoffstaedter 1986) and literary theory (cf. Culler 1975, Arrivé 1979, Hardt 1976). The semiotic study of poetry in the narrower sense is part of the semiotics of literature. Poetry is also sometimes the topic of studies under the title of semiotics and poetics (Kloepfer 1975, Hardt 1976), but for others (cf. Todorov 1968, Culler 1975), poetics covers the whole field of literature (cf. Rhetoric 1.1). Poeticalness is also defined as a more general phenomenon of semiosis, occurring in and outside of literature and even outside of language (see, e.g., Film; cf. Ejxenbaum, ed. 1927). Jakobson defined it as a pansemiotic phenomenon (1960: 351). In this wider sense, the semiotics of poeticalness converges with semiotic aesthetics. These manifold points of contact make it impossible to delimit poeticalness clearly from the related areas of the semiotic field.

Two fundamental positions have basically dominated the semiotic debate on the essence of the poetic (cf. Koch 1983). One considers poeticalness a textual function or a mode of communication; the other describes it as a textual structure. For the integration of both principles within one semiotic model of poeticalness, see 3.

1. Functional Views of Poetry and Poeticalness

Pure functionalist views of poeticalness reject the assumption of a poetic language having characteristic structural features (cf. Pratt's [1977] and Posner's [1982: 125] arguments against the "poetic language fallacy"). Instead, the theory of the poetic function (cf. Pelletier 1977) defines poeticalness as a specific act of communication. In the functionalist view, poeticalness is not a matter of syntax and semantics, but one of pragmatics.

Semiotic research in poeticalness was initiated by Roman Jakobson. He was the dominant proponent of a functionalist view of the poetic. In Jakobson's view, however, the functional explanation of poeticalness was not irreconcilable with a structural principle, which he proposed at the same time. Jakobson's functionalist views are closely related to theories of poeticalness developed by the Russian Formalists and Prague structuralists (q.v.).

1.1 Poetry and Poeticalness

In continuation of the Formalist search for literariness (see Literature 1.3), Jakobson (1933a) introduced the concept of poeticalness. For him, *poeticalness* was a synonym of *poetic function*, the definition of which Jakobson later discussed more extensively in his famous paper on linguistics and poetics (1960). Both concepts are clearly distinguished from that of poetry. According to Jakobson,

> the concept of *poetry* is unstable and tied to specific times, but *poeticalness* [. . .] is an element sui generis, [. . .] usually the component of a complex structure, yet a component which necessarily transforms the other elements. [. . .] Whenever poeticalness, the poetic function, becomes dominant in a literary work, we speak of poetry. (1933a: 123–24)

In this view, poeticalness is a general semiotic phenomenon which may occur to various degrees as a function of any text. Poetry, on the other hand, presupposes poeticalness, but, in addition, the evaluation of a text as poetry depends on literary conventions of a given epoch. Jakobson therefore concluded: "The linguistic study of the poetic function must overstep the limits of poetry, and, on the other hand, the linguistic scrutiny of poetry cannot limit itself to the poetic function" (1960: 357).

1.2 The Poetic Function

In accordance with the semiotic theory of literary and aesthetic autonomy, Jakobson defined the poetic message as *autotelic*, i.e., as having no other function besides itself. At the same time, Jakobson repudiated the critique of aestheticism raised against his position. The poetic, in this view, has certain affinities with metalanguage.

1.2.1 THE AUTOTELIC MESSAGE
According to Jakobson, poeticalness "manifests itself in that the word is perceived as a word, and not only as a mere substitute for the named object or as an outburst of feeling. [. . .] Poetic words and their combination [. . .] are not indifferent indices of reality, but they attain their own importance and independent value" (1933a: 124). And in his classical manifesto on poeticalness, Jakobson states: "The set (*Einstellung*) toward the MESSAGE as such, focus on

the message for its own sake, is the POETIC function of language. [. . .] Poetic function is not the sole function of verbal art but only its dominant, determining function, whereas in all other verbal activities it acts as a subsidiary, accessory constituent" (1960: 356).

1.2.2 THE SOCIAL DIMENSION
The theory of poetic autonomy has often been criticized for being aestheticistic and for neglecting the social dimension of the poetic. Jakobson countered such objections with reference to his distinction between poetry and poeticalness, and more generally between art and the aesthetic. It is poetry that changes with social reality, not the poetic function:

> It is said that the formalist school of literature does not understand the relation between art and social life. Allegedly it proclaims the ism of l'art pour l'art following in the footsteps of Kant's aesthetics. [. . .] Neither Tynjanov, nor Mukařovský, nor Šklovskij nor I myself proclaim the self-sufficiency of art. But we emphasize to the contrary that art is a constituent part of the social system, an element in connection with other elements, a variable element, because both the sphere of art and its relation to the other sectors of social structure are in a permanent dialectical change. What we emphasize is not the separatism of art, but the autonomy of the aesthetic function. (1933a: 123)

1.2.3 THE POETIC AND THE METALINGUISTIC
In Jakobson's theory, the poetic function is both opposed and similar to the metalinguistic function (see Function 3.2). Both similarity and difference are apparent with respect to Jakobson's structural principle of poetic equivalence:

> It may be objected that metalanguage also makes a sequential use of equivalent units when combining synonymic expressions into an equational sentence: A = A ("Mare is the female of the horse"). Poetry and metalanguage, however, are in diametrical opposition to each other: in metalanguage sequence is used to build an equation, whereas in poetry the equation is used to build a sequence. (1960: 358)

Besides this structural difference between the

poetic and the metalinguistic function, Jakobson implicitly also recognized a fundamental heuristic similarity between the poetic and the metalinguistic. Jakobson pointed out that insight into the autonomous structure of the poetic sign results in a metalinguistic insight into the structure of the linguistic sign in general. It demonstrates that "the sign does not fuse with the referential object," and shows that

> besides the immediate consciousness of identity of sign and object (A equals A_1) the immediate consciousness of the incomplete identity (A is not equal to A_1) is necessary; this antinomy is inevitable, since without contradiction there is no movement of concepts, no movement of signs. The relation between concept and sign becomes automatized, the course of events stops, the consciousness of reality dies. (1933a: 124)

With these observations, Jakobson raised the more fundamental question of the relation between poetry and semiotics, more generally between poetry and science. A semiogenetic theory of correspondence between these two fields has been developed by Koch (1983).

1.3 "Estrangement," Deautomatization, and Foregrounding

The communicative and the conventional, thus social, aspects of the poetic function were a central topic of the poetics of Russian Formalism and Prague structuralism. In contradistinction to the structural explanation, functional theories permit explanations of the potential poeticalness of minimal art poems.

1.3.1 "MAKING STRANGE"
According to Šklovskij (1916) and Tynjanov (1924), the typical device of poetry (and art in general) is that of "making strange" (*ostranenie*; cf. Russian Formalism 1.). "Estrangement," later called *deautomatization*, is the process of perceiving differences in comparison with the habitual semiotic patterns of everyday communication. Such patterns, perceived without special attention, are de-

scribed as being automatized. Perceptual deautomatization (ultimately caused by structural deviation; cf. 2.2) results not only in an awareness of the creative difference but also in a "new way of seeing" and that autotelic awareness of language described by Jakobson.

1.3.2 POETIC FOREGROUNDING
A further development of this functional view of poeticalness was the theory of *foregrounding* in Mukařovský's aesthetics (q.v. 3.2.2). Poetic language is defined by Mukařovský as follows:

> The function of poetic language consists in the maximum of foregrounding of the utterance. Foregrounding is the opposite of automatization, that is, the deautomatization of an act; the more an act is automatized, the less it is consciously executed; the more it is foregrounded, the more completely conscious does it become. [. . .] In poetic language foregrounding achieves maximum intensity to the extent of pushing communication into the background as the objective of expression and of being used for its own sake; it is not used in the services of communication, but in order to place in the foreground the act of expression, the act of speech itself. (1932: 19)

For further aspects of Mukařovský's functional poetics, see Mukařovský (1939; 1976).

1.3.3 THE FUNCTIONALIST EXPLANATION OF MINIMAL ART POEMS
The poetic avant-garde has raised texts whose poeticalness cannot be explained by structural features to the rank of poetry. Found objects and trivial events have been acclaimed as objects or performances of representational art (cf. Nöth 1972). Catalogue excerpts and cooking recipes have been included in anthologies of poetry under the label of *found poems* (cf. Nöth 1978a). All these examples of concrete poeticalness require a functional approach. They demonstrate how a "new way of seeing" can be achieved even with texts that have no evident aesthetic features.

2. Structural Features of Poeticalness

Traditionally, the structural devices of poetry have been located at two levels of linguistic analysis (e.g., Cohen 1966). At the level of expression, the specific feature of poetry has traditionally been phonetic recurrence in the form of rhyme, alliteration, or other prosodic structures. (Jakobson, however, extended the principle of recurrence also to the level of content; cf. 2.1.1). At the level of content, poetry has traditionally been defined in terms of semantic deviation, particularly within rhetoric and stylistics. An attempt to define poeticalness as a specific correlation between expression and content is made by those who propose the theory of poetic convergence.

2.1 Poeticalness of Recurrence

Repetition, parallelism, symmetry, similarity, equivalence, and variation are variants of poetic recurrence which can be detected on the levels both of expression and of content. The semiotic foundation of recurrence is Jakobson's thesis of poetic equivalence.

2.1.1 JAKOBSON'S THESIS OF EQUIVALENCE
Besides his functional criterion of the poetic, Jakobson also proposed a structural ("empirical linguistic") principle of poeticalness (1960: 358). The point of departure of Jakobson's theory of the poetic is the distinction between the paradigmatic and the syntagmatic dimensions of semiosis (see Structure 2.1). The former describes the process of selection, the latter that of combination of linguistic items. According to Jakobson, "selection is produced on the base of equivalence, similarity and dissimilarity, synonymity and antonymity" (ibid.). In everyday language, this paradigmatic dimension is only a potential structure of discourse. It refers only to linguistic alternatives which are not actualized in speech. Once the speaker's selection has taken place, the equivalent forms which he or she could (e.g., synonyms) or could not (e.g., antonyms) have chosen are lost in the chain of discourse. In poetry, however, these equivalences reappear in the text and are thus preserved in the axis of combination. Jakobson's thesis is: "*The poetic function projects the principle of equivalence from the axis of selection into the axis of combination*. Equivalence is promoted to the constitutive device of the sequence" (1960: 358).

2.1.2 RECURRENCE OF EXPRESSION
The reiteration of phonetically similar or even identical forms of expression in "I like Ike" or "Veni, vidi, vici" conveys a certain degree of poeticalness to these phrases from contexts outside of poetry (cf. Jakobson 1960: 356–57). The pansemiotic phenomenon of poeticalness also manifests itself in other substances of expression. Graphemic recurrences are a constitutive device of visual poetry. Other visual and acoustic recurrences determine the pansemiotic poeticalness of media such as film, painting, and music. Koch extends the pansemiotic research in poeticalness even to the sphere of the presemiotic, where he discovers *biopoetic* structures in symmetries and other recurrences within nature (1983: e.g., 436).

2.1.3 RECURRENCE AND STRUCTURES OF CONTENT
The semantic principle of poetic recurrence was formulated by Jakobson as follows: "In poetry not only the phonological sequence but in the same way any sequence of semantic units strives to build an equation. Similarity superimposed on contiguity imparts to poetry its thoroughgoing symbolic, multiplex, polysemantic essence" (1960: 370). Forms of semantic recurrence ("topical recurrence") have been studied by Koch as a mode of poeticalness (1966: 32–34; 1968). With his study in poetic isotopies (following Greimas 4.), Rastier (1972b) proposed a related approach to semantic recurrences in poetry. Nevertheless, Koch concludes that semantic ("informational") poeticalness remains a major neglected area of semiotic poetics (1983: 72).

2.2 Poeticalness of Deviation

Innovation and creativity are concepts which refer to forms of deviation from a given semiotic norm. The classical field of poeticalness by deviation is rhetoric, stylistics, and metaphor. For some authors, deviation is the foundation of all forms of poeticalness. Cohen (1966), for example, even explains phonetic recurrences as a systematic violation of the laws of ordinary language use. Every deviation presupposes a norm. The norm from which poetical structures are assumed to be deviating has been conceived either in terms of the language system or in terms of the readers' expectations.

2.2.1 DEVIATION AND THE GRAMMATICAL NORM

Especially in the tradition of generative grammar, several attempts were made to define poeticalness in terms of a deviation from the rules of language (cf. Ihwe, ed. 1971). Some have described how poetic structures infringe the generative rules of normal language. Others have attempted to formulate the rules proper by which those poetic structures were generated. One of the problems with these attempts was the difficulty of distinguishing between linguistic errors and poetic creativity by these procedures. Critics of these methods have also questioned the possibility of establishing a nonpoetic language norm in the first place. Should it be the everyday language, the written, the literary, or any other language norm? Posner, for example, has rejected the assumption that rules could ever determine the structures of poeticalness, because a system of rules would be the death of poetry (1982: 125). Yet, while a system of rules generating poetry may be an illusion (or at best a tautology because every new poetical structure would require a new rule), the category of deviation, or at least difference (cf. Rhetoric 2.3.1) from a semiotic norm, seems to be indispensable in semiotic rhetoric and stylistics.

2.2.2 DEVIATION FROM EXPECTATION

The difficulties with an abstract language norm were avoided in Riffaterre's structural stylistics (see Rhetoric 3.3.1) by the assumption of certain contextual expectations of an average reader. In *Semiotics of Poetry* (1978: 1–2), Riffaterre continues to develop and to expand this idea, beginning with the assumption that "poetry expresses concepts and things by indirection," occurring in several forms of grammatical and semantic deviation. On this premise, Riffaterre develops a two-phase model of the reading of poetry (ibid.: 4–5): In the first phase, the reader encounters poetic ungrammaticalities on the basis of his or her linguistic competence. At this stage of *heuristic reading*, a coherent referential (mimetic) interpretation of the poem is still prevented because of the difficulties which result from the textual indirection ("saying one thing and meaning another"). Only at a second stage, called *retroactive reading*, does the reader succeed in resolving the mimetic deviations by integrating them into a new semantic system in which the text acquires its poetic function. At this higher level, mimetic ungrammaticalness turns into poetic grammaticalness.

2.2.3 AMBIGUITY AND POETICALNESS

Supporting Empson's (1930) theory of poetic ambiguity, Jakobson also characterized poeticalness as fundamentally ambiguous: "The supremacy of poetic function over referential function does not obliterate the reference but makes it ambiguous. The double-sensed message finds correspondence in a split addresser, in a split addressee, and besides in a split reference" (1960: 371). Eco interprets this poetic ambiguity in terms of deviation: "Semiotically speaking ambiguity must be defined as a mode of violating the rules of the code" (1976: 262–63). Eco furthermore characterizes the device of poetic ambiguity as "a sort of introduction to the aesthetic experience" because it focuses the reader's attention and "incites me toward the discovery of an unexpected flexibility in the language." Poetic deviation thus leads to the recognition of poetic auto-reflexivity.

2.3 Poetics of Convergence

While poeticalness has so far been studied on the expression and the content planes separately, the poetics of convergence assumes a fundamental correlation between these two planes of poetic semiosis.

2.3.1 SEMANTICS OF EXPRESSION-FORM

The assumption of a semantic value for the poetic form of expression is a variant of the theory of literary iconicity. Jakobson shared this assumption and claimed: "Rhyme necessarily involves the semantic relationship between rhyming units." And still more generally: "In poetry, any conspicuous similarity in sound is evaluated in respect to similarity and/or dissimilarity in meaning" (1960: 367, 372). Lotman has frequently insisted on the semantic function of rhyme and other recurrences of expression-form in poetry, but for him such recurrences are only a part of a more global system of correspondences: In poetry "the phenomenon of structure in a line always, in the final analysis, turns out to be a phenomenon of meaning" (1970: 119).

2.3.2 COUPLING

Levin (1962) developed a structuralist theory of poeticalness in which he describes the specific fusing of form and meaning in poetry by the concept of *coupling*. Coupling is the structural parallelism between syntactically equivalent positions in the text, on the one hand, and semantic or phonetic equivalences, on the other (cf. ibid.: 33, 36): For example, in Pope's line "A Soul as full of Worth as void of Pride," the modifiers "full of Worth" and "void of Pride" are the syntactically equivalent positions in which the adjectives *full* and *void* exhibit the additional phonetic (both are monosyllabic) and semantic (they are antonyms) parallelism. Levin summarizes this principle of poeticalness as follows: "The individual items occurring in the coupling are positionally equivalent in the message and naturally [i.e., semantically or phonetically] equivalent in the code" (1962: 38). Coupling is thus a specific form of the Jakobsonian projection of paradigmatic structures into the syntagmatic axis of the poem. The poetic convergence which is achieved by coupling is not simply an iconic mapping of content structures into language form (cf. ibid.: 37; Literature 2.1)

but is the creative process of generating a textual structure of a higher order, namely, the structure of poetic unity.

2.3.3 CONVERGENCE BY ISOMORPHY

Greimas (1972: 13–15) and other semioticians of the Paris School consider the relationship of isomorphism between structures of the expression and of the content plane to be the specific feature of poeticalness. Greimas postulates a parallel development of the phonetic and the semantic structures in poetry and describes the formal equivalence between the two planes of discourse in terms of his formula of *homologation* A : B :: A' : B' (ibid.; cf. Greimas & Courtés 1979: 144): A and A', two phonetic elements of expression, are considered to be homologous with the two semantic structures B and B' which they express. Coquet describes homologations between elements at several levels of the poetic text, e.g., A : A' (a syntactic parallelism) :: B : B' (a metric p.) :: C : C' (a prosodic p.) :: D : D' (a semantic p.), and concludes that such homologies in poetry occur as points of equivalence without constituting a system of equivalences (1973: 102).

3. Poeticalness and Poetry

In spite of Jakobson's early plea for an integrated view of the poetic, many semioticians have taken sides for either the functional or the structural view of poeticalness. Yet, only the consideration of both structure and function seems to allow a satisfactory explanation of poeticalness in all of its modes of appearance in poetry.

3.1 Structural and Functional Poeticalness

Koch criticizes the "pernicious onesidedness" of theories that "try to outlaw either function or morphology" (i.e., structure) as determinants of the poetic (1983: 39). Based on the assumption of a mutual feedback relationship between poetic structure and function, Koch attempts to integrate both principles in his own semiogenetic poetics (1966; 1968; 1983: 40). Structure *and* function determine his three modes of the poetic (e.g., Koch 1983: 124–29), the *stylistic* (mode of deviation; cf. 2.2), the *aesthetic* (mode of phonetic or morphological recurrence; cf. 2.1.2), and the *informational* (mode of content). According to Koch, this latter mode of semantic poeticalness comprises not only recurrences of sememes (cf. 2.1.3) but also more fundamental dimensions of content (such as meanings concerning man and life in the universe) which he calls *metaphysical* poeticalness (ibid.: 63–65, 80–89). Besides these modes of poeticalness, Koch's poetics furthermore distinguishes three phases of the poetic process which correspond to the order of poetogenesis: the phase of symmetry (*prosphory*), the phase of asymmetry (*diaphory*), and the phase of integration (*symphory*) (ibid.: 281, 383).

3.2 Poeticalness as Potential Poetry

While for Jakobson texts of the genre of poetry were characterized by the dominance of poeticalness, Koch proposes a different delimitation (1966: 22; 1983: 45). For him, poeticalness "refers to the structural properties susceptible of being universally regarded as potentially pertaining to poetry." Poeticalness is thus *potential poetry*. While poeticalness is amenable to structural analysis, poetry depends on additional literary conventions and evaluations. Poets, readers, and literary critics are the ones who by their selection and evaluation transform the potential structures of poeticalness into poetry. Poetry is thus not a matter of a certain quantity of poeticalness. It is the functional act of aesthetic perception which turns the structures of poeticalness into poetry.

Theater and Drama

The theater is a topic of many semiotic dimensions. Barthes describes it as an "informational polyphony" and characterizes theatricality by its particular "density of signs" (Barthes 1964b: 262). As presentation, theater has the character of a sign, showing one thing instead of another (Eco 1975: 34). As sign, it participates in processes of aesthetic communication. As play and show, it exhibits iconic and indexical signs; as drama, it has specific actantial structures; as written text and visual and nonverbal performance, theater is a code participating in still other modes of semiosis. Because of these numerous intersections with topics and codes discussed in the sections on aesthetics and visual and nonverbal communication, the semiotics of theater transcends the field of text semiotics in its narrower sense.

1. The State of the Art

Contributions to the semiotics of theater have come from individual schools of semiotics, and more recently from authors who have attempted pluralistic syntheses of various approaches. General surveys of the whole field are given by Wittig (1974), De Marinis & Magli (1975), Ertel (1977), de Lauretis (1979), Elam (1980), Lewis (1981), De Marinis (1982: 9–23), Pavis (1982: 11–21), and Esslin (1987).

1.1 Schools of Semiotics in Theatrical Research

Early explicitly semiotic studies of theater were pursued in the 1930s and '40s within the aesthetics of the Prague School. Among the contributors were Zich (1931; cf. Steiner & Volek 1978), Bogatyrev (1936; 1938; 1940), Brušák (1939), Honzl (1940), Veltruský (1940; 1978; 1984a), and Mukařovský (1941). For general surveys see Deák (1976), Matejka & Titunik, eds. (1976: xi–xv), Slawinska (1978), Elam (1980: 5–19), and Veltruský (1981). Other schools of semiotics developed new contributions to the study of theater only decades later.

Information theory and mathematical linguistics were the models of analysis for a series of studies: Frank (1959), Balcerzan & Osiński (1966), Dinu (1968; 1972), Schraud (1966), Marcus (1970: 287–370; 1975), Ruffini (1973), and Marcus, ed. (1977). From the point of view of Hjelmslev's glossematics, Jansen (1968) outlines a semiotics of drama. While his study is concerned primarily with the written text, Kowzan (1968; 1975), inspired by Saussure's semiology, launched a theory of theatrical codes.

Various schools of text semiotics have influenced to different degrees semiotic theater studies in France (Hamon 1972, Corvin 1973, Ertel 1977, Ubersfeld 1977), Belgium (Helbo 1975a; b; 1981; 1983a; 1987), Canada (Pavis 1976;

1982; 1985), Germany (Koch 1969; 1988, Nöth 1972, Eschbach 1979, Fischer-Lichte 1983a–c, Lohr 1987), Spain (Tordera 1978), England (Elam 1980, Esslin 1987), and the productive research in Italy (Pagnini 1970, Eco 1975; 1977c, De Marinis 1975; 1982, Ruffini 1978). Few studies have analyzed theater on the basis of Peircean semiotics (Bayer 1975; 1980, and partly see 3.3.2). A contribution of Soviet semiotics to the study of drama is Scheglov (1977).

1.2 Pluralistic Approaches

According to Alter, semiotic approaches to theater have to deal with "two categories of signs," which the author calls *verbal signs* and *staging signs* (1981: 113–14). Theater studies have often neglected one of these two semiotic dimensions and have thus become the victim of one of two "fallacies": "The literary fallacy leads to the assimilation of theater to the text only and results in its reduction to the status of a particular *genre* of literature. The performing fallacy, increasingly popular, leads to the assimilation of theater to the performance only, and results in its reduction to the status of a particular *genre* of show" (ibid.). The attempt to overcome such fallacies in a holistic approach to the medium is perhaps one of the most general characteristics of semiotic approaches to theater.

With the increase of interest in this field of research, pluralistic and sometimes even encyclopedic studies have attempted various syntheses of the field, in particular Pavis (1976; 1985), Ubersfeld (1977), Ruffini (1978), Eschbach (1979), Molinari & Ottolenghi (1979), Elam (1980), De Marinis (1982), Fischer-Lichte (1983), and Esslin (1987). Handbooks of theater studies covering in part semiotic aspects of the field are Pfister (1977) and Pavis (1980). Monographs with applied semiotic studies of individual authors, works, and epochs or special topics of the theater are Schmid (1973), Castagnano (1974), Relyea (1976), Canoa Galiana (1977), Scheglov (1977), Russell (1978), and Lewis (1981). Closely related to the semiotics of theater is the

semiotics of film (cf. Bettetini 1975) and the semiotics of circus (Bouissac 1973; 1976a).

Classical theories of drama are interpreted in semiotic terms by Bayer (1975), Fischer-Lichte (1983b), and Lohr (1987). Collections of papers dealing with the semiotics of theater are the volumes by Díez Borque & García Lorenzo, eds. (1975), Helbo et al. (1975), Hess-Lüttich, ed. (1982b), Schmid & Van Kesteren, eds. (1984), and in the special issues of the journals *Degrés* 6.13 (1978), *Poetics* 6.2 (= Marcus, ed. 1977), *Poetics Today* 2.3 (1981), *Modern Drama* 25.1 (1982), *Kodikas/Code* 7.1/2 (1984), and *Zeitschrift für Semiotik* 11.1 (1989).

---

2. Communication in Theater

Mounin (1970b) put forward the provocative thesis that there is no communication in theatrical semiosis. This argument led to an extensive discussion about the communication theoretical bases of theater (De Marinis 1975, Helbo 1975a, Ubersfeld 1977: 40–57, Ruffini 1978: 71–79, Elam 1980: 32–38, Helbo 1981, Fischer-Lichte 1983a: 189–94).

2.1 Theater and the Semiotics of Communication

Denying the communicative nature of theatrical semiosis is understandable only in terms of the concepts of communication and signification evolved by the functional school of semiotics of Buyssens, Prieto, and Mounin. This theory postulates *intentionality*, *bidirectionality*, and a code common to addresser and addressee as criteria of a semiotics of communication (q.v. 2.4). Mounin claims that such semiotic interaction does not occur between the audience and the actors in a theatrical performance (1970b: 91). With reference to Eco, Kirby proposed a similar thesis (1982: 110). In his view, theater is nonsemiotic because the audience does not decode but only interprets the theatrical message.

Such arguments may be objected to on both

terminological and material grounds. Terminologically, there is communication in theater for all those who define this concept in the broader sense which includes also unidirectional forms of semiosis (cf. Helbo 1975a: 14). On material grounds, Mounin's arguments neglect a plurality of interactions between actors and audience. These interactions existed in conventional forms of theater where the audience always had some "secondary role" (Campeanu 1975, Veltruský 1978: 576–92) in the performance. They emerged more strongly in anti-illusionist performances and reached their climax in "living theater" and "happenings" (cf. Nöth 1972).

2.2 Models of Theatrical Communication

Prototypically, theatrical semiosis comprises two interlocking systems or frames of communication (cf. Pfister 1977: 21, Koch 1988: § 4). The inner frame is the communication on stage. This is an essentially bidirectional exchange of messages between at least two actors. The outer frame consists of the author's message (whose signs are the actors) to the theatrical audience. This communication flow is superficially unidirectional, but if the various feedback messages from spectators to the author are taken into consideration, this outer system has bidirectional aspects, too. More comprehensive analyses of communication in theater have frequently been carried out on the basis of Jakobson's model of *communicative functions* (e.g., Revzine & Revzine 1971). For these functions in theatrical semiosis, see also Pavis (1976: 23–25), Pfister (1977: 149–68), Ubersfeld (1977: 42–44), and Veltruský (1978: 576–92). Elam develops a more complex "theatrical communication model" (1980: 39).

---

3. The Theatrical Sign

Which objects, events, and acts on the stage have the character of a sign, what is the structure of such signs, and what types of signs are used in theatrical performances?

3.1 The Semiotic Transformation on the Stage

The essence of the theatrical sign and its semiotic dynamics was a recurrent topic of Prague text semiotics (cf. Bogatyrev 1936; 1938, Veltruský 1940, 1981; for a summary see Elam 1980: 3–19). For the Prague structuralists, theater is a place of *semiotic transformation*: Material objects, events, and behavior which have a practical, nonsemiotic function in everyday life are transformed into signs by being presented in the aesthetic context of the stage. This process of transformation of a practical action into a theatrical sign is described by Veltruský as follows:

> The properties of an action directed toward a practical objective are determined by this objective, irrespective of the perceiver [. . .]. In the theater, however, the action is an end in itself and it lacks an external practical purpose which might determine its properties. [. . .] The properties of the action are thus pure meanings, just as its purpose is a semiological matter and not a matter of practical life. (1940: 83)

Bogatyrev considered the process of semiotic transformation to be the specific feature of theatricality (1940: 51). In poetic or epic literature, he argues, the author writes about himself or some other person, which results in a certain aesthetic distance between author and narrated events. In theater, however, the actor is obliged to identify himself completely with the person he represents by transforming his own self into the theatrical sign of that person. By such semiotizations, everything on the stage can finally turn into a sign (Veltruský 1940: 84). Moreover, one and the same material object can be used to refer to several objects (especially in Chinese theater), and it can acquire a plurality of connotations. The Prague structuralists have discussed this semiotic flexibility under the concept of the *communicative dynamics* of signs in theater (cf. Honzl 1940).

3.2 Structure of the Theatrical Sign

Objects, persons, and their behavior are the signifiers of theatrical signs formed by stage properties, actors, and actions.

3.2.1 SIGNS OF OBJECTS AND SIGNS OF SIGNS

With respect to signs formed by objects, Bogatyrev distinguishes between *signs of objects* and *signs of signs* (1938: 33–34). Signs of objects, e.g., a cardboard set signifying a 'stone house,' imply only a single transformation from the nonsemiotic to the semiotic. Signs of signs, e.g., a folk costume signifying first a nationality and secondly a social status, transform the nonsemiotic object ("piece of clothing") twice into units of cultural meaning. This is the semiotic process which Hjelmslev has characterized as a *connotative semiotics*. On such connotative levels of meaning in theater, see also Ubersfeld (1977: 33–35) and Elam (1980: 10).

3.2.2 THE SELF-REFERENTIAL ACTOR

With respect to actors and acting, Veltruský points out that "the material the actor uses is the actor himself, his own properties and abilities" (1978: 554). Signifier, the human being and his behavior, and signified, the represented person and his actions, are thus of the same nature: "Even the concept of similarity in its simplest semiotic sense of resemblance tends, therefore, to give way to the idea of sameness." This aspect of self-referentiality is also emphasized by Ubersfeld, who claims that the theatrical sign has three referents, (1) within the theatrically represented world, (2) in the extratheatrical world, and (3) in its own material existence (1977: 37).

3.2.3 MULTIMEDIAL POLYSEMY

Theatrical signs are thus basically polysemous. As a source of this polysemy, Ubersfeld discusses the possible semiotic discrepancies between the theatrical text as written script, on the one hand, and as performance, on the other (1977: 35–36). In her interpretation, both forms of the theatrical constitute two po-

tentially independent triadic signs (with signifiers, signifieds, and referents). While the "classical" concept of theater postulates a congruence of the signifieds and referents of these two signs, contemporary theater has emphasized the potential differences between the written and the staged signs.

3.3 Typologies of Theatrical Signs

Typological considerations of theatrical signs have been based on two main types of classification, the dichotomy between natural and artificial signs and the Peircean icon-index-symbol trichotomy.

3.3.1 NATURAL OR ARTIFICIAL SIGNS?

The discussion about the naturalness and artificiality of the theatrical sign was already a major topic of the literary theories of the classics (cf. Fischer-Lichte 1983b). More recently, Kowzan resumed the discussion, applying different criteria of naturalness (cf. Elam 1980: 20). He argues that "the spectacle transforms natural signs into artificial ones. [. . .] It has thus the power to 'artificialize' signs" (1968: 68). Kowzan's "artificialization" is basically the Prague structuralists' semiotic transformation. He defines "artificial" signs as those whose communicative function is higher than that of "natural" signs.

3.3.2 ICONS AND SYMBOLS

Several authors have discussed the theatrical sign with respect to Peirce's trichotomy of icon, index, and symbol (cf. Kott 1969, Helbo 1975b: 68–71, Pavis 1976: 13–18, Elam 1980: 21–30, Pladott 1982, Esslin 1987). In accordance with Peirce's functional conception of this typology, Ubersfeld points out that every theatrical sign is to some degree icon, index, and symbol at the same time (1977: 30). Nevertheless, the dominance of these sign types in theater may vary.

The symbolic, thus arbitrary and conventional, and the iconic, thus motivated, are two modes of theatricality which are characteristic of different theatrical traditions and genres.

Prototypical of the symbolic is the Balinese, the Chinese, or the Japanese theater (cf. Brušák 1939, Ertel 1977: 134, Veltruský 1978: 564ff.), while the naturalistic theater is the prototype of the iconic on stage. But there are many intermediate degrees of arbitrariness in the diverse epochs and traditions of theater (cf. Kott 1969). For the conventionality of theater, see also 4.1.

Pavis considers the iconic to be the basic mode of theatricality (1976: 13). It is the basis of theatrical mimesis, the imitation of persons and acts by the actor (the "mime"). Iconic signs in theater are not only visual and nonverbal (actors, stage props, costumes, gestures, etc.) but also acoustic and verbal (theatrical sounds and words imitate extratheatrical events and persons).

3.3.3 OSTENSION AND INDEXICALITY

Eco considers the *ostensive* sign to be "the most basic instance of performance" (1977c: 110; cf. De Marinis 1979: 11–16, Elam 1980: 29–30). This mode of semiosis by showing an object or event vicariously for a class of referents (cf. Eco 1973b: 63–67) is sometimes interpreted as being iconic. Yet, a distinction has to be made between the act of showing, which is an index, and the object shown, which is an icon of the referent. The indexical mode of theatricality is present both in the inner and in the outer frame of theatrical communication. In the outer frame, indexicality dominates in the above-mentioned act of ostension. In its inner frame, the actors' interpersonal, spatial, and temporal orientation presupposes indexical signs. This indexicality is reflected in the highly deictic language of dramatic discourse (cf. Elam 1980: 138–48).

4. Theatrical Code and Codes in Theater

The conventions of theatrical performances constitute the theatrical code, but theater is a medium which makes use of many codes which have a semiotic existence outside the stage.

4.1 Theatrical Code

The semiotic conventions which constitute the code and system of theater are discussed in detail by Ertel (1977), Elam (1980: 49–87), De Marinis (1982: 113–38), and Esslin (1987).

4.1.1 CODE AND SYSTEM

Following Coseriu (see System 2.2.3), Fischer-Lichte differentiates between the theatrical code as system, as norm, and as speech (1983a: 21–23). As system, the theatrical code comprises all those semiotic elements, codes, and subcodes which can possibly be used in theatrical performances. As norm, a theatrical code consists of the acting conventions of a given epoch. This norm is only a selection from the potentialities of the theatrical system. At the level of speech, the theatrical code is finally formed by the specific theatrical performance.

4.1.2 PROBLEMS OF SEGMENTATION

The structures, units, and segments of the theatrical code are the topic of several semiotic studies (Koch 1969, Hein 1976, Pavis 1976: 8–10, Ertel 1977: 134–39, Ruffini 1978: 123–73, De Marinis 1978–79, Serpieri et al. 1981, and Fischer-Lichte 1983c: 76–96). The procedures proposed for the discovery of *minimal units* and larger *autonomous segments* of theatrical performances are related to those discussed in the semiotics of film (q.v. 5.). Critics of the attempts at theatrical segmentation have discovered "little progress" in this field of study (Elam 1980: 46). Particular criticism has been directed at the attempts to discover minimal units of theatrical code (cf. Ertel 1977: 134–36, De Marinis 1979: 3–7, Ubersfeld 1977: 32–33, Elam 1980: 48). On the other hand, it is true that the principles of segmentation (into such units as scenes, acts, etc.) have been a central topic of the theory of drama since ancient poetics and rhetoric (cf. Lausberg 1960: 565–71, Pfister 1977: 307–318). The methods of theatrical segmentation are relevant to the problem of the transcription of performances into a dramatological *score*. Such a score is proposed by Elam (1980: 184–207).

4.2 Codes in Theater

Kowzan considers the following codes to be typical constituents of theatrical performances (1968; 1975: 167–221): (1) word, (2) tone (see Paralinguistics), (3) facial mime (see Facial Signals), (4) gesture (q.v.), (5) movement (see Kinesics), (6) makeup, (7) hairstyle, (8) costume, (9) props, (10) decor, (11) lighting (cf. Russell 1978), (12) music (q.v.), and (13) sound effects. This model of theatrical codes has influenced a number of semiotic studies in theater (Eschbach 1979: 148–71, Molinari & Ottolenghi 1979, Fischer-Lichte 1983a). Elam, criticizing among other things Kowzan's neglect of the architectural, pictorial, and proxemic codes, expands this model to a system of twenty-nine codes which he describes as specifically theatrical and dramatic derivatives of more general cultural codes (1980: 49–87). Esslin (1987) proposes a typology which distinguishes five groups of theatrical codes: (1) framing systems outside the drama proper, (2) sign systems at the actor's disposal, (3) visual sign systems, (4) the text, and (5) aural sign systems.

For a more elementary model of codes in theater see Rovenţa-Frumuşanti (1982). Specific nonverbal codes in theatrical performance are discussed by Pavis (1982) and Poyatos (1982b). For the theatrical codes of gestures see Pavis (1981; 1985: 83–134) and Gesture (2.3.4).

---

5. Actantial Constellations in Drama

A number of studies have developed or applied text semiotic models for the analysis of dramatic actions and processes. Souriau's (1950) model of *dramatic functions* is discussed by Greimas (1966: 201–215) as a precursor of a text semiotics of drama. A discussion of Souriau's actantial constellations is also included in Elam's semiotics of theater (1980: 126–34). Pavis (1976: 67–78) and Segre (1981) study dramatic structures of action from the point of view of semiotic *narratology*. Ubersfeld applies Greimas's actantial model in her more comprehensive study of dramatic constellations (1977: 58–150) and gives also the outline of a text semiotic theory of *character*, a topic to which Hamon (1972) dedicated an earlier study. Elam (1980) extends the research in the logic of drama by applying models from the logic of *possible worlds* and the philosophical *theory of action*.

Narrative

The semiotics of narrative has become a classical area of text semiotics. Its closest neighboring field is the semiotics of literature, but *narratology*, the theory of narrative, is also concerned with nonliterary narratives. In its foundations, semiotic narratology was also influenced by the structural analysis of myth. Pursuing a tradition beginning with Russian Formalism (Propp) and structuralism in anthropology (Lévi-Strauss; see Myth 2.), text semiotic research has given special attention to the *minimal units* of a narrative and the principles of their combination into a *grammar of the plot*. Extending these approaches, narrative pragmatics and the study of visual narratives are further topics of semiotic narratology.

1. Foundations of Narratology

Narrativity, the specific feature of a narrative text, is a subject of interdisciplinary research which has also become known as narratology.

1.1 Survey of Narratology

Narrativity extends beyond the scope of a specific genre and medium of expression. Within the interdisciplinary field of narratology, several approaches have been distinguished besides the semiotic ones.

1.1.1 THE SCOPE OF NARRATIVITY

The semiotic universality of narratives has been pointed out in a definition given by Barthes:

> Narrative is first and foremost a prodigious variety of genres, themselves distributed amongst different substances. [. . .] Able to be carried by articulated language, spoken or written, fixed or moving images, gestures, and the ordered mixture of all these substances, narrative is present in myth, legend, fable, tale, novella, epic, history, tragedy, drama, comedy, mime, painting [. . .], stained glass windows, cinema, comics, news item, conversation. (1966a: 79)

1.1.2 THE SCOPE OF NARRATOLOGY

A new discipline to study this extended field of narrative discourse was first proposed by Todorov under the designation of *narratology* (1969: 10), a term which has now become established within the sciences of discourse (cf. Genette 1972: 22, Chatman 1978: 9, Bal 1977, Prince 1982). Ihwe introduced the term *narrativics* (1972b: 6), probably in order to emphasize the parallelism with *poetics*. This term became widely adopted in German narratology (cf. Haubrichs, ed. 1976–78, Sparmacher 1981). Genot, however, distinguishes between the two terms, defining narrativics as the discipline "charged with the elaboration, the criticism and the comparison of narratological models" (1979: v).

Theoretical and applied narratology is a transdisciplinary field of research (cf. the bibliographical surveys in Haubrichs, ed. 1976–78, and by Mathieu 1977 and Gülich & Quasthoff 1985). Beyond the "theory of literature" (cf. Lämmert 1955, Scholes & Kellogg 1966, Lämmert, ed. 1982, Stanzel 1979), structures of narrativity are objects of study in anthropology (Jason & Segal, eds. 1977), the philosophy of history (Danto 1965, Miguelez 1971), theology (q.v. 2.2), journalism, text linguistics, and the social sciences (ethnomethodology) (cf. Gülich & Quasthoff 1985). Within the latter field, the scope of narratology has been extended from oral and written literature to everyday conversational narratives (cf. ibid.; cf. also Labov & Waletzky 1967). Two more recent interdisciplinary fields of research which are contributing to narratology are discourse analysis (*Textwissenschaft*; cf. van Dijk 1980b, van Dijk, ed. 1985) and cognitive science, which extends from cognitive psychology to artificial intelligence (cf. van Dijk 1980a, Beaugrande 1982).

1.1.3 SEMIOTIC APPROACHES TO NARRATIVITY

Gülich (1973) and Haubrichs (1976: 8) have suggested typologies of approaches to narratology which locate semiotic narratology basically within the French structuralist posterity of Propp and Lévi-Strauss (cf. Myth 2. and Sparmacher 1981). Following Ihwe (1972b: 6), both consider text linguistics as a major approach to narrativity separate from the semiotic one. For Gülich (cf. Gülich & Raible 1977: 192), the third major approach is represented by Wienold's "reception theoretical" approach. However, it should be pointed out that the latter was developed within Wienold's *Semiotics of Literature* (1972) and that the former, the text linguistic approach, is not always programmatically differentiated from the semiotic approaches either (besides Wienold 1972 see also Hendricks 1973). For text linguistic approaches see Dijk (1972), Dijk et al. (1972), Prince (1973; 1982), Baum (1977), Dijk & Petöfi, eds. (1977), Gülich & Raible (1977), Genot (1979), Ryan (1979). Even the more re-

cent trend in narratology, the cognitive science approach, has already been subsumed under the semiotic framework (Maranda 1985).

For surveys of semiotic approaches to and studies in narratology (besides the ones discussed in detail below), see Chabrol (1971), Chabrol, ed. (1973), Pavel (1973), Scholes (1974), Culler (1975), Bal (1977), Hawkes (1977), Fokkema & Kunne-Ibsch (1977), Kloepfer (1977b), Chatman (1978), Grosse (1978), Hornung (1978), Marcus, ed. (1978), Dorner-Bachmann (1979), Blanchard (1980), Sparmacher (1981), Hendricks (1982), Ricoeur (1984: 29–60), Stewart (1987), and Everaert-Desmedt (1988). Special mention is due to Saussure (q.v. 2.2.2). In a way, he deserves to be called the first semiotic narratologist, but his narratological studies have had almost no influence on current semiotic narratology.

1.2 Narrative and Narrativity

With reference to the Formalists' theory of literariness, semiotic narratologists have proposed to study narrativity (instead of "the narrative") as the specific feature of narrative discourse (cf., e.g., Cerisola 1980: 109). The essence of narrative has been defined in relation to various other modes of discourse. While most narratologists define it in terms of content, Plato characterized narrativity with reference to the act of narrating (*Republic* 392c–395). He distinguished between pure narrative (*diegesis*), in which the author is speaking himself without pretending to be a fictive character, and imitation (*mimesis*), in which the author is speaking as someone else (cf. Genette 1972: 162–63). An influential linguistic characterization of narrativity has been proposed by Benveniste (1966: 205–216). He opposes historical narrative to nonnarrative discourse according to criteria of tense and person. (E.g., indexical words, such as *I, you, here*, characterize nonnarrative discourse, while the pronoun *he* is typical of narrative.)

The closest rivals to the concept of narrative are those of fiction and epic. But besides the fact that there are also historical and "true" narratives (cf. Miguelez 1971), fiction also includes the mode of description as a nonnarrative form of discourse (cf. Todorov 1971b: 38). In any case, narrativity is not the feature of a specific genre. It transcends the traditional genre of the epic. Narrativity is furthermore *translinguistic* (in the sense of Greimas [1971: 793]: "common to cultures with different natural languages").

It should not be ignored, at this point, that the narrative vs. nonnarrative distinction has also been challenged (cf. Rauch 1981: 172). However, such a challenge is based on an unusually abstract and extended concept of narrativity, such as the one proposed by Greimas, for whom "narrativity is [. . .] the organizing principle of *all* discourse" (Greimas & Courtés 1979: 210).

1.3 Narrativity in Story and Discourse

Narratologists early recognized the necessity of distinguishing between narrative discourse and narrated events. This distinction was first discussed in the form of dichotomies, such as Aristotle's *mythos* vs. *mimesis* (cf. Ricoeur 1983: 31–51) or more recently *story* and *plot* (or *discourse*). Later, various expansions of this basic distinction were proposed (cf. Stierle 1975: 49–55, Segre 1979c: 1–56, Schmid 1984).

1.3.1 STORY AND DISCOURSE (OR PLOT)

The basic dichotomy of narratology is defined by Chatman as follows:

> A story (*histoire*) [is] the content or chain of events (actions, happenings), plus what may be called the existents (characters, items of setting); and a discourse (*discours*) [. . .] is the expression, the means by which the content is communicated. In simple terms, the story is the *what* in a narrative that is depicted, discourse is the *how*. (1978: 19)

Chatman traces this narratological dichotomy back to Aristotle's distinction between *mythos* and *logos* (see Myth 1.2). The most influential version of this dichotomy is the distinction between *fabula* and *sjužet* (mostly translated as *story* vs. *plot*), introduced by the Russian Formalists V. Šklovskij and B. Tomaševskij (cf. Chatman 1978: 20, Segre 1979c: 4–24). According to this theory, story is the basic succession of events, the author's raw material, so to speak, and plot is the result of the author's creative (trans)formation of these events in the narrative.

Semiotic narratologists have partly transformed, partly adopted (cf. Gülich & Raible 1977: 216) the story-plot dichotomy. Bremond distinguishes between *récit raconté* (narrated story) and *récit racontant* (the narrative message) (1964: 4; 1973: 12, 102), and Todorov (1971a) between *histoire* (story) and *discours* (narrative discourse). Other concepts which have been interpreted as corresponding to this dichotomy are Greimas's dichotomy of *immanence* vs. *manifestation* and Kristeva's distinction between *genotext* and *phenotext*, but these two dichotomies are elements of much more complex text semiotic theories.

1.3.2 BARTHES'S LEVELS OF NARRATOLOGICAL ANALYSIS

Barthes proposed a hierarchy of three levels forming a narrative code (1966a: 88). At the lowest level, that of *functions* and indices, there are the minimal units of the narrative. At the next higher level, that of *actions*, these elements are integrated in a functional syntax of actions. The third level is that of *narrative communication* between a narrator and a listener.

1.3.3 GENETTE'S THEORY OF NARRATIVE DISCOURSE

Genette replaces the story-plot dichotomy by the following three levels of narrativity (1972: 27): (1) *story*, "the signified of narrative content" (comprising Barthes's first two levels of functions and actions), (2) *narrative*, "the signifier, statement, discourse or narrative text itself," and (3) *narrating*, "the producing narrative action" ("l'acte narratif producteur"). Focusing on the second level, Genette develops a theory of narrative discourse based on the assumption that the essence of narrativity can be studied with reference to categories borrowed from the grammar of verbs (ibid.: 30–31): Under the aspect of *tense*, the temporal relations between narrative and story are studied. The modalities (e.g., perspective, distance) of narrative representation are revealed from the category of *mood*. Finally, *voice*, the category referring to the subject (person) of the verb, refers to the act of narrating within the narrative.

2. In Search of the Narreme

Motif, motifeme (Dundes 1962: 101; Doležel 1972), *mytheme, narreme, minimal narrative* (Labov & Waletzky 1967, Dorfman 1969), *minimal story*, and *kernel story* (Prince 1973; 1982) are concepts which have been proposed in the search for a minimal constituent of the narrative (cf. Köngäs & Maranda 1971: 21). Two approaches to this problem may be distinguished: The first is the *a priori* determination of the narreme on the basis of an elementary logic of action, and the second is an *a posteriori* approach, which derives the narreme by deduction from a corpus of narratives.

2.1 Elementary Unit of Action

From the point of view of the logic of action, narratologists have defined narremes as units corresponding approximately to one, two, or three propositions.

2.1.1 THE MONADIC VIEW
The monadic view is based on an elementary unit which corresponds referentially to an event (Prince 1973: 17) and linguistically to a proposition. Todorov (1967; 1969; 1970b; 1971a; b), Doležel (1972; 1976), Güttgemanns (1977: 80), and Greimas (cf. Greimas & Courtés 1979: 203) have taken monadic approaches to the narreme. Within his grammar of the narrative, Todorov defines the basic element of narrative syntax as a proposition corresponding to an "irreduc-ible" action (1969: 19). Such narrative propositions are formed by a proper name (corresponding to an agent) plus a predicate, consisting of either a verb (of action) or an attributive adjective (ibid.: 27). Narrative propositions are furthermore characterized by secondary categories such as that of mode (ibid.: 46–52). They may express facts (indicative mode), volition (obligatory and optative modes), or hypotheses (conditional and predicative modes).

Doležel expresses the monadic view of the narreme in the following logical form: "A *motifeme* (M) is a proposition predicating an act (Act) to an actant (Ant): M = Ant + Act" (1972: 59). Essentially, however, this concept of motifeme was not developed within an elementary logic of action, but is derived from Propp's corpus-based tradition.

2.1.2 DYADIC AND TRIADIC VIEWS OF THE NARREME
The dyadic and triadic views expand the narrative monad by a dimension of *process*, expressed in categories of *time* (Danto 1965: 236), *causality* (van Dijk et al. 1972: 16), or, more generally, *transformation* (cf. Todorov 1971b: 39). If the narreme is to be defined in terms of action and not only in terms of events, the dimension of process is logically presupposed. For action, in a definition given by van Dijk, is "a change of state brought about intentionally by a (conscious) human being in order to bring about a preferred state or state change" (1976: 550).

An example of a dyadic view is Labov's definition of the "minimal narrative as a sequence of two clauses which are temporally ordered" (1972: 360). The triadic view is formulated by Danto (1965: 236), who characterizes the structure of a story (and of "narrative explanation") by the sequence (1) x is F at t–1. (2) H happens to x at t–2. (3) x is G at t–3 (where F, G, and H are predicate variables and x is an individual variable designating the subject of change). Triadic views of elementary narrativity, however, refer elsewhere also to narrative sequences or even macrostructures.

2.2 Corpus-Based Definitions of the Narreme

Propp's *Morphology of the Folktale* (1928) is the point of departure of a narratology which derives its elementary units from the narrative text as a whole and/or from a corpus of narratives. With his formalist method, Propp founded a structural narratology which turned from an etic to an emic approach to narrative structure (Dundes 1962; cf. Structuralism 1.1.3). For Propp's influence on Lévi-Strauss and the structural study of myth, see Lévi-Strauss (1973: 115–45) and Myth (2.)

2.2.1 PROPP'S FUNCTIONS

Traditional motif research, e.g., Stith Thompson (cf. Dundes 1962: 97), considers actors, items (objects), and incidents as minimal units of narrative analysis. Propp rejects such an approach as too surface-oriented. His minimal unit, called *function*, is one of action, and "an action cannot be defined apart from its place in the course of narration" (Propp 1928: 21). "Functions of characters serve as stable, constant elements in a tale, independent of how and by whom they are fulfilled" (ibid.). Functions as units of action are narrative invariants, while the agents performing those actions are textual variables. Within his corpus of one hundred fairy tales, Propp discovered a relatively small number of thirty-one such invariant functions, as opposed to a large number of persons, objects, or events (corresponding to the traditional motif).

2.2.2 MOTIF AND MOTIFEME

Propp's basic functional (emic) principles of analysis have influenced most semiotic narratologists, although many improvements and further developments were proposed. The basic distinction between variable and invariant elements of content, for example, was reinterpreted in terms of the categories motif and motifeme (Dundes 1962). In the interpretation of Doležel (1972: 59–60), motifemes ("acts of an actant," see 2.1.1) are entities of an abstract, deep level of analysis, thus corresponding to Propp's functions. At a higher level, closer to the textual surface structure, motifemes correspond to motifs (*m*), defined as propositions predicating an action (*a*) to a character (*c*). For example, the motifeme "The hero defeated the villain" could correspond to the motif "Ivan killed the dragon."

2.2.3 BARTHES'S FUNCTIONS

Within his narratological model, Barthes distinguished between *functions* and *indices* as minimal units of narrative. Following Propp, Barthes described functions as units of content in syntagmatic correlation with other narrative elements representing a course of action (1966a: 89–90). Functions which concern the semantic kernel of a narrative are defined as *cardinal functions*. Less important functions are called *catalyzers* (ibid.: 93). Barthes called functions *distributional* units and distinguished them from indices, which he characterized as *integrational* units. Indices have a low degree of narrative functionality (ibid.: 96). Instead of structuring the chain of events, indices proper refer "to the character of a narrative agent, a feeling, an atmosphere (for example suspicion) or a philosophy." A second class of indices, called *informants*, "serves to identify, to locate in time and space."

---

3. Narrative Syntax and Macrostructure

The rules by which narremes may be combined into a narrative form the *narrative syntax*. The global semantic structure of a narrative, as it may, for example, be expressed in the form of a summary, is often referred to as its *macrostructure* (cf. Dijk 1972; 3.2).

3.1 Narrative Syntax

The influential point of departure is again Propp. His narrative syntax was developed further by Bremond, Greimas, and many other narratologists.

3.1.1 PROPP'S NARRATIVE SEQUENCES

Within his corpus of one hundred fairy tales, Propp discovered that a sequence of altogether thirty-one functions was always identical (1928: 25ff.). To illustrate this narrative syntax, the first three functions (after one called α, "initial situation") and the last four may be quoted: (1) β, absentation (One of the members of a family leaves home.), (2) γ, interdiction (addressed to the hero), (3) δ, violation (of the interdiction) . . . , (28) Ex, exposure (of the villain), (29) T, transfiguration (The hero is given a new appearance.), (30) U Punishment, (31) W, Wedding.

Not all thirty-one functions have to be present in every tale, but "the absence of certain functions does not change the orders of the rest" (Propp 1928: 22). Propp further argues that the thirty-one functions are distributed among seven *spheres of action*, which may be performed by varying characters (ibid.: 79). These spheres give the fairy tale the following actantial framework: (1) the villain, (2) the donor, (3) the helper, (4) the sought-for person, (5) the dispatcher, (6) the hero, (7) the false hero.

3.1.2 BREMOND'S DECISIONAL SYNTAX

Bremond (1964; 1966; 1970; 1973) objects to Propp's principle of strict linearity in the combination of functions. Against the assumption of a logically necessary connection between each two functions in the sequence, Bremond argues that every function opens a set of alternative consequences. (E.g., a "fight" may be followed either by "victory" or by "defeat.") With this principle of *narrative alternatives*, narrativity is described as a process reflecting the reader's narrative expectations.

While Bremond's model of narrative is dyadic in its paradigmatic dimension (reflecting the alternatives), it is triadic in its syntagmatic dimension. An elementary narrative sequence, according to Bremond, consists of the following triad of phases describing a narrative process (1970: 249; 1973: 131): (1) situation opening a *potentiality*, (2) its *actualization* (alternative: lack of a.), (3) *success* (alternative: failure). Various possibilities of combining

these phases lead to a typology of complex sequences.

3.1.3 GREIMAS'S ACTANTIAL MODEL

Greimas's actantial model has three major sources: Propp, Souriau's theory of dramatic constellations (1950: 117), and Tesnière's (1959) dependency grammar. Greimas reduces Propp's seven spheres of action and Souriau's six dramatic functions to a basic inventory of narrative actants forming three binary oppositions (1966: 197–207): (1) *subject* vs. *object* (Propp's hero vs. sought-for person), (2) *sender* vs. *receiver*, and (3) *helper* vs. *opponent*. These actantial functions form an elementary narrative constellation which Greimas represents in his ("mythical") *actantial model* (Fig. N 1).

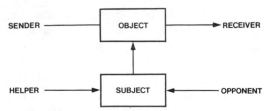

Fig. N 1. Greimas's actantial model (1966: 207).

The syntactic order of these actantial categories is basically as follows: a subject wants an object, encounters an opponent, finds a helper, obtains the object from a sender, and gives it to the receiver. This narrative syntax, originally derived only from the structure of myth (or fairy tales), describes the structure of many other types of text, from ideologies (Greimas 1966: 208) to the messages of advertising (q.v. 3.).

In the further development of his actantial model, Greimas later abandoned the helper-opponent dichotomy as a major category of actants (cf. Courtés 1976: 68ff, Coquet et al. 1982: 54). He now describes narrative sequences as processes of value transfer among four agents related by *disjunction* (e.g., separation, fight) and *conjunction* (e.g., union, reconciliation) (see Greimas 3.1). Accordingly, narrative sequences begin with a relation of conjunction between two actants, followed by a disjunction. The end of the narrative is a new conjunction resulting in a redistribution of semantic values (Greimas 1970: 182; cf. 1966: 234). In this form, the narrative is already described in its macrostructure.

3.2 Narrative Macrostructures

Time and causality as basic dimensions of the narrative process (cf. Ricœur 1983–84) suggest a linear macrostructure of the narrative. Sequences such as "initial state → transition → final state" (cf. Dijk et al. 1972: 17) or "problem → solution" (cf. Todorov 1969: 76) suggest linearity in the narrative macrostructure. Most narratologists, however, agree that narratives essentially refer to sequences of events of which the final event is semantically connected with the initial event. This idea has led to cyclical models of narrative macrostructure. These models are based either on a full cycle or on a semicycle. Semicyclical, for example, is Prince's model of narrative macrostructure (1973: 31). Prince defines a *minimal story* as a sequence of three temporally and causally conjoined events, of which the third event is the inverse (e.g., wealth) of the first (e.g., poverty).

In further development of Greimas, Bremond proposes a cyclical model of the narrative with four phases beginning either with a state of deficiency or with a satisfactory state (1970: 251) (Fig. N 2). Todorov also adopts this model (1971b: 39). A different cyclical model is proposed by Labov & Waletzky (1967: 41; cf. Labov 1972: 369) for the mac-

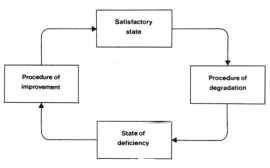

Fig. N 2. Bremond's narrative cycle (1970: 251).

rostructure of oral narratives. Its phases are: (1) orientation, (2) complicating action, (3) evaluation, (4) resolution, and (5) coda.

4. Beyond Syntax, Semantics, and Verbal Structure

Beyond narrative syntax and semantics, semiotic approaches to narratology have dealt with the pragmatics of narrative discourse and with narrativity in nonlinguistic media.

4.1 Pragmatics of Narrativity

Recent developments toward a pragmatics of narrativity are discussed by Prince (1983). An approach to the structures of narrative communication, based on Hjelmslev's glossematics, is outlined by Janik (1985). Wienold (1972) developed a pragmatics of narrativity within his theory of text processing, which is a text semiotic variant of literary reception theory (cf. Holub 1984). Wienold is concerned not with "text structures" but rather with the structures of the readers' reactions to the narrative (1972: 65, 82; cf. Gülich & Raible 1977: 280–305). Two strategies of text processing are described as typical of narrativity by Wienold: *textual rearrangement*, by which the reader reconstructs the narrated events in their logical sequence, and *recipient commitment* (*Rezipientenengagement*), which describes the reader's emotional involvement in narrative situations such as horror or suspense. For a semiogenetic theory of narrative suspense and tension, see Koch (1985).

4.2 Narrativity in the Media

In the semiotics of visual communication, the specifics of narrativity have been studied especially in the fields of film (Metz 1968, Chatman 1978; 1980, Scholes 1982: 57–72) and comics (Hünig 1974, Mathieu 1977: 257 with bibliography). For narrativity in advertising, see Advertising (3.).

Myth

Myth is a basic phenomenon of human culture. Its fundamental relevance to the sciences of man has made it an object of study of interdisciplinary research. Modern interpretations of myth begin in 1725 with Vico's *New Science* (cf. Hawkes 1977: 11–15). With Lévi-Strauss, myth becomes a privileged object of text semiotics. Beginning with Barthes, myth has been interpreted as a semiotic phenomenon of everyday culture. For surveys of research in myths and mythology see Sebeok, ed. (1955), Maranda, ed. (1972), Dupré (1973), Bolle (1974), Calame (1982), Hendricks (1982), and Hübner (1985).

1. General Definition of Myth

Myth (from Gr. μῦθοσ, 'word', 'speech', 'tale of Gods') "may be defined as a story or a complex of story elements taken as expressing, and therefore as implicitly symbolizing, certain deep-lying aspects of human and transhuman existence" (Wheelwright 1974: 538).

1.1 Myth as a Metaphorical Narrative

The above definition characterizes myth as a metaphorical narrative, a text that is to be interpreted on two levels. One is a surface level, referring to actions of mythical agents. (Greimas & Courtés [1979] call this the *practical* level of myth.) The other is a deep level, referring to existential questions (cf. Jolles 1930) concerning man and cosmos. Examples from Greek and Christian mythology are the myths of the origin and end of man, cosmos, or natural elements (e.g., fire or water), myths of time and eternity, or myths of rebirth and renewal.

1.2 Myth, Science, and Truth

The transcendental character of these questions has made mythology a topic in the study of religions. Its cosmological dimension brought mythology (like magic, q.v. 3.–4.) into conflict with science. The Greeks (cf. Nestle 1942) distinguished between *mythos* (possibly fictive discourse) and *logos* (rational discourse). In the ages of Enlightenment and Positivism, *myth* even became opposed to *reality*. *Mythical* was a synonym of *false*. After having designated the "absolute truth" and "sacred history," *myth* was now an antonym of *science* and *reality* (cf. Eliade 1957: 23–24). Yet, modern theology (e.g., Eliade), psychoanalysis (Freud, C. G. Jung), the philosophy of symbolic forms (E. Cassirer, S. Langer), literary criticism (N. Frye), and finally structural anthropology (Lévi-Strauss) have contributed to the understanding of myth as a constant dimension of the human mind (cf. Hübner 1985).

2. Lévi-Strauss's Structural Analysis of Myths

Lévi-Strauss developed a structural method of myth analysis which became paradigmatic for text semiotics, in particular Greimas's structural semantics and the semiotic theory of narrativity. For surveys and applications of this method see Greimas (1970: 117–34), Köngäs Maranda & Maranda (1971), Culler (1975), and Hawkes (1977).

2.1 Myth as a Sign System

For Lévi-Strauss, myths are messages based on a code with structures similar to those of a language (1958: 206–231). Methods of linguistic structuralism, such as segmentation, classification, and the search for binary oppositions, are therefore his tools of analysis. In his study of the Oedipus myth, Lévi-Strauss begins by breaking down the text into basic units consisting of summarizing sentences. These express a relation in the form of a subject-predicate structure. "Bundles" of such relations within a myth and its variants form the "gross constituent units" of myth analysis, which Lévi-Strauss calls *mythemes* (ibid.: 211). In myth, these constituents function like phonemes in language: They are "made up of all their variants" (ibid.: 212). In a two-dimensional notational system, which Lévi-Strauss likens to an orchestra score (ibid.: 213), the mythemes are arranged on a syntagmatic and a paradigmatic axis. The former follows the narrative sequence of mythical events shown in the textual combination of the mythemes. The latter represents the semantic equivalences of the textual units in the form of columns. Especially with its paradigmatic dimension, this method of structural text analysis provided a new approach to the analysis of narratives. Propp, Lévi-Strauss's predecessor in the history of text semiotics (see Narrative 2.2), had developed a model of analysis that was still predominantly syntagmatic.

A myth, like the Oedipus myth, which contains four mythemes (1, 2, 3, 4) occurring in the textual sequence 1, 3, 2, 4, 2, 4, 3, 4, 1, 2, 1, is then represented in the following chart:

By this analysis, a semantic reduction of the text from eleven to four content units becomes possible. With such procedures of textual reduction, Lévi-Strauss arrives at specific deep structures in which he discovers a hidden logic of myth.

2.2 Mythological Logic

The final sequence of textual units can be reduced still further. According to Lévi-Strauss (ibid.: 228), every myth contains a kernel of four mythemes related by opposition and equivalence:

$$F_x(a): F_y(b) \simeq F_x(b): F_{a^{-1}}(y)$$

In this formula, a and b refer to two terms representing agents; x and y are functions representing actions. The formula states that term a is replaced by its opposite a^{-1} and that an inversion occurs between the function value y and the term value a. In the Oedipus myth this means, for example, that the killing (F_x) done by the Sphinx (a) is related to the rescue of the men (F_y) by Oedipus (b) as the murder (F_x) committed by Oedipus (b) is related to the final rescue of the men (y) by the destruction of the Sphinx (a^{-1}) (cf. Köngäs Maranda & Maranda 1971: 26–34). More generally: $F_x : F_y$ is the conflict between evil and good. It is resolved by the hero committing a negative act, the destruction of the villain. This nevertheless results in the inverse, namely, a victory. In this way, "mythical thought always progresses from the awareness of oppositions toward their resolution. — The purpose of myth is to provide a logical model capable of overcoming a contradiction" (Lévi-Strauss 1958: 224, 229).

3. Everyday Myths

With his *Mythologies* (1957), Barthes founded a semiotic approach to modern culture which defines myth not as a form of narrative, but as a phenomenon of everyday life (see Barthes 2., Hervey 1982: 139–48, Lavers 1982: 113–27).

3.1 Myth as a Secondary Semiotic System

According to Barthes (1957), myth is a "second order semiotic system" built on the principle of connotation (see Barthes 1.). Myths consist of connotative meanings which are, so to speak, engrafted in a parasitic fashion onto a denotational level of meaning. As such, myths appear in advertising (q.v. 3.), films (cf. Drummond 1984), business life (cf. Broms & Gahmberg 1981), or the daily food of a given culture (e.g., wine or steak and chips in France).

3.2 From Mythoclasm to Semioclasm

In this tradition, the concept of myth becomes an instrument of cultural criticism (Barthes 1957: 151–53). Myth serves to "naturalize" the messages of the bourgeois class by using factual messages (on the denotational level) as a vehicle for hidden (connotational) ideological meanings. Myths deprive their object of their history and avoid questioning the present state of affairs by disguising particular statements as universal truths. "Under the effect of mythical inversion, the quite contingent foundations of the utterance become [. . .] the Norm, General Opinion, in short the *doxa*" (Barthes 1977: 165). Thus, "myth is always a stolen language" (Barthes 1957: 131). A crucial point of this theory of myth is its probably naive assumption of an ideologically "innocent" primary level of meaning onto which the myth is grafted as a secondary system. In a later revision of his own theory, Barthes seems to have recognized this problem. Barthes concludes:

> The new semiology — or the new mythology — can no longer, will no longer be able to, separate so easily the signifier from the signified, the ideological from the phraseological. [. . .] A mythological doxa has been created: [. . .] demythification has itself become discourse, stock phrases. [. . .] It is no longer the myths which need to be unmasked [. . .], it is the sign itself which must be shaken. [. . .] In an initial moment, the aim was the destruction of the (ideological) signified; in a second, it is that of the destruction of the sign: "mythoclasm" is succeeded by a "semioclasm." (1977: 166–67)

4. Mythological Consciousness

Myth and mythology are also among the dominant topics of Soviet semiotics (cf. Ivanov 1978b). In this tradition, Lotman & Uspenskij define mythological thought as a general phenomenon of human consciousness (1974: 5): The mythological world seems to be composed of holistic objects which are (a) not integrated into hierarchies, (b) without structural features, and (c) singular. In such a world, signs appear as analogous to proper nouns. Names are without semantic features, merely denote objects, and, according to Lotman & Uspenskij, are identified with the named (ibid.: 8; cf. Magic 3.2). With these characteristics, the mythological consciousness is interpreted as *asemiotic*: "Myth and name are directly connected in their nature [. . .]: Myth is personal (nominational), and name is mythological" (ibid.). In this perspective, the mythological consciousness in the history of culture "began to be perceived as an alternative to semiotic thinking," sometimes even as a negation of sign systems.

Ideology

The study of ideologies brings semiotics into interdisciplinary contact with philosophy and the social sciences. As a science, ideology has been connected with modern semiotics since its early history. Today, the semiotic analysis of ideologies is a recurrent topic of theoretical semiotics and of text semiotics, especially in the critical semiotic study of the mass media.

1. The Meaning of Ideology

The term *ideology* was first used in 1796 by A. L. C. Destutt de Tracy to designate a new empiricist "science of ideas" (cf. Rastier 1972a). In the Age of Enlightenment, the French *idéologues* (see History 3.3.4; Busse & Trabant, eds. 1986) developed this "study of the origins of ideas" as a science free from metaphysical and religious prejudices. When Napoleon later attacked and ridiculed these philosophers, the concept of ideology began to acquire a negative connotation. Until today, the meanings of ideology have continued to be situated between these early positive and negative evaluations. In current usage, two main versions of the concept and a third, less frequent one may be distinguished (for more comprehensive surveys see Plamenatz 1970, Dierse & Romberg 1976, Williams 1977: 55–71).

1.1 *The Value-Neutral Concept*

In a value-neutral sense, ideology is any system of norms, values, beliefs, or *weltanschauungen* directing the social and political attitudes and actions of a group, a social class, or a society as a whole. In this value-neutral sense, ideology is mostly defined by American sociologists (e.g., Parsons; cf. Dierse & Romberg 1976: 178), but even Lenin uses a value-neutral term when he speaks of the "socialist ideology." Thus, both socialism and capitalism, nationalisms and religions are ideologies in this sense.

1.2 *The Pejorative Sense*

The pejorative sense of ideology goes back to Marx and Engels, who defined ideologies as systems of false ideas, representing the false consciousness of a social class, in particular of the ruling class, the bourgeoisie. The ideas are false because they promote the interest of a particular class while pretending to be in the interest of the society as a whole. In this sense, ideology is seen as an instrument of deceit. It is sometimes associated with myth and opposed to science and truth. Those who adopt this evaluative concept of ideology have always refused to consider their own system of ideas an ideology. For them, ideology is the thought of the others (cf. Nattiez 1973a: 72).

1.3 The Universalistic Sense

The universalistic sense is a less frequent version of the concept. It identifies ideology with the sphere of ideas in general. In Marxist contexts, ideology in this sense sometimes refers to the superstructures in opposition to the material basis of a society. Bakhtin (under the pseudonym Vološinov) uses ideology in this sense when he writes: "Everything ideological [. . .] is a *sign*; *without signs, there is no ideology.* [. . .] The domain of ideology coincides with the domain of signs. [. . .] Wherever a sign is present, ideology is present, too. *Everything ideological possesses semiotic value*" (1930: 9–10). In this sense, the study of ideology merges with semiotics.

---

2. Semiotic Approaches to Ideology

With exceptions, such as Bakhtin, semiotics has discussed ideology mostly as a concept with negative connotations. (For surveys see Carontini & Péraya 1975: 133–73, Nattiez 1973a, Larrain 1980, Zima 1981, Heim 1983: 261–311, Nicholson 1986.) The tenor of the arguments is that semiotics should provide scientific instruments to destroy or at least reveal ideologies. In applied semiotics, text semiotic studies were for some time pursued with the conviction of the former possibility. Theoretical or metasemiotic studies, however, have often acknowledged the impossibility of an escape from ideology.

2.1 Applied Semiotic Analyses of Ideologies

The interest of text semiotics in ideology as an object of analysis is expressed by Rossi-Landi as follows: "It is by means of sign systems that ideologies are transmitted and by reflecting on sign systems that it becomes possible to demystify them in their internal mechanisms" (1972: 9). Two prominent semioticians who have made proposals for such a program of ideological demystification are Barthes and Eco.

2.1.1 IDEOLOGY AS A SECONDARY SEMIOTIC SYSTEM

In his critical studies of messages in the mass media, Barthes describes ideology as a secondary semiotic system based on the principle of connotation (see Barthes 1.): The "common domain of the signifieds of connotation is that of *ideology*, which cannot but be single for a given society and history, no matter what signifiers of connotation it may use" (1964c: 49). In this description, the concept of ideology merges with that of myth (q.v. 3.), and it remains unclear whether Barthes intends any difference between the two concepts (cf. Silverman 1983: 30). A possible differentiation and a further parallel between ideology and myth are suggested by Larrain (1980: 145, 150) with reference to Lévi-Strauss's theory (see Myth 2.): "The difference is located in the fact that ideology tries to solve social contradictions and myth tries to solve contradictions with nature." But both myth and ideology are phenomena operating in the unconscious. (Cf. also Althusser's position; Structuralism 4.1.)

Barthes understood ideology in the pejorative sense outlined above. A logical problem with this definition of myth and ideology is therefore the normative value which denotation assumes when it is seen as nonideological and nonmythological. Does not this distinction between an "innocent denotation" and a "biased connotation" presuppose an ideological point of view itself? Barthes's later revision of his own concepts (see Myth 3.2, Barthes 2.) took this dilemma into consideration. For an extensive discussion of the theories of ideological connotations, see Kerbrat-Orecchioni (1977: 208–233).

2.1.2 THE IDEOLOGICAL CODE

Eco (1970) describes ideologies as codes which generate messages with connotations of a particular kind. According to Eco, ideological connotations form "sclerotically hardened messages, which become the signifying unit of a rhetorical subcode" (1968: 173). Ideologies "prevent us from seeing the various semantic systems in the totality of their mutual relations" by restricting the field of possible connotations to the ones determined by the ideological subcode and by concealing all other connotations. Later, Eco describes ideology as an instance of *overcoding*, i.e., a process where (secondary) meanings are assigned to messages generated by a basic (primary) code (1976: 135, 290, cf. Code 3.3.4).

2.1.3 IDEOLOGEMES

For the study of ideology in (literary) texts, Kristeva introduces the term *ideologeme* (1969c: 113–14). It is defined as that intertextual function (cf. Kristeva 2.3) which gives a text its historical and social coordinates and which relates the text to the other signifying practices which make up its cultural space. Kristeva's (1970) textual analyses show that her ideologemes are something like a semiotic paradigm (in the sense of Kuhn) or the episteme (in the sense of Foucault; see Structuralism 4.2.2) of a cultural epoch.

2.2 Metasemiotic Reflections

Several metasemiotic studies start out with the assumption of the "ideological character of every discourse" (Rossi-Landi 1968: 95). In this perspective, semiotic discourse becomes itself a potentially ideological activity. From the double encounter of semiotics and ideology, on the object- and on the metalevel, Rossi-Landi concludes "on the one hand that a doctrine of ideologies without semiotics is incapable of articulating itself sufficiently. [. . .] On the other hand, a semiotics, without the support of a doctrine of ideologies, remains a specialized discipline, separated from praxis, in spite of its claim to be a general theory of signs" (1972: 9). While most metasemiotic studies agree on the impossibility of an escape in principle from one's own ideological bias, they nevertheless suggest that a scientific semiotics might be able to "neutralize" this bias.

2.2.1 IDEOLOGY AS A DISGUISE OF STRUCTURAL ALTERNATIVES

Prieto gives an account of ideology based on the structuralist principle of pertinence (1975b: 143–65) (see Structuralism 1.1.3). In semiotic research, this principle reveals that distinctive features, and thus the structures of an object, never have their foundation in the material object itself: "The way a subject perceives a material object [. . .] presupposes a particular way of perceiving another object deriving from another universe of discourse" (ibid.: 147). In accordance with this Saussurean principle of structure as difference, Prieto argues that objective knowledge in the sciences of man requires reference to the historicity and arbitrariness of knowledge, a reference which reveals the alternatives to the object of analysis. In contradistinction to such differential procedures of analysis, ideologies attempt to "naturalize" the cognition of a material reality, i.e., to make knowledge appear as a necessary consequence of its object (cf. ibid.: 160). Ideology thus disguises its own semiotic foundations.

2.2.2 THE SCIENTIFIC NEUTRALIZATION OF IDEOLOGY

Verón, too, admits that the ideal of pure, objective scientific knowledge can never be attained but suggests that scientific research may nevertheless be able to neutralize its ideological bias. According to Verón, an ideology is not a message but "a system of semantic rules to generate messages," which are transmitted through the "communicational dimension" of connotation (1971: 67–68; cf. 1973b; 1978). Ideology is both similar and opposed to science (1971: 71): Whenever the scientist makes choices the bases for which are scientifically unverifiable, his or her decisions are ideological. But science, unlike ideology, makes an "effort towards a neutralization of connotative meanings by making explicit the decisions that generate them."

2.2.3 AUTOCRITICAL SEMIOTICS

In a metasemiotic perspective, Kristeva criticizes certain formalistic tendencies in semiotics for neglecting "the question of the presuppositions or the ideology which authorize the application of this formalization, and ultimately its validity and its truth" (1975: 703). At the same time, she points out that by investigating that ideology, semiotics "attacks itself at those same matrices which allow the process of cognition: the sign, the subject, and its sociohistorical position." Her own escape from this metatheoretical dilemma is outlined in her proposals for an autocritical research, constantly reflecting upon its own theoretical and ideological presuppositions (see Kristeva 1.).

Theology

Although semiotic theology has so far been concerned mainly with the semiotics of texts, it belongs only in part to the field of text semiotics. If theology is research in religious texts and their exegesis, and if the semiotics of religion is to be defined as "a science which studies religious discourse within religious praxis" (Davidsen 1981: 79), then theological semiotics is a branch of text semiotics. From this point of view, theology is also discussed in the chapter on hermeneutics and exegesis. But there are aspects of theology which transcend the field of text semiotics in the narrower sense, in particular the concept of the religious sign and the semiotics of liturgy. Further topics which have been discussed in the interdisciplinary context of semiotics and theology are the semiotics of translation (see Güttgemanns 1982: 156–57) and more generally the topic of intertextuality (see Compagnon 1979: 155–232, Delorme & Geoltrain 1982: 113–17).

This chapter will be restricted to Christian theology. For the semiotics of religions in general see Ogibenin (1979), Gay & Patte (1986), and the special issue of *Le bulletin du groupe de recherche sémio-linguistique* 8 (April 1979) entitled *Sémiotique du domaine religieux*. For the philosophical theology of Peirce, another related topic of interest to semioticians, see Orange (1984).

1. Theology of the Sign

E. Cassirer, M. Eliade, and Meschonnic (1975: 48) have pointed out a fundamental affinity between the sign and the dimension of the sacred: "The model of the sign is the model of the sacred: a relation to the Absent, to the Other." It is thus not surprising that the essence of signs has been a topic of theological concern since the early patristic writings. Specifically theological dimensions of the sign are a central topic of biblical exegesis and the medieval pansemiotic vision of the universe.

1.1 Church Fathers as Semioticians

The history of semiotics from the late ancient to medieval times is part of Church history. There was a unity of philosophy and theology in this epoch, so that significant contributions to the theory of signs could be made by the Church Fathers. For the discussion of this early Christian semiotics, see History (2.1.5–2.2.1).

1.2 The Sign as a Key Concept of the Bible

Semeion (σημεῖον; cf. Charlier 1959, Rengstorf 1971), *eikon* (εἰκών; cf. Eltester 1958), and *imago* (cf. Dürig 1952, Otto 1963, Lange 1969) are semiotic key concepts of the Scriptures referring to signs, symbols, and images. In the Old Testament, signs are mostly indices or symbols. Indices occur in the form of natural signs of orientation in time and space (e.g., "lights in the firmament" as signs "to divide the day from the night," Genesis 1:14), prophetic signs of future events, and signs of proof of the presence of God (Judges 6:17: "show me a sign that thou talkest with me."). Among the latter group of signs are miracles, taken as proofs of the will of God (Exodus 4:17: "And thou shalt take this rod in thine hand, wherewith thou shalt do signs."). Besides these indices explicitly called "signs," the pansemiotic sphere of universal symbolism is one of implicit indexicality.

Examples of conventional symbols in the Old Testament are the signs of the covenant between the people of Israel and God (e.g., circumcision, Genesis 17:11; blood at the door, at Passover, Exodus 12:13). In Genesis (9:12–13), a natural phenomenon, the rainbow, is interpreted as a conventional sign, "a token of covenant between me and the earth." In the New Testament, the concept of sign is central to the Gospel of Saint John (cf. Charlier 1959). The miracles performed by Christ are interpreted as manifestations of God's glory (John 2:11) and thus as indexical signs. In contradistinction to the Old Testament, the New Testament puts more emphasis on reporting the effects of the signs on the minds of their addressees (ibid.: "and his disciples believed on him."). There seems to be a shift toward the pragmatic dimension of theological semiosis.

1.3 The Medieval Pansemiotic View of the Universe

"The heavens declare the glory of God" (Psalm 19:1) and "the God of glory thundereth" (Psalm 29:3): such messages express Old Testament views of the universe as a sign of God's power. In the Middle Ages, this view developed into an elaborate pansemiotic system of world interpretation. Not only the words of the Bible but also the objects designated by those words (thus Thomas Aquinas, *Summa Theologicae* I,

9.1, art. 10) and finally the whole universe became signs of divine revelation. Medieval theology interpreted these universal signs on the basis of the exegetic codes of manifold scriptural meaning (see Hermeneutics 1.2). The medieval doctrine of *universal symbolism* (cf. Dunbar 1961: 19–20, Białostocki 1973: 20ff.), which ascribed pansemiotic meanings to natural objects in the universe, became codified in lapidaries, bestiaries, and other pseudoscientific treatises. In this theological interpretation of nature, a rock, for example, could have the following three spiritual meanings (cf. Dunbar 1929: 19): In a tropological sense it was 'that which each soul should be to its fellows'; allegorically it referred to Christ, and anagogically to 'the foundation of the heavenly kingdom.'

In the pansemiotic theological exegesis, the natural signs of the universe are either symbols or icons. These types of sign are implied in two topoi of medieval universal symbolism, namely, those of the world as a book and as a mirror of God. The book metaphor (cf. Curtius 1948: 323–29) of the world as a *codex vivus* written by God is based on an arbitrary system of symbols, which could be deciphered only by an exegetic code. The mirror metaphor implies iconicity in a world which was considered to be an image or even an imitation of God (cf. Gilbert & Kuhn 1939: 147–50).

2. Religious Discourse and Theological Text Semiotics

Following the structuralist debate (Schiwy 1969b; 1971: 167–87) and the "linguistic theology" founded by Güttgemanns (cf. his journal *Linguistica Biblica* 1 [1970]ff., and see also Berger [1977] on linguistic exegesis), an explicitly semiotic theology has developed since the 1970s (cf. Grabner-Haider 1973, Boff 1976, Güttgemanns 1982; 1983; 1989, Volp, ed. 1982, and the journals *Semeia*, Chicago 1 [1974]ff., and *Sémiotique et bible*, Lyon 1 [1975]ff.). Its major fields of interest are religious language, biblical narratives, and practical theology. A text semiotic theology transcending these topics by a special emphasis on psychoanalytic (Lacan) and other dimensions (e.g., Derrida's grammatology) of theological hermeneutics has been developed by Güttgemanns (1983).

2.1 Religious Discourse

According to Grabner-Haider, semiotics can contribute to theology in its "urgent task" of the "development of a metalanguage of religious discourse" (1973: 209). This goal has been pursued in several semiotic studies. Morris, in his behavioristic semiotics, classifies religious discourse as being prescriptive and incitive (of behavior). A more differentiated semiotic typology of religious discourses (including prophetic, apocalyptic, epistolary, liturgic, theological, and mystic discourse) is discussed by Delorme & Geoltrain (1982: 112).

Following Morris, Grabner-Haider (1973) gives a general outline of the syntactic, semantic, and pragmatic dimensions of religious discourse and develops a "theological theory of language" on the basis of analytic, hermeneutic, and transcendental philosophy. Analytical philosophy of language (Austin, Searle), in addition to the semiotics of Peirce, is also the basis of Almeida's (1978) study of religious discourse. Hermeneutical questions about the interrelation of written and spoken theological discourse are discussed by Magaβ (1983). Goldschläger (1980) discovers the foundation of religious rhetoric in a "vertical reasoning" in which all argumentation is subordinated to a superior, divine principle.

2.2 Semiotics of Biblical Narratives

Biblical narratives are the topic to which most semiotic studies have been dedicated in the field of theology. A comprehensive survey of semiotic research methods in this field since structuralism is given by Greenwood (1985). An earlier review is included in McKnight (1978). Early semiotic approaches to biblical narratives were based on Lévi-Strauss's structural model of myth (e.g., Leach 1962) and structuralist approaches to narrativity from Propp to Barthes and Ricœur (Barthes et al. 1971a; b). Later, Greimas's text semiotics became the dominant model of research in biblical texts (Chabrol & Marin, eds. 1971; 1974) in France. This direction of study was intensified at the *Centre pour l'analyse du discours réligieux* (Lyon). Authors from this center (Groupe d'Entrevernes 1977; 1979) give an introduction to Greimas's text semiotics with applications to the Tower of Babel narrative and present further analyses of biblical parables. An exemplary study in the spirit of Greimas is also Courtés (1985). Delorme and Geoltrain give a survey of the Paris School approaches to biblical texts. Marin (1971c) extends semiotic research in narrativity from actantial constellations to the function of personal and place names in the logic of biblical narratives.

In the United States, studies such as Culley (1976), Patte (1976), Patte, ed. (1976), McKnight (1978), Patte & Patte (1978), and papers in *Semeia* have applied models of structuralist and text semiotic narratology. In Belgium and France, Almeida (1978) pursued a pluralistic semiotic approach to biblical parables. Numerous German contributions to the field were published in *Linguistica Biblica*.

3. Semiotics of Religious Praxis

Against logocentric theories of religion, theologians have consulted semiotic models to underline the importance of nonlinguistic signs, codes, and communication in religious praxis (cf. Güttgemanns 1982: 152; 1986: 472).

3.1 Divine Communication

According to Schiwy, the founding of the Christian religion constituted a specific communicative act (1975: 245): The addresser, the sign, and the first addressee merge in the person of the founder, who declared, "I am the way, and the truth, and the life" (John 14:6). Accordingly, the religious sign given by Jesus of Nazareth refers back to itself, since being a "sign of God," Christ is at the same time the first addressee of this message. Schiwy further argues that in this act of divine communication, Christ is a sign whose signifier is his human shape and whose signified is his divinity (1975: 245–48). The decoding of Christ's message is finally possible on the basis of several codes, which allows a plurality of interpretations.

3.2 Sacraments as Signs

Thomas Aquinas (1225–1274) in his *Summa Theologiae* (III, 60–84) discussed the Christian sacraments in terms of a theory of signs. Schiwy resumes this discussion in explicitly semiotic terms (1969b: 58–62). One of the most disputed topics in the history of Christianity has been the semiotic status of the signs of "wine" and "bread" within the sign system of "the Holy Communion." During the Reformation, the question of the substance of the Eucharist developed into a theological dispute which Güttgemanns interprets in semiotic terms (1982: 153; 1983: 228–30): Are "wine" and "bread" indexical (*pars pro toto*) signs of the "real presence" of Christ, as Luther argued with his "hoc est" thesis, or are they, following Zwingli's "hoc significant" thesis, natural icons of the divine?

3.3 Liturgical Semiotics

Proposals for an applied semiotics in practical theology have been presented in a volume by Schiwy et al. (1976). The authors examine liturgy as processes of semiosis and demonstrate the possibilities of applying semiotic insights in the course of the planning and practical innovations in church services. Semiotic implications of the mass, prayers, and the Eucharist are also discussed in several papers in Volp, ed. (1982), with special attention to the various liturgical codes and subcodes. For a study of liturgy from the point of view of Greimas's text semiotics, see Calloud (1973). Güttgemanns (1986; 1989) gives a more comprehensive survey of the semiotics of liturgy since its Jewish origins.

Nonverbal Communication: Introduction

Pursuing Saussure's program for the extension of research from linguistics to "a science that studies the life of signs within society," semioticians have turned to the study of nonverbal communication as the semiotic field most closely connected with verbal behavior (cf. Rossi-Landi 1968: 66). The core of nonverbal communication is the semiotic function of the human body in time and space, but there is some vagueness in its delimitation against visual and vocal communication. The conditions under which nonverbal behavior becomes sign or communication are of central interest to the foundations of semiotics.

1. Survey of the Field

Nonverbal communication is a transdisciplinary field of research. Its branches are commonly determined according to the parts of the human body functioning as a signifier in semiosis, but some authors have proposed alternative classifications of the field according to criteria such as the relation to verbal behavior (Ehlich & Rehbein 1982), channels, and psychological or semiotic functions (Poyatos 1982a; 1983, Patterson 1983, Tantam 1986).

1.1 State of the Art

Nonverbal communication research is a rapidly expanding field of transdisciplinary interest.

1.1.1 SOURCES OF RESEARCH

The state of the art in nonverbal research is documented in a number of textbooks (Eisenberg & Smith 1971, Harrison 1974, Leathers 1976, Knapp 1978), surveys, reviews, handbooks, and state-of-the-art reports (Scherer 1970, Mehrabian 1972, McCardle 1974, Spiegel & Machotka 1974, Argyle 1975, Key 1975, Poyatos 1976, Henley 1977, Harper et al. 1978, LaFrance & Mayo 1978, Burgoon 1980, Helfrich & Wallbott 1980, Scherer & Ekman, eds. 1982, Bull 1983, Posner 1985a, Kendon 1986a), individual approaches and research reports (Heslin & Patterson 1982, Patterson 1983, Poyatos 1983, Tantam 1986), anthologies of research papers and conference proceedings (Laver & Hutcheson, eds. 1972, Weitz, ed. 1974, Kendon et al., eds. 1975, Benthall & Polhemus, eds. 1975, Siegman & Feldstein, eds. 1978, Scherer & Wallbott, eds. 1979, Raffler-Engel, ed. 1980, Kendon, ed. 1981, Key, ed. 1982, Wiemann & Harrison, eds. 1983, Wolfgang, ed. 1984), and bibliographies (Davis, comp. 1972, Key 1977, Obudho, comp. 1979, Davis & Skupien, comps. 1982). Popular but richly illustrated books on nonverbal behavior are Morris (1978; 1985).

1.1.2 TRANSDISCIPLINARY CONNECTIONS

The transdisciplinary interest in nonverbal communication research was evident from its earliest precursors, which are in the fields of theater (Engel 1785), rhetoric (Bell 1806), biology and ethology (Darwin 1872), and cultural history (Kleinpaul 1888). Today, nonverbal communication research is an established branch of social psychology. One of the more specific topics within this field is the study of sex differences in nonverbal behavior (cf. Henley 1977, Mayo & Henley 1981). There are many other transdisciplinary contributions to the field, in particular from psychology and psychiatry (Ruesch & Kees 1956, Scheflen 1972; 1973, Wolfgang, ed. 1984: 203–252), sociology, anthropology (Goffman 1963; 1971, La Barre 1964, Birdwhistell 1970, Benthall & Polhemus, eds. 1975), and ethology (Eibl-Eibesfeldt 1967, Hinde, ed. 1972, Cranach & Vine, eds. 1973, Krames et al., eds. 1974, McCardle 1974).

1.1.3 NONVERBAL BEHAVIOR RESEARCH AND LINGUISTICS

The most important contribution of linguistics to the study of nonverbal communication is Pike's (1967) *Unified Theory of Human Behavior*. Pike's work is an attempt to develop a unified structural framework for the analysis of both verbal and nonverbal behavior. His aim is the extension of language studies to a theory of culture. His methods are those of structural linguistics, *tagmemics*, as his approach is called. In analogy to the *phonemes* and *utteremes* (utterances) of language, Pike postulates such general behavioral units as the *acteme* and the *behavioreme*. Outside of the school of tagmemics, these proposals have not yet had a great impact on nonverbal behavior research, but Pike's principles of emic and etic research (cf. Structuralism 1.1.3) have been highly influential in many fields. For further studies of nonverbal behavior in the context of linguistics

and discourse analysis, see Duncan & Fiske (1977), Key, ed. (1980), Goodwin (1981), and Scherer & Wallbott (1985).

1.1.4 NONVERBAL COMMUNICATION AND THE SEMIOTIC FIELD

Applied research in nonverbal behavior is of interest to several other areas of the semiotic field such as literature (Poyatos 1983), narratives (Müller 1981), rhetoric (McCroskey 1968; see Gesture 2.3.3), theater (see Gesture 2.3.4), the comics (q.v. 3.), advertising (Goffman 1976, Umiker-Sebeok 1979), other media (Bosmajian 1971, Böhme 1982), and teaching (Smith 1984).

1.2 Extension of the Field

There are broad and narrow definitions of the field of nonverbal communication (cf. Harrison 1974: 27–29, Harper et al. 1978: 2–4, Patterson 1983: 1–11). In its broadest definition, nonverbal communication has been determined according to the formula "communication minus language," thus including animal and visual communication. In its narrowest definition, it is restricted to behavior which is concomitant of verbal communication (cf. Kendon 1981: 3–4, Posner 1985a: 241–42). In this handbook, nonverbal communication is any nonlinguistic human somatic mode of semiosis.

Central domains of the field are those included in this section: gesture, kinesics, and "body language," facial signals, gaze, tactile communication, and proxemics. Only *chronemics* is less often discussed as a domain of nonverbal communication. Mostly, paralinguistics is also considered a central domain of the field, but in this handbook vocal communication is discussed as an area of language studies. Several surveys of nonverbal communication include research on bodily appearance and clothing (Argyle 1975: 323–44, Key 1975: 27–29; 1977: 116–17, Leathers 1976: 85–115, Knapp 1978: 152–95, Kendon 1986a). Among the topics of study in appearance are physical attractiveness (Adams 1977), hair (Firth 1973: 262–98, Knapp 1978: 171–75), cosmetics, and other artifacts as by-elements of the human body. On the semiotics of clothing and fashion see Bogatyrev (1936), Barthes (1967b), Sahlins (1976: 179–204), Hoffmann (1985), *Kodikas/Code* 8 (1985: 81ff.), and Sebeok, ed. (1986: 252–55).

In spite of the fact that Wescott (1966) has proposed to study the communicative functions of taste and odor in disciplines for which he proposed the designations of *geustics* and *osmology*, these areas have remained marginal domains of research. For discussions of olfactory signals see Key (1975: 110–14; 1977: 113), Leathers (1976: 155–65), Poyatos (1976; 1983), Knapp (1978: 169–71), and Sebeok, ed. (1986: 647–48). For a few remarks on gustatory signals see Eisenberg & Smith (1971: 119–20) and Poyatos (1976; 1983). The related topic of culinary semiotics has been given more attention (Sebeok, ed. 1986: 157–62, *Zeitschrift für Semiotik* 4.4 [1982]). More exotic topics which some authors have studied within the field of nonverbal communication include telepathy (Leathers 1976: 169–98) and extraterrestrial communication (Key 1977: 37).

1.3 Neighboring Fields

Some taxonomies of nonverbal communication include domains which have a different systematic place in this handbook. Thus, topics of zoosemiotics are discussed in the context of nonverbal communication by Hinde, ed. (1972), Krames et al., eds. (1974), and Argyle (1975: 18–49). Topics from the semiotic field of language studies which appear in nonverbal communications research (cf. Key 1977) are paralinguistics (frequently; cf. 2.1), sign languages, and language substitutes. One of the earliest books on nonverbal communication (Ruesch & Kees 1956) also includes portions of the semiotic field of visual communication, namely, "messages through objects and pictures." Except for Harrison (1974), this view is not adopted by other researchers in the field, but the view that all nonlinguistic messages

should be defined as nonverbal is also taken by semioticians such as Rossi-Landi (1968: 66–82). Lange-Seidl (1975) has a similarly broad concept of the sphere of nonverbal signs.

---

2. Terminological Considerations

There has been some terminological criticism of the concept of "nonverbal communication." It has been deplored that it gives only a negative characterization of a field of research, that it is often too broad or too vague in its scope, and finally that the nonverbal cannot be successfully separated from other modes of communication. In view of the high degree of acceptance which this designation has found in the research field under discussion, the total rejection of the term, which Sebeok proposes in view of the "morass of nomenclature" (1976: 158; 1977: 1065–66), has found little resonance. Evidently, terms cannot be expected to derive their definition from their own etymology.

2.1 Verbal, Vocal, and Nonverbal

Some authors have discussed or proposed the terms *vocal* vs. *nonvocal* as an alternative to the *verbal-nonverbal* dichotomy (Laver & Hutcheson, eds. 1972: 12, Poyatos 1976: 23–25; 1983: 66–69), but these are in fact overlapping categories. *Verbal* means "of words," which can be acoustic (vocal) or visual signs (see Writing). Thus, the two fields of communication by language and by somatic (bodily) signs can be subdivided as follows (cf. Poyatos 1976: 23–25):

1. *Verbal-vocal* communication comprises messages of a spoken natural language.

2. *Nonverbal-vocal* communication (cf. Helfrich & Wallbott 1980: 268) comprises the field of paralinguistics and some other nonlinguistic uses of the human voice (e.g., screaming, laughing, etc.).

3. *Verbal-nonvocal* communication is carried

on by writing systems, language substitutes, and sign languages (see also Stokoe 1978).

4. *Nonverbal-nonvocal* communication (cf. Helfrich & Wallbott 1980: 268) comprises the somatic signs in time and space dealt with in this section.

2.2 Communication Excluding and Including Language

Studies which "insist on viewing nonverbal communication as 'communication minus language'" have been criticized by Sebeok for "encompassing an astounding congeries of topics" (1977: 1065). In agreement with this criticism, the field of nonverbal communication is restricted in this handbook to nonlinguistic somatic modes of communication (cf. 1.2).

Another criticism of nonverbal communication research has been that its establishment as a separate field of study threatens to separate artificially language from concomitant modes of semiotic behavior (cf. Kendon 1977: 211; 1980b: 30–31, Sebeok 1977: 1065, Knapp 1978: 3). A number of authors have consequently preferred the term *face-to-face-interaction* (e.g., Kendon et al., eds. 1975, Duncan & Fiske 1977) for their approach to the field. This criticism is justified as a memento for the necessity of an integrated view of semiotic behavior in all of its contexts but cannot discredit attempts at the analytic isolation of the various components of semiosis. There are furthermore various degrees of autonomy of the codes of nonverbal communication in relation to language (cf., e.g., the relative autonomy of gestural emblems in Gesture 2.2).

3. Nonverbal Behavior, Sign, and Communication

Nonverbal behavior raises the question of the threshold of semiosis: According to which criteria is human behavior to be considered as sign or communication? (Cf. Gesture 2.1, Tactile Communication, and Communication 2.) The answers depend, of course, on the definitions of these terms. As discussed in the chapters on sign and communication, the plurality of criteria which may be valid independently suggests an approach which determines semiosis according to various degrees of semioticity. The lowest degree of semiosis would be the pansemiotic position, and the highest degree would include all of the additional restrictive criteria discussed in the following. For good surveys of and proposals for the solution of these questions at issue, see Knapp (1978: 2–12), Patterson (1983: 37–55), and Posner (1985a).

3.1 The Pansemiotic View

According to the pansemiotic view, all nonverbal behavior is communication (cf. Patterson 1983: 37–38). This is basically the position of the proponents of the metacommunicative axiom of the impossibility of not communicating (see Communication 2.6). Goffman, for example, argues that "although an individual can stop talking, he cannot stop communicating through body idiom; he must say either the right thing or the wrong thing. He cannot say nothing" (1963: 35). Those who reject this very broad concept of communication will have to admit that nonverbal behavior is a permanent source of potential messages (cf. Communication 2.6.2).

3.2 Unilateral Semiosis

In unilateral semiosis, the nonverbal behavior is a sign either only to the receiver or only to the sender. In the first case, semiosis is observation, diagnosis, or interpretation (see Communication 2.1). In the second case a sign is intended, but the receiver is not aware of it. This situation is also defined as "unsuccessful communication" (cf. Posner 1985a: 243). To many semioticians, unilateral semiosis implies a sign but is not yet communication.

Intentionality and *awareness* are two related

categories of behavior which may be present independently in the production and in the reception of signs. Intentional (also *goal-directed* or *purposive*) behavior is described from the sender's perspective. Only bilateral communication is intended *and* interpreted as intended (''successful communication''; cf. Posner 1985a: 243). In unilateral communication, intentionality may be present in the following types of situation (cf. MacKay 1972: 24): The sign is (1) intended but not interpreted as intended, or (2) not intended, but interpreted as intended. (Nonintentional behavior which is not interpreted as such would not qualify as semiosis at all.)

Awareness describes the degree to which signs may be conscious or unconscious to the receiver (R) or to the sender (S). According to Argyle, this feature is mostly unilateral in nonverbal semiosis (1975: 7). The following cases may be distinguished (cf. ibid.): (1) Both S and R are mostly unaware of the sign. (According to Argyle, this situation is typical of most nonverbal modes of semiosis.) (2) S is unaware and R is aware of the nonverbal sign (e.g., in diagnosis). (3) S is unaware and R is unaware but influenced (e.g., gaze shifts or pupil dilation). (4) S is aware but R is unaware (as, e.g., an actor employing certain gestures).

3.3 Bilateral Communication

According to Wiener et al., nonverbal behavior is communicative only when it is bilateral (cf. Communication 2.3). To these authors, nonverbal communication involves ''(a) a socially shared [. . .] code, (b) an encoder who makes something public via that code, and (c) a decoder who responds systematically to that code'' (1972: 186). To these and other authors (Posner 1985a: 243), unilateral semiosis can imply only nonverbal signs but no communication. An additional criterion of bilaterality in nonverbal communication is *interaction* (Ekman & Friesen 1969: 56, Posner 1985a: 243): The nonverbal behavior of an agent is interactive if it influences or modifies the behavior of other persons. Since many modes of semiosis studied in the field of nonverbal communication are clearly unilateral, the requirement of bilaterality seems to be too strong as a criterion for a definition of the field.

Gesture, "Body Language," and Kinesics

This chapter deals with the semiotic potential of the human body from hand and arm gestures to posture and body movements. Following Birdwhistell, this field of research is often subsumed under the designation of *kinesics*, but many social psychologists use this term only for Birdwhistell's own structuralist approach to the field. The study of gesticulation (parallel to speech) and of spontaneous and coded gestures is of concern to many fields of semiotic research, in particular to rhetoric, theater, ritual, and to language, speech and its origins. Special gestural languages are discussed in the chapters on sign languages and language substitutes.

1. Survey of the Field

The "language of the body" is a field which extends from subconscious emotional expressions to highly conventional and ritualized forms of behavior. The diversity of approaches to and research interest in this field of study is reflected by differences in terminology.

1.1 State of the Art

A survey of the state of the art in this vast field of research must remain far from comprehensive. In addition to monographs, anthologies, and bibliographies on nonverbal communica-

tion in general, which deal extensively with this field, the following more specialized publications may be consulted: On gestures, see Critchley (1975), Nespoulous et al., eds. (1986), and Kendon's (1986b) survey in the special issue of *Semiotica* (62.1/2) entitled *Approaches to Gesture*. A popular but richly illustrated account of gestures is Morris et al. (1979). Classics in the history of research in gestures are Darwin (1872), Wundt (1900), Bühler (1933a), Wolff (1945), and Efron (1941). On posture and body movement see Scheflen (1972; 1973), Argyle (1975), Morris (1978), and Lamb & Watson (1979). Bibliographies are Davis, comp. (1972) and Davis & Skupien, comps. (1982). For kinesics see 3.

1.2 Terminology and Scope

The subdivision of the field of nonverbal communication varies considerably with respect to gesture and kinesics, at least from a terminological point of view.

1.2.1 GESTURE

A gesture in the narrower sense is bodily communication by means of hands and arms and to a lesser degree by the head. This narrower concept excludes nonverbal communication by posture and body movement (see 1.2.2) and facial expression (cf., e.g., Abercrombie 1954: 3, Morris et al. 1979). But in a broader sense of gesture, not adopted here, the latter modes of expression are also included, for example, when Hayes defines gestures as "any bodily movement excepting that of vocalization made consciously or unconsciously to communicate either with one's self or with another" (1966: 627).

In a still broader sense, *gesture* has been used by some authors as a fundamental term for any act of communication. Such broad definitions include the concept of vocal gesture. Mead (1934) uses the term *gesture* in this broad sense as a key concept of his theory of symbolic interaction to describe communicative acts of humans or of animals. In his behavioristic framework, Mead defines gestures in terms of their effect on the receiver: "The gesture is that phase of the individual act to which adjustment takes place on the part of other individuals in the social process of behavior" (1934: 46). Mead further distinguishes between unconscious and conscious gestures. Only the latter are "significant *symbols*," but "a gesture is not significant when the response of another organism to it does not indicate to the organism making it what the other organism is responding to" (ibid.: 81).

The concept of vocal gesture has also been used to refer to the expressive function of language in general. In this sense, Sapir defines the paralinguistic characteristics of a speaker's voice as "a form of gesture" (1949: 535). Within poetics, a theory of language as gesture has been developed by Blackmur, based on the argument that "when the language of words most succeeds it *becomes* gesture in its words" (1935: 3).

1.2.2 "BODY LANGUAGE"
For lack of a better term, bodily communication by posture, body motion, and orientation will be subsumed under the designation of *body language*. Although this term is rather controversial (cf. Sebeok 1976: 160), it is used not only by popular authors (Fast 1970, Bonnafont 1977) but also by scholars such as Scheflen (1972), Birdwhistell (1974), Key (1975: 76–106), Dittmann (1978), and Raffler-Engel, ed. (1980:

2). The major objection against this term is that bodily communication has only few features in common with linguistic codes (cf. Dittmann 1978: 81–93, Scherer et al. 1979: 178). An older term for the field of bodily communication is *pantomime* (cf. Frijda 1965, Adler 1979: 8–30), but generally this concept is restricted to theatrical performances.

1.2.3 KINESICS
The concept of kinesics is derived from the Greek κίνησις 'movement.' Birdwhistell, the founder of kinesics, defined it as the "systematic study of how human beings communicate through body movement and gesture" (1952; 1955: 10) and also as the "systematic study of the visually sensible aspects of nonverbal interpersonal communication" (ibid.: 12; 1960: 54). In this definition, the scope of kinesics covers most of the field of nonverbal communication. In this sense, Duncan, for example, enumerates "gestures and other body movements, facial expression, eye movement and posture" as modalities of kinesic behavior (1969: 118), excluding only paralanguage, proxemics, olfactive and tactile communication, as well as dress and cosmetics. Key (1975), Harper et al. (1978: 119), and Knapp (1978: 12) give a similar outline of the scope of kinesics. Raffler-Engel, ed. (1980: 3) even includes proxemics. Other authors, however, prefer to define kinesics not as a field of study but as the specific approach to nonverbal communication developed by Birdwhistell (e.g., Argyle 1975, Scherer & Wallbott, eds. 1979, Scherer & Ekman, eds. 1982). As such, kinesics will be surveyed in this chapter.

1.2.4 KINEMICS
Because of its foundations in linguistic structuralism, kinesics was early included in the field of semiotics (cf. Sebeok et al., eds. 1964 and Eco 1968). Birdwhistell's emic principles of research made it seem consistent to suggest the term *kinemics* for this approach to nonverbal communication, analogous to *phonemics* and *proxemics* (cf. Lange-Seidl 1975: 246). This term appears in the dictionaries of Pei & Gay-

nor (1954) and Hartmann & Stork (1972) but was not widely adopted elsewhere. An independent approach to the study of body movements is proposed by Schutz (1976) under the designation of *kinesiology*. It includes a surface structure representation called *kinetics* and an underlying representation of movement called *kinemics*.

1.3 *The Sign Repertoire*

A preliminary survey of the sign repertoire of the human body shows that the major communicative potential of the human body is by gestures, whereas only weakly coded messages can be conveyed by "body language."

1.3.1 GENERAL TYPOLOGY OF GESTURES

One of the most influential classifications of gestures was developed by Ekman & Friesen (1969; 1972; Ekman 1976; 1980b). In further development of Efron's (1941) theory of gesture, this classification comprises the following five categories of nonverbal behavior:

1. *Emblems* are gestures "which have a direct verbal translation, or dictionary definition" (Ekman & Friesen 1969: 63). They are conventional and generally intended signs which are autonomous in relation to language. But "an emblem may repeat, substitute, or contradict some part of the concomitant verbal behavior" (ibid.). For a survey of emblematic codes, see 2.2.

2. *Illustrators* are speech-related gestures serving to illustrate what is being said verbally. A less technical term for this type of nonverbal communication is *gesticulation* (cf. Kendon 1986b: 7). For these gestures see 2.3.1.

3. *Affect displays* are nonverbal (mostly facial) expressions of emotions and affects.

4. *Regulators* are speech-related gestures which regulate the verbal interaction between speakers and listeners (see 2.3.2).

5. *Body manipulators* are movements of touching or manipulating one's own body (e.g., scratching the head, licking the lips) or an object (e.g., playing with a pencil). Such acts of subconscious autocommunication are interpreted as adaptive efforts to satisfy self or bodily needs or to manage emotions (cf. Ekman & Friesen 1969: 84). For further studies and illustrations see Kiener (1962: 239–344), Feyereisen (1974), and Morris (1978: 102–105).

1.3.2 "BODY LANGUAGE"

Postures, body orientation, and body movement form the sign repertoire of the human "body language." On the basis of anthropological data from different cultures, Hewes (1957) has developed a typology of postures which distinguishes no fewer than one thousand static positions (such as standing, sitting, squatting, kneeling, and lying) of the human body. Body motion and orientation have also been the subject of elaborate systems of description (Rosenfeld 1982). Yet, the communicative function of these etic modes of behavior is far from certain. Interpretations of "body language" have focused on the following dimensions of significance.

1. *Cultural specificity*: The number and form of conventional and socially acceptable bodily postures vary cross-culturally (cf. Hewes 1957, Scheflen 1964: 152). Differences in the evaluation of the same postures by males and females from different cultures have been studied by Perrino (1981). Mauss (1935) argued that "the techniques of the body," the simple and practical everyday activities, are not natural but are learned. An example of such culturally determined body movements is the walking styles discovered by La Barre (1964: 195).

2. *Ethological significance*: The degree to which bodily behavior is culturally coded is still disputed. Ethological interpretations of nonverbal behavior give evidence for the universality of bodily behavior (cf. Grant 1968). But most ethological research in body language has so far been concerned with gestures and facial expressions (see 2.5).

3. *Psychoanalytic significance* (cf. Deutsch 1952, Mahl 1968, Feyereisen 1974): Postural behavior of patients during interviews has been interpreted as a symptom of unconscious emotional needs.

4. *Interpersonal relations*: Bodily behavior as an expression of social relations such as status, power, preference, or affiliation has been studied by Scheflen (1964; 1972) and Mehrabian (1969; 1972).

5. *Expressive functions*: Bodily movements as expressions of emotional states have been studied by Ekman & Friesen (1967) and others.

2. Gestures

The semiotics of gestures covers three major areas of study: gestures as autonomous signs or even "languages," gestures in contiguity with other modes of sign behavior, and the role of gestures in the evolution of sign behavior (semiogenesis).

2.1 Gestures as Signs

The human body is acting at all times. This ubiquity of the body as a medium of expression has given rise to the metacommunicative axiom of the impossibility of not communicating, which was modified elsewhere into an axiom of the merely potential (not necessary) semioticity of behavior, objects, and events (see Communication 2.6.3). The semioticity of the human body in a given situation depends on several pragmatic factors. While there is little doubt about conventional gestures being signs, the semioticity of practical behavior has been questioned.

Cultural differences in the meaning and use of gestures (cf. La Barre 1947, Kendon 1986b: 15–20), even in such widely distributed gestures as those for "yes" and "no" (cf. Jakobson 1972), characterize gestures as arbitrary and in this respect similar to linguistic signs. On the other hand, ethologists have emphasized the universal character of the origin of gestures, which brings gestures closer to natural than to conventional signs.

2.1.1 PRACTICAL AND COMMUNICATIVE GESTURES

The question whether everyday practical behavior is communicative or whether a dividing line can be drawn between praxis and semiosis has been raised by semioticians such as Rastier (1968), Kristeva (1969c: 90–112), Greimas (1970: 57–82), and Mukařovský (see Prague School). Mukařovský (e.g., 1978: 40), in his theory of semiotic functions, draws a clear dividing line between praxis and semiosis (cf. Aesthetics 3.2.2). According to this theory, praxis is "immediate self-realization vis-à-vis reality." This occurs "when man reorganizes reality with his own hands so that he can immediately use this reorganization to his own advantage. (He breaks branches in order to start a fire by rubbing them together.)"

With reference to Mauss (1935) and theories of cultural anthropology, Greimas bases his theory of gesturality on the assumption of cultural determination and thus semioticity of all human actions (1970: 60). Nevertheless, Greimas also distinguishes between *gestural praxis* and *gestural communication*: Gestural praxis describes behavior whose intention is to "transform the world" and not to communicate any message to those who observe it (ibid.: 69). This criterion, according to Greimas, characterizes two modes of behavior, *practical gestures* (such as acts performed by a cook in a kitchen) and *mythical* (e.g., ceremonial, ritual, or magic) *gestures*.

A basic distinction between gestural praxis and gestural communication, according to Greimas, is in the role of the acting subject (1970: 66–67). In gestural communication, the agent has the role of a sender and is thus the subject of a communicative act of enunciation (cf. Text Semiotics 3.1.2). In gestural praxis, the agent is the subject of the utterance. While the agent of communicative gestures is a "you" for the addressee, the agent of the utterance of gestural praxis remains "he or she" for those who observe it.

The field of communicative gestures according to Greimas is further subdivided as follows (1970: 70–81): (1) *attributive gestures*, expressions of attitudes and inner states, (2) *modal gestures*, expressing phatic (communication-related) and metasemiotic (text-related) functions (see Function 3.2), (3) *mimetic gestures*, bodily icons of visual events, and (4) *playful gestures (gestualité ludique)*, e.g., dance.

2.1.2 SEMIOTIC TYPOLOGY

From a semiotic point of view, gestures have been classified with respect to their function and their object relation (see Peirce 3.). In a functional view, gestures are *referential* when they refer to an extracommunicative object. Gesticulation is *emotive* when it expresses the sender's feelings, and it is *appellative* when it is directed toward the receiver. A fourth important type of function is the *phatic* gesture. It indicates interest in maintaining and regulating the communicative interaction (e.g., turn taking; see 2.3.2). Typologies of gestures from the point of view of their object relation were set up by Wundt (1900) and Bühler (1933a). In terms of Peirce's typology, these and other studies of gestures have distinguished between *indexical* (pointing), *iconic* (representing), and *symbolic* (conventional) gestures. For an attempt at a synthesis of semiotic typologies of gestures, see Nespoulous & Lecours (1986).

2.2 Conventional Gestures (Emblems)

Gestures of the type which Efron (1941: 96) and Ekman & Friesen (see 1.3.1) have classified as emblems have been collected and described lexicographically, which raises the question whether such gestures can be considered codes.

2.2.1 GESTURAL "LANGUAGES"

Like languages, gestural emblems are restricted in their occurrence to specific cultures, but the geographical distribution of gestures according to Morris et al. (1979) does not coincide with language boundaries. Gestural emblems in everyday communication can function as substitutes for single words or sentences. But these gestures hardly form a system of elements in opposition, and gestures are generally not combinable into texts. The sign repertoire of emblematic gestures is rather restricted. Except for special gestures, emblematic gestures have a high variability in usage, conventionality, and distribution (cf. Johnson et al. 1975, Morris et al. 1979). Because of these characteristics, gestural emblems can hardly be considered to form codes. For the comparison of emblematic gestures with language codes, see also Vendryes (1950), Greimas (1970: 57–82), Ekman (1976: 22–24), and Dittman (1978: 81–94).

2.2.2 LEXICOGRAPHY OF GESTURAL EMBLEMS

The lexicography of emblematic gestures in various cultures is still in its beginnings (see Abercrombie 1954). Early international dictionaries of gestures (cf. Brun 1969, Bauml & Bauml 1975) still lack a scholarly foundation. A comprehensive lexicographic survey of the origins and distribution of gestures in Europe is Morris et al. (1979). In Italy Neapolitan gestures and gesticulations have been studied in detail since the nineteenth century (cf. Wundt 1900: 80–96). For gestures in modern Italy see Munari (1963). A lexicon of Italian gestures is also included in Efron's (1941) influential comparative study of Italian and Jewish gestures in New York City. In the context of the teaching of the French language and culture, Brault (1962) and Wylie (1977) give an introduction to gestures in France. German emblems in contrast to gestures used in other countries are studied by Loof (1981) and Kirch (1987).

Flachskampf (1938) collected and commented on gestures in Spain. Green (1968) set up a gesture inventory for the teaching of Spanish. Under the influence of Coseriu's linguistic structuralism, a systematic study of gestures in Uruguay and Argentina was published by Meo-Zilio (1961; 1962). A contrastive study of gestures in Colombia and in the United States is Saitz & Cervenka (1972; cf. Teaching 2.2.1). For gestural emblems in the United States and the methods of gestural lexicography, see Johnson et al. (1975) and the studies by Ekman & Friesen. A contrastive study of emblems in the United States of America and in other countries in addition to Saitz & Cervenka (1972) is Loof (1981). Gestures in Arab countries are described and discussed by Goldziher (1886) and Barakat (1973). For gestures in Iran and Russia see Sparhawk (1978) and Eismann (1983).

For the study of emblematic and other gestures in literature and folklore, see Wespi (1949) and Röhrich (1967). Gestures in historical paintings are discussed by Siger (1968). On symbolic gestures in medieval iconography, see Garnier (1982). The history of some gestural emblems is discussed by Bates (1975) and Kirch (1987).

2.2.3 SPECIAL GESTURAL CODES
Some types of emblematic gestures are restricted in their usage to special situations, activities, groups, or professions. Such gestures, being highly conventional and necessarily unambiguous, might be considered codes. Some of them come close to being a sign language. Examples of such specialized codes are the gestures used by French transport workers (Cuny 1972), by Canadian sawmill workers (Meissner & Philpott 1975), and by German automobilists (Savigny 1980: 16–20). For references to further specialized gestural codes employed by grain merchants, skin divers, truck drivers, baseball umpires, and hitchhikers, see Kendon (1986b: 8).

2.3 Speech-Related Gestures

Speech-related gestures have been studied in everyday face-to-face interactions and in special rhetorical discourse.

2.3.1 ILLUSTRATORS
Within the class of gesticulations which Ekman & Friesen (1969; 1972) have classified as illustrators, Ekman distinguishes the following eight subtypes (1980b: 98): (1) *batons* (gestures which emphasize words; see esp. Scheflen 1972: 51–66, Morris 1978: 56–63), (2) *underliners* (emphasizing sentences), (3) *ideographs* (sketching a direction of thought), (4) *kinetographs* (depicting actions), (5) *picto-*graphs (showing objects), (6) *rhythmics* (depicting the rhythm or tempo of an event), (7) *spatials* (depicting spaces), and (8) *deictics* (pointing to objects). While batons have generally only an expressive function, all other illustrators have an indexical or iconic function of reference (cf. 2.1.2). The semantic relation between language and illustrators can be one of emphasis, repetition, substitution, complementation, or contradiction (cf. Mahl 1968).

2.3.2 REGULATORS
Regulators are gestures of a predominantly phatic function. Head gestures, body movement, and body orientation indicate the speaker's desire for consent and turn taking. Often these gestural regulators run parallel with the linguistic syntax of the discourse. Detailed research in the "grammar" of regulators has been done by Scheflen (1964; 1972; 1973), Duncan (1973; 1975a; b), Duncan & Fiske (1977), Kendon (1972; 1977; 1980c), and Goodwin (1981).

2.3.3 RHETORICAL GESTURES
Pronuntiatio, the art of the gesturally and vocally efficient delivery of a speech, was a constituent part of ancient rhetoric (q.v. 2.1.2). Quintilian discusses it at length in *De institutione oratoria* (I, 11, 17), where he defines the rhetorical study of gestures as *chironomy* or the law of gesture. Renaissance scholars led the study of gestural rhetoric to a new climax. Bulwer's *Chirologia: or the Natural Language of the Hand* (1644) contains a comprehensive dictionary of illustrative and emblematic gestures (e.g., for "threatening," "despair," "imploring," etc.) which indicate a high degree of codification in oratorical gesticulation. Bulwer's *Chirologia* is also a treatise on the natural and universal character of gesticulation (cf. Sign Language 2.1.3, Universal Language 1.3.4). For further accounts of the history of gestural rhetoric, see also Joseph (1951) and Siger (1968).

Manuals of rhetoric continued to include instructions on rhetorical gesticulation until the nineteenth century (e.g., Bell & Bell 1884).

During this time, there were first attempts at the development of a system of notation of gestures and body movements in public speech (cf. ibid.: 29–31 and Austin 1806). For oratorical gesticulation in modern times, see also Morris (1978: 56–63) and Morris et al. (1979).

2.3.4 THEATRICAL GESTURES

Gesticulation and "body language" in theater have a twofold sign character (cf. Skwarczyńska 1974: 343): on the one hand, they are emblems, illustrators, or regulators with semiotic functions like everyday gestures. On the other hand, they are iconic signs representing the behavior of persons in an extratheatrical world. Theatrical gesture and "body language" thus permanently have a semiotic function, whereas gestures in everyday communication are only potentially communicative. For a more comprehensive account of gestures and "body language" in the history of theater, see Joseph (1951), Pavis (1981), Poyatos (1982b), Fischer-Lichte (1983a: 60–87; 1983b: 45–56; 1983c), and Helbo (1983a).

2.4 Gestural Texts: Rituals and Artistic Performances

Gestural texts (cf. Greimas & Courtés 1979: 136) are language-independent modes of nonverbal semiosis comprising aesthetic and artistic performances (e.g., dance, ballet, acrobatic numbers, pantomime) as well as rituals and ceremonies.

2.4.1 NONVERBAL ARTISTIC AND AESTHETIC PERFORMANCES

Semiotic approaches to aesthetic and artistic gestures have been developed by Ikegami (1971) in a stratificational analysis of hand gestures in Indian classical dancing, by Bouissac (1973) in his study of body movements in acrobatics, and by Scotto di Carlo (1973) and Shapiro (1981) in studies on ballet and gestures in operas. A recurring topic of the semiotics of artistic gestures is the development of a notational system for gestures and body movements. For the field of dance, such a notational

system was introduced under the designation of *labonotation* (Hutchinson 1954).

2.4.2 RITUALS AND CEREMONIES

Gestures are a dominant feature of religious rites and secular ceremonies, even where these are accompanied by language. Ritual and ceremonial gestures are distinct from practical as well as from communicative gestures (cf. Langer 1942: 49, Trabant 1976a: 92–97). Their function is mainly a phatic one: They serve to establish, change, confirm, or restore social relationships (cf. Argyle 1975: 172–92). The form of rituals and ceremonies is strictly determined by cultural convention and regular repetition. Because of these characteristics, the term *ritual* has been extended to common acts of everyday phatic interaction which are neither religious nor ceremonial in the narrower sense, e.g., greeting and farewell gestures, social meetings, or family reunions. For these and other aspects of ritual, see Goffman (1967), Shaughnessy (1973), D'Aquili et al., eds. (1979), Knuf & Schmitz (1980), Werlen (1984), and Klein, ed. (1987).

Ritual has been described both as being a language and as being superior to verbal communication. Thus, Langer defines ritual as "the language of religion" but emphasizes that "ritual is a symbolic transformation of experiences that no other medium can adequately express" (1942: 52). In its social function, ritual is related to magic. Langer considers magic a form of ritual (ibid.). But while ritual has primarily the function of social confirmation, magic aims at the transformation of the world of objects.

2.5 Gestures and Semiogenesis

Two topics of major semiogenetic relevance in the study of gestures and nonverbal behavior in general are the phylogenesis of gestures and the theory of a gestural origin of language.

2.5.1 PHYLOGENY OF GESTURES

After Darwin (1872), several contemporary ethologists have emphasized the natural and prehuman origin of some universally distributed gestures and other modes of nonverbal behavior (cf. Hinde 1974: 125–46). Darwin saw the origin of the affirmative nodding and the negative shaking of the head in the infant's inclining its head forward to accept food or withdrawing its head laterally from the breast (1872: 286). Hooff (1972) explains the phylogenetic development of smiling and laughter from the gestures of silent bared-teeth display and relaxed open-mouth display by which subhuman primates express affinity and play. Eibl-Eibesfeldt (1970; 1972; 1984) discusses the evolution of eyebrow movements from an earlier attention signal associated with the widening of the eyes for better vision to various display signals of surprise or interest in humans (see Zoosemiotics 5.2.4).

A key concept in this discussion of the phylogeny of gestures is *ritualization*, basically the process by which an original behavior becomes a "fixed pattern," often simplified and amplified, and changes or loses its original function. Such processes are studied by human ethologists in the evolution from animal to human behavior and by cultural ethologists (e.g., Koenig 1970) in the history of human cultures. Critics of the phylogenetic study of human gestures have emphasized the cross-cultural differences in the functions of nonverbal behavior (cf. Leach 1972), but in analogy to language it can certainly be argued that the phylogenetic study of gestures can at least reveal evidence about the "etymology" of nonverbal behavior (cf. Zoosemiotics 5.2.1).

2.5.2 GESTURAL ORIGIN OF LANGUAGE

Comparative studies of the vocal systems of primates and humans have suggested that the vocal tracts of chimpanzees and also of Neanderthal man are or were unsuitable for the development of speech. But while attempts at teaching words of vocal language to nonhuman primates have therefore failed, the teaching of gestural and visual sign languages has been rather successful (cf. Zoosemiotics 2.3.1–2). Such biological and anthropological findings as well as earlier assumptions of or observations about the universality of gestures in humans

(Hewes 1974) have given rise to theories of a gestural origin of language (Lurçat 1972, Hewes 1973; 1976, Kendon 1975). Some authors have discussed *vocal gestures* (see 1.2.1 and La Barre 1964: 206) as a possible connecting link in a phylogenetic evolution from gestures to language. The hypothesis of the evolution of speech from gestures has also been adduced in favor of proposals for the development of an international gestural universal language (cf. Knowlson 1975: 211–23).

The importance of manual gestures in the evolution of language has also been emphasized by the anthropologist Leroi-Gourhan (1964–65). But in his view, there was basically a parallel development of manual activities and vocal language in the phylogeny of man (cf. ibid.: 54–55, 147–53). When the hand became liberated from the task of locomotion, the face became free from the performance of the technical task of collecting food. Thus, the evolution of the hand into the major instrument of *homo faber* left the speech organs free for the development of an oral language.

3. Kinesics

As discussed above, the concepts of kinesics and kinemics are sometimes used to refer to the whole field of gestures and "body language." But in accordance with an equally current usage, this chapter discusses kinesics only as the particular approach to nonverbal communication developed by Birdwhistell (1952; 1955; 1960; 1961; 1963; 1968; 1970; 1974; 1979).

3.1 Outline of Kinesic Research

Kinesics, the "systematic study of those patterned and learned aspects of body motion which can be demonstrated to have communicative value" (Birdwhistell 1963: 125), is a research program which Birdwhistell (1955; 1960) divides into the following areas of analysis:

3.1.1 PREKINESICS

This first field of research, prekinesics, deals with the physiology of body motion. Similar to phonetics, which studies the physiology and acoustics of sounds, the approach is etic and concerned with presemantic structures. Prekinesics isolates the minimal elements of nonverbal behavior which have a differential value within a given context. These distinctive elements are defined as *kines*.

3.1.2 MICROKINESICS

A class of kines with the same social meaning, e.g., a "head nod," is defined as a *kineme*. The variants belonging to this class are the *allokines* of the kineme. The study of kinemes constitutes the *microkinesic* level of research. It presupposes a cultural evaluation of nonverbal behavior since the social meaning of human behavior is culturally variable. Kinemes furthermore combine into larger configurations (see 3.3.2).

3.1.3 SOCIAL KINESICS AND KINESIC CONTEXT

At the stage of social kinesic research, the meaning of body motion within its social and temporal context is studied. Birdwhistell proposes a radically contextual theory of *kinesic semantics* (1970: 96, 185). No kineme may be said to have any definite meaning irrespective of its context. Only the social context may resolve the question whether, for example, the gesture of a clenched fist is a gesture of anger or the imitation of someone else's behavior, or whether it represents, ironically, a friendly attitude (cf. Kendon 1977: 217). Birdwhistell (1961: 55; 1970: 119) underlines his contextual theory of kinesic meaning by defining gestures as *bound morphs* (such as -*cept*, *pre-*, *con-*, or -*tion* in English): "Gestures are forms which are incapable of standing alone." As bound morphs, gestures require a morphological context to achieve identity. A logical consequence of this radically contextual theory of kinesic meaning would be the impossibility of setting up sign repertoires of kinesic codes. Research and results in the lexicography of gestural emblems contradict this assumption.

3.1.4 PARAKINESICS

In analogy to paralinguistics, the parakinesic level of analysis studies modifiers of kinemes occurring in allokinetic variations of nonverbal behavior. At this level, Birdwhistell distinguishes between *motion qualifiers* (of intensity, range, and velocity of the movement) and *activity modifiers*, which characterize the mode of an entire body in motion (1961: 56; 1963: 135).

3.2 Kinesic Notation

Birdwhistell's kinesics also comprises a notation system for body movements (1952; 1970: 257–82). Using base symbols for eight body sections (head, face, trunk, shoulder, hands, legs, feet, and neck), the author develops a complex system of *kinegraphs* for kinesic recording. Studies such as Pittenger et al. (1960) and McQuown, ed. (1971) have applied this kinesic notation system in integrated analyses of language and nonverbal behavior in psychoanalytic interviews. For other notation systems and the history of recording nonverbal behavior, see Key (1977: 61–91) and Scherer et al. (1979).

3.3 The Kinesic Code

One of Birdwhistell's aims is the discovery of a kinesic code of American everyday life. According to his research program, language is the model of this nonverbal code. Although Birdwhistell is aware of the limitations of the linguistic-kinesic analogy, he considers the model of language to be a useful heuristic device in kinesic research (1970: 82–84, 197, 229).

3.3.1 AMERICAN KINEMES

Birdwhistell sets up a list of fifty or sixty kinemes which he considers to be basic elements of the nonverbal behavior of an average American (1970: 99; 1974: 218). For example, among thirty-two kinemes of the face and head area, he distinguishes three kinemes of head nod and four of brow behavior. The semiotic status of these kinemes, however, remains uncertain. On the one hand, the kineme seems to be structurally analogous to the phoneme when it is described as an element of a differential value without a meaning of its own (cf. Birdwhistell 1955: 13; 1968: 198, and 3.1.1–2). Elsewhere, however, Birdwhistell (e.g., 1968: 199; 1970: 100) describes kinemes as significant units of behavior, e.g., when he associates kinemes of brow behavior with semantic modes such as ''doubt'' or ''questioning.'' This interpretation characterizes the kineme rather in analogy to linguistic morphemes.

3.3.2 FROM KINEMORPHOLOGY TO KINESIC TEXTS

Kinemes combine hierarchically to form higher levels of the kinesic code (cf. Birdwhistell 1968: 198; 1970: 101, 195). After the kinemic level comes a morphological level, where kinemes combine into *kinemorphs*. A class of such units with the same communicative function is defined as a *kinemorpheme*. The next level of the kinesic code consists of *complex kinemorphs*. Their linguistic analogy is the word. The kinesic analogy to the linguistic level of the sentence is called a *kinemorphic construction*. Sequences of such kinesyntactic constructions could be defined as a *kinetext* (thus Koch 1971b: 222).

3.4 Kinesics and Semiotics

Birdwhistell's approach to nonverbal communication has been criticized from empirical (cf. Harper et al. 1978: 125–26) as well as methodological (cf. Scherer & Wallbott, eds. 1979: 188) points of view. There are doubts about the possibility of discovering a finite list of kinemes and objections against the structuralist segmentation of body motions. Kristeva even raises the objection of a positivistic neglect of the acting subject (1969c: 112). Nevertheless, the importance of kinesics to semiotics is widely acknowledged (cf. Kendon 1977; 1982: 456). Within semiotics, kinesics has provided significant heuristic impulses (cf. Sebeok et al., eds. 1964, Eco 1968). It has shown ways to analyze culturally determined modes of nonverbal behavior as a semiotic system and has thus stimulated methods of research in nonlinguistic codes.

Facial Signals

Long before scholars began to study the "language of the face" (Darwin 1872, Nummenmaa 1964, Kirchhoff, ed. 1965, Izard 1971, Ekman 1980a; 1982, Ekman et al. 1972, Ekman, ed. 1973, Ekman & Friesen 1975, Harper et al. 1978: 77–118), artists, poets, and actors had recognized the semiotic potential of facial expression (cf. Engel 1785, Bell 1806). The face is the medium of relatively permanent signals in the human physiognomy and of the temporarily variable signals of facial expressive movements. Facial expressions seem to be largely universal but are nevertheless culturally variable to a certain degree.

1. Physiognomy

The permanent features of the face contain essential indices for the identification of a person. These features of an individual's physiognomy form, on the one hand, an *autological* sign, an index of a person's identity. On the other hand, the same features can be interpreted as a *heterological* sign indicating the age, sex, or ethnic or family origin of a person. Only some of these features can be individually or culturally changed by cosmetic or other means (cf. Harrison 1974: 115). On the extended

possibilities of adopting a new physiognomy by means of a mask in theatrical performances, see Fischer-Lichte (1983a: 100–111).

The history of physiognomics since ancient times has been outlined by Bühler (1933a). In the eighteenth century, Johann K. Lavater (1741–1801) founded a doctrine of physiognomics, followed by Franz J. Gall's (1758–1828) *phrenology*. Both scholars believed in the possibility of discovering psychological characteristics of a personality from the physiology and anatomy of his or her face and head. Although these assumptions have long since been rejected (cf. Piderit 1867: 149), the popular belief in a correlation between physiognomy and personal character (e.g., "high forehead" as an index of 'intelligence') is a semiotic fact documented both in literature and the visual arts (cf. Kleinpaul 1888: 92ff.) and in empirical investigations of personality judgments by test persons (cf. Argyle 1975: 223–26).

A related assumption about a correlation between human physiognomy and psychology is that in the course of time, habitual facial expressions leave permanent physiognomic traces in a person's face. Verifications of this assumption held by some traditional psychologists (Piderit 1867: 157, Lersch 1932: 21, Leonhard 1976: 251) will hardly be possible.

2. Facial Expression

The variable semiotic potential of the face is usually studied under the heading *facial expression*. Eyebrows and forehead, eyes (see Gaze), nose, lips and jaw, cheeks, and skin are the regions by which facial signals can be transmitted (cf. Nummenmaa 1964, Leonhard 1976).

2.1 Functions

The major functions of facial signals are expressive (of emotions), phatic, and conative (in communicative interactions). With these functions, facial expressions occur independently of speech, parallel with speech (as interactional signals; cf. Argyle 1975: 213), and dependent on or even derived from speech (e.g., facial movements in connection with phonetic articulation; cf. Vendryes 1950: 12ff., Sarles 1977: 214). In their primary function, spontaneous or intended signals of the face are indexical signs. But derived from such primary situations of semiosis, facial signals also occur as mimic behavior transmitting signals by imitation (cf. Morris 1978: 28–29). In these cases, facial signals are iconic signs.

2.2 Research Strategies

Facial expression has been the topic of an intensive research tradition (cf. Vine 1970, Harper et al. 1978: 77–118, Wallbott 1979, Ekman 1982). The major research methods for the exploration of the "language of the face" (thus Nummenmaa 1964, Izard 1971, Ekman et al. 1972, Stringer 1973) have made use of an indirect semiotic strategy: The researchers do not investigate the *producer* but the *receiver* of facial signals. Usually, test persons are asked to describe their evaluations of facial expressions presented to them (often in the form of photos). Such research in facial expression does not directly investigate the expression of emotions but rather the discourse about expressed facial emotions. A more objective system of notation of facial action, the *Facial Action Coding System* (FACS), has been developed by Ekman & Friesen (1978). It is based on a technique of describing facial movements as a result of the actions of the facial muscles involved.

2.3 Elements of Expression and Content

Facial signals are usually evaluated on the basis of (pictures of) the whole face. Some authors have experimentally isolated the forehead and eyebrows, eyes, nose, and mouth as regions of the face where emotional meanings may be discovered independently (Nummenmaa 1964, Ekman et al. 1971). For experiments in evaluating emotions on the basis of a commutation test in which elements of schematic drawings of faces are permutated, see Argyle (1975: 217). An attempt at setting up an inventory of facial elements of expression together with a proposal for a notation system has been made by Birdwhistell (1970: 260).

The semantic space of facial signals has been described in various emotional categories (cf. Izard 1971, Ekman et al. 1972, Ekman & Friesen 1975). While the free verbalization of facial expressions by test persons could yield an almost unlimited number of emotional meanings, the *a priori* reduction of possible responses to basic categories of emotion such as fear, disgust, happiness, anger, or interest usually results in a relatively high agreement in the evaluation of facial signals.

3. Universality and Cultural Determination

Since Darwin (1872; cf. Ekman, ed. 1973), ethological research has emphasized the phylogenetic determination and thus the universality of facial expressions of primary affects such as happiness, fear, or anger (cf. Eibl-Eibesfeldt 1967; 1972, Vine 1970, Chevalier-Skolnikoff 1973; see also Gesture 2.5.1). On the other hand, cultural anthropologists such as La Barre, Birdwhistell, and Mead (cf. Ekman 1972) have considered culture to be the major determinant of facial expression.

A synthesis between the positions of universal invariance and cultural determinacy of facial expressions has been outlined by Ekman (1972; Ekman et al. 1972: 153–68). According to his *neuro-cultural* theory of facial expressions of emotion, the signals of the human face are determined both by nature and by culture. On the one hand, the movements of the facial muscles resulting from primary emotions are controlled by a neurological facial "affect program" which constitutes the pancultural basis of facial expressions. On the other hand, this neurological basis is culturally modified by the following factors: (1) The elicitors causing an emotional reaction can become individually and culturally variable by learning experiences. (2) The universal facial affect program can be modified by cultural display rules by which felt emotions are intensified, deintensified, neutralized, or masked. On the latter processes of nonverbal masking and deceit, see Ekman (1985).

Gaze

In a cliché of popular culture, the eye is "the mirror of the soul," and archaic cultures believe in the magic power of the "evil eye." Such views epitomize the great social significance of gazing behavior. Semiotic functions of the eye and of visual interaction have been explored by cultural ethologists (Koenig 1975), social psychologists (Ellgring 1975, Argyle & Cook 1976), linguists (Ehlich & Rehbein 1982), and many other interdisciplinary researchers in nonverbal communication (cf. Harper et al. 1978: 171–245, Exline & Fehr 1978, Knapp 1978: 294–321, Scherer & Wallbott, eds. 1979: 59–102).

1. The Sign Repertoire of the Eye

Gazing behavior is one of the most impressive examples for illustrating Watzlawick's metacommunicative axiom of the impossibility of not communicating (see Communication 2.6.2). In social interaction, both gazing and not gazing at the other person may be equally communicative. Communication by gazing has been analyzed according to three major variables: frequency, duration, and gaze direction. For the frequency and duration of gazing in verbal interaction, see Duncan & Fiske (1977: 80–88). Modes of gaze direction, as discussed by Cranach & Ellgring (1973: 421–22), are one-sided gaze, mutual gaze (eye contact), gaze shift, one-sided and mutual omission and avoidance of gaze. For the further development of the typology of gazing behavior into a more comprehensive taxonomy of the sign repertoire of the eye, see Ehlich & Rehbein (1982: 48–77).

Apart from these studies in eye movements and the research in eyebrow behavior (see Facial Signals), the eyelids and the pupils are two further domains of potential semiotic significance in gazing. Little research has been done on the significance of lid movements (cf. Ehlich & Rehbein 1982: 23–42, and see Maranda 1986 on the semiotics of blinking), but studies on pupillary reactions claiming that pupil dilation and constriction can be interpreted as an index of the degree of emotional arousal and interest (cf. Hess & Petrovich 1978) have caused a vivid debate (cf. Harper et al. 1978: 228–33).

2. Functions of Gaze

The primary functions of gaze are phatic, expressive, and conative.

2.1 Phatic Function

In verbal interaction, the phatic function of gaze lies in its monitoring role in the initiation and maintenance of conversation. Among several other functions of gazing discussed by Argyle & Dean (1965: 303), the following three refer to such phatic functions: (1) signaling that the channel is open (for further interaction), (2) information seeking, and (3) establishment and recognition of social relationship (cf. also Argyle et al. 1973). The phatic function of gaze is more apparent in the gaze patterns which accompany conversational turn taking (Kendon 1977, Goodwin 1981). For example, it has been shown that the avoidance of eye contact in conversation is an index of the speaker's desire to continue speaking, while the prolonged looking at another person is a signal for this person to speak next (cf. Kendon 1977: 48). For more detailed studies in the correlation between gaze and speaking, see Ellgring (1975), Harper et al. (1978: 184–89), Ekman (1980a), and Ehlich & Rehbein (1982).

2.2 Expressive and Conative Functions

Nummenmaa (1964) conducted tests in which photographs of eyes isolated from the rest of the face were presented to test persons. The results showed a significant agreement in the evaluations of emotions such as 'pleasure,' 'surprise,' and 'anger' which were attributed to the eyes (see also Argyle & Cook 1976: 75). Such gazes testify to the expressive function of looking behavior. On the less certain assumption that eyes might also express personality traits, see Piderit (1867: 42–52), Lersch (1932: 40–81), and Leonhard (1976: 120–36). For racial and sex differences in gazing, see Henley (1977: 151–67).

While gazes with an expressive function convey information about the addresser, the conative function dominates when the message focuses on the addressee. Such functions of gazing are less clearly identifiable in isolation from the facial and social context of the eye. Nevertheless, not only the proverbial phrase "if looks could kill" but also research on gazes as indices of intimacy, sympathy, hos-

tility, aggression, or dominance (Argyle & Cook 1976, Ellsworth & Langer 1976, Harper et al. 1978: 189–215) testify to the conative function of gaze.

3. Culture and Nature in Gazing

Like other facial signals, gaze has both a biological and a cultural basis (cf. Argyle & Cook 1976: 1–34). Phylogenetically, staring eyes are a threat signal for many animal species. For several primate species, the glance has been shown to be a signal by which social dominance is established or strengthened. For the glance as signal of power and preference in humans and nonhuman primates, see Exline (1971). Several species have developed eye rings to augment the semiotic function of their eyes, and the eyespots on the wings of butterflies and the bodies of birds and fish have been interpreted as examples of mimicry, instances of protective resemblance (cf. Eibl-Eibesfeldt 1967, Koenig 1975). In human cultures, the motif of the evil eye (cf. ibid.) seems to be an archetypical pattern of a threat signal. On the ontogenetic functions of gaze in the development of the human infant, see Argyle & Cook (1976: 9–16).

Cultural differences in gazing behavior appear in both frequency and length of eye contact (cf. Argyle & Cook 1976: 26–34). These differences show that looking at each other is socially more acceptable in some cultures than in others. Eibl-Eibesfeldt reports similar cultural differences in eyebrow behavior (1967: 467). Correlations which exist between eye contact and interpersonal distance (cf. Argyle & Dean 1965) have also been studied as an indicator of proxemic behavior. On sex differences in looking and on possible personality differences, see Henley (1977) and Harper et al. (1978: 216–26).

Tactile Communication

Tactile information transfer is one of the most primitive forms of communication. Its semiotic importance decreases in moving from zoo- to anthroposemiotics. Nevertheless, many social psychologists have considered bodily contact as an autonomous mode of nonverbal communication (cf. Argyle 1975: 286–99, Leathers 1976: 141–68, Henley 1977: 94–123, Knapp 1978: 242–62). Occasionally, tactile communication is subsumed under proxemics (cf. Kauffman 1971, Harper et al. 1978: 295–302). From semiotic points of view, tactile information raises the question whether touching can be a sign, communication, or even a code. A specialized use of the tactile channel is for the purpose of a speech surrogate.

1. Tactile Semiosis

Information via the tactile channel becomes less significant in the course of onto- and phylogenetic evolution. Culturally, touch has become not only restricted in its communicative potential but also repressed by the norms of societies.

1.1 The Tactile Channel

The receptors of tactile information are sensory cells of the skin. The tactile channel is therefore also defined as the *cutaneous* channel (Geldard 1977: 212). Physiological classifications of the cutaneous sensory channels (Moles 1986: 1073) distinguish between sensitivity to pressure (touch) and pain, thermal, sensual (erogenous), and vibrational sensitivity, and muscular reactivity. The tactile channel of communication belongs to the physiochemical channels which further comprise the two chemical channels of smell and taste. Compared to other channels, the skin has the following advantages as a medium of communication: It is the largest human sense organ, relatively "traffic-free," freely oriented toward potential sources of information, and less vulnerable than the eye or ear. "As with audition, there is little redundancy in cutaneous information . . . [and] it can be presented only when needed" (Geldard 1977: 213–14).

1.2 Semiogenetic Functions

Basic phylogenetic functions of cutaneous information are biological protection and reproduction (cf. Zoosemiotics 3.4.2). Ontogenetically, the importance of touch is evident from the infant's basic need of body contact. In the course of biological evolution, visual and auditory information becomes more important than the tactile channel. The advantage of sight and hearing over touch is that they permit communication at distance. Yet, in the case of the loss of sight and hearing, the skin remains the only channel of communication which is able to substitute visual and acoustic information. As the life of Helen Keller proves, even language can be transmitted by tactile information.

1.3 Cultural Semiotics of Touch

Bodily contact is culturally coded with respect to its quality and quantity (Frank 1957: 237–43, Montagu 1971: 220–92, Argyle 1975: 286–99). An extreme form of reglementation of bodily communication is the cultural repression of touch (cf. Montagu 1971: 236–40). Empirical investigations into the frequency of bodily contact in public places (cf. Harper et al. 1978: 296–97) in different countries have confirmed Hall's (see Proxemics 2.) distinction between *contact* and *noncontact* types of culture. Arabs, Latin Americans, and Southern Europeans belong to the former cultures with relatively high degree of bodily contact, while Asians, Indians, and Northern Europeans are noncontact cultures (cf. Watson 1970: 115). For the low degree of bodily contact in the Japanese culture, see also Barnlund (1975: 444–47). Argyle reports that in English-speaking countries bodily contact is more frequent in working-class families than in other social groups (1975: 290). Other variables of bodily contact are age, sex, relationship of the persons involved, and place and time of the encounter. For specific tactile codes of different cultures, see 2.3.

---

2. Tactile Signs and Codes

The semiotics of touch raises the question whether and under which conditions tactile information can be sign, communication, or even code.

2.1 Communication

Tactile information is *precommunicative* when there is contact with an object without a sender (e.g., hitting a stone; cf. Communica-

tion 2.1). Whenever touch is caused by a human being, the act of touching is potentially communicative. It may then be perceived as *noncommunicative* when it is unintentional and uncoded (e.g., body contact in a crowd). But occasionally, unintentional touching may nevertheless communicate subconscious intentions and/or be interpreted as such an intention. When touching deviates from cultural norms (cf. 1.3) or when it is coded (cf. 2.3), it is usually interpreted as an act of communication.

2.2 The Tactile Sign

Tactile communication raises the question of meaning and of the tactile sign. The most general meanings of uncoded bodily signals are various modes of interpersonal relationships such as nurture, affiliation, friendship, aggression, or sexuality. Whether a punch in the face is a sign or not, is a popular test question for semioticians. Bodily aggression is evidently more than a verbal threat or insult, but both may be interpreted very similarly (also in court). Both may cause the same "disposition to respond," as Morris would say. The semiotic difference between verbal and bodily aggression has to do with the difference between meaning and reference. The meaning of both acts ('threat,' 'danger') and the "disposition to respond" are similar or even identical. But the distinction is one of reference. In bodily attack, the signifier, which is the act of physical aggression, has as its referent the tactile experience of pain connected with this very aggression. In verbal "attacks," the linguistic signifier is only a semiotic means which inflicts no immediate physical pain, but its referent includes a potential physical attack.

2.3 Codes of Tactile Behavior

Although most interpersonal tactile forms of behavior are culturally determined and thus coded, the semioticity of psychosemiotic and sociosemiotic acts such as aggression and stroking is relatively low because of the high universality of their occurrence. A number of tactile signs, however, have a higher degree of semioticity and may be considered to belong to weak codes. Examples (cf. Argyle 1975: 294–96) are signs of greeting (shaking hands, embracing, or kissing), congratulating, attention, and guiding, and finally, with a further semiotic dimension, ceremonies. For the semiotics of such interactional signals, see also Morris (1978: 86–101).

2.4 Tactesics and Tactemics

In analogy to kinesics and as an extension of proxemics, Kauffman (1971) proposes a program of research in tactile communication which she calls *tacesics*. The term should be corrected to *tactesics* (from Lat. *tactus* 'touch,' not from *tacere* 'to be silent'). Another designation for this field of research, proposed by Wescott (1966), Key (1975), and Raffler-Engel, ed. (1980: 3), is *haptics*. Kauffman proposes to apply an emic framework to the study of touch (1971: 156). In her view, a system of tactile communication consists of *tactemes*, *tactemorphs*, *tactemorphic constructions*, and finally *tactevents*. But such analogies to the structural patterning of language, kinesic, and proxemic codes remain largely programmatic. It is doubtful whether systemic properties of tactile communication can ever be discovered which justify the application of these categories.

3. Tactile Language Substitutes

In case of the loss of vision and hearing, the tactile channel is the only one by which language can be transmitted. Most tactile language substitutes are codes that translate the letters of the alphabet into tactile stimuli. The classical and still the most widely used tactile language of this type is Braille. But several alternative digital and analog methods of tactile language substitution have been developed. Geldard (1977) gives a survey of such tactile languages: The channels of communication are *mechanical* (touching of surfaces, and feeling of vibrations), *electromechanical*, and *electrical*. The three major methods of tactile speech encoding are (1) *direct speech mediation* such as "speech feeling," a technique of feeling amplified sound waves by the skin, (2) *pictorial display*, devices of cutaneous recognition of tactile patterns analogous to the visual form of letters and images (e.g., tactile TV), and (3) *coded languages*, e.g., Braille, finger spelling, and electrotactile Morse, including several experimental developments of alphabetic codes such as electrocutaneous "vibratese."

Proxemics: The Semiotics of Space

Proxemics in its broadest sense is the semiotics of space. Originally developed by Hall in the context of cultural anthropology, proxemics was early based on semiotic principles. Proxemics in its narrower sense is usually studied as a mode of nonverbal communication, but the semiotics of space is a topic of many more interdisciplinary concerns.

1. Aspects of the Semiotics of Space

Hall's program of proxemic research is concerned with the communicative function of space. The focus of his studies is on differences in spatial behavior between members of different cultures. For empirical results see also Watson (1970), Loof (1976). Later studies have revealed the significance of further determinants of proxemic behavior such as sex differences, age, personality differences, and psychiatric conditions (Harper et al. 1978: 246–70). Such studies are generally carried out within social psychology (reviewed by Sundstrom & Altman 1976). As a special branch of this field, Mehrabian (1976) has proposed a study of space which he calls *environmental psychology*. Approaches to the cognitive psychology of space were developed by Canter (1977) and Moles & Rohmer (1978). Within this research, a new field of study has emerged which is concerned with the semiotics of geographical spaces. The semiogenetic extension of research in spatial behavior leads to interdisciplinary connections between proxemics and zoosemiotics, namely, the study of territorial behavior in men and animals.

The most fundamental dimensions of space have been studied within philosophy (Bollnow 1963, Gosztonyi 1976). For progress in the anthropology of space after Hall, see Segaud (1973), Pinxten et al. (1983), and Watson & Anderson (1987). For the semiotics of places (cf. Boudon 1981) and of space, see also Architecture (1.).

While space in the research fields discussed above is the primary visual or tactile signifier within communicative processes, space is also a topic of semiotic study in the form of linguistically or textually represented space. For various aspects of the semiotics of space, see also the special issue of *Degrés* 35/36 (1983).

2. Hall's Program of Proxemics

Hall popularized his program of proxemic research in his two best-selling books entitled *The Silent Language* (1959) and *The Hidden Dimension* (1966). His seminal ideas were developed more systematically in articles (Hall 1963a; b) and his *Handbook for Proxemic Re-*

search (1974). Many of Hall's early programmatic suggestions only later became the subject of empirical investigation. For the state of the art see also Argyle (1975: 300–22), Baldassare & Feller (1975), Harper et al. (1978: 246–317), and Patterson (1978).

2.1 Definitions of Proxemics

Hall (1963a; b) coined the term *proxemics* from the Latin root *prox-* (as in *proximity*) and the suffix *-emic* (as in *systemic, phonemic*). The term indicates the programmatic relationship of his research program to the principles of linguistic structuralism. Watson quotes the following definitions by Hall describing the scope of proxemics (1974: 312):

1. "... the study of how man unconsciously structures microspace—the distance between men in conduct of daily transactions, the organization of space in his houses and buildings, and ultimately the layout of his towns" (Hall 1963b: 1003).

2. "... the study of ways in which man gains knowledge of the content of other men's minds through judgments of behavior patterns associated with varying degrees of proximity to them" (1964: 41).

3. "... the interrelated observations and theories of man's use of space as a specialized elaboration of culture" (1966: 1).

4. "... the study of man's perception and use of space ..." (1968: 83).

5. "... [proxemics] deals primarily with out-of-awareness distance-setting" (1968: 83).

2.2 Dimensions of Research

Hall (1966) and Watson (1974) propose a classification of proxemic behavior according to its spatial extension and its cultural or semiogenetic level. In its extension, proxemic behavior occurs in dimensions which cover micro-, meso-, and macrospace. *Microspace* is the individual's immediate surroundings, which constitutes a sphere of privacy. *Mesospace* is the further proximate environment within the person's reach. *Macrospace* extends over larger territories from settlements to cities and beyond.

Within the cultural dimension, Hall (1966) and Watson (1970: 34–43) distinguish infra-, pre-, and microcultural levels of proxemic behavior. *Infracultural* proxemic behavior is "rooted in man's biological past" (Hall 1966: 95). It is usually described as territorial behavior. *Precultural* proxemics refers to man's sensory (tactile, visual, etc.) perception of space. Only at the *microcultural* level is spatial behavior determined by cultural conventions.

2.3 Categories of Proxemic Analysis

Hall proposes three categories of proxemic description, distance, space, and a third category which comprises the modes of behavior and perception for which he develops his proxemic notation system (1966: 101ff.).

2.3.1 CATEGORIES OF INTERPERSONAL DISTANCE

Hall distinguishes four categories of interpersonal distance, each with a close (c) and a far (f) phase (1966: 116–29). For North American culture, the distances according to Hall are (1) *intimate distance* (c: 0–6 inches, f: 6–18 in.), (2) *personal distance* (c: 18–30 in., f: 30–48 in.), (3) *social distance* (c: 4–7 ft., f: 7–12 ft.), and (4) *public distance* (c: 12–25 ft., f: 25– ft.). For methods and results of empirical studies in interpersonal distances, see Forston (1975) and Scherer (1975).

2.3.2 CATEGORIES OF SPACE

Hall distinguishes three categories of space according to the degree to which cultures treat spatial constellations as *fixed, semi-fixed,* or *variable* (1963a: 429–41; 1966: 103–112; cf. Watson 1970: 39–43): Fixed feature space is formed by walls and territorial boundaries. Semi-fixed features are spatial constellations formed by mobile elements such as curtains, screens, movable partitions, and furniture arrangement. Space is informal or dynamic when a person varies the spatial features of his or her surroundings or the interpersonal distances.

2.3.3 PROXEMIC NOTATION SYSTEM

Hall develops a system for the notation of proxemic behavior in microspace which comprises eight variables (1963b: 1006–1014):

1. *postural-sex identifiers* (e.g., female, standing)
2. *sociofugal-sociopetal orientation* (from face-to-face to back-to-back)
3. *kinesthetic code* (describing the distances of body parts, from "reaching" to "contact")
4. *touch code* (from "caressing and holding" to "no contact whatever")
5. *visual code* (see Gaze)
6. *thermal code* (whether radiated heat is detected or not)
7. *olfaction code* (detection of odor or breath)
8. *voice loudness* (see Paralinguistics)

The empirical relevance of these categories for the determination of cultural differences within an international group of students was tested in a study by Watson (1970).

3. Proxemics and Semiotics

Hall did not explicitly study proxemics in the framework of semiotics, but his attempts to analyze spatial behavior as an autonomous communicative system with analogies to language characterize his program of research as one of applied semiotics. With Eco (1968: 344–49) and Watson (1970; 1974), proxemics began to be studied explicitly as a branch of semiotics.

3.1 Analogies between Spatial Behavior and Language

Proxemics aims at the discovery of codes of spatial behavior valid for different cultures, similar to linguistics, which studies the grammars of different languages. But how far do the analogies between language and proxemic behavior extend? Hall examines proxemic behavior on the basis of the design features which Hockett has set up as characteristics of language (q.v. 3.1) and discovers such features as *arbitrariness, interchangeability, displacement,*

specialization, and even *duality* in proxemic codes (1963b: 1018–19). While arguing that "proxemic behavior parallels language, feature for feature," he nevertheless has to admit that "proxemic behavior is obviously *not* language and will not do what language will do."

The feature of duality or *double articulation* is for many semioticians the strongest criterion for the semioticity of a code (see Language 4.1). It refers to two levels of structures in a semiotic system, the first consisting of meaningful elements and the second of nonsemantic distinctive elements (like the phonemes of a language). Hall claims that the proxemic code has these two levels and describes them as *sets* and *isolates* (1963b: 1018; cf. Hall 1959; cf. also Chronemics 2.). However, the term *proxeme*, introduced in this context (ibid.: 1021–22, Watson 1974: 339), is not always clearly defined with respect to these two levels. Sometimes it is discussed in analogy to the phoneme, thus as an element of second articulation (Hall 1963b: 1022), but elsewhere the discussion of "the meaning of proxemes" (Watson 1974: 339) suggests an element of first articulation.

3.2 Proxemics and Proxetics

Most individuals are generally unaware of the norms of proxemic behavior within their culture, but they do become conscious of them when these norms are violated or when they notice differences in spatial behavior due to the norms of foreign cultures (cf. Watson 1974: 328–29). By descriptive and contrastive procedures, the proxemic norms of a culture can be discovered. But in spite of the relatively elaborate system of proxemic description, a "lexicon" of proxemic behavior does not yet exist. The semantics of proxemic behavior remains largely unexplored. In view of this research situation, Hall concludes that his system of proxemic analysis is still mostly restricted to the etic level of analysis and has not yet reached an emic level, i.e., proxemic behavior is objectively measurable and describable, but its cultural function cannot yet be sufficiently specified (1963b: 1021). Such studies are therefore more concerned with *proxetics*, which is only the first step toward research in proxemics.

4. Territorial Behavior

Hall's proxemics deals with space mainly in categories of distance. Research in human and animal territoriality (cf. Esser, ed. 1971) and personal space (Sommer 1969) extends the scope of analysis into three-dimensional space.

4.1 Animal Territoriality

The concept of territoriality (cf. Hall 1966: 7–40, Ardrey 1967, Watson 1970: 20–33, Vine 1975) is a concept of zoosemiotics which was developed within ethology. In Hediger's definition (quoted by Altman 1975: 106), "territories are geographical areas where an animal lives and from which it prevents others of the same species from entering." Territories fulfil several biological functions, "such as feeding, mating, and rearing of the young" (ibid.). They are often demarcated by optical, acoustical, and olfactory signals (cf. ibid.) which indicate possession and the willingness to defend against invasion.

4.2 Human Territoriality

Human territorial behavior has been described by Sommer in his theory of *personal space* (1969: 26). This term "refers to an area with invisible boundaries surrounding a person's body into which intruders may not come." Such areas are built up either temporarily or permanently by individuals who consider them their personal property and who are willing to defend them in certain ways (cf. Goffman 1963, Lyman & Scott 1967, Altman 1975, Vine 1975). A specific form of human territoriality is also evident in the seating preferences of individuals within a group, which are often an index of those individuals' roles within the group (cf. Sommer 1969: 58–73, Henley 1977: 27–42).

4.2.1 TYPOLOGY OF HUMAN TERRITORIES

Lyman & Scott (1967) distinguish four types of human territories: *public*, *home*, *interactional*, and *body* territories. Public territories are places such as streets or parks where everybody has free access. Home territories "are areas where the regular participants have a relative freedom of behavior and a sense of intimacy and control over the area" (ibid.: 238). Examples can be offices, libraries, club houses, and similar meeting places. Interactional territories are zones of temporary social gatherings, and body territories refer to the space encompassed by the human body. Within nonpublic space, Altman further distinguishes between *primary* and *secondary* territories (1975: 111–18). Primary territories are strictly private. They are claimed exclusively by one individual or group. Secondary territories are semipublic and are temporarily open for other people. For further aspects of the typology of territories, see Goffman (1963; 1971).

4.2.2 TERRITORIAL SIGNS

Boundaries of territories are signaled by *indexical markers*. Primary territories are marked by walls, fences, hedges, "private property" signs, or warnings against trespassing. Secondary territories, e.g., seats or tables in libraries, are marked by books, coats, or briefcases. Sometimes neighbors are asked to reserve a seat and thus protect the territory (cf. Sommer 1969: 52–57, Altman 1975: 129–33).

The meaning of a territorial sign is related both to the addresser, whose possession it indicates, and to the addressee, who is warned against intrusion. These are its denotational meanings. In addition, territorial signs may connote further meanings such as prestige, power, affective relations (such as the preferred armchair), and even a more profound field of archetypal meanings such as those suggested by Bachelard (1938) in his poetics of space.

4.2.3 TERRITORIAL INVASION AND DEFENSE

A proof of the existence of a human territory is the individual's willingness to defend his or her area against intrusions. Lyman & Scott (1967) distinguish three forms of such territorial encroachments: *violation* (by intrusion), *invasion* (by taking over the territory), and *contamination* (e.g., by destruction or pollution). Reactions against such forms of encroachment extend from a reproachful glance to defense or flight.

---

5. The Representation of Space

The communication of space, as it is experienced via the visual, tactile, or acoustic channel, is a mode of nonverbal communication. While the semiosis of space is here experienced at an object level, the representation of space by means of language or visual communication is a study at a *meta*level. It is concerned not with space as a sign but with signs about space.

5.1 Space in Language, Literature, and Painting

The representation of space is only briefly dealt with in Hall's proxemics (1966: 79–100): He discusses how the evolution of painting and literature illustrates the historical changes of proxemic norms in different cultures. Furthermore, Hall interprets the representation of space in language from the point of view of Whorf's theory of linguistic relativity. The claim is that the perception of space is determined by the morphological and semantic categories which a particular language provides for the representation of space.

A central topic in research on spatial representation in language is prepositional and adverbial *deictics*, indexical words whose referent depends on and shifts with the location of the interlocutors (e.g., *this/that, here/there*) (cf. Goeppert 1970). Although temporal deixis, in the form of tense, is morphologically much more diversified in most languages, Wunderlich (1982) has argued that spatial deixis is nevertheless more fundamental for the organization of language. At any rate, the linguistics of space has more than a morphological or lexical dimension. The verbalization of space has therefore become a field of research for text linguistics and linguistic pragmatics (Wunderlich 1982, Schweizer, ed. 1985).

5.2 The Semiotics of Geographical Spaces

Both the study of space as a mode of nonverbal communication and the topic of verbal deixis focus on the meaning of space in interpersonal semiosis. But space also has cognitive dimensions which are not based primarily in social interaction. People associate their spatial environment, landscapes, cities, and other geographical regions with typical connotations which have become a more recent topic of study, extending proxemics into a semiotics of geographical spaces. This development takes place within new interdisciplinary research by geographers, psychologists, and architects, the so-called cognitive geography (cf. Gould & White 1974, Canter 1977, Downs & Stea 1977, Schweizer, ed. 1985).

Cognitive geography represents visual conceptualizations which individuals or social groups have developed about geographical spaces by means of *cognitive maps*. Such a map shows, for example, how the geography of Britain is seen differently by inhabitants from North and South England. Other cognitive maps represent the degree of preference for certain geographical regions, the knowledge about routes connecting streets or cities, and also the linguistic and visual symbols of cities and countries (cf. Downs & Stea 1977: 93ff.). Thus, cognitive cartography provides empirical tools for the expansion of proxemics to a semiotics of geographical space.

Chronemics: The Semiotics of Time

Chronemics, the semiotics of time, is a relatively recent branch of semiotics, although concern with the temporal dimension of human behavior and existence is as old as philosophy. As a branch of semiotics, chronemics is closely related to proxemics, the semiotics of space. But the semiotics of time transcends the field of nonverbal communication in also being fundamental to *all* processes of semiosis. The basic questions are whether the dimension of time is emic or only etic to communication, whether there is such a thing as a chronemic sign, and at what levels time could be relevant to semiosis.

1. The Scope of Chronemics

Early considerations of the semiotics of time are outlined in the context of Hall's proxemics. From the study of space, Hall's (1959) cultural anthropological studies gradually shifted to the study of time (Hall 1976; 1983).

Chronemics as an extension of proxemics was explicitly proposed by Poyatos (1972; 1976) and Bruneau (1977; 1980; 1985). Bruneau defines chronemics as "the study of human temporality as it relates to human communication at the intrapersonal, interpersonal, and socio-cultural levels of ontogenetic integration and interaction" (1985: 286). Time-experiencing accordingly involves the follow-

ing levels: "biological, physiological, perceptual, objective, conceptual, psychological, social, and cultural" (ibid.). This scope of chronemics indicates its transdisciplinary character. Chronemics is thus closely related to studies in time which have been developed within philosophy (Whitrow 1961, Kümmel 1962, Gonseth 1964, Gale 1968, Mellor 1981), psychology (Fraisse 1963, Doob 1971), psychopathology (Yaker et al., eds. 1972), linguistic and literary studies (see 4.2), sociology (Zerubavel 1981) and social history (Wright 1968), anthropology, and many other transdisciplinary contexts (see the following anthologies: Meyer, ed. 1964, Fraser, ed. 1966, Fraser & Müller, eds. 1972, Fraser & Lawrence, eds. 1975, Patrides, ed. 1976, Fraser et al., eds. 1978, and Fraser 1988).

2. The Chronemic Code

Chronemic analysis presupposes an emic approach to time. Cultures have developed different attitudes toward time which have been interpreted as chronemic codes.

2.1 Emic and Etic Time

So-called objective time, which is measurable in terms of seconds, minutes, and hours, forms the etic (cf. Structuralism 1.1.3) frame of reference of chronemic research. The study of time becomes emic when it is concerned with culture-specific and thus arbitrary segmentations and conceptualizations of the temporal continuum. (For the dialectics between objective and cultural time, see Bruneau 1980: 102). Hall distinguishes between *technical*, *formal*, and *informal* time (1959: 127–45). Technical time may be measured by chronometrically exact methods. It is thus etic time. Formal time is the system of measurement which in a given culture has been developed to regulate the course of work and public life. It is structured by means of calendars and clocks. Informal time consists of less precise, impressionistic units such as "soon," "a while," or "later" which vary much more with situations and cultures. Both formal and informal time are thus emic frames of reference of chronemics.

2.2 Is There a Chronemic System?

Hall even believes in the possibility of an emic segmentation of time in cultural systems (1959: 96, 130). His model of chronemic analysis proposes three segmental units in analogy to the model of language: *isolates*, *sets*, and *patterns*. These units are described as the "phonemes," the "morphemes," and the "sentences" of a chronemic message (but see 3.). According to Hall, Americans' informal time consists of a "vocabulary" of eight or nine sets (from "very short" to "forever"), while for the Mediterranean Arab informal time is restricted to only three sets ("no time," "now," and "forever") (ibid.: 135–37). The basis of this particular analysis may be questionable in detail, but the differences referred to illustrate that chronemic codes may underlie culturally different attitudes toward time.

3. The Semiotic Function of Time

According to Hall "time talks" and "speaks more plainly than words" (1959: 15). These metaphors illustrate the undeniable communicative function of time. But can units of time ever be autonomous signs? Against Hall's assumption of time as a system of relatively autonomous signifiers within a chronemic code, the following considerations suggest that time can be a system only of distinctive but not of autonomously signifying units.

3.1 Time as an Indexical Sign

Since Leibniz (cf. Böhme 1974: 202–204), philosophers have acknowledged the relativity of time. Time is a one-dimensional phenomenon (Bunn 1981: 108–132) which never occurs in any absolute or isolated form. Instead, time is always perceived as a manifestation of the change of objects in space or of persons in actions. Only as a mode of appearance of other semiotic substances can time ever become communicative. Being an aspect of a semiotic object, time can never be the autonomous signifier of a symbol or an icon. Time can only be the signified of a linguistic or pictorial representation which may be symbolic (words designating time) or iconic, as in metaphors and similes (such as "time is money"; cf. Lakoff & Johnson 1980: 7–9). As a primary signifier, measurable in terms of minutes or hours, time can function only as an indexical sign which differentiates between actions or objects (of different length or speed).

3.2 The Chronemic Signifier

Time (priority, duration, or frequency) can be an index of the value which a person ascribes to an activity (cf. Doob 1971: 63–66). Punctuality, the degree of congruence between an arranged and the observed point of time, can be an index of personal appreciation. Television programs show a clear correlation between time and value: Time and length of a news story or an interview indicate the importance of the report or the interviewed personality. In TV commercials, these temporal factors are directly correlated to their costs. The popularity and public importance of TV series are moreover evident from their rhythm and frequency within the monthly program. Time, duration, frequency, and rhythm are thus the signifying substances of differential chronemic contents.

3.3 The Chroneme

Time as a chronemic signifier has no context-independent signified. The duration of an hour is short for a feature film but long for an interview. This chronemic relativity prevents the formation of chronemic signs as temporal units (signifiers) with fixed signifieds. But, as outlined above, time may have the indexical function of differentiating meanings. The temporal index or *chroneme* thus corresponds only to the suprasegmental phonemes in language. They serve to distinguish meanings without being meaningful themselves. The chronemes of a culture thus form a code (q.v. 4.2) which has only the second and no first articulation.

4. Levels of Chronemic Analysis

Time has a semiotic function within several spheres of semiosis.

4.1 Bio- and Psychosemiotics of Time

Biological time is articulated by the so-called physiological clock. Its units are biorhythmic phases and hormonal and metabolic periodicities. Those who restrict semiotics to the criterion of arbitrariness and to cultural determinants have to consider biological time a presemiotic phenomenon. Yet, besides the many culturally determined forms of behavior associated with biorhythms (from daily sleep to the rites of passage), even the individual biological clock may acquire psychosemiotic relevance, in particular when circumstances of social activities ("stress") enter into conflict with biological time.

4.2 Time in Language, Texts, and Communication

Time is relevant to language and communication on an object- and a metalevel. On the object level, time structures language and communication. On the metalevel, time is represented by means of language and texts.

4.2.1 TIME STRUCTURING COMMUNICATION

The semiotic function of time in linguistic communication is a phenomenon of paralinguistics. For the temporal variables in speech and in particular the semantic functions of pauses, see Dechert & Raupach, eds. (1980). On the semiotics of silence, see Tannen & Saville-Troike, eds. (1985). For the paralinguistic and nonverbal temporal factors of communication, see Feldstein & Welkowitz (1978). Time as a factor of communication in American sign language (ASL) is studied by Stokoe (1975: 322–30). Research in temporal factors of communication such as duration, rhythm, or pauses is a semiotic study of time at the object level of analysis.

4.2.2 SEMIOTIC REPRESENTATION OF TIME

Research in semiotic representations of time (signs about time) in language and texts is a study of time at the metalevel. Various semiotic codes have specific means of representing time. Tense, the morphological representation of time, is not available in all languages, but past, present, and future can also be expressed by lexical or other means. At the level of the text, Greimas and Courtés describe temporalization, the representation of temporal sequences in texts, as a fundamental feature of narrativity (1979: 337). For the representation of time in language and literature in general, see, e.g., Gonseth (1964), Meyer, ed. (1964), Fraser, ed. (1966), Gale (1968), Fraser & Lawrence, eds. (1975: 122–35), Patrides, ed. (1976), Fraser et al., eds. (1978), Jakobson (1985: 11–24), and Pinto (1989).

Specific means of representing time are also available to drama (scenes and acts; cf. Theater) and film (e.g., slow motion, quick motion, cutting, and editing). The temporal dimensions of music (tempo, rhythm) are possibly based on an iconic mapping of biological and psychological time. In painting, the possibilities of representing time are rather restricted. For a bibliography on temporal representation in art, film, and music, see Patrides, ed. (1976:258–59).

4.3 Evolution of Codes

The temporal dimensions of speech and communication discussed above belong to the synchronic dimension of semiotics. The changes in time implied by this dimension are the trivial prerequisite of communication and do not affect the semiotic code. Only when code changes take place is time a feature of the diachronic dimension of semiotics. Linguistic evolution and stylistic innovations in the arts are examples of code changes. The transformation of code structures is emic and thus of diachronic relevance whenever the structural difference is interpreted as being a result of differences between historically distinguishable codes (cf. Koch 1971b: 525; 1974b: 242–49). Chronemic signs are metasigns. They refer to the historical dimension of a sign and thus to a code (cf. Function 3.2).

Aesthetics

Originally, aesthetics was the study of beauty in works of art and in nature. Following Plato, many philosophers considered beauty to be an intrinsic property of objects. In contrast to this view, semiotic approaches to aesthetics consider works of art as signs and texts whose production and reception are a specific process of semiosis. Classical theories of the essence of art were based on two seemingly incompatible principles, *mimesis* and *l'art pour l'art*. Semiotic aesthetics has reinterpreted these principles in terms of semantics and pragmatics. Some defined the aesthetic sign as being iconic; others characterized it as being autotelic or *self-referential*. Further models of semiotic aesthetics have been derived from the theory of codes.

Basic problems of aesthetics are also a topic of several related chapters in this handbook (see Music and Painting in this section). Most theories of the verbal arts are discussed in the section on text semiotics, especially in the chapters on literature and poetics. While this chapter focuses on aesthetics at its most general level, it also includes some topics of particular concern to the visual arts.

1. Semiotic Aesthetics

Semiotic aesthetics has both developed its own theories of art and aimed at a reinterpretation of the history of aesthetics from a semiotic point of view (cf. Fischer-Lichte 1983d, Paetzold 1983).

1.1 Semiotic Origins of Aesthetics

Theories of the arts are as old as the history of philosophy (cf. Gilbert & Kuhn 1939), but as a separate discipline of philosophy, aesthetics was proposed only in 1735 by Alexander G. Baumgarten (1714–1762).

1.1.1 BAUMGARTEN'S AESTHETICS
Baumgarten (cf. 1750/58: §§ 1–2, 9, 13) coined the term *aesthetics* from the Greek αἴσθησις, 'perception by the senses,' in order to designate his idea of a "science of *perceptual* cognition" (*scientia cognitionis sensitivae*), as opposed to logic, the science of rational knowledge. His system of theoretical aesthetics (ibid.: § 13) also postulated a *semiotics* as its branch of study concerned with "the beautifully conceived and arranged" (*de signis pulchre cogitatorum et dispositorum*). The origin of aesthetics is thus closely connected with the history of semiotics. As Todorov points out, this origin coincided with the end of (classical) rhetoric, that other precursor of semiotics (1977: 111)

The subsequent prehistory of semiotic aesthetics cannot be outlined here. For chapters of this history see, for example, Eco (1954; 1978), Todorov (1977), and Eschbach (1981). A milestone in the semiotic history of aesthetics was Lessing's *Laokoon* (1766), which has been the subject of various semiotic interpretations (cf. Bayer 1975, Gebauer, ed. 1984, Wellbery 1984; see also Literature 2.1.1).

1.1.2 BEAUTY IN NATURE AND ART
In its classical definition, aesthetics was the theory of beauty in nature *and* art. During the history of aesthetics this definition has undergone two essential changes concerning the criteria of beauty and nature. The first change was partially due to the evolution of the arts themselves. Beauty could no longer be considered an essential feature of the arts. The second change was less programmatic. Aesthetics became more and more the study of objects of art, to the neglect of aesthetic objects of nature. Only recently have semioticians shown a renewed interest in aesthetic features of nature. Thus, Sebeok (1981) has studied prefigurations of visual art and music with animals, and Koch (1984) has developed a phylogenetic theory of the evolution of the arts, based on earlier universal theories of aestheticalness (cf. Koch 1971b).

1.2 Trends in Semiotic Aesthetics

Excluding the current trends discussed in the context of the more specific branches of aesthetics (see esp. Literature), five major semiotic approaches to, or even schools of, aesthetics in general may be distinguished: approaches following Peirce and Morris, the Prague School, semiotic studies based on mathematical models, and studies that will be discussed under the heading of code theoretical approaches. For surveys of the whole field of aesthetic semiotics, see the monographs by Eco (1978; 1979), Busse & Riemenschneider (1979), Fischer-Lichte (1979), Kiefer (1982), and Faltin (1985), the papers by Rudner (1951), Volli (1972a), Steiner (1977), Paetzold (1983), and Morawski (1984), the collections of papers edited by Chatman et al. (1979), Lange-Seidl (1981), Sturm & Eschbach (1981), and Oehler (1984), and the special issue of *Bulletin du groupe de recherches sémio-linguistiques* 35 (1985).

1.2.1 THE PEIRCEAN FOUNDATION
Although aesthetics is not a central topic in the philosophy of Peirce, his writings deal with aesthetic problems at several points (cf. Schulz 1961, Kent 1976, Kaelin 1983). Peirce's theory of signs, in conjunction with a numerical theory of the aesthetic object, became the basis of the semiotic school of aesthetics founded by Bense (1965a; 1969; 1971; 1975; 1977a; 1979; cf. Walther 1974: 132–36, Plebe, ed. 1981). Bense's semiotic studies of aesthetic objects are concerned primarily with the classification of aesthetic signs according to Peirce's typology of signs. For studies in this tradition see, for example, Brög (1968; 1979), Bayer (1975), Schmalriede (1981), and many papers published in the journal *Semiosis*. Peirce's theory of signs is also a basis of the semiotic aesthetics developed by Nadin (1981). See also Peirce (4.2–4).

1.2.2 MORRIS'S SEMIOTIC AESTHETICS
From 1939, Charles Morris (see also Morris & Hamilton 1965) developed a behaviorist theory which characterizes art as an iconic sign of value. This aesthetic semiotics became the topic of an extensive debate (cf. Rudner 1951, Roberts 1955) whose history is outlined by Rossi-Landi (1972: 75–82) and Dutz (1983: 78–99). Steiner (1977) discusses Morris's semiotic aesthetics in comparison with Mukařovský's approach.

1.2.3 PRAGUE SCHOOL AESTHETICS
The semiotic aesthetics of the Prague School is a functional theory which defines the essence of art within the pragmatic dimension of semiosis. Sources with contributions to this school of aesthetics are Garvin, ed. (1964), Matejka & Titunik, eds. (1976), and Matejka, ed. (1978). Reviews and general discussions are Schmid (1978), Fischer-Lichte (1979: 138–80), Garvin (1981), Holmes (1981), and Fietz (1982: 70–104). A dominant figure of this school of aesthetics is Mukařovský (esp. 1936; 1978). For special studies of his theories, see Steiner (1977), Winner (1979), and Chvatík (1983). Important contributions to Prague School aes-

thetics were also made by Jakobson (cf. Winner 1987, Poetry 1.3).

1.2.4 NUMERICAL AND INFORMATION THEORETICAL APPROACHES

Mathematical approaches to aesthetics were developed on a numerical basis within Bense's school and on an information theoretical basis in other studies. A further mathematical approach to aesthetics proposed by Nadin (1981; 1984) is based on the theory of *fuzzy sets*. The numerical component of Bense's aesthetics is based on Birkhoff's (1932) formula of the *aesthetic measure* (cf. also Gunzenhäuser 1962, Maser 1970). It determines the aestheticalness of an object of art in relation to its degree of complexity (*C*) and its features of harmony, symmetry, or order (*O*). Aestheticalness, the aesthetic measure *M*, is thus calculated by the formula $M = \frac{O}{C}$. On this basis, Bense pursues the goal of an "objective" science whose object of study is the work of art in its "materiality," "irrespective of a particular mode of perception" (1969: 8, 45; 1971: 65). On statistical grounds, Bense (1979) argues that the improbability of an event is a defining criterion of its aestheticalness. The objectivist approach of this theory is probably able to characterize universal features of beauty in art and nature. With its programmatic exclusion of the pragmatic dimension of aesthetic semiosis (cf. 3.), however, this approach can hardly account for the dynamic processes in the perception and evaluation of art.

Approaches to the semiotics of the arts based on information theory have attempted a reinterpretation of phenomena such as harmony, originality, and innovation in terms of redundancy, information, and entropy (Moles 1958, Frank 1959, Gunzenhäuser 1962, Bense 1969). In an independent development, information theory has also influenced the aesthetics of Soviet semiotics. Thus, Lotman elaborates the thesis that the transformation of noise (i.e., disorder and entropy) into information is the specific feature of art (1970: 75). The mathematical models applied in Lotman's calculations of aesthetic entropy (ibid.: 25–31) were developed by A. M. Kolmogorov.

1.2.5 FURTHER SEMIOTIC APPROACHES TO AESTHETICS

Further semiotic approaches to aesthetics can be only briefly enumerated. Most of them are discussed in more detail in the context of the verbal arts (see Text Semiotics):

1. For Soviet contributions to the semiotics of art and their Russian Formalist precursors, see Sklovskij (1916), Uspenskij (1977b), Ivanov (1976), and Matejka (1978). On Lotman's theories see also 4.2.

2. Goodman's *Languages of Art* (1968) has been interpreted as a new semiotic aesthetics (Ihwe 1985), although other semioticians have claimed that it "contributes almost nothing to the understanding of art" (Schnelle 1980: 387) (see 2.3).

3. Attempts at a pluralistic synthesis of various currents in the semiotics of art have been made by Garroni (1968, especially with reference to film semiotics), Volli (1972a), Busse & Riemenschneider (1979), Kiefer (1982, with special reference to teaching), and Faltin (1985, whose study also includes a chapter on Wittgenstein's aesthetics).

4. For the comparative semiotics of the various branches of art (music, painting, poetry, etc.) see Veltruský (1981).

5. For Eco's and other code theoretical approaches to art, see 4. On Jakobson's semiotic aesthetics see Winner (1987).

---

2. Semantics of the Aesthetic Sign

Many semioticians have defined art as a particular type of sign characterized by a specific mode of reference.

2.1 Art in the Peircean Semiotic Framework

In the semiotics of Peirce, the referential function of signs is defined by the icon-index-symbol trichotomy, but a holistic interpretation must also determine the sign as *representamen* (*quali-*, *sin-*, or *legisign*) and as *interpretant* (*rheme*, *dicent*, or *argument*).

2.1.1 ICON, INDEX, SYMBOL

Not all semioticians have followed Morris's standard interpretation of art as an iconic sign. Shapiro, for example, claims that "the relation of the art-sign to its object is not iconic or indexical but *symbolic*; it represents by means of a conventional symbolism rather than by being a natural sign" (1975: 35). In a different framework, this aspect of conventionality in art is also emphasized by Goodman (1968).

The aspect of indexicality has also been discussed as a distinctive feature of art (e.g., Bense 1977a: 204). Peirce himself ascribed features of indexicality to works of the visual arts (§ 1.176; cf. Bense 1979: 5): "Works of sculpture and painting can be executed for a single patron and must be by a single artist. A painting always represents a fragment of a larger whole. It is broken at its edges. [. . .] In such a work individuality of thought and feeling is an element of beauty." The categories of exemplification or ostension by which others have characterized art are also modes of indexicality in the sense of Peirce.

These divergent interpretations of the semantics of art are not necessarily contradictory, since Peirce himself declared (cf. Schulz 1961: 103): "The most perfect of signs are those in which the iconic, indicative and symbolic characters are blended as equally as possible" (§ 4.448). Following this line, Bense discusses the work of art in its "iconic semblance," "indexical reality," and "symbolic being" and characterizes the aesthetic condition as the "iconic probability of the indexical reality" (1975: 145–46).

2.1.2 ART AS REPRESENTAMEN AND INTERPRETANT

Aspects of the first and third trichotomies of the aesthetic sign are also discussed in various writings by Bense (1971; 1975; 1977a). With respect to its interpretant, the work of art is characterized as a rheme, a sign of "qualitative possibility" which does not affirm anything. This classification of art is closely related to its feature of interpretative openness. As a representamen, the aesthetic sign is less determined. With reference to its "creative-innovative nature and its indeterminacy of production" (1971: 69), Bense characterizes art as a sinsign, but with respect to its materiality he defines it as a qualisign, and concerning its "formal" characteristics he classifies it as a legisign. Bense explains this indeterminacy by the "extreme ambiguity" in the definition of the aesthetic between its qualitative and its conventional characteristics (1977a: 202–203).

2.2 Morris's Aesthetic Sign

The theory of the iconic character of art has a precursor in the more specific field of literature, namely, the theory of mimesis. But Morris gave this ancient theory a new interpretation.

2.2.1 ICONICITY AND VALUE

Morris specified the differentia of the aesthetic sign by two features, *iconicity* and *value* (1939: 420–21). Iconicity, according to Morris, is more than mere similarity: "An iconic sign denotes any object which has the properties (in practice, a selection from the properties) which it itself has. Hence, when an interpreter apprehends an iconic sign vehicle, he apprehends directly what is designated" (ibid.). But iconicity is not a sufficient characteristic of art since it also defines pictorial representation in general. Only when the designatum of the iconic sign is a value does the sign become aesthetic: "The aesthetic sign is an iconic sign whose designatum is a value" (ibid.).

The concept of value was central to Morris's behavioristic theory of semiosis. It characterizes a value as "a property of an object or situation relative to an interest." It is not "located in the objects" but depends on the perceiver's "interested act" (ibid.: 418). Hence, the aesthetic sign can exist only in a process of interpretation, and in this definition the semantic dimension of art has a necessary counterpart in a pragmatic dimension. To Morris, the role of the interpreter in aesthetic semiosis was no less essential than it is in the aesthetics of Mukařovský (cf. Steiner 1977).

The theory of aesthetic iconicity seems to contradict the assumption of aesthetic autonomy. While the former is based on a criterion of reference, the latter seems to refute the very idea of a referential object. Morris, however, argued that his theory of aesthetic iconicity could solve even this paradox of the self-referential sign: Since in aesthetic signs "there is the direct apprehension of value properties through the very presence of that which itself has the value it designates [. . .] aesthetic perception is tied to the work itself and does not use this merely as a springboard for evoking reveries and recollections" (1939: 420). The paradox of aesthetic self-reference or of "disinterested interest" is thus "accounted for in the fact that in the apprehension of the iconic sign there is both a mediated and an immediate taking account of certain properties." Morris later modified his position somewhat in response to criticism of the concept of iconicity. For details see Morris (1946: 276, 296) and Morris & Hamilton (1965).

2.3 Goodman's Symptoms of Art

Goodman distinguishes five "symptoms" of the aesthetic (1968: 252; 1978: 67–68; cf. Image 3.4). Three of them characterize features of the aesthetic code or symbol system: (1) *syntactic density* (the symbols lack finite articulation or differentiation), (2) *semantic density* (the symbols are differentiated by minimal differences), and (3) *syntactic repleteness* (relatively many features of the symbols are significant). The two further criteria are of particular interest in this context dealing with the referential function of art: (4) *exemplification* and (5) *multiple* and *complex reference*.

By exemplification, as opposed to denotation, Goodman describes a mode of reference which also characterizes the difference between *showing* and *telling* (1968: 253). It includes expression, which Goodman defines as metaphorical or figurative exemplification. In exemplification, a symbol refers to properties which the symbol itself "possesses and shows forth," although not every one of its properties has this function of exemplification (e.g., not the size of a sample). A sign by exemplification has thus both iconic (by having common features; cf. 2.2.1) and indexical characteristics (since the referential object is present in the act of semiosis).

Goodman, however, is cautious not to call his "symptoms" criteria of art and argues that these symptoms "are neither a necessary nor a sufficient condition for, but merely tend in conjunction with other such symptoms to be present in, aesthetic experience" (ibid.: 252). He proposes that the question "What is art?" should be replaced by the question "When is art?" to remind the aesthetician of the necessary pragmatic conditions under which objects actually function as works of art (1978: 57). A related theory of aesthetic reference was proposed by Faltin (1972). He characterizes art by the category of *ostension*.

3. Pragmatics of Aesthetic Semiosis

The classical theory of aesthetic autonomy leads to a semantic paradox. Semiotic aesthetics has tried to solve this paradox by criteria of the pragmatic dimension of semiosis. Among the first who developed a semiotic aesthetics on this basis was Mukařovský. His theory of the aesthetic function is closely related to Jakobson's poetic function. Other pragmatic criteria of art have been developed in Schmidt's (1971) theory of aesthetic *polyfunctionality* and *polyvalence* and Eco's theory of aesthetic openness. Based on his philosophy of action, Danto (1981) has developed an aesthetics which is closely related to some pragmatically oriented semiotic theories of art. On aesthetic autonomy see also Literature (2.2) and Poetry (1.2).

3.1 Art for Art's Sake

The traditional version of the theory of aesthetic autonomy reached its climax in the romantic *l'art pour l'art* aesthetics (cf. Egan 1921). An early explicit formulation of this doctrine was given by Augustine, who defined beauty as something which pleases in itself (*per se ipsum*) (cf. ibid.: 7). In Kant's *Critique of Judgement* (1790), this exclusion of reference in aesthetic experience is implied in his classical criteria of "disinterested pleasure" ("interesseloses Wohlgefallen") and "purposiveness without purpose" ("Zweckmäßigkeit ohne Zweck"). In parenthesis it may be added that it is precisely this ideal of the detachment of the aesthetic from its referential (and sociological) context which attracted the criticism of sociologically oriented aestheticians. See in particular Bourdieu's (1979) "anti-Kantian" aesthetics.

The traditional theories of aesthetic autonomy did not maintain that art excludes reference in principle. The argument is rather that the aestheticalness of art cannot lie in any referential function. This negative characterization of art in its semantic dimension has always led to the search for specific aesthetic features in the pragmatic dimension of art. One of the early theories focusing on this dimension is the theory of *aesthetic distance*, which according to Gilbert & Kuhn (1939: 269) was proposed earlier by G. V. Gravina (1664–1718). In a psychological interpretation, Bullough defined this phenomenon in the perception of art as "the cutting out of the practical sides of things and of our practical attitudes to them" (1912: 89). This view comes close to Mukařovský's aesthetic function.

3.2 Mukařovský's Aesthetic Function

In his paper "Art as a Semiotic Fact" (1934) and his book *Aesthetic Function* (1936), Mukařovský gives a first outline of his semiotic theory of aesthetic autonomy (cf. 1.2.3 and Function 3.3).

3.2.1 AESTHETIC VS. COMMUNICATIVE SIGNS
Mukařovský contrasts the aesthetic or *autonomous* sign function with the *communicative* function of signs (1934: 85). Both functions may be present in a work of art (e.g., in a realistic painting), but only the autonomous function constitutes the specificity of art: "The significance of a work of art as a work of art per se does not lie in communication" (Mukařovský 1966: 237). While the communicative sign has a referential function, the autonomous sign "does not refer to a distinct existence but to the total context of social phenomena of the given milieu." Instead by a lack of reference, Mukařovský thus characterizes the aesthetic autonomy by the feature of *fictionality* (cf. Literature 2.3): "It is impossible to postulate the documentary authenticity of the subject of a work of art as long as we evaluate the work as a product of art" (1934: 88). With this characteristic, Mukařovský's aesthetics turns out to be a rather moderate version of the theory of autonomy. More radical theories have gone further by defining the aesthetic sign as being autotelic or self-referential (thus, Jakobson in the context of poetry, Poetry 1.2). For a more recent pragmatic theory of aesthetics which emphasizes the noncommunicative character of art in the framework of the theory of action, see Trabant (1980).

3.2.2 PRAGMATICS OF THE AESTHETIC FUNCTION
Mukařovský determines the pragmatic essence of aesthetic perception within the larger framework of his functional theory of human behavior. In this theory (1942: 38), functions are "attitudes toward the external world," and the aesthetic function is one of two semiotic functions which are both opposed to nonsemiotic (especially practical) functions (see Function 3.3). The attitude described as aesthetic renders an object of perception "a *sign*, not subordinated to any external purpose but self-sufficient and evoking in man a certain attitude toward all of reality" (Mukařovský 1966: 240).

A basic feature of the aesthetic function is its "ability to *isolate* an object" and to "cause maximal focus of attention on a given object" (Mukařovský 1936: 21). These are the characteristics which, in the poetics of the Russian Formalist and Prague schools, have been described by the principles of *estrangement*, *deautomatization*, and *foregrounding* (see Poetry 1.3). With special reference to the visual arts, Mukařovský emphasizes that the difference between a natural object and an object of art is essentially "based on the way in which the perceiver approaches it" (1966: 230–31). The perceiver can even approach objects of nature aesthetically and thus discover features of art in nature.

4. Aesthetic Codes

The concept of code has undergone remarkable transformations. Borrowed from information theory, where it refers to precise rules for the correlation of signals, it has become a key concept in the field of text semiotics (cf. Fokkema 1985) and aesthetics, where creativity and thus deviations from rules have to be accounted for. A symptomatic climax of this terminological transformation is Barthes's semiotics of literature (1970b: 23–25). Here a code has become "a perspective of quotations, a mirage of structures," and a network of literary associations with the effect of a filter in the reading of a text. In the field of aesthetics, two semiotic theories have been based on a more elaborate theory of codes.

4.1 Eco's Theory of Aesthetic Codes

Within Eco's (1968; 1976; 1979) theory of codes, innovative texts are described as *open* messages generated in a process of *coding* or *overcoding*.

4.1.1 THE AESTHETIC MESSAGE AS A PROCESS OF CODING

Eco describes the aesthetic code as the result of a dialectics between the (conventional) code and the innovative *message* (1968: 162–66). By their innovative character, aesthetic messages infringe the rules of their genre and thus negate the code. But at the same time, the new message creates a new aesthetic code: "Every work

[of art] upsets the code but at the same time strengthens it, too; [. . .] by violating it, the work completes and transforms the code" (ibid.: 163).

Eco describes this innovative process as one of overcoding, i.e., the creation of new rules on the basis of preestablished rules (1976: 155, 268–70). Aesthetic overcoding generates a semiotic "surplus" on the level both of content and of form. By this surplus of expression and of content, the text becomes open to multiple interpretations (ibid.: 270). More recently, Eco (1985c) considers the ideal of *innovation* to be a characteristic of modern aesthetics since Mannerism and Romanticism, whereas postmodern aesthetics, in this interpretation, has developed a new aesthetics of *iteration* and *repetition*.

4.1.2 THE OPEN MESSAGE

An essential feature of aesthetic codes and messages, according to Eco (1962; 1968; 1979), is openness. Because of its ambiguity and the plurality of cultural subcodes (Eco 1968: 134, 143, 163), the aesthetic message has the character of an "empty form," into which the recipient inserts meanings. The interpreter "tries to accept the challenge posed by this open message and to fill the invisible form by his or her own codes" (ibid.: 165). However, the openness is counteracted by the "logic of the signifier." This opposed principle is the requirement of interpretative "fidelity to the structured context of the message" (ibid.: 163), which depends on the historically given conventional codes. Besides the dialectics of message and code, the aesthetic message is therefore also determined by a dialectics between openness and closure due to conventional codes.

4.2 Lotman's Plurality of Aesthetic Codes

Based on models of the theories of information and communication, Lotman develops his theory of the plurality of artistic codes (1970: 23ff.; cf. Soviet Semiotics).

4.2.1 THE COMMON CODE AND THE AESTHETICS OF IDENTITY

Like any other message, the artistic message can be decoded only on the basis of a common code shared by both the sender and the receiver. In literature, for example, this code consists of a standard language, but also of the traditional literary conventions which have become codified in normative poetics and rhetoric. Messages generated only from these common codes follow an *aesthetics of identity* (ibid.: 24).

4.2.2 CODE DIFFERENCES AND AESTHETICS OF OPPOSITION

Aesthetically innovative messages, according to Lotman, are based on an *aesthetics of opposition* (1970: 292–96). With such messages, the receiver "tries to decipher the text using a code different from the one that the creator uses" (ibid.: 24–25). As a result, the text is either recoded by the receiver (which occasionally involves its aesthetic destruction, when the text is treated as though it were nonaesthetic), or it is interpreted as an artistic text, which requires the creation of an as yet unknown aesthetic code. In this case, the receiver recognizes in the course of decoding that he or she has to work out a new code for deciphering the message. This new aesthetic code can be either the author's code or a transformation of it. Such transformations often occur as "creolizations," i.e., assimilations with other codes of the interpreter. Therefore, the artistic text may acquire different meanings for sender and receiver. Even fortuitous elements of the text may be interpreted as meaningful. Lotman calls this "the ability of an artistic text to amass information" (ibid.: 25).

The preference for either an aesthetics of identity or an aesthetics of innovation is a matter of cultural tradition or aesthetic fashion. According to Ikegami (1989), the Japanese culture traditionally emphasized the principle of imitation, whereas Western art has set store by the principles of creativity and innovation. This means that Japanese aesthetics is one of identity, whereas Western aesthetics is one of innovation. However, if Eco is right, the new trend in postmodern Western aesthetics is also one of an aesthetics of identity.

Music

The semiotics of music raises the question whether sounds can be studied as signs, compositions as messages, and music as a semiotic system. The answers have been controversial. Although some have rejected the concept of a musical sign (Benveniste 1969: 238), many scholars have accepted music as an object of semiotic study. Nevertheless, some have defined music as *asemantic* (Ruwet 1975: 33, Faltin 1985: 72), whereas others have characterized it as *asemiotic* (Benveniste 1969: 236). But the difference between these evaluations is in part one of terminology.

1. Survey of the Semiotics of Music

Traditional aesthetics and musicology have already raised the implicitly semiotic question about meaning in music, often under the metaphorical heading of the "language of music," but an explicitly semiotic theory of music has developed only since the early 1970s. Its beginning was an interdisciplinary dialogue between linguists and musicologists.

1.1 The State of the Art

The dialogue between linguists and musicologists began with a contribution by Jakobson (1932) and was resumed by Springer (1956),

Nettl (1958), Bright (1963), Harweg (1968), Koch (1971b: 283–95), and Bierwisch (1979). While these contributions discussed analogies between signs and systems in language and in music, the linguist Ruwet (1972; 1975) turned to analogies between poetics and music. "What is the semiotics of music?" was first asked explicitly in articles by Nattiez (1973b) and Kneif (1974). Special issues of journals such as *Musique en jeu* 5 (1971), 10 (1973), 12 (1973), 17 (1975), *Degrés* 18 (1978), *Bulletin du groupe de recherches sémio-linguistiques* 28 (1983), *Semiotica* 66.1/3 (1987), and *Zeitschrift für Semiotik* 9.3/4 (1987) and conference proceedings (cf. Stefani 1975) testify to an increasing interest in the new field of research. Nattiez (1975) became the main proponent of the semiotics of music, followed by Stefani (1976), Martin (1978), Schneider (1980), and Faltin (1985). General surveys are also given by Nattiez (1973c), Molino (1975), Keiler (1981), Orlov (1981), Tarasti (1986), and Tarasti et al. (1987).

1.2 Trends in the Semiotics of Music

Approaches to the semiotics of music have been developed by various schools and tendencies of semiotics. Linguistic structuralism is the starting point of many of these approaches (e.g., Firca 1972). Nattiez (1973d) distinguishes three structuralist models underlying the major semiotic approaches to music, Prague School *functionalism* (see also Jiranek 1975), *distributionalism* (including Lévi-Strauss's text structuralism), and *generative grammar* (cf. Structuralism 1.–2.). Further approaches to the semiotics of music have been based on Morris (cf. Coker 1972, Boilès 1973), Peirce, and Greimas (cf. Tarasti 1982) and on mathematical linguistics (Cazimir 1976). Several contributions are by Barthes (1985b: 245–312). Precursors of the explicit semiotics of music are studies based on communication and information theory (e.g., Moles 1958, Meyer-Eppler 1962).

1.3 Semiotics and Semiography

Nattiez (1973b) distinguishes two branches within the semiotics of music concerned with different types of signs. The first and major branch, to which this chapter will be restricted, studies music as an acoustic system of signs. The second branch studies the systems of musical notation, which consist of graphic signs representing acoustic signs. For the semiography of music see also Moutard (1974) and Göschl (1980).

1.4 Excursus: Opera and Ballet

The semiotics of opera and ballet, situated between the study of music and of theater, requires taking into account additional dimensions of semiotic research such as gestures, facial expressions (Scotto di Carlo 1973), kinesics, myth, and narrativity (Tarasti 1979). For the semiotics of opera see Noske (1977). For preliminaries to a semiotics of ballet, see Koch (1971b: 263–82) and Shapiro (1981).

2. The Musical Sign

The question about meaning in music (Coker 1972) and the search for the musical symbol (Epperson 1967) have been of concern to mu-

sicology and aesthetics (Langer 1942) for a long time. Gatz distinguished two major trends in the aesthetics of music according to the answers given to this question (1929: 11–13): The first is the *aesthetics of heteronomy*. It interprets music as an expression of extramusical content. The second is the *aesthetics of autonomy*. It prefers to define music as a phenomenon *sui generis*, without any semantic dimension. The assumption of meaning in music necessarily implies the acceptance of a musical sign. Some have argued that the aesthetics of autonomy refutes the existence of such a sign (cf. Nattiez 1977: 124), but in terms of a concept developed within semiotic aesthetics, music has been interpreted as an autonomous sign.

2.1 Autonomy of the Musical Sign

According to Stravinsky, "music is, by its very nature, essentially powerless to *express* anything at all, whether a feeling, an attitude of mind, a psychological mood, a phenomenon of nature, etc." (1936: 53). This thesis reflects a radical view of musical autonomy. In a more moderate view, Jakobson describes the autonomy of music as a matter of the dominance of the poetic (more generally: aesthetic) function over possible referential or other functions of the musical message (1968: 703–704). Ruwet, Nattiez, and Faltin (1972) have elaborated the theory of the autonomous musical sign which refers only to itself. Ruwet interprets this semiotic autonomy in terms of Jakobson's theory of poetic equivalence, defining the aesthetic essence of music by the feature of the recurrence of equivalent sounds (1972: 10, 135).

Faltin (1972; 1985: 96ff.) discusses the apparent semiotic paradox of musical *autoreflexivity* and the question whether communication without reference deserves to be called a sign on the basis of the distinction between meaning and reference (cf. Sign 2.). While Faltin agrees with those who deny reference to the musical sign, he argues that music nevertheless carries meaning. In this view, the musical sign is similar to ostensive signs which carry no message beyond their own reality either. The semiotics of the musical sign is furthermore similar to fictional proper names (cf. Literature 2.3), which have meaning within a text but no extratextual reference (cf. Faltin 1972: 208–209).

2.2 Semantics of the Musical Sign

In the discussion about the meaning and reference of the musical sign, different concepts of "semantics" are used so that arguments for or against the semanticity of music may imply very different claims. The basic semantic distinction in musicology is between meanings that are inherent in music and those which have some extramusical reference. Related problems are the verbalization of musical experience and the type of object relation of musical signs.

2.2.1 SEMANTICS AND SEMIOTICS IN MUSIC

Following Morris and the tradition of logical semantics, some restrict the concept of semantics to the sphere of reference. For this reason, Faltin, who denies referentiality to music, concludes that music is asemantic, although it has meaning and is thus an object of semiotic study (1985: 100). In a quite different sense, Benveniste uses the same terms when he concludes that music is a semantic but an asemiotic phenomenon (1969: 238, 242; see also Barthes 1985b: 311–12). "Asemiotic" in this theory means that the elements of this system have no meaning (or reference) in isolation and are therefore not signs. The argument is that single musical sounds are always meaningless in this sense. "Semantic," on the other hand, refers to meanings as differential functions generated by and within a discourse. A composition, being a discourse whose sound elements are interrelated to form a coherent whole, is certainly "semantic" in this sense. This conclusion of Benveniste's describes basically the same state of affairs which Faltin defines in the opposite terminology (see also Semantics 1.4.3). Ignoring these terminological differences between some schools of semi-

otics, the following paragraphs will discuss the semantic dimension of music in the broadest sense, including reference, meaning, and contextual (or "discoursive") functions of music.

2.2.2 ENDOSEMANTIC FUNCTIONS OF MUSIC

Benveniste's and Faltin's twofold characterizations of musical content correspond to two different domains of the semantics of music (in the broader sense), which musicologists have distinguished in different terms. Bright, for example, introduced the distinction between *endosemantic* and *exosemantic* structures of music (1963: 29). Exosemantic content structures within music refer to extramusical sound events. Coker calls such forms of reference *extrageneric musical meanings* (1972: 61). Endosemantic content structures consist of musical references to sound structures (e.g., motifs or themes) which exist within music only. Coker defines them as *congeneric musical meanings* (ibid.). The discussion of these structures is sometimes restricted to *intramusical* references (to sound structures within one composition). But the endosemantics of music also comprises *intermusical* references (to elements of other compositions). Coker considers both, pointing out that in these two forms of musical semiosis "someone interprets one part of a musical work as a sign of another part of that same work *or* a diverse musical work" (ibid.).

Style, epoch, and genre of a piece of music are recognizable by intermusical reference to other compositions of the same kind or period. In this sense, they are an endosemantic structure of music. However, if the style of a composition is interpreted as a reference to the culture of a whole epoch (e.g., to the Romantic culture in Germany), then this reference becomes exosemantic.

2.2.3 MUSICAL REFERENCE AND EXOSEMANTIC CONTENT

The referential potential of music (for those who accept any) has only a rather restricted scope. But if the category of musical reference is expanded from the perception of extramusical sound events to other forms of experience which music may evoke, this category is considerably expanded. The major categories of such exosemantic musical contents are the following (cf. Osmond-Smith 1972, Jiranek 1975):

1. *Sound events*: Onomatopoeic representations of bird songs, hunting horns, thunderstorms, bells, battle cries, or cannonades, which characterize the genre of program music, are typical examples of musical sounds referring to extramusical acoustic events. Such forms of exosemantic reference are only marginally relevant to music on the whole. Only acoustic events can be represented denotatively in music. All other forms of reference are possible only by connotation.

2. *Emotions*: The most important semantic field studied in traditional musicology is emotional meaning. The content of the musical sign in this case is the emotion evoked within the hearer. Langer argues that music is the "logical expression" of feelings, a "symbolic form" (1942: 185, 204), whose significance can be felt, but not defined because it is only "implicit, but not conventionally fixed." Musicologists who have attempted to discover correlates between musical form and content are Meyer and Cooke. Meyer (1956) developed a theory of correspondence between patterns of tension, delay, and release in rhythm or harmony and in human emotions. Cooke (1959) even attempts to establish a musical "vocabulary" correlating musical phrases and harmonic sequences to emotions such as joy, pleasure, sorrow, etc.

3. *Synaesthetic and associative contents*: By synaesthesia, the hearer perceives impressions of the visual, tactile, or other channels of perception concomitantly with the musical sounds, e.g., light colors with clear sounds. Such connotations are usually highly ideosyncratic. Associative meanings, on the other hand, as they may be experimentally derived from word associations in reaction to music, constitute a statistically more significant area of musical semantics (cf. Knobloch et al. 1968, Nattiez 1973d). However, as also in linguistic

psychosemantics, the results obtained from such tests may reflect meanings imposed by the analyst, which do not have to correspond with any "inherent" meanings in music.

4. *Musical meanings sui generis*: A borderline case of musical semantics is those meanings of music which are said to be inexpressible or untranslatable into language. In this vein, Langer argues that "music articulates forms which language cannot set forth" (1942: 198), and Eggebrecht claims that access to music is possible only by "understanding without concepts" (1973: 52). The borderline which these theories touch is the one between the heteronomy (and thus semanticity) and the autonomy (and thus asemanticity) of music. The topos of inexpressibility raises the question of the possibilities of a verbalization of musical meanings.

2.2.4 VERBALIZATION OF MUSICAL MEANINGS

Ruwet, a proponent of an endosemantic interpretation of music, considers verbalizations to be the only possible form of content in music: "If it is necessary at all to assume a signifier and signified in music, one could say that the signified in music (the 'intelligible' or 'translatable' aspect, according to Jakobson) is the description of the signifier (the 'perceivable' aspect)" (1972: 12). Nobody will claim that the verbalizations of musical semantics correspond or are equivalent to musical meanings in a way in which linguistic paraphrases or synonyms may be mutually equivalent. According to Benveniste, there is a basic asymmetry between language and music (1969: 10, 130). While language generates its own metalanguage, music cannot be analyzed by means of music. The analytical metalanguage (more precisely: *metasemiotic*) of music is language, while this language itself is not translatable into music. This is why a semantics of music is impossible without language, although such verbalizations, being a metasemiotic, cannot be considered equivalent to their object of description.

2.2.5 OBJECT RELATION OF THE MUSICAL SIGN

According to its object relation, the musical sign is basically an icon or an index (cf. Coker

1972, Osmond-Smith 1972, Bierwisch 1979: 43–49, Tarasti 1982). Symbols in the sense of Peirce, conventional signs, are only marginally important in music (e.g., in the case of a national anthem referring to the particular nation). All musical references to extramusical acoustic events are iconic signs. Endosemantic references, such as indicators of style, are indexical insofar as they establish a connection between elements of semiotic messages. At the same time, such references also imply an icon since the connection presupposes the recognition of a similarity: Thus, any variation is an icon of its theme, but the intramusical reference from the variation back to the original occurrence of the theme is an index (cf. Tarasti 1982: 504).

How are emotions related to the musical signs which evoke them? Apparently, there is no relation of similarity. Nevertheless, Osmond-Smith considers the evocation of emotions by means of music to be an unconsciously iconic process (1972: 39–40). His argument is that an emotional reaction to music (e.g., joy or sorrow) has physiological features which equally occur in human reactions to equivalent (joyful or sad) nonmusical events. For such iconic correspondences between music and human biorhythms, see also Meyer (1956) and McLaughlin (1970).

3. Music as a Semiotic System

Paradoxically, there is more agreement about music being a semiotic system than about musical sounds being signs. The discussion about the systematic nature of music focuses on both analogies and differences between music and language.

3.1 Language and Music

The traditional metaphor of the "language of music" (cf. D'Ollone 1952, Mayer 1970, Martin 1978) was used in musicology to refer generally to the meaningful character of music.

Semiotics, however, has shown interest in more systematic correspondences and other points of contact between language and music. A first common feature of language and music is their linear and acoustic manifestation (cf. Bierwisch 1979). Both language and music are cultural systems of arbitrary, recurrent, and structured sounds (Springer 1956: 504). Both systems make differential use of acoustic phenomena such as pitch, duration, quality, and intensity of sounds (ibid. and Nettl 1958). But the function of these structures is quite different within their respective systems (cf. Nattiez 1971: 57). By its own system of acoustic differential values, music, like language, proves to be a semiotic system of values (Jakobson 1932, Kristeva 1969a: 305).

Besides the potential similarities or analogies between language and music, a second type of relation is that of *contiguity* (Harweg 1968: 276). Essential contiguities between the two modes of expression, according to Harweg (ibid.), exist in songs and in metrical and rhythmically spoken language. In both cases, the influence of music on language is one of *parole* but not of *langue*. For the mutual influences between music and spoken language in vocal music, see also Georgiades (1954), Bright (1963), and Hall (1964: 413–14).

3.2 Minimal Units of Music

The question about the minimal units of the semiotic system of music remains undecided in spite of the fact that Lefebvre attempted to introduce the term *meleme* for such a unit (1971: 57). It is uncertain whether the tone, the interval, or the chord should constitute such a unit and how tone color, rhythm, and tempo should be classified. There has been extensive discussion of the question whether a tone in music has the same semiotic function as a phoneme in language. Analogies already pointed out by Jakobson (1932) are that both tones and phonemes are elements of cultural systems in which they have functional values which vary with these cultures. Springer (1956: 509), Nettl (1958: 39), Lévi-

Strauss (1964), and Nattiez (1975: 196–99) dealt more extensively with the analogies between the function of tones within their keys and phonemes within their languages. An objection against considering tones as "musical phonemes" within a given key is that with the change of the key one would have to assume the beginning of a new "musical language." Thus, a musical composition, unlike most verbal texts, would appear to be written in several "languages."

3.3 Double Articulation

Lévi-Strauss (1964) and other semioticians (cf. Nattiez 1975: 199–208) ascribe a *double articulation* (cf. Language 4.1) to music. This assumption presupposes a level of musical signs with meanings, like the morphemes (or words) of a language, a level of musical "phonemes," and the possibility of generating new musical "morphemes" by the exchange of "phoneme-tones." Benveniste (1969), Ruwet (1972: 36), and many others (cf. Schneider 1980: 205–208) reject the assumption of double articulation in music. Ruwet considers music to be a semiotic system with one articulation only, since "the elements and the groups differentiated by them are of the same kind" (1972: 36). For further analogies and differences between the elementary signs and the syntax of language and music, see Bierwisch (1979: 64–84).

3.4 Structures of the Musical Text

Traditional musicology used linguistic metaphors such as *phrase* and *sentence* to designate segments of musical compositions. Following the model of language, the semiotics of music developed further criteria of segmentation and classification of works of music. Thus, Ruwet (1972) applied principles of distributional linguistics to determine syntagmatic and paradigmatic structures of compositions. Nattiez (1975) follows the model of generative linguistics to develop a system of rules for the analysis and synthesis of musical texts. Narrative structures in works of music are studied by Tarasti (1979) on the basis of Lévi-Strauss's structural model of myth.

Architecture

The semiotics of architecture, a branch of the semiotics of visual communication, is closely related to aesthetics, to the semiotics of objects, and to proxemics, the semiotics of space (see esp. Eco 1968: 344ff.). Preziosi (1979a) even discovers connections to zoosemiotics when he talks about "zooarchitectonics." According to Barthes, the semiotics of architecture begins where mere metaphorical discussions of the "language of the city" are replaced by analytic and systematic research in architectonic signs and codes (1967a: 12). Such research originated mostly in the 1960s. It was discussed both at a theoretical level at international semiotic conferences (e.g., Chatman et al., eds. 1979: 901–978) and by practitioners of architecture. Some of them considered semiotics a tool "to overcome the crisis in the methodology of design" (Schneider 1977: 50) or "a way out of naive functionalism" (Sipek 1981: 86–87). According to Sipek (1980; 1981), for example, semiotics can contribute to solving the problems of architectural practice by pointing out the pluralities of interpretation and by thus placing man in the center of architectural concern.

1. State of the Art

Studies under the more or less metaphorical heading of "the language of architecture" (cf. Prak 1968, Reinle 1976) are precursors of the semiotics of architecture. Collins traces the history of this metaphor back to 1750 (1965: 173–84). After an early discussion of architecture within Mukařovský's semiotic aesthetics, explicitly semiotic approaches to architecture originated in the 1960s with a number of studies in the context of structuralism (Koenig 1964; 1970, Eco 1968: 293–356, Jencks & Baird, eds. 1969; cf. Tafuri 1968: 183–216). Hjelmslev, Peirce, and Morris provided different models of analysis for various approaches to the architectural sign.

In France, a school of architectural semiotics developed on the basis of Hjelmslev and Greimas (cf. Greimas 1976b: 129–58, Groupe 107 [1973], Boudon 1981, Hammad et al. 1977, and the volume *Sémiotique de l'espace* [1979]). A special issue of *Communications* 27 (1977) is entitled *Sémiotique de l'espace*, and special issues of *Bulletin du groupe de recherches sémio-linguistiques* 10 (1979) and 18 (1981) are entitled *Sémiotique de l'architecture* and *Parcours et espace*. A semiotic and ideological study of historical architecture in England and its representation in poetry is Wayne (1984). The history and the state of the art in the semiotics of architecture are documented in surveys, studies, and anthologies by Agrest & Gandelsonas (1973; 1977), Krampen (1979a; b), Preziosi (1979a; b), Broadbent et al., eds. (1980a; b), Tafuri (1980: 121–237), Dreyer (1984), Minai (1984), and Gottdiener & Lagopoulos, eds. (1986). A bibliography is Gwin & Gwin (1985).

2. Meaning and Functions of Architecture

In its cultural origins, architecture had the practical function of providing shelter, and nobody will deny that the roofs and windows of most contemporary buildings serve such primary functions as protecting against rain and providing light (cf. Eco 1968: 296). At first sight, architecture seems neither to be communicative nor to represent anything except itself. Traditional aesthetics therefore used to classify architecture together with music as an *asemantic* art (see Wallis 1975: 40 for a survey of such theories). Yet, architecture is not restricted to its utilitarian function. It is polyfunctional and may have several dimensions of meaning. Even doors (Seligmann 1982, Gandelman 1984) and windows (Sebeok & Margolis 1982) may evince a multiplicity of meanings.

2.1 Functional Views of Architecture

Within his structuralist aesthetics, Mukařovský gave an outline of a polyfunctional view of architecture in which he opposes the *aesthetic* function of architecture to the following four *functional horizons* (1937: 241–44): (1) the immediate *practical* function, (2) the *historical* function relating to previous modes of building, (3) the *social* function relating to the social status and economic resources of the builder, and (4) the *individual* function relating to his individual style. In contradistinction to these four specifically architectonic functions which relate buildings to entities beyond themselves, the aesthetic function of a building is autotelic. It refers only to itself and is thus a dialectic negation of the other four functions.

Later functional semiotic descriptions of architecture were based on Jakobson's models of the six functions of communication (Schiwy

1973: 117–19, Preziosi 1979a: 49–55; 1979b: 68–72; see Function 3.2). Preziosi defines these functions of architecture as follows: (1) the *expressive* function dominates in the personal style, the mode of architectonic self-representation of a builder. (2) The *conative* function of architecture addresses its user, suggesting orientations, interpretations, and his spatial behavior. (3) The *phatic* function is the environmental framing of interpersonal interactions, the aspect of architectural "territoriality." (4) The *aesthetic* function predominates when architecture is oriented toward its own mode of construction. (5) The *meta-codal* function is realized through historical reference or illusion and "quotations." (For such modes of architectonic self-reference see Wittig 1979.) (6) The *referential* function is defined by Preziosi as being its contextual utility or immediate purpose.

2.2 Semantics of Architecture

Architectural form has many dimensions of meaning. Eco sees here an example of Peirce's principle of unlimited semiosis (1972a; 117). In this uncertain semantic space there is no final signified, as Barthes points out (1967a: 40).

2.2.1 ARCHITECTURAL DENOTATIONS AND CONNOTATIONS

One attempt to structure the semantic space of architecture is by means of the dichotomy of connotation and denotation (cf. Hjelmslev 4.). Eco interprets the primary (utilitarian) functions of buildings as their denotation and the secondary functions as the infinite domain of connotation (1968: 306–311; 1972: 98): A domestic residence, for example, denotes its utility and connotes by its historical, aesthetic, and anthropological contents an ideology of living (Eco 1968: 334). (For the ideological dimension of architecture see also Agrest & Gandelsonas 1977: 100–104.) The denotation-connotation dichotomy has been used in many other semiotic interpretations of architecture (e.g., Dorfles 1969: 44, Seligmann 1982). Scalvini (1971; 1979) reinterprets C.

Brandis's dichotomy of the *tectonic* vs. the *architectonic* in terms of connotation and denotation.

2.2.2 DIMENSIONS OF ARCHITECTONIC MEANINGS

Two methods of research in architectural meanings deserve special mention at this point: *iconology* and *psychosemiotics*. Iconology, the method of studying icons and symbols within the history of art, is a tool of research in architecture for Wallis (1975), Reinle (1976), and Pochat (1982: 177–85). In contradistinction to this hermeneutic and diachronic approach to architecture, Krampen (1979b) proposes a synchronic and empirical study of architectural meanings. His method is psychosemiology. On the basis of semantic differential analyses, verbalized meanings are studied to test what persons associate with buildings or architectural elements.

The relationships between architectural meanings and the language describing these meanings have been evaluated differently. If architectural meaning comprises such contents as 'practical utility' or stylistic references to, and thus differences from, other architectural forms, then architectural meanings do not seem to presuppose any verbalization (unless for sake of scientific description). Against this view, Martinidis seems to see no difference between architectural meanings and their verbalizations when he claims that "architectural 'language' consists mainly of the verbal language, which comments on built space, criticizes its forms and evaluates its styles" (1986: 371).

3. The Architectural Sign and Code

Approaches to the interpretation of architecture as a system of signs have been based on different models from the major traditions of semiotics. The code (or system) of these signs was mostly interpreted according to the semiotic model of the code of language.

3.1 Models of the Architectural Sign

Analyses of the architectural sign have followed the semiotics of Morris, Saussure, Hjelmslev, and Peirce.

3.1.1 MORRIS'S BEHAVIORISTIC MODEL

Koenig (1964; 1970: 30–31, 254) defines the architectural sign in Morris's behavioristic categories as something that directs behavior with respect to an absent stimulus object which is its denotatum. In this interpretation, the semiotic function of a building is the behavior which it imposes on its inhabitants. The (not necessarily) absent denotata of a building are the human beings "whose existence permits the completion of the response sequences." The denotata of a school, for example, are the children who study there. The significatum of this building is the fact that these children go to school.

3.1.2 SAUSSURE'S DYADIC MODEL

Many semioticians of architecture have based their study on Saussure's dyadic sign model (cf. Scalvini 1971, Ledrut 1973: 18). A specific interpretation of architecture in terms of this model is proposed by De Fusco (1971), who relates the dichotomy of *signifier* and *signified* to the architectonic categories of *outer* and *inner space*. The inner space (signified), according to De Fusco, embodies the essence of architecture, the motive for the creation of a building, because in it the practical and representative functions of life are developed.

3.1.3 HJELMSLEV'S GLOSSEMATIC MODEL

Eco has always defended the dyadic sign model, namely, in its more elaborate form developed by Hjelmslev. Against a triadic model of the architectural sign, Eco objects that in architecture a distinction between a material sign vehicle (or signifier) and its referential object appears to be impossible because both entities have the same physical existence, namely, architectonic matter (1968: 301).

Following Hjelmslev, Eco defines the architectural sign as having the following four levels

(1972: 101): The *expression-substance* is the sum total of all possibilities which can articulate space and matter. The *expression-form* is the system of architectonic oppositions and thus structures of form. The *content-substance* is all possible architectural functions in a given culture. Its *content-form* is the system of meanings which a culture associates with architecture. Eco gives the outline of such a system of architectonic sememes, which he studies by the semantic method of componential analysis (ibid.). In this analysis, the units of architectonic expression form are called *morphemes*. They are correlated with units of content-form, called *sememes*, which are further structured by semantic components.

3.1.4 PEIRCE'S TRIADIC SIGN MODEL

Peirce's triadic sign model and typology of signs are the basis of several other studies in the semiotics of architecture (e.g., Kiefer 1970, Dreyer 1979, and Arin 1981, and see Krampen 1979a: 42–50 for a survey). Following Peirce, Walther determines the factually existing building as a dicent indexical sinsign (1974: 140–41). Being a singular object fixed with respect to time and space makes it a sinsign. By referring to the architect who designed it, the building becomes an index, and as a cultural object which evokes judgments and evaluations, the building is a dicent.

3.2 Architecture as a Code

According to Eco, architectural codes originated when man began to form architectural concepts (1968: 297). When cave man learned that a cave could have various forms of existence, the idea of the cave became an abstract model of the singular occurrences of caves, a code which generated messages about the potential functions of the cave. As in the case of other visual codes (cf. Image 3.3, Comics 2.2, Film 5.), principles for describing the architectural code have been derived mainly by analogy from the code of language. Such procedures have not remained undisputed (cf. Dorfles 1969: 40, Preziosi 1979a: 3). Criticism is particularly appropriate (cf. Agrest & Gandelsonas 1973: 254) where analogies are based on misconceptions of semiotic terms.

3.2.1 ARCHITECTURE AND LANGUAGE

Broadbent (1969) and others discuss the question whether the architectural code is a *langue* in the sense of Saussure by which architects produce a *parole* of individual buildings. Schiwy pursues the idea of analogies between language and architecture further by postulating ideolects, dialects, sociolects, and even language barriers of architecture (1973: 121–23). Among the systemic characteristics of architecture which have been described in analogy to language are the syntagmatic and paradigmatic relations between architectural elements (cf. Broadbent 1969: 51ff., Koenig 1970) and their hierarchical structure. Further analogies between the two semiotic codes have been derived from Chomsky's concepts of linguistic creativity and generativity. The application of these notions to the interpretation of architectural design processes has led to proposals for a "generative grammar of architecture" (cf. Krampen 1979a: 179–81, Ghioca 1983).

3.2.2 DOUBLE ARTICULATION

The possibility of a *double articulation* of the architectural code has been discussed by Eco (1968: 327), Koenig (1970: 159ff.), and Preziosi (1979a: 60; 1979b: 103). In analogy to the double articulation into signifying elements (morphemes), on the one hand, and nonsignifying phonemes, on the other, Eco (1968: 326) and Koenig (1970) introduce the concepts of *choreme* for an architectural element with an elementary signified and *archeme* (Koenig) or *stoicheia* (Eco) for differential elements without a signified. For a different approach to the minimal units of architecture, see also Vallier (1981). Eco considers the architectonic code to be a system of two semiotic dimensions (1972a: 102–103). Its relevant units are, on the one hand, elements (choremes or stoicheia) of prearchitectural geometrical and spatial configurations. On the other hand, they are elements of an anthropological (proxemic) system of functions which Eco defines as *morphemes* (first articulation) and *morphological markers* (second articulation).

3.2.3 HIERARCHICAL STRUCTURE

In further development of the thesis of double articulation in architecture, Preziosi (1979a; b) postulates a hierarchical structure of the architectural code in analogy to further levels of the language system. In this interpretation, architecture and language show the following analogies in their hierarchy of code elements (Preziosi 1979a: 67):

		Architecture	Language
I. Sense-discriminative units:	A	distinctive features	distinctive features
	B	forms	phonemes
	C	templates	syllables
II. Sense-determinative units:	D	figures	morphemes
	E	cells	words
III. Patterns of aggregation	F	matrices	phrases
	(G)	compounds structures settlements etc.	sentences texts discourses etc.

4. The City as a Text

In his *Cours de linguistique générale* (1916a), Saussure discussed remarkable analogies between the city and the sign system of language (see Trabant 1976b). Barthes (1967a), Choay (1972), Schneider (1976), and others (cf. Krampen 1979a: 175–76) have studied further systemic relations and semantic structures which might justify the description of the city as a semantic field or a text. Choay (1972) interprets the development of the urban space from the Middle Ages to modern times as a process of semantic reduction. Ledrut (1973) studies the images which inhabitants associate with their city as semantic fields. Fauque (1973) analyzes the semantization of the urban space in terms of structural semantics (cf. Greimas). Following ideas developed by Bense (e.g., 1968), Kiefer (1970) presents a semiotic study of signs and signals in traffic and urban space in general, which he defines as "secondary architecture."

Objects

The semiotics of objects studies the communicative potential of cultural artifacts and natural objects. The possibility of a semiotics of the natural world (Greimas 1970: 49–92), the transformation of real-world objects into signs, and the so-called language of objects raise the question of the semiotic threshold from the nonsemiotic to the sphere of semiosis. A paradigm of object semiosis is the "language of commodities." Except for culinary semiosis (cf. Herzfeld 1986), most object messages are instances of visual communication. Within this section, more specific semiotic aspects of visual objects are also discussed in the chapters on aesthetics and architecture. A special subfield of the semiotics of natural objects is the study of mantic signs (see Magic 2.3.4).

1. Semiotics of Objects: State of the Art

In his *Language without Words* (1888), Kleinpaul discusses among other things a language of facts, of stamps, of flowers, and even "of fans and gloves." These examples refer to a folkloristic field of objects whose semiotic potential is popularly circumscribed by the metaphor of language. In the beginnings of nonverbal communication research, Ruesch &

Kees proposed to study the message of objects in everyday life as object languages (1956: 87–107). Later, however, the field of nonverbal communication was restricted mostly to messages of the human body. The state of the art in the semiotics of objects is reviewed by Krampen (1979b: 6–20). Objects as signs are a topic of special concern to three fields of semiotic research, aesthetics, culture, and, in the borderland between semiotics and political economy, the semiotics of commodities.

1.1 Aesthetic Objects

Semiotic aesthetics raises the question of how objects of everyday life become aesthetic signs. This question is studied in the semiotics of art, architecture, and industrial design. A first outline of a semiotic aesthetics of object messages was given by Maltese (1970). As Mukařovský pointed out, not only artifacts but also natural objects, such as rocks or pieces of wood, may be viewed as aesthetic signs (1966: 230–31). The semiotic transformation of artifacts of everyday life into pieces of art, radically demonstrated with Marcel Duchamp's *objets trouvés* and Andy Warhol's *Brillo boxes*, has led to a reconsideration of the fundamental conditions of aesthetic semiosis (cf. Nöth 1972; 1987b, Danto 1981). The climax of this dynamic process seems to be the transformation of trash objects into aesthetic signs, as analyzed by Thompson (1979).

1.2 Objects of Cultural Praxis

A pioneer work in the semiotics of cultural objects is Barthes's study of the *Fashion System* (1967b; cf. 3.2). Following this approach, Imbert (1978) gives a thorough analysis of the furniture system in the world of Balzac's novels. Both studies are concerned with texts (fashion journals or novels) about cultural objects and do not study these objects directly. Among the few attempts at a semiotics of everyday objects not based on texts about such objects are studies by Boudon (1969) and Moles (1972a; cf. 3.1). A major interest of these studies is the possibility of a systematic taxonomy of artifacts. A promising perspective for the semiotics of objects is the research in *The World of Goods* and *The Meaning of Things* carried out in cultural anthropology (Douglas & Isherwood 1979 and Csikszentmihalyi & Rochberg-Halton 1981). The focus of these empirical studies is on the cultural and psychological significance of objects in domestic life (cf. 4.2.3).

2. Objects as Signs

The features of object signs may be characterized in comparison with language signs and in opposition to their referents.

2.1 The "Language of Objects"

The impracticability of an attempt to develop a universal language on the basis of a sign repertoire of objects was demonstrated in J. Swift's satire of the Academy of Lagado (*Gulliver's Travels* V. 3). The mere metaphorical nature of expressions such as "the language of flowers" is apparent from a comparison of natural languages with "object languages." The design features of phonetic languages from which "object languages" differ most typically are *specialization, rapid fading, arbitrariness*, and *duality of patterning* (the lack of distinctive features and of an object syntax). Cf. Language 3.1.

Specialization refers to the fact that language is exclusively or at least primarily communicative in its function. Speech production requires little energetic effort, and man is free to perform other activities while speaking. Object languages are not specialized in this sense. If there are systems of objects such as a "language of flowers" (Billig & List, eds. 1974), a "language of the automobile" (cf. Zygulski 1973, Aronoff 1985), or a "language of clothes" (Lurie 1981, Hoffmann 1985, and McCracken 1988: 57–70), it is clear that these classes of objects are not designed primarily for the purpose of communication. As shown in Swift's satire, one of the major disadvantages of object languages would be the lack of the feature of rapid fading (cf. Harrison 1974: 147). Objects cannot be accumulated and dispensed with as quickly as words can be uttered.

2.2 Objects as Sign Vehicles and as Referents

In epistemology and semiotics, *object* is a relational term, defined with reference to a perceiving subject and to other semiotic entities within the semiotic system (cf. Greimas & Courtés 1979: 216). However, the subject-object dyad is really a semiotic triad in which the object occurs twice, once in the form of a sign vehicle and once as the referential correlate of this sign vehicle.

2.2.1 SIGN VEHICLE VS. REFERENT
Objects in the function of signs raise the semiotic question of the difference between sign vehicle (signifier or representamen) and its referent (denotatum). While in natural languages this difference is characterized by the principle of arbitrariness, the referential motivation of object signs implies a reduction of the distance between sign vehicle and referential object. Borderline cases of object semiosis, where the sign vehicle seems to merge with its referent, are *autotelic signs* (see Aesthetics 2.2.2) and *exemplifications*.

2.2.2 OBJECTS AS SAMPLES

In exemplification, according to Goodman, a sign vehicle, e.g., a *sample*, is an example of what it is. It refers to properties which it possesses itself. Thus, the direction of reference in exemplification is opposed to that in denotation (1968: 52–57). Denotation is the reference of a sign vehicle to a referent, while in exemplification (e.g., in a sample) there is reference both from the sign vehicle to its referent and from the referent back to the sign vehicle. Goodman illustrates this difference as follows: "For a word, say, to denote red things requires nothing more than letting it refer to them; but for my green sweater to exemplify a predicate, letting the sweater refer to that predicate is not enough. The sweater must also be denoted by that predicate; that is, I must also let the predicate refer to the sweater" (ibid.: 59).

---

3. Semiosis vs. Praxis

The semiotic process by which objects of practical usage, such as tools (cf. Eco 1976: 22–24) or food, become signs raises the question of the "semiotic threshold" from the nonsemiotic to the semiotic (cf. ibid.: 19–28). One of the attempts to determine this threshold was Mukařovský's distinction between (presemiotic) *practical* and *semiotic* functions. Does this distinction mean that the sphere of human praxis is by definition presemiotic? Nöth (1988) argues that praxis and semiosis are two perspectives from which the same event may be perceived. Thus, even practical objects and actions may be perceived as signs, while they may have a nonsemiotic dimension at the same time.

3.1 The Semiotization of Praxis

The semiotic sphere has rarely been extended to the realm of utilitarian praxis and functionality, but Moles has proposed such an extension in his *Theory of Objects* (1972a). Moles defines the meaning of an object as being "largely attached to its *function*, its utility in relation to the repertoire of human needs" (1972a: 48). To him, the practical function of a commodity is its denotative meaning. In his study of such meaning, he combines principles of structural semantics with methods of psychosemantics. The meaning of an object thus discovered is similar to the lexicographical meaning of the word by which the object is designated. For example, the meaning of the object "knife," according to this theory, could be 'sharp blade with a handle, used as a cutting instrument.' In addition to this primary layer of meaning, Moles also studies secondary layers of meaning which he defines as "aesthetic or connotative."

3.2 Sociocultural Semiotization of Objects

A further semiotic dimension of the sphere of human praxis was postulated by Barthes (cf. 1964a: 41–42). To him, the threshold from the nonsemiotic to the semiotic seems to lie above the "utilitarian or functional" aspect of objects (although he calls these aspects of objects sign-functions; cf. ibid.: 41, 68). Barthes acknowledges that utilitarian objects "have a substance of expression whose essence is not to signify." For example, "clothes are used for protection and food for nourishment even if they are also used as signs." But in an "inevitable" process of semantization, this utilitarian object becomes "pervaded with meaning: [. . .] As soon as there is a society, every usage is converted into a sign of itself." Barthes discusses two aspects of this semiotization (ibid.: 41). The first might be called the *sociocultural sign*. (His example: "The use of a raincoat . . . cannot be dissociated from the very signs of an atmospheric situation" [ibid.].) The second might be called the *economic sign*. Its frame of reference is the system of commodities (cf. 4.): "Since our society produces only standardized, normalized objects, these objects are unavoidably realizations of a model, [. . .] the substance of a significant form. To rediscover a non-signifying object, one would have to imagine a utensil absolutely improvised and with no similarity to an existing model" (ibid.: 41–42).

4. The Language of Commodities

A field of object semiotics in which the topic of the semiotic threshold between utilitarian praxis and semiosis has been discussed from various perspectives is the "language of commodities" (cf. Nöth 1988).

4.1 Commodity Exchange as Communication

According to Lévi-Strauss, the exchange of goods and services, the exchange of women, and the exchange of messages are the three basic modes of social communication (1958: 296). In this view, economic and kinship systems (cf. Structuralism 2.2) evince analogies to the system of language. Following this guideline, and in connection with a semiotic interpretation of Marx's political economy, Rossi-Landi (1968; 1975a) developed one of the first explicitly semiotic approaches to economy on the basis of linguistic homologies.

4.2 The Commodity as a Sign

Semiotic aspects of commodities have become apparent in research carried out in marketing research, political economy, and anthropology. A related field of study is the semiotics of advertising, i.e., of messages *about* commodities.

4.2.1 SEMIOTICS OF THE COMMODITY IN MARKETING RESEARCH

In addition to the study of advertising, marketing research has been concerned with two types of commodity messages, the brand image and the "consumption symbol." Brand image research studies meanings which consumers typically associate with a given brand. Semantic components of a brand image, according to Levy, include 'technical matters,' 'product

characteristics,' 'financial value,' and 'social suitability' (1978: 168). Semiotically, such components constitute the signified (or content) of the product, while the material object is the signifier of the commodity as a sign.

"Symbolic consumption" (cf. Hirschman & Holbrook, eds. 1981), already discovered by Veblen (1899) in the form of "conspicuous consumption," is an act of communication, not between producer and consumer but between the consumer and any other member of society, possibly also between the consumer and that consumer's self. The sign in symbolic consumption is less the commodity itself than the act of its consumption. As summarized by Belk et al., the theory of symbolic consumption makes the following assumption about the meaning of such a sign: "Whether or not consumption communicates status as clearly as was once the case, it is clear that there are still a number of inferences about people which are affected by the goods and services that they presumably have selected" (1982: 6). If inferences are thus made from goods (e.g., cars) to their users (e.g., their personality type), the commodities are interpreted as indexical signs. The meaning of such an index is not a characteristic feature of the commercial object itself (e.g., its usefulness or stylistic beauty). The commodity, taken as an index, refers to an attribute which supposedly characterizes its consumer. A language of commodities based on such indexical signs is a language about commodity users.

4.2.2 POLITICAL ECONOMY AND THE SEMIOTICS OF THE COMMODITY

Within the framework of political economy, the semiotic essence of the commodity was first sought in its use- and exchange-value. An implicitly semiotic interpretation of the commodity along these lines was given by Marx (*Capital*, bk. 1.1, chap. 1.3.2a), who discusses the (relational) "meaning" and even the "language of commodities." In explicitly semiotic terms, Lefebvre, for example, argues that a commodity is a sign whose signifier is the "object susceptible of exchange" and whose signified is the "potential satisfaction" which the consumer might derive from it (1966: 342). Rossi-Landi, while accepting this use-value aspect of the commodity as "a sign function which exists already at the product level," argues that the specific sign value of an object as commodity is its exchange-value because only by this value does a useful object become a commodity (1975a: 128).

Baudrillard (1968; 1972) developed a semiotics of consumer goods which defines both the use- and the exchange-value of commodities as values within a system of commercial signs. According to Baudrillard (1968: 276–77), commodities become signs within the process of consumption, which he considers "an activity of systematic sign manipulation." In this view, the material and functional object acquires meaning in an "abstract systematic relation to all other object-signs, [. . .] never in its materiality, but in its difference" from all other commodities. Like linguistic signs whose value is determined by their difference from other elements of a language, commodities are thus defined as elements of a semiotic system. As in language, where the material (phonetic or written) substance of words is essentially irrelevant ("arbitrary") to their content, commodities are seen as signs whose material substance is equally arbitrary: "Evidently, it is never the objects which are consumed, but it is [. . .] the *idea of the relation* which is consumed in the series of objects which give rise to this idea." With this radical view of the semiotics of consumption, the semiotization of the commodity has reached an unsurpassable climax: the commodity has become a pure sign. There seems to be no material trace of practical functionality.

4.2.3 THE COMMODITY IN CULTURAL ANTHROPOLOGY

Baudrillard's extreme insistence on the semiotic essence of commodities to the neglect of their utilitarian function (cf. Krampen 1979b: 7) is paralleled by theses proposed independently by anthropologists. As outlined by Sahlins, anthropological theory has for a long time oscillated between the two poles of a utilitarian

and a symbolic account of the goods and activities. The former pole is that of *culture*, while the latter is that of *practical reason* (1976: 55). While a cultural interpretation ascribes a sign value to goods, "practical reason" interprets goods as having a nonsemiotic, utilitarian function. Sahlins's own position in this debate is that objects of consumption are always permeated by cultural meanings both in their practical utility and in their social and commercial context: "The social meaning of an object that makes it useful to a certain category of persons is no more apparent from its physical properties than is the value it may be assigned in exchange. Use-value is not less symbolic or less arbitrary than commodity-value" (ibid.: 169).

This radical thesis of the semiotic character of commodities has no less vigorously been defended by Douglas & Isherwood, who programmatically declare that "the essential function of consumption is its capacity to make sense. Forget the idea of consumer irrationality. Forget that commodities are good for eating, clothing, and shelter; forget their usefulness and try instead the idea that commodities are good for thinking; treat them as a nonverbal medium for the human creative faculty" (1979: 62). Following these guidelines, further psycho- and sociosemiotic dimensions of *The Meaning of Things* in everyday life have been explored in empirical and theoretical studies by Csikszentmihalyi & Rochberg-Halton (1981) and Appadurai, ed. (1986).

4.3 The Language of Commodities as a System

If commodities deserve to be called a language, they should be analyzable in terms of paradigmatic and syntagmatic relations, those two basic types of relation which form the two classical axes of linguistic structure. While the paradigmatic axis of a language refers to the possible (e.g., lexical or semantic) alternatives of and oppositions to a sign, the syntagmatic axis refers to its syntax, the rules for the combination of the signs.

4.3.1 THE PARADIGMATIC DIMENSION

Barthes was among the first to propose an analysis of the paradigmatic dimension of commodities (1964a: 63; 1967). More recently, American consumer research has begun with the empirical exploration of this dimension of the market (cf. Mick 1986: 202–203). The study of the paradigmatic dimension of a semiotic system has to explore both similarities and differences between the objects under consideration. By semantic likeness, the units of a system are grouped together to form classes of signs. The classification of commodities by brands and kinds of goods performed by any manager of a supermarket reflects a possible semiotic classification of commodities as utilitarian signs. By the differences between these signs, commodities enter into oppositions which constitute the structure of the semiotic system. In the language of commodities, these structures of opposition are emphasized by the competition between brands and classes of goods. Saussure's thesis that a semiotic system, and with it the meanings of its signs, is constituted only by the differences between its elements, is particularly true of the language of commodities. Since competition is the motor of a free market, it should be evident that the language of commodities is a semiotic system *par excellence*. In the intention of the advertisers and producers of goods, this language is even a system of a radically semiotic nature. The language of commodities strives to maximize the differences and to minimalize the similarities between competing goods. The most convincing illustration of this thesis is the competition between the so-called generic brands and their materially identical counterparts sold in a different package, under a different name, and at a higher price.

4.3.2 THE SYNTAX OF COMMODITIES

If commodities are combined by the producer and the consumer in a meaningful way, similar to the combination of words into sentences and texts, this combination will result in a commodity message. The rules which determine these combinations in space and time form the syntagmatic dimension of the language of commodities. Barthes proposed to study such combinations of clothes into garments, foods into menus, or pieces of furniture into the furnishing of a room as syntagmatic structures (1964a: 63). More recently, Kehret-Ward (1987), too, has proposed to study product combinations as the syntax of commodities. However, the studies of product combinations have so far resulted only in the discovery of a very rudimentary product syntax. At least in comparison to the one-dimensional (surface) syntax of language, the pluridimensional space of possible combinations of commodities is much less structured. In contradistinction to its highly structured paradigmatic dimension, it must then be concluded, the language of commodities has only a rather weak syntax.

Image

Images cover a broad spectrum of phenomena, of which many are also discussed elsewhere in this handbook. This chapter will therefore focus only on the two extremes of this spectrum, pictures and mental images.

1. Images and Signs

A survey of the broad field of phenomena defined as images indicates a variety of semiotic topics extending beyond this article.

1.1 Variety of Images and Icons

Mitchell proposes a "typology of images" which distinguishes the following five classes (1986: 10): (1) *graphic* (pictures, statues, designs), (2) *optical* (mirrors, projections), (3) *perceptual* (sense data, "species," "appearances"), (4) *mental* (dreams, memories, ideas, fantasmata), and (5) *verbal* images (metaphor, descriptions). (For the definition of images see also Thibault-Laulan 1972: 20–25.) All of these phenomena are traditionally defined by features such as likeness, resemblance, or similitude. Owing to these characteristics, images belong to the class of icons.

Often a difference between icons and images is hardly discernible. While the concept of image generally refers to visual phenomena (and their mental representations), icons, at least in the definition of Peirce, cover a broader class of signs by likeness which includes signs by non-visual channels. The feature of likeness defining both images and icons also raises a number of more fundamental semiotic questions which justify a discussion in a separate chapter (Icon and Iconicity).

1.2 The Study of Images and Semiotics

Within the field of aesthetics and visual communication, a number of proposals have been made to establish an autonomous, albeit transdisciplinary, field of research in images. Some authors have proposed to designate this field by the term *iconics* (Huggins & Entwistle 1974: 3, Cossette 1982). Mitchell introduces the term *iconology* for the study of the discourse of (and about) images (1986: 1). (For a different concept of iconology, cf. Painting 2.1.) These and other studies in the "language of images" (thus: Thibault-Laulan 1971, Mitchell, ed. 1974, Eco 1985a, Saint-Martin 1987) are sometimes explicitly, sometimes implicitly semiotic in their approach.

In addition to the topics of this chapter and the one on icons, various other subjects of the spectrum of imagery are discussed elsewhere in this handbook. Within this section, the chapters on painting and photography deal with special types of pictures. The relationship between pictures and language is among the topics of the chapters on comics, film, and advertising. Special pictorial signs which form codes of their own (e.g., traffic signs or playing cards) are discussed in the section on codes. Verbal images (for this concept see especially Furbank 1970) are the subject of the chapter on metaphors and the paragraph on iconicity in Literature (2.1). For visual metaphors see Metaphor (∅).

A few other subjects within the semiotics of images can be covered only by means of bibliographic reference: On the semiotics of cartography and graphics, see Bertin (1967), Krampen (1985); on design see Bense (1971), Walther (1974: 136–39), Berger (1979); on colors see Bense (1971: 92–98), Thürlemann (1984), Eco (1985a), and Saint-Martin (1987); on mirrors see Eco (1984b, where the author argues that mirror images cannot be signs). On the whole field of visual images see Lindekens (1976), Krampen, ed. (1983), Baker (1985), Sauerbier (1985), Floch (1985), Mitchell (1986), Muckenhaupt (1986), Saint-Martin (1987), special issues of the journals *Communications* (29 [1978]), *Degrés* (34 [1982]), and *Semiotica* (52.3/4 [1984]), and the relevant sections on the semiotics of visual communication in collective volumes such as Chatman et al., eds. (1979), Helbo, ed. (1979), Oehler, ed. (1984), and Sebeok & Umiker-Sebeok, eds. (1986).

2. Mental Images

The relevance of mental images to human thought has been investigated since antiquity. In Plato's idealist philosophy, the sphere of ideas consisted in the first place of words (λόγος) and only in the second place of images (εἰκών; cf. Eltester 1958: 3–4). To him, images were not the result of sense impressions (αἴσθησις) but had their origin within the soul itself. Aristotle (*On Memory* 450ª, trans. Beare), initiating the empiricist tradition, attached more importance to mental imagery when he

argued that "without an image thinking is impossible." The issue became central to the history of philosophical epistemology (Hogrebe 1971, Manser 1973) and to cognitive psychology (Block, ed. 1981).

From a semiotic point of view, two topics have emerged in the course of this discussion which are particularly relevant to a general theory of signs: the theory that mental images are signs of reality, and the question whether meanings of words (and other signs) should be considered as mental images. The first topic is one of philosophical and psychological epistemology, the second is one of semantics. Only a few exemplary answers to these problems of the history of semiotics can be discussed here.

A much more comprehensive view of the mental image, which cannot be discussed in the following, has been developed by Boulding (1961). His vision of a new science of the image, called *eiconics*, may perhaps be characterized as a sociobiological and transdisciplinary theory of knowledge.

2.1 Mental Images as Iconic Signs

The view of the mental image as an icon or even a copy of reality has been expressed in various schools of thought.

2.1.1 THE EMPIRICIST HERITAGE
The Epicureans believed in mental images as copies of the external world, εἴδωλα or *simulacra*, which resulted from the reception of invisible atoms emitted by the physical object. At the climax of the empiricist tradition, Hume defined ideas as the result of sense impressions, as "a copy taken by the mind, which remains after the impression ceases" (*Treatise of Human Nature* I, 1.2). According to such views, the image is not only an icon, but, being an "imprint" caused by the original object, it is also an index (in the sense of Peirce).

2.1.2 THE MATERIALIST COPY THEORY
A modern materialist version of the empiricist copy theory of cognition is defended by Marxist semioticians (Klaus & Segeth 1962, Klaus

1963, and Resnikow 1977). According to the official Marxist-Leninist epistemology (Klaus & Buhr, eds. 1964: 31–33), every act of cognition results in a mental image in the form of an ideational copy (*Abbild*). These mental representations are said to be formed in a process of reflection (*Widerspiegelung*) during which the individual acquires knowledge of the "objective reality." The resulting copies are characterized as being different from the depicted object (since they are transformed by perceptual coding and information processing), but at the same time dependent on it and congruent with it (ibid.). The relation between mental copy (*Abbild*) and the "reality" it reflects is further specified as a *similarity* (Neumann et al. 1976: 334–39) or as an objective relation of *homomorphy* (Klaus 1969). These features characterize the materialist *Abbild* as an iconic sign (see also 2.2.2).

2.1.3 PIAGET'S MENTAL IMAGERY

From a psychological point of view, Piaget has given a semiotic interpretation of the mental image. In his genetic epistemology, Piaget characterizes mental imagery as the "interiorized imitation" and transformation of reality (1970: 14–15, 45). He describes this process of internal imitation as an aspect of the general semiotic function, the ability to represent something by a sign: the mental image is a signifier which represents the exterior signified.

Piaget rejects the naive picture theory of the mental image as a kind of "trace" resulting from a passive perception of an objectively given reality. While criticizing the "knowledge-as-copy hypothesis," Piaget & Inhelder propose an assimilation theory of the image according to which the inner image is the product of an internalized imitation (1966: xiii, xix). Thus, the inner image becomes a "semiotic instrument necessary in order to evoke and to think what has been perceived" (ibid.: 381). Piaget characterizes this image as a symbol (ibid.), which in his definition is a sign that presupposes a mental differentiation between its signifier and the signified. More specifically, this image is defined as a figural signifier whose

figural signified is the object it refers to (ibid.: 383).

Piaget's inner image is based on a sign model which differs both from the dyadic Saussurean and from the triadic Peircean tradition. The referential object which is the signified of Piaget's mental image is an extrasemiotic entity to Saussure. In his dyadic model both components of the sign are psychic entities. In analogy to his theory of the verbal signifier as a "sound image," the signifier of a picture is a mental "visual image" in the Saussurean tradition, which is not incompatible with Piaget's signifier. But the Saussurean signified is also a mental "concept," and this makes it incompatible with Piaget's characterization of the object as a signified. In terms of Peirce's triadic semiotics, Piaget's inner image comes close to the interpretant, and its corresponding "exterior event" would be a Peircean object.

2.2 Mental Images as Meanings of Signs

In the history of semantics, the essence of meaning has occasionally been assumed to be a mental image. Philosophically, such images were first discussed as ideas, psychologically also as mental associations. The crudest form of this assumption, namely, that words generally evoke visual concepts, must certainly be rejected (cf. Palmer 1981: 25), but some of the issues raised by the *ideational* or *conceptual theory of meaning* should be discussed briefly. For mentalist and other theories of meaning, see also Meaning (1.4).

2.2.1 MEANING AS IDEA

In Locke's semantics, the meanings of words are characterized as "invisible ideas": "The use, then, of words is to be sensible marks of ideas; and the ideas they stand for are their proper and immediate signification" (1690: III 2.1). The nature of Locke's empiricist ideas is not clearly defined in his philosophy. Sometimes they seem to be mental pictures, but mostly they are defined as more abstract entities (cf. Woozley 1967: 199–200). Against the assumption that such ideas could have the form of a mental picture, Berkeley argued that a picture, e.g., of a triangle, always has a particular visual form so that a general, abstract idea of all possible triangles could never be represented in one visual image (1710: Intro. §§ 15–16).

2.2.2 THE MATERIALIST PICTURE THEORY OF MEANING

Marxist semantics ascribes to meaning the character of a picture (*Abbild*) which reflects objectively the material reality (cf. Neumann et al. 1976: 392–98). This picture is taken to be the result of the more general process of cognition (cf. 2.1.2). Therefore, there are more mental pictures than there are meanings. Only those mental pictures which have become associated with the words of a language are defined as meanings. As long as the character of those mental pictures that are said to occur in the black box of the human brain cannot be further specified, the picture theory of meaning is at risk of becoming circular (cf. Palmer 1981: 26). The inaccessible mirror image of meaning which is connected with the occurrence of words seems like the ancient phlogiston, which was believed to explain the occurrence of fire.

2.2.3 WITTGENSTEIN'S PICTURE THEORY OF MEANING

Wittgenstein (1922; 1953) developed a theory of pictorial meaning and picture thinking (cf. Aldrich 1958) which has given rise to some interpretative controversies (cf. Stegmüller 1969a: 539, Kutschera 1971: 52). According to his *Tractatus*, "We make ourselves pictures of facts," "The picture is a model of reality," and "The logical picture of the facts is the thought" (§§ 2.1, 2.12, 3.). Here, *picture* does not refer to a visual mental image or naturalistic representation but rather to the abstract logical relation of *mapping*: Wittgenstein's picture is a mental representation whose inner structure is isomorphic with the facts of the world (Stenius 1969). As a result of this process of mapping, "The proposition *shows* its sense" (§ 4.022), i.e., "we read from its exterior structure the corresponding exterior structure of the fact" (Stegmüller 1969a: 555).

In his later philosophy, Wittgenstein (1953) proposed a new interpretation of meaning based on the pragmatic conditions of language use. He no longer referred to ontological facts which are mapped by means of logical pictures. Instead of considering the reality as ontologically given, he showed that the world is always the result of linguistic interpretations (cf. Kutschera 1971: 133–34): Since ontological facts are no longer the point of departure in a process of mapping, they become, instead, interpreted as "*projections* of the primarily given *linguistic* structures by which we speak about the world" (ibid.).

---

3. Semiotics of Pictures

The semiotics of pictures is closely related to a number of other topics within the semiotic field (cf. 1.2). In particular, the chapter on iconicity, dealing with more general aspects, and the chapters on painting and photography, dealing with more specific topics of pictorial representation, must be referred to in this context. Among the major semiotic topics not discussed in those chapters are the question of the *semiotic autonomy* of pictures, the search for a *pictorial grammar*."

3.1 *Schools and Trends in Pictorial Semiotics*

Contributions to the study of pictorial representation have been made by various schools of semiotics. Barthes (e.g., 1964c) developed his own semiology of pictures based on Saussure and Hjelmslev (cf. Naville 1970, Baker 1985). Following Hjelmslev more closely, Lindekens (1976) develops a glossematic semiotics of visual images (cf. Photography). For further approaches in the tradition of French semiology, see Marin (1971a), Thibault-Laulan (1973), Porcher (1976), Baticle (1977), and Saint-Martin (1987). A functional interpretation of visual images in the sense of Jakobson is outlined by Thibault-Laulan (1972), and Veltruský (1976) studies pictorial signs based on functional views of the Prague School of semiotics. The model of structuralist rhetoric is being applied in a new semiotic program of research in pictures developed by the Liège Group μ (Klinkenberg et al. 1980; 1985).

Whether or not Goodman's (1968) philosophy of pictorial representation should be considered a semiotic approach (cf. Mitchell 1986: 63), his philosophy of pictures can certainly not be ignored in semiotic research. For approaches to pictorial semiotics based on Peirce, Greimas, structuralism, and information theory, see also Painting (3.) and Photography.

3.2 Semiotic Autonomy of the Picture

Is an autonomous semiotics of pictorial perception possible, or does the semiotic analysis of pictures always require recourse to the model of language? This question has been a recurrent topic of semiotics.

3.2.1 PICTURES AND LANGUAGE

Arguments for the dependence of pictures on language are of two kinds. One concerns the role of verbal commentaries accompanying pictures (see also 4.); the other concerns the necessity of recourse to language in the process of analysis. Barthes rejected the assumption of a semiotic autonomy of pictures (cf. Barthes 4.). He argued that the pictorial message in advertising or press photography is decoded primarily on the basis of its verbal commentary:

> Images [. . .] can signify [. . .], but never autonomously; every semiological system has its linguistic admixture. Where there is a visual substance, for example, the meaning is confirmed by being duplicated in a linguistic message [. . .] so that at least a part of the iconic message is [. . .] either redundant or taken up by the linguistic system. (1964a: 10)

Barthes's argument has been criticized as being logocentric. Proponents of the semiotic auton-

omy of pictures (esp. Lindekens 1971; 1976) have objected that commentaries, however important they may be in multimedial contexts (cf. 4.), do not prove the semiotic priority of the verbal over the visual message.

A different trace of logocentrism is apparent in the various proposals for a pictorial grammar, e.g., when Eco (1976: 231, similarly: Metz 1968: 71–72) argues that a picture showing a man is a semiotic entity corresponding to a verbal sentence because it means not only 'person x' but 'so and so is walking.' In such analyses, the semiotic structure of the picture seems to be derived from the structure of (one of) its verbal paraphrase(s). Since pictures have no visual metalanguage of their own, it is true that language is always necessary as an instrument of pictorial analysis (see also Benveniste 1969: 239). However, the structure of the verbal metalanguage must not be projected onto the semiotics of the visual object under consideration. But is there any semiotically relevant preverbal level of visual perception and analysis?

3.2.2 GESTALTEN AS SIGNS

Proponents of an autonomous pictorial semiotics have turned to the theory of visual perception in search of language-independent entities which might be interpreted as semiotic elements of visual cognition. Dominant paradigms of research have been gestalt psychology and information theory (cf. Lindekens 1971: 38–58, Krampen 1973, Mateescu 1974: 46–49). To Piaget, gestalt psychology is one of the sources of structuralism (1968: 52). According to this theory of perception, the organism does not obtain its environmental visual data atomistically. The scanning of the visual field rather generates organized forms called *gestalten*. A gestalt is a holistic perceptual structure. Being more than only the sum total of its elements, it is an invariant shape, a figure which tends to contrast against its (back)ground.

Gestalten have been interpreted as signs. Thus, for example, Arnheim argues that "no visual pattern is only itself. It always represents something beyond its own individual existence—which is like saying that all shape is the form of some content" (1954: 65). And Klaus & Buhr (1964: 497) interpret gestalten as the semiotic invariance of a perceived sign, its emic aspect (cf. Structuralism 1.1.3) or its being a type (see Peirce 3.1).

3.2.3 PERCEPTUAL SUPERSIGNS

In the context of information theory, semioticians have interpreted gestalten as *supersigns* (e.g., Dörner 1977, Maser 1977), holistic elements of information processing whose building blocks are sign elements, called *subsigns*. According to Moles, the perception of a visual image is a process of integrating such subsigns and supersigns within the pictorial whole (1972b: 65). More specifically, he proposes a hierarchy of perceptual levels extending from a differential optical element, a geometrical morpheme, a partial image of a signifying object to an iconic phrase and discourse.

3.2.4 GIBSON'S INVARIANTS

Within the theory of perception, gestalt theory has not remained unchallenged. In his influential ecological theory of perception, Gibson (1966; 1979) argues that not figures or colors but more abstract formless invariants are the elementary units of perception. Gibson defines stimulus invariants as being related to their environmental sources by laws of physics which cause a percept as their psychological resonance (1966: 244). This concept of invariance seems to refer to a presemiotic level of perception.

3.3 Pictorial Grammar

Can the metaphor of the "language of pictures" be taken literally to such a degree that levels of pictorial structure may be discovered which correspond to levels of the grammar of language? This question has been a major topic in the semiotics of visual communication.

3.3.1 OBJECTIONS

Benveniste argues that a semiotic system presupposes a finite repertoire of signs with rules of order governing its figures (differential elements) existing independently of the number of discourses that the system allows to be produced (1969: 237). He concludes that the visual arts do not fulfil these criteria. Although there is a semantic dimension to the arts (ibid.: 242), pictures thus cannot be characterized as semiotic systems according to Benveniste. For related objections raised by Goodman, see 3.4. In spite of such objections, semioticians have pursued the search for structural equivalents to the linguistic principle of *double articulation* (cf. Language 4.1) in pictures. Although the "naive verbocentric" approach to pictorial articulation was soon abandoned (cf. Calabrese 1980: 8), "its ingeniousness," as Eco puts it, "conceals a serious problem" (1976: 213).

3.3.2 SECOND ARTICULATION

In search of structures which might constitute a pictorial code, many semioticians have postulated elements of a first articulation, but only few believe in a second articulation of pictorial representation. In analogy to the level of phonemes in language, a second articulation of pictures would consist of a system of elements without meaning but with the function to differentiate meaningful visual elements. In the terminology of Hjelmslev, such elements have been defined as *figurae*. Besides Lindekens (cf. Photography 3.2), Carter (1972; 1976) is one of the few who believe in such a visual counterpart to verbal phonemes. He characterizes his minimal pictorial elements as invariants of *shape* (1976: 115). A different approach to the analysis of minimal elements of pictorial semiosis is proposed by Saint-Martin (1987). She postulates a unit called coloreme as the minimal unit of visual semiosis.

Eco also discusses the possibility of a pictorial second articulation (1968: 243–47). In a first approach, he defines the conditions of visual perception such as figure-ground relations, light contrast, or geometrical elements as constituents (figurae) of a second articulation of pictures. On the other hand, he argues that these phenomena are not really part of a (semiotic) iconic code but rather belong to a presemiotic code of perception to be studied within the psychology of perception (cf. ibid.: 244). Later, Eco states that pictures are not further analyzable into figurae: Although "one can isolate pertinent discrete units within the iconic continuum," these elements "do not correspond to linguistic phonemes because they do not have positional and oppositional value" (1976: 215).

3.3.3 FIRST ARTICULATION

Eco discusses two candidates for elements of a first pictorial articulation: the *sign* (corresponding to a morpheme or word) and the *sema*, a visual "proposition" (1968: 236). In his view, pictures are not analyzable into signs but are always semata. Lindekens (e.g., 1971: 241), in contradistinction, defends the view of a first pictorial articulation into minimal meaningful units, signs in Eco's sense. To him such units can be determined by methods of semantic differential analysis. Porcher (1976) proposes empirical methods of determining the "lexical" units of visual images. His procedure is a kind of a visual commutation test based on principles of structural semantics (see Greimas).

3.3.4 VISUAL SYNTAX

Several semioticians have postulated structural homologies between the syntax of sentences and the structure of pictures. In the context of the semiotics of painting, Zemsz (1967), Marin (1971a), and Paris (1975) see analogies between pictorial forms, lines, and colors and verbal syntax: Zemsz postulates an analogy between the sentence and visual forms, since the latter represent an object and its attributes (1967: 42). But Schefer sees an analogy between the pictorial figure-space relation and the verbal subject-predicate structure (1969: 171, 177).

Bense postulates a "visual semiotics as the embodiment of the problems of a visual language" (1971: 92–93). In his view, the constituents of any perception are color and form. Bense therefore postulates two basic elements (*perceptemes*) of visual perception which he

calls *chromemes* and *formemes*. Chromemes are the elements of color perception. Formemes are geometrical-typological elements such as points, lines, surfaces, or bodies. According to Bense, the conjunction of formemes and chromemes constitutes a visual sign in which the duality of form and color functions like the subject and predicate of a verbal proposition. Homologies between verbal syntax and pictorial representations are also the topic of the debate over the question whether pictures can be assertions and thus express true or false statements (cf. Korsmeyer 1985). For a language-independent model of visual syntax, see Saint-Martin (1987).

3.3.5 THE PICTORIAL TEXT

Koch (1971b: 38–42, 478–91; 1973: 98–126) proposes a model of pictorial semiotics with visual units corresponding to all levels of language structure, from the phoneme to the "texteme" (see Comics 2.2). But his "pictorial grammar" is not the sign repertoire of a visual code (cf. Koch 1971b: 306–309). Instead, Koch argues that the rules of pictorial segmentation can be determined only within a particular picture. Only the model of the individual pictorial text determines pertinence and structural value of its visual elements. A textual theory of pictorial articulation is also proposed by Eco (1976) and Calabrese (1980). Eco argues that structural units in a picture can be determined only with reference to their pictorial context, so that pictures are not articulated by a code but "the iconic text is an act of *code-making*" (1976: 213–16).

3.4 Goodman's Theory of Pictorial Representation

Goodman's (1968) influential theory of pictorial representation is of particular concern to two topics in the semiotics of pictures, the essence of the pictorial sign and the similarities and differences between verbal and pictorial representation. Other topics of Goodman's theory, discussed elsewhere, are pictorial iconicity and the aesthetic essence of paintings.

3.4.1 THE PICTORIAL SIGN

Goodman first emphasizes the similarities between linguistic and pictorial representation (1968: 5). He claims that pictures are conventional symbols related to their referential object like a predicate is related to what it applies to. Furthermore, both visual depiction and verbal description have a function of denotation. But as a nominalist, Goodman argues that neither verbal depiction nor visual representation can denote by simply mirroring the structure of the world since "there is no such thing as the structure of the world for anything to conform to" (1972: 31–32). Based on these similarities between language and pictures, Goodman proposes a "language theory of pictures" (ibid.).

3.4.2 PICTURES AS A SYSTEM

Considering pictures as a system of representation, Goodman (1968) emphasizes the differences between linguistic and pictorial representation. He discusses the similarities and differences of the various modes of representation on the basis of five criteria by which he characterizes the features of notational systems (such as musical notation; ibid.: 130–54): two syntactic criteria of disjointness and finite differentiation and three further semantic features of unambiguity, disjointness, and finite semantic differentiation. He concludes that ordinary languages usually fulfil the syntactic criteria but violate the semantic ones, whereas language, pictures, and other nonlinguistic notational systems violate all of these criteria. Thus, pictures are characterized by "a lack of differentiation—indeed through density (and consequent total absence of articulation)—in the general symbol scheme" (ibid.: 226).

---

4. Picture, Text, and Context

Compared to verbal texts, pictures have been characterized as being typically polysemous (Barthes 1964c: 39, Sullerot 1964: 280, Bardin 1975: 99, Moles 1978: 25) or even as being open messages (Marin 1971a: 26, Brög 1978,

Sauerbier 1978: 43). In most cases, the semiotic context of pictures has the function to reduce this interpretative openness.

4.1 Picture and Word

The function of pictures in the context of words, already briefly discussed above from Barthes's point of view, has become a topic of increasing semiotic and other research interests (Schapiro 1973, Schöberle 1984, Langner 1985, Sauerbier 1985, Muckenhaupt 1986, Hupka 1989, and the journal *Word and Image* 1 [1985]ff.).

4.1.1 FUNDAMENTAL ISSUES

A basic question concerning the contextual relationship between picture and word was formulated by Barthes as follows: "Does the image duplicate certain of the informations given in the text by a phenomenon of redundancy or does the text add a fresh information to the image?" (1964c: 38) However, both addition and duplication are unduly simplified characterizations of the text-image relation. Instead, the juxtaposition of picture and word usually results in a new holistic interpretation of the scripto-pictorial or the audiovisual message (cf. Bardin 1975: 111). In illustrations in the print media, the dialectics between word and image is even further extended to a triadic network of interrelationships between text, legend, and figure, where "the legend comments on the image which cannot be properly understood by itself, the image or figure comments on the text and, in some cases the image also comments on its own legend" (Moles 1978: 22).

4.1.2 ANCHORAGE AND RELAY

Barthes distinguished two main types of text-image relationship, which he called *anchorage* and *relay* (1964c: 38; see also Bassy 1974): In anchorage, "the text directs the reader through the signifieds of the image, causing him to avoid some and receive others. [. . .] It remote-controls him towards a meaning chosen in advance" (ibid.: 40). In relay, "text and image stand in a complementary relationship; the words, in the same way as the images, are fragments of a more general syntagm and the unity of the message is realized at a higher level" (ibid.: 41). Considering the interpretation of the message as a whole, anchorage is thus the case of a picture-word dependency, while relay is the complementarity of both text constituents.

4.1.3 FURTHER PICTURE-WORD RELATIONSHIPS

Without wanting to propose a comprehensive typology of picture-text relationships (for such proposals see, e.g., Bardin 1975, Moles 1978, Spillner 1982), a few other types of relationship will be mentioned which either are not covered by the anchorage-relay dichotomy or might be classified as subtypes of these:

1. *Illustration*. The picture-word relationship in textual illustrations is characterized by the semiotically subordinate function of the picture in relation to the text it illustrates. Book illustrations exemplify this relationship: while some editions of literary works are printed with illustrations, other editions of the same work are printed without such pictures.

2. *Pictorial exemplification*. Such picture-word relationships are a subtype of relay. In contrast to illustrations, pictorial exemplifications retain a higher informational autonomy in relation to the verbal message which they exemplify visually. An example is the photo in an encyclopedic article which illustrates the definition of a rare animal species.

3. *Labeling*. The indexical reference of a label to a picture may be either a case of anchorage (e.g., the titles of most pictures in art galleries) or a type of relay (e.g., the name under a photographic portrait). On the naming and labeling of pictures, see also Goodman (1968) and Muckenhaupt (1986: 35–70).

4. *Mutual determination* (cf. Spillner 1982: 96). This type of picture-word relationship is a mixture of relay and anchorage. The verbal text directs the interpretation of the picture, but the picture is equally necessary to the understanding of the words. The device is popular in advertising. For example, the verbal text for-

mulates a question to which the product shown in the picture is the answer.

5. *Contradiction* (cf. Rokem 1986). This rare text-picture relation was made famous by R. Magritte's pictures of the type "ceci n'est pas une pipe" (showing a pipe).

4.2 Word and Picture in the Arts

There have been several significant transformations of the word-picture relationship during the history of the visual arts which have reached a climax in the avant-garde of this century (see Faust 1977). A semiotic study of (mostly) medieval examples of paintings in the context of religious narratives is Schapiro (1973). The author shows that text illustrations could be either "extreme reductions of a complex narrative" or an "enlargement of the text, adding details, figures, and a setting not given in the written source" (ibid.: 11). The illustrations refer both to the literal and to the spiritual senses of the words whose interpretation depended on the medieval codes of scriptural exegesis (cf. Hermeneutics 1.2). A classical painting is the subject of studies in which Marin (1970) discusses further semiotic aspects of the text-image relationship. Among his topics are the transformational rules for the intersemiotic transposition of a myth into a painting and the relationship of later literary descriptions of the mythological picture to elements of the painting.

4.3 Picture-Picture Contexts

The interpretation of a picture can be influenced by the content of another picture placed in contiguity with it. The classical demonstration of this contextual influence is the so-called Kuleshov effect of film montage (cf. Levaco 1971). Kuleshov showed that the meaning which an audience associated with a picture A (of a man's face) changed significantly when it was presented in contiguity to pictures B (of a plate of soup), C (of a dead woman), or D (of a playing girl). In continuation of this tradition, the semiotic effect of the juxtaposition of photographs is studied by Tardy (1964). In a study of the contextual effect of pictures in sequences, Thibault-Laulan argues that pictures in spatial juxtaposition are connected semantically by a logic of *attribution*, while pictures in temporal sequence (as in films) tend to be connected by a logic of *implication* since the sequence typically gives the impression of a consequence (1971: 27).

Painting

This chapter is, in a way, an appendix to the one on images and a subchapter to the one on aesthetics. Two more general topics, the essence of pictorial representation and the aesthetic value of paintings, are discussed there, while the present chapter gives only a survey of the precursors of, the major approaches to, and some topics in the semiotics of painting.

tions are given by Kristeva (1969a: 308–311), Toussaint (1978: 116–31), Innis, ed. (1985: 206–225), and Mounin (1985: 101–117). Programmatic papers on the semiotics of painting are Marin (1971a) and Damisch (1978). Many current topics in the semiotics of painting are discussed in Steiner's (1982) semiotic study of the relation between painting and literature.

1. State of the Art

The state of the art in the semiotics of painting can still be characterized as being in its beginnings (cf. Gerlach 1977: 262). As Calabrese argues, progress in the semiotics of painting has been impeded by a number of delimitational obstacles but also by some unproductive approaches (1980: 3–6). One of the former problems is a general tendency to discuss painting under the designation of art and thus not to differentiate between the semiotics of art (see Aesthetics) and the semiotics of painting. Another problem is the delimitation of semiotic studies of painting and their precursors from other approaches to the theory of painting.

One of the few critical surveys of the field is Calabrese (1980). Calabrese, ed. (1980) and Steiner, ed. (1981a) are anthologies of papers on the semiotics of painting. Brief introduc-

2. From Iconology to the Semiotics of Painting

Iconology is both a precursor of an explicit semiotics of painting (cf. Calabrese 1980: 11–12) and a field of research within semiotics (cf. Damisch 1975, Calabrese 1986).

2.1 Iconological Art Criticism

As a hermeneutics of the arts, iconology was founded by Panofsky (1939; 1955; cf. Kaemmerling, ed. 1979, Gombrich 1972, Gerlach 1978). Panofsky distinguishes *iconography* and *iconology* as two successive stages in the act of art interpretation (1955: 66). In his definition (ibid.: 51, 66), iconography "concerns itself with the [. . .] meaning of works of art, as opposed to their form." At this stage, the art historian studies "the world of images, stories and allegories." At the next stage of iconology, the interpretation is concerned with the "intrinsic meaning [. . .] constituting the world of 'symbolical' values." This deeper level of research brings "insight into the manner in which, under varying historical conditions, essential tendencies of the human mind were expressed by specific themes and concepts."

In this orientation, iconology has common goals with the semiotics of art, namely, the interest in the semantic dimension of art. But semiotics does not exclude the aspect of form and is concerned with further dimensions of aesthetic semiosis. As Damisch puts it, "whereas iconography attempts essentially to state what the images *represent*," semiotics aims at "stripping down the mechanisms of signifying" and of the "signifying process" (1975: 29). Nevertheless, as Veltruský remarks, "most studies in the semiotics of the picture do not go much beyond iconology" (1976: 252).

2.2 Gombrich's Conventionalism

An important precursor of explicitly semiotic theories of painting is Gombrich (1960; 1972; 1981). His studies of pictorial illusion became particularly influential in the semiotic discussion of iconicity, so that Calabrese considers Gombrich "a true 'bridge' between iconology and semiotics" (1986: 331). For reviews of Gombrich's work, see also Tomas (1965) and Mitchell (1986: 75–94).

Gombrich (1960) emphasizes the feature of *conventionality* in paintings and agrees with the painter Constable, to whom "the art of seeing nature is a thing almost as much to be acquired as the art of reading the Egyptian hieroglyphs" (ibid.: 12). In his own theory, painters have never had the "natural optics" of an "innocent eye." Instead, as the history of painting shows, their view of the world was always determined and mediated by what Gombrich defines as *schemata*, stylistic and other conventional modes, or, as semioticians would say, codes of perception and representation. From these premises, Gombrich concludes that "the

phrase 'the language of art' is more than a loose metaphor" (ibid.: 76).

2.3 Semiotic Iconology

Within the semiotics of painting, the iconological tradition is resumed and developed further by Schapiro (1969; 1973; cf. Image 4.2), Uspenskij (1971b; 1972), and Wallis (1975). Wallis, for example, interprets medieval painting as a system of iconic and symbolic signs with a syntax and a lexical dimension. He shows how medieval paintings were structured into "semantic fields," zones of signification (such as right vs. left, above vs. below, centrum vs. periphery) which codify the meaning of their pictorial elements. Schapiro (1969) and Uspenskij (1972: 16–19) show that even the picture frame has changed in its semiotic function in the course of art history. For this topic see also Marin (1979).

In his *Semiotics of the Russian Icon*, Uspenskij describes the "language of icon painting" as a semiotic system of four levels (1971: 12–17). The first level of this language, the very pictorial *alphabet*, is "the system of optical-geometrical restrictions determined by the perspectival system." (For the semiotics of perspective in painting, see also Gerlach 1978 and Uspenskij 1972, whose study is also concerned with isomorphisms between pictorial and literary perspective.) In further analogy to language, the *semantic* level articulates the "specificity of the objects represented," the *grammatical* level is constituted by the ideographic representational devices of the icon, and the *phraseological* level corresponds to the symbolic level of the icon.

3. Approaches and Topics

French structuralism was the source of explicitly semiotic research in painting. The structuralist debate was first about the question of analogies between painting and language. After this search for a pictorial code, semiotics began to study paintings as discourse and as an intertextual system of readings. Other approaches cover the broad spectrum from rhetoric and structuralism to the theory of information.

3.1 Painting, Language, Code, and Style

In response to Barthes's early semiological program, structuralists began a controversial discussion about the question "Is Art Language?" (Dufrenne 1966) or even "Is Painting a Language?" (Zemsz 1967, Barthes 1969). Most scholars answered in the negative to the question thus posed, but the underlying problem was soon accepted as worth debating: Is painting a system of signs (cf. Damisch 1978: 2), and what is its structure in comparison to language (Paris 1975)?

Among the critics of a language-painting homology, Dufrenne formulates two major objections, a structural and an aesthetic one (1966: 20–23). The structural argument is that painting, unlike language, is not a system with two articulations. (For this argument see Image 3.3). A corollary of this thesis is that art "does not write its own grammar. It invents it and betrays it in its invention." The aesthetic argument says that painting does not have the function to signify but to show: The semantic function of a painting "is not a criterion of its aesthetic quality" (ibid.: 20).

Among the proponents of far-reaching homologies between the verbal and the pictorial code (see also Image 3.3.4), Zemsz describes paintings as "being articulated by the systems of pertinence characterizing a given stylistic convention" and argues that these conventions constitute a "coherent coded optics" (1967: 46, 54). Painting is thus not a language, but there are as many pictorial languages as there are styles. Pictorial styles are defined as "systems of rules which permit to give meaning to represented and visible events" (ibid.: 59). By referring implicitly to its own stylistic code, a painting contains "a partial summary of the system of contrasts characteristic of its style": "Without the relay of language," a painting

"thus contains its own commentary" (ibid.: 46–47, 65).

3.2 Painting as Discourse and System of Reading

In his "Elements of a Pictorial Semiotics," Marin describes painting as "an open system of readings" (1971a: 28): Although subject to "the constraints of a 'pictorial grammar,' " the "trajectory of the viewer's gaze," from one reading to another, detects always new differences in pictorial articulation. On the basis of a "primary level of readability," the pictorial elements, at a second level of reading, become associated with an unlimited potential of figures 'in absentia' (ibid.: 26). This paradigmatic dimension of painting opens up a third dimension of pictorial codes which is its cultural space (ibid.).

A central topic of Marin's (1971a; 1978) semiotics of painting is again the role of language in pictorial analysis. Following Hjelmslev, he defines the discourse about painting as a scientific metalanguage (1971a: 19). The apparent gulf between the visual object of study and its verbal articulation, according to Marin, is bridged by his axiom of "the indissociability of the visible and the namable as source of meaning" (ibid.: 23). It says that meaning exists only by verbalization and "the world of the signifieds is nothing but the one of language." Therefore, it is the verbal discourse about a painting which "permits its articulation and constitutes it as a signifying whole" (ibid.: 24). Many of the semiotic categories which Marin (1978) applies in his studies of paintings are consequently categories of discourse analysis and structural semantics.

3.3 Painting and the Semiotics of Its Description

Based on the premise that painting is not a language, Schefer develops a semiotics of painting to which language is nevertheless of central concern (1969: 7; cf. Barthes 1969, Marin

1971b). He rejects the heuristics of the language-painting analogy and the search for a pictorial code, turning instead to the study of the discourse about painting in order to describe "the system" formed by "the relationship between painting, reading and text" (ibid.: 167). To Schefer, a painting is always the sum total of its own descriptions: "The picture has no a priori structures. It has textual structures [. . .] of which it is the system" (ibid.: 162). By these logocentric theses, this approach reveals its debt to the poststructuralist thought of Derrida and Kristeva. When Schefer nevertheless analyzes system and structure of painting, his premises are diametrically opposed to static structuralism. To Schefer, "the structure of a painting is defined by its mobility. It is the system which permanently modifies its apparatus of analysis" (1969: 158). The structure is "not the invariant but the diagram of a variability."

3.4 Further Approaches to the Semiotics of Painting

A number of further approaches to the semiotics of painting can only briefly be enumerated in the following:

1. Semiotic studies of painting in the tradition of the Marxist picture theory of meaning (cf. Image 2.2.2) are Kondratow (1964), Bassin (1965), and Karbusicky (1973).

2. A semiotic study of works by Dürer based on information theory and numerical aesthetics is Brög (1968).

3. Burnham (1971; 1974) applies methods of structuralism and Lévi-Strauss's model of mythological logic in his studies of modern paintings (cf. Myth 2.2).

4. For a Prague structuralist approach to painting, see Veltruský (1976).

5. Derrida (1978) gives the outline of a poststructuralist semiotic philosophy of painting.

6. Structural semantic rhetoric is the method of research in painting developed by Group μ (Klinkenberg et al. 1980; 1985). The authors aim at the discovery of a "zero degree" of painting on the basis of which its aesthetic and stylistic features can be determined by means of "rhetorical operations" such as addition, omission, or permutation.

7. Thürlemann (1981a; b) applies Greimas's model of generative discourse analysis in his studies of paintings by Paul Klee.

8. Further French semiotic approaches to painting which are characterized by their authors as being structural and generative are Paris (1978) and Floch (1985).

9. For an evolutionary perspective of the semiotics of painting, see Schenk (1982).

Photography

Photographs are pictures which have many features in common with other images (cf. McLean 1973). Beyond these general characteristics (also discussed in the context of iconicity, film, and advertising), the semiotics of photography has tried to determine the specificity of the photographic sign.

1. Topics and Approaches

One of the most distinctive characteristics of a photograph is its quasi-mechanical production—Tomas (1982) even interprets it as a *ritual*—in a physico-chemical process where the referent is a cause of the pictorial signifier. This characteristic has dominated the discussion of two topics in this field of study, the photographic sign and referent, and the photographic message and code. The contributions have come from several schools of semiotics. In the tradition of Peirce and Bense (1965b), an elaborate typology of photographic signs has been developed by Brög (1979) and Schmalriede (1981). Barthes's (1961; 1964c; 1980) semiotics of photography deals with topics such as the photographic denotation, its connotation, and the text-image relationship (cf. Keim 1963 and Barthes 4.). Lindekens's semiotics of photography is based on Hjelmslev's glossematics and the theory of codes. For a short study of photo-graphic poetics in the spirit of Greimas's structural semantics and semiotics, see Floch (1985). Several papers on the semiotics of photography are included in Burgin, ed. (1982).

2. The Photographic Sign

"Photography and reality" is a topic to which semiotics has contributed by its study of the relationship between the photographic signifier and its referential object.

2.1 Iconicity or Arbitrariness?

Two positions are opposed in the discussion of the referential function of photography (cf. Barthes 1980: 88): The "realists" believe in an essential iconicity of photography, but the "cultural relativists" emphasize its features of arbitrariness.

2.1.1 ICONICITY

Like all other images, the photograph is an icon of the reality it depicts. As Martino points out, geometrical *invariance* is an essential feature of photographic iconicity: "When a three-dimensional object is mapped onto the surface of a photograph, a set of projective transformations is applied that leaves certain attributes of the object unchanged" (1985: 9). Such invariance is optical evidence of iconicity. There is, of course, a loss of features in the photographic transformation of reality which reduces the iconicity of the photographic analogon. Gubern, for example, enumerates such aniconic features as (a) the loss of the third dimension, (b) the limitation by the frame, (c) the loss of movement, (d) the loss of color and the granular surface structure of the picture, (e) the change of scale, and (f) the loss of nonvisual stimuli (1974: 50–52). This feature of selectivity in relation to reality has not changed the popular belief in the essential iconicity of photography, the assumption that the photographic signifier is an *analogon* of reality. Barthes supports this view: "Certainly the image is not the reality but at least it is its perfect *analogon* and it is exactly this analogical perfection which, to common sense, defines the photograph" (1961: 17).

2.1.2 ARBITRARINESS

The two basic arguments for the arbitrariness of photography are the photographer's manipulation of reality and the cultural and ontogenetic determination in the perception of a photograph. The modes and techniques of photographic distortion were adduced by Goodman as an argument against iconicity in photography (1968: 15–16). Eco argues that a photograph can lie: "We know that, through staging, optical tricks, emulsion, solarization, and the like, someone could have produced the image of something that did not exist" (1984b: 223). The result of this element of arbitrariness due to the manipulation of reality is that, to a certain degree, "the photographer *creates* the reality of the photograph" (Berger 1984: 120). The perception of photographs has to be learned both by children (cf. Eco 1984b: 223) and by cultures. Cultural evidence for the arbitrariness of photography is reported by anthropologists who have observed members of remote tribes being unable to identify themselves in photographs (cf. Goodman 1968: 15).

2.2 Peirce on Photography

Peirce characterized photographs both as icons and as indices (§ 2.281). On the one hand, "they are in certain respects exactly like the objects they represent," and on the other, they are in "physical connection" with their object, since photographs "were physically forced to correspond point by point to nature." From the point of view of its material characteristics (Peirce's "firstness"), the photograph is essentially a *legisign* if one considers the negative from which countless instances ("replicas") of positive prints can be made. The individual print in its material singularity is then a *sinsign* (cf. Peirce § 2.246). As to its "thirdness," Peirce classified the photograph as a *dicent* sign (like a proposition):

> The mere print does not, in itself, convey any information. But the fact that it is virtually a section of rays projected from an object *otherwise known*, renders it a Dicisign. [. . .] This connection of the print, which is the quasi-predicate of the photograph, with the section of the rays, which is the quasi-subject, is the Syntax of the Dicisign. (§ 2.320)

(For further aspects of Peirce's semiotics of photography, cf. Brög 1979 and Schmalriede 1981.)

2.3 Indexicality of Photography

Without reference to Peirce, the indexical specificity of the photographic sign has been acknowledged by several semioticians. Eco, for example, characterizes the photograph as an *imprint* or a *trace*, a "motivated but heteromaterial" sign, since "the plate turns light rays into different matter" (1984b: 223). In the interpretation of Barthes, photography "always carries its referent with itself" since it is "an emanation of *past reality*" (1980: 5, 88). A different aspect of indexicality is the photographic reference to personal experience. As Berger puts it, private photos "have an existential significance. They say, 'look, we exist! [. . .] I've seen things, I've done things'" (1984: 121).

2.4 A Glossematic Model

Lindekens (1971; 1973; 1976; 1978) proposes a glossematic model of the photographic sign.

In the dyadic tradition of Hjelmslev, he considers the photographic sign to be semiotically autonomous in relation to its referential object (1971: 11; 1976: 15). While the photographic sign derives from an iconic code, its referential analogon should be studied at a different level of research, namely, within the semiotics of the natural world (for this topic see Objects).

The photographic signifier is structured into its substance and a form of expression (Lindekens 1971: 250; 1976: 97; 1978: 17–18): The physico-chemical manifestation of the photographic picture is its expression-substance. Its expression-form consists of the iconically pertinent features which "select" from that perceptual substance the traits by which the meaning of the photographic message is constructed (see also Mounin 1980: 122). The photographic content-form is in the conceptual schemes on which the verbalization or the interpretation of the image is based. This content form is ultimately derived from the sphere of ideas which constitutes its content-substance.

---

3. Photographic Message and Code

The alleged "objectivity" of the photographic image and its indexical dependence on its referential object has been reflected in the theory of the uncoded nature of photography. The opposite view, which assumes photography to be selective and unobjective, has given rise to an attempt to discover the code underlying the photographic message.

3.1 Barthes's Photographic Paradox

Barthes claimed that the photographic image, being "the perfect analogon of reality," is a message without a code (1961: 16–20). By its analogy or even "objectivity," the photograph is a denotative message. But in the case of press photography, the message has also been "treated according to professional, aesthetic or ideological norms which are so many factors of *connotation*." (For an empirical study of such photographic connotations, see Espe 1985.) Since connotations are always derived from a code, Barthes concluded that in (press) photography there is a "co-existence of two messages, the one without a code (the photographic analogue), the other with a code." To Barthes, the generation of a "connoted message on the basis of a message without a code" constituted the specific *photographic paradox*.

3.2 Lindekens's Photographic Code

In opposition to Barthes's belief in an uncoded denotative level of photography, Lindekens assumes photography to be strictly coded, even at its perceptual iconic level. Photography, according to Lindekens, is an iconic code whose semiotic structure even justifies its being defined as a language (1971: 263; 1976: 17). Based on analytic principles of linguistic structuralism, Lindekens (e.g., 1971: 247) proceeds to reveal the feature of *double articulation* (cf. Image 3.3) within this photographic code. At the level of second articulation, he postulates *iconemes* (1976: 81), distinctive minimal units of photography without meaning but with the function to differentiate visually the meaningful elements of a photograph (as the phonemes do in language). The units with meaning are located at the level of first articulation of the photographic code. These *iconic morphemes* combine into still larger units of content.

Film

Film semiotics, or the semiotics of cinema, has become a major trend in film theory. The search for the structures of a filmic code began with the hypothesis of homologies between language and film. In addition to this research in the "grammar of film," the study of the filmic sign and communication are among the central topics of film semiotics. Many filmologists agree that the essence of film cannot be exhausted by the study of its "syntax" but requires research at the text semiotic level.

1. The Semiotics of Film: State of the Art

The history of the semiotics of film began in the structuralist era of the 1960s in Italy and France. Earlier, implicitly semiotic approaches to film are among the classics of film theory.

1.1 Research Surveys

The development and the state of the art in the semiotics of film have been reviewed in a series of articles by West (1968), Worth (1969), Bettetini & Casetti (1973), Hanhardt & Harpole (1973), Ivanov (1973), Hoensch (1976), Harman (1977), Odin (1977), and Bentele (1978; 1980). Comprehensive critical surveys

are also included in the monographs on the semiotics of film by Wollen (1969; 1982), Chateau & Jost (1979), Carroll (1980), Henderson (1980), Presnell (1983), Chateau (1986), and Möller-Naß (1986). Anthologies are Knilli, ed. (1971) and Heath & Mellencamp, eds. (1983). The bibliography on film semiotics by Eschbach & Rader, comps. (1978) comprises almost twenty-five hundred titles. For more recent bibliographical information and reviews, see the bibliographical newsletter *Film Theory* (Horak et al., eds. [1] 1983ff.) and Sebeok & Umiker-Sebeok, eds. 1986.

1.2 Film Theory and Precursors of Film Semiotics

Film semiotics has become acknowledged as a major branch of film theory. Its place in relation to other approaches to film is outlined in studies on the history of film theory by Andrew (1976), Monaco (1977), Casetti (1978), and Henderson (1980).

1.2.1 PRECURSORS

Precursors of the semiotics of film can be found in the tradition of aesthetics (Arnheim 1957, Mitry 1963; 1965), formalism (Eisenstein 1942–49, Balázs 1930; 1952; cf. 1.2.2), and film criticism (Bazin 1958–65, Kracauer 1960). (For surveys of these film theories, see Tudor 1973 and Andrew 1976. For semioticians referring to this tradition, cf. Metz 1972: 195, Eagle 1978, Bentele 1980: 122, and Möller-Naβ 1986). Within this tradition, theories evoking the metaphor of the "language of film" are of special interest to the semiotics of film.

1.2.2 FILM AS LANGUAGE, MONTAGE AS GRAMMAR

The history of the metaphor of the "language of film" (e.g., Whitaker 1970) or the "grammar of film" (Spottiswoode 1935) has been outlined by Pryluck (1975), Chateau (1986), and Möller-Naβ (1986). Balázs, for example, argued that film was a new language that the spectators of the early twentieth century had to learn first before they could understand it (1930: 3–8). The "grammar" of this language, according to Balázs, consisted of the techniques of close-up, shot, and montage.

Many early filmologists defined the principles of montage as the syntax of film. Pudovkin considers the filmic image the *words* and the combination of these pictures the *phrases* of film language (1928: 100). Eisenstein also compares the shot to a word and the filmic "montage phrase" to a sentence (1942–49: 236–37). In an essay of 1929, he likens montage to the combination of "depictable hieroglyphs" into "undepictable ideograms" (i.e., concepts) in Chinese writing (ibid.: 28–30; cf. Ivanov 1985). A further presemiotic filmologist who deals extensively with film-language analogies is Mitry (1963). He describes film as a language, "a system of signs or symbols which permits designating the things by naming them, to signify ideas, to translate thoughts" (ibid.: 48). But the language of film, according to Mitry, is not like a common spoken language. It is a language of art whose elements become meaningful only at a higher level (cf. Andrew 1976: 209).

1.3 The Development of Film Semiotics

One of the first explicitly semiotic studies of film is a study in Dutch by Peters (1950; cf. Peters 1981 for a later English publication). His first research is based on the semiotics of Mor-

ris. Peters defines film language as a system of iconic film signs (1950: 145) and studies its morphology, syntactics, semantics, and pragmatics. This study remained largely unnoticed by later semioticians of film (cf. Schneider 1978).

The further development of film semiotics began with the era of structuralism. After early contributions by Jakobson (e.g., 1933b; 1967), systematic research in the sign systems of film began with Barthes (1960) and Metz (cf. Mrulik 1970). (For later contributions by Barthes, see also Barthes 1977: 52–78.) Subsequent studies by Metz, Eco, and Bettetini developed film semiotics into a major branch of applied semiotics in France and Italy. The theories of Metz in particular became a central topic of discussion or criticism in British (Wollen 1969; 1972, Hervey 1982: 234–43) and American (cf. Andrew 1976, Carroll 1980, Henderson 1980) film semiotics. The first monograph on film semiotics in Germany is Knilli, ed. (1971). The further development of German film semiotics is outlined by Bentele (1980). For Soviet film semiotics see 1.4.2, and for film semiotics in other countries cf. Sebeok & Umiker-Sebeok, eds. (1986).

1.4 Trends, Schools, and Topics

Only some of the research in film semiotics has gained the importance of a school. Other studies have remained isolated trends in the field or have focused on single topics.

1.4.1 FRANCO-ITALIAN FILM SEMIOTICS

This most influential branch of film semiotics began with the hypothesis of language-film homologies and the search for the structures of a filmic code. The linguistic structuralism of Saussure, Hjelmslev, and A. Martinet was the theoretical foundation of this research. Within a few years, no fewer than four influential monographs were dedicated to the search for the language of film (Bettetini 1968, Garroni 1968, Metz 1968; 1971; cf. Mrulik 1970). Other contributors to this phase of "filmolinguistic research" were Pasolini (1966; 1967) and Eco (1968; but for a different approach see Eco 1977b). Metz's first semiotics of film has been extensively reviewed by Cegarra (1970), Andrew (1976: 212–41), Henderson (1980: 160–200), Carroll (1980: 29–45), and Hervey (1982: 234–43).

In a second phase of development, Franco-Italian film semiotics dissociated itself from the earlier filmolinguistic approach, and a "new semiotics" of film (cf. Casetti 1974, Chateau & Jost 1979) was proposed. Bettetini (1975), for example, turns to the study of new topics such as the arbitrariness and iconicity of the filmic image, communication and signification in cinema, and the generative process of film production. Metz (1977b) gives a new direction to his research by turning to psychoanalytic interpretations of films. Lacan's semiological psychoanalysis (see Structuralism 3.) is one of the foundations of this "second film semiotics," whose topics include dream, fantasy, voyeurism, fetishism, and the principles of metaphor and metonymy in film. A filmologist who follows Metz's approach in many respects is Bellour (1979).

1.4.2 FROM FORMALISM TO SOVIET FILM SEMIOTICS

The semiotics of film in the Soviet Union has two precursors. One is the *film theory* of pioneer film makers such as Pudovkin (1928), Kuleshov (cf. 1974), and Eisenstein (cf. 1942–49; see 1.2.1–2). The other is the *poetics of film* developed by Russian Formalists such as Ejxenbaum, ed. (1927), Tynjanov, and Sklovskij (cf. Beilenhoff, ed. 1974). In this tradition, the work of Sergei Eisenstein (1898–1948) plays a central role. Semioticians such as Ivanov (1976: 158–378; 1985), Eagle (1978), and Zholkovsky (1981) have interpreted Eisenstein's writings as a semiotics of film *avant la lettre*.

Current trends in the Soviet semiotics of film can be studied from Lotman (1973), Ivanov (1973; 1975; 1976), and O'Toole & Shukman, eds. (1981). Ivanov (1973; 1975) discusses the relation between sign and reality in the filmic sign system. Following Jakobson, he further studies the metaphoric and metonymic princi-

ples as foundations of a typology of filmic narrativity. Lotman studies cinema as a language of art, a secondary system which models the world (1973: 77). He describes cinema as a system of iconic and conventional signs whose structure consists of binary elements of marked and unmarked filmic forms. Among the specific features of film studied by Lotman is the particular tension between the impression of reality and the awareness of artistic illusion (ibid.: 10–22). Film uses both reality as signs and signs as reality (ibid.: 84). And yet, the filmic message is coded on several levels (ibid.: 85). Central to cinema are the *directional* code (which generates shots and combines them in montage), the code of *everyday behavior*, and the code of the actor's *acting*.

1.4.3 FURTHER TRENDS AND TOPICS

Further trends and topics in film semiotics can be treated only very summarily in the following:

1. There is not yet a school of *Peircean film semiotics*, but several authors have taken Peirce's icon-index-symbol trichotomy as a point of departure of film semiotic studies. Outlines of a film semiotics based on Peirce and Bense's Stuttgart School are given by Beckmann (1974), Hoensch (1976), and Burzlaff (1978).

2. In addition to Garroni (1968) and Lotman, contributors to a *semiotic aesthetics* of film are the Prague structuralist Mukařovský (1933), Beckmann (1974), from the point of view of information theoretical aesthetics, and Wuss (1986), who develops a semiotics of the *open form* in cinema (cf. Aesthetics 4.1.2).

3. *Rhetoric* is an approach to film semiotics chosen by authors such as Kaemmerling (1971) and Knilli & Reiss (1971).

4. A *generative grammar* of film has been developed by Carroll (1980) on a psychological basis. Colin (1980) gives the outline of a generative text grammar of film.

5. *Communication theory* is the basis of film semiotic studies by Worth (1969), Schanz (1974), and Bentele (1978).

6. Film semiotic research based on W. A.

Koch's *socio-semiotic structuralism* is Koch (1969; 1971b), Zurlo (1976), and Lindemann (1977).

7. Lacan's *semiotic psychoanalysis* has influenced film semiotic studies such as Metz (1977b), Bellour (1979), Presnell (1983), and de Lauretis (1984). Presnell's further background is semiotic phenomenology. De Lauretis's central topic is feminism in cinema.

8. The *semiotics of film sound* is the topic of a special study by Andrews (1979).

2. Filmic Communication

The specific features of filmic semiosis have been characterized in comparison to spoken, written, and theatrical messages.

2.1 Asymmetry of Semiosis

Like a book, but unlike spoken language, the film conveys messages to which the spectator cannot give an immediate response in the same code (Metz 1968: 83; cf. Worth 1969: 292). Cinema is thus largely unilateral communication, more so than theater, where the public may have some influence on the performance. Feedback messages from the spectator's reactions and critical reviews reach the film producers only with considerable delay. In viewing a film, the spectator is in a communicative isolation which Metz interprets as voyeurism: "there is no need for him to be seen [. . .], no need for a knowing object, or rather an object that wants to know, an object-subject to share the activity of the component drive" (1977b: 96).

2.2 Medium and Message

In its visual and acoustic expression-form, the film cannot be altered during performance and is endlessly repeatable (cf. Bettetini 1968: 21–22). This is another characteristic by which cinema resembles more closely the book than theater. Both film and book, more generally writing, are semiotic recording techniques. (Cf.

Metz 1971: 254–88 for these and further similarities but also on differences between film and writing.)

Another characteristic of filmic semiosis is the psychosemiotic impression of a reduced difference between the filmic signifier and its referential object. This illusion of immediate reality, which is stronger than in theater or photography, is the source of a high degree of empathy and psychic participation on the part of the spectators (cf. Bettetini 1968: 20, Metz 1968: 3–15, Lotman 1973: 10–22 on the filmic illusion of reality). The more the distance between signifier and signified is reduced in filmic empathy, the more film approaches magic communication (q.v.).

3. Sign, Motivation, and Reference

The "imaginary signifier" (Metz 1977b) of the filmic image, its illusionary character of being, and not only representing, "reality," raises the question of the nature of the filmic sign, its motivation and modes of reference.

3.1 The Filmic Sign

The dyadic sign of the Saussurean and Hjelmslevian tradition has been the major model in the semiotic discussion about the essence of the filmic sign. This dyadic model programmatically excludes the dimension of reference, as emphasized in Eco's semiotics of film (1977b: 4). Nevertheless, the relation between the filmic signifier and its referential reality plays a central role in the study of the filmic sign.

3.1.1 BARTHES'S SAUSSUREAN MODEL
Barthes (1960) described the filmic sign in Saussurean categories as a unity of a signifier and a signified. In his interpretation, filmic signifiers are not screenic images, but rather elements of filmic representation, such as actors, costumes, set, landscape, gestures, and music. These signifiers are characterized by heterogeneity (since they are visual and acoustic signs),

polyvalence (they may have multiple meanings), and their syntagmatic dimension.

Concerning the signified of the filmic sign, Barthes's definitions show an essential ambiguity (1960: 87). On the one hand, he defined the signified as a conceptual entity existing in the spectator's mind. On the other hand, he characterized it as "everything that is outside of the film and needs to be actualized in it." In his context, he distinguished between filmic *expression*, where "reality" (invented or not) is directly shown to the spectator, and filmic *signalization* or *signification*, where the spectator apprehends events which take place outside of visible filmic scenes. In this sense, he defined signification as a marginal process of filmic semiosis. Barthes further considered motivation by analogy and a "very short distance between signifier and signified" to be characteristics of the filmic sign (ibid.: 88). For the thesis of the "short distance" between signifier and signified in film, see also Metz (1968: 62–63).

3.1.2 IN SEARCH OF THE FILMIC SIGNIFIER

Like Barthes, Pasolini considers the elementary filmic sign to belong to the level of represented reality (1967: 171; cf. 5.3.1). In his view, filmic signifiers are the "objects, forms, and acts of reality" which compose a filmic image. Yet, as Mitry pointed out, the film does not present an unmediated copy of reality (1967: 145). The filmic image "is not a natural sign, but a sign of representation by which the world receives a secondary meaning." The "language" of objects and nonverbal acts consists of signs which are constituted outside of filmic representation (cf. also Möller-Naβ 1986: 156). In contradistinction to Barthes and Pasolini, Mitry therefore describes the image as the primary filmic sign (1967: 143). Metz supports this view and defines the filmic signifier as the image and its signified as "what the image represents" (1968: 62).

3.1.3 METZ'S HJELMSLEVIAN APPROACH

Metz further elaborates the dyadic model of the filmic sign in Hjelmslevian categories (1971: 208–212). Within this model, the signs of the referential reality are assigned to extrafilmic codes. In a Hjelmslevian view, the expression-matter of the filmic signifier is a combination of audiovisual "raw materials" which are structured in their expression-form by extrafilmic phonetic, visual, musical, or nonverbal *expression-codes* (cf. Metz 1971: 248–49). The content-matter of the filmic signified is equally unspecific; the signifieds are unspecialized and structured into content-form within several *content-codes*. For, like literature and theater, film is in principle capable of saying anything (ibid.: 39). The system of relations between filmic contents, the internal thematic organization of films (ibid.: 16), constitutes the content-form of the filmic sign. The network of relations between the elements of expression-matter in film constitutes the expression-form of filmic signs.

3.2 *Motivation, Iconicity, and Indexical Signs*

According to Metz, "cinematographic signification is always more or less motivated, never arbitrary" (1968: 108). On the basis of Peirce's categories of icon and index, several authors have studied aspects of the motivation of the filmic signifier (Bettetini 1968: 180–90, Wollen 1969: 120–54, Hoensch 1976, Monaco 1977: 133–44, Peters 1981, Presnell 1983: 134–55).

3.2.1 FILMIC ICONICITY

According to Bettetini, "the iconic motivation [of the cinematographic sign] is almost complete, because the sign is constructed around the object in a deeply analogical relationship" (1968: 186). And yet, under the influence of Eco's criticism of iconicity, film semiotics has focused mostly on the noniconic aspects of film. Thus, Eco emphasizes the cultural and cinematographic conventions by which the filmic image is coded (1968: 251). And Metz assumes that "analogy is itself coded without, however, ceasing to function authentically as analogy in relation to the [cultural] codes" (1968: 111). Nevertheless, iconicity remains a cornerstone of Metz's film semiotics even though he describes essential aspects of film as being situated "beyond the principle of analogy" (1972: 151–62). On a text semiotic level, filmic metaphors (cf. Jakobson 1967, Ivanov 1973, Metz 1977b: 149ff.) and textual diagrams (Möller 1978) are further aspects of filmic iconicity. On filmic iconicity, see also the volume *papmaks* 7 (Münster, 1978).

3.2.2 FILMIC INDICES

Like a photograph, the filmic image is an indexical sign since, in its origin, the filmic picture is causally connected with the light reflections emanating from its referential object. This indexical connection of the sign to its referent is one of the foundations of cinematographic realism (Bettetini 1971). In addition to referential indices, there are intrafilmic indices in the form of metonymies (cf. Jakobson 1967, Ivanov 1973, Metz 1977b), and of connectors linking shots or sequences. Hoensch furthermore interprets the various types of filmic movement (of events, actions, and camera) and commentary as examples of cinematographic indexicality (1976: 48).

4. Film and Cinematographic Codes

The cinematographic message is not based on a homogeneous filmic code (cf. 1.4.2, 3.1.3). Its structure is "orchestral," "plurisemiotic" (Chateau & Jost 1979: 280), and based on a heterogeneity of codes.

4.1 Film and Cinema

Some semioticians of film distinguish between film and cinema (Metz 1971: 50–55) or between filmic and cinematographic codes (Eco 1968: 250). In this terminological distinction, *a* film is a particular filmic message which has its own beginning and ending, and *film* in general designates "one or more specific messages proper to all films" (Metz 1971: 53). *Cinema*, however (like *movies*), is "the filmic fact in its most general sense," which connotes technology and economy (cf. ibid.). According to Eco, the technological devices by which reality is reproduced in cinema are codified in the *cinematographic code*, while the *filmic code* generates narrative messages in filmic communication (1968: 250). These distinctions broadly refer to two codes or groups of codes involved in cinematographic communication: cinema, the audiovisual medium, and film as a specific text. However, this terminological distinction between *film* and *cinema* is not always strictly observed. (Metz's *Langage et cinéma* [1971], for example, was translated as *Language and Cinema*, while his *Essais sur la signification au cinéma I* [1968] was translated as *Film Language*.) In this chapter, *film* and *cinema* are used interchangeably.

4.2 Cinematographic and Other Codes

Metz (1971: 61–69) describes cinema as a plurality of cinematographic codes, and the totality of these codes as the *cinematographic language* ("*langage*"; cf. 5.2). He distinguishes between *general* cinematographic codes, whose structures are common to all films, and *particular* cinematographic codes, whose features appear only in certain types of film (ibid.: 62). While cinematographic codes are multiple and evolve in the course of film history, the cinematographic language, being the "common denominator of all individual codes," remains basically invariant (ibid.: 68–69).

The specifically cinematographic means of codification, such as camera movement or montage, is only one of several sources of filmic codification. "A film is not 'cinema' from one end to another" (Metz 1971: 63): it is also codified by many noncinematographic codes. Film semiotics has never attempted to set up a complete list of the codes which contribute to filmic communication. The openness of this genre would require the inclusion of most verbal, nonverbal, visual, and acoustic codes, from architecture to zoosemiotics. Metz distinguishes between general *cultural* codes and *specialized* codes and enumerates codes such as visual perception and recognition, cultural symbols, objects, gestures, and narrativity as examples of extrafilmic codes (1968: 62, 112–14). Eco discusses a similar typology of codes (1968: 252). Cf. also Bitomsky (1972: 39–82).

5. The Grammar of Film

Semiotic attempts at a grammar of film have been guided by the model of the grammar of language. For precursors of this idea, cf. 1.2.2. For the topic of the cultural relativity of the language and grammar of film, see Worth & Adair (1972).

5.1 The Tradition of "Filmolinguistic" Research

In the tradition of "filmolinguistic" research, some semioticians have discovered major differences, while others have maintained essential homologies between language and film. The extent of these homologies ranges from the level of *minimal units* and *double articulation* to assumptions of total analogies at several levels and strata (Koch 1969; 1971b) and the strong claim of a generative transformational grammar of film (Carroll 1980).

In the development of the semiotic debate on the grammar of film, Möller distinguishes between a "classical" and a "new" semiotics of film (1981: 253). While the "classics" until the mid–1970s followed the language model of Saussurean structuralism, the "new" film semioticians (cf. also Chateau & Jost 1979) have largely abandoned this guideline and have turned to models such as generative grammar, text linguistics, and linguistic pragmatics. Even though some of the early structuralist proposals for a grammar of film may now be rejected by many semioticians of film, the following discussion will deal mainly with the "classics," whose contributions have meanwhile become part of the history of (film) semiotics.

5.2 Language or Language System?

Metz is mostly critical toward the assumption of language-film homologies. In his view, the cinematographic language has nothing which corresponds to the double articulation of language (Metz 1968: 7, 114). Because of the motivation of the film sign, there is nothing which corresponds to linguistic phonemes (second articulation), since "it is impossible to break up the signifier without getting isomorphic segments of the signified" (ibid.: 63). Nor does Metz admit any first articulation of film into units corresponding to words (ibid.: 114–16). To him, the basic unit of cinema is the shot, which he considers more similar to a statement than to a word. Nevertheless, Metz concludes that

> the methods of linguistics—commutation, analytical breakdown, strict distinction between signifier and signified, between substance and form, between the relevant and the irrelevant etc.— provide the semiotics of the cinema with a constant and precious aid in establishing units that, though they are still very approximate, are liable over time to become progressively refined. (ibid.: 107)

Metz answers the question of the "logomorphic" nature of the film in terms of Saussure's *langue-langage* dichotomy: cinema is a *langage*, i.e., a semiotic faculty and habit to generate messages (cf. Saussure 1916b: 9, 77). But cinema is unlike a specific language system (*langue*) "because it contradicts three important characteristics of the linguistic fact: a language (langue) is a system of signs used for intercommunication" (1968: 44). But to Metz, "the cinema is one-way communication, [. . .] only partly a system [. . .] and uses only very few true signs" (ibid.: 75).

5.3 Theories of Filmic Articulation

Filmolinguistic proposals for a grammar of film have focused on the question of the minimal units of cinematographic analysis. In the history of film theory, the shot was frequently interpreted as the basic unit of film. Worth, for example, proposes a semiotics of film and defines its elementary unit, the shot, as the *videme* (1969: 299); but he does not decide to which level of language this unit might correspond. Film semioticians such as Pasolini (1966; 1967), Bettetini (1968: 36–44), and Eco (1968) have oriented their search for minimal units of film by Martinet's theory of double articulation (see Language 4.1.1) and have searched for elementary units at more than one level of linguistic structure (cf. Image 3.3).

5.3.1 SECOND ARTICULATION
Second articulation is the level of minimal distinctive elements corresponding to the phonemes of language. Pasolini postulates such minimal units of film and defines them as *cinemes* (*cinèmi*) (1967: 171–72). In his view, the various objects depicted in a shot are filmic cinemes. Pasolini admits, however, that these cinemes, in contradistinction to phonemes, are unlimited in number. In contrast to Pasolini, Eco maintains that objects cannot be elements of second articulation since, unlike phonemes, they represent already meaningful elements (1968: 256). In his own analysis (ibid.: 258), the presemantic units of second articulation in film are defined as *figurae*. These are differential units of visual communication (cf. Image 3.3.2).

5.3.2 FIRST ARTICULATION
In Pasolini's interpretation (1967: 171–74), the basic element of first articulation in film, corresponding to meaningful units of language, is the shot (*inquadratura*). Pasolini argues that, unlike in language, there is no finite lexicon of meaningful elements in film, but like the lexicon of possible words, the repertoire of images is infinite (1966: 50; for a different view of the filmic lexicon see Lotman 1973: 44–46). Bettetini argues that the minimal significant unit of film, which he calls *cineme* (or *iconeme*), is the filmic image and corresponds to a sentence in language rather than to a word (1968: 35–36).

Eco, too, contributed to the discussion of filmic articulation but later dissociated himself from his own proposals in self-irony (1977b: 12). Eco argues that a filmic image (e.g., of a human face) is made up of still smaller word-like units (such as eyes, nose, hair, etc.). He defines these smallest meaningful units as *iconic signs* (cf. Image 3.3.3) and argues that their combination within the image results in a more complex meaningful unit, called *seme*, which corresponds to a verbal *sentence* (1968: 236, 258). The level of first articulation is thus made up of iconic signs combined into semes.

5.3.3 THIRD ARTICULATION
Against Pasolini, Bettetini, and Metz, Eco argues that the film, unlike language, has *three* levels of articulation (1968: 257–62). In addition to the double articulation of the filmic image into *signs* and *figurae*, the third articulation of film lies in its dynamic dimension of *motion*. Eco argues that meanings of dynamic gestures, for example, can be determined only at this third level. He calls these dynamic units of third articulation *cinemorphs*.

5.3.4 TEXTUAL RELATIVITY OF FILMIC ARTICULATION
Progress in the search for units of filmic articulation has been impeded by the failure to distinguish between filmic articulation and the articulation of other codes (cf. 4.2 and Lindemann 1977: 235). In his attempts at focusing on the specificity of filmic articulation, Koch (1969; 1971b) therefore proposes a (con)textual theory of filmic articulation. In his view, the relevant elements of filmic structure cannot be determined in a context-free grammar of minimal units. Only the textual recurrence of visual elements decides on their structural value within a given film. The various levels of filmic articulation can thus be determined only within the framework of a text semiotic analysis.

5.4 Filmic Syntax

The semiotic syntax of film has its precursor in the theory of montage. Metz developed a theory of syntagmatic film analysis which is basically a taxonomy of cinematographic segments (1968: 119–82; cf. Henderson 1980: 144–59, Möller[-Naβ] 1981; 1986). The further development from syntagmatic film analysis to a syntax of film takes place in studies by Bitomsky (1972), Schanz (1974), Chateau (1978), Fledelius (1978), Carroll (1980), Möller[-Naβ] (1981; 1986), and Elling & Möller, eds. (1985).

6. Film as Text

Text semiotic research in film has given priority to the study of narrative films (cf. Metz 1968: 96, 185–227, Chateau 1978, Chatman 1978, Heath 1981, Scholes 1982: 57–72, Branigan 1984). Most of these studies analyze narrative structures which are unspecific of films (cf. Hervey 1982: 239). Thus, Wollen discovers Propp's narrative functions of the fairy tale in a film by Hitchcock (1982: 18–39). Chateau (1978), however, studies the cinematographic structure of narrative sequences in films, and Chatman (1980) focuses on the specific differences between verbal and filmic narratives (q.v. 2.2.1).

Related topics in the text semiotics of films are the study of movies as myth (Drummond 1984) and ideology (Baudry 1970, Nichols 1981). Little research has been done in the study of filmic poeticalness (e.g., Lindemann 1977), but for rhetorical approaches see 1.4.3. From the point of view of text grammar, Odin (1979) studies the aspect of coherence in films.

Comics

Comic strips are a mass medium in which several semiotic codes are transformed in genre-specific ways. The study of this medium transcends the field of visual communication. Its specific features are also in the fields of non-verbal communication, language, narrativity, and hence text semiotics.

1. State of the Art

General research in comics has been carried out from a number of perspectives. Histories, handbooks (Fuchs & Reitberger 1978), and encyclopedias (Horn, ed. 1970) of the genre have traced its development to cave paintings (Hogben 1949) or to the medieval Bayeux Tapestry (Kunzle 1973), to Leonardo da Vinci and Hogarth (Horn, ed. 1970), to Wilhelm Busch, or only to the American mass media of the 1890s (Daniels 1971, Berger 1973). After much dispute about the presumed triviality and educational dangers of this genre (cf. Wermke 1973), comics began to be discovered as art or at least popular art (Becker 1959, Metken 1970, Zimmermann, ed. 1973, Gubern & Moliterni 1978). Pedagogical projects for the use of comics in education were developed (Gaupp et al. 1978), and teaching programs for their study in school were proposed (Wermke 1973, Pforte, ed. 1974, Kowalski 1975, Vogel 1975, Baur 1977, Grünewald 1982). At the same time, literary criticism began to discover comics as a topic of interpretation and analysis (Baumgärtner 1965, Stoll 1974, Kagelmann 1976), often with special attention to psychological, sociological, and ideological implications of the genre (Drechsel et al. 1975). Special techniques of research were content analysis (e.g., Barcus 1961) and semantic differential analysis (Trabant 1971). An as yet largely unexplored genre closely related to the comics is the photo romance (cf. Sempre 1976).

Early semiotic approaches to the comics appeared with Eco (1964). Special attention was soon directed to the mythological structures in the narrative content of comic strips (Eco 1964, Baumgärtner 1970). For further topics of semiotic research in comics, see 2.–4. Among the few monographs which follow a semiotic approach to the study of comics are Cirne (1972), Fresnault-Deruelle (1972; 1977), Gubern (1972), Hünig (1974), Krafft (1978), Rey (1978b), and Wienhöfer (1979).

2. The Iconic Code

The graphic elements in the nonlinguistic part of the comic strip, elements of visual communication, are often subsumed under the designation of the *iconic* (Bremond 1968, Martinez 1972: 172) or the *visual code* (Oomen 1975: 50). Both concepts are terminological compromises since on the one hand these visual elements are not exclusively iconic, and on the other hand the verbal elements appear in writing, and thus visually, too. Moreover, there are also the codes of nonverbal communication whose structures are both depicted and transformed within the visual part of the genre.

2.1 Elements of Graphic Representation

Graphic elements such as line drawings and blots, colors, panels, and visual symbols are the basic elements of the iconic code of the comic strip.

2.1.1 GRAPHIC ELEMENTS

The semiotic means used in comic strips to depict "real world" events are either of a general graphic nature or specific to the genre. Line drawings and the resulting visual figures are the general iconic elements. Also, the technique of drawing in perspective imposed on the figure-ground relations of the drawings belongs to a more general code of western graphic representation of which the comics make use (cf. Fresnault-Deruelle 1972: 22). Among the graphic elements which have become specific to the genre are the so-called speed lines or action lines. These serve to convey a dynamic dimension to the otherwise static drawing. Contents of such lines are direction, mode, and intensity of movements (see Gubern 1972: 155–56, Kowalski 1975: 144–45).

2.1.2 COLOR

Colors in comics are not only represented iconically, referring to similar colors of the objects represented. Some comics (cf. Martinez 1972: 173) have made use of cultural color symbols to represent emotions or atmospheres (e.g., green/bluish referring to 'dangerous malice' or black/grey to a 'mysterious character'). Some of these color symbols may be of synaesthetic origin and thus partially iconic. For the

functions of colors in comics, see also Fresnault-Deruelle (1977: 143–68).

2.1.3 PANELS

In contradistinction to the film, comics can vary their picture frames and use this variation as an expressive element. Changes in panel size, framing, and succession are then used as iconic means of representing the changing dynamics of action (cf. Gubern 1972: 113ff., Riha 1974: 165, Fresnault-Deruelle 1977: 53–71). For the specific syntagmatic conventions of panel sequences which have been developed in the history of comics, see Gubern (1972: 161–75) and Krafft (1978).

2.1.4 VISUAL METAPHORS AND SYMBOLS

Visual metaphors translate linguistic metaphors, mostly those of emotions, into the form of an image (e.g., stars, spirals, etc.; cf. Gubern 1972: 148–51, Kowalski 1975: 147–48). Such "intersemiotic translations" (Jakobson 1959a: 261) imply a twofold iconicity, one in the linguistic code (e.g., the metaphor "to see stars") and one in the visual code, where the referential object of the nonmetaphorical object is depicted (drawing of stars). Visual symbols are derived mostly from popular culture in general (e.g., the drawing of a heart representing 'love'). They often merge with the graphemic symbols within the balloons.

2.2 Segmentation

While some semioticians consider the panel to be the ultimate and irreducible unit of the genre (Fresnault-Deruelle 1972: 20), others have suggested further principles of segmentation in analogy to the structures of the language code (cf. Image 2.3). Koch (1971b: 37–42) and Hünig (1974: 32–42) suggest the following levels of segmentation: The whole sequence of the comic strip is a *text*. Every panel is one of its *syntactemes*, equivalent to sentences of a linguistic text. Recurrent units such as persons, objects, or behaviors constitute the *logemes* of comics (units corresponding to words in a linguistic text). Visual *morphemes* are the minimal meaningful units within these visual logemes (e.g., eye or mouth drawings within the logeme of a face). In analogy to the phonemes of language, Koch also postulates minimal differential units (*representemes*) of the visual code of comics which he identifies as lines, contours, colors, or shadings (ibid.). For the discussion of such minimal units, see also Gubern (1972: 108–109). He postulates *iconemes* as minimal units, differentiating units of form (*morphemes*) or of color (*chromemes*). In an analysis of the "Peanuts" comics, Oomen (1975) studied the techniques of representing facial expression in this genre and discovered a limited inventory of visual morphemes with typical variants (*allo-forms*). For further principles of segmentation, see Krafft (1978).

3. Nonverbal Communication

Within comics, facial expression, gestures, body language, and other forms of nonverbal communication are graphically transformed (see also Krafft 1978: 74–81).

3.1 *Graphic Reduction and Hyperbole*

The visual transformation of nonverbal communication in the comics may be characterized by *reduction*, on the one hand, and *hyperbole*, on the other. Reduction is first due to the representational economy of the genre of drawing (the three-dimensional visual space is reduced to lines) and to the necessity of translating movements into static images. A second source of reduction is the stereotypes of the genre (cf. Bremond 1968: 96), which are evident in the limitation of comics to a restricted inventory of nonverbal expressions of elementary feelings (such as fear or anger), of human relations (such as love or aggression), or of everyday body movements (walking, running, etc.). For the elements of a gestural code of comics, see also Gubern (1972: 136–37).

3.2 *The Proxemic Code*

Fresnault-Deruelle studied the dimension of space in comics, distinguishing between expression-form and content-form (see Hjelmslev 3.) within three dimensions of the *proxemic code*, the acoustic, the visual, and the tactile space (1977: 117ff.).

3.2.1 THE ACOUSTIC SPACE

The expression-form of the acoustic space of the comics is the balloons. Their size, their form, and the direction of their arrows indicate the distance between speakers in space. In addition, the size and form of the letters may be used as an iconic means of representing loudness within this space. The content-form of the acoustic space is structured by oppositions between various modes of appeal, such as threats, warnings, or cries for help. Curses and imprecations are "hurled" into the acoustic space as if to "conjure the separating distance" (ibid.: 125).

3.2.2 THE VISUAL SPACE

The expression-form of the visual space is determined by various representational means of perspective. The techniques are influenced by the camera work and perspective in modern film. Unlike film, the contiguity of panels in comics permits the representation of eye contact between protagonists across the panel frames. Such experimental means of representation destroy the conventional unity of space. Within the content-plane of visual space, Fresnault-Deruelle describes the forms of suspense created by expressive eye contact and by spatial obstacles such as walls, houses, or rocks separating the protagonists.

3.2.3 THE TACTILE SPACE

The tactile space comprises modes of direct touching or body contact by means of weapons. The content-form of this space is structured by meanings ranging from love to aggression. Action lines and visual metaphors representing strikes or kisses are means of the expression-form within the tactile space.

4. Language

The most characteristic features of language use in comics are at the graphemic and the lexical level. At the textual level, the language of this genre can be described as a restricted code. Its restrictions are dictated on the one hand by the taste of its mass public (often children), and on the other by the limited graphic space available for dialogues and narrative commentaries.

4.1 Graphemics of the Comics

The "ideographic" techniques of writing in comics have been studied by Caprettini (1970), Fresnault-Deruelle (1972: 29ff.), Gubern (1972: 139ff.), Toussaint (1976), and Wienhöfer (1979). The specific graphemic characteristics of the genre appear both in the outer frames which delimit the written text from the iconic illustrations and in the visual form of writing itself.

4.1.1 THE FRAMING OF WRITTEN LANGUAGE
The two basic types of framing are (a) the usually rectangular frames for captions and narrative commentaries, and (b) the balloons as frames of the dialogues (or monologues). Words without framing within the panels usually indicate nonlinguistic sounds. Variations in the forms of balloons and their arrows indicate different speech acts. Balloons and arrows in "normal" line drawings indicate direct speech, "cloudlets" indicate unspoken thoughts, balloons in broken lines indicate whispering, and jagged balloons indicate angry utterances.

4.1.2 ICONIC LETTERS AND SPELLINGS
Creative variations of typography are used to represent meanings which correspond to the content of the written word, e.g., boldface letters indicating 'loud speech,' trembling handwriting indicating 'fear,' etc. Also, the unusual spellings of words in comics are mostly attempts at an iconic rendering of expressive forms of spoken language, for example, when prolonged cries are expressed by multiple graphemes (e.g., "awaaaay"). A specific invention of the comics is further the lexicalization of graphemes (e.g., ? meaning 'surprise,' ! 'attention,' and zzz 'sleep'). For the onomatopoeic function of words in comics, see Wienhöfer (1979).

4.2 Lexical Characteristics

Interjections and onomatopoeic words are a specially creative domain of the comics (cf. Sornig 1986). They are used to render expressions of feelings and to imitate voices and noises. Besides the characteristic onomatopoeic neologisms (such as *goink* or *zonk*), a typical word formation pattern of the genre is deverbal root morphemes (such as *gulp*, *sob*, etc.) used as interjections.

5. Comics as Narratives

Both adventure comics and the "funnies" are an essentially narrative genre (cf. Bremond 1968: 94). Narrative structures of comics have been studied by Cirne (1972), Fresnault-Deruelle (1972), and Hünig (1974). These studies analyze elementary narrative functions, sequences, and actantial constellations of comics, revealing both similarities to and differences from other narrative genres. Another text semiotic approach to the comics has been Barthes's model of myth. Following this model, Baumgärtner (1970) and Baur (1977) have studied adventure comics as a secondary semiotic system in which a first level of narrative events refers to a secondary level of archetypical contents such as "the fight between good and bad" or "nature vs. civilization."

Advertising

The semiotics of advertising offers interdisciplinary perspectives on the study of sign exchange and research in commodity exchange (economics). In this interdisciplinary field, semiotics contributes to advertising research with respect both to methodology and to the object of investigation. Concerning the former, semiotics provides the theoretical tools for the analysis of signs and communication processes in advertising. Concerning the latter, semiotics expands the analytic horizon from the verbal message in the narrower sense to the multiplicity of codes used in persuasive communication.

Various schools of semiotics have developed quite different approaches to the study of advertising. Yet, there seems to be a common denominator in these approaches: the extension of the analysis from the linguistic message to larger spheres of semiosis, such as meanings on various levels, textual structures, functions, and typical forms of sign manipulation. The early history of the semiotics of advertising, especially in the Romance countries, has been reviewed by Victoroff (1972), Spillner (1980), Dyer (1982: 114–38), and Pérez Tornero (1982). The still growing number of monographs based on semiotic approaches to advertising in recent years (Williamson 1978, Everaert-Desmedt 1984, Magariños de Morentín 1984, Handl, ed. 1985, Leiss et al. 1986, Henny, ed. 1987, Umiker-Sebeok, ed. 1987) indicates that this topic constitutes one of the major fields of applied semiotic research.

1. Interdisciplinary Connections

Advertising is an area of research in a field lying between the two seemingly unrelated academic disciplines of economics and semiotics. For economics, advertising is a factor in the process of the exchange of *goods*. For semiotics, advertising is a process of the exchange of *messages*. The research which has traditionally been conducted independently in these two fields has recently become the object of interdisciplinary semiotic investigations.

1.1 Advertising and the Exchange of Goods

In the economic process, advertising is both a means and an object of exchange. It is a means of exchange insofar as the advertising message influences people to buy goods. As such, the advertisement is a sign of the product. It is an object of exchange insofar as the advertising message is an economic good itself, sold by advertising agencies and bought by the producers of goods. The fact that in 1983 about $75 billion was spent on advertising in the United States (cf. Bogart 1984: 1) illustrates the economic importance of this latter aspect of advertising.

1.2 Advertising and the Exchange of Messages

As a process of message exchange (or *semiosis*), advertising has been the object of explicitly semiotic studies since the 1960s. Related disciplines that have traditionally taken an interest in the study of advertising messages are psychology (often in a more popular vein; cf. Dichter 1960), sociology (e.g., Berman 1981), anthropology (cf. Leiss 1983), marketing (Dunn & Barban 1986), journalism, visual (Millum 1975) and mass communication research (cf. Moragas Spa 1976, Durand 1981, Dyer 1982), traditional rhetoric, stylistics (Spitzer 1949, Galliot 1955, Corti 1973), and linguistics. Among these various approaches to advertising are many studies that can be characterized as implicitly semiotic, particularly in the fields of marketing and linguistics (if this discipline is not considered a branch of semiotics anyhow). In linguistics, several studies of the "language of advertising" deserve to be mentioned: Penttilä (1962), Leech (1966), Römer (1968), Block de Behar (1973), Garfinkel (1979), Geis (1982), Everaert-Desmedt (1984), and Schöberle (1984). In the field of marketing, those approaches are closest to semiotics that study the selling, purchasing, and consumption of products as a process of communication (cf. DeLozier 1976) or as a "symbolic activity" (Levy 1978). The latter approaches have been grouped together under the headings *symbolic consumption research* and *consumer aesthetics* (Hirschman & Holbrook, eds. 1981).

1.3 Semiotics and Marketing

The study of signs and persuasive strategies in advertising has traditionally been carried out at the two extreme poles of ideological criticism and positivistic marketing statistics. While at the one pole a lack of insight into economic necessities has been deplored, research at the other pole has been accused of a naive approach to the complex field of meaning and communication. Between these two extremes, applied semiotics (Le Boeuf 1979) and consumer symbolism research have established a more fruitful middle field. Yet, an intensification of the dialogue between semiotic and marketing approaches to advertising still seems desirable. With this goal, a first workshop and an international conference on semiotics and marketing have been organized (Umiker-Sebeok 1985, Umiker-Sebeok, ed. 1987), and the newsletter *Marketing Signs* (1 [1987]ff.), edited by Umiker-Sebeok at the Bloomington Research Center for Language and Semiotic Studies, is to keep track of future developments in this interdisciplinary endeavor.

---

2. Levels of Meaning

Popular writers on advertising like to discover hidden (sometimes called *subliminal*) meanings in this text genre. Ideologists have criticized advertising for manipulating the public with such secretive strategies. In semiotics, various layers or levels of meaning of advertisements have been discussed. In a first phase of research, the semiotic concepts of connotation and ideology were considered to be the key to advertising analysis. Later, the genre was discussed with respect to various codes which determine its structure. Even in the determination of the semantic core of the text genre, the distinction between overt and hidden meanings in advertising is decisive.

2.1 Semantics of Connotation and Ideology

Since the earliest semiotic studies of advertising, Hjelmslev's semantic concepts of denotation and connotation have been used as tools of analysis (see Barthes 1.). Since denotation comprises the literal meaning of a sign, and connotation refers to units of content which lie beyond this primary level of meaning, the theory of connotation appears to be a most appropriate tool for the discovery of "hidden" layers of meaning in advertising. Barthes (1964c) further argues that connotations depend on cultural knowledge and are thus coded. The signifiers of connotative signs are defined as *connotators*. In advertising and in the mass media in general, connotators, like fields of associations, amalgamate into *systems of connotations*. The totality of such connotators form the rhetoric of advertising. Rhetoric in this definition refers to the level of expression (or to the signifiers). On the corresponding level of content (the signifieds), such systems of connotation appear as the ideology of a given society. Rhetoric and ideology thus form a sign of which the former is the expression (or signifier) and the latter is the content (or signified) (cf. Barthes 1964a: 93).

Barthes's semiological approach has stimulated a number of advertisement analyses. Ehmer (1971b), Péniou (1972), Pérez Tornero (1982), and others have studied systems of connotation in advertisements. An important work in this context is Barthes's own study of a related genre, the fashion system (in fashion journals). Semantic studies of ideological systems in advertising have been carried out by Williamson (1978), Wernick (1983), Rabelo Campos (1984), and in part by Vestergaard & Schrøder (1985). Williamson, in her detailed text analyses, also uses the Saussurean dyadic sign model, but gives the concept of ideology an additional Marxist interpretation.

2.2 Codes, Visual and Nonverbal Messages

The concept of code is frequently used to describe the plurality of channels and semiotic systems used in the multimedial messages of advertising. Barthes (1964c) distinguishes three types of messages in an illustrated advertisement. Only two of them are coded. The first is the *linguistic* message, which depends on the code of language. It consists of the brand name and the verbal commentary. The two other messages inhere in the visual image: one is the *uncoded iconic* message, in which the photographic image analogously denotes the "real" objects in such a manner that the signifier and the signified are "quasi-tautological," and the

other is a *coded iconic* or *symbolic* message. The latter includes the connotations of the picture which form the "image" of the product.

Eco speaks of advertising codes with double *registers*, one *verbal* and one *visual*, and distinguishes five levels of visual codification (1968: 271): (1) the *iconic* level, similar to Barthes's uncoded iconic messages; (2) the *iconographic* level, based upon historical, cultural traditions and genre conventions (cf. Barthes's coded iconic message); (3) the *tropological* level, with the visual equivalents of rhetorical figures; (4) the *topic* level, with the premises and topoi of argumentation; and (5) the *entymematic* level, with the actual structure of the visual argumentation. For more detailed analyses of rhetorical figures in the visual images of advertising, see Bonsiepe (1966), Durand (1970; 1978), Dyer (1982: 158–82), Förster (1982), Magariños de Morentin (1984: 245–312), and Spang (1987).

The extension of analysis from the verbal to the visual and the nonverbal messages is of central interest in semiotic advertising research. Further semiotic foundations of the visual messages in advertising are discussed by Nöth (1975b; 1977a), Porcher (1976), Magariños de Morentín (1984), Cornu (1985; 1987), and Vestergaard & Schrøder (1985). Binder (1975), Kloepfer (1976), Spillner (1982), Schöberle (1984), and Langner (1985) focus on the interrelationships between the verbal and visual messages. Exemplary analyses of the nonverbal messages in advertising are Goffman (1976) and Umiker-Sebeok (1979).

2.3 The Prototypical Advertising Message

Despite the multiplicity of semiotic means and strategies, advertisements remain a text genre with a rather invariant semantic and pragmatic core (cf. Nöth 1987a). In the pragmatic perspective, every process of advertising implies a semiotic act of message exchange with the goal of an economic act of commodity exchange. Semantically, an advertisement is a message about a commodity combined with a sales (or purchase) appeal. With these simple (and here further simplified) textual invariants, advertising appears as an extremely semantically *closed* text, diametrically opposed to poetry, which is a semantically *open* text (see Aesthetics 4.1).

Every consumer is well acquainted with these core messages of the genre of advertising. Yet, some of its invariants are typically hidden or masked in the surface structure of an advertisement. There is a "strategy of occultation" (Charaudeau 1983: 124), according to which any reference to the economic interests of the advertiser is avoided or carefully masked in the advertising message. For example, the purchase appeal ("Buy X!"), which would express most directly the advertiser's intention, is either avoided or replaced by a consumption appeal ("Enjoy X!"). Also, the advice given to the consumer in an advertisement is never uttered by the advertiser in person, but by a substitute personality, who is likely to convey the message with more impartiality and authority. For a semiotic study of the speech acts involved in these strategies, see Everaerdt-Desmedt (1984).

Advertising is thus a text type which is interpreted by the consumer on two levels, the level of an overt or surface message and the level of a hidden message. The hidden message in this sense is not about any subliminal meaning (as described by some advertising psychologists) but about the economic realities of selling and buying. These realities are only hidden in the surface text. They are not unknown to the consumer. Reference to the economic interests of the advertiser is avoided in the overt message because it seems to be detrimental to the effects of persuasion. Therefore, a typical conflict exists between the contents of the overt and the hidden messages in advertising.

---

3. Structural Semantics, Myth, and Narrative Structures

An attempt to investigate semantic deep structures and even semantic universals of advertising is undertaken by Langholz-Leymore (1975). Her text semiotic approach follows Lévi-Strauss's model of the structural analysis of myths and Greimas's text semiotics. According to this study, advertising is a mediator between the concrete (the product) and the abstract (the signs). The semantic characteristics of the advertisement appear as a binary structure in which an opposition between the positive properties of the advertised product and the negative properties of competing products are explicitly or implicitly contrasted. The two products and their positive/negative properties form a twofold sign, of which the former are the signifiers and the latter are the signifieds. Within this twofold sign, an equivalence relation holds between the two opposed products and their two qualities. The analysis of these binary oppositions leads to the conclusion that advertising, just like myth, is concerned with finding answers to universal human problems such as 'life/death,' 'happiness/misery,' 'war/peace,' and 'hate/love.' These universal themes are present with the same regularity in the deep structures of both advertising and myth. But because advertising works with simpler means, it appears as a degenerate form of myth.

The approach of structural semantics to advertising has also been pursued by Lindekens (1974; 1975) and Porcher (1976). Chébat & Lindekens (1975) further argue that the oppositional positive/negative structure in commercial persuasion implies a fundamental logical and pragmatic paradox. Another area of research, inspired by Greimas's text semiotics, especially his actantial model, is the analysis of narrative constellations in advertisements. First steps in this direction have been taken by Charaudeau (1983: 122–30), Everaert-Desmedt (1984: 97–129; 247–52), Vestergaard & Schrøder (1985: 27–32; 93–97), and Broms & Gahmberg (1987). For an independent approach to narrativity in advertising, see Kloepfer (1986b) and Mick (1987).

4. Functions of the Advertising Message

On the basis of Bühler's and Jakobson's functional models of communication (see Function 3.1–2), the functions of the advertising message have been studied by Péniou (1972), Bachand (1978), Nöth (1983a), Vestergaard & Schrøder (1985: 15–18), and Cornu (1987). Although all six communicative functions distinguished by Jakobson can be found in advertisements, only the *conative* (or *appellative*) function is specific to the genre. This function has traditionally (since Strong 1925: 348–59) been expressed in terms of the popular "AIDA formula," according to which advertising wants to capture *attention*, maintain *interest*, create *desire*, and get *action*. This basic appellative function may be more or less dominant in a particular advertisement. The dominance of communicative functions becomes important for the typology of advertisements. Thus, for example, informative advertisements are messages with a predominantly *referential* function.

Although not a distinctive feature of the genre, the *poetic* function is among the most remarkable features within the mass media. Poetic and aesthetic aspects of advertising have often been commented on (cf. Januschek 1976, Nöth 1983a, Moeran 1985), but from the point of view of semiotic aesthetics and poetics, little research has been done in this field so far. Kloepfer (1975) shows how principles of semiotic poetics can be applied to the study of the language of advertising and is now working on a new project on the aesthetics of advertising (Kloepfer 1986a). Nöth discusses the aesthetic effects of *deviation* and *recurrence* in advertising (1975b: 87–91) and proposes to study the relationship between advertising, poetry, and art on the basis of the semiotic distinctions between poeticalness and poetry, or aestheticalness and art (Nöth 1987b). For other relationships between advertising and the visual arts, see also Ehmer (1971a).

5. Indexical Semiosis and Meaning Transfer

Peirce's "most fundamental division of signs" between icon, index, and symbol has frequently been applied to the study of advertisements (Bense 1965c, Nöth 1975b, Magariños de Morentin 1984: 139–96, Vestergaard & Schrøder 1985: 36–42). Pictures of the product and its consumers, comparisons, metaphors, and other signs referring to their object by similarity belong to the domain of the icon in advertising. Symbols appear in the language, brand names, trademarks, and visual logos. In its most prototypical function, however, the advertiser's attempt to draw the consumer's attention to the product implies an act of pointing, which is the sign type of an index.

Indexical semiosis also takes place in the more subtle strategies of meaning attribution and image creation. Nöth (1975b; 1977a) describes these processes as *indexical feature transfer*. Instead of showing the positive features of the product iconically, which is often impossible, the product is represented in contiguity to valuable objects, film stars, or similar entities whose desirable attributes are well known. By means of this contiguity relation, a semantic transfer occurs. The well-known features of the "valuable," "famous," or "desirable" entity become associated with the less well known product. This feature transfer implies an indexical sign relation: the features transferred to the product refer to it as an index. Most connotations with which products are associated in an advertising campaign are generated by this process of indexical semiosis. For the semantic process of meaning transfer in advertising, see also Chébat & Hénault (1974: 6), Williamson (1978: 19), Spillner (1982: 99), Vestergaard & Schrøder (1985: 152). Lindekens describes this process from the point of view of structural semantics and interprets meaning transfer as a process of "assimilation of initially asemantic contents" (1975: 8).

BIBLIOGRAPHY

Aarsleff, Hans. 1975. The eighteenth century, including Leibniz. In Sebeok, T. A., ed., *Current Trends in Linguistics*, vol. 13, pp. 383–480. The Hague: Mouton.

———. 1982. *From Locke to Saussure*. Minneapolis: Univ. of Minnesota Press.

Abercrombie, David. 1948. Forgotten phoneticians. In *Transactions of the Philological Society* (Oxford), pp. 1–34.

———. 1954. Gesture. *English Language Teaching* 9: 3–12.

———. 1967. *Elements of General Phonetics*. Edinburgh: Univ. Press.

———. (1968) 1972. Paralanguage. In Laver, John, and Hutcheson, Sandy, eds., *Communication in Face to Face Interaction*, pp. 64–70. Harmondsworth: Penguin.

———. 1981. Extending the Roman alphabet. In Asher, R. E., and Henderson, J. A., *Towards a History of Phonetics*, pp. 206–24. Edinburgh: Univ. Press.

Abish, Walter. 1977. *In the Future Perfect*. New York: New Directions.

Abrams, M. H. 1953. *The Mirror and the Lamp*. London: Oxford University Press.

Acree, Terry E., and Soderlund, David M., eds. 1985. *Semiochemistry*. Berlin: de Gruyter.

Adams, Gerald R. 1977. Physical attractiveness. *Human Development* 20: 217–39.

Adler, Max K. 1979. *Non-Vocal Language and Language Substitutes*. Hamburg: Buske.

Adriaens, Mark. 1981. Ideology and literary production: Kristeva's poetics. In Zima, Peter W., ed., *Semiotics and Dialectics*, pp. 179–220. Amsterdam: Benjamins.

Agrest, Diana, and Gandelsonas, Mario. 1973. Critical remarks on semiology and architecture. *Semiotica* 9: 252–71.

———. 1977. Semiotics and the limits of architec-

ture. In Sebeok, Thomas A., ed., *A Perfusion of Signs*, pp. 90–120. Bloomington: Indiana Univ. Press.

Aichler, Otl, and Krampen, Martin. 1977. *Zeichensysteme der visuellen Kommunikation*. Stuttgart: Koch.

Aitchinson, Jean. 1976. *The Articulate Mammal*. London: Hutchinson.

Akmajian, Adrian, et al. 1979. *Linguistics*. Cambridge, Mass.: MIT Press.

Alarcos Llorach, Emilio. 1968. Communication orale et graphique. In Martinet, André, ed., *Le langage*, pp. 515–68. Paris: Gallimard.

Albone, Eric S. 1984. *Mammalian Semiochemistry*. Chichester: Wiley.

Aldrich, V. C. 1958. Pictorial meaning and picture thinking in Wittgenstein's philosophy. *Mind* 67: 70–79.

Allan, Keith. 1986. *Linguistic Meaning*. 2 vols. London: Routledge.

Almeder, Robert F. 1980. *The Philosophy of Charles S. Peirce*. Oxford: Blackwell.

Almeida, Yván. 1978. *L'opérativité sémantique des récits-paraboles*. Louvain: Peeters.

Alston, R. C. 1971. Note. In Dalgarno, George, *Didascalocophus*, pp. iv-vi. Menston: Scolar Reprint, (1680) 1971.

Alston, William P. 1956. Pragmatism and the theory of signs in Peirce. *Philosophy and Phenomenological Research* 17: 79–88.

———. 1967. Sign and symbol. In Edwards, Paul, ed., *Encyclopedia of Philosophy*, vols. 7–8, pp. 437–41. New York: Macmillan.

Alter, Jean. 1981. From text to performance. *Poetics Today* 2: 113–40.

Althaus, Hans Peter. 1973. Graphetik, Graphemik. In *Lexikon der germanistischen Linguistik*, pp. 105–10 and 118–32. Tübingen: Niemeyer.

Althaus, Hans Peter, and Henne, Helmut. 1971.

Sozialkompetenz und Sozialperformanz. *Zeitschrift für Dialektologie und Linguistik* 38: 1–15.

Althaus, Hans Peter, et al., eds. 1980. *Lexikon der germanistischen Linguistik*, 2nd ed. Tübingen: Niemeyer.

Althusser, Louis. (1965) 1972. *For Marx*. New York: Pantheon.

Althusser, Louis, and Balibar, Etienne. (1968) 1970. *Reading Capital*. London: New Left Books.

Altman, Irwin. 1975. *The Environment and Social Behavior*. Monterey, Calif.: Brooks/Cole.

Altmann, Stuart A. 1967. The structure of primate social communication. In Altmann, Stuart A., ed., *Social Communication among Primates*, pp. 325–62. Chicago: Univ. Press.

Altmann, Stuart A., ed. 1967. *Social Communication among Primates*. Chicago: Univ. Press.

Andersen, Henning. 1979. Phonology as semiotic. In Chatman, Seymour, et al., eds., *A Semiotic Landscape*, pp. 377–81. The Hague: Mouton.

Andrew, J. Dudley. 1976. *The Major Film Theories*. Oxford: Univ. Press.

Andrews, Ben. 1979. *The Semiotics of Film Sound*. Columbia: Univ. of Missouri Ph.D.

Antezana, J. Luis H. 1977. *Elementos de semiótica literaria*. La Paz: Instituto Boliviano de Cultura.

Anttila, Raimo. 1972. *An Introduction to Historical and Comparative Linguistics*. New York: Macmillan.

———. 1976. Who is a structuralist? In *Linguistics and Literary Studies in Honor of Archibald A. Hill I.*, pp. 63–73. Lisse: de Ridder.

Apel, Karl-Otto. (1963) 1975. *Die Idee der Sprache in der Tradition des Humanismus von Dante bis Vico*. Bonn: Bouvier.

———. (1967) 1981. *Charles S. Peirce: From Pragmatism to Pragmaticism*. Amherst: Univ. of Massachusetts Press.

———. 1973. Charles W. Morris und das Programm einer pragmatisch integrierten Semiotik. In Morris, C. W., *Zeichen, Sprache und Verhalten*, pp. 9–66. Düsseldorf: Schwann.

———. 1976. *Transformation der Philosophie, vol. 1: Sprachanalytik, Semiotik, Hermeneutik*. Frankfurt: Suhrkamp.

Aphek, Edna, and Tobin, Yisshai. 1986. The semiology of cartomancy. *American Journal of Semiotics* 4.1–2: 73–98.

Apostel, Leo; Mandelbrot, B.; and Morf, A. 1957. *Logique, langage et théorie de l'information*. Paris: Presses Univ. de France.

Appadurai, Arjun, ed. 1986. *The Social Life of Things*. Cambridge: Univ. Press.

Apter, Michael J. 1982. Metaphor as synergy. In Miall, David S., ed., *Metaphor: Problems and Perspectives*, pp. 55–70. Brighton: Harvester.

Ard, Josh. 1983. The semiotics of mathematical symbolism. *Kodikas/Code* 6: 3–14.

Ardener, Edwin, ed. 1971. *Social Anthropology and Language*. London: Tavistock.

Ardrey, Robert. 1967. *The Territorial Imperative*. London: St. James.

Arens, Hans. (1969) 1974. *Sprachwissenschaft. Der Gang ihrer Entwicklung von der Antike bis zur Gegenwart*. 2 vols. Frankfurt: Athenäum.

Argyle, Michael. 1975. *Bodily Communication*. London: Methuen.

Argyle, Michael, and Cook, Mary. 1976. *Gaze and Mutual Gaze*. Cambridge: Univ. Press.

Argyle, Michael, and Dean, J. (1965) 1972. Eye contact, distance, and affiliation. In Laver, John, and Hutcheson, Sandy, eds., *Communication in Face to Face Interaction*, pp. 301–16. Harmondsworth: Penguin.

Argyle, Michael, et al. 1973. The different functions of gaze. *Semiotica* 7: 19–32.

Arin, Ertekin. 1981. *Objekt und Raumzeichen in der Architektur*. Stuttgart: Diss. Ing.

Aristotle. (ca. 335–34 B.C.) 1960. *The Poetics*, trans. Fyfe, W. Hamilton. London: Heinemann.

———. 1984. *Rhetoric*, rev. trans. Roberts, W. Rhys. In *The Complete Works of Aristotle*, vol. 2, ed. Barnes, Jonathan, pp. 2152–269. Princeton, N.J.: Univ. Press.

Armstrong, Daniel, and Schooneveld, C. H. van, eds. 1977. *Roman Jakobson: Echoes of His Scholarship*. Lisse: de Ridder.

Armstrong, E. A. 1963. *A Study of Bird Song*. London: Oxford Univ. Press.

Arnauld, Antoine, and Nicole, Pierre. (1662) 1965. *La logique ou l'art de penser*, crit. ed. [including the additions of 1683] by Freytag Löringhoff, B. von, and Brekle, H. E. 2 vols. Stuttgart: Frommann. (An English translation which appeared in 1685 under the title *The Art of Thinking* [London] is available from University Microfilms, Ann Arbor, Mich. and in the following edition.)

———. (1685) 1964. *The Art of Thinking*. Indianapolis: Bobbs-Merrill.

Arndt, Hans Werner. 1979. Die Semiotik Christian Wolffs als Propädeutik der ars characteristica. *Zeitschrift für Semiotik* 1: 325–31.

Arnheim, Rudolf. 1954. *Art and Visual Perception*. Berkeley: Univ. of California Press.

———. 1957. *Film as Art*. Berkeley: Univ. of California Press.

———. 1971. *Entropy and Art*. Berkeley: Univ. of California Press.

Arnold, Erwin. 1952. Zur Geschichte der Suppositionstheorie. *Symposion: Jahrbuch für Philosophie* 3: 5–134.

Aronoff, Mark. 1985. Automobile semantics. In

Clark, V. P., et al., eds., *Language*, 4th ed., pp. 401–421. New York: St. Martin's Press.

Arrivé, Michel. 1972. *Les langages de Jarry—Essai de sémiotique littéraire*. Paris: Klincksieck.

———. 1973. Pour une théorie des textes poly-isotopiques. *Langages* 31: 53–63.

———. 1974. Sémiologie ou sémiotique? *Le Monde*, June 7, p. 28.

———. 1979. Poétique et rhétorique. In Helbo, André, ed., *Le champ sémiologique*, J1–26. Bruxelles: Ed. Complexe.

———. 1981. Le concept de symbole en sémiolinguistique et en psychanalyse, 1: Approche lexicologique. In *Actes sémiotiques—Documents* 3.25, 5–31.

———. 1982a. La sémiotique littéraire. In Coquet, J. C., et al., *Sémiotique: L'école de Paris*, pp. 127–50. Paris: Hachette.

———. 1982b. Le concept de symbole en sémiolinguistique et en psychanalyse, 2: Le symbole chez Freud. In *Actes semiotiques—Documents* 4.36, 5–35.

Arrivé, Michel, and Coquet, Jean-Claude, eds. 1987. *Sémiotique en jeu*. Amsterdam: Benjamins.

Asbach-Schnitker, Brigitte. 1984. Introduction. In Wilkins, John, *Mercury: or the Secret and Swift Messenger*, pp. ix-cix. Amsterdam: Benjamins, (1641) 1984.

Ashworth, E. Jennifer. 1974. *Language and Logic in the Post-Medieval Period*. Dordrecht: Reidel.

———. 1985. *Studies in Post-Medieval Semantics*. London: Variorum.

———. 1988. The historical origins of John Poinsot's *Treatise on Signs*. *Semiotica* 69: 129–47.

Assmann, Aleida; Assmann, Jan; and Hardmeier, Christof, eds. 1983. *Schrift und Gedächtnis*. München: Fink.

Attneave, Fred. 1959. *Applications of Information Theory to Psychology*. New York: Holt.

Auerbach, Erich. (1946) 1964. *Mimesis*. Bern: Francke.

Augst, Gerhard, ed. 1985. *Graphematik und Orthographie*. Frankfurt: Lang.

———. 1986. *New Trends in Graphemics and Orthography*. Berlin: de Gruyter.

Augustine, Aurelius. (397) 1952. *On Christian Doctrine*, trans. J. F. Shaw. In St. Augustine, *Confessions . . .* , pp. 619–98. Chicago: Encyclopedia Britannica.

Auroux, Sylvain. 1979. *La sémiotique des encyclopédistes*. Paris: Payot.

Austin, Gilbert. 1806. *Chironomia; or, a Treatise on Rhetorical Delivery*. London.

Austin, J. L. 1962. *How to Do Things with Words*. Oxford: Univ. Press.

Auzias, Jean-Marie. (1967) 1971. *Clefs pour le structuralisme*. Paris: Seghers.

Avalle, d'Arco Silvio. 1973a. La sémiologie de la narrativité chez Saussure. In Avalle, d'Arco Silvio, et al., *Essais de la théorie du texte*, pp. 17–49. Paris: Galilée.

———. 1973b. *L'ontologia del segno in Saussure*. Torino: Giappichelli.

———. 1975. *Modelli semiologici nella Commedia di Dante*. Milano: Bompiani.

Ayer, Alfred J. (1936) 1974. *Language, Truth, and Logic*. Harmondsworth: Penguin.

———. 1968. *The Origins of Pragmatism*. London: Macmillan.

Bachand, Denise. 1978. Opération Solidarité Economique (OSE): une analyse sémiologique. *Communication et information* 3.3: 99–142.

Bachelard, Gaston. (1938) 1969. *The Poetics of Space*. Boston: Beacon.

Bacon, Francis. (1605) 1973. *The Advancement of Learning*, ed. Kitchin, G. W. London: Dent.

Bailey, Richard W. (1978) 1980. William Dwight Whitney and the origins of semiotics. In Bailey, R. W., et al., eds., *The Sign: Semiotics around the World*, pp. 68–80. Ann Arbor: Michigan Slavic Pub.

Baker, Steve. 1985. The hell of connotation. *Word and Image* 1: 164–75.

Bakhtin, Mikhail. (1929) 1984. *Problems of Dostoevsky's Poetics*. Minneapolis: Univ. of Minnesota Press.

———. See also Vološinov, Valentin Nikolaevič.

Bal, Mieke. 1977. *Narratologie*. Paris: Klincksieck.

Balázs, Béla. (1930) 1972. *Der Geist des Films*. Frankfurt: Makol.

———. 1952. *Theory of the Film*. London: Dobson.

Balcerzan, Edward, and Osiński, Zbigniew. (1966) 1974. Die theatralische Schaustellung im Lichte der Informationstheorie. In Kroll, Walter, and Flaker, Aleksandar, eds., *Literaturtheoretische Modelle und kommunikatives System*, pp. 371–411. Kronberg: Skriptor.

Baldassare, Mark, and Feller, Susan. 1975. Cultural variations in personal space. *Ethos* 3/4: 481–503.

Baldinger, Kurt. (1970) 1980. *Semantic Theory*. Oxford: Blackwell.

Bally, Charles. (1909) 1951. *Traité de stylistique française*. Paris: Klincksieck.

Bann, Stephen, and Bowlt, John E., eds. 1973. *Russian Formalism*. New York: Barnes & Noble.

Bär, Eugen. 1974. Understanding Lacan. *Psychoanalysis and Contemporary Science* 3: 473–544.

———. 1975. *Semiotic Approaches to Psychotherapy*. Bloomington: Indiana Univ. Press.

———. (1981) 1984. Thomas A. Sebeok's doctrine of signs. In Krampen, et al., eds., *Classics of Semiotics*, pp. 181–210. New York: Plenum.

———. 1982. The medical symptom. *American Journal of Semiotics* 1.3: 17–34.

———. 1983. A semiotic history of symptomatology. In Eschbach, Achim, and Trabant, Jürgen, eds., *History of Semiotics*, pp. 41–66. Amsterdam: Benjamins.

———. 1987. Grasping semiotics. *Semiotica* 65: 157–61.

———. 1988. *Medical Semiotics*. Lanham: University Press of America.

Barakat, Robert A. 1973. Arabic gestures. *Journal of Popular Culture* 6: 749–87.

———. 1975. *The Cistercian Sign Language*. Kalamazoo, Mich.: Cistercian Pub.

Baran, Henryk, ed. (1974) 1976. *Semiotics and Structuralism: Readings from the Soviet Union*. White Plains, N.Y.: Int. Arts and Sciences Press.

Barash, David. 1981. *Sociobiology*. Glasgow: Fontana.

Barcus, Francis E. 1961. A content analysis of trends in Sunday comics, 1900–1959. *Journalism Quarterly* 38: 171–80.

Bardin, Laurence. 1975. Le texte et l'image. *Communication et langages* 26: 98–112.

Bar-Hillel, Yehoshua. 1954. Indexical expressions. *Mind* 63: 359–74.

———. 1964. *Language and Information*. Reading, Mass.: Addison-Wesley.

Bar-Hillel, Yehoshua, and Carnap, Rudolf. 1953. Semantic information. In Jackson, Willis, ed., *Communication Theory*, pp. 503–12. London: Butterworth.

Barley, Nigel F. 1974. Two Anglo-Saxon sign systems compared. *Semiotica* 12: 227–37.

Barnlund, Dean C. 1975. Communicative styles in two cultures: Japan and the United States. In Kendon, Adam, et al., eds., *Organization of Behavior in Face-to-Face Interaction*, pp. 427–56. The Hague: Mouton.

Baron, Naomi S. 1981. *Speech, Writing, and Sign*. Bloomington: Indiana Univ. Press.

———. 1984. Speech, sight, and signs: The role of iconicity in language and art. *Semiotica* 52: 187–211.

Barth, Erhard, and Harras, Gisela. 1974. Zur Sprachtheorie von Louis Hjelmslev. In Hjelmslev, L., *Aufsätze zur allgemeinen Sprachwissenschaft*, pp. v–xxiii. Stuttgart: Klett.

Barthes, Roland. (1957) 1987. *Mythologies*. New York: Hill & Wang.

———. 1960. Le problème de la signification au cinéma. *Revue internationale de filmologie* 10: 83–89.

———. (1961) 1977. The photographic message. In Barthes, R., *Image—Music—Text*, pp. 15–31. Collins: Fontana.

———. (1963) 1964. *On Racine*. New York: Hill & Wang.

———. (1964a) 1967. *Elements of Semiology*. London: Cape.

———. (1964b) 1972. *Critical Essays*. Evanston: Northwestern Univ. Press.

———. (1964c) 1977. Rhetoric of the image. In Barthes, Roland, *Image—Music—Text*, pp. 32–51. New York: Hill & Wang.

———. (1966a) 1977. Introduction to the structural analysis of narratives. In Barthes, R., *Image—Music—Text*, pp. 79–124. New York: Hill & Wang.

———. 1966b. *Critique et vérité*. Paris: Seuil.

———. (1967a) 1971. Sémiologie et urbanisme. *L'architecture d'aujourd'hui (La ville)* 153: 11–13.

———. (1967b) 1983. *The Fashion System*. New York: Hill & Wang.

———. (1969) 1985. Is painting a language? In Barthes, R., *The Responsibility of Forms*, pp. 149–52. Oxford: Blackwell.

———. 1970a. L'ancienne rhétorique. *Communications* 16: 172–229.

———. (1970b) 1974. *S/Z*. New York: Hill & Wang.

———. 1971a. Réponses. *Tel Quel* 47: 89–107.

———. 1971b. Style and its image. In Chatman, Seymour, ed., *Literary Style*, pp. 3–15. London: Oxford Univ. Press.

———. 1972. Sémiologie et médicine. In Bastide, Roger, ed., *Les sciences de la folie*, pp. 37–46. The Hague: Mouton.

———. (1975a) 1977. *Barthes by Barthes*. New York: Hill & Wang.

———. (1975b) 1985. Texte (théorie du). In *Encyclopaedia universalis* (Paris), vol. 7, pp. 996–1000.

———. 1977. *Image—Music—Text*. New York: Hill & Wang.

———. (1980) 1982. *Camera Lucida: Reflections on Photography*. London: Cape.

———. (1984) 1986. *The Rustle of Language*. Oxford: Blackwell.

———. 1985a. *L'aventure sémiologique*. Paris: Seuil.

———. 1985b. *The Responsibility of Forms*. Oxford: Blackwell.

Barthes, Roland, et al. 1971a. *Analyse structurale et exégèse biblique*. Neuchâtel: Delachaux.

———. 1971b. *Exégèse et herméneutique*. Paris: Seuil.

Barwick, Karl. 1957. *Probleme der stoischen Sprachlehre und Rhetorik*. Berlin: Akademie Verlag.

Bassin, J. 1965. Die Semiotik über Darstellung und Ausdruck in der Kunst. *Kunst und Literatur* 13: 1259–69.

Bassy, Alain-Marie. 1974. Du texte à l'illustration: Pour une sémiologie des étapes. *Semiotica* 11: 297–334.

Bastide, Françoise. 1985. Linguistique et génétique. *Bulletin du Groupe de Recherches sémio-linguistiques* (EHESS) 8 [33]: 21–28.

Bastide, Roger, ed. 1962. *Sens et usages du terme 'structure' dans les sciences humaines et sociales.* The Hague: Mouton.

Bates, J. A. 1975. The communicative hand. In Benthall, J., and Polhemus, T., eds., *The Body as a Medium of Expression*, pp. 175–94. London: Allen & Unwin.

Bateson, Gregory, et al. 1956. Toward a theory of schizophrenia. *Behavioral Science* 1: 251–62.

Bateson, Mary Catherine. 1968. Linguistics in a semiotic frame. *Linguistics* 39: 5–17.

Bateson, Paul Patrick Gordon, and Klopfer, Peter H., eds. 1973–81. *Perspectives in Ethology.* 4 vols. New York: Plenum.

Baticle, Yveline. 1977. Le verbal, l'iconique et les signes. *Communication et langages* 33: 20–35.

Baudrillard, Jean. 1968. *Le système des objets.* Paris: Gallimard.

―――. (1972) 1981. *For a Critique of the Political Economy of the Sign.* St. Louis: Telos.

Baudry, Jean-Louis. (1970) 1974–75. Ideological effects of the basic cinematographic apparatus. *Film Quarterly* 28.2: 39–47.

Baum, Richard. 1977. Narrativik und Sprachwissenschaft. In Haubrichs, Wolfgang, ed., *Erzählforschung. Theorien und Modelle der Narrativik*, vol. 2, pp. 16–45. Göttingen: Vandenhoeck.

Baumgarten, Alexander Gottlieb (1750/58) 1983. *Theoretische Ästhetik*, trans. and ed. Schweizer, H. R. Hamburg: Meiner.

Baumgärtner, Alfred Clemens. (1965) 1972. *Die Welt der Comics.* Bochum: Kamp.

―――. (1970) 1973. Die Welt der Comics als semiologisches System. In Zimmermann, H. D., ed., *Vom Geist der Superhelden*, pp. 98–111. München: dtv.

Baumgärtner, Klaus. 1969. Der methodische Stand einer linguistischen Poetik. *Jahrbuch für Internationale Germanistik* 1.1: 15–43.

Bauml, B. S., and Bauml, F. H. 1975. *A Dictionary of Gestures.* Metuchen: Scarecrow.

Baur, Elisabeth Katrin. 1977. *Der Comic. Strukturen—Vermarktung—Unterricht.* Düsseldorf: Schwann.

Baur, Rupprecht S., and Grzybek, Peter. 1989. Language teaching and semiotics. In Koch, W. A., ed., *Semiotics in the Individual Sciences.* Bochum: Brockmeyer.

Bausani, Alessandro. 1970. *Geheim- und Universalsprachen.* Stuttgart: Kohlhammer.

Baxtin, M. See Bakhtin, M.

Bayer, Udo. 1975. *Lessings Zeichenbegriffe und Zeichenprozesse im 'Laokoon' und ihre Analyse nach der modernen Semiotik.* Stuttgart: Diss. Phil.

―――. 1980. Theater als Superisationsprozeß über einem heterogenen Mittelrepertoire. In Eschbach, A., and Rader, W., eds., *Literatursemiotik*, vol. 2, pp. 203–59. Tübingen: Narr.

Bazin, André (1958–65), 1967, 1971. *What Is Cinema?* 2 vols. Berkeley: Univ. of California Press.

Beaugrande, Robert de. 1980. *Text, Discourse, and Process.* Norwood, N.J.: Ablex.

―――. 1982. The story of grammars and the grammars of stories. *Journal of Pragmatics* 6: 383–422.

―――. 1985. Text linguistics and discourse studies. In Dijk, Teun A. van, ed., *Handbook of Discourse Analysis*, vol. 1, pp. 41–70. London: Academic Press.

―――. 1986. Artificial intelligence. In Sebeok, Thomas A., ed., *Encyclopedic Dictionary of Semiotics*, pp. 56–58. Berlin: Mouton de Gruyter.

Beaugrande, Robert de, and Dressler, Wolfgang. 1981. *Introduction to Text Linguistics.* London: Longman.

Becher, Johann Joachim (1661) 1962. *Character, pro Notitia Linguarum Universali*, partial reprint and trans.: *Zur mechanischen Sprachübersetzung*, ed. Waffenschmidt, W. G. Stuttgart: Kohlhammer.

Beck, Cave. 1657. *The Universal Character, by Which All the Nations in the World May Understand One Another's Conceptions.* London.

Beck, Götz. 1980. *Sprechakte und Sprachfunktionen.* Tübingen: Niemeyer.

Becker, Stephen. 1959. *Comic Art in America.* New York: Simon & Schuster.

Beckmann, Peter. 1974. *Formale und funktionale Film- und Fernsehanalyse.* Stuttgart: Diss. Phil.

Beilenhoff, Wolfgang, ed. 1974. *Poetik des Films.* München: Fink.

Belk, Russell W.; Bahn, K. D.; and Mayer, R. N. 1982. Developmental recognition of consumption symbolism. *Journal of Consumer Research* 9. 4–17.

Bell, Charles. 1806. *The Anatomy and Philosophy of Expression as Connected with the Fine Arts.* London: Murray.

Bell, David Charles, and Bell, Alexander Melville. 1884. *Bell's Standard Elocutionist.* London: Hodder.

Bellert, Irena, and Ohlin, Peter, eds. 1978. *Selected Concepts in Semiotics and Aesthetics.* Montreal: McGill Univ.

Bellour, Raymond. 1979. *L'analyse du film.* Paris: Albatros.

Ben-Amos, Dan, and Goldstein, Kenneth S., eds. 1975. *Folklore.* The Hague: Mouton.

Bennett, James R. 1985. *A Bibliography of Stylistics and Related Criticism, 1967–83.* New York: Modern Language Association.

Benoist, Jean-Marie. 1970. The end of structuralism. *Twentieth Century Studies* 3: 31–53.

Bense, Elisabeth; Eisenberg, Peter; and Haberland, Hartmut, eds. 1976. *Beschreibungsmethoden des amerikanischen Strukturalismus*. München: Hueber.

Bense, Max. 1962. *Theorie der Texte*. Köln: Kiepenheuer & Witsch.

———. (1965a) 1982. *Aesthetica*. Baden-Baden: Agis.

———. 1965b. Fotoästhetik. In Pawek, Karl, ed., *Panoptikum oder Wirklichkeit*, pp. 144–47. Hamburg: Gruner & Jahr.

———. 1965c. *Kommunikationsforschung und Werbung*. Düsseldorf: Troost. Also as Ästhetik und Werbung, in Bense, Max, *Aestetica*, pp. 303–14. Baden-Baden: Agis, (1965) 1982.

———. 1967. *Semiotik*. Baden-Baden: Agis.

———. (1968) 1971. Urbanismus und Semiotik. In *Konzept I: Architektur als Zeichensystem*, pp. 99–104. Tübingen: Wasmuth.

———. 1969. *Einführung in die informationstheoretische Ästhetik*. Reinbek: Rowohlt.

———. 1971. *Zeichen und Design: Semiotische Ästhetik*. Baden-Baden: Agis.

———. 1975. *Semiotische Prozesse und Systeme*. Baden-Baden: Agis.

———. 1977a. Die semiotische Konzeption der Ästhetik. *Zeitschrift für Literaturwissenschaft und Linguistik* 27/28: 188–201.

———. 1977b. Pädagogische Intentionen in der Semiotik. In Brög, Hans, ed., *Probleme der Semiotik unter schulischem Aspekt*. Ravensburg: O. Maier.

———. 1979. *Die Unwahrscheinlichkeit des Ästhetischen*. Baden-Baden: Agis.

———. 1981. *Axiomatik und Semiotik in Mathematik und Naturerkenntnis*. Baden-Baden: Agis.

———. 1983. *Das Universum der Zeichen*. Stuttgart: Agis.

———. 1986. *Repräsentation und Fundierung der Realitäten: Fazit semiotischer Perspektiven*. Baden-Baden: Agis.

Bense, Max, and Walther, Elisabeth, eds. 1973. *Wörterbuch der Semiotik*. Köln: Kiepenheuer & Witsch.

Bentele, Günter. 1978. The functions of a semiotic of film. *Kodikas/Code* 1: 78–93.

———. 1980. Filmsemiotik in der Bundesrepublik Deutschland. *Zeitschrift für Semiotik* 2: 119–38.

———. 1985. Audio-visual analysis and a grammar of presentation forms in new programs: Some mediasemiotic considerations. In Dijk, Teun A. van, ed., *Discourse and Communication*, pp. 159–84. Berlin: de Gruyter.

Bentele, Günter, ed. 1981. *Semiotik und Massenmedien*. München: Ölschläger.

Bentele, Günter, and Bystrina, Ivan. 1978. *Semiotik*. Stuttgart: Kohlhammer.

Bentele, Günter, and Hess-Lüttich, Ernest W. B., eds. 1985. *Zeichengebrauch in den Massenmedien*. Tübingen: Niemeyer.

Benthall, Jonathan, and Polhemus, Ted, eds. 1975. *The Body as a Medium of Expression*. London: Lane.

Bentley, Arthur F. 1947. The new "semiotic." *Philosophy and Phenomenological Research* 8.1: 107–31.

Benveniste, Emile. (1939) 1971. The nature of the linguistic sign. In Benveniste, E., *Problems in General Linguistics*, pp. 43–49. Coral Gables: Univ. of Miami Press.

———. (1966) 1971. *Problems in General Linguistics*. Coral Gables: Univ. of Miami Press.

———. (1969) 1985. The semiology of language. In Innis, Robert E., ed., *Semiotics*, pp. 226–46. Bloomington: Indiana Univ. Press.

———. 1974. *Problèmes de linguistique générale*, vol. 2. Paris: Gallimard.

Berger, Arthur Asa. 1973. *The Comic-Stripped American*. New York: Walker.

———. 1982. *Media Analysis Techniques*. Beverly Hills: Sage.

———. 1984. *Signs in Contemporary Culture*. New York: Longman.

———. 1987. Semiotics and popular culture. In Sebeok, T. A., and Umiker-Sebeok, J., eds., 1987, *The Semiotic Web, 1986*, pp. 355–66. Berlin: Mouton de Gruyter.

Berger, Charles R., and Chaffee, Steven H., eds. 1987. *Handbook of Communication Science*. Newbury Park: Sage.

Berger, Christel. 1979. Semiotik und Design—Theorie und Praxis. *Ars Semeiotica* 2: 1–22.

Berger, Christian G. 1779. *Plan zu einer... allgemeinen Sprache*. Berlin.

Berger, Klaus. 1977. *Exegese des Neuen Testaments*. Heidelberg: Quelle & Meyer.

Berkeley, George. (1710) 1969. *The Principles of Human Knowledge*, ed. Warnock, G. J. London: Fontana.

Berlyne, D. E. 1974. Information and motivation. In Silverstein, Albert A., ed., *Human Communication*, pp. 19–45. Hillsdale, N.J.: Erlbaum.

Berman, Ronald. 1981. *Advertising and Social Change*. Beverly Hills: Sage.

Bernard, Jeff, ed. 1983. *Didaktische Umsetzung der Zeichentheorie*. Wien: Österr. Ges. Für Semiotik (= Angewandte Semiotik 2).

Bernard, Jeff, and Withalm, Gloria. 1986. Ferruccio Rossi-Landis dialektisch-materialistische Zeichentheorie. In Dutz, K. D., and Schmitter, P., eds., *Geschichte und Geschichtsschreibung der Semiotik*, pp. 329–66. Münster: MAkS.

Berry, Margaret. 1975. *Introduction to Systemic Linguistics I*. London: Batsford.

Bertalanffy, Ludwig von. (1968) 1971. *General Systems Theory*. London: Allen Lane/Penguin.

———. 1975. *Perspectives on General Systems Theory*. New York: Braziller.

Bertin, Jacques. (1967) 1983. *Semiology of Graphics*. Madison: Univ. of Wisconsin Press.

Bettetini, Gianfranco. (1968) 1973. *The Language and Technique of the Film*. The Hague: Mouton.

———. 1971. *L'indice del realismo*. Milano: Bompiani.

———. 1975. *Produzione del senso e messa in scena*. Milano: Bompiani.

———. 1986. La semiotica nella didattica e la didattica della semiotica. In Arlandi, G. F., ed., *Incontro con la semiotica*, pp. 65–69. Como: Centro Stampa Comunale.

Bettetini, Gianfranco, and Casetti, Francesco. 1973. La sémiologie des moyens de communication audio-visuels. *Revue d'Esthétique* 2.4: 87–96.

Betti, Emilio. 1962. *Die Hermeneutik als allgemeine Methodik der Geisteswissenschaften*. Tübingen: Mohr.

Białostocki, Jan. (1973) 1979. Skizze einer Geschichte der beabsichtigten und der interpretierenden Ikonographie. In Kaemmerling, Ekkehard, ed., *Ikonographie und Ikonologie—Bildende Kunst als Zeichensystem*, vol. 1, pp. 15–63. Köln: DuMont.

Bierman, Arthur K. 1962. That there are no iconic signs. *Philosophy and Phenomenological Research* 23: 243–49.

Bierwisch, Manfred. 1979. Musik und Sprache. In *Jahrbuch Peters 1978*, pp. 9–102. Leipzig: Edition Peters.

Billig, Ilse, and List, Sylvia, eds. 1974. *Neue vollständige Blumensprache*. München: Piper.

Binder, Harald. 1975. Zum Verhältnis von verbaler und visueller Kommunikation in Werbebildern. *Linguistik und Didaktik* 21: 85–102.

Birdwhistell, Ray L. (1952) 1954. *Introduction to Kinesics*. Louisville: University, and Ann Arbor: University Microfilm.

———. 1955. Background to kinesics. *ETC* 13: 10–18.

———. 1960. Kinesics and communication. In Carpenter, Edmund, and McLuhan, Marshall, eds., *Explorations in Communication*, pp. 54–64. New York: Beacon.

———. (1961) 1972. Paralanguage 25 years after Sapir. In Laver, John, and Hutcheson, Sandy, eds., *Communication in Face to Face Interaction*, pp. 82–100. Harmondsworth: Penguin.

———. 1963. The kinesic level in the investigation of the emotions. In Knapp, P., ed., *Symposium on Expressions of the Emotions in Man*, pp. 123–39. New York: Int. Univ. Press.

———. 1968. Kinesics. In *International Encyclopedia of the Social Sciences*, vol. 8, pp. 379–85. New York: Macmillan.

———. (1970) 1973. *Kinesics and Context*. Harmondsworth: Penguin.

———. 1974. The language of the body. In Silverstein, Albert, ed., *Human Communication*, pp. 203–220. Hillsdale, N.J.: Erlbaum.

———. 1979. Kinesics. In *International Encyclopedia of the Social Sciences*, vol. 8, pp. 379–85.

Birkhoff, George D. 1932. A mathematical theory of aesthetics. In *The Rice Institute Pamphlets* 5.19, pp. 189–342.

Bitomsky, Hartmut. 1972. *Die Röte des Rots von Technicolor*. Neuwied: Luchterhand.

Black, Max. 1962. *Models and Metaphors*. Ithaca, N.Y.: Cornell Univ. Press.

———. 1968. *The Labyrinth of Language*. New York: Praeger.

———. 1979. More about metaphor. In Ortony, Andrew, ed., *Metaphor and Thought*, pp. 19–43. Cambridge: Cambridge Univ. Press.

Blackmur, Richard P. (1935) 1952. *Language as Gesture*. New York: Harcourt.

Blanchard, Jean-Marc (= Marc Eli). 1975. Sémiostyles: Le rituel de la littérature. *Semiotica* 14: 297–328.

Blanchard, Marc Eli. 1980. *Description: Sign, Self, Desire*. The Hague: Mouton.

Blanke, Detlev. 1985. *Internationale Plansprachen*. Berlin: Akademie-Verlag.

Blest, A. D. 1961. The concept of ritual. In Thorpe, W. H., and Zangwill, D. L., eds., *Current Problems of Animal Behavior*, pp. 102–24. Cambridge: Univ. Press.

Bliss, Charles K. (1949) 1965. *Semantography*. Sydney: Semantography Publications.

Block, Ned, ed. 1981. *Imagery*. Cambridge, Mass.: MIT Press.

Block de Behar, Lisa. 1973. *El lenguaje de la publicidad*. Buenos Aires: Siglo XXI, 1976.

Blonsky, Marshall, ed. 1985. *On Signs*. Baltimore: Johns Hopkins.

Bloomfield, Leonard. 1933. *Language*. New York: Allen & Unwin.

———. (1939) 1974. *Linguistic Aspects of Science*. Chicago: Univ. Press (= Int. Encyclopedia of Unified Science: Foundations 1.4).

Blum, Herwig. 1969. *Die antike Mnemotechnik*. Hildesheim: Olms.

Blumensath, Heinz, ed. 1972. *Strukturalismus in der Literaturwissenschaft*. Köln: Kiepenheuer & Witsch.

Bobes Naves, María del Carmen. (1973) 1979. *La semiótica como teoría lingüística*. Madrid: Gredos.

Bocheński, Joseph M. (1956) 1970. *Formale Logik.* Freiburg: Alber.

———. 1968. *Ancient Formal Logic.* Amsterdam: North Holland.

Boesch, Ernst E. 1983. *Das Magische und das Schöne.* Stuttgart: Frommann-Holzboog.

Boff, Leonardo. 1976. Teología e semiótica. *Vozes* (Petrópolis) 70: 325–34.

Bogart, Leo. 1984. *Strategy in Advertising.* 2nd ed. Chicago: Crain.

Bogatyrev, Petr. (1936) 1976. Costume as a sign. In Matejka, Ladislav, and Titunik, Irwin R., eds., *Semiotics of Art*, pp. 13–19. Cambridge, Mass.: MIT Press.

———. (1937) 1971. *The Functions of Folk Costume in Moravian Slovakia.* The Hague: Mouton.

———. (1938) 1976. Semiotics in the folk theater. In Matejka, Ladislav, and Titunik, Irwin R., eds., *Semiotics of Art*, pp. 33–50. Cambridge, Mass.: MIT Press.

———. (1940) 1976. Forms and functions of folk theater. In Matejka, Ladislav, and Titunik, Irwin R., eds., *Semiotics of Art*, pp. 51–56. Cambridge, Mass.: MIT Press.

Boge, Herbert. 1974. *Griechische Tachygraphie und Tironische Noten.* Hildesheim: Olms.

Böhme, Gernot. 1974. *Zeit und Zahl.* Frankfurt: Klostermann.

Böhme, Karin. 1982. Nonverbale Kommunikation. In Kalgelmann, H. Jürgen, and Wenninger, Gerd, eds., *Medienpsychologie*, pp. 127–33. München: Urban.

Bohn, Volker, ed. 1980. *Literaturwissenschaft. Probleme ihrer theoretischen Grundlegung.* Stuttgart: Kohlhammer.

Boilès, Charles L. 1973. Sémiotique de l'ethnomusicologie. *Musique en jeu* 10: 34–41.

Bolinger, Dwight. 1965. The atomization of meaning. *Language* 41: 555–73.

———. 1975. *Aspects of Language.* 2nd ed. New York: Harcourt.

Bolinger, Dwight, ed. 1972. *Intonation.* Harmondsworth: Penguin.

Bolle, Kees W. 1974. Myth and mythology. In *Encyclopaedia Britannica*, vol. 12, pp. 793–804.

Bollnow, Otto F. 1949. *Das Verstehen.* Mainz: Kirchheim.

———. (1963) 1980. *Mensch und Raum.* Stuttgart: Kohlhammer.

Bolzano, Bernard. (1837a) 1971. *Semiotik*, ed. & intro. Walther, E. Stuttgart: Ed. Rot.

———. (1837b) 1970. *Wissenschaftslehre.* 4 vols. Aalen: Scientia.

———. (1837c) 1973. *Theory of Science*, trans. Terrell, B., ed. Berg, J. Dordrecht: Reidel.

Bonet, Juan Pablo. 1620. *Reduction de las letras, y arte para enseñar a ablar los mudos.* Madrid: F. Abarca de Angulo. (Eng. trans 1890: *Simplification of the Letters of the Alphabet and Method of Teaching Deaf-Mutes to Speak.* Harrogate: Farrar.)

Bonnafont, Claude. 1977. *Les silencieux messages du corps.* Paris: Buchet-Chastel.

Bonner, John Tyler. 1980. *The Evolution of Culture in Animals.* Princeton: Univ. Press.

Bonsiepe, Gui. 1966. Visuell/verbale Rhetorik. *Ulm* (= *Journal of the Ulm School for Design*) 14: 23–40.

Borbé, Tasso, ed. 1984. *Semiotics Unfolding.* 3 vols. Berlin: Mouton.

Bormann, Ernest G. 1980. *Communication Theory.* New York: Holt, Rinehart & Winston.

Born, Karl Erich. 1973. Der Strukturbegriff in der Geschichtswissenschaft. In *Der Strukturbegriff in den Geisteswissenschaften* (= Abhandlungen der Akademie der Wiss. und Lit., Geistes- und Sozialwiss. Klasse 1973, 2), pp. 17–30.

Bosmajian, Haig A. 1971. *The Rhetoric of Nonverbal Communication.* Glenview: Scott.

Boudon, Pierre. 1969. Sur le statut de l'objet: différer l'objet de l'objet. *Communication* 13: 66–86.

———. 1981. *Introduction à une sémiotique des lieux.* Paris: Klincksieck & Montréal: Presses univ.

Bouissac, Paul. 1973. *La mesure des gestes.* The Hague: Mouton.

———. 1976a. *Circus and Culture.* Bloomington: Indiana Univ. Press.

———. 1976b. The "golden legend" of semiotics. *Semiotica* 17: 371–84.

Bouissac, Paul; Herzfeld, Michael; and Posner, Roland, eds. 1986. *Iconicity: Essays on the Nature of Culture; Festschrift for T. A. Sebeok.* Tübingen: Stauffenburg.

Boulding, Kenneth E. (1961) 1977. *The Image.* Ann Arbor: Univ. of Michigan Press.

———. 1968. General systems research: overview. In Buckley, W. E., ed., *Modern Systems Research for the Behavioral Scientist*, pp. 3–10. Chicago: Aldine.

Bourdieu, Pierre. (1970) 1974. *Zur Soziologie der symbolischen Formen.* Frankfurt: Suhrkamp.

———. 1979. *La distinction critique sociale du jugement.* Paris: Minuit.

Bowie, Malcolm. 1979. Jacques Lacan. In Sturrock, John, ed., *Structuralism and Since*, pp. 116–53. Oxford: Univ. Press.

Branigan, Edward. 1984. *Point of View in the Cinema: A Theory of Narration.* Berlin: Mouton.

Brault, Gerard J. 1962. Kinesics and the classroom: Some typical French gestures. *The French Review* 36: 374–82.

Bréal, Michel. (1897) 1924. *Essai de sémantique: Science des significations.* Paris: Hachette.

Brekle, Herbert E. 1964. Semiotik und linguistische

Semantik in Port-Royal. *Indogermanische Forschungen* 69: 103–21.

———. 1972. *Semantik*. München: Fink.

———. 1975. The seventeeth century. In Sebeok, Thomas A., ed., *Current Trends in Linguistics*, vol. 13, pp. 277–382. The Hague: Mouton.

———. 1985. *Einführung in die Geschichte der Sprachwissenschaft*. Darmstadt: Wiss. Buchges.

Bremond, Claude. 1964. Le message narratif. *Communications* 4: 4–32.

———. 1966. La logique des possibles narratifs. *Communications* 8: 60–76.

———. 1968. Pour un gestuaire des bandes dessinées. *Langages* 3: 94–100.

———. 1970. Morphology of the French folktale. *Semiotica* 2: 247–76.

———. 1973. *Logique du récit*. Paris: Seuil.

Bremond, J. C. 1963. Acoustic behavior of birds. In Busnel, R.-G., ed., *Acoustic Behavior of Animals*, pp. 709–750. Amsterdam: Elsevier.

Bright, Michael. 1984. *Animal Language*. Ithaca: Cornell Univ. Press.

Bright, William. 1963. Language and music. *Ethnomusicology* 7: 26–32.

Brinkmann, Hennig. 1975. Kritische Sprachanalyse im Lichte der Zeichentheorie. *Wirkendes Wort* 25: 289–323.

Broadbent, Geoffrey. 1969. Meaning into architecture. In Jencks, Charles, and Baird, George, eds., *Meaning in Architecture*, pp. 51–75. London: Barrie & Jenkins.

Broadbent, Geoffrey, et al., eds. 1980a. *Meaning and Behaviour in the Built Environment*. Chichester: Wiley.

———. 1980b. *Signs, Symbols, and Architecture*. Chichester: Wiley.

Brög, Hans. 1968. *Semiotische und numerische Analyse zweier Holzschnitte von Albrecht Dürer*. Stuttgart: Diss. Phil.

———. 1978. Einige Aspekte zur Bild-Text-Korrelation. In Arbeitsgruppe Semiotik, ed., *Die Einheit der semiotischen Dimensionen*, pp. 11–26. Tübingen: Narr.

———. 1979. *Erweiterung der allgemeinen Semiotik und ihre Anwendung auf die Live-Photographie*. Kastellaun: Henn.

Brög, Hans, ed. 1977. *Probleme der Semiotik unter schulischem Aspekt*. Ravensburg: O. Maier.

Broich, Ulrich, and Pfister, Manfred, eds. 1985. *Intertextualität*. Tübingen: Niemeyer.

Broms, Henri, and Gahmberg, Henrik. 1981. The mythology of the Chrysler crisis. *Kodikas/Code* 3. 233–40.

———. 1987. The grammar of myths—The new cutting edge of marketing. In Umiker-Sebeok, Jean, ed., *Marketing and Signs: New Directions in the Study of Signs for Sale*. Berlin: Mouton de Gruyter.

Bronowski, Jacob. 1967. Human and animal languages. In *To Honor Roman Jakobson*, pp. 374–94. The Hague: Mouton.

Brooke-Rose, Christine. 1958. *A Grammar of Metaphor*. London: Secker & Warburg.

Brown, James W. 1984. Semiotics and foreign language pedagogy. *Degrés* 38, a 1–20.

Brown, Roger L. 1967. *Wilhelm von Humboldt's Conception of Linguistic Relativity*. The Hague: Mouton.

Browne, Robert M. 1971. Typologie des signes littéraires. *Poétique* 2: 334–53.

Brun, Theodore. 1969. *The International Dictionary of Sign Language*. London: Wolfe.

Bruneau, Charles. 1952. Euphémie et euphémisme. In *Festgabe Ernst Gamillscheg*, pp. 11–23. Tübingen: Niemeyer.

Bruneau, Thomas J. 1977. Chronemics: The study of time in human interaction. *Communication, Journal of the Communication Association of the Pacific* (Univ. of Hawaii) 6: 1–30.

———. 1980. Chronemics and the verbal-nonverbal interface. In Key, Mary Ritchie, ed., *The Relationship of Verbal and Nonverbal Communication*, pp. 101–17. The Hague: Mouton.

———. 1985. Silencing and stilling process: The creative and temporal bases of signs. *Semiotica* 56: 279–90.

Brušák, Karel. (1939) 1976. Signs in the Chinese theater. In Matejka, L. and Titunik, I. R., eds., *Semiotics of Art: Prague School Contributions*, pp. 59–73. Cambridge, Mass.: MIT Press.

Bruss, Elizabeth W. 1978. Peirce and Jakobson on the nature of the sign. In Bailey, Richard W., et al., eds., *The Sign: Semiotics around the World*, pp. 81–98. Ann Arbor: Michigan Slav. Pub.

Brütting, Richard. 1975. Linguistische Poetik, Semiotik, Semanalyse. In Brutting, Richard, and Zimmermann, Bernhard, eds., *Theorie—Literatur—Praxis*, pp. 10–30. Frankfurt: Athenäum.

———. 1976. *"écriture" und "texte". Die französische Literaturtheorie "nach dem Strukturalismus"*. Bonn: Bouvier.

Buczyńska-Garewicz, Hanna. 1984. The degenerate sign. In Borbé, Tasso, ed., *Semiotics Unfolding*, vol. 1, pp. 43–50. Berlin: Mouton.

Bühler, Karl. (1933a) 1968. *Ausdruckstheorie*. Stuttgart: Fischer.

———. (1933b) 1982. *The Axiomatization of the Language Sciences*. In Innis, Robert E., *Karl Bühler*, pp. 75–164. New York: Plenum.

———. (1934) 1965. *Sprachtheorie*. Stuttgart: Fischer.

Bühler-Oppenheim, Kristin. 1971. *Zeichen, Marken, Zinken*. Stuttgart: Hatje.

Bühring, Karin. 1973. *Allgemeine Semantik: Sprachkritik und Pädagogik*. Düsseldorf: Schwann.

Bull, Peter. 1983. *Body Movement and Interpersonal Communication*. Chichester: Wiley.

Bullough, E. 1912. "Psychical distance" as a factor in art and as an aesthetic principle. *British Journal of Psychology* 5.2: 87–118.

Bulwer, John. (1644) 1974. *Chirologia: or The Natural Language of the Hand, and Chironomia: or the Art of Manual Rhetoric*. Carbondale: Univ. of Southern Ill. Press.

Bunge, Mario. 1974. *Treatise on Basic Philosophy: I. Semantics I: Sense and Reference*. Dordrecht: Reidel.

Bunn, James H. 1981. *The Dimensionality of Signs, Tools, and Models*. Bloomington: Indiana Univ. Press.

Bureau, Conrad. 1976. *Linguistique fonctionnelle et stylistique objective*. Paris: Presses Univ.

Burghardt, Gordon M. 1970. Defining "Communication." In Johnston, James W., et al., eds., *Communication by Chemical Signal*, pp. 5–18. New York: Appleton.

Burgin, Victor, ed. 1982. *Thinking Photography*. London: Macmillan.

Burgoon, Judee K. 1980. Nonverbal communication research in the 1970s. *Communication Yearbook* 4: 179–97.

Burke, Kenneth. (1950) 1969. *A Rhetoric of Motives*. Berkeley: Univ. of California Press.

Burke, Peter. 1985. *Vico*. Oxford: Univ. Press.

Burkhardt, Dietrich; Schleidt, Wolfgang; and Altner, Helmut, eds. 1966. *Signale der Tierwelt*. München: Moos.

Burkhardt, Hans. 1980. *Logik und Semiotik in der Philosophie von Leibniz*. München: Philosophia.

Burks, Arthur W. 1949. Icon, index, and symbol. *Philosophy and Phenomenological Research* 9: 673–89.

———. 1981. Man: Sign, or algorithm. In Steiner, Wendy, ed., *Image and Code*, pp. 57–70. Ann Arbor: Univ. of Michigan.

Burnham, Jack. (1971) 1973. *The Structure of Art*. New York: Braziller.

———. 1974. *Great Western Salt Works*. New York: Braziller.

Bursill-Hall, G. L. 1971. *Speculative Grammars of the Middle Ages*. The Hague: Mouton.

———. 1976. Some notes on the grammatical theory of Boethius of Dacia. In Parret, H., ed., *History of Linguistic Thought*, pp. 164–88. Berlin: de Gruyter.

Burzlaff, Werner. 1978. Semiotische Taxonomie des kinetischen Bildes. In Arbeitsgruppe Semiotik, ed., *Die Einheit der semiotischen Dimension*, pp. 217–32. Tübingen: Narr.

Busnel, René-Guy. 1977. Acoustic communication. In Sebeok, Thomas A., ed., *How Animals Communicate*, pp. 233–51. Bloomington: Indiana Univ. Press.

Busnel, René-Guy, ed. 1963. *Acoustic Behaviour of Animals*. Amsterdam: Elsevier.

Busnel, René-Guy, and Classe, André. 1976. *Whistled Languages*. Berlin: Springer.

Busse, Klaus-Peter, and Riemenschneider, Hartmut. 1979. *Grundlagen semiotischer Ästhetik*. Düsseldorf: Schwann.

Busse, Winfried. 1971. Das literarische Zeichen. In Ihwe, Jens, ed., *Literaturwissenschaft und Linguistik*, vol. 2, pp. 437–53. Frankfurt: Athenäum.

———. 1975. Funktionen und Funktion der Sprache. In Schlieben-Lange, Brigitte, ed., *Sprachtheorie*, pp. 207–240. Hamburg: Hoffmann & Campe.

Busse, Winfried, and Trabant, Jürgen, eds. 1986. *Les idéologues*. Amsterdam: Benjamins.

Buyssens, Eric. 1943. *Les langages et le discours*. Bruxelles: Office de la Publicité. (Revised ed.: *La communication et l'articulation linguistique*. Bruxelles and Paris: Presses Universitaires, 1967.)

———. 1956. Le langage par gestes chez les moines. *Revue de l'Institut de Sociologie* 29: 537–45.

———. 1967. *La communication et l'articulation linguistique*. Bruxelles and Paris: Presses Universitaires. (Revised ed. of *Les langages et le discours*. Bruxelles: Office de la Publicité, 1943.)

Bystrina, Ivan. 1989. *Kultursemiotik*. Tübingen: Stauffenburg.

Calabrese, Omar. 1980. From the semiotics of painting to the semiotics of pictorial text. *Versus* 25: 3–27.

———. 1986. Iconology. In Sebeok, Thomas A., ed., *Encyclopedic Dictionary of Semiotics*, pp. 330–32. Berlin: Mouton de Gruyter.

Calabrese, Omar, ed. 1980. *Semiotica della pittura*. Milano: Il Saggiatore.

Calabrese, Omar, and Mucci, Edigio. 1975. *Guida a la semiotica*. Firenze: Sansoni.

Calame, Claude. 1982. Le discours mythique. In Coquet, Jean-Claude, et al., *Sémiotique. L'école de Paris*, pp. 85–102. Paris: Hachette.

Callaghan, William J. 1986. Charles Sanders Peirce: His general theory of signs. *Semiotica* 61: 123–61.

Calloud, Jean. 1973. Sémio-linguistique et texte liturgique. *La Maison Dieu* 114: 36–58.

Calvet, Louis-Jean. 1975. *Pour et contre Saussure*. Paris: Payot.

Calvet de Magalhaes, Teresa. 1981. *Signe ou symbole: Introduction à la théorie sémiotique de C. S. Peirce*. Louvain-la-Neuve: Cabay.

Camhy, Daniela. 1984. Sematologie als Grundlagenwissenschaft. In Eschbach, A., ed., *Bühler-Studien*, vol. 1, pp. 98–114. Frankfurt: Suhrkamp.

Campeanu, Pavel. 1975. Un rôle secondaire: le spectateur. In Helbo, André, et al., *Sémiologie de la représentation*, pp. 96–111. Brüssel: Ed. Complexe.

Cannon, Walter B. (1932) 1960. *The Wisdom of the Body*. New York: Norton.

Canoa Galiana, Joaquina. 1977. *Semiología de las "Comedias bárbaras."* Madrid: Cupsa.

Canter, David. 1977. *The Psychology of Place*. London: Architectural Press.

Caprettini, Gian Paolo. 1970. Grammatica del fumetto. *Strumenti critici* 4 (13): 318–26.

———. 1980. *Aspetti della semiotica*. Torino: Einaudi.

Capurro, Rafael. 1978. *Information*. München: K. G. Saur.

Carillo, Francisco. 1982. *Semiolingüística de la novela picaresca*. Madrid: Ed. Cátedra.

Carnap, Rudolf. (1928) 1961. *Der logische Aufbau der Welt*. Hamburg: Meiner.

———. (1942/43) 1975. *Introduction to Semantics and Formalization of Logic*. 2 vols. in 1. Cambridge: Harvard Univ. Press.

———. 1947. *Meaning and Necessity*. Chicago: Univ. Press.

———. (1954) 1958. *Introduction to Symbolic Logic and Its Applications*. New York: Dover.

Carontini, Enrico. (1983) 1984. *L'action du signe*. Louvain-la-Neuve: Cabray.

Carontini, Enrico, and Péraya, Daniel. 1975. *Le projet sémiotique*. Paris: Delarge.

Carroll, John M. 1980. *Toward a Structural Psychology of Cinema*. The Hague: Mouton.

Carter, Curtis L. 1972. Syntax in language and painting. *The Structurist* 12: 45–50.

———. 1976. Painting and language. *Leonardo* 9: 111–18.

Carzo, Domenico, and Jackson, Bernard, eds. 1985. *Semiotics, Law, and Social Science*. Roma: Gagnemi & Liverpool: Liv. Law Review.

Casetti, Francesco. 1974. "Nuova" semiotica, "nuovo" cinema. *Ikon* 88–89: 275–346.

———. 1977. *Semiotica*. Milano: Edizione Academica.

———. 1978. *Teorie del cinema: Dal dopoguerra a oggi*. Milano: Espresso.

Cassirer, Ernst A. (1922–38) 1969. *Wesen und Wirkung des Symbolbegriffs*. Darmstadt: Wiss. Buchges.

———. (1923, 1925, 1929) 1957. *The Philosophy of Symbolic Forms*. 3 vols. New Haven: Yale Univ. Press.

———. (1935–45) 1979. *Symbol, Myth, and Culture*. New Haven: Yale Univ. Press.

———. (1944) 1948. *An Essay on Man*. New Haven: Yale Univ. Press.

———. 1945. Structuralism in modern linguistics. *Word* 1: 99–120.

Castagnano, Raúl H. 1974. *Semiótica, ideología y teatro hispanoamericano contemporáneo*. Buenos Aires: Nova.

Catford, J. C. 1965. *A Linguistic Theory of Translation*. London: Oxford Univ. Press.

Cazimir, Bogdan. 1976. Sémiologie musicale linguistique mathématique. *Semiotica* 15: 48–57.

Cebik, L. B. 1984. *Fictional Narrative and Truth*. Lanham, Md.: Univ. Press of America.

Cegarra, Michel. 1970. Cinéma et sémiologie. *Cinétique* 7–8: 25–63.

Cerbrián-Herreros, Mariano. 1978. *Introducción al lenguaje de la televisión: Una perspectiva semiótica*. Madrid: Pirámide.

Cerisola, Pier Luigi. 1980. *La critica semiotico-strutturalistica*. Roma: Edizioni studium.

Chabrol, Claude. 1971. *Le récit féminin*. The Hague: Mouton.

Chabrol, Claude, ed. 1973. *Sémiotique narrative et textuelle*. Paris: Larousse.

Chabrol, Claude, and Marin, Louis, eds. 1971. *Sémiotique narrative: récits bibliques* (= *Langages* [Paris] 22).

———. 1974. *Le récit évangélique*. Paris: Aubier Montaigne.

Chao, Yuen Ren. 1968. *Language and Symbolic Systems*. Cambridge: University Press.

Charaudeau, Patrick. 1983. *Langage et discours: Eléments de sémiolinguistique*. Paris: Hachette.

Chateau, Dominique. 1986. *Le cinéma comme langage*. Paris: Editions l'Association Internationale pour la Sémiologie du Spectacle/Publications de la Sorbonne ACEV.

Chateau, Dominique, and Jost, François. 1979. *Nouveau cinéma, nouvelle sémiologie*. Paris: Union Générale d'Editions.

Chatman, Seymor. 1974. Rhetoric and semiotics. In Chatman, Seymor, et al., eds., *A Semiotic Landscape*, pp. 103–12. The Hague: Mouton.

———. 1978. *Story and Discourse*. Ithaca: Cornell Univ. Press.

———. 1980. What novels can do that films can't. *Critical Inquiry* 7.1: 121–40.

Chatman, Seymour, ed. 1971. *Literary Style*. London: Oxford Univ. Press.

Chatman, Seymour, et al., eds. 1979. *A Semiotic Landscape*. The Hague: Mouton.

Chébat, Jean-Charles, and Hénault, Georges M. 1974. L'apport de la perception séquentielle et de la théorie de l'information á la sémiologie publicitaire. *Canadian Journal of Research in Semiotics* 2.1: 3–13.

Chébat, Jean-Charles, and Lindekens, René. 1975. Les paradoxes logico-sémantiques en publicité. *Canadian Journal of Semiotics* 3.1: 37–50.

Cherry, Colin. (1957) 1970. *On Human Communication*. Cambridge, Mass.: MIT Press.

———. 1980. The communication explosion. In Foster, Mary LeCron, and Brandes, Stanley H., eds., *Symbol as Sense*, pp. 249–67. New York: Academic Press.

Chetwynd, Tom. 1982. *A Dictionary of Symbols*. London: Granada.

Chevalier-Skolnikoff, Suzanne. 1973. Facial expression of emotion in nonhuman primates. In Ekman, Paul, ed., *Darwin and Facial Expression*, pp. 11–89. New York: Academic Press.

Choay, Françoise. (1972) 1976. Semiotik und Urbanismus. In *Konzept 3: Die Stadt als Text*, pp. 43–60. Tübingen: Wasmuth.

Chomsky, Noam. 1979. Human language and other semiotic systems. *Semiotica* 25: 31–44.

Chouinard, Timothy. 1970. The symbol and the archetype. *Journal of Analytical Psychology* 15: 155–67.

Christensen, Bjarne Westring. 1967. Glossématique, linguistique fonctionnelle, grammaire générative et stratification du langage. *Word* 23: 57–73.

Chvatík, Květoslav. 1983. Die ästhetische Einstellung. *Zeitschrift für Semiotik* 5: 229–42.

———. 1984. Jan Mukařovský, Husserl, and Carnap. *Zeitschrift für Semiotik* 6: 421–31.

Chydenius, Johan. 1960. *The Theory of Medieval Symbolism*. Helsingfors: Centraltryckeriet (= Societas Scientiarium Fennica, Commentationes Humanarum Litterarum 27.2).

Cirne, Moacy. 1972. *Para ler os quadrinhos*. Petrópolis: Ed. Vozes.

Clarke, D. S., Jr. 1987. *Principles of Semiotic*. London: Routledge & Kegan.

Clarke, Simon. 1981. *The Foundations of Structuralism*. Totowa, N.J.: Barnes & Noble.

Cohen, Einya; Namir, Lila; and Schlesinger, I. M. 1977. *A New Dictionary of Sign Language*. The Hague: Mouton.

Cohen, Jean. 1966. *Structure du langage poétique*. Paris: Flammarion.

Cohen, Jonathan. 1954. On the project of a universal character. *Mind* 63: 49–63.

Cohen, Marcel. 1958. *La grande invention de l'écriture et son évolution*. Paris: Klincksieck.

Coker, Wilson. 1972. *Music and Meaning*. New York: Free Press.

Colin, Jean-Paul. 1973. Rhétorique et stylistique. In Pottier, Bernard, ed., *Le langage*, pp. 254–71. Paris: CEPL.

Colin, Michel. 1980. 'Deux ou trois choses que je sais d'elle' (Notes pour une grammaire du texte filmique). *Kodikas/Code* 2.1: 27–38.

Collins, Peter. 1965. *Changing Ideals in Modern Architecture*. London: Faber & Faber.

Collis, Dermot Ronán F. 1971. *Pour une sémiologie de l'esquimau*. Paris: Dunod.

Comenius, Johann Amos. (1668) 1938. *The Way of Light*. Liverpool: Univ. Press.

Compagnon, Antoine. 1979. *La seconde main*. Paris: Seuil.

Comrie, Bernard. 1981. *Language Universals and Linguistic Typology*. Oxford: Blackwell.

Condillac, Etienne B. de. (1746) 1947. *Essai sur l'origine des connaissances humaines*. In Condillac, E. B. de, *Oeuvres philosophiques*, vol. 1, pp. 1–118. Paris: Presses Univ. de France.

Condon, John C. 1977. When people talk with people. In Civikly, Jean M., ed., *Messages*, 2nd ed., pp. 68–82. New York.

Conklin, Harold C. 1959. Linguistic play in its cultural context. *Language* 35: 631–35.

Conte, Maria-Elizabeth. 1976. Semantische und pragmatische Ansätze in der Sprachtheorie Wilhelm von Humboldts. In Parret, H., ed., *History of Linguistic Thought and Contemporary Linguistics*, pp. 616–32. Berlin: de Gruyter.

Cook, Daniel J. 1973. *Language in the Philosophy of Hegel*. The Hague: Mouton.

Cooke, Deryk. 1959. *The Language of Music*. Oxford: Univ. Press.

Cooper, David E. 1986. *Metaphor*. Oxford: Blackwell.

Cooper, William E., and Ross, John Robert. 1975. World order. In Grossman, R. E., et al., eds., *Papers from the Parasession on Functionalism*, pp. 63–111. Chicago: Ling. Society.

Coppieters, Frank, and Goyvaerts, Didier L., eds. 1978. *Functional Studies in Language and Literature*. Ghent: Story-Scientia.

Coquet, Jean-Claude. 1973. *Sémiotique littéraire*. Tours: Mame.

———. 1985. Eléments de bio-bibliographie. In Parret, Herman, and Ruprecht, Hans-George, eds., *Aims and Prospects of Semiotics*, pp. liii–lxxxv. Amsterdam: Benjamins.

Coquet, Jean-Claude, et al. 1982. *Sémiotique. L'école de Paris*. Paris: Hachette.

Corbett, Edward P. J. 1965. *Classical Rhetoric for the Modern Student*. New York: Oxford Univ. Press.

Corder, S. Pit. 1966. *The Visual Element in Language Teaching*. London: Longman.

Cornelius, Paul. 1965. *Languages in the 17th- and Early 18th-Century Imaginary Voyages*. Genève: Droz.

Corner, John, and Hawthorn, Jeremy, eds. 1980. *Communication Studies*. London: Arnold.

Cornett, R. Orin. 1967. Cued speech. *American Annals of the Deaf* 112: 3–13.

Cornu, Geneviève. 1985. La lecture de l'image publicitaire. *Semiotica* 54: 405–28.

———. 1987. L'évolution des pôles de la communication: L'idée de publicité. *Semiotica* 63: 269–97.

Corti, Maria. 1973. Il linguaggio della publicita. In Beccaria, Gian Luigi, ed., *I linguaggi settoriale in Italia*, pp. 119–39. Milan: Bompiani.

———. 1978. *An Introduction to Literary Semiotics*. Bloomington: Indiana Univ. Press.

Corvez, Maurice. 1969. *Les structuralistes*. Paris: Aubier-Montaigne.

Corvin, Michel. 1973. Approche sémiologique d'un texte dramatique. *Littérature* 9: 86–100.

Coseriu, Eugenio. (1962) 1975. *Sprachtheorie und allgemeine Sprachwissenschaft*. München: Fink.

———. 1967. L'arbitraire du signe. *Archiv für das Studium der neueren Sprachen und Literaturen* 204: 81–112.

———. (1970) 1975, and 1972. *Die Geschichte der Sprachphilosophie von der Antike bis zur Gegenwart*. 2 vols. Tübingen: TBL.

———. 1973. *Probleme der strukturellen Semantik*. Tübingen: Narr.

———. 1975. *Sprachtheorie und allgemeine Sprachwissenschaft*. München: Fink.

———. 1981. *Textlinguistik*. 2nd ed. Tübingen: Narr.

Coseriu, Eugenio, and Geckeler, Horst. 1974. Linguistics and semantics. In Sebeok, Thomas A., ed., *Current Trends in Linguistics*, vol. 12, pt. 1, pp. 103–171. The Hague: Mouton.

Cossette, Claude. 1982. *How Pictures Speak: A Brief Introduction to Iconics*. Québec: Ed. Riguil Int.

Costadeau, Alphonse. (1917) 1983. *Traité des signes*, vol. 1, ed. Le Guern-Forel, O. Bern: Lang.

Coulmas, Florian. 1981. *Über Schrift*. Frankfurt: Suhrkamp.

Coulmas, Florian, and Ehlich, Konrad, eds. 1983. *Writing in Focus*. Berlin: de Gruyter.

Count, Earl W. 1973. *Being and Becoming Human*. New York: Van Nostrand.

Courtés, Joseph. 1976. *Introduction à la sémiotique narrative et discursive*. Paris: Hachette.

———. 1985. Sémiotique et théologie du péché. In Parret, Herman, and Ruprecht, Hans-George, eds., *Exigences et perspectives de la sémiotique*, pp. 863–903. Amsterdam: Benjamins.

Couturat, Louis. (1901) 1961. *La logique de Leibniz*. Hildesheim: Olms.

Couturat, Louis, and Leau, Léopold. (1903) 1979. *Histoire de la langue universelle*. Hildesheim: Olms.

Coward, Rosalind, and Ellis, John. 1977. *Language and Materialism: Developments in Semiology and the Theory of the Subject*. London: Routledge.

Cram, David. 1985. Language universals and 17th century universal language schemes. In Dutz, K. D., and Kaczmarek, L., eds., *Rekonstruktion und Interpretation*, pp. 243–57. Tübingen: Narr.

Cranach, Mario von, and Ellgring, Johann Heinrich. 1973. Problems in the recognition of gaze direction. In Cranach, Mario von, and Vine, Jan, eds., *Social Communication and Movement*, pp. 419–43. London: Academic Press.

Cranach, Mario von, and Vine, Jan, eds. 1973. *Social Communication and Movement [. . .] in Man and Chimpanzee*. New York: Academic Press.

Cranach, Mario von, et al., eds. 1979. *Human Ethology*. Cambridge: Univ. Press.

Critchley, MacDonald. 1975. *Silent Language*. London: Butterworths.

Croy, Peter. 1972. *Signs and Their Messages: Signs, Symbols, Trade Marks*. Göttingen: Musterschmidt.

Crystal, David. 1969. *Prosodic Systems and Intonation in English*. Cambridge: Univ. Press.

———. 1975. *The English Tone of Voice*. London: Arnold.

———. 1980. *Introduction to Language Pathology*. London: Arnold.

———. 1987. *The Cambridge Encyclopedia of Language*. Cambridge: Univ. Press.

Crystal, David, and Craig, Elma. 1978. Contrived sign language. In Schlesinger, I. M., and Namir, Lila, eds., *Sign Language of the Deaf*, pp. 141–68. New York: Academic Press.

Crystal, David, and Davy, Derek. (1969) 1976. *Investigating English Style*. London: Longman.

Crystal, David, and Quirk, Randolph. 1964. *Systems of Prosodic and Paralinguistic Features in English*. The Hague: Mouton.

Csikszentmihalyi, Mihaly, and Rochberg-Halton, Eugene. 1981. *The Meaning of Things*. Cambridge: Univ. Press.

Cullen, J. M. 1972. Some principles of animal communication. In Hinde, R. A., ed., *Non-Verbal Communication*, pp. 101–25. Cambridge: Univ. Press.

Culler, Jonathan. 1975. *Structuralist Poetics*. London: Routledge.

———. 1976. *Saussure*. Glasgow: Collins.

———. (1981a) 1983. *The Pursuit of Signs*. Ithaca: Cornell Univ. Press.

———. 1981b. Semiotics: Communication and signification. In Steiner, Wendy, ed., *Image and Code*, pp. 78–84. Ann Arbor: Univ. of Michigan.

———. (1982) 1983. *On Deconstruction*. London: Routledge & Kegan.

———. 1983. *Barthes*. Glasgow: Fontana.

Culley, Robert C. 1976. *Studies in the Structure of Hebrew Narrative*. Philadelphia: Fortress Press.

Cunningham, Donald J. 1985. Semiosis and learning. In Deely, J., ed., *Semiotics 1984*, pp. 427–34. Lanham: Univ. Press of America.

———. 1987a. Semiotics and education. In Sebeok, Thomas A., and Umiker-Sebeok, Jean, eds., *The*

Semiotic Web, 1986, pp. 367–78. Berlin: Mouton de Gruyter.

———. 1987b. Outline of an education semiotic. *American Journal of Semiotics* 5: 201–216.

Cuny, Xavier. 1972. L'approche psycho-sémiologique: étude d'un code gestuel de travail. *Cahiers de linguistique théorique appliquée* 9: 261–75.

Curtius, Ernst Robert. (1948) 1969. *Europäische Literatur und lateinisches Mittelalter*. Bern: Francke.

Dalgarno, George. (1661) 1968. *Ars signorum, vulgo character universalis et lingua philosophica*. Menston: Scolar.

———. (1680) 1971. *Didascalocophus*. Menston: Scolar..

Damisch, Hubert. 1975. Semiotics and iconography. In Sebeok, Thomas A., ed., *The Tell Tale Sign*, pp. 27–36. Lisse: de Ridder.

———. 1978. Eight theses for (or against?) a semiology of painting. *Enclitics* 3.1: 1–15.

Damm, Janne. 1876. *Praktische Pasigraphie*. Leipzig: Douffet.

Daniels, Les. 1971. *Comix: A History of Comic Books in America*. New York: E. P. Dutton.

Danto, Arthur C. 1965. *Analytical Philosphy of History*. Cambridge: Univ. Press.

———. 1981. *The Transfiguration of the Commonplace*. Cambridge, Mass.: Harvard Univ. Press.

D'Aquili, Eugene G., et al., eds. 1979. *The Spectrum of Ritual*. New York: Columbia Univ. Press.

Darrault, Ivan. 1985. La psychosémiotique. In Parret, H., and Ruprecht, H.-G., eds., *Exigences et perspectives de la sémiotique*, pp. 583–92. Amsterdam: Benjamins.

Darwin, Charles. (1872) 1892. *The Expression of the Emotions in Man and Animals*. London: Murray.

Dascal, Marcelo. 1978. *La sémiologie de Leibniz*. Paris: Aubier-Montaigne.

———. 1983. Signs [. . .] in the history of semiotics. In Eschbach, A., and Trabant, J., eds., *History of Semiotics*, pp. 169–90. Amsterdam: Benjamins.

———. 1987. *Leibniz: Language, Signs, and Thought*. Amsterdam: Benjamins.

Daube-Schackat, Roland. 1988. Zur Verhältnisbestimmung von Semiotik und Hermeneutik. In Claussen, R., and Daube-Schackat, R., eds., *Gedankenzeichen*, pp. 123–34. Tübingen: Stauffenburg.

David, Madeleine V.-. 1965. *Le débat sur les écritures et l'hiéroglyphe au XVIIᵉ et XVIIIᵉ sciècles*. Paris: S.E.V.P.E.N.

Davidsen, Ole. 1981. Der Status der Religionssemiotik als autonomer Wissenschaft. *Linguistica Biblica* 49: 71–84.

Davidson, Donald. (1967) 1971. Truth and meaning. In Rosenberg, Jay F., and Travis, Charles,

eds., *Readings in the Philosophy of Language*, pp. 450–65. Englewood Cliffs, N.J.: Prentice Hall.

———. 1978. What metaphors mean. *Critical Inquiry* 5: 31–47.

Davidson, Julian M., and Davidson, Richard J., eds. 1980. *The Psychobiology of Consciousness*. New York: Plenum.

Davies, H. Neville. 1967. Bishop Godwin's "lunatic language." *Journal of the Warburg and Cortauld Institute* 30: 296–316.

Davis, Martha, comp. (1972) 1982. *Understanding Body Movement: An Annotated Bibliography*. Bloomington: Indiana Univ. Press.

Davis, Martha, and Skupien, Janet, comps. 1982. *Body Movement and Nonverbal Communication: An Annotated Bibliography, 1971–81*. Bloomington: Indiana Univ. Press.

Dawkins, Richard. (1976) 1981. *The Selfish Gene*. Oxford: Univ. Press.

Dawkins, Richard, and Krebs, John R. 1978. Animal signals: Information or manipulation. In Krebs, J. R., and Davies, N. B., eds., *Behavioral Ecology*, pp. 282–309. Oxford: Blackwell.

Deák, František. 1976. Structuralism in theatre: The Prague School contribution. *The Drama Review* 20.4: 83–94.

de Beaugrande, Robert. See Beaugrande, Robert de.

Dechert, Hans W., and Raupach, Manfred, eds. 1980. *Temporal Variables in Speech*. The Hague: Mouton.

Deely, John N. 1974. The two approaches to language . . . Jean Poinsot's semiotic. *The Thomist* 38: 856–907.

———. 1982. *Introducing Semiotic: Its History and Doctrine*. Bloomington: Indiana Univ. Press.

Deely, John. 1985. Semiotic and the liberal arts. *The New Scholasticism* 59: 296–322.

———. 1986a. On the notion of phytosemiotics. In Deely, J., et al., eds., *Frontiers in Semiotics*, pp. 96–103. Bloomington: Indiana Univ. Press.

———. 1986b. Semiotic as framework and direction. In Deely, J., et al., eds., *Frontiers in Semiotics*, pp. 264–71. Bloomington: Indiana Univ. Press.

Deely, John N. 1988. The semiotic of John Poinsot: Yesterday and tomorrow. *Semiotica* 69: 31–127.

Deely, John, ed. 1986. *Semiotics 1985*. Lanham, Md.: Univ. Press of America.

Deely, John, et al., eds. 1986. *Frontiers in Semiotics*. Bloomington: Indiana Univ. Press.

De Fusco, Renato. 1971. Eine Vorausschau auf die architektonische Semiotik. *werk* 58: 251–53.

Degérando, M.-J. 1800. *Des signes et de l'art de penser considérés dans leurs rapports mutuels*. Paris: Etienne.

De Lacy, Estelle. 1938. Meaning and methodology

in Hellenistic philosophy. *Philosophical Review* 47: 390–409.

De Lacy, Phillip H. 1986. Plato. In Sebeok, Thomas A., ed., *Encyclopedic Dictionary of Semiotics*, pp. 735–36. Berlin: Mouton de Gruyter.

De Lacy, Phillip H., and De Lacy, Estelle A., eds. 1941. *Philodemus: On Methods of Inference*. Philadelphia: American Philological Association (= Philological Monographs 10).

Delahaye, Yves. 1977. *La frontière et le texte: Pour une sémiotique des relations internationales*. Paris: Payot.

Delas, Daniel, and Filliolet, Jacques. 1973. *Linguistique et poétique*. Paris: Larousse.

De Lauretis, T. See Lauretis, T. de.

Deledalle, Gérard. 1979. *Théorie et pratique du signe*. Paris: Payot.

––––––. 1981. Le representamen et l'objet dans la *semiosis* de Charles S. Peirce. *Semiotica* 33: 195–200.

––––––. 1987. *Charles S. Peirce*. Amsterdam: Benjamins.

Delorme, Jean, and Geoltrain, Pierre. 1982. Le discours religieux. In Coquet, Jean-Claude, ed., *Sémiotique: L'école de Paris*, pp. 103–126. Paris: Hachette.

Delormel, Jean. 1795. *Projet d'une langue universelle*. Paris.

DeLozier, M. Wayne. 1976. *The Marketing Communication Process*. New York: McGraw Hill.

De Marinis, Marco. 1975. Problemi e aspetti di un approccio semiotico al teatro. *Lingua e Stile* 10: 343–57.

––––––. 1978–79. Lo spettacolo come testo. *Versus* 21: 66–104, and 22: 3–31.

––––––. 1982. *Semiotica del teatro*. Milano: Bompiani.

De Marinis, Marco, and Magli, Patrizia. 1975. Materiali bibliografici per una semiotica del teatro. *Versus* 11: 53–128.

De Mauro, T. See Mauro, T. de.

DeMott, Benjamin. 1955. Comenius and the real character in England. *PMLA* 70: 1068–81.

Derossi, Giorgio. 1965. *Segno e struttura linguistici nel pensiero de Ferdinand de Saussure*. Udine: del Bianco.

Derrida, Jacques. (1967a) 1976. *Of Grammatology*. Baltimore: Johns Hopkins Univ. Press.

––––––. (1967b) 1973. *Speech and Phenomena and Other Essays on Husserl's Theory of Signs*. Evanston: Northwestern Univ. Press.

––––––. (1967c) 1978. *Writing and Difference*. Chicago: Univ. Press.

––––––. 1968. Sémiologie et grammatologie. *Information sur les sciences sociales* 7: 135–48.

––––––. 1978. *La vérité en peinture*. Paris: Flammarion.

Descartes, René. 1629. Lettre à Mersenne, 20 nov. 1629. In Descartes, René, *Oeuvres et Lettres*, pp. 911–15. Paris: Gallimard, 1953.

Descombes, Vincent. (1983) 1986. *Objects of All Sorts*. Oxford: Blackwell.

Detel, Wolfgang. 1982. Zeichen bei Parmenides. *Zeitschrift für Semiotik* 4: 221–39.

Deuchar, Margaret. 1984. *British Sign Language*. London: Routledge & Kegan.

Deutsch, F. 1952. Analytic posturology. *Psychoanalytic Quarterly* 21: 196–214.

DeVore, Irven, ed. 1965. *Primate Behavior*. New York: Holt.

Dewey, John. 1946. Peirce's theory of linguistic signs, thought, and meaning. *Journal of Philosophy* 43: 85–95.

Dichter, Ernest. 1960. *The Strategy of Desire*. Garden City: Doubleday.

Dierkes, Hans, and Kiesel, Helmuth. 1973. Interpretative Bemerkungen zu A. J. Greimas: "Strukturale Semantik." *Linguistik und Didaktik* 14: 146–61.

Dierse, U., and Romberg, R. 1976. Ideologie. In Ritter, Joachim, ed., *Historisches Wörterbuch der Philosophie*, vol. 4, pp. 158–86. Basel: Schwabe.

Díez Borque, José M., and García Lorenzo, Luciano, eds. 1975. *Semiología de teatro*. Barcelona: Planeta.

Dijk, Teun A. van. 1972. *Some Aspects of Text Grammars*. The Hague: Mouton.

––––––. 1976. Narrative macro-structures: Logical and cognitive foundations. *PTL: Journal for Descriptive Poetics and Theory of Literature* 1: 547–68.

––––––. 1980a. Story comprehension. *Poetics* 9: 1–21.

––––––. 1980b. *Textwissenschaft*. München: dtv.

Dijk, Teun A. van, ed. 1985. *Handbook of Discourse Analysis*. 4 vols. London: Academic Press.

Dijk, Teun A. van, et al. (1972) 1974. *Zur Bestimmung narrativer Strukturen auf der Grundlage von Textgrammatiken*. Hamburg: Buske.

Dijk, Teun A. van, and Petöfi, János S., eds. 1977. *Grammars and Descriptions*. Berlin: de Gruyter.

Dik, Simon C. 1978. *Functional Grammar*. Amsterdam: North Holland.

Dilthey, Wilhelm. (1892) 1968. Die drei Epochen der modernen Ästhetik. In Dilthey, W., *Gesammelte Schriften*, vol. 6, 5th ed., pp. 242–87. Göttingen: Vandenhoeck & Ruprecht.

––––––. (1900) 1968. Die Entstehung der Hermeneutik. In Dilthey, W., *Gesammelte Schriften*, vol. 5, 5th ed., pp. 317–31. Göttingen: Vandenhoeck & Ruprecht.

––––––. (1905) 1958. Der psychische Strukturzusammenhang. In Dilthey, W., *Gesammelte*

Schriften, vol. 7, pp. 3–23. Göttingen: Vandenhoeck & Ruprecht.

———. 1958. *Gesammelte Schriften*, vol. 7. Göttingen: Vandenhoeck & Ruprecht.

Dingwall, William Orr. 1980. Human communicative behavior. In Rauch, Irmengard, and Carr, Gerald F., *The Signifying Animal*, pp. 51–86. Bloomington: Indiana Univ. Press.

Dinu, Mihai. 1968. Structures linguistiques probabilistes issues de l'étude du théâtre. *Cahiers de lingusitique théorique et appliquée* 5: 29–46.

———. 1972. L'interdépendance syntagmatique des scènes dans une pièce de théâtre. *Cahiers de linguistique théorique et appliquée* 9: 55–69.

Diringer, David. 1962. *Writing*. London: Thames & Hudson.

Dittmann, Allen T. 1978. The role of body movement in communication. In Siegman, Aron W., and Feldstein, Stanley, eds., *Nonverbal Communication*, pp. 69–95. Hillsdale: Erlbaum.

Dobnig-Jülch, Edeltraud, et al. 1981. Videoeinsatz bei der Erforschung asymmetrischer Kommunikation. In Lange-Seidl, A., ed., *Zeichenkonstitution*, vol. 2, pp. 159–67. Berlin: de Gruyter.

Doležel, Lubomír. 1972. From motifemes to motifs. *Poetics* 4: 55–90.

———. 1976. Narrative semantics. *PTL: Journal for Descriptive Poetics and Theory of Literature* 1: 129–51.

Doležel, Lubomír, and Kraus, Jiří. 1972. Prague School stylistics. In Kachru, Braj B., and Stahlke, Herbert F. W., eds., *Current Trends in Stylistics*, pp. 37–48. Edmonton, Alta.: Ling. Research, Inc.

D'Ollone, Max. 1952. *Le langage musical*. 2 vols. Paris: La Palatine.

Donato, Eugenio. 1967. Of structuralism and literature. *Modern Language Notes* 82: 549–74.

Doob, Leonard. 1971. *Patterning of Time*. New Haven: Yale Univ. Press.

Dorfles, Gillo. 1969. Structuralism and semiology in architecture. In Jencks, Charles, and Baird, George, eds., *Meaning in Architecture*, pp. 39–49. London: Barrie & Jenkins.

Dorfman, Eugene. 1969. *The Narreme in the Medieval Romance Epic*. Toronto: Univ. Press.

Dörner, Dietrich. 1977. Superzeichen und kognitive Prozesse. In Posner, Roland, and Reinecke, Hans-Peter, eds., *Zeichenprozesse*, pp. 73–82. Wiesbaden: Athenaion.

Dorner-Bachmann, Hannelotte. 1979. *Erzählstruktur und Texttheorie*. Hildesheim: Olms.

Douglas, Mary. (1970) 1982. *Natural Symbols*. New York: Pantheon.

Douglas, Mary, and Isherwood, Baron. (1979) 1982. *The World of Goods*. New York: Norton.

Downs, Roger M., and Stea, David. 1977. *Maps in Minds*. New York: Harper & Row.

Drechsel, Wiltrud Ulrike, et al. 1975. *Massenzeichenware: Die gesellschaftliche und ideologische Funktion der Comics*. Frankfurt: Suhrkamp.

Dressler, Wolfgang U., et al. 1987. *Leitmotifs in Natural Morphology*. Amsterdam: Benjamins.

Dreyer, Claus. 1979. *Semiotische Grundlagen der Architekturästhetik*. Stuttgart: Diss. Phil.

———. 1984. Neuere Tendenzen in der Architektursemiotik. *Zeitschrift für Semiotik* 6: 331–39.

Dreyfuss, Henry. 1972. *Symbol Sourcebook*. New York: McGraw-Hill.

Droixhe, Daniel. 1983. Diderot: les signes du portrait. In Eschbach, A., and Trabant, J., eds., *History of Semiotics*, pp. 147–67. Amsterdam: Benjamins.

Droste, Flip G. 1972. The grammar of traffic regulations. *Semiotica* 5: 257–63.

———. 1985. Semiotic principles and semantic theory. *Semiotica* 54: 429–58.

Drummond, Lee. 1984. Movies and myth. *American Journal of Semiotics* 3.2: 1–32.

Dubois, Jacques, et al. (= Group μ). (1970) 1981. *A General Rhetoric*. Baltimore: Johns Hopkins Univ. Press.

Dubois, Jean, et al. 1973. *Dictionnaire de linguistique*. Paris: Larousse.

Ducrot, Oswald. 1976. Quelques implications linguistiques de la théorie médiévale de la supposition. In Parret, H., ed., *History of Linguistic Thought and Contemporary Linguistics*, pp. 189–227. Berlin: de Gruyter.

Ducrot, Oswald, and Todorov, Tzvetan. (1972) 1981. *Encyclopedic Dictionary of the Sciences of Language*. Oxford: Blackwell.

Ducrot, Oswald, et al. 1968. *Qu'est-ce que le structuralisme?* Paris: du Seuil.

Dufrenne, Mikel. 1966. L'art est-il langage? *Revue d'Esthétique* 19: 1–43.

Dummett, Michael. 1973. *Frege: Philosophy of Language*. London: Duckworth.

———. 1976. What is a theory of meaning? In Evans, Gareth, and McDowell, John, *Truth and Meaning*, pp. 67–137. Oxford: Clarendon.

Dunbar, H. Flanders. (1929) 1961. *Symbolism in Medieval Thought*. New York: Russell & Russell.

Duncan, Starkey, Jr. 1969. Nonverbal communication. *Psychological Bulletin* 72: 118–37.

———. 1973. Toward a grammar of dyadic conversation. *Semiotica* 9: 29–46.

———. 1975a. Interaction units during speaking turns in dyadic, face-to-face conversations. In Kendon, Adam, et al., eds., *Organization of Behavior in Face-to-Face Interaction*, pp. 199–213. The Hague: Mouton.

———. 1975b. Language, paralanguage, and body motion in the structure of conversations. In Williams, Thomas R., ed., *Socialization and Commu-*

nication in Primary Groups, pp. 286–311. The Hague: Mouton.

Duncan, Starkey, Jr., and Fiske, Donald W. 1977. *Face-to-Face Interaction*. Hillsdale, N.J.: L. Erlbaum.

Dundes, Alan. 1962. From etic to emic units in the structural study of folktales. *Journal of American Folklore* 75: 95–105.

Dunn, S. Watson, and Barban, Arnold M. 1986. *Advertising: Its Role in Modern Marketing*. 6th ed. Chicago: Dryden.

Dupré, Wilhelm. 1973. Mythos. In Krings, Hermann, et al., eds., *Handbuch der Philosophischen Grundbegriffe*, pp. 948–56. München: Kösel.

Dupriez, Bernard. 1986. The semiotics of rhetoric: Definition. In Sebeok, Thomas A., ed., *Encyclopedic Dictionary of Semiotics*, 3 vols., pp. 819–31. Berlin: Mouton de Gruyter.

Durand, Gilbert. 1964. *L'imagination symbolique*. Paris: Presses Universitaires.

Durand, Jacques. 1970. Rhétorique et image publicitaire. *Communications* 15: 70–95.

———. 1978. Figures de rhétorique et image publicitaire. *Humanisme et entreprise* 54.2: 78–110.

———. 1981. *Les formes de la communication*. Paris: Dunod.

Dürig, Walter. 1952. *Imago*. München: Zink.

Dutz, Klaus D. 1979. *Glossar der semiotischen Terminologie Charles W. Morris'*. Münster: Arbeitskreis für Semiotik (= papmaks 9).

———. 1983. Die Semiotiken des Charles W. Morris und ihre Rezeption. In Dutz, K. D., and Wulff, H. J., eds., *Kommunikation, Funktion und Zeichentheorie*, pp. 47–109. Münster: MAkS (= papmaks 15).

———. 1985. Schlüsselbegriffe einer Zeichentheorie bei G. W. Leibniz. In Dutz, K. D., and Kaczmarek, L., eds., *Rekonstruktion und Interpretation*, pp. 259–310. Tübingen: Narr.

———. 1986. Historiographie der Semiotik. In Dutz, K. D., and Schmitter, P., eds., *Geschichte und Geschichtsschreibung der Semiotik*, pp. 11–37. Münster: MAkS.

Dutz, Klaus D., and Schmitter, Peter, eds. 1985. *Historiographia Semioticae*. Münster: MAkS.

———. 1986. *Geschichte und Geschichtsschreibung der Semiotik*. Münster: MAkS.

Dyer, Gillian. 1982. *Advertising as Communication*. London: Methuen.

Eagle, Herbert. (1978) 1980. Eisenstein as a semiotician of the cinema. In Bailey, Richard W.; Matejka, L.; and Steiner, P., eds., *The Sign: Semiotics around the World*, pp. 173–93. Ann Arbor: Michigan Slavic Pub.

Eakins, Barbara W. 1972. *Charles Morris and the Study of Signification*. Univ. of Iowa: Ph.D. diss.

Ebbesen, Sten. 1983. The odyssey of semantics from the Stoa to Buridan. In Eschbach, Achim, and Trabant, Jürgen, eds., *History of Semiotics*. pp. 67–85. Amsterdam: Benjamins.

Ebeling, Gerhard. 1959. Hermeneutik. In Galling, K., *Die Religion in Geschichte und Gegenwart*, 3rd ed., pp. 241–62. Tübingen: Mohr.

Eberlein, Gerald. 1961. Ansätze einer allgemeinen Zeichen- und Kommunikationstheorie bei Francis Bacon. *Grundlagenstudium aus Kybernetik und Geisteswissenschaften* 2.1: 1–6.

Eco, Umberto. (1954) 1988. *The Aesthetics of Thomas Aquinas*. Cambridge, Mass.: Harvard Univ. Press.

———. (1962) 1973. [*Opera aperta*, trans.] *Das offene Kunstwerk*. Frankfurt: Suhrkamp.

———. (1964) 1984. [*Apocalittici e integrati*, trans.] *Apokalyptiker und Integrierte*. Frankfurt: S. Fischer.

———. (1968) 1972. [*La struttura assente*, trans.] *Einführung in die Semiotik*. München: Fink.

———. 1970. Codes and ideology. In *Linguaggi nella società e nella tecnica*, pp. 545–57. Milano: Ed. Comunità.

———. 1972a. A componential analysis of the architectural sign /column/. *Semiotica* 5: 97–117.

———. 1972b. Introduction to a semiotics of iconic signs. *Versus* 2: 1–15.

———. 1973a. *Il costume di casa*. Milano: Bompiani.

———. (1973b) 1977. *Zeichen: Einführung in einen Begriff und seine Geschichte*. Frankfurt: Suhrkamp.

———. 1975. Paramètres de la sémiologie théâtrale. In Helbo, André, ed., *Sémiologie de la représentation*, pp. 33–41. Bruxelles: Ed. Complexe.

———. (1976) 1979. *A theory of Semiotics*. Bloomington: Indiana Univ. Press.

———. 1976a. Peirce's notion of the interpretant. *Modern Language Notes* 91: 1457–72.

———. 1977a. The influence of Roman Jakobson on the development of semiotics. In Armstrong, D., and Schooneveld, C. H. van, eds., *Roman Jakobson: Echoes of His Scholarship*, pp. 39–58. Lisse: de Ridder.

———. 1977b. On the contribution of film to semiotics. *Quarterly Review of Film Studies* 2.1: 1–14.

———. 1977c. Semiotics of theatrical performance. *The Drama Review* 21: 107–117.

———. 1978. *La definizione dell' arte*. Milano: Mursia.

———. 1979. *The Role of the Reader*. Bloomington: Indiana Univ. Press.

———. (1980a) 1983. *The Name of the Rose*. New York: Secker & Warburg.

———. 1980b. Towards a semiotic inquiry into the television message. In Corner, J., and Hawthorn, J., eds., *Communication Studies*, pp. 131–49. London: Arnold.

_____. 1984a. Proposals for a history of semiotics. In Borbé, Tasso, ed., *Semiotics Unfolding*, pp. 75–89. Berlin: Mouton.

_____. 1984b. *Semiotics and the Philosophy of Language*. Bloomington: Indiana Univ. Press.

_____. 1985a. How culture conditions the colors we see. In Blonsky, Marshall, ed., *On Signs*, pp. 157–75. Baltimore: Johns Hopkins Univ. Press.

_____. 1985b. *Sugli specchi e altri saggi*. Milano: Bompiani.

_____. 1985c. Innovation and repetition: Between modern and post-modern aesthetics. *Daedalus* 11: 161–84.

_____. 1989. Über die Unmöglichkeit, eine 'Ars obliovinalis' zu konstruieren. To appear in *Carte Semiotiche 5*.

Eco, Umberto, ed. 1984. *Semiotica medievale*. Milano: Bompiani (= *Versus* 38/39).

Eco, Umberto, and Marmo, Constantino, eds. 1989. *On the Medieval Theory of Signs*. Amsterdam: Benjamins.

Eco, Umberto, and Sebeok, Thomas A., eds. 1983. *The Sign of Three: Dupin, Holmes, Peirce*. Bloomington: Indiana Univ. Press.

Eco, Umberto, et al. 1986. "Latratus canis" or: The dog's barking. In Deely, J., et al., eds., *Frontiers in Semiotics*, pp. 63–73. Bloomington: Indiana Univ. Press.

Edwards, Paul, ed. 1967. *Encyclopedia of Philosophy*. New York: Macmillan.

Efron, David. (1941) 1972. *Gesture, Race, and Culture*. The Hague: Mouton.

Egan, Rose Frances. (1921) 1969. *The Genesis of the Theory of "Art for Art's Sake" in Germany and in England*. Folcroft, Pa.: Folcroft Press.

Ege, Niels. 1949. Le signe linguistique est arbitraire. *Travaux du Cercle Linguistique de Copenhague* 5: 11–29.

Eggebrecht, Hans Heinrich. 1973. Über begriffliches und begriffsloses Verstehen in der Musik. In Faltin, Peter, and Reinecke, Hans-Peter, eds., *Musik und Verstehen*, pp. 48–57. Köln: Volk/Gerig.

Ehlich, Konrad. (1980) 1983. Development of writing as social problem solving. In Coulmas, Florian, and Ehlich, Konrad, eds., *Writing in Focus*, pp. 99–130. Berlin: Mouton.

Ehlich, Konrad, and Rehbein, Jochen. 1982. *Augenkommunikation*. Amsterdam: Benjamins.

Ehmer, Hermann K. 1971a. Von Mondrian bis Persil. In Ehmer, Hermann K., *Visuelle Kommunikation*, pp. 180–212. Köln: DuMont.

_____. 1971b. Zur Metasprache der Werbung. In Ehmer, H. K., ed., *Visuelle Kommunikation*, pp. 162–78. Köln: DuMont.

Ehmer, Hermann K., ed. 1971. *Visuelle Kommunikation*. Köln: DuMont.

_____. 1973. *Kunst: Visuelle Kommunikation, Unterrichtsmodelle*. Steinbach/Gießen: Anabas.

Ehrmann, Jacques, ed. (1966) 1970. *Structuralism*. Garden City: Doubleday.

Eibl-Eibesfeldt, Irenäus. (1967) 1975. *Ethology: The Biology of Behavior*, 2nd ed. New York: Holt, Rinehart & Winston.

_____. (1970) 1971. *Love and Hate*. London: Methuen.

_____. 1972. Similarities and differences between cultures in expressive movements. In Hinde, R. A., ed., *Non-Verbal Communication*, pp. 297–314. Cambridge: Univ. Press.

_____. 1984. *Die Biologie des menschlichen Verhaltens*. München: Piper.

Eikhenbaum, B. M. See Èjxenbaum, B. M.

Eimermacher, Karl. 1975. Zum Verhältnis von formalistischer, strukturalistischer und semiotischer Analyse. In Kimpel, Dieter, and Pinkerneil, Beate, eds., *Methodische Praxis der Literaturwissenschaft*, pp. 259–83. Kronberg: Scriptor.

Eimermacher, Karl, comp. 1974. *Arbeiten sowjetischer Semiotiker der Moskauer und Tartuer Schule (Auswahlbibliographie)*. Kronberg: Scriptor.

Eimermacher, Karl, ed. 1971. *Teksty sovetskogo literaturovedčeskogo strukturalizma—Texte des sowjetischen literaturwissenschaftlichen Strukturalismus*. München: Fink.

_____. 1986. *Semiotica Sovietica*. 2 vols. Aachen: Rader.

Eimermacher, Karl, and Eimermacher, Renate, eds. 1982. *Fragestellungen sowjetischer Semiotiker* (= *Zeitschrift für Semiotik* 4.1/2: 1–134).

Eimermacher, Karl, and Shishkoff, Serge, comps. 1977. *Subject Bibliography of Soviet Semiotics*. Ann Arbor: Univ. of Michigan.

Eisenberg, Abne M., and Smith, Ralph R., Jr. 1971. *Nonverbal Communication*. Indianapolis: Bobbs-Merrill.

Eisenstein, Sergei. (1942–49) 1957. *Film Form and Film Sense*. Cleveland: Meridian.

Eismann, Wolfgang. 1983. Russische Gesten im Sprachunterricht. In Baur, Ruprecht S., ed., *Materialen zur Landeskunde der Sowjetunion*, vol. 1, pp. 93–109. München: Sagner.

Èjxenbaum, Boris M. (1927) 1971. The theory of the formal method. In Matejka, Ladislav, and Pomorska, Krystyna, eds., *Readings in Russian Poetics*, pp. 3–37. Cambridge, Mass.: MIT Press.

Èjxenbaum, Boris M., ed. (1927) 1982. *The Poetics of Cinema*. Oxford: RPT Publications (= Russian Poetics in Translation 9).

Ekman, Paul. 1972. Universals and cultural differences in facial expression of emotion. In Cole, James, ed., *Nebraska Symposium on Motivation*, pp. 207–283. Lincoln: Univ. of Nebraska Press.

_____. 1976. Movements with precise meanings. *Journal of Communication* 26: 14–26.

_____. 1980a. Facial signals. In Rauch, Irmengard, and Carr, Gerald F., eds., *The Signifying Animal*, pp. 227–39. Bloomington: Indiana Univ. Press.

_____. 1980b. Three classes of nonverbal behavior. In Raffler-Engel, Walburga, ed., *Aspects of Nonverbal Communication*, pp. 89–102. Lisse: Swets & Zeitlinger.

_____. 1982. Methods for measuring facial action. In Scherer, Klaus R., and Ekman, Paul, eds., *Handbook of Methods in Nonverbal Behavior*, pp. 45–90. Cambridge: Univ. Press.

_____. 1985. *Telling Lies*. New York: Norton.

Ekman, Paul, ed. 1973. *Darwin and Facial Expression*. New York: Academic Press.

Ekman, Paul, and Friesen, Wallace V. 1967. Head and body cues in the judgement of emotion. *Perceptual and Motor Skills* 24: 711–24.

_____. 1969. The repertoire of nonverbal behavior: Categories, origins, usage, and coding. *Semiotica* 1: 49–98.

_____. 1972. Hand movements. *Journal of Communication* 22: 353–74.

_____. 1975. *Unmasking the Face*. Englewood Cliffs, N.J.: Prentice Hall.

_____. 1978. *Facial Action Coding System*. Palo Alto: Consulting Psychologists Press.

Ekman, Paul; Friesen, Wallace V.; and Ellsworth, Phoebe. 1972. *Emotion in the Human Face*. New York: Pergamon.

Ekman, Paul; Friesen, Wallace V.; and Tomkins, Silvan S. 1971. Facial affect scoring technique: A first validity study. *Semiotica* 3: 37–58.

Elam, Keir. 1980. *The Semiotics of Theatre and Drama*. London: Methuen.

Eliade, Mircea. 1952. *Images et symboles*. Paris: Gallimard.

_____. (1957) 1967. *Myths, Dreams, and Mysteries*. New York: Harper.

Elias, Peter. 1958. Information theory. In Grabbe, Eugene M., et al., eds., *Handbook of Automation, Computation, and Control 1*, 16–01–48. New York: Wiley.

Ellgring, Johann Heinrich. 1975. *Blickverhalten und Sprechaktivität*. Marburg: Diss. Phil.

Elling, Elmar. 1978. Zum Begriff des ikonischen Zeichens bei Charles Sanders Peirce. *Papmaks* (Münster) 7: 21–36.

Elling, Elmar, and Möller[-Naβ], Karl-Dietmar, eds. 1985. *Untersuchungen zur Syntax des Films II*. Münster: MAkS.

Ellis, Jeffrey. 1987. The logical and textual functions. In Halliday, M.A.K., and Fawcett, Robin P., eds., *New Developments in Systemic Linguistics*, vol. 1, pp. 107–129. London: F. Pinter.

Ellsworth, Phoebe C., and Langer, Ellen J. 1976.

Staring and approach. *Journal of Personality and Social Psychology* 33: 117–22.

Eltester, Friedrich-Wilhelm. 1958. *Eikon im Neuen Testament*. Berlin: Töpelmann.

Emanuele, Pietro. 1982. Präsemiotik und Semiotik in Heidegger. *Semiosis* 25/26: 140–44.

Empson, William. (1930) 1970. *Seven Types of Ambiguity*. London: Chatto & Windus.

Eng, Jan van der, and Grygar, Mojmír, eds. 1973. *Structure of Texts and Semiotics of Culture*. The Hague: Mouton.

Engel, Johann Jakob. (1785) 1971. *Ideen zu einer Mimik*. Frankfurt: Athenäum (Reprint).

Engels, Leopold K. 1978. *Pedagogical Grammar as Applied Semiotics*, Paper B 38. Trier: L.A.U.T.

Engler, Rudolf. 1962. Théorie et critique d'un principe saussurien: L'arbitraire du signe. *Cahiers Ferdinand de Saussure* 19: 5–66.

_____. 1968. *Lexique de la terminologie saussurienne*. Utrecht: Spectrum.

_____. 1970. Semiologische Lese. In Dierickx, Jean, and Lebrun, Yvan, eds., *Linguistique contemporaine: Hommage à Eric Buyssens*, pp. 61–73. Bruxelles: Ed. de l'Institut de Sociologie.

_____. 1975a. European structuralism: Saussure. In Sebeok, Thomas A., ed., *Current Trends in Linguistics* 13.2: 829–86.

_____. 1975b. Sémiologies saussuriennes I. *Cahiers Ferdinand de Saussure* 29: 45–73.

_____. 1980. Sémiologies saussuriennes II. *Cahiers Ferdinand de Saussure* 34: 1–16.

Englert, Klaus. 1987. *Frivolität und Sprache: Zur Zeichentheorie bei Jacques Derrida*. Essen: Blaue Eule.

Enkvist, Nils Erik. 1973. *Linguistic Stylistics*. The Hague: Mouton.

_____. 1981. Experimental iconism in text strategy. *Text* 1: 97–111.

Enkvist, Nils Erik, et al. (1964) 1971. *Linguistics and Style*. London: Oxford Univ. Press.

Entrevernes Group. See Groupe d'Entrevernes.

Epperson, Gordon. 1967. *The Musical Symbol*. Ames: Iowa State Univ. Press.

Erlich, Victor. (1955) 1969. *Russian Formalism*. The Hague: Mouton.

Ertel, Evelyne. 1977. Eléments pour une sémiologie du théâtre. *Travail théâtral* 28/29: 121–50.

Ertel, Suitbert. 1969. *Psychophonetik*. Göttingen: Verlag für Psychologie.

Esbroeck, Michel van. 1968. *Herméneutique, structuralisme et exégèse*. Paris: Desclée.

Escal, Françoise. 1978. Musique et icone: l'illusion du cratylisme. *Degrés* 15: 1–23.

Escarpit, Robert. 1976. *Théorie générale de l'information et de la communication*. Paris: Hachette.

Eschbach, Achim. 1975a. Charles W. Morris'

dreidimensionale Semiotik und die Texttheorie. In Morris, C. W., *Zeichen, Wert, Ästhetik*, pp. 7–68. Frankfurt: Suhrkamp.

———. 1975b. Bibliographie der Publikationen von Charles W. Morris und Auswahlbibliographie der Sekundärliteratur. In Morris, C. W., *Zeichen, Wert, Ästhetik*, pp. 334–50. Frankfurt: Suhrkamp.

———. 1977. Pragmatische Semiotik und Handlungstheorie. In Morris, C. W., *Pragmatische Semiotik und Handlungstheorie*, pp. 11–76. Frankfurt: Suhrkamp.

———. 1978. Einleitung. In Smart, B. H., *Grundlagen der Zeichentheorie*, pp. 7–36. Frankfurt: Syndikat.

———. 1979. *Pragmasemiotik und Theater*. Tübingen: Narr.

———. 1980. Semiotik. In Althaus, Hans Peter, et al., eds., *Lexikon der germanistischen Linguistik*, 2nd ed., pp. 41–57. Tübingen: Niemeyer.

———. 1981. Die Objektivität von Perspektiven. In Sturm, Hermann, and Eschbach, Achin, eds., *Ästhetik & Semiotik*, pp. 29–40. Tübingen: Narr.

———. 1986. Überlegungen im Anschluß an Georg J. Hollands . . . allgemeine Zeichenkunst. . . . In Dutz, K. D., and Schmitter, P., eds., *Geschichte und Geschichtsschreibung der Semiotik*, pp. 151–62. Münster: MAkS.

———. 1987. Bildsprache: Isotype und die Grenzen. In Brög, Hans, and Eschbach, Achim, eds., *Die Tücke des Objekts* (= Festschrift H. Sturm), pp. 258–97. Aachen: Rader.

Eschbach, Achim, comp. 1974. *Zeichen, Text und Bedeutung*. München: Fink.

Eschbach, Achim, ed. 1981. *Zeichen über Zeichen über Zeichen*. Tübingen: Narr.

———. 1984. *Bühler Studien*. 2 vols. Frankfurt: Suhrkamp.

Eschbach, Achim, and Eschbach-Szabó, Viktória, comps. 1986. *Bibliography of Semiotics 1975–1986*. 2 vols. Amsterdam: Benjamins.

Eschbach, Achim, and Koch, Walter A., eds. 1987. *A Plea for Cultural Semiotics*. Bochum: Brockmeyer.

Eschbach, Achim, and Rader, Wendelin, comps. 1976. *Semiotik-Bibliographie I*. Frankfurt: Syndykat.

———. 1978. *Film Semiotik. Eine Bibliographie*. München: Verlag Dokumentation Saur.

Eschbach, Achim, and Rader, Wendelin, eds. 1980. *Literatursemiotik*. 2 vols. Tübingen: Narr.

Eschbach, Achim, and Trabant, Jürgen, eds. 1983. *History of Semiotics*. Amsterdam: Benjamins.

Espe, Hartmut. 1985. Konnotationen als Ergebnisse fotografischer Techniken. *Zeitschrift für Semiotik* 7: 63–71.

Esposito, Joseph L. 1980. *Evolutionary Metaphysics*. Athens: Ohio Univ. Press.

Esser, Aristide, ed. 1971. *Behavior and Environment: The Use of Space by Animals and Men*. New York: Plenum.

Esslin, Martin. 1987. *The Field of Drama*. London: Methuen.

Evans, Gareth, and McDowell, John, eds. 1976. *Truth and Meaning*. Oxford: Clarendon.

Evans, William F. 1968. *Communication in the Animal World*. New York: Crowell.

Evans-Pritchard, E. E. 1937. *Witchcraft, Oracles, and Magic among the Azande*. Oxford: Clarendon.

Everaert-Desmedt, Nicole. 1984. *La communication publicitaire. Etude sémio-pragmatique*. Louvain-la-Neuve: Cabay.

Ewert, Jörg-Peter. (1976) 1980. *Neuroethology*. New York: Springer.

Exline, Ralph V. (1971) 1974. Visual interaction: The glances of power and preference. In Weitz, Shirley, ed., *Nonverbal Communication*, pp. 65–92. New York: Oxford Univ. Press.

Exline, Ralph V., and Fehr, B. J. 1978. Applications of semiosis to the study of visual interaction. In Siegman, Aron W., and Feldstein, Stanley, eds., *Nonverbal Behavior and Communication*, pp. 117–57. Hillsdale, N.J.: Erlbaum.

Fabbri, Paolo, et al. 1976. Rassegna critica sulla nozione di codice. In *Intorno al "Codice"* (= Atti del III Convegno della Associazione Italiana di Studi Semiotici [AISS] Pavia 1975), pp. 151–222. Firenze: La Nuova Italia.

Faber, Helm von. 1981. Der Einfluß unterschiedlicher Kommunikationsebenen beim Einsatz von Videoprogrammen im Fremdsprachenunterricht. In Lange-Seidl, A., ed., *Zeichenkonstitution*, vol. 2, pp. 168–73. Berlin: de Gruyter.

Fages, Jean-Baptiste. 1968. *Comprendre le structuralisme*. Toulouse: Privat.

Fährmann, Rudolf. (1960) 1967. *Die Deutung des Sprechausdrucks*. Bonn: Bouvier.

Faltin, Peter. 1972. Widersprüche bei der Interpretation des Kunstwerks als Zeichen. *International Review of the Aesthetics and Sociology of Music* 3: 199–213.

———. 1985. *Bedeutung ästhetischer Zeichen: Musik und Sprache*. Aachen: Rader.

Fast, Julius. 1970. *Body Language*. New York: Evans.

Fauque, Richard. 1973. Pour une nouvelle approche sémiologique de la ville. *Espaces et sociétés* 9: 15–27.

Faur, José. 1986. *Golden Doves with Silver Dots: Semiotics and Textuality in Rabbinic Tradition*. Bloomington: Indiana Univ. Press.

Faust, Wolfgang Max. 1977. *Bilder werden Worte*. München: Hanser.

Fawcett, Robin P. 1982. Language as a semiological system. In Morreall, John, ed., *The Ninth Lacus Forum, 1982*, pp. 59–125. Columbia: Hornbeam.

Fawcett, Robin P., et al., eds. 1984. *The Semiotics of Culture and Language.* 2 vols. London: F. Pinter.

Feibleman, James U. 1970. *An Introduction to the Philosophy of Charles S. Peirce.* Cambridge, Mass.: MIT Press.

Feldstein, Stanley, and Welkowitz, Joan. 1978. A chronography of conversation: In defense of an objective approach. In Siegman, Aron W., and Feldstein, Stanley, eds., *Nonverbal Behavior and Communication*, pp. 329–78. Hillsdale, N.J.: L. Erlbaum.

Fellinger, Raimund. 1980. Probleme einer Semiotik der Literatur. In Bohn, Volker, ed., *Literaturwissenschaft. Probleme ihrer theoretischen Grundlegung*, pp. 217–50. Stuttgart: Kohlhammer.

Féral, J. 1978. Kristevian Semiotics. In Bailey, Richard W., et al., eds., *The Sign: Semiotics around the World*, pp. 271–79. Ann Arbor: Michigan Slavic Pub.

Ferguson, George. 1954. *Signs and Symbols in Christian Art.* New York: Oxford Univ. Press.

Février, James G. (1948) 1959. *Historie de l'écriture.* Paris: Payot.

Feyereisen, Pierre. 1974. Théories de certains mouvements expressifs: les comportements d'autocontact. *Revue de psychologie et des sciences de l'éducation* 9: 89–113.

Fiesel, Eva. 1927 (1973). *Die Sprachphilosophie der deutschen Romantik.* Hildesheim: Olms.

Fietz, Lothar. 1976. *Funktionaler Strukturalismus.* Tübingen: Niemeyer.

———. 1982. *Strukturalismus.* Tübingen: Narr.

Figge, Udo L. 1973. Strukturale Linguistik. In Koch, Walter A., ed., *Perspektiven der Linguistik I*, pp. 1–36. Stuttgart: Kröner.

———. 1986. Bienentanz und Menschensprache. In Eschbach, A., ed., *Perspektiven des Verstehens*, pp. 42–71. Bochum: Brockmeyer.

Fillmore, Charles J. 1968. The case for case. In Bach, Emmon, and Harms, Robert T., eds., *Universals in Linguistic Theory*, pp. 1–88. New York: Holt, Rinehart & Winston.

Finlay-Pelinski, Marike. 1982. Semiotics or history. *Semiotica* 40: 229–66.

Finter, Helga. 1980. *Semiotik des Avantgardetextes.* Stuttgart: Metzler.

Fiordo, Richard. 1977. *Charles Morris and the Criticism of Discourse.* Bloomington: Indiana Univ. Press.

Firca, Gheorghe. 1972. Struktur and Strukturalismus in der Musikforschung. *International Review of the Aesthetics and Sociology of Music* 3: 247–52.

Firth, John R. (1930, 1937) 1966. *The Tongues of Men and Speech.* London: Oxford Univ. Press.

———. 1957. *Papers in Linguistics, 1934–1951.* London: Oxford Univ. Press.

Firth, Raymond. (1973) 1975. *Symbols.* London: Allen & Unwin.

Fisch, Max H. 1978. Peirce's general theory of signs. In Sebeok, Thomas A., ed., *Sight, Sound, and Sense*, pp. 31–70. Bloomington: Indiana Univ. Press.

———. 1986. *Peirce, Semiotic, and Pragmatism.* Bloomington: Indiana Univ. Press.

Fischer-Jørgensen, Eli. 1965. Louis Hjelmslev. *Acta Linguistica Hafniensia* 9.1: 3–23.

———. 1966. Form and substance in glossematics. *Acta Linguistica Hafniensia* 10: 1–33.

Fischer-Lichte, Erika. 1979. *Bedeutung: Probleme einer semiotischen Hermeneutik und Ästhetik.* München: Beck.

———. 1980. Zum Problem der Bedeutung ästhetischer Zeichen. *Kodikas/Code* 2: 269–83.

———. 1983a, b, c. *Semiotik des Theaters*, vols. 1, 2, 3. Tübingen: Narr.

———. 1983d. Kunst und Wirklichkeit. *Zeitschrift für Semiotik* 5: 195–216.

Fiske, John, and Hartley, John. (1978) 1980. *Reading Television.* London: Methuen.

Fitzgerald, John F. 1966. *Peirce's Theory of Signs as Foundation for Pragmatism.* The Hague: Mouton.

Flachskampf, Ludwig. 1938. Spanische Gebärdensprache. *Romanische Forschungen* 52: 205–58.

Flechtner, Hans-Joachim. (1966) 1972. *Grundbegriffe der Kybernetik.* Stuttgart: Hirzel.

Fledelius, Karsten. (1978) 1979. Syntagmatic film analysis. In *Untersuchungen zur Syntax des Films* (= papmaks 8), pp. 33–68. Münster: MAkS.

Fleischer, Michael. 1987. *Hund und Mensch: Eine semiotische Analyse ihrer Kommunikation.* Tübingen: Stauffenburg.

———. 1989. *Die sowjetische Semiotik.* Tübingen: Stauffenburg.

Floch, Jean-Marie. 1985. *Petites mythologies de l'oeil et de l'esprit.* Paris-Amsterdam: Hadès-Benjamins.

Florkin, Marcel. 1974. Concepts of molecular biosemiotics and of molecular evolution. In Florkin, M., and Stotz, E. H., eds., *Comparative Biochemistry.* Amsterdam: Elsevier (= Comprehensive Biochemistry 29A).

Fokkema, Douwe W. 1985. The concept of code in the study of literature. *Poetics Today* 6: 643–65.

Fokkema, D. W., and Kunne-Ibsch, Elrud. 1977. *Theories of Literature in the Twentieth Century.* London: Hurst.

Földes-Papp, Károly. (1966) 1975. *Vom Felsbild zum Alphabet.* Bayreuth: Gondrom.

Fónagy, Ivan. 1971. Le signe conventionnel motivé. *Linguistique* 7.2: 55–80.

Fontanille, Jacques, ed. 1984. *Sémiotique et enseignement du français* (= Langue Française 61) Paris: Larousse.

Formigari, Lia. 1970. *Linguistica ed empirismo nel seicento inglese.* Bari: Laterza.

———. 1976. Sprache und Philosophie im Zeitalter der Aufklärung. In Sulowski, J., ed., *Semiotic-Historical Studies*, vol. 3, pp. 125–60. Wrocław: Zakład Narodowy.

Förster, Uwe. 1982. Moderne Werbung und antike Rhetorik. *Sprache im technischen Zeitalter* 81: 59–73.

Forston, Robert F. 1975. Proxemic research. In Williams, Thomas R., ed., *Socialization and Communication in Primary Groups*, pp. 339–45. The Hague: Mouton.

Foster, Mary LeCron, and Brandes, Stanley H., eds. 1980. *Symbol as Sense.* New York: Academic Press.

Foucault, Michel. (1966a) 1970. *The Order of Things.* London: Tavistock.

———. 1966b. Interview with Madeleine Chapsal. *Quinzaine Littéraire* 5: 14–15.

———. (1969) 1972. *The Archeology of Knowledge.* New York: Pantheon.

Fouts, Roger S. 1974. Language: Origins, definitions, and chimpanzees. *Journal of Human Evolution* 3: 475–82.

Fouts, Roger S., et al. 1978. Studies of linguistic behavior in apes and children. In Siple, Patricia, ed., *Understanding Language through Sign Language Research*, pp. 163–85. New York: Academic Press.

Fraisse, Paul. 1963. *The Psychology of Time.* New York: Harper & Row.

François, Denise. 1969. Fonctions du langage. In Martinet, André, ed. *La linguistique*, pp. 103–110. Paris: Denoël.

Frank, Helmar. (1959) 1968. *Grundlagenprobleme der Informationsästhetik und erste Anwendung auf die mime pure.* Quickborn: Schnelle.

———. 1964. Informationspsychologie. In Frank, H., ed., *Kybernetik: Brücke zwischen den Wissenschaften*, pp. 259–71. Frankfurt: Umschau Verlag.

Frank, Lawrence K. 1957. Tactile communication. *Genetic Psychology Monographs* 56: 209–55.

Frank, Manfred. 1984. *Was ist Neostrukturalismus?* Frankfurt: Suhrkamp.

Frank-Böhringer, Brigitte. 1963. *Rhetorische Kommunikation.* Quickborn: Schnelle.

Franke, Ursula. 1979. Die Semiotik als Abschluß der Ästhetik. *Zeitschrift für Semiotik* 1: 345–59.

Fraser, Julius Thomas. 1988. *Time, the Familiar Stranger.* Amherst: Univ. of Massachusetts Press.

Fraser, Julius Thomas, ed. (1966) 1981. *The Voices of Time.* Amherst: Univ. of Massachusetts Press.

Fraser, Julius Thomas; Haber, F. C.; and Müller, G. H., eds. 1972. *The Study of Time.* Berlin: Springer.

Fraser, Julius Thomas, and Lawrence, Nathaniel, eds. 1975. *The Study of Time II.* Berlin: Springer.

Fraser, Julius Thomas; Lawrence, Nathaniel; and Park, D., eds. 1978. *The Study of Time III.* New York, Berlin: Springer.

Frazer, James George. (1922) 1967. *The Golden Bough.* Abr. ed. London: Macmillan.

Freedman, Joseph S. 1986. Signs within 16th and 17th century philosophy: The case of Clemens Timpler (1563–1624). In Dutz, K. D., and Schmitter, P., eds., *Geschichte und Geschichtsschreibung der Semiotik*, pp. 101–18. Münster: MAkS.

Freeman, Donald C., ed. 1970. *Linguistics and Literary Style.* New York: Holt.

Freeman, Eugene, ed. 1983. *The Relevance of Charles Peirce.* La Salle, Ill.: Monist Library.

Frege, Gottlob. (1892) 1974. On sense and reference. In Zabeeh, Farhang, et al., ed., *Readings in Semantics*, pp. 118–40. Urbana: Univ. of Illinois Press.

French, M. A. 1976. Observations on the Chinese script and the classification of writing-systems. In Haas, W., ed., *Writing without Letters*, pp. 101–29. Manchester: Univ. Press.

Fresnault-Deruelle, Pierre. 1972. *La bande dessinée.* Paris: Hachette.

———. 1977. *Récits et discours par la bande.* Paris: Hachette.

Freud, Sigmund. (1900–01) 1973. *The Interpretation of Dreams* (= Standard Edition, vols. 4–5). London: Hogarth.

———. (1913) 1962. *Totem and Taboo.* New York: Norton.

———. (1916–17) 1973. *Introductory Lectures on Psycho-analysis* (= Standard Edition, vols. 15–16). London: Hogarth.

Freudenthal, Hans. 1960. *Lincos: Design of a Language for Cosmic Intercourse.* Amsterdam: North Holland Pub.

Fricke, Harald. 1981. *Norm und Abweichung.* München: Beck.

Friedman, Lynn A. 1977. Formational properties of American Sign Language. In Friedman, Lynn A., ed., *On the Other Hand*, pp. 13–56. New York: Academic Press.

Friedman, Lynn A., ed. 1977. *On the Other Hand.* New York: Academic Press.

Friedman, Norman. (1965) 1974. Symbol. In Preminger, Alex, ed., *Princeton Encyclopedia of Poetry and Poetics*, pp. 833–36. Princeton: Univ. Press.

Friedman, William F. 1974. Cryptology. In *Encyclopedia Britannica*, 15th ed., vol. 5, pp. 844–51.

Friedrich, Johannes. 1966. *Geschichte der Schrift.* Heidelberg: Winter.

Frier, Wolfgang. 1977. Ansätze einer Semiotik des Sprachgebrauchs. *Lingua* 43: 313–37.

Frijda, Nico H. 1965. Mimik und Pantomimik. In Kirchhoff, Robert, ed., *Ausdruckspsychologie*, pp. 351–421. Göttingen: Hogrefe.

Frings, Hubert, and Frings, Mable. 1964. *Animal Communication.* New York: Blaisdell.

Frisch, Joseph C. 1969. *Extension and Comprehension in Logic.* New York: Philosophical Library.

Frisch, Karl von. (1965) 1967. *The Dance Language and Orientation of Bees.* Cambridge, Mass.: Harvard Univ. Press.

Frishberg, Nancy. 1978. Code and culture. In Peng, Fred C. C., ed., *Sign Language and Language Acquisition in Man and Ape*, pp. 45–85. Boulder: Westview.

———. 1979. Historical change: From iconic to arbitrary. In Klima, Edward S., and Bellugi, Ursula, et al., *The Signs of Language*, pp. 67–83. Cambridge, Mass.: Harvard Univ. Press.

Fromkin, Victoria, and Rodman, Robert. 1983. *An Introduction to Language.* 3rd ed. New York: Holt.

Fronval, George, and Dubois, Daniel. 1985. *Indian Signals and Sign Language.* New York: Bonanza.

Frutiger, Adrian. 1981. *Zeichen, Symbole, Signete, Signale.* Echzell: Heiderhoff.

Fry, Virginia H. 1986. A juxtaposition of two views of rhetoric: Charles Peirce's semiotic and Kenneth Burke's dramatism. In Deely, John, ed., *Semiotics 1985*, pp. 431–39. Lanham, Md.: Univ. Press of America.

Frye, Northrop. 1957. *Anatomy of Criticism.* Princeton: Univ. Press.

Fuchs, Wolfgang J., and Reitberger, Reinhold. 1978. *Comics-Handbuch.* Reinbek: Rowohlt.

Funke, Otto. 1926. Sprachphilosophische Probleme bei Bacon. *Englische Studien* 61: 24–56.

———. 1929. *Zum Weltsprachenproblem in England im 17. Jh.* Heidelberg: Winter.

Furbank, Philip N. 1970. *Reflections on the Word "Image."* London: Secker & Warburg.

Füssel, Kuno. 1983. *Zeichen und Strukturen.* Münster: Ed. Liberación.

Gabler, Darius. 1987. *Die semantischen und syntaktischen Funktionen im Tractatus "De modis significandi."* Bern: Lang.

Gabriel, Gottfried. 1975. *Fiktion und Wahrheit. Eine semantische Theorie der Literatur.* Stuttgart: Frommann-Holzboog.

Gadamer, Hans-Georg. (1960) 1975. *Wahrheit und Methode.* Tübingen: Mohr.

———. 1974. Hermeneutik. In Ritter, Joachim, ed., *Historisches Wörterbuch der Philosophie*, vol. 3, pp. 1061–73. Basel: Schwabe.

Gadamer, Hans-Georg, and Boehm, Gottfried, eds. 1976. *Seminar: Philosophische Hermeneutik.* Frankfurt: Suhrkamp.

Gale, Richard M. 1967. Indexical signs. In Edwards, Paul, ed., *The Encyclopedia of Philosophy*, pp. 151–55. New York: Macmillan.

———. 1968. *The Language of Time.* London: Routledge.

Gallie, W. B. 1966. *Peirce and Pragmatism.* New York: Dover.

Galliot, Marcel. 1955. *Essai sur la langue de la réclame contemporaine.* Toulouse: Privat.

Gamkrelidze, Thomas V. 1974. The problem of 'l'arbitraire du signe.' *Language* 50: 102–10.

Gandelman, Claude. 1984. Doors in painting: The semiotics of liminality. *Versus* 37: 55–70.

Gandelsonas, Mario. 1974. Linguistic and semiotic models in architecture. In Spillers, William R., ed., *Symposium on Basic Questions of Design Theory*, pp. 39–54. New York.

Gandillac, Maurice de; Goldmann, Lucien; and Piaget, Jean, eds. 1965. *Entretiens sur les notions de genèse et de structure.* Paris: Mouton.

Gardiner, Alan H. (1932) 1969. *The Theory of Speech and Language.* Oxford: Clarendon.

———. 1944. De Saussure's analysis of the signe linguistique. *Acta Linguistica Hafniensia* 4: 107–110.

Gardner, Howard. 1973. *The Quest for Mind.* New York: Knopf.

Gardner, Robert Allen, and Gardner, Beatrice T. 1969. Teaching sign language to a chimpanzee. *Science* 165: 664–72.

Garfinkel, Andrew D. 1979. *Sociolinguistic Analysis of the Language of Advertisement.* Ann Arbor: University Microfilms.

Garnier, François. 1982. *Le langage de l'image au moyen âge.* Paris: Léopard d'or.

Garrido Gallardo, Miguel Ángel. 1982. *Estudios de semiótica literaria.* Madrid: Consejo superior de investigaciones científicas.

Garroni, Emilio. 1968. *Semiotica ed estetica: L'eterogeneità del linguaggio e il linguaggio cinematografico.* Bari: Laterza.

Garvin, Paul L. 1977. Linguistics and semiotics. *Semiotica* 20: 101–110.

———. 1981. Structuralism, esthetics, and semiotics. In Steiner, Wendy, ed., *Image and Code*, pp. 97–108. Ann Arbor: Univ. of Michigan.

Garvin, Paul L., ed. 1964. *A Prague School Reader on Esthetics, Literary Structure, and Style.* Washington, D.C.: Georgetown Univ. Press.

Gary-Prieur, Marie-Noëlle. 1971. La notion de connotation(s). *Littérature* 4: 96–107.

Gätschenberger, Richard. (1901) 1987. *Grundzüge einer Psychologie des Zeichens*, ed. Eschbach, A. Amsterdam: Benjamins.

Gatz, Felix M. 1929. *Musik-Ästhetik.* Stuttgart: Enke.

Gaupp, Berthold, et al. 1978. *Phänomen Comics—transparent gemacht.* Fellbach: Bonz.

Gay, Volney P., and Patte, Daniel. 1986. Religious studies. In Sebeok, Thomas A., ed., *Encyclopedic Dictionary of Semiotics*, pp. 797–807. Berlin: Mouton de Gruyter.

Geach, Peter Thomas. (1962) 1970. *Reference and Generality*. Ithaca, N.Y.: Cornell Univ. Press.

Gear, Maria Carmen, and Liendo, Ernesto Cesar. 1975. *Sémiologie psychanalytique*. Paris: Minuit.

Gebauer, Gunter, ed. 1984. *Das Laokoon-Projekt: Pläne einer semiotischen Ästhetik*. Stuttgart: Metzler.

Geis, Michael L. 1982. *The Language of Television Advertising*. New York: Academic Press.

Geißner, Hellmut. 1969. Rhetorische Kommunikation. *Sprache und Sprechen* 2: 70–81.

Gelb, Ignace J. 1952. *A Study of Writing*. Chicago: Univ. Press.

————. 1980. Principles of writing systems within the frame of visual communication. In Kolers, Paul A., et al., eds., *Processing Visible Language*, vol. 2, pp. 7–24. New York: Plenum.

Geldard, Frank A. 1977. Tactile communication. In Sebeok, Thomas A., ed., *How Animals Communicate*, pp. 211–32. Bloomington: Indiana Univ. Press.

Genette, Gérard. (1972) 1980. *Narrative Discourse*. Oxford: Blackwell.

————. 1976. *Mimologiques*. Paris: Seuil.

Genot, Gérard. 1979. *Elements of Narrativics*. Hamburg: Buske.

Gentry, George. 1952. Habit and the logical interpretant. In Wiener, Philip P., and Young, Frederic H., eds., *Studies in the Philosophy of Charles Sanders Peirce*, pp. 75–90. Cambridge, Mass.: Harvard Univ. Press.

George, Emery E. (1978) 1980. Ernst Cassirer and neo-Kantian aesthetics. In Bailey, R. W., et al., eds., *The Sign: Semiotics around the World*, pp. 132–45. Ann Arbor: Michigan Slavic Pub.

Georgiades, Thrasybulos. 1954. *Musik und Sprache*. Berlin: Springer.

Gerhardt, Marlis. 1969. *Die Sprache Kafkas*. Stuttgart: Diss. Phil.

Gerlach, Peter. 1977. Probleme einer semiotischen Kunstwissenschaft. In Posner, Roland, and Reinecke, Hans-Peter, eds., *Zeichenprozesse*, pp. 262–92. Wiesbaden: Athenaion.

————. 1978. "Panofsky: Perspektive als symbolische Form" in semiotischer Sicht. In Arbeitsgruppe Semiotik, ed., *Die Einheit der semiotischen Dimensionen*, pp. 319–36. Tübingen: Narr.

Gesellschaft für Symbolforschung, ed. 1984. *Symbolforschung: Akten des 1. Symposiums*. Bern: Lang.

Gessinger, Joachim, and Rahden, Wolfert von, eds. 1988. *Theorien vom Ursprung der Sprache*. 2 vols. Berlin: de Gruyter.

Geyer, Bernhard, ed. 1951. *Die patristische und scholastische Philosophie*, 12th ed. (= Friedrich Ueberwegs Grundriß der Geschichte der Philosophie 2). Tübingen: Mittler.

Ghioca, Gabriela. 1983. A generative model in architecture. *Semiotica* 45: 297–305.

Gibson, James J. 1966. *The Senses Considered as Perceptual Systems*. Boston: Mifflin.

————. 1979. *The Ecological Approach to Visual Perception*. Boston: Mifflin.

Gilbert, Katherine Everett, and Kuhn, Helmut. (1939) 1972. *A History of Esthetics*. Westport, Conn.: Greenwood.

Gillan, Garth. 1982. *From Sign to Symbol*. Brighton: Harvester.

Gimson, A. C. (1962) 1970. *An Introduction to the Pronunciation of English*. London: Arnold.

Gipper, Helmut. 1978. *Sprachwissenschaftliche Grundbegriffe und Forschungsrichtungen*. München: Hueber.

Gipper, Helmut, and Schmitter, Peter. 1975. Sprachwissenschaft und Sprachphilosophie im Zeitalter der Romantik. In Sebeok, T. A., ed., *Current Trends in Linguistics*, vol. 13, pp. 481–606. The Hague: Mouton.

Gleason, Henry A., Jr. (1955) 1967. *An Introduction to Descriptive Linguistics*. New York: Holt, Rinehart & Winston.

Glück, Helmut. 1987. *Schrift und Schriftlichkeit*. Stuttgart: Metzler.

Godel, Robert (1957) 1969. *Les sources manuscrites du cours de linguistique générale*. Genève: Droz.

————. 1975. La semiologia saussuriana. *Lingua e stile* 10: 1–16.

Goeppert, Herma C. 1970. *Die sprachliche Strukturierung des Raums*. Tübingen: Diss. Phil.

Goffman, Erving. 1963. *Behavior in Public Places*. New York: Free Press.

————. 1967. *Interaction Ritual*. New York: Pantheon.

————. 1971. *Relations in Public*. New York: Basic Books.

————. (1976) 1979. *Gender Advertisements*. London: Macmillan.

Goldschläger, A. 1980. Rhétorique et esprit religieux. *Ars Semeiotica* 3.1: 47–60.

Goldschmidt, Victor. 1940. *Essai sur le "Cratyle."* Paris: Libr. H. Champion (= Bibliothèque de l'Ecole des Hautes Etudes, Sciences historiques et philologiques 279).

Goldziher, I. 1886. Über Geberden- und Zeichensprache bei den Arabern. *Zeitschrift für Völkerpsychologie und Sprachwissenschaft* 16: 369–86.

Göller, Thomas. 1986. *Ernst Cassirers kritische Sprachphilosophie*. Würzburg: Königshausen.

Gombrich, Ernst H. (1960) 1968. *Art and Illusion*. London: Phaidon.

————. (1972) 1975. *Symbolic Images*. Edinburgh: Phaidon.

————. 1981. Image and code: Scope and limits of conventionalism in pictorial representation. In

Steiner, Wendy, ed., *Image and Code*, pp. 11–42. Ann Arbor: Univ. of Michigan.

Gomperz, Heinrich 1908. *Weltanschauungslehre*, vol. 2: *Noologie*, pt. 1: *Einleitung und Semasiologie*. Jena: Diederichs.

Gonseth, Ferdinand. (1964) 1972. *Time and Method*. Springfield: Thomas.

Goodall, Jane. 1986. *The Chimpanzees of Gombe*. Cambridge, Mass.: Belknap/Harvard Univ. Press.

Goodman, Nelson. 1968. *Language of Art*. Indianapolis: Bobbs-Merrill.

———. 1972. *Problems and Projects*. Indianapolis: Bobbs-Merrill.

———. 1978. *Ways of Worldmaking*. Indianapolis: Hackett.

Goodrich, Peter. 1986. *Reading the Law*. Oxford: Blackwell.

———. 1987. *Legal Discourse*. London: Macmillan.

Goodwin, Charles. 1981. *Conversational Organization*. New York: Academic Press.

Gordon, W. Terrence. 1982. *A History of Semantics*. Amsterdam: Benjamins.

Göschl, Johannes B. 1980. *Semiologische Untersuchungen zum Phänomen der gregorianischen Liqueszenz*. Wien: Verband der Wiss. Ges.

Gosztonyi, Alexander. 1976. *Der Raum*. 2 vols. Freiburg: Alber.

Gottdiener, Mark, and Lagopoulos, Alexandros Ph., eds. *The City and the Sign*. New York: Columbia Univ. Press.

Goudge, Thomas A. (1950) 1969. *The Thought of C. S. Peirce*. New York: Dover.

———. 1965. Peirce's index. *Transactions of the Charles S. Peirce Society* 1: 52–70.

Gould, Peter, and White, Rodney. 1974. *Mental Maps*. Harmondsworth: Penguin.

Grabner-Haider, Anton. 1973. *Semiotik und Theologie*. München: Kösel.

Graeser, Andreas. 1978. The Stoic theory of meaning. In Rist, J., ed., *The Stoics*, pp. 77–100. Berkeley: Univ. of California Press.

Granger, Gilles-Gaston. 1968. *Essai d'une philosophie du style*. Paris: A. Colin.

Grant, E. C. 1968. An ethological description of non-verbal behavior during interviews. *Journal of Medical Psychology* 41: 177–84.

Graumann, Carl Friedrich, and Herrmann, Theo, eds. 1984. *Karl Bühlers Axiomatik*. Frankfurt: Klostermann.

Gray, Bennison. 1969. *Style: The Problem and Its Solution*. The Hague: Mouton.

Green, Jerald R. 1968. *A Gesture Inventory for the Teaching of Spanish*. Philadelphia: Chilton.

Greenberg, Joseph H. 1966. *Language Universals*. The Hague: Mouton.

Greenlee, Douglas. 1968. The similarity of discernibles. *The Journal of Philosophy* 65: 753–63.

———. 1973. *Peirce's Concept of Sign*. The Hague: Mouton.

Greenwood, David. 1985. *Structuralism and the Biblical Text*. Berlin: Mouton.

Gregory, Michael, and Carroll, Susanne. 1978. *Language and Situation*. London: Routledge & Kegan Paul.

Greimas, Algirdas Julien. (1966) 1983. *Structural Semantics*. Lincoln: Univ. of Nebraska Press.

———. 1970. *Du sens*. Paris: Seuil.

———. 1971. Narrative grammar: Units and levels. *Modern Language Notes* 86: 793–806.

———. 1972. Pour une théorie du discours poétique. In Greimas, Algirdas Julien, ed., *Essais de sémiotique poétique*, pp. 5–24. Paris: Larousse.

———. 1974a. Dialogue with Herman Parret. In Parret, Herman, ed., *Discussing Language*, pp. 55–79. The Hague: Mouton.

———. 1974b. Sémiotique. In *Grande Encyclopédie Larousse*, vol. 18, pp. 10987–88. Paris: Larousse.

———. (1976a) 1988. *Maupassant: The Semiotics of Text*. Amsterdam: Benjamins.

———. 1976b. *Sémiotique et sciences sociales*. Paris: Seuil.

———. 1979. Pour une sémiotique didactique. *Bulletin du Groupe de recherches sémio-linguistiques* 7: 3–8.

———. 1983. *Du sens II*. Paris: Seuil.

———. 1987. *On Meaning*. Minneapolis: Univ. of Minnesota Press.

Greimas, Algirdas Julien, ed. 1972. *Essais de sémiotique poétique*. Paris: Larousse.

Greimas, Algirdas Julien, and Courtés, Joseph. (1979) 1982. *Semiotics and Language*. Bloomington: Indiana Univ. Press.

———. 1986. *Sémiotique: Dictionnaire raisonné de la théorie du langage*, vol. 2. Paris: Hachette.

Greimas, Algirdas Julien, and Landowski, Eric. 1976. Analyse sémiotique d'un discours juridique. In Greimas, A. J., *Sémiotique et sciences sociales*, pp. 79–128. Paris: Seuil.

Greimas, Algirdas Julien, and Nef, Frédéric. 1977. Essai sur la vie sentimentale des hippopotames. In Dijk, Teun A. van, and Petöfi, János S., eds., *Grammars and Descriptions*, pp. 85–104. Berlin: de Gruyter.

Grolier, Eric de, ed. 1983. *Glossogenetics: The Origin and Evolution of Language*. Chur: Harwood.

Gröschel, Bernhard. 1983. Sprachliche Kommunikation und Sprachfunktionen. In Dutz, Klaus D., and Wulff, Hans J., eds., *Kommunikation, Funktion und Zeichentheorie*, pp. 15–45. Münster: MAkS.

Grosse, Ernst Ulrich. 1971. Zur Neuorientierung der Semantik bei Greimas. *Zeitschrift für romanische Philologie* 87: 359–93.

———. 1978. French structuralist views on narrative grammar. In Dressler, Wolfgang U., ed., *Current Trends in Textlinguistics*, pp. 155–73. Berlin: de Gruyter.

Groupe d'Entrevernes. (1977) 1978. *Signs and Parables*. Pittsburgh: Pickwick.

————. 1979. *Analyse sémiotique des textes*. Lyon: Presses Univ.

Groupe 107. 1973. *Sémiotique des plans en architecture*. Paris: Groupe 107.

Group(e) μ. See Dubois, Jacques, et al.; Klinkenberg, Jean Marie, et al.

Grünewald, Dietrich. 1982. *Comics: Kunst oder Kitsch?* Weinheim: Beltz.

Grzybek, Peter. 1988. *Studien zum Zeichenbegriff der sowjetischen Semiotik*. Bochum: Diss. Phil.

Gubern, Román. 1972. *El lenguaje de los comics*. Barcelona: Ed. Península.

————. 1974. *Mensajes icónicos en la cultura de masas*. Barcelona: Lumen.

Gubern, Román, and Moliterni, Claude. 1978. *Comics. Kunst und Konsum der Bildergeschichten*. Reinbek: Rowohlt.

Guillén, Claudio. 1971. *Literature as System*. Princeton, N.J.: Univ. Press.

Guiraud, Pierre. (1954) 1967. *La stylistique*. Paris: Presses Univ. de France.

————. 1968. Langage et théorie de la communication. In Martinet, André, ed., *Le langage*, pp. 145–68. Paris: Gallimard.

————. 1969. *Essais de stylistique*. Paris: Klincksieck.

————. (1971) 1975. *Semiology*. London: Routledge & Kegan.

————. 1973. La sémiologie. In Pottier, Bernard, ed., *Le langage* (= Les dictionnaires du savoir moderne), pp. 454–83. Paris: CEPL.

————. 1974. Rhetoric and stylistics. In Sebeok, Thomas A., ed., *Current Trends in Linguistics*, vol. 12, pt. 2, pp. 943–55. The Hague: Mouton.

————. 1978. *Sémiologie de la sexualité*. Paris: Payot.

Guiraud, Pierre, and Kuentz, Pierre. 1970. *La stylistique*. Paris: Klincksieck.

Gülich, Elisabeth. 1973. Erzähltextanalyse. *Linguistik und Didaktik* 16: 325–28.

Gülich, Elisabeth, and Quasthoff, Uta M. 1985. Narrative analysis. In Dijk, Teun A. van, ed., *Handbook of Discourse Analysis*, vol. 2, pp. 169–97. London: Academic Press.

Gülich, Elisabeth, and Raible, Wolfgang. 1977. *Linguistische Textmodelle*. München: Fink.

Gumbrecht, Hans Ulrich. 1975. Algirdas Julien Greimas. In Lange, Wolf-Dieter, ed., *Französische Literaturkritik der Gegenwart*, pp. 326–50. Stuttgart: Kröner.

Gumpel, Liselotte. 1984. *Metaphor Reexamined*. Bloomington: Indiana Univ. Press.

Günther, Hans. 1972. Struktur als Prozeß. *Archiv für Begriffsgeschichte* 16: 86–92.

Günther, Hartmut. 1983. Charakteristika von schriftlicher Sprache und Kommunikation. In Günther, Klaus B, and Günther, Hartmut, eds., *Schrift, Schreiben, Schriftlichkeit*, pp. 17–39. Tübingen: Niemeyer.

Gunzenhäuser, Rul. 1962. *Ästhetisches Maß und ästhetische Information*. Quickborn: Schnelle.

Gutiérrez López, Gilberto A. 1975. *Estructura de lenguaje y conocimiento. Sobre la epistemología de la semiótica*. Madrid: Fragua.

Gutterer, Dietrich. 1983. Ansätze zu einer Zeichentheorie bei Hegel. In Eschbach, A., and Trabant, J., eds., *History of Semiotics*, pp. 191–204. Amsterdam: Benjamins.

Güttgemanns, Erhardt. 1977. Fundamentals of a grammar of oral literature. In Jason, Heda, and Segal, Dimitri, eds., *Patterns in Oral Literature*, pp. 77–97. The Hague: Mouton.

————. 1982. Semiotik und Theologie. *Zeitschrift für Semiotik* 4: 151–68.

————. 1983. *Fragmenta semiotico-hermeneutica*. Bonn: Linguistica biblica.

————. 1986. Liturgy. In Sebeok, Thomas A., ed., *Encyclopedic Dictionary of Semiotics*, pp. 467–73. Berlin: Mouton.

————. 1989. Semiotik und Theologie. In Koch, Walter A., *Semiotik in den Einzelwissenschaften*. Bochum: Brockmeyer.

Gwin, William R., and Gwin, Mary M. 1985. *Semiology, Symbolism, and Architecture*. Monticello, Ill. (= Vance Bibliographies, Architecture Series A 1346).

Haag, Karl. 1930. *Die Loslösung des Denkens von der Sprache durch Begriffsschrift*. Stuttgart: Kohlhammer.

Haas, W. 1956. Concerning glossematics. *Archivum linguisticum* 8: 93–110.

Haas, W., ed. 1976. *Writing without Letters*. Manchester: Univ. Press.

Habermas, Jürgen. (1968) 1971. *Knowledge and Human Interest*. Boston: Beacon.

————. 1971. Vorbereitende Bemerkungen zu einer Theorie der kommunikativen Kompetenz. In Habermas, Jürgen, and Luhmann, Niklas, *Theorie der Gesellschaft oder Sozialtechnologie*, pp. 101–41. Frankfurt: Suhrkamp.

Hafner, Heinz. 1982. *Prolegomena zu einer linguistisch–literaturwissenschaftlichen Zeichentheorie*. Heidelberg: Groos.

Hager, Frithjof, et al. (1973) 1975. *Soziologie und Linguistik*. Stuttgart: Metzler.

Haidu, Peter. 1982. Semiotics and history. *Semiotica* 40: 187–228.

Hailman, Jack P. 1977a. Communication by reflected light. In Sebeok, Thomas A., ed., *How Ani-*

mals Communicate, pp. 184–210. Bloomington: Indiana Univ. Press.

———. 1977b. *Optical Signals*. Bloomington: Indiana Univ. Press.

Haiman, John. 1980. The iconicity of grammar: Isomorphism and motivation. *Language* 56: 515–40.

Haiman, John, ed. 1985. *Iconicity in Syntax*. Amsterdam: Benjamins.

Haken, Hermann. (1981) 1984. *The Science of Structure: Synergetics*. New York: Van Nostrand.

Hale, Kenneth. 1971. A note on a Walbiri tradition of antonymy. In Steinberg, Danny D., & Jakobovits, Leon A., eds., *Semantics,* pp. 472–82. Cambridge: Univ. Press.

Hall, A. D., and Fagen, R. E. 1956. Definition of system. *General Systems Yearbook* 1: 18–28.

Hall, Edward T. 1959. *The Silent Language*. Greenwich: Fawcett.

———. 1963a. Proxemics—the study of man's spatial relations. In Galdston, Iago, ed., *Man's Image in Medicine and Anthropology*, pp. 422–45. New York: Int. Univ. Press.

———. 1963b. A system for the notation of proxemic behavior. *American Anthropologist* 65: 1003–1026.

———. 1964. Silent assumptions in social communication. *Disorders of Communication* 42: 41–55.

———. 1966. *The Hidden Dimension*. Garden City: Anchor Books.

———. 1968. Proxemics. *Current Anthropology* 9: 83–108.

———. 1974. *Handbook for Proxemic Research*. Washington, D.C.: Society for the Anthropology of Visual Communication.

———. 1976. *Beyond Culture*. Garden City: Doubleday.

———. 1983. *The Dance of Life*. Garden City: Anchor Press.

Hall, Robert A., Jr. 1964. *Introductory Linguistics*. Philadelphia: Chilton.

Halle, Morris, and Matejka, Ladislav, eds. 1984. *Semiosis: Semiotics and the History of Culture; In Honorem Georgii Lotman*. Ann Arbor: Univ. of Michigan.

Halle, Morris, et al. 1983. *A Tribute to Roman Jakobson, 1896–1982*. Berlin: Mouton.

Haller, Rudolf. 1959. Das 'Zeichen' und die 'Zeichenlehre' in der Philosophie der Neuzeit. *Archiv für Begriffsgeschichte* 4: 113–57.

Hallett, Garth. 1967. *Wittgenstein's Definition of Meaning as Use*. New York: Fordham Univ. Press.

Halliday, Michael A. K. 1970. Language structure and language function. In Lyons, John, ed., *New Horizons in Linguistics*, pp. 140–65. Harmondsworth: Penguin.

———. 1973. *Explorations in the Functions of Language*. London: Arnold.

———. 1978. *Language as Social Semiotic*. London: Arnold.

———. 1985. *An Introduction to Functional Grammar*. London: Arnold.

Halliday, Tim R., and Slater, Peter J. B., eds. 1983a. *Communication* (= *Animal Behavior*, vol. 2). New York: Freeman.

———. 1983b. *Animal Behavior*. 3 vols. New York: Freeman.

Hamburger, Käthe. 1957 (1968). *Die Logik der Dichtung*. Stuttgart: Klett.

Hammad, Manar, et al. 1977. L'espace du séminaire. *Communications* 27: 28–54.

Hamon, Philippe. 1972. Pour un statut sémiologique du personnage. *Littérature* 6: 86–110.

Handl, Haimo L., ed. 1985. *Werbung: Rollenklischee—Produktkultur—Zeichencharakter*. Wien: Österr. Ges. für Semiotik.

Hanhardt, John G., and Harpole, Charles H. 1973. Linguistics, structuralism, and semiology. *Film Comment* 9: 52–59.

Hansen, Bert. 1986. The complementarity of science and magic before the scientific revolution. *American Scientist* 74.2: 128–36.

Hantsch, Ingrid. 1975. *Semiotik des Erzählens*. München: Fink.

Harari, Josué V., ed. 1979. *Textual Strategies: Perspectives in Post-Structuralist Criticism*. London: Methuen.

Hardenberg, Christine. 1979. G. E. Lessings Semiotik als Propädeutik einer Kunsttheorie. *Zeitschrift für Semiotik* 1: 361–76.

Hardt, Manfred. 1975. Julia Kristeva. In Lange, Wolf-Dieter, ed., *Französische Literaturkritik der Gegenwart*, pp. 309–25. Stuttgart: Kröner.

———. 1976. *Poetik und Semiotik*. Tübingen: Niemeyer.

Harland, Richard. 1987. *Superstructuralism*. London: Methuen.

Harman, Gilbert. 1977. Semiotics and the cinema. *Quarterly Review of Film Studies* 2.1: 15–24.

Harnad, Stevan R., et al., eds. 1976. *Origins and Evolution of Language and Speech* (= Annals of the New York Academy of Sciences 280). New York: N.Y. Academy of Sciences.

Harper, Robert G.; Wiens, Arthur N.; and Matarazzo, Joseph D. 1978. *Nonverbal Communication: The State of the Art*. New York: Wiley.

Harris, Roy. 1986. *The Origin of Writing*. London: Duckworth.

Harris, Zellig S. 1951. *Methods in Structural Linguistics*. Chicago: Univ. Press.

Harrison, Randall P. 1974. *Beyond Words*. Englewood Cliffs: Prentice Hall.

Hartley, R. V. L. 1928. Transmission of information. *Bell System Technical Journal* 7: 535–63.

Hartmann, Peter. 1971. Texte als linguistische

Objekte. In Stempel, Wolf-Dieter, ed., *Beiträge zur Textlinguistik*, pp. 9–29. München: Fink.

Hartmann, R. R. K., and Stork, F. C. 1972. *Dictionary of Language and Linguistics*. London: Applied Science Pub.

Harweg, Roland. 1968. Language and music: An immanent and sign theoretic approach. *Foundations of Language* 4: 270–81.

———. 1973. Phonematik und Graphematik. In Koch, W. A., ed., *Perspektiven der Linguistik 1*, pp. 37–64. Stuttgart: Kröner.

Hasenmueller, A. Christine. 1981. The function of art as "iconic text." *Semiotica* 36: 135–52.

Haubrichs, Wolfgang. 1976. Einleitung. In Haubrichs, W., ed., *Erzählforschung*, vol. 1, pp. 7–28. Göttingen: Vandenhoeck.

Haubrichs, Wolfgang, ed. 1976–78. *Erzählforschung. Theorien, Modelle und Methoden der Narrativik*, vols. 1–3 (= LiLi, Zeitschrift für Literaturwissenschaft und Linguistik, Beihefte 4 [1976], 6 [1977], 8 [1978]). Göttingen: Vandenhoeck.

Hauff, Jürgen. 1971. Hermeneutik. In Hauff, J., et al., *Methodendiskussion*, vol. 2, pp. 1–82. Frankfurt: Athenäum.

Haupenthal, Reinhard, ed. 1976. *Plansprachen*. Darmstadt: Wiss. Buchges.

Hauptmeier, Helmut, and Schmidt, Siegfried J. 1985. *Einführung in die empirische Literaturwissenschaft*. Braunschweig: Vieweg.

Havelock, Eric A. 1963. *Preface to Plato*. Oxford: Blackwell.

———. 1976. *Origins of Western Literacy*. Toronto: Ontario Institute for Studies in Education.

Hawkes, Terence. 1977. *Structuralism and Semiotics*. London: Methuen.

Hayakawa, Samuel I. (1941) 1974. *Language in Thought and Action*. London: Allen & Unwin.

Hayes, Alfred S. (1964) 1972. Paralinguistics and kinesics: Pedagogical perspectives. In Sebeok, Thomas A.; Hayes, Alfred S.; and Bateson, Mary Catherine, eds., *Approaches to Semiotics*, pp. 145–72. The Hague: Mouton.

Hayes, Catharine H. 1951. *The Ape in Our House*. New York: Harper & Row.

Heath, Stephen. 1971. Towards textual semiotics. In Heath, Stephen, et al., eds., *Signs of the Times*, pp. 16–36. Cambridge: Granta.

———. *Questions of Cinema*. London: Macmillan.

Heath, Stephen, and Mellencamp, Patricia, eds. 1983. *Cinema and Language*. Frederick, Md.: Univ. Publications of America.

Hediger, Heini. 1970. Zur Sprache der Tiere. *Der Zoologische Garten* (NF) 38: 171–80.

Hegel, Georg Wilhelm Friedrich. (1817) 1916. *The Philosophy of Fine Art*. 4 vols. London: Bell.

———. (1830) 1970. *Enzyklopädie der philosophischen Wissenschaften*. 3 vols. Frankfurt: Suhrkamp.

Heim, Robert. 1983. *Semiologie und historischer Materialismus*. Köln: Pahl-Rugenstein.

Hein, Norbert 1976. Ansatz zur strukturellen Dramenanalyse. In Koch, Walter A., ed., *Textsemiotik und strukturelle Rezeptionstheorie*, pp. 119–213. Hildesheim: Olms.

Heinekamp, Albert. 1975. Natürliche Sprache und Allgemeine Charakteristik bei Leibniz. In *Akten des 2. Internationalen Leibniz-Kongresses* (Hannover 1972), pp. 257–86. Wiesbaden: Steiner.

———. 1976. Sprache und Wirklichkeit nach Leibniz. In Parret, H., ed., *History of Linguistic Thought*, pp. 518–70. Berlin: de Gruyter.

Helbig, Gerhard. 1969. Zum Funktionsbegriff in der modernen Linguistik. *Wissenschaftliche Zeitschrift der Humboldt-Universität zu Berlin, Ges.-Sprachw. R.* 18: 241–49.

———. 1974. *Geschichte der neueren Sprachwissenschaft*. Reinbek: Rowohlt.

Helbo, André. 1975a. Le code théâtral. In Helbo, André, et al., *Sémiologie de la représentation*, pp. 12–27. Bruxelles: Ed. Complexe.

———. 1975b. Pour un proprium de la représentation théâtrale. In Helbo, André, et al., *Sémiologie de la représentation*, pp. 62–72. Bruxelles: Ed. Complexe.

———. 1981. The semiology of theater. *Poetics Today* 2.3: 105–111.

———. 1983a. *Les mots et les gestes*. Lille: Presses Univ.

———. 1983b *Sémiologie des messages sociaux*. Paris: Edilig.

———. 1987. *Theory of Performing Arts*. Amsterdam: Benjamins.

Helbo, André, ed. 1979. *Le champ sémiologique. Perspectives internationales*. Bruxelles: Ed. Complexe.

Helbo, André, et al. 1975. *Sémiologie de la représentation*. Brüssel: Ed. Complexe.

Helfman, Elizabeth S. 1981. *Blissymbolics*. New York: Elsevier.

Helfrich, H., and Wallbott, Harald G. 1980. Theorie der nonverbalen Kommunikation. In Althaus, Hans Peter, et al., eds., *Lexikon der germanistischen Linguistik*, 2nd ed., pp. 267–75. Tübingen: Niemeyer.

Hempfer, Klaus W. 1976. *Poststrukturale Texttheorie und narrative Praxis*. München: Fink.

Hénault, Anne. 1979. *Les enjeux de la sémiotique*. Paris: Presses Univ. de France.

———. 1983. *Narratologie, sémiotique générale*. Paris: Presses Univ. de France.

Henckmann, Wolfhart. 1985. Oswald Külpes Beitrag zu einer Erkenntnistheorie der Zeichen. In Dutz, K. D., and Schmitter, P., eds., *Historiographia Semioticae*, pp. 69–132. Münster: MAkS.

Henderson, Brian. 1980. *A Critique of Film Theory*. New York: Dutton.

Hendricks, William O. 1973. *Essays on Semiolinguistics and Verbal Art*. The Hague: Mouton.

———. 1976. *Grammars of Style and Styles of Grammar*. Amsterdam: North Holland.

———. 1982. Structure and history in the semiotics of myth. *Semiotica* 39: 131–65.

Henle, Paul. 1958. Metaphor. In Henle, Paul, ed., *Language, Thought, and Culture*, pp. 173–95. Ann Arbor: Univ. of Michigan Press.

Henley, Nancy M. 1977. *Body Politics*. Englewood Cliffs, N.J.: Prentice Hall.

Henne, Helmut, and Wiegand, Herbert Ernst. 1973. Pleremik: Sprachzeichenbildung. In Althaus, Hans Peter, et al., eds., *Lexikon der Germanistischen Linguistik* I, pp. 132–44. Tübingen: Niemeyer.

Henny, Leonard M., ed. 1987. *The Semiotics of Advertisements*. Aachen: Rader.

Herculano de Carvalho, José G. 1961. Segno e significazione in João de São Tomás. In Flasche, Hans, ed., *Aufsätze zur portugiesischen Kulturgeschichte*, vol. 2, pp. 152–78. Münster: Aschedorff.

Herder, Johann Gottfried. 1768 (1877). *Über die neuere deutsche Literatur. Fragmente* (= *Sämtliche Werke*, ed. Suphan, B., vol. 2), pp. 1–108. Berlin: Weidmann.

———. 1769 (1878). *Kritische Wälder* (= Sämtliche *Werke*, ed. Suphan, B., vol. 3). Berlin: Weidmann.

———. 1784–85 (1887). *Ideen zur Philosophie der Geschichte der Menschheit* (= *Sämtliche Werke*, ed. Suphan, B., vol. 13). Berlin: Weidmann.

Heringer, Hans Jürgen, ed. 1974. *Seminar: Der Regelbegriff in der praktischen Semantik*. Frankfurt: Suhrkamp.

Herman, Louis M.; Richards, Douglas G.; and Wolz, James P. 1984. Comprehension of sentences in bottlenosed dolphins. *Cognition* 16: 129–219.

Hermes, Hans. (1938) 1970. *Semiotik. Eine Theorie der Zeichengestalten als Grundlage für Untersuchungen von formalisierten Sprachen*. Hildesheim: Gerstenberg.

Herrick, Marvin T. (1965) 1974. Rhetoric and poetics. In Preminger, Alex, ed., *Princeton Encyclopedia of Poetry and Poetics*, pp. 702–705. Princeton: Univ. Press.

Hervey, Sándor G. J. 1982. *Semiotic Perspectives*. London: Allen & Unwin.

Herzfeld, Michael. 1986. Culinary semiotics. In Sebeok, Thomas A., ed., *Encyclopedic Dictionary of Semiotics*, pp. 157–59. Berlin: Mouton de Gruyter.

Heslin, Richard, and Patterson, Miles L. 1982. *Nonverbal Behavior and Social Psychology*. New York: Plenum.

Hess, Eckhard, and Petrovich, Slobodan B. 1978. Pupillary behavior in communication. In Siegman, Aron W., and Feldstein, Stanley, eds., *Nonverbal Behavior and Communication*, pp. 159–79. Hillsdale, N.J.: Erlbaum.

Hess-Lüttich, Ernest W. B. 1984. *Kommunikation als ästhetisches Problem*. Tübingen: Narr.

Hess-Lüttich, Ernest W. B., ed. 1982a, b. *Multimedial Communication*, vol. 1: *Semiotic Problems of Its Notation*, vol. 2: *Theatre Semiotics*. Tübingen: Narr.

Hewes, Gordon W. 1957. The anthropology of posture. *Scientific American* 196: 123–32.

———. 1973. Primate communication and the gestural origin of language. *Current Anthropology* 14: 5–24.

———. 1974. Gesture language in culture contact. *Sign Language Studies* 4: 1–34.

———. 1976. The current status of the gestural theory of the language origin. In Harnad, Stevan R., et al., eds., *Origins and Evolution of Language and Speech* (= Annals of the New York Academy of Sciences 280), pp. 482–504.

Heymer, Armin. 1977. *Ethological Dictionary*. Berlin: Parey.

Hiersche, Rolf. 1974. Zur Entstehung von F. de Saussures Konzeption vom arbitraire du signe linguistique. *Archiv für das Studium neuerer Sprachen* 211: 1–17.

Hill, Archibald A. 1958. *Introduction to Linguistic Structures*. New York: Harcourt.

Hill, Elizabeth K. 1970. What is an emblem? *Journal of Aesthetics and Art Criticism* 29: 261–65.

Hinde, R. A. 1974. *Biological Bases of Human Social Behavior*. New York: McGraw-Hill.

———. 1975. The comparative study of non-verbal communication. In Benthall, J., and Polhemus, T., eds., *The Body as a Medium of Expression*, pp. 107–42. London: Allen & Unwin.

Hinde, R. A., ed. 1972. *Non-Verbal Communication*. Cambridge: Univ. Press.

Hintikka, Jaakko. 1968. The varieties of information and scientific explanation. In Van Rootselaar, B., and Staal, J. F., eds., *Logic, Methodology, and Philosophy of Science* 3, pp. 311–31. Amsterdam: North Holland.

Hirsch, Eric D., Jr. (1967) 1971. *Validity in Interpretation*. New Haven: Yale Univ. Press.

Hirschman, Elizabeth C., and Holbrook, Morris B., eds. 1981. *Symbolic Consumer Behavior* (= Proceedings of the Conference on Consumer Esthetics and Symbolic Consumption). Ann Arbor: Association for Consumer Research.

Hjelmslev, Louis. (1937) 1973. On the principles of phonematics. In Hjelmslev, L., *Essais linguistiques II*, pp. 157–62. Copenhagen: Nordisk Sprog- og Kulturforlag.

———. (1943) 1961. *Prolegomena to a Theory of Language*. Madison: Univ. of Wisconsin Press.

———. (1943a) 1974. *Prolegomena zu einer Sprachtheorie*. München: Hueber.

———. (1948) 1959. Structural analysis of language. In Hjelmslev, L., *Essais linguistiques*, pp. 27–35. Copenhagen: Nordisk Sprog- og Kulturforlag.

———. (1954) 1959. La stratification du langage. In Hjelmslev, L., *Essais linguistiques*, pp. 37–68. Copenhagen: Nordisk Sprog- og Kulturforlag.

———. (1957) 1959. Pour une sémantique structurale. In Hjelmslev, L., *Essais linguistiques*, pp. 96–112. Copenhagen: Nordisk Sprog- og Kulturforlag.

———. 1959. *Essais linguistiques* (= Travaux du Cercle linguistique de Copenhague 12). Copenhagen: Nordisk Sprog- og Kulturforlag.

———. 1973. *Essais linguistiques II* (= Travaux du Cercle linguistique de Copenhague 14). Copenhagen: Nordisk Sprog- og Kulturforlag.

———. 1975. *Resumé of a Theory of Language,* ed. and trans. Whitfield, Francis J. Madison: Univ. of Wisconsin Press.

Hobbes, Thomas. (1640) 1966. *Human Nature*. In Hobbes, T., *The English Works*, vol. 4. Aalen: Scientia (Reprint of the 1839 ed.).

———. (1655) 1966. *Elements of Philosophy 1: Concerning Body*. In Hobbes, T., *The English Works*, vol. 1. Aalen: Scientia (Reprint of the 1839 ed.).

Hockett, Charles F. (1948) 1957. A note on "structure." In Joos, Martin, ed., *Readings in Linguistics I*, pp. 279–80. Chicago: Univ. of Chicago Press.

———. 1958. *A Course in Modern Linguistics*. New York: Macmillan.

———. (1960) 1977. Logical considerations in the study of animal communication. In Hockett, Charles F., *The View from Language*, pp. 124–43. Athens: Univ. of Georgia Press.

———. (1963) 1977. The problem of universals in language. In Hockett, Charles F., *The View from Language*, pp. 163–86. Athens: Univ. of Georgia Press.

———. (1974) 1977. Information, entropy, and the epistemology of history. In Hockett, C. F., *The View from Language*, pp. 290–322. Athens: Univ. of Georgia Press.

———. 1977. Review of T. A. Sebeok's 'Current Trends in Linguistics, vol. 12.' *Current Anthropology* 18: 78–82.

Hockett, Charles F., and Altmann, Stuart. 1968. A note on design features. In Sebeok, Thomas A., ed., *Animal Communication*, pp. 61–72. Bloomington: Indiana Univ. Press.

Hoensch, Jarmilla. 1976. Fragen an die Filmsemiologie. *Semiosis* 3: 42–53.

Hoffmann, Hans-Joachim. 1985. *Kleidersprache*. Frankfurt: Ullstein.

Hofstadter, Douglas R. 1980. *Gödel, Escher, Bach: An Eternal Golden Braid*. New York: Vintage.

Hogben, Lancelot. 1949. *From Cave Painting to Comic Strip*. London: Parrish.

Hogrebe, W. 1971. Bild. In Ritter, Joachim, Ed., *Historisches Wörterbuch der Philosophie*, pp. 915–19. Basel: Schwabe.

Holenstein, Elmar. (1974) 1976. *Roman Jakobson's Approach to Language: Phenomenological Structuralism*. Bloomington: Indiana Univ. Press.

———. 1976. *Linguistik, Semiotik, Hermeneutik*. Frankfurt: Suhrkamp.

———. 1978a. Präliminarien zu einer Theorie der funktionalen Aspekte der Sprache. In Seiler, Hansjakob, ed., *Language Universals*, pp. 33–52. Tübingen: Narr.

———. 1978b. Semiotic philosophy. In Bailey, R. W., et al., eds., *The Sign: Semiotics around the World*, pp. 43–67. Ann Arbor: Michigan Slavic Pub.

———. 1980. Double articulation in writing. In Coulmas, Florian, and Ehlich, Konrad, eds., *Writing in Focus*, pp. 45–62. Berlin: Mouton.

———. 1985. *Sprachliche Universalien*. Bochum: Brockmeyer.

Holmes, Wendy. 1981. Prague School aesthetics. *Semiotica* 33: 155–68.

Hołówka, Teresa. 1981. On conventionality of signs. *Semiotica* 33: 79–86.

Holub, Robert C. 1984. *Reception Theory*. London: Methuen.

Honzl, Jindřich. (1940) 1976. Dynamics of the sign in the theater. In Matejka, Ladislav, and Titunik, Irwin R., eds., *Semiotics of Art*, pp. 74–93. Cambridge, Mass.: MIT Press.

Hooff, J. A. R. A. M. van. 1972. A comparative approach to the phylogeny of laughter and smiling. In Hinde, R. A., ed., *Non-Verbal Communication*, pp. 209–238. Cambridge: Univ. Press.

Hookway, Christopher. 1985. *Peirce*. London: Routledge & Kegan.

Hopkins, Carl D. 1977. Electric communication. In Sebeok, Thomas A., ed., *How Animals Communicate*, pp. 263–89. Bloomington: Indiana Univ. Press.

Horak, Jan-Christopher, et al., eds. 1983ff. *Film Theory: Bibliographical Information and Newsletter* 1ff. (Münster: MAkS).

Hörmann, Hans. (1967) 1971. *Psycholinguistics*. Heidelberg: Springer.

Horn, Maurice, ed. 1970. *The World Encyclopedia of Comics*. New York: Chelsea Pub.

Hornung, Alfred. 1978. *Narrative Struktur und Textsortendifferenzierung*. Stuttgart: Metzler.

Householder, Fred Walter. 1971. *Linguistic Specula-tions*. Cambridge: Univ. Press.

Houser, Nathan. 1987. Toward a Peircean semiotic theory of learning. *The American Journal of Semiotics* 5: 251–74.

Hovland, Carl I., et al. (1953) 1966. *Communication and Persuasion*. New Haven: Yale Univ. Press.

Howell, Kenneth. 1987. Two aspects of Roger Bacon's semiotic theory in "De Signis." *Semiotica* 63: 73–81.

Hoy, David Couzens, ed. 1986. *Foucault: A Critical Reader*. Oxford: Blackwell.

Hsu, Francis L. K. 1983. *Exorcising the Trouble Makers*. Westport, Conn.: Greenwood.

Hubig, Christoph. 1979. Die Zeichentheorie Johann Heinrich Lamberts. *Zeitschrift für Semiotik* 1: 333–44.

Hübner, Kurt. 1985. *Die Wahrheit des Mythos*. München: Beck.

Hudson, R. A. 1968. Linguistic form: System and structure. In Meetham, A. R., and Hudson, R. A., eds., *Encyclopedia of Linguistics, Information, and Control*, pp. 278–80. Oxford: Pergamon.

Hufnagel, Erwin. 1976. *Einführung in die Hermeneu-tik*. Stuttgart: Kohlhammer.

Huggins, W. H., and Entwistle, Doris R. 1974. *Iconic Communication*. Baltimore: Johns Hopkins Univ. Press.

Hüllen, Werner. 1987. Semiotics narrated: Umberto Eco's "The Name of the Rose." *Semiotica* 64: 41–57.

———. 1989. Linguistik und Semiotik. In Koch, Walter A., ed., *Semiotics in the Individual Sciences*. Bochum: Brockmeyer.

Hünig, Wolfgang K. 1974. *Strukturen des Comic Strip*. Hildesheim: Olms.

Hupka, Werner. 1989. *Wort und Bild*. Tübingen: Niemeyer.

Husserl, Edmund. (1890) 1970. Zur Logik der Zeichen. In Husserl, Edmund, *Gesammelte Werke*, vol. 12, pp. 340–73. The Hague: Nijhoff.

———. (1900–01) 1970. *Logical Investigations*, vol. 1. London: Routledge & Kegan.

———. (1913) 1950. *Ideen zu einer reinen Phänome-nologie I* (= Husserliana, vol. 3). The Hague: Nijhoff.

Hutchinson, Ann. 1954. *Labonotation: The System for Recording Movement*. London: Phoenix.

Hutt, Clélia. 1968. Etude d'un corpus: Dictionnaire du langage gestuel chez les Trappistes. *Langages* 10: 107–18.

Huxley, Julian S. (1914) 1968. *The Courtship Habits of the Great Crested Grebe*. London: Cape.

———. 1966. Introduction. In Huxley, J. S., ed., *A Discussion of Ritualization of Behavior in Animals and Man* (= Philos. Transact. Royal Society [London], ser. B, 251 [772], 247–526), pp. 249–71.

Hymes, Dell H. 1962. The enthnography of speak-ing. In Gladwin, Thomas, and Sturtevant, William C., eds., *Anthropology and Human Behavior*, pp. 13–53. Washington, D.C.: Anthropol. Society.

———. 1972. On communicative competence. In Pride, J. B., and Holmes, Janet, eds., *Sociolinguis-tics*, pp. 269–93. Harmondsworth: Penguin.

Hymes, Dell H., and Fought, John. 1975. American structuralism. In Sebeok, Thomas A., ed., *Current Trends in Linguistics* 13.2, pp. 903–1209.

Ihwe, Jens. 1972a. *Linguistik in der Literaturwissen-schaft*. München: Bayerischer Schulbuchverlag.

———. 1972b. On the foundations of a general the-ory of narrative structure. *Poetics* 3: 5–14.

———. 1985. *Konversation über Literatur*. Braun-schweig: Vieweg.

Ihwe, Jens, ed. 1971. *Literaturwissenschaft und Lin-guistik*. 3 vols. Frankfurt: Athenäum.

Ikegami, Yoshihiko. 1971. A stratificational analysis of hand gestures in Indian classical dancing. *Semi-otica* 4: 365–91.

———. 1989. In defense of "imitation." To appear in *Proceedings of the 5th International Congress of the Deutsche Gesellschaft für Semiotik*.

Imbert, Patrick. 1978. *Sémiotique et description balzacienne*. Ottawa: Ed. de l'université.

———. 1980. Multidisciplinarity, semiotics, and pedagogy. *Ars Semeiotica* 3: 275–81.

Immelmann, Klaus. 1976. *Einführung in die Verhaltensforschung*. Berlin: Parey.

Innis, Robert E. 1981. *Karl Bühler: Semiotic Founda-tions of Language Theory*. New York: Plenum.

Innis, Robert E., ed. 1985. *Semiotics: An Introductory Anthology*. Bloomington: Indiana Univ. Press.

Isačenko, A. V. 1964. On the conative function of language. In Vachek, Josef, ed., *A Prague School Reader in Linguistics*, pp. 88–97. Bloomington: In-diana Univ. Press.

Ivanov, Vjačeslav Vsevolodovič. (1973) 1986. Der strukturale Zugang bei der Untersuchung der Sprache des Films. In Eimermacher, Karl, ed., *Se-miotica Sovietica*, pp. 729–53. Aachen: Rader.

———. (1975) 1981. Functions and categories of film language. In O'Toole, L. M., and Shukman, Ann, *Film Theory and General Semiotics*, pp. 1–35. Oxford: Holdan.

———. (1976) 1985. *Einführung in allgemeine Probleme der Semiotik*. Tübingen: Narr.

———. (1978a) 1983. *Gerade und Ungerade*. Stutt-gart: Hirzel.

———. 1978b. The structure of the Ket myth. *Working Papers of the Centro Internazionale di Se-miotica e di Linguistica* 78–79/D.

———. 1979. Nejrosemiotika ustnoj reči i funk-cional'naja asimetrija mozga [Neurosemiotics of oral speech and the functional asymmetry of the brain]. *Učenye zapiski Tartuskogo gosudarstvennogo universiteta* 481: 121–42.

———. 1985. Eisenstein's montage of hieroglyphic signs. In Blonsky, Marshall, ed., *On Signs*, pp. 221–35. Baltimore: Johns Hopkins.

Izard, Carroll E. 1971. *The Face of Emotion*. New York: Appleton.

Izutsu, Toshihiko. 1956. *Language and Magic*. Tokyo: Keio Inst.

Jachnow, Helmut. 1981. Sprachliche Funktionen und ihre Hierarchiegefüge. In Esser, Jürgen, and Hübler, Axel, eds., *Forms and Functions*, pp. 11–24. Tübingen: Narr.

Jackson, B. Darrell. 1969. The theory of signs in St. Augustine's *De doctrina christiana*. *Revue des études augustiniennes* 15: 9–49.

Jackson, Bernhard S. 1985. *Semiotics and Legal Theory*. London: Routledge & Kegan.

Jacquinot, Geneviève. 1977. *Image et pédagogie*. Paris: Presses Univ. de France.

Jadacki, J. 1986. Conceptualism, Nominalism, Realism. In Sebeok, Thomas A., ed., *Encyclopedic Dictionary of Semiotics*. Berlin: Mouton de Gruyter.

Jaeggi, Urs. 1968. *Ordnung und Chaos—Strukturalismus als Methode und Mode*. Frankfurt: Suhrkamp.

Jäger, Ludwig, and Stetter, Christian, eds. 1986. *Zeichen und Verstehen. Akten des Aachener Saussure-Kolloquiums 1983*. Aachen: Rader.

Jaglom, Akiva M., and Jaglom, Isaak M. (1967) 1984. *Wahrscheinlichkeit und Information*. Berlin: Deutscher Verlag der Wissenschaften.

Jakob, François. 1974. Le modèle linguistique en biologie. *Critique* 30 [322]: 197–205.

Jakobson, Roman. (1932) 1971. Musikwissenschaft und Linguistik. In Jakobson, R., *Selected Writings II*, pp. 551–53. The Hague: Mouton.

———. (1933a) 1973. Qu'est-ce que la poésie? In Jakobson, R., *Questions de poétique*, pp. 113–26. Paris: Seuil.

———. (1933b) 1968. Verfall des Films? *Sprache im technischen Zeitalter* 27: 185–91.

———. (1956) 1971. Two aspects of language and two types of aphasic disturbances. In Jakobson, R., *Selected Writings II*, pp. 239–59. The Hague: Mouton.

———. (1959a) 1971. On linguistic aspects of translation. In Jakobson R., *Selected Writings II*, pp. 260–66. The Hague: Mouton.

———. (1959b) 1971. Zeichen und System der Sprache. In Jakobson, R., *Selected Writings II*, pp. 272–79. The Hague: Mouton.

———. 1960. Linguistics and poetics. In Sebeok, Thomas A., ed., *Style in Language*, pp. 350–77. Cambridge, Mass.: MIT Press.

———. (1961) 1971. Linguistics and communica-tion theory. In Jakobson, R., *Selected Writings II*, pp. 570–79. The Hague: Mouton.

Jakobson, Roman (1965) 1971. Quest for the essence of language. In Jakobson, R., *Selected Writings II*, pp. 345–59. The Hague: Mouton.

———. 1966–1988. *Selected Writings*. 8 vols. The Hague & Berlin: Mouton de Gruyter.

———. (1967) 1973. Entretien sur le cinéma avec Adriana Aprá et Luigi Faccini. In Noguez, Dominique, ed., *Cinéma: théorie, lectures*, pp. 61–68. Paris: Klincksieck (= *Revue d'Esthétique* 26.2–4).

———. (1968) 1971. Language in relation to other communication systems. In Jakobson, R., *Selected Writings II*, pp. 697–708. The Hague: Mouton.

———. 1971. *Roman Jakobson: A Bibliography of His Writings*. The Hague: Mouton.

———. 1972. Motor signs for 'Yes' and 'No.' *Language in Society* 1: 91–96.

———. 1973a. *Main Trends in the Science of Language*. London: Allen & Unwin.

———. 1973b. *Questions de poétique*. Paris: Seuil.

———. (1975) 1980. A glance at the development of semiotics. In Jakobson, Roman, *The Framework of Language*, pp. 1–29. Ann Arbor: Michigan Slavic Pub. (= Mich. Studies in the Humanities 1).

———. (1976) 1978. *Six Lectures on Sound and Meaning*. Hassocks: Harvester Press.

———. 1980. *The Framework of Language*. Ann Arbor: Michigan Slavic Pub. (= Mich. Studies in the Humanities 1).

———. 1982. Einstein and the science of language. In Holton, Gerald, and Elkana, Yehuda, eds., *Albert Einstein*, pp. 139–50. Princeton: Univ. Press.

———. 1985. *Verbal Art, Verbal Sign, Verbal Time*. Minneapolis: Univ. of Minnesota Press.

Jakobson, Roman; Gadamer, Hans-Georg; and Holenstein, Elmar. 1984. *Das Erbe Hegels II*. Frankfurt: Suhrkamp.

Jakobson, Roman, and Waugh, Linda. (1979) 1988. *The Sound Shape of Language*. In Jakobson, R., *Selected Writings VIII*, pp. 1–315. Berlin: Mouton de Gruyter.

Jameson, Frederic. 1972. *The Prison-House of Language: A Critical Account of Structuralism*. Princeton: Univ. Press.

Jander, Rudolf. 1981. General semiotics and biosemiotics. In De George, Richard T., ed., 1981, *Semiotic Themes*, pp. 225–50. Lawrence: Univ. of Kansas Pub.

Janik, Dieter. 1985. *Literatursemiotik als Methode*. Tübingen: Narr.

Jansen, Steen. 1968. Esquisse d'une théorie de la forme dramatique. *Langages* 12: 71–93.

Jantsch, Erich. 1980. *The Self-Organizing Universe*. Oxford: Pergamon.

Januschek, Franz. 1976. *Sprache als Objekt: Sprech-*

handlungen in Werbung, Kunst und Linguistik. Kronberg: Scriptor.

Janzen, Daniel H. 1980. When is it coevolution? *Evolution* 34: 611–12.

Jason, Heda, and Segal, Dimitri, eds. 1977. *Patterns in Oral Literature.* The Hague: Mouton.

Jaspers, Karl. (1947) 1958. *Von der Wahrheit.* München: Piper.

Jaulin, Robert. 1970. Formal analysis of geomancy. *Semiotica* 2: 195–246.

Jencks, Charles, and Baird, George, eds. 1969. *Meaning in Architecture.* London: Barrie & Rockliff.

Jens, Walter. (1971) 1977. Rhetorik. In *Reallexikon der deutschen Literaturgeschichte,* 2nd ed., vol. 3, pp. 432–56. Berlin: de Gruyter.

Jensen, Hans. (1935) 1958. *Die Schrift in Vergangenheit und Gegenwart.* Berlin: Dt. Verlag der Wiss.

Jespersen, Otto. 1894. *Progress in Language.* London: Sonnenschein.

Jiranek, Jaroslav. 1975. The development and present situation of the semiotics of music in Czechoslovakia. In *Proceedings of the 1st International Congress on Semiotics of Music,* pp. 28–38. Pesaro: Centro di Iniziativa Culturale.

Johannesen, Richard L., ed. 1971. *Contemporary Theories of Rhetoric.* New York: Harper & Row.

Johansen, Jørgen Dines. 1986a. The place of semiotics in the study of literature. In Evans, Jonathan D., and Helbo, André, *Semiotics and International Scholarship,* pp. 101–126. Dordrecht: Nijhoff.

———. 1986b. Semiotics in Denmark. In Sebeok, T. A., and Umiker-Sebeok, J., eds., *The Semiotic Sphere,* pp. 115–43. New York: Plenum.

Johansen, Svend. 1949. La notion de signe dans la glossématique et dans l'esthétique. In *Recherches structurales* (= Travaux du cercle linguistique de Copenhague 5), pp. 288–303. Copenhagen

John of St. Thomas. See Poinsot, J.

Johnson, Harold G.; Ekman, Paul; and Friesen, Wallace V. 1975. Communicative body movements: American emblems. *Semiotica* 15: 335–53.

Johnston, James W., Jr.; Moulton, David G.; and Turk, Amos, eds. 1970. *Communication by Chemical Signals.* New York: Appleton.

Joia, Alex de, and Stenton, Adrian. 1980. *Terms in Systemic Linguistics.* London: Batsford.

Jolles, André. (1930) 1974. *Einfache Formen.* Tübingen: Niemeyer.

Joly, André. 1986. Descartes. In Sebeok, T. A., ed., *Encyclopedic Dictionary of Semiotics,* pp. 183–85. Berlin: Mouton de Gruyter.

Jones, Daniel. (1914) 1956. *Outline of English Phonetics.* London: Heffer.

Jones, Daniel, and Passy, Paul Edouard. (1907)

1971. Alphabet organique. In *Le Maître phonétique* 22.11–12, *Supplément,* pp. 1–8.

Joos, Martin. 1958. Semology: A linguistic theory of meaning. *Studies in Linguistics* 13: 53–70.

Joseph, B. L. 1951. *Elizabethan Acting.* Oxford: Univ. Press.

Jules-Rosette, Bennetta. 1986. Sociosemiotics. *International Semiotic Spectrum* 6 (June): 1–2.

Jung, Carl Gustav. 1956. *Symbols of Transformation* (= *Collected Works,* vol. 5). New York: Pantheon.

Kachru, Braj B., and Stahlke, Herbert F. W., eds. 1972. *Current Trends in Stylistics.* Edmonton, Alta.: Linguistic Research, Inc.

Kaczmarek, Ludger. 1983. Significatio in der Zeichen- und Sprachtheorie Ockhams. In Eschbach, A., and Trabant, J., eds., *History of Semiotics,* pp. 87–104. Amsterdam: Benjamins.

———. 1986. Quid sit aliquid representari in verbo. In Dutz, Klaus D., and Schmitter, Peter, eds., *Geschichte und Geschichtsschreibung der Semiotik,* pp. 85–100. Münster: MAkS.

Kaelin, E. F. 1983. Reflections on Peirce's aesthetics. In Freeman, Eugene, ed., *The Relevance of Charles Peirce,* pp. 224–37. La Salle, Ill.: Monist Library.

Kaemmerling, Ekkat (= Hans-Ekkehard). 1971. Rhetorik als Montage. In Knilli, Friedrich, ed., *Semiotik des Films,* pp. 94–112. München: Hanser.

Kaemmerling, Hans-Ekkehard. 1973. Aspekte einer semiotischen Rhetorik und Stilistik. *Sprachkunst* 4: 189–201.

Kaemmerling, Hans-Ekkehard, ed. 1979. *Ikonographie und Ikonologie* (= *Bildende Kunst als Zeichensystem,* vol. 1). Köln: DuMont.

Kagelmann, H. Jürgen. 1976. *Comics.* Bad Heilbrunn: Klinkhardt.

Kahn, David. 1966. *The Codebreakers: The Story of Secret Writing.* London: Weidenfeld.

Kainz, Friedrich. 1961. *Die "Sprache" der Tiere.* Stuttgart: Enke.

Kalinowski, Georges. 1985. *Sémiotique et philosophie.* Paris-Amsterdam: Hadès-Benjamins.

Kalkofen, Hermann. 1979. Die Einteilung der Semiotik bei Georg Klaus. *Zeitschrift für Semiotik* 1: 81–91.

———. 1983. Bestimmungselemente der Kommunikation. In Dutz, Klaus D., and Wulff, Hans J., eds., *Kommunikation, Funktion und Zeichentheorie,* pp. 111–63. Münster: MAkS.

———. 1985. *Signalverhalten und Signalstrukturen* (= Publikationen zu Wissenschaftlichen Filmen, Sektion Biologie, 17.22 [D 1339]). Göttingen: Inst. für Wiss. Film.

Kalmár, Georgius. 1774. *Grammatische Regeln zur philosophischen oder allgemeinen Sprache.* Wien.

Kalmus, H. 1962. Analogies of language to life. *Language and Speech* 5: 15–25.

Kalverkämper, Hartwig. 1983. Antike Rhetorik und Textlinguistik. In Faust, Manfred, et al., eds., *Allgemeine Sprachwissenschaft, Sprachtypologie und Textlinguistik*, pp. 349–72. Tübingen: Narr.

Kamlah, Wilhelm, and Lorenzen, Paul. 1967. *Logische Propädeutik*. Mannheim: Bibl. Inst.

Kapp, Volker, ed. 1973. *Aspekte objektiver Literaturwissenschaft*. Heidelberg: Quelle & Meyer.

Karbusicky, Vladimir. 1973. *Widerspiegelungstheorie und Strukturalismus*. München: Fink.

Katz, Jerrold J. (1971) 1972. *Linguistic Philosophy*. London: Allen & Unwin.

Kauffman, Lynn E. 1971. Tacesics, the study of touch: A model for proxemic analysis. *Semiotica* 4: 149–61.

Kehret-Ward, Trudy. 1987. Combining products in use: How the syntax of product use affects product design and promotion. In Umiker-Sebeok, Jean, ed., *Marketing and Semiotics*. Berlin: Mouton de Gruyter.

Keiler, Allan R. 1981. Two views of musical semiotics. In Steiner, Wendy, ed., *The Sign in Music and Literature*, pp. 138–68. Austin: Univ. of Texas Press.

Keim, Jean A. 1963. La photographie et sa légende. *Communications* 2: 41–55.

Kelemen, János. 1976. Locke's theory of language and semiotics. *Language Sciences* 40: 16–24.

Kelkar, Ashok R. 1984. Prolegomena to an understanding of semiotics and culture. In Fawcett, Robin P., et al., eds., *The Semiotics of Culture and Language*, vol. 2, pp. 102–134. London: F. Pinter.

Kellogg, Winthrop N., and Kellogg, Louise. (1933) 1967. *The Ape and the Child*. New York: Hafner.

Kempski, Jürgen von. 1952. *Charles Sanders Peirce und der Pragmatismus*. Stuttgart: Kohlhammer.

Kempson, Ruth. 1977. *Semantic Theory*. Cambridge: Univ. Press.

Kendon, Adam. 1972. Some relationships between body motion and speech. In Siegman, Aron Wolfe, and Pope, Benjamin, eds., *Studies in Dyadic Communication*, pp. 177–210. New York: Pergamon.

_____. 1975. Gesticulation, speech, and the gesture theory of language origins. *Sign Language Studies* 9, 349–73.

_____. 1977. *Studies in the Behavior of Social Interaction*. Lisse: de Ridder.

_____. 1980a. A description of a deaf-mute sign language from the Enga Province of Papua New Guinea. *Semiotica* 31: 1–34 and 32: 87–117.

_____. 1980b. Features of the structural analysis of human communicative behavior. In Raffler-Engel, Walburga von, ed., *Aspects of Nonverbal Communication*, pp. 29–44. Lisse: Swets & Zeitlinger.

_____. 1980c. Gesticulation and speech. In Key,

Mary Ritchie, ed., *The Relationship of Verbal and Nonverbal Communication*, pp. 207–27. The Hague: Mouton.

_____. 1980d. The sign language of the women of Yuendumu. *Sign Language Studies* 27: 101–12.

_____. 1982. Organization of behavior in face-to-face interaction. In Scherer, Klaus R., and Ekman, Paul, eds., *Handbook of Methods in Nonverbal Behavior Research*, pp. 440–505. Cambridge: Univ. Press.

_____. 1986a. Nonverbal communication. In Sebeok, Thomas A., ed., *Encyclopedic Dictionary of Semiotics*, pp. 609–22. Berlin: Mouton de Gruyter.

_____. 1986b. Some reasons for studying gesture. *Semiotica* 62: 3–28.

Kendon, Adam, ed. 1981. *Nonverbal Communication, Interaction, and Gesture*. The Hague: Mouton.

_____. 1989. *Sign Languages of Aboriginal Australia*. Cambridge: Cambridge Univ. Press.

Kendon, Adam; Harris, Richard M.; and Key, Mary Ritchie, eds. 1975. *Organization of Behavior in Face-to-Face Interaction*. The Hague: Mouton.

Kennedy, George A. 1963. *The Art of Persuasion in Greece*. Princeton: Univ. Press.

_____. (1972) 1983. *The Art of Rhetoric in the Roman World*. Princeton: Univ. Press.

_____. 1980. *Classical Rhetoric and Its Christian and Secular Tradition from Ancient to Modern Times*. Chapel Hill: Univ. of North Carolina Press.

_____. 1983. *Greek Rhetoric under Christian Emperors*. Princeton: Univ. Press.

Kennedy, John M. 1982. Metaphor in pictures. *Perception* 11: 589–605.

Kent, Beverly. 1976. Peirce's esthetics: A new look. *Transactions of the Charles Sanders Peirce Society* 12: 263–83.

Kerbrat-Orecchioni, Catherine. 1976. L'isotopie. *Linguistique et sémiologie* (Lyon) 1: 11–34.

_____. 1977. *La connotation*. Lyon: Presses Univ.

Kerner, Günter, and Duroy, Rolf. 1977. *Bildsprache 1*. München: Don Bosco.

Ketner, Kenneth L., and Kloesel, Christian J. W. 1975. The semiotics of Charles Sanders Peirce and the first dictionary of semiotics. *Semiotica* 13: 395–414.

Ketner, Kenneth L., et al., comps. 1977. *A Comprehensive Bibliography and Index of the Published Works of Charles S. Peirce with a Bibliography of Secondary Studies*. Greenwich, Conn.: Johnson (Microfiche).

Ketner, Kenneth L., et al., eds. 1981. *Proceedings of the C. S. Peirce Bicentennial International Congress*. Lubbock: Texas Tech Univ.

Kevelson, Roberta. 1986. Prolegomena to a comparative legal semiotics. In Deely, John, et al., eds., *Frontiers in Semiotics*, pp. 191–98. Bloomington: Indiana Univ. Press.

——. 1987. *Charles S. Peirce's Method of Methods*. Amsterdam: Benjamins.

——. 1988. *The Law as a System of Signs*. New York: Plenum.

Kevelson, Roberta, ed. 1987. *Law and Semiotics*. New York: Plenum.

Key, Mary Ritchie. 1975. *Paralanguage and Kinesics*. Metuchen, N.J.: Scarecrow.

——. 1977. *Nonverbal Communication: A Research Guide and Bibliography*. Metuchen: Scarecrow.

Key, Mary Ritchie, ed. 1980. *The Relationship of Verbal and Nonverbal Communication*. The Hague: Mouton.

——. 1982. *Nonverbal Communication Today*. Berlin: Mouton.

Kiefer, Georg R. 1970. *Zur Semiotisierung der Umwelt*. Stuttgart: Diss. Phil.

Kiefer, Klaus H. 1982. *Ästhetik—Semiotik—Didaktik*. Tübingen: Narr.

Kiener, Franz. 1962. *Hand, Gebärde und Charakter*. München: Reinhardt.

Kiesow, Karl-Friedrich. 1986. . . . Semasiologie von Heinrich Gomperz. In Dutz, K. D., and Schmitter, P., eds., *Geschichte und Geschichtsschreibung der Semiotik*, pp. 223–34. Münster: MAkS.

Kirby, Michael. 1982. Nonsemiotic performance. *Modern Drama* 25: 105–11.

Kirch, Max S. 1987. *Deutsche Gebärdensprache*. Hamburg: Buske.

Kircher, Athanasius. 1663. *Polygraphia nova et universalis ex combinatoria arte detecta*. Roma. Reprint of part 1 in Schott, Caspar, *Technica Curiosa*, pp. 482–579. Hildesheim: Olms, (1664) 1977.

Kirchhoff, Robert, ed. 1965. *Ausdruckspsychologie*. Göttingen: Hogrefe.

Kirshenblatt-Gimblett, Barbara, ed. 1976. *Speech Play*. Philadelphia: Univ. of Pennsylvania Press.

Kirstein, Boni. 1982. Peircean semiotic concepts applied to stylistic analysis. *Kodikas/Code* 4/5: 9–20.

Klanfer, Julius. 1934. *Sematologie Der Wappenzeichen*. Wien: Diss. Phil.

——. 1935. Theorie der heraldischen Zeichen. *Archiv für die gesamte Psychologie* 34: 413–45.

Klaus, Georg. (1963) 1973. *Semiotik und Erkenntnistheorie*. München: Fink:

——. (1964) 1972. *Die Macht des Wortes*. Berlin: DEB.

——. 1969. *Wörterbuch der Kybernetik*. Frankfurt: Fischer.

Klaus, Georg, and Buhr, Manfred, eds. (1964) 1976. *Philosophisches Wörterbuch*. Berlin: Verlag das europäische Buch.

Klaus, Georg, and Segeth, Wolfgang. 1962. Semiotik und materialistische Abbildtheorie. *Deutsche Zeitschrift für Philosophie* 10: 1245–60.

Klein, Josef. 1983. *"Denken" und "Sprechen." Nach Aspekten der theoretischen Semiotik unter besonderer Berücksichtigung der Phänomenologie Edmund Husserls*. Stuttgart: Diss. Phil.

——. 1984. Vom Adel des Gesetzes. *Semiosis* 33: 34–69.

Klein, Wolfgang, ed. 1987. *Sprache und Ritual* (= Zeitschrift für Literaturwissenschaft und Linguistik 65). Göttingen: Vandenhoeck.

Kleinpaul, Rudolf. (1888) 1972. *Sprache ohne Worte*. The Hague: Mouton.

Kleinschmidt, Gert. 1973. Welt durch Zeichen. *Praxis Deutsch* 1/73: 17–20.

Klima, Edward S., and Bellugi, Ursula, et al. 1979. *The Signs of Language*. Cambridge, Mass.: Harvard Univ. Press.

Klinkenberg, Jean-Marie. 1973. Le concept d'isotopie. *Le français moderne* 41: 285–90.

——. 1986. Style. In Sebeok, Thomas A., ed., *Encyclopedic Dictionary of Semiotics*, pp. 1022–25. Berlin: Mouton de Gruyter.

Klinkenberg, Jean-Marie, et al. (Groupe μ). 1980. Plan d'une rhétorique de l'image. *Kodikas/Code* 2: 249–68.

——. 1985. Structure et rhétorique du signe iconique. In Parret, H., and Ruprecht, H.-G., eds., *Exigences et perspectives de la sémiotique*, pp. 449–61. Amsterdam: Benjamins.

Klix, Friedhart. 1971. *Information und Verhalten*. Berlin: Verlag der Wissenschaften.

Kloepfer, Rolf. 1975. *Poetik und Linguistik*. München: Fink UTB.

——. 1976. Komplementarität von Sprache und Bild am Beispiel Comic, Karikatur und Reklame. *Sprache im technischen Zeitalter* 57: 42–56.

——. 1977a. Tendenzen der Literatursemiotik in der Bundesrepublik Deutschland. *Romanistische Zeitschrift für Literaturgeschichte* 1: 247–64.

——. 1977b. Zum Problem des "narrativen Kode." *Zeitschrift für Literaturwissenschaft und Linguistik* 27/28: 69–90.

——. 1986a. Die zunehmende Orientierung des europäischen Fernsehens an der Ästhetik des Werbespots. *Mannheimer Berichte* 29: 13–18.

——. 1986b. Mimesis und Sympraxis: Zeichengelenktes Mitmachen ım erzählenden Werbespot. In Kloepfer, R., and Möller, K. D., eds., *Narrativität in den Medien*. Mannheim: MANA, and Münster: MAkS.

Klopfer, Peter H., and Hailman, Jack P., eds. 1972. *Function and Evolution of Behavior*. Reading, Mass.: Addison-Wesley.

Kluge, F. 1885. Zur Geschichte der Zeichensprache. *Internationale Zeitschrift für allgemeine Sprachwissenschaft* 2: 116–40.

Knapp, Mark L. 1978. *Nonverbal Communication in Human Interaction*. 2nd ed. New York: Holt.

Kneale, William, and Kneale, Martha. (1962) 1978. *The Development of Logic*. Oxford: Clarendon.

Kneif, Tibor. 1974. Was ist Semiotik der Musik? *Neue Zeitschrift für Musik* 135: 348–53.

Knilli, Friedrich. 1970. *Deutsche Lautsprecher. Versuche zu einer Semiotik des Radios*. Stuttgart: Metzler.

———. 1979. Medium. In Faulstich, Werner, ed., *Kritische Stichwörter zur Medienwissenschaft*, pp. 230–51. München: Fink.

Knilli, Friedrich, ed. 1971. *Semiotik des Films*. Frankfurt: Athenäum.

Knilli, Friedrich, and Reiss, Erwin. 1971. *Einführung in die Film- und Fernsehanalyse*. Steinbach: Anabas.

Knobloch, Ferdinand, et al. 1968. On an interpersonal hypothesis in the semiotic of music. *Kybernetika* (Číslo) 4: 364–82.

Knowlson, James. 1975. *Universal Language Schemes in England and France*. Toronto: Univ. Press.

Knowlton, James Q. 1966. On the definition of "picture." *Audio Visual Communication Review* 14: 157–83.

Knuf, Joachim, and Schmitz, H. Walter. 1980. *Ritualisierte Kommunikation und Sozialstruktur*. Hamburg: Buske.

Koch, Rudolf. (1930) 1955. *The Book of Signs*. New York: Dover.

Koch, Walter A. 1963. On the principles of stylistics. *Lingua* 12: 411–22.

———. 1966. *Recurrence and a Three-Modal Approach to Poetry*. The Hague: Mouton.

———. 1968. Linguistische Analyse und Strukturen der Poetizität. *Orbis* 17: 5–22.

———. (1969) 1973. Le texte normal, le théâtre et le film. In Koch, Walter A., *Das Textem*, pp. 99–126. Hildesheim: Olms.

———. 1971a. *Taxologie des Englischen*. München: Fink.

———. 1971b. *Varia Semiotica*. Hildesheim: Olms.

———. 1973. *Das Textem*. Hildesheim: Olms.

———. 1974a. Semiotik und Sprachgenese. In Koch, Walter A., ed., *Perspektiven der Linguistik II*, pp. 312–46. Stuttgart: Kröner.

———. 1974b. Tendenzen der Linguistik. In Koch, Walter A., ed., *Perspektiven der Linguistik II*, pp. 190–311. Stuttgart: Kröner.

———. 1976. Ontologiethese und Relativitätsthese für eine Textlinguistik. In Koch, Walter A., ed., *Textsemiotik und strukturelle Rezeptionstheorie*, pp. 1–38. Hildesheim: Olms.

———. 1981. Roman Jakobson. In Schnelle, H., ed., *Sprache und Gehirn*, pp. 223–35. Frankfurt: Suhrkamp.

———. 1983. *Poetry and Science: Semiogenetical Twins*. Tübingen: Narr.

———. 1984. Art: Biogenesis and semiogenesis. *Semiotica* 49: 283–304.

———. 1985. Tension and suspense: On the biogenesis and semiogenesis of the detective novel, soccer, and art. In Ballmer, Thomas T., ed., *Linguistic Dynamics*, pp. 279–321. Berlin: de Gruyter.

———. 1986a. *Evolutionary Cultural Semiotics*. Bochum: Brockmeyer.

———. 1986b. *Genes vs. Memes*. Bochum: Brockmeyer.

———. 1986c. *Philosophie der Philologie und Semiotik. Literatur und Welt: Versuche zur Interdisziplinarität der Philologie*. Bochum: Brockmeyer.

———. 1987. First draft of a curriculum in semiotics. In Eschbach, A., and Koch, W. A., eds., *A Plea for Cultural Semiotics*, pp. 146–63. Bochum: Brockmeyer.

———. 1988. The biology of the theatre: On the semiogenesis of drama and related cultural events. Bochum: Ms.

Koch, Walter A., ed. 1972. *Strukturelle Textanalyse*. Hildesheim: Olms.

———. 1976. *Textsemiotik und strukturelle Rezeptionstheorie*. Hildesheim: Olms.

———. 1979. *Semiotische Versuche zu literarischen Strukturen*. Hildesheim: Olms.

———. 1982. *Semiogenesis*. Frankfurt: Lang.

———. 1989a. *The Nature of Culture*. Bochum: Brockmeyer.

———. 1989b. *Geneses of Language*. Bochum: Brockmeyer.

———. 1989c. *Semiotics in the Individual Sciences*. Bochum: Brockemeyer.

Köck, Wolfram K. 1980. Autopoiesis and communication. In Benseler, Frank; Heijl, Peter M.; and Köck, Wolfram, K., eds., *Autopoiesis, Communication, and Society*, pp. 87–112. Frankfurt: Campus.

Koenig, Giovanni Klaus. 1964. *Analisi del linguaggio architettonico*. Firenze: Fiorentina.

———. 1970. *Architettura e comunicazione*. Firenze: Fiorentina.

Koenig, Otto. 1970. *Kultur und Verhaltensforschung: Einführung in die Kulturtheologie*. München: dtv.

———. 1975. *Urmotiv Auge*. München: Piper.

Koerner, Ernst F. Konrad. 1972a. *Bibliographia saussureana 1870–1970*. Metuchen: Scarecrow.

———. 1972b. *Contribution au débat post-saussurien sur le signe linguistique*. The Hague: Mouton.

———. 1973. *Ferdinand de Saussure*. Braunschweig: Vieweg.

———. 1975. European structuralism: Early beginnings. In Sebeok, Thomas A., ed., *Current Trends in Linguistics* 13.2: 717–827. The Hague: Mouton.

Köhring, Klaus Heinrich, and Schwerdtfeger, Inge Christine. 1976. Landeskunde im Fremdsprachenunterricht: Eine Neubegründung unter semiotischem Aspekt. *Linguistik und Didaktik* 7/ 25: 55–84.

Kolers, Paul A., et al., eds. 1979–80. *Processing of Visible Language 1–2*. New York: Plenum.

Köller, Wilhelm. 1975. *Semiotik und Metapher.* Stuttgart: Metzler.

———. 1977. Der sprachtheoretische Wert des semiotischen Zeichenmodells. In Spinner, Kaspar H., ed., *Zeichen, Text, Sinn—Zur Semiotik des literarischen Verstehens*, pp. 7–77. Göttingen: Vandenhoeck.

———. 1980. Der Peircesche Denkansatz als Grundlage für die Literatursemiotik. In Eschbach, Achim, and Rader, Wendelin, eds., *Literatursemiotik I*, pp. 39–64. Tübingen: Narr.

———. 1986. Dimensionen des Metaphernproblems. *Zeitschrift für Semiotik* 8: 379–410.

Kolschanski, Gennadij V. (1984) 1985. *Kommunikative Funktion und Struktur der Sprache.* Leipzig: Bibl. Inst.

Komar, Gerhard. 1985. *Ansatz zu einer zeichentheoretisch orientierten Wirtschaftsdidaktik.* München: Minerva.

Komenský. See Comenius.

Kondratow, A. 1964. Semiotik und Kunsttheorie. *Kunst und Literatur* 12: 519–30.

Köngäs-Maranda, Elli, and Maranda, Pierre. 1971. *Structural Models in Folklore.* The Hague: Mouton.

Kopperschmidt, Josef. (1973) 1976. *Allgemeine Rhetorik.* Stuttgart: Kohlhammer.

Korsmeyer, Carolyn. 1985. Pictorial assertion. *Journal of Aesthetics and Art Criticism* 43.3: 257–65.

Korzybski, Alfred. 1933. *Science and Sanity.* Lakeville, Conn.: Int. Non-Aristotelian Library.

Kott, Jan. 1969. The icon and the absurd. *The Drama Review* 14: 17–24.

Kowalski, Klaus. 1975. *Die Wirkung visueller Zeichen.* Stuttgart: Klett.

Kowzan, Tadeusz. 1968. Le signe au théâtre. *Diogène* 61: 59–90.

———. 1975. *Littérature et spectacle.* The Hague: Mouton.

Kracauer, Siegfried. (1960) 1973. *Theorie des Films.* Frankfurt: Suhrkamp.

Krafft, Ulrich. 1978. *Comics lesen.* Stuttgart: Klett-Cotta.

Krames, Lester; Pliner, Patricia; and Alloway, Thomas, eds. 1974. *Nonverbal Communication.* New York: Plenum.

Krampen, Martin. 1965. Signs and symbols in graphic communication. *Design Quarterly* 62: 3–31.

———. 1979a. Survey on current work in semiology of architecture. In Chatman, Seymour, et al., eds., *A Semiotic Landscape*, pp. 169–94. The Hague: Mouton.

———. 1979b. *Meaning in the Urban Environment.* London: Pion.

———. 1973. Iconic signs, supersigns, and models. *Versus* 4: 101–108.

———. 1981a. A bouquet for Roman Jakobson. *Semiotica* 33: 261–99.

———. 1981b (1987). Ferdinand de Saussure and the development of semiology. In Krampen, Martin, et al., eds., *Classics of Semiotics*, pp. 59–88. New York: Plenum.

———. 1981c. Phytosemiotics. *Semiotica* 36: 187–209.

———. 1983. *Icons of the Road.* Berlin: de Gruyter (= *Semiotica* 44. 1/2).

———. 1985. Leistung und Grenzen der Grafik. *Zeitschrift für Semiotik* 7: 3–8.

———. 1986. Phytosemiotics. In Sebeok, T. A., ed., *Encyclopedic Dictionary of Semiotics*, pp. 726–30. Berlin: Mouton de Gruyter.

Krampen, Martin, ed. 1983. *Visuelle Kommunikation und/oder verbale Kommunikation.* Hildesheim: Olms.

Krampen, Martin, et al., eds. (1981) 1987. *Classics of Semiotics.* New York: Plenum.

Krebs, J. R., and Davies, N. B., eds. 1978. *Behavioral Ecology.* Oxford: Blackwell.

Kretzmann, Norman. 1967. History of semantics. In Edwards, Paul, ed., *Encyclopedia of Philosophy*, vols. 7–8, pp. 358–406. New York: Macmillan.

———. 1974. Aristotle on spoken sound significant by convention. In Corcoran, J., ed. *Ancient Logic*, pp. 3–21. Dordrecht: Reidel.

———. 1976. The main thesis of Locke's semantic theory. In Parret, Herman, ed., *History of Linguistic Thought and Contemporary Linguistics*, pp. 331–47. Berlin: de Gruyter.

Kretzmann, Norman, et al., eds. 1982. *The Cambridge History of Later Medieval Philosophy.* Cambridge: Univ. Press.

Krippendorff, Klaus. 1986. *Information Theory: Structural Models for Qualitative Data* (= Quantitative Applications in the Social Sciences 62). Beverly Hills: Sage.

Kris, Ernst. 1952. *Psychoanalytic Explorations in Art.* New York: Int. Univ. Press.

Kristeva, Julia. (1969a) 1981. *Le langage, cet inconnu.* Paris: Seuil.

———. 1969b. La sémiologie comme science des idéologies. *Semiotica* 1: 196–204.

———. 1969c. Σημειωτική: *Recherches pour une sémanalyse.* Paris: Seuil.

———. (1970) 1976. *Le texte du roman.* The Hague: Mouton.

———. (1974) 1984. *Revolution in Poetic Language.* New York: Columbia Univ. Press.

———. (1975) 1985. Sémiologie. In *Encyclopaedia universalis*, vol. 16, pp. 703–706.

———. 1977. *Polylogue.* Paris: Seuil.

———. 1980. *Desire in Language: A Semiotic Approach to Literature and Art.* New York: Columbia Univ. Press.

———. 1982. *Powers of Horror: An Essay on Abjection.* New York: Columbia Univ. Press.

———. 1986. *The Kristeva Reader,* ed. Moi, Toril. New York: Columbia Univ. Press.

Kristeva, Julia, and Coquet, Jean-Claude. 1972. Sémanalyse: Conditions d'une sémiotique scientifique. *Semiotica* 5: 324–49.

Kritzman, Lawrence. 1978. A. J. Greimas and narrative semiotics. In Bailey, Richard W., et al., eds., *The Sign: Semiotics around the World,* pp. 258–70. Ann Arbor: Michigan Slavic Pub.

Kröber, Günter. 1968. Die Kategorie "Struktur" und der kategorische Strukturalismus. *Deutsche Zeitschrift für Philosophie* 16: 1310–25.

Kroeber, A. L. 1928. Subhuman culture beginnings. *The Quarterly Beginnings of Biology* 3: 325–42.

———. 1958. Sign language inquiry. *International Journal of American Linguistics* 24: 1–19.

Kroeber, Burkhart, ed. 1987. *Zeichen in Umberto Ecos Roman "Der Name der Rose."* München: Hanser.

Kroepsch, Rainer A. 1976. Zur strukturellen Theorie der Massenkommunikation. In Koch, Walter A., ed., *Textsemiotik und strukturelle Rezeptionstheorie,* pp. 214–355. Hildesheim: Olms.

Kröhnert, Otto. 1966. *Die sprachliche Bildung des Gehörlosen.* Weinheim: Beltz.

Krois, John Michael. 1984a. Cassirers semiotische Philosophie. In Oehler, K., ed., *Zeichen und Realität,* vol. 1, pp. 361–67. Tübingen: Stauffenburg.

———. 1984b. Ernst Cassirers Semiotik der symbolischen Formen. *Zeitschrift für Semiotik* 6.4: 433–44.

Kronasser, Heinz. (1952) 1968. *Handbuch der Semasiologie.* Heidelberg: Winter.

Kroodsma, Donald E., and Miller, Edward H., eds. 1982. *Acoustic Communication in Birds.* 2 vols. New York: Academic Press.

Kuleshov, Lev. 1974. *Kuleshov on Film,* trans. & ed. Levaco, Ronald. Berkeley: Univ. of California Press.

Kümmel, Friedrich. 1962. *Über den Begriff der Zeit.* Niemeyer: Tübingen.

Kuno, Susumu. 1987. *Functional Syntax.* Chicago: Univ. Press.

Kunzle, David. 1973. *History of the Comic Strip.* Berkeley: Univ. of California Press.

Kurz, Gerhard. 1976. Warnung vor dem Wörtchen "Kode." *Linguistik und Didaktik* 26: 154–64.

Kurzweil, Edith. 1980. *The Age of Structuralism: Lévi-Strauss to Foucault.* New York: Columbia Univ. Press.

Kutschera, Franz von. (1971) 1975. *Sprachphilosophie.* München: Fink.

Kuwayama, Yasaburo. 1973. *Trademarks and Symbols.* 2 vols. New York: Van Nostrand.

Kuypers, K. 1934. *Der Zeichen- und Wortbegriff im Denken Augustins.* Amsterdam: Swets & Zeitlinger.

Kyle, Jim G., and Woll, Bencie, eds. 1983. *Language in Sign.* London: Croom Helm.

La Barre, Weston. (1947) 1972. The cultural basis of emotions and gestures. In Laver, John, and Hutcheson, Sandy, eds., *Communication in Face to Face Interaction,* pp. 207–224. Harmondsworth: Penguin.

———. (1964) 1972. Paralinguistics, kinesics, and cultural anthropology. In Sebeok, Thomas A., et al., eds., *Approaches to Semiotics,* pp. 191–220. The Hague: Mouton.

Labov, Williams. 1972. *Language in the Inner City.* Philadelphia: Univ. of Pennsylvania Press.

Labov, William, and Waletzky, Joshua. 1967. Narrative analysis: Oral versions of personal experience. In Helm, June, ed., *Essays on the Verbal and Visual Arts.* Seattle: Univ. of Washington Press.

Lacan, Jacques. (1949) 1968. The mirror phase. *New Left Review* 51: 71–77.

———. (1956) 1968. *The Language of the Self,* trans. and annot. Wilden, Anthony. Baltimore: Johns Hopkins.

———. (1966) 1980. *Ecrits: A Selection.* London: Tavistock.

———. (1973) 1977. *The Four Fundamental Concepts of Psycho-analysis.* London: Hogarth.

Laferrière, Daniel. 1979. Structuralism and quasi-semiotics. *Semiotica* 25: 307–17.

LaFrance, Marianne, and Mayo, Clara. 1978. *Moving Bodies.* Monterey, Calif.: Brooks/Cole.

Lagrange, Marie-Salomé. 1973. *Analyse sémiologique et historie de l'art.* Paris: Klincksieck.

Lakoff, George, and Johnson, Mark. 1980. *Metaphors We Live By.* Chicago: Univ. of Chicago Press.

Lamb, Sydney M. 1984. Semiotics of language and culture. In Fawcett, Robin P., et al., eds., *The Semiotics of Culture and Language,* vol. 2, pp. 71–100. London: F. Pinter.

Lamb, Warren, and Watson, Elizabeth. 1979. *Body Code.* London: Routledge & Kegan.

Lambert, Johann Heinrich. (1764) 1965. *Neues Organon oder Gedanken über die Erforschung und Bezeichnung des Wahren und dessen Unterscheidung vom Irrthum und Schein (= Philosophische Schriften,* vol. 1–2). Hildesheim: Olms.

Lamizet, Bernard. 1984. Sémiotique du nombre. In

Borbé, T., ed., *Semiotics Unfolding*, vol. 3, pp. 1483–91. Berlin: Mouton.

Lämmert, Eberhard. (1955) 1975. *Bauformen des Erzählens*. Stuttgart: Metzler.

Lämmert, Eberhard, ed. 1982. *Erzählforschung*. Stuttgart: Metzler.

Land, Stephen K. 1974. *From Signs to Propositions*. London: Longman.

Landowski, Eric. 1980. *Le devoir de français*. Paris: Ed. pédagogie moderne.

Landsberg, M. E., ed. 1988. *The Genesis of Language*. Berlin: Mouton de Gruyter.

Lane, Harlan. 1980. A chronology of the oppression of sign language in France and the United States. In Lane, Harlan, and Grosjean, François, eds., *Recent Perspectives on American Sign Language*, pp. 119–61. Hillsdale, N.J.: Erlbaum.

Lane, Harlan, and Grosjean, François, eds. 1980. *Recent Perspectives on American Sign Language*. Hillsdale, N.J.: Lawrence Erlbaum.

Lane, Michael, ed. 1970. *Introduction to Structuralism*. New York: Basic Books.

Langer, Susanne K. (1942) 1951. *Philosophy in a New Key*. New York: Mentor.

Lange-Seidl, Annemarie. 1985 and 1988. Semiotik an den Universitäten der Bundesrepublik Deutschland, Österreichs und der Schweiz. *Zeitschrift für Semiotik* 7: 465–76 and 10: 291–310.

———. (1975) 1977. *Approaches to Theories for Nonverbal Signs*. Lisse: de Ridder.

Lange-Seidl, Annemarie, ed. 1981. *Zeichenkonstitution*. 2 vols. Berlin: de Gruyter.

———. 1988. *Zeichen und Magie*. Tübingen: Stauffenburg.

Langholz-Leymore, Varda. 1975. *Hidden Myth: Structure and Symbolism in Advertising*. London: Heineman (and New York: Basic Books).

Langner, Paul Werner. 1985. *Strukturelle Analyse verbal-visueller Textkonstitution in der Anzeigenwerbung*. Frankfurt: Lang.

Lanigan, Richard I. 1972. *Speaking and Semiology*. The Hague: Mouton.

———. 1977. *Speech Act Phenomenology*. The Hague: Nijhoff.

Lanyon, W. E., and Tavolga, W. N., eds. 1960. *Animal Sounds and Communication*. Washington: American Inst. of Biol. Sciences.

Large, Andrew. 1985. *The Artificial Language Movement*. Oxford: Blackwell.

Larrain, Jorge. 1980. *The Concept of Ideology*. Athens: Univ. of Georgia Press.

Lasso [Licenciado]. (1550) 1919. *Tratado legal sobre los mudos*. Madrid: Minuesa.

Laszlo, Ervin. (1972) 1973. *Introduction to Systems Philosophy*. New York: Gordon & Breach.

———. 1983. *Systems Science and World Order*. Oxford: Pergamon.

Laughlin, Charles D., Jr., and Stephens, Christopher D. 1980. Symbolism, canalization, and *p*-structure. In Foster, Mary LeCron, and Brandes, Stanley H., eds., *Symbol as Sense*, pp. 323–63. New York: Academic Press.

Lauretis, Teresa de. 1979. Semiotics of the theatre: Some theoretical problems. *Canadian Journal of Research in Semiotics* 6: 171–86.

———. 1984. *Alice Doesn't*. Bloomington: Indiana Univ. Press.

Lausberg, Heinrich. 1960. *Handbuch der literarischen Rhetorik*. 2 vols. 2nd ed. München: Hueber.

Laver, John. (1968) 1972. Voice quality and indexical information. In Laver, John, and Hutcheson, Sandy, eds., *Communication in Face to Face Interaction*, pp. 189–203. Harmondsworth: Penguin.

———. 1975. Communicative functions of phatic communion. In Kendon, Adam, et al., eds., *Organization of Behavior in Face-to-Face Interaction*, pp. 215–38. The Hague: Mouton.

———. 1976. Language and nonverbal communication. In Carterette, Edward C., and Friedman, Morton P., eds., *Handbook of Perception VII*, pp. 345–61. New York: Academic Press.

———. 1980. *The Phonetic Description of Voice Quality*. Cambridge: Univ. Press.

Laver, John, and Hutcheson, Sandy, eds. 1972. *Communication in Face to Face Interaction*. Harmondsworth: Penguin.

Laver, John, and Trudgill, Peter. 1979. Phonetic and linguistic markers in speech. In Scherer, Klaus R., and Giles, Howard, eds., *Social Markers in Speech*, pp. 1–32. Cambridge: Univ. Press.

Lavers, Annette. 1982. *Roland Barthes: Structuralism and After*. London: Methuen.

Lavis, Georges. 1971. Le texte littéraire, le référent, le réel, le vrai. *Cahiers d'analyse textuelle* 13: 7–22.

Lawendowski, Bogusław P. 1978. On semiotic aspects of translations. In Sebeok, Thomas A., ed., *Sight, Sound, and Sense*, pp. 264–82. Bloomington: Indiana Univ. Press.

Leach, Edmund R. (1962) 1967. Genesis as myth. In Middleton, John, ed., *Myth and Cosmos*, pp. 1–13. Garden City: Natural History Press.

———. (1970) 1974. *Lévi-Strauss*. New York: Viking.

———. 1972. The influence of cultural context on non-verbal communication in man. In Hinde, R. A., ed., *Non-Verbal Communication*, pp. 315–47. Cambridge: Univ. Press.

———. 1976. *Culture and Communication*. Cambridge: Univ. Press.

Leathers, Dale G. 1976. *Nonverbal Communication Systems*. Boston: Allyn & Bacon.

Le Boeuf, Claude. 1979. Les apports de la sémiotique au marketing. *Humanisme & Entreprise* N.S. 55: 13–31.

Ledrut, Raymond. 1973. *Les images de la ville*. Paris: Anthropos.

Leech, Geoffrey N. 1966. *English in Advertising*. London: Longman.

———. 1974. *Semantics*. Harmondsworth: Penguin.

———. 1983. *Principles of Pragmatics*. London: Longman.

Lees, Robert B. 1980. Language and the genetic code. In Rauch, Irmengard, and Carr, Gerald F., eds., *The Signifying Animal*, pp. 218–26. Bloomington: Indiana Univ. Press.

Lefebvre, Henri. 1966. *Le langage et la société*. Paris: Gallimard.

———. 1971. Musique et sémiologie. *Musique en jeu* 4: 52–62.

Leff, Gordon. 1975. *William of Ockham*. Manchester: Rowman & Littlefield.

Le Guern, Michel. 1973. *Sémantique de la métaphore et de la métonymie*. Paris: Larousse.

Lehner, Ernst. 1950. *Symbols, Signs, & Signets*. New York: Dover.

Leisi, Ernst. 1973. *Praxis der englischen Semantik*. Heidelberg: Winter.

Leiss, William. 1983. The icons of the marketplace. *Theory Culture and Society* 1.3: 10–21.

Leiss, William; Kline, Stephen; and Jhally, Sut. 1986. *Social Communication in Advertising*. New York: Methuen.

Lekomceva, M. J., and Uspenskij, B. A. 1977. Describing a semiotic system with a simple syntax. In Lucid, Daniel P., ed., *Soviet Semiotics*, pp. 65–76. Baltimore: Johns Hopkins Univ. Press.

Lemke, J. L. 1987. Social semiotics and science education. *American Journal of Semiotics* 5: 217–32.

Lenneberg, Eric Heinz. 1967. *Biological Foundations of Language*. New York: Wiley.

Leonhard, Karl. 1976. *Der menschliche Ausdruck in Mimik, Gestik und Phonetik*. Leipzig: Barth.

Leont'ev, A. A. (1969) 1971. *Sprache—Sprechen—Sprechtätigkeit*. Stuttgart: Kohlhammer.

Lepschy, Giulio C. 1975. European structuralism: Post-Saussurean schools. In Sebeok, Thomas A., ed., *Current Trends in Linguistics* 13.2: 887–902. The Hague: Mouton.

Leroi-Gourhan, André. 1964–65. *Le geste et la parole*. 2 vols. Paris: Albin.

Lersch, Philipp. (1932) 1961. *Gesicht und Seele*. München: Reinhardt.

Levaco, Ronald. 1971. Kuleshov. *Sight and Sound*. 40.2: 86–91 and 109.

Levin, Samuel R. 1962. *Linguistic Structures in Poetry*. The Hague: Mouton.

———. 1977. *The Semantics of Metaphor*. Baltimore: Johns Hopkins Univ. Press.

Lévi-Strauss, Claude. (1958) 1963. *Structural Anthropology*. New York: Basic Books.

———. (1962) 1966. *The Savage Mind*. Chicago: Univ. Press.

———. (1964) 1970. *The Raw and the Cooked*. London: Cape.

———. (1973) 1976. *Structural Anthropology*, vol. II. New York: Basic Books.

Levy, Sidney J. 1978. *Marketplace Behavior*. New York: AMACOM.

Lewis, C. I. 1918. *A Survey of Symbolic Logic*. Berkeley: Univ. of Calif. Press.

Lewis, David. 1969. *Convention*. Cambridge, Mass.: Harvard Univ. Press.

Lewis, Ioan M., Ed. 1977. *Symbols and Sentiments*. New York: N.Y. Press.

Lewis, Philip E. 1974. Revolutionary semiotics. *Diacritics* 4 (Fall): 28–32.

Lewis, William R. 1981. *A Semiotic Model for Theatre Criticism*. Ann Arbor, Mich.: Univ. Microfilms Int.

Lhoest, Françoise. 1979. Regards sur la sémiotique soviétique. In Helbo, André, ed., *Le champ sémiologique*, pp. R1–22. Bruxelles: Ed. Complexe.

Libéria, Alain de. 1976. La sémiotique d'Aristote. In Nef, Fréderic, ed., *Structures élémentaires de la signification*, pp. 28–55. Bruxelles: Ed. Complexe.

Liddell, Scott K. 1980. *American Sign Language Syntax*. The Hague: Mouton.

Lieb, Hans-Heinrich. 1964. *Der Umfang des historischen Metaphernbegriffs*. Köln: Diss. Phil.

———. 1971. On subdividing semiotic. In Bar-Hillel, Yehoshua, ed., *Pragmatics of Natural Languages*, pp. 94–119. Dordrecht: Reidel.

———. 1981a. Das 'semiotische Dreieck' bei Ogden und Richards: eine Neuformulierung des Zeichenmodells von Aristoteles. In Geckeler, Horst, et al., eds., *Logos Semanticos*, pp. 137–56. Berlin: de Gruyter.

———. 1981b. Sprachwissenschaft semiotisch gesehen—aktuelle Probleme. In Lange-Seidl, Annemarie, ed., *Zeichenkonstitution*, vol. 1, pp. 147–54. Berlin: de Gruyter.

Lieberman, Philip. 1972. *The Speech of Primates*. The Hague: Mouton.

———. 1984. *The Biology and Evolution of Language*. Cambridge, Mass.: Harvard Univ. Press.

Lilly, John Cunningham. 1967. *The Mind of the Dolphin*. Garden City: Doubleday.

———. 1978. *Communication between Man and Dolphin*. New York: Crown.

Lindauer, Martin. (1961) 1971. *Communication among Social Bees*. Cambridge, Mass.: Harvard Univ. Press.

Lindekens, René. 1971. *Eléments pour une sémiotique de la photographie*. Paris: Didier.

———. 1973. Eléments pour une analyse du code de l'image photographique. In Rey-Debove,

Josette, ed., *Recherches sur les systèmes signifiants*, pp. 505–34. The Hague: Mouton

———. 1974. Sémiotique d'un type de discours: l'annonce publicitaire. *Canadian Journal of Semiotics* 2: 7–21.

———. 1975. *Sémiotique du discours publicitaire* (= Documents de Travail 45 B, Centro Internazionale di Semiotica e di Linguistica, Università di Urbino).

———. 1976. *Essai de sémiotique visuelle*. Paris: Klincksieck.

———. 1978. Sémiotique de l'image fixe et informations scientifiques. In *Colloque international: Aspects de la photographie scientifique: Actes*, pp. 11–19. Paris: Centre National de la Recherche Scientifique.

Lindemann, Bernhard. 1972. L'arbitraire du signe: Zur Neubestimmung eines Saussureschen Begriffs. *Orbis* 21: 275–88.

———. 1977. *Experimentalfilm als Metafilm*. Hildesheim: Olms.

Linden, Eugene. 1976. *Apes, Men, and Language*. Harmondsworth: Penguin.

Lindner, Monika, and Pfister, Manfred. 1984. Structuralism in Germany. *Structuralist Review* 2: 88–119.

Linke, Detlef. 1981. Ganzheit und Teilbarkeit des Gehirns. In Schnelle, Helmut, ed., *Sprache und Gehirn*, pp. 81–109. Frankfurt: Suhrkamp.

Linsky, Leonard. 1967. *Referring*. London: Routledge & Kegan Paul.

Lipski, John M. 1976. On the meta-structure of literary discourse. *Journal of Literary Semantics* 5: 53–61.

Ljung, Magnus. 1965. Principles of a stratificational analysis of the Plains Indian Sign Language. *International Journal of American Linguistics* 31: 119–27.

Lloyd, James E. 1977. Bioluminescence and communication. In Sebeok, Thomas A., ed., *How Animals Communicate*, pp. 164–83. Bloomington: Indiana Univ. Press.

Locke, John. (1690) 1973. *An Essay concerning Human Understanding*. London: Collins.

Lodwick, Francis. (1647) 1969. *A Common Writing: Whereby Two, Although Not Understanding One the Others Language, Yet by the Helpe thereof, May Communicate Their Minds One to Another*. Menston: Scolar Reprint.

Lohr, Günther. 1987. *Körpertext: Historische Semiotik der komischen Praxis*. Opladen: Westdt. Verlag.

Loof, Dennis de. 1976. Some American and German customs compared. *Le Langage et l'Homme* 30: 37–46.

———. 1981. A comparison of selected German and American emblems. *Kodikas/Code* 3: 99–118.

Lorenz, Konrad. 1978. *Vergleichende Verhaltensforschung*. Wien, New York: Springer.

Lorenz, Wolfgang, and Wotjak, Gerd. 1977. *Zum Verhältnis von Abbild und Bedeutung*. Berlin: Akademie Verlag.

Lotman, Jurij M. (1970) 1977. *The Structure of the Artistic Text*. Ann Arbor: Univ. of Michigan.

———. (1972) 1976. *The Analysis of the Poetic Text*. Ann Arbor: Univ. of Michigan.

———. (1973) 1976. *Semiotics of Cinema*. Ann Arbor: Univ. of Michigan.

Lotman, Jurij M., and Pjatigorskij, A. M. 1977. Text and function. In Lucid, Daniel P., ed., *Soviet Semiotics*, pp. 125–35. Baltimore: Johns Hopkins Univ. Press.

Lotman, Jurij M., and Uspenskij, Boris A. (1974) 1976. Myth—name—culture. In Baran, Henryk, ed., *Semiotics and Structuralism*, pp. 3–32. White Plains, N.Y.: Int. Arts and Sciences Press.

Lotman, Jurij M., and Uspenskij, Boris A., eds. 1973. *Ricerche semiotiche*. Torino: Einaudi.

Lotz, John. 1966. Adolf Noreen. In Sebeok, Thomas A., ed., *Portraits in Linguistics*, vol. 2, pp. 56–65. Bloomington: Indiana Univ. Press.

Lubac, Henri de. 1959–64. *Exégèse médiévale*. 4 vols. Paris: Aubier.

Lucas, Yvette. 1974. *Codes et machines: Essai de sémiologie industrielle*. Paris: Presses Univ. de France.

Lucid, Daniel P., ed. 1977. *Soviet Semiotics*. Baltimore: Johns Hopkins Univ. Press.

Lullus, Raymundus. (1308) 1970. *Ars Generalis Ultima*. Frankfurt: Minerva.

Lumsden, Charles J. 1986. The gene and the sign. *Semiotica* 62: 191–206.

Lumsden, Charles J., and Wilson, Edward O. 1981. *Genes, Mind, and Culture*. Cambridge, Mass.: Harvard Univ. Press.

Lurçat, Liliane. 1972. Du geste au langage. *Bulletin de psychologie* 26: 501–50.

Lurie, Alison. 1981. *The Language of Clothes*. New York: Random House.

Lurker, Manfred. 1968. *Bibliographie zur Symbolkunde*. Baden-Baden: Heitz.

———. 1979. *Wörterbuch der Symbolik*. Stuttgart: Kröner.

Lüthe, Rudolf. 1974. Fiktionalität als konstitutives Element literarischer Rezeption. *Orbis Litterarum* 29: 1–15.

Lyman, Stanford M., and Scott, Marvin B. 1967. Territoriality: A neglected sociological dimension. *Social Problems* 15: 236–49

Lyons, John (1963) 1972. *Structural Semantics*. Oxford: Blackwell.

———. 1968. *Introduction to Theoretical Linguistics*. Cambridge: Univ. Press.

———. 1977. *Semantics*. 2 vols. Cambridge: Univ. Press.

———. 1981. *Language and Linguistics*. Cambridge: Univ. Press.

MacCannell, Dean. 1986. Semiotics and sociology. *Semiotica* 61: 193–200.

MacCannel, Dean, and MacCannell, Juliet Flower. 1982. *The Time of the Sign*. Bloomington: Indiana Univ. Press.

MacCannell, Juliet Flower. 1986a. *Figuring Lacan*. Beckenham: Croom Helm.

———. 1986b. Kristeva's horror. *Semiotica* 62: 325–55.

McCardle, Ellen. 1974. *Nonverbal Communication*. New York: Decker.

McCracken, George E. 1948. Athanasius Kircher's universal polygraphy. *Isis* 39: 215–28.

McCracken, Grant. 1988. *Culture and Consumption*. Bloomington: Indiana Univ. Press.

McCroskey, James C. (1968) 1978. *An Introduction to Rhetorical Communication*. Englewood Cliffs, N.J.: Prentice-Hall.

McGill, Thomas E., ed. 1965. *Readings in Animal Behavior*. New York: Holt, Rinehart & Winston.

Mack, Dorothy. 1975. Metaphoring as speech act. *Poetics* 4: 221–56.

MacKay, Donald M. 1969. *Information, Mechanism, and Meaning*. Cambridge, Mass.: MIT Press.

———. 1972. Formal analysis of communicative processes. In Hinde, R. A., ed., *Non-Verbal Communication*, pp. 3–25. Cambridge: Univ. Press.

McKnight, Edgar V. 1978. *Meaning in Texts*. Philadelphia: Fortress Press.

Macksey, Richard, and Donato, Eugenio, eds. (1970) 1979. *The Structuralist Controversy*. Baltimore: Johns Hopkins Univ. Press.

McLaughlin, Terence. 1970. *Music and Communication*. London: Faber & Faber.

McLean, William P. 1973. Propositions for a semiotical definition of the photograph. *Versus* 6: 59–67.

McLuhan, Marshall. (1962) 1969. *The Gutenberg Galaxy*. New York: Signet.

———. 1964. *Understanding Media*. New York: McGraw-Hill.

McNeill, David. 1979. *The Conceptual Basis of Language*. Hillsdale, N.J.: Lawrence Erlbaum.

———. 1980. Iconic relationships between language and motor action. In Rauch, Irmengard, and Carr, Gerald F., eds., *The Signifying Animal*, pp. 240–51. Bloomington: Indiana Univ. Press

McQuown, Norman A., ed. 1971. *The Natural History of an Interview*. Chicago: Microfilm.

Maddox, Donald. 1984. *Semiotics of Deceit*. London: Associated University Presses.

Magariños de Morentin, Juan A. 1984. *El mensaje publicitario*. Buenos Aires: Hachette.

Magarotto, Cesare. 1974. Eine internationale Gebärdensprache. *Unesco-Kurier* 15.3: 20–21.

Magaβ, Walter. 1983. *Hermeneutik und Semiotik*. Bonn: Linguistica Biblica.

Mahl, George F. 1968. Gestures and body movements in interviews. In Shlien, J., ed., *Research in Psychotherapy III*, pp. 295–346. Washington: Am. Psych. Ass.

Mahl, George F., and Schulze, Gene. (1964) 1972. Psychological research in the extralinguistic area. In Sebeok, Thomas A., ed., *Approaches to Semiotics*, pp. 51–124. The Hague: Mouton.

Maimieux, Joseph de. 1797. *Pasigraphie*. Paris.

Makridakis, Spyros. 1977. The second law of systems. *International Journal of General Systems* 4: 1–12.

Malinowski, Bronislaw. (1923) 1946. The problem of meaning in primitive languages. Supplement to Ogden, C. K., and Richards, I. A., *The Meaning of Meaning*, pp. 296–336. New York: Harcourt.

———. (1925) 1954. *Magic, Science, and Religion*. Garden City, N.Y.: Doubleday.

Mallery, Garrick. (1881) 1972. *Sign Language among North American Indians*. The Hague: Mouton.

———. 1893. *Pictographs of the North American Indians*. Washington (= Fourth Annual Report of the Bureau of Ethnology, Smithsonian Institute).

Malmberg, Bertil. 1974. Derrida et la sémiologie. *Semiotica* 11: 189–99.

———. 1977. *Signes et symboles*. Paris: Picard.

Maltese, Corrado. 1970. *Semiologia del messaggio oggettuale*. Milano: Mursia.

Man, Paul de. (1979) 1980. Semiology and rhetoric. In Harari, Josué V., ed., *Textual Strategies*, pp. 121–40. London: Methuen.

Mandel, Mark. 1977. Iconic devices in American Sign Language. In Friedman, Lynn A., ed., *On the Other Hand*. New York: Academic Press.

Manser, A. R. 1973. Images. In *The Encyclopedia of Philosophy*, vol. 4, pp. 133–36. New York: Macmillan.

Maranda, Pierre. 1985. Semiography and artificial intelligence. *International Semiotic Spectrum* 4 (June): 1–3.

———. 1986. Physiosemiotics: The iconicity of blinking. In Bouissac, Pierre, et al., eds., *Iconicity*, Festschrift for T. A. Sebeok, pp. 463–67. Tübingen: Stauffenburg.

Maranda, Pierre, ed. 1972. *Mythology*. Harmondsworth: Penguin.

Marchand, Hans. (1960) 1969. *The Categories and Types of Present-Day English Word-Formation*. München: Beck.

Marchese, Angelo. 1981. *Introduzione alla semiotica della letteratura*. Torino: Società Editrice Internazionale.

Marcus, Solomon. (1970) 1973. *Mathematische Poetik*. Frankfurt: Athenäum.

———. 1974. Linguistics as a pilot science. In Sebeok, Thomas A., ed., *Current Trends in Linguistics,* vol. 12, pp. 2871–87. The Hague: Mouton.

———. 1975. Stratégies des personnages dramatiques. In Helbo, André, ed., *Sémiologie de la représentation,* pp. 73–95. Bruxelles: Ed. Complexe.

Marcus, Solomon, ed. 1977. *The Formal Study of Drama* (= Special issue of *Poetics* 6.2).

———. 1978. *La sémiotique formelle du folklore*. Paris: Klincksieck.

Mariani Ciampicacigli, Franca. 1980. *Semiotica della letteratura*. Milano: F. Angeli.

———. 1985. *Guida a una semiotica per la scuola*. Roma: Riuniti.

Marin, Louis. 1970. La description de l'image. *Communications* 15: 186–206.

———. 1971a. Eléments pour une sémiologie picturale. In Marin, L., *Etudes sémiologiques,* pp. 17–43. Paris: Klincksieck.

———. 1971b. Le discours de la figure. In Marin, L., *Etudes sémiologiques,* pp. 45–99. Paris: Klincksieck.

———. (1971c) 1980. *The Semiotics of the Passion Narrative*. Pittsburgh: Pickwick Press.

———. 1978. *Détruire la peinture*. Paris: Galilée.

———. 1979. The frame of the painting or the semiotic functions of boundaries. In Chatman, S., et al., eds., *A Semiotic Landscape,* pp. 777–82. The Hague: Mouton.

Maritain, Jacques. (1938) 1948. Sign and symbol. In Maritain, J., *Ransoming the Time,* pp. 217–54, 305–315. New York: Scribner's.

———. 1957. Langage and the theory of signs. In Anshen, Ruth Nada, ed., *Language: An Enquiry into its Meaning and Function,* pp. 86–101. New York: Harper.

Markowicz, Harry. (1977) 1980. Myths about American Sign Language. In Lane, Harlan, and Grosjean, François, eds., *Recent Perspectives on American Sign Language,* pp. 1–6. Hillsdale, N.J.: Erlbaum.

Markus, R. A. 1957. St. Augustine on signs. *Phronesis* 2: 60–83.

Marler, Peter. 1961. The logical analysis of animal communication. *Journal of Theoretical Biology* 1: 295–317.

———. 1965. Communication in monkeys and apes. In DeVore, Irven, ed., *Primate Behavior,* pp. 544–84. New York: Holt.

———. 1968. Visual systems. In Sebeok, T. A., ed., *Animal Communication,* pp. 103–126. Bloomington: Indiana Univ, Press

———. 1969. Animals and man. In Roslansky, J. D., ed., *Communication,* pp. 23–62. Amsterdam: North Holland Pub.

———. 1974. Animal communication. In Krames, Lester, et al., eds., *Nonverbal Communication,* pp. 25–50. New York: Plenum.

———. 1977. The evolution of communication. In Sebeok, T. A., ed., *How Animals Communicate,* pp. 45–70. Bloomington: Indiana Univ. Press.

Marquardt, Beate. 1984. *Die Sprache des Menschen und ihre biologischen Voraussetzungen*. Tübingen: Narr.

Marshall, J. C. 1970. The biology of communication in man and animals. In Lyons, J., ed., *New Horizons in Linguistics,* pp. 229–41. Harmondsworth: Penguin.

Martin, Richard. 1986. Semiotics in Belgium. In Sebeok, T. A., and Umiker-Sebeok, J., eds., *The Semiotic Sphere,* pp. 19–45. New York: Plenum.

Martin, Richard M. 1978. *Semiotics and Linguistic Structure*. Albany: State University of New York Press.

Martin, Richard M., ed. 1988. *Logical Semiotics and Merology*. Amsterdam: Benjamins.

Martin, Serge. 1978. *Le langage musical: Sémiotique des systèmes*. Paris: Klincksieck.

Martinet, André. (1949) 1965. La double articulation linguistique. In Martinet, A., *La linguistique synchronique,* pp. 1–41. Paris: Presses Universitaires de France.

———. (1955) 1964. *Economie des changements phonétiques*. Bern: Francke.

———. 1957. Arbitraire linguistique et double articulation. *Cahiers Ferdinand de Saussure* 15: 105–16.

———. (1960) 1967. *Elements of General Linguistics*. Chicago: Univ. Press.

———. 1962. *A Functional View of Language*. Oxford: Clarendon.

———. 1967. Connotations, poésie et culture. In *To Honor Roman Jakobson II,* pp. 1288–94. The Hague: Mouton.

———. 1978. Les termes "fonction" et "fonctionnel" dans l'usage linguistique. In Coppieters, Frank, and Goyvaerts, Didier L., eds., *Functional Studies in Language and Literature,* pp. 99–107. Gent: Ed. Story-Scientia.

———. 1979. Grammatical function. In Allerton, D. J.; Carney, E.; and Holdcroft, D., eds., *Function and Context in Linguistic Analysis,* pp. 142–47. Cambridge: University Press.

Martinet, Jeanne. 1973. *Clefs pour la sémiologie*. Paris: Seghers.

———. 1974. La sémiologie du numéro. *La linguistique* 10.2: 47–61.

———. 1982. From linguistics to semiology. In Morreall, John, ed., *The Ninth Lacus Forum,* pp. 169–74. Columbia: Hornbeam.

Martinez, Léa. 1972. Analyse structurale des bandes dessinées. In Thibault-Laulan, Anne-Marie, ed.,

Image et communication, pp. 171–81. Paris: Ed. univ.

Martinidis, Petros. 1986. Semiotics of architectural theories. *Semiotica* 59: 371–86.

Martino, Emanuele. 1985. Referenz und Invarianz in der Photographie. *Zeitschrift für Semiotik* 7: 9–25.

Maruyama, Magoroh. 1963. The second cybernetics: Deviation-amplifying mutual causal processes. *American Scientist* 51: 164–79.

Maser, Siegfried. 1970. *Numerische Ästhetik*. Stuttgart: Krämer.

————. 1971. *Grundlagen der allgemeinen Kommunikationstheorie*. Stuttgart: Kohlhammer.

————. 1977. Arten der Superzeichenbildung. In Posner, Roland, and Reinecke, Hans-Peter, eds., *Zeichenprozesse*, pp. 83–108. Wiesbaden: Athenaion.

Masters, Roger M. 1970. Genes, language, and evolution. *Semiotica* 2: 295–320.

Mateescu, Catalina Anca. 1974. Toward a structural approach to pictorial language. *Poetics* 11: 46–61.

Matejka, Ladislav. 1978. The roots of Russian semiotics of art. In Bailey, Richard W., et al., eds., *The Sign: Semiotics around the World*, pp. 146–72. Ann Arbor: Michigan Slavic Pub.

Matejka, Ladislav, ed. 1978. *Sound, Sign, and Meaning*. Ann Arbor: Univ. of Michigan.

Matejka, Ladislav, and Pomorska, Krystyna, eds. 1971. *Readings in Russian Poetics: Formalist and Structuralist Views*. Cambridge, Mass.: MIT Press.

Matejka, Ladislav, and Titunik, Irwin R., eds. 1976. *Semiotics of Art: Prague School Contributions*. Cambridge: MIT Press.

Matejka, Ladislav, et al., eds. 1977. *Readings in Soviet Semiotics*. Ann Arbor: Univ. of Michigan.

Mates, Benson. 1953. *Stoic Logic*. Berkeley: Univ. of California Press.

Mathieu, Michel. 1977. Analyse du récit. *Poétique* 8: 226–59.

Maturana, Humberto R. 1978. Biology of language: The epistemological reality. In Miller, George A., and Lenneberg, Elizabeth, eds., *Psychology and Biology of Language and Thought*, pp. 27–63. New York: Academic Press.

Maturana, Humberto R., and Varela, Francisco. 1972. *Autopoiesis and Cognition*. Dordrecht: Reidel.

Mauro, Tullio de. 1967. *Ludwig Wittgenstein: His Place in the Development of Semantics*. Dordrecht: Reidel.

————. 1969. *Une introduction à la sémantique*. Paris: Payot.

————. 1975. The link with linguistics. In Sebeok, Thomas A., ed., *The Tell-Tale Sign*, pp. 37–46. Lisse: de Ridder.

Mauss, Marcel. (1902) 1950. Les éléments de la magie. In Mauss, M., *Sociologie et anthropologie*, pp. 17–141. Paris: Presses Univ. de France.

————. (1935) 1973. Techniques of the body. *Economy and Society* 2.1: 70–88.

Mayer, Cornelius Petrus. 1969. *Die Zeichen in der geistigen Entwicklung und in der Theologie des jungen Augustinus*. Würzburg: Augustinus Verlag.

Mayer, Günter. 1970. Semiotik und Sprachgefüge der Kunst. *Beiträge zur Musikwissenschaft* 3: 112–21.

Mayerthaler, Willi. (1981) 1988. *Morphological Naturalness*. Ann Arbor: Karoma.

Mayo, Clara, and Henley, Nancy M., eds. 1981. *Gender and Nonverbal Behavior*. New York: Springer.

Mead, George Herbert. 1934. *Mind, Self, and Society: From the Standpoint of a Social Behaviorist*, ed. Morris, C. W. Chicago: Univ. Press.

Mehrabian, Albert. 1969. Significance of posture and position. *Psychological Bulletin* 71: 359–72.

————. 1972. *Nonverbal Communication*. New York: Aldine.

————. 1976. *Public Places and Private Spaces*. New York: Basic Books.

Meier, Georg Friedrich. (1756) 1965. *Versuch einer allgemeinen Auslegungskunst*. Düsseldorf: Stern.

Meier, Georg F. 1969. Wirksamkeit der Sprache. *Zeitschrift für Phonetik, Sprachwissenschaft und Kommunikationsforschung* 22: 474–92.

Meissner, Martin, and Philpott, Stuart B. 1975. The sign language of sawmill workers in British Columbia. *Sign Language Studies* 9: 291–347.

Melazzo, Lucio. 1975. La teoría de segno linguistico negli Stoici. *Lingua e stile* 10: 199–230.

Melenk, Hartmut. 1980. Semiotik als Brücke: Der Beitrag der angewandten Semiotik zur vergleichenden Landeskunde. *Jahrbuch Deutsch als Fremdsprache* 6: 133–48.

Meletinsky, Elizar, and Segal, Dmitri. 1971. Structuralism and semiotics in the USSR. *Diogenes* 73: 88–115.

Mellor, David H. 1981. *Real Time*. Cambridge: Univ. Press.

Mendelson, Jack H., et al. 1964. The language of signs and symbolic behavior of the deaf. In Rioch, David McK., and Weinstein, Edwin A., eds., *Disorders of Communication*, pp. 151–70. Baltimore: William & Wilkins.

Menninger, Karl. (1958) 1970. *Number Words and Number Symbols*. Cambridge, Mass.: MIT Press.

Meo-Zilio, Giovanni. 1961. *El lenguaje de los gestos en el rio de la Plata*. Montevideo: Imp. Libertad.

————. 1962. El lenguaje de los gestos en el Uruguay. *Boletin de Filología* (Santiago de Chile) 13 (1961): 75–163.

Merrell, Floyd. 1982. *Semiotic Foundations*. Bloomington: Indiana Univ. Press.

————. 1983. How general should/can rhetoric be? *Pre-text* 4: 139–62.

————. 1985. *A Semiotic Theory of Texts*. Berlin: Mouton de Gruyter.

Mertz, Elizabeth, and Parmentier, Richard J., eds. 1985. *Semiotic Mediation*. Orlando, Fla.: Academic Press.

Mertz, Elizabeth, and Weissbourd, Bernard. 1985. Legal ideology and linguistic theory: Variability and its limits. In Mertz, Elizabeth, and Parmentier, Richard J., eds., *Semiotic Mediation*, pp. 261–85. Orlando, Fla.: Academic Press.

Meschonnic, Henri. 1975. *Le signe et le poème*. Paris: Gallimard.

Mesnil, Marianne. 1974. *Trois essais sur la Fête*. Bruxelles: Editions de l'université.

Mestrallet, R. 1980. *Communication, linguistique et sémiologie: Etude sémiologique des systèmes de signes de la chimie*. 2 vols. Barcelona: Universidad Autónoma.

Metken, Günter. 1970. *Comics*. Frankfurt: Fischer.

Metz, Christian. 1967. Remarque sur le mot et sur le chiffre. A propos des conceptions sémiologiques de Luis J. Prieto. *La linguistique* 2: 41–56.

————. (1968) 1974. *Film Language: A Semiotics of the Cinema* (= trans. of *Essais sur la signification au cinéma I*). New York: Oxford Univ. Press.

————. 1970a. Au-delà de l'analogie, l'image. *Communications* 15: 1–10.

————. 1970b. Images et pédagogie. *Communications* 15: 162–68.

————. (1971) 1974. *Language and Cinema* (= trans. of *Langage et cinéma*). The Hague: Mouton.

————. 1972. *Essais sur la signification au cinéma II*. Paris: Klincksieck.

————. 1977a. *Essais sémiotiques*. Paris: Klincksieck.

————. (1977b) 1982. *The Imaginary Signifier*. Bloomington: Indiana Univ. Press.

Metzger, Johann Daniel. 1785. *Grundsätze der allgemeinen Semiotik und Therapie*. Königsberg: G. L. Hartung.

Meyer, Leonard B. 1956. *Emotion and Meaning in Music*. Chicago: Univ. Press.

Meyer, R. W., ed. 1964. *Das Zeitproblem im 20. Jahrhundert*. München: Francke.

Meyer-Eppler, Werner. (1959) 1969. *Grundlagen und Anwendungen der Informationstheorie*. Berlin: Springer.

————. 1962. Informationstheoretische Probleme der musikalischen Kommunikation. *Die Reihe* 8: 7–10.

Michaelis, Ad. Alf. 1940. *Semiotik*, 2nd ed. Radebeul: Rohrmoser.

Mick, David G. 1986. Consumer research and semiotics. *Journal of Consumer Research* 13: 196–213.

————. 1987. Toward a semiotic of advertising "story grammars." In Umiker-Sebeok, Jean, ed., *Marketing and Signs: New Directions in the Study of Signs for Sale*. Berlin: Mouton de Gruyter.

Mignolo, Walter. 1978. *Elementos para una teoria del texto literario*. Barcelona: Ed. Crítica.

Miguelez, Roberto. 1971. Le récit historique: légalité et signification. *Sémiotica* 3: 20–36.

Mill, John Stuart. (1843) 1905. *A System of Logic*. London: Routledge.

Miller, George A. (1951) 1963. *Language and Communication*. New York: McGraw-Hill.

Millet, Louis, and Varin d'Ainvelle, Madeleine. 1970. *Le structuralisme*. Paris: Ed. Univ.

Millum, Trevor. 1975. *Images of Women*. London: Chatto & Windus.

Minai, Asghar Talaye. 1984. *Architecture as Environmental Communication*. Berlin: Mouton.

Mininni, Giuseppe. 1982. *Psicosemiotica*. Bari: Adriatica.

Miškovská, V. T. 1959. La panglottie de J. A. Komenský. *Philologia Pragensia* 2: 97–106.

————. 1962. Comenius (Komenský) on lexical symbolism in an artificial language. *Philosphy* 37: 238–44.

Mitchell, W. J. Thomas. 1986. *Iconology: Image, Text, Ideology*. Chicago: Univ. Press.

Mitchell, W. J. Thomas, ed. (1974) 1980. *The Language of Images*. Chicago: Univ. Press.

Mitry, Jean. 1963, 1965. *Esthétique et psychologie du cinéma*. 2 vols. Paris: Ed. Universitaires.

————. 1967. D'un langage sans signes. *Revue d'esthétique* NS 2–3: 139–52.

Modley, Rudolf. 1966. Graphic symbols for worldwide communication. In Kepes, Gyorgy, ed., *Sign, Image, Symbol*, pp. 108–25. New York: Braziller.

Moeran, Brian. 1985. When the poetics of advertising becomes the advertising of poetics. *Language and Communication* 5.1: 29–44.

Moles, Abraham A. (1958) 1968. *Information Theory and Esthetic Perception*. Urbana: Univ. of Illinois Press.

————. 1972a. *Théorie des objets*. Paris: Ed. Universitaires.

————. 1972b. Vers une théorie écologique de l'image. In Thibault-Laulan, Anne-Marie, ed., *Image et Communication*, pp. 49–73. Paris: Editions Universitaires.

————. 1976. De la corruption nécessaire de la science des signes. *Degrés* 9: b1–b5.

————. 1978. L'image et le texte. *Communication et langages* 38: 17–29.

Moles, Abraham. 1986. Tactile communication. In Sebeok, Thomas A., ed., *Encyclopedic Dictionary of Semiotics*, pp. 1072–74. Berlin: Mouton de Gruyter.

Moles, Abraham, and Rohmer, Elisabeth. 1978. *Psychologie de l'espace*. Tournai: Casterman.

Molinari, Cesare, and Ottolenghi, Valeria. 1979. *Leggere il teatro*. Firenze: Vallecchi.

Molino, Jean. 1971. La connotation. *La linguistique* 7.1: 5–30.

————. 1975. Fait musical et sémiologie de la musique. *Musique en jeu* 17: 37–62.

Möller[-Naβ], Karl-Dietmar. 1978. Diagrammatische Syntagmen und einfache Formen. In *Untersuchungen zur Syntax des Films* (= papmaks 8), pp. 69–115. Münster: MAkS.

————. 1981. Syntax und Semantik in der Filmsemiotik. In Bentele, Günter, ed., *Semiotik und Massenmedien*, pp. 243–79. München: Ölschläger.

Möller-Naβ, Karl-Dietmar. 1986. *Filmsprache*. Münster: MAkS.

Monaco, James. (1977) 1978. *How to Read a Film*. New York: Oxf. Univ. Press.

Monnerot-Dumaine, M. 1960. *Précis d'interlinguistique générale et spéciale*. Paris: Maloine.

Montagu, Ashley. 1971. *Touching: The Human Significance of the Skin*. New York: Columbia Univ. Press.

Mooij, J. J. A. 1975. Tenor, vehicle, and reference. *Poetics* 4: 257–72.

Moragas Spa, Miquel de. (1976) 1980. *Semiótica y comunicación de masas*. Madrid: Ed. Península.

Morawski, Stefan. 1984. Concerning the so-called structuralist-semiotic esthetics. In Pelc, Jerzy, et al., eds., *Sign, System, and Function*, pp. 169–86. Berlin: Mouton.

Morris, Charles W. 1925. *Symbolism and Reality: A Study in the Nature of Mind*. Chicago: Ph.D. diss.

Morris, Charles W. (1938) 1970. *Foundations of the Theory of Signs*. Chicago: Univ. Press (= Foundations of the Unity of Science: Towards an International Encyclopedia of Unified Science, vol. 1.2).

————. (1939) 1971. Esthetics and the theory of signs. In Morris, C. W., *Writings on the General Theory of Signs*, pp. 415–33. The Hague: Mouton.

————. (1946) 1971. *Signs, Language, and Behavior*. In Morris, C. W., *Writings on the General Theory of Signs*, pp. 73–398. The Hague: Mouton.

————. (1948) 1971. Signs about signs about signs. In Morris, C. W., *Writings on the General Theory of Signs*, pp. 434–55. The Hague: Mouton.

————. (1957) 1971. Mysticism and its language. In Morris, C. W., *Writings on the General Theory of Signs*, pp. 456–63. The Hague: Mouton.

————. 1964. *Signification and Significance: A Study of the Relations of Signs and Values*. Cambridge, Mass.: MIT Press.

————. 1970. *The Pragmatic Movement in American Philosophy*. New York: Braziller.

————. 1971. *Writings on the General Theory of Signs*. The Hague: Mouton.

Morris, Charles W., and Hamilton, Daniel J. 1965. Aesthetics, signs, and icons. *Philosophy and Phenomenological Research* 25: 356–64.

Morris, Desmond. 1978. *Manwatching*. Frogmore: Triad.

————. 1985. *Bodywatching*. London: Cape.

Morris, Desmond, et al. 1979. *Gestures: Their Origins and Distributions*. London: Cape.

Morton, John, ed. 1971. *Biological and Social Factors in Psycholinguistics*. London: Logos.

Moser, Bruno. 1986. *Bilder, Zeichen und Gebärden*. München: Südwest.

Mottron, Laurent, and Wildgen, Wolfgang. 1987. *Dynamische Sprachtheorie*. Bochum: Brockmeyer.

Mounin, Georges (1964) 1985. Communication, linguistics, and information theory. In Mounin, G., *Semiotic Praxis*, pp. 33–49. New York: Plenum.

————. 1967. Les fonctions du langage. *Word* 23: 396–413.

————. (1968a) 1971. *Clefs pour la linguistique*. Paris: Seghers.

————. 1968b. *Ferdinand de Saussure ou le structuraliste sans le savoir*. Paris: Seghers.

————. 1970a. *Introduction à la sémiologie*. Paris: Minuit.

————. 1970b. La communication théâtrale. In Mounin, Georges, *Introduction à la sémiologie*, pp. 87–94. Paris: Minuit.

————. 1970c La sémiologie chez Hjelmslev. In Mounin, G., *Introduction à la sémiologie*, pp. 95–102. Paris: Minuit.

————. 1970d. Linguistique et sémiologie. In Mounin, G., *Introduction à la sémiologie*, pp. 67–76. Paris: Minuit.

————. 1970e. Sémiologie de la communication et sémiologie de la signification. In Mounin, Georges, *Introduction à la sémiologie*, pp. 11–15. Paris: Minuit.

————. (1980) 1985. Semiology and scientific photography. In Mounin, G., *Semiotic Praxis*, pp. 119–25. New York: Plenum.

————. 1981. L'intention de communication. In Lange-Seidl, Annemarie, ed., *Zeichenkonstitution 1*, pp. 16–18. Berlin: de Gruyter.

————. 1985. *Semiotic Praxis*. New York: Plenum.

————. 1986. Héraldique et sémiologie. *La linguistique* 22.1: 47–56.

Moutard, Nicole. 1974. Sémiologie de la notation musicale. *La linguistique* 10.2: 63–70.

Mrulik, Barbara. 1970. The film as language. In Greimas, A. J., et al., eds., *Sign, Language, Culture*, pp. 440–50. The Hague: Mouton.

Muckenhaupt, Manfred. 1986. *Text und Bild*. Tübingen: Narr.

Mueller-Vollmer, Kurt, ed. (1985) 1986. *The Hermeneutics Reader*. Oxford: Blackwell.

Mukařovský, Jan. (1932) 1964. Standard language and poetic language. In Garvin, Paul L., ed., *A Prague School Reader on Esthetics, Literary Structure, and Style*, pp. 17–30. Washington, D.C.: Georgetown University Press.

———. (1933) 1978. A note on the aesthetics of film. In Burbank, John, and Steiner, Peter, eds., *Structure, Sign, and Function*, pp. 178–200. New Haven: Yale Univ. Press.

———. (1934) 1978. Art as a semiotic fact. In Mukařovský, Jan, *Structure, Sign, and Function*, pp. 82–88. New Haven: Yale Univ. Press.

———. (1936) 1970. *Aesthetic Function, Norm, and Value as Social Facts*. Ann Arbor: Univ. of Michigan.

———. (1937) 1978. On the problem of functions in architecture. In Mukařovský, Jan, *Structure, Sign, and Function*, pp. 236–50. New Haven: Yale Univ. Press.

———. 1939. Le langage poétique. In *Vème Congrès International des Linguistes, Bruxelles; Rapports*, pp. 94–102. Bruges: St. Catherine.

———. (1941) 1978. On the current state of the theory of theater. In Mukařovský, Jan, *Structure, Sign, and Function*, pp. 201–19. New Haven: Yale Univ. Press.

———. (1942) 1977. The place of the aesthetic function among the other functions. In Mukařovský, Jan, *Structure, Sign, and Function*, pp. 31–48. New Haven: Yale Univ. Press.

———. (1966) 1976. The essence of the visual arts. In Matejka, Ladislav, and Titunik, Irwin L., eds., *Semiotics of Art*, pp. 229–44. Cambridge, Mass.: MIT Press.

———. 1976. *On Poetic Language*. Lisse: de Ridder.

———. 1977. *The Word and Verbal Art*. New Haven: Yale Univ. Press.

———. 1978. *Structure, Sign, and Function*. New Haven: Yale Univ. Press.

Mulder, Jan W. F., and Hervey, Sándor G. J. 1972. *Theory of the Linguistic Sign*. The Hague: Mouton.

———. 1980. *The Strategy of Linguistics*. Edinburgh: Scottish Academy Press.

Müller, Arno. 1970. *Probleme der behavioristischen Semiotik*. Frankfurt/Main: Diss. Phil.

Müller, Horst M. 1987. *Evolution, Kognition und Sprache*. Berlin: Parey.

Müller, J. E. 1981. Face-to-Face-Situation und narrativer Text. In Winkler, Peter, ed., *Methoden der Analyse von Face-to-Face-Situationen*, pp. 168–99. Stuttgart: Metzler.

Müller, Wolfgang G. 1981. *Topik des Stilbegriffs*. Darmstadt: Wiss. Buchges.

Munari, Bruno. 1963. *Supplemento al dizionario italiano*. Milano: Muggiani.

Murphey, Murray G. 1961. *The Development of Peirce's Philosophy*. Cambridge, Mass.: Harvard Univ. Press.

Mysak, Edward. 1970. Speech system. In Sereno, K. K., and Mortensen, C. D., eds., *Foundations of Communication Theory*, pp. 40–54. New York: Harper & Row.

Nadin, Mihai. 1981. *Zeichen und Wert*. Tübingen: Narr.

———. 1984. On the meaning of the visual. *Semiotica* 52: 335–77.

Namir, Lila, and Schlesinger, I. M. 1978. The grammar of sign language. In Schlesinger, I. M., and Namir, Lila, eds., *Sign Language of the Deaf*, pp. 97–140. New York: Academic Press.

Nattiez, Jean-Jacques. (1971) 1975. Musicology and linguistics. *Canadian Journal of Research in Semiotics* 3: 51–71.

———. 1973a. Problèmes sémiologiques de l'analyse des idéologies. *Sociologie et sociétés* 5.2: 71–89.

———. 1973b. Sémiologie et sémiographie musicales. *Musique en jeu* 13: 78–85.

———. 1973c. Sémiologie musicale. *Encyclopaedia universalis (Organum)* 17: 560–63.

———. 1973d. Trois modèles linguistiques pour l'analyse musicale. *Musique en jeu* 10: 3–11.

———. 1975. *Fondements d'une sémiologie de la musique*. Paris: Union générale d'éditions.

———. 1977. The contribution of musical semiotics to the semiotic discussion in general. In Sebeok, Thomas A., ed., *A Perfusion of Signs*, pp. 121–42. Bloomington: Indiana Univ. Press.

———. 1979. Zum Problem der Zeichenklassifikation. *Zeitschrift für Semiotik* 1: 389–99.

Naumann, Hans, ed. 1973. *Der moderne Strukturbegriff*. Darmstadt: Wiss. Buchges.

Nauta, Doede, Jr. 1972. *The Meaning of Information*. The Hague: Mouton.

Naville, Pierre. 1970. Recherches pour une sémiologie de l'image optique. *Epistémologie sociologique* 9: 95–119.

Nef, Frédéric. 1976. La philosophie du langage et la sémiotique de J. H. Lambert à la lumière de son époque. In Sulowski, Jan, ed., *Semiotic-Historical Studies*, pp. 161–209. Wrocław: Zakład Narodowy.

———. 1977. Introduction to the reading of Greimas. *Diacritics* 7 (March): 18–22.

Nef, Frédéric, ed. 1976. *Structures élémentaires de la signification*. Bruxelles: Ed. Complexe.

Nehring, Alfons. 1945. Plato and the theory of language. *Traditio* 3: 13–48.

Nespoulous, Jean-Luc, and Lecours, André Roch. 1986. Gestures: nature and function. In Nespoulous, J.-L., et al., eds., *The Biological Foundations of Gestures.*, pp. 49–62. Hillsdale, N.J.: Erlbaum.

Nespoulous, Jean-Luc; Perron, Paul; and Lecours, André Roch, eds. 1986. *The Biological Foundations of Gestures*. Hillsdale, N.J.: L. Erlbaum.

Nestle, Wilhelm. (1942) 1966. *Vom Mythos zum Logos*. München: Oldenbourg.

Nettl, Bruno. 1958. Some linguistic approaches to music. *Journal of the International Folk Music Council* 10: 37–41.

Neubert, Albrecht. 1962. *Semantischer Positivismus in den USA*. Halle: Niemeyer.

Neumann, Werner, et al. 1976. *Theoretische Probleme der Sprachwissenschaft*. 2 vols. Berlin: Akademie.

Neuner, Gerhard, ed. 1979. *Pragmatische Didaktik des Englischunterrichts*. Paderborn: Schöningh.

Nichols, Bill. 1981. *Ideology and the Image*. Bloomington: Indiana Univ. Press.

Nicholson, Jane A. 1986. The ideological function in semiosis. In Deely, John, ed., *Semiotics 1985*, pp. 382–89. Lanham, Md.: University Press of America.

Nida, Eugene A. 1952. A problem in the statement of meanings. *Lingua* 3: 121–37.

Niebel, Wilhelm Friedrich. 1984. Descartes' Mathesis universalis . . . : Das semiotische Paradigma. In Oehler, K., *Zeichen und Realität*, vol. 1, pp. 389–98. Tübingen: Stauffenburg.

Nieraad, Jürgen. 1977. *"Bildgesegnet und bildverflucht"—Forschungen zur sprachlichen Metaphorik*. Darmstadt: Wiss. Buchges.

Nketia, J. H. K. (1971) 1976. Surrogate languages of Africa. In Sebeok, Thomas A., and Umiker-Sebeok, Donna Jean, eds., *Speech Surrogates: Drum and Whistle Systems*, pp. 825–64. The Hague: Mouton.

Noppen, Jean Pierre van, comp. 1985. *Metaphor: A Bibliography of Post–1970 Publications*. Amsterdam: Benjamins.

Normand, Claudine. 1974. L'arbitraire du signe comme phénomène de déplacement. *Dialectiques* 12: 109–26.

Norrick, Neal R. 1981. *Semiotic Principles in Semantic Theory*. Amsterdam: Benjamins.

Norris, Christopher. 1982. *Deconstruction: Theory and Practice*. London: Methuen.

Norrman, Ralf, and Haarberg, Jon. 1980. *Nature and Language: A Semiotic Study of Cucurbits in Literature*. London: Routledge.

Noske, Frits. 1977. *The Signifier and the Signified: Studies in the Operas of Mozart and Verdi*. The Hague: Nijhoff.

Nöth, Winfried. 1972. *Strukturen des Happenings*. Hildesheim: Olms.

———. 1975a. Homeostasis and equilibrium in linguistics and text analysis. *Semiotica* 14: 222–44.

———. 1975b. *Semiotik. Eine Einführung mit Beispielen für Reklameanalysen*. Tübingen: Niemeyer.

———. 1977a. *Dynamik semiotischer Systeme. Vom altenglischen Zauberspruch zum illustrierten Werbetext*. Stuttgart: Metzler.

———. 1977b. Semiotics of the Old English charm. *Semiotica* 19: 239–59.

———. 1978a. The semiotic framework of textlinguistics. In Dressler, Wolfgang U., ed., *Current Trends in Textlinguistics*, pp. 21–34. Berlin: de Gruyter.

———. 1978b. Systems analysis of Old English literature. *Journal for Descriptive Poetics and Theory of Literature (PTL)* 3: 117–37.

———. 1980. *Literatursemiotische Analysen zu Lewis Carrolls Alice-Büchern*. Tübingen: Narr.

———. 1983a. Illustrierte Werbetexte: Appell- und Darstellungsstrukturen. *Anglistik und Englischunterricht* 21: 87–102.

———. 1983b. Systems theoretical principles of the evolution of the English language and literature. In Davenport, Michael; Hansen, Erik; and Nielsen, Hans Frede, eds., *Proceedings of the Second International Conference on English Historical Linguistics*, pp. 103–22. Odense: Univ. Press.

———. 1985. *Handbuch der Semiotik*. Stuttgart: Metzler.

———. 1986. Semiotics of magic in children's folklore. In Deely, John, ed., *Semiotics 1985*, pp. 390–400. Lanham, Md.: University Press of America.

———. 1987a. Advertising: The frame message. In Umiker-Sebeok, Jean, ed., *Marketing and Semiotics: New Directions in the Study of Signs for Sale*, pp. 279–94. Berlin: Mouton de Gruyter.

———. 1987b. Advertising, poetry, and art: Semiotic reflections on aesthetics and the language of commerce. *Kodikas/Code* 10: 53–81.

———. 1988. The language of commodities. *International Journal of Research in Marketing* 4: 173–86.

———. 1989. Systems theory and semiotics. In Koch, Walter A., *Semiotics in the Individual Sciences*. Bochum: Brockmeyer.

Nummenmaa, Tapio. 1964. *The Language of the Face*. Jyväskylä: Kustantajat Pub.

Nykrog, Per. 1968. Strukturbegrebet i analyse af narrativ litteratur. In *Romanproblemer. Festskrift til Hans Sørensen*, pp. 45–53. Odense: Univ.-Forlag. German summary in *Archiv für Begriffsgeschichte* 13 (1969): 102–103.

Obudho, Constance E., comp. 1979. *Human Nonverbal Behavior*. Westport, Conn.: Greenwood.

Odin, Roger. 1977. Où en est l'analyse sémiologique des films. *Degrés* 11–12: fl-f9.

———. 1979. Quelques jalons pour une réflexion sur la notion de cohérence au cinéma. *Canadian Journal of Research in Semiotics* 6.3/7.1: 175–88.

Odmark, John, ed. 1979–80. *Language, Literature, & Meaning I-II*. Amsterdam: Benjamins.

Oechslin, Werner. 1982. Architektur und Alphabet. In Braegger, Carlpeter, ed., *Architektur und Sprache*, pp. 216–54. München: Prestel.

Oehler, Klaus. (1981a) 1987. An outline of Peirce's semiotics. In Krampen, M., et al., eds., *Classics of Semiotics*, pp. 1–21. New York: Plenum.

——. 1981b. Ein in Vergessenheit geratener Zeichentheoretiker des Deutschen Idealismus: Johann Gottlieb Fichte. In Lange-Seidl, Annemarie, ed., *Zeichenkonstitution*, vol. 1, pp. 75–81. Berlin: de Gruyter.

——. 1982. Die Aktualität der antiken Semiotik. *Zeitschrift für Semiotik* 4: 215–19.

Oehler, Klaus, ed. 1984. *Zeichen und Realität*. 3 vols. Tübingen: Stauffenburg.

Ogden, Charles Kay. (1930) 1968. *Basic English International Second Language*, rev. ed. New York: Harcourt.

——. 1934. The magic of words. *Psyche* 14: 9–87.

Ogden, Charles Kay, and Richards, Ivor Armstrong. (1923) 1946. *The Meaning of Meaning*. New York: Harcourt.

Ogibenin, Boris. 1979. A semiotic approach to religion. In Sebeok, Thomas A., ed., *Sight, Sound, and Sense*, pp. 232–43. Bloomington: Indiana Univ. Press.

Oldani, Louis. 1981. Literary language and postmodern theories of semiotics. In De George, Richard T., ed., *Semiotic Themes*, pp. 95–108. Lawrence: Univ. of Kansas Pub.

Oléron, Pierre. 1978. *Le langage gestuel des sourds: syntaxe et communication*. Paris: Ed. CNRS.

Olson, David R. 1977. From utterance to text. *Harvard Educational Review* 47: 257–81.

O'Mahony, Brendan E. 1964. A medieval semantic. *Laurentianum* 5: 448–86.

Oomen, Ursula. 1972. Systemtheorie der Texte. *Folia linguistica* 1: 12–34.

——. 1975. Wort—Bild—Nachricht: Semiotische Aspekte des Comic Strip "Peanuts." *Linguistik und Didaktik* 23: 247–59.

——. 1979. Modelle der linguistischen Poetik. In Frier, Wolfgang, and Labroisse, Gerd, eds., *Grundfragen der Textwissenschaft*, pp. 173–93. Amsterdam: Rodopi.

Opie, Iona, and Opie, Peter. (1959) 1977. *The Lore and Language of Schoolchildren*. Frogmore: Paladin.

Orange, Donna M. 1984. *Peirce's Conception of God*. Lubbock, Texas: Institute for Studies in Pragmatics (= Peirce Studies 2).

Orlov, Henry. 1981. Toward a semiotics of music. In Steiner, Wendy, ed., *The Sign in Music and Literature*, pp. 131–37. Austin: Univ. of Texas Press.

Osgood, Charles E. 1976. *Focus on Meaning 1: Explorations in Semantic Space*. The Hague: Mouton.

——. 1980. What is language? In Rauch, Irmen-gard, and Carr, Gerald F., eds., *The Signifying Animal*, pp. 9–50. Bloomington: Indiana Univ. Press.

Osgood, Charles E.; Suci, G. J.; and Tannenbaum, P. H. 1957. *The Measurement of Meaning*. Urbana: Univ. of Illinois Press.

Osgood, Charles E., and Sebeok, Thomas A., eds. (1965) 1969. *Psycholinguistics*. Bloomington: Indiana Univ. Press.

Osmond-Smith, David. 1972. The iconic process in musical communication. *Versus* 3: 31–42.

Osolsobě, Ivo. 1973. Czechoslovak semiotics past and present. *Semiotica* 9: 140–56.

Ostwald, Peter F. 1973. *The Semiotics of Human Sound*. The Hague: Mouton.

Ota, Yukio. 1973. LoCoS. *Bild der Wissenschaft* 10.1: 152–59.

O'Toole, L. M., and Shukman, Ann, eds. 1981. *Film Theory and General Semiotics* (= Russian Poetics in Translation, vol. 8). Oxford: Holdan.

Otto, Stephan. 1963. *Die Funktion des Bildbegriffes in der Theologie des 12. Jahrhunderts*. Münster: Aschendorf.

Padley, G. A. 1976. *Grammatical Theory in Western Europe, 1500–1700*. Cambridge: Univ. Press.

Paetzold, Heinz. 1981. Ernst Cassirers "Philosophie der symbolischen Formen" und die neuere Entwicklung der Semiotik. In Lange-Seidl, Annemarie, ed., *Zeichenkonstitution*, pp. 90–100. Berlin: de Gruyter.

——. 1983. Semiotik und Ästhetik. *Zeitschrift für Semiotik* 5: 243–57.

——. 1985. Locke und Berkeley über Zeichen. In Dutz, K. D., and Schmitter, P., eds., *Historiographia Semioticae*, pp. 149–81. Münster: MAkS.

Paget, Richard A. 1943. A world language. *Nature* 151: 80.

Pagnini, Marcello. 1970. Per una semiologia del teatro classico. *Strumenti critici* 12: 121–40.

Palmer, Frank R. 1981. *Semantics*. 2nd ed. Cambridge: Univ. Press.

Palmer, Richard E. 1969. *Hermeneutics: Interpretation Theory in Schleiermacher, Dilthey, Heidegger, and Gadamer*. Evanston: Northwestern Univ. Press.

Panaccio, Claude. 1985. Der Nominalismus Ockhams. In Dutz, K. D., and Kaczmarek, L., eds., *Rekonstruktion und Interpretation*, pp. 1–22. Tübingen: Narr.

Panofsky, Erwin. (1939) 1962. *Studies in Iconology*. New York: Harper.

——. (1955) 1970. *Meaning in the Visual Arts*. Harmondsworth: Penguin.

Paprotté, Wolf, and Dirven, René, eds. 1985. *The Ubiquity of Metaphor*. Amsterdam: Benjamins.

Paradis, Michel; Hagiwara, Hiroko; and Hildebrandt, Nancy. 1985. *Neurolinguistic As-*

pects of the Japanese Writing System. Orlando: Academic Press.

Paris, Jean. 1975. *Painting and Linguistics*. Pittsburgh, Pa.: Carnegie-Mellon University (= Praxis/ Poetics Series 1/75).

———. 1978. *Lisible, Visible*. Paris: Seghers.

Parmentier, Richard J. 1985. Signs' place in medias res: Peirce's concept of semiotic mediation. In Mertz, E., and Parmentier, R. J., eds., *Semiotic Mediation*, pp. 23–48. Orlando: Academic Press.

Parret, Herman. 1969. In het taken van het teken. *Tijdschrift voor Filosofie* 31: 232–60.

———. 1975. *Idéologie et sémiologie chez Locke et Condillac*. Lisse: de Ridder.

———. 1983. *Semiotics and Pragmatics*. Amsterdam: Benjamins.

Parret, Herman, ed. 1976. *History of Linguistic Thought and Contemporary Linguistics*. Berlin: de Gruyter.

Parret, Herman, and Ruprecht, Hans-George, eds. 1985. *Aims and Prospects of Semiotics: Essays in Honor of Algirdas Julien Greimas*. Amsterdam: Benjamins.

Pasch, Georges. 1975. Drapeaux nationaux. *Semiotica* 15: 285–95.

Pasolini, Pier Paolo. 1966. Die Sprache des Films. *Film* 4.2: 49–56.

———. (1967) 1976. La langue écrite de la réalité. In Pasolini, P. P., *L'expérience hérétique: langue et cinéma*, pp. 167–96. Paris: Payot.

Patrides, C. A., ed. 1976. *Aspects of Time*. Manchester: Univ. Press.

Patte, Daniel. 1976. *What is Structural Exegesis?* Philadelphia: Fortress Press.

———. 1984. The semantic function in narrative semiotics. In Pelc, Jerzy, et al., eds., *Sign, System, and Function*, pp. 281–96. Berlin: Mouton.

Patte, Daniel, ed. 1976. *Semiology and Parables*. Pittsburgh: Pickwick Press.

Patte, Daniel, and Patte, Aline. 1978. *Structural Exegesis: From Theory to Practice*. Philadelphia: Fortress Press.

Patterson, Francine. 1978. Linguistic capabilities of a lowland gorilla. In Peng, F. C. C., ed., *Sign Language and Language Acquisition in Man and Ape*, pp. 161–201. Boulder, Colo.: Westview Press.

Patterson, Miles L. 1978. The role of space in social interaction. In Siegman, Aron W., and Feldstein, Stanley, eds., *Nonverbal Behavior and Communication*, pp. 265–90. New York: Wiley.

———. 1983. *Nonverbal Behavior*. New York: Springer.

Paulus, Jean. 1969. *La fonction symbolique et le langage*. Bruxelles: Dessart.

Pavel, Thomas G. 1973. Some remarks on narrative grammars. *Poetics* 8: 5–30.

———. 1976. "Possible worlds" in literary semantics. *Journal of Aesthetics and Art Criticism* 34: 165–76.

Pavis, Patrice. 1976. *Problèmes de sémiologie théâtrale*. Montréal: Presses de l'Université du Québec.

———. 1980. *Dictionnaire du théâtre*. Paris: Ed. Sociales.

———. 1981. Problems of a semiology of theatrical gesture. *Poetics Today* 2: 65–94.

———. 1982. *Languages of the Stage*. New York: Performing Arts Journal Publications.

———. 1985. *Voix et images de la scène: Vers une sémiologie de la réception*. Lille: Presses Univ.

Pazukhin, Rościsław. 1972. The concept of signal. *Lingua Posnaniensis* 16: 25–43.

Peckham, Morse. (1965) 1967. *Man's Rage for Chaos*. New York: Schocken.

Pei, Mario. 1958. *One Language for the World*. New York: Devin-Adair.

Pei, Mario, and Gaynor, Frank. 1954. *A Dictionary of Linguistics*. New York: Philosophical Library.

Peirce, Charles Sanders. 1931–58. *Collected Papers*. Vols. 1–6 ed. Hartshorne, Charles, and Weiss, Paul; vols. 7–8 ed. Burks, Arthur W. Cambridge, Mass.: Harvard Univ. Press. (Reference is made to vols. and paragraphs.)

———. 1940. *The Philosophy of Peirce: Selected Writings*, ed. Buchler, J. New York: Harcourt.

———. 1958. *Values in a Universe of Chance*, ed. Wiener, Philip P. Stanford, Calif.: Univ. Press.

———. 1963–66. *The Charles S. Peirce Papers*. 30 reels, microfilm edition. Cambridge, Mass.: The Houghton Library of University Microproduction.

———. 1972. *Charles S. Peirce: The Essential Writings*, ed. Moore, Edward C. New York: Harper & Row.

———. 1975–79. *Charles Sanders Peirce: Contributions to "The Nation,"* ed. Ketner, K. L., and Cook, J. E. 3 vols. Lubbock: Texas Tech Press.

———. 1976. *The New Elements of Mathematics*, ed. Eisele, Carolyn. 4 vols. The Hague: Mouton.

———. 1977a. *Complete Published Works, Including Secondary Materials*, Microfiche Edition, ed. Ketner, Kenneth L., et al. Greenwich, Conn.: Johnson.

———. 1977b. *Semiotic and Significs: The Correspondence between Charles S. Peirce and Victoria Lady Welby*, ed. Hardwick, C. S. Bloomington: Indiana Univ. Press.

———. 1982–89. *Writings of Charles S. Peirce: A Chronological Edition*. Vol. 1: 1857–66; vol. 2: 1867–71; vol. 3: 1872–78; vol. 4: 1879–84. Bloomington: Indiana Univ. Press.

Pelc, Jerzy. 1961. Semantic functions as applied to the analysis of the concept of metaphor. In Davie, Donald, et al., eds., *Poetics—Poetyka—Poetika*, pp. 305–39. The Hague: Mouton.

_____. 1971. *Studies in Functional Logical Semiotics of Natural Language*. The Hague: Mouton.

_____. 1981a. Prolegomena zu einer Definition des Zeichenbegriffs. *Zeitschrift für Semiotik* 3: 1–9.

_____. 1981b. Theoretical foundations of semiotics. *American Journal of Semiotics* 1: 15–45.

_____. 1982. Semiotic and nonsemiotic concepts of meaning. *American Journal of Semiotics* 1.4: 1–19.

_____. 1984a. Preface. In Pelc, Jerzy, et al., eds., *Sign, System, and Function*, pp. v-x. Berlin: Mouton.

_____. 1984b. Sign and inference. In Pelc, Jerzy, et al., eds., *Sign, System, and Function*, pp. 319–27. Berlin: Mouton.

Pelc, Jerzy, ed. (1971) 1979. *Semiotics in Poland, 1894–1969*. Dordrecht: Reidel.

Pelc, Jerzy, et al., eds. 1984. *Sign, System, and Function*. Berlin: Mouton.

Pelletier, Anne-Marie. 1977. *Fonctions poétiques*. Paris: Klincksieck.

Peña-Marín, Cristina, and Lozano y Gonzalo Abril, Jorge. 1978. Bibliografía sobre análisis semiótico de las comunicaciones de masas. *Revista Española de investigaciones sociológicas* 3: 209–26.

Peng, Fred C. C., ed. 1978. *Sign Language and Language Acquisition in Man and Ape*. Boulder, Colo.: Westview Press.

Péniou, Georges. 1972. *Intelligence de la publicité*. Paris: Laffont.

Penttilä, Erkki. 1962. *Advertising English*. Helsinki (= Mémoires de la Société Néophilologique de Helsinki 25.2).

Pépin, Jean. 1975. L'herméneutique ancienne. *Poétique* 6: 291–300.

Percival, W. Keith. 1975. The grammatical tradition and the rise of the vernaculars. In Sebeok, T. A., ed., *Current Trends in Linguistics*, vol. 13, pp. 231–76. The Hague: Mouton.

_____. 1981. Ferdinand de Saussure and the history of semiotics. In De George, Richard T., ed., *Semiotic Themes*, pp. 1–32. Lawrence: Univ. of Kansas Pub.

Perelman, Chaim, and Olbrechts-Tyteca, Lucie. (1958) 1969. *The New Rhetoric*. Notre Dame: Univ. Press.

Pérez Tornero, J. M. 1982. *La semiótica de la publicidad*. Barcelona: Mitre.

Perrino, Benedict. 1981. Evaluation of postures. *Semiotica* 37: 27–38.

Perron, Paul, and Collins, Frank, eds. 1988. *Paris School Semiotics*, vol. 1: *Theory*. Amsterdam: Benjamins.

Pesaresi, Massimo. 1981. Signale und Symbole. In Eschbach, Achim, ed., *Zeichen über Zeichen über Zeichen*, pp. 145–60. Tübingen: Narr.

Pesot, Jurgen. 1979. *Silence, on parle: Introduction à la sémiotique*. Montreal: Guérin.

_____. 1980. Ikonismus in der Phonologie. *Zeitschrift für Semiotik* 2: 7–18.

Peters, Jan Marie. 1950. *De taal van de film*. The Hague: Govers.

_____. 1981. *Pictorial Signs and the Language of Film*. Amsterdam: Radopi.

Peters, Johannes. 1967. *Einführung in die allgemeine Informationstheorie*. Berlin: Springer.

Peters, K. 1898. *Illustrierte Briefmarkensprache*. Mülheim/Ruhr: Bagel.

Petitot, Jean. 1987. Sur le réalisme ontologique des universaux sémio-linguistiques. In Arrivé, M., and Coquet, J.-C., eds., *Sémiotique en jeu*, pp. 43–63. Amsterdam: Benjamins.

Petitot-Cocorda, Jean. 1985. *Morphogénèse du sens*. Paris: Presses Univ. de France.

Petöfi, János S. 1986. Text, discourse. In Sebeok, Thomas A., ed., *Encyclopedic Dictionary of Semiotics*, 3 vols., pp. 1080–87. Berlin: Mouton de Gruyter.

Petrovich, Slobodan B., and Hess, Eckhard H. 1978. An introduction to animal communication. In Siegman, Aron W., and Feldstein, Stanley, eds., *Nonverbal Behavior and Communication*, pp. 17–53. Hillsdale, N.J.: Erlbaum.

Pettit, Philip. 1975. *The Concept of Structuralism*. Berkeley: Univ. of California Press.

Petzoldt, Leander, ed. 1978. *Magie und Religion*. Darmstadt: Wiss. Buchges.

Pfeifer, David E. 1981. George Berkeley: Precursor of Peircean semiotic. In Lange-Seidl, Annemarie ed., *Zeichenkonstitution*, vol. 1, pp. 67–74. Berlin: de Gruyter.

Pfister, Manfred. 1977. *Das Drama*. München: Fink.

Pforte, Dietger, ed. 1974. *Comics im ästhetischen Unterricht*. Frankfurt: Athenäum.

Pharies, David A. 1985. *Charles S. Peirce and the Linguistic Sign*. Amsterdam: Benjamins.

Piaget, Jean. (1946) 1962. *Play, Dreams, and Imitation in Childhood* (= Trans. of *La formation du symbole*). New York: Norton.

_____. (1968) 1971. *Structuralism*. London: Routledge & Kegan.

_____. (1970) 1971. *Genetic Epistemology*. New York: Norton.

Piaget, Jean, and Inhelder, Bärbel. (1966) 1971. *Mental Imagery in the Child*. London: Routledge & Kegan.

Piderit, Theodor. (1867) 1925. *Mimik und Physiognomik*. Detmold: Meyersche Hofbuchhndlg.

Pierce, John R. 1962. *Symbols, Signals, and Noise*. London: Hutchinson.

Pignatari, Décio. 1974. *Semiótica e literatura*. São Paulo: Ed. Perspectiva.

Pike, Kenneth L. (1943) 1971. *Phonetics*. Ann Arbor: Univ. of Michigan Press.

———. 1967. *Language in Relation to a Unified Theory of the Structure of Human Behavior*. 2nd rev. ed. The Hague: Mouton.

Pinborg, Jan. (1967) 1985. *Die Entwicklung der Sprachtheorie im Mittelalter*. Münster: Aschendorff.

———. 1972. *Logik und Semantik im Mittelalter*. Stuttgart: Frommann.

———. 1982. Speculative grammar. In Kretzmann, N., et al., eds., *The Cambridge History of Later Medieval Philosophy*, pp. 254–69. Cambridge: Univ. Press.

———. 1984. Modus significandi. In Ritter, J., ed., *Historisches Wörterbuch der Philosophie*, vol. 6, pp. 68–72. Basel: Schwabe.

Pinborg, Jan, et al. 1974. Konnotation. In Ritter, Joachim, ed., *Historisches Wörterbuch der Philosophie*, pp. 975–77. Basel: Schwabe.

Pinsker, Harold M., and Willis, William D., Jr. 1980. *Information Processing in Nervous Systems*. New York: Raven.

Pinto, Julio C.M. 1989. *The Reading of Time*. Berlin: Mouton de Gruyter.

Pinxten, Rik, et al. 1983. *Anthropology of Space*. Philadelphia: Univ. of Pennsylvania Press.

Pittenger, Robert E.; Hockett, Charles F.; and Danehy, John J. 1960. *The First Five Minutes*. Ithaca, N.Y.: P. Martineau.

Pittenger, Robert E., and Smith, Henry Lee, Jr. 1957. A basis for some contributions of linguistics to psychiatry. *Psychiatry* 20: 61–78.

Pladott, Dinnah. 1982. The dynamics of the sign systems in the theatre. In Hess-Lüttich, Ernest W. B., ed., *Multimedial Communication*, vol. 2, pp. 28–45. Tübingen: Narr.

Plamenatz, John. (1970) 1971. *Ideology*. London: Macmillan.

Plank, Frans. 1979. Ikonisierung und De-Ikonisierung als Prinzipien des Sprachwandels. *Sprachwissenschaft* 4: 121–58.

———. 1981. *Morphologische (Ir-)Regularitäten*. Tübingen: Narr.

Plebe, Armando, ed. 1981. *Semiotica ed Estetica—Semiotik und Ästhetik*. Roma: Libro-Field, and Baden-Baden: Agis.

Plett, Heinrich. 1975. *Textwissenschaft und Textanalyse—Semiotik-Linguistik-Rhetorik*. Heidelberg: Quelle & Meyer UTB.

Plett, Heinrich, ed. 1977. *Rhetorik*. München: Fink.

Ploog, Detlev. 1974. *Die Sprache der Affen*. München: Kindler.

Pochat, Götz. (1982) 1983. *Der Symbolbegriff in der Ästhetik und Kunstwissenschaft*. Köln: DuMont.

Podlewski, Regina. 1982. *Rhetorik als pragmatisches System*. Hildesheim: Olms.

Pogorzelski, H. A., and Ryan, W. J. 1982. *Foundations of Semiological Theory of Numbers*. Orono: Univ. of Maine Press.

Pohl, Jacques. 1968. *Symboles et langages 1: Le symbole*. Paris: Sodi.

Poinsot, John. (1632) 1985. *Tractatus de signis*, ed. & trans. Deely, J. N. Berkeley: Univ. of California Press.

Polenz, Max. 1948. *Die Stoa*. 2 vols. Göttingen: Vandenhoeck.

Pomorska, Krystyna, et al., eds. 1987. *Language, Poetry, and Poetics*. Berlin: Mouton de Gruyter.

Popper, Karl Raimund, and Eccles, John C. 1977. *The Self and Its Brain*. Berlin: Springer.

Porcher, Louis. 1976. *Introduction à une sémiotique des images*. Paris: Didier.

Poser, Hans. 1979. Signum, notio und idea. *Zeitschrift für Semiotik* 1: 299–303.

Posner, Roland. (1969) 1982. Structuralism in the interpretation of poetry. In Posner, R., *Rational Discourse and Poetic Communication*, pp. 129–59. Berlin: Mouton.

———. (1981) 1987. Charles Morris and the behavioral foundations of semiotics. In Krampen, M., et al., eds., *Classics of Semiotics*, pp. 23–57. New York: Plenum.

———. 1982. *Rational Discourse and Poetic Communication*. Berlin: Mouton.

———. 1984. Die Zahlen und ihre Zeichen. In Oehler, Klaus, ed., *Zeichen und Realität*, vol. 1, pp. 235–48. Tübingen: Stauffenburg.

———. 1985a. Nonverbale Zeichen in öffentlicher Kommunikation. *Zeitschrift für Semiotik* 7: 235–71.

———. 1985b. La syntactique, sa relation à la sémantique et la pragmatique, à la morphologie et la syntaxe, et à la syntagmatique et la paradigmatique. In Parret, H., and Ruprecht, H.-G., eds., *Exigences et perspectives de la sémiotique*, vol. 1, pp. 73–96. Amsterdam: Benjamins.

———. 1986. Iconicity in syntax. In Bouissac, P., et. al., eds., *Iconicity*, pp. 305–37. Tübingen: Stauffenburg.

Posner, Roland, and Reinecke, Hans-Peter, eds. 1977. *Zeichenprozesse*. Wiesbaden: Athenaion.

Posner, Roland, et al. 1983. Diskussion: Systemhaftigkeit. *Zeitschrift für Semiotik* 5: 401–431.

Poyatos, Fernando. 1972. The communication system of the speaker-actor. *Linguistics* 83: 64–84.

———. 1976. *Man beyond Words*. Oswego, N.Y.: State Univ. Coll.

———. 1982a. New perspectives for an integrative research of nonverbal systems. In Key, Mary Ritchie, ed., *Nonverbal Communication Today*, pp. 121–38. Berlin: Mouton.

———. 1982b. Nonverbal communication in the theater. In Hess-Lüttich, Ernest W. B., ed., *Multimedial Communication 2, pp. 75–94. Tübingen: Narr.

———. 1983. New Perspectives in Nonverbal Communication. Oxford: Pergamon.

Prak, Niels Luning. 1968. The Language of Architecture. The Hague: Mouton.

Pratt, Mary Louise. 1977. Toward a Speech Act Theory of Literary Discourse. Bloomington: Indiana Univ. Press.

Premack, David. 1976. Intelligence in Ape and Man. Hillsdale, N.J.: Erlbaum.

———. 1986. Gavagai! or the Future History of the Animal Language Controversy. Cambridge, Mass.: MIT Press.

Premack, David, and Premack, Anne J. 1983. The Mind of an Ape. New York: Norton.

Preminger, Alex, ed. (1965) 1974. Princeton Encyclopedia of Poetry and Poetics. Princeton: Univ. Press.

Presnell, Michael. 1983. Sign, Image, and Desire: Semiotic Phenomenology and the Film Image. Ann Arbor: Univ. Microfilms Int.

Prevignano, Carlo, ed. 1979. La semiotica nei Paesi slavi. Milano: Feltrinelli.

Preziosi, Donald. 1979a. Architecture, Language, and Meaning. The Hague: Mouton.

———. 1979b. The Semiotics of the Built Environment. Bloomington: Indiana Univ. Press.

Pribram, Karl H. 1971. Languages of the Brain. Englewood Cliffs, N.J.: Prentice-Hall.

Price, H. H. 1953. Thinking and Experience. New York: Hutchinson.

Prieto, Luis J. 1966. Messages et signaux. Paris: Presses Universitaires.

———. 1968. La sémiologie. In Martinet, André, ed., Le langage (Encyclopédie de la Pléiade), pp. 93–144. Paris: Gallimard.

———. 1975a. Etudes de linguistique et de sémiologie générales. Genève: Droz.

———. 1975b. Pertinence et pratique. Paris: Minuit.

———. 1975c. Sémiologie de la communication et sémiologie de la signification. In Prieto, Luis J., Etudes de linguistique et de sémiologie générales, pp. 125–41. Genève: Droz.

Prigogine, Ilya, and Stengers, Isabelle. (1979) 1984. Order Out of Chaos. New York: Bantam.

Prince, Gerald. 1973. A Grammar of Stories. The Hague: Mouton.

———. 1982. Narratology. Berlin: Mouton.

———. 1983. Narrative pragmatics, message, and point. Poetics 12: 527–36.

Prodi, Giorgio. 1988. Material bases of signification. Semiotica 69: 191–241.

Propp, Vladimir Jakovlevič. (1928) 1968. Morphology of the Folktale. 2nd ed. Austin: Univ. of Texas Press.

Pryluck, Calvin. 1975. The film metaphor metaphor. Literature Film Quarterly 3.2: 117–23.

Pudovkin, Vsevolod I. (1928) 1958. Film Technique and Film Acting. London: Vision/Mayflower.

Pulgram, Ernst. 1951. Phoneme and grapheme: A parallel. Word 7: 15–20.

Pulman, S. G. 1982. Are metaphors "creative"? Journal of Literary Semantics 11: 78–89.

Püschel, Ulrich. 1980. Linguistische Stilistik. In Althaus, Hans Peter, et al., eds., Lexikon der germanistischen Linguistik, 2nd ed., pp. 304–13. Tübingen: Niemeyer.

Pütz, Hans-Henning. 1973. Das Zeichensystem Sprache—Zur Behandlung zeichentheoretischer Fragestellungen auf der Unterstufe. Linguistik und Didaktik 4: 83–98.

Quine, Willard Van Orman. (1960) 1976. Word and Object. Cambridge, Mass.: MIT Press.

———. (1968) 1971. The inscrutability of reference. In Steinberg, Danny D., and Jakobovits, Leon A., eds., Semantics, pp. 142–54. Cambridge: Univ. Press.

———. 1981. Theories and Things. Cambridge, Mass.: Belknap Press.

Rabelo Campos, María Helena. 1984. Advertising and ideology: A semiotic approach. In Borbé, Tasso, ed., Semiotics Unfolding, pp. 977–90. Berlin: Mouton.

Raffler-Engel, Walburga von, ed. 1980. Aspects of Nonverbal Communication. Lisse: Swets.

Ramat, Paolo. 1975. Semiotics and linguistics. Versus 10: 1–16.

Rambosson, J. 1853. Langue universelle, langage mimique mimé et écrit. Paris: Garnier.

Rancour-Laferrière, Daniel. 1980. Semiotics, psychoanalysis, and science. Ars Semeiotica 3: 181–240.

Ranea, Alberto Guillermo. 1986. Zeichen, Symbol, Begriff. In Dutz, K. D., and Schmitter, P., eds., Geschichte und Geschichtsschreibung der Semiotik, pp. 303–16. Münster: MAkS.

Ransdell, Joseph. 1980. Semiotic and linguistics. In Rauch, Irmengard, and Carr, Gerald F., The Signifying Animal, pp. 135–85. Bloomington: Indiana Univ. Press.

———. 1986. On Peirce's conception of the iconic sign. In Bouissac, P., et al. eds., Iconicity, pp. 193–213. Tübingen: Stauffenburg.

Rapoport, Anatol. (1952) 1965. What is semantics? In Hayden, Donald E., and Alworth, E. Paul, Classics in Semantics, pp. 337–54. New York: Philosophical Library.

Rastier, François. 1968. Comportement et signification. Langages 10 (1968): 76–86.

———. 1972a. Idéologie et théorie des signes. The Hague: Mouton.

———. 1972b. Systématique des isotopies. In

Greimas, A. J., ed., *Essais de sémiotique poétique*, pp. 80–106. Paris: Larousse.

——. 1973. *Essais de sémiotique discursive*. Tours: Mame.

——. 1981. Le développement du concept d'isotopie. *Documents de recherche du Groupe de recherches sémio-linguistiques* 3.29: 5–29.

Rauch, Irmengard. 1980. Between linguistics and semiotics: Paralanguage. In Rauch, I., and Carr, Gerald F., eds., *The Signifying Animal*, pp. 284–89. Bloomington: Indiana Univ. Press.

——. 1981. Semiotics in search of method: Narrativity. *Semiotica* 34: 167–76.

Read, Allen Walker. 1948. An account of the word "semantics." *Word* 3/4: 78–98.

Rehbock, Helmut. 1980. Rhetorik. In Althaus, Hans Peter, et al., eds., *Lexikon der Germanistischen Linguistik*, 2nd ed., pp. 293–303. Tübingen: Niemeyer.

Reichenbach, Hans. (1947) 1966. *Elements of Symbolic Logic*. New York: Free Press.

Reinle, Adolf. 1976. *Zeichensprache der Architektur*. Zürich: Artemis.

Relyea, Suzanne. 1976. *Signs, Systems, and Meanings: A Contemporary Reading of Four Molière Plays*. Middleton, Conn.: Wesleyan.

Rengstorf, K. H. 1971. Semeion. In Kittel, G., et al., eds., *Theological Dictionary of the New Testament*, pp. 1015–24. Grand Rapids: Eerdmans.

Renský, Miroslav. 1966. The systematics of paralanguage. *Travaux de linguistique de Prague* 2: 97–102.

Resnikow, Lasar Ossipowitsch. (1964) 1969. *Erkenntnistheoretische Fragen der Semiotik*. Berlin: Deutscher Verlag der Wissenschaften.

——. 1977. *Zeichen, Sprache, Abbild*. Frankfurt: Syndikat.

Révész, Géza. (1946) 1970. *The Origins and Prehistory of Language*. Westport, Conn.: Greenwood.

Revzine, Olga, and Revzine, Isaak. 1971. Expérimentation sémiotique chez Eugène Ionesco. *Semiotica* 4: 240–62.

Rewar, Walter. 1976. Semiotics and communication in Soviet criticism. *Language and Style* 9: 55–69.

Réthoré, Joëlle. 1978. Semiotik und Pädagogik der Fremdsprachen: Audiovisuelle Hilfsmittel in Frage gestellt? In *Die Einheit der semiotischen Dimensionen*, pp. 251–55. Tübingen: Narr.

Rey, Alain. 1971. La théorie positiviste des langages: Auguste Comte et la sémiotique. *Semiotica* 4: 52–74.

——. 1973 and 1976. *Théories du signe et du sens*. 2 vols. Paris: Klincksieck.

——. 1978a. Communication vs. semiosis: Two conceptions of semiotics. In Sebeok, Thomas A., ed., *Sight, Sound, and Sense*, pp. 98–110. Bloomington: Indiana Univ. Press.

——. 1978b. *Les spectres de la bande*. Paris: Minuit.

——. 1984. What does semiotics come from? *Semiotica* 52: 79–93.

Rey-Debove, Josette. 1971. Notes sur une interprétation autonymique de la littérarité. *Littérature* 4: 90–95.

——. 1974. Autonomie et sémiotique littéraire. *Littérature* 16: 107–16.

——. 1979. *Lexique sémiotique*. Paris: Presses Univ.

Richards, Ivor Armstrong. 1928. *Principles of Literary Criticism*. New York: Harcourt.

——. (1936) 1979. *The Philosophy of Rhetoric*. Oxford: Univ. Press.

Ricœur, Paul. 1965. *L'interprétation*. Paris: Seuil.

——. 1969. *Le conflit des interprétations: Essais d'herméneutique*. Paris: Seuil.

——. (1975a) 1978. *The Rule of Metaphor*. London: Routledge.

——. (1975b) 1985. Signe et sens. In *Encyclopaedia universalis*, vol. 16, pp. 881–95.

——. (1983–84) 1984–85. *Time and Narrative*. 2 vols. Chicago: Univ. Press.

Riffaterre, Michael. 1959. Criteria for style analysis. *Word* 15: 154–74.

——. 1971. *Essais de stylistique structurale*. Paris: Flammarion.

——. 1978. *Semiotics of Poetry*. Bloomington: Indiana Univ. Press.

Riha, Karl. 1974. Technik der Fortsetzung im Comic strip: Zur Semiotik eines Massenmediums. In Pforte, D., ed., *Comics im ästhetischen Unterricht*, pp. 151–71. Frankfurt: Athenäum.

Rijk, L. M. de. 1967. *Logica modernorum*, vol. 2, pt. 1. Assen: van Gorcum.

Rijnberk, Gérard A. van. 1953. *Le langage par signes chez les moines*. Amsterdam: North Holland.

Rissom, Ingrid. 1979. Zum Begriff des Zeichens in den Arbeiten Vygotskijs. In Geier, Manfred, et al., eds., *Sprachbewußtsein*, pp. 9–31. Stuttgart: Metzler.

Roberts, Louise Nisbet. 1955. Art as icon: An interpretation of C. W. Morris. *Tulane Studies in Philosophy* 4: 75–82.

Robertson, D. W., Jr. 1951. Historical criticism. *English Institute Essays, 1950* (New York): 3–31.

Robertson, D. W., Jr. and Huppé, Bernard F. 1951. *Piers Plowman and Scriptural Tradition*. Princeton, N.J.: Univ. Press.

Robey, David, ed. 1973. *Structuralism: An Introduction*. Oxford: Clarendon.

Robins, Robert Henry. (1951) 1971. *Ancient and Medieval Grammatical Theory in Europe*. Port Washington: Kennikat.

——. 1967. *A Short History of Linguistics*. London: Longman.

Robinson, W. P. 1972. *Language and Social Behavior*. Harmondsworth: Penguin.

Rochberg-Halton, Eugene, and McMurtrey, Kevin. 1983. The foundations of modern semiotic: Charles Peirce and Charles Morris. *American Journal of Semiotics* 2.1–2: 129–56.

Rodriguez Adrados, Francisco. 1981. La teoría del signo en Georgias de Leontinos. In Geckeler, H., et al., eds., *Logos Semantikos*, pp. 9–19. Berlin: de Gruyter.

Roeder, Werner. 1927. *Beiträge zur Lehre vom Zeichen in der deutschen Philosophie des 18. Jahrhunderts*. Berlin: Diss. Phil.

Roggenhofer, Johannes. 1987. Sprache und Kultur: Linguistisch-semiotische Anmerkungen zu Ernst Cassirer. In Asbach-Schnitker, B., and Roggenhofer, J., eds., *Neuere Forschungen zur Wortbildung and Historiographie der Linguistik*. 387–97. Tübingen: Narr.

Röhrich, Lutz. 1967. *Gebärde—Metapher—Parodie*. Düsseldorf: Schwann.

Rokem, Freddie. 1986. The death of the apple or contradictions between the visual and verbal. In Deely, John, ed., *Semiotics 1985*, pp. 139–48. Lanham, Md.: Univ. Press of America.

Rollin, Bernard E. 1976. *Natural and Conventional Meaning*. The Hague: Mouton.

Romeo, Luigi. 1977. The derivation of "semiotics" through the history of the discipline. *Semiosis* 6.2: 37–49.

———. 1979a. Charles S. Peirce in the history of semiotics. *Ars Semeiotica* 2: 247–52.

———. 1979b. The bivium syndrome in the history of semiotics. *The Canadian Journal of Research in Semiotics* 6: 93–111.

———. 1979c. Pedro da Fonseca in Renaissance semiotics. *Ars Semeiotica* 2: 187–204.

———. 1979d. *Ecce Homo: A Lexicon of Man*. Amsterdam: Benjamins.

Römer, Ruth. 1968. *Die Sprache der Anzeigenwerbung*. Düsseldorf: Schwann.

Rónai, Paulo. 1967. *Homens contra Babel*. Rio de Janeiro: Zahar Ed.

Rosenfeld, Howard M. 1982. Measurement of body motion and orientation. In Scherer, Klaus R., and Ekman, Paul, eds., *Handbook of Methods in Nonverbal Behavior Research*, pp. 199–286. Cambridge: Univ. Press.

Rosenfeld, Lawrence William. 1971. *Aristotle and Information Theory*. The Hague: Mouton.

Rosenkranz, Bernhard. 1961. *Der Ursprung der Sprache*. Heidelberg: Winter.

Rösler, Wolfgang. 1983. Schriftkultur und Fiktionalität. In Assmann, A., et al., eds., *Schrift und Gedächtnis*, pp. 109–22. München: Fink.

Rosnay, Joël de. (1975) 1979. *The Macroscope*. New York: Harper & Row.

Ross, John R. 1983. Ikonismus in der Phraseologie. *Zeitschrift für Semiotik* 2: 39–56.

Rossi, Ino, ed. 1974. *The Unconscious in Culture: The Structuralism of Claude Lévi-Strauss in Perspective*. New York: Dutton.

Rossi, Paolo. (1957) 1968. *Francis Bacon*. London: Routledge.

———. 1960. *Clavis universalis: arti mnemoniche e logica combinatoria de Lullo a Leibniz*. Milano: Ricciardi Editore.

Rossi, Raymond. 1987. Semiotics in the classroom. *American Journal of Semiotics* 5: 303–13.

Rossi-Landi, Ferruccio. 1953. *Charles Morris*. Roma: Fratelli Bocca.

———. (1968) 1983. *Language as Work and Trade*. South Hadley, Mass.: Bergin & Garvey.

———. (1972) 1976. [*Semiotica e ideologia*, trans.] *Semiotik, Ästhetik und Ideologie*. München: Hanser.

———. 1975a. *Linguistics and Economics*. The Hague: Mouton.

———. 1975b. Signs about a master of signs. *Semiotica* 13: 155–97.

———. 1984. Wittgenstein: Old and new. In Borbé, T., ed., *Semiotics Unfolding*, pp. 327–44. Berlin: Mouton.

Rössler, Gerda. 1979. *Konnotationen*. Wiesbaden: Steiner.

Rothschild, Friedrich S. 1968. Concepts and methods of biosemiotic. *Scripta Hierosolymitana* 20: 163–94.

Rovența-Frumușanti, Daniela. 1982. The articulation of the semiotic codes. In Hess-Lüttich, E. W. B., ed., *Multimedial Communication*, vol 2., pp. 313–26. Tübingen: Narr.

Rudner, Richard, 1951. On semiotic aesthetics. *Journal of Aesthetics and Art Criticism* 10: 67–77.

Ruef, Hans. 1981. *Augustin über Semiotik und Sprache*. Bern: Wyss Erben.

Ruesch, Jurgen. 1972. *Semiotic Approaches to Human Relations*. The Hague: Mouton.

Ruesch, Jurgen, and Kees, Welden. (1956) 1974. *Nonverbal Communication*. Berkeley: Univ. of California Press.

Ruffini, Franco. 1973. Semiotica del teatro: la stabilizzazione del senso: Un approccio informazionale. *Biblioteca teatrale* 10: 205–39.

———. 1978. *Semiotica del testo: l'esempio teatro*. Roma: Bulzoni.

Rumbaugh, Duane M., ed. 1977. *Language Learning by a Chimpanzee*. New York: Academic Press.

Runggaldier, Edmund. 1985. *Zeichen und Bezeichnetes*. Berlin: de Gruyter.

Russell, Bertrand. (1905) 1974. On denoting. In Zabeeh, Farhang, et al., eds., *Readings in Semantics*, pp. 143–58. Urbana: Univ. of Illinois Press.

Russell, Claire, and Russell, W. M. S. 1971. Language and animal signals. In Minnis, Noel, ed., *Linguistics at Large*, pp. 159–94. London: Gollancz.

Russell, Sharon A. (1978) 1981. *Semiotics and Lighting*. Ann Arbor, Mich.: Univ. Microfilms Int.

Ruwet, Nicolas. 1972. *Langage, musique, poésie*. Paris: Seuil.

———. 1975. Théorie et méthodes dans les études musicales. *Musique en jeu* 17: 11–36.

Ryan, Marie-Laurent. 1979. Linguistic models of narratology: From structuralism to generative semantics. *Semiotica* 28: 127–55.

Saarnio, Uuno. 1959. Betrachtungen über die scholastische Lehre der Wörter als Zeichen. *Acta Academica Paedagogica Jyväskyläensis* 17: 215–49.

Sahlins, Marshall. 1976. *Culture and Practical Reason*. Chicago: Univ. Press.

Saint-Martin, Fernande. 1987. *Sémiologie du langage visuel*. Sillery: Presses de l'Université du Québec.

Saitz, Robert L., and Cervenka, Edward J. 1972. *Handbook of Gestures: Colombia and the United States*. The Hague: Mouton.

Sakaguchi, Alicja. 1983. Plansprachen . . . , Semiotik und Interlinguistik. *Zeitschrift für Semiotik* 5: 331–51.

Salmon, Vivian. 1972. *The Works of Francis Lodwick*. London: Longman.

———. 1979. *The Study of Language in Seventeenth Century England*. Amsterdam: Benjamins.

Sampson, Geoffrey. 1985. *Writing Systems*. London: Hutchinson.

Sanders, Gary. 1970. Peirce's sixty-six signs? *Transactions of the Charles S. Peirce Society* 4.1: 3–16.

Sanders, Willy. 1973. *Linguistische Stiltheorie*. Göttingen: Vandenhoeck.

Sangster, Rodney B. 1982. *Roman Jakobson and Beyond: Language as a System of Signs*. Berlin: Mouton.

Sapir, Edward. (1921) 1949. *Language*. New York: Harcourt.

———. 1949. *Selected Writings*. Berkeley: Univ. of California Press.

Sarles, Harvey. 1977. *After Metaphysics*. Lisse: de Ridder.

Sauerbier, Samson Dietrich. 1978. Wörter bildlich/Bilder wörtlich. In Arbeitsgruppe Semiotik, ed., *Die Einheit der semiotischen Dimensionen*, pp. 27–94. Tübingen: Narr.

———. 1985. *Wörter, Bilder und Sachen*. Heidelberg: Winter.

Šaumjan, S. K. See Shaumyan.

Saussure, Ferdinand de. (1916a) 1986. *Cours de linguistique générale*, ed. Bally, Charles, and Sechehaye, Albert. 25th ed. Paris: Payot.

———. (1916b) 1969. *Course in General Linguistics*, trans. Baskin, Wade. New York: McGraw-Hill.

———. (1916c) 1972. *Cours de linguistique générale*, ed. de Mauro, Tullio. Paris: Payot.

———. (1916d) 1968, 1974. *Cours de linguistique générale*, ed. Engler, Rudolf. Vol. 1 (1968), vol. 2, part 4 (1974). Wiesbaden: Harrassowitz.

———. (1916e) 1986. *Course in General Linguistics*, trans. Harris, Roy. La Salle, Ill.: Open Court.

Savage-Rumbaugh, E. Sue. 1986. *Ape Language*. New York: Columbia Univ. Press.

Savan, David. 1980. La séméiotique de Charles S. Peirce. *Langages* 58: 9–23.

Savigny, Eike von. 1974. Zeichen. In Baumgartner, Hans Michael, and Krings, Hermann, *Handbuch philosophischer Grundbegriffe*, pp. 1787–98. München: Kösel.

———. 1980. *Die Signalsprache der Autofahrer*. München: dtv.

Scalvini, Maria Luisa. 1971. Über das Signifikat in der Architektur. *werk* 58: 390–93.

———. 1979. A semiotic approach to architectural criticism. In Chatman, Seymour, et al., eds., *A Semiotic Landscape*, pp. 965–69. The Hague: Mouton.

Schäfer, Michael. 1974. *Die Sprache des Pferdes*. München: Nymphenburger.

Schaff, Adam. (1960) 1973. *Einführung in die Semantik*. Reinbek: Rowohlt.

———. 1964 (1974). *Sprache und Erkenntnis*. Reinbek: Rowohlt.

Schanz, Gunter. 1974. Filmsprache und Filmsyntax. In Buselmeier, Michael, ed., *Das glückliche Bewußtsein*, pp. 80–122. Darmstadt: Luchterhand.

Schanze, Helmut. 1974. *Medienkunde für Literaturwissenschaftler*. München: Fink.

Schapiro, Meyer. 1969. On some problems in the semiotics of visual art. *Semiotica* 1 (1969): 223–42.

———. 1973. *Words and Pictures*. The Hague: Mouton.

Schauenberg, Paul. 1972. *Les animaux et leurs langages*. Paris: Hachette (English trans. 1981 as *Animal Communication*. London: Burke.)

Scheerer, Eckhart. 1983. Probleme und Ergebnisse der experimentellen Leseforschung. In Günther, Klaus B., and Günther, Hartmut, eds., *Schrift, Schreiben, Schriftlichkeit*, pp. 89–118. Tübingen: Niemeyer.

Scheerer, Thomas M. 1980. *Ferdinand de Saussure*. Darmstadt: Wiss. Buchges.

Schefer, Jean-Louis 1969. *Scénographie d'un tableau*. Paris: Seuil.

Scheffler, Israel. 1986. Ten myths of metaphor. *Communication and Cognition* 19: 389–94.

Scheflen, Albert E. 1964. The significance of posture in communication systems. *Psychiatry* 27: 316–31.

———. 1972. *Body Language and Social Order.* Englewood Cliffs, N.J.: Prentice-Hall.

———. 1973. *How Behavior Means.* New York: Gordon & Breach.

Scheglov, Yu. K. (1977) 1979. *The Poetics of Molière's Comedies.* Colchester: Univ. of Essex (= Russian Poetics in Translation 6).

Schenk, Brigitte. 1982. The phylogeny of art. In Koch, Walter A., Ed., *Semiogenesis*, pp. 417–46. Frankfurt: Lang.

Scherer, Bernd Michael. 1984. *Prolegomena zu einer einheitlichen Zeichentheorie.* Tübingen: Stauffenburg.

Scherer, Klaus R. 1970. *Non-verbale Kommunikation.* Hamburg: Buske.

Scherer, Klaus R., ed. 1982. *Vokale Kommunikation.* Weinheim: Beltz.

Scherer, Klaus R., and Wallbott, Harald G. 1985. Analysis of nonverbal behavior. In Dijk, Teun A. van, ed., *Handbook of Discourse Analysis*, vol. 2, pp. 199–230. London: Academic Press.

Scherer, Klaus R.; Wallbott, Harald G.; and Scherer, Ursula. 1979. Methoden zur Klassifikation von Bewegungsverhalten: Ein funktionaler Ansatz. *Zeitschrift für Semiotik* 1: 177–92.

Scherer, Klaus R., and Ekman, Paul, eds. 1982. *Handbook of Methods in Nonverbal Behavior Research.* Cambridge: Univ. Press.

Scherer, Klaus R., and Giles, Howard, eds. 1979. *Social Markers in Speech.* Cambridge: Univ. Press.

Scherer, Klaus R., and Wallbott, Harald G., eds. 1979. *Nonverbale Kommunikation.* Weinheim: Beltz.

Scherer, Shawn E. 1975. A photographic method for the recording and evaluation of proxemic interaction patterns. In Williams, Thomas R., ed., *Socialization and Communication in Primary Groups*, pp. 347–54. The Hague: Mouton.

Schippan, Thea. (1972) 1975. *Einführung in die Semasiologie.* Leipzig: Bibl. Inst.

Schiwy, Günther. (1969a) 1984. *Der französische Strukturalismus.* Reinbek: Rowohlt.

———. 1969b. *Strukturalismus und Christentum.* Freiburg: Herder.

———. 1971. *Neue Aspekte des Strukturalismus.* München: Kösel.

———. 1973. *Strukturalismus und Zeichensysteme.* München: Beck.

———. 1975. Zeichen und Bedeutung. In Volp, Rainer, ed., *Chancen der Religion.* pp. 244–52. Gütersloh: Mohn.

———. 1985. *Poststrukturalismus und "Neue Philosophen."* Reinbek: Rowohlt.

Schiwy, Günther, et al. 1976. *Zeichen im Gottesdienst.* München: Kaiser/Kösel.

Schleiermacher, Friedrich D. E. (1838) 1977. *Hermeneutik und Kritik.* Frankfurt: Suhrkamp.

Schleifer, Ronald. 1983. Introduction. In Greimas, Algirdas Julien, *Structural Semantics*, pp. xi-lvi. Lincoln: Univ. of Nebraska Press.

———. 1987. *A. J. Greimas and the Nature of Meaning.* London: Croom Helm.

Schlesinger, Hilde S. 1978. The acquisition of bimodal language. In Schlesinger, I. M., and Namir, Lila, eds., *Sign Language of the Deaf*, pp. 57–93. New York: Academic Press.

Schlesinger, I. M., and Namir, Lila. 1978. Introduction. In Schlesinger, I. M., and Namir, Lila, eds., *Sign Language of the Deaf*, pp. 1–8. New York: Academic Press.

Schlesinger, I. M., and Namir, Lila, eds. 1978. *Sign Language of the Deaf.* New York: Academic Press.

Schlieben-Lange, Brigitte. 1975. Metasprache und Metakommunikation. In Schlieben-Lange, Brigitte, ed., *Sprachtheorie*, pp. 189–205. Hamburg: Hoffmann & Campe.

Schmalriede, Manfred. 1981. Ästhetische Funktionalität. Gestalten der Objekte der Fotografie. In Sturm, Hermann, and Eschbach, Achim, eds., *Ästhetik & Semiotik*, pp. 71–80. Tübingen: Narr.

Schmandt-Besserat, Denise. 1978. The earliest precursors of writing. *Scientific American* 238.6: 38–47.

Schmid, Georg, ed. 1986. *Die Zeichen der Historie: Beiträge zu einer semiologischen Geschichtswissenschaft.* Wien: Böhlau.

Schmid, Herta. 1973. *Strukturalistische Dramentheorie.* Kronberg: Scriptor.

———. 1978. Aspekte und Probleme der ästhetischen Funktion im tschechischen Strukturalismus. In Matejka, Ladislav, ed., *Sound, Sign, and Meaning*, pp. 386–424. Ann Arbor: Univ. of Michigan.

Schmid, Herta, and Van Kesteren, Aloysius, eds. 1984. *Semiotics of Drama and Theatre.* Amsterdam: J. Benjamins.

Schmid, Wolf. 1984. Der semiotische Status der narrativen Ebenen. In Oehler, Klaus, ed., *Zeichen und Realität*, vol. 2, pp. 477–86. Tübingen: Stauffenburg.

Schmidt, Bernd. 1984. *Malinowskis Pragmasemantik.* Heidelberg: Winter.

Schmidt, Siegfried J. 1968. *Sprache und Denken . . . von Locke bis Wittgenstein.* The Hague: Nijhoff.

———. 1969. *Bedeutung und Begriff.* Braunschweig: Vieweg.

———. 1971. *Ästhetizität.* München: Bayer. Schulbuch-Verlag.

———. 1973. *Texttheorie.* München: Fink.

———. 1974 *Elemente einer Textpoetik.* München: Bayerischer Schulbuch-Verlag.

———. 1980. *Grundriß der Empirischen Literaturwissenschaft.* Braunschweig: Vieweg.

———. 1984. *Vom Text zum Literatursystem (=*

Lumis Publications 1). Siegen: University, Institute for Empirical Literature and Media Research.

Schmidtbauer, Wolfgang. (1971) 1975. *Psychotherapie. Ihr Weg von der Magie zur Wissenschaft.* München: dtv.

Schmidt-Radefeldt, Jürgen 1984. Sémiologie et langage(s). *Oeuvres et critiques* 9.1: 127–54.

_____. 1987. Der erste Entwurf einer Zeichentheorie von Paul Valéry (1901). In Toro, A. de, ed., *Texte, Kontexte, Strukturen*, pp. 139–56. Tübingen: Narr.

Schmitt, Alfred. 1980. *Entstehung und Entwicklung von Schriften.* Köln: Böhlau.

Schmitter, Peter. 1980. Semiotische Theoreme im Bereich der Textsemantik. In Eschbach, Achim, and Rader, Wendelin, eds., *Literatursemiotik*, vol. 2, pp. 99–120. Tübingen: Narr.

_____. 1983. Plädoyer gegen die Geschichte der Semiotik. In Eschbach, A., and Trabant, J., eds., *History of Semiotics*, pp. 3–23. Amsterdam: Benjamins.

_____. (1984) 1985. Zum Heraklitverständnis in der gegenwärtigen Geschichtsschreibung der Linguistik. In Dutz, K. D., and Schmitter, P., eds., *Fallstudien zur Historiographie der Linguistik* (= Arbeitsberichte 2), pp. 3–20. Münster: Inst. für Allg. Sprachwiss.

_____. 1985. Ein transsemiotisches Modell: Wilhelm von Humboldts Auffassung von Kunst und Sprache. In Dutz, K. D., and Kaczmarek, L., eds., *Rekonstruktion und Interpretation,* pp. 311–34. Tübingen: Narr.

_____. 1986. Wilhelm von Humboldt. In Sebeok, T. A., ed., *Encyclopedic Dictionary of Semiotics*, pp. 317–23. Berlin: Mouton de Gruyter.

_____. 1987. *Das sprachliche Zeichen.* Münster: Inst. für Allg. Sprachwissenschaft & MAkS Pub.

Schmitz, Heinrich Walter. 1975. *Ethnographie der Kommunikation.* Hamburg: Buske.

_____. 1985. Victoria Lady Welby's Significs. In Welby, V., *Significs and Language*, pp. ix-cclxvii. Amsterdam: Benjamins.

Schneider, Reinhard. 1980. *Semiotik der Musik.* München: Fink.

Schnelle, Helmut. 1962. *Zeichensysteme zur wissenschaftlichen Darstellung.* Stuttgart: Frommann.

_____. 1976. Information, Informationstheorie. In Ritter, Joachim, ed., *Historisches Wörterbuch der Philosophie*, pp. 355–59. Basel: Schwabe.

_____. 1980. Notationssysteme. *Zeitschrift für Semiotik* 2: 387–96.

Schnelle, Helmut, ed. 1981. *Sprache und Gehirn: Roman Jakobson zu Ehren.* Frankfurt: Suhrkamp.

Schöberle, Wolfgang. 1984. *Argumentieren— Bewerten—Manipulieren.* Heidelberg: Groos.

Scholes, Robert. 1974. *Structuralism in Literature.* New Haven: Yale Univ. Press.

_____. 1982. *Semiotics and Interpretation.* New Haven: Yale Univ. Press.

Scholes, Robert, and Kellogg, Robert. 1966. *The Nature of Narrative.* New York: Oxford Univ. Press.

Scholz, Gunther. 1969. "Struktur" in der mittelalterlichen Hermeneutik. *Archiv für Begriffsgeschichte* 13: 73–75.

Schonauer, Klaus. 1986. *Signal, Symbol, Symptom: Alte und neue Aspekte der medizinischen Semiotik.* Münster: Institut für Allg. Sprachwiss. & MAkS.

Schrader, W. H. 1976. Konvention. In Ritter, Joachim, ed., *Historisches Wörterbuch der Philosophie*, vol. 4. Basel: Schwabe.

Schramm, Wilbur, ed. 1963. *The Science of Human Communication.* New York: Basic Books.

Schraud, Peter. 1966. *Theater als Information: Kommunikation und Ästhetik.* Wien: Diss. Phil.

Schreckenberger, Waldemar. 1978. *Rhetorische Semiotik.* Freiburg: K. Alber.

Schröder, Ernst. 1890. *Über das Zeichen.* Karlsruhe: Braun.

Schrödinger, Erwin. 1947. *What Is Life?* Cambridge: Univ. Press.

Schuh, Hans-Manfred. 1977. Semiotische Analyse literarischer Texte. In Schröder, Konrad, and Weller, Franz-Rudolf, eds., *Literatur im Fremdsprachenunterricht*, pp. 20–39. Frankfurt: Diesterweg.

_____. 1982. Aspekte semiotischer Stilbeschreibung. *Kodikas/Code* 4/5: 21–37.

Schult, Joachim. 1986. Zeichenvermitteltes Verhalten bei Spinnen. *Zeitschrift für Semiotik* 8: 253–76.

Schulz, Theodore Albert. 1961. *Panorama der Ästhetik von Charles Sanders Peirce.* Stuttgart: Diss. Phil.

Schutz, Noel W. Jr. 1976. *Kinesiology: The Articulation of Movement.* Lisse: de Ridder.

Schwarze, Christoph, and Wunderlich, Dieter, eds. 1985. *Handbuch der Lexiokologie.* Königstein: Athenäum.

Schwarz-Winklhofer, Inge, and Biedermann, Hans. (1972) 1975. *Das Buch der Zeichen und Symbole.* München: Droemer Knaur.

Schweizer, Harro. 1979. *Sprache und Systemtheorie.* Tübingen: Narr.

Schweizer, Harro, ed. 1985. *Sprache und Raum.* Stuttgart: Metzler.

Schwidetzky, Ilse, ed. 1973. *Über die Evolution der Sprache.* Frankfurt: Fischer.

Scotto di Carlo, Nicole. 1973. Analyse sémiologique des gestes et mimiques des chanteurs d'opéra. *Semiotica* 9: 289–318.

Scragg, D. G. 1974. *A History of English Spelling.* Manchester: Univ. Press.

Searle, John R. 1970. *Speech Acts.* Cambridge: Univ. Press.

_____. 1979. Metaphor. In Ortony, Andrew, ed.,

Metaphor and Thought, pp. 92–123. Cambridge: Univ. Press.

Sebeok, Thomas A. 1972. *Perspectives in Zoosemiotics*. The Hague: Mouton.

———. (1976) 1985. *Contributions to the Doctrine of Signs*. Lanham, Md.: Univ. Press of America.

———. 1977. Zoosemiotic components of human communication. In Sebeok, Thomas A., ed., *How Animals Communicate*, pp. 1055–77. Bloomington: Indiana Univ. Press.

———. 1979. *The Sign and Its Masters*. Austin: Univ. of Texas Press.

———. 1981. *The Play of Musement*. Bloomington: Indiana Univ. Press.

———. 1984. Sympton. In Copeland, James E., ed., *New Directions in Linguistics and Semiotics*, pp. 211–30. Amsterdam: Benjamins.

———. 1986a. An evolving theory of mind. *Times Literary Supplement*, July 4, p. 740.

———. 1986b. *I Think I Am a Verb*. New York: Plenum.

———. 1988. Linguistik und Semiotik. In Claussen, R., and Daube-Schackat, Roland, eds., *Gedankenzeichen: Festschrift für Klaus Oehler*, pp. 193–203. Tübingen: Stauffenburg.

Sebeok, Thomas A., ed. (1955) 1958. *Myth*. Bloomington: Indiana Univ. Press.

———. (1960) 1968. *Style in Language*. Cambridge, Mass.: MIT Press.

———. 1966. *Portraits of Linguists*. vol. 2. Bloomington: Indiana Univ. Press.

———. 1968. *Animal Communication*. Bloomington: Indiana Univ. Press.

———. 1975. *Current Trends in Linguistics 13: Historiography of Linguistics*. The Hague: Mouton.

———. 1977. *How Animals Communicate*. Bloomington: Indiana Univ. Press.

———. 1986. *Encyclopedic Dictionary of Semiotics*. 3 vols. Berlin: Mouton de Gruyter.

Sebeok, Thomas A.; Lamb, Sydney M.; and Regan, John O. 1988. *Semiotics and Education: A Dialogue*. Claremont, Calif.: Claremont Graduate School (= Issues of Communication 10).

Sebeok, Thomas A., and Margolis, Harriet. 1982. Captain Nemo's porthole. *Poetics Today* 3: 110–39.

Sebeok, Thomas A.; Hayes, Alfred S.; and Bateson, Mary Catherine, eds. (1964) 1972. *Approaches to Semiotics*. The Hague: Mouton.

Sebeok, Thomas A., and Ramsay, Alexandra, eds. 1969. *Approaches to Animal Communication*. The Hague: Mouton.

Sebeok, Thomas A., and Rosenthal, Robert, eds. 1981. *The Clever Hans Phenomenon: Communication with Horses, Whales, Apes, and People*. New York: N.Y. Academy of Sciences.

Sebeok, Thomas A., and Umiker-Sebeok, Jean, eds.

1976. *Speech Surrogates: Drum and Whistle Systems*. The Hague: Mouton.

———. 1980. *Speaking of Apes*. New York: Plenum.

———. 1986. *The Semiotic Sphere*. New York: Plenum.

———. 1987. *The Semiotic Web, 1986*. Berlin: Mouton de Gruyter.

Segaud, Marion. 1973. Anthropologie de l'espace. *Espaces et Sociétés* 9: 29–38.

Segre, Cesare. 1973. *Semiotics and Literary Criticism*. The Hague: Mouton.

———. 1979a. Du structuralisme à la sémiologie en Italie. In Helbo, André, ed., *Le champ sémiologique*, pp. L 1–29. Bruxelles: Ed. Complexe.

———. 1979b. *Semiotica filologica*. Torino: Einaudi.

———. 1979c. *Structures and Time*. Chicago: Univ. Press.

———. 1980. *Literarische Semiotik*. Stuttgart: Klett-Cotta.

———. 1981. Narratology and theater. *Poetics Today* 2.3: 95–104.

Seibert, Thomas M., ed. 1980. *Der Kode—Geheimsprache einer Institution* (= *Zeitschrift für Semiotik* 2.3). Wiesbaden: Athenaion.

Seiffert, Helmut. 1968. *Information über Information*. München: Beck.

Seligmann, Claus. 1982. What is door? Notes toward a semiotic guide to design. *Semiotica* 38: 55–76.

Semiotique de l'espace: Architecture, urbanisme, sortir de l'impasse. Paris: Denoël, 1979.

Sempre, Pedro. 1976. *Semiología del infortunio: Lenguaje e ideología de la fotonovela*. Madrid: Ed. Felmar.

Serpieri, Alessandro, et al. 1981. Toward a segmentation of the dramatic text. *Poetics Today* 2.3: 163–200.

Serrano, Sebastià. (1980) 1981. *Signos, lengua y cultura*. Barcelona: Ed. Anagrama.

———. 1981. *La semiótica*. Barcelona: Montesinos.

Seung, T. K. 1982. *Semiotics and Thematics in Hermeneutics*. New York: Columbia Univ. Press.

Shands, Harley C. 1970. *Semiotic Approaches to Psychiatry*. The Hague: Mouton.

———. 1977. *Speech as Instruction*. The Hague: Mouton.

Shannon, Claude E., and Weaver, Warren. 1949. *The Mathematical Theory of Communication*. Urbana: Univ. of Illinois Press.

Shapiro, Gary. 1975. Intention and interpretation in art: A semiotic analysis. *Journal of Aesthetics and Art Criticism* 33: 33–42.

Shapiro, Marianne. 1981. Preliminaries to a semiotics of ballet. In Steiner, Wendy, ed., *The Sign in Music and Literature*, pp. 216–27. Austin: Univ. of Texas Press.

Shapiro, Michael. 1976. *Asymmetry*. Amsterdam: North Holland.

——. 1983. *The Sense of Grammar*. Bloomington: Indiana Univ. Press.

Shapiro, Michael, and Shapiro, Marianne. 1976. *Hierarchy and the Structure of Tropes*. Lisse: de Ridder.

Shaughnessy, J. D. 1973. *The Roots of Ritual*. Grand Rapids, Mich.: W. Eerdmans.

Shaumyan, Sebastian K. 1987. *A Semiotic Theory of Language*. Bloomington: Indiana Univ. Press.

Shaw, Bernard. 1962. *Androcles and the Lion with a Parallel Text in Shaw's Alphabet*. Harmondsworth: Penguin.

Sheriff, John K. 1981. Charles S. Peirce and the semiotics of literature. In De George, Richard T., ed., *Semiotic Themes*, pp. 51–74. Lawrence: Univ. of Kansas Pub.

Shibles, Warren. 1971. *Metaphor: An Annotated Bibliography and History*. Whitewater, Wis.: Language Press.

Shklovsky. See Šklovskij.

Shorey, H. H. 1976. *Animal Communication by Pheromes*. New York: Academic Press.

Shukman, Ann. 1977. *Literature and Semiotics*. Amsterdam: North Holland.

Siegman, Aron W., and Feldstein, Stanley, eds. 1978. *Nonverbal Behavior and Communication*. Hillsdale, N.J.: Erlbaum.

Siertsema, B. (1954) 1965. *A Study of Glossematics*. The Hague: Nijhoff.

Sievers, Eduard. 1924. Ziele und Wege der Schallanalyse. In *Stand und Aufgaben der Sprachwissenschaft* (= Festschrift Wilhelm Streitberg), pp. 65–111. Heidelberg: Winter.

Siger, Leonard. 1968. Gestures, the language of signs, and human communication. *American Annals of the Deaf* 113: 11–28.

Silverman, Kaja. 1983. *The Subject of Semiotics*. New York: Oxford Univ. Press.

Simone, Raffaele. 1972. Sémiologie augustienne. *Semiotica* 6: 1–31.

Simpson, M. J. A. 1973. Social displays and the recognition of individuals. In Bateson, P. P. G., and Klopfer, P. H., eds., *Perspectives in Ethology*, vol. 1, pp. 225–79. New York: Plenum.

Singer, Milton. 1984. *Man's Glassy Essence: Explorations in Semiotic Anthropology*. Bloomington: Indiana Univ. Press.

Sipek, Borek. 1980. *Architektur als Vermittlung. Semiotische Untersuchung der architektonischen Form als Bedeutungsträger*. Stuttgart: Krämer.

——. 1981. Ästhetische Funktionalität gestalteter Objekte. In Sturm, Hermann, and Eschbach, Achim, eds., *Ästhetik und Semiotik*, pp. 81–92. Tübingen: Narr.

Siple, Patricia, ed. 1978. *Understanding Language through Sign Language Research*. New York: Academic Press.

Skelly, Madge. 1979. *Amer-Ind Gestural Code*. New York: Elsevier.

Skidmore, Arthur. 1981. Peirce and semiotics. In De George, R. T., ed., *Semiotic Themes*, pp. 33–50. Lawrence: Univ. of Kansas Pub.

Šklovskij, Viktor. (1916) 1969. Kunst als Verfahren. In Striedter, Jurij, ed., 1969, *Russischer Formalismus*, pp. 3–35. München: Fink.

Skwarczyńska, Stefania. 1974. Anmerkungen zur Semantik der theatralischen Gestik. In Kroll, Walter, and Flaker, Aleksander, eds., *Literaturtheoretische Modelle und kommunikatives System*, pp. 328–70. Kronberg: Scriptor.

Slaughter, M. M. 1982. *Universal Languages and Scientific Taxonomy in the Seventeenth Century*. Cambridge: Univ. Press.

Slawinska, Irena. 1978. La semiologia del teatro in statu nascendi: Praha 1931–41. *Biblioteca teatrale* 16: 114–35.

Sless, David. 1986. *In Search of Semiotics*. London: Croom Helm.

Smart, Benjamin Humphrey. 1831, 1837. *Outline of Sematology & Sequel to Sematology*. London: Longman.

Smith, Barbara Herrenstein. 1968. *Poetic Closure*. Chicago: Univ. Press.

Smith, Howard A. 1984. State of the art of nonverbal behavior in teaching. In Wolfgang, Aaron, ed., *Nonverbal Behavior*, pp. 171–202. Lewiston: Hogrefe.

Smith, W. John. 1974. Zoosemiotics: Ethology and the theory of signs. In Sebeok, Thomas A., ed., *Current Trends in Linguistics* 12: 561–626.

——. 1977a. *The Behavior of Communicating: An Ethological Approach*. Cambridge, Mass.: Harvard Univ. Press.

——. 1977b. Communication in birds. In Sebeok, Thomas A., ed., *How Animals Communicate*, pp. 545–74. Bloomington: Indiana Univ. Press.

Solbrig, David. 1726. *Allgemeine Schrift, Scriptura oecumenica*. Salzwedel.

Sommer, Robert. 1969. *Personal Space*. Englewood Cliffs, N.J.: Prentice Hall.

Sommerfeld, Reinhard. 1980. *Evolution, Kommunikation und Sprache: Versuch einer Synthese ethologischer und linguistischer Semiotik*. München: Tuduv.

Sontag, Susan, ed. 1982. *A Barthes Reader*. New York: Hill & Wang.

Sørensen, Hans. 1958. Littérature et linguistique. In *Orbis Litterarum*, suppl. 2 (Copenhagen), pp. 182–97.

Sornig, Karl. 1986. *Holophrastisch-expressive Äußerungsmuster (Anhand . . . der trivial-narra-*

tiven Gattung "fumetti"). Graz: Universität (= Grazer Linguistische Monographie 3).

Souriau, Etienne. 1950 (1970). *Les deux cent mille situations dramatiques.* Paris: Flammarion.

Spang, Kurt. 1987. *Grundlagen der Literatur- und Werberhetorik.* Kassel: Reichenberger.

Spang-Hanssen, Henning. 1954. *Recent Theories on the Nature of the Language Sign.* Copenhagen: Nordisk Kulturforlag.

———. 1966. Glossematics. In Mohrmann, C., et al., eds., *Trends in European and American Linguistics, 1930–1960*, pp. 128–64. Utrecht: Spectrum.

Sparhawk, Carol M. 1978. Contrastive identificational features of Persian gestures. *Semiotica* 24: 49–86.

Sparmacher, Angelika. 1981. *Narrativik und Semiotik.* Bern: Lang.

Speciale, Emilio. 1986. Emilio Tesauro. In Sebeok, T. A., ed., *Encyclopedic Dictionary of Semiotics*, pp. 1078–79. Berlin: Mouton de Gruyter.

Sperber, Dan. 1968. Le structuralisme en anthropologie. In Wahl, François, ed., *Qu'est-ce que le structuralisme?* Paris: Seuil.

———. (1974) 1984. *Rethinking Symbolism.* Cambridge: Univ. Press.

Spiegel, John, and Machotka, Pavel. 1974. *Messages of the Body.* New York: Free Press.

Spillner, Bernd. 1974. *Linguistik und Literaturwissenschaft.* Stuttgart: Kohlhammer.

———. 1980. Über die Schwierigkeiten der semiotischen Textanalyse. *Die Neueren Sprachen* 79: 619–30.

———. 1982. Stilanalyse semiotisch komplexer Texte. *Kodikas/Code* 4/5: 91–106.

Spinner, Kaspar H. 1977. Semiotische Grundlegung des Literaturunterrichts. In Spinner, K. H., ed., *Zeichen, Text, Sinn. Zur Semiotik des literarischen Verstehens*, pp. 125–64. Göttingen: Vandenhoeck.

———. 1980. Die Aporien des Konnotationsbegriffs in der Literatursemiotik. In Eschbach, Achim, and Rader, Wendelin, eds., *Literatursemiotik I*, pp. 65–84. Tübingen: Narr.

Spitzer, Leo. 1949. American advertising explained as popular art. In Spitzer, Leo, *A Method of Interpreting Literature*, pp. 102–49. Northampton, Mass.: Smith College.

Spottiswoode, Raymond. (1935) 1973. *A Grammar of the Film.* Berkeley: Univ. of California Press.

Sprengel, Kurt. 1801. *Handbuch der Semiotik.* Halle: Gebauer.

Springer, George P. 1956. Language and music. In *For Roman Jakobson*, pp. 504–13. The Hague: Mouton.

Staiano, Kathryn Vance. 1986. *Interpreting Signs of Illness: A Case Study in Medical Semiotics.* Berlin: Mouton de Gruyter.

Stankiewicz, Edward. 1960. Linguistics and the study of poetic language. In Sebeok, Thomas A., ed., *Style in Language*, pp. 69–81. Cambridge, Mass.: MIT Press.

Stanzel, Franz K. (1979) 1984. *A Theory of Narrative.* Cambridge: Univ. Press.

Stappers, J. G. 1966. *Publicistiek en Communicatiemodellen.* Nijmegen: Busser.

Starobinski, Jean. (1971) 1979. *Words upon Words: The Anagrams of Ferdinand de Saussure.* New Haven: Yale Univ. Press.

Stefani, Gino. 1975. Situation de la sémiotique musicale. In *Proceedings of 1st International Congress on Semiotics in Music*, pp. 9–25. Pesaro: Centro di Iniziativa Culturale.

———. 1976. *Introduzione alla semiotica della musica.* Palermo: Sellerio.

Stéfanini, Jean. 1976. Jules César Scaliger et son De causis linguae Latinae. In Parret, H., ed., *History of Linguistic Thought*, pp. 317–30. Berlin: de Gruyter.

Stegmüller, Wolfgang. 1969a. *Hauptströmungen der Gegenwartsphilosophie.* 4th ed. Stuttgart: Kröner.

———. (1969b) 1974. *Wissenschaftliche Erklärung und Begründung.* Berlin: Springer.

Steiner, George. 1972. After the book. *Visible Language* 6: 197–210.

Steiner, Peter. 1977. Jan Mukařovský and Charles W. Morris: Two pioneers of the semiotics of art. *Semiotica* 19: 321–34.

Steiner, Peter, and Volek, Bronislava. 1978. Semiotics in Bohemia in the 19th and early 20th centuries. In Bailey, R. W., et al., eds., *The Sign: Semiotics around the World*, pp. 207–26. Ann Arbor: Michigan Slavic Pub.

Steiner, Wendy. (1978) 1980. Modern American Semiotics. In Bailey, R. W., et al., eds., *The Sign: Semiotics around the World*, pp. 99–118. Ann Arbor: Michigan Slavic Pub.

———. 1982. *The Colors of Rhetoric.* Chicago: Univ. Press.

Steiner, Wendy, ed. 1981a. *Image and Code.* Ann Arbor: Univ. of Michigan.

———. 1981b. *The Sign in Music and Literature.* Austin: Univ. of Texas Press.

Steinfeld, Thomas. 1984. *Symbolik, Klassik, Romantik: Kritik der Literaturphilosophie Hegels.* Königstein: Hain.

Steinmann, Martin, ed. 1967. *New Rhetorics.* New York: Scribner's.

Steinmeyer, Elias, and Sievers, Eduard, eds. 1895 (1969). *Die althochdeutschen Glossen.* Dublin: Weidmann.

Stempel, Wolf-Dieter, ed. 1972. *Texte der russischen Formalisten II.* München: Fink.

Stender-Petersen, Adolf. 1949. Esquisse d'une théorie structurale de la littérature. In *Recherches struc-*

turales (= Travaux du Cercle Linguistique de Copenhague 5), pp. 277–87. Copenhagen.

———. (1958) 1971. Zur Möglichkeit einer Wortkunst-Theorie. In Ihwe, Jens, ed., *Literaturwissenschaft und Linguistik* 2.2, pp. 454–71. Frankfurt: Athenäum.

Stenius, Erik. 1969. *Wittgensteins Traktat*. Frankfurt: Suhrkamp.

Stern, Theodore. (1957) 1976. Drum and whistle 'languages': An analysis of speech surrogates. In Sebeok, Thomas A., and Umiker-Sebeok, Donna Jean, eds., *Speech Surrogates: Drum and Whistle Systems*, pp. 124–48. The Hague: Mouton.

Sternberg, Martin L. A. 1981. *American Sign Language: A Comprehensive Dictionary*. New York: Harper & Row.

Stetter, Christian. 1979. Peirce und Saussure. *Kodikas/Code* 1: 124–49.

Stewart, Ann Harleman. 1987. Models of narrative structure. *Semiotica* 64: 83–97.

Stierle, Karlheinz. 1975. *Text als Handlung*. München: Fink.

Stock, Alex. 1978. *Textentfaltungen—Semiotische Experimente mit einer biblischen Geschichte*. Düsseldorf: Patmos.

Stockinger, Peter. 1983. *Semiotik. Beitrag zu einer Theorie der Bedeutung*. Stuttgart: Akad. Verl. H.-D. Heinz.

Stokoe, William C., Jr. 1960. *Sign Language Structure* (= Studies in Linguistics, Occasional Papers 8). Buffalo: Univ.

———. 1972. *Semiotics and Human Sign Languages*. The Hague: Mouton.

———. 1974. Classification and description of sign languages. In Sebeok, Thomas A., ed., *Current Trends in Linguistics* 12: 345–71. The Hague: Mouton.

———. 1975. Face-to-face interaction: Signs to language. In Kendon, Adam; Harris, Richard M.; and Key, Mary Ritchie, eds., *Organization of Behavior in Face-to-Face Interaction*, pp. 315–37. The Hague: Mouton.

———. 1976. Sign language autonomy. *Annals of the New York Academy of Sciences* 280: 505–13.

———. 1978. Sign languages and the verbal/nonverbal distinction. In Sebeok, Thomas A., *Sight, Sound, and Sense*, pp. 157–72. Bloomington: Indiana Univ. Press.

———. 1980. Sign language structure. *Annual Review of Anthropology* 9: 365–90.

Stokoe, William C., Jr.; Croneberg, C.; and Casterline, D. 1965. *A Dictionary of American Sign Language*. Washington: Gallaudet Coll. Press.

Stoll, André. (1974) 1977. *Asterix*. Köln: DuMont.

Stravinsky, Igor. (1936) 1962. *An Autobiography*. New York: Norton.

Strawson, P. F. 1950. On referring. *Mind* 59: 320–44.

Strickland, Geoffrey. 1981. *Structuralism or Criticism?* Cambridge: Univ. Press.

Striedter, Jurij, ed. 1969. *Russischer Formalismus*. München: Fink.

Stringer, Peter. 1973. Do dimensions have face validity? In Cranach, Mario von, and Vine, Jan, eds., *Social Communication and Movement*, pp. 341–85. London: Academic Press.

Strombach, Werner. 1983. Wholeness, gestalt, system. *International Journal of General Systems* 9: 65–72.

Strong, Edward K. 1925. *The Psychology of Selling and Advertising*. New York: McGraw-Hill.

Studnicki, Frantiszek. 1970. Traffic signs. *Semiotica* 2: 151–72.

Sturm, Hermann, and Eschbach, Achim, eds. 1981. *Ästhetik und Semiotik*. Tübingen: Narr.

Sturrock, John, ed. 1979. *Structuralism and Since*. Oxford: Univ. Press.

Suhor, Charles. 1984. Towards a semiotics-based curriculum. *Journal of Curriculum Studies* 16: 247–57.

Sullerot, Evelyne. 1964. De la lecture de l'image. *Terre d'images* 4/5: 279–83.

Sullivan, Scott. 1986. Master of the signs. *Newsweek (International)*, Dec. 22, pp. 46–50.

Sulowski, Jan, ed. 1971, 1973, 1976. *Semiotic-Historical Studies*, vols. 1–3. Wrocław: Zakład Narodowy.

Sundstrom, Eric, and Altman, Irwin. 1976. Interpersonal relationships and personal space: Research review and theoretical model. *Human Ecology* 4: 47–67.

Sweet, Henry. 1890. *Primer of Phonetics*. Oxford: Clarendon.

Swiggers, P. 1981. La théorie du signe à Port-Royal. *Semiotica* 35: 267–85.

———. 1986. Port-Royal: Autour du signe. In Dutz, K. D., and Schmitter, P., eds., *Geschichte und Geschichtsschreibung der Semiotik*, pp. 119–32. Münster: MAkS.

———. 1987. Eric Buyssens. In Sebeok, T. A., and Umiker-Sebeok, J., *The Semiotic Web, 1986*, pp. 103–119. Berlin: Mouton de Gruyter.

Szemerényi, Oswald. 1971. *Richtungen der modernen Sprachwissenschaft*. Heidelberg: Winter.

Szondi, Peter. 1975. *Einführung in die literarische Hermeneutik*. Frankfurt: Suhrkamp.

Tafuri, Manfredo. (1968) 1980. *Theories and History of Architecture*. London: Granada.

Talens, Jenaro, et al. 1978. *Elementos para una semiótica del texto artístico*. Madrid: Ed. Cátedra.

Tallis, Raymond. 1988. *Not Saussure: A Critique of Post-Saussurean Literary Theory*. Houndmills: Macmillan.

Tambiah, S. J. 1968. The magical power of words. *Man* 3: 175–208.

Tannen, Deborah, and Saville-Troike, Muriel, eds. 1985. *Perspectives on Silence*. Norwood: Ablex.

Tantam, Digby. 1986. A semiotic model of nonverbal communication. *Semiotica* 58: 41–57.

Tanz, Christine. 1971. Sound symbolism in words relating to proximity and distance. *Language and Speech* 14: 266–76.

Tarasti, Eero. 1979. *Myth and Music*. The Hague: Mouton.

———. 1982. Peirce and Greimas from the viewpoint of musical semiotics. In Herzfeld, Michael, and Lenhart, Margot D., eds., *Semiotics 1980*, pp. 503–11. New York: Plenum.

———. 1986. Music as sign and process. In Evans, Jonathan D., and Helbo, André, *Semiotics and International Scholarship*, pp. 127–51. Dordrecht: Nijhoff.

Tarasti, Eero, et al. 1987. Basic concepts of studies in musical signification. In Sebeok, Thomas A., and Umiker-Sebeok, eds., *The Semiotic Web, 1986*, pp. 405–581. Berlin: Mouton de Gruyter.

Tardy, Michel. 1964. Le troisième signifiant. *Terre d'images* 4–5: 313–22.

Tarski, Alfred. (1944) 1974. The semantic conception of truth. In Zabeeh, Farhang, et al., eds., *Readings in Semantics*, pp. 677–711. Urbana: Univ. of Illinois Press.

Tavolga, William N. 1974. Application of the concept of levels of organization to the study of animal communication. In Krames, Lester, et al., eds., *Nonverbal Communication*, pp. 51–76. New York: Plenum.

Taylor, Allan Ross. 1975. Nonverbal communications systems in native North America. *Semiotica* 13: 329–74.

Tembrock, Günter. 1971. *Biokommunikation*. 2 vols. Berlin: Akademie-Verlag.

———. 1973. Aktuelle Probleme der Zoosemiotik im Bereich der Bioakustik. In Rey-Debove, J., ed., *Recherches sur les systèmes signifiants*, pp. 635–49. The Hague: Mouton.

Terrace, Herbert S. 1979. *Nim*. New York: Knopf.

Tesnière, Lucien. 1959. *Eléments de syntaxe structurale*. Paris: Klincksieck.

Thayer, Lee. 1972. Communication system. In Laszlo, Ervin, ed., *The Relevance of General Systems Theory*, pp. 93–121. New York: Braziller.

———. 1982. Human nature: Of communication, of structuralism, of semiotics. *Semiotica* 41: 25–40.

Thibault-Laulan, Anne-Marie. 1971. *Le langage de l'image*. Paris: Editions Universitaires.

———. 1972. Image et communication. In Thibault-Laulan, Anne-Marie, ed., *Image et communication*, pp. 19–47. Paris: Editions Universitaires.

———. 1973. Image et langage. In Pottier, Bernard, ed., *Le langage*, pp. 148–215. Paris: Centre d'Etude et de Promotion de la Lecture.

Thom, Martin. 1981. The unconscious as a language. In MacCabe, Colin, ed., *The Talking Cure*. pp. 1–44. London: Macmillan.

Thom, René, and Marcus, Solomon. 1986. Mathematics and semiotics. In Sebeok, T. A., ed., *Encyclopedic Dictionary of Semiotics*, pp. 487–97. Berlin: Mouton.

Thoma, Werner. 1976. Ansätze zu einer sprachfunktional-semiotisch orientierten Stilistik. *Zeitschrift für Literaturwissenschaft und Linguistik (LiLi)* 22: 117–41.

Thomas, Donald W. 1984. Project Semiotics and the schools. In Borbé, T., ed., *Semiotics Unfolding*, vol. 1, pp. 631–38. Berlin: Mouton.

———. 1987. Semiotics: The pattern which connects. *American Journal of Semiotics* 5: 291–302.

Thomas, Donald W., ed. 1980–83. *Semiotics 1–4*. 5 vols. Lexington, Mass.: Gin Press.

Thompson, Michael. 1979. *Rubbish Theory*. Oxford: Univ. Press.

Thompson, Roger M. 1982. Language planning in frontier America: The case of the Deseret Alphabet. *Language Problems and Language Planning* 6.1: 46–62.

Thompson, Stith. 1966. *Motif-Index of Folk-Literature*. Bloomington: Indiana Univ. Press.

Thorndike, Lynn. (1923) 1943. *A History of Magic and Experimental Science*. New York: Columbia Univ. Press.

Thorpe, W. H. 1961. *Bird-Song*. Cambridge: Univ. Press.

———. 1972a. The comparison of vocal communication in animals and man. In Hinde, R. A., ed., *Non-Verbal Communication*, pp. 27–47. Cambridge: Univ. Press.

———. 1972b. Vocal communication in birds. In Hinde, R. A., ed., *Non-Verbal Communication*, pp. 153–75. Cambridge: Univ. Press.

———. 1974. *Animal Nature and Human Nature*. Garden City, N.Y.: Anchor Press.

Thürlemann, Felix. 1981a. Bildbedeutung jenseits der Ikonizität. In Lange-Seidl, Annemarie, ed., *Zeichenkonstitution II*, pp. 3–11. Berlin: de Gruyter.

———. 1981b. Überlegungen zur Bedeutungskonstitution in der Malerei. In Sturm, Hermann, and Eschbach, Achim, eds., *Ästhetik und Semiotik*, pp. 59–70. Tübingen: Narr.

———. 1984. Die Farbe in der Malerei. In Borbé, Tasso, ed., *Semiotics Unfolding*, pp. 1389–96. Berlin: Mouton.

Tiefenbrun, Susan W. 1980. *Signs of the Hidden*. Amsterdam: Rodopi.

———. 1984. The state of literary semiotics: 1983. *Semiotica* 51: 7–44.

Tinbergen, Niko. 1965. *Animal Behavior*. New York: Time-Life.

Tobin, Yishai, ed. 1988. *The Prague School and Its Legacy*. Amsterdam: Benjamins.

Todorov, Tzvetan. 1967. *Littérature et signification*. Paris: Larousse.

———. (1968) 1981. *Introduction to Poetics*. Brighton: Harvester Press.

———. 1969. *Grammaire du Décaméron*. The Hague: Mouton.

———. 1970a. Les études du style. *Poétique* 1: 224–32.

———. (1970b) 1973. *The Fantastic*. Cleveland: Case Western Univ. Press.

———. 1970c. Synecdoques. *Communications* 16: 26–35.

———. (1971a) 1977. *The Poetics of Prose*. Oxford: Blackwell.

———. 1971b. The two principles of narrative. *Diacritics*, Fall, pp. 37–44.

———. 1972. Introduction à la symbolique. *Poétique* 3: 273–308.

———. 1973. Discours de la magie. *L'Homme* 13.4: 38–65.

———. 1974. On linguistic symbolism. *New Literary History* 6: 111–34.

———. 1975. Literature and semiotics. In Sebeok, Thomas A., ed., *The Tell-Tale Sign*, pp. 97–102. Lisse: de Ridder.

———. (1977) 1982. *Theories of the Symbol*. Ithaca, N.Y.: Cornell Univ. Press.

———. (1978) 1983. *Symbolism and Interpretation*. London: Routledge & Kegan Paul.

———. (1981) 1984. *Mikhail Bakhtin: The Dialogical Principle*. Minneapolis: Univ. of Minnesota Press.

Todorov, Tzvetan, ed. 1965. *Théorie de la littérature. Textes de formalistes russes*. Paris: Seuil.

Tomas, David. 1982. The ritual of photography. *Semiotica* 40: 1–25.

Tomas, Vincent. 1965. Is art language? *The Journal of Philosophy* 65: 559–74.

Tomkins, Gordon M. 1975. The metabolic code. *Science* 189: 760–63.

Tordera Sáez, Antonio. 1978. Teoría y técnica del análisis teatral. In Talens, J., et al., *Elementos para una semiótica del texto artístico*, pp. 157–202. Madrid: Ed. Cátedra.

Tort, Patrick. 1976. Dialectique des signes chez Condillac. In Parret, Herman, ed., *History of Linguistic Thought and Contemporary Linguistics*, pp. 488–502. Berlin: de Gruyter.

Toumajian, T.-S. 1986. *The Semiotics of Printed Instructions*. St. Andrews: Ph.D. Diss. (abstracted in *Index to Theses* 35.4–A7, p. 1488).

Toussaint, Bernard. 1976. Idéographie et bande dessinée. *Communications* 24: 81–93.

———. 1978. *Qu'est-ce que la sémiologie*. Toulouse: Privat.

Toussaint, Maurice. 1983. *Contre l'arbitraire du signe*. Paris: Didier.

Trabant, Jürgen. 1970. *Zur Semiologie des literarischen Kunstwerks*. München: Fink.

———. 1971. Superman: Das Image eines Comic-Helden. In Ehmer, Hermann K., ed., *Visuelle Kommunikation*, pp. 251–76. Köln: DuMont.

———. 1976a. *Elemente der Semiotik*. München: Beck.

———. 1976b. Die Stadt und die Sprache: eine Saussuresche Analogie. In *Konzept 3: Die Stadt als Text*, pp. 79–88. Tübingen: Wasmuth.

———. 1980. Zeichen in ästhetischen Handlungen. In Eschbach, A., and Rader, W., eds., *Literatursemiotik I*, pp. 85–102. Tübingen: Narr.

———. (1981a) 1987. Louis Hjelmslev: Glossematics as general semiotics. In Krampen, M., et al., eds., *Classics of Semiotics*, pp. 89–108. New York: Plenum.

———. 1981b. Monumentalistische, kritische und antiquarische Historie der Semiotik. *Zeitschrift für Semiotik* 3: 41–48.

———. 1983. Ideelle Bezeichnung. In Eschbach, A., and Trabant, J., eds., *History of Semiotics*, pp. 251–76. Amsterdam: Benjamins.

———. 1986. *Apeliotes oder Der Sinn der Sprache*. München: Fink.

Trager, George L. 1950. *The Field of Linguistics*. Norman, Okla.: Battenburg Press (= Studies in Linguistics: Occasional Papers 1).

———. 1958. Paralanguage: A first approximation. *Studies in Linguistics* 13: 1–12. (Also in Hymes, Dell, ed., *Language in Culture and Society*, pp. 274–88. New York: Harper & Row, 1964.)

———. 1961. The typology of paralanguage. *Anthropological Linguistics* 3: 17–21.

———. 1974. Writing and writing systems. In Sebeok, Thomas A., ed., *Current Trends in Linguistics* 12.1: 373–496. The Hague: Mouton.

Trendelenburg, Adolf. 1856. *Über Leibnizens Entwurf einer allgemeinen Charakteristik*. Berlin: Dümmler.

Trojan, Felix. 1975. *Biophonetik*. Mannheim: Bibliog. Inst.

Trubetzkoy, Nicolaj. (1939) 1958. *Grundzüge der Phonologie*. Göttingen: Vandenhoeck.

Tudor, Andrew. 1973. *Theories of Film*. New York: Viking.

Turbayne, Colin Murray. (1962) 1970. *The Myth of Metaphor*. Columbia: Univ. of South Carolina Press.

Turner, Victor. 1975. Symbolic studies. *Annual Review of Anthropology* 4: 145–61.

Tversky, Amos. 1977. Features of similarity. *Psychological Review* 84: 327–52.

Tylor, Edward B. 1871. *Primitive Culture*. 2 vols. London: Murray.

Tynjanov, Jurij. (1924) 1969. Das literarische Faktum. In Striedter, Jurij, ed., *Russischer Formalismus*, pp. 394–431. München: Fink.

———. (1927) 1971. On literary evolution. In Matejka, Ladislav, and Pomorska, Krystyna, eds., *Readings in Russian Poetics*, pp. 66–78. Cambridge, Mass.: MIT Press.

Ubersfeld, Anne. 1977. *Lire le théâtre*. Paris: Ed. sociales.

Ueding, Gert, and Steinbrink, Bernd. 1986. *Grundriß der Rhetorik*. Stuttgart: Metzler.

Uexküll, Jakob von. (1928) 1973. *Theoretische Biologie*. Frankfurt: Suhrkamp. (Trans.: *Theoretical Biology*. New York: Harcourt, 1962.)

———. (1940) 1982. The Theory of Meaning. *Semiotica* 42: 25–82.

Uexküll, Thure von. 1978. Autopoietisches oder autokinetisches System? In Heijl, Peter M.; Köck, Wolfram K.; and Roth, Gerhard, eds., *Wahrnehmung und Kommunikation*, pp. 141–49. Frankfurt: Lang.

———. 1981a (1984). The sign theory of Jakob von Uexküll. In Krampen, M., et al., eds., *Classics of Semiotics*, pp. 147–79. New York: Plenum.

———. 1981b. System and crisis in human physical and mental development. In Roth, Gerhard, and Schwegel, Helmut, eds., *Self-Organizing Systems*, pp. 132–44. Frankfurt: Campus.

Uhlenbeck, E. M. 1978. The communicative function of language and speech. In Coppieters, Frank, and Goyvaerts, Didier L., eds., *Functional Studies in Language and Literature*, pp. 109–17. Ghent: Story-Scientia.

Uldall, Hans Jørgen. 1944. Speech and writing. *Acta Lingusitica* 4: 11–16.

———. 1967. *Outline of Glossematics* (= Travaux du Cercle linguistique de Copenhague 10.1). Copenhagen: Nordisk Sprog- og Kulturforlag.

Ullmann, Ingeborg. 1975. *Psycholinguistik, Psychosemiotik*. Göttingen: Vandenhoeck.

Ullmann, Stephen. (1962) 1972. *Semantics*. Oxford: Blackwell.

———. 1966. *Language and Style*. Oxford: Blackwell.

———. 1975. Natural and conventional signs. In Sebeok, Thomas A., ed., *The Tell Tale Sign*, pp. 103–110. Lisse: de Ridder.

Ulmer, Gregory L. 1985. *Applied Grammatology*. Baltimore: Johns Hopkins Univ. Press.

Umiker, Jean. 1974. Speech surrogates: Drum and whistle systems. In Sebeok, Thomas A., ed., *Current Trends in Linguistics* 12: 497–536. The Hague: Mouton.

Umiker-Sebeok, Jean. 1977. Semiotics of culture: Great Britain and North America. *Annual Review in Anthropology* 6: 121–35.

———. 1979. Nature's way? Visual images of childhood in American culture. In Winner, Irene Portis, and Umiker-Sebeok, Jean, eds., *Semiotics of Culture*, pp. 173–220. The Hague: Mouton.

———. 1985. Workshop on semiotics and marketing. *Semiotica* 57: 189–96.

Umiker-Sebeok, Jean, and Sebeok, Thomas A. 1978. Introduction. In Umiker-Sebeok, D. J., and Sebeok, T. A., eds., *Aboriginal Sign Languages of the Americas and Australia*, 2 vols., pp. xiii–xxxii. New York: Plenum.

Umiker-Sebeok, Jean, ed. 1987. *Marketing and Semiotics: New Directions in The Study of Signs for Sale*. Berlin: Mouton de Gruyter.

Umiker-Sebeok, Jean, and Sebeok, Thomas A., eds. 1978. *Aboriginal Sign Languages of the Americas and Australia*. 2 vols. New York: Plenum.

———. 1987. *Monastic Sign Languages*. Berlin: Mouton de Gruyter.

Ungeheuer, Gerold. 1981. De Wolfii Significatu Hieroglyphico. In Geckeler, Horst, et al., eds., *Logos Semanticos*, vol. 1, pp. 57–67. Berlin: de Gruyter.

Urquhart, Sir Thomas. (1652) 1971. Εκσκυβαλαυρον. In Urquhart, Sir T., *The Works*, pp. 177–294. New York: Johnson Reprint (1834).

———. (1653) 1970. *Logopandecteision, or An Introduction to the Universal Language*. Menston: Scolar Reprint.

Uspenskij, Boris A. 1971a. Les problèmes sémiotiques du style à la lumière de la linguistique. In Kristeva, Julia, et al., eds., *Essays in Semiotics*, pp. 447–66. The Hague: Mouton.

———. (1971b) 1976. *The Semiotics of the Russian Icon*. Lisse: de Ridder.

———. 1972. Structural isomorphism of verbal and visual art. *Poetics* 5: 5–39.

———. 1977a. Historia sub specie semioticae. In Lucid, Daniel P., ed., *Soviet Semiotics*, pp. 107–15. Baltimore: Johns Hopkins Univ. Press.

———. 1977b. Semiotics of art. In Lucid, Daniel P., ed., *Soviet Semiotics*, pp. 171–73. Baltimore: Johns Hopkins Univ. Press.

Uspenskij, Boris A., et al. 1973. Theses on the semiotic study of cultures. In Eng, Jan van der, and Grygar, Mojmír, eds., *Structure of Texts and Semiotics of Culture*, pp. 1–28. The Hague: Mouton.

Uspensky. See Uspenskij.

Vachek, Josef. (1939) 1976. Zum Problem der geschriebenen Sprache. In Vachek, J., *Selected Writings in English and General Linguistics*, pp. 112–20. The Hague: Mouton.

Vachek, Josef, ed. 1964. *A Prague School Reader in Linguistics*. Bloomington: Indiana Univ. Press.

Valdman, Albert, ed. 1977. *Pidgin and Creole Linguistics*. Bloomington: Indiana Univ. Press.

Valen, Leigh van. 1955 (1976). Talking drums and similar African tonal communication. In Sebeok, Thomas A., and Umiker-Sebeok, Donna Jean, eds., *Speech-Surrogates: Drum and Whistle Systems*, pp. 746–56. The Hague: Mouton.

Valesio, Paolo. 1980. *Novantiqua: Rhetorics as a Contemporary Theory*. Bloomington: Indiana Univ. Press.

Vallier, Dora. 1981. Minimal units in architecture. In Steiner, Wendy, ed., *Image and Code*, pp. 139–46. Ann Arbor: Univ. of Michigan.

Valsiner, Jaan, and Allik, Jüri. 1982. General semiotic capabilities of the higher primates. In Key, Mary Ritchie, ed., *Nonverbal Communication Today*, pp. 245–57. Berlin: Mouton.

Varela, Francisco J. 1981. Autonomy and autopoiesis. In Roth, Gerhard, and Schwegel, Helmut, eds., *Self-Organizing Systems*, pp. 14–23. Frankfurt: Campus.

Veblen, Thorstein. (1899) 1934. *The Theory of the Leisure Class*. New York: Modern Library.

Veith, Werner H. 1973. Graphetik. In *Lexikon der germanistischen Linguistik*, pp. 105–18. Tübingen: Niemeyer.

Veltruský, Jiří. (1940) 1964. Man and object in the theater. In Garvin, Paul, ed., *A Prague School Reader on Esthetics, Literary Structure, and Style*, pp. 83–91. Washington, D.C.: Georgetown Univ. Press.

———. 1976. Some aspects of the pictorial sign. In Matejka, Ladislav, and Titunik, Irwin R., eds., *Semiotics of Art*, pp. 245–64. Cambridge, Mass.: MIT Press.

———. 1978. Contribution to the semiotics of acting. In Matejka, Ladislav, ed., *Sound, Sign, and Meaning*, pp. 533–606. Ann Arbor: Univ. of Michigan.

———. 1981. The Prague School theory of theater. *Poetics Today* 2.3: 225–35.

———. 1984a. Acting and behavior: A study in the *signans*. In Schmid, Herta, and Van Kesteren, A., eds., *Semiotics of Drama and Theatre*, pp. 393–441. Amsterdam: Benjamins.

———. 1984b. Bühlers Organon-Modell und die Semiotik der Kunst. In Eschbach, Achim, ed., *Bühler-Studien*, vol. 1, pp. 161–205. Frankfurt: Suhrkamp.

Vendryes, J. 1950. Langage oral et langage par gestes. *Journal de psychologie normale et pathologique* 44: 7–33.

Venezky, Richard L. 1970. *The Structure of English Orthography*. The Hague: Mouton.

Ventola, Eija. 1987. *The Structure of Social Interaction: A Systemic Approach to the Semiotics of Service Encounters*. London: Pinter.

Verburg, Pieter Adrianus. 1952. *Taal en functionaliteit*. Wageningen: Veenman & Zonen.

Verdiglione, Armando, ed. 1975. *Psychanalyse et sémiotique*. Paris: Union Générale.

Verón, Eliseo. 1970. L'analogique et le contigu (Note sur les codes non digitaux). *Communications* 15: 52–69.

———. 1971. Ideology and social sciences. *Semiotica* 3: 59–76.

———. 1973a. Pour une sémiologie des opérations translinguistiques. *Versus* 4: 81–100.

———. 1973b. Remarques sur l'idéologique comme production de sens. *Sociologie et sociétés* 5.2: 45–70.

———. 1978. Sémiosis de l'idéologique et du pouvoir. *Communications* 28: 7–20.

Vestergaard, Torben, and Schrøder, Kim. 1985. *The Language of Advertising*. Oxford: Blackwell.

Vico, Giambattista. (1725) 1984. *The New Science*, trans. of the 3rd ed. of 1744 by Bergin, T. G., and Fish, M. H. Ithaca: Cornell Univ. Press.

Victoroff, David. 1972. Nouvelle voie d'accès à l'étude de l'image publicitaire: l'analyse sémiologique. *Bulletin de psychologie* 25: 521–32.

Vigener, Gerhard. 1979. *Die zeichentheoretischen Entwürfe von F. de Saussure and Ch. S. Peirce als Grundlagen einer linguistischen Pragmatik*. Tübingen: Narr.

Vincent Ferrer. (ca. 1400) 1977. *Tractatus de suppositionibus*, ed. Trentman, J. A. Stuttgart: Frommann.

Vine, Jan. 1970. Communication by facial-visual signals. In Crook, J. H., ed., *Social Behavior in Birds and Mammals*, pp. 279–354. New York: Academic Press.

———. 1975. Territoriality and the spatial regulation of interaction. In Kendon, Adam, et al., eds., *Organization of Behavior in Face-to-Face Interaction*, pp. 357–87. The Hague: Mouton.

Voegelin, C. F. 1958. Sign language analysis, on one level or two? *International Journal of American Linguistics* 24: 71–76.

Voegelin, C. F., and Harris, Zellig S. 1945. Linguistics in ethnology. *Southwestern Journal of Anthropology* 1: 455–65.

Vogel, Harald. 1975. Comics im Deutschunterricht. *Der Deutschunterricht* 27: 6–33.

Voigt, Jürgen; Gericke, Fritz E.; and Genth, Diedrich. 1973. *Sprachen der Zeichen*. Köln: VGS.

Voigt, Vilmos. 1979. Semiotik in Osteuropa. *Zeitschrift für Semiotik* 1: 267–75, 401–16.

Volli, Ugo. 1972a. È possibile una semiotica dell'arte? In Volli, U., ed., *La scienza e l'arte*, pp. 87–112. Milano (= Antologie e saggi 4).

————. 1972b. Some possible developments of the concept of iconism. *Versus* 3: 14–30.

Vološinov, Valentin Nikolaevič (= Bakhtin, Mikhail). (1930) 1973. *Marxism and the Philosophy of Language*. New York: Seminar Press.

Volp, Rainer. 1982. Die Semiotik Friedrich Schleiermachers. In Volp, R., ed. *Zeichen*, pp. 114–45. München: Kaiser.

Vygotsky, Lev Semenovich. (1930) 1981. The instrumental method in psychology. In Wertsch, James V., ed., *The Concept of Activity in Soviet Psychology*, pp. 134–43. Armonk, N.Y.: Sharpe.

Waddington, Conrad H. 1957. *The Strategy of the Genes*. London: Allen & Unwin.

Wagner, Roy. 1986. *Symbols That Stand for Themselves*. Chicago: Univ. Press.

Wahl, François. 1968a. Introduction. In Ducrot, Oswald, et al., *Qu'est ce que le structuralisme?* pp. 7–12. Paris: Seuil.

————. 1968b. La philosophie entre l'avant et l'après du structuralisme. In Ducrot, Oswald, et al., *Qu'est-ce que le structuralisme?* pp. 299–442. Paris: Seuil.

Wald, Henri. 1969. Structure, structural, structuralisme. *Diogène* 66: 20–30.

Wallbott, Harald G. 1979. Gesichtsausdruck: Einführung. In Scherer, Klaus R., and Wallbott, Harald G., eds., *Nonverbale Kommunikation*. Weinheim: Beltz.

Wallis, Mieczysław. 1975. *Arts and Signs*. Bloomington: Indiana Univ.

Walther, Elisabeth. 1962. Textsemiotik. In Bense, Max, ed., *Theorie der Texte*, pp. 65–69. Köln: Kiepenheuer & Witsch.

————. 1965a. *Francis Ponge*. Köln: Kiepenheuer & Witsch.

————. 1965b. Semiotische Analyse. In Kreuzer, Helmut, and Gunzenhäuser, Rul, eds., *Mathematik und Dichtung*, pp. 143–57. München: Nymphenburger Verlag.

————. 1971. Interpretation—ein semiotisches Phänomen. In Martini, Fritz, ed., *Festschrift für Käte Hamburger*, pp. 422–29. Stuttgart: Klett.

————. 1974. *Allgemeine Zeichenlehre*. Stuttgart: dva.

————. 1984. Die Beziehung zwischen Semiotik und Linguistik. *Semiotica* 52: 111–17.

————. 1985. Semiotik der natürlichen Sprache. *Semiosis* 10.3–4: 46–61.

Walther, Fritz R. 1984. *Communication and Expression in Hooved Mammals*. Bloomington: Indiana Univ. Press.

Ward, Leo, and Raffler-Engel, Walburga. 1980. The impact of nonverbal behavior on foreign language teaching. In Raffler-Engel, Walburga von, ed., *Aspects of Non-Verbal Communication*, pp. 287–304. Lisse: Swets & Zeitlinger.

Warning, Rainer, ed. 1975. *Rezeptionsästhetik*. München: Fink.

Watson, O. Michael. 1970. *Proxemic Behavior*. The Hague: Mouton.

————. 1974. Proxemics. In Sebeok, Thomas A., ed., *Current Trends in Linguistics* 12: 311–44. The Hague: Mouton.

Watson, O. Michael, and Anderson, Myrdene. 1987. The quest for coordinates in space and time. *Reviews in Anthropology* 14.1: 78–89.

Watt, William C. 1975. What is the proper characterization of the alphabet? Part 1: Desiderata. *Visible Language* 9: 293–327.

————. 1980. What is the proper characterization of the alphabet? Part 2: Composition. *Ars Semeiotica* 3: 3–46.

————. 1981. What is the proper characterization of the alphabet? Part 3: Appearance. *Ars Semeiotica* 4: 269–313.

————. 1983. Grade der Systemhaftigkeit. Zur Homogenität der Alphabetschrift. *Zeitschrift für Semiotik* 5: 371–99.

————. 1984. As to psychosemiotics. In Fawcett, Robin P., et al., eds., *The Semiotics of Culture and Language*, vol. 2, pp. 3–28. London: Pinter.

————. 1988. What is the proper characterization of the alphabet? Part 4: Union. *Semiotica* 70: 199–241.

Watzlawick, Paul; Beavin, Janet H.; and Jackson, Don D. 1967. *Pragmatics of Human Communication*. New York: Norton.

Waugh, Linda R. 1976. *Roman Jakobson's Science of Language*. Lisse: de Ridder.

————. 1983. Possibilities and limitations of verbal communication: Language and reality. In Krampen, Martin, ed., *Visuelle Kommunikation*, pp. 178–98. Hildesheim: Olms.

————. 1984. Some remarks on the nature of the linguistic sign. In Pelc, Jerzy, et al., eds., *Sign, System, and Function*, pp. 389–438. Berlin: Mouton.

Wayne, Don E. 1984. *Penshurst: The Semiotics of Place and the Poetics of History*. Madison: Univ. of Wisconsin Press.

Weidemann, Hermann. 1982. Ansätze zu einer semantischen Theorie bei Aristoteles. *Zeitschrift für Semiotik* 4: 241–57.

Weinreich, Uriel. 1968. Semantics and semiotics. *International Encyclopedia of the Social Sciences* 14: 164–69. New York: Macmillan.

Weinrich, Harald. 1963. Semantik der kühnen Metapher. *Deutsche Vierteljahresschrift für Literaturwissenschaft und Geistesgeschichte* 37: 325–44.

Weiss, Paul, and Burks, Arthur. 1945. Peirce's sixty-six signs. *Journal of Philosophy* 42: 383–89.

Weitman, Sasha R. 1973. National flags: A sociological overview. *Semiotica* 8: 328–68.

Weitz, Shirley, ed. 1974. *Nonverbal Communication.* New York: Oxford Univ. Press.

Weizsäcker, Ernst von. 1984. Überraschung und Bestätigung gibt Information. In Schaefer, Gerhard, ed., *Information und Ordnung,* pp. 89–98. Köln: Aulis.

Welby, Victoria Lady. (1903) 1983. *What is Meaning?* ed. Eschbach, A. Amsterdam: Benjamins.

———. (1911) 1985. *Significs and Language,* ed. Schmitz, H. W. Amsterdam: Benjamins.

Wellbery, David E. 1984. *Lessing's Laokoon: Semiotics and Aesthetics in the Age of Reason.* Cambridge: Univ. Press.

Wellek, René. 1969. *The Literary Theory and Aesthetics of the Prague School.* Ann Arbor: Univ. of Michigan.

———. 1973. Symbol and symbolism in literature. In Wiener, Philip, ed., *Dictionary of the History of Ideas,* vol. 4, pp. 337–45. New York: Scribner's.

Wells, Rulon S. 1947. De Saussure's system of linguistics. *Word* 3: 1–31.

———. 1977. Criteria for semiosis. In Sebeok, Thomas A., ed., *A Perfusion of Signs,* pp. 1–21. Bloomington: Indiana Univ. Press.

Werlen, Iwar. 1984. *Ritual und Sprache.* Tübingen: Narr.

Wermke, Jutta. 1973. *Wozu Comics gut sind?* Kronberg: Scriptor.

Wernick, Andrew. 1983. Advertising and ideology. *Theory Culture and Society* 2.1: 16–33.

Wescott, Roger W. 1966. Introducing coenetics. *American Scholar* 35: 342–56.

———. 1967. The evolution of language. *Studies in Linguistics* 19: 67–81.

———. 1971. Linguistic iconism. *Language* 47: 416–28.

———. 1984. Semiogenesis and paleogenesis. *Semiotica* 48: 181–85.

Wescott, Roger W., ed. 1974. *Language Origins.* Mintwood, Md.: Linstock.

Wespi, Hans-Ulrich. 1949. *Die Geste als Ausdrucksform und ihre Beziehung zur Rede.* Zürich: Diss. Phil.

West, Frank. 1968. Semiology and the cinema. In Wollen, Peter, *Working Papers on the Cinema: Sociology and Semiology,* pp. 23–30. London: British Film Institute.

West, LaMont. 1960. *The Sign Language Analysis.* Bloomington: Indiana Univ. Diss. (Microfilm).

Wheelwright, Philip. 1974. Myth. In Preminger, Alex, ed., *Princeton Encyclopedia of Poetry and Poetics,* pp. 538–41. Princeton: Univ. Press.

Whitaker, Rod. 1970. *The Language of Film.* Englewood Cliffs, N.J.: Prentice Hall.

Whitehead, Alfred North. 1928. *Symbolism: Its Meaning and Effect.* Cambridge: Univ. Press.

Whiteside, Anna. 1988. Verbal icons and self-reference. *Semiotica* 69: 315–29.

Whitney, William Dwight. 1875 (1970). *The Life and Growth of Language.* Hildesheim: Olms.

Whitrow, Gerald J. (1961) 1980. *The Natural Philosophy of Time.* Oxford: Clarendon.

Wichelhaus, Barbara. 1979. *Zeichentheorie und Bildsprache mit Lehrplananalysen und Unterrichtsmodellen.* Königstein: Forum Academicum.

Wickler, Wolfgang. (1970) 1975. *Stammesgeschichte und Ritualisierung.* München: dtv.

———. 1971. *Mimikry.* München: Kindler.

———. 1972. *Verhalten und Umwelt.* Hamburg: Hoffmann & Campe.

Widmaier, Rita. 1986. Die Idee des Zeichens bei Locke und Leibniz. In Dutz, K. D., and Schmitter, P., eds., *Geschichte und Geschichtsschreibung der Semiotik,* pp. 133–49. Münster: MAkS.

Wiegand, Herbert Ernst. 1970. Synchronische Onomasiologie und Semasiologie. *Germanistische Linguistik* 3/70: 243–384.

Wiemann, John M., and Harrison, Randall P., eds. 1983. *Nonverbal Interaction.* Beverly Hills: Sage.

Wiener, Linda. 1986. Song learning in birds. *Word* 37: 159–75.

Wiener, Morton, et al. 1972. Nonverbal behavior and nonverbal communication. *Psychological Review* 79: 185–214.

Wiener, Norbert. (1948) 1961. *Cybernetics or Control and Communication in the Animal and the Machine.* Cambridge, Mass.: MIT Press.

Wienhöfer, Friederike. 1979. *Untersuchungen zur semiotischen Ästhetik des Comic Strip.* Dortmund: Diss. Phil.

Wienold, Götz. 1972. *Semiotik der Literatur.* Frankfurt: Athenäum.

Wilbur, Ronnie Bring. 1979. *American Sign Language and Sign Systems.* Baltimore: Univ. Park Press.

Wilden, Anthony. 1972. *System and Structure.* London: Tavistock.

Wildgen, Wolfgang. 1983. Dialogdynamik. *Papiere zur Linguistik* 29: 3–21.

Wilkins, John. (1641) 1984. *Mercury: or the Secret and Swift Messenger.* Amsterdam: Benjamins.

———. (1668) 1968. *An Essay towards a Real Character and a Philosophical Language.* Menston: Scolar (Reprint).

Williams, Brooke. 1985. What has history to do with semiotics? *Semiotica* 54: 267–333.

Williams, Raymond. 1977. *Marxism and Literature.* Oxford: Univ. Press.

Williamson, Judith. 1978. *Decoding Advertisements.* London: Boyars.

Wilson, Edward O. 1975. *Sociobiology.* Cambridge, Mass.: Belknap/Harvard Univ. Press.

Wilss, Wolfram, ed. 1980. *Semiotik und Übersetzen.* Tübingen: Narr.

Wimmer, Rainer. 1979. *Referenzsemantik*. Tübingen: Niemeyer.

Wimsatt, William K. Jr., and Brooks, Cleanth. (1957) 1970. *Literary Criticism*. London: Routledge.

Winner, Irene Portis, and Winner, Thomas G. 1976. The semiotics of cultural texts. *Semiotica* 18: 101–56.

Winner, Irene Portis, and Umiker-Sebeok, Jean, eds. 1979. *Semiotics of Culture*. The Hague: Mouton.

Winner, Thomas G. 1978. On the relation of verbal and nonverbal art in early Prague semiotics: Jan Mukařovský. In Bailey, R. W., et al., eds., *Semiotics around the World*, pp. 227–37. Ann Arbor: Univ. of Michigan.

———. 1979. Jan Mukařovský: The beginnings of structural and semiotic aesthetics. In Odmark, John, ed., *Language, Literature, and Meaning* I: *Problems of Literary Theory*, pp. 1–34. Amsterdam: Benjamins.

———. 1987. The aesthetic semiotics of Roman Jakobson. In Pomorska, Krystyna, ed., *Language, Poetry, and Poetics*, pp. 257–74. Berlin: Mouton de Gruyter.

Withalm, Gloria. 1988. Depictions—reflections—perspectives. *Semiotica* 69: 149–78.

Wittgenstein, Ludwig. (1922) 1971. *Tractatus Logico-Philosophicus*. London: Routledge & Kegan Paul.

———. 1953. *Philosophische Untersuchungen—Philosophical Investigations*. Oxford: Blackwell.

———. (1964) 1975. *Philosophical Remarks*. Chicago: Univ. Press.

Wittig, Susan. 1974. Toward a semiotic theory of the drama. *Educational Theatre Journal* 26: 441–54.

———. 1976. Semiology and literary theory. In Garvin, Harry R., ed., *Phenomenology, Structuralism, Semiology*, pp. 140–50 (= *Bucknell Review*, April 1976). Lewisburg: Bucknell Univ. Press.

———. 1979. Architecture about architecture: Self-reference as a type of architectural signification. In Chatman, Seymour, et al., eds., *A Semiotic Landscape*, pp. 970–78. The Hague: Mouton.

Wolff, Charlotte. (1945) 1972. *A Psychology of Gesture*. New York: Arno.

Wolff, Christian. (1720) 1983. *Vernünfftige Gedancken von Gott, der Welt und der Seele des Menschen, auch allen Dingen überhaupt* (= *Gesammelte Werke* I. 2). Hildesheim: Olms.

———. (1730) 1962. *Philosophia prima sive ontologica*. Darmstadt: Wiss. Buchgesellschaft.

Wolfgang, Aaron, ed. 1984. *Nonverbal Behavior*. Lewiston: Hogrefe.

Wolke, Christian Heinrich. 1797. *Erklärung, wie die wechselseitige Gedanken-Mitteilung oder die Pasiphrasie möglich ist*. Dessau & Leipzig: S. L. Crusius.

Wollen, Peter. (1969) 1972. *Signs and Meaning in the Cinema*. Bloomington: Indiana Univ. Press.

———. 1982. *Readings and Writings*. London: Verso.

Woodward, James. 1978. Historical bases of American Sign Language. In Siple, Patricia, ed., *Understanding Language through Sign Language Research*, pp. 333–48. New York: Academic Press.

Woolley, Dale E. 1977. Iconic aspects of language. In Beansitt, E. L., and di Rheto, G., eds., *The 3rd Lacus Forum*, pp. 287–94. New York: Columbia Univ. Press.

Woozley, A. D. 1967. Universals. In Edwards, Paul, ed., *Encyclopedia of Philosophy*, vol. 8., pp. 194–206. New York: Macmillan.

Worth, Sol. 1969. The development of a semiotic of film. *Semiotica* 1: 282–321.

Worth, Sol, and Adair, John. (1972) 1974. *Through Navajo Eyes*. Bloomington: Indiana Univ. Press.

Wright, Edmond L. 1976. Arbitrariness and motivation: A new theory. *Foundations of Language* 14: 505–523.

Wright, Lawrence. 1968. *Clockwork Man*. London: Elek.

Wulff, Hans J. 1979. Medium und Kanal. *Papiere des Münsteraner Arbeitskreises für Semiotik* 10: 38–67.

———. 1988. Neue enzyklopädische und bibliographische Hilfsmittel der Semiotik. *Zeitschrift für Semiotik* 10: 113–32.

Wunderli, Peter. 1981a. *Saussure-Studien*. Tübingen: Narr.

———. 1981b. Saussure und die "signification." In Geckeler, Horst, et al., eds., *Logos Semantikos*, pp. 267–84. Berlin: de Gruyter.

Wunderlich, Dieter. 1969a. Karl Bühlers Grundprinzipien der Sprachtheorie. *Muttersprache* 79: 52–62.

———. 1969b. Unterrichten als Dialog. *Sprache im technischen Zeitalter* 32: 263–86.

———. 1971. Terminologie des Strukturbegriffs. In Ihwe, Jens, ed., *Literaturwissenschaft und Linguistik*, pp. 91–140. Frankfurt: Athenäum.

———. 1972. Zur Konventionalität von Sprechhandlungen. In Wunderlich, Dieter, ed., *Linguistische Pragmatik*, pp. 11–58. Frankfurt: Athenäum.

———. 1982. Sprache und Raum. *Studium Linguistik* 12: 1–19; 13: 37–59.

Wundt, Wilhelm. (1900) 1973. *The Language of Gestures*. The Hague: Mouton.

Wuss, Peter. 1986. *Die Tiefenstruktur des Filmkunstwerks*. Berlin: Henschelverlag.

Wylie, Laurence W. 1977. *Beaux Gestes: A Guide to French Body Talk*. Cambridge, Mass.: Undergraduate Press.

Yaker, Henri; Osmond, Humphry; and Cheek, Frances, eds. 1972. *The Future of Time*. London: Hogarth.

Yamada-Bochynek, Yoriko. 1985. *Haiku East and West: A Semiogenetic Approach*. Bochum: Brockmeyer.

Yates, Frances A. 1954. The art of Ramon Lull. *Journal of the Warburg and Courtauld Institutes* 17: 115–67.

———. 1966. *The Art of Memory*. Chicago: Univ. Press.

Young, Robert, ed. 1981. *Untying the Text: A Post-Structuralist Reader*. Boston: Routledge & Kegan Paul.

Zarcadoolas, Christina. 1984. *How to Do Things with Linguistics: Semiotics, Speech Acts, and Phenomenology*. Ann Arbor: Univ. Microfilms Int.

Zellmer, Siegfried. 1979. *Pädagogische Semiotik in der Mathematik-Didaktik*. Baden-Baden: Agis.

Zeman, J. Jay. 1977. Peirce's theory of signs. In Sebeok, Thomas A., ed., *A Perfusion of Signs*, pp. 22–39. Bloomington: Indiana Univ. Press.

Zemsz, Abraham. 1967. Les optiques cohérentes (La peinture est-elle langage?). *Revue d'Esthétique* 20: 40–73.

Zerubavel, Eviatar. 1981. *Hidden Rhythms*. Chicago: Univ. Press.

Zholkovsky, A. 1981. Generative poetics in the writings of Eisenstein. In O'Toole, L. M., and Shukman, Ann, eds., *Film Theory and General Semiotics*, pp. 40–61. Oxford: Holdan.

Zich, Otakar. 1931. *Estetika dramatického umění* [The Aesthetics of Dramatic Art]. Praha: Melantrich.

Zima, Peter V. 1981. Semiotics, dialectics, and critical theory. In Zima, Peter V., ed., *Semiotics and Dialectics*, pp. 3–36. Amsterdam: Benjamins.

Zimmermann, Albert, ed. 1971. *Der Begriff der Repraesentatio im Mittelalter*. Berlin: de Gruyter.

Zimmermann, Hans Dieter, ed. 1973. *Vom Geist der Superhelden: Comic Strips*. München: dtv.

Zipf, George K. (1935) 1968. *The Psycho-Biology of Language*. Cambridge, Mass.: MIT Press.

Zisterer, Sylvia. 1975. Probleme der phylogenetischen Sprachentstehung. In Leist, Anton, ed., *Ansätze zur materialistischen Sprachtheorie*, pp. 156–205. Kronberg: Scriptor.

Zito, George V. 1984. *Systems of Discourse: Structures and Semiotics in the Social Sciences*. London: Greenwood.

Zobel, Arthur. 1928. Darstellung und kritische Würdigung der Sprachphilosophie John Lockes. *Anglia* 52: 289–324.

Zoest, Aart J. A. van. 1974. Eine semiotische Analyse von Morgensterns Gedicht "Fischers Nachtgesang." *Zeitschrift für Literaturwissenschaft und Linguistik* 16: 49–67.

———. 1978. *Semiotiek*. Baarn: Ambo.

Zurlo, Georg. 1976. Strukturelle Untersuchungen zu Western-Texten. In Koch, Walter A., ed., *Textsemiotik und strukturelle Rezeptionstheorie*, pp. 407–565. Hildesheim: Olms.

Żygulski, Kazimierz. 1973. Le problème de la genèse des signes dans la civilisation technique—L'auto comme signe. In Rey-Debove, Josette, ed., *Recherches sur les systèmes signifiants*, pp. 605–23. The Hague: Mouton.

INDEX OF SUBJECTS AND TERMS

asymmetry, 360
asyndeton, 341
attention, 26–27
attribute, 115
attribution (semantic), 455
audiolingual, 223
audiovisual, 223, 453
audition, 177
auspices, 189
author, 337
auto-communication, 159, 394
autocriticism, 380
automatization (vs. foregrounding), 307–8, 344, 356
automobile, language of the, 441
autonomy, aesthetic, 35, 307, 349, 355, 425–26, 430; musical, 432; poetic, 349, 355–56; semantic, 350; semiotic, 178–80, 187, 204, 208, 239, 261, 269, 280–82, 287, 290–91, 303, 313, 390, 394–95, 449–50, 462; (structural), 196; systemic, 200, 202; textual, 332
autonymy, 349
autopoiesis, 178–80, 200, 203–4, 303
auto-reflexivity, 349, 358, 430
autotelic (sign), 30, 355–56, 436
auxiliary speech, 289
awareness, 35, 391
axiological, 102

back-slang, 289, 398
ballet, 430
Basic English, 276–77
baton, 397
beauty, 421–23, 426
bees, "language" of, 150–55, 159, 163
behavior, 82, 157, 364, 390, 394; animal, 149; bodily, 394–95; and communication, 157, 171; ethology of, 165; -family, 53; vs. nonbehavior, 173; nonverbal, 390, 394 (see also nonverbal communication); verbal, 388
behavioreme, 388
behaviorism, 48–55, 88, 99–100, 157, 301; social, 48
belief, 141
Benedictine sign language, 286
bestiary, 382
bidirectionality (in communication), 362
bi-isotopy, 319
bilateral interaction, 171–72
binary (structure), 135, 300, 302; binarism, 76, 300; binarization, 138; code, 138–39; opposition, 217
bioacoustics, 161
biochemistry, 161
biocommunication, 148, 167–68
biogenesis, 164
biography, 337
biology, 49, 81, 147–50, 170, 180, 306; molecular, 148, 171
bioluminescence, 162
biophonetics, 161
biopoetic, 357
biorhythm, 417, 433
biosemiotics, 36–37, 148, 417

biosocial, 159
biplanar (semiotics), 71, 110
bird(s): calls, 151, 154–55; "language" of, 151, 154–55, 161; songs, 148, 151
bit, 137–38, 142
Blissymbolics, 277
bodily communication, 392–401; bodily movement, 392, 394–95, 400; body contact, 161, 407; **body language**, 388, **392–401**; body manipulator, 394; body motion, 393, 400
boustrophedon, 260
brachigraphy, 271
braille (alphabet), 57, 219, 290, 409
brand, 115, 219
brand image, 443
broadcast transmission, 154, 156, 161, 235, 260

calculus, rational, 22, 274
camouflage, 163
car system, 204. *See also* automobile
cartography, 220, 447; cognitive, 414
cartomancy, 189
catalyzer, 371
catastrophe theory, 203–4
category, conceptual, 29; universal (*see* universal c.)
causality, 25, 86, 113, 370, 373; and semiosis, 176
cell (architectural), 439
cells, interaction of, 170
ceneme, 71; cenematics, 238; cenemic, 71, 252
censure, 323
ceremony, 398
channel, 109–10, 137, 160–62, 174–77, 185–87, 214, 235–37, 259; acoustic 175 (*see also* acoustic semiosis); auditory, 157, 407; chemical, 161–62, 175; electric, 161, 175, 409; energetic, 175; gustatory, 161, 175, 389; material, 175; olfactory (*see* olfactory s.); optical, 162, 175; physical, 175; tactile (*see* tactile c.); thermal, 161, 175, 412; visual, 154, 175, 260, 407 (*see also* visual s.); vocal-auditory, 154–57, 161, 235–60
chaos, 192, 194, 200, 203
character (sign), 91
character (theatrical), 366
characteristica universalis. See universal character
charm, 188–89
chemical semiosis, 161–62
chemoreceptor, 161
chereme, 184, 284, 286
Cherokee writing, 256
cherology, 284
chimpanzees. *See* apes
Chinese writing, 254, 268, 271–72
chirogram, 283
chirology, 397
chiromancy, 189
chironomy, 397
choice, 201, 343–44
choreme, 184, 438
chromeme, 452, 474

chromosome, 217
chroneme, 417
chronemics, 388, **415–18**
Church Fathers, 381
cinema, 463, 468; vs. film, 468 (*see also* film)
cineme, 470
cinemorph, 470
cipher, 29, 137–38, 289–90; alphabet, 207; code, 57; ciphertext, 290
circus, 362
Cistercian sign language, 286
city, 439
civilization, 31
clarity, 28
classeme, 318
classification, 301
clay token, 252
Clever Hans phenomenon, 153–54
cloak, 207
closure: semiotic, 179–80; textual, 322, 332, 352, 479
clothing, 389, 441
Cluniac sign language, 286
coats of arms, 31, 115, 220
code, 63, 76, 135–42, 172, 175–80, 184–86, **205–20**, 238, 306, 331, 343–44, 362, 391, 478; in advertising, 478; aesthetic, 213, 427–28; alphabetical, 138–39, 218, 287, 290; analogic, 208; *a posteriori*, 344; *a priori*, 344; architectural, 437–39; articulation, 215–20; asystematic, 214; binary, 23, 208, 219, 290; book, 269, 290; cinematographic, 468; cipher, 57; commercial, 290; complementary, 292; as correlational device, 210; cryptographic (*see* cryptography); cultural, 97, 133, 211, 394; definition of, 211; difference(s), 239, 428; digital, 208; direct, 219; epistemological, 213; exegetic, 382; extrinsic, 214; filmic, 465, 468–69; flag (*see* flags); genetic, 37, 81, 171, 213, 217; graphic, 220; iconic, 451, 472; ideological, 378; incomplete, 211; institutional, 206; intrinsic, 214; kinesic, 401; kinesthetic, 412; language and (/as) c., 209–11, 236–39; language-based, 287; vs. language, 210; legal, 206, 213; literary, 427; logical, 212; mantic, 213; metabolic, 217; mythic, 214; nonlinguistic, 37, 210, 401; nonsignificant, 209, 218; number, 207; numerical, 217–18; parallel, 262; phonological, 212; photographic, 462; perceptual, 457; pictorial, 451–52, 457–59; practical, 213, 217; preliminary, 211; primary, 210, 218, 287, 291; proper, 212; proxemic, 412; rhetorical, 312; scientific, 213–14; secondary, 210–11, 287, 290, 341, 350; selective, 209; semiotic, 210; significant, 209, 218; and (sign) system, 205, 209–12, 238; social, 210, 213; structure, 214,

93–96, 101–2, 118, 311–12, 376,
378, 425, 442, 453; architectural,
436–37; deconstruction of, 102;
vs. connotation, 351; denotative
fallacy, 72, 191 denotatum, 53–54,
60, 88–94, 108–9, 117, 123–24,
437
density (,aesthetic), 425
deontic, 206
dependence, dependency, 182, 196
dependency grammar, 372
depiction, 453
description, descriptive, 47, 95, 369,
453
descriptivism, 300–1
descriptor, 109, 114
design, 447
designation, 19, 86, 93–94;
designative, 55; designator, 108–9,
162, 284; designatum, 50, 52–53,
104, 108, 424
design features of language, 59, 154–
56, 159, 161, 170, 235–36, 259,
286, 412, 441
destination, 174–77, 179
detractio, 341
deviation (poetic, stylistic), 341–44,
356–58, 427
device, 307
diachronic, diachrony, 62–63, 147–
48, 183, 295–96, 299, 301
diagnosis, 159, 170–72, 390–91
diagnostics, 13, 114
diagram (graphic), 220
diagram (iconic), 22, 47, 73, 122–
26, 133, 151, 163, 258, 468
dialectic(s), 323, 339
dialects of animals, 151, 154–55, 163
dialogue, 43, 176, 178–80, 323
dianoiology, 28
diaphory, 360
dicent, 45, 47, 438, 461; indexical
legisign, 45; (indexical) sinsign,
45, 438; symbol, 45
dicisign, 45, 461
dictio, 19
didactic(s), 222–23, 340
diegesis, 368
difference, 23, 61, 193–95, 201,
266, 324; *différance,* 266, 306;
différence, 266, 306; difference,
stylistic, 343–45, 358;
differentiation, 324
directional reception, 161, 235, 260
disambiguation, 319
discourse, 33, 169, 305–6, 315–16,
319, 322, 451; analysis, 330, 368;
analysis, generative, 315;
deliberative, 340; forensic (or
judiciary), 340; function, 340;
pictorial, 458; religious, 381–83;
and (vs.) story, 352, 369; and text,
332; theory of, 330; typology, 54–
55, 340; universe of, 210;
discursive structure, 315–16
discreteness, 154, 156, 161, 236–37
disequilibrium, 204
disjointness, 453
disjunction, 317; narrative, 372
disorder, 138, 200
displacement [design feature of
language], 155–56, 163, 236, 412

displacement (psychoanalytic), 323
displacement activity (,zoosemiotic),
165
display behavior, 165
display rules, 404
display signal, 399
dispositio, 340, 342
dissipative structure, 200, 203
distance, 411
distinctive feature (analysis), 35, 76,
106, 183, 217, 219, 284, 299–
300, 312, 400, 439
distinctiveness, 183
distinguisher, 318
distributional analysis, 301, 312
distributionalism, 300–1, 430
disturbance (,informational), 140
divination, 104, 334
divine. *See also* theology; age, 31;
meanings, 116
divisio, 340
doctrine of signs, 24, 33. *See also*
semiotics, d. of documentation, 314
dogs, "language" of, 150
dolphins, "language" of, 150
dominance, 185–86
double articulation, 65, 80, 110,
117, 139–40, 151, 153–55, 184,
209, 215–20, 236–38, 258, 273,
284, 286, 289, 298, 412, 434,
438–39, 451–52, 458, 462, 469–
70. *See also* articulation, duality of
patterning; of writing, 264
doxa, 376
drama, 315, 349, **361–66**
dramatic constellations, 372
dream, dream symbol, 120, 122, 303
drum languages, 75, 287–89, 291
duality of patterning, 156, 217, 236–
38, 412, 441. *See also* double
articulation
dyad, semiotic. *See* sign, dyadic
model of
dynamics, 192–93, 204, 239, 299
dynamism, communicative, 363

echolocation, 159
ecology, behavioral, 149, 164
economics 6, 76, 223, 305, 442,
476–77
economy (of coding), 137–38, 140,
208, 215, 219; linguistic, 141
economy, political, 306
education. *See* teaching
effector (organ), 158, 208
efficiency, 178
effort (communicative), 138, 140;
least, 237
eiconics, 447
eidos, 35, 67
electrical semiosis. *See* channel, e.
element, 194, 196, 198–99
elocutio, 339–40, 344
eloquence, 338
emblem, 31, 115, 396; emblem
(gestural), 394, 396, 400
emic, 183–84, 244, 284, 300, 371,
388, 394, 409, 412, 415–16, 418,
451
emitter, 176
emotion(s), 394, 403–4, 433
empathy, 466

empiricism, 20, 23, 25, 48, 76, 84,
306
empirism, 35
empty form, 427
encoding, 206–7, 238–39, 243;
encoder, 176, 391; stylistic, 344;
symbolic, 288
encyclopedians, 25–26
endosemantic, 431, 433
endosemiotics, 37, 81, 148, 159,
171, 217
energeia, 33
Enlightenment, 20, 25, 27, 305
enphrasing, 288
ensign, 31
enthymeme, 339
entropy, 138, 194, 199–200, 203,
423; negative, 199
entymematic, 478
enunciation, 332, 395
environment, 36–37, 54, 149, 151,
155–58, 162, 165, 172, 179, 199–
200, 436; environmental
psychology, 410
epic, 368
Epicureans, 16–17, 85, 87, 447
epideictic, 340
episteme, 305, 379
epistemology, 16, 34–35, 81, 447;
genetic, 112, 448
equilibrium, 141, 199–200, 203,
308; dynamic, 299
equivalence, 195; cognitive, 100;
poetic, 357, 359, 430;
substitutional, 100
ergon, 33
Eskimo, 314
Esperanto, 269, 276–77
esse est percipi, 25
estrangement, 307–8, 356, 426
ethnography, 119
ethnomethodology, 368
ethnosemiotics, 5, 34
ethogram, 164
ethology, 147–50, 164–65, 388,
394, 398, 403, 413; cultural, 399,
405; human, 399
etic, 183, 284, 300, 371, 388, 394,
412, 415–16
etiquette, 211, 213, 241
etymology, 241, 245
Eucharist, 384
euphemism, 189
event, 370
event [art performance], 356
evidence, 87
evolution, 148; cultural, 166–67;
genetic, 166–67; linguistic (*see*
language, evol.); literary, 204, 307,
353; of semiosis, 147; systemic,
200; theory of, 203; evolutionary
semiotics, 83
example, 29
exchange, social, 323
exchange-value, 444
exegesis (scriptural), 17, **334–37,**
346, 381–82
exemplification, 95, 425, 441–42,
454
existentialism, 298
exordium, 340
exosemantic, 431–32

happening [art form], 363
haptics, 409
harmony, 423, 432; prestabilized, 22
helper vs. opponent, 372
heraldic sign, 28; heraldry, 220
hermeneutic(s), 11, 27, 30–31,
192, 211, 304, 330, **334–37**, 340;
circle, 194, 336; theological, 383
Hermes, 334
heroic age, 31
heterogeneity, 202
heteronomy: aesthetic, 430; of codes,
291; musical, 432; semiotic, 287
hierarchy, 202
hieroglyphics, 23, 28, 31, 253–54,
260, 268, 272; filmic, 464
hiranaga, 256
historicism, 301, 306
history, 6, 31, 36, 66, 304–5, 368; of
ideas, 304; natural, 305; semiotics
of, 329–30; **history of semiotics**,
11–38, 48, 62–65, 83–87, 381,
421, 447
holism, 82–83, 194, 199
homeorhesis, 200
homeostasis, 178, 200, 203–4
homo: faber, 150, 399; *habilis,* 150;
loquens, 150; *ludens,* 150; *politicus,*
150; *prometheus,* 150; *ridens,* 150;
sapiens, 150
homogeneity, 202
homologation (discursive), 359
homology, 231, 296
homomorphy, 448
horses, "language" of, 150
human age, 31
humanism, 20, 305
hydromancy, 189
hyle, 67
hyperbole, 128, 474
hyperonomy, 102
hypoicon, 122–23
hyponomy, 102

icon(ic), 23, 27, 29, 32, 44–46, 54,
106–10, **121–27**, 133, 153, 189,
246, 382, 384, 422, 424, 432–33,
446, 480; natural, 21; pure, 121–
22; Russian, 457; theatrical, 364–
65; legisign, 45, 122; qualisign,
122; sinsign, 45, 122; iconeme,
462, 470, 474
iconicity, 19, 30, 118, **121–127**,
151, 163–64, 223, 382, 424–25,
449, 457; acoustic, 124; of art, 30;
of content, 349; degrees of, 123–
24, 132, 349; diagrammatic *(see
diagram, i.)*; of expression, 349; in
language, 20, 33, 124–25; literary,
348–49; metaphorical, 133;
nonverbal, 124–25; in
photography, 460–61; primary,
125; quantitative, 126–27;
secondary, 125–26; in scientific
signs, 28; of sign languages, 283;
textual, 47, 126; visual, 124
iconics, 446
iconism, critique of, 127
iconization, 125
iconographic, 478; iconography, 397,
456–57
iconology, 212, 437, 446, 456–57

idea, 21–27, 33–34, 61, 67, 87–90,
98, 111, 122, 305, 447–48, 471
idealism, 25, 32, 43
identificative, 55
identifior, 54, 114, 162–63
identity, 162; aesthetics of, 428
ideogram, 254, 277; filmic, 464
ideograph(y), ideographic, 122, 252–
55, 257, 475; gestural, 397
ideologeme, 379
idéologues, 25, 27, 34, 275, 377
ideology, 47, 102, 212, 304, 311–
12, 322, 342, 372, **377–80**, 437,
477–78; and science, 379
idiom, 120, 126
idiomorphic systems, 75
Ido, 276
idol, 23
illocutionary act, 241
illusion, 466
illustration, 454
illustrator (gestural), 394, 397
image, 47, 73, 95, 122–27, 133,
188, 303, 446–56, 460. *See also*
picture; [eidolon]; 16; filmic, 467;
inner, 448; mental, 447–48; in
Romanticism, 32; vs. schema, 29;
verbal, 447; visual, 447, 452;
language of, 446; typology of, 446
imaginary, the, 116; filmic, 466
imagination, 26, 31, 47
imitation, 30, 163, 166, 296, 338,
428, 448
immanence, 295–96, 317–18, 396
immediacy (vs. mediation), 190–91
immunology, 37
immutability (of language), 59, 242–
43
immutatio, 341
implication, 318, 455
imposition, 19
impression, 82
imprint, 461
incitive, 55
index(icality), 21, 44–46, 54, 86,
106, 108–17, 123, 151, 153, 161–
64, 185–86, 223, 246, 344, 382,
384, 402, 416–17, 424, 432–33,
438, 443, 480; field, 36; filmic,
468; intentional, 111, 113;
narrative, 369, 371; natural, 111,
113; non-intentional, 111, 113;
photographic, 461; vs. sign, 111;
and signal, 112, 172; of sign
languages, 284; theatrical, 365
indication, 86, 108, 111
indicator, 109–14, 163
indicium, 114
induction, 23, 336, 339
inference, 86–87, 113
infinite regression, 306
informant (narrative), 371
information, 122, **134–43**, 172,
194, 199, 203, 207, 299, 423,
428; exchange of, 170–71; flow,
174, 178, 180; linguistic, 139;
logical theory of, 141; and
meaning, 135; pragmatic, 141;
processing, 141–42, 168, 170,
178; psychology, 141–42;
quantification of, 135; quantity,
140; selective, 142; semantic, 135,

141; signal, 135, 139; source, 142,
174; storage, 166, 260; syntactic,
135, 139; theory, 81, **134–43**,
168, 203, 210, 309, 344, 361,
423, 427, 450–51, 459, 465;
transfer, 139, 148, 166, 179;
value, 135–36, 140
informative, 55
informativity, 134, 141, 143, 184,
333
infracultural, 411
innate, 151, 164–65; ideas, 21, 26
innovation, 142, 204, 423, 427–28
inscription, 266
insignia, 213
instability, 200, 204
instinctive, 165
institution, social, 58–60
instruction, 179
instrumental, 82; instrumentality,
181
integration: poetic, 360; structural,
202, 295
intension, 16, 22, 53, 94, 102, 108
intention, 98–99, 107–9, 113, 172,
174, 336–37, 394; intentional
fallacy, 180; intentionality, 34,
100, 107, 109, 113, 157, 159,
164, 172–73, 210, 214, 332–33,
362, 391
interaction, 391; bilateral, 170;
communicative, 403; levels of,
170; mutual, 171; social, 161,
173; symbolic, 393; systemic, 170;
in zoosemiosis, 159
interchangeability, 154, 156, 159,
235, 237, 412
interdependence, 70
interest, 425
interjections and language origins, 31
Interlingua, 276
interlinguistics, 276
International Association for Semiotic
Studies (IASS), 7, 38
international auxiliary language,
267–69, 275–76
interoceptivity, 318
interpersonal relations, 395
interpretant, 41–47, 50, 53, 89–90,
94, 96, 121–22, 448; defined, 43;
dynamical, 44, 47; emotional, 44;
energetic, 44; final, 44; 47;
immediate, 43; logical, 44;
Morris's definition of, 53
interpretation, 30, 43–44, 47, 73,
87, 99, 119–20, 180, 211–12,
220, 306, 334–37, 346, 358, 390;
vs. decoding, 362
interpreter, 42–43, 47–53, 81–86,
90, 94, 101, 113, 336–37, 343;
autonomy of, 180
intersemiotic. *See* translation, i.;
transmutation, 230;
intersemioticity, 82, 98
intertextuality, 322–23, 333, 352,
379, 381
intonation, 248
intrafilmic, 468
intramusical, 433
intrasemiotic, 93, 431
intraspecific, 157, 165
intrinsic signal, 162

introjection, 350
intuition, 35
invariance, 195, 199, 451
invariant, 76, 183; perceptual, 451; pictorial, 451
invasion (,territorial), 414
inventio(n), 109, 127, 340
isolate (,proxemic), 412, 416
isomorphism, 126, 231
isomorphy, 449; poetic, 359
isotopy, 319–20, 333, 357
Isotype, 278
iterativity, 319

Jewish hermeneutics, 334
joke, 120
journalism, 169
juncture, 248
jurisprudence, 334

Kabbala, 261
kana, 256
kanji, 256
katakana, 256
key stimulus, 165
kine, 400
kinegraph, 400
kineme, 184, 286, 400–1
kinemics, 394, 399
kinemorph(eme), 401
kinesic(s), 211, 388, **392–401**; notation, 400; text, kinetext, 401
kinesiology, 394
kinetics, 394
kinetograph, 397
kinship (system), 76, 301–2, 433
knowledge, 305
Kuleshov effect, 454

labeling, 454
labonotation, 398
langage, 469
language, 57–59, 63–66, 112, 154, 173, 186, 193–96, 217, 227, **229–39**, 240, 291, 305–6, 313; acquisition, 236; "language" of animals, 147–50; and architecture, 435, 437–39; of art, 457; artificial 153, 269–70; arts, 338; "language" of bees. *See* bees; biological foundations of, 233; change, 141, 202–4; cinematographic, 468; and code (*see* code, l.); cosmic, 276; criterion of acoustic manifestation, 59; criticism, 23; and culture, 233; definitions of, 33, 65; design features of (*see* design f.); "language" of dolphins, 150; dynamics, 239, 299; evolution, 125, 155, 399, 204, 216, "language" of the face, 402; and (/of) film, 463–64, 469; "language" of flowers, 215; formal, 276; genesis of, 26; gestural, 279, 396 (*see also* gestures, language of; sign language); gestural origins of, 16, 156, 398–99; Herder on, 29; Hjelmslev's definition of, 65–66; "language" of horses, 150; human vs. animal, 150; iconicity (*see* iconicity in l.); "language" of

images, 446; and information, 136–37, 139, 141–42; as instrument, 185; and kinesics, 400; vs. *langage,* 469; vs. *langue* (see *langue*); linearity of, 26, 30; logical, 141; model of, 309; Modist view of, 20; Morris's definition of, 54; and (/of) music, 429, 432–34; natural, 271; nonlinguistic, 232; nonvocal, 233; norm, 202; of objects, 440–41; origins of, 26, 30, 156; *patron général* of semiotics, 58–59; philosophical, 29, 271–73; phylogeny, 155; and photography, 462; pictorial, 450–51, 453, 457–59; planned, 276; reform, 105; scientific, secret (*see* cryptography); and semiotics, 58, 75, 227, 229–39 (*see also* linguistics and semiotics); sign (*see* sign, linguistic); and space, 412; subcodes of, 239; **language substitutes,** 37, 75, 207, 212, 280–81, **287–92**, 389–90, 409; system, 61, 131, 201–3, 299; system of values, 61; taboo (*see* taboo); teaching; 222–23; and thought, 21; transforms, 75; universals (*see* universals, linguistic); use, 202, 449; visual, 452

langue, 62, 76, 131, 210, 238, 299, 303–4, 312, 316, 438, 469
lansign-system, 54
lapidary, 382
Latino sine flexione, 276
laughter, 156
law [legal semiotics], 6, 314, 329, 342
law [rule], 44–45, 206
learnability, 155–56, 236
learning, 166, 180, 221–22
legal semiotics. *See* law
legend, 120, 453
legisign, 44–46, 110, 114, 424, 461
lektón, 15–16, 85, 90–91
letter. *See* grapheme; information value of, 134, 138, 140
lexeme, 317–18
lexical field, 69
lexicography, 99
lexicology, 83, 106, 124, 315
lexicon, 318
lexigram, 154
life, 171
likeness, 119, 126, 128, 133, 446
Lincos, 276
linearity (of language), 236, 260
lingua franca, 285–86
linguistic relativity, 234, 414
linguistics, 34, 56, 58, 76, 330; distributional, 100; formalist, 182; functional, 140, 182; history of, 12; and literature, 374; and nonverbal behavior, 387–88; and paralinguistics, 248; and pragmatics, 232; semiotic, 231 35, 238; and semiotics, 75, 227, 229–31, 313, 330 (*see also* language and semiotics; semiotics and linguistics); structural(ist), 51, 64–65, 298; systemic, 68, 182, 201

literal. *See* meaning, l.; literariness, 307, 346, 348–49, 368
literary: communication, 204; criticism, 330, 346, 374; science, 346
literature, 38, 46–47, 58, 65–66, 73, 180, 306, 313, 343, **346–53**; evolution of, 204; and nonverbal behavior, 388; pragmatics of, 350; semantics of, 350; theory of, 346
littera, 335
liturgy, 384
living theater, 363
LoCoS, 277
logarithm, 136–37
logic, 11–12, 34, 50, 93, 338–39, 343; and semiotics, 5; symbolic, 274, 276; logistics, 66
logo, 115, 219
logocentrism, 313, 383, 450, 459
logogram, 254, 288
logograph(y), 252–54, 265
logos vs. *mythos,* 374
lottery, 136

machines and communication, 170, 172
macrospace, 411
macrostructure, narrative, 371, 373
magic, 83, **188–91**, 260, 398, 466; black, 189; contagious, 189; homeopathic, 189; of names, 189; verbal, 189; white, 189; and writing, 260–62
maieutic, 222
manifestation, 69, 318, 369
manipulation, 477
mantic(s), 189–90, 213, 334, 440
manual alphabet. *See* alphabet, m.
map, 220; cognitive, 414
mapping, 182, 331, 449
mark, 24–25, 28, 90, 115, 219, 259
markedness, 76, 237
marker, 318
marketing (research), 223, 443, 477
Markoff chain, 137
Marxism 52, 105, 304; Marxist semiotics, 38, 52, 96, 448–49, 459
mask, 402
masking, 404
mass communication, 211
mass media, 38, 175, 329–30, 342; semiotics of the, 5
materialism, dialectical, 321
mathematics, 6, 40, 66, 135–38, 142; semiotic, 217; and teaching, 223
matrix (architectural), 439
matter, 25, 32, 66–69
meaning, 21, 33–34, 36, 43–44, 50–53, 61–62, 68, 70, 73, 79, 90–91, **92–102**, 202, 302, 430–31. *See also* content; absolute, 101; acquisition of, 101; affective, 102; associative, 432; behaviorist account, 100; biological theory of, 158, 167; broad sense, 93; carrier of, 158; causal theory of, 100; collocative, 102; conceptual, 102; connotative (*see* connotation); contextual, 104; contextual theory

pleroma, 124
plot (vs. story), 308, 369
poetic, 30, 46, 162, 324. *See also*
function, p.; negativity, 324
poeticalness, 354–60, 480; filmic,
465, 471; metaphysical, 360;
stylistic, 360
poetics, 309, 337–38, 343, 346,
354; generative, 347; normative,
428; of writing, 260–61
poetogenesis, 360
poetry, 30–31, 37, 46–47, 55, 73,
338, **354–60**; and metalanguage,
355; potential, 360; and science,
356; visual, 47, 375
political economy, 433, 440, 443
polyfunctional(ity), 436; aesthetic,
425; literary, 350
polygraphia, 271
poly-isotopy, 320
polyphony (textual), 323, 337, 352,
361
polysemic, 34
polysemy, 131, 318–19, 364;
literary, 351–52; textual, 336–37
polyvalence, aesthetic, 425
popular culture, 5
portrait, 122–23
Port Royal, 21–22, 25, 62, 87, 305
positivism (,logical), 48, 96–97
possible worlds, 97, 350, 366
possibility, 45, 47
post-modernism, 427–28
post-structuralism, 58, 266, 296–98,
304, 321, 347, 459
posture(s), 392–94
potential(ity): (category of), 44;
(narrative), 372; sign, message (*see*
sign, p.)
practical. *See also* praxis; function (*see*
function, p.); gesture, 395; reason,
444
practice, signifying, 322, 379
pragma, 90
pragmatics, 33, 47, 50–51, 54, 65,
83, 86, 97, 100, 109, 114, 123,
127, 130, 148, 157, 168, 232,
235, 241; defined, 52
pragmatism, 41, 48
Prague School, 35, 64, 75, 181, 193,
299, **307–9**, 344, 363, 422, 430,
450, 459, 465
praxis, 343, 395, 433, 442. *See also*
practical; gestural, 395; religious,
383
precommunicative, 180
preconception, 336
precultural, 411
predicate, 97
predictability, 344
prekinesics, 400
prelinguistic, 26–27, 116, 250, 323
premise, 87
preparatory-stimulus, 53
prescriptive, 55
prescriptor, 109, 162
presemiotic, 61, 66, 82–83. *See also*
nonsemiotic
presentation, 179, 361
prevarication, 156, 236
primates (nonhuman), 153, 157, 406
primitive concept. *See* concept p.

primitives, semantic, 274
printing, 265
probability (of signals), 134–42
process, 46, 201, 332
productivity, 59, 155–56, 218, 236–
37, 286, 290, 322–23, 337
prognostics, 13
prolongation, 236
pronoun, pronominalization, 20,
333
pronuntiatio, 340, 397
propaganda, 55, 169
proper name, proper noun, 45, 376
proposition, 45, 87, 214
prosodic, prosody, 247–48
prosphory, 360
proto-language, 268, 272
proverb, 120
proxeme, 184, 412
proxemics, 148–49, 388, 394, 406–
7, **410–14**, 415, 435, 438, 474;
proxetics, 412–13
psychiatry, 6, 169, 250, 388
psychoanalysis, 6, 115, 119, 169,
302–3, 321, 323, 374, 383, 394,
465–66
psychobiology, 164
psychogenesis, 164
psychology, 169–70, 388; cognitive,
410, 447; social, 58, 60, 168, 388,
405, 407, 410
psychopathology, 169
psychophonetics, 245
psychosemantics, 103, 432
psychosemiology, 104, 437
psychosemiotics, 6, 26, 239, 417
psychosocial, 159
psychotherapy, 6, 169, 174, 191
public opinion research, 169
purport, 66–69, 71
purpose, purposiveness, 157, 181,
391

qualisign, 44–46, 110, 424
quality, 29, 102
quantity, 29
quipu, 252

rank, 140
rapid fading, 154, 156, 161, 235,
260, 441
ratio difficilis, 127
ratio facilis, 127
rationalism, 20–23, 27, 87
reader, 331; average, 344
reading, 260, 263; of poetry, 358
real, the, 116
real character, 271–73
realism, 17–18, 82–84, 87, 98, 196;
cinematographic, 468; in
literature, 47; ontological, 43, 96,
326; semantic, 84, 98
reality, 84, 196, 244, 461, 465–67
rearrangement, 341
reason, age of, 31
reason, pure, 29
rebus principle, 254
receiver, 138–41, 174–80, 186, 390.
See also recipient
reception, literary, 73
reception theory, 180, 347, 368, 373
receptor, 158, 176–77, 179, 208, 407

recipient, 176; commitment, 373
reciprocity, 159
recoding, 428
recognition, 109, 171
reconstruction, hermeneutic, 336–37
recurrence: poetic, 357, 430;
semantic, 333, 357; textual, 320
redundancy, 137–39, 141, 268, 407,
423
redundantia, 137
reference, 17, 21, 52–53, 59, 83–87,
89, 90, 92–94, 104–5, 155, 242–
44, 425–26, 430–31, 442. *See also*
object, referential; function,
referential; aesthetic, 425–26;
double, 129; dualist theory of, 96;
fictional, 349; filmic, 466;
imaginary, 350; inscrutability of,
95; literary, 350; multiple, 425;
musical, 431, 433; split, 358;
theatrical, 364
referent, 16, 19, 22, 42, 84–86, 89–
90, 94–96, 102, 109, 185–86,
441–42. *See also* object, referential;
as context, 97; deconstruction of,
97; elimination of, 97–98, 127;
ontology of, 96
referential, 162–63; fallacy, 96;
function (*see* function, r.); object
(*see* object, r.)
referral, 70, 85
referring, 94
reflection, 24, 26
reflexiveness, 155–56, 236
refutatio, 340
register, 478
regulator (gestural), 394, 397
relation, 29, 181, 193–96, 198–99,
201, 301–2; elementary, 317
relativism, 126
relativity: linguistic, 33, 70, 234,
414; semantic, 22
relatum, 196
relay, 453–54, 458
releaser, 165–66
releasing mechanism, 165
relevance, 183, 300; abstractive, 186
religion, 36, 211, 374, 381. *See also*
theology; and teaching, 223;
religious discourse, 383
remetaphorization, 131
reminiscence, 26
Renaissance, 305
repetition, 427
replacement, metaphorical, 128
repleteness (aesthetic), 425
replica, 44, 109, 461
replicability, 109–10
representamen, 42, 44, 46, 50, 80,
85, 89–90, 123, 424; vs. sign, 79
representation, 17, 21, 28, 32, 36,
43, 85, 87–88, 94–95, 108, 111–
12, 117, 122, 179, 185–86, 233,
305, 450, 453; conceptual, 120;
indirect, 118; partial, 119
representeme, 474
res, 82, 85, 88, 91
resemblance, 123, 305
response, 53, 82, 100, 112;
conditioned, 53; disposition to,
53, 55
revelation, 382

rhematic indexical legisign, 45
rhematic indexical sinsign, 45
rhematic symbol, 45
rheme, 45, 47, 424
rhetoric, 11, 34, 46, 126, 137, 143, 211–12, 282, 312, 330, **338–45**, 450, 478; filmic, 465, 471; gestural, 397; literary, 338; new, 340; and nonverbal communication, 388; pictorial, 459; and pragmatics, 339; pure, 50–51; religious, 383; speculative, 342
rhetorical figures. *See* figures, rh.
rhyme, 357, 359
rhythm, 248, 432
rhythmics (gestural), 397
rite, 57, 205
ritual, 31, 166, 213, 398
ritualization, 164–66, 399
romanticism, 32
round dance, 151
rule, 241; constitutive, 241; regulative, 241; system, 201
rune(s), 188, 256, 260
Russian Formalism, 75, **307–9**, 347–48, 423, 465

sacraments, 384
Safo, 277
Sanskrit hermeneutics, 334
schema, 29, 124, 457; vs. image, 29; vs. symbol, 29
scheme (rhetorical), 341
schizophrenia, 169, 173
scholastics, 17–20, 84–85, 87, 101
science, 36, 377; and ideology, 379; vs. magic, 188, 190; and myth, 374; and teaching, 223; sciences, classification of, 58, 63
s-code, 212
script, theatrical, 364
scripto-pictorial, 453
scriptures, 334–35
secondary (semiosis): coding, 350; modeling system, 309, 349; semiotic system, 259, 311–12, 376, 378
secondness, 41, 44, 121, 222, 343
secret language, 288–90. *See also* cryptography
segmental, 247
segmentation, 296, 301, 473. *See also* articulation, double articulation
selection, 142, 176, 195, 344–45; axis of, 357; natural, 166–67
self-adaptation, 178
self-correction, 178
self-generation, 180
self-maintenance, 199–200
self-organization, 200–1, 203
self-realization, 187
self-reference, self-referential(ity), 42, 200, 349, 364, 425–26, 436
self-reflexivity, 105
self-regulation, 193, 195
self replication, 166
self-stabilization, 200, 203–4
self-transformation, 180
sema, 452
sēmainómenon, 15, 62, 90
sēmáinon, 15, 62, 90

semanalysis, 321–24
semantic: axis, 103, 317–18; categories, 316; change, 125; components, 71, 106, 315, 317, 438; decomposition, 274; differential, 103, 437, 452, 472; fallacy, 189; feature (analysis), 19, 317, 342; field, 210, 439, 457; primitives (*see* primitives, s.); vs. semiological, 105, 318; space, 103; sphere, 130; tension, 129; universe, 317
semanticity, 156, 235
semantics, 11, 13, 22, 32, 34, 50–53, 57, 61–62, 93, 96, **103–6**, 130–31, 148, 301, 318, 431–32, 436; anthropological, 103; behaviorist, 101; cognitive, 99; definition of, 104; descriptive, 104; diachronic, 106; discourse, 103; general (*see* General Semantics); history of, 12, 14, 34, 104; linguistic, 104–6, 130; logical, 37, 53, 97, 104; philosophical, 98, 103, 105; psychological, 103; pure, 104; referential, 96–97; and semiotics, 103; vs. semiotics, 104, 431; structural, 61, 65, 71, 96–97, 106, 194, 196, 234, 267, 269, 314, 341–42, 439, 452, 460, 479–80; synchronic, 106; term of, 104; text, 106; truth conditional, 97
semantization, 309, 349, 439, 442
Semantography, 277
semasiographic, 253
semasiology, 13, 37, 94, 104, 106
sematology, 13, 34, 36–37, 104, 273
seme, 71, 84, 88, 214–20, 315, 317–19, 470
sémeiologie, 37
semeion, 90
semeiosis, 13, 42
semeiotic(s), 14
sememe, 83, 317–19, 438
sememographic, 252
semeotic, 14
semic: act, 88; analysis, 317; articulation, 317; category, 317; system, 317
sémie, 214–15
semiobiology, 148
semiochemicals, 161
semiochemistry, 161
semioclasm, semioclastry, 313, 376
semiogenesis, 26, 36, 38, 69, 112, 147, 154–57, 164, 233, 236, 398, 407. *See also* phylogeny
semiography, 430
semiolinguistics, 233
semiological vs. semantic, 105, 318. *See also* semiotics vs. semantics
semiology, 3, 5, 13, 56–66, 104, 220, 229–30, 244, 313; and linguistics, 58; definition of, 57; and semiotics, 14 (*see also* semiological vs. semantic), and sociology, 58
semio-narrative, 315
semiophysis, 313
semiosis, 16–17, 35, 42–43, 49–50, 52–53, 65, 69, 81–82, **168–80**,

388, 390–91, 433, 442; asymmetrical, 466; causal, 171; and cognition, 60; definition of, 50, 170, 343; dimensions of, 50; (in)direct, 23, 208, 218, 291; levels of, 26, 159; natural, 81, 86–87, 210, 213–14 (*see also* nature; sign, natural); and praxis (*see* praxis); unilateral, 141, 165, 170, 363, 390–91; unlimited, 43, 436
semiostyles, 343
semiotic. *See also* semiotics; vs. communicative, 171; denotative, 72; fallacy, 190; field, 4–5, 11, 38, 75, 87, 211–13; Hjelmslev's definition, 65; vs. nonsemiotic, 35. *See also* nonsemiotic; specificity, 109; square, 317–19; vs. symbolic, 116, 323; as a synonym of semiotics, 14; system, 210, 311–12, 315, 317, 323; system, secondary, 210; therapy (*see* therapy, s.); threshold, 82, 170, 213, 390, 433, 440, 442; transformation, 363, 398; triangle, 37, 86, 89–90
semiotica, 13
semioticity, 390, 395
semiotics, ix, 3, 49, 168; applied, 5, 34, 48, 65, 75, 222, 325; autocritical, 5, 321–22, 379; axiomatic, 38; behaviorist, 111–12 (*see also* behaviorism); bibliography of, 6; biological basis of, 53; Christian, 381; of communication (*see* communication, s. of); connotative, 71–72, 345, 364; and creativity, 313; crisis of, 4; cultural, 213; definitions of, 3, 49, 104, 315, 326; denotative, 72; descriptive, 5, 50; dimensions of, 49–51; a discipline, 4, 224; a doctrine, 4–5, 33, 42; empirical science, 53; encyclopedia of, xi; explicit, 3, 11–12; field of (*see* semiotic field); functional, 38, 181, 214, 231, 436; general, 5, 40; "geography" of, 38; glossaries of, xi; heuristics of, 63; history (*see* history of s.); historiography of, 11–12, 34, implicit, 4, 11–12; instrument of science, 49; an interdiscipline, 4, 7, 49, 224; introductions to, 6; journals of, 6–7; and language, 58, 75, 227, 229–39; and linguistics, 13–14, 39–40, 58, 63, 227, 229–30, 234, 313, 315; literary (*see* literature); logical, 232; Marxist (*see* Marxism, s.); medical (*see* medicine and s.); medieval, 17, 85, 107, 382; a metadiscipline, 4; a metalanguage, 5; a metatheory, 321; a method, 4; monistic approaches to, xi; a movement?, 4; natural, 98; an object language, 5; philosophical, 13, 39, pluralistic approaches to, x, xi, 3, 12; *a priori*, 29; a project, 4, 314; pure, 5, 50; revolution of, 4; in school, 222, 224; science of man, 49; science (of signs), 3–5, 17, 49, 57–58; science of the text,

322; scope of, 3, 49 (*see also* semiotic field); self-reflexivity of, 5; vs. semantics, 104, 431 (*see also* semiological vs. semantic); and semiology, 14; special, 5; structuralist, x, 40; systematics of, 63; teaching of, 221, 223; term of, 12; terminology of, xi, 40; theoretical, 5, 325; a theory of language, 232; a theory of signs, 4–5; as translinguistics, 331

sémiotique, 37

semiotization, 363, 442, 444

semiotropy, 313, 337

semology, 13

sender, 142, 175–77, 179, 186, 390–91; actantial, 372

sensation, 24–29, 88

sense, 21, 33, 52–53, 66, 83–86, 89–90, 92, 242–44, 266; datum, 82; figurative and literal (*see* meaning, f. *and* l.); original, 336

sensifics, 13

sensory-motor, 112

sensualist, 25

sensus, 335

sensus allegoricus, 335; *sensus anagogicus*, 335; *sensus historicus*, 335; *sensus litteralis*, 335; *sensus tropologicus*, 335

sententia, 335

set (proxemic), 412, 416

set theory, 193, 198

sham behavior, 163

shorthand. *See* stenography

showing, 425

sickle dance, 151

sigmatics, 52, 96

sign(s), 13, 24, 32, 41–45, 50, 53–54, 70–71, **79–91**, 94, 174, 186, 263, 304–5, 315, 390, 430, 451; abstract, 31; accidental, 26, 34; actual, 81; aesthetic, 30, 32, 73, 187, 421–26; ambiguous, 54, 109; analogue, 27; animal, 110; arbitrary, 21, 23, 26–28, 30–31, 34, 45, 110, 117–18, 348–49 (*see also* arbitrariness); architectural, 437; articulation, 100 (*see also* articulation); artificial, 28, 113, 364; auditory, 33; autological, 402; autonomous, 32, 426, 430; autotelic, 421, 425–26, 441; biblical, 381–82; bilateral, 67 (*see also* sign, dyadic model of); causal, 171; chemical, 28; chronemic, 417; classification of, 44–45 (*see also* typology of signs); as a class of index, 111; as a class of "signs," 110; as a class of symbols, 110; commemorative, 15; communicative, 171, 426; complex, 110; component, 70; compound, 110; connotative, 71–73 (*see also* connotation); context-bound, 111; context-free, 111; conventional, 17, 19, 21–22, 44–45, 81, 107–10, 112–13, 117, 394–95 (*see also* convention); correlates of, 44–46, 87; definitions of, 15, 21–22, 26–33, 36, 42, 49, 52–53, 70, 79–80,

84–85, 87, 104, 110, 310; degenerate, 122–23; demonstrative, 86; denotative, 71–73 (*see also* denotation); derivative, 110; derived, 28; dyadic model of, 16, 21, 23, 25, 36, 59–62, 66–67, 83–89, 96, 122, 243, 305, 437, 448, 467; element, 80, 208; evolution of, 26, 31 (*see also* semiogenesis); -family, 54; figurative, 27, 34, 128 (*see also* meaning figurative); filmic, 466–67, 469–70; function, 42, 70, 97, 182, 442, 444; general, 54, 109; genuine, 122; gestural, 33, 284, 395 (*see also* gesture); heterological, 402; Hjelmslev's definition, 66, 70–71; iconic (*see* icon); -image, 118; vs. index, 111; indicative, 15, 27 (*see also* index); by institution, 26; integral, 333; intentional, 107–9 (*see also* intention); interpersonal, 54, 109; **sign language**, 23, 34, 37, 57, 68, 150, 153–54, 157, 205, **279–86**, 287, 291, 389–90, 399; linguistic, 59, 130, 133, 186, 232, 239–44 (*see also* language); literal, 31; magic, 190; vs. mark (*see* mark); as a medical term, 114; mentalist concept of, 23, 60; models, 59, 62, 83, 86; monadic (monolateral) view of, 62, 83, 122; Morris's definition, 52; motivated (*see* motivation); musical, 430; natural, 17, 21–23, 26–28, 30–31, 34, 58, 86–88, 107–13, 116, 213, 232, 245–46, 348–49, 364, 382, 395 (*see also* nature; signs, natural); necessary, 28; nonlinguistic, 59, 63, 71, 215, 230; nonverbal (*see* nonverbal (communication)); and object, 191, 356; as an objective category (*Zeichen an sich*), 33; object, 441; ontology of, 17, 33, 80; ostensive, 430; pathic, 109; Peirce's definition of, 42; personal, 54, 109; photographic, 460–61; pictorial, 450, 452; plurisituational, 54, 109; polysemic, 34; potential, 81, 158, 390, 395; pragmatics of, 33; precise, 54, 109; primitive, 28, 110; process, 49–50; production, 109, 127; prognostic, 86; proper, 34; prophetic, 382; psychological entity, 59; psychology of the, 37; relation, 86; reliable, 54, 109; religious, 384; rememorative, 86; repertoire, 135, 138, 176–77, 207–9, 236, 239; asystematic, 205; systematic, 205; and representamen, 42, 60; and the sacred, 381; Saussure's definition, 60; scientific, 28; secondary, 208, 263; vs. seme, 215–17; vs. signal, 117, 174; vs. sign element, 80; vs. signified, 32; and signifier, 60; vs. sign vehicle, 79, 88; simple, 110; singular, 54, 109; social, 28; socio-cultural, 442; substitutive, 112, 117, 291; and symbol, 32, 54, 71,

110, 120; symbolic, 119, 187 (*see also* symbol); synonymous, 54; system, 57, 61, 63, 65, 70, 175, 201, 209–11, 310 (*see also* system; system, semiotic); system vs. code, 205; system, nonlinguistic, 229–30; tetradic model of, 83; theatrical, 363–64; theory of, 4–5, 17, 20, 22, 29, 33–37, 39–40, 48–49, 315; token, 108; trapezium model of, 83; triadic model of, 22, 41–42, 59–62, 83–90, 96, 122, 244, 305, 437–38, 448 (*see also* semiotic triangle); trichotomies of, 44–45; typology of (*see* typology of signs); unambiguous, 54, 109; unilateral model of, 62; unisemic, 34; unisituational, 54, 109; universal, 382; unreliable, 54, 109; use, 54–55; user, 100; vague, 54, 109; -vehicle, 42, 50, 52–54, 60, 62, 79–80, 83, 85–90, 110, 112, 124, 441–42; defined, 80; verbal, 15, 19, 33; visual, 33–34; vs. word, 33;

signal, 54, 57, 72–73, 80, 101, 108–13, 116–17, 134–38, 157–60, 165, 170, 172–75, 177, 179, 185–86; function, 166; and index, 112, 172; vs. sign, 80, 117, 174; source, 170; vs. symbol, 54, 108, 117; transmission, 137–38, 142, 174

signalization, filmic, 467

signans, 62, 88

signation, 284

signatum, 28, 62, 88

signatures, doctrine of, 32

signet, 115, 219, 220

signifiant, 57, 60, 80, 88, 91. *See also* signifier

significance, 33–34, 43, 87, 322; vs. meaning, 337

significatio, 85–86, 89

signification, 18, 24, 31, 36, 43, 52–53, 57, 60–61, 79, 86, 88, 93–95, 98, 111, 117, 167, 172, 266, 303, 306, 315–18; accessory, 22; and communication, 168, 172, 362; elementary structure of, 316; filmic, 467; natural, 31; proper, 22; semiotics of, 172–73

significatum, 19, 53–54, 90, 437

significatus, 28

signific (character), 254

signific(s) (movement), 13, 34, 104

signifié, 57, 60, 88, 91

signified, 15, 32, 59, 60–62, 66, 86–88, 91, 93–94, 99, 112, 117–18, 243–44, 291, 296, 303, 306, 437, 448

signifier, 15, 21, 42, 59–62, 66, 79–80, 83, 86–88, 91, 93–94, 112, 116–18, 243–45, 263, 296, 303, 437. *See also* signifiant, sign vehicle; vs. sign, 79; and signified, 22, 24, 32–33, 35–36

signifying practice, 322, 379

signifying system, 230

signologie, 57

signum [sign], 62, 82, 88, 91, 111; *demonstrativum*, 27, 109; *naturale*,

107; *ad placidum,* 107; *prognosticum,* 28, 109; *rememorativum,* 28, 110;
silence, 286, 417
similarity, 18, 76, 108, 121–24, 126–33, 305, 341, 357
simile, 132
similitude, 132, 446
simulacrum, 350, 447
simultaneity, 202
singular description, 97
sinsign, 44–46, 110, 114, 424, 438, 461
situationality, 333
social psychology. *See* psychology, s.
social science(s), 169, 314
sociobiology, 149, 164
sociogenesis, 164
sociolinguistics, 239
sociology, 6, 58, 169, 388
sociosemiotic(s), 6, 234
solidarity, 70, 72
somatic (signs), 288, 389
Sorésol, 270
soul, 90
sound change, 125
sound-image, 59–62, 66, 177–78
sound symbolism, 126, 272
source, 110, 174, 176–79
Soviet semiotics, 307–9, 331, 362, 376, 423, 465
space, 410–14, 435, 437, 474. *See also* proxemics
spatials (gestural), 397
specialization (design feature), 156, 161, 235, 260, 412, 441
spectator, 363
speech, 63, 248–50; act, 131, 232, 241; -circuit, 59, 176–77; code, 239; disguise, 289; evolution of, 399; signal, 80; substitutes, 288; surrogates, 287–89, 291, 407
spell, 188, 260
spelling: pronunciation, 262; reform, 257
stability, 199–200, 203
stage, 364
stamps, 440
stare pro, 85
static(s), 192, 299
statistics and information, 134–35, 138, 142
steady state, 200
steganography, 207
stenography, 270–71, 291
stereotypes, 474
stimulator, 166
stimulus, 53, 82, 100, 112, 165, 172; preparatory, 114
stochastic process, 137
stoicheia, 438
Stoics, 15–17, 62, 85, 87, 90–91, 104, 305
story, 370; and discourse, 352, 369; and plot, 308, 369
stratificational linguistics, 286
streptistics, 249
stress, 248
structural semantics. *See* semantics, s.
structuralism, 31, 35, 38, 56, 58, 63–64, 75–76, 81, 84, 192–94, 196, **295–306,** 310, 315, 325,

429, 435, 450, 457, 459, 464; American, 300–1; critique of, 326; dynamic, 75–76; functional(ist), 82, 299; genetic, 195; in linguistics, 298–301; methodological, 196, 326; ontological, 326; and semiotics, 297; Soviet, 309; static, 304
structuralist activity, 296
structure, 51, 61–62, 64, 71, 96, **192–97,** 198–99, 201–2, 244, 306, 317, 326, 450, 459; absent, 326; actual, 197; binary, 317; deep, 301, 316–17, 319, 323; definitions of, 192; dissipative, 200, 203, dynamic, 193, 308; elementary, 194, 302, 304; and form, 61, 68; and function, 182; ontology of, 196, 326; potential, 131, 197, 202; semantic, 61; semiotic, 68; surface, 301, 316, 318–19, 323
stuff, 33
Stuttgart School, 40, 46
style, 46, 72, 345; definition of, 343–44; philosophy of, 343; pictorial, 458–59; stylistic function, 184; stylistic stimulus, 344
stylistics, 46, 114, 212, 247, **338–45,** 358; generative, 345; genetic, 344; and information, 143
subject [person], 187, 303–4, 323; actantial, 372
subjectivity, 187, 337
subsegmental phonemes, 249
subsign, 451
substance, 19, 25, 61, 65–73, 244, 262, 296, 310; formed, 69; phonetic, 68, 71
substitute stimulus, 53
substitution, 86, 128, 195, 207, 290, 341–42. *See also* code, substitutive
supersign, 333, 451
superstructuralism, 298, 304, 306
supposition, 17–18, 85
suppression, 342
suprasegmentals, 248, 285
surface structure. *See* structure, s.
suspense, 142, 373
syllabary, 256
syllogism, 45, 339
symbiosis, 167
symbol(s), 21, 29–32, 35–36, 42–46, 54, 58, 70–71, 80, 83, 88, 90, 96, 101, 108–13, **115–20,** 123, 150–53, 163–64, 174, 185–87, 246, 382, 424–25, 433, 448, 480; in aesthetics, 115–16, 118; in anthropology, 115; chemical, 217; as connotation, 118; conventional sign, 116; cryptic (*see* cryptic); defined, 54, 115; dream (*see* dream s.); field, 36; gestural, 393; graphic, 115, 219–20, 259; in hermeneutics, 115; Hjelmslev's definition, 70–71; as icon, 117–18, vs. index, 116, irrational, 119; literary, 116, 118; and metaphor, 119; motivated, 110; musical, 430; acc. to Peirce, 44–46; in philosophy, 115; pictorial, 115; in poetics, 115; in psychoanalysis,

115, 119; and sign, 32, 54, 71, 110, 115–16, 120; vs. signal, 108, 116–17; in sociology, 115; substitutional definition, 117; theatrical, 364; ubiquity of, 115; verbal, 115–16; visual, 116, 153, 259
symbolic, 187, 323; the, 116; code, 120; cognition, 116; consumption, 443, 477; form, 35–36, 88, 116, 374, 432; interaction, 48; vs. semiotic, 116, 323; level of semiosis, 159–60
symbolics, 36
symbolism, 115, 119–20; universal, 29, 382; visual (*see* symbol v.)
symmetry, 357, 360; communicative, 159
symphory, 360
symptom, 17, 21, 32, 86, 101, 108–11, 113–16, 185–86, 213
symptomatology, 13
synaesthesia, 124, 126, 133, 432
synchronic, 147–48, 243, 296, 299, 301, 312
synchrony, 62–63, 69, 183, 296; dynamic, 203
synecdoche, 128
synergetics, 200
synergy, cognitive, 130
syntactics, 50–51, 148
syntagm, 205; syntagmatic, 51, 135, 183, 195, 201, 204, 312, 332, 375, 438, 444
syntax, 51; of film, 470; functional, 184; fundamental, 316, 317; narrative, 316
synthesis, 41
synthetic, 29, 141
system(s), 37, 46, 64, 69, 193–95, **198–205,** 210, 244, 297, 299, 304. *See also* sign system; system, semiotic; autopoietic, 200, 204; closed, 179, 199, 332; and code, 209, 211, 238; cybernetic, 37, 200; definition of, 198; dynamic, 195, 199, 202–3, 307; evolution of, 200; and function, 183; language as (*see* language s.); and norm (*see* norm); open, 199–200, 239; secondary (*see* secondary s.); semiotic, 61–62, 75–76, 202, 205, 209, 232, 238, 311–12, 433–34, 444–45, 451; social, 304; and text, 104, 201, 322, 332; theatrical, 365; theory, 143, 169–71, 178, 193, 198, 200, 203, 309
systematic vs. asystematic, 205, 214
systemic, 55

taboo, 189, 285, 302
tabula, 284
tachygraphy, 271
tacteme, 409
tactemics, 409
tactemorph, 409
tactesics, 409
tactile communication, 151, 161, 175, 388, **407–9,** 412, 474
tagmemics, 233, 388
tally stick, 252
taste, 389

tautology, 141
taxic, 159
taxonomic, taxonomy, 199, 301
teaching, 221–24, 388
tectonic, 437
telecommunication, 287, 290
telegraphy, 270
telepathy, 389
television, 5
template, 439
tempo, 248
tenor (metaphorical), 129
tense, 370, 414, 417
tension, 142, 373
term, 45
territoriality, 410–11, 413, 436
text, 33, 46–47, 64, 73, 131, 174, 184, 204, 217, 306, 309, 314–15, 319, 322, 331–32, 439; constitution, 319; definition of, 331; descriptive, 47; and discourse, 332; textual function, 182, 184; grammar, 330; iconicity of, 124; and image, 453–54, 460; legal, 47; linguistics, 330–31, 347; nonlinguistic, 329; pictorial, 452; polyfunctionality, 46; pragmatics, 297, 331–32; processing, 139, 348; production, 46, 142; reception, 46, 331; science(s) of, 322, 330; semantics, 315, 331; **text semiotics,** 45–46, 54, 75, 103, 211, 213, 222, 228, 233, **295–97,** 301, 307–8, 310, 313–14, 319, 325, **329–33,** 334, 338, 343, 471; structuralism, 73, 295, 307; syntax, 331; and system, 104, 201, 203, 322, 332; theory, 330; typology, 297
textuality, 143, 204, 331–33
theater, 30, 65, **361–66,** 388, 398; and communication, 171
theatricality, 361, 363
thematization, 316
theology, 17, 81, 334, 374, **381–84**
therapy, semiotic, 189, 191
thermic semiosis. *See* channel, th.
thermodynamics, 138, 199–200
thesaurus, 269
thetic, 323
thing, 29, 50, 60, 82, 87–91, 94, 99, 244, 305–6, 444. *See also* object; in itself, 36
thinking, 43
thirdness, 41, 44, 121, 222, 343
thought, 41, 94
time, 370, 373, 415–18
token, 44, 81, 110, 127, 136–37, 140, 282
tone (musical), 433–34
tone language, 288
tonic, 159–60
tools, 442
totality, 194–95, 201
totemism, 302
touch, 407–8
trace, 113, 266, 306, 461
trade mark, 220, 223
trade name, 223
tradition, 155–56, 236
traffic lights, 137, 212, 215

traffic signs, 183, 205, 210, 216, 220, 254
transcription, paralinguistic, 250
transfer, metaphorical, 128–29
transformation, 193–95, 199, 239, 370; semiotic, 363, 398
translatability, 230, 237
translation, 72, 231, 257, 381; interlingual, 99, 291; intersemiotic, 98, 102, 290–91, 431; intralingual, 99
translinguistic(s), 227, 313, 322, 330–31, 338, 369
transliteration, 257, 291
transmitter, 174–75, 177, 179
transmutatio, 341
transmutation. *See* intersemiotic t.
transparency (semantic), 131, 244–45
transphrastic, 332
transposition, 207
transsemiotic, 33, 81
trash, 440
triad, semiotic. *See* sign, triadic model
trivium, 50
tropes, 128, 339–42
trophic, 159
tropological, tropology, 335, 382, 478
truth, 22, 45, 96–97, 305, 326, 337, 374, 377; and fiction, 350
turn taking, 397, 406
type, 44, 81, 110, 127, 136–37, 140
typography, 47
typology of signs, 20–22, 26–27, 40, 44, 46, 52–54, 63, **107–14,** 127, 185. *See also* signs, classification of
Tyronian notes, 271

ultrasonic, 159
umwelt, 158. *See also* environment
uncertainty, 142
unconscious, 120, 303–4, 394
undercoding, 212
underliner (gestural), 397
understanding, 335–37
unified science, 48, 50, 278
unilateral semiosis, 170–71
unity, 195
universal(s), 17–18, 21, 24–25, 35, 84, 306; categories, 20, 41, 49, 121; character, 270–71, 274; gestural, 394; grammar (*see* grammar, u.); **universal language,** 17, 21–22, 207, 253, 257, **267–278,** 282–87, 441; language, gestural, 399; linguistic, 70, 237, 268, 300; ontological, 17–18
universe, 382
usage, 69
use, 69, 96, 101
use-value, 444
utility, utilitarian, 436, 442–45
utterance, 332
uttereme, 388

valuation, valuative, 55
valuator, 109

value, 61, 424–25; aesthetic, 422, 424; structural, 23, 193, 195, 201, 244; transfer, 372
vegative, 159–60
vehicle (of metaphor), 129
verb, 20
verbal, 247–48, 389; **verbal communication,** 387, 173, 185, **227–28,** 388 (*see also* language)
verificationism, 97
vesteme, 312
videme, 470
vision, 157
visual. *See also* channel, vis.; communication, 124, 211, 223–24, 228, 388–89, 421–47, 470, 472; semiosis, 154, 162–63; syntax, 452; tropes, 342
vocal (-auditory), 247–50, 388–89. *See also* channel, v.-a.; gesture, v.; vocalization, 250
voice, 91. *See also* vox; quality, 72, 247, 249–50; set, 72, 250
Volapück, 276
vox, 19, 85, 88, 91

wagging (waggle) dance, 151–52
Walbiri, 289
wampum belt, 252
whistle language, 75, 287–88, 291
wholeness, 194, 196, 199
Widerspiegelung, 448
wig-wag, 290
world, 82
word(s), 23–24, 28, 87–90, 217, 305–6; association, 103; code, 290; information value of, 140; lexical, 270; magic, 188, 190–91; and picture, 453–54; vs. sign, 33; as symbol, 116
work, 323, 343
writing, 37, 57, 68, 71, 75, 154, 188, 202, 209, 214, **251–66,** 289, 390, 475; alphabetic (*see* alphabet); autonomy of, 261–63, 269; cenemic, 252–53, 256, 262; and culture, 265; directionality of, 260; evolution of, 251–54; and film, 466; heteronomy of, 263, 291; iconic, 475; philosophy, 265; pleremic, 252–54, 262–63; poetics of, 260–61; and speech, 262; substitutes of, 290–91; as a substitutive system, 261; syllabic, 256

Yerkish, 153, 155

zero degree: language, 341, 344; of painting, 459
zero sign, 81
zooarchitectonics, 435
zoopragmatics, 148, 157
zoosemantics, 148, 162
zoosemiosis, 159
zoosemiotics, 16, 21, 25, 37, 49, 58, 87, **147–68,** 170–71, 211, 213, 235–36, 247, 389, 413, 435; definition of, 147; history of, 149
zoosyntactics, 148

INDEX OF NAMES

Beaufront, L. de, 276
Beaugrande, R. de, 143, 184, 204, 330, 333, 368
Becher, J. J., 269, 271–72
Beck, C., 269, 271–72
Beck, G., 182, 184–85
Becker, S., 472
Beckmann, P., 465
Beilenhoff, W., 465
Belk, R. W., 443
Bell, A. M., 258, 397
Bell, C., 388, 402
Bell, D. C., 397
Bellert, I., 299
Bellour, R., 465–66
Bellugi, U., 124, 281, 283–84
Ben-Amos, D., 6
Bennett, J. R., 343
Benoist, J.-M., 298
Bense, E., 300
Bense, M., xi, 6, 40, 46–47, 143, 217, 221–22, 233, 422–24, 439, 447, 452, 460, 465, 480
Bentele, G., 6, 35, 38, 49, 52, 169, 175, 330, 463–65
Benthall, J., 387–88
Bentham, J., 34
Bentley, A. F., 49
Benveniste, E., 14, 104–5, 112, 150, 159, 182, 195, 230–31, 236, 242–44, 321, 332, 368, 429–34, 450–51
Berger, A. A., 5–6, 461, 472
Berger, C., 261, 447
Berger, C. G., 276
Berger, C. R., 169
Berger, K., 382
Berkeley, G., 23–25, 84, 240, 449
Berlyne, D. E., 142
Berman, R., 477
Bernard, J., 38, 221–22
Bernstein, B., 212, 238–39
Berry, M., 201
Bertalanffy, L. v., 198, 200
Bertin, J., 220, 447
Bettetini, G., 47, 221–23, 362, 463–70
Betti, E., 335–37
Białostocki, J., 382
Bibliander, T., 271
Biedermann, H., 220
Bierman, A. K., 126
Bierwisch, M., 429, 433–34
Bilfinger, W. G. B., 29
Billig, I., 215, 441
Binder, H., 478
Birdwhistell, R. L., 249, 388, 392–93, 399–404
Birkhoff, G. D., 423
Bitomsky, H., 469, 471
Black, M., 93, 95–97, 100, 129–30, 133
Blackmur, R. P., 393
Blanchard, J.-M., 343, 347
Blanchard, M. E., 368
Blanke, D., 268–69, 276–77
Blest, A. D., 165
Bliss, C. K., 277
Block, N., 447
Block de Behar, L., 477
Blonsky, M., 4–6
Bloomfield, L., 88, 100, 102, 112, 231, 251, 261, 300–301

Blum, H., 340
Blumensath, H., 295
Bobes Naves, M. del C., 232
Bocheński, J. M., 12, 15, 17
Boeckmann, J. L., 34
Boehm, G., 336
Boesch, E. E., 191
Boethius [Ancius Manlius Severinus], 15, 85, 90–91
Boethius of Dacia, 19
Boff, L., 382
Bogart, L., 476
Bogatyrev, P., 6, 182, 307–8, 361, 363–64, 389
Boge, H., 271
Böhme, G., 416
Böhme, K., 388
Bohn, V., 374
Boilès, C. L., 430
Bolinger, D., 125–26, 227, 248–50, 318
Bolle, K. W., 374
Bollnow, O. F., 337, 410
Bolzano, B., 13, 33–34, 84
Bonet, J. P., 281
Bonnafont, C., 393
Bonner, J. T., 156, 164, 166
Bonsiepe, G., 341, 478
Boole, G., 276
Borbé, T., 4, 7, 12, 230, 348
Bormann, E. G., 168, 340
Born, K. E., 193
Bosmajian, H. A., 388
Boudon, P., 264, 410, 435, 441
Bouissac, P., 11, 37, 121, 124, 331, 362, 398
Boulding, K. E., 199, 447
Bourdieu, P., 115, 425
Bowie, M., 302
Bowlt, J. E., 307
Braille, L., 257
Brandes, S. H., 115
Brandis, C., 437
Branigan, E., 471
Brault, G. J., 396
Bréal, M., 13, 34, 106
Brekle, H. E., 20–21, 23, 62, 93–94, 106, 270, 272
Bremond, C., 352, 369, 371–73, 473–75
Bremond, J. C., 151
Brentano, F., 34, 84
Bright, M., 150
Bright, T., 271
Bright, W., 429, 431, 433
Brinkmann, H., 28
Broadbent, G., 435, 438
Brög, H., 221–23, 422, 453, 459–61
Broich, U., 323
Broms, H., 376, 479
Brøndal, V., 75
Bronowski, J., 150, 163, 235–37
Brooke-Rose, C., 130
Brooks, C., 339
Brosses, C. de, 240, 258
Brown, J. W., 223
Brown, R. L., 33
Browne, R. M., 46–47
Brun, T., 396
Bruneau, C., 189
Bruneau, T. J., 415–16
Brušák, K., 361, 365

Bruss, E. W., 40
Brütting, R., 297, 321, 347
Buczyńska-Garewicz, H., 122
Bühler, K., 13, 36, 85, 88, 107–9, 113–16, 130, 174, 184–87, 216, 220, 234, 392, 396, 402, 480
Bühler-Oppenheim, K., 220
Buhr, M., 182, 448, 451
Bühring, K., 105
Bull, P., 387
Bullough, E., 426
Bultmann, R., 335
Bulwer, J., 282–83, 397
Bunge, M., 95
Bunn, J. H., 416
Bureau, C., 343
Burghardt, G. M., 157, 159–60
Burgin, V., 460
Burgoon, J. K., 387
Burke, K., 340
Burke, P., 31
Burkhardt, D., 150
Burkhardt, H., 22, 274
Burks, A. W., 39, 41, 44
Burnham, J., 459
Bursill-Hall, G. L., 17, 19, 85
Burzlaff, W., 465
Busch, W., 472
Busnel, R.-G., 161, 287–88, 291
Busse, K.-P., 223, 422–23
Busse, W., 73, 182, 185, 377
Buyssens, E., 37, 63, 88, 172, 181–83, 205, 210, 214–15, 231, 236–38, 261, 286, 291, 362
Bystrina, I., 5–6, 35, 38, 49, 52

Cabanis, P., 27
Calabrese, O., 6, 12, 451–52, 456–57
Calame, C., 374
Callaghan, W. J., 41
Calloud, J., 384
Calvet, L.-J., 57
Calvet de Magalhaes, T. C., 41
Camhy, D., 13
Campanella, T., 14, 20
Campeanu, P., 363
Cannon, W. B., 200
Canoa Galiana, J., 362
Canter, D., 410, 414
Caprettini, G. P., 37, 214, 475
Capurro, R., 134
Carillo, F., 348
Carnap, R., 5, 37, 51–53, 94, 97, 104, 141, 196, 232
Carontini, E., 6, 321, 378
Carroll, J. M., 463–65, 469, 471
Carroll, S., 102
Carter, C. L., 451
Carzo, D., 329
Casetti, F., 6, 463, 465
Cassirer, E. A., 21, 31, 35–36, 88, 94, 107–12, 115–16, 229, 374, 381
Castagnano, R. H., 362
Catford, J. C., 264
Cazimir, B., 430
Cebik, L. B., 350
Cegarra, M., 465
Cerbrían-Herreros, M., 5
Cerisola, P. L., 296, 347, 368
Cervenka, E. J., 396–97

Durand, J., 477–78
Dürer, A., 459
Dürig, W., 381
Duroy, R., 233–34
Dutz, K. D., 12, 22, 49, 52, 422
Dyer, G., 476–78

Eagle, H., 464–65
Eakins, B. W., 49
Ebbesen, S., 18, 85
Ebeling, G., 334
Eberlein, G., 23
Eccles, J. C., 82
Eckardt, A., 277
Eco, U., 12–17, 65–66, 74–76, 87, 102, 107–21, 127–33, 172–73, 196, 209–18, 319–20, **325–26**, 330–31, 335, 340–41, 352–53, 358, 378–79, 421–28, 435–38, 442, 450–52, 464–72, 478 *passim*
Edwards, P., 18
Efron, D., 392, 394, 396
Egan, R. F., 425
Ege, N., 242
Eggebrecht, H. H., 432
Ehlich, K., 254, 263, 387, 405–6
Ehmer, H. K., 223, 478, 480
Ehrmann, J., 298, 302
Eibl-Eibesfeldt, I., 156, 164, 283, 388, 399, 403, 406
Eichenbaum, B. M. *See* Ėjxenbaum
Eikhenbaum, B. M. *See* Ėjxenbaum, B. M.
Eimermacher, K., 307–9
Eimermacher, R., 308
Eisenberg, A. M., 387, 389
Eisenstein, S., 463–65
Eismann, W., 397
Ėjxenbaum, B. M., 307, 348, 354, 465
Ekman, P., 124, 387, 391–97, 402–6
Elam, K., 361–66
Eliade, M., 115, 374, 381
Elias, P., 309
Eliot, T. S., 349
Ellgring, J. H., 405–6
Elling, E., 121, 471
Ellis, J., 6, 38, 182, 184, 302, 304, 310, 321
Ellsworth, P. C., 406
Eltester, F.-W., 381, 447
Emanuele, P., 35
Empson, W., 358
Eng, J. van der, 309
Engel, J. J., 30, 388, 402
Engels, L. K., 223, 377
Engler, R., 57–59, 195, 230, 242–43, 298
Englert, K., 306
Enkvist, N. E., 125–26, 343–44
Entrevernes Group. *See* Groupe d'Entrevernes
Entwistle, D. R., 121, 124, 446
Epicurus, 16
Epperson, G., 430
Erfurt, T. *See* Thomas of E.
Erlich, V., 307
Ertel, E., 361, 365
Ertel, S., 245
Esbroeck, M. van, 304, 335
Escarpit, R., 143
Eschbach, A., 5, 6, 12, 29–30, 34–

37, 48–49, 84, 185, 234, 277–78, 348, 362, 366, 421–22, 463
Eschbach-Szabó, V., 6
Espe, H., 462
Esposito, J. L., 41
Esser, A., 413
Esslin, M., 361–66
Estoup, J. B., 140
Euler, L., 29
Evans, G., 96–97
Evans, W. F., 149–50
Evans-Pritchard, E. E., 191
Everaert-Desmedt, N., 368, 476–79
Ewert, J.-P., 164
Exline, R. V., 405–6

Fabbri, P., 212
Faber, H. von, 223
Fagen, R. E., 198
Fages, J.-B., 295–98
Fährmann, R., 249–50
Faltin, P., 84–85, 422–25, 429–31
Fast, J., 393
Fauque, R., 439
Faur, J., 334
Faust, W. M., 454
Fawcett, R. P., 5, 233–34
Fehr, B. J., 405
Feibleman, J. U., 41
Feldstein, S., 249, 387, 417
Feller, S., 411
Fellinger, R., 347
Féral, J., 321
Ferguson, G., 115
Ferrer, V. *See* Vincent Ferrer
Février, J. G., 251
Feyereisen, P., 394
Fichte, J. G., 32
Fiesel, E., 32
Fietz, L., 187, 295, 298, 422
Figge, U. L., 150, 193
Filliolet, J., 354
Fillmore, C. J., 184
Finlay-Pelinski, M., 330
Finter, H., 348
Fiordo, R., 49, 54
Firca, G., 429
Firth, J. R., 100–103, 126
Firth, R., 115, 119, 169, 174, 220, 389
Fisch, M. H., 40–42
Fischer-Jørgensen, E., 64–68
Fischer-Lichte, E., 26, 30, 38, 83, 95, 97, 362–66, 398, 402, 421–22
Fiske, D. W., 388–90, 397, 405
Fiske, J., 5
Fitzgerald, J. F., 41, 44
Flachskampf, L., 396
Flechtner, H.-J., 143, 209
Fledelius, K., 471
Fleischer, M., 150, 308
Floch, J.-M., 447, 459–60
Florkin, M., 148
Fodor, J. D., 315, 318–19
Fokkema, D. W., 180, 307–8, 347, 368, 427
Földes-Papp, K., 251
Fónagy, I., 242
Fonseca, P. de, 20
Fontanille, J., 222
Formigari, L., 21–26, 240, 270–71
Förster, U., 478

Forston, R. F., 411
Foster, M. L., 115
Foucault, M., 21, 62, 94, 304, 379
Fought, J., 300
Fouts, R. S., 153, 155
Fowler, H. N., 265
Fraisse, P., 415
François, D., 173, 182
Frank, H., 141–43, 361, 423
Frank, L. K., 408
Frank, M., 298, 304–6
Frank-Böhringer, B., 143, 340
Franke, U., 30
Fraser, J. T., 415, 417
Frazer, J. G., 120, 189, 191
Freedman, J. S., 20
Freeman, D. C., 343
Freeman, E., 41
Frege, G., 34, 84, 93–94, 276
Fresnault-Deruelle, P., 472–75
Freud, S., 120, 191, 303, 321, 323, 374
Freudenthal, H., 276
Fricke, H., 344
Friedman, L. A., 281, 284
Friedman, N., 119
Friedman, W. F., 206
Friedrich, J., 251
Frier, W., 232
Friesen, W. V., 124, 391, 394–97, 402–3
Frijda, N. H., 393
Frings, H., 149, 157, 160–61, 167
Frings, M., 149, 157, 160–61, 167
Frisch, J. C., 93
Frisch, K. von, 150–52, 164
Frishberg, N., 282–83
Fromkin, V., 149–50, 227
Fronval, G., 285
Frutiger, A., 220
Fry, V. H., 342
Frye, N., 116, 119, 374
Fuchs, W. J., 472
Funke, O., 23, 270, 273
Furbank, P. N., 447
Füssel, K., 298, 304, 310

Gabler, D., 19, 85
Gabriel, G., 350
Gadamer, H.-G., 334–37, 340
Gahmberg, H., 376, 479
Gale, R. M., 113, 415, 417
Galen, 13, 15
Gall, F. J., 402
Gallaudet, T. H., 282
Gallie, W. B., 41, 43
Galliot, M., 477
Gamillscheg, E., 489
Gamkrelidze, T. V., 125, 242
Gandelman, C., 436
Gandelsonas, M., 435–36, 438
Gandillac, M. de, 193
Gäng, P., 30
García Lorenzo, L., 362
Gardiner, A. H., 182, 244
Gardner, B. T., 153
Gardner, H., 301
Gardner, R. A., 153
Garfinkel, A. D., 477
Garnier, F., 397
Garrido Gallardo, M. A., 347